THINKING
AND
DESTINY

BOOKS by HAROLD W. PERCIVAL

THINKING AND DESTINY

Deluxe One Vol. hardcover edition, complete
Quality Softcover edition, complete

ADEPTS, MASTERS AND MAHATMAS
Library of Congress 92-082024
ISBN: 0-911650-11-3

MASONRY AND ITS SYMBOLS
In the Light of Thinking and Destiny
Library of Congress 52-2237
ISBN: 0-911650-07-5

MAN AND WOMAN AND CHILD
Library of Congress 52-6126
ISBN: 0-911650-08-3

DEMOCRACY IS SELF-GOVERNMENT
Library of Congress 52-30629
ISBN: 0-911650-10-5

Available from:
THE WORD FOUNDATION, INC.
P.O. Box 180340
Dallas, Texas 75218
Website: www.word-foundation.com

THINKING

AND

DESTINY

With a brief account of

THE DESCENT OF MAN

into this Human World,
and,
How he will return to

THE ETERNAL ORDER OF PROGRESSION

By HAROLD W. PERCIVAL

SYMBOLS, ILLUSTRATIONS and CHARTS,
and
DEFINITIONS and EXPLANATIONS of Terms and Phrases,
as used in this book.

This edition published by arrangement with
The Word Foundation, Inc. of Dallas, Texas

by

Motilal Banarsidass Publishers
Private Limited ● Delhi

First Indian Edition: Delhi, 2001
First Edition: USA, 1946
Reprint: USA 1950, 1954, 1961, 1966, 1971, 1974, 1978, 1981, 1987, 1995

ISBN: 81-208-1783-4 (Cloth)
ISBN: 81-208-1809-1 (Paper)

Library of Congress 47-1811

Also available at:

MOTILAL BANARSIDASS

236, 9th Main III Block, Jayanagar, Bangalore 560 011
41 U.A. Bungalow Road, Jawahar Nagar, Delhi 110 007
8 Mahalaxmi Chamber, Bhulabhai Desai Rd., Mumbai 400 026
120 Royapettah High Road, Mylapore, Chennai 600 004
Sanas Plaza, 1302 Baji Rao Road, Pune 411 002
8 Camac Street, Kolkata 700 017
Ashok Rajpath, Patna 800 004
Chowk, Varanasi 221 001

Printed in India
BY JAINENDRA PRAKASH JAIN AT SHRI JAINENDRA PRESS,
A-45 NARAINA, PHASE-I, NEW DELHI 110 028.
PUBLISHED BY ARRANGEMENT WITH THE WORD FOUNDATION, INC.
BY NARENDRA PRAKASH JAIN FOR
MOTILAL BANARSIDASS PUBLISHERS PRIVATE LIMITED,
BUNGALOW ROAD, DELHI 110 007

TABLE OF CONTENTS

List of SYMBOLS, ILLUSTRATIONS AND CHARTS.

PREFACE TO THE ELEVENTH EDITION

GREETINGS! Gentle Reader, and welcome on your way home! For those who read this book *are* on their way home already.

When THINKING AND DESTINY was first published forty-nine years ago, the author stated that "the book was ahead of its time, and that it would not come into its own until the last part of this century". He evidently foresaw that it would take all of the dramatic developments in the destinies of individuals, families, groups and nations during these many years, to give rise to the unprecedented quest for truth and knowledge that is everywhere apparent now.

So you embarked on your search, and eventually were led to this book. As you begin to read it, you will probably find it to be unlike anything you have ever read before. Most of us did. Many of us had difficulties, at first, in comprehending. But as we read on, a page at a time, we discovered that Percival's unique system of conveying his knowledge called into use faculties long dormant within us, and that our capacity to understand grew with each reading. Ultimately, we KNEW — and then wondered how it could be that we had been without this knowledge for so long. Then we understood the reasons for that, also.

We trust that THINKING AND DESTINY will help you to learn who you are, where you are and what your destiny may be. We hope that it will inspire you with new understanding of your own power to direct your destiny. We feel sure that it will satisfy the longing in your heart to know why man is as he is, and how—by thinking—he may enrich and ennoble his life evermore.

If you are among those who wish to help spread The Word, or you desire contact with fellow students, you are cordially invited to write to us. THE WORD FOUNDATION, INC. is a nonprofit organization established in 1950 to make known to the people of the world all books written by Harold W. Percival, and to ensure the perpetuation of his legacy to humanity.

Dallas, Texas
May, 1995

THE WORD FOUNDATION, INC.
P.O. Box 180340
Dallas, Texas 75218

HAROLD W. PERCIVAL
1868 –1953

AUTHOR'S FOREWORD

This book was dictated to Benoni B. Gattell at intervals between the years 1912 and 1932. Since then it has been worked over again and again. Now, in 1946, there are few pages that have not been at least slightly changed. To avoid repetitions and complexities entire pages have been deleted, and I have added many sections, paragraphs and pages.

Without assistance, it is doubtful whether the work would have been written, because it was difficult for me to think and write at the same time. My body had to be still while I thought the subject matter into form and chose appropriate words to build out the structure of the form: and so, I am indeed grateful to him for the work he has done. I must also here acknowledge the kind offices of friends, who desire to remain unnamed, for their suggestions and technical assistance in completing the work.

A most difficult task was to get terms to express the recondite subject matter treated. My arduous effort has been to find words and phrases that will best convey the meaning and attributes of certain incorporeal realities, and to show their inseparable relation to the conscious selves in human bodies. After repeated changes I finally settled on terms used herein.

Many subjects are not made as clear as I would like them to be, but the changes made must suffice or be endless, because on each reading other changes seemed advisable.

I do not presume to preach to anyone; I do not consider myself a preacher or a teacher. Were it not that I am responsible for the book, I would prefer that my personality be not named as its author. The greatness of the subjects about which I offer information, relieves and frees me from self-conceit and forbids the plea of modesty. I dare make strange and startling statements to the conscious and immortal self that is in every human body; and I take for granted that the individual will decide what he will or will not do with the information presented.

Thoughtful persons have stressed the need of speaking here of some of my experiences in states of being conscious, and of events of my life which might help to explain how it was possible for me to be acquainted with and to write of things that are so at variance with present beliefs. They say this is necessary because no bibliography is appended and no references are offered to substantiate the statements herein made. Some of my experiences have been unlike anything I have heard of or read. My own thinking about human life and the world we live in has revealed to me subjects and phenomena I have not found mentioned in books. But it would be unreasonable to suppose that such matters could be, yet be unknown to others. There must be those who know but cannot tell. I am under no pledge of secrecy. I belong to no organization of any kind. I break no faith in telling what I have found by thinking; by steady thinking while awake, not in sleep or in trance. I have never been nor do I ever wish to be in trance of any kind.

What I have been conscious of while thinking about such subjects as space, the units of matter, the constitution of matter, intelligence, time, dimensions, the creation and exteriorization of thoughts, will, I hope, have opened realms for future exploration and exploitation. By that time right conduct should be a part of human life, and should keep abreast of science and invention. Then civilization can continue, and Independence with Responsibility will be the rule of individual life and of Government.

Here is a sketch of some
experiences of my early life:

Rhythm was my first feeling of connection with this physical world. Later on I could feel inside the body, and I could hear voices. I understood the meaning of the sounds made by the voices; I did not see anything, but I, as feeling, could get the meaning of any of the word-sounds expressed, by the rhythm; and my feeling gave the form and color of the objects which were described by words. When I could use the sense of sight and could see objects, I found the forms and appearances which I, as feeling, had felt, to be in approximate agreement with what I had apprehended. When I was able to use the senses of sight, hearing, taste and smell and could ask and answer questions, I found myself to be a stranger in a strange world. I knew I was not the body I lived in, but no one could tell me who or what I was or where I came from, and most of those whom I questioned seemed to believe they were the bodies in which they lived.

I realized that I was in a body from which I could not free myself. I was lost, alone, and in a sorry state of sadness. Repeated happenings and experiences convinced me that things were not what they appeared to be; that there is continued change; that there is no permanence of anything; that people often said the opposite of what they really meant. Children played games they called "make-believe" or "let us pretend".

Children played, men and women practiced make-believe and pretense; comparatively few people were really truthful and sincere. There was waste in human effort, and appearances did not last. Appearances were not made to last. I asked myself: How should things be made that will last, and made without waste and disorder? Another part of myself answered: First, know what you want; see and steadily hold in mind the form in which you would have what you want. Then think and will and speak that into appearance, and what you think will be gathered from the invisible atmosphere and fixed into and around that form. I did not then think in these words, but these words express what I then thought. I felt confident I could do that, and at once tried and tried long. I failed. On failing I felt disgraced, degraded, and I was ashamed.

I could not help being observant of events. What I heard people say about things that happened, particularly about death, did not seem reasonable. My parents were devout Christians. I heard it read and said that "God" made the world; that he created an immortal soul for each human body in the world; and that the soul who did not obey God would be cast into hell and would burn in fire and brimstone for ever and ever. I did not believe a word of that. It seemed too absurd for me to suppose or believe that any God or being could have made the world or have created me for the body in which I lived. I had burned my finger with a brimstone match, and I believed that the body could be burned to death; but I knew that I, what was conscious as I, could not be burned and could not die, that fire and brimstone could not kill me, though the pain from that burn was dreadful. I could sense danger, but I did not fear.

People did not seem to know "why" or "what", about life or about death. I knew that there must be a reason for everything that happened. I wanted to know the secrets of life and of death, and to live forever. I did not know why, but I could not help wanting that. I knew that there could be no night and day and life and death, and no world, unless there were wise ones who managed the world and night and day and life and death. However, I determined that my purpose would be to find those wise ones who would tell me how I should learn and what I should do, to be entrusted with the secrets of life and death. I would not even think of telling this, my firm resolve, because people would not understand; they would believe me to be foolish or insane. I was about seven years old at that time.

Fifteen or more years passed. I had noticed the different outlook on life of boys and girls, while they grew and changed into men and women, especially during their adolescence, and particularly that of my own. My views had changed, but my purpose—to find those who were wise, who knew, and from whom I could learn the secrets of life and death—was unchanged. I was sure of their existence; the world could not be, without them. In the ordering of events I could see that there must be a government and a management of the world, just as there must be the government of a country or a management of any business for these to continue. One day my mother asked me what I believed. Without hesitation I said: I know without doubt that justice rules the world, even though my own life seems to be evidence that it does not, because I can see no possibility of accomplishing what I inherently know, and what I most desire.

In that same year, in the spring of 1892, I read in a Sunday paper, that a certain Madam Blavatsky had been a pupil of wise men in the East who were called "Mahatmas"; that through repeated lives on earth, they had attained to wisdom; that they possessed the secrets of life and death, and that they had caused Madam Blavatsky to form a Theosophical Society, through which their teachings could be given to the public. There would be a lecture that evening. I went. Later on I became an ardent member of the Society. The statement that there were wise men—by whatever names they were called—did not surprise me; that was only verbal evidence of what I inherently had been sure of as necessary for the advancement of man and for the direction and guidance of nature. I read all that I could about them. I thought of becoming a pupil of one of the wise men; but continued thinking led me to understand that the real way was not by any formal application to anybody, but to be myself fit and ready. I have not seen or heard from, nor have I had any contact with, "the wise ones" such as I had conceived. I have had no teacher. Now I have a better understanding of such matters. The real "Wise Ones" are Triune Selves, in The Realm of Permanence. I ceased connection with all societies.

From November of 1892 I passed through astonishing and crucial experiences, following which, in the spring of 1893, there occurred the most extraordinary event of my life. I had crossed 14th Street at 4th Avenue, in New York City. Cars and people were hurrying by. While stepping up to the northeast corner curbstone, Light, greater than that of myriads of suns opened in the center of my head. In that instant or point, eternities were apprehended. There was no time. Distance and dimensions were not in evidence. Nature was composed of units. I was conscious of the units of nature and of units as Intelligences. Within and beyond, so to say, there were greater and lesser Lights; the greater pervading the lesser Lights, which revealed the different kinds of units. The Lights were not of nature, they were Lights as Intelligences, Conscious Lights. Compared with the brightness or lightness of those Lights, the surrounding sunlight was a dense fog. And in and through all Lights and units and objects I was conscious of the Presence of Consciousness. I was conscious of Consciousness as the Ultimate and Absolute Reality, and conscious of the relation of things. I experienced no thrills, emotions, or ecstasy. Words fail utterly to describe or explain CONSCIOUSNESS. It would be futile to attempt description of the sublime grandeur and power and order and relation in poise of what I was then conscious. Twice during the next fourteen years, for a long time on each occasion, I was conscious of Consciousness. But during that time I was conscious of no more than I had been conscious of in that first moment.

Being conscious of Consciousness is the set of related words I have chosen as a phrase to speak of that most potent and remarkable moment of my life.

Consciousness is present in every unit. Therefore the presence of Consciousness makes every unit conscious as the function it performs in the degree in which it is conscious.

Being conscious of Consciousness reveals the "unknown" to the one who has been so conscious. Then it will be the duty of that one to make known what he can of *being conscious of Consciousness.*

The great worth in being conscious of Consciousness is that it enables one to know about any subject, by thinking. Thinking is the steady holding of the Conscious Light within on the subject of the thinking. Briefly stated, thinking is of four stages: selecting the subject; holding the Conscious Light on that subject; focussing the Light; and, the focus of the Light. When the Light is focussed, the subject is known. By this method, *Thinking and Destiny* has been written.

The special purpose of this book is: To tell the conscious selves in human bodies that we are inseparable doer parts of consciously immortal *individual* trinities, Triune Selves, who, within and beyond time, lived with our great thinker and knower parts in perfect sexless bodies in the Realm of Permanence; that we, the conscious selves now in human bodies, failed in a crucial test, and thereby exiled ourselves from that Realm of Permanence into this temporal man and woman world of birth and death and re-existence; that we have no memory of this because we put ourselves into a self-hypnotic sleep, to dream; that we will continue to dream through life, through death and back again to life; that we must continue to do this until we de-hypnotize, wake, ourselves out of the hypnosis into which we put ourselves; that, however long it takes, we must awake from our dream, become conscious *of* ourselves *as* ourselves in our bodies, and then regenerate and restore our bodies to everlasting life in our home—The Realm of Permanence from which we came—which permeates this world of ours, but is not seen by mortal eyes. Then we will consciously take our places and continue our parts in the Eternal Order of Progression. The way to accomplish this is shown in chapters which follow.

*　　*　　*

At this writing the manuscript of this work is with the printer. There is little time to add to what has been written. During the many years of its preparation it has been often asked that I include in the text some interpretations of Bible passages which seem incomprehensible, but which, in the light of what has been stated in these pages, make sense and have meaning, and which, at the same time, corroborate statements made in this work. But I was averse to make comparisons or show correspondences. I wanted this work to be judged solely on its own merits.

In the past year I bought a volume containing "The Lost Books of the Bible and The Forgotten Books of Eden." On scanning the pages of these books, it is astonishing to see how many strange and otherwise incomprehensible passages can be comprehended when one understands what is herein written about the Triune Self and its three parts; about the regeneration of the human physical body into a perfected, immortal physical body, and the Realm of Permanence,—which in the words of Jesus is the "Kingdom of God."

Again requests have been made for clarifications of Bible passages. Perhaps it is well that this be done and also that the readers of *Thinking and Destiny* be given some evidence to corroborate certain statements in this book, which evidence may be found both in the New Testament and in the books above mentioned. Therefore I will add a fifth section to Chapter X, "Gods and their Religions," dealing with these matters.

H.W.P.

New York, March 1946

CHAPTER I

INTRODUCTION

This first chapter of *Thinking and Destiny* is intended to introduce to you only a few of the subjects that the book deals with. Many of the subjects will seem strange. Some of them may be startling. You may find that they all encourage thoughtful consideration. As you become familiar with the thought, and think your way through the book, you will find that it becomes increasingly clear, and that you are in process of developing an understanding of certain fundamental but heretofore mysterious facts of life—and particularly about yourself.

The book explains the purpose of life. That purpose is not merely to find happiness, either here or hereafter. Neither is it to "save" one's soul. The real purpose of life, the purpose that will satisfy both sense and reason, is this: that each one of us will be progressively conscious in ever higher degrees in being conscious; that is, conscious of nature, and in and through and beyond nature. By nature is meant all that one can be made conscious of through the senses.

The book also introduces you to yourself. It brings you the message about yourself: your mysterious self that inhabits your body. Perhaps you have always identified yourself with and as your body; and when you try to think of yourself you therefore think of your bodily mechanism. By force of habit you have spoken of your body as "I", as "myself". You are accustomed to use such expressions as "when I was born," and "when I die"; and "I saw myself in the glass," and "I rested myself," "I cut myself," and so on, when in reality it is your body that you speak of. To understand what you are you must first see clearly the distinction between yourself and the body you live in. The fact that you use the term "my body" as readily as you use any of those just quoted would suggest that you are not altogether unprepared to make this important distinction.

You should know that you are not your body; you should know that your body is not you. You should know this because, when you think

1

about it, you realize that your body is very different today from what it was when, in childhood, you first became conscious of it. During the years that you have lived in your body you have been aware that it has been changing: in its passing through its childhood and adolescence and youth, and into its present condition, it has changed greatly. And you recognize that as your body has matured there have been gradual changes in your view of the world and your attitude toward life. But throughout these changes you have remained *you:* that is, you have been conscious of yourself as being the same self, the identical I, all the while. Your reflection on this simple truth compels you to realize that you definitely are not and cannot be your body; rather, that your body is a physical organism that you live in; a living nature mechanism that you are operating; an animal that you are trying to understand, to train and master.

You know how your body came into this world; but how *you* came into your body you do not know. You did not come into it until some time after it was born; a year, perhaps, or several years; but of this fact you know little or nothing, because your memory of your body began only after you had come into your body. You know something about the material of which your ever-changing body is composed; but what it is that *you* are you do not know; you are not yet conscious *as what* you are in your body. You know the name by which your body is distinguished from the bodies of others; and this you have learned to think of as *your* name. What is important is, that you should know, not who you are as a personality, but what you are as an individual—conscious *of* yourself, but not yet conscious *as* yourself, an unbroken identity. You know that your body lives, and you quite reasonably expect that it will die; for it is a fact that every living human body dies in time. Your body had a beginning, and it will have an end; and from beginning to end it is subject to the laws of the world of phenomena, of change, of time. *You,* however, are not in the same way subject to the laws that affect your body. Although your body changes the material of which it is composed oftener than you change the costumes with which you clothe it, your identity does not change. You are ever the same *you.*

As you ponder these truths you find that, however you might try, you cannot think that you yourself will ever come to an end, any more than you can think that you yourself ever had a beginning. This is because your identity is beginningless and endless; the real I, the Self that you feel, is immortal and changeless, forever beyond the reach of the phenomena of change, of time, of death. But what this your mysterious identity is, you do not know.

When you ask yourself, "What do I know that I am?" the presence of your identity will eventually cause you to answer in some such manner as this: "Whatever it is that I am, I know that at least I am conscious; I am conscious at least of being conscious." And continuing from this fact you may say: "Therefore I am conscious that I am. I am conscious, moreover, that I am I; and that I am no other. I am conscious that this my identity that I am conscious of—this distinct I-ness and selfness that I clearly feel—does not change throughout my life, though everything else that I am conscious of seems to be in a state of constant change." Proceeding from this you may say: "I do not yet know what this mysterious unchanging I is; but I am conscious that in this human body, of which I am conscious during my waking hours, there is something which is conscious; something that feels and desires and thinks, but that does not change; a conscious something that wills and impels this body to act, yet obviously is not the body. Clearly this conscious something, whatever it is, is myself."

Thus, by thinking, you come to regard yourself no longer as a body bearing a name and certain other distinguishing features, but as the conscious self in the body. The conscious self in the body is called, in this book, *the doer-in-the-body*. The doer-in-the-body is the subject with which the book is particularly concerned. You therefore will find it helpful, as you read the book, to think of yourself as *an embodied doer;* to look upon yourself as an immortal doer in a human body. As you learn to think of yourself as a doer, as the doer in your body, you will be taking an important step toward understanding the mystery of yourself and of others.

You are aware of your body, and of all else that is of nature, by means of the senses. It is only by means of your body senses that you are able at all to function in the physical world. You function by thinking. Your thinking is prompted by your feeling and your desire. Your feeling and desiring and thinking invariably manifest in bodily activity; physical activity is merely the expression, the exteriorization, of your inner activity. Your body with its senses is the instrument, the mechanism, which is impelled by your feeling and desire; it is your individual nature machine.

Your senses are living beings; invisible units of nature-matter; these start forces that permeate the entire structure of your body; they are entities which, though unintelligent, are conscious *as* their functions. Your senses serve as the centers, the transmitters of impressions between the objects of nature and the human machine that you are operating. The senses are nature's ambassadors to your court. Your body and its senses have no power of voluntary functioning; no more than your glove through which you are able to feel and act. Rather, that power is you, the operator, the conscious self, the embodied doer.

Without you, the doer, the machine cannot accomplish anything. The involuntary activities of your body—the work of building, maintenance, tissue repair, and so forth—are carried on automatically by the individual breathing machine as it functions for and in conjunction with the great nature machine of change. This routine work of nature in your body is being constantly interfered with, however, by your unbalanced and irregular thinking: the work is marred and nullified to the degree that you cause destructive and unbalancing bodily tension by allowing your feelings and desires to act without your conscious control. Therefore, in order that nature might be allowed to recondition your machine without the interference of your thoughts and emotions, it is provided that you shall periodically let go of it; nature in your body provides that the bond which holds you and the senses together is at times relaxed, partially or completely. This relaxation or letting go of the senses is sleep.

While your body sleeps you are out of touch with it; in a certain sense you are away from it. But each time you awaken your body you are immediately conscious of being the selfsame "I" that you were before you left your body in sleep. Your body, whether awake or asleep, is not conscious *of* anything, ever. That which is conscious, that which thinks, is you yourself, the doer that is in your body. This becomes apparent when you consider that you do not think while your body is asleep; at least, if you do think during the period of sleep you do not know or remember, when you awaken your body senses, what you have been thinking.

Sleep is either deep or dream. Deep sleep is the state in which you withdraw into yourself, and in which you are out of touch with the senses; it is the state in which the senses have stopped functioning as the result of having been disconnected from the power by which they function, which power is you, the doer. Dream is the state of partial detachment; the state in which your senses are turned from the outer objects of nature to function inwardly in nature, acting in relation to the subjects of the objects that are perceived during wakefulness. When, after a period of deep sleep, you re-enter your body, you at once awaken the senses and begin to function through them again as the intelligent operator of your machine, ever thinking, speaking, and acting as the feeling-and-desire which you are. And from lifelong habit you immediately identify yourself as and with your body: "*I* have been asleep," you say; "now *I* am awake."

But in your body and out of your body, alternately awake and asleep day after day; through life and through death, and through the states after death; and from life to life through all your lives—your identity and your feeling of identity persist. Your identity is a very real thing, and always a presence with you; but it is a mystery which one's intellect cannot comprehend. Though it cannot be apprehended by the senses you are nevertheless conscious of its presence. You are conscious of it as a feeling; you have a feeling of identity; a feeling of I-ness, of selfness; you *feel*, without question or rationalizing, that you are a distinct identical self which persists through life.

This feeling of the presence of your identity is so definite that you cannot think that the *you* in your body ever could be any other than yourself; you know that you are always the same you, continuously the same self, the same doer. When you lay your body to rest and sleep you cannot think that your identity will come to an end after you relax your hold on your body and let go; you fully expect that when you again become conscious in your body and begin a new day of activity in it, you will still be the same you, the same self, the same doer.

As with sleep, so with death. Death is but a prolonged sleep, a temporary retirement from this human world. If at the moment of death you are conscious of your feeling of I-ness, of selfness, you will at the same time be conscious that the long sleep of death will not affect the continuity of your identity any more than your nightly sleep affects it. You will feel that through the unknown future you are going to continue, even as you have continued day after day through the life that is just ending. This self, this you, which is conscious throughout your present life, is the same self, the same you, that was similarly conscious of continuing day after day through each of your former lives.

Although your long past is a mystery to you now, your previous lives on earth are no greater wonder than is this present life. Every morning there is the mystery of coming back to your sleeping body from you-do-not-know-where, getting into it by way of you-do-not-know-how, and again becoming conscious of this world of birth and death and time. But this has occurred so often, has long been so natural, that it does not seem to be a mystery; it is a commonplace occurrence. Yet it is virtually no different from the procedure that you go through when, at the beginning of each re-existence, you enter a new body that has been formed for you by nature, trained and made ready by your parents or guardians as your new residence in the world, a new mask as a personality.

A personality is the persona, mask, through which the actor, the doer, speaks. It is therefore more than the body. To be a personality the human body must be made awake by the presence of the doer in it. In the ever-changing drama of life the doer takes on and wears a personality, and through it acts and speaks as it plays its part. As a personality the doer thinks of itself as the personality; that is, the masquerader thinks of itself as the part that it plays, and is forgetful of itself as the conscious immortal self in the mask.

It is necessary to understand about re-existence and destiny, else it is impossible to account for the differences in human nature and character. To assert that the inequalities of birth and station, of wealth and poverty, health and sickness, result from accident or chance is an affront to law and justice. Moreover, to attribute intelligence, genius, inventiveness, gifts, faculties, powers, virtue; or, ignorance, ineptitude, weakness, sloth, vice, and the greatness or smallness of character in these, as coming from physical heredity, is opposed to sound sense and reason. Heredity has to do with the body; but character is made by one's thinking. Law and justice do rule this world of birth and death, else it could not continue in its courses; and law and justice prevail in human affairs. But effect does not always immediately follow cause. Sowing is not immediately followed by harvesting. Likewise, the results of an act or of a thought may not appear until after a long intervening period. We cannot see what happens between the thought and an act and their results, any more than we can see what is happening in the ground between seeding time and harvest; but each self in a human body makes its own law as destiny by what it thinks and what it does, though it may not be aware when it is prescribing the law; and it does not know just when the prescription will be filled, as destiny, in the present or in a future life on earth.

A day and a lifetime are essentially the same; they are recurring periods of a continuous existence in which the doer works out its destiny and balances its human account with life. Night and death, too, are very much alike: when you slip away to let your body rest and sleep, you go through an experience very similar to that which you go through when you leave the body at death. Your nightly dreams, moreover, are to be compared with the after-death states through which you regularly pass: both are phases of subjective activity of the doer; in both you live over your waking thoughts and actions, your senses still functioning in nature, but in the interior states of nature. And the nightly period of deep sleep, when the senses no longer function—the state of forgetfulness in which there is no memory of anything—corresponds to the blank period in which you wait on the threshold of the physical world until the moment you re-connect with your senses in a new body of flesh: the infant body or child body that has been fashioned for you.

When you commence a new life you are conscious, as in a haze. You feel that you are a distinct and definite something. This feeling of I-ness or selfness is probably the only real thing of which you are conscious for a considerable time. All else is mystery. For a while you are bewildered, perhaps even distressed, by your strange new body and unfamiliar surroundings. But as you learn how to operate your body and use its senses you tend gradually to identify yourself with it. Moreover, you are trained by other human beings to feel that your body is yourself; you are made to feel that you are the body.

Accordingly, as you come more and more under the control of your body senses, you become less and less conscious that you are something distinct from the body that you occupy. And as you grow out of childhood you will lose touch with practically everything that is not perceptible to the senses, or conceivable in terms of the senses; you will be mentally imprisoned in the physical world, conscious only of phenomena, of illusion. Under these conditions you are necessarily a lifelong mystery to yourself.

A greater mystery is your real Self—that greater Self which is not in your body; not in or of this world of birth and death; but which, consciously immortal in the all-pervading Realm of Permanence, is a presence with you through all your lifetimes, through all your interludes of sleep and death.

Man's lifelong search for something that will satisfy is in reality the quest for his real Self; the identity, the selfness and I-ness, which each one is dimly conscious of, and feels and desires to know. Hence the real Self is to be identified as Self-knowledge, the real though unrecognized goal of human seeking. It is the permanence, the perfection, the fulfillment, which is looked for but never found in human relations and effort. Further, the real Self is the ever-present counsellor and judge that speaks in the heart as conscience and duty, as rightness and reason, as law and justice—without which man would be little more than an animal.

There is such a Self. It is of the *Triune Self,* in this book so called because it is one indivisible unit of an *individual* trinity: of a knower part, a thinker part, and a doer part. Only a portion of the doer part can enter the animal body and make that body human. That embodied part is what is here termed the doer-in-the-body. In each human being the embodied doer is an inseparable part of its own Triune Self, which is a distinct unit among other Triune Selves. The thinker and knower parts of each Triune Self are in the Eternal, the Realm of Permanence, which pervades this our human world of birth and death and time. The doer-in-the-body is controlled by the senses and by the body; therefore it is not able to be conscious of the reality of the ever-present thinker and knower parts of its Triune Self. It misses them; the objects of the senses blind it, the coils of flesh hold it. It does not see beyond the objective forms; it fears to free itself from the fleshly coils, and stand alone. When the embodied doer proves itself willing and ready to dispel the glamour of the sense illusions, its thinker and knower are always ready to give it Light on the way to Self-knowledge. But the embodied doer in search for the thinker and knower looks abroad. Identity, or the real Self, has always been a mystery to thinking human beings in every civilization.

Plato, probably the most illustrious and representative of the philosophers of Greece, used as a precept to his followers in his school of philosophy, the Academy: "Know thyself"—*gnothi seauton.* From his writings it would appear that he had an understanding of the real Self, although none of the words that he used has been rendered into English as anything more adequate than "the soul". Plato used a method of inquiry concerning the finding of the real Self. There is great art in the exploiting of his characters; in producing his dramatic effects. His method of dialectics is simple and profound. The mentally lazy reader, who would rather be entertained than learn, will most likely think Plato tedious. Obviously his dialectic method was to train the mind, to be able to follow a course of reasoning, and to be not forgetful of the questions and answers in the dialogue; else one would be unable to judge the conclusions reached in the arguments. Surely, Plato did not intend to present the learner with a mass of knowledge. It is more likely that he intended to discipline the mind in thinking, so that by one's own thinking he would be enlightened and led to knowledge of his subject. This, the Socratic method, is a dialectical system of intelligent questions and answers which if followed will definitely help one to learn how to think; and in training the mind to think clearly Plato has done more perhaps than any other teacher. But no writings have come down to us in which he tells what thinking is, or what the mind is; or what the real Self is, or the way to knowledge of it. One must look further.

The ancient teaching of India is summed up in the cryptic statement: "that art thou" (*tat tvam asi*). The teaching does not make clear, however, what the "that" is or what the "thou" is; or in what way the "that" and the "thou" are related, or how they are to be identified. Yet if these words are to have meaning they should be explained in terms that are understandable. The substance of all Indian philosophy—to take a general view of the principal schools—seems to be that in man there is an immortal something which is and always has been an individual part of a composite or universal something, much as a drop of sea water is a part of the ocean, or as a spark is one with the flame in which it has its origin and being; and, further, that this individual something, this the embodied doer—or, as it is termed in the principal schools, the *atman,* or the *purusha,*—is separated from the universal something merely by the veil of sense illusion, maya, which causes the doer in the human to think of itself as separate and as an individual; whereas, the teachers declare, there is no individuality apart from the great universal something, termed Brahman.

The teaching is, further, that the embodied fragments of the universal Brahman are all subject to human existence and coincident suffering, unconscious of their supposed identity with the universal Brahman; bound to the wheel of births and deaths and re-embodiments in nature, until, after long ages, all the fragments gradually will have been re-united in the universal Brahman. The cause or the necessity or the desirability of Brahman's going through this arduous and painful procedure as fragments or drops is not, however, explained. Neither is it shown how the presumably perfect universal Brahman is or can be benefitted by it; or how any of its fragments profit; or how nature is benefitted. The whole of human existence would seem to be a useless ordeal without point or reason.

Nevertheless, a way is indicated by which a properly qualified individual, seeking "isolation," or "liberation" from the present mental bondage to nature, may by heroic effort pull away from the mass, or nature illusion, and go on ahead of the general escape from nature. Freedom is to be attained, it is said, through the practice of yoga; for through yoga, it is said, the thinking may be so disciplined that the *atman*, the *purusha*—the embodied doer—learns to suppress or destroy its feelings and desires, and dissipates the sense illusions in which its thinking has long been entangled; thus being freed from the necessity of further human existence, it is eventually reabsorbed into the universal Brahman.

In all of this there are vestiges of truth, and therefore of much good. The yogi learns indeed to control his body and to discipline his feelings and desires. He may learn to control his senses to the point where he can, at will, be conscious of states of matter interior to those ordinarily perceived by the untrained human senses, and may thus be enabled to explore and become acquainted with states in nature that are mysteries to most human beings. He may, further, attain to a high degree of mastery over some forces of nature. All of which unquestionably sets the individual apart from the great mass of undisciplined doers. But although the system of yoga purports to "liberate," or "isolate," the embodied self from the illusions of the senses, it seems clear that it actually never leads one beyond the confines of nature. This is plainly due to a misunderstanding concerning the mind.

The mind that is trained in yoga is the sense-mind, the intellect. It is that specialized instrument of the doer that is described in later pages as the body-mind, here distinguished from two other minds heretofore not distinguished: minds for the feeling and the desire of the doer. The body-mind is the only means by which the embodied doer can function through its senses. The functioning of the body-mind is limited strictly to the senses, and hence strictly to nature. Through it the human is conscious of the universe in its phenomenal aspect only: the world of time, of illusions. Hence, though the disciple does sharpen his intellect, it is at the same time evident that he is still dependent upon his senses, still entangled in nature, not freed from the necessity of continued re-existences in human bodies. In short, however adept a doer may be as the operator of its body machine, it cannot isolate or liberate itself from nature, cannot gain knowledge of itself or of its real Self, by thinking with its body-mind only; for such subjects are ever mysteries to the intellect, and can be understood only through the rightly coordinated functioning of the body-mind with the minds of feeling and desire.

It does not seem that the minds of feeling and of desire have been taken into account in the Eastern systems of thinking. The evidence of this is to be found in the four books of Patanjali's *Yoga Aphorisms,* and in the various commentaries on that ancient work. Patanjali is probably the most esteemed and representative of India's philosophers. His writings are profound. But it seems probable that his true teaching has been either lost or kept secret; for the delicately subtle sutras that bear his name would seem to frustrate or make impossible the very purpose for which they are ostensibly intended. How such a paradox could persist unquestioned through the centuries is to be explained only in the light of what is put forth in this and later chapters concerning feeling and desire in the human.

The Eastern teaching, like other philosophies, is concerned with the mystery of the conscious self in the human body, and the mystery of the relation between that self and its body, and nature, and the universe as a whole. But the Indian teachers do not show that they know what this the conscious self—the atman, the purusha, the embodied doer—is, as distinguished from nature: no clear distinction is made between the doer-in-the-body and the body which is of nature. The failure to see or to point out this distinction is evidently due to the universal misconception or misunderstanding of feeling and desire. It is necessary that feeling and desire be explained at this point.

A consideration of feeling and desire introduces one of the most important and far reaching subjects put forth in this book. Its significance and value cannot be overestimated. The understanding and use of feeling and desire may mean the turning point in the progress of the individual and of Humanity; it can liberate doers from false thinking, false beliefs, false goals, by which they have kept themselves in darkness. It disproves a false belief that has long been blindly accepted; a belief that is now so deeply rooted in the thinking of human beings that apparently no one has thought of questioning it.

It is this: Everybody has been taught to believe that the senses of the body are five in number, and that feeling is one of the senses. The senses, as stated in this book, are units of nature, elemental beings, conscious *as* their functions but unintelligent. There are only four senses: sight, hearing, taste, and smell; and for each sense there is a special organ; but there is no special organ for feeling because feeling—though it feels through the body—is not of the body, not of nature. It is one of the two aspects of the doer. Animals also have feeling and desire, but animals are modifications from the human, as explained later on.

The same must be said of desire, the other aspect of the doer. Feeling and desire must always be considered together, for they are inseparable; neither can exist without the other; they are like the two poles of an electric current, the two sides of a coin. Therefore this book makes use of the compound term: *feeling-and-desire.*

Feeling-and-desire of the doer is the intelligent power by which nature and the senses are moved. It is within the creative energy that is everywhere present; without it all life would cease. Feeling-and-desire is the beginningless and endless creative art by which all things are perceived, conceived, formed, brought forth, and controlled, whether through the agency of doers in human bodies or of those who are of The Government of the world, or of the great Intelligences. Feeling-and-desire is within all intelligent activity.

In the human body, feeling-and-desire is the conscious power which operates this individual nature machine. Not one of the four senses—feels. Feeling, the passive aspect of the doer, is that in the body which feels, which feels the body and feels the impressions that are transmitted to the body by the four senses, as sensations. Further, it can in varying degrees perceive supersensory impressions, such as a mood, an atmosphere, a premonition; it can feel what is right and what is wrong, and it can feel the warnings of conscience. Desire, the active aspect, is the conscious power that moves the body in the accomplishment of the doer's purpose. The doer functions simultaneously in both its aspects: thus every desire arises from a feeling, and every feeling gives rise to a desire.

You will be taking an important step on the way to knowledge of the conscious self in the body when you think of yourself as the intelligent feeling present through your voluntary nervous system, as distinct from the body which you feel, and simultaneously as the conscious power of desire surging through your blood, yet which is not the blood. Feeling-and-desire should synthesize the four senses. An understanding of the place and function of feeling-and-desire is the point of departure from the beliefs which for many ages have caused the doers in human beings to think of themselves merely as mortals. With this understanding of feeling-and-desire in the human, the philosophy of India may now be continued with new appreciation.

The Eastern teaching recognizes the fact that in order to attain to knowledge of the conscious self in the body, one must be freed from the illusions of the senses, and from the false thinking and action that result from failure to control one's own feelings and desires. But it does not transcend the universal misconception that feeling is one of the senses of the body. On the contrary, the teachers state that touch or feeling is a fifth sense; that desire is also of the body; and that both feeling and desire are things of nature in the body. According to this hypothesis it is argued that the *purusha,* or *atman*—the embodied doer, feeling-and-desire—must completely suppress feeling, and must utterly destroy, "kill out," desire.

In the light of what has been shown here concerning feeling-and-desire, it would seem that the teaching of the East is advising the impossible. The indestructible immortal self in the body cannot destroy itself. If it were possible for the human body to go on living without feeling-and-desire, the body would be a mere insensible breathing-mechanism.

Aside from their misunderstanding of feeling-and-desire the Indian teachers give no evidence of having a knowledge or understanding of the Triune Self. In the unexplained statement: "thou art that," it must be inferred that the "thou" who is addressed is the atman, the purusha—the individual embodied self; and that the "that" with which the "thou" is thus identified is the universal self, Brahman. There is no distinction made between the doer and its body; and likewise there is a corresponding failure to distinguish between the universal Brahman and universal nature. Through the doctrine of a universal Brahman as the source and end of all embodied individual selves, untold millions of doers have been kept in ignorance of their real Selves; and moreover have come to expect, even to aspire, to lose in the universal Brahman that which is the most precious thing that anyone can have: one's real identity, one's own individual great Self, among other individual immortal Selves.

Although it is clear that the Eastern philosophy tends to keep the doer attached to nature, and in ignorance of its real Self, it seems unreasonable and unlikely that these teachings could have been conceived in ignorance; that they could have been perpetuated with the intention of keeping people from the truth, and so in subjection. Rather, it is very probable that the existing forms, however ancient they may be, are merely the vestigial remnants of a much older system that had descended from a civilization vanished and almost forgotten: a teaching that may have been truly enlightening; that conceivably recognized feeling-and-desire as the immortal doer-in-the-body; that showed the doer the way to knowledge of its own real Self. The general features of the existing forms suggest such a probability; and that in the course of the ages the original teaching imperceptibly gave way to the doctrine of a universal Brahman and the paradoxical doctrines that would do away with the immortal feeling-and-desire as something objectionable.

There is a treasure that is not entirely hidden: *The Bhagavad Gita,* the most precious of India's jewels. It is India's pearl beyond price. The truths imparted by Krishna to Arjuna are sublime, beautiful, and ever-lasting. But the far-off historical period in which the drama is set and involved, and the ancient Vedic doctrines in which its truths are veiled and shrouded, make it too difficult for us to understand what the characters Krishna and Arjuna are; how they are related to each other; what the office of each is to the other, in or out of the body. The teaching in these justly venerated lines is full of meaning, and could be of great value. But it is so mixed with and obscured by archaic theology and scriptural doctrines that its significance is almost entirely hidden, and its real value is accordingly depreciated.

Owing to the general lack of clearness in the Eastern philosophy, and the fact that it appears to be self-contradictory as a guide to knowledge of oneself in the body and of one's real Self, the ancient teaching of India seems to be doubtful and undependable. One returns to the West.

Concerning Christianity: The actual origins and history of Christianity are obscure. A vast literature has grown out of centuries of effort to explain what the teachings are, or what they originally were intended to be. From the earliest times there has been much teaching of doctrine; but no writings have come down that show a knowledge of what was actually intended and taught in the beginning.

The parables and sayings in *The Gospels* bear evidence of grandeur, simplicity, and truth. Yet even those to whom the new message first was given appear not to have understood it. The books are direct, not intended to mislead; but at the same time they state that there is an inner meaning which is for the elect; a secret teaching intended not for everyone but for "whosoever will believe." Certainly, the books are full of mysteries; and it must be supposed that they cloak a teaching that was known to an initiated few. The Father, the Son, the Holy Ghost: these are mysteries. Mysteries, too, are the Immaculate Conception and the birth and life of Jesus; likewise his crucifixion, death, and resurrection. Mysteries, undoubtedly, are heaven and hell, and the devil, and the Kingdom of God; for it is scarcely likely that these subjects were meant to be understood in terms of the senses, rather than as symbols. Moreover, throughout the books there are phrases and terms that plainly are not to be taken too literally, but rather in a mystical sense; and others clearly could have significance only to selected groups. Further, it is not reasonable to suppose that the parables and miracles could have been related as literal truths. Mysteries throughout—but nowhere are the mysteries revealed. What is all this mystery?

The very evident purpose of *The Gospels* is to teach the understanding and living of an inner life; an interior life which would regenerate the human body and thereby conquer death, restoring the physical body to eternal life, the state from which it is said to have fallen—its "fall" being "the original sin." At one time there certainly must have been a definite system of instruction which would make clear exactly how one might live such an interior life: how one might, through so doing, come into the knowledge of one's real Self. The existence of such a secret teaching is suggested in the early Christian writings by references to secrets and mysteries. Moreover it seems obvious that the parables are allegories, similes: homely stories and figures of speech, serving as vehicles for conveying not merely moral examples and ethical teachings, but also certain inner, eternal truths as parts of a definite system of instruction. However, *The Gospels,* as they exist today, lack the connections which would be needed to formulate a system; what has come down to us is not enough. And, concerning the mysteries in which such teachings supposedly were concealed, no known key or code has been given to us with which we might unlock or explain them.

The ablest and most definite expositor of the early doctrines that we know of is Paul. The words he used were intended to make his meaning clear to those to whom they were addressed; but now his writings need to be interpreted in terms of the present day. "The First Epistle of Paul to the Corinthians," the fifteenth chapter, alludes to and reminds of certain teachings; certain definite instructions concerning the living of an interior life. But it is to be assumed that those teachings either were not committed to writing—which would appear understandable—or· else that they were lost or have been left out of the writings that have come down. At all events, "The Way" is not shown.

Why were the truths given in the form of mysteries? The reason might have been that the laws of the period prohibited the spreading of new doctrines. The circulating of a strange teaching or doctrine could have been punishable by death. Indeed, the legend is that Jesus suffered death by crucifixion for his teaching of the truth and the way and the life.

But today, it is said, there is freedom of speech: one may state without fear of death what one believes concerning the mysteries of life. What anyone thinks or knows about the constitution and functioning of the human body and of the conscious self that inhabits it, the truth or opinions that one may have concerning the relation between the embodied self and its real Self, and regarding the way to knowledge—these need not be hidden, today, in words of mystery requiring a key or a code for their understanding. In modern times all "hints" and "blinds," all "secrets" and "initiations," in a special mystery language, should be evidence of ignorance, egotism, or sordid commercialism.

Notwithstanding mistakes and divisions and sectarianism; notwithstanding a great variety of interpretations of its mystical doctrines, Christianity has spread to all parts of the world. Perhaps more than any other faith, its teachings have helped to change the world. There must be truths in the teachings, however they may be hidden, which, for nearly two thousand years, have reached into human hearts and awakened the Humanity in them.

Everlasting truths are inherent in Humanity, in the Humanity which is the totality of all the doers in human bodies. These truths cannot be suppressed or entirely forgotten. In whatever age, in whatever philosophy or faith, the truths will appear and reappear, whatever their changing forms.

One form in which certain of these truths are cast is Freemasonry. The Masonic order is as old as the human race. It has teachings of great value; far greater, in fact, than is appreciated by the Masons who are their custodians. The order has preserved ancient bits of priceless information concerning the building of an everlasting body for one who is consciously immortal. Its central mystery drama is concerned with the rebuilding of a temple which was destroyed. This is very significant. The temple is the symbol of the human body which man must rebuild, regenerate, into a physical body that will be eternal, everlasting; a body that will be a fitting habitation for the then consciously immortal doer. "The Word" which is "lost" is the doer, lost in its human body—the ruins of the once great temple; but which will find itself as the body is regenerated and the doer takes control of it.

This book brings you more Light, more Light on your thinking; Light to find your "Way" through life. The Light that it brings, however, is not a light of nature; it is a new Light; new, because, although it has been a presence with you, you have not known it. In these pages it is termed the Conscious Light within; it is the Light that can show you things as they are, the Light of the Intelligence to which you are related. It is because of the presence of this Light that you are able to think in creating thoughts; thoughts to bind you to objects of nature, or to free you from objects of nature, as you choose and will. Real thinking is the steady holding and focussing of the Conscious Light within on the subject of the thinking. By your thinking you make your destiny. Right thinking is the way to knowledge of yourself. That which can show you the way, and which can lead you on your way, is the Light of the Intelligence, the Conscious Light within. In later chapters it is told how this Light should be used in order to have more Light.

The book shows that thoughts are real things, real beings. The only real things which man creates are his thoughts. The book shows the mental processes by which thoughts are created; and that many thoughts are more lasting than the body or brain through which they are created. It shows that the thoughts man thinks are the potentials, the blue prints, the designs, the models from which he builds out the tangible material things with which he has changed the face of nature, and made what is called his way of living and his civilization. Thoughts are the ideas or forms out of which and upon which civilizations are built and maintained and destroyed. The book explains how the unseen thoughts of man exteriorize as the acts and objects and events of his individual and collective life, creating his destiny through life after life on earth. But it also shows how man can learn to think without creating thoughts, and thus control his own destiny.

The word *mind* as commonly used is the all-inclusive term which is made to apply to all kinds of thinking, indiscriminately. It is generally supposed that man has only one mind. Actually three different and distinct minds, that is, ways for thinking with the Conscious Light, are being used by the embodied doer. These, previously mentioned, are: the body-mind, the feeling-mind, and the desire-mind. Mind is the functioning of intelligent-matter. A mind therefore does not function independently of the doer. The functioning of each of the three minds is dependent upon the embodied feeling-and-desire, the doer.

The body-mind is that which is commonly spoken of as the mind, or the intellect. It is the functioning of feeling-and-desire as the mover of physical nature, as the operator of the human body machine, and hence is here called the body-mind. It is the only mind that is geared to and that acts in phase with and through the senses of the body. Thus it is the instrument by means of which the doer is conscious of and may act upon and within and through the matter of the physical world.

The feeling-mind and the desire-mind are the functioning of feeling and of desire irrespective of or in connection with the physical world. These two minds are almost completely submerged in and controlled and subordinated by the body-mind. Therefore practically all human thinking has been made to conform to the thinking of the body-mind, which ties the doer to nature and prevents its thinking of itself as something distinct from the body.

That which today is called psychology is not a science. Modern psychology has been defined as the study of human behavior. This must be taken to mean that it is the study of impressions from objects and forces of nature that are made through the senses upon the human mechanism, and the response of the human mechanism to the impressions thus received. But that is not psychology.

There cannot be any kind of psychology as a science, until there is some kind of understanding of what the psyche is, and what the mind is; and a realization of the processes of thought, of how the mind functions, and of the causes and results of its functioning. Psychologists admit that they do not know what these things are. Before psychology can become a true science there must be some understanding of the interrelated functioning of the three minds of the doer. This is the foundation upon which can be developed a true science of the mind and of human relations. In these pages it is shown how the feeling and desire are directly related to the sexes, explaining that in a man the feeling aspect is dominated by desire and that in a woman the desire aspect is dominated by feeling; and that in every human the functioning of the now dominant body-mind is more nearly attuned to the one or the other of these, according to the sex of the body in which they are functioning; and it is shown, further, that all human relations are dependent upon the functioning of the body-minds of men and women in their relations to each other.

Modern psychologists prefer not to use the word *soul,* although it has been in general use in the English language for many centuries. The reason for this is that all that has been said concerning what the soul is or what it does, or the purpose that it serves, has been too unclear, too doubtful and confusing, to warrant the scientific study of the subject. Instead, the psychologists have therefore taken as the subject of their study the human animal machine and its behavior. It has long been understood and agreed by people generally, however, that man is made up of "body, soul, and spirit." No one doubts that the body is an animal organism; but concerning spirit and soul there has been much uncertainty and speculation. On these vital subjects this book is explicit.

The book shows that the living soul is an actual and literal fact. It shows that its purpose and its functioning are of great importance in the universal plan, and that it is indestructible. It is explained that that which has been called the soul is a nature unit—an elemental, a unit of an element; and that this conscious but unintelligent entity is the furthest advanced of all the nature units in the make-up of the body: it is the senior elemental unit in the body organization, having progressed to that function after a long apprenticeship in the myriad lesser functions comprising nature. Being thus the sum of all of nature's laws, this unit is qualified to act as the automatic general manager of nature in the human body mechanism; as such it serves the immortal doer through all its re-existences by periodically building a new fleshly body for the doer to come into, and maintaining and repairing that body for as long as the destiny of the doer may require, as determined by the doer's thinking.

This unit is termed the *breath-form.* The active aspect of the breath-form is the breath; the breath is the life, the spirit, of the body; it permeates the entire structure. The other aspect of the breath-form, the passive aspect, is the form or model, the pattern, the mold, according to which the physical structure is built out into visible, tangible existence by the action of the breath. Thus the two aspects of the breath-form represent life and form, by which structure exists.

So the statement that man consists of body, soul, and spirit can readily be understood as meaning that the physical body is composed of gross matter; that the spirit is the life of the body, the living breath, the breath of life; and that the soul is the inner form, the imperishable model, of the visible structure; and thus that the living soul is the perpetual breath-form which shapes, maintains, repairs, and rebuilds the fleshly body of man.

The breath-form, in certain phases of its functioning, includes that which psychology has termed the subconscious mind, and the unconscious. It manages the involuntary nervous system. In this work it functions according to the impressions which it receives from nature. It also carries out the voluntary movements of the body, as prescribed by the thinking of the doer-in-the-body. Thus it functions as a buffer between nature and the immortal sojourner in the body; an automaton blindly responding to the impacts of objects and forces of nature, and to the thinking of the doer.

Your body is literally the result of your thinking. Whatever it may show of health or disease, you make it so by your thinking and feeling and desiring. Your present body of flesh is actually an expression of your imperishable soul, your breath-form; it is thus an exteriorization of the thoughts of many lifetimes. It is a visible record of your thinking and doings as a doer, up to the present. In this fact lies the germ of the body's perfectibility and immortality.

There is nothing so very strange today in the idea that man will one day attain to conscious immortality; that he will eventually regain a state of perfection from which he originally fell. Such a teaching in varying forms has been generally current in the West for nearly two thousand years. During that time it has spread through the world so that hundreds of millions of doers, re-existing on earth through the centuries, have been brought into recurrent contact with the idea as an inwardly apprehended truth. Though there is still very little understanding of it, and still less thinking about it; though it has been distorted to satisfy the feelings and desires of different people; and though it may be regarded variously today with indifference, levity, or sentimental awe, the idea is a part of the general thought pattern of present day Humanity, and therefore is deserving of thoughtful consideration.

Some statements in this book, however, will quite possibly seem strange, even fantastic, until enough thought has been given to them. For instance: the idea that the human physical body may be made incorruptible, everlasting; may be regenerated and restored to a state of perfection and eternal life from which the doer long ago caused it to fall; and, further, the idea that that state of perfection and eternal life is to be gained, not after death, not in some far away nebulous hereafter, but in

the physical world while one is alive. This may indeed seem very strange, but when examined intelligently it will not appear to be unreasonable.

What is unreasonable is that the physical body of man must die; still more unreasonable is the proposition that it is only by dying that one can live forever. Scientists have of late been saying that there is no reason why the life of the body should not be extended indefinitely, although they do not suggest how this could be accomplished. Certainly, human bodies have always been subject to death; but they die simply because no reasonable effort has been made to regenerate them. In this book, in the chapter *The Great Way*, it is stated how the body can be regenerated, can be restored to a state of perfection and be made a temple for the complete Triune Self.

Sex power is another mystery which man must solve. It should be a blessing. Instead, man very often makes of it his enemy, his devil, that is ever with him and from which he cannot escape. This book shows how, by thinking, to use it as the great power for good which it should be; and how by understanding and self-control to regenerate the body and accomplish one's aims and ideals in ever progressive degrees of accomplishment.

Every human being is a double mystery: the mystery of himself, and the mystery of the body he is in. He has and is the lock and key to the double mystery. The body is the lock, and he is the key in the lock. A purpose of this book is to tell you how to understand yourself as the key to the mystery of yourself; how to find yourself in the body; how to find and know your real Self as Self-knowledge; how to use yourself as the key to open the lock which is your body; and, through your body, how to understand and know the mysteries of nature. You are in, and you are the operator of, the individual body machine of nature; it acts and reacts with and in relation to nature. When you solve the mystery of yourself as the doer of your Self-knowledge and the operator of your body machine, you will know—in each detail and altogether—that the functions of the units of your body are laws of nature. You will then know the known as well as the unknown laws of nature, and be able to work in harmony with the great nature machine through its individual body machine in which you are.

Another mystery is time. Time is ever present as an ordinary topic of conversation; yet when one tries to think about it and tell what it really is, it becomes abstract, unfamiliar; it cannot be held, one fails to grasp it; it eludes, escapes, and is beyond one. What it is has not been explained.

Time is the change of units, or of masses of units, in their relation to each other. This simple definition applies everywhere and under every state or condition, but it must be thought of and applied before one can understand it. The doer must understand time while in the body, awake. Time seems to be different in other worlds and states. To the conscious doer time seems not to be the same while awake as while in dreams, or while in deep sleep, or when the body dies, or while passing through the after-death states, or while waiting for the building and the birth of the new body it will inherit on earth. Each one of these time periods has an "In the beginning," a succession, and an end. Time seems to crawl in childhood, run in youth, and race in ever increasing speed until death of the body.

Time is the web of change, woven from the eternal to the changing human body. The loom on which the web is woven is the breath-form. The body-mind is the maker and operator of the loom, spinner of the web, and weaver of the veils called "past" or "present" or "future". Thinking makes the loom of time, thinking spins the web of time, thinking weaves the veils of time; and the body-mind does the thinking.

CONSCIOUSNESS is another mystery, the greatest and most profound of all mysteries. The word Consciousness is unique; it is a coined English word; its equivalent does not appear in other languages. Its all-important value and meaning are not, however, appreciated. This will be seen in the uses that the word is made to serve. To give some common examples of its misuse: It is heard in such expressions as "my consciousness," and "one's consciousness"; and in such as animal consciousness, human consciousness, physical, psychic, cosmic, and other *kinds* of consciousness. And it is described as normal consciousness, and greater and deeper, and higher and lower, inner and outer, consciousness; and full and partial consciousness. Mention is also heard of the beginnings of consciousness, and of a change of consciousness. One hears people say that they have experienced or caused a growth, or an extension, or an expansion, of consciousness. A very common misuse of the word is in such phrases as: to lose consciousness, to hold to consciousness; to regain, to use, to develop consciousness. And one hears, further, of various states, and planes, and degrees, and conditions of consciousness. Consciousness is too great to be thus qualified, limited, or prescribed. Out of regard for this fact this book makes use of the phrase: to be *conscious of,* or *as,* or *in.* To explain: whatever is conscious is either

conscious *of* certain things, or *as* what it is, or is conscious *in* a certain degree of being conscious.

Consciousness is the ultimate, the final Reality. Consciousness is that by the presence of which all things are conscious. Mystery of all mysteries, it is beyond comprehension. Without it nothing can be conscious; no one could think; no being, no entity, no force, no unit, could perform any function. Yet Consciousness itself performs no function: it does not act in any way; it is a presence, everywhere. And it is because of its presence that all things are conscious in whatever degree they are conscious. Consciousness is not a cause. It cannot be moved or used or in any way affected by anything. Consciousness is not the result of anything, nor does it depend on anything. It does not increase or diminish, expand, extend, contract, or change; or vary in any way. Although there are countless degrees *in* being conscious, there are no degrees of Consciousness: no planes, no states; no grades, divisions, or variations of any sort; it is the same everywhere, and in all things, from a primordial nature unit to the Supreme Intelligence. Consciousness has no properties, no qualities, no attributes; it does not possess; it cannot be possessed. Consciousness never began; it cannot cease to be. Consciousness IS.

In all your lives on earth you have been indefinably seeking, expecting or looking for someone or something that is missing. You vaguely feel that if you could but find that for which you long, you would be content, satisfied. Dimmed memories of the ages surge up; they are the present feelings of your forgotten past; they compel a recurring world-weariness of the ever-grinding treadmill of experiences and of the emptiness and futility of human effort. You may have sought to satisfy that feeling with family, by marriage, by children, among friends; or, in business, wealth, adventure, discovery, glory, authority, and power—or by whatever other undiscovered secret of your heart. But nothing of the senses can really satisfy that longing. The reason is that you are lost—are a lost but inseparable part of a consciously immortal Triune Self. Ages ago, you, as feeling-and-desire, the doer part, left the thinker and knower parts of your Triune Self. So you were lost to yourself because, without some understanding of your Triune Self, you cannot understand yourself, your longing, and your being lost. Therefore you have at times felt lonely. You have forgotten the many parts you have often played in this world, as personalities; and you have also forgotten the real beauty and power of which you were conscious while with your thinker and knower in the Realm of Permanence. But you, as doer, long for balanced union of your feeling-and-desire in a perfect body, so that you will again be with your thinker and knower parts, as the Triune Self, in the Realm of Permanence. In ancient writings there have been allusions to that departure, in such phrases as "the original sin," "the fall of man," as from a state and realm in which one is satisfied. That state and realm from which you departed cannot cease to be; it can be regained by the living, but not after death by the dead.

You need not feel alone. Your thinker and knower are with you. On ocean or in forest, on mountain or plain, in sunlight or shadow, in crowd or in solitude; wherever you are, your really thinking and knowing Self is with you. Your real Self will protect you, in so far as you will allow yourself to be protected. Your thinker and knower are ever ready for your return, however long it may take you to find and follow the path and become at last again consciously at home with them as the Triune Self.

In the meantime you will not be, you cannot be, satisfied with anything less than Self-knowledge. You, as feeling-and-desire, are the responsible doer of your Triune Self; and from what you have made for yourself as your destiny you must learn the two great lessons which all experiences of life are to teach. These lessons are:

What to do;
and,
What not to do.

You may put these lessons off for as many lives as you please, or learn them as soon as you will—that is for you to decide; but in the course of time you will learn them.

CHAPTER II

THE PURPOSE AND PLAN
OF THE UNIVERSE

SECTION 1

*There is a purpose and a plan in the Universe. The law of thought.
Religions. The soul. Theories concerning the destiny of the soul.*

The Universe is guided according to a purpose and a plan. There is a simple law by which the purpose is accomplished and according to which the plan is carried out. That law is universal: it reaches all entities without exception. Gods and the weakest beings are equally powerless against it. It rules this visible world of change, and it affects the worlds and spheres beyond. At present it can be understood by man only as it affects human beings, though it is possible that its operations in animate nature may be seen. It affects human beings according to the responsibility which can be charged to them; and it determines their duty, measured by their responsibility.

This is the law: Every thing existing on the physical plane is an exteriorization of a thought, which must be balanced through the one who issued the thought, and in accordance with that one's responsibility, at the conjunction of time, condition, and place.

This law of thought is destiny. It has aspects which have been expressed by such terms as kismet, nemesis, karma, fate, fortune, foreordination, predestination, Providence, the Will of God, the law of cause and effect, the law of causation, retribution, punishment and reward, hell and heaven. The law of thought includes all that is in these terms, but it means more than all of them; it means, essentially, that thinking is the basic factor in shaping human destiny.

25

The law of thought is present everywhere and rules everywhere; and is the law to which all other human laws are subservient. There is no deviation from, no exception to, this universal law of thought. It adjusts the mutually interdependent thoughts and plans and acts of the billions of men and women who have died and lived and who will continue to live and die on this earth. Happenings beyond number, some apparently accounted for, some apparently inexplicable, are marshalled to fit into the limiting framework of time and place and causation; facts innumerable, near and far, apposite and contradictory, related and unrelated, are worked into one whole harmonious pattern. It is only by the operation of this law that people exist together on the earth. Not only physical acts and their results are thus ordered; the invisible world in which thoughts originate is likewise adjusted. All this adjustment and universal harmony out of selfish discord is brought about by the action of universal forces operating under the law.

The mechanical part of the operation of this law in the physical world may not be apparent. Yet, every stone, every plant, every animal, every human, and every event has a place in the great machinery for the working out of the law of thought, as destiny; each performs a function in the machine, whether as a gear, a gauge, a pin, or a transmission. However insignificant a part a man may seem to play, he starts the machinery of the law when he starts to think; and by his thinking he contributes to its continued operation. The machinery of the law is nature.

Nature is a machine composed of the totality of unintelligent units; units which are conscious as their function only. The nature machine is a machine composed of laws, through the worlds; it is perpetuated and operated by intelligent and immortal Ones, complete Triune Selves, who administer the laws from their individual university machines through which as unintelligent nature units they have passed; and as intelligent units in the Realm of Permanence (Fig. II-G; H), they have qualified as Governors, in The Government of the world.

The university machines are perfect physical bodies composed of balanced nature units; all units are related in and organized into the four systems of the perfect body and are coordinated as one entire and perfect whole mechanism; each unit is conscious as its function only, and each function in the university machine is a law of nature through the worlds.

Only the phenomena of the machinery are seen; the nature machine itself is not seen by mortal eyes; neither are the forces which work it. The

Intelligences and complete Triune Selves who direct the operation cannot be seen by the human. Hence come the many theories about the creation of the human world, and about the nature and powers of gods and the origin and nature and destiny of the human. Such theories are furnished by various systems of religion.

Religions center about a God or gods. These deities are credited with universal powers to account for the operation of universal forces. Gods and forces alike, however, are subject to the Intelligences and the complete Triune Selves, who rule this world according to the law of thought. It is due to the operation of this law as destiny that events occur on the physical plane in the harmonious manner which makes certain the continuance of the law's operation so that the plan of the Universe may be carried out and its purpose accomplished.

Religions have been substitutes for what a knowledge of the law of thought should be, and for what it eventually will be to man, when the human is able to stand more Light. Among such substitutes is a belief in a God who is supposed to be all-wise, all-powerful, ever-present; but whose alleged actions are arbitrary and capricious and show jealousy, vindictiveness, and cruelty. Such religions have held the minds of men in bondage. In this bondage they have received fragmentary and distorted information about the law of thought; what they received was all they could stand at the time. In every age one of the Gods was represented as a ruler, and as the giver of a law of justice; but his own acts did not seem just. A solution of this difficulty was sometimes found in an after death adjustment in a heaven or a hell; at other times the matter was left open. As the human becomes more enlightened he will find in the clear and precise understanding of the law of thought that which will satisfy his sense and reason; and he will accordingly outgrow the need for belief in the doctrine, or of fear and faith in the decrees of a personal God.

The rationality of the law of thought is in marked contrast to the various contradictory or irrational teachings concerning the origin and nature and destiny of that which has been called the soul; and it should dissipate the general ignorance that has existed concerning the soul. An error is commonly made in believing that the soul is something above or superior to that which is conscious in the human. The fact is that the conscious self in the body is of the doer of the Triune Self and that the "soul" is merely the form of the breath-form or "living soul", which still belongs to nature but which must be advanced beyond nature by the

Triune Self. In that sense only is it correct to speak of the need of "saving one's soul".

Concerning the origin of the soul, there are two principal theories: one is that the soul is an emanation from the Supreme Being or One, as the source of all creatures and from whom all come into existence and into whom all return; the other theory is that the soul comes from a previous existence—either down from a superior state or up from a lower. There is another belief, current mainly in the West, that each soul lives but one life on earth and is a special, fresh creation furnished by God to every human body brought into the world by a man and a woman.

As to the destiny of the soul after death, the theories are chiefly these: that the soul is annihilated; that it returns to the essence from which it came; that it goes back to the God by whom it was created; that it goes immediately either to heaven or hell; that before going to its final destination it enters a purgatory; that it sleeps or rests until it is resurrected on the Day of Judgment when it is examined and sent forthwith to hell or to paradise. Then there is also the belief that the soul returns to earth for experience necessary to its progress. Of these, the belief in annihilation is favored among materialists, while the beliefs in resurrection and in heaven and hell are held by most religions, both of the East and the West.

The religions which teach of emanation and reincarnation include not only the worship of a godhead, but the doctrine of the improvement of the conscious self in the body and the corresponding improvement of the nature-matter with which the embodied self comes into contact. The religions which are based upon a personal God are primarily for the purpose of glorifying the God, the improvement of the embodied doer being secondary and acquired as a reward for worshipping that God. The nature of a religion and of its God or gods is indicated unequivocally by the requirements of the worship; and by the symbols, hymns, rites, ornaments, vestments, and edifices that are used in its practice.

No teaching has been generally accepted which states that the individual is solely responsible for whatever happens to him. This is due to the fact that a vague sentiment of fear, arising from religious teachings, affects all persons who share the notions of the majority of their contemporaries concerning the origin and nature, the purpose and destiny, of the human.

SECTION 2

The soul.

Nearly everyone who hears or uses the word soul fancies that he knows what it means. But he cannot define it or explain it because he does not know what the soul is, or what it does or does not do. As to the meaning of soul no religion makes any clear statement of what it is; yet if it were not for that unknown and undescribed something there would be no reason or excuse for a religion. The something called the soul was not suddenly spoken into being; nor was it created in any other way.

The soul is not intelligent, but it is indispensable to the human. It is a unit of nature-matter; and it is the result of a long course of progression which will be properly explained in later pages. For the moment it will be enough to say that the processing of a unit of nature-matter results in its being finally the breath-form of a physical body. The breath-form, as already stated in the introductory chapter, is the living soul of the body. The form aspect of the breath-form is the progressed nature unit referred to above, and is the passive or formative aspect of the breath-form. The active aspect of the breath-form is the breath; this breath aspect is the life of the form and the builder of the body to be. Originally the form, the soul, was perfect; it was a balanced nature unit in a perfect, immortal physical body in and of the nature Realm of Permanence. Nothing in nature could deform that perfect form; its perfect body was inhabited and operated by the doer part of an immortal Triune Self. That doer was feeling-and-desire; it had charge of the breath-form, and it alone could change the form aspect of the breath-form; only the doer could change that perfect physical body. That its body is now human, mortal, and imperfect is the result of the doer's action.

The doers which are now in the imperfect bodies of men and women on this earth once made a fatal mistake. In passing through the necessary trial test of bringing feeling-and-desire into balanced union, they allowed themselves to succumb to the spell cast by the natural functioning of the body-mind through the senses. As feeling-and-desire, those doers lost their balance, their self-control, that is, control of their feeling-and-desire minds, and of the body-mind by which they had maintained their body of units in balance. Control passed to the body-mind of each of these doers, and the doers thereby fell under the illusion of the senses, and thereafter thought only in the terms of the phenomena of time, of birth and death. All doers now in human bodies are among those who made that mistake. Those who did not make that mistake, those who maintained their balance, their self-control, who controlled the body-mind by their feeling- and desire-minds, passed the test and qualified as high officers of nature; they have their parts in The Government in the Realm of Permanence, and of this human world of change, (Fig. V-B,a).

Every human body that comes into this world is fashioned in its mother according to the form, the soul, which enters her body through her breath and causes the conception of the body which is to be fashioned. At birth the physical life-breath of the breath-form enters the infant body, and in the heart it unites with the form aspect and then is the breath-form; thereupon the breath-form performs its functions as the "living soul" of the body. The form is, and throughout that lifetime it will be, the type or pattern according to which the living breath of the breath-form will build out into a visible structure the units of nature-matter—solid, fluid, airy, and radiant—of which that changing body is composed. When the doer separates from the body at death the breath-form leaves with it. The nature units of which the body is composed return to the four states or elements to which they belong. The form aspect of the breath-form, that is, the "soul", accompanying the doer portion that had been in the body, passes through the various after-death states, (Fig. V-D); and according to the doer's destiny it will in due time be again the form which will be the cause of the conception and the form for the building up of another human body, another nature machine in which the re-existing doer will resume its work in the world, and live out that portion of its destiny which it had made, by its thinking.

From these statements it will be seen that the vague and indeterminate, equivocal and bewildering term soul alludes to that very important elemental entity, the breath-form—a nature unit which is conscious as its function—in the most advanced degree in nature, (Fig. II-H).

To briefly restate at this point certain facts made evident in the Introduction: The doer is feeling-and-desire in the body. Feeling, though generally believed to be a fifth sense as touch, is not a sense; it is not of nature. Feeling is the passive side, or aspect, of the doer; desire is the active side. Feeling-and-desire in the body are not two or separate: they blend into each other and are always functioning together, an inseparable twain, the opposites in the doer. One dominates the other and had determined the sex of the body.

That which feels and desires and thinks in the human body, that which experiences and does the things that are done in the world, is the doer. That doer-in-the-body, however, is only one of twelve portions of the entire doer. These twelve portions are inseparable, but each portion re-exists separately; the twelve re-exist successively, one after another, one at a time, in life after life.

The entire doer is only one part, the psychic part, of the three integral parts of its immortal Triune Self. The other two are the thinker, the mental part, and the knower, the noetic part. Because of the imperfections and limitations of the human body, the thinker and knower parts of the Triune Self do not dwell in the body as does the embodied portion of the doer part; they merely contact the body by means of nerve centers. Hereafter, for the sake of brevity when the meaning of the text is clear, the single word doer will be used instead of such words as doer-in-the-body, embodied doer portion, the portion of the doer existing in the human body.

SECTION 3

Outline of a system of the Universe. Time. Space. Dimensions.

In this section is presented a comprehensive system of the Universe,—a system of development by progression, not evolution.

This system takes in the Universe in its entirety, in its largest divisions and in its smallest parts; it shows the place of the human body in relation to the physical universe, and of the human in relation to his Triune Self and the Supreme Intelligence of the Universe; and, finally, Consciousness, the ultimate One Reality.

The system is all-inclusive; yet it is compact, logical and easy to apprehend or imagine. It can be tested by its scope, by its unity, by its simplicity, its analogies, its interrelations, and by the absence of contradictions.

Current classifications, such as God, nature, and man; body, soul, and spirit; matter, force, and consciousness; good and evil; the visible and the invisible, are insufficient; they are makeshifts, not parts of a system, yet these various entities and things have each a place in the vast scheme, but what place has not been shown.

This system shows a Universe which consists of nature-matter and intelligent-matter, and Consciousness which is the same in both kinds of matter. Matter differs in the degree in which it is conscious. All matter as units on the nature-side is conscious, but merely conscious—each unit being conscious *as* its function only; all matter on the intelligent-side at least can be conscious that it is conscious; that is the distinction between the units of unintelligent nature-matter and of intelligent-matter. The purpose of the Universe is to make all units of matter conscious in progressively higher degrees, so that nature-matter shall become intelligent-matter; and, further, so that intelligent-matter shall increase in being conscious until ultimately it becomes Consciousness. The purpose of the Universe may be comprehended by distinguishing beings, that is, units of the elements, elementals, out of the mass of matter, as they progress through the various stages or states in which matter is conscious. The progression of these nature units is accomplished while they are on ground which is common to all nature units. In the world of birth and death the common ground is the human body.

The human body is on the lowest degree of the physical plane of all the worlds and spheres. The units of the matter of the world of birth and death are kept circulating through, or in contact with, human bodies. By means of this circulation all physical acts, objects, and events are brought about.

In order to understand the human body and its relation to this complex Universe and the relation of the doer in that body to the nature-side and to the intelligent-side of the Universe, it is well to examine the Universe as a whole and in all its parts. In the following propositions certain words are given specific meanings; they are used for lack of more adequate terms, for example: fire, air, water, earth, for the spheres; and light, life, form, physical, for the worlds and planes.

The spheres, worlds, and planes have each an unmanifested and a manifested side; the unmanifested side permeates and sustains the manifested, (Fig. I-A, B, C). In the diagrams they are shown as an upper and a lower half. Let it be understood that the point of coincidence of the spheres, worlds, and planes is their common center, and not at the lowest part of the circles. The diagrams are drawn as they are in order to show relations, which cannot well be done with a set of concentric circles.

Concerning the nature-side of the Universe:

1) The Universe exists in four vast primordial and fundamental spheres: the spheres of fire, air, water, and earth, as elements, (Fig. I-A). The fire element permeates the air element, that reaches through the water element and that passes into the earth element. The units of the matter of the four spheres are conscious as fire, air, water, and earth units. These units of the elements are behind and are the basis of manifestation of the units of the worlds.

2) In the manifested part of the sphere of earth is the light world; in the manifested part of the light world is the life world; in the manifested part of the life world is the form world; and in the manifested part of the form world is the physical world, (Fig. I-B). In other words, the physical world is permeated, supported, and surrounded by three other worlds. The physical world may be considered from two viewpoints, (Fig. II-G): As the Realm of Permanence, and, as the temporal human world which is in part visible to the eye,—as is being done in the following pages.

3) In each of the four worlds there are four planes, namely, the light plane, the life plane, the form plane, and the physical plane. Each of these planes corresponds and relates to one of the four worlds, (Fig. I-C).

4) The physical plane of the human physical world contains all that is spoken of as the physical universe. It is made up of four states of matter, namely, the radiant, the airy, the fluid, and the solid states, (Fig. I-D). Each of these states of physical matter is of four substates, (Fig. I-E). Only the solid state and its four substates are at present subject to physical and chemical investigation.

5) In the physical universe that is visible to the human eye is the earth, the world of time, of sex, of birth and death; it is made up of and its human bodies are composed of unbalanced units, (Fig. II-B); that is, units that are either active-passive or passive-active, male or female; bodies that alternate, that die. Within and beyond and pervading this physical world of time is the permanent physical world, invisible to us, the Realm of Permanence, (Fig. II-G); it is made up of balanced units, units that are balanced and therefore do not alternate from passive to active, and the reverse, (Fig. II-C). Bodies of balanced units of the Realm of Permanence do not die; they are perfect and everlasting; they do not change in the sense that unbalanced units do; they progress in being conscious in successively higher degrees, according to the Eternal Order of Progression.

Concerning the human body:

6) A human body is the model or plan of the changing universe; in it nature units pass through series of the fourfold states of nature-matter.

7) Thus four physical masses of units constitute the human body, (Fig. III): the visible, solid-solid body, and three inner, invisible, unformed masses or potential bodies, namely, the fluid-solid, the airy-solid, and the radiant-solid, which are at present beyond scientific investigation. Among this fourfold constitution of the human body and the fourfold constitution of the spheres, worlds, and planes there is an interrelation, an action and reaction.

8) Radiations from these four masses or bodies extend as zones around the solid-solid body; together they make up the physical atmosphere of the human body, (Fig. III; V-B). In addition to this physical atmosphere, which is made up of nature units, there are three other atmospheres, the psychic, mental, and noetic atmospheres of the Triune Self, which reach into the physical atmosphere and relate to the form, life, and light planes of the physical world, (Fig. V-B). Further, those parts of the noetic, mental, and psychic atmospheres of the Triune Self, which are within the radiations of the fourfold, visible, solid-solid body, are here spoken of as the atmospheres of the human.

9) The human body is built in four sections or cavities: the head, the thorax, the abdomen, and the pelvis. These relate to the four planes of the physical world, to the four worlds of the sphere of earth, and the four great spheres of the elements of fire, air, water, and earth. That is:

10) The pelvic cavity relates to the physical plane; the abdominal cavity relates to the form plane; the thoracic cavity relates to the life plane, and the head relates to the light plane of the physical world. Similarly, these four cavities of the body relate respectively to the physical, form, life, and light worlds, and to the four spheres of earth, water, air, and fire.

11) In the body there are four systems. The systems relate respectively to the same planes and worlds and spheres as do the sections. The digestive system is of the physical plane, of the physical world, and of the earth; the circulatory system is of the form plane, the form world, and the water; the respiratory system is of the life plane, the life world, and the air; and the generative system is of the light plane, the light world, and the fire.

12) Each system is governed by one of the four senses. The senses are elemental beings, nature units. The digestive system is governed by

the sense of smell; the circulatory system by the sense of taste; the respiratory system by the sense of hearing; and the generative system by the sense of sight. Each of these senses is affected by its respective element in outside nature: the sense of smell is operated by the element of earth, taste is operated by the water, hearing by the air, and sight by the fire.

13) Each of the four senses is passive and active. To illustrate: in seeing, when the eye is turned toward an object the sense of sight passively receives an impression; by the active light, or fire, this impression is aligned so that it is seen.

14) Throughout the body nature operates through the involuntary nervous system for communication with all parts of the body and for the performance of the involuntary functions of the four systems, (Fig. VI-B).

15) All these phenomena belong and relate to the nature-side of the universe; so, too, the matter of which the body is built and by which it is maintained is of the nature-side.

16) A human body is the meeting ground of the nature-side and the intelligent-side of the changing universe; and in the body there is a continuous interaction between the two.

Concerning the intelligent-side of the Universe:
17) The Triune Self represents the intelligent-side of the Universe. A Triune Self has three parts, and three atmospheres, and three breaths, (Fig. V-B). The three parts are: the psychic or doer part, which in its passive aspect is feeling and in its active aspect is desire; the mental or thinker part, which is passively rightness and actively reason; and the noetic or knower part, which passively is I-ness and actively selfness. Each of the three parts has, in a measure, the aspects of the other two parts. Each part is in an atmosphere; thus there are the psychic, mental, and noetic atmospheres of the Triune Self, which relate to the form world, the life world, and the light world. Through each atmosphere a portion of that atmosphere flows as a breath, just as there are currents which move in the air and which are the air, yet are at the same time distinct from the air. Of this complex Triune Self, only a portion of the doer part exists in the human body. It governs the body mechanism by means of the voluntary nervous system.

18) That portion of the doer part has its station in the kidneys and adrenals. The other two parts of the Triune Self are not in the body but merely contact it: the thinker part contacts the heart and lungs; the knower part barely contacts the rear half of the pituitary body and the

pineal body in the brain. The Triune Self contacts the voluntary nervous system as a whole, (Fig. VI-A). The thinker of each human is his individual divinity.

19) The vertical line that divides or connects the two sides of the universe, and the upper and lower points, are the symbol of the aia and of the breath-form, (Fig. II-G, H). The upper point of the line is the aia, representing the intelligent-side to the right of the line; the lower point is the breath-form, which stands for nature, on the left side of the line. The two points and the line relate the aia for the intelligent-side with the breath-form for the nature-side, so that there can be immediate action and reaction on each other. The aia belongs to the Triune Self, as the breath-form belongs to nature. The aia is without dimension; it is not destroyed; it is always in the psychic atmosphere of the doer part. Prior to conception the aia revivifies a nature unit, the form, with the breath of the breath-form, which will be the "living soul" of the body during life. The breath-form is the cause of conception. The breath-form is stationed in the front half of the pituitary body, and lives in the involuntary nervous system. It is an automaton, and is the means of communication between the Triune Self and nature.

20) The Triune Self receives Light from an Intelligence. The Intelligence is the next higher degree in being conscious, beyond the Triune Self, (Fig. V-C). The Light of an Intelligence is a Conscious Light. By its Conscious Light, an Intelligence is related to the Triune Self, and through the Triune Self the Intelligence maintains contact with the four worlds. In the noetic atmosphere the Conscious Light, so to say, is clear, and it is likewise clear in that portion of the mental atmosphere which is in the noetic atmosphere of the Triune Self. But in the mental atmosphere of the human, (Fig. V-B), the Conscious Light is diffused and more or less obscured. The Light does not enter the psychic atmosphere. The use of the Conscious Light makes the doer intelligent.

21) An Intelligence unit is the highest degree in which a unit can be conscious as a unit. An Intelligence was a primordial unit of matter in the sphere of fire, there conscious as its function only; it progressed through the spheres and many cycles in the worlds to the degree where it has at last become an ultimate unit, a unit conscious as an Intelligence, (Fig. II-H). An Intelligence is self-conscious, individuated, has identity as an Intelligence, and has seven inseparable parts or faculties, each of the seven being a conscious witness to the unity of the seven, (Fig. V-C).

22) The Supreme Intelligence is the highest in degree of all Intelligences; is chief of the Intelligences governing the Universe; and is in relation with the Universe through the individual Intelligences and their complete Triune Selves. Each Triune Self is in conscious relation to the Supreme Intelligence through the individual Intelligence to whom it is related.

Concerning The Government of the world:
23) Complete Triune Selves constitute The Government of the world. They are in everlasting, perfect bodies of the, to mortals, invisible, physical Realm of Permanence. They govern the physical, the form, the life, and the light worlds. Complete Triune Selves are the active agents of Intelligences who supervise, but take no active part in, The Government.

Concerning Consciousness:
24) Consciousness is that by the presence of which all things are conscious. Consciousness is the same in all matter and in all beings. Consciousness is changeless. Matter changes as it becomes increasingly conscious in successive degrees. Beings are conscious in varying degrees; but Consciousness is the same in all beings, from the least nature unit to the Supreme Intelligence. Consciousness has no states, is not conditioned, is without attributes, does not act, cannot be acted upon, cannot be separated, cut up or divided, does not vary, does not develop, and is the completion of all becoming. By the presence of Consciousness all there is in the Universe is conscious according to its capacity to be conscious.

Concerning units:
25) All nature-matter is of units. A unit is an indivisible, irreducible one; it has an active and a passive side, either of which dominates the other. There are four kinds of units: nature units, aia units, Triune Self units, and Intelligence units, (Fig. II-A). The term nature units includes all units of the spheres, worlds, planes, and states of matter. Units are beyond the reach of chemistry and physics; they can be dealt with only by the mind.
26) A unit begins its development as a primordial unit on the unintelligent nature-side; that is, as a fire unit of the fire sphere, (Fig. II-H). The unit progresses as a unit on the intelligent-side; that is, as first a Triune Self and ultimately as an Intelligence. Between these two stages

are innumerable conditions of units. The purpose is to develop a primordial unit of the fire sphere until it is an Intelligence. The purpose is achieved by the passage of the unit through all stages of units on the nature-side, then through the aia kind, and then through all the degrees on the intelligent-side as a Triune Self and then as an Intelligence. In the changing universe, all this is done according to the plan of a human body, by re-existences of the doer portions until the doer is consciously one with its Triune Self.

27) A unit of nature goes through four conditions, always of a fiery, airy, fluid, and earthy kind, before it can be changed. In the world of time the active or the passive side dominates the other until the unit is ready to be changed, at which time the active side and the passive side are equal. Then the change is made through the unmanifested, which pervades the manifested, of the unit that disappears from the state in which it is and reappears through the unmanifested as that which it becomes. When a unit changes from one state or plane or world to another, the change is made through the unmanifested during all manifestations.

28) Changes of units in this manner occur throughout nature in chemical processes; but only while a unit is in a perfect body can it progress.

The foregoing plan presents the Universe as it appears to the doers in human bodies existing on the earth crust who are confined to sensuous perceptions and whose understanding is accordingly restricted.

Nerve centers of the body are at present used for the pleasure of the human and the housekeeping of the body; but potentially they are centers for the exercise of mental and noetic powers undreamed of.

Time is the change of units or of masses of units in their relation to each other. On the earth crust, where time is measured as the earth mass changes in its relation to the sun mass, time is not the same as time in other states and worlds. Time applies only to units that have not been balanced. In the Realm of Permanence, where the units do not change alternately from active-passive to passive-active, that is, where the units are balanced, there is no time as known to humans.

Space is related to time as the unmanifested is related to the manifested. Time is of nature units; it can be measured; space is not matter, it is not of units, and cannot be measured. Space has no dimensions. Distance has no relation or application to space. The manifestation of the Universe is in space, but space is not affected by it. Space is unconscious Sameness. To the sensuous perceptions of doers on the earth crust, space is no thing.

Dimensions are conditions of physical matter, and do not relate to space. The doers on the earth crust are limited to the four senses for perception. These senses can at present perceive only one dimension: the dimension of on-ness, that is, surfaces. What are called three dimensions—length, breadth, and thickness—are only surfaces. The senses do not perceive the other three dimensions. Though the doers cannot see the next dimension, which is in-ness, they are aware that there is a dimension beyond their sense perception. The doers are not aware of a third and a fourth dimension, but they guess about them.

SECTION 4

Plan relating to the earth sphere.

The following is a partial outline of the plan of the Universe relating to the earth sphere. This outline, though sketchy and incomplete, indicates enough to show what the plan is, and to explain the working of the law of thought in so far as it relates to man.

Only a small portion of this immense sphere is familiar to the human, namely, the physical, visible universe, which is in the solid state of the physical plane of the human physical world in the sphere of earth. Beyond this state the ordinary human does not even think, (Fig. V-B).

By thinking there is precipitated onto our earth into visibility, through the four worlds, that portion of the four spheres which is within and blended into the sphere of earth, as fire, air, water, and earth. The nature-matter thus concreted may be perceived by the four senses of man in the forms and structures of the human, animal, vegetable and mineral kingdoms.

The senses of the body are elemental beings, nature units; they are personalized parts of the four elements of invisible nature. The senses are developed and drawn and bound into the human body and bear the seal of the doer that inhabits it. The senses do not feel; neither does nature feel, but through the senses the doer in the human feels and desires.

The matter which composes the human body is impressed directly by the thinking and the thoughts of the doer in the human body. All the matter in the human world has passed, does pass and will again and again pass through human bodies in streams of units, cyclically by circulations.

Thus there is kept up a continual circulation of the units of nature through human bodies; it is kept going by thinking and breathing, by which the matter is taken in and returned to the states and planes. It is only while matter is in a human body that it can be raised or lowered from the condition in which it is, by thinking. It is thus that the units of the human world descend and ascend continually.

After the death of the body and the dispersion into nature of the senses and the other nature units there remains the form of the breath-form; this form stays in the psychic atmosphere of the doer and is later used as a model or pattern to build a new body for the doer. By this process innumerable bodies will be built successively for a re-existing doer. As a result of the experiences and learning of the doer in these bodies, the units of which the bodies are composed are eventually equilibrated and the feeling-and-desire of the doer of the Triune Self are in balanced union in a regenerated and perfected physical body.

The part of the plan which is outlined in this section relates merely to the operation of the law of thought as destiny, in so far as the operation of the law is the rule of life for man. As the purpose of the Universe is unfolded in these pages, additional features of the plan are given which affect nature, the Triune Self and the Intelligence.

SECTION 5

Transition of a breath-form unit to the state of aia. Eternal Order of Progression. The Government of the world. The "fall of man." Regeneration of the body. Passage of a unit from the nature-side to the intelligent-side.

From the universal plan outlined in the foregoing pages it will be seen that the sphere of earth is of nature-matter and intelligent-matter; and that Consciousness, unchangeable and the same throughout, is present everywhere.

In order that a nature unit may become an intelligent unit, it must have reached the limit of progression on the nature-side; that is, it must have become the breath-form unit in a perfect body. The next degree takes the breath-form unit beyond the bounds of nature. Then it is an aia unit, as the intermediary point or line between nature and the intelligent-side, (Fig. II-G, H), belonging however to the intelligent-side.

The transition of the breath-form unit to the degree of aia, is made while the doer is in its perfect, immortal physical body in the Realm of Permanence; that is, according to the Eternal Order of Progression, as follows:

The unmanifested of a unit is Sameness,—which is in and through the manifesting active and passive aspects of the unit, (Fig. II-C). The manifesting active and passive aspects alternately change until each is adjusted to the other by the unchanging Sameness, so that they are equalized and balanced, and the unit is Sameness throughout.

It is so with the breath-form unit: its unmanifested is the sum of all functions as which it was successively conscious during its entire progress through all preceding degrees as a nature unit in that perfect body. As the sum those degrees do not function; they are neutral; they are as Sameness. But those degrees qualify the manifesting aspects as breath-form to function: to keep in operation and functioning all the units in that perfect body. And the aia unit is in the perfect body, in the transitional state and degree to which the breath-form is developing.

The breath-form is the most advanced degree to which a nature unit can progress, always in a perfect body. By the doer of the Triune Self that dwelt in that perfect body the breath-form was balanced. And at the same time all other units in the perfect body were ready to advance one degree in being conscious. So the breath-form was made ready to be advanced to the neutral state, the transitional state, between nature-matter and intelligent-matter.

When the Triune Self of that perfect body becomes an Intelligence it raises the aia of that body to take its place and degree as Triune Self, which then advances the breath-form to the state of aia, as stated; and, that new Triune Self takes charge of the body. But in doing this all the units of that perfect body have advanced one higher degree in being conscious. Therefore there must be an alignment of units in their advanced degrees, especially with the new breath-form and its senses and their organs. And there must be an adjustment by the doer of the Triune Self through which it will maintain and keep the perfect body in operation. This adjustment is a critical and most important process.

Some advancements made by units in the perfect body are: The unit of the sense of smell, that is, its active aspect, breath, is, together with the passive aspect, form, advanced to be the breath-form of the perfect body. Taste is advanced to the degree of smell. Hearing is advanced to the degree of taste. Sight is advanced to the degree of hearing. And the unit of the organ of the eye is advanced to be the sense of sight. These four advanced sense units are to act as intermediaries between outside nature and the perfect body. The control and maintenance of that body would be by means of the breath-form, and the doer of the Triune Self would keep the body in balance; and the doer, in addition, would be active in administering affairs of the human world. The Triune Self would then be a Triune Self complete, and as such it would be one of The Government of the world, according to the Eternal Order of Progression.

However, before all this could come about, the doer of the Triune Self had to pass the trial test of balance; that is, it had to bring its feeling aspect and its desire aspect into balanced union. In order to do this, the doer's perfect sexless body is divided into a male body and a female body; the feeling aspect of the doer then dwells in the female body and the desire aspect in the male body. The two bodies are the balances. Then, with feeling and desire in the two bodies of opposite sexes, as the balances, the doer was to preserve the oneness of itself as feeling-and-desire while it was present in both halves of the divided one body. This would be done by thinking, by the proper adjustment of the three minds of the doer, under control of the doer. Then, feeling-and-desire thinking together as the doer, could not think other than as one doer. Thus thinking, the body-mind would be attuned to and controlled by the feeling-and-desire minds thinking together as one, and would also think of feeling-and-desire as one. Thus, by the three minds unitedly thinking as one, the male and female half-bodies would be again united, and feeling-and-desire, by thinking together, would be in balanced and inseparable union. Such united thinking of the three minds would also adjust the units of the four systems of the perfect body through the four senses of the body by means of the breath-form under control of the doer, who would then be in right relation to its thinker and knower.

But the doers of all human beings failed to pass that test and trial. They did not balance the newly advanced units in their proper relation. Feeling-and-desire allowed the body-mind to control their thinking. So the body-mind thinking through the senses of the male body and the female body hypnotized desire-and-feeling into seeing and believing that they were bodies, and they forgot that they were the desire and the feeling of one doer, and not bodies. The Conscious Light was withdrawn. They were in darkness of the senses; and then they did not think of themselves as feeling-and-desire—similarly as most humans now think of them-

selves as bodies instead of as the doers in their bodies. They lost the
government of the body and could not remain in the Realm of Permanence. Their thinking took them out of the Realm of Permanence. They
could only see and sense and think of this world of birth and death. This
is the basis of the legend of the "fall of man".

To understand the Eternal Order of Progression it is necessary here
to consider The Government of the world by complete Triune Selves in
the Realm of Permanence. As heretofore stated, the Triune Self is a unit
of three inseparable knower, thinker, and doer parts. The knower and
thinker parts are qualified and perfect, but the doer part must be qualified
by taking over and consciously operating the perfect immortal physical
body, to train and keep units of nature poised in perfect balance. To
operate and take charge of the perfect body machine the doer must have
its feeling-and-desire in balanced union. For this every doer must pass
the trial test of balance, the balancing of the sexes. In the orderly course
of progress, the doer passes the test and, with its thinker and knower,
makes its Triune Self complete. Then, after serving in the high office as
one of The Government of the world in the Realm of Permanence, and
as one of The Government of the human world and of the destinies of
the nations, the Triune Self complete goes on to the degree of an
Intelligence, with other Intelligences in the spheres: the spheres of earth,
of water, of air, and of fire, and it goes on and on in higher degrees of
being conscious, towards the ultimate—Consciousness.

This in brief is the perpetual progressive development which has
always been going on, and will go on, according to the Eternal Order of
Progression. But this book does not deal in detail with that; it is
particularly concerned with the destinies of human beings, whose doers
left the orderly course of the doers that passed the test and that continued
to advance.

By failing in that test, the doers of mankind departed from that
Eternal Order of Progression. Instead of continuing in everlasting physical bodies in the Realm of Permanence, they exiled themselves to exist
and re-exist in human bodies on the earth crust, this human world. They
now tread the path of birth and life and death in man and woman bodies,
and periodically live and die and re-exist. By failing in their test they did
not keep in balance the perfectly balanced units which composed their
perfect bodies. And those unbalanced compositor units now compose
the bodies in which they re-exist in this world. They are now imperfect,
human beings; that is, the feeling aspect and the desire aspect of the doers

have fallen under the glamour of the sexes and are ruled by their senses and sensations and sexes; they are not self-controlled; they have forgotten their knowers; the Light of their Intelligences in them is obscured.

The doer will continue to re-exist until it regenerates the imperfect mortal body into a perfect and immortal physical body, such as it originally had; more precisely, until the doer restores the breath-form unit and the compositor units of the body to their original perfect state of balance. The regeneration and restoration of the perfect body is the duty of every doer; this duty must be and ultimately will be performed, as described in Chapter XI, "The Great Way".

In this system all parts of the whole are related in a definite plan and for a definite purpose. The plan and the purpose show that nature in the human world of time is in states toward progression by constant cycles or circulations of the units through human bodies; when the doers of the Triune Selves progress and the complete Triune Selves advance to the degree of Intelligences, the units are balanced. The Intelligences charged with the responsibility of this education, free themselves in the discharge of this duty. The circulation of nature, the development of the doers, the freeing of the Intelligences, are done owing to the presence of Consciousness through all. Because of the presence of Consciousness, each unit of nature, each aia, each Triune Self, and each Intelligence, is conscious in and as the different degrees of matter which it is. Thus the link connecting intelligent-matter and nature-matter is kept unbroken.

To present this intricate subject from the symbolic point of view: The progression of unintelligent units from the nature-side to be intelligent units of the intelligent-side of the universe, (uninterrupted by the fall of the doer part of the Triune Self into the human world of change), is shown by Figure II-G. This progressive development is accomplished by the functioning of the nature units composing the complete and perfect physical bodies of the physical Realm of Permanence. Those perfect bodies of nature units are occupied and operated by the units that had graduated from the nature-side and that had become Triune Self units on the intelligent-side. The unintelligent nature units differ from the intelligent units in that they are conscious as their functions only,—nothing more; whereas, the Triune Self units are conscious as themselves, Triune Selves, and are also conscious of the functioning of the units of their perfect bodies, as laws of nature. They are the governors of the worlds, under their Intelligences in the spheres. By dwelling in and operating the individual perfect bodies, through which they as units had progressed, the Triune Selves keep and train the units of the bodies in the Eternal Order of Progression; and, by governing the units of their bodies (to which the units of the outside forces of nature are attuned and directed), the Triune Selves govern the bodies and, through them, control the forces of nature.

If the successive progress of any Triune Self unit is interrupted by the failure of its doer part to pass the trial test of balance, with the consequent fall of the doer part into the human world, the progress of that Triune Self is halted until its doer part regenerates the human body to the perfect state, and in it reestablishes itself in the Realm of Permanence and continues its course as one of the governors, in The Government of the world.

CHAPTER III

OBJECTIONS TO THE LAW OF THOUGHT

SECTION 1

The law of thought in religions and in accidents.

The objections to the doctrine that man is the maker of his destiny are that men have no choice in being created, and no choice concerning their destiny; and that there is not more than one life on earth. Their experience would show that justice is seldom meted out; that the good often suffer misfortune, and that the wicked often prosper; that rewards and afflictions generally come to mankind without wise dispensation; that the weak and poor are oppressed, and that the strong and rich can get with impunity what they want; and that there is not an equal opportunity for all. Another factor militating against the acceptance of the law of thought as destiny is the belief in vicarious atonement. If individuals may be relieved of the consequences of their sins by the sacrifice of another, there is no reason for a belief in justice.

The hope of eternal bliss in heaven, and the fear of eternal suffering in hell, as a reward or punishment for the acts of one short life on earth, and based upon the mere acceptance or rejection of a doctrine, dull the perception and stagger the understanding. Predestination means that each doer is at birth arbitrarily created for good or ill: a vessel for shame or honor. This idea, when believed without question, enslaves the believers.

Those who accept an only God who, at will, dispenses blame or favor, raises or puts down, and gives life or death; those who are satisfied with the explanation that every event is the will of God or the ways of Providence, are, merely by holding such beliefs, unable to apprehend the law of thought as destiny. Some people believe in many gods, and others in a particular god, who will grant their wishes and condone their sins if propitiated by offerings and supplications. People who believe that they have such a god, do not want a law to which they cannot appeal for their selfish ends and get a desired response.

No religion can dispense with the law of thought, as destiny: it is the basis of moral law. No religion is without moral law; it must be in every religious system; and in some form it is. Therefore the moral aspects of every religion are shared in some degree by all. For this reason efforts have been successfully made to show the identity of religions in fundamentals, their moral code being the bond between them. Each religion, however, puts the administration of the moral law into the hands of that particular God whose religion it is. His power is believed to be so great that he himself is not bound by the moral law, being above it; hence the belief in the will of God and the ways of Providence; hence also, in some persons, some doubt of the management of that God, and eventually a belief in blind force and chance.

Another reason why some people may not wish to accept the law of thought as destiny is that they do not grasp it. They know of no system of the Universe; they know nothing of the nature of the gods, or of the parts which the gods play in creating, maintaining and changing the physical world; they know little about the nature of the doer and its connection with the gods. The failure of people to grasp these points is due to the absence of a standard measure by which the nature and relations of all matter and beings in the invisible worlds and their planes, and on the visible physical plane, can be estimated. Owing to his weakness and selfishness, man accepts force as that measure; his moral code therefore is practically that might is right. Man sees in his God a magnified man; thus he is prevented from seeing a system of thinking, without which he cannot have a key to the mysteries of the visible plane.

No religion can dispense with the law of thought as destiny. Yet theological doctrines are often incompatible with it. They make it appear in strange disguises, stories and teachings that conceal the law. Nevertheless these are forms used by Triune Selves to teach their doers as much of the law of thought as the doers can acquire. The faith which holds to "ways of Providence," the "wrath of God" and "original sin" to mention but these few, even as the skepticism which speaks of mere chance and accident, is a station through which the doer passes while it is being educated by the Light of the Intelligence.

The law of thought as destiny works in silence and is unseen. Its course is not perceptible by the senses. Even its results on the physical plane attract no attention unless they are unusual or unexpected. Then by some persons they are called accidents, and are attributed to chance; by others, miracles or the will of God, and an explanation is sought in religions. It is not generally understood that religion is the relation between doers and the gods they have fashioned out of nature. The God or the gods which men worship are nature gods. This fact is apparent from the symbols by which they demand to be adored. These nature gods, however, are subject to complete Triune Selves: they are created by the embodied doers of Triune Selves. Triune Selves furnish to the embodied portions of their doers the means of accomplishing the worship due to—and even the worship demanded by—the nature gods. The "divinity" of each human, speaking within, is the thinker of his own Triune Self. Triune Selves educate their doers, and use religions as a means of teaching. Thus the doer in a human body is allowed to consider a personal God as its creator and source of power, and as the administrator of justice according to a moral code. In so far as the God's acts or omissions do not fall in with the moral code—the very code which is attributed to the God—the doer believes in the "inscrutable ways of Providence".

Sometimes small parts of the law of thought are to be found in religions; but then they are colored to fit in with the body of the theology. When the doer matures sufficiently to see that it is sense-bound in a body which is personalized nature, and to distinguish between the gods or God on the one hand, and, on the other, the Light it receives from its Intelligence, then by that Light will the doer understand the innate idea of justice, the real meanings of the "wrath of God" and of the doctrine of original sin.

Accidents and chance are words used by persons who do not think clearly when they attempt to account for certain happenings. Anyone who thinks must be convinced that in a world as orderly as this there is no room for the words accident and chance. Every natural science depends upon the recurrence of certain facts in a certain order. A physical law means facts observed and the assurance of their recurrence in orderly sequence. Such physical laws govern all physical actions, from sowing to harvesting, from boiling water to sailing a vessel, from playing a fiddle to the electrical transmission of sound and images by radio.

Can it be that there is no certainty of the orderly sequence of facts and events when we search for moral law, for moral order? There is such a law, and it accounts for so-called accidents: Everything existing on the physical plane is an exteriorization of a thought which must be adjusted through the one who issued the thought, in accordance with his responsibility and at the conjunction of time, condition and place.

SECTION 2

An accident is an exteriorization of a thought. Purpose of an accident. Explanation of an accident. Accidents in history.

An "accident" is an event which happens to one or more persons or things unexpectedly, without being foreseen and without intention. Therefore the accident stands out from the general and foreseen order of events as unusual or separate. A so-called accident is, like any other event on the physical plane, a thought in a certain part of its course.

A thought is a being created by the Conscious Light and desire; and which, when issued, has in it an aim, a potential design, and a balancing factor—which balancing factor, like the needle of a compass, points to the final balance of the thought as a whole. The thought endures until the balancing factor has brought about an adjustment through the one who issued the thought. The balancing factor causes exteriorizations as long as the thought endures. Whenever the thought, moving in its courses, approaches the physical plane, it causes the one who issued it to be in place for an exteriorization of that thought. An exteriorization can happen only when there is a juncture of time, condition and place. The laws which control the exteriorization do not always fit in with the intention and expectation of the persons concerned; and the exteriorization is then called an accident. An accident is a perceived physical part of a thought which is proceeding on its otherwise invisible course. The exteriorization makes visible that part of the thought which touches the physical plane and is not yet balanced. The demonstration is made on or through the person who is concerned in the accident.

Accidents such as a personal injury, or a barn being struck by lightning, or an occurrence which prevents one from embarking on a ship that is to be wrecked, come only to those whose thoughts are thereby partially exteriorized to them. An accident presents to the one to whom it happens something of his past, either distant or recent. The accident is a part of one of his own thoughts that he has not balanced, and which will endure and, from time to time, meet him face to face as a physical event, until he has paid or received payment through the direct exteriorization of the design, learns his lesson from that child of his mind and desire, and has satisfied his conscience. Often accidents come to injure him, often to help him, and sometimes as protections.

The reasons why events happen to him in the form of accidents, in an exceptional, unforeseen manner, are that a man would not do certain things to himself, like breaking an arm, or that circumstances do not call for a commission of a crime against him, that is, an intentional injury; or finally that the happening accidentally is the easiest and most direct way to bring about the juncture of time, condition and place for the exteriorization.

Further, there is in the happening of an accident a special call for attention. An accident rather than an ordinary event, produces this, because the accident is unlooked for, startling.

An accident is brought about in the ordinary course of the law of thought as destiny. Every man has a vast number of thoughts cycling in his mental atmosphere toward and away from exteriorization on the physical plane. The thoughts live on with a tendency to exteriorize in the events which the balancing factor in each of them requires and projects.

The thoughts begin and continue their cycles from the time a person issues them. Whenever they approach the physical plane, they seek to exteriorize; but they are often held back by the exteriorizations of his present design. When there is an opportunity, be it ever so slight, the whole nature of the man seizes upon it and uses it to precipitate an event which will bring about one of these exteriorizations. Every thought, once it is issued, endures and appears cyclically, exteriorized as a physical event. For that purpose, the one who issued the thought calls mentally or psychically on other persons concerned with the thought, through their atmospheres. If a cycle of one of those persons' thoughts coincides with a cycle of one of his own, this will produce, unintentionally to the first one, the event which is called an accident.

Another manner in which accidents are brought about is by elementals, nature units. They follow and are bound by a man's thought, and rush with it into his body as an impulse, so that he unexpectedly performs an act which results in an accident to him; he may, for instance, cut himself; or may fall in front of a fast moving car. Another way in which elementals may act to precipitate a thought, is by producing an occurrence without human intervention, as where fire burns a man, or a cinder gets into his eye, or melting ice drops on him from a roof, or he finds articles of value. In every instance his own thought, seeking exteriorization, is the means of precipitating upon him the event which he calls an accident.

The purpose of an accident is to call one's attention to the thought of which it is one of the exteriorizations. One to whom an accident happens can always, by searching, find out something about that. Though the event may not reveal the whole past to him, it may reveal that portion of the past which it is necessary for him to know. If he tries to understand, he will learn, and he will learn more, if he is willing to pay,—he must pay anyway. What he learns will bring him nearer to the adjustment.

Suppose two men are traveling in a mountainous country. By placing his foot on an insecure stone, one of them slips and falls into a ravine. His companion goes to the rescue, finds the mangled body below, among rocks; and close at hand he discovers, cropping out from the side of the ravine, a vein of gold. The death of the one impoverishes his family and causes failure to some with whom he was in business. Because of that fall, the other discovers an ore deposit which becomes a source of wealth. Such an occurrence is said to be an accident, bringing death to one, sorrow and poverty to some, failure to others, and "good luck" to the comrade whose wealth is gained by chance.

There is no accident or chance connected with such occurrences. Each of the events is in accordance with the working out of the law as destiny, and is an exteriorization of some thought, issued by the person affected, though beyond the limits of perception.

The one who was killed was a man whose allotted time had run its course, though his death could have occurred a little sooner or might have been postponed for a short time. The manner of his death had been predetermined to be sudden. Further, it was necessary, on account of his family and his business connections, that his relations to them be severed abruptly. Therefore he suffered sudden death.

Whether the poverty awakens self-reliance in those who have been dependent on the deceased and brings out traits which could not be seen while they were dependent on another, or whether they become disheartened, give up to despair or become paupers, rests largely upon the past of those concerned. Whether the one who discovers the gold improves the opportunity of wealth to be honest, to better the conditions of himself and others, to relieve suffering, or to support educational work; or whether, on the other hand, he does none of these, but uses his wealth and the power which it gives him for the oppression of others; or whether he becomes morally corrupt and urges others to lives of dissipation, is all according to the law of thought, and has been largely determined by previous thoughts of those concerned.

If the deceased had been more careful in the selection of his path, he might not have fallen, though his death, as it was required by the law, would merely have been postponed a short time. If his companion had not descended the perilous path in the hope of rendering assistance, he would not have found the means by which he acquired his wealth. Yet, even if fear should have kept him from going to the aid of his comrade, he would only have deferred his prosperity, because wealth was to be his as the result of his past thoughts and works. By not letting pass an opportunity which duty presented, he hastened his prosperity.

It is injurious to speak of accident and chance as events happening without cause and irrespective of law. Such unthinking use of the words fosters in people the belief that they may act or fail to act, and not be held accountable. They come to believe that things may happen to them without cause. So they may dull their moral conceptions. They limit their views and reasoning to things on the physical plane; they trust to chance, and are liable to become irresponsible.

Events which affect a few or many, or a race or a continent, or the whole world, arrive to those whom they benefit or afflict according to the working of the law of thought as destiny. To each individual are exteriorized some of his past thoughts. The thoughts press for an opening for exteriorization. If there are many people whose thoughts tend towards a similar event, they are gathered even from the ends of the earth to bring about the so-called accidents. To everyone comes the advantage or loss that exteriorizes some of his past thoughts.

Accidents which happen to a community, like a conflagration, cyclone, inundation or pestilence, are likewise the exteriorizations of thoughts of those affected. Under this head fall also the destruction of hamlets and cities, and the devastation of countries, like the ruthless razing of Carthage, the sacking of Rome, the plundering of the Spanish settlements by the buccaneers, or the conquest of Peru. In these cases the "just" suffer with the "unjust". The "unjust" are the evil ones in the present; the "just" are the unrighteous of the past. Such destinies have been made by the action and inaction, the participation and indifference, of the inhabitants in times such as those of the persecution of the Huguenots, or of the Netherlands by Alva, or of the Quakers by the Puritans in New England. They will be brought together in the course of time, and their thoughts will lead them to the place and time of the exteriorization of those past thoughts. That place may be the same locality; or the people may be brought together in another, and there live in prosperity or in trouble, and share in the accidents of the final disaster.

The reckoning may be held up for a long time; but it is sure to come. The United States of America was set apart by Intelligences to try out self-government by the multitude, and so they have been led to success in their various wars, their political institutions and their economic undertakings, notwithstanding the actions of the people. In peace and in war, their escape from the natural consequences of their selfishness and indifference is striking. But this protection and universal success, which school histories and orators seem to take as a matter of course, may not last. There must be an accounting for all that these people did tolerate and do in violation of their great responsibility. The New England bigots, the Massachusetts slave traders, the Southern slave drivers, the oppressors of the Indians, the political and other corruptionists will at some time meet and suffer at the reckoning which is sure to come.

In every life there are numerous events which are generally regarded as accidents. Such events are, to mention a few: birth at a particular time into a certain country, race, family and religion; birth into favorable or unfavorable conditions; birth into a sound or a diseased body; birth with certain psychic tendencies and mental endowments. Peoples' lives are largely made up of events which they cannot choose, and which seem to be determined by accident. Among these are opportunities offered to enter a trade, a business or a vocation; chance acquaintances who cause, prevent or end associations in work or commerce; and conditions which lead to or hinder marriage and friendship.

People, if they do not look upon events as happenings by chance, explain them as the will of God and seek consolation in their religion.

SECTION 3

Religions. Gods. Their claims. The need of religions. The moral code.

Religions, which turn around personal gods, seem incompatible with the law of thought as destiny. Some of their doctrines are particularly designed to settle inquiries into the mysteries of the law by statements which must be accepted by faith and without contradiction.

A religion is the relation between man and a God or gods, which he has helped to fashion or maintain, largely for the purpose of getting comfort and protection. The religion into which a man is born, or which he accepts during life, indicates the stage of his development. The commands of the god whom he worships, the form of the worship, the punishments threatened, and the rewards promised, show the particular element of nature to which his doer is attuned.

Nature is the nature-matter in those parts of the spheres of fire, air, and water which reach into the sphere of earth; a part of which earth sphere is the human physical world in which is the visible universe, including the moon, sun, planets and stars, (Fig. I-E). A part of the human world is personalized in the organs, systems and senses in the human body. All these are made up of matter belonging to the four elements. Each of the senses is a nature unit, doing service in a human body. The four senses of seeing, hearing, tasting and smelling are the connections which relate the doer in the human as a distinct entity, to nature as a whole through its four elements.

There is a constant pull, on the one hand, by each of the four elements of nature on its particular sense in the human body, and, on the other hand, by nature on the doer through the connection of the four senses with the doer-in-the-body. The senses are the emissaries of nature: the messengers, agents, priests, through which nature speaks to the doer. The pull is like a call from nature to man; it is experienced as a feeling, an emotion, a sentiment, a longing. The human is overwhelmed by uncertainty and the fear of powers against which he is helpless. He responds to that call, and to his wish for comfort and protection, by worship. That worship must take some form. The form is the religion of the particular human.

The human worships nature in terms of personality. The reason for this is that the human identifies himself with his body, and so does not think of nature, power, love, or intelligence, except as proceeding from a personality. Man cannot conceive of anything without identity or form; therefore, when he wants to worship nature he gives to nature form and identity. So he creates gods which are nature gods—magnified men and women. His religion is the tie between him and his gods.

These nature gods cannot continue to exist without worship, for they need and depend on human thought for nourishment. That is why they are continually crying for and commanding worship. There are ceremonies and symbols with which they demand to be adored; and certain places, temples and buildings for their worship. The symbols appear in ornaments on, or in the very form of, vestments, temples, and structures; or in dances or rites performed in these by worshippers.

The symbols represent chiefly procreation, food and punishment. Among such religious symbols are, for the male deities, the sun and the rays of the sun; fire and that which carries fire—as a torch or a candle; and for the goddesses, the earth, the moon and water. Then there are directly the generative parts of the human body, and the symbols which indicate them; as, for the male, the stem of a palm-tree, conifers, a shaft, a pillar, a staff, an obelisk, an arrow, a lance, a sword, an erect serpent, a bull, a goat and other animals. The female is represented by a woman holding a child; and by a vessel, an arch, a grove, a door, a lozenge, a shell, a boat, a rose, a pomegranate, a cow, a cat, and similar fertile animals. The parts of man are made to appear in the conventional forms of the male triad, trefoil and bishop's crook; and the female symbols are such things as the vesica pisces, a bowl, a goblet or an urn. These symbols are used alone or jointly. The conventional forms appear in many combinations, generally in cross or star forms, indicating junction.

Nature and the nature gods have no feeling and no desire in themselves; but they feel and desire with human feelings and desires. They get these through human bodies. That is not to say that these gods are subservient to man, or that they are powerless. They are beings of splendor and of vast power: the force of nature is behind them. They can and they do punish and reward. Their worshippers they reward with the objects of the worship. They are as faithful to man as he is to them. They reward a man or a people as far as they can. There is a limit to their powers; but they can bestow strength and beauty of body, and health, possessions, worldly power, success in undertakings, long life, and posterity. The gods do this as long as a man or a people are faithful in worship and obedient to their commands. However, the power of these gods is limited in a twofold way: by the worship of the people, and by the boundaries set by the law of thought.

None of these gods has intelligence of his own; a god is not an Intelligence and has no Light of an Intelligence, except what he gets in the thoughts of human worship. All the intelligence a god has he gets through doers in human bodies. Such a nature god is subject to the Intelligences which rule the earth sphere. Yet each nature god desires to be considered by his human servitors as the Supreme Intelligence of the Universe. It is from the doer that the god gets the idea of being worshipped as the Supreme Intelligence. The god desires such worship because, if the doer feels so about him, it will be faithful to him. The god is what the human beings make him. They actually endow him with all their ambitions and desires, their brutality and revenge, their mercy, kindness and love. Nature gods crave Light of an Intelligence. It is impossible for them to receive it except as they get control of doers in human bodies.

When the doer responds to the claims of the god, Light of the Intelligence goes out in the doer's thought which follows the pull of nature. Light of its Intelligence furnishes the doer with the means of accomplishing the doer's worship. But the doer is not aware of this. The great effort of nature gods is to obtain the subjugation and service of human thinking. Therefore it is represented by the priests of a religion that the thinking is inferior to belief. The believer is given to believe that feeling is superior to thinking, and that, in religion, thinking should follow the promptings of feeling.

The priests may say that thinking leads the soul away from the god. They say that if the soul gives up its devotion to the god it will be led away from him and be lost to God as a soul. This is quite true. When the doer follows the Light of the Intelligence, it is led away from nature and from the gods it has fashioned out of nature.

The nearer an embodied doer is to nature, the more quickly will that doer respond to the pull of nature by religious worship; and it is proper that such a doer should worship in this way while it is sense-bound. As a doer responds more to the Light of its Intelligence, it begins to question. The questions are about power, right and wrong, God and man, the visible and invisible, the real and unreal. These a nature god answers through the senses; his messages are interpreted in terms of feeling, and they affect the heart. By contrast, the Triune Self answers with the Light, showing to the doer the solution by the Light. At the proper time, the doer must choose between the worship of nature and that of the Triune Self and Light. Every doer knows when that time has come.

As the doer advances in development, it recedes from belief until it may reach through agnosticism and denial to disbelief in any god. Disbelief usually comes through progress in the natural sciences and through thinking, which disprove some of the assertions of theology, discredit some of the sources of revelation, question the motives of the revealers and of the priesthood, and lead to disbelief in everything that cannot be verified by physical measurements and the reactions of science. Disbelief also comes when thinking is developed in the doer to the extent that it realizes the injustice of a god who disobeys the moral code which he proclaims for his children, and who demands that the "will of God", the "wrath of God", and the "ways of Providence" be accepted as an excuse or explanation of his iniquities.

Disbelief, however, is wrong. It is worse for one to break away from religion, deny the existence of a god and assert that death ends all, than to share the naive belief in the "ways of Providence" and the "will of God". The gods do exist; and they can furnish to the body food and things that make physical life pleasant. They are entitled to gratitude for what they give: but not to worship as the Supreme Intelligence.

The manner in which humans are taught the law of thought is the way in which they want to think or learn. That way is to let the doer, so long as it remains sense-bound, consider a personal God as its creator, a God of mercy and love, the source of power, and the administrator of justice according to a moral code. Complete Triune Selves, The Government of the world, provide the code of morals by influencing the human beings who develop a religion. This code is suited to the requirements of the people who look to their God as their creator, preserver, destroyer and lawgiver. Without religions, the doers in human beings would have nothing to hold them in check. Each feels the presence of his Triune Self, but in their sensuous stages people do not sense its qualities and power, and in their ignorance they seek in nature for their God.

The threatenings of a god cause fear. The human fears that he is not immortal. He fears the wrath of his God. He senses that he does wrong, and that he cannot help but do wrong when temptation beckons. These conditions of the human are permitted by the Triune Selves to impress a moral code upon him. The gods are quite willing to pose as the lawgivers and dictators. Human priests are ready to take advantage of the ignorance and the fear of the human beings. So the moral code given by the Triune Selves is used at the same time by nature gods and their priests to maintain themselves and to keep the doers in human beings in dependence. The teaching of the "wrath of God" and the doctrine of "original sin", are illustrative of this. Yet these doctrines have a meaning.

SECTION 4

The wrath of God. The destiny of humanity. The innate faith in justice.

The thoughts of one life which have not been adjusted are carried over by the doer to the next life, and to the next; and from one civilization to another, until they are adjusted. Families, tribes, cities, nations, civilizations and the whole of humanity have their destiny. The presence of the destiny of humanity is one of the sources from which comes the feeling of assurance that justice rules the world. The other source is the idea of justice. This idea is inherent in the doer of every human; and because of it, man fears the "wrath of God" and asks for "mercy".

The wrath of God is the accumulation of wrong actions which, like Nemesis, pursues ready to overtake, as soon as the conditions are ripe. This feeling of the destiny of humanity is shared by all its members; it causes mankind to try to propitiate some unseen being, and is made one of the foundations of religion.

The mercy which man seeks is likewise a source of religion; he seeks it that he may have his just deserts removed. Removal is impossible, but the pressure of one's thoughts towards exteriorization may be held back for a time until the suppliant for mercy is able to meet the exteriorizations of his thoughts. Mercy is asked by those who feel themselves too weak, or who are too fearful or too selfish to let the law be fulfilled.

Besides the fear of the "wrath" or "vengeance" of God, and in addition to the desire for "mercy", there is in man a faith that somewhere in the world—notwithstanding all the seeming injustice—there is, though unseen and not understood, adjustment and justice. This inherent faith in justice is self-existent in the doer of man. It blossomed when the aia was raised to be a Triune Self. But to evoke this faith it requires some crisis in which man is thrown upon himself by the seeming injustice of others. The faith in justice is part of the intuition of immortality, which persists in the heart of man despite his agnosticism and materialism, and adverse conditions which harden him.

The intuition of immortality is the underlying knowledge that the doer comes into being in the Eternal, not in time; that it has fallen into time; that man is able to live and will live through the seeming injustice that is imposed upon him; and that he will live to right the wrongs which he has done. The idea of justice, innate in the heart of man, is the one thing which saves him from cringing for the favor of a wrathful god. The idea of justice causes a man to look fearlessly into another's eye, even though he may be conscious that he must suffer for a wrong he has done. The fear of the wrath and vengeance of God, the desire for mercy, faith in the eternal justice of things—these are evidences of the doer's recognition of the destiny of humanity.

SECTION 5

The story of original sin.

The story of original sin is not without basis; it is a fable which conceals some true traditions. One of these has to do with the procreation of the bodies of human beings. Many events are covered by this mythology. The doers who were affected by the events feel a truth under the story of original sin. The details of the story are in some ways related to the original events, but are twisted, inaccurate and childish. Nevertheless the story has power because doers are conscious of truths which are concealed in it.

The naive story covers a history of disquieting results. The use of the procreative power was the "original sin". The result following the procreative act was to give to the human race the tendency to unlawful procreation; and this tendency was one of the means of bringing on ignorance and death in the world.

The penalty of the original sin of the doers is that they are now dominated by that which they originally refused to govern. When they could govern they would not; now that they would govern, they cannot. One proof of that ancient sin is present with every human in the sorrow that follows an act of mad desire which, even against his reason, he is driven to commit. Another evidence is the existence on earth of what today is spoken of as the lower human races.

This and other events which underlie the legend of original sin have consequences which reach the present day. They all come from times when doers knew right from wrong and were therefore responsible. They could not stand still, but had to go on or back, one way or the other. They had to decide; and they gave in to the temptation of pleasure. They now give way to sensation and assent to their desires. They look into darkness rather than into the Light. Their destiny has followed them through the ages; it has led them deeper into wrong until now the degree of doers in human bodies is that of sense-bound doers; their feelings and desires are ruled and enfeebled by sensations, and the Light of the Intelligence is obscured in them. They are dimly conscious of events for which they were responsible. This is one of the reasons why the doctrine of original sin has found a response in the hearts of so many.

But the origin of the story of original sin was when the doer in its perfect body was in the Realm of Permanence. There, in the trial test for bringing its feeling-and-desire into balanced union, it failed. Therefore it came into this world of birth and death, and it periodically re-exists in a man body or in a woman body.

SECTION 6

The moral code in religions.

The unit which is now the Triune Self of the doer-in-the-body was once a primordial unit in nature, and later progressed through all stages in a perfect body in the Realm of Permanence before its doer "fell" and came into a human body in this human world of change; that is, it functioned in all parts and systems of the perfect nature university machine, the perfect body. Thus it functioned successively as the organ unit of each of the organs in each of the four systems of that perfect body; then it became the manager of each system in succession, and at the same time functioned as, and was one of, the four senses; eventually the unit became the breath-form; and as breath-form it managed the four systems and the body as a whole. The breath-form unit became the aia. Finally, because of the guidance and the Light of its Intelligence, the aia in turn became a Triune Self—the Triune Self of the Intelligence which had previously been a Triune Self, (Fig. II-G, H).

The Triune Self is not nature, but it progressed through and advanced beyond nature. The Triune Self is not an Intelligence; but it is always within the sphere of its Intelligence, and the Light of its Intelligence is in it. The four senses are the roots of nature in or around the doer now in the human body. Nature draws nourishment from the doer-in-the-body and the doer gets experience from nature. This exchange is made possible by the Light of the Intelligence which is with the Triune Self, not with nature. The voice or pull of nature is experienced as a feeling, a longing. The doer responds by worship and belief and fashions for itself gods out of nature.

The reason that nature gods desire worship from the doer in a human is that this is the only way by which they can receive the Light of an Intelligence. Religions exist because there is this tie or pull of nature on the doer; and Triune Selves use this relation for the development and education of their doers. Religions are allowed by Triune Selves for the purpose of letting their doers learn the law of thought as destiny, though the teaching is not under that name. Simple teachings only can be received by childish doers. Therefore the doers have been allowed to believe that their God is the administrator of justice according to a moral code, and that he speaks to them through their conscience. The code of morals is furnished by Triune Selves; and, by means of that code, responsibility of the doers is developed.

The doer, because it is tied to nature, readily credits to its nature god more than is due. The nature gods, dependent as they are upon worship for their nourishment and existence, wish to figure as the supreme lords of justice. Priests also take advantage of the needs and sentiments of the doers. So the moral code given by Triune Selves is, for ecclesiastical purposes, supplemented by theological doctrines and ceremonial homage; and is used by the gods and their priests to keep doers in subjection.

As the doer advances it begins to inquire. The arbitrary and quite human injustice shown in the management of worldly affairs may bring about disbelief, agnosticism and atheism; but only for a time. During such a period of transition, the rulers of the world seem to be blind chance and fortune; and the explanation of everything that is unusual, unrelated, and unexpected is that it happened as an accident.

So doers pass through the various stages of belief: they believe that man is born without having made his own destiny; that he has but one life on earth, in which he sees justice unequally meted out; that man is born in sin; that he may be saved from the consequences of his faults by vicarious atonement since he has no moral responsibility; that all depends upon the arbitrary will of God; that everything is the result of chance and accident. These doctrines are contrary to reason. In time men will see that these credulously accepted beliefs are not valid objections to the law of thought, when they understand the whole plan of the development of the doer with all its unity, simplicity, analogies and interrelations.

CHAPTER IV

OPERATION OF THE
LAW OF THOUGHT

SECTION 1

Matter. Units. An Intelligence. A Triune Self. A human being.

Into the physical world of the earth sphere reach the form, life and light worlds of the sphere, (Fig. I-B), and through and around all of these are the spheres of water, air and fire, (Fig. I-A).

The physical plane of the human physical world exists in four states of matter: the radiant, airy, fluid, and solid states, (Fig. I-D). The solid state in its radiant-solid, airy-solid, fluid-solid, and solid-solid substates, makes up the visible, physical universe, (Fig. I-E). The fluid, airy, and radiant states of matter of the physical plane of the human physical world are invisible and are at present beyond the reach of chemistry and physics. In other words, all that is subject to the investigation by the natural sciences is the solid state with its four substates, of the physical plane of the physical world, and that only in small part. However, the spheres and worlds, the light, life and form planes, and the radiant, airy and fluid states of matter of the physical plane reach into, affect, and are affected by those small portions of them which are in the solid state of the physical plane of the human physical world, (Fig. I-E). In this fourfold solid, visible, physical plane of the physical world are the earth crust and the moon, planets, sun and stars, of which the fourfold physical body of man is a plan, pattern or model, and a condensation.

The light, life, form and physical planes referred to hereafter are those of the human physical world; the law of thought affects more immediately the matter and the beings functioning in that world. But the whole

63

plan is here recalled because eventually the law of thought affects the matter of the whole Universe.

In the entire universe of which the human may become conscious all changes in degrees in which nature-matter is conscious, must be accomplished during the passage of that matter through a human body; there it comes directly under the Light of an Intelligence, or under reflected or diffused parts of that Light. The Light of an Intelligence does not affect nature directly or by reflection. While nature as streams of transient units is passing through a human body, the doer, by thinking, disperses some of the Light with the nature-matter. The Light which thus goes out stimulates the manifested side of nature-matter and keeps nature going as instinct, natural selection, chemical reaction and other manifestations of intelligence, usually attributed to a god.

Nature is here a name for matter which is a manifestation of Substance. The nature-matter manifesting is fourfold in the four elements: free units, which belong to all the spheres and worlds and have not formed a constituent part of a human body; transient units, which are the material used in building the physical body of man and of outside visible nature; compositor units, which are or were units in a human body catching and composing the transient units into form and visibility; and sense units, which control or govern the four systems in a human body.

An Intelligence is on the intelligent-side of the Universe and is a self-conscious unit of the Eternal, acting in the spheres which may operate in the four worlds of the sphere of earth through the Triune Self to which it is related. An Intelligence is immortal, individuated, has unbroken identity as an Intelligence and never loses its knowledge of this identity. It has seven inseparable faculties: The light, time, image, focus, dark, motive and I-am faculties, each faculty being forever a conscious witness to the unity of the seven, (Fig. V-C). An Intelligence differs from nature in that an Intelligence is an ultimate unit which has passed through all departments and degrees as a nature unit, an aia unit, a Triune Self unit, and as an Intelligence it has reached the ultimate degree of progression in being conscious which a unit can attain, that is, it is conscious as an Intelligence.

All units in nature are conscious, but not conscious that they are conscious, whereas an Intelligence is conscious that it is conscious and knows that it is conscious as an Intelligence. Between nature and an Intelligence is that which is not nature-matter, nor yet an Intelligence;

it is of intelligent-matter. This is the Triune Self. A Triune Self is a self-knowing unit of the Eternal and is to act in the four worlds of the earth sphere. The Triune Self knows itself to be an eternal knower and thinker and doer, as a Triune Self. Each of these three parts of a Triune Self has a double office. The offices of the knower are actively selfness or knowledge and passively I-ness or identity; the offices of the thinker are actively reason and passively rightness; and the offices of the doer are actively desire and passively feeling, and the duty of each office is to think.

A portion of the doer operates periodically in the physical world while it is in a flesh body. While that portion is in a flesh body its interests are on the physical plane of the physical world, and it is ignorant of itself as the doer. It is earthbound and is conscious only as a human being.

At the human stage the law of thought has the aspect of adjustment, as destiny. At this stage of the doer's development, man can without much difficulty understand the constitution of the Triune Self and its relation to its Intelligence and something about thinking and the nature and properties of a thought and the generation, the course, the exteriorization, the results and the adjustment of a thought.

SECTION 2

Mind. Thinking. A thought is a being. The atmospheres of the Triune Self. How thoughts are generated.

Thoughts are generated and must be balanced through the action of mind and desire concerning objects of nature. By mind is meant that which uses the Conscious Light of an Intelligence loaned to its Triune Self. The general belief is that there is one mind,—no other is spoken of. Actually there are three minds that are available to the human, that is, three channels along which that Light flows. There is the body-mind, which operates through the senses concerning all things pertaining to nature. Then there is the feeling-mind which is concerned with sentiments and feelings; and there is the desire-mind which has to do with action and with desires. The subject of which a person thinks indicates which one of the three minds he is using; thus, when one thinks along the line of feeling, he is using the feeling-mind, controlled, however, by the body-mind and interpreted in terms of the senses. Besides these there are four minds that are used by the reason and the rightness of the thinker, and by the I-ness and the selfness of the knower of the Triune Self, but these four minds are not available to the doer.

Thinking is the steady holding of the Conscious Light within on the subject of the thinking. Because the functions of the knower, the thinker and the doer are to think, the I-ness of the knower thinks as identity and the selfness thinks as knowledge, the rightness of the thinker thinks as law and the reason thinks as justice; the feeling of the doer should think as beauty and the desire should think as power. But because of the reduced and imperfect condition of the doer-in-the-body, the feeling of the doer in the human thinks from feeling and the desire thinks from desire. And feeling-and-desire are both compelled by the body-mind and the senses to think of themselves as the senses and as sensation. So that the feeling of the doer-in-the-body thinks with the feeling-mind subject to the body-mind, and the desire thinks with the desire-mind subject to the body-mind, and both are made to think in terms of the senses.

Thoughts on subjects in the physical world are of four classes. They are sexual, elemental and emotional thoughts, all of which are stimulated by sensations, that is, elementals, nature units, coming from outside the human; and intellectual thoughts which may come from without or from within, but are always stimulated by sensations. The thoughts that are started from without or start from within are caused by the action of nature upon the breath-form, through the four senses and their systems, the representatives of nature. Thoughts of subjects in the light, life and form worlds are conceived of by men only as they are able to apply them to physical things. There can be thinking about the Triune Self, but thoughts are always concerned with nature and are the result of thinking with attachment to objects of nature. Therefore thinking which creates thoughts holds the human being to nature. That is the reason why freedom of the doer-in-the-body and immortality of the body can be attained only by the thinking which does not create thoughts or destiny, that is, thinking which is not attached to objects.

Thoughts on subjects in the physical world are those which have filled the heads and hearts of men. These kinds of thoughts includes religions and even the metaphysics of religions, such as speculations about the Trinity and the nature of God. It includes politics, government, customs, literature, art; in short, everything that there is on the earth. In this book chiefly sexual, elemental, emotional and intellectual thoughts are dealt with, because they have made men what they are, and will for some time to come make the world and the men and the creatures in it and bring on the events which are usually ascribed to God, destiny or chance.

Thinking of time, of space, of mathematics or of any subjects in the life world or the light world of the earth sphere is not particularly dealt with here. Such thinking need have no direct physical expression and is not exteriorized, unless a thought is created that relates to the physical plane. The body will have to be cleansed, its centers brought to life and its channels opened, before thoughts of the life and light worlds can be had. Most men and women are merely doers whose feeling-and-desire are ruled by sensations and who refuse to be ruled by the thinker and knower parts of the Triune Self. They have few, if any, ideals. So thoughts of a sexual, elemental and emotional nature hold the stage, together with a few intellectual thoughts which are entertained to be the servants of the three other kinds.

As to the nature and properties of thoughts there is nothing on the visible plane to which a thought can be compared. This makes it hard to describe the nature and properties of a thought, even though all physical things are exteriorized parts of thoughts.

A thought is a being. It has a system, though only a rudimentary one. The system is made up of Light of the Intelligence, which represents some of the faculties of the Intelligence; of projections from the doer, thinker and knower; and of units from the four elements of nature. It is made up of and clothed in all the grades of nature-matter in varying proportions. It has in it matter of the four states of physical matter drawn through the four senses and their systems in the body; it has nature-matter of the form, life and light worlds, drawn from them in the same way through the breath; and it has intelligent-matter from the Triune Self itself, principally feeling-and-desire, and matter conscious in the degree called Light of the Intelligence.

A thought has no size in the physical sense but it is vast as compared to the physical acts and objects into which it is later precipitated. The power of a thought is enormous and superior to all the successive physical acts, objects and events that body forth its energy. A thought often endures for a time much greater than the whole life of the man who thought it. A thought summons and directs units as elemental beings which have to build out the design of the thought. The power of a thought when compared to the visible effect produced by it is of an enormous, towering quality; and indeed it must be so, because one of the parents is the Intelligence, which by its Light lends to the thought some of its creative power, while the other parent is the doer of the Triune Self, and behind the thought stands the whole force of nature.

The power of a thought is expressed in the acts, objects and events in which it is made manifest. Great or small, they are shadows on the physical plane, projections of projections by the thought.

In such a vast, powerful and lasting being are potentially a great many physical acts, objects and events, which gradually appear out of it, like all that comes out of a seed. There are many more thoughts generated than there are men, animals, plants and things in this world. Some thoughts are insignificant, like that of plucking an apple, or of saying "How are you?" habitually. Some thoughts are important, such as the definite and far reaching thought of William Penn, the philanthropist, or of Camillo Cavour, the statesman. It is therefore difficult to cover the whole field accurately and completely. The statements here made must of necessity be general, incomplete and subject to explanations and exceptions.

Thoughts are either conceived, gestated and born, or are former thoughts of the same or another person, which are received, entertained and issued again. Usually a thought conceived and born is entertained and issued many times before it is exteriorized.

There is a nature organization as well as the constitution of a Triune Self for thinking and the consequent production and exteriorizations of thoughts. The nature organization in the body comprises the four senses, their systems and organs and the physical atmosphere. The constitution of the Triune Self comprises the portions of its doer, its thinker and knower and their atmospheres and breaths.

The nature organization in the body is arranged to receive the impulse, pull and pressure of nature which come through the openings and nerve centers in the body. Through these the four senses are reached and compelled. The senses act on their respective four systems through the sympathetic or involuntary nervous system. All of this is the natural and involuntary activity of the body.

A Triune Self has three parts: the psychic part or doer, the mental part or thinker, and the noetic part or knower. A portion of the doer is in the kidneys and adrenals, the thinker contacts the heart and lungs, and the knower contacts the pituitary body and the pineal body. These three parts are active parts of the psychic, mental and noetic atmospheres, and are only partially connected with these organs.

There are four atmospheres: the physical atmosphere of the body, and the psychic, mental, and noetic atmospheres of the Triune Self, (Fig. V-B). The atmospheres of the Triune Self relate to the form, life, and light worlds of the earth sphere, and to the psychic, mental, and noetic atmospheres of the human, which in turn relate to the form, life, and light planes of the physical world. The physical atmosphere consists of units of the solid-solid, fluid-solid, airy-solid, and radiant-solid substates of matter, (Fig. III). These are kept in circulation in and through the physical body by the physical breath, which is the active side of the breath-form. With each inhalation there is an exhalation of matter through the openings of the body, including the pores of the skin. This physical atmosphere is usually invisible, though the sense of sight can be adjusted to perceive some of its radiations. It is not like a cloud of dust, but has a definite boundary in which are zones and a whirling through them. The physical atmosphere does not continue after death.

The psychic, mental and noetic atmospheres of the Triune Self are intelligent-matter, not nature-matter, (Fig. V-B). The psychic atmosphere surrounds and pervades the physical atmosphere of the body during life, and is spherical with a definite boundary; it corresponds to the matter of the form world and is conscious in the degree of feeling-and-desire. Throughout the psychic atmosphere of the Triune Self is a definite circulation and surging, carried on through the blood and the physical atmosphere. Surrounding and passing through the psychic atmosphere is the mental atmosphere, which is spherical and with a definite boundary. It corresponds to the matter of the life world and is conscious in the degree of rightness-and-reason. That portion which is in the psychic atmosphere contracts and expands and in it is diffused Light of the Intelligence, like sunlight in a heavy fog. This Light comes from the noetic atmosphere which surrounds and is present throughout the mental atmosphere. The noetic atmosphere corresponds to the matter of the light world, and is conscious in the degree of I-ness-and-selfness or identity and knowledge. This atmosphere is clear; it is a colorless sphere of shadowless Light, which comes from its source directly into the noetic atmosphere.

Circulations of units are carried on through the four atmospheres by the breaths. The physical breath connects the three atmospheres of the Triune Self with the corresponding three atmospheres of the human, (Fig. V-B), and, through the physical atmosphere, with the four systems, and it further connects all these atmospheres with their respective planes and worlds. So the physical breath connects the constitution of the Triune Self, by way of the atmospheres of the human, with the nature organization in the physical body. By means of the physical breath there is a current between the human and the corresponding planes and worlds and the fire, air, water, and earth elementals in them.

Now, concerning the generation of a thought. In or through the physical atmosphere there is a constant pressing by elementals of the different worlds, to reach the organs and centers of the physical body so as to affect the feeling of the doer and get sensation through it. They throng this way because they seek sensation, for they themselves have no feeling, no sensation through feeling, except as they can get it through the feeling of an animal or a human. They are repelled or attracted by the character, good or bad, of the physical atmosphere. Elementals of the physical world are attracted or kept away particularly by the condition of the body, enfeebled, exhausted and unhealthy, or strong and vigorous. The elementals of the different worlds meeting and thronging around the physical atmosphere enter and leave it with the physical breathing, which takes them in and out through the openings and nerve centers of the body. With the elementals throng the thoughts of other persons. Elementals and thoughts of a sexual nature enter through the sex opening.

Elementals and thoughts of another kind having other aspects of sensation and excitement, enter through the navel and the pores. These are here called simply elemental, because they are especially connected with romping or playing rather than with lust. Such elementals and thoughts are those of hunger, thirst, running to see fires or accidents, doing such things as looking out of or into a window without having an object, splashing in water, dancing, making a noise, running, joining in a crowd, inquisitiveness without reason, mischief, traveling with swift movement, doing what gives a thrill or makes fun. Through the navel enter also elementals and thoughts of anger, fear, malice, hatred and drunkenness.

Emotional elementals and thoughts enter through the openings in the breasts. They are of ordinary religious exercises, of social activities at dances, card games, races and banquets, of oratory, of music, of sympathy, of suffering, of tolerance, of pathos, of kindliness, of fanaticism and of prejudice. In addition, elementals and thoughts may enter through the eye, ear, mouth or nose, which four organs of sense are common to all four classes of elementals.

Intellectual thoughts may enter from without or come from within. If they come from without they enter through the openings in the head; if they come from within they arise in the head. Of this order are intellectual thoughts concerned with sense perceptions, all thoughts of business, law, architecture, theology, chemistry and other branches of the natural and social sciences and speculations of a philosophical kind.

Elementals and thoughts of these various kinds enter through their appropriate gates at the proper swing of the breath. Once in the body, to which they can gain access only through their likeness to the mental, psychic and physical atmospheres surrounding it, they stir the astral body, which is a body of radiant-radiant, airy-radiant, fluid-radiant and solid-radiant units of physical matter, which are shaped into form by the much finer matter of the breath-form. The astral body puts the elementals or the thoughts in touch with the sensory side of the involuntary nervous system which connects with the opening or nerve center. The astral body also connects the elementals or the thoughts with the breath-form, while they are still in the nerve center. The breath-form is throughout the involuntary nervous system and is in this way reached by the elementals or the thoughts. The breath-form, when touched by the elementals or thoughts, acts automatically through the motor fibers of the involuntary nerve, on the sensory fibers of the voluntary nerve, which corresponds to the nerve by which the elementals or the thoughts entered. The elemental or thought travels with this communication and arrives at the sensory side of the voluntary system. There the breath-form puts the elemental or the thought in touch with feeling.

The seat of feeling is in the kidneys, at present. Feeling is usually not felt there; it extends throughout the body wherever the blood goes and nerves are. There is no feeling in the involuntary nervous system, but only in the voluntary system; however, there are reactions between the voluntary and the involuntary systems, which let it appear that feeling is in the involuntary system. But nature has no feeling and the system through which it works in the body has none. The other side of feeling is desire. Desire has its center in the adrenals, but is not noticed there any more than feeling, its counterpart, is noticed in the kidneys. Desire responds to feeling, into which it shades imperceptibly, so that at no time a clear line can be drawn between the two. There can be no feeling without some desire and no desire without some feeling. When feeling is affected desire acts from its seat in the adrenals and sends an adrenal secretion into the venous bloodstream and so to the heart and lungs. This secretion causes the blood in the lungs to take up oxygen, and so desire from the psychic atmosphere enters the arterial bloodstream, through the breath. Feeling and desire· travel along the bloodstream and the nerves.

Up to the time when the breath-form puts elementals and thoughts in touch with feeling in the voluntary nervous system, in the kidneys, the procedure is the same, but after that a distinction must be made between the area of elementals and that of thoughts. When elementals have come into touch with the feeling aspect of the doer, they act from the kidneys, where they are, however, not felt. They travel along the sensory nerves of the voluntary system. There they are the sensations in the parts to which they are attracted. They dance and play and sport, so to speak, on the nerves there. The doer feels their action and they share in that feeling. They produce the sensations; they are the sensations as long as they are in touch with feeling.

The sensations mostly produced are of a sensual and simple elemental kind. They affect the nerves in the pelvic and the abdominal sections. Elementals come because they want fun, activity, sensation and excitement, and they want to come under the Light of Intelligence. They will swarm into one's body when his psychic and physical atmospheres permit. These atmospheres always permit one or another species to enter. Therefore elementals are always in the body. What kind can come in and the length of time they may stay in the body, depends on one's thinking. Elementals want continuous sensation. One sensation cannot last long; it has to give way to another. It matters not to the elementals whether the sensations are pleasant or unpleasant to the human. They are as much thrilled by pain as by pleasure. They leave a body when they are crowded out by other elementals, or when thinking shuts them out.

The feeling caused by the action of elementals starts desire, which is as continuous as the sensations. Desire carries the impressions into the mental atmosphere. It reaches that in the heart with which a portion of the thinker of the Triune Self is in contact. Desire, the active side of the doer, rushes to the passive side of the thinker, rightness. Through the heart, the blood and the nerves, flows a stream of desires aroused by elementals. The desire comes from the psychic atmosphere with the intake of the breath and enters the heart with arterial blood from the lungs. When the sensory nerves of the voluntary system are affected by feeling, in the kidneys, they start the motor nerves connecting with the adrenals and reaching the heart. With the nerve action there is a flow of secretions from the adrenals to the heart. The motor nerves from the adrenals affect the sensory nerves of the heart which belong to rightness, the passive side of the thinker. The action causes a mild emotion of approval or disapproval, which is the response of rightness. If no action is taken against these impressions, feeling and desire begin to work some of the motor nerves of the heart and lungs belonging to the thinker, and these communicate back to the sensory nerves of the voluntary system in the kidneys, which belong to the doer. Some of the nerves of the lungs which belong to reason, the active side of the thinker, are then concerned with the feeling. The flow from feeling-and-desire of the doer to rightness-and-reason of the thinker, and back to feeling, that is, from the kidneys and adrenals to the heart and lungs, and back to the kidneys, is passive thinking.

Passive thinking is the play of desire and mind, that is to say, the play of desire in the Light of the Intelligence, which is diffused in a part of the mental atmosphere. It is the haphazard, purposeless, unintentional, random thinking which fills nearly all the waking hours of the run of human beings. It is produced by pictures, sounds, tastes, odors and contacts which strike the four senses, and by elementals which enter the openings of the body. It goes on without sequence, without reasoning, and it changes with each new impression that comes into the body. By this flaccid and aimless thinking, a little of the Light that is found in the mental atmosphere is drawn off into nature by elementals as they leave through the openings. Only feeling and desire are concerned in this kind of thinking.

Passive thinking leaves impressions on the breath-form. When these become strong enough a different kind of thinking is started. When an impression is marked distinctly and deeply enough it suggests the subject of thought for which it stands. If this is in accord with reason, reason directs Light of the Intelligence on the subject of thought. The I-ness of the knower is a witness to the thinking. Thus passive thinking may induce and compel active thinking. The motor nerves of the voluntary nervous system in the heart and lungs act on the sensory nerves in the pituitary body and the cerebrum, and the motor nerves from the hemispheres of the cerebrum react on the sensory nerves in the heart, which start again the motor nerves in the heart and lungs.

By this continuing process certain thinking on the subject of thought is urged on by desire and an effort is made to focus Light. This is active thinking. It continues for a short time only, is intermittent and is the effort to hold the diffused Conscious Light of the Intelligence steadily on a given subject of thought.

Through active thinking thoughts are produced by the union of desire and an impression of nature with Light of the Intelligence. In passive thinking, thinking merely plays in the Light, but by active thinking the Light is sought to be held on the subject of thought. During this effort a thought is conceived when Light unites with desire, that is, with the subject of thought. The union is made in a point of nature-matter which has been carried by desire into the mental atmosphere. Union can occur only when Light is sufficiently focussed, and this happens at the moment between the inbreathing and the outbreathing of the physical breath, at which time all the breaths are in phase.

Desire comes into the heart impressed with getting or avoiding an act, an object or an event. This desire is the subject of the thought, and it has in it nature-matter of the physical world furnished by the senses of the body. The desire itself is matter of the psychic atmosphere; rightness-and-reason allow the drawing in of matter of the mental atmosphere; and the knower allows the drawing in of matter of the noetic atmosphere. Then there is the Light of the Intelligence.

Therefore, when a thought is conceived in the heart it has in it actually matter of all the worlds, of all the atmospheres of the Triune Self, and Light of the Intelligence. It has further potentially a structure, which though yet non-existent will accord later with the systems of the three factors of which it is composed. The desire is no longer desire, but is a part of a new entity and can therefore, when it is united to Light, ascend in the body to regions to which it could not go as desire.

The newly conceived thought goes by the joint action of the blood, the breath and the nerves in both systems, to the cerebellum. There the thought is gestated for a short or for a long time. Then it passes into the cerebrum and into the ventricles of the brain, where it is elaborated and matured. Finally it is born and sent forth through the frontal sinuses at a point above the nose.

Not only elementals and one's own thoughts but thoughts from other persons enter through the openings and nerve centers in the body. By whatever gate elementals enter, they cannot go farther than the adrenals. The last thing they do is to leave their impress on desire before it starts toward the heart. It is different with thoughts from others. They go beyond the adrenals and enter the heart itself, because in them is Light of an Intelligence. In the heart they are either approved or disapproved by rightness.

If they are disapproved they are expelled through one of the openings with the outward breath. If they are approved, or if rightness suffers desire to have its way, they are entertained in the heart and then pass on to the cerebellum, as does a newly conceived thought. In the brain they can be nourished, weakened or slightly modified. Their aim cannot be changed, but their design can be varied. They are issued through the frontal sinuses, like thoughts that are newly born.

Thoughts of one's own return to him from time to time. Once a thought has been conceived, gestated and issued, it remains in the mental atmosphere of the one who created it. It circulates in the atmosphere and may re-enter the body from time to time. It enters through the breath and does not again pass through the lower stages of thinking by which it became a thought.

This ends the description of the generation of a thought, which may be the conception, gestation and birth of one's own thought, or the reception, entertainment and issue of a thought generated by someone else or by oneself, in the past.

SECTION 3

Course and exteriorization of a thought. The innate idea of justice.

Next comes the course of the thought towards its exteriorization.

The law is that thinking of physical things tends to be objectified into acts, objects or events on the physical plane. Not every thought that is generated is exteriorized. Some lack vitality to go on towards the physical plane; they have not the force to develop. Such thoughts die out and the desire in them returns into the matter of the psychic atmosphere, but the Light remains in the mental atmosphere. Some thoughts are changed before they are exteriorized. This can occur during any part of their course before exteriorization. The change occurs when the aim in the thoughts is changed; those thoughts will be exteriorized not as originally generated, but as changed by the new aim. Some thoughts are revoked before they are issued; this is so if the doer has disapproved of the thought and its purpose, after the thought has been generated. When the doer refuses it exteriorization, it is dissipated. The reason may be fear of discovery or of the consequences or it may be a change of aim.

Often the human broods over certain subjects of thought in gloom, misery or despondency, without conceiving a thought. He merely creates and dwells in a drab atmosphere and entertains thoughts without issuing them. Sometimes he plays with light fancies, castles in the air, daydreams. These occupations do not at once produce thoughts. Yet all of this kind of thinking has a tendency to influence the mental atmosphere and to determine the aim when a thought is generated.

Everything that is on the physical plane is an exteriorization of a thought, and in order to be so exteriorized that thought has to go through a certain course. Thoughts are conceived in the heart, that is, on the light plane of the life world. They are born or issued through the brain, that is, on the light plane of the light world, and this is so even though they are thoughts of low, disgusting physical things. Thoughts when born contain four factors, an aim, a plan or design, an effect or effects of the design, and the balancing factor. These will become actual in the course of the thought. A thought issues as a thought, but it is still far from being a physical thing. It issues as a point on the light plane of the light world, on the nature-side. A thought is intelligent-matter of the degree called feeling-and-desire and of the degree called Light of the Intelligence and is clothed in nature-matter of all the four worlds, but these clothes, potential as a structure within the point, become actual in its course toward exteriorization, when the structure within the point develops outward from the point.

A thought tends to carry out the potential design within it; as soon as it issues as a point it carries within it also that which will eventually balance it. This balancing factor is related to conscience, that is, a man's knowledge of his departure from rightness, the man's moral standard of right. The design is a cause, its exteriorization is an effect, which, owing to factors beyond one's control, is not always carried out as he desires. The exteriorization of the design is one thing, the exteriorization of the thought as a whole quite another. If the exteriorization of its design is also the exteriorization of the whole thought, the thought is balanced at once. This is the case if one does what he knows to be right because it is right, without attachment to the results of his actions. It is also the case in trivial affairs where conscience does not warn against the thought or action.

But if the thought is not balanced at that exteriorization, then exteriorizations must continue until in time by some one exteriorization the whole thought has been exteriorized and is itself balanced by the doer.

A thought may find exteriorization either as an act of the one who thought it, or as an event, a happening to him because of the exteriorization of the thought of another person, which his own past thought brings about.

To balance a thought is to return to nature all that is nature-matter in the thought, and to return to the doer all that belongs to the doer. The balance is made at one of the exteriorizations of the thought. Then the thought is abrogated, it ceases to exist and is balanced. A human balances a thought when he performs a duty willingly and intelligently without attachment to the results. He may not know about the thought or the method by which he balances it. Nevertheless, the thought is balanced by him.

The knower and the thinker of the Triune Self are always ready. The doer is not ready because it is not willing to let go of that in the thought which is nature-matter and which it tries to make a part of itself. The doer portion makes itself ready, though the human does not know it, when it desires to be honest and to do right and to be informed of its ignorance about itself and about what it wants.

Some of the events which will exteriorize the design, may follow only after long periods. The mystery of the physical world is caused by this separation of cause and effect. Though cause and effect become separated, there is an indissoluble connection between them and a tendency towards balancing at every stage. Conditions and opportunities do not always permit an immediate balance, but the tendency to bring one about is there in the thought and will fulfill itself in the end. The energy in a thought is not exhausted until the thought is balanced. Usually there are no outward indications of the connection between results and a still existing thought; and though a thought is a part of the man who issued it, there is then no physical evidence to show his connection with the belated or outstanding exteriorization. But whenever an exteriorization of a thought occurs, as an event in the life of someone, and results of joy or sorrow follow, his thought is there, and brings about the event to him.

When a thought issues on its way to be exteriorized it is actually a point of matter on the light plane of the light world, having latent in it matter of the three lower worlds, and is therefore still potential, that is, its inherent possibilities have not become physical things. It is on the nature-side and is guided by its aim. A thought has in itself the tendency to unfold the structure within the point, and so to express itself in physical matter, out of which the generating desire was aroused and to which it is directed by the aim, (Fig. IV-A). The course may be devious, may be delayed or may be interfered with, but it descends to the physical plane and will arrive there at last.

The term "descends" is figurative; it does not mean moving down. All the worlds intermingle in a human body. When it is said that a thought descends from one world or plane to another it means that the thought affects, and is itself affected by, different kinds of matter in a human body, and that it changes from the finer kind that clothed it to a coarser kind.

From the light plane of the light world the thought descends to the light plane of the life world, and there the potential life matter grows from the point outward, and clothing the thought becomes actual on that plane. Then the thought descends into the form world where the form matter becomes actual; then it descends to the light plane of the physical world. The descent in each case is made when the matter grows from a point to the quarter circle.

Then the thought enters the body or bodies through which it is to be exteriorized. It passes from the light plane to the radiant-radiant state on the physical plane of the physical world. There in the head it takes on radiant matter from the generative system. Then it descends to the airy state in the thorax and takes on airy matter from the respiratory system. If the thought is to be exteriorized in speech or in an act not connected with food, smell or sex, it does not go below the heart, and there it draws from the circulatory and digestive systems, by means of the blood, fine fluid and solid matter, and is exteriorized with that. If the thought is one concerned with eating or smelling or sex, it goes below into the abdominal or the pelvic section and receives there the matter that will clothe it to become an act, an object or an event. If the thought affects many, as the prosperity which comes from a harvest or a new road, or as the calamity which follows the sweep of a disease or a devastation, it is built into the event in the bodies of all the people, near and distant, who are touched by it.

This concretion of a thought may happen instantly or it may take a long time. If there is a delay the thought does not reach the physical plane, but waits on the radiant-form plane, in the abdomen. This is so even though the thought is to be manifested as speech and does not go below the heart. It is nevertheless on the radiant-form plane in the region of the kidneys.

When the thought has arrived on the radiant-physical plane, that is, in a state of radiant-radiant or astral matter, it is well defined and is the counterpart of what it is intended to be as a physical act, object or event. This is why events can sometimes be foretold.

When the astral form becomes the physical act, object or event, a part of the thought is exteriorized. It may take many physical efforts and a long series of physical events before the balance with the physical event is made by the doer in itself, as it inevitably must be made. Because of the factors in the generation of a thought, the balancing depends on conscience and responsibility. At present only the course of a thought will be kept in view.

The astral form of the thought which is in the radiant-radiant state of matter on the physical plane becomes visible when time, place and circumstances are provided for it to appear in the solid-solid state of matter, and then the act, object or event takes place. But it is to be remembered that the thought survives and survives, and that the potential exteriorization is not complete until the balancing factor which was and remains in the thought and is an essential part of it, is satisfied. The acts, things and events on earth are but partly exteriorized thoughts; an invisible part remains behind.

Therefore it often happens that many physical effects are necessary in order that one thought may be balanced. Each man must reap all the physical results which come from the act which he thought into the world, though the reaping be separated from the sowing by a life or lives. A man conceives thoughts and issues them apart from earthly time and place. Their materialization into physical acts, objects and events cannot take place except as conditions on the earth permit. When a design is exteriorized there may be a number of other exteriorizations before the thought is balanced. The joyful and sorrowful events into which thoughts exteriorize may have to wait long before circumstances occur which will give a suitable experience.

Numerous difficulties must be adjusted before an exteriorization can take place. Some of these are: The problem of placing in physical time the many physical effects which are to unfold out of one thought. There is the difficulty of a physical manifestation, in one place, of the several effects which are to follow out of one thought. There is the sequence of exteriorizations into physical matter under physical laws, which may take many years. The laws of the growth and maturing of the bodies or conditions connected with the exteriorization may make impossible a contemporaneous manifestation of a physical cause and the physical effects produced by it. It often takes a long time to produce and mature the instruments through which the balance is made. The unresponsiveness of physical matter to thought is another difficulty. Further, there is the long past of the doer, who waits to have balanced causes which have not yet been compensated. Moreover, there are thoughts, due to hostile interests of others, which oppose the exteriorization. The difficulties thus presented in the case of one man are correspondingly multiplied when the thoughts of others, or those of all people living in the world, or those of all human beings that have ever lived, are to be considered. Another consideration is that thoughts move in cycles, and that the intersection of cycles governs exteriorization into solid matter. These are some of the difficulties to be adjusted before an exteriorization can take place.

When a thought has taken form, it is halted in its course and lies on the threshold of the physical plane, ready to be externalized. It is right here in the radiant-radiant state on the physical plane, but cannot be seen. It has no solid clothes to make it visible as act, object or event. In this same sense it may be said to be halted in its course of exteriorization. Four factors, time, condition, place, and a human body, form the matrix through which a thought is exteriorized.

All acts, objects and events that were on the physical plane in the past, that are here now and that will appear here in the future, were, are and will be thoughts built into visibility. They cannot come into being in any other way. This world is the visible appearance of the result of the action of mind and desire, the exteriorizations of human thought. This ends the description of the course of a thought up to the time when the design is exteriorized.

With the exteriorization of a thought are connected physical, psychic, mental and noetic results, each of which may be followed by an almost unending chain of physical effects. There are results which will naturally follow the physical act.

The decrees of the law determine the physical results only, but through these physical results man will be compelled by that law to fulfill the psychic, mental and noetic requirements. The law does not determine these; the doer in the man does that. The physical results of an exteriorized thought are produced under the laws of physics, chemistry and the natural sciences generally. These laws are subservient to the law of thought, and it works only through them. Only such results are of interest here as are produced under these physical laws for the purpose of making the generator of a thought pay or receive payment, of giving him experience, of making him learn a lesson and of making him get a certain knowledge, and so to balance the thought through the exteriorization and its results in the doer.

Physical results happen at the conjunction of time and place and when the conditions are mature, and are then inevitably produced by causes that may have no seemingly reasonable or necessary connection with their occurrence. Herein lies the secret of the management of the physical world. This lack of apparent reason or justice is a mystery of life. Yet the world goes on as it has for untold years, and how could that be without any fundamental rule and equilibrium? The balancing is done through physical results. Every act done affords an opportunity to restore a balance.

The intention of the person who does the act is usually to further his own interests in a particular manner, but whether he succeeds or not, the consequences of his act are used to afford to persons with whom he may or may not be concerned, an opportunity to balance their past thoughts. The lives of men and the history of peoples show unmistakably that individuals act chiefly for their own selfish purposes, and that in every case the forces which are thus released or set in motion are taken charge of by some intelligent powers and used to bring about events not wished for, not contemplated, not even dreamed of and hardly appreciated at the time by anybody. So is made and accomplished the destiny of men and nations; not as the individuals would have it, but by a mysterious management, whose ultimate plan is to obtain a balance of thoughts by means of acts and events.

The present is the manifestation of a hold-over from the past. An immeasurable accumulation of events waits for time and place to burst into visibility and to cause joy or grief to those whom these events will affect. These exteriorizations will affect those for whom they have not yet had a chance to appear, face to face, clothed in solid matter. Events continue to come to a person until through exteriorizations he pays for the past exteriorization, learns the lessons required by the stage of his growth, gets a certain amount of knowledge and so balances in the psychic, mental and noetic states the thoughts which caused these events.

There is in the doer-in-the-body of every human a desire for justice, an innate idea in the doer. What is considered justice varies with the varied development of different human beings. Savages have crude notions of justice, conscience, right; as man becomes more civilized, his vision changes, his knowledge of what is right increases, and more and more things which to the savage seem right, stand out to him as wrong. All events in a man's life are offered to him, allure him, please him, annoy him, force him on, overwhelm him, for the purpose of letting him have an opportunity to satisfy his desire for justice by right thinking; or else to make him pay for wrong action and reward him for right, so as to give him a chance to learn to distinguish right from wrong, through experience and observation. The law of thought, as destiny, uses all manner of agencies to bring about these results. The results of a person's thoughts and acts have to fit in with this universal arrangement. Man does not balance his thought in an instant; he does not do it even in many lives. Therefore he must learn; and he learns by the experiences which life brings to him and by his observations of the experiences of others.

SECTION 4

The law of thought. Exteriorizations and interiorizations. Psychic, mental, and noetic results. The power of thought. Balancing a thought. Cycles.

The law is: Everything existing on the physical plane is an exteriorization of a thought, which must be balanced through the one who issued the thought, in accordance with his responsibility, and at the conjunction of time, condition and place. Thus are explained the seemingly unjust, arbitrary or accidental events in a person's life. Whatever happens to one, happens at the conjunction of time, condition and place. The physical events which occur to a man may or may not be exteriorizations of his own thoughts. But the psychic events, the feelings of joy or sorrow which he experiences from each and every event in his life are the results of his own thinking.

These are interiorizations—psychic, mental and noetic. They tend towards balancing the thought. Psychic results are the first interiorizations. Joys and sorrows, sensations and emotions, are furnished to the human as experiences. Through them he should learn, that is, get mental results. If he will not learn, the experiences are repeated and repeated and intensified until he does learn. All joys and sorrows are the results of events which are exteriorizations of prior thoughts. The sensations are produced by physical means, slight or potent, and the physical events and conditions are called physical destiny.

So come about the sale of worthless shares and the loss by investors, the dishonest conduct of a business and the ruin of innocent partners, the courageous deed of a lifesaver and his rescue of the doomed, and the act of a murderer and the death of his victim. So come about individual accidents as well as universal calamities, crop failures, famines and pests, strikes and wars and the subsequent shifting of the layers of society. These events produce sensations of joy or sorrow, and these come to each one as the reaping of his former sowing, as a result of his thoughts, that survive for him. So come about births of persons with strong or infirm characters, good or evil inclinations; so also the attraction exercised by religion, sport, gambling, drinking or by certain trades and lines of business. So comes about birth with the mental endowments and moral qualities that adorn or disgrace a man. So originate the treasures of insight and innate knowledge.

How do thoughts call for the happening of events which will permit them to be exteriorized? The answer to this explains the bringing about of such events as the Hundred Years War between France and England, the conquests of Mexico and of Peru, the Napoleonic wars, and the World Wars, which caused the death of millions and which have affected other millions favorably or unfavorably. It explains how some persons at the last moment get on a ship that will be lost, while others get off before it sails; how a merely inquisitive person gets into a crowd and is seriously hurt; how some survive unharmed all manner of dangers in an adventurous life, and how others are led into trouble by unexpected events. Physical events, no matter how great they seem to be, are small and like bits of straw blown by the wind, when they are compared with the thought that caused them or calls for them.

Thoughts live and last until they are adjusted. They are powerful beings, though not as men know beings. Thoughts urge, pull and press in on a person or set of persons who allow them to be exteriorized in an event that will affect physically the person or set of persons responsible for them. This urging and pressing by a thought can affect only those who will entertain the thought or who will allow themselves to be influenced by it. Persons who will not entertain or allow themselves to be influenced cannot be affected, or induced to commit acts. The thought lives in the mental atmospheres of persons or communities and is entertained or refused audience in the hearts. When it is entertained or allowed to enter, it suggests action; and when time, condition and place are fit the thought issues from the brain of someone, the design in it is exteriorized, and the person or persons will do an act which in turn will be an event in the life of the person or community whose thought is exteriorized through that event.

Events bring sensations, that is, results upon the doer-in-the-body and the psychic atmosphere of the human. These sensations, whether they come from physical or psychic causes, are experiences of a psychic kind and are content or discontent, well-being or uneasiness, delight or weariness, gladness or a heavy heart. These experiences are caused by the exteriorizations of a present or a past thought of the one who has the experience. A trifling event may bring on a tremendous sensation. The sensation is what counts. The event is negligible compared with the sensation. The importance of a thing or event is found in the sensation, the psychic result it produces. Any event that will lend itself to bring about the sensation required will suffice, but the sensation must be produced. Sensations mean paying or receiving pay for acts done or left undone. They may be the means of learning, which is a mental result.

If men would learn from experience, get learning from psychic results, they need not have the same experiences over again. But men will not learn from their experiences and so continue in the same round of thoughts and have the same experiences in life after life. Out of these repeated experiences is built up the psychic nature or character of man, with certain tendencies to criminality, selfishness, carelessness, lack of consideration for the feelings of others, or the reverse of all these. This psychic nature is expressed later in the physical body. So people are born afflicted with certain diseases, or develop them later. As thoughts enter the body and affect one of the four systems, so the elementals building out the thoughts carry with them and build out the disease which is called for by the thought. In turn, diseases are among the chief causes for sensation. They are the experiences of nearly everyone. On the other hand, events which are welcome are often a punishment in disguise, as will soon appear to those concerned, just as unwelcome events are often blessings in disguise. Such are the psychic results following the exteriorization of a thought. Mental results follow from the pleasure or pain of experiences.

Mental results will follow sooner or later. The Light of the Intelligence is on the doer which the Triune Self has in charge. By the use of that Light the doer is developed to value the fitness of things. Moral lessons are taught through religions and at the mother's knee. The laws of a country also present a ready code for conduct. Further, there are the laws of nature which let him learn concerning digestion, breathing and disease. By all these means a human is taught directly.

He also learns by observing facts. When he has gathered enough facts, even though he may not know why or how he observed them, a desire to learn from them is awakened because the doer is in the Light of its Intelligence. Then the human begins to think, infer, combine and separate, by Light of the Intelligence. So he works with theories concerning his problems. He will feel what event has some meaning for him when it occurs, even though it be not perceptibly connected with him. Most events have a meaning for the one who experiences them or who observes them. While the doer-in-the-body is learning from a set of experiences it is like a man groping around in the dark trying to find out what the different things he contacts are, and who sees the objects from time to time by flashes of light. The events which come to the human in life cannot be related until he receives Light. By the Light, he learns. From learning many things and seeing them verified, the doer acquires a certain amount of knowledge of what is right. The amount of knowledge of what is right is his conscience.

The mental results are different in different cases. They are impressions that the act or event is right or wrong, and that it carries or does not carry a lesson for the thinking doer. When the impression is that the act or event was right or wrong, this mental impression is one of the factors in forming one's opinions on right and wrong as to things in general. Even if the event was not due perceptibly to any act of his, there will be some indication that the occurrence has a meaning for him and some suggestion to make him look into it.

Every event has a meaning for the one to whom it comes, even though he rarely pays attention to the call. A man often tries to hide from himself the facts, when disagreeable, and so prevents himself from seeing what is right and what he should or should not do. From the manner in which one looks mentally upon acts and events and their psychic results to him, he creates or strengthens mental tendencies and confirms mental attitudes with which he regards those lines of right or wrong action; this causes the recurrence of thoughts with the same or a similar aim.

Noetic results, that is, results in the noetic atmosphere of the human come from the mental results which follow the psychic results of pleasure or pain from the experience of physical events. The noetic results are extracts of mental results, which contain the essence of the psychic results, and are the record of what the doer of the Triune Self has done with itself towards being conscious of what the knower already knows. What the doer has become conscious of as being morally right or wrong is kept as a record in the noetic atmosphere and is to the doer conscience. Conscience speaks only from or through rightness of the thinker of the Triune Self. Noetic results are the essence of what people learn, but as they learn so very little the noetic results from exteriorizations are meager.

A thought is exteriorized until there is a balancing of it by means of its physical, psychic, mental and noetic results. The physical results are the exteriorizations which were potentially in the thought from the beginning. Exteriorizations continue until the potential balance contained in the thought is made an actual one. The balancing factor in the thought by which the potential balance is forced on and exteriorized is conscience, which speaks as the result of knowledge and of departure from what is known to be right.

The actual balance of a thought is made when at last the noetic, mental, psychic and physical results are in agreement, that is, when the knower, the thinker and the doer are satisfied through the particular event which is an exteriorization of the thought. This exteriorization may mean much or little in the world, but it means much to the doer. The exteriorization is the only thing the world can see; but the Triune Self desires or thinks or knows what that event is to it. The important thing for the doer to do, after it has created a thought, is to desire to balance it in the three parts of the Triune Self with any physical event which is an exteriorization of the thought.

The balancing proceeds from the doer of the Triune Self. There takes place an accomplishment by and from all the experiences concerned with all the events that were potentially in and developed actually out of that thought. The doer is ready when it has had enough experiences through the thought; when it sees that what it actually wants is in itself, not in possessions; when it sees that it as desire cannot judge; when it desires the thinker to do the judging; when it wants to let go. The knower, as knowledge, and the thinker, as justice, are at all times ready for the balancing. They wait for the doer to be in the condition where it is willing to have the adjustment between itself and nature made. This adjustment is the balancing of the thought, and is made by returning to nature that in the thought which belongs to nature and by freeing the desire from its attachment to it. When the desire is to let go and to be guided by the thinker, the human is unattached to the event and is happy in the feeling of freedom. He is satisfied with the exteriorization even if it be the loss of everything, or the hardest fate. Though the human is not necessarily conscious of the balancing he is conscious of what his attitude towards the exteriorization means to him. This is in every case a step towards thinking without creating thoughts, destiny, that is, without attachment to objects of nature. The knower disapproves of every thought which is created, because this attaches the desire of the doer to the results of the thought.

Though the doer-in-the-body is not conscious of what goes on in the Triune Self, one does the acts which are the balancing when he performs his duties gladly, without attachment to their results. Few persons balance their thoughts, because most people are not willing to perform their duties and they refuse to understand that the doer-in-the-body must be willing to be guided by the thinker and not by sensations. Yet they are generating new thoughts without balancing many and they go through life like comets, with enormous tails of unbalanced thoughts following them.

In the course of making the adjustment of a thought a man has to pay his old debts, and he receives compensation for what is due him. A thought cannot be balanced without payment having been made or received and the accounts settled in connection with that particular thought. The payment may be made in pain, sorrow, terror or despair, for payment is always made in psychic coin, but the psychic conditions result from physical conditions. Likewise, payment is received always in psychic coin as pleasure, well-being, serenity.

Payment alone is not enough. A man must pay whether he wills to or not; he will continue to pay over and over again until he learns why the payment must be made. This does not mean that he must know the one whom he wronged and where and when he became a debtor, but that he must learn how not to injure others and how not to allow others to injure him; how to be considerate of the rights and feelings of others without becoming their prey. Payment and learning alone are not enough. There must be a noetic enlightenment accomplished by the results of what he has learned from his experiences. This is usually shown by his attitude of mind towards his duties. Duties performed with willingness and understanding effect a balance of the thought of which they are an exteriorization.

A thought must be balanced by the one who issued it according to the responsibility which was his at the time he generated or entertained it. His responsibility is his appreciation of right and wrong, his standard of right. He is informed of this responsibility not by reason, but by direct warning from his conscience, given through the rightness of his thinker. This warning stamps the thought for life through death, and throughout the existence of the thought. The thought will continue until that stamp is matched. The stamp is the balancing factor, that compels cyclic exteriorizations out of the thought until the thought is balanced by the agreement of the physical, psychic, mental and noetic results. One's responsibility is his knowledge as the result of all that his doer has learned from all its experiences through all its lives. This knowledge is abstract; but a concrete expression of this abstraction is found in the duty which is his at any given time. That duty is a mirror of his responsibility.

A thought once issued moves in a cycle. It is issued from the light world and its course is towards exteriorization. It is exteriorized on the physical plane as an act, an object or an event that produces results which are interiorized as psychic, mental and noetic results in Triune Selves.

If no balance of the thought is made, desire starts the action of the thinking and desire on a new cycle of the same thought. Frequently the old thought which has not been balanced returns. It is not again conceived, but is entertained in the heart, reinforced through the brain and reissued, and then it seems to be a new thought. That is one reason why one's thoughts run along certain lines and are related to each other. The aim always brings the thought back to where it started, and then the aim may be slightly changed as the thought is sent on its new cycle. A thought once issued has a tendency to cause continued similar thinking to reinforce it.

If a thought, when its results are interiorized in the psychic, mental and noetic atmospheres of the human, be not balanced, it has while it is going through its cycles, decided effects upon the human. The results on the human are feelings of joy or sorrow and desire for continuance or cessation of the results and, further, sharpening, dulling or control of that desire. The human senses the desire as being right or wrong. If the desire wants to be right, rightness strengthens it; if desire insists on the wrong, rightness gives way. Yet the thinking may be active and effective. That is very often so when the personality is by the cycles of a thought built up on a morally wrong basis, as of cunning, selfishness or crookedness. In such cases the human regards everything as right that he desires, and everything that stands in his way as wrong.

The cycle of a thought has a certain path. At one point in its path the thought is exteriorized. Here the cycle is dealt with only in so far as it produces the exteriorization in orderly succession. One part of the path is toward exteriorization, the other part of the path is interior and subjective and comes after the part that appears as the exteriorization. Of course, when a thought issues on the light plane of the light world, which is formless, the thought is formless and its movements are not cyclic in the same sense in which they are when the thought has form and cycles in the physical world. For simplicity the term cycle is applied also to the prior stages.

Within the larger course of the thought from issuance to exteriorization are many smaller cycles, so that in one cycle from the mental atmosphere in the life world by way of the physical plane of the physical world and back to the mental atmosphere in the life world there may be many lesser cycles. These are produced by desires and thinking toward the exteriorization of that thought. The act, object or event may be followed by other cycles within the greater cycle of the thought, the smaller cycles producing feelings, sensations and emotions. These may be followed by innumerable cycles of mental processes. A thought cycles downward by mental activities to find a way toward exteriorization. As it takes on a definite design, plan and form by which it will be exteriorized it approaches and finally appears on the physical plane. After this exteriorization of a part of the thought it goes on, affecting the doer subjectively, first by feeling, sensation, emotion and sentiment, all flowing as results from the exteriorization. This is a cycle of experiences, (Fig. IV-A).

So the course of the thought continues until the doer learns from its experiences through these exteriorizations. After the doer has learned and there is a willingness and readiness in the doer to do what it feels it should, there is a noetic, mental and psychic agreement between knowledge, conscience, desiring and doing or suffering in relation to the exteriorization of that thought, and the cycle of the thought is completed—balanced in the mental atmosphere.

The length of the cycle and the number of the lesser cycles within its path are determined by the responsibility of the doer and its willingness to learn and perform its duties. No one thought can be exteriorized separately from everything else, because no thought or thing can act independently of its relation to another thought or thing. Two or more thoughts of the same person, or a thought of one person and at least one thought of another person are necessary to bring about an exteriorization. Two or more thoughts must touch or cross each other for the exteriorization of either or both. When at least two thoughts make such a junction, coalescing, intersecting or coinciding, one or both are ready for exteriorization, if place and condition can be found. The time is determined by the fact that the thought is on the form plane of the physical world. Only there thoughts can meet for exteriorization.

A thought, once it is issued and exteriorized in part, continues its cyclic paths after the death of the body of the one who generated it. It goes with the doer-in-the-body and stays in the mental atmosphere of the human, (Fig. V-B). It appears cyclically in that portion of the doer after death during the different after-death states. Its thoughts are the accusers and witnesses that come to the doer for or against it in the Hall of Judgment and the states of expiation and purification. The cycles continue. Only portions of the best thoughts accompany the doer into its heaven and stay with it there, (Fig. V-D). When the doer portion returns to physical life and enters a human body, its former thoughts continue to cycle around the human. The human in the early stages of life is not conscious of the cycling thoughts. As the body matures and the doer finds itself, it has thoughts. These thoughts which come to it in cyclic recurrence are its former thoughts. They are not conceived anew but are entertained in the heart, reinforced in the brain and from there reissued. The cycles of a person's thoughts determine the length and nature of his hell and his heaven and approximately the time between re-existences.

So far past thoughts of a single individual have been considered; but that is not enough. All human beings are generating thoughts. Their thoughts, like those of the individual, are condensed and so gradually exteriorized.

All these thoughts have formed the conditions of the past with its savagery, despotism, slavery; its feudal and absolute monarchies, with its serfs and peasants subject to forced labor, tithes and taxes; with its nobles and their right to jurisdiction and to the services of those who belonged to the land; and then the changing conditions in the nineteenth century, when thoughts found expression in wider education, united nations, bureaucracies and in manufacture and commerce, with railroads, telegraph and further inventions, whereby the middle classes and laborers came to the front and education became common in all civilized lands.

If others' thoughts were not opposed to his, the individual could nearly always count upon a realization of his own thoughts in the physical world, though not always as he wishes it to be, because no man can consider all of the factors in the light, life, form and physical worlds; nor can he know when the cycles will meet, favorably or unfavorably, to permit exteriorizations. All human beings are issuing thoughts. Many of these run counter to the thoughts of any one; some coincide with them. When thoughts of people cross each other or coincide there is usually an encounter or a coinciding on the physical plane, in acts and in things. So friends, business associates, persons thinking of a common cause or occupation, adherents of church or political movements meet; their thoughts bring them together. In the same way enemies, individuals struggling or races warring meet, because of their conflicting thoughts. So nations are divided, as was Poland, and united, as was Italy after her long struggle.

Thoughts do not usually result in exteriorization as a person would wish, because he cannot consider the unknown factors. Important among these are his past thoughts which have not yet come into realization, and the results of which may prevent the immediate exteriorization of his present thought. Another factor is that out of the millions of thoughts, his own and those of others, only a small number can be realized in the physical world at any one time, as place and time on the physical plane condition the exteriorization of thoughts. Then exteriorization into physical acts and events can take place only under physical laws, and further, when the meeting of cycles of thoughts permits. Moreover, no thought could be exteriorized if it were not for present thinking. So there are many obstacles which are not known and overcome. But the most mysterious of all factors is the balancing factor in the thought, which is connected with the universal tendency to adjustment and continues to impel exteriorizations of the thought until it is balanced.

Because these factors are unperceived and because it appears that there is no immediate, just retribution, it seems that moral acts do not produce the effect which they should produce. Acts worthy and noble often appear to be without reward, and mean and unjust acts to be crowned with worldly success. In this way the moral requirements which men feel as the rule of their own lives appear to be absent in the management of the world.

Justice on the physical plane cannot be had at once because of people's unwillingness to have justice done to them; because of the unresponsiveness of physical matter to thought; because of the hindrances on the physical plane to immediate exteriorization of everything that is required for adjustment; because the cross-currents of various persons' thoughts interfere; because the time is not ripe for those involved to come together; and, because of other difficulties indicated.

SECTION 5

How exteriorizations of a thought are brought about. Agents of the law. Hastening or delaying destiny.

These difficulties, hindering the exteriorizations of a thought, are resolved in a marvelous way by a proper marshalling of the successive exteriorizations of every thought into events, which appear in an orderly way under the certain laws governing the conduct of physical matter. The certainty of the operation of these laws, such as those of chemistry, physics and the procreation, growth, disease, death and decay of organic bodies, is not interfered with; indeed these very laws are subservient to the law of thought.

The marshalling is done by agents of the law. Every being is an agent of the law, but not every being knows that it is. These agents may be elementals, nature units of the nature-side; or they may be on the intelligent-side; these range from the Supreme Intelligence of the sphere of earth, through lesser Intelligences, to Triune Selves, down to the doer-in-the-body in the lowest human being.

Among the conscious agents are three orders of Intelligences, named respectively Desirers, Thinkers and Knowers, (Fig. V-C); then there are Triune Selves who have not quite attained to the stage of an Intelligence. Besides these there are doers of Triune Selves that may have many weaknesses, but are at times aware that they have definite parts to take and things to do, in public and in private life. It is likely that such men in public life were William Penn, Benjamin Franklin, Alexander Hamilton, Abraham Lincoln, Theodore Roosevelt, Voltaire, Napoleon, Disraeli and Lord Shaftesbury; in private life, men like Emerson and Kerning are likely to have been conscious agents of their Triune Selves.

Then there are the unconscious agents of the law, either willing or unwilling. The unconscious but willing are those who wish to do right, like Luther; the unwilling are those who are self-seekers and do not want to do anything but what serves their interest and purpose, like Richard III, or Henry VIII. Among these agents again there are two kinds, the slothful, lazy ones, and such as are actually and actively disposed to do evil.

All these agents, the conscious as well as the unconscious, occupy their positions because they have earned them by thinking. The doers of Triune Selves operate the mechanism; the unconscious agents form the human part of it and are used for the ends of the law of thought while they are carrying out their own plans. Unconscious agents as well as conscious, always have a choice as to what they will and will not do. Nero, Attila, Pizarro, Genghis Khan, and the host of cruel despots were agents of the law as destiny; so is a pickpocket snatching a purse and a murderer striking his blow. They all act to carry out their own plans, inconsiderate of others. Such as these are parts of the machinery of the law. That does not mean that they deserve any credit, or will be excused for stealing, corruption or killing. Their motives and desires are used in the intelligent administration, as is a tiger that devours a child, or a saw that injures a laborer.

The beings on the nature-side which are agents of the law are in the four elements of the sphere of earth. The beings in the unmanifested part of the worlds do not usually come into manifestation and into relation with man. They are named the upper elementals, to distinguish them from the elementals, large and small, in the manifested part of the worlds.

These upper elementals are spoken of as angels and archangels and rulers over the four elements. To them the plan of worlds is outlined by complete Triune Selves under the Great Triune Self of the worlds; and the upper elementals give directions to be executed by the lower. There is the Great Triune Self of the worlds present in the unmanifested and the manifested, who keeps in unity and relation all the complete Triune Selves acting in the worlds. The upper elementals are called into existence by complete Triune Selves; they are pure, untainted by the world's lust or ambition. They respond perfectly to the complete Triune Selves whom they worship but cannot sense. The upper elementals serve the purpose of these Triune Selves to control the elemental gods; they are the intermediaries and messengers to them from the complete Triune Selves. At special conjunctions of cycles in the history of the human race, the upper elementals, one or more, may appear to an individual or to a number of people, to issue an order to human beings as coming from the God of the particular religion these humans believe in. At certain crises of a nation's history, these elemental messengers may appear and change the course of events.

They are the only nature beings that come under the Light of an Intelligence, without human beings as go-betweens. They differ from doers in that they act absolutely according to the behest of the Light and cannot use the Light for themselves. They are, and cannot be more than, messengers of the Light.

The lower elementals are of four groups, named the causal, portal, form and structure elementals, all in the manifested part of the sphere of earth, each group having in it elementals of the fire, air, water and earth. Causal elementals belong to creation and bring all things into existence, and also destroy them; they are the cause of change in substances and in structures. The portal elementals stir up things in nature and keep up a state of constant circulation in all things. Form elementals hold things together as they are in visible nature. These three groups do all things in visible nature, but cannot be seen. They do their work in the structures built by the fourth group. The structure elementals, in their mass, are the apparent forms of things. They are the builders and are the structure of the visible universe. They make things solid. They are surfaces. By these descriptions some of the activities of the lower elementals are shown. And each elemental is a nature unit of the element to which it belongs.

All material things are produced, maintained, changed, destroyed and reproduced by elementals of these four groups. The matter-force of the sphere of earth is under the rule of the great elemental Earth Spirit; and under it each element is under the rule of a great elemental God, the God of Fire, the God of Air, the God of Water and the God of Earth, which are not referred to in any religion and are not worshipped. Under each of these Gods are elemental beings in hierarchies, in and of the god of the element, diminishing in power from the greatest to the infinitesimal. There is the great God of Fire, who may cause the consuming of the earth crust by fire, and there is the elemental of a bacillus of fever, belonging to one of his hierarchies. All operations of nature are carried on by elementals under their rulers who receive the plan from upper elementals under the direction of an Intelligence of the sphere of earth. These operations are guided by an Intelligence according to the general definite plan. So elementals bring rescues, accidents, diseases, success, money and quarrels to individuals, and general calamities, storms, earthquakes, famines, epidemics and periods of opulence.

A thought issued comes into touch with elementals in the life world. Its soundless sound impresses some of them into its plan and there it takes life. Then the thought sounds in the form world. There elementals give it form. Then it comes to the physical world, where the four orders of earth elementals begin to give materiality to its form. The elementals which give this physicality are worked through the body of man. The beginnings are made on the light plane through the brain which summons and attracts radiant, astral matter. Then the heart and lungs, on the life plane, working with the brain, bind and change the particles of radiant matter into airy. The kidneys and adrenals, on the form plane, draw airy matter into the fluid state and hold it so. Finally, the organs of the digestive system consolidate fluid matter into the cellular or solid state. The breath-form, through the breath, organizes and coordinates these workings and their effects so as to produce the physicality of the thought, which will be exteriorized later at the conjunction of time, condition and place as an act, an object or an event. This is true where the thought of one man only is active, as well as where the thoughts of thousands are involved in the exteriorization. In this way everything in the physical world is brought about. Every structure that is built, every institution that is founded, every law that is enacted, all events in public and in private life, are so exteriorized.

Out of the thoughts available, some are selected to appear in form, others often contribute thereto. The selection of what act is produced physically cannot be made by elementals, for none of them are intelligent. The selection is made by complete Triune Selves according to the law and according to the possibilities permitted by the limitations of time and place and of existing conditions, and at their conjunction the elementals carry out the bidding of the Triune Selves, and in this way successive acts fit naturally into and develop from existing conditions.

Each man has stored up many thoughts which have not been given form, and many more have form and are thronging on the physical plane but have not yet been given physical expression. The Triune Selves administering the law and marshalling the order of exteriorization of effects, have to hold back on the radiant-physical plane many acts and events which will appear when place, time and conditions permit.

A man hastens or postpones the exteriorization of his past thoughts by his general mental attitude and definite mental set as to a certain course of action. All things which suit that course are drawn in whether they have been held back for a long or a short time. His thinking and acting make the time, place and conditions for events about to happen to him. He may postpone exteriorizations of his thoughts by trying to

ward off events which threaten as natural consequences, just as he is able
to put off a trial in a court or an appointment to meet a creditor. He may
postpone by planning, but though a man may put off the events which
are to come he cannot avoid them forever. If he succeeds in postponing
what is unpleasant to him, he interferes with the Triune Selves who
arrange the actions of the elementals and who see to the arrival of events
at the proper conjunction of time, place and condition. If he is successful,
many of the conditions which are due him accumulate. The tendency of
the accumulated energy is to increase their pressure. The longer he
continues his accumulating the greater is the pressure, until finally vast
elemental powers may be disturbed, and they react on him and will force
him to make an opening through which the accumulated destiny will
pour in on him.

Every one knows as much of his destiny as is necessary. It is his good
fortune that he does not know more than that, because knowledge of
unpleasant things about to happen might prevent him from doing his
present duty, and knowledge of agreeable things to come might cause
him to neglect it. All that is necessary for one to know is his present duty.
He can always know it if he wishes. Duty is that part of his destiny
selected by his Triune Self from all of his past, which he should dispose
of in the present. His Triune Self marshalled his past and present and
some of his future destiny so that all three converge into the duty of the
present moment. If one refuses to do his duty, he merely postpones it; it
must be performed by him in time. The performance of duty opens the
road to other duties leading into larger fields. So the willing performance
of duty allows him to see his duties more clearly and to come more under
the Light of the Intelligence.

SECTION 6

Duties of a human being. Responsibility. Conscience. Sin.

The human has duties to nature, to his breath-form, to his Triune
Self, to the Intelligence from whom the Triune Self receives its Light,
and to the Supreme Intelligence.

The duties to nature are, to nature in the human body and to nature
outside. While nature-matter is in the human body it is the doer's duty
to improve it so that the nature-matter becomes conscious in higher
degrees. In most of this improvement, as that through the progression

of the nature units in the body, the doer in the human is unconscious, but senses a duty to keep the body whole, sound and clean; this includes the duty to care for the four beings which are the four senses. To outside nature the human has the duties to worship it according to the religion into which he is born or which he chooses, and to be true to that religion while he believes in it; to worship, pay tribute to and to nourish a nature god or the nature gods, so long as the human believes him or them to be the source of his being. This is the case chiefly while the doer is in the stage of the run of human beings. When the human advances he has the duty to see and understand nature in his own body.

The duty of the human to his breath-form begins when he discovers that nature and the nature gods are not the source of his being. The duty is to restore his breath-form to the Realm of Permanence so that it will take its place in the Eternal Order of Progression when his Triune Self becomes an Intelligence.

The duties of the doer in a human to its Triune Self are to learn what the three parts of the Triune Self are, as doer, thinker and knower, and what their proper relation is, and not to allow itself to be lost into nature. The doer must learn the nature and functions of itself as feeling-and-desire, of the thinker as rightness-and-reason, and of its knower as I-ness-and-selfness. Feeling must be kept sensitive, so that it may receive accurately impressions from nature and from the other parts of the Triune Self. Desire must be restrained so as not to strive against rightness-and-reason. Thus rightness should be made safe against the pressure of desire. Rightness should receive the respect due it for showing the standard of what is right, and reason should receive the reverence due it as the guide of the doer in the human who should learn to communicate with rightness-and-reason. The human should revere the I-ness of his knower as his unchanging identity, and the selfness of his knower as his Self-knowledge and as his bringer and dispenser of Light of the Intelligence. It is the duty of the doer-in-the-body to distinguish itself as that which is not the body with a name, but as desire-and-feeling in the body, and to adjust each to the other towards a final balanced union.

The duties of the doer in the human to the Intelligence are to recognize it as its Conscious Light, as different from nature, as the source of the Light that is in the Triune Self. The human should preserve the Light and not lose it into nature. One should try to become conscious of the Light and to be conscious of the Intelligence through the Light of the Intelligence. The duty of the human to the Supreme Intelligence is to become conscious of it through the Light of the Intelligence which gives its Light to the Triune Self. When these duties are comprehended they will be done as naturally as are the bodily duties of eating and drinking and bathing and breathing and sleeping, and as gladly as one communicates with those whom he respects and loves.

Responsibility is closely connected with duty. A man's duty, the decree of the law of thought, is measured by his responsibility and this is based on his standard of right, his appreciation of right and wrong, that is, on the amount of knowledge of what is morally right or wrong which he has acquired through the doer-in-the-body. A man is responsible to the degree of his knowledge in a given situation and of his ability to perform the duties of that situation. The law of thought centers upon the doer of the Triune Self. Under that law is made the advance of the human or by that law he is cast into nature and imprisoned as a "lost" doer portion.

What the human has become conscious of as morally right or wrong, finds its expression as conscience, which is man's knowledge of his departure from what he knows is right for him, that is, his duty. In any given case, his duty to do or not to do, to suffer or not to suffer, is shown to him by his conscience. If he thinks about doing what he knows to be a positive wrong, his conscience will tell him "Don't." If he is in doubt about the rightness of his doing or not doing, suffering or not suffering, conscience will advise him as he keeps on thinking.

Conscience will never show the way, nor will it give an explanation, but it will say: "Do not" or "No" as often as necessary to let him find the way. He must find the way himself through the maze of life. Conscience will protect him from going wrong by telling him whenever he is about to do so. That is enough. His conscience makes him responsible. His conscience will speak, whether he listens or not. He must listen to the voice, if he wants to know. The voice of conscience becomes the balancing factor in thoughts which are conceived or entertained and issued notwithstanding the warning.

Thoughts against which conscience does not warn make no destiny. In them the balancing factor, which is conscience, is satisfied at once by the issuing of the thought. It ends when its design is exteriorized.

Intending to violate one's duty, conscience and responsibility, is sin and will be exteriorized in a sinful act or omission. Sin originates in ignorance, that is, a man's act is a sin not because he does not know better but because he does what he knows to be wrong. Acts done without knowing that they are wrong, are not sins, though harmful results may follow, as where one poisons another accidentally, or unintentionally causes him to fall under a train. If these acts are done with the intent of producing the result, they are sins; if not, they are done in ignorance. The difference under the law that demands that adjustment be made lies in the fact that in the second case conscience does not warn and no duty is violated; but in the first, responsibility attaches. The ignorance out of which sins originate is different from that which causes ignorant action. The ignorance from which sin springs is due chiefly to obstinate prejudices and one's refusal to see his own mistakes.

A man may sin in various ways. He sins first in thinking, and then the thought is exteriorized as a physical sin. There are sins against bodies and against doers, his own or those of others. Further, there are sins against outside nature and against his own Intelligence and the Supreme Intelligence.

Sins against one's own body are all acts or omissions by which its well-being and usefulness are interfered with; as, sexual sins, overfeeding or eating unwholesome food, drunkenness, uncleanliness, not taking care of one's eyes, teeth or any part, not attempting to cure disease once it is noticed, inflicting a physical injury and murder of one's own body.

Some of these sins, like injury and murder, may be inflicted also directly upon the body of another. However, many more sins, which will demand a serious discipline and retribution, are inflicted indirectly upon the bodies of others. Such sins are the manufacture or sale of adulterated foods and drinks and of narcotics, sins of indifference, or extortions which cause poverty, overcrowding, disease and indecency in miserable dwellings, sins of employers who do not provide safe and sanitary places to work, and who pay insufficient wages. These sins, too, may be chargeable to those who are not directly interested as employers but are their agents, and to persons in public office, through whose connivance such conditions are allowed to exist. Revolutionists who fish in troubled waters also belong here. In the same way the people at large are responsible if they know of such facts and do not do what they can to remedy conditions by which sins against the body are committed. In this way a community as well as its party politicians may commit sins, as by permitting abuse of convicts or by allowing rivers and lakes to be polluted by sewage or by not insisting upon laws to compel sanitary food, dwellings and travel.

The physical body is the house of the doer and should become the temple of the Triune Self; into a physical body are solidified the four elements and the beings in them. Matter and beings travel in the body and are there affected by the conditions in which it exists and then are transformed, transmuted, etherealized and go back into the kingdoms of physical nature. In a human body the four great spheres are together and there they may be affected. In a human physical body the Great Universe and all its many beings can be brought together and focussed. Therefore by sins against a human body, one's own or another's, nature is more directly affected than by any other sins of man.

Sins against the Triune Self are giving free rein to one's desires and appetites, in disregard of what one senses or knows to be wrong. The desires may be for physical enjoyments, as overeating or laziness, or for psychic enjoyments, as sensuality or pleasure generally, or they may be for mental enjoyments as ambition, arrogance and selfishness generally.

There are sins against the thinker. They are the denial of the existence of the Light of the Intelligence, the intentional shutting out the Light so that one may remain in desired darkness. Then there are the sins against the doer of another. These are the encouragement or seduction or coercion of him to acts or indulgences that are sins against his Triune Self. Sins against the thinker of another are keeping him in darkness, shutting out the Light of his Intelligence for him, preventing him from reaching out for knowledge and generally seducing or forcing him to do or suffer sins against his own thinker, as by encouraging infantile belief, lying, perjury and otherwise acting against his conscience.

One commits a sin against his Intelligence by denying the existence of that Intelligence. The intentional shutting out of the Light of the Intelligence may appear in the form of bigotry, as the refusal to think about or examine religious problems, or as the clinging to an ancestral creed when one has outgrown it, or because of mental laziness. As conscience is the knowledge in the doer of its contemplated departure from what is its standard of right, the stifling of conscience is a crime against the Intelligence. Lying, which is the intentional statement of a falsehood, and perjury, which is a similar statement after a solemn invocation of the deity, are crimes against the Intelligence because they flout its Light. Though a liar is often a clear thinker, yet he blurs his own thinking and dims the Light that is in his atmosphere, because only to the degree that one sees a lie to be true can one lie most successfully and influence others. Though a lie is known to be a lie, it nevertheless beclouds the mental outlook of him who utters it.

Sins against nature may be sins against nature or sins against nature gods. The sins against nature are committed by sinning against one's own body or the body of another. The matter circulating through human physical bodies is affected, improved or vitiated, while under the influence of the Light that is with the portions of doers inhabiting them.

It is a sin against the Supreme Intelligence to deny that there is law and order in the Universe. If one is not sufficiently enlightened to believe in the Supreme Intelligence, that is no sin; but everyone has enough knowledge to believe in some kind of a God or an Intelligence. Whatever God a man worships as the author of his being and intelligence, by that form he worships the Supreme Intelligence, the highest source of his conscience, duty and responsibility.

Sins, here put into these classes, are a disturbance of order, and an adjustment follows automatically. The adjustment originates inside of the man, and at once provides in the thought itself the balancing factor, and causes exteriorizations in events on the physical plane until a balance is made to the satisfaction of conscience. This satisfaction is at the same time sufficient for universal adjustment and the tendency to maintain order in the Great Universe.

True repentance is the recognition of having done wrong, coupled with the will to compensate by doing or suffering to adjust and to do one's duty. Forgiveness of sin can be had only from one's conscience and only at the completion of the compensation, that is agreement, which must inevitably have been made in all four atmospheres. Salvation is being free from the consequences of continued exteriorizations flowing out of all sinful thoughts. It can only be the result of adjustment. This is the meaning of the doctrines of repentance, forgiveness of sins and salvation.

SECTION 7

The law of thought. Physical, psychic, mental, and noetic destiny.

Thus the Great Law by which the plan is worked for lowering, condensing and materializing spirit or force into matter through the beings and forms of nature until these are fashioned into a human body, and then for raising and sublimating that matter which becomes an aia and then a Triune Self until that Triune Self becomes an Intelligence, has at the human stage the aspect of the law of thought, as destiny.

The law of thought centers on the rightness of the thinker of the Triune Self, under the circumstances of a given situation. Physical conditions offer to the human an opportunity to perform his duty. Duty is measured by responsibility and determined by conscience. Duty is that part of the doer's destiny selected from all its past as necessary to be disposed of in the present; responsibility is the degree of knowledge in the particular situation; and conscience, when selfness sends the message through rightness, is the knowledge which warns of departure from right. In every situation in life there is a duty, easy or hard, of action or inaction. When the duty is presented the human does it or fails to do it. The doing or not doing is the result of the action of mind with desire.

The Light of the Intelligence which is diffused in a part of the mental atmosphere of the human combines with desire into thinking and then into a thought. Certain mental operations of the body-mind are what are commonly called mind. From such thinking and thoughts come all physical acts or omissions, the creation, existence and destruction of all the objects and institutions which are man-made, all physical events and also the forms and beings in the animal, vegetable and mineral kingdoms—everything on the physical plane. Everything existing on the physical plane is the exteriorization of a thought, and must be balanced through the one who issued the thought, in accordance with his responsibility, and at the conjunction of time, place and condition. These results must by interiorizations be brought back to their source, to the end that by the effect on the doer there shall be an adjustment. The adjustment is brought about by a balancing factor which is in the thought as soon as it is issued and is connected with the tendency of the Great Universe to remain in equilibrium.

The operation of this law affects the conception or entertainment of a thought in the heart, its issue through the brain and its externalization through the breath-form and the physical body as an immediate act and possibly as many events produced by the thought, the energy of which is not exhausted until it is balanced. From the exteriorizations come results. Only the physical results are determined by the law of thought and are physical destiny. The psychic, mental and noetic results upon the one who generated the thought (while they are a purpose of the law of thought) are balanced not exclusively by the decrees of the law, but are largely determined by the man himself and are the conditions under which he exists.

There are four things involved or concerned in the creation and exteriorization and balancing of a thought as destiny. These are: A unit of nature, a desire, Conscious Light, and a balancing factor. The unit of nature represents the object of nature desired by that desire, and to which it is bonded by the Conscious Light. The exteriorization is the physical act, object or event which is the result of the thinking and attachment to the object of nature. The balancing factor brings about an adjustment of all things involved and restores the four to their proper sources, thus freeing the Light and the desire from their bondage to nature.

A thought is conceived by the bonding of a desire and an object of nature when a human wants to get something or to do or avoid acts as they are pleasant or unpleasant, and which bring him the feeling of comfort, well-being, joy or satisfaction, or of pain, grief, or dissatisfaction. This affects the doer as a feeling of right or wrong. Conscience warns of a departure from the standard of right.

Once issued, a thought tends to exteriorization as a physical act, object or event. Its course runs to the nature-side of the light plane of the light world. The thought may at first be too weak for materialization. But one thought is usually related to another. They run along the same line, getting their aims from a certain desire. Soon the first is reinforced sufficiently for materialization. Then it proceeds to the light plane of the light world, then moves down the nature-side until it reaches the life world, then the form world and then the physical world. There it waits in the radiant state until it can become physical as an act, an object or an event or as many events.

Events continue to occur as exteriorizations of a thought as long as its energy endures and that continues until the thought is balanced in the physical, form, life and light worlds. These physical effects are perceived by the human through the four senses and may be felt in a fourfold way: as a result of a disturbance of physical well-being through pain, or by psychic feeling as grief or as fear, or by a moral feeling as of shame or disgrace, or by a mental disturbance as from loss of money or influence, or by a combination of some or all of these four kinds of feeling affecting the personality. Agreeable sensations are felt in the same way by the human. These four kinds of feelings, especially if painful, teach the human; they pay him and make him pay, and tend to bring about an adjustment of the action of the Conscious Light with desire and an object of nature. These objects may not be attained at once or in a lifetime, or even in many lives.

There are many factors which interfere with the speedy attainment of these purposes. Some of them are the factors mentioned which hold back exteriorizations on the physical plane. Then there is ignorance and unwillingness to pay, to learn and to adjust, which retard the action of the law on all planes. Also it takes much longer for matter to advance in the form and physical worlds than it does for thought to impress matter in the life world. But paying, learning and adjusting have to wait for and follow upon the events on the physical plane. Therefore there are in the form world and life world conditions in which the flow and progress is restrained until there is an outlet into the physical world. These conditions of inhibition and retardation cause the accumulation of forces in the life world and the form world while they have to wait for the time, place and condition that will permit their orderly appearance on the physical plane. These states in the various worlds are a man's future, his destiny. They are of his own making, but his destiny nevertheless, and they determine to a large degree his thinking, his feelings and his acting.

So there are four kinds of destiny: physical, psychic, mental and noetic destiny. They are the conditions under which the human lives on the physical plane and in the psychic, mental and noetic atmospheres of his Triune Self.

This destiny is sometimes spoken of as good or bad, but such terms are unfit. Destiny in itself is neither good nor bad. It is agreeable or disagreeable, acceptable or not acceptable. The question is that of balancing and so ending the exteriorizations, or of not balancing. The question is not of good or bad. So-called good destiny may be bad and bad destiny may be good—according to what use is made of it.

CHAPTER V

PHYSICAL DESTINY

SECTION 1

What physical destiny includes.

Physical destiny is everything that affects flesh. and blood and nerves. It includes the features, frame and fabric of the physical body, the skin, the outer organs of sense and of action, and the inner organs of the generative, respiratory, circulatory and digestive systems. It also includes all physical causes that affect the body agreeably or otherwise. Physical circumstances that carry with them opportunity or the lack of it, environment of all kinds, food and the means of work or of leisure, are physical destiny. It includes, moreover, birth, family connections, health, money and the need of it, the span of life and manner of death of the body. Group destiny affects those who are drawn together into families or held together by social, political or religious ties.

Men see the world, but not the causes that bring about what they see. Upon examination into the factors which make up the race, environment, features and habits of even a single man, it is wonderful how these factors were worked together as the exteriorizations of so many conflicting thoughts.

It is difficult to follow the thoughts which elementals as nature units had to build into these healthy, diseased or deformed bodies, and into the daily events amidst which people exist, as well as into the epochal facts that mark periods in their common history. Though the real causes producing these results will not be seen at once, what can be understood is the law of thought, as destiny, according to which they are produced.

The entire physical world is made up of exteriorized parts of human thoughts. Not only the direct and intended results of human action, but the physical facts generally attributed to the gods of religions are exteriorized human thoughts.

Thoughts are produced by the thinking of the doer-in-the-body concerning objects of nature; and they are the cause of all physical acts, objects and events. These physical results are not always intended. Usually they are not, and would be avoided if that were in the power of the person who issued the producing thought. Neither the creator of the thought nor any other being can stop the further exteriorizations of a thought once it has been exteriorized in part.

A thought is a being, conceived by thinking, with a purpose and a plan. It is like an invisible blueprint to be exteriorized as an act or an object. The exteriorized action is physical destiny.

The first exteriorization is physical destiny and, as such, produces its results. Even the first exteriorization is the concretion of many thoughts, all having a similar aim and flowing from the same motive.

One does not murder or steal or commit any dishonest action without having thought of murder, or planned to steal or harbored dishonest thoughts. One who thinks upon murder, theft or lust will find a way to put his thoughts into deeds. If of too cowardly a nature to do this he will become the prey to others' thoughts, or to invisible inimical influences which may, even against his wish, possess him at some critical time and urge him to perform the kind of act which he thought of as desirable and revolved in his brain, yet was too timid to execute. In the same way acts of goodness, courtesy, delicacy, service or gratitude do not come out of thin air, but are the form in which long continued thinking of the same kind is expressed. Over weakness and hesitation at the critical time one may be helped by thoughts of others and by friendly influences which seize him and decide him to do the kind of act which he had thought of as ideal.

Physical destiny is, however, not only what results from that first act. The physical destiny of that thought comprises all the successive exteriorizations which are projected out of it. These take place whenever its cycle has led it again to the radiant-solid plane, and whenever on that plane it intersects one or more thoughts, whether of the one who created it, or of other persons. These precipitations are from thoughts; from them there is no permanent escape. There must be exteriorizations until adjustment is made. Everything existing on the physical plane is an exteriorization of a thought which must be balanced through the one who issued the thought, in accordance with his responsibility, and at the conjunction of time, condition and place. That, in each instance, is the decree of the law. The destiny and decree do not reach beyond the physical plane.

Some psychic results are inevitable, as joy or sorrow; mental results are uncertain because they depend on the mental attitude. Neither, however, is a physical result. But they are to be considered because physical conditions continue on account of them. There are three purposes in the operation of the law of thought, and they cause exteriorizations of thoughts as physical acts, objects and events.

The first purpose is to let the doer-in-the-body learn what thoughts are, their meaning and how the physical world is built by them; that it is responsible for its thoughts and will be rewarded and punished for them and that it can attain conscious immortality only by thinking. The second purpose is payment. Therefore a doer pays and is paid in the equivalent of what physical actions and conditions it caused or permitted. This does not mean that if a man beats a boy the boy will sometime beat the man, or if a wife nags a husband that the husband has formerly jarred the person now his wife. It means that the man who put the stripes on the boy will himself suffer stripes, but not necessarily from that boy, and that the present husband has nagged someone, but not necessarily that same woman. The third purpose is the adjustment between the desire of the doer and the exteriorization, the balancing of the thought.

The adjustment must be made by the doer understandingly; not necessarily with knowledge of the past, but with an understanding, for example, that a certain suffering is merited, and so must be borne willingly. This decision makes the adjustment, and that thought is then balanced. Usually a man refuses to take that attitude. Thoughts are created and accumulated without an adjustment being made. So these thoughts become the hard circumstances that envelop so many. In each of these thoughts the balancing factor causes exteriorization after exteriorization. Little is learned and few adjustments are made out of the multitude of accumulating thoughts.

The three purposes are interrelated. By paying and receiving payment a man learns about his thoughts and his duties. Without payment he does not usually learn. In most cases he does not learn even by being made to pay repeatedly. He must continue to pay until he learns what he should do or not do in a particular case. Even after he has learned what is wrong he has not learned well enough to resist temptation;

therefore the condition of the world is what it is. But there is a bright future ahead if people are willing to learn and to adjust.

All worlds depend on the physical plane of the physical world of the sphere of earth for their development. Progress of the matter in any sphere can be made only while the matter of that sphere is in the physical bodies of doers. There only is it under the influence of the Light of an Intelligence, and there only do all the worlds and spheres meet.

There matter circulates through the corresponding four zones of the physical atmosphere of the body. The circulation is kept up by the swing of the breath as it comes and goes. The matter then circulates through the four systems of the fourfold body. The reason all matter can come together there is that there the physical planes of the four worlds interlock. By these circulations this body is built, maintained, made coarser or finer, kept in health or afflicted with disease, according to the thinking of the doer which inhabits it. A thought is built into the body through nature units, elementals, which rush into the form which the thought assumes. They build it out and precipitate it, as a handsome feature, a malformed part or a disease of the body; or they bring about actions and accidents as exteriorizations of the thought.

Beyond the physical plane the law of thought does not decree or compel results; however, the results not directed or compelled by the law of thought, namely, the results on the doer which are produced by the physical events, are also means for teaching the doer. Life in a human body affords opportunities by which the doer is to be taught, trained and disciplined to be in union with his Triune Self. The doer can become thus conscious only while living in a human body, never after the death of the body. Only while it is in its fleshly body is the doer in contact with all the worlds and spheres. The commingling of all the worlds and spheres is necessary as a condition under which a Triune Self can be raised to become conscious as an Intelligence.

The body is the result of the work of the doer during aeons. There are in human bodies doer portions of various degrees, on the descent and on the ascent. Both classes need physical bodies to work out their destiny. No two bodies are equal in any sense; the doers in them are not equal in development, nor are their thoughts, which make the bodies. People who look at a human body cannot tell what is in it. Position in life will not tell; a man of education may be rapidly descending, one who appears to be lowly may be advanced. In these physical bodies, however, all receive the destiny they have made for themselves, and through these crucibles passes the whole of nature in the human world of birth and death.

SECTION 2

Outward circumstances as physical destiny.

Physical conditions begin with birth onto the physical plane. The sex, family, race, country and environment are determined by previous thoughts.

The parents of whom one is born may be his old friends or his bitter enemies. Whether birth be attended by rejoicing or regrets, the doer comes into its appropriate body and in it has to work out old antagonisms and assist and be assisted by old friends.

Birth of the body represents a budget of debit and credit accounts of thoughts. The manner in which the budget will be dealt with depends upon the dweller in the body. Birth of a body to obscure parents in an out-of-the-way place, where the necessities of life are obtained with difficulty, birth in a notable family well stationed, birth under conditions of frugality and simplicity which from the start throw the doer on its own resources, or birth where the child has at first a life of ease and leisure, but later on in life meets with reverses of fortune which require the development of strength of character—all will provide opportunities necessary to carry on the work in the world which the dweller in the body has yet to perform. Birth into galling, uncongenial surroundings, such as obscurity, squalor, depravity or oppression is the result of past oppression of others, or of callousness to their conditions; or it is due to laziness of body and slothfulness in thinking. Such a birth may be the result of a need to live under adverse conditions, by the overcoming of which alone strength of character may be attained.

As the infant grows through childhood and develops into youth, the manner of life, habits of body, breeding and education form the physical capital with which he begins the present life. He enters into business, politics, a profession, a trade or servitude, according to the tendencies of his past and according to the class or party spirit to which he had then adhered.

All of this physical circumstance is destiny, yet not any destiny arranged for him by some arbitrary, extraneous power or by force of outside circumstances, but offered to, or made easy or forced upon him by his past thoughts.

Out of the mass of factors which the past holds ready for demonstration, those only are used which admit of being assembled and worked out in harmony with the destiny of the millions of other doers in bodies at the same time. One cannot change destiny already made; it is the field of action provided by one's thoughts. The future may be changed by submitting to the destiny already provided, by working out duties and changing one's thinking.

In all the varied conditions of life it is true that the environment in which one is born is due to those desires, ambitions and ideals for which he has worked in the past; or it is the result of that which he has forced upon others and which it is necessary for him to feel and understand; or it is the means for the beginning of a new line of effort to which his past actions have led.

Environment is one of the means by which physical conditions of life are brought about. Environment is not a cause in itself, it is an effect, but as an effect it is often the origin of action and tendencies. The human body, born into a certain environment, is there born because the environment furnishes the conditions through which the doer and body must work, and should learn. Environment controls animals; the human changes his environment according to his thinking and choosing. That may be limited, but every human has some choice and some power to engage in mental activities. A physical life may be led in accordance with the tendencies due to birth and environment; in that case the man's development along those lines will go on and he will continue to be born in like environment. Or he may use up all the credit which birth and position have given him as the result of past works, and at the same time refuse to honor the claims of birth, position and race. In that case he will leave that sphere of activity.

The features and form of the body are true records of the thoughts which made them. Lines, curves and angles in their relation to one another, are like so many written words which the thoughts and actions have formed. Each line is a letter, each feature a word, each organ a sentence, each part a chapter, and all make up a story of the past, fashioned by thinking and expressed in the human body. The lines and features are changed by and with one's efforts at thinking. The kind of body which is born is the kind the doer has determined as a result of past thoughts.

SECTION 3

Physical heredity is destiny. Healthy or sickly bodies. Unjust perse-cutions. Errors of justice. Congenital idiots. The span of life. Manner of death.

Heredity is destiny. Physical endowments, habits and traits, may seem to be clearly those of one's parents, especially in early youth. Yet ultimately these physical peculiarities, habits of snuffling, whining, blinking, walking with hands in the pockets; or traits like a tendency to baldness, defective sight, gout, clubfoot or soft bones, are expressions of the thoughts of one's previous lives. Inclinations may be modified or accentuated by the tendencies of the parents, and sometimes close association causes the features of two or more persons to resemble each other, yet all was regulated by one's own thinking. What is called heredity of the body is only the medium through which the physical destiny is produced, the loom on which it is woven. Parentage is selected because of the special properties inherent in the germs of the father and mother.

Whether the new body is diseased or healthy depends among other things upon the abuse or care that was given to the past body. If the body inherited is healthy, it means sobriety, frugality, work in the past; if sickly or diseased, it means that it is the result of gluttony, drunkenness, laziness or neglect. A healthy or a diseased body is primarily and ultimately due to the antecedent use or abuse of the sex function. Another antecedent cause is the proper or improper use of food. Disorders, if they exist when life is ended, are brought into the next physical life, at birth or later, and are what is called hereditary. Such affections as soft bones, poor teeth, imperfect sight and cancerous growths, are due to the causes mentioned.

Blindness may result from many cumulative causes in former lives, like carelessness of one's own sight or destruction of another's. Former inordinate indulgence of sex may produce in this life paralysis of the optic nerve. Former misuse or abuse of the eye by overtaxing it or neglecting it may bring on blindness in the present life. Blindness at birth may be caused by having inflicted upon others diseases of sex, or by having wilfully or carelessly deprived another of his sight.

He who is born deaf or dumb may be one who has wilfully listened to and acted upon lies told by others, or who has wronged others by spreading spiteful scandal, by lying or by bearing false witness. Dumbness may also have its cause in the abuse of sex.

One of the reasons for blindness is that the sense of sight has its roots in the generative system, and the other senses are vitally connected with it. The life of the physical body depends on the vitality and powers elaborated in the sex organs and distributed through the body. Eventually man will learn that it is necessary to check indulgence and waste in order to give power to the senses, and beauty, health and strength to the body.

Deformities, impairments and afflictions are often blessings in disguise. They may be checks which prevent one from doing things which he longs for or might do, and which if done would prevent him from doing that work in the world which is his particular duty. They may interrupt a tendency which, if not stopped, would acquire such force as to lead him into idiocy, as in the case of a glutton or a rake. These checks are designed to give the doer an opportunity to reflect, to recuperate, to limit the tendency to self-indulgence and disregard of others' needs and rights. So a doer is often saved from its destructive bent by an affliction which checks its ignorant belief in its own almightiness, and turns it onto the way of rectitude and honor.

Forms of grace and beauty are externalized thoughts. As to beauty, two kinds may be distinguished. That a face or figure is beautiful does not necessarily signify that the thoughts are beautiful, they are often quite the reverse. The beauty of many men and women in youth is the elemental beauty of nature, not the direct result of the presence of the Light of the Intelligence. When the thinking has not opposed nature, the lines are well-rounded and graceful, and the features are even and well-adjusted, like particles which are grouped together in symmetrical regularity by sound. This is elemental beauty; it is the beauty of the daisy or the rose, of childhood and of youth. From this elemental beauty is to be distinguished beauty issuing from strong, intelligent mental activities. This kind of beauty is seldom seen. Between the two extremes, beauty of elemental innocence and that of serenity and of knowledge, are faces and forms of innumerable varieties. When thinking is first practiced, the elemental beauty of face and figure may be lost. Then the lines become irregular, harder and more angular, and this continues during the process of training. But when the doer is at last beyond the control of the four senses and its thinking is done intelligently, the severe lines are again changed; they are softened and express the beauty of peace, derived from a cultured, balanced, strong and virtuous doer.

The limbs and organs of the body are instruments for using great powers in the Universe. One may not misuse or leave unused the instrument of a universal power without paying the penalty; for each one has these organs in order that he may put them to physical use to further universal purposes, and become conscious of the connection between his body and the Universe. When these organs are misused, or used to injure others, it is a more serious thing than at first appears. It is an interference with the plan of the Universe by turning the individual against the whole.

The hands are organs of executive power. One is deprived of the use of the hands as a result of not having used them when they should have been, or if they have served against the bodies or interests of others. Employing a hand to abuse another's body by breaking his limb, or by signing unjust orders, or employing the hand generally in acts of oppression, extortion and crooked dealing, may result in deprivation of the use of the hand for some time, or in its loss. Loss of the use of a limb may result from any kind of "accident".

Immediate physical causes are not the real or ultimate, but only the apparent causes. In the case of one who loses a limb by the unhappy mistake of a surgeon or nurse, the immediate cause of the loss is said to be carelessness or accident; but the real cause is some past action or inaction of the maimed himself, which is exteriorized by means of the carelessness. It is in just payment that he is deprived of the use of his limb. A surgeon and nurse too careless of or inattentive to their patients will themselves sometime suffer at the hands of others. The pain is for the purpose of teaching how others have felt under like conditions; of preventing them from repeating similar actions and of making them value more the power which may be used through the limb. If they do not learn from the loss, they will again suffer.

He who inflicts wilful injury upon others, who forces or inveigles others into plots or fights where physical suffering results, and who seems to benefit from the wrong done them and to enjoy prestige and unjust gains, may live out his life unharmed, but the thought of the wrong is still with him; his thought is not fully exteriorized; from it he cannot escape.

He who is unjustly persecuted, convicted or imprisoned, is he who in a past life, or even in the present one, has, through malice, greed or indifference, caused others to be deprived unjustly of their liberty. He suffers captivity and its horrors of diseases, of an enfeebled body, of vitiated morals, so that he may experience and sympathize with such sufferings and may avoid false accusation or causing others to be coerced and to lose their liberty and health. Many are today the victims of errors of justice, who deserve this galling fate because of the wantonness with which they discharged their duties while they had power, sat in the judgment seat or refrained through indolence or selfishness from doing what they might have done to bring about fair judgment. The wardens of prisons, of poorhouses and insane-asylums, the guardians of infants, in short all in whose charge are placed the life, health and fate of others, are held to the strictest account for their acts and omissions in the performance of their duty. Neglect, rancor or venality in the discharge of one's duty, will draw him inevitably into the position of his victims, there to undergo the wrongs he has done or has allowed to be done, to them. Escape for a day or for a life is not escape forever.

A special case of physical retribution is that of a congenital idiot. His condition is the result of past actions in many lives in which there have been only physical indulgences of the appetites, actions which are all debits and no credits. The congenital idiot has no drawing account, all physical credits having been used up. He is likely to be the last appearance for an indefinite period of a portion of the doer in human form. Before this last appearance the doer has lived many lives of depravity and decadence, in neglected districts of cities or in the country, among peons, cretins and the backward dwellers on mountain sides. Finally comes the last appearance as a hopeless idiot. The chief producing causes of this fate are sexual abuses, narcotics and drunkenness.

Such an anomaly as an idiot who has some one faculty abnormally developed, is the remnant of a man who has indulged the senses and the abnormalities of sex, but who has carried on the study of one particular subject, such as music or mathematics, and devoted himself to that.

Idiots, congenital or otherwise, become so by the withdrawal of the doer portion from the human, as a result of opportunities persistently neglected or misused. With the doer portion goes the Light of the Intelligence.

The span of life of every human is already determined at the close of his previous life, but the period may be sometimes lengthened or shortened. The length of the span was marked on the form of the breath-form at death, and that impresses the sign on the first cell with which the building of the new body begins. Accordingly a coil is developed in the astral body, by elementals. The coil will let a certain amount of life force pass, namely, enough for the span of the person's life.

The length of the span is predetermined so as to let the person do the work and pass through the events called for by his destiny. Within the span he generates new thoughts, does or refuses to do the work, makes new destiny, and he puts off some minor events. In a general way the course of his life and the salient events, and the time within which he must finish, are laid out for him, but he has choice as to how he will act in details and with what mental attitude he will view these salient events.

The manner of death is physical destiny, and is already predetermined at the end of the preceding life. There is one exception, suicide. The mere disposition to commit suicide is predetermined, but even in that case the man can choose whether or not he will die by his own hand. He may have contemplated the act and refused to do it, but if he continues to think and plan about suicide, the predetermined tendency together with his continued thinking will be exteriorized in the act of self-murder.

By committing suicide one does not escape from the allotted span of life or from the sorrow, dread, pain or disgrace he feared to endure by living on. Death by one's own hand is not like the ordinary case of dying. In the case of self-murder the doer remains with the breath-form in the radiant state of the physical plane, experiencing all it dreaded to meet in life, and does not go into the after-death states until after the allotted span of life ends. In the next life on earth he will have the same inclination to commit suicide, but coupled with that will be a dread of it. In that life he is liable to be murdered. In no case can he escape by suicide that which he feared to suffer. The conditions from which he sought escape will confront him again, because they are exteriorizations of his own thoughts.

The physical body is the fulcrum on which thoughts are balanced. It is without feeling—almost as dead in life as it is after death. Decay, impermanence and corruption are almost synonymous with the human body. It is the sediment of all the worlds, their dregs and lees. The doer during its life on earth feels and desires through such a body, and after death it is confronted with what it has felt and desired through the body during life. The activity and vigor, the breath and life of the body, are due to the presence of the doer. The involuntary functions of the body continue only as long as the doer and its breath-form inhabit it. What seems to be a lasting body is a moving mass, constantly changing, always coming and going and held in visibility only while it is in passage through the shape of the astral body, according to the breath-form. A human body, however, is the thing on which all is set, around which all turns, upon which all that the doer longs for and hopes to have or to be is centered.

Though a human body has no permanence or existence in itself, by means of it the doer is put into touch with matter of the worlds and even of the spheres. By means of such a body the doer takes form, learns what its feelings and desires are and how to refine them, and what the feelings of others are and how to feel with them. By means of this body the doer learns how to think.

SECTION 4

Money. The money god. Poverty. Reversals. The born thief. There is no accident of wealth or inheritance.

The subject of money and what has monetary value deserves special attention. The possession and the lack of money create today the thousand and one conditions through which the ways of destiny lead. Independence, servitude, fatigue, checks on development, choice of associates, power, opportunity, duty, most of the innumerable predetermined aspects of life in the world, are related to money.

Everybody needs money. It is proper that everybody should have some. Indeed one of the tests of a good government is that all people under it should have the opportunity to earn enough for food, clothes and shelter. Beyond these needs some wants are justifiable according to the position a man holds in the world. If one has no wife or children, less is needed. But the thoughts of man go beyond and demand not only what would be sufficient for their needs and reasonable wants. They want money for luxury and display, for power over others, and some want money for money's sake. However much they may have, they still want more. Often money, after it has been acquired, has little value. It will not buy health, honor, self-respect; it cannot buy love nor life; nor independence, ease or knowledge.

True independence is what money should help to bring, and little money is enough for that. Though independence varies with one's position and work in the world, little money is needed to establish it. Cares, troubles and intrigues surround those who desire more than enough. Money does not enlarge the range of independence. Happiness within and assurance without is what all men want, but life never gives them. The nearest approach is independence, however modest it be. Money is one of the smallest requirements. The less one needs and the less he wants from the money god, the more independent that one is.

The money god is a powerful earth spirit, created, kept alive and given his power, like other gods, by the worship of doer portions in human bodies. Under this great earth god are little money gods, special deities for each of the worshippers. Each little money god, in the heart and on the hearth, is nourished by the worshipper, and stands for the great god. The individual gods pass the worship on to the composite great god. This one, in turn, through the hierarchy, aids his worshippers in obtaining money and avoiding losses, in helping them into successful enterprises and lucrative positions, or in keeping them out of financial disasters. But this god cannot give health, comfort or esteem; nor love, cheer or hope; nor can it give protection in the end, when destiny cannot be held back. Often a worshipper having obtained the money worships other gods and uses the money to gratify other desires which his wealth permits. The money god is tolerant while he holds the first place in the heart, but if the new worship, such as that of voluptuousness, drunkenness, ambition interferes, he is a jealous god and revenges himself not only by the loss of money, but by the loss of the things that the money had bought.

He who is born in poverty, who feels at home in poverty and makes no effort to overcome his poverty, is a feeble, indolent and ignorant person, who has done little in the past and so has little in the present. He will be driven by hunger and want or be brought by love of those dependent upon him to work, as the only escape from the dull treadmill of poverty. He who is born in poverty with ideals, talents or high ambitions, may be one who has ignored physical conditions and spent his energies in dreaming and in castle building.

He who suddenly suffers reversals of fortune may be one who in the past has deprived others of their property, or who has neglected to protect his own. The present experience is a lesson necessary to make him feel the physical want and suffering which loss of prosperity brings, and to make him sympathize with others who experience it. Or the loss of fortune may be required by destiny as a check on developing tendencies, or as preparation for other work.

The possession of wealth is the result of work or worship in the present or in the past life. Physical labor, intense desire, worship of the money god, and continual thought, are the means by which money is obtained. Upon the predominance of any one factor will depend the amount.

The unskilled laborer in field, mine or shop, who uses little thought and does not carefully direct his desire, must work hard and long to earn enough for a scanty existence. With more intense desire and more thought, the laborer becomes skilled and is able to earn more. When money itself—not merely food, clothing and shelter—is the object of desire, thinking provides the means by which it may be obtained. Then wider fields are sought, where money is to be made and greater opportunities are seen and taken advantage of.

To obtain vast sums of money a man must have made money the chief object of his life and have sacrificed other interests to the worship of the money god. When he has paid the price in worship, the money god will put him in touch with other men having the same aims, whom he will be able to use in getting the money he craves, or the money god will put him into a position where he can levy directly or indirectly upon a multitude as in the case of tax-eaters, bondholders, army contractors, government builders or franchise owners. Sometimes the money does not come soon, but then it comes in another life in the shape of inheritance, good fortune, gifts, sinecures or pensions, without present work or worship. Yet such things do not happen except for the work and worship of the past.

According to the right or wrong use of money will one suffer or enjoy what money brings. When money is the chief object of one's existence, he is unable to enjoy fully the physical things which its use can provide, and money makes him indifferent to the wrongs he does, deaf to the sorrows of others and careless of his own true needs. Money, again, is the Nemesis which is the close and constant companion of those who pursue it. So one who finds pleasure in the hunt for money continues the hunt until it becomes a mad chase. Frequently the long hours of thought and labor required to amass his riches have ruined his health and he dies a discontented man.

Money may open up other sources of misery to the money worshipper. He may use his money in ostentation or vice. He often neglects his children and leaves them to be cared for by others. It may be noticed that insanity and degeneracy are frequent among the idle and luxurious offspring of the rich. In their turn, these degenerate children are the money worshippers of other days. The love of money drew them into a rich family, but money is now a curse.

Different from the future of the mere miser or dollar-hunter is that of those who are unscrupulous and dishonest in the acquisition of money. The lot of successful usurers, engrossers of necessaries, sellers of adulterated food, schemers, promoters and floaters of financial bubbles, is in the future that of common thieves or robbers. Persons who individually or as members of privileged classes obtain through force or corruption special privileges to the injury of others, are legalized robbers. These characters, of thieves and oppressors, which they developed, will find their true expression later, when they are externalized.

Then without the cover of legality, money, station or influence, they are born as rogues, and complain of the injustice of their lot. The born thief who is hounded from birth and soon comes to grief is the successful thief of a past life who plundered or defrauded others without then suffering the consequences. He is now paying the debts which he then incurred, whether he was a pilfering servant, a pickpocket, a common spoiler, a robber baron, a tax-eater, a food engrosser, a bribe-taker or any other kind of a cheat or fraud; whether his acts were labelled as crime or not, they were dishonest, that was enough. If he has had the character of a thief, that character eventually becomes externalized physically, when he is the "born thief", who "never had a chance". He is marked, outlawed, convicted and caged as a rogue.

The physical suffering which one may have caused, the poverty which he may have brought to others by outwitting them or by depriving them of their property, must all in turn be suffered by him.

One who overvalues the pleasures and indulgences which money can buy, and uses his money to procure these, must be without money at some time, and feel the need of it. The misuse of money brings poverty; the right use of money brings independence and honest wealth. Money properly procured gives physical conditions for comfort, enjoyment and work for self and others. One who is born of honorable and wealthy parents, or who inherits money, has earned it by his thought and actions; there is no accident of wealth or of inheritance by birth.

SECTION 5

Group destiny. Rise and fall of a nation. The facts of history. Agents of the law. Religions as group destiny. Why a person is born into a religion.

Group destiny is a destiny which affects alike a certain number of people. Their thoughts have made that destiny for them. Members of a family may have a certain destiny in common. They have the same ancestry, traditions and honor, are related to a locality and share to a certain extent social and cultural connections. Often their common destiny is the lack of all this except locality and ancestry. Sometimes, similar physical features appear among the members of a family and are designated as hereditary. In some families the members continue to be reborn through several lives. They receive what they have given to the family name and standing or have allowed to happen to it. Group destiny may affect the members of a family for one or two generations only, or may extend through centuries. People are drawn into a family and kept there by similarity of thought; as long as that similarity lasts the family is held together. Formerly land ownership with entail, or the mere living in a locality was the means of establishing and perpetuating a family. In modern times the thought has changed and land is no longer the chief means of continuing a family. Sometimes mutually hostile thoughts draw people into the same family and its group destiny.

Persons share in the group destiny, that is, the physical conditions, of their community because their thoughts had or have something in common; these bring them into the same hamlet or town, with common conditions and interests. Though the separate destinies in such communities vary, there is some bond of common thought that draws persons into and keeps them in the locality. There they have a common language, physical environment, neighborhood, customs and pleasures; there they intermarry and there meet a common fate in times of prosperity, adversity, epidemic, fire, inundation or war. What each person receives in a common disaster is an exteriorization of his own past thoughts. If the common fate does not coincide with the cycle of any thought of those present in such a locality, they escape. So it is that there are miraculous exceptions from the general fate when many are brought together and made to suffer, as in a shipwreck, a burning theater, a collapsing building, a flood or in religious or political persecutions.

People are born into a nation or race because their thoughts, and the disposition and character made by them, draw them there. They make the general spirit, character, peculiarities and tendencies of the race, and develop, strengthen or change them. The people make the spirit which is the god of the race, they create it by their thought. It breathes through the representatives of that race; hence comes indifference towards or prejudice against those who do not belong to or who oppose the national spirit. All who think similarly are drawn to the spirit and are eventually born into the race, where they share its group destiny to the extent to which their thoughts can be exteriorized at the time, condition and place.

Generally the people who are of any race belong there naturally, by the degree of development of their doers and bodies. Some, however, are born into a race to get special training; some because they have persecuted the race; some because they are entitled to special benefits from it; and some because they have to do a certain work for it: all share the group destiny.

At the time of an unusual calamity, as in periods of famine, defeat in war, oppression by a hostile nation, uprisings and lawlessness, outsiders are there to share the group destiny. These outsiders are born into a race as naturally as those who belong to it, so as to be there at the time when these disasters happen. They have exteriorized to them through the public calamity what they have attracted to themselves by their own thoughts. The same is true of those doers who come in to participate in a period of achievement, refinement and splendor.

The rise or fall of a nation is due to a particular thought which becomes the national thought. The same thought that is exteriorized in the power and greatest achievement of a nation is often the cause of its decline, fall and disappearance. A set of people generates the thought and develops it. Others are drawn in by the similarity of their thoughts and aid in the building of a nation through the exteriorization of its dominating thought. Some thoughts are powerful enough to keep a nation up for centuries before it is given over to inferior doers or sinks away or is effaced. The complete disappearance of a people like the Carthaginians, the Egyptians or the ancient Greeks, is evidence that at the crucial times there were not enough people to give to the national thought a new impetus that would carry the nation through the accumulating exteriorizations of its past thoughts.

There is a time, and its span does not exceed fifty years, in which every nation might have disappeared as a political entity under the weight of its destiny. The thoughts of every nation, whether it be a republic or a monarchy, are the collective thoughts of its people. If these thoughts are, and have been in the past, directed towards individual advantage or public conquest, to deceit or oppression, they are exteriorized in public calamities. These thoughts would make an end of the political entity as a state. But nearly always there is someone who has broader vision and creates a new thought or a new feeling or a modification of those which exist. In this he is assisted by some of the complete Triune Selves who watch and help the world. Thus the nation gets over the critical period. Of course no one man alone could save a nation; there must be a sufficient number of persons who support the regenerating thought, and if they can obtain a preponderance of thought the nation goes on, otherwise it declines.

Men are self-indulgent and act with selfish ends in view. To acquire and increase possessions, to have personal comfort and safety and to wield power, are the motives of their thoughts. Treason and evasion of military duty in war, monopolies, tax-dodging and special privileges in peace, are extreme cases. And almost everyone is interested in public matters only to the extent of the personal advantages he expects. Men seek little favors here and big gifts there, knowing that they will profit thereby at the expense of the public or of justice. Almost everyone adds to the general tendency toward corruption in public institutions. Some persons are active under the sting of selfish interest, most are indolent and inert from love of ease. There are many men who would be good officials, but they are not available. The people do not appreciate and will not uphold a just official, but they forsake him and leave him a disappointed man. So they do not get the best men, and if they do get well-intentioned men, they usually force them to protect themselves by complaisance or by corruption.

Therefore public officials in monarchies, oligarchies and democracies, are as bad as they are. They are the representatives of the people; in them the thoughts of the people have taken form. Those who are not in office would do as the present officials do, or even worse, if they had the opportunity. Corrupt officials can hold office and sinecures only so long as the thoughts of the people are depraved. Cruel barons could oppress the people only as long as the majority of the people, if they had been in the barons' place, would have done as the barons did. Despots have lived only because they embodied the ambitions and desires of the people over whom they ruled. The Catholic Inquisition to suppress heresy existed as long as it expressed the thoughts of the people.

When the thoughts of the people demand a change for the better a man usually appears to fight for it. He expresses their thoughts; but usually they forsake him when his actions need their support. When it is a question of choice between the public interest and their private interests, the private interests prevail. Usually those who complain of misrule, taxes, extortion or other injustice, would themselves be guilty of such wrongs if only they could commit them with impunity. The persons in power, whether in a despotism or in a democracy, are those who can discern and use human weaknesses, and at the same time have more vigor and are willing to take more risks than the multitude.

The actual facts of history are little known. Glorification of their nation and religion in schoolbooks, selection of favorable topics on public occasions, suppression of facts, a catch phrase here and there, are what all who are not close observers of history get concerning it. The weaknesses and misdeeds of individuals, and the inertia, incompetence and corruption of those engaged in public and national affairs, usually remain hidden—from all but the law. Largely from these unobserved facts come the group destiny of oppression, injustice, war, revolutions, heavy taxes, strikes, pauperism and epidemics. Those who complain of these misfortunes are among their contributory causes.

Seemingly unimportant things may be factors in physical destiny. Only a portion of what man eats can be used by him; that which he cannot use belongs to the earth. He should return to the earth, in a sanitary way, the refuse of the body after he has used the food which the earth has yielded for him. A community which conducts its waste and putrescent matter into a river or lake, does a wrong. Such matter befouls the water. Many diseases and epidemics in cities have been caused thereby. This is group destiny.

At critical times certain men arise and accomplish unusual results. Such men are generally unconscious agents of the law. The group destiny of their people calls for an instrument by which the people's thoughts can be exteriorized. A man appears when the thoughts of his people demand him. To no one man of this kind should be attributed all of what he does. He acts because he is impelled to act and because he is allowed to see the way to accomplish his purpose. Some such men in the last century were Palmerston, Bismarck, Cavour, Mazzini and Garibaldi.

The English spirit of the past made Lord Palmerston, kept him in office and produced during his long rule the results obtained for Britain through him. Bismarck was a Prussian; he was in himself an able and powerful man; but what made him successful was the time, the place, and the conditions, which allowed the thought of Prussian schooling, administration, militarism and power, to be exteriorized as the thought of the whole of Germany. In the same way the Italian thoughts of nationalism and of freedom from Austrian tyranny and Papal misrule, were expressed in the success of Cavour, Mazzini and Garibaldi.

Sometimes the agents of the law are conscious agents. Washington, Hamilton, Lincoln and Napoleon were of this kind. Washington knew that he was to be the true leader of men and the founder of a new nation. Hamilton actually knew that he had to lay truly the foundations of American finance in government. Lincoln knew that he had to preserve the Union, and he acted as best he could with the selfish and fanatical forces surrounding him. He accomplished the purpose with which he was charged by the Intelligence he spoke of as God.

Napoleon's mission to Europe was to remove the old ghosts of dynasties which had kept Europe in turmoil, bloodshed and servitude for centuries. He was to give these countries an opportunity for a government by the people as a whole. He failed because the French people, though they said they wanted liberty, equality and fraternity, were quite willing to let Napoleon create a new dynasty and conquer the world for them. He received instruction from some of the agents of complete Triune Selves; he was to give France a model government; and Europe was to pattern after it, if the people would. He was to leave no royal issue, so that he could found no dynasty. His ambition overcame him; he divorced his barren wife and married again, so as to have issue. After he had determined on this course, his power began to diminish and he could no longer discern opportunities or provide against dangers. The destiny of the people of Europe exteriorized for him his own weakness and ambition, to bring on the reactionary period which lasted there for nearly a hundred years.

Group destiny is particularly manifest at times when there are sudden changes in methods of government, as when there is a rising of slaves or a revolution, and mob rule in the wake of such convulsions.

Religions, too, belong to group destiny. They develop out of prior religious institutions, which no longer fit the times and the thoughts of the people. Gradually new views spread, and provision has to be made to allow the former thoughts of coming generations to be exteriorized. Then the subversive attitude of mind spreads until it is so general that the new religion can be supported by it. Upon the scene so prepared appears a founder of the new religion. Sometimes he remains unknown. The new phase of religion succeeds where many attempts had failed because the time was not yet ripe to allow them to take hold.

A theocracy is the rule by priests in the name of their God or gods. The priests rule; if the gods ever do rule by direct mandate, they soon leave all to their priests, who attend to mundane affairs for the benefit of the priestly hierarchy. The priests look after the welfare of the people chiefly for their own prosperity. For backward doers some features of a theocracy permit a good schooling in morals, just as slavery was permitted to let doers get a training. The morals taught are substantially the same in all religious systems, and are no worse in a theocracy than in other systems.

The group destiny of those who live under a theocracy is notable. There all worldly and ecclesiastical power is in the hands of priests. Lands, offices, possessions, revenues and exactions of all kinds are obtained by priests in a measure unnecessary for "spiritual" guides. Their real object is to satisfy their human love of power, luxury and lust. As long as they unite temporal power with their priestly office, they hold the common people in ignorance, credulity, bondage, poverty and fear, and cow powerful nobles. So it was in India, in Judea, in Egypt, with the Aztecs, and during the Dark Ages in countries where the Roman Catholic Church had temporal power. The group destiny of the common people is the exteriorization of their childish thoughts. These keep them in subjection to priests, whom they believe to be representatives of God. However, that is usually the only way in which backward doers can be taught morals and can progress at all.

The persons belonging to such a religion are born into it because they belong to it. They are marked by the God of that religion before birth. They can emancipate themselves only by individual thinking. Aside from the group destiny, the individuals of course have their own thoughts of greed, hypocrisy and oppression exteriorized to them in the events which are their destiny. If they have engaged in persecutions as joint enterprises, it may be that they will be together in groups when the arm of the law smites.

The priests of any particular religion are not exceptional in the desire to maintain themselves in power by whatever means they can. The

French priest Calvin, the Scotch Presbyterians, priests of the English Church, the Puritans of Massachusetts, including the witch-killers of Salem, all were eager to stamp out heresies and were oppressors. Everyone who persecutes others and seeks the supremacy of his own doctrines, justifies his atrocity by the claim that he benefits those whom he tortures. However, hypocrisy and the arguments which were a screen in days of theocratic domination, are no protection when payment is exacted, and the lesson of tolerance and broad sympathy with humanity has to be learned in the school of the law. The priests, executioners and mobs meet their destiny singly or in groups. As to any theocracy, monotheistic or polytheistic, none of them is, as far as the persons who live under it are concerned, any better or more lenient than the most brutal of barbarous despots.

Each god is jealous of power, and the priests of one religion declare war on the worshippers of other gods. The gods are not the ones that are killed; the people have to pay with their lives during the cruel religious wars of the priests. The gods at the heads of all religions are nature gods created by men; they are not Intelligences. This is indicated by the fact that they have priests who represent them; by the element of fire, air, water or earth, to which they belong; by the sense or senses to which they are related, as sights, sounds, tastes or odors, which are used in rites and symbols in their worship; and, by the fact that each of the gods is worshipped collectively and is believed to be exterior.

All this may be learned by one or a few in a lifetime, but the majority of the adherents of any religion remain together and experience in groups whatever destiny their devotion, sincerity and honesty, or their prejudice, bigotry and hypocrisy, or their arrogance, fanaticism and cruelty in their religious belief brings to them. Thus religions provide group destiny.

The group destiny of those who live under a clerical oligarchy is governed by the same law as that which affects the group destiny of those who live under other forms of oligarchical government. Oligarchies of aristocratic landowners, of soldiers, of bureaucrats, of money-kings, of political bosses and of labor leaders, all have similar aspects. Sometimes there are hereditary features in these institutions; however, here as well as in the so-called heredity of a physical body, the hereditary feature is merely a means of working out the destiny which is always a precipitation and concretion of the thoughts of those who are affected by these forms of government.

SECTION 6

The Government of the world. How the destinies of the individual, the community, or the nation are made by thinking; and how destiny is administered.

Concerning The Government of this world, the destinies of nations, of communities, and of individual human beings, can there be any doubt that these mysterious problems are determined by law? For if chance is to be considered as a determining factor in bringing about events, there must of necessity be a law of chance. And chance then becomes a law which must fit in with other laws and be related to them, or else the established laws would be jostled around and overthrown. As nature is governed by law, so also mankind and human relations must be governed by law. And law dissipates the thought of chance. Chance is only a word used as an escape from the inability to understand and to explain law.

Is there a government of this world? And if so, what is it? How is it constituted? What is law, and how are laws made? Who or what is the authority for the law? And for justice in administering the law? By whom are the laws administered, and, what is justice? Are the laws just, and if so how is justice shown to be just? How are the destinies of nations, of communities, and of individuals administered?

The answer to these questions is: Yes, there is a Government of this changing world. The Government is not in the changing world. It is in the Realm of Permanence, and though the Realm of Permanence pervades this world of change, it cannot be seen by mortal eyes.

The Government of the world is made up of complete Triune Selves. They are constituted to be The Government by the Conscious Light, which is Truth, endowed to them by their Intelligences who are under the Supreme Intelligence.

Law is the prescription for performance, made by the thoughts and acts of its maker or makers, and to which those who subscribe are bound. The laws for the individual human are made by the thinking of the human, during the creation of his thoughts. These thoughts are his laws, prescribed by his thinking. Other human beings who subscribe to these thoughts by their own thoughts, are bound thereby. When the individual thoughts created bring the human beings together, the human beings are bound by verbal or written contracts. Then, or later, the thoughts exteriorize as physical destiny to those concerned. The breaking of these contracts causes disorder and confusion.

The authority for law is the Self-knowledge of the Triune Self. Self-knowledge of the Triune Self is the real and unchanging order of Self-conscious being, which includes all laws of nature. That authority for law is inexhaustible and immeasurable; it is at once available to the knowers and thinkers of all Triune Selves: in detail, and as one related and coordinated whole.

Justice is the action of knowledge in relation to the subject judged; and the judgment determines its administration as prescribed by the law. Justice is just because those who are concerned are the makers of the law for which the human is responsible. The thought and act begin with the human. The human is judged by the knowledge of his own knower. The judgment is administered by the doer's own thinker. This cannot be otherwise than just.

The destinies of human relations, and of communities and of nations, are exteriorized by the human beings themselves, operated by the doers in their bodies, directed by the thinkers as the judges of their doers by the knowledge of the knowers of the humans, as arranged and ordered by The Government of the world, and as determined by the peoples of the world as their destiny.

The complete Triune Selves comprise The Government which is established in the Realm of Permanence. They occupy and operate perfect and immortal physical bodies. Their bodies are organized and composed of balanced nature units. These nature units are unintelligent, but conscious. They are not conscious *of* anything,—they are conscious *as* their functions only; they are conscious of nothing more or less than their functions. Therefore their functions are laws of nature, always constant; they cannot act or perform any functions other than their own; that is why laws of nature are constant and dependable.

Balanced units, (Fig. II-C), are trained to function as laws of nature during their service in a perfect immortal body of a complete Triune Self which is serving as one of The Government of the world in the Realm of Permanence. Each such perfect body is a living university machine. From the admission of the unit into the perfect body and its being a constituent part thereof, until it is qualified to leave the body, the unit successively progresses in its development, from each degree to each next higher degree in that university machine. The unit is conscious as its

function only, in each degree; and in each degree its function is a law of
nature.

When the unit has qualified in being conscious successively as each
and every function of that immortal body of balanced units, it is
potentially conscious as every law of nature. It has finished its course as
an unintelligent nature unit, and is ready to be advanced beyond nature,
to become an intelligent Triune Self unit. When it is advanced beyond
nature it is an aia, and is later raised to the degree of, translated into, the
Triune Self unit. As a Triune Self unit it is to be the successor to the
Triune Self who was its predecessor in training the nature units in the
perfect body, in which it has been educated. Thus all stages are as links
in the chain of being progressively conscious in higher degrees; and this
chain, made up of units that are conscious in progressively higher degrees,
is kept unbroken.

The Triune Self is an indivisible unit, an *individual* trinity of three
parts: I-ness-and-selfness are identity and knowledge, as knower of the
Triune Self; rightness-and-reason are law and justice, as thinker of the
Triune Self; feeling-and-desire are beauty and power, as doer of the
Triune Self. The knower as the authority of knowledge, and the thinker
as justice in relation to whatever subject is judged, are complete, perfect.
But the doer, to be an operator of the body, must prove its ability to
manage and maintain its perfect body whose functions are laws of nature.
Every unit in that body is a balanced unit. Through the breath-form unit
of the perfect body, all other units in that body are kept in balance. The
doer part of the Triune Self is to be operator and manager of the perfect
body. For this purpose it has been trained and educated in that university
machine. The doer as feeling-and-desire must equalize and balance itself
in beauty and power, in an inseparably balanced union, else the units of
the perfect body would become unbalanced, imperfect, and would leave
the Realm of Permanence. In the Eternal Order of Progression the doer
does balance its feeling-and-desire, and so completes its Triune Self.
Then the Triune Self, complete, is constituted as one of The Governors
of the world in the Realm of Permanence.

The doers which are at present in human bodies have failed to unite
their feeling-and-desire in balanced union. In the trial test of the sexes
they unbalanced the balanced units which composed their perfect physical bodies. The composing units were then unbalanced and were active-
passive man bodies, and passive-active woman bodies. And the doers in
their imperfect man bodies and woman bodies lost the direct and

continuous use of the Conscious Light. They ceased to be conscious of their thinkers and knowers in the Realm of Permanence; they were conscious only of this human world of birth and death.

And although its thinker and knower are always present with it, the doer is not conscious of their presence, nor of the Realm of Permanence. It is not even conscious of itself as the immortal feeling-and-desire which it is. The doer-in-the-body does not know who or what it is, although it may mistakenly suppose that it is the body which it inhabits during about sixteen of the twenty-four hours of a day. The body-mind controls the minds of feeling and of desire. The body-mind can think only about things of the senses, and so binds feeling-and-desire to nature through the senses.

The doer is immortal; it cannot cease to be. It has the right to choose what it will do and will not do; because only by choosing to do, and by doing, what is right, will it become independent and responsible. Its destiny requires it to be eventually conscious *of* itself, and *as* itself in the body; to be in conscious relation with its thinker and knower, and by their guidance to find and travel The Way to conscious immortality. That is the situation in which all doers are, who are in human bodies in this human world.

By thinking, the doer in every human creates thoughts. These thoughts are its own prescriptions; its own laws, to which and by which the human, as the maker of the laws, is bound. Then at the right time, condition and place, and with the authority of the knower, the thinker causes its doer in the human to bring about, by act or object or event, what its thoughts have prescribed for performance. That is its destiny. Therefore, all that does happen to the human for good or ill is of his own thinking and doing, and for which he must be responsible. This applies to the individual of every human being. The happenings cannot be otherwise than just.

In the destiny of individuals and of social intercourse, thinking establishes human relations. How then is justice as destiny in human affairs administered? Individual human beings do not know the law. They may or may not agree about acts or objects or events. But the thinkers and knowers of all the individual doers in human bodies have real knowledge; they do know what the human thoughts are, as laws. The thinker and knower of each doer knows what is justice for its doer; and all the thinkers and knowers concerned agree to what happens to humans in relation to other humans, as individuals and as communities.

In this way the thinkers and knowers of the individual doers in human bodies bring about the destiny of human relations in communities.

The Government of this world and of the destinies of the nations starts and is concerned with the government of oneself in one's relation to others. The doer is pulled or driven by its numerous desires responding or opposed to the impressions received by feeling from the objects of nature coming into the body through the senses, as sights, sounds, tastes or smells, and by the thoughts that are cycling in its atmosphere. Each doer is holding open court; impressions and thoughts clamor for one's attention. Before sanctioning the desires which appeal for or demand their objects, one should listen to the voice of conscience or consider the advice of reason. Otherwise one will act on impulse in responding to the most impressive claimant. Whatever one does, he thereby prescribes the law which will be administered to him, in the near or distant future, as his destiny. These proceedings are carried on around the "judgment seat" in each human heart, in the court of its own atmosphere, where the feelings and desires and the thoughts assemble.

That which one doer does, in making its individual destiny in its relations with other human beings, every other embodied doer is likewise doing. And while the doer is holding open court, its ever present knower and thinker is witnessing the recording of its laws as its own conditions, as its own prescriptions to be administered to it as future destiny, and also in its relation to the destiny of others. And in the same way the knowers and thinkers of other embodied doers are the witnesses of the laws made by those others:—all concerning the destinies of human beings in their human relations, as communities and as nations.

The doers in human bodies do not know this, nor do they always agree or keep their agreements, because their Conscious Light is obscured by sense impressions. But their knowers and thinkers always have the clear Conscious Light, as Truth; and know at once what is right and just concerning each human. There is never any doubt. They are always in agreement concerning human destiny.

The Triune Selves of human beings are not of The Government of the world, but they are always in agreement with the complete Triune Selves who constitute The Government. The knowledge of each knower is at the service of all knowers; knowledge of all the knowers is common to every knower. Therefore, through the knowers of the human beings, The Government can at once know the individual destiny of every human being. So it should not be difficult to understand that the destiny of nations, which is determined by The Government of the world, is brought about by the agencies of the human beings through their Triune Selves. Every act, object and event on the physical plane is an exteriorization of a thought, which must be balanced by the one who created the thought, according to his responsibility and at the conjunction of time, condition and place. The knowers and thinkers see to it that their individual doers bring about the events as destiny in their relation to each other in communities.

Complete Triune Selves, as The Government of the world, cause destiny as justice to be administered in the nations through the agencies of the Triune Selves by their embodied doers.

The destiny of each of the nations is made by what the individuals of the nation think and do. By the thoughts and acts of its people, each nation has its destiny prescribed for it as law, by which the peoples of nations are bound. And The Government of the world sees to it that the destiny as law is executed through the individual knowers and thinkers of their doers in human bodies.

All the acts, objects, and events in the make-up of the life and relations of human beings are woven into a pattern as the panorama of life on the background of the world. Sections of the panorama are seen. But the causes that keep the figures moving, that bring about the events in the orderly performance, and that relate the sectional views into series, as an endless panorama of human life,—these are not seen. Therefore the human is unable to account for the acts and events in life. To understand why things happen as they do, one must first understand that he is the immortal doer, comprising feeling-and-desire; and that he operates the bodily machine. Then he should understand that as a doer he is inseparably related to his thinker and knower, and that they know, and determine the happenings caused by his thoughts and acts—which bring about the happenings in the orderly series of acts and events that unfold and make up his life.

The acts, objects, and events of life are exteriorizations of thoughts. Thoughts are created by the thinking of men and women, as destiny. The acts, objects, or events are the results of what human thoughts have prescribed. It is their thinking through the four senses that relates the men and women to objects of nature. Feeling-and-desire keeps the machinery of the body in action,—the machinery by which their thoughts are exteriorized as acts, objects, and events. The design or pattern woven is in the thought. The men and women are related to each other by the nature and character of their thoughts.

The thinkers of the embodied doers are the real administrators who relate the thoughts and arrange the time, condition and place for the precipitation of the thoughts. The acts, objects and events exteriorized are the physical destiny prescribed by the men or women who made them. The acts and objects experienced cause other thoughts to be created and exteriorized. The cyclic recurrence of the creation and exteriorizations of thoughts in small events, leading to great events, keep up the perpetual performance. Their recurrence must be by law, because the human chooses what he will or will not think or do; and because the unknown thinker arranges what its doer chooses into orderly series of events as individual destiny,—and at the same time arranges them in relation with the thinkers of the doers in other human beings who are related by their thoughts.

The individual patterns of thoughts are arranged in the lives which are related to each other. And these are arranged into larger patterns by the individual thinkers of the individual humans, unknown to the humans, but known to the thinkers in larger and larger groups, until the individual thinking affects the law and destinies of peoples and nations.

The Government of the world is in the administration of justice as destiny; and the relations of the peoples, races and nations are determined by them respectively. The Government at once has knowledge of all particulars from the knowers, and the determination by the thinkers of the individual doers concerning their human beings, among whatever races or nations they are placed. And each individual, and each group, and each state or nation has its destiny administered in time, condition and place in justice to each, and in relation to the whole. And so the performance goes on.

SECTION 7

Possible chaos in the world. Intelligences govern the order of events.

Human thoughts, the very large majority of human thoughts, are opposed to universal law and order. Man's desires are mostly lawless, frivolous or vicious, and he gives rein to them when he thinks he can. Most people would, if they could, restrain others and be unrestrained themselves.

Where the acts of every person are limited by ignorance and inertia and often stimulated by self-interest, and most people desire laws for protection on the one hand, and on the other are not unwilling to break them if they can do so without too much danger to themselves, there would soon be chaos in this world and a breaking up of all institutions if men were left to themselves. Intelligences and complete Triune Selves govern affairs according to the law of thought. Elemental beings under their direction do the mechanical part, and are the material with which they work. Every thinking man sees that intelligence of some kind must be behind or within the working of the visible universe. Some assume that there is a single Intelligence whom they call God. The difference between that idea and this system is that the gods of religions are described as personal and as arbitrary in the creation and government of the world, whereas the real "God" of every human is directly related to the conscious doer within him. The Light of his Intelligence is the Light through which alone he can see into the Light of the Supreme Intelligence. The visible world outside is built and destroyed by upper elementals which obey the orders of Intelligences and complete Triune Selves, under the Supreme Intelligence and see to it that the law of thought is carried out.

The Triune Selves and Intelligences are the managers of the continuing play. They arrange the scene, call the players and let them act. Every human is an actor in some spot of the world's stage. At a certain time and place which the Triune Selves or the Intelligences determine, they let him play the part he has prepared himself to play. He is not aware of this preparation made by his thinking. He has forgotten the design and the way in which he designed, but he finds himself on the stage, and is buffeted, coddled, led or lured by others who are in the same or a similar position as he is. His actions may affect himself alone or a few or hosts. The Triune Selves and Intelligences cannot change the destiny of an individual or of a group; all they can do is to retard or accelerate the exteriorizations that would produce chaos and destruction of the human race in less than fifty years if not timed intelligently. They do not interfere with any cycle in its working, but at critical times they guide the course of a cycle so as to allow or prevent an intersection with another cycle or cycles.

Men think and act for their own selfish ends. They have little control over the result of their action beyond their immediate object. Only the Triune Selves and Intelligences know what men's thoughts call for, and the destiny of the greater and smaller groups to which people belong. They manage the order of events by selecting time and place for them, so that the human race will be preserved and continued opportunity will be given to the doers in human beings.

But this opportunity can be continued only upon one condition. That is, that in the sum of human thought the good shall outweigh the bad. What is here spoken of as weight is determined not by quantity but by quality of thought. While it is true that the majority of men are uninformed and their thoughts are largely superficial, callous or vicious, yet there are among humanity many who have fundamental and rugged virtues, whose thoughts have made them honest, self-respecting and self-sacrificing, so that they receive more Light from their Intelligences. Usually such men play no public part, for the public would not have them. However, they turn the balance and so furnish a condition which permits the Intelligences to regulate the time and place of events in orderly succession. They go on as long as there are a few sincere and honest men and women, the power of whose virtuous thoughts is greater than that of the inert, selfish, corrupt and vicious multitude. This condition of the human race is not surprising. Their thinking does not focus Light of the Intelligence; it is limited by the four senses. So they do not know what they are or where they are going.

If there comes a time when the power of the thoughts of the vicious so preponderates as to make any recovery hopeless, then an Intelligence lets a fire god or a water god give to the race what its thoughts have called for. Then follows the destruction of the race by water or volcanic action: the crust of the earth shakes and opens, flames pour forth, and the earth crust sinks while the waters sweep over the land and submerge it. New land rises out of the ocean and awaits the coming of a new race.

That is what happens when the people of a country or of the world determine by their thoughts and acts that they will not live by law and order; that they will use force against law and justice; or that they will give reign to the senses and indulge in debauchery, lawlessness, drunkenness. That would be the beginning of the end of civilization.

But the people of the world are giving evidence of awakening to their responsibilities in life. They begin to understand that as individuals they cannot live and enjoy separately or in separate communities, that their lives are related to the lives of others, and of other peoples. Individuals of different countries are understanding that as they desire independence, so also do the peoples of other countries desire independence. And that if any one people were to deprive another people of their independence, they are in turn liable to lose their own independence. Individuals among different peoples are awakening to the fact that independence, as individuals or as a people, is dependent on their responsibility; that individuals of a people cannot have independence without responsibility; that the degree of their independence is limited to the degree of their responsibility. Independence and responsibility are inseparable. Independence with responsibility will open the way and bring with it more light, the Conscious Light, which will be the entrance into a new Way of life: The Way of life that can eventuate in the establishment of a permanent civilization of Self-Government on this earth.

CHAPTER VI

PSYCHIC DESTINY

SECTION 1

Form destiny. Strictly psychic destiny. Six classes of psychic destiny. The aia. The breath-form.

The law of thought does not decree events beyond the physical plane, that is, beyond physical destiny. What then is psychic destiny?

Psychic destiny is a name for two kinds of destiny. One kind, form destiny, affects nature-matter on the form plane, and has to do chiefly with prenatal influences. The other, strictly psychic destiny, has to do with states in the psychic atmosphere of the doer, and affects the doer after the birth of the body. This is what is here called psychic destiny.

Form destiny is a thought so far advanced toward exteriorization that elementals have already built out the form of it as a future physical act, object or event. This form abides on the form plane of the physical world, ready for appearance on the physical plane when there is a juncture of time, condition and place to give it entrance; then it takes a set and is fixed in the radiant substates of the physical plane as physical destiny. This happens when the cycle of the thought, thus partly in form, intersects the cycle of at least one other thought of the same or of some other person. All physical destiny comes out of the ether, which is the solid state of matter on the form plane. It comes through the radiant, airy and fluid states of the physical plane into the solid state of the physical plane. There it appears in sensible, tangible actions and conditions, produced by elementals of the causal, portal, form and structure kinds under the control of structure elementals. The fluid, plastic form matter is hardened from the ether into the stiff material world. Only a

137

small part can be precipitated at one time, because time, condition and place, which are different on the physical plane, limit the amount of form destiny that can come through. All in a thought that has become form is destiny; its arrival in the physical state may be postponed, but cannot be permanently avoided.

Psychic destiny is all that relates to the human who is conscious as feeling-and-desire. Such psychic destiny comprises all the states and powers of the doer in its psychic atmosphere.

Psychic destiny is of six classes. The first class is the feeling of pleasure or pain when the physical body is affected by contact. The second is the feeling of joy or sorrow when the doer is affected without physical contact, as by receipt of a message or by anticipation of a pleasure or of a calamity. The third class of psychic destiny, and the most important, is the character of the human, his disposition, endowments, sentiments, instincts, virtues and vices. This make-up comes into being before birth and lasts through life and for some time after death. The fourth class is sleep with its restoration of bodily energy, dreams, the adjustment of the doer during sleep, and states similar to sleeping and dreaming, where the doer relaxes its hold on the senses. The fifth class is death itself and the processes of death. The sixth class is shown in the psychic conditions through which the doer passes after death during the periods of its metempsychosis, heaven, transmigrations and re-existence, (Fig. V-D).

Three things are directly affected by psychic destiny: the aia, the breath-form and the doer.

The first of these three things, the aia, is the principle of form for a human. It is matter in a neutral state, matter which is no longer nature-matter but is not yet intelligent-matter and does not belong to any one of the four worlds of the earth sphere. The aia, like the mathematical point, is without dimension; it is not a form; it has neither parts nor size; it cannot be perceived by any of the four senses. The aia came out of Substance as a unit of fire, progressed through all the degrees of nature-matter until it became an aia, and is destined to become a Triune Self. Beings below the human stage have no aias. At the time of conception the aia which is itself without form and without dimension revivifies the form of the breath-form, which is to be distinguished from the radiant or astral body of the human.

The second of the three things affected by psychic destiny, the breath-form, has an active side which is the physical breath, and a passive side, the form, which receives impressions from the senses, and from the doer when it thinks. The aia stands back of the breath-form through life and after death until the breath of the breath-form is put out of phase with the form. The breath-form is an automaton; it is a harlot and an angel for nature and for the doer. It goes with that which is the stronger; it responds to the call that makes the strongest impression; it obeys man's basest desires, yet it is his angel because, after it has been purified, it takes him into heaven. It is most delicately sensitive. It has no inclination to right or wrong, good or bad, health or disease. It responds to impressions made upon it, and then projects them and gives them form.

The breath-form does with the physical body whatever it is bidden to do by the senses or by the doer. It offers no resistance unless it is bidden to resist. It lives in the involuntary nervous system. From its station in the brain, the front half of the pituitary body (Fig. VI-A,a), it operates automatically the involuntary functions of the body. The physical destiny of the body is worked through the breath-form. Elementals build out the radiant-solid or astral body, and therefrom the airy-, fluid-, and solid-solid bodies or masses from invisible marks impressed on the breath-form.

All living beings or things that have form in the world of change, from a gnat to an elephant, from a toadstool to a star, from a devil to a god, get their forms through the breath-forms of human beings after death. These breath-forms express in nature the impressions they have borne as the record of human thinking and thoughts. Expression into nature forms is automatic; elementals of the causal, portal, form and structure kinds have to obey, build out and body forth the signatures on the breath-form. Each breath-form has issued millions of forms in and for nature and continues to issue them.

The breath-form cannot be seen by clairvoyants. That which is sometimes seen as phosphorescent, luminous or star-like, is the astral or radiant-solid body, which must not be mistaken for the breath-form.

Before conception of the physical body, the aia is in the psychic atmosphere. There it revivifies the form with its breath as the breath-form unit. Gradually the breath-form sinks to the light plane of the physical world. As it is lowered, life matter from the life plane and form matter from the form plane of the physical world collects around the invisible breath-form, which begins to glow. The breath-form is then like an ember that is coming to life, and this ember is the breath-form of the future physical human being. The breath-form is an invisible physical unit.

At the time of copulation of the parents, this breath-form enters their joined physical atmospheres—flashing with lightning speed through their breaths and blood and along all the nerves—and then or later the form of the breath-form blends the radiant part of the seed cell with the radiant part of the soil cell. A vortex is formed at the blending. Radiant matter begins to flow into the vortex and so builds up the radiant or astral body. The physical cells divide, multiply by division and make up the fleshly body according to the model of the radiant body, made by the form of the breath-form. This astral body is radiant matter which now begins to change and take on the visible embryonic forms leading eventually to the human form. The general form has remained and will remain the same throughout the present period of human progress and is not carved out by the thoughts of each person in the preceding life. People cannot think of themselves except as in this form; so they perpetuate the type. An individual determines by his thoughts in one life the changes which will be brought about through his aia for the succeeding life; thus an athlete may become a hunchback, a beauty a hag, and vice versa.

From the time of conception the form grows from the state of the glowing ember and gives form to the radiant matter of the cells of the embryo which is drawn into the vortex, so it builds up the radiant body and according to that the airy, the fluid and the fleshly bodies. The form which expands is the reproduction of the form of the last life of the doer, with the variations as to feature, habits and rudimentary tendencies to health and disease, into which past thoughts will be exteriorized at the proper age of the fleshly body. During fetal development the breath of the breath-form is separated from its form, but will again unite with it at the birth of the body.

In the prenatal state the aia reawakens some of the impressions of the past lives, and so provides for the signatures on the form of the breath-form which will be quickened at the proper season into the characteristics of the human being. Not only the future physical formation and psychic traits are on the form of the breath-form in rudimentary, symbolic, magic outlines, but there also are sketched the signatures for future success or failure. As called for by the symbolic lines on the form of the breath-form, elementals come in from nature and build up the finer bodies and then the fleshly body, and the form coordinates them. This goes on until the fleshly body is born; then the breath enters into and unites with its form and they are the breath-form.

From birth to death the breath-form is the coordinating formative unit, which gives form to and holds the four senses, the systems, organs, cells, molecules, atoms, and particular elementals which are, or function through, these, into one complete organization, and through the fourfold physical body keeps them in proper relation. It causes all involuntary movements of the body in waking or sleeping and also obeys the directions of the doer for voluntary movements. The breath-form does what some people attribute to the "subconscious mind," the "unconscious mind," the "subconscious self" or the "inner consciousness." It obeys whatever makes the clearest and the deepest impression. So it obeys the impulses of nature in carrying on the involuntary functions; it obeys conscious or unconscious self-suggestion; or it will act on a lie, such as that a rooted disease does not exist. But it will only obey an impression as long as that is the strongest. In this way it may seem to go against the law for a while, but in time that impression which has behind it the universal law of thought must become the strongest.

The breath-form plays an important part in feeling. The doer can feel a physical object only when its physical body contacts the object and this contact is transmitted through the nerves to the finer bodies, which transmit the impressions to the breath-form. The doer makes the contact through the breath-form. This lines up and relates to the doer the impression received. During waking life the breath-form is connected with the doer. During deep sleep the doer is out of touch with it. The breath-form holds the same general shape throughout life, but it changes from youth to age and assumes the features revealed by the changing appearance of the human. These changes come, not because the breath-form itself grows old, but because of man's thinking and mode of living. By different thinking the breath-form could be kept young forever and be made exempt from death.

The breath-form is for communication of the doer with nature by the body-mind, through the senses. Animals do not have a breath-form; they do not need a breath-form, because they do not think—though it is often supposed that animals do think. How then, it may be asked, can animals feel and desire without the breath-form? The answer is that the feelings and desires of animals are automatically put directly in touch with nature through the four senses of nature, by sight and hearing, and by taste and smell. The animal feels and desires with that portion of the feeling-and-desire of the doer, cast off after death, which animates and is the type of the animal. While having modified characteristics of human beings, animals are relieved from the restrictions of human thinking according to human customs; they are dependent on the senses in their relation to nature. They are impressed by nature directly through the senses and respond immediately to the impressions received. Thinking would inhibit their immediate response to impressions. Animals are specialists in response to nature impressions through the senses, without inhibitions.

After death the breath-form remains for a while with the doer, but later is separated from it. The doer and its breath-form unit are in touch and out of touch at various times after death. At the end of the heaven period, the breath and form of the breath-form unit are out of phase and are quiescent. When it is time for the new life on earth, the aia stimulates the breath, which revivifies its form and then is the breath-form for the next physical body.

The aia is not the astral or radiant-solid body, nor is the breath-form the astral body. The astral body is a body of radiant matter, not a unit. It is made of radiant matter of the physical plane, of the same matter as are the stars and lightning. It may be seen at times as separate from the physical body, but the aia and the breath-form cannot be seen at all. The astral body grows with the fetus and after birth surrounds the nerves through which the breath-form lives. The destruction and dissipation of the astral body, as by burning or decay, does not affect the aia or the breath-form.

The astral body has little more permanence than has the gross physical body. However, it is nearly as different from the solid-solid as is the breath-form from it. The astral body is the means by which figure is transmitted from the breath-form to the fleshly body. It is plastic, elastic and electric. It can exhibit tremendous strength, can extend beyond or out of the physical body, and get away from it for some distance. It can be molded into any shape and take any color. It may diminish or increase in size. Physical bodies cannot be mutilated without destroying them; thus the head cannot be flattened or elongated, or a sword cannot be pushed through the heart without causing death. But the astral body can for a time assume any shape and return uninjured to its physical body. So it is possible that a person while walking through a garden may reach out his astral arm and pluck an apple or a flower, or in a room apport objects, which then come to him through the air by means invisible to one who cannot see the operator's astral body. The astral body of a medium furnishes the matter in which materializing entities clothe themselves; when they cease to use it, it reenters the body of the medium. In these and other respects the astral body differs from the breath-form.

The third of the three things affected by psychic destiny, the doer, and the manner in which it is so affected, are discussed in subsequent pages.

SECTION 2

Form destiny. Prenatal influences. Six classes of psychic destiny.

The first kind of psychic destiny, form destiny, comprises the prenatal influences which mold the physical body. These influences are the doer's past desires while in animal forms, which come together again when summoned for the descent of the doer. The mother and heredity are merely the channels for the shape and endowments of the newborn. The period of prenatal development subjects the mother as well as the child to influences from the form world, for childbearing is a distinctly psychic period.

The second kind of psychic destiny, strictly psychic destiny, becomes manifest after birth, in the endowments and conditions under which the doer works in life. Formative influences appear in the first years, others come later in life; all are exteriorizations of thoughts. So come cheerfulness, content, courage, modesty, frankness, and their opposites.

In a few instances special features appear as psychic destiny, as in mediumship and the premature development of functioning on the form plane. But since men are unable to govern their feelings and desires it is well that they do not develop along these lines. Among practices to force such a development are postures and breathing in a certain way. They usually end disastrously, for interference with the physical breath brings on far-reaching disturbances. The psychic nature should not be dreaded because of these dangers; many benefits may be derived from a normal and natural development of the psychic powers, now latent in most people.

The ability to diagnose and prescribe for diseases, the acquisition of personal magnetism and the power to heal by laying on of hands, are advantages which may accrue because of psychic development. Some space is given to those who explain all things by the law of vibrations, and to those who believe that a study of colors is a key to occult powers, and to those who want to be astrologers. Sensing astrally that which is ordinarily concealed comes as the result of natural growth of the sense of sight. If the development is premature or is abused, the doer instead of controlling forces and beings in the elements will be controlled by them.

Religions are psychic, and are psychic destiny. They affect the emotions and satisfy the need of the suffering doer and the demand for being saved, that is, that it may not perish after death.

Government, institutions, laws and politics are largely psychic destiny, and changes in them are due to emotional reactions of those who are affected by them. Party spirit is not merely a figure of speech; it is an entity which represents the feelings and desires of many, united in one form. Likewise there are spirits of definite classes clinging to their special conservatism and prejudices. These spirits make an impression on the astral body of the embryo of one who belongs to them, and so comes the inborn predisposition for or against certain institutions. Habits, customs and fashions are psychic effects. These various aspects of psychic destiny relate to form destiny and to the first and second classes of psychic destiny, those which comprise feeling through the physical body and feeling by the doer without contact.

The six classes of strictly psychic destiny are all subjective states. These, as well as mental and noetic destiny, are the interiorizations and their effects, which are produced upon a doer by what happens to its body on the physical plane.

Some of the interior effects of the first class, which are those of pleasure and pain from physical contact, result with certainty. These are directly reward and punishment and, while they are not decreed by the law of thought, they result necessarily. They are used to make or enforce payment and to teach lessons. While it does not follow that there can be no learning without previous payment, there is in most cases no learning without it. Besides, the paying is a part of universal adjustment and, as it consists in having pleasure or pain as the immediate result of exteriorizations in physical events, it cannot be avoided.

Psychic destiny of the second class—joy or sorrow without physical contact—is also unavoidable.

The third class relates to the character of the human being, his disposition, endowments, sentiments, instincts, virtues and vices. While the make-up of the doer portion in the body is stamped in rudimentary form on the aia, the human can exercise a right of choice whether he will submit to or fight against his temperament, disposition and desires. Therefore character does not necessarily result from exteriorizations of thinking and thoughts alone. The character brought over from the past life was impressed upon the aia, and when time, condition and place are fit, the traits will appear in physical actions. Psychic effects appear also in some of the vices, such as drunkenness and gambling, and in certain psychic states, as gloom, pessimism, malice, fear and despair and, on the other hand, as hopefulness, joyousness, trust and ease.

The fourth class of psychic destiny is sleep and other states where the doer is not in control of the four senses, as hallucinations, somnambulism, hypnosis and self-suggestion.

The fifth class is death and the process of death.

The sixth class relates to states after death, (Fig. V-D), the Judgment, the hells and heaven. From heaven the doer sinks at last at the fullness of its eternity, onto the light plane of the form world and there awaits connection with the physical body which is being prepared for it and in which it will re-exist.

The psychic destiny of the fourth, fifth, and sixth classes is unavoidable.

With these preliminary remarks on psychic destiny as a basis, we can now proceed to a more detailed discussion of form destiny and strictly psychic destiny.

SECTION 3

Form destiny. Prenatal influences. Conception. Fetal development.

One's form destiny begins with prenatal influences on the body in which he will dwell, and lasts through life and beyond death until the end of his heaven period. The race to which the body will belong had been determined at the end of the previous life. The family in that race in which the body will be formed is selected to meet the requirements of the doer's destiny. The doer portion which is to re-exist brings about the influences which will affect its body during formation, and will provide it through the family with such tendencies as are the result of its past thoughts and fit the opportunities of the present.

Hardly ever is anyone in after life conscious of the suffering incident to the formation of the body in its place in the womb. He who does remember is one who understands his own shortcomings and his duties and the failings of his fellows, who sympathizes with the weakness of others and who endeavors to assist in the difficulties of life.

The selection of a family and of the time for building the body often involves many problems. The physical destiny of the doer-in-the-body must fit in with innumerable events in the lives of others and with public matters. Time, condition and place are all-important. To be born too soon or too late would mean being a misfit in the social order. The time for the beginning of a certain body must be selected so as to allow the cycles of its own life to intersect cycles in the lives of others with whom it is to be connected. When the selection has been made and at the time of conception, the breath-form enters the atmosphere of the father and mother.

Conception is caused by the presence of the form of the breath-form. It binds their two germs in the body of the woman by fusing the radiant matter in both germs and is the center at which universal forces begin the building of the new physical body. This radiant matter develops into a small astral or radiant-solid body which takes on the impressions from the form. The expansion of the radiant-solid body within the fused cells causes the physical cells to divide and so to multiply until the potential form within the radiant-solid body is gradually built out into the growing embryo.

The bonding is the union of the three and is like a gong, a summons or a trumpet blast. Inaudible to physical ears, the summons brings in the elementals which are directly concerned with the building, in their order.

Hundreds of these gongs resound through the world every minute. But each call is answered by those elementals only which are to build that particular body. Only those build who were connected in a certain way as elementals with the previous physical body of the owner of the new body. When the summons comes to them, some are free in the elements, some are bound in plants and some in animals. They must obey the summons. Those that are free go at once; those that are in plants are set free. Those that are in animal bodies are set free by the natural death or the destruction of the animals in which they are. In this way the elementals which once operated in parts of a human body come together in the physical atmosphere of the mother, and pass into her body through light, breath, water and food.

Gradually they are built into the body of the embryo. Those which are built in before the placenta is developed, during the amniotic period, come in by osmosis; those which make up the fetus after placental development has begun are breathed by the mother from her atmosphere into her lungs, enter her bloodstream, pass through the umbilical cord and are built into the fetus. This taking on by the breath-form of a new carnal body is a resurrection of the former body.

The flora and fauna of the world do not spring into existence at the order of a personal God; they are created by the thoughts of man. A part of this subject has a bearing upon psychic destiny at the time of the birth of a new body. During the previous life the doer had desires for prey, cruelty, squalor or venom. These desires bond the union of male and female animals, and are later embodied in the offspring. In this manner human feelings and desires become pigs, cats, fish and other animals. Cattle, sheep, deer, zebras, horses and dogs are of a different kind, and are the embodiment of a better class of desires. Animals have no indwellers in the sense of doers in human bodies, nor have they aias. They are feelings and desires and their bodies are made up of elementals. Some of these animals are formed during the lifetime of the man, some after his death.

When the call is sent out at conception, these former desires, in their animal garbs, have to obey the call. The animal bodies in which they are, die so as to have the animal-like feelings and desires present in the order in which they are needed for the new human body that is being built. These animal types are built into the radiant-solid body and partly into the flesh body, and are later in life the basis for thoughts like those of which these animal shapes were the exteriorizations.

So the cycles go on and the circulations from man to nature and from nature to man are kept up; the thoughts take form in animal shapes, and upon the destruction of the shapes the indwelling feelings and desires seek the source of their existence. They return to the psychic atmosphere of which they are a part. In this way animals transmigrate from nature into man.

Malformations, defects, diseases and disposition to ailments which come in later life, are built by elementals from impressions upon the breath-form into the radiant-solid body at about the time that they appear in the flesh. These formations are forms of thoughts. In a former life repetition of some thought or a sudden energy concentrated and poured into a thought, gave it a mold, which made an impression upon the aia. Elementals now sense the mark which is projected upon the new breath-form and build it into the radiant-solid and then into the flesh body. The thought is exhibited now in that part of the body or connected with the center through which the thoughts of that particular kind usually come into the human system when a man thinks.

The physical body is prepared and built in the prenatal state by the four classes of elementals. According as one class predominates in the combination, the man is endowed with certain abilities or disabilities which come out in his youth or in later years. Where the fire elementals prevail, the man will be agile and quick in his movements; where the air elementals prevail, he will be graceful, a dancer, a jumper or a runner, and can pass over heights without fear of falling; the water elementals give a love for water, swimming and bathing; the earth elementals make him heavy in body, so that he prefers to keep on solid ground. These four classes of elementals are combined in different proportions; where one class is lacking the person will fear the conditions which the lacking class would have made agreeable to him.

So the lack of fire elementals causes fear of fire and inability to deal with it and danger of being burnt. The lack of air elementals will cause a dread of dizzy heights or any heights, of looking into deep places or of walking on a trestle. Such a person will never make a good dancer or a swift runner. The lack of water elementals becomes evident by dislike of the water and by misgivings where water is concerned. Such a person will not really enjoy bathing or make a good swimmer. Lack of the earth element will cause one to get away from the land and seek the water; he will be ever moving about, restless and seeking change.

According to the predominance or absence of a certain class of elementals one will select or be attracted to or led into a vocation and certain events will happen to him. Those who become firemen, stokers, smelters, electricians, fighters, actors or astronomers by choice do so because in them the fire elementals predominate. In dancers, mountain climbers, aeronauts, athletes, musicians, poets and singers, the air element prevails. The water elementals make men sailors, fishermen, boatmen or good cooks. The earth elementals make men workers of the soil, miners, farmers or masons.

The four temperaments are due to the prevalence of elementals of a particular class in the personal make-up. Fire elementals make men ardent, irascible and quarrelsome; air elementals make them dreamers and light-hearted; water elementals make them restless, adventurous and changeable; and earth elementals make them heavy, stolid and materialistic.

Worldly success and failure are determined and foundations for them are built into the embryo by these four classes of elementals, from the magic symbols on the breath-form. Each class of elementals represents its own great sphere of fire, air, water or earth; but in the earth sphere the other three worlds are subordinated to the physical world, where the great Spirit of the Earth rules, and where the most concrete form of his rule is money. For one to have material success the earth elementals must be powerful in his make-up.

The building of the body in its prenatal state is thus done by elementals that work out in physical matter the lines on the breath-form made by previous thinking and thoughts.

Among peculiar prenatal influences are those exerted by several kinds of creatures that have thrown themselves out of the stream of human progress. These beings were human, but have foresworn their humanity. They lost it because they were enemies of humanity or because they fell below a certain level. Shedding blood for the pleasure of it, inflicting injury for the delight of seeing the victim suffer, extorting money from the helpless or delight in ruining the lives of others, and excessive sexual indulgence practiced for many lives, will put one out of the stream of humanity.

Then there are those who are not so much a danger to others, but who have fallen below the standard. Such are the persons who are degenerate through drinking alcohol to excess, using narcotics, or through excessive or abnormal sexuality. These creatures have lost the right to be born in human shape and are debarred from lawful entrance through normal copulation. They can come only if they can bond a couple uniting out of season or while drunk or during menstruation. Such a couple sponsor the creature for which they furnish a body, and are responsible for bringing into the world one who would have been barred from the human family except for the manner of their admittance. The prenatal influences which these creatures bring to bear result in acts of depravity by the mothers.

SECTION 4

Prenatal influences of parents. Thoughts of the mother. Inheritance of former thoughts.

It is supposed that the child's future character depends upon the mother and her environment. This is not entirely true. The mother is but the willing or unwilling instrument who works according to the form destiny of the future child.

Experiments have been tried to produce offspring that would fulfill certain hopes. Most of them have failed. Among the Greeks, expectant mothers were surrounded by objects conducive to the production of healthy, beautiful and noble children. Such children were frequently produced, as far as physical qualities were concerned; but parents cannot produce noble characters and intellects. The best way for a woman to assure herself of a child which will have noble qualities and intellectual powers is to have these herself, to control her desires and think on lofty subjects before conception. However, women with strong desires or holding tenaciously to a thought have shown that strange results may sometimes be produced by the invisible and psychic influences prevailing on the form plane during fetal development. Marks have been made on the body of the child, due to a picture held in the thoughts of its mother and then built out by elementals. Strange appetites have been impressed, fierce desires engendered and peculiar tendencies implanted in the child; or birth was accelerated or retarded in consequence of some thought of its mother.

This interference would at first seem to disprove the law of thought, as destiny; but there is no real contradiction. Often when the mother supposes that she is the cause of birth marks or tendencies in the child, she has been impelled to act by the child's own past thoughts. The child whose destiny seems to have been interfered with by the action of the mother is receiving just payment for a similar act done to another in a prior life, while the mother is either paying the child for a like interference with her or another's psychic destiny in a previous life, or is setting up for reasons of the law a new score which must and will be paid in the future. When the doer to whom such form or psychic destiny is due is ready to re-exist, it will be attracted to parents who have these notions about prenatal development.

If a man and his wife are pure in their bodies and their thoughts, they will attract a doer about to come into a body whose destiny requires such conditions. The destiny is decided before pregnancy. After the impregnation is made, the mother cannot change the character and psychic tendencies of the doer which is to re-exist; the utmost that she can do is to interrupt or postpone their expression, if such is the destiny of the child.

The mother has no right to say what the features of the child shall be, or what position in life it shall hold. Nor has she the right to attempt to determine its sex. The sex has been determined before pregnancy; any attempt to change it is against the law and injures the child.

With the beginning of pregnancy, the mother is brought more closely into touch with the form plane. She should hold herself to a pure life and think on lofty subjects, thereby avoiding improper thoughts. Her right to change these thoughts, appetites and desires which come to her depends on how they affect herself. She has the right to refuse to obey any impressions felt which would tend to lower her in her own estimation or to injure her present or future health.

Prenatal development opens the psychic nature of the prospective mother and makes her sensitive to influences from the form plane. If she is of sound health, mind and morals, the uncommon emotional phases which she experiences come to her because of the thoughts of the doer which will be in the child. If she is a medium or of weak mind, lax morals or unsound body, she may be beset by all manner of beings of the form plane, which desire to obsess or control her and to have the sensations which her condition affords them. Nature ghosts, ghosts of dead men and morbid desires of the living and "lost" portions of doers, may crowd in upon her. If her body is not strong enough or her desires not opposed to them or if she is not high-minded enough to resist their urgings and does not know how to keep them away, these creatures in search of sensation may control her. Sudden debauchery, fits of drunkenness and morbid fancies may be indulged in; bestial appetites gratified; revolting practices allowed; explosive outbursts of anger which lead to killing and messing in blood may take place; paroxysms of delirious fury, frenzied hilarity or intense gloom, may obsess the mother irregularly or with cyclic frequency. Such conditions are usually caused by creatures who have been thrown out of the stream of human progress.

On the other hand, the prenatal period may be one of satisfaction, one in which the mother feels sympathy for everyone; a period of mental exhilaration, buoyancy and life, of happiness, aspiration and high-mind-edness, and she may gain knowledge of things not usually known. The atmospheres of the incoming doer blend with the atmospheres of the mother, and thoughts whirling in the atmospheres of the fetus affect her. The atmosphere of the doer of the fetus acts upon it through the atmospheres of the mother, and all connections are made through the breath.

All this is the psychic destiny of the doer who will live in the body which is being prepared, and at the same time it fits the mother and is her destiny. This period of a woman's life is distinctly psychic. She may learn much by studying her emotions and thoughts during that time, for by doing so she may follow not only the processes of nature within herself, but may see these in operation in the external world. Moreover, it is her duty to protect the body in her charge from evil influences which may beset it through her.

As soon as placental development begins and circulation is established between the fetus and the mother, the four atmospheres of the mother and the breath-form of the fetus are mutually connected. The food she takes becomes part of her blood and that carries her breath into the fetus, where the doer's own thoughts are thereby implanted. Desire in the mother for wholesome food or for liquors or for strange foods and drinks, comes from the thoughts of the doer which thus express themselves in the physical body later in life as proneness to virtues or vices.

The father's heredity is stamped on his germ cell, the mother's on her germ cell, and the doer's own heredity on its breath-form. But nothing can come as heredity from father or mother that does not coincide with the heredity of the breath-form. This heredity, which controls like a screen what will be let through from father and mother, consists of the impressions made on the aia by previous thoughts of the doer and is transferred to the breath-form at conception or during gestation. Thoughts are precipitated as tendencies into the fetus in a twofold way: firstly as impressions transferred from the breath-form through heredity from the parents, and secondly directly from the breath-form as exteriorizations from thoughts in the mental atmosphere of the doer. After the child is born, the tendencies implanted in the fetus and re-existing in the child gradually develop into the physical form and features, the psychic inclinations and the mental qualities and powers. Finally, the body comes into the world with the desires and tendencies which have been transferred by the doer to the child through the father and mother.

All those who "inherit" propensities to shed blood, to rape, lie and steal; tendencies to madness, fanaticism or epilepsy; inclinations to be hypochondriacs, freaks or rogues, or to be mild-mannered, easy-going, matter-of-fact or jolly; a bent towards religious fervor or artistic ideals; who inherit unaffected, modest, upright, considerate and well-bred natures—all possess such traits as a result of their own former thinking and thoughts.

SECTION 5

The first few years of life. Psychic inheritance.

When a child is born, its breath-form contains the rudimentary psychic destiny to be experienced during life. This psychic destiny is held in germ, ready to grow as soon as season and conditions are propitious. The conditions and the season for the development of the psychic destiny are brought about by the growth, maturity and aging of the physical body, in conjunction with the mental attitude of the doer connected with that body. The destiny to be experienced in adult life is distant while the body remains that of a child. As the body develops, the conditions are furnished by which the old desire seeds take root and grow. The growth is retarded or accelerated, continued or changed, according to the manner in which the doer thinks about these conditions.

The first few years of life, up to about the seventh, soon pass out of the memory of most people. These years are spent in adapting the physical body to its breath-form through the astral body. Although forgotten, they are among the most important in the life of a human being.

As a tree is shaped, trained and pruned by the gardener, so the desires, appetites and psychic proclivities impressed on the breath-form are encouraged, restrained or changed by parents and teachers. The child has fits of temper, meanness and viciousness, which are curbed by the parent or teacher who protects the young from noxious influences. The training, care or abuse of the psychic nature which are experienced in early life are the direct inheritance of the doer. The surroundings furnished, with their psychic influences, the vicious or pure minded temperaments of those to whom a child is entrusted and the manner in which its wants, desires and needs are treated, are just returns for its past thinking.

While desire is usually attracted by a like desire and a doer seeking re-existence is guided to those parents who have similar desires, yet owing to the interblending of the different kinds of destiny, a doer is often connected with those whose desires and thoughts are different. The stronger the character, the better and more readily will the doer overcome any evil psychic tendencies acquired in early life; but as there are comparatively few strong characters, the early psychic training generally gives direction to the entire life.

A parent or guardian who is vapid, who loves the glitter of baubles, who panders to the appetites and seeks sensation, will instill similar inclinations into the growing child and stimulate its desires to a wild, luxuriant growth. This is the fate of those who in the past have not cared to restrain their desires. The child who is allowed to bawl and fret inconsiderate of others, and whose parents allow it to have whatever it cries for, is one of those unfortunates who live on the surface of life; these are the barbarians of society who, however numerous they may be at present, will as humanity grows out of its child state, be fewer, and will be considered wild specimens of an undeveloped tribe. Theirs is a troublesome destiny, as they must awaken to a knowledge of their own ignorance and taint before they can so adjust themselves as to become orderly, inconspicuous members of civilized society.

The encouragement or restraint of its emotional nature which a child receives is either the return for its past treatment of others, or an opportunity to learn control of its feelings and desires. A child who gives evidence of talents, but who, owing to circumstances such as the disapproval of its parents, is discouraged from developing them, may find this not a misfortune but a benefit, if certain other tendencies are present, like a desire for narcotics or drink. For the artistic temperament, if allowed to express itself then, would make the psychic nature more susceptible, would encourage drunkenness and would injure the astral body by opening it to vagabonds in the astral states. Not to allow artistic training in such a case will only defer this development and help the child to resist more easily the demon of intoxication. At the same time, parents who either through lack of means or without apparent reason offer opposition to a child's psychic inclinations, often furnish such opposition in payment of an old score or because the doer did not make use of the opportunities which it had before.

Those who encourage its appetites, or who aid to develop its cunning or its wish for that which does not belong to it, or who do not discountenance its tendency to self-indulgence, laziness or greed, are made to offer such conditions as the natural psychic inheritance of the child's past. With these conditions the child should work in the present in order to overcome and control them.

SECTION 6

Mediumship. Materializations. Seances.

Peculiar phases of form destiny and psychic destiny are furnished by persons in whom "astral senses" are developed prematurely or improperly, as in cases of mediumship, clairvoyance and the practice of certain breathing exercises; and, on the other hand, by those who are endowed with personal magnetism as the result of right living.

It is dangerous to develop away from the physical towards the ethereal, which is the solid state of the form plane. One needs a gross or solid physical body to be on the physical plane and to protect his fluid-solid, airy-solid, and radiant-solid bodies from the forces which are concentrated in the solid-solid state, (Fig. III). When lust, anger, vanity, envy and greed are controlled according to the dictates of reason and morals, the physical body is able to withstand inimical forces of the finer states of the physical plane.

As an immortal doer now comes to life in the solid state of the physical plane and becomes aware of it, so the doer will at some time become conscious in and aware of the finer, the fluid, airy, and radiant states of the physical plane. To do this with safety, the doer must become alive to these finer states in the regular course of development and without leaving the fourfold physical body.

Since the finer bodies or masses develop as the solid-solid physical grows, any attempt to give them special attention and to develop them is not only injurious to the solid-solid physical body, but calls upon the finer bodies to do more than they ought. Until the feelings and desires are mastered any attempt to force an entrance into the finer states of the physical plane is almost certain to end in control and obsession in that life, followed by a similar fate in the next.

One phase of psychic destiny is mediumship. The differences in degree and development of mediums are many, but generally speaking there are two kinds. One is the medium whose feelings and desires are under his control, whose astral body and breath-form are trained and whose doer remains conscious and in control of the body while that body reports the impressions which the doer would have it receive. The second kind abandons the body to outside controlling entities and is ignorant of what is done with it while the human is in the mediumistic state and under the control of spooks or elementals. Mediums of the first kind are few and not likely to be known to the world; the second kind is becoming more numerous, because of influences of discarnate beings to lead the human race into ancestor worship.

Mediums radiate a peculiar and subtle odor in their physical atmosphere, as a flower emits a perfume which attracts insects. Elementals, spooks, shells, dwellers and vampires seek the physical atmosphere of a medium and through his body as a channel to reach the physical plane in order to satisfy themselves. Such a medium is one who has in the past or in the present life desired the inner use of his senses, principally sight and hearing. Nearly every medium thinks that he is specially favored by the "spirits", who tell him that he, the medium, has some special and important mission in the world.

One who desires to develop mediumship frequents seance rooms and desires apparitions; or, sitting in the dark in a negative condition, waits for impressions, the appearance of colored lights or spectral forms. Or he gazes at a bright spot so as to become negative and unconscious in order to induce control. He may sit as one of a circle where all desire communication of some kind with the "spirit world"; or he may use a planchette or ouija board to get into such communication, or hold a pencil and yearn to have something push it. He may gaze into a crystal to throw the vision into focus with astral pictures. Or he may take narcotics to have his nerves affected and put in touch with the radiant-solid, or astral, state of the physical plane.

The psychic destiny of all who trespass upon this state, is the same, whether these practices are followed or whether one chooses to be hypnotized and so forced into the astral state by the will of another. They become slaves of irresponsible beings of that state. The known history of some of those who kept open house for unknown beings, which have then obsessed and controlled them, should be a lesson to others who want to be mediums and to all those who desire to develop their senses astrally.

It is hardly possible for one in a thousand to escape the clutches of the inimical creatures which are likely to obsess the unprotected on the form plane or on the astral plane. At seances, public or private, there may be present elementals of the four elements, or mere astral forms, or wraiths of dead men and desire ghosts of dead men, called spooks, shells, monsters, cloaks of vices or elementaries, which may be either feeble and innocuous or strong and malignant. Desire ghosts of still living men may be there too, but this happens rarely. All these entities crave sensation through the activities of living beings. They want to bathe in and absorb the feelings and force of the living, which they cannot do in their own state but only through a human body. The desire ghosts of living men want more power to add to their own. If the moral nature of the medium is strong, the unseen entities that may enter are either of a better class or are too cunning to oppose at once his moral standards. As the astral body of the medium is used by these entities, it loses its force and its power of resistance until there is no opposition to the controlling influence, which is seldom the same for any length of time.

When the astral counterparts of organs are weakened and broken down, the entities which have used them discard the medium's body for other bodies furnished by new persons longing to be mediums. So that even if a medium is at first controlled by an entity which seems above the usual inane beings which are called controls, this entity will discard the medium when he is run down. Then creatures of still lower orders will in turn obsess the medium. Finally there is the sorry spectacle of a human ridden by creatures less than human, which goad him in various directions, as a monkey astride a pig will bite and drive it. The medium and the control both desire sensation, and both get it.

The entities that come from the other side of death are exceptions to the multitude of doers who have passed on. Death is followed by a coma from which some doers do not recover for a long time. After the coma some dream, and some live over events of the past life. But all awaken at some time, become conscious that they have passed through death, and after a time they are judged; then they go through purifications, and then into a state called heaven, or rest, (Fig. V-D). While they are being judged and while they are being purified, they cannot return to earth. But before their judgment, some of them may on rare occasions return to the radiant-solid state of the physical plane.

Sometimes if the departed doer dreams of one of those present, it may drift into the physical atmosphere of the medium. But then its whisperings and breathings will be only the vaporings of the dreamer. After waking from the dream and before going to its judgment the departed doer may, on rare occasions, come or be drawn into the atmosphere of the medium to communicate with one of the living, either to give some information or to express regret; it appears when its breath-form is clothed with matter taken from the medium's astral body.

Another class, few in number, of doers that may return, are doers who when overtaken by death know that they have left undone something which they had wished to do. Another class are suicides, drunkards, murderers, misers and those with whom money was almighty; their dreams bind them closely to the earth. Another class are doers who have thought little in life, and will not have much of an after-death state. All these are at least doers. Also, doers that are in a coma or in a dream may be awakened by the strong desires of the living who would hold converse with them. So a husband would disturb the doer of his wife, or a mother that of her child. If they come into contact with a medium, they, because of their strong desires, can, through the atmosphere of the medium, reach and pull on the departed doer and bring it back to the radiant-solid state.

There the doer is like one suddenly awakened from a dream, confused, uncertain and unfamiliar with its surroundings, and so can give little information as to its condition, though it may be able to answer some questions. Such doers are ignorant of their own status and of their future. They do not know any more than they did in life—they do not know as much. The doers of the restless and the worried, who have left something undone and therefore seek the earth, are sometimes allowed to come back to have what they wished carried out. The great majority, however, are the earth-bound doers, those of the hard-hearted, inhuman and fiendish and with them suicides and drunkards. These often seek the earth through the atmosphere of a medium. After a while they are taken away and so deprived of the means of satisfying their greed, lust and cruelty. No doer can return after the judgment.

The desires that were shaken off are nothing more than cloaks of vices, without conscience and without a form, but are venom, lust and greed. These are again earth-bound, but they are not doers; they are writhing, shapeless or monstrous things, which seek the earth to fasten on a human and obsess him. They are sometimes called elementaries, or "soulless" beings. They seek the atmosphere of a medium so that they can fasten on it or on some other human through it. If they get a human they lay hold of him at the sex part or the solar plexus, like a poultice or a crab, and ooze in, or they jump on the neck like a cat and eat into it and disappear, sinking into the body.

What is called materialization takes place through the preparation of an atmosphere and a channel through which the creatures which manifest pass from the radiant-solid to the solid-solid state. The atmosphere is made by the audience; the friendlier its attitude the more complete and easy will be the materialization. These persons think: "What will come?"—"I want to see my husband."—"I want Black Hawk, the control."—"Will my investment in Blue Sky Petroleum shares pay?"—"Is my lover faithful?"—"Shall I make the voyage to Brazil?"—"Will Bright Eyes tell me if I have a tumor?"—"Who stole the silk from Weaver's store?"—"Was Mabel murdered or has she eloped?"—"Is Johnny safe in Heaven?"—"What do the spirits do in Summerland?"—"Where do we go when we die?"—"Have the spirits any message for me?" These thoughts, selfish, inquisitive, emotional and silly, are so many currents in the room. They revolve around the medium and they may interfere with each other. Sometimes it is asked that a melody be sung. A melody produces a magnetic bath and arranges the currents so as to prevent their crossing. The thoughts roll around the medium, and soon create a whirl which is drawn into the medium as a center. Then the conditions are ready for a materialization. The atmosphere has been created and the channel is ready.

Like a mob no longer restrained by gates, swarms of spooks and elementals are ready to rush in. But there is a law that too many cannot come at once, else they would destroy the medium. Usually the medium has a so-called control which protects him after a fashion against the onrush.

Then there issues, usually from the side of the medium, a soft, bluish, phosphorescent, plastic stream, which is matter withdrawn from the fourfold physical body, and visible because of the radiant matter. This stream gives body to the materializing spook or elemental, then called a "spirit". This may have an entire human form, or only a head or a hand or other part. One or two or even more forms may be manifested at the same time, depending upon the vitality furnished by the medium and the audience. Not only human bodies, but fabrics, flowers, musical instruments, bells, tables or other things may be manifested. These bodies and things are hard or flexible to the touch. They can be examined. The "spirits" may lift someone in the audience, or they may be lifted themselves. All these manifestations are made of the material furnished by the medium, and reinforced by effluvia drawn off from the fourfold physical bodies of the sitters through their physical and psychic atmospheres.

The manifestations may last for a few seconds or for hours, depending upon the vitality of the medium and audience and upon the harmonious wish to have that particular form remain. Skepticism, ridicule, disbelief and opposition to the manifestation will interfere with or dissipate it. The manifestations cannot usually be done by daylight, any more than a photographic negative can be satisfactorily developed in sunlight. Sunlight and strong artificial light interfere because such lights are harsh in their action on this finer matter, preventing its expansion and formation. The manifestations are easier and better in the dark, or by soft moonlight or low artificial light and in a cloudy or moist air. Such air furnishes a better magnetic condition.

A seance is like a play in which the actors converse with the audience. The medium furnishes the costumes in which the actors appear, and the audience, though unknowingly, decides what characters the spooks shall assume. Sometimes the characters represented are genuine spooks; then, if anyone in the audience will help them, they can tell about their own past experiences and present condition. They can do this, however, only because of the Light available through the thinking of the audience. Most frequently the spooks or elementals masquerade as the person desired by the audience. Frequently thoughts are in the atmospheres of people in the audience, of which they themselves are not conscious. But the spooks and elementals sense these thoughts and impersonate them. So the ordinary Bills and Janes, the many Napoleons, Shakespeares, Cleopatras and Queen Marys, appear. The spooks have no intelligence, nor have the elementals. Whatever reasonable information is given is developed from such intelligence as the audience may furnish. In rare instances a disembodied doer may impart information of moral value. It is possible that information of a higher order may be given at certain periods. It is possible, but actually has been so rare as to be negligible.

Everyone taking part in such materializations gives something and gets something. The sitters, be they one or many, give a portion of their finer bodies and vitality, whether they will or not; and they get the entertainment, such as it is, and the experience; but they get no information except such as may be brought out from the other sitters; no new information is given. The elementals and spooks give amusement and pretend to give whatever the sitters desire, and get the sensations afforded them by direct association with human beings. At seances the admonition is given to believe in "spiritualism", in order to excite the curiosity of the sitters, to hold their thoughts and to get them to think of the departed as also living but in the "summerland", another world connected with the earth. The purpose is to raise recruits for mediumship, and to open the partition between the physical and form planes and let the ghosts of dead men partake of the desires of the living. The medium gives his personality for exploitation by the spooks, and they give to the medium thrills and stimulation. This is at the seance; when the medium is later alone the body may be simply obsessed and the elementals and spooks do with it what they want, to get sensation.

At seances another class of entities may appear; they are nature elementals. There are hosts of them, too numerous to classify, but one category will illustrate. In one of the after-death states, during the purification of the doer, the scenes which were lived through and which are made up of elementals are separated and thrown off by the doer. Other nature elementals seeking sensation and fun will coalesce with these ejected bits of scenery and will appear at a seance to enact them through the finer bodies of the medium.

A danger that faces the present race as its possible psychic destiny is that, like many older races, it may adopt a new form of ancestor worship, which is a worship either of the shades, that is, the astral bodies or of the desire bodies of the disembodied doers. In the growth of human races there is a tendency to leave the normal path of progress and to branch off towards the worship of ghosts of the dead. Such worship has always been disastrous to a race; not only would it stop civilization, as it did with those who worshipped the spirits of ancestors in China and parts of India, but it would shut out the light of knowledge. This condition, however impossible it may seem, might be brought about by the increase of what is called communication with the dead or the "dear departed." Fortunately the great majority are against the ghastly and ghoulish practices at materialization seances.

SECTION 7

Clairvoyance. Psychic powers.

Clairvoyance, which is desired by some, is usually an abnormal development. Such development at present is like gigantism, a disease where one part of the body grows to enormous size while the other parts remain normal. Where one develops clairvoyance only, the sense of sight functions astrally or on the form plane while the other senses do not. Inasmuch as such a clairvoyant has not the companion senses to balance it, or the psychic power so trained as to work it, or the knowledge to judge concerning his experience, he is deluded and confused. This is the form destiny attendant on premature development of the astral or radiant aspect of the senses, organs and nerves of the body so as to see or hear that which is concealed.

"Astral senses" are usually used to astonish the credulous and to satisfy the curiosity of the skeptics, or to feed the psychic hunger of the spook seeker, or to gratify those who want to have "spiritual husbands" or "spiritual wives", or to make money.

The term "astral senses" is not accurate. There are no astral senses any more than there are physical senses. The term is used for brevity to indicate the functioning in any state other than the solid-solid state, of the same elementals that work as the four senses in seeing, hearing, tasting, smelling and contacting. Astral vision of a future event, for example, refers to the functioning of the same elemental, in radiant matter on the physical or any other plane, which works as the sense of sight in looking at a ball game, in solid-solid matter. To see a thing astrally means in common speech to see the thing in a state of matter or on a plane other than the solid-solid. There are on the physical plane three other states and on the form plane four states. Beyond these even the best clairvoyant cannot go.

The sense of sight is a fire elemental of the light world, the sense of hearing an air elemental of the life world, the sense of taste a water elemental of the form world and the sense of smell an earth elemental of the physical world. While these elementals are in a body they function on the physical plane and there only in the solid state and not in their own worlds. Only things in the solid state can be seen, heard, tasted, smelled and contacted.

The things which they perceive they transmit through the finer physical bodies or masses to the breath-form. When the sense of sight perceives a thing it can perceive it in two ways, negatively or positively, depending on the attitude of the human. When one is negative, his sense of sight merely receives the impressions which come in a fourfold stream of fine matter emitted by the objects seen. When he is positive and bent on making an observation, his sense of sight sends something of its own nature of fire out to meet the stream of matter coming from the objects seen. The sense of sight usually does this sending out for a distance of from three inches to three feet. In both cases, that of the negative and of the positive perception, the sense of sight aligns the particles of matter and transmits its alignment, as a point, to the breath-form as a perception.

There are limits to this functioning of the sense of sight. It can see only things outside the body. It can see only in a curve called a straight line. It can see only matter in the solid state. Matter in the radiant, in the airy and in the fluid states of the physical plane is not visible. Seeing at a distance is limited by the size of the object and by the nature of the intervening matter. Things which are too small cannot be seen. Another limitation is that the sense cannot perceive unless there is sufficient light, that is, light of the kind that can be seen by. Nor can it see colors beyond a limited range. It cannot see through opaque matter. It can see only surfaces and not the interior of things. Such are some of its limitations. It is true of all the four senses that the range of their functioning is very limited.

The limitations are not inherent in the senses, but are due to the organs and nerves through which they have to work. The functioning of the senses is intimately related to the universe in which man is, that is, the universe which his senses show him, the universe as it appears. Little of the universe stands out before his senses, and that little the senses report as the whole. Only a small part is open to view, to hearing, to taste, and to contact by smell; the greater part is imperceptible and therefore concealed from the senses and not reported by them. The senses are deceived by appearances and report things as they are not, because they perceive them not as they are but subject to their own limitations. Man accepts the testimony which comes through the senses because he has no other witnesses to what exists outside of him. He believes his senses. The further result is that he is ignorant of what the senses do not bring in. This ignorance causes misconceptions of the universe in which he lives. He does not see it as it really is, as a huge being, made up of four states of matter which are in constant flux, change and transformation, inside and outside the shell that he now beholds.

The perception of the senses would be different if the finer physical bodies or masses were built up, if the sense organs and nerves were more sensitive and could be better focussed and if the nervous systems were less dull, heavy and choked up. Then perceptions by the senses would not be limited as they are. Vision, for instance, could be focussed to see inside the body and to see the very eye itself; to see not only some of the matter, but to see the flow of all of the matter in the four states of the physical plane; to see any object irrespective of distance and of intervening solid matter; to see things so small as to be imperceptible through any microscope; to see in the absence of ordinary light; to see colors other than those now visible; to see not only surfaces but to see between and inside and through surfaces. The eye is now normally focussed to see by sunlight, and by the other kinds of light, like candle and electric light, in which sunlight is stored. Sunlight is matter in the airy state or dominated by matter in the airy state. When the eye can be focussed so as to see by radiant matter, which is also physical, it can see without sunlight and can see between and through the surfaces of solid objects. Such vision is as physical as seeing by sunlight, but it is called astral vision or clairvoyance, though the things seen are physical.

True astral vision or clairvoyance is the clear seeing of things that are on the astral-form plane, that is, in the radiant or astral state of matter on the form plane of the physical world. These are not things of the physical plane. The physical things are seen, but in another medium, and so they appear different, as a man in the water appears different from the same man on land. If things are seen in the present or in the past by contacting an object, as in psychometry, the vision may be either astral-physical or on the astral-form plane of the physical world. The vision is on the astral-form plane if things are seen which will happen in the future. Such things are on the form plane and have not yet come to the physical plane for exteriorization. True seeing in the astral state of matter on the form plane is done by the same sense of sight which sees physically through the eye. When it sees on the form plane it does not necessarily use the organism of the eye. It can perceive directly without the use of the organ, as it does in deep sleep, in dreams, or after death when it beholds the scenes of the life that has passed.

Usually no distinction is made between the clairvoyance which is astral-physical and that which is on the astral-form plane. The term clairvoyance is generally used to cover the seeing of things which are ordinarily not visible to the naked eye in the waking state.

Some persons have the gift of clairvoyance from birth, others acquire it through certain practices, others through diseases, and others are clairvoyant when they are in trance states into which they go or into which they have been put. Then they see, hear, taste, and smell things concealed from the average man. Those who are natural clairvoyants should not practice their gifts for amusement or money. Those who have not the gift should not attempt to develop it prematurely.

Until a man knows something definite about the properties of the doer, of the breath-form, of the astral and the other inner bodies and of the four senses, the development of the sense organs and of the nervous systems, so as to let the senses see, hear, taste, smell and contact that which to the ordinary man is concealed, will bring confusion and may bring injury. It is fortunate that people have not developed their organs and nerves so as to use their senses astrally, else they would in their present state, become the prey of irresponsible or inimical beings and would be in greater troubles than they are in now.

When a man rules his feelings and desires, his voluntary nervous system comes under his control and changes go on in his fourfold physical body. Among these changes are that the nerves of the sense organs are cleansed, strengthened and keyed up to impressions of finer and finer matter. These nerves belong to the involuntary nervous system. This system becomes less dull, heavy and choked up as the voluntary nervous system comes under control.

As the nerves in the sense organs become keyed up to matter that is finer than the matter ordinarily perceived, the senses perceive matter within the matter which they have so far perceived and which was their limitation. The gross matter is then no obstruction. On the physical plane, things unsuspected will come within the ken of man as he perceives new dimensions of physical matter and is no longer limited by the on-ness or surface matter spoken of as length, breadth and thickness. That one may then see solid objects and within the solid matter finer matter that is circulating through it; he can watch the sap flowing through plants, the digestion of food and the circulation in his own body and in other bodies, the currents of the breath going through the body and its physical atmosphere, the currents in the air and in the water. Distance will not interfere with sight. He may see through the crust of the earth into the interior. Then the shape of the earth crust will not be that of a globe or of a plane. He will see the sun and moon through the earth crust as he now sees them above it. He will see the planets working through the earth as he now sees them cycling around the sun. He will see the stars not as millions of miles away and of fantastic size but as they are and connected with the nerves of human bodies.

Then he will hear what he sees in plants and in human and animal bodies, the circulation of sap and blood and nervous fluid. He will hear finer matter flowing through the coarser matter that forms solid objects. He will hear the sound made by the earth and other celestial bodies as they move in their courses. He will so see and hear by focussing his sight and hearing on the objects and their movements. Sight and hearing work together; so do taste and smell. Without physical contact he will sense the properties of any thing as being palatable, poisonous, fragrant, friendly or inimical. All this can be done by the four senses acting as reporters, on the physical plane. No exercise of psychic power should be required.

The senses can be used as instruments and agents for the exercise of psychic powers in the control of physical matter. One could act upon radiant matter through his sense of sight, and so cause lightning, or might set fire to anything, or break up solid objects by dispersing the causal elementals in them. With the air elemental that is his hearing, he may, if the organ and nerves are attuned, create sounds in the world outside and can shake and vibrate things to destruction by disorganizing their portal elementals, so that they break up the cohesive power of the form elementals that hold the particles together. He may contact the sun or the moon as he may now touch a boulder.

While man is unable to govern his appetites and restrain his feelings and desires and he has not his voluntary nervous system under his control, it is well that he has not organs and nerves that would enable him to let his senses deal with the finer matter on the physical plane, as each organ so developed would be like a road left open for forces to sweep through and wreck his body.

SECTION 8

Pranayama. Psychic phenomena by wonder-workers.

Psychic results may be obtained by breathing exercises known as pranayama, or inhalation, retention, and exhalation of the breath, to acquire occult powers; but one who advises another to practice these usually cannot foretell how such exercises will affect the nervous system and the doer of the one who practices them. The pupil knows less than his teacher. Both will suffer certain psychic and physical consequences of such practices. The teacher will suffer some psychic injury and will be held to account for the injury done to his follower. Those who practice such exercises have particularly a mental destiny.

The involuntary movements of the physical body, such as respiration, circulation and digestion, are operated by the breath-form. They are due to impressions made continually by the four elements of nature through the four senses, which communicate these impulses to the breath-form. The volitional impulses come from the doer. They, too, must act on the breath-form before physical organs can move. Nature acts on the breath-form and thereby on the physical body, through the involuntary nervous system, and the doer acts through the voluntary system. Man may by his consent subordinate that which is called his will which is really desire, to control by nature, and he may to some degree subordinate the involuntary functions of the body to his will, as is done by those who can stop respiration, circulation and digestion temporarily. Practice of certain exercises by the ignorant is intended to gain such mastery and to give them occult powers. The practices are concerned with breathing, sitting in postures, repeating words and phrases and the starting and stopping of currents in the body.

Centers for breathing are located in physical organs, principally in the throat, lungs, heart and sex organs. The doer-in-the-body is in the kidneys and adrenals; the field of operation of feeling is in the voluntary nervous system, and that of desire in the blood. Through the breath the thinker may contact the heart and lungs, and the knower may contact the pituitary body and the pineal body. Except for the portion of the doer in the kidneys and adrenals, all parts of the Triune Self are outside the body in their respective atmospheres. There are circulations in these atmospheres. They are kept up by three inner breaths, the psychic, mental, and noetic breaths, which run usually through the physical breath, and can continue when the body appears to be dead, as in trance states.

Breath is not breathing; that is merely the movement of the air through lung action. The physical breath is the movement of the physical atmosphere into and out of the body. It moves in paths of lemniscates, figures of 8. The paths are not noticed; only the air passing through the lungs and nostrils is noticed. The physical breath is the effect of the action of the three inner breaths flowing through the physical body. These matters are too far removed from the subject for detailed treatment, and are mentioned only to show the connections of the breaths of the Triune Self with physical breathing.

The psychic breath, which is the lowest of the three inner breaths, has many phases; in one of these it is a revolution, in another it acts like the swing of a pendulum, in another it is like the movement of the walking-beam which turns the paddle wheels of a steam boat. One cycle or swing of the psychic breath may comprise several cycles of the physical breath. The lesser cycles of the physical breath are related to their dominating psychic breath cycle. There is one center of the psychic breath in the kidneys and adrenals, and another in the psychic atmosphere. The psychic breath can be made to coincide with a cycle of the physical breath, and so the physical breath can be made to affect the psychic breath and by that affect thinking.

From these few statements it will be seen that there must be a science of the breath. It will be plain that any interference with normal breathing is dangerous, because it affects the physical breath and through that the psychic breath. If they are thrown out of phase it is likely that digestive, kidney, heart, skin and nervous disorders will follow.

Connected with practices for the suppression of the breath is that of sitting in postures to start certain at present inactive currents, which run through the fourfold physical body along the nerves.

One of the main hopes of such practitioners is to open channels in their bodies to allow a certain universal force, in Sanskrit, Kundalini, to flow through them, thereby giving to the practitioners occult power. If that force did really pass through them prematurely it would burn out their nerves. The experiments, while not likely to produce this extreme result, because they are more or less desultory, generally undermine physical health, loosen the finer bodies in the flesh body and disorder the morals.

Tales told about unusual phenomena produced by negro sorcerers, dancing dervishes, medicine and miracle men of various tribes, conjurers, fakirs, ascetics and holy men, either alone, in company, during religious orgies of an ecstatic assembly or among a band wallowing in debauch, are sometimes true. Deception practiced by the wonder-workers themselves, credulity of the observers or exaggeration by the narrators, do not overcome the fact that some people possess extraordinary psychic powers. Some of them can exercise their powers at any time and place, and some only under certain conditions. These people require for their sorcery, charms and fascination, certain phases of the moon or seasons of the year, caves or mountains, forests or groves, fires, sounding of instruments, chanting, dancing, blood-letting, incense and symbols, which have a magic power.

In every case the phenomena are produced by mysterious powers, that is, an unusual development of feeling and desire, and a manipulation of the breath by feeling and desire. In some cases feeling and desire, in addition, compel the four senses to obey them, thereby reversing the usual relation, which is a control of feeling and desire by these senses. In some cases feeling and desire and the breath, working through these senses or some of them, control elementals and through them parts of the elements. In almost every case thinking is necessary and it also is controlled by feeling and desire. Certain organs of the body and symbols are also used. So are produced such phenomena as eating coals of fire from a burning stick, walking through flames or over red hot coals, making people see living pictures of persons and scenes, rising or floating in the air, traveling through it, producing without instruments sounds in the air, ringing astral bells, transporting huge stones through the air and precipitating flowers, letters, pictures, food and other objects out of it. So, too, are performed walking on water, precipitating rain, locating springs, increasing or decreasing a quantity of water in a vessel. Making the earth to undulate, causing a landslide, making precious stones, transmuting lower metals into gold, making plants grow rapidly to giant size, or dwarfing trees like pines to the size of mushrooms, and passing one solid object through another, are done in the same manner. And so also men are enabled to slash the flesh and pierce the bones of their own bodies or those of others, without pain and without leaving an injury; to be entombed or buried in the ground, to become as a wolf or a tiger, to reanimate a dead form, to take possession of another's body and operate it, to summon elementals and compel them to render service, to have them as familiars, messengers, reporters and as guards, to cast evil spells over people or places and to bring back the dead by necromancy.

SECTION 9

Personal magnetism.

Benefits may be derived from psychic development, as well as harm. The psychic nature enables one to come more closely into touch with humanity, to share in the joys and sorrows of others, to sympathize with and assist them. When one has his feelings and desires and prejudices under control, it is safe to begin the use of psychic powers; they will grow and develop and will not then need special urging, but rather the training which all new growths require.

A knowledge of the psychic nature, the breath-form and the astral body of man, together with a less limited use of the senses, would enable physicians to diagnose and treat diseases more accurately. They would then also know the properties and uses of plants, and how medicines should be compounded and administered to heal the sick. These powers are not used at present, because physicians ignore them or are limited by professional pride and prejudice or are too eager for money. This hunger, itself a psychic force, confuses the understanding, and so does not permit a calm and intelligent use of the senses.

Psychic powers are even now manifesting in some. The circulation of the psychic breath produces some striking characteristics. Among them is personal magnetism, which if increased may become the power to heal by the laying on of hands. Personal magnetism is a radiation from feeling-and-desire through the astral body, and is the attraction or repulsion of other astral bodies. As vibrations of heat are thrown out by hot iron, so the magnetic psychic force radiates from individuals. It affects other human beings through their psychic atmospheres. Personal magnetism is expressed through manner, movement and speech, which charm and fascinate, or irritate and repel. Magnetism is in the physical atmosphere of a human and tells its quality, as the odor of a flower will tell what the flower is.

One kind of personal magnetism is the result of having strong and finer physical bodies through which strong desire forces operate. Such finer bodies result when the sex power developed in prior lives was not wasted. One whose magnetism is strong is prompted by a double force to express his sex nature.

The power to heal by laying on of the hands is the psychic quality of one who has used or desired to use his magnetic power to help others. Power to heal by touch comes with the strengthening of the finer inner bodies so that they serve as a reservoir filled by strong desire. Thereby one can come into correlation with the form and life forces and will be the means to lead their forces into the body of the afflicted. In the case of a healer who places his hands on the centers in a human body which is out of order, the finer inner bodies of the healer guide healing elementals of outside nature into the weak inner bodies of the other and start them into orderly operation. The healing is effected by removing obstacles from the clogged and diseased inner bodies or by connecting nerves, doers and their atmospheres so that there is a proper circulation. Those who are devitalized after healing do not heal as effectively as do those who feel no exhaustion. When one uses up one's own magnetism he depletes his reservoir and will give temporary relief only. He should not make a special effort to force his own magnetism into the diseased body. He will be most effective when he places his hands on the centers of the sick one and feels the magnetic currents flowing into the other. A spirit of goodwill and feeling the currents flowing in the other, produce the best results.

If they are natural and come without training, personal magnetism, the power to heal and other psychic powers, such as that of levitation, the power to increase or decrease in weight, to remain immovable, to produce phenomena, such as precipitation of writing or of pictures, are a capital of psychic power to start with. One's progress depends on how they are used. If the motive is unselfish, these powers, even though unwisely applied, will not result in serious harm. But if the motive is one of self-seeking, the results, whether or not he thinks it possible, will be harmful to him.

In no case should personal magnetism or the power to heal or any of the other powers mentioned be employed to obtain money. The thought of getting money in this connection acts like an infection, and as such affects him who uses the power as well as the one on whom it is used.

SECTION 10

Vibrations. Colors. Astrology.

Among current tendencies is that to explain invisible things by the "law of vibrations" and to speak of "spiritual vibrations" and "thought vibrations." These phrases sound well and mean little. They are generally used by those who know nothing about the difference between the doer and nature, and who are carried along on emotional currents into psychism of one kind or another, by those who understand little about what vibrations are, where they are and about the laws which control vibrations.

There are laws under which the four elements combine according to number, power and form, that is, the numbers one, two, three and four, the power which the combinations attain under these numbers, and the form of the expression of the combinations.

A vibration is the name given to a movement back and forth or wave-like, or to shake or tremble. It is said that a violin string vibrates in the air. The movement is one of matter in a mass which consists of a different state of matter, as the swinging of the violin string in the air, that is, the movement of solid matter in airy matter. A vibration is an elemental or a mass of elementals, a nature unit or a mass of nature units, moving in another state of matter.

This term, vibrations, is used by those who would explain all invisible things as being caused by vibrations. They do not explain in what manner, by what means and with what results.

There are no actual vibrations in the sense of those of a violin string or even of a wireless current of electricity, beyond the four states of matter on the physical plane. Vibrations relate to only one dimension, on-ness, of physical matter. The term has no application and cannot possibly have any to the doer or its feeling, desiring or thinking. There are no vibrations of a doer or in a doer or in an Intelligence. There are no vibrations apart from the matter that vibrates. Vibrations cease when that matter stops vibrating.

Another class of people believe that colors are a key to occult knowledge and power. A study of colors will not give knowledge of the doer or more than a minimum of occult information. What people call color is limited to the physical plane of the physical world. Colors depend on sunlight. Pigments and the colors of the spectrum are elementals manifesting as surface matter on that plane. Those who see colors cannot see them above the radiant-solid state of physical matter. No one can derive information about the nature of the doer merely by color, and color will tell him nothing whatever about the Intelligence. People who talk about the colors of "Masters" or about seeing the auras of Masters, or about telling a Master by his aura or its color, show ignorance. A mere spook can take on a brilliant and attractive so-called "spiritual" red or yellow or blue. Elementals do appear in glorious colors. Nor will a color or set of colors lead to correspondences or parallelisms of any value.

In order that a human may know something about vibrations, color, sound or number, he must be mentally trained. He must be shown the way to so-called occultism by the Light of the Intelligence. He must use a particular method of thinking. Clairvoyance cannot guide him. His reason, however, will not teach with the Light of the Intelligence unless he is safe, that is, has his sight, hearing, taste, and smell so under control that they cannot mislead or deceive him; and, with feeling-and-desire under control so that they do not leave their appointed stations in the body and act from wrong centers. When the human is so far along the way, colors will not be a lure. Occult colors, "soul" colors, affinities, "spiritual" colors and auras, as well as vibrations are often lures to immorality.

Astrology, the science of the stars, is sometimes sought by persons who wish to have a part of the future revealed to them. If they are about to venture on something or if they want to know their destiny or to learn about the fate of a ship, a country, a city or a speculation, they have a figure of the heavens erected and read for them by an astrologer.

The astrologer acts according to mechanical rules, sometimes called grammar of astrology. He considers the signs of the zodiac, the sun, moon and planets, their natures, aspects and relations as they appear in the figure of the heavens, which he erects. The conclusions he draws therefrom are sometimes wrong, sometimes vague, sometimes right. They are usually right if he reads from the event after it has happened.

Astrology is not a strictly physical science, nor can it be worked by facts revealed in the physical heavens alone. It is the occult science of astronomy and therefore two rules apply, namely, that one who practices it for gain or idle curiosity will be deceived in the end, and that the doer-in-the-body must be able to think with the feeling-mind and the desire-mind in conjunction with the body-mind, so that by their powers the astrologer can use and check the sense organs and nerves, which must also have been developed sufficiently.

There is a connection between the breath-form having on it the impressions of its destiny and the sidereal universe. Astrology is a science which is based upon the fact that all acts, things and events are exteriorized thoughts. To cast and read a horoscope is equivalent to following the exteriorizations of a person's thoughts. Of course a mere contemplation of the starry heavens will not do this, especially if one is ignorant of the origin of the stars. The horoscope found in the heavens is an extension of the design on the breath-form at the time of the birth or event inquired into. Just as the designs on the breath-form of a newborn are exteriorized into the carnal body and the events in its life, so they are still further extended till they reach the heavens and beyond.

The paths of the sun, moon and planets have been and will be followed regularly; that regularity is the standard of regularity and certainty on earth. Yet these stars and their paths were and are the extensions and will be the extensions of the designs or horoscopes on the invisible breath-form of billions of human beings. How is that possible?

Thoughts about to exteriorize can move on certain lines only. The courses of thought are as fixed as is the path of the blood, the course of digestion, the movements of the breath, the currents of the nerves, the production of the seed and the courses of the stars. There are comparatively few paths along which thoughts travel.

Nothing seems more real than the sun, moon and stars, time and space and the positions of the stars in space. Astronomers even weigh celestial bodies, calculate their courses and know their constituents. Who doubts that the earth is solid?

Yet the sun is not where it is seen, or where the astronomers have claimed it to be. Nor is the sun a burning body—it is not a solid body and is not even hot. It is a focus of forces from which light, heat and power are developed as with a burning-glass. If this is so, it becomes questionable whether the celestial universe is what it appears to be. The moon is a body but is not where it is seen to be. Its fluid matter predominates over its solid side. It is a sort of clearing house for streams of units from the sun and from the earth. The sun sends matter to the earth and the earth sends matter to the sun, and the moon screens and circulates the forces which they exchange.

The earth is in the solid state of physical matter. This solid state is fourfold and is itself of an earthy, fluid, airy and fiery nature. Within, through and beyond this solid state of matter, is matter in the fluid, airy and radiant states, which four states, constantly circulating, make up the matter of the physical plane of the physical world of the sphere of earth. The solid earth, so-called, is only a crust, though many miles deep. The other states of physical matter are constantly flowing through it. On both sides of the solid or crust layer, is a layer of matter in the fluid state and beyond that a layer of matter in the airy state and beyond that a layer of matter in the radiant state. To sensuous perception there are thus seven planes. In fact, however, there are only four, because the inner and the outer layer of each of the three states are one. The sense of sight with its present limitations cannot see this, and it will not be able to see this constitution of the earth until it can perceive the four dimensions of physical matter, and so will not be limited to surface matter.

At the present stage the universe is anthropocentric, because human bodies are the fulcrum on which everything rests. This should not seem so strange when one considers that out of the millions of heavenly bodies our earth is the only one known to support life. At the same time the universe is heliocentric, because the matter of which it is composed circulates from and to the sun. The matter of which the solid earth is composed is precipitated by the sun and goes back to it. The earth and the planets revolve about the sun, but the earth and the planets are not where they appear to be in the heavens. Some planets are solid bodies, some are not. The fixed stars, so-called, are not solid bodies, and are not where they are seen to be. Yet there is a "Milky Way" and there are constellations and star clusters, but they are extensions or projections in starry matter, of nerve centers in human bodies and they are in a different density than are the sources of their projections; and the human bodies are the condensations of them.

Hence comes the influence which they are said to exert on human destiny. The heavens, like a mirror, return the reflections of the persons moving within the constellations. These are like ganglia in the celestial body, receiving and sending forth influences from and to the persons on the earth.

Time is changeable and is not fixed. Space is conceived of as distance, but space itself is not conceived. Distance is relative and is not fixed. It changes. Nor is what is called space empty. The substance of space is more solid as to permanence than is the solid earth.

The heavenly bodies move through a universe of dense matter, as fish move in water. That is, the matter in which they move is to them as dense as water is to the fish. The fish are not aware that they are moving in dense matter, any more than men know that what they call space, in which they and the stars are moving, is dense matter. The difference between the paths of the sun, moon, planets, and the paths of the fish, is that the paths of heavenly bodies are certain and regulated in their smallest deviations.

To be an astrologer one would have to know all about this as the skeleton of his science. However, then it is not likely that he would spend his time in casting horoscopes.

SECTION 11

Religions, as psychic destiny.

A religion is a part of the psychic destiny of a human and the religions of any time are those which are suited to the feelings and desires of the people and give them the training they need. A human is generally attracted to that religion which offers him bargains here and hereafter or which causes him to fear. Persons seeking power over others, and who are more familiar with the psychic nature, its weaknesses and its needs, will guarantee their religion to fill these wants. Man continues or changes his religious belief according to his understanding of nature, but he does not know this.

Religions are concerned with the emotions and the four senses. Their range is from the belief of the lowest savage to the refined emotions of the cultured. A religion may be known by what it offers to its adherents. It offers always things of the senses, beauties to the eye, music to the ear, feasts for the palate, incense for the nostrils and, for the emotions, joyful and tragic feelings and consolation. Fasts and penances and asceticism are things of the senses. The vast majority cannot get along without this kind of religion. It gives them a moral code, teaches them to distinguish right from wrong and consoles them in their moments of anguish. Such religions were necessary in the past and they are necessary at this time. It is a mistake for those who are or think they are more enlightened, who may themselves get on without it, to persuade others that such a religion is unnecessary. It is necessary until people outgrow it.

These psychic religions set up a standard of morals and offer training. for the emotions. While religions allow the play of these emotions in an etherealized state after death, they put a restraint upon their wild and selfish tendencies during life. Different religions are fitted for different peoples and different classes. According to the psychic needs of a people a religion will be furnished. If they follow the best of its teachings and keep to the highest standards that it sets, that religion will be a blessing to them. If they practice the worst phases, it and its priests will prey upon their weaknesses; then that religion will be to them a tax, a burden and a curse, from which they will find it difficult to escape. Even if a religion is more than a psychic religion, as when it takes on mental and noetic aspects, it will be applied psychically by persons in whom the psychic nature predominates, and these are the vast majority.

Psychic aspects of religions are seen in missions, camp meetings, revivals and cures. There the convert is usually worked up to and kept in a psychic condition before he can be cured or "saved." This takes place at a meeting where the evangelist is of a magnetic and emotional nature, starting and keeping up an emotional whirl which acts upon the psychic natures of those present. The new sensation appeals to their feelings, and "conversion" follows.

Other phases of the psychic aspect of religions are masses, hymns, liturgies, creeds, prayers, ceremonies and ornaments, which all affect the psychic nature. But there the effect is steady or at least seasonal, while at the revival it is spasmodic.

To raise humanity, religions should not appeal to the selfish instincts in man by fostering a belief that he need not pay his debts, since some man or God has suffered or will suffer for his sins. Religions should elevate him from the sordid business world of profit and loss and the whirl of psychic attractions to a moral standard, where deeds are done for the sake of right and duty, not from the fear of punishment or hope of reward. The moral education of the doer must be carried on in a manner which will affect it.

Just how undeveloped human beings are, can best be seen in their religious beliefs and in their stories and scenes that have given them religious comfort in the hour of need or have kept them, as far as possible, on the path of virtue. They worship nature gods whom they themselves have made by their thinking, and cling to a particular form of nature worship until the cycle changes. Then the old traditions are taken away, and new names are given to beliefs and institutions which stretch back to earlier times. After new names and personalities are substituted, these are declared by the priests to be a divine revelation and made to center around a new God or set of gods. The old beliefs are denounced and the old gods are vilified as devils. Bloodshed, war and struggle are the means of educating these doers because of their desires.

Such are the ways by which the human beings try to work themselves out of their ignorance. When human beings worship in sincerity, not with mere formality, they worship the Intelligence, in whatever form they worship nature gods. If they do not worship sincerely, but for self-interest and with hypocrisy and deceit, they have taken the road back to nature.

All religions then come into existence and continue their central deity or deities and heaven and hell, as long as they are desired, for the education of human beings along moral lines. Science and intelligence and knowledge are not essential to religions.

Owing to the doer's choice and action in its early human history it is nourished from the four elements, the nature-mother, through a religion, as the fetus is nourished through the umbilical cord. When the fetus has attained its growth, the child is born and the cord is severed. A religion is like the umbilical cord; it connects the doer with nature. The four senses serve as an umbilical cord. Through a religion the doer wants to be nourished and to grow. When it has received all that a religion can give it and has attained its growth, then, for its development, there must be a severance from that religion. But, unlike the fetus, the doer must sever itself. It does this by a new growth. This is the effort to see and understand. Understanding is to the doer as taking breath is to the newborn babe. The child by taking breath changes its circulation and establishes it in its relation to its new source of life. By taking Light the doer severs itself, and changes its nourishment from feeling or belief to understanding, and so it, as the psychic part of the Triune Self, makes its connection with reason. Its understanding is by the Light it receives from rightness-and-reason of its Triune Self. This is a part of the degree of the Entered Apprentice in true Freemasonry.

SECTION 12

Psychic destiny comprises government and institutions.

The psychic destiny of a nation largely makes its government. Many of the aspects of the government are mental, but the destiny of the governed is largely psychic. A government which would care for its soldiers and the weak, which would make provision for those who have grown old in its service and would enforce laws for the safety of its people from foreign and internal enemies and educate its citizens not to do what they would not like to suffer, would be the kind of government that its people had desired and deserved. It would be united and long lived and an instrument for good among other nations. History shows no such government. All paternal governments have been for the benefit of the ruler and the ruling class. Countries were mere lands, possessed and bartered by kings and nobles, and the people went with the land. When the change came in the eighteenth century from home manufacture in villages to congregation in city factories, the welfare of the laborers was again ignored until degeneration and revolution threatened.

A government which, even though under the label of a democracy, exploits its citizens for the benefit of a few individuals or of a class, which is careless of its wards, soldiers and public servants, which does not look after the health and welfare of all, will be short lived. Either the ruling class or traitors will be the cause of its downfall. Some of its own people may betray it to others, just as it has betrayed its own.

Similar to religious fervor at revival meetings is political enthusiasm, the jingo love of one's own country and of one's particular social and economic institutions, as a landed nobility, clerical hierarchy, labor union or "big business" combinations. In modern democracies this political force is important inasmuch as the people now express themselves without the disabilities of the past. All this is of the psychic nature.

In political campaigns people become agitated about their party rather than about the interests of good government. Men will shout over issues they do not understand, and they will shift in their arguments and accusations with little or no reason; and they will adhere to a party even though they know that its policy is wrong. Ignorance and selfishness permit the psychic nature to rule without restraint.

The most successful party politicians are those who can best reach, agitate and control the psychic nature of the people through their appetites, weaknesses, selfishness and prejudices. After all, these politicians are only means to exteriorize the thoughts of the people to the people. A party politician haranguing an audience, appeals to its special interests or he whispers to some clique. He uses his personal influence, which is his psychic nature, to reach the prejudices of his hearers, under pretense of loyalty to people and country. His love is for power and the gratification of his own ambitions, and using his own psychic influence he enlists the prejudices of others by appealing to their desires, fears and sentiments.

Bad government must continue while those who are governed are selfish, indifferent and uninformed. Such a government is their psychic destiny. This must be so long as the people remain blind to the fact that they get what they give, individually or as a whole, and that what they get is an exteriorization of their own thoughts. The desires of individuals and the collective desire of the people are what brings about these things. They will be changed only when people refuse to countenance the party politician who appeals to them for what they know to be wrong, even when what he promises appears to be to their personal advantage. If it is to injure others it is wrong and will surely react upon themselves. Reading history with understanding will teach this lesson.

The man who attempts to enforce the law is quite frequently downed. The statesman or political reformer who offers amelioration of conditions is usually doomed to disappointment, because he is attempting to remodel forms and physical conditions while the causes which brought and bring about these effects continue. Politics, institutions and customs are what they are because they are the psychic destiny of individuals who are immoral, selfish, ignorant and hypocritical.

SECTION 13

Psychic destiny comprises party and class spirits.

When people bind themselves together for special interests, their united thoughts take form. This form is more or less defined according to the definiteness of the thinking. It is energized and actuated by the desire which they entertain, and so is brought into existence the party spirit. The party or political spirit is not a mere figure of speech, it is a psychic entity which represents the psychic destiny of a large or small party. From local party spirits the spirit of state and national politics is made up. Party politics is an enemy to democracy because it divides the people, causes them to be against each other and prevents them from having a strong and united government.

Similarly there are spirits of definite classes, like those of the professions, with their characteristic prejudices, conservatism and privileges. During prenatal development, politics and patriotism are implanted in the astral body of the fetus, and this class impression is part of the psychic destiny of the individual. So persons have predispositions to callings and inborn prejudices for or against institutions. This impression gives the tendency to their lives which thus decides their entering politics, civil, military, clerical or other class life.

The more strongly the astral body is impressed before birth by the psychic entity that rules a nation, party, church or class, the stronger will be the love for these things. This adherence has its good and its bad sides. It is wrong for one to allow any of these spirits to influence him to act against his standard of right. When one's prejudice is aroused, he should see whether the principle involved is right. If so, he should support it; if not, he should discountenance it, even though he may be frowned on or injured. To the degree of his opposition he frees himself from the destiny of the selfish multitude who remain subject to the class, church and similar spirits.

SECTION 14

Habits, customs and fashions are psychic destiny.

The habits, customs and fashions of an individual and of a people are psychic destiny; they depend upon the bent of feeling-and-desire. The thought connected with the desire gives them the astral form in which they are then expressed as fashions and customs.

Personal habits may be attributes at birth; in such case they were transferred to the astral body in its formation and manifest later in life. If they are acquired during life, the breath-form was impressed by a thought along a certain line and this then finds vent through some organ of the body. A habit is an elemental. The elemental finding an opportunity to become a sensation, continues as habit often against the person's wish. Instances are blinking the eyelids, twisting the mouth, raising the eyebrows, clearing the throat. Other instances are certain cases of stammering, whistling without intent, touching gateposts or stepping on certain parts of the pavement, clenching the hands, spreading the fingers, wabbling the knees—all these habits, when against the wish of the person, are elementals taking possession of the part in question. Offensive or peculiar habits or mannerisms are the reflex action of like offensive or peculiar feelings or desires given form by thought. However trifling a habit may seem it is the outcome of one's thinking which permits an elemental to become a habit. It is psychic destiny exteriorized onto the physical plane.

The fashions of dress, superficial manners, furniture, songs, dances and slang phrases, which appear and change and reappear, are caused by the effort of thinking to give expression to varying emotions. So there are extremes of fashion, from a clinging gown to a balloon-like dress, from flowing folds to a tight-fitting garment; or headgear varying from a close cap to a structure of great width or height. A style can no longer remain permanently in fashion than there can be a permanent emotion. Sentiments and emotions change and their changes are expressed in fashions.

SECTION 15

Gambling. Drinking. The spirit of alcohol.

So far space has been given to form destiny, that is, that which affects the astral body and the senses, and to two classes of strictly psychic destiny, those which relate to feeling through the physical body and to feeling by the doer directly. The third class of psychic destiny relates to traits, qualities and endowments of the doer and to forces and feelings like anger, lust, sympathy and sorrow.

After the unit has left nature and becomes a Triune Self, it has three parts, the doer, the thinker and the knower. The doer may use from one to three minds. The doer has good and bad desires. It depends upon the make-up of the human which of these it will identify with itself and manifest. Manifested, they are expressions of the desires or feelings of the doer.

Among the desires that violate a duty to oneself, are greed, lust, gluttony, and sloth. Anger, hatred, cruelty and revenge break a duty to another. These are primary and crude evidences of desire and are animal in their nature. Goodly expressions relate to control of one's own body and also relate to others, as fellow-feeling, helpfulness and good nature. As the doer develops, the natural expressions of its feelings and desires change from bad to good or from good to bad. The Light which is in the mental atmosphere mixing with natural desires, adds foresight, comparison, planning, combining, inventing and refining. Right thinking improves the crude desires, such as malice, cruelty, avarice and envy, which are immoral toward another, and gluttony, gambling, drunkenness and lasciviousness which wrong oneself. The virtues are courage, temperance and chastity, and are essentially restraints of selfish indulgence in vices, and mastery of temptation. In addition to these active desires there are states of the doer, as joyousness, ease, trust, cheerfulness and hope, and on the other hand, gloom, pessimism, fear and despair.

All these forces which are sent out towards others or centered on oneself, as well as these states or attitudes of the doer, appear in cycles, because they are guided by thoughts. These desires or states begin feebly, increase, wane and disappear periodically. The ill will as well as the goodwill sent out, returns to the sender in a double way; one phase of the psychic force sent out by a human does not leave his own psychic atmosphere, reverts to him and acts on him much as he would have it act on others. The force sent out is of course connected with a thought, and that thought is later exteriorized into physical actions and events and from these exteriorizations follow psychic results of joy or sorrow to the one who issued the thought. Beside these two effects, which result in joy or sorrow sooner or later, there is a third. This is that the psychic force which he sends out is identified with him, builds up his character and helps to make the ground from which his future desires rise.

Character is a predisposition for like desires and the desires generate like thoughts. Character is impressed upon the aia. When the breath-form is built up again, it has the impress of the character. This is the reason why people have their characters when they come into life and why unexpected traits appear in later life, when time, condition and place bring them out. Hence come the predisposition to oppression, theft, malice, gambling and drunkenness, and to helpfulness, fellow feeling, courage, loyalty and chastity. By way of examples the vices of gambling and drunkenness and the psychic states of gloom, pessimism, malice, fear and despair will be considered in some detail, as will also the states of hope, joyousness, trust and ease.

One who gambles desires the money at stake which, will-o'-the-wisp like, leads him on, and is intoxicated by the chance of gain. The money is the chief object with a gambler, while a sport seeks to win, to excel, money being secondary. A sport prefers games of skill, a gambler games of chance. Be the gambling with dice or cards, betting on races, specu-lating in stocks, or any venture without engaging in industry, it is all of a psychic nature. One who plays horses, cards or the stock market, will be played by these in turn. His sensations will be varied by gain and loss, exultation and disappointment, but the result must be eventually that he will be deluded with the idea of getting something for nothing. He will be taught that no one can get something for nothing; that willingly or unwillingly, all that men get they must pay for in some way, and that taking a risk of losing is not paying. Force of circumstances will compel the gambler to lose his gains. What he wins today he will lose tomor-row—be the tomorrow after a day or after many days. Winning or losing will goad him on to win again and so deluded he turns the treadmill, until he learns that the belief that he can get something for nothing is a delusion. He is driven on until he learns his lesson fully. If he has learned it, circumstances will, though unnoticed, surely change and lead him into fields of honest effort.

Some of the most despicable gambling is that in foodstuffs and other necessaries. The interference of the gamblers makes the cost of staples unsteady and often deprives producers of their just rewards. Such interference with the necessaries of physical life is the cause of hunger, want and misery for many. The food gambler is an enemy of mankind. He takes no part in the actual production or distribution of the foods in which he gambles. Moreover, he breeds in others the psychic disease of gambling and by his example causes them also to be intoxicated. To cure him of the psychic disease of gambling, the food gambler will suffer the hunger and want, which his speculations have caused to others. He may starve because of actual lack or because of some disease.

Food gambling, and all other gambling, is due to the spirit of gambling present among mankind. The spirit of gambling is an entity, without definite form. It is a nefarious thing which likes intoxication and gets it through its adherents. It is a god, though its religion has no recognized dogmas, rites or symbols. It has a fraternity which supports and worships it. The members recognize each other through that god which is in them and whose worship is their psychic destiny. Their worship is often more devoted than the lip service paid to other gods who have a regular religious system. This gambling god is created and nourished by the greed and selfishness of men.

The desire to be drunk is one of the worst and deadliest of psychic forces. Though alcohol belongs to the world and the processes of physical nature, there works through it an entity, a spirit, which does not belong to the present period, is an enemy to the doer and to the Intelligence and can reach the doer only through alcohol, when the doer is in the body. It cannot reach the Intelligences, but is as death to the doers; it can affect an Intelligence only in so far as it suspends the progress of the doer by preventing the re-existing portion from continuing its orderly return to earth life. It hinders the Intelligence in the help that it would give to the doer.

Temperate drinking of wine and other intoxicants does not immediately in itself harm the drinker. In no case did it or does it or can it benefit the doer, though an alcoholic drink may stimulate the body in a crisis; but even then other stimulants might serve as well. Alcoholic drinks are not necessary for the maintenance of health. Wine is desired for its taste and aroma and for the psychic effect it has of magnifying and intensifying sensation. Temperate drinking mingles the psychic atmospheres and produces a sort of geniality.

It is difficult to draw the line at temperate drinking. At social gatherings this line is crossed, else the drinkers would not be convivial. People who drink lightly now and then or who regularly take a limited allowance, may not become actual and habitual drunkards. From life to life the tendency is to increase the sensations which alcohol produces. In time, as the liking of the doer for drink becomes stronger, the entity that works through alcohol, as the enemy of every human, may claim the doer. In the following life the breath-form bears the mark of this spirit. This spirit breaks down physical health and moral restraint, opens the barriers between the four states of physical matter and lets in the play of emotional currents and elemental beings. If not overcome the bondage becomes ever more pronounced, until in some life what was once a temperate drinker may be a periodic or habitual drunkard. At some time the doer must conquer or be conquered. If the doer loses, the human is lost and cut off from the Light of the Intelligence. The history of doers, if it were ever written, would show that more doers have failed through the spirit of alcohol than bodies were ever slain in all the battles of the world.

SECTION 16

Gloom, pessimism, malice, fear, hope, joyousness, trust, ease,—as psychic destiny.

Gloom is a psychic state, a state of feeling and of unsatisfied desires. It is not a state created in the present, but comes from the past. It was there created by brooding over unsuccessful attempts to satisfy a desire, without understanding the reason for the lack of success. A person busy with attempts to satisfy an appetite has no chance to brood. No matter what other trouble he will get into, if he keeps busy he will keep away gloom. At any period in the present when he is disappointed or depressed by acts or events, his gloom comes over him and envelops him. Gloom overtakes a person in cyclic periods. If he welcomes it, broods over the present and feels dissatisfied, that feeling feeds and adds to the gloom, which becomes ever deeper and its cycle more frequent. Finally gloom is always with him. Some people may even enjoy it as a steady companion, but this cannot last. The accumulation of gloom, an undefined, indistinct feeling, will lead to tangible and definite despondency and despair.

The cure for gloom is resolution and action. Desire cannot be satisfied or put down or killed; but it can be changed. It can be changed only by thinking. The best way to dissipate gloom is to inquire into it and try to see how and why it came. This very inquiry will tend to drive it away and it is at once weakened by resolution and action. At each return of the gloom its force will be lessened, if it is so met. Finally this treatment will dissipate it.

Pessimism, though a state of the feelings, is more mental in its nature than gloom. Pessimism results from thinking to satisfy desires. When the doer-in-the-body discovers that the desires cannot be satisfied, the discovery reacts on it and produces a psychic state of dissatisfaction. Everything is then felt by the doer-in-the-body as an illusion of the senses and a delusion of itself. The doer seeks happiness. But it cannot attain to happiness through the gratification of its feelings and desires and cannot realize the futility of trying to do so. Its dissatisfaction with itself and the world and the expectation of the worst in every situation comes from this failure of the doer to get what will satisfy its feelings and desires and from its not knowing that desires must be changed. It is subjected to a continuous urge, without having the means of satisfying it and therefore it feels that everything is wrong. Pessimism may be overcome by refusing to entertain gloom, despondency and malice and by seeing when it can be seen—and that is very often—cheer, hope, generosity and goodwill in the world. Pessimism is driven out when one is able to feel himself in the hearts of others and others in his own heart. Then one will soon discover that all things are not running on to ultimate doom, but that there is a bright and glorious future for the doers in human beings.

Malice is a state of the doer in which without provocation it desires harm to another or to people in general. The malice in revenge, jealousy, envy and anger is not referred to here. There are people who rejoice at the loss or injury that befalls others and who delight in doing harm and causing pain, injury or loss. This general state comes on by continual indulgence in anger, envy, jealousy, hatred and revenge. From the temporary outburst of these passions, the doer gradually becomes the channel through which malignant creatures opposed to humanity work. Then such a man will himself be cut off from the Light of his Intelligence and become a human aligned with evil forces against other human beings. This destiny can be prevented by checking the continual indulgence in anger and the other outbursts of passion. This is not saying that a man should not be angry under provocation, but refers to giving way to bursts of malignant passion. Besides checking the outbursts, he should put himself in the other's place and try to be just, after having ascertained all the facts. Very often he himself is to blame. He should try to have a feeling of forbearance and goodwill.

Fear is a state of the doer due to its ignorance and to wrong acts done. Fear is the feeling of impending disaster. This ignorance relates to the uncertainty of time and place when the misfortune will come and what the thing that is to come will be. By fear is not meant the anxiety of going to a surgeon or of walking across a high trestle or of losing a sum of money, but is a state of constant dread, during certain periods, of some unknown disaster. It is a vague, harrowing oppression, a shrinking and drawing back, a feeling as of guilt though there is apparently nothing of which one is guilty. Sometimes the dread is definite, as of imprisonment, becoming a pauper, blindness. These feelings are psychic results of exteriorizations of past thoughts; namely, a feeling of the unbalanced remnants which must be balanced at the conjunction of time, condition and place. The unbalanced thoughts cycle in the mental atmosphere and at times affect the psychic atmosphere outside of the body. The human may feel the thoughts cycling in a general way and when there is a coincidence of cycles which will allow a manifestation, the feeling becomes more pronounced and special and is experienced as fear, which itself may be the means of drawing on the disaster.

This feeling is retribution for sins committed, and offers in every case an opportunity to balance some of the exteriorizations and to atone for the sins. If the doer shrinks from the apprehended disaster, wants to run away and refuses to meet it, it may escape for a time. It cannot escape forever because the sins go with it, as they are a part of it. If it continues to run away, it will be overtaken by the disaster as an actual physical punishment. When stricken by disgrace, disease, imprisonment or loss of fortune, the doer is less likely to balance and the tendency is to commit other sins.

If the doer does not run away from the indistinct apprehension of some disaster or from the fear of some definite calamity, it has an opportunity to change the desire that helped to conceive or entertain the thought that has to be balanced. All the doer need or can do, is to feel that it wants to do right and is willing to do or to suffer whatever is necessary to that end. When the doer gets itself into that feeling, it has strength; strength comes to it. If it holds that feeling of strength it will be able to go through any disaster. The duty of the present moment will be the means of precipitating the seeming disaster or a new duty will be made clear to the human, though it may not be clear to anyone else. The performance of his duty enables the human to defeat fear and throw off dread, because he has performed his part towards balancing the thought the cycling of which was felt as fear.

Despair is the ultimate state of fear, when the doer has not balanced the part it had in issuing a thought. Despair is giving up to fear without further effort to overcome or escape it.

Hope, which is concerned chiefly with feelings and desires, is born with the doer and is its companion. It is like a flash or reminiscence from the unmanifested. Hope is one of the great things in the experiences of the doer. It is linked with Intelligence and with ignorance. This is one of the mysterious things about hope. It connects the unmanifested with the manifested. It is that which does not change when Substance manifests in a primordial unit, nor does it change during all the changes of the unit, nor even after it becomes part of the doer in a human. The doer in the human is the first stage in which it may be perceived and where it can be felt as a state. It is in the Intelligence also and affects it. In the human it is a foretaste of conscious immortality. When the doer tries to grasp it, it disappears, but it soon reappears and then the human chases after it. It is often accused of deceiving, because the thing on which it seemed to rest has failed the human. This is not the fault of hope, but of the human, who must learn that he cannot depend upon things of sense. Hope remains with the doer to teach it this through all its lives in joy or sorrow, ease or discontent. So it performs a mighty function.

Hope is undying. As soon as the doer has failed to learn and is sunk in the slough of despondency and gloom, hope comes again and, like a beam of light, leads the doer out if the doer will follow. Without hope the human could not remain human. When the human is exhausted by grief or remorse, covered with shame and abandoned by the world, hope glimmers and brightens into a ray of light. The doer, in its darkest hours, looks for hope. While it looks for hope it cannot fail altogether. Hope cannot save the human, but it shows the way by which one can save himself and earn his conscious immortality.

Hope cannot give the doer wisdom or knowledge. It cannot give anything, but it can dimly show the way to everything that is attained, and to everything that fails; but the human must learn which is the way to failure and which the way to knowledge, immortality and wisdom. To the embodied doer hope is a feeling. While the doer seeks sensation hope must remain a feeling. To know hope the human must follow it out of the senses and into the Light of the Intelligence.

Joyousness is the sparkling good spirits that flow out of a healthy disposition. This comes as the natural expression of good feeling and continued activities without intent to do wrong. It is characteristic of the youth of the doer, but the doer may carry its joyousness with it through ages of bitter experiences. It pours out like the full-throated melody of the thrush, or enters into the feelings of others like the mimicry of the mockingbird or rises out of itself like the song of the skylark. It drives away gloom, melancholy and dull care as sunshine melts mists and darkness away. Joyousness remains with the doer as long as the doer has no settled intent to harm anyone. The thing that shuts out joyousness is malice. Feelings of hatred, envy, bitterness or ill-will, drive joyousness away and keep it out. It should be a natural part of the disposition of the doer, and while it is kept it attracts elementals which are sprightly, graceful, well disposed, like fun and carry life. They pour into the doer and keep up the wellspring of life. The age of the body is no bar to them, though they are chiefly attracted to youth. But young or old, it depends upon the doer, for joyousness is with the doer and is not a matter of the body.

Trust is a natural feeling of the doer that it can depend upon life, that it will not be harmed, that it can get along and find its way, that whatever the conditions are it will be borne over them, that it will swim and not sink.

Trust sometimes is an indication that the human is innocent, without a wide experience, that he has not come into contact with all phases of life. When trust that is due to innocence is betrayed or fails, the human will show feelings of rancor, bitterness, gloom, doubt and suspicion. On the other hand, trust may be an evidence that the doer has had a wide, deep, lasting experience and that it can be depended upon by other doers. The doer itself will show by its speech and actions whether the state of trust is due to innocence or is its character as the result of long experience.

Eventually the human learns that he can trust and that it is better to trust and that there is a law that works for betterment, even though he cannot quite understand it. This is one of the reasons for religious faith. Trust is a reward for duties well performed, for goodwill, generosity and helpfulness. Trust is an expression of fundamental inclination to honesty. Even if this quality of trust seems at times out of place and without foundation, yet when the doer feels forsaken or cast down, it will bear it up and carry it along. The doer's periods of dejection, if any, will be very short and it will never entertain bitterness or doubt. There will be always an underlying feeling that there is something to rely on, something that is beyond vicissitudes and all changes, and that it is with the doer.

Ease is a further development of trust. Only a developed doer can feel at ease in riches or in poverty, in sickness or in health. Ease comes to a doer only after it has been the victor in many battles and difficulties and has learned their ways and how to live with them. Ease does not depend on easy circumstances, but the doer maintains its ease notwithstanding any outward conditions, favorable or adverse. Ease is a feeling of confidence that the doer will find its way through life, and is a compensation for work well done in prior lives.

SECTION 17

Sleep.

The fourth class of strictly psychic destiny relates to sleep and to other states where the doer-in-the-body is not in full control of the four senses; the thinker and knower are not concerned with the senses.

Going to sleep is the withdrawal of the doer from directing the breath-form. The breath-form is the automaton and obeys the orders of nature and of the doer. The breath-form is in the involuntary nervous system as a whole. The orders of nature are given through the four senses and their systems to the involuntary nervous system. Each nerve has a sensory and a motor part. The order is given by nature to the breath-form through the sensory part, and then the breath-form by means of the fourfold physical body makes the motor part carry out the order. This applies to all the involuntary functions of the body. In sleep the breath-form causes all involuntary functions to continue, but there is no conscious feeling, because the doer has withdrawn from contact with the breath-form.

If a cold draught blows upon the uncovered body of the sleeper, it irritates the skin and affects the circulation. The irritation is conveyed by the sensory nerves through their connections to a sensory nucleus in the front half of the pituitary body which is the seat of the breath-form. The breath-form, from that center, can make the motor nerves of the involuntary nervous system cause the body of the sleeper to turn away from the draught. The breath-form is not aware of the draught. The movement is not made with any intelligence, nor is it made because of feeling. It is simply an impulse to protect the body against the irritation. The impulse comes from nature, namely, from the circulatory system which registers like a thermometer the change in temperature, and the sensory nerves notify the breath-form which responds to the disturbance mechanically and automatically and turns the physical body. If the doer were present the irritation would be felt, the doer would at once see the cause and would by voluntary movements close the window or cover the body.

The time for sleep is announced to the doer when the senses lose their grip on their respective organs and the breath-form has difficulty in coordinating the four senses. This happens when atoms notify their molecules, the molecules notify their cells, the cells notify their organs, the organs notify their systems and their senses, and the systems and senses notify the breath-form that they need a rest for readjustment. Then the breath-form produces yawning, a feeling of tiredness or a feeling of being run down. This is an automatic notification that it is time for sleep and rest and becomes in the doer a feeling. The doer has the power to resist the feeling of sleepiness and to compel the breath-form, the systems, organs, cells, molecules and atoms to continue. It does this by commanding the general manager of the body, that is, the breath-form, and each governor in turn notifies the entities under him and in him. This shows the behavior of the breath-form, which will obey the commands of nature or of the doer, whichever is the more imperative.

When the doer has the feeling of approaching sleep, it withdraws more or less from its touch with the breath-form. The rear half of the pituitary body is the nervous governing center contacted by the I-ness of the knower, the front half is the seat of the breath-form. As long as the doer maintains its grip on the breath-form, there can be no sleep. As soon as the doer lets go, sleep comes.

Sleep is a loosening of the doer from the body. During sleep forces are at work to repair the damage sustained by the body during working hours while it was driven by the double commands of nature and the doer. The forces can repair only when there is no interference by the doer. Then electrical currents stimulate and magnetic waves bathe the atoms, molecules, cells, organs and systems; waste is removed, parts are properly related to each other and the systems are keyed up. And the doer should be away while bodily repairs are going on. The body, rested and refreshed, is ready for the senses to begin new activities. Sleep of the body has to do with nature alone.

When the doer withdraws, it lets go its contact with both nervous systems. Then it is out of touch with nature, because it is out of touch with the four senses. It cannot feel anything physical, and cannot see, hear, taste or smell. This is its condition in deep sleep. When the doer awakens it does not remember. All that it may bring back is an indistinct feeling of the nature of what it has gone through. The period of deep sleep may begin a few minutes after the doer has withdrawn from its touch with the pituitary body and continue until a few minutes before the awakening, or it may be intermittent during the night. As soon as the repairs in the physical structure are made and the body is thereby rested, the senses notify the breath-form of their readiness for activity. When the body is restored and refreshed the doer is attracted to it, reenters its stations in the body, returns to the waking state and suddenly or gradually becomes conscious of its feeling in the physical world and of the action of the senses on its feeling. This is the natural course of awakening. However, a shock, the name being called or a strong smell of some thing, may summon the doer back to the waking state suddenly.

SECTION 18

Dreams. Nightmares. Obsessions in dreams. Deep sleep. Time in sleep.

Dreams occur during the time when the doer is withdrawing from the four senses into the state of deep sleep, and during the time when the doer is returning from deep sleep to its connection with these four senses. Dreams may or may not occur. If they occur they may or may not be remembered. When they are remembered the record may be accurate or imperfect. The doer dreams while it is in connection with the nerve centers of seeing, hearing, tasting and smelling and their areas in the brain. Most dreams have to do with seeing. While dreaming, the doer does not go away from the body; dreams of places or persons, near or distant, occur in the body, nowhere else.

Dreams begin when the doer has let go the hold it has, through the breath-form, on the physical plane and abandons the organs of the four senses, but still lingers in the areas of the optic, auric, gustatory and olfactory nerves and remains, through the breath-form, in touch with the areas and sees, hears, tastes and smells and contacts by means of them. Dreams are usually connected with seeing. Sometimes, but rarely, people hear in dreams; they hardly ever taste or smell and hardly ever dream of touching anything, or of feeling warm or cold.

The reason is that the organs and nerves of sight and hearing are more developed than those of taste and smell, and that there is no special organ for feeling, because feeling is an aspect of the doer, not a part of nature.

The sense of sight is a fire elemental and when the doer is in the dream state this elemental brings before the doer the picture it has recorded in the waking state, on the same day or years before. The pictures may be alive and move, and so form actions or events. If the pictures are of a distant past, they usually represent the events as they were, but if they are of recent events or are caused by physiological disturbances, they may be distorted. The pictures brought up depend upon the coincidence of the cycles of thought. Whether the pictures are vivid or indistinct depends upon the closeness of contact between the doer and the nerve centers, and the ability of the sense to register the picture.

The pictures or sounds may be produced by many causes. One of these is the interest of the dreamer in continuing the activities of the day or of some past time. Hope, expectation, anxiety and fear make up the dream and give it its direction. Another cause may be something that others think about the dreamer, which reaches him and coincides with one of the cycles of his own thoughts; or his own mental nature, reason, may cause a dream to give him a warning as to his conduct. Sometimes elementals show him pictures which have become destiny, are waiting at the threshold of the physical plane and will appear there, as the burning of a house, the sinking of a ship, the death of a person, the finding of some article. There can be physical causes due to physiological disturbances—like indigestion, pressure of some object upon the sleeping body, the slamming or rattling of a door, cold air striking the body or a pain. Another cause may be the presence of astral entities which prey upon the vitality of the sleeper. These are a few of the causes that produce dreams.

The ways in which pictures and sounds and in rare cases tastes and odors are produced vary. One way is that a thought present or past, held in the waking state, is followed by the elemental serving as the sense in the body. When sleep comes, the fire elemental serving as sight, for example, follows the thought and gathers the material for the dream. The material may be the matter that was perceived as the picture, or matter from the four elements taken from the fourfold body of the dreamer. Sometimes also material of part of the dream is furnished by the bodies of persons concerned in the dream, or by elementals not one's own. When the bodies of other persons are a part of the picture, these bodies remain where they are, and when distant places are seen they are not brought near nor does the dreamer go to them. The reason persons and places though distant can be seen in the dream, is that the barriers of what is called distance disappear and leave the vision or hearing unobstructed, or clairvoyant or clairaudient. The elementals of sight or hearing producing the dream, work and adjust all this material into a present, harmonious, acting picture of near or distant scenes or events.

The subjects of dreams may be of any activities the dreamer has had or thought of in the waking state. It may be that the dreamer lives through scenes entirely foreign to any experience in his life or anything he has read or thought of. In this case he sees something that has happened, is going on, or will happen in a distant place, or the scene and the dream experience may be from a past life. This is unusual and happens only when the cycles of his past thoughts coincide with his thoughts and conditions of the present.

Dreams are usually confused, topsy-turvy and indistinct. There is no consecutiveness or any connection between one scene and another. It is rare that one related series of events is followed through one dream, where the sky is blue, the objects clear in color and outline, where the water shimmers and sparkles and the boats rise and fall on it, where the things done follow each other for a purpose, and the persons seem real. The reason for this is that the thoughts of the dreamer in the waking state were nearly as disconnected and indistinct as in the dream. The clear and distinct dreamer is the clear and distinct observer and thinker.

It is possible to make dreaming a means of learning. One may carry a subject of thought from the waking into the dream state and consider it in that state. In this way he may consider the subject from two states in which he is conscious. In the dream state many of the obstacles of the waking state are absent. To do this one must charge his breath-form to bring up the subject for consideration at a certain time during sleep. The subject must be fixed on the breath-form by clear thinking and then it may be followed night after night. The main thing is to be clearly conscious, not drowsily but fully, both in the waking and in the dream state.

In passing from the waking to the dream state there is a period of darkness, forgetfulness, in which the sleeper is unconscious. It is best not to continue the waking thought into the first part of the night, but to instruct the breath-form to call the doer from the deep sleep into the dream state, and to present to the doer the subject of thought, when the physical body has rested and is refreshed. It should be impressed upon the breath-form that the doer should be fully conscious of the subject and of the dream. One can also learn to be conscious in the dream state that he is dreaming. In fact, the waking state is a dream, but the doer is not conscious that it is a dream.

Different from the learning which the dreamer continues from his waking activities when the breath-form calls him at his request, is the instruction which he gets at times from his non-embodied doer portions. Men do not take cognizance of the doer while they are awake, nor do they pay much attention to what happens. Therefore the doer sometimes uses a dream, because that is an unusual thing, to call attention to some fact. This warning, instruction, or illumination, may be given by symbol, or as a vision, or a phrase; the person will or should know the meaning for him.

Nightmares are an unusual phase of dreams. They may be due to the physical causes already mentioned, which interfere with digestion, circulation or respiration. A late supper may cause congestion of some organs, pressure on the nerves which suggest to the sense elementals a cause for the pressure, which the elementals then show to the dreamer distorted and exaggerated. The cause seen or felt in the dream may be some animal, but the picture of it is a hallucination. On the other hand, nightmares may also be due to actual entities trying to obsess the sleeper, as a pig astride the stomach, or a crab or spider clawing the abdomen, or a demon gripping the throat, or a creature in animal or human shape at the sex. Such entities may be evil-disposed elementals, or mixtures of elementals and disembodied entities. These entities attack humans to obtain their vital force, for by means of it they can prolong their own existence. They can approach a person in sleep when his thoughts in the waking state were about sexual practices and so tempered his psychic and physical atmospheres that such beings could approach through them.

One of the worst phases of psychic destiny connected with dreams is the creation of an incubus or a succubus, or obsession by one created by another person. Such phases are fortunately unusual in modern times.

An incubus is a male created by a woman, a succubus is a female created by a man. These creatures are created by a person having no sexual intercourse, but thinking, while the sex force accumulates, about a form of the opposite sex which has the features and traits most desired. The thought is built into a form by elementals, and in time it appears to the person in a dream. Then or later the person has intercourse in dream with that form. The appearance and relation continue, until there is a definite presence at night.

Every human has two sides; the female side is suppressed in the man, and the male side is suppressed in the woman. To carnalize the entity there must be a physical germ, as in the case of any physical body to be born. The suppressed woman is called upon by the man, or the suppressed man by the woman, to furnish this germ, which is astral. Then this unites with the solid germ of the vitality, and so there is a basis for the building of a physical body which is gradually made more solid by its absorption of vitality. The desire attracts to this basis a nature unit from one of the elemental races, a disembodied sense elemental which belonged to another human. This elemental having, as all elementals have, the form of a human, had gone back into its element, after the breath-form of the human to whom it had belonged, was divided. It attaches itself to the germ. As it becomes more physical it continues the relation with the person in the waking state. It partakes of all of the four elements through their systems in the fourfold physical body; so it gets its breath and blood and nourishment in addition to the generative force with which the thing started. Ultimately it appears to its creator during waking hours as a fleshly, palpitating being of the other sex and is a succubus or incubus, endowed by the elementals with even more beauty, grace, strength, amorousness and desire than its creator thought of. If the thought was of something brutish, fierce, bestial, then the succubus or incubus will present that in a greater degree than desired.

Seen by any other person the thing would seem like a human being, solid and real, but there would be something strange about it. The cause of the strangeness would be that the thing has no atmosphere of its own, as it can only exist in the atmospheres of its creator, or in those of another human.

At first the thing comes only in dreams, but as it becomes more established in the psychic atmosphere of its creator, it can appear to him or her in daylight. It may appear gradually or suddenly, at first only when it is desired, but later even when it is not desired. It can disappear gradually or suddenly, as it is only half physical. It explains its existence according to the nature of the individual. If its creator is religiously inclined, it may say that it is a saint or an angel; if the human likes art or aesthetics, it may claim to be a god or goddess appearing by special favor.

In the early stages of association, the thing will be affectionate and loving, and wait on its lover. Then it demands more, grows insistent and commanding. It may show jealousy, revenge and anger, and may harm its lover. Often the human would like to get rid of it, but cannot, not knowing how. Then fear comes. As the human grows weaker because of loss of vitality, a nameless dread begins to overshadow him and insanity or suicide may be the end. That may be the end of the physical life, but not the end of the demon and of the relationship. After death the incubus or succubus may persecute the doer that created it. However, the demon cannot continue its existence unless it can get vitality from a living human being. It may get this vitality from sleepers in their dreams, or it may obsess one of its own sex; then the obsessed is driven by the obsession to intercourse with the other sex.

"Religious" cults have been founded on the worship of incubi and succubi. These may then be called "spiritual husbands" or "spiritual wives." Such cults idealize and intensify sexual relations without the responsibility of physical progeny. Ascetics, hermits and men and women in monasteries, nunneries and other "holy" places, with whom sex expression is restrained but in whom such thoughts find lodgment, have created incubi and succubi and believed them to be heavenly beings. The more ignorant they are, the more certain they are of the "spirituality" and saintliness of their visitors.

Dreams occur during the intervals between deep sleep and waking. Dreams may be remembered, but what occurs in deep sleep is not. The reason why the doer does not remember what happens to it in deep sleep is that the doer is out of touch with the four senses and their areas in the brain and has no way of attaching its feelings in deep sleep to the memory of sights, of sounds, of tastes and of smells. Feelings must be connected with perceptions through these four senses for the doer to remember anything when it is in a physical body. When the doer dreams, it may be on the form plane of the physical world, though it usually is on the invisible side of the physical plane. These are the dreams that have been referred to and which may be remembered.

After the doer-in-the-body has withdrawn from the sense areas and nerve centers it may pass into and remain in the voluntary nerves of the cervical region during sleep. This region is as far as ordinary doers go, some do not even go as far.

Deep sleep is a forgetfulness of all sights, sounds, tastes and smells, and which may be the being conscious by the doer in its own state; this has three degrees, psychic, mental, and noetic. In deep sleep the doer may go over and continue activities of the day or of the past, without relating them to seeing, hearing, tasting or smelling.

In the first degree the feelings and desires that go on in the doer are of a sensuous kind, or they are related to sensations painful or pleasant, as of anger or of affection. The feelings and desires are simple, not associated with external objects. So a person who likes money and deals with it cannot hear the jingle of coins or the crackling of notes, nor can he see the money. He cannot touch the money, or see or hear or taste or smell the objects which he buys or sells, yet the feelings and desires which these transactions produce in his doer are there, and usually they are the only things that are there. A feaster cannot see the choice morsels or the table decoration, or smell the appetizing odors of food or wine, or hear the voices of his companions, or make a clever turn in conversation; nor can he feel the pains of indigestion, yet of the separate feelings and desires which are produced by all of these he can be conscious. They may be there. A person who likes the dance cannot see her preparation and dressing up, the lights, the dresses of the other dancers or of the moving figures, or hear the music or the compliments paid her, or smell the perfumes or feel the pressure of bodies, but the feelings and desires coming from these perceptions of the outer world are often there in deep sleep and with them, perhaps, jealousy and greed.

In the second degree, the feelings and desires of the doer are concerned with rightness, with the righteousness or wrongfulness of the acts and omissions of the day or of the past, and with the rightness or incorrectness of abstract thinking. Perturbations come upon the doer, arising from outward activities when there are no longer any activities, or anything that seeing, hearing, tasting, smelling or contact can enter into. The neglect of duty or duty well done are here felt as remorse, anguish, regret and fear, or as peace, content and ease.

In the third degree, the feelings and desires are concerned with identity. They are again feelings and desires alone, without any association with external objects. The "I" and the feelings are the only things which exist for the doer in that degree. In the waking state the doer says: "*I* did that; *I* made that speech; *I* hit him; *I* will do this or that; *I* got the best of that bargain. This is *my* property, *my* shop, *my* estate, *my* husband, *my* wife, *my* child, *my* dog. *I* shall take that office, that property, that woman. *My* opinion is right. *My* plans must be carried out. *My* name will be famous. He wronged *me*. He hurt *me*. *I* lost that." It says, too: "*I* am great; *I* am generous; *I* was not considered." But in the third degree of deep sleep there is only the identity with the feelings and desires of doing, making, hitting, getting, owning, taking, intending, suffering, losing and being. The persons, objects and events which produced the feelings and desires do not exist for the doer in this degree.

The persons, the happenings, the objects which evoked these feelings have disappeared and the feelings of "I", of the power of the "I", of the loss to the "I", of the injury to the "I", remain. The objects—enemies, competitors, audiences, property, husband, wife, child, dog, injuries, praise and blame—have disappeared, but the feelings and desires produced by them remain as the feelings and desires of the "I" and "mine". Of these the doer is conscious.

These three phases in which the doer is conscious, feelings-and-desires, rightness-and-reason and I-ness, are commingled in deep sleep, as they were in the waking state. One phase usually dominates the other two. The Light of its Intelligence is on the doer, and the doer is therefore conscious of its feelings and desires. These states of the doer are the result of the activities in the daytime. They are not a cause of future action, but are a reward or punishment for the acts and omissions of the doer in the waking state. Nor does the doer learn anything in sleep, unless the desire for learning existed in the waking state and the necessary work was then done. In that case, the Light of the Intelligence may aid in solving problems that were worked over, or give illumination. A great deal may be learned in sleep if one will charge himself in the waking state to be informed on certain points.

The time spent in deep sleep depends upon the length of time the physical body needs in which to be repaired and refreshed, upon the digestion and assimilation by the doer, apart from the four senses, of its experiences during the waking state and upon the refreshment the embodied doer portion needs. When the body is fit for new activities and the doer is ready, nature and the doer seek each other. The doer returns by way of the medulla and the cerebellum to the sense nerve areas, and connects with the rear half of the pituitary body and then takes up its stations in the body. The eyes open, sounds are heard and the doer is conscious of this. Then it becomes conscious of where it is and of the identity or name of the body by which it is known in the world.

Time seems to be different in deep sleep, in dreaming and in the waking state. The difference lies in the standard of measurement. The essence of time is accomplishment, and this is measured differently in each of the three states. The accomplishment is a result that is brought about by the change of the relation of things to each other. In the waking time, the accomplishment by which time is measured is the movement of the earth in relation to the sun. A revolution of the earth around its axis in relation to the sun is the measure of a day, a revolution of the earth around the sun is the measure of a solar year, and a revolution of the pole of the equator around the pole of the ecliptic is the measure of a sidereal year. This kind of time is measured by the eye, is objective, external and the same for all on the surface of the earth. In waking life man is guided by this kind of time and so far as he can think of time he measures it by this standard. This time is the phase of time for those who are conscious of matter in the solid state of the physical plane, that is, time which they measure as earthly time of the physical plane.

In a dream one may live through many years crowded with events, and on awakening find that he has slept only a few seconds. Therefore the dream time seems unreal when compared with his measure of waking time. He does not and cannot compare the waking time and the dream time and judge, in the dream state. However, if during a dream one is conscious of the experiences of his waking time, those waking experiences seem as unreal in the dream time as his dream experiences seem unreal in the waking time. In deep sleep he cannot compare the waking time and the dreaming time with the time in deep sleep, nor can he compare the time in deep sleep with the waking time and the dreaming time, because in deep sleep the four senses of the waking and the dream states are out of touch with the doer and the doer is unconscious of them. The accomplishments measured in deep sleep time are results brought about by the changes of feelings and desires, rightness-and-reason, and I-ness-and-selfness, in their relations to each other from the beginning to the end of deep sleep. On awakening the waking time cannot be compared with the deep sleep time because the measures are so different. In dream states the doer measures not according to earthy time of the physical plane, but usually according to the fluid, airy and fiery time of that plane; in deep sleep the doer measures according to the changes in its feelings and desires produced by the things that happened to it while with the senses. Sometimes the feeling brought back from deep sleep is one of peace, confidence and ease; sometimes it is the reverse; in either case, it is an indication of the thing accomplished in the deep sleep.

Reality is for a man what he experiences or knows at the present moment. The experiences of yesterday are as unreal as are dreams, as long as he does not live them over again in feeling and desiring. If he lives them over, they are in the present moment, and become real again. Thoughts of the future are only dreams, unless these thoughts are felt and lived. To the degree that they are felt and lived they make the present disappear, take its place and are reality.

Dreams seem to be unreal because one cannot bring them into the present moment and he cannot put himself into the state in which he was in dream. Man has not built up his four senses so that he can act with them on the form plane of the physical world; he cannot even use them on the astral or radiant side of the physical plane. At present these senses cannot act independently of the physical organs and nerves. In the waking state they need these organs and nerves; in the dream state they need only the sense nerves. If man had these four senses so developed that they could act on the form plane, what he could see in dream would be more real to him than the things he now perceives in his waking hours.

The material on the form plane is finer and firmer, and the senses are sharper, more sensitive and more far reaching when acting on that plane than when acting on the physical plane. If the senses were properly developed they would have a consecutiveness and order in their functioning, which would permit man to perceive consecutiveness in events and to remember them in his waking state. Instead, he now remembers only topsy-turvy and distorted patches. At present when the doer dreams and is not definite in its purpose, and when the senses are not coordinated and controlled, nature ghosts rush into, around and out of the atmosphere like a lot of noisy children, and help to make the unrelated shifting scenes.

SECTION 19

Hallucinations. Somnambulism. Hypnosis.

Hallucinations in the waking state, in fever, in narcotic and hypnotic states, are like impressions produced by dreams. Objects are seen, heard, tasted, smelled and touched when there are no such objects as on the solid physical plane. Hallucinations are of many kinds and are produced in many different ways. Alcohol affects the nerves in such a way that the doer receives from the astral and airy states of matter reflections of all kinds of sights and sounds, such as bugs, vermin or beasts, and so senses these things. In narcotic states the sense organs are opened to pleasant and sometimes gorgeous scenes, sounds and sensations, which are reported by the senses; and later, hideous creatures appear, terrifying sounds are heard, uncanny things are touched. In fever states the nerves are overwrought and the senses get in touch with elementals which convey pictures and sounds of a distorted nature. The senses are not properly correlated with the doer, and the reports they make are partial, exaggerated and incoherent.

Hallucinations of these various kinds are produced when the nerves of the body are affected by outside influences, are no longer under the proper control of the breath-form, and the elementals functioning as the four senses and as the rulers of the four systems in the body are no longer checked but function uncontrolled. Improper acts or habits will reduce the nerves to this condition, and then elementals of various kinds that like fun and sensation, pour in and affect the already disordered senses.

Hallucinations induced by hypnosis are different. There a man's psychic nature or his breath-form or both are partially or entirely under the control of another person, and the senses and the doer of the hypnotized obey the command of the hypnotizer.

Other psychic states which are related to sleep and to hallucinations in the waking state, are somnambulism, hypnosis, self-hypnosis and conditions due to self-suggestion in the waking state.

Somnambulism is a state resulting usually from unintended self-suggestion. In somnambulism there is no intention to compel the body to do what it does later in the somnambulic sleep. In that state the doer is in deep sleep, while its body walks, rides or climbs, often in dangerous places, and then returns to normal sleep in bed. The cause of somnambulism is, that the doer in the waking state thought of certain acts. These thoughts were impressed upon the breath-form. The physical body was restrained from doing the acts by the doer, which, though it wanted to do them, was prevented by the fear of danger or by conventionality. When the doer has retired and is in deep sleep and the body is no longer restrained, the breath-form, obeying the impression received, causes the physical body to do the acts. Whatever the senses and the organs do is merely the carrying out of the impression made by that thought. Somnambulic walking is a concrete illustration of the exteriorization of a thought. Somnambulism can be prevented by self-suggestion, that is, by forbidding the breath-form to perform in sleep any such suggestions made to it in the waking state and charging it to awaken the doer if it should be impelled to carry out the impression.

Hypnosis is an artificial sleep brought about by the command of one doer-in-the-body acting on the doer-in-the-body of another. This cause is a subject of mental destiny, but the phenomena are psycho-physical. The phenomena preceding natural sleep are produced artificially to put a person into the hypnotic state. The hypnotist causes a feeling of drowsiness to creep over the senses of sight and hearing of his subject, and then suggests or commands that the subject go to sleep and then asserts that he is asleep. This suggestion or command is obeyed. The phenomena of sleep are produced. The doer withdraws from the pituitary body and the senses, or from the pituitary body alone, and then the thought of the hypnotist takes the place of the doer and so controls the breath-form and through that the voluntary movements and the senses. The doer is usually disconnected from its breath-form and its body and is in deep sleep. The operator having taken the place of the other's doer, dictates the movements of the breath-form and so can affect even involuntary movements, suspend respiration and heartbeat and compel the senses to see, hear, taste, smell and contact what he suggests. Beside the stage tricks usually compelled, the operator may throw the subject into trance states, in which the subject may relate his visions, undergo surgical operations without feeling pain, or receive suggestions for his moral improvement, which he will later carry out.

One should never under any condition consent to be hypnotized by anyone. The hypnotic state once permitted has a tendency to loosen the hold of the doer on its breath-form and to make the breath-form and the doer negative and subject to the magnetic influences of others. The hypnotizer, elementals or disembodied beings may take hold of the breath-form and keep the doer out. All sorts of hallucinations, delusions and moral obliquity may follow for the unfortunate, whose body may become the plaything of any entity. No one can hypnotize another if the other refuses. No experiments should be permitted.

SECTION 20

The process of dying. Cremation. To be conscious at the moment of death.

Death is the fifth class and is especially psychic destiny. It marks the end of the period during which the embodied doer works through the four senses in the physical world. The time of death had been determined at the end of the previous life. Usually the place and manner of death are also decided by the thoughts in the previous life.

Fear of death is caused by a feeling of the doer that it has not earned its conscious immortality, and it dreads its ignorance and the unknown. There are other causes for the fear of death. The doer has been through the experience of death so often that it fears the experience, because it means a break in the continuity of life, a parting from things it has held dear and uncertainty of the future. The doer feels that there is to be an accounting, something that it must pass through.

Dying is the withdrawal or rolling up of the three inner bodies or masses, (Fig. III), from the extremities toward the heart. As they recede, rigor mortis sets in; the regions which they leave become cold and there is no feeling in them. Then these masses hover or flutter over the heart and puff themselves out of the mouth with the last breath, causing a slight gurgle or rattle in the throat. With them go the breath-form and the doer, which is the cause of the rolling up of the inner bodies. They hover over the physical body like a bird, a cloud or a globe, or they may stand in human form beside or above the body for a while. Usually the doer does not see its body or anything else. If death has not yet taken place, there is a slight line or ray or cord that connects these finer inner bodies with the heart or some other part. While this connection remains it is possible for these finer bodies and the doer with the breath-form to reenter the body. There is no actual death until this connection is broken. The connection is broken when the breath-form leaves. It leaves when the doer desires, consents or wills to die. The doer that is attached to life at first refused to desire to die. But when it knows, by the Light of the

Intelligence, that it is useless to cling to the body, it wills, and death is instantaneous. The time taken to reach the decision is not measured by the standard of external time. According to that, death is always instantaneous.

At death the four senses and the breath-form and the doer leave and are separated from the flesh body. The four senses remain with the breath-form which usually leaves the three inner bodies. These remain with the physical body and in none of them is there seeing, hearing, tasting, smelling or feeling. Nothing that may be done to the flesh body or to the finer bodies can be felt in any way by the doer, the only entity that can feel.

Cremation is the best disposition of the body after death. By burning, the material of the body is soon restored to the elements from which it came and the three inner bodies or masses are dissipated; and so the magnetic connection between them and the breath-form and the remains of the flesh body ceases. The physical atmosphere is also destroyed. Where a body is devoured by birds, fishes and animals, the three finer bodies are destroyed as soon as the flesh is digested. The radiant, airy and fluid bodies go with the solid fragments like smoke or a shadow. It is different in life, where the breath-form is present and holds the inner bodies intact. Burial and embalming are the worst methods. These customs, bad for the doer and for the community, hold the inner bodies with the flesh body for a long time, namely, until the flesh body has decayed. As the physical atmosphere is not destroyed by burial, it is possible for the doer with its breath-form to go back to its old haunts. It cannot find them without its physical atmosphere.

Death is a friend to the doer. Death frees it from the turmoil, changes and uncertainties of physical life, so that it may have a rest before it is drawn back for another life on earth.

During life it is well to set the thought upon being conscious at the time of death and to charge the breath-form to remind the doer to be conscious of the passing over and of its identity with its thinker and knower. The doer will not be conscious at the time of death, unless this has been impressed upon the breath-form by many repetitions during life. The doer ought to be conscious of the Light of the Intelligence, but unless it was conscious of the presence of the Light during life, it will not be conscious of it at death. If it has been conscious of the Light during life and if it is reminded by the breath-form of its passing, it will be conscious at the time of its death and will also be conscious of the Light of the Intelligence. Then it will understand what is before it and will go through it more easily.

SECTION 21

After death. Communications with the dead. Apparitions. The doer becomes conscious that its body has died.

The sixth class of psychic destiny is of the states through which the doer passes after death, (Fig. V-D). After death the various entities that were combined into a human being gradually separate. The more quickly the fourfold physical body is disposed of the better it is for the entities composing it, for the doer and for the people in the world. When the physical body is consumed, the elementals, nature units, which are its atoms, molecules and cells, are freed and return to their respective four elements, that is, states of matter, in the earth sphere. From there they are drawn into other bodies, mineral, vegetable, animal and human. So they continue their constant circulation during the life and the dissolution of the different bodies of which they form a part.

The radiant-solid or astral body, which was during life the matter that contacted the invisible breath-form, took its form from that and was visible to clairvoyants, is now only the shadow of the physical body. During life the fluid body was the carrier of life to the physical body from the food that the four states of matter furnished. In a physical body each cell is insulated and is not in touch with any other cell. The astral, airy, and fluid bodies pass through these cells and connect them with each other, so that a current of life can flow through them. After death the astral body has lost touch with the breath-form and is as dead as the solid body. It decays in the astral state of the physical plane as the flesh decays in the airy, fluid and solid states of the physical plane. The places are now reversed. In life the grosser physical body depended on the astral, but after death the astral depends on the grosser physical and so can last only as long as that does. This disposes of the fourfold physical body, which is dissipated after death and takes no part in any of the after-death states of the doer.

The breath-form with its four senses and the portion of the doer remain together in the atmospheres of the doer and go together through a process usually called hell. This entity is the human without the fourfold physical body.

After death there is a period of unconsciousness, that separates the doer from the physical world and the state in which it finds itself. The period may last less than an hour, or it may be many years.

The doer becomes conscious again in different ways. It may become conscious in a dream without being aware of its identity, as a person dreams during ordinary sleep. These dreams are usually incoherent; the scenes in them lack sequence and tangibility and are generally scenes without sounds. Or the doer may become conscious of one of the very early conditions of its life; so a middle-aged man may be conscious as what he was when he was ten years old and remain in that state, playing marbles or on his way to school, for a long, long time. Or the doer may become conscious in one of the positions which it filled in life and continue going over the same acts for a long time. So a messenger may deliver his parcels, a clerk may make his entries, a librarian may sort over his books, a banker may make his loans, a milliner trim hats, a housewife look after her household, a prisoner serve over his sentence in jail, a soldier fight over a battle, an invalid go through his period of illness, and a fisherman catch fish. In these cases they follow the occupations which engrossed one period of their lives on earth and do them over and over again. The rich continue their activities and the poor theirs. Or the doer may wake up as though from a sleep and continue a number of activities, either with or without the feeling of identity. So a fisherman catches his fish, takes them to market, sells them, goes to a tavern, and mends his nets and boat. Another case is where the doer just continues all its ordinary activities. These are a few illustrations out of many.

In all these states the doer lives over scenes from the life it left. Nothing new is done. There is no new thinking. A feeling of identity may or may not be present; if it is present it is the false "I," the ego, of the human. Other persons may seem to take part in these scenes, but in that case they are not those who actually did take part in the scenes in life. In none of these instances does the doer do anything that it has not done before in life and in none of them is the doer aware, at first, that it has passed through death and has lost its physical body, or that the world it lives in is not the physical world. Questions such as these do not come up, any more than in ordinary life. The bookkeeper did not ask himself in life whether he was awake or dreaming, dead or alive and no more does he ask that in the states described.

The characteristics of these and other such states are that the flesh body is dead, and the doer is not yet aware that it has passed through death and does no new thinking; that what it does it does automatically, with only dreamy sensuous perceptions; and that all seems as real as though it were done for the first time. The condition may be illustrated by scenes that have once been acted and which are reproduced by cinema a thousand times. These states if passed through at all, are passed through by the bad and the good alike; so far there is no reward or punishment.

Not all doers pass through these states, but only those in whose lives strong impressions have been made on the breath-form and who have to wait some time before the judgment. In these states, the doer is with its breath-form on the astral form plane of the physical world. The breath-form cannot be seen by any clairvoyant if the astral body has been sloughed off. If the astral body is still connected with the breath-form the astral body may be seen clairvoyantly. However, while the doer is in the states mentioned it cannot communicate by any means with any one on earth, and it cannot know what is happening on earth. It does not know that the body has died and it cannot do anything but work off the impressions on the breath-form.

If anyone tried to communicate with a doer in one of these states and had power to do it, either directly or through the astral body of a medium, there would either be an interference with that state without the doer's coming out of it, or else the interference would bring the doer out of the state. That would he a premature announcement to the doer that its physical body was dead. Then the condition in which the doer was automatically living over scenes would cease, and the doer would receive a shock, untimely and cruel, which would cause it to have a longing to return to the earth, or a fear of the earth, and to go through a period of suffering and uncertainty until its time for judgment came. This is the destiny that is experienced by some of those who in life have tried to communicate with the departed. It is one thing for the doer to try to come back; to force it to come back is quite another.

Apparitions of the dead are not incompatible with these statements. The doer cannot be seen; the doer is not the apparition or specter, which may be seen. There are various kinds of apparitions; some have more or less of a connection with a doer, and some have none.

Some apparitions take place because a medium draws them to his body, sometimes aided by the thoughts of those attending a seance. So a doer, dreaming of one who is present at a sitting, may be attracted to the medium; or after waking from the dream and before the judgment a doer may on rare occasions be drawn to a medium, to give information or express regret to one who is living; or attempt to have something done which the doer had wished to have done before it departed; or a doer may be attracted to the atmosphere of the medium if the dreams of the doer are of a mean, low or brutal nature, such as those of drunkards, criminals or misers; or if the dreams are crude and about things of the earth only, as are the dreams of doers that thought little and only of things of the body. The apparitions caused by these doers come about when the breath-forms of the departed doers get astral matter from the astral body of the medium or of the sitters, and are clothed with that sufficiently to be visible and sometimes tangible. In none of these cases is the doer fully awake; hence come the confused, incoherent and inane effusions of the "departed souls."

Most apparitions which come through mediums have, however, no connection with departed doers. Such are mere spooks, that is, shells, or rarely cloaks of vices sloughed off by doers during their purifications; or the apparitions are due to elementals which sport and thrill at the expense of the medium and the sitters.

Then there are apparitions seen occasionally at certain times and places. Some of them are seen by anybody and some by certain persons who are mediumistic, or who have the astral use of the sense of sight and who are called clairvoyants. In these cases the specters sometimes use for materialization the astral body of the beholder, without his knowledge. In some cases the specters use the astral body of a nearby animal, which is still or sleeps during the manifestation; or they may use astral matter of their own astral body, if the physical is not too much decayed; or the breath-form may, when the doer dreams vividly, draw astral matter from the radiant state of matter and so become visible, without the aid of any flesh body.

Among such apparitions are shades or wraiths, that is, the astral of the physical body disconnected from the human. They are specters which glide or float along. Usually they do not walk. Often they wear a white sheet or shroud. The reason for this is that a sheet or shroud was placed over the dead body and the astral body soaked through and was impressed by the sheet or the shroud. When it drifts away from the corpse it appears in the garment of death. If burial clothes were used, the wraith appears in burial clothes. Wraiths are senseless; they cannot see or hear, and cannot make any more contact than a fog or a breeze. They drift along magnetic currents as thistledown floats in the air. They may go through a door, a wall or other solid objects.

Then there are apparitions that are seen in some costume worn during life. In such case the doer is dreaming and the breath-form is automatically enacting the dream, astral matter being attracted to and giving visibility to the breath-form which is vivified by the dreaming. Such specters perform the same thing over and over again or they may do different things on different occasions. Sometimes the specter seems to be acting with other beings which are not visible. Usually the specters do not see and are not aware of the beholder.

Another kind of apparition is one which may occur either while the doer does not know of the death of the body and before it enters the dreaming, or before the judgment when the doer has finished the dreaming and may or may not know of having passed through death. The doer is there partly awake; the record on the breath-form may bring up a memory of something which the doer was set upon having done; and the desire to have it done vivifies the breath-form so that it may go to the locality thought of and act to attract the attention of a living person. Such may be cases where the specter appears lifelike and raises a hand to warn or beckons to be followed, or leads to a place where a letter, a document, a treasure, or a murdered or lost body lies. The specter is likely to continue its visits and actions until that which the doer was set upon having done is accomplished. Then the magnetic connections between the breath-form and the letter, document, treasure, or other object cease. There belong also apparitions or presences felt where the mark on the breath-form is set to protect a person in danger, prevent a marriage, or revenge a wrong.

The time during which unconsciousness and such dream and com- atose states last, was determined during life by the impressions which thoughts made on the breath-form of the doer. Eventually the doer becomes aware that it has passed through death. It is awakened by its own breath-form or by the Light of its own Intelligence or by entities appointed for the purpose.

When the doer is awakened it connects with its four senses which are in the breath-form. It is awake as it was in the waking state on earth, but it cannot do any thinking other than the very thoughts it had during its earth life. The doer may in this way go over its past life, which is as real or even more intense than it was on earth. Then comes the judgment, which is followed by two distinct stages of suffering in a "hell" which the doer created while it lived on earth. One stage is a suffering by the doer through the senses which are in the breath-form; the other stage is a suffering by the doer itself after it has parted from the breath-form. Both these stages are purifying. At the end of the second state the purified doer arises, meets and unites with its breath-form which has also been purified and enters the state called heaven.

SECTION 22

The twelve stages of the doer, from one earth life to the next. After death the doer leads a composite life. The judgment. Hell is made by desires. The devil.

There are twelve states, stages, or conditions constituting one round which each doer portion passes through from one life to its next life on earth, (Fig. V-D).

When the doer eventually becomes conscious that its body has died, it awakens as after sleep. If the fourfold physical body has not yet been dissipated by cremation or by the decay of the flesh body, the doer may be held by its desires on the form plane of the physical world. If the body has been dissipated, the doer when it awakens is in its psychic atmosphere on the physical or the form plane of the physical or the form world. The doer does not know any more of these planes than it knew of them in life.

In either case the doer is with its breath-form and its four senses. It can see, hear, taste, smell and feel, and it is conscious in its breath-form. It lives over its past life, not from childhood to the time of death, but its entire life is made a composite and it lives that composite. It is in its own world, in its psychic atmosphere. Its acts, its events and its environments are those they were on earth and as real as it perceived and felt them to be in life. It is dressed in a favorite dress as in dreams, or with the composite dress. It meets the people it met on earth and speaks and acts with them and they with it, similarly as in a dream on earth. These are not the earth people or doers, but a reproduction of them as impressed on the breath-form, by thoughts of them during life. The doer does not in this state go through extreme sorrow or extreme joy. Some doers go through this state for an hour, and others for many years of earth time before going to judgment. Some receive their judgment as soon as they awaken. Nothing more is there known about the after-death states than was known during life.

Sooner or later in this way the doer becomes aware that it is to be judged for its thoughts and deeds on earth. It goes through what impresses it to be a passage, and emerges in what seems to be a hall of Light, which is present in every part of the doer. The doer would retreat into the passage to escape the Light, but the passage has disappeared. It seeks a way to escape from the Light; it seeks something to shield it from the Light; but the Light is everywhere; there is nowhere for the doer to go and nothing that can intercept the Light. It tries to call upon God, as it thought of God during life, to save it, but it cannot pronounce his name. It calls upon its friends, its protectors, its dependents, its money, its power, its good works, but none can enter the Light. It would accept the help of the very devil, if it believed in a devil, to get out of that Light; if its bad works would convict it and damn it into hell it would summon them, but it is conscious that not even these would take it out of the Light. It feels that this Light, the Conscious Light of Intelligence, is conscious of everything, and that it is now alone in this. Gradually the Light makes the doer aware that it does not even own the form it is in. Then the doer and the breath-form separate.

The doer feels naked, stripped of its very breath-form, but is conscious. The breath-form with its four senses stands before it. There is silence. The doer cannot see or hear. The Light which is through the breath-form brings out all the thoughts that were invisibly impressed upon it during the life which has passed. The deeds in life, the objects with which the doer and the body were concerned, the persons and the places and the settings, are brought out by the Light and shut off from the doer. They appear with the thoughts which the doer issued about them during life. These thoughts in their stages toward exteriorization are shown through the breath-form. The doer feels as though it saw and heard all that appears upon the breath-form that was its own. The entire life passes and is felt by the doer.

The Conscious Light is Truth. It reveals and makes the doer conscious of what the Light is conscious of. As each thought, act and event is brought out, the doer is aware of the Judgment of the Light and that the judgment is true, without favor or ill-will, and is the judgment of the doer itself. This, too, is impressed upon the breath-form. It is as though judgment were pronounced and recorded—and the doer feels naked, in the Light, and without its breath-form.

The Light withdraws. The doer reenters its breath-form and is in darkness and unconscious of the judgment through which it has passed, though it feels that it has been judged. All that the doer had or did in its past life and that was made invisible and inaudible by the Light in the Hall of Judgment, rushes in and makes the world in which the doer then is. The world changes at once and instead of being the physical world as it appeared to the doer on earth, becomes the world in which it really was, but which the doer did not then know. A period of suffering begins as the doer now enters the first stage of hell.

There are in hell no torturers, no fire, no brimstone, no foul smelling waters, nor any of the infernal agonies which theologians of various religions have fabricated for a multitude whom they have damned to suffer them. Nor is there a cloven-hoofed, fork-tailed devil. Yet there is suffering in hell for sinful thoughts and acts while on earth; there is also a devil, its own devil.

The breath-form, on which all thoughts, their exteriorizations, and their effects had left their marks, which were illuminated and adjudged by the Light at the time of judgment, now shows the pictures one by one. As they come the doer lives through the desires it then had. The persons and objects connected with the desires are there, but there is no physical body and no means of satisfying the desires. Desires can never be satisfied; they can be weakened for the time by the exhaustion of the physical means of gratification. The more desires are fed, the stronger they get and the more the means of gratification are weakened. That was so in the physical world, but now on the form plane of the physical or the form world, the doer has the desires again and no means of gratifying them. They rage.

The ordinary person with his desires for food, for sexual intercourse, for drink and for comfort, in their various forms, suffers by having these desires without any means of gratifying them. There is a hunger, a burning desire for satisfaction which eats into the doer without destroying it. Normal and moderate appetites do not produce this suffering in hell, but only the inordinate, intemperate, vicious desires which the doer felt to be wrong. Selfishness and covetousness in the past life, the desire to possess the things of others and to hold them for oneself, return to the doer in hell, but all physical things have been swept away together with the means of getting them. The doer longs and this longing pains like the pangs of hunger. Arrogance in life will come back to the doer after death and then the doer has the arrogant desires, but where there is no wealth, power or station, there is an emptiness which consumes the doer itself. These feelings of hunger, of burning, of being consumed, are similar to the physical states. The difference is that the fleshly body is not there, but the doer has its breath-form with its four senses, and it feels and yet it is not destroyed by the feeling.

The devil that accompanies the doer through hell is its ruling and chief desire, which was its evil genius in life and is its devil after death. The lesser desires are the little devils under the chief. None of the devils has form here; they cry, they pull on the doer; they goad, strain and burn, each according to its own appetite, longing or lust.

Of the sins against one's own body and against itself the doer lives over only the desires in this psychic state. The sins against the bodies and doers of others produce a different effect. The doer lives over not only the desires which were involved in those sinful thoughts and acts, it is accused by the people whom it wronged. Those who inflicted injuries or death by violence, by criminal negligence or by adulterated food; landlords or employers who caused the degradation of their tenants' or workers' bodies; the rulers, statesmen and party politicians who connived at such wrongs; cruel prison keepers, hard or indifferent judges, and those who sinned against the doers of others by encouragement to acts of indulgence: these hear again the accusations and the things they knew of in life; they see their victims, sacrificed to their greed, selfishness, corruption and indifference; they see them and they feel what the victims felt—pain, disease, shame, degradation and despair. This phase of hell is worse than the sufferings of those who wronged only themselves.

All the doers in hell suffer, but they do not learn anything there, they do not repent, they have no remorse. The opportunity for learning can come only on earth in the next life. The suffering is not for the sake of punishment but to purify the breath-form. Punishment also is reserved for the next life on earth.

After the doer has suffered from its desires it remains on the form plane of the physical world or of the form world. The doer so far has experienced only its feelings and desires—its psychic destiny. It now begins to exercise one of its phases of thinking, which is mental destiny. The doer feels itself; it is conscious of itself as the human. Thoughts it had in the past life come to it, of the stifling of conscience, of mental laziness, of clinging to ancient creeds when outgrown, of bigotry, of lying, of perjury, of denial of a life after death, of time-serving, of treason and of ingratitude, all thoughts by which it sinned against itself and thoughts by which it sinned against the doers of others, by which it kept other doers in darkness and delusion. The doer feels the presence of its conscience. Its thoughts which conscience in life told it were wrong, cry out against it. It feels anguish, remorse, a mental agony. In that state of hell the doer feels that it must make reparation for these sins. It only suffers; it does not learn anything. Life in a physical body on earth is the time for learning.

In both of these states, those of living over again the feelings and the desires and the thoughts the doer has had, it has its breath-form and its four senses. The anguish, remorse and suffering from its feelings and desires and from its thoughts, loosen the doer from its breath-form. During the loosening process the elemental beings which built up the scenes made by the feelings and desires and thoughts are perceived by the doer. These elementals are the various colors, forms, movements and actions in the scenes. Now as the doer is loosening from its breath-form and everything is breaking up, separating and vanishing, the doer perceives that the things which seemed to be real in life and in hell were made up of these elementals. The doer fears; things seem unreal; it passes through another after death stage.

The doer may try to hold on to its breath-form or to any of the objects in the dissolving scenes, but it cannot grasp or hold. The forms change into other forms even while it tries to hold them. Then the breath-form itself seems to dissolve into the other forms and disappears. At the time of parting and disappearance those feelings and desires which were associated with the four senses and are attached to outward things, assume a few or numerous animal forms, of beasts, birds, fishes or reptiles, of ever changing types. The doer feels at the same time that it is, and that it is not, these feelings and these desires. The doer struggles with itself. This continues until the doer distinguishes and refuses to identify itself as these animal forms. Then the forms of the feelings and desires disappear and the doer is free from them.

The desire forms coalesce. There is usually one dominating desire form, into which the multitude of lesser desires merge. There are other desire forms which remain separate. Now that the conscious doer has withdrawn, these desires no longer change the forms they have become. These forms, few or many, are now ready to leave the radiant state whenever there is a time and place for the physical animals of which they are types, to be conceived. At the birth of the animals they go into the bodies and are the animals.

The doer, now without the breath-form and the senses, is in its psychic atmosphere, on the form plane of the form or of the physical world. It is no longer conscious as the past human. It is conscious as the doer portion that was in the body. It goes through the feelings and desires and acts which engaged its thoughts during life. Only the feelings and desires come, without the persons, objects and events that caused them. The doer cannot see, hear, taste, smell or touch, but it feels the feelings unmixed and apart from the things which produced them. The feelings are affection, passion, anger, need, envy, hate or greed. The feelings and desires only are there, turbulent and strong. They move and fluctuate, they rise and fall, they turn and whirl and simmer. The doer is in this state with itself and only feels and desires.

Gradually another kind of feeling comes. This is the feeling of right and wrong. The doer is conscious of the righteousness or wrongfulness of these feelings and desires, and this starts the turmoil again. Now feelings of remorse, repentance and sorrow are added; feelings of duties not done or violated are felt.

Gradually a different feeling comes—the feeling of I-ness. First there was only the raging desire without objects or form, then came the feeling of remorse, now the third is the feeling that identifies the raging passions and weighty sorrows with the doer itself. The doer feels then that the passions and the sorrow are itself, and it suffers.

The fires of the raging desires and the sorrow for the duties violated, purify the doer and separate the feelings and desires, the sinful from the righteous. The sinful roll away when the righteous part refuses to identify itself as these desires; and they form the basis for the desire body of the doer, to haunt the earth or to lie in wait to be re-embodied with the doer. These feelings and desires are not attached to outward things, but seek an interior gratification and want to absorb, to hold or to control. They are the selfish attitude of the doer, which is gratified by the "outward" desires that went into animal forms. Throughout all the stages in hell, that which is now the desire body or cloak of vices, was the cause of its chief suffering. This was the devil, the ruling desire of the doer. Those feelings that conform to the standard of duty, being now purified and free from dross and slag, rise to the light plane of the form or the physical world. They are the doer that has passed through hell and is purified.

SECTION 23

Heaven is a reality. Re-existence of the succeeding doer portion.

On the light plane the doer meets and feels the presence of what is to it an angel. It becomes one with that angel and finds itself in heaven (Fig. V-D). When the doer parted from its breath-form and during the doer's struggle with its desires before it separated from them, the breath-form seemed to dissolve. The struggle of the doer was also a purification of the breath-form, and a burning away from it of all that suffering could dissolve or burn away, and then the breath-form rose to the light plane of the physical world. There it awaited and met the doer and was the purified angelic being, the doer's own glorified form, his breath-form, which the doer took on and with which it entered heaven.

In heaven the doer is a glorified being; it has its breath-form and senses and can see, hear, taste, smell and touch. It continues its earth life as if there had never been any interruption. But the life is idealized. No sins, no trouble, no sorrow, no poverty, no loss, no sickness, no death; no anger, no greed, no envy and no selfishness will be found in heaven. Heaven is a state of happiness and everything that mars unalloyed happiness is absent. There is no sex, no thought of sex; no shame and nothing to be ashamed of. The relations of sweethearts, husbands and wives are there, but idealized. Carnal thoughts, sensuality and dross were burned off in hell. Mothers have their children, whom they lost on earth. It seems as if there had never been any loss. Friends find their friends; there are no enemies. The doers in heaven carry on the occupations they had on earth, but only if their occupations were ideals to them. The good country priest or pastor is the shepherd of his flock and takes care of them as he did on earth; the kindly physician is happy because of the recovery of his patients. The chemist discovers new things which he sees are of benefit to the people. The statesman works in his ideal government. All occupations are free from the thought of gain through loss by others; the heavenly joy lies in the service which is rendered.

There is no sleep, no darkness and no weariness in heaven. There is no eating and drinking for its own sake. There may be eating and drinking if that was a part of the ideal occupation, as a mother's or a host's preparations to give enjoyment to others.

There are rivers, beautiful scenes, flowers and verdure, if the doer longed for them. There are lights, jewels, decorations and heavenly music for those whom this will make happy. The dress of the beings in heaven is as they conceived it as their ideal dress, while they were on earth. The doers in heaven have their religion in heaven if they had it on earth, purified from sordidness, commercialism, bigotry and fanaticism. God will be there in heaven in whatever form he was conceived on earth and the Christ and saints and angels, all will be in heaven as they were believed in on earth, but in an idealized, glorified, exalted state.

There is nothing tame, colorless or inane about heaven. The pulse of life and enjoyment runs higher than it does on earth, for there are no drawbacks or obstacles to lessen enjoyment. In life on earth things are so mixed that there is usually some interference with full enjoyment, but in heaven the interfering sentiments are screened off from the doer, therefore the feelings, affections and joys in heaven are keener and more alive than on earth. These are things the doer longed for, yet they could not be realized because of impediments on earth. Now, while it rests in heaven, the realization of every good thing it thought or worked for, comes without drawbacks.

Heavenly enjoyment is the result of what the doer thought and did in the earth life. Nothing is added to what the doer wished for or aspired to while on earth. The doer learns nothing new in heaven; the earth and the earth only is the place for learning, because there all the spheres and worlds intermingle on the physical plane.

Heaven is not a mere belief, a fancy, a beautiful mirage. It is nearer to reality than anything on earth. A doer interprets as realities that which it is thinking and experiencing at the time and under the conditions in which the doer is.

On earth there are flesh and blood relations between the doer in its body and parents, husband, wife or child; and relations of friend, neighbor or acquaintance; and relations to those whom one sees, hears about, reads about and thinks about. These relations make up the physical world while the doer is on earth. They are not merely physical, they are psychic, and some may be mental. After death the physical world and the physical body with its physical atmosphere have gone; in hell the grosser, sinful feelings have been burned out, but the relationships remain. When the grossness has been removed and the doer enters heaven, the relationships which have remained with the doer are realities to it, and are more real than they were on earth.

The Intelligence has no heaven as has the doer, yet there would be no heaven for the doer if the Light of the Intelligence did not fill heaven. Heaven is a part of the psychic atmosphere of the doer, at any rate for the vast majority of doers. This part was unmanifested during earth life. During life the Light of the Intelligence is not in the psychic atmosphere, but when the doer is in the heaven state the Light of the Intelligence is there. The doer in heaven is back in its original happy state for which it longed during its earth life.

Heaven is not a community heaven, or a theological heaven. It would be impossible as a community heaven, because no two heavens could be alike. The ideals of earth life are different to everyone, and although each one includes many others in his ideals, his ideals of them to him are different from their ideals concerning themselves. If they were to carry out their ideals, that would interfere with the carrying out of his, and then there would be no heaven for him; but there would be the discords of earth. In order for each to be in heaven, it is necessary that it should be in his own heaven and not in that of someone else, because then neither would have one. But each can be in the other's heaven according to the ideals of that other.

Heaven is not made up of successive scenes and events, of growing and aging, of changes, of beginnings and endings. Heaven is a composite of all these. It would not be heaven if there were a succession of changes in people or events. The changes are there, but they are there only in the composite, which is a whole. So a mother would not see or think of her son as the baby, the child, the bridegroom, the head of the family and the man of affairs, but she would see him as a composite of all these. The absence of change makes heaven completeness and eternity.

There is no time in heaven. Heaven is an eternity. There is no time and no eternity in the doer itself, but only in so far as it sees time and eternity in nature.

The doer is in its psychic atmosphere at all times, in life and after death, but it is conscious in one part during life and in another after death. During life it has a mixed hell and heaven; after death there is a sorting out and a separation of the doer from its garment of lower feelings and desires, and a passing in a purified state to its own heaven, all within its own psychic atmosphere. In rare cases it may also pass into its mental atmosphere and enjoy a mental heaven in the contemplation of mental problems.

The three atmospheres of the Triune Self (Fig. V-B) are within the sphere of its Intelligence, and the Intelligence by its Light brings about all these experiences. Whatever the doer's ideal as to time or eternity had been on earth, will be carried out in heaven. If one believes that heaven is eternal and without an end, it will be so to the doer. To those who do not pay much attention to the thought of heaven, as such, their ideals make their heaven.

There is an end to heaven for every doer when it has lived out in heaven all the ideals it had on earth. Then there comes a state of sweet rest without activities and without any appearance of ending. The doer separates from its breath-form as it did in deep sleep on earth and in the second stage of purification, and remains in its psychic atmosphere until it is again to return to earth. Gradually it passes from the form world to the light plane of the physical—the Light of its Intelligence is obscured by the physical world and that doer portion is in a state of forgetfulness.

When the breath-form with the four senses parted from the doer, the breath was disunited from the form and the senses were loosed. The four elemental beings which had served as the senses then returned to their respective elements and acted with the elemental races. The doer portion remains in the state of rest until each other doer portion has lived its life on earth, each in its turn. Then when the time of its appearance in a human body fits in with the lives of those whom it has to meet, the form of the breath-form is activated by the aia which causes the breath-form to enter the atmospheres of the future parents; the form enters the mother and then or later bonds the seed with the soil. Then elemental beings are summoned in their order and build up and fill out the astral, then the airy, the fluid and the solid parts of the fourfold physical body, in fetal development, according to the model of the astral, furnished by the form of the breath-form. The summons is answered by the different entities in nature, whether they are in the four elements, or in vegetable or animal bodies. The animal feelings and desires themselves begin to come in from nature with the beginning of placental development. They are the same feelings and desires with which the doer struggled and which were loosened by its suffering in hell and from which the doer separated when it separated from its breath-form. These feelings and desires, of which the new breath-form bears a symbolic record, are built into the astral body accordingly. With these feelings and desires the doer must deal again at the seasons when they manifest in later life.

The fetus gradually develops and is prepared for birth. It waits for the right swing of the breath—this may be for hours or for days or weeks—and is then born into the world. Up to the time of birth the fetus has no distinctive physical atmosphere. Only the form of the breath-form is in the fetus. The fetus is developed in the mother's physical atmosphere. The breath of the breath-form enters with the intake of the breath into its form as the breath-form, and the breath-form is then the living soul of the newborn infant body. With the intake the physiological change of breathing takes place. Then the infant begins to live in its own physical atmosphere. Later, the doer portion enters and lives in the body, and the three atmospheres of the Triune Self penetrate and surround the physical atmosphere of the child.

The desire body or cloak of vices which rolled away from the doer when it entered heaven, may have passed through many conditions, but it awaits the doer and oozes or is breathed into the physical body at a later period of life.

This is the course of the doer from the time of death to the beginning of re-existence of the succeeding doer portion on earth. Ancient initiations related to this course of the doer in the after-death states. Some initiations were into metempsychosis only, some were into the heaven period and others included transmigration and resurrection.

There is, and has been for ages, much confusion about such terms as reincarnation, transmigration, and metempsychosis. They have been used as synonyms, but while they have been related they mark twelve different stages in the history of the doer and of the entities composing the body, from the time of the death of the body until the doer returns to earth.

Metempsychosis comprises certain after-death states and nothing else, namely, the states of the doer after death while it goes through its changes, struggles and purification before its heaven period begins. Transmigration is to be understood in three aspects: the wandering of the feelings and the desires and of the units of matter through different worlds and the kingdoms of nature, after death; the coming together of some of them and their growing into a human body after the form of the breath-form begins to glow; and the passage of the fourfold physical body from the time of conception, through the mineral, vegetable and animal forms into the human form of the fetus. Re-existence, heretofore called reincarnation, is the return of the doer portion into a human body made up from elementals that composed the body in the past life on earth. It is the doer portion that re-exists. Resurrection—incorrectly used with regard to the doer—is its coming into and taking on again the breath-form with the four senses and a fourfold physical body, after which the doer re-exists. Resurrection applies: first, to the fleshly body in so far as the breath-form calls and draws together the compositor units which made up the body in the former life; and, second, to the raising of the breath-form when it will have been regenerated and restored to its original and perfect form in a perfect physical body.

The time between re-existences varies with the needs of the doer, with the parts it has to take in the succeeding life, with the readiness of the world to let it play those parts and with the coming of other doers it has to meet on earth. A doer portion may go through all the after-death states and be reborn on earth within a few hundred years, or not until a thousand or many thousand earthly years have elapsed. There is no fixed period, nor any average period at which a doer portion will return to earth. Within one year of earth time the doer may go through what by its feeling and measurement of time would be countless years or an eternity. Indeed, the period in heaven is always an eternity to the doer, because there is no beginning and no end; beginning and end are united in completeness.

Here has been given an outline of the passage of a portion of the average doer through the after-death states. This outline is simplified. Complications, variations and special cases have been omitted, so as not to disturb the plainness. It can be compared to a brief description of the life of man on earth; what would be true of one would be in a measure true of all.

CHAPTER VII

MENTAL DESTINY

SECTION 1

The mental atmosphere of the human.

All destiny begins with thinking. When the thought is developed to exteriorization, that is the physical result; from that comes a psychic result, from that a mental result and from that a noetic result, for the human. All this is done by his thinking around the thought. A thought as a whole is his mental destiny, and his other three kinds of destiny and their results come out of it by thinking. These four kinds of destiny are the destiny of the human, not of the Triune Self. The thinker and the knower have no destiny, because they do not create thoughts when they think.

The mental destiny of a human is his predisposition to think as he does. It is the state of the mental atmosphere of the human, (Fig. V-B). It is his mental character, his mental endowments, which are used by his feelings and desires.

The active part of the mental atmosphere is represented in the human by three of the minds of the thinker of the Triune Self which are put at the service of the doer. There is the body-mind, with which feeling-and-desire should think to care for and to control the physical body and nature. Then there is the feeling-mind, which feeling should use to find and distinguish itself from the body, and also to give forms to the matter of nature—by thinking. And there is the desire-mind, which desire should use to control its feelings and desires, to distinguish itself as desire from the body in which it is, and to have union with feeling. But feeling-and-desire, the doer in the human, usually think with the body-mind and in the service of nature. In the run of human beings the

223

doer works chiefly with its body-mind for its feelings and desires, as a laborer, a trader, a lawyer, a manager, an accountant, an inventor, a builder. The use of the three minds lowers or elevates feeling-and-desire. Feeling-and-desire are concerned with physical things; they are busy with material things; they live in them, are bound up with them and do not leave them. They are the servants of the body. The thinking which the three minds do is that which is and makes mental destiny.

Thinking is of two kinds: real thinking, which is the steady holding of the Conscious Light within on the subject of the thinking, and the ordinary human thinking, which is either passive or active to the subject of thought. Passive thinking is of objects of the senses, merely listless and casual, and without effort to hold the Light. Active thinking is the effort to hold the Light. Passive thinking begets active thinking. In consequence, thoughts are conceived and issued. They are beings and have in them something which, once they have been exteriorized, requires their successive projections until they are balanced.

Thinking, and the thoughts which follow it, depend on the condition of the mental atmosphere, which is the mental destiny of the person. The atmosphere has a moral aspect and is dominated by a ruling thought. It has mental attitudes and mental sets, a certain amount of knowledge which is based on experiences through the four senses, and warnings of conscience. In its most general aspect the atmosphere is either honest or dishonest and has accordingly a tendency to truthfulness or to lying. The atmosphere shows what the human is responsible for. The good and evil thinking that men have done remains with them in their mental atmospheres until removed by thinking. Certain mental attitudes towards responsibility will raise the thinking from servitude and interference to a mental excellence which in later lives appears as an endowment.

Responsibility is connected with duty, the present duty, the doing of which leads to the balancing of a thought. One of the objects of life is to think without creating thoughts, that is, without being attached to the object for which the thought is created, and can be attained only when desire is self-controlled and directed by thinking. Until then thoughts are created, and are destiny.

SECTION 2

An Intelligence. The Triune Self. The three orders of Intelligences.
The Light of the Intelligence.

It is important to understand the distinction between an Intelligence
and a Triune Self, (Fig. V-C). The Intelligence lends its Conscious Light
to its Triune Self. Without the Conscious Light, the Triune Self has no
means of thinking. Though the Triune Self is conscious of itself as the
doer, the thinker, and the knower, it cannot relate, coordinate, work or
use these parts without the Light. The Light of the Intelligence is merely
loaned to the Triune Self and never becomes a part of it. The Light is
that which relates and, so to speak, links the Intelligence which is in the
spheres, with the Triune Self which is in the worlds. The Light is
potential in the Triune Self; it will become actual when the Triune Self
becomes an Intelligence.

Ordinarily, when the senses receive impressions from nature, feeling-and-desire of the doer-in-the-body merely respond to the impressions without thinking. But when feeling-and-desire *as* the doer thinks,
the feelings and desires will be guided and raised and refined according
to the thinking done. Then thinking with the body-mind will be done
for the advancement of nature; thinking with the feeling-mind, for the
development of beauty in character and form; thinking with the desire-
mind for the discipline and exercise of power.

The term "mind" will be used as that with which thinking is done.
The doer as feeling-and-desire uses the body-mind and may use the
feeling-mind and the desire-mind. The thinker as rightness-and-reason
uses the mind of rightness and the mind of reason; and the knower as
I-ness-and-selfness uses the mind of I-ness and the mind of selfness. It is
to be remembered that by mental destiny is meant the mental destiny of
the portion of the doer that has entered into the human, not destiny of
the thinker or knower; by mental operations is meant that they are mental
performances of that portion of the doer which is in the body; by mental
set, by attitude of mind, and by actions of the mind is meant that they
are of the doer in so far as it is in the human being; by a thought is meant
the result of the action of mind and desire; by Self-knowledge is meant
knowledge of the Triune Self. Knowledge of the Intelligence is so far
beyond ordinary humanity that it is useless to speculate about it.

The loose use of the term intelligence is due to the fact that people do not know about a real Intelligence. Therefore, no words are ready to designate the Intelligence as beyond the Triune Self, or its spheres, or the various degrees of the Light of the Intelligence, when it is, metaphorically speaking, direct, diffused, reflected or focussed, or to name the parts and the functions of the thinker and the knower of the Triune Self.

All these spheres, degrees, parts and functions are distinct, and they are as different from each other as is the sun from its reflections in a mirror, and from the mirrored reflection imposed upon a picture on a wall, which reflection lights up the picture. They are as different each from the other as an oyster from its shell, the electric current from the wire, and as both from the voice heard over the telephone; as different as printed words are from the brain through which they were thought. In these examples there is some connection, but to speak of the doer as the Intelligence would be like identifying the picture made visible with the sun, and the voice heard over the telephone with the source of electricity.

When the Light which an Intelligence loans to its Triune Self has been sent into nature by the doers in human beings, it is the intelligence that is everywhere manifesting in the order and the laws of nature. An Intelligence is not in a body. It is in one or any of the three spheres, which surround the three atmospheres of the Triune Self.

Some information as to the nature of the Intelligence, its faculties and the manner of some of their functionings, and on the other hand the receptive and responsive reactions of the doer, is necessary in order to understand what thinking means, what it is and how it is done.

The doer is always within the spheres of the Intelligence, in life and after the death of the body. A human body is in its own physical atmosphere and stands within the three atmospheres of the Triune Self and in the three spheres of the Intelligence. In such a body and its atmospheres the three atmospheres of the Triune Self and the four spheres of nature intermingle, (Fig. V-B, C).

An Intelligence is a consciously immortal ultimate unit, that is, it has developed to be the highest kind of unit that it is possible for a unit to become, and it has power and jurisdiction in the spheres and worlds. Such a One has passed through all stages of nature and of a Triune Self and is an Intelligence under the Supreme Intelligence. There are many stages in the development of Intelligences, but all Intelligences are conscious of their identity, immortality and indestructibility; they are conscious of all other Intelligences, of all things in nature, and of the Triune Selves in their charge.

An Intelligence started as a primordial unit in the sphere of fire and progressed through all stages of nature until it became an aia and then a Triune Self. Then it progressed until it became an Intelligence, that is, became conscious as an Intelligence and knew itself to be an Intelligence. It will continue its progress as an Intelligence until it knows the entire manifested Universe with its four spheres in their entirety.

The Intelligences are connected with the earth of the doers by furnishing the Light to their Triune Selves and by directing the activities of that Light when it has gone into nature, and by serving under the Supreme Intelligence to carry out the purpose of the Universe. Every ultimate unit that is conscious in the degree called an Intelligence has certain qualities which distinguish it as an Intelligence. An Intelligence is one unit having seven faculties, which are inseparable, make up the sevenfoldness of it as an Intelligence as a whole and are conscious immortal witnesses to its unity as an Intelligence. Its seven faculties act in four spheres; the light and I-am faculties in the sphere of fire, the time and motive faculties in the sphere of air, the image and dark faculties in the sphere of water and the focus faculty in the sphere of earth, (Fig. V-C).

Each faculty has a special function and power and is represented in each other faculty, any of which it may reinforce or modify. The light faculty sheds Light into the worlds through its Triune Self. The time faculty regulates and measures the changes of units or bodies in their relations to each other. The image faculty gives form to matter. The focus faculty centers other faculties upon the subject to which it is directed. The dark faculty resists or gives strength to the other faculties. The motive faculty gives purpose and direction to thought. The I-am faculty is the real Self of the Intelligence.

These statements about the seven faculties of an Intelligence are mere suggestions by which the faculties may be thought of. The faculties are not things of the senses or even of the Triune Selves. Only one of them, the focus faculty, comes into contact with the body. Even this faculty reaches the body only through the doer. The six other faculties can act on the Triune Self but only through the focus faculty; and through the same faculty only does an Intelligence receive reactions from its Triune Self until feeling-and-desire of the doer are in union. The focus faculty transmits the Light of the Intelligence to the noetic atmosphere of the Triune Self.

The term "faculty" as here used is therefore not to be understood in the ordinary meaning of "faculty of mind." The faculties here referred to are far removed from the mental powers, properties or operations of the human, original or acquired, which are generally spoken of as "faculties of the mind." The phrase is here adopted because it is in common usage, and because it is suited to characterize the constitution of an Intelligence.

As the worlds in the earth sphere are to the Triune Selves, so the great spheres of earth, water, air and fire are to the Intelligences. An Intelligence is One in the fire sphere, as a Triune Self is a One in the light world of the earth sphere. The Triune Self is to the Intelligence somewhat as the doer is to its knower.

Somewhat as an aia when it became a Triune Self, was at once taken to the light plane of the light world and had there made actual by the direct Light of the Intelligence its potential knowledge as a Triune Self, so the Triune Self, when it is raised and becomes an Intelligence, is at once in the sphere of fire. There in the Light of the Supreme Intelligence of the Universe, what was potential in the Triune Self becomes actual knowledge as an Intelligence. It is its own immense Light and knows itself as the identity of that Light, in the presence of the Supreme Intelligence. It is conscious of certain truths: let them be called Substance, Conscious Sameness, or I-Am-Thou-And-Thou-Art-I-ness, Motion, Pure Intelligence, and Consciousness. These words are merely markers to complete a system, only the sensuous part of which in the sphere of earth relates to human interests, but the whole of which is required to show the difference between the Triune Self and the Intelligence.

In this state the Intelligence is as though it had always been an Intelligence. Time does not exist for it; it knows what its purpose is; all things and their possibilities are present and are as one. This is the state of knowledge as an Intelligence. It is in the Eternal of the spheres of the Great Universe. The Intelligence begins to think, and this thinking takes all but the Light and the I-am faculties out of the eternality of the fire sphere into the spheres of air and water. This is the downward path and leads to the boundary where the sphere of water and the sphere of earth meet.

Just as the Triune Self has three beings or material aspects potentially in the worlds, so the Intelligence is as three eternal beings in the spheres of water, air and fire. These are not three distinct Intelligences, but three distinct stages or orders of the same Intelligence. As the parts of the Triune Self are the doer, the thinker, and the knower, so the dark faculty, the motive faculty and the I-am faculty of the Intelligence are three related orders of one Intelligence, the Desirer, the Thinker and the Knower. These terms are used relatively to knowledge as an Intelligence, which is quite different from knowledge as a Triune Self. Knowledge as a Triune Self is knowledge of the four worlds; knowledge as an Intelligence is knowledge of the four spheres. The majority of human beings now on the outer crust of the earth are sense-bound and the Intelligences connected with them are of the order of the Desirers.

These Intelligences, even of the order of the Desirers, are superior Ones, far beyond the present comprehension of ordinary men. Men do not know of them, but they are the real givers of the Conscious Light to human beings on earth. The relative distance between a human and an Intelligence is greater than the distance between the human and the being he conceives as the omniscient, omnipresent and omnipotent God.

These three orders of Intelligences and the complete Triune Selves are those who order and direct the operations in universal nature. Their thinking contacts the form world and the physical world through their Triune Selves and is sufficient to compel elementals to carry out the law under their directions. Both the machinery of nature and the operators of it are elementals, units or masses of units of the elements. The Intelligences direct certain of the nature gods, the upper elementals, which control the lower elementals. The Intelligences, with the assistance of their Triune Selves, carry out the purpose of the physical world by thus controlling the elementals, called the forces of nature and the material universe.

This range of visible and invisible activity includes the powers ascribed to God in many religions. In these three orders the difference between the Intelligences is correspondingly as great as the difference in development of human beings. A Knower is in the sphere of fire, a Thinker works in the sphere of air and a Desirer works in the spheres of water and of earth.

Besides superintending collectively the plan of operating physical nature, each of these Intelligences has its related Triune Self in charge, which it had raised from the state of aia. The Intelligences have the double aspect of being the Light in the Triune Self, and of being the directors with their Triune Selves, of the forces of outer nature to produce physical results as exteriorizations of thoughts.

The Light of the Intelligence, in the Triune Self, is conscious as Light. In the noetic atmosphere the Light is clear, self-luminous and self-conscious; in the mental atmosphere it is also clear; but in that portion of the mental atmosphere which is in the psychic atmosphere of the human, it is diffused, obscured, dimmed. Desires for objects interact there with this diffused Light.

There are no limitations to the Light. It can go through everything in nature and can make known to the searcher everything for which he searches. The power of the Light is available to the human to the degree that he can hold the Light steady on the subject of his thinking.

SECTION 3

Real thinking. Active thinking; passive thinking. The three minds of the doer. About lack of terms. Rightness-and-reason. The seven minds of the Triune Self. A human thought is a being and has a system. Exteriorizations of a thought.

There are two kinds of thinking, real thinking and human thinking, and human thinking is either passive or active. Human thinking is concerned with physical things almost exclusively. In human thinking the subjects of thought are usually objects of the senses, and the thinking is of sexual, elemental, emotional and intellectual subjects, all directly connected with or indirectly originating from physical things. Human beings do not want to think about things as they are; they are attached to the results of their thinking. The thinking done by human beings differs as to amount, quality and aim and so divides them into four classes.

Real thinking is the steady holding of the Conscious Light of the Intelligence on the subject of the thinking. It is intentional, is self-moved and not moved by nature. It is done only with clear Light of the Intelligence, which reason by its mind focusses on the subject. The thinking must be steady, else it cannot form a channel by or through which the Light is conducted. The thinking of the knower is the conductor along which the Light comes from the noetic atmosphere. Real thinking stills the perturbations and pains in the body, stops breathing and makes known the subject to which it is directed. It shows the reality and the illusions connected with the subject of thinking. It is used to administer justice or to give knowledge. Such thinking does not result in a thought, unless the thinker wishes to create one. Then he conceives the thought and carries it from its conception to its completion.

Some few men have had thoughts which were the results of real thinking. The pre-existent ideas of Plato, the thought of The Way to eternal life in St. Paul's teaching, and the thought of Union in the pre-Brahminical portion of the Bhagavad-Gita are real thoughts. Those who conceived and gave birth to these thoughts did real thinking at the time those thoughts were created.

At times real thoughts might have been created, but instead thoughts have been born into the world undeveloped, malformed monstrosities. Among them are the modern thoughts of the Superman and Monopoly.

Real thoughts have an existence independent of those who created them. Real thoughts make no destiny for their creators, because the creators of real thoughts are not selfishly interested in the results which will flow from them; they show a true way; no one is bound by them; they lead the thinker from bondage to freedom.

Human thinking is quite different from real thinking, because it is not done with the clear but with diffused Light; because usually only the body-mind is active; because its mental operations do not work together, being perturbed by the influence of various and often opposite desires; and especially because a human is attached to the object of his thinking and the result of his thought.

Human thinking is either passive or active. Thinking of one of these two kinds goes on continuously, even during automatic work, such as house work or labor in office, field or factory. Passive thinking is the play of desires around or with the body-mind, in the diffused Light of the Intelligence. This is the kind of purposeless play that goes on almost uninterruptedly in the mental atmosphere of the human, (Fig. V-B).

There is in the mental atmosphere of the human a constant feeble current in which desires play in the Light of the Intelligence. The current passes with the breath through the physical body and back into the mental atmosphere. In this current are impressions of objects, brought in by the four senses and feelings and memories, anything at all that one is conscious of. When anything in this current attracts the attention of the body-mind, because of feelings and desires, a passive, listless, haphazard sort of thinking starts and goes on. When diffused Light of the Intelligence is turned towards (not focussed upon) any set of things in this current, the current becomes a stream of passive thinking, that is, the passive thinking becomes stronger.

Passive thinking is aided .by memories, the memories of sense impressions which are transmitted from the breath-form and engage the desires in the play. Everything coming from nature tends to aid in this way. Stray thoughts of one's own or of others are drawn into the current of passive thinking and strengthen it. All involuntary impressions serve passive thinking. Anything, however, that compels attention interferes with passive thinking, such as a sudden noise or contact or remembering something that must be done. Active thinking checks and even stops it, according to the degree of attention that is given to the subject engaging the attention.

The feeling-and-desire of the doer in the human are affected by passive thinking. When feeling is impressed it starts desire, which carries the impression into the mental atmosphere. There they engage in a play around, about or with the body-mind. The body-mind is affected by the impressions but does not take any active part in the play as long as the thinking remains passive. The reason why the doer in the human is thus affected is that its feeling-and-desire are under the domination of nature and not under the rule of rightness-and-reason. So feeling-and-desire are moved, stirred, thrilled.

Passive thinking goes on continuously through the entire life, except when active thinking takes its place, suppresses or stops it. It goes on during dreams in sleep. There it is kept up by memories and is one of the causes of dreams. It goes on also at intervals after death.

Passive thinking turns into active thinking when one of the subjects in the stream has sufficiently attracted the attention of feeling-and-desire, around which the play went on, and desire compels its mind to show how to be, to get or to act with the subject in order to satisfy the feeling or desire.

Active thinking is an effort to focus and hold steadily the Light of the Intelligence diffused in the mental atmosphere on the subject of the thinking. Passive thinking is not the only method by which active thinking is developed, but is the substratum of most active thinking. Active thinking is done by one or more of the three minds used by the doer.

The thinker is that part of the Triune Self which really thinks. It is in its mental atmosphere, (Fig. V-B). Only a part of it contacts the doer in the human through the heart and lungs and works also through the brain. There are nerves in the brain and spinal cord which belong to the thinker, but which are practically unused. The nerves in use there are those of the doer. When physical things are felt, feeling is located distinctly as being in the skin or affected organs. When psychic things are felt, the feeling is located in the heart, the pit of the stomach and sometimes in the sexual organs. But there is no feeling or recognition or even location by the human when he reacts mentally. Some of the nerves for the thinker of the Triune Self are not used at all. Some of them are used by the doer when it attempts to use the feeling-mind or the desire-mind. If the nerves for the thinker were called into use, there would be an airiness in the body and a lightness in the bones, and people could converse by thinking, without words. At present the human, except in physical sciences, depends on feeling what is correct and what is wrong, rather than on rightness and reason. If the body-mind now used by the feeling of the doer had free action the human would be able to feel the right or wrong in calculations, measurements and comparisons at once, as he now feels a pain or pleasure. The mind used by a human is as impotent and out of touch with the nerves as is a hand that is asleep or numbed with cold. Rightness, the passive side of the thinker, should be located in the heart, and reason, the active side, in the lungs, instead of merely contacting them. The knower stands behind the thinker and the doer. So the thinker is in communication with and acts according to the knowledge of the knower, which issues no orders but knows what the thinker and the doer do. But the thinker is not in the same manner in communication with the doer. It knows everything the doer in the human does or inclines or intends to do, but the doer knows practically nothing of the thinker. The thinker has no direct relation to nature, except through the body-mind which it lets the doer use for the purpose of controlling the body and nature, though actually the senses now use it to control the doer. The thinker is related to the Intelligence, for, in a manner of speaking, it walks in the Light of its Intelligence.

The thinker guides the cyclic movements of the thoughts in the mental atmosphere. It brings about an exteriorization of thoughts, in conformity with the thinking of the doer in the human. Therefore the destiny of a human is directly dispensed to it by a part of its very Self, by the thinker under the Light of the Intelligence.

The thinker lets the doer have the use of three minds, the body-mind, the feeling-mind, and the desire-mind, to the end that the doer in the human may use these minds to distinguish between itself and nature, and that the doer may of its own free will come into harmony with and be guided by rightness-and-reason, the thinker. The doers in the run of human beings ordinarily use only one of the three minds, and that one is the body-mind, in answering to the needs and wants of the body and to follow the attractions of nature.

How little these minds have been used by the doer in the human for the purposes of itself and of the Triune Self can be seen by the lack of words having relation to noetic, mental or psychic things. Another and a telling fact is that mental activities are described as if they were physical or extensions of physical or psychic things. In nearly all instances the use of words is suggested by feelings and desires, and mental actions are merely translations of acts and states to the life plane of the physical world. Some such words are conscious, understanding, perceiving, conceiving, speculating, analyzing, comparing, comprehension, attention, intuition, intelligence, enlightened, and hunger for knowledge. Transcendental activities are treated as extensions of physical and psychic things. If the physical base were taken away the words would have no meaning as related to mental action, because as descriptions of mental activities they are inapplicable. No mental action has anything to do or can be compared with conscious, understanding, conceiving, speculating, judging and similar words. The mental actions by themselves are described by these words in an infantile way. For what is here called rightness-and-reason, and for mental operations as the activities of the mind, there are no words.

Because of this lack of terms, there are no words to designate the seven "minds" of the thinker with their many functions, or the knower and its powers and attributes, or the nature and actions of the psychic, the mental and noetic atmospheres, or the nature of the Light of the Intelligence, or the degrees in which matter is conscious. It is because there are no words with a definite meaning, that phrases like psychic atmosphere, mental operations, noetic world, knowledge of the Triune Self, knowledge of the Intelligence, faculties of the Intelligence, nature-side and intelligent-side have to be used.

If the doer in the human could use one of the three minds at its disposal to work independently of physical things there would be a vocabulary of thousands of words, where now there are fewer than a dozen. There would be in the language a particular word for each of the seven minds, and for each of their many functions and results in the Triune Self, in the atmospheres, in the body, on the breath-form and on each of the senses. There would be a special word for each stage of each function of the doer in each of the after-death states; and a word for each of the particular effects produced by the Light of the Intelligence in each of the atmospheres of the Triune Self, and in nature through the thinking of the doer. Also there would be words to describe in some way each of the faculties of the Intelligence in relation to the sphere of earth; and a word to designate each stage in which matter is conscious from the time it is a fire unit in the light world of the earth sphere until it is conscious as a Triune Self in the noetic world and until it reaches the degree of an Intelligence.

In the physical world feeling has needed, and the doer has caused the body-mind to provide for it, words to distinguish the various visible states in the development of the body from birth to old age, the forms and appearance of bodies and distinctions as to trade, work and rank. So one gets a different impression when he hears of a Kaffir baby, an American colonel or a French cook. In contrast to the wealth of descriptive terms available to indicate any person, place, power or condition in the physical world, there is nothing to identify the life world or any being or condition in it. It is the same as to the light world. It is as if there were no word to show any difference among a fat general, a crying schoolgirl, a parrot, a pine tree and alcohol, and yet the origins of all the beings and things that have been and are in the visible world, are in the life world, and these origins are as different from each other as are their manifestations on earth. This condition of the language and the absence of words show the incapacity and weakness of the thinking which the human does.

Rightness-and-reason have to each other a relation similar to that which feeling has to desire. The mutual action of feeling-and-desire is unrestrained and is done without effort when nature calls for a response, but one is always dominated by the other. The interaction of rightness-and-reason is harmonious and continuous. Rightness does not always sanction the thinking of feeling-and-desire, and often does interfere with and restrict it.

A person does not distinguish where one set of functions in him ends and the other begins. The interplay between the two sides of the thinker is immediate and harmonious, whereas feeling-and-desire often oppose each other.

Rightness is the passive side of the thinker. As related to the doer in a human rightness is in the diffused Light of the mental atmosphere; it has a spark of the pure Light in it, is the custodian of that spark, and because of it knows when the thinking on a subject is correct, and when it departs from what the spark shows to be right. This spark affecting the diffused Light in the mental atmosphere causes something like a flame, like the flame of a candle, in the heart of every human. Ordinarily, the flame, the representative of rightness, is not calm. It flickers because desire rushes into the heart and agitates the flame so as to disturb thinking. This is especially so with anything that has a moral aspect. The flame is calm at the instant between inbreathing and outbreathing and between outbreathing and inbreathing and when breathing is suspended by real thinking. If the subject of thought has no moral aspect, as when it relates to measuring or reckoning and is not connected with emotions, the flame in the heart will be steady, till thinking begins. If the operations of measuring or of calculating are correct, the flame does not flicker, but if they are incorrect or other operations interfere with them, the flame in the heart flickers. Sometimes a person is conscious of a doubt or uncertainty, as soon as he adds a column of figures. Then the doubt is caused by the flickering. But persons are not conscious of the flame or that the flame flickers. The active thinking which has resulted from passive thinking is in practically every case concerned with objects of the senses. Thinking is the reaction which nature obtains from the doer.

Reason is the active side of the thinker. In reason are centered the seven minds. The term mind as used by everybody is the body-mind; it is the lowest of the seven minds and is that which is used by the doer-in-the-body to think with about the objects of nature through the four senses of the body. It is the only mind that is spoken of or known. Each of the other six minds is for the use of one of the six aspects of the Triune Self. The feeling-mind is that with which feeling should think, to know what feeling is in itself as apart from the body, and its relation to desire and nature, and its relation to the thinker and knower as the Triune Self. The desire-mind is that with which desire should think, to know what it is apart from nature and in its relation to feeling and to its Triune Self. These three minds may be used by the doer; the remaining four cannot be used by the doer. They are the mind of rightness, the mind of reason, the mind for I-ness and the mind for selfness. The three which may be used by the doer are weak, inefficient and lack exercise and discipline. The minds of feeling-and-desire are not usually exercised for feeling and for desire and are therefore not independently active. They serve as auxiliaries to the body-mind. The doer in the human does not control them. The subject of the thinking determines which of the three minds is being used.

Human active thinking is an interaction between rightness and the mind or minds with which the doer makes the effort to hold the Light of the Intelligence steadily on a subject. While the doer tries to hold the Light steady, rightness shows whether and how far it is correct or incorrect. The interaction goes on while the thinking lasts. The body-mind is devoid of feelings and desires. Its thinking may be of a mathematical nature, like calculations; or of a literary nature as to words, style, clarity; or of an intellectual nature, like searches, distinctions and speculations. The thinking of the minds of feeling and of desire may be of a moral kind, concerning moral right and wrong according to the voice of conscience. Or the thinking may be tinged by emotions, like pity, shame, anger or greed. The thinking of all three may be about travel, work, a business deal, a person, an invention or a religion. In all these instances rightness shows to the feeling or to the desire what is correct or incorrect. A moral question is dealt with in the same manner as a mathematical calculation. There is no argument any more than there is with a compass.

Processes of intending, comparing, analyzing, distinguishing, speculating, imagining and determining, are aspects of thinking, checked up by reasoning, while efforts are made to focus and hold the Light of the Intelligence. These processes are with the run of human beings done usually by one, and sometimes by two or three of the minds, which are judged by reasoning as to correctness.

The manner in which the body-mind acts is like getting matter in which is diffused Light, fashioning that matter into building material of points, lines, angles, curves and surfaces, building up a structure for the subject and tearing it down, trying at the same time to exclude obscuring matter from interfering with the building and keeping the structure in the Light. They do all this until they are near what they are after. The brightness or dimness of the Light available depends upon the length of time attention is given, and upon the degree of attention, that is, its steadiness.

Thinking gets the building material from matter of the mental atmosphere, and at times also from various planes of the physical, the form and the life worlds. The structure built may thus be made of intelligent-matter and of nature-matter and therefore can be exteriorized as an act, an object or an event.

Human thinking is faulty and inefficient for many reasons. It is hard to get the Light of the Intelligence, that is, to get it out from the matter among which it is diffused in the mental atmosphere. It is harder to hold the Light, for the mind lets go quickly and is not steady. It is still harder to hold the Light steadily on a subject, because the mind tries to hold the subject in the Light instead of holding the Light on the subject. Other reasons are that the mental activities do not cooperate, that they are severally directed to different subjects and so interfere with each other instead of agreeing and working in harmony; that there is not enough understanding concerning what is being done or how to do it properly; and that only some activities are developed.

Without a physical body the doer in a human cannot do any active thinking. Though after death there is a kind of thinking, it is only an automatic, mechanical reproduction, entirely caused by the thoughts which were created and entertained during life, and which revolve in the mental atmosphere. A human is a laboratory in which nature does the chemical part and thinking carries on the alchemical work.

The places where thinking goes on are in the mental atmosphere about the heart, the lungs and the brain. The subject of the thinking comes through one of the openings in the body, along nerves or other passages, into the kidneys, then into the adrenals and then into the heart, where rightness is. When the desire is strong enough the subject of the thinking is in the lungs. There, in the mental atmosphere, thinking is carried on. Then the subject is carried by the breathing, along the blood and the nerves, into the brain, first into the cerebellum, then into the cerebrum, and possibly into one or all of the lobes and then into the frontal sinuses. In the mental atmosphere in these parts of the brain thinking tries to focus diffused Light of the Intelligence into an area, large or small, as on a screen in a cinema show. The thinking builds the structures or makes the pictures on this area in the brain. The illuminated space is large or small according to the range of the thinker's subject of thought. The energy which he uses in directing the light is drawn from the adrenals into the heart and into the voluntary nervous system.

Thinking does not turn into a thought, but it prepares for the conception of a thought and goes on after the conception. A thought, as soon as conceived, has in it Light of the Intelligence, desire and the physical matter which was carried to the doer in the impression made from nature. A thought is conceived in the heart and on the life plane of the light world, as soon as the choice is made to be or to do or to have the subject of the thought The knower is not affected. The witnessing by the thinker stamps the thought, identifying it with the one who is responsible for it.

If the entertainment is not a suggestion from one of the senses but a thought already issued, there is not again a conception, but the entertainment in the heart will be nourished and reinforced by the thinking. The thoughts conceived or entertained in the heart are, after gestation or elaboration, issued or reissued from the brain.

Thinking follows as the return action of the doer in a human when the senses report an object. The reactions of the doer are efforts made by the mind to focus the diffused Light on the object of the senses, to interact with rightness and to communicate with feeling on these objects.

To illustrate a set of mental activities and the part they play in the actions and interactions of the four senses and of the three parts of the Triune Self, the mental processes incident to making a loan may be considered.

The owner of a piece of property approaches a money lender with the request for a mortgage. The lender looks at the property. His sense of sight informs him of the nature and state of the building on it, the class of tenants, the character of the neighborhood and the transportation facilities. His sense of smell reports the nearness to a pickle factory and a brewery. His sense of hearing reports the noise of children and of heavy traffic. The reports of these senses are made on his breath-form which communicates them to his feeling. His feeling starts desire. Desire carries the reports, mixed with feeling, to rightness. Rightness shows the fitness or unfitness of the loan and feeling-and-desire start thinking as the reports of the senses continue.

His body-mind gathers modified and diffused Light in the mental atmosphere and by that Light sorts, arranges, works over and examines the reports now tinged with feelings and desires and impressed by rightness and then begins to paint and build and tear down over and over, as the reports continue and after they have ceased. I-ness witnesses without interest and by so noticing gives identity to the transaction.

Rightness-and-reason merely observe with impartiality. There will be an agreement or a disagreement between his feelings and desires and the judgment as the result of his thinking. If the judgment is against the loan and his feelings and desires are also against it, the loan will be refused. If the judgment is against the loan and his feelings and desires favor it, the decision of the lender will depend on whether feeling-and-desire will be guided by the judgment or will overrule it.

Likes, prejudices and emotions may strengthen feeling-and-desire. In a mere business, like lending money, where no personal element as of relation or friendship enters, a man will decide according to the judgment of his thinking made upon the reports of the senses. These transmissions by the parts of the Triune Self are instantaneous.

Before the decision, the lender may try to remember other investments of a like nature which he has made or of which he has heard. Remembering, which is an automatic process and requires no thinking, is done by the human by calling upon the breath-form to produce the memories of sight, hearing, taste, smell and touch, that bear upon the subject. The lender in this way remembers facts which are relevant to the loan.

The ordinary path of the impressions from and the reactions to the reports of the senses is like the lines of an hourglass or of a figure eight. Nature by means of the senses conveys impressions to feeling, feeling conveys them to desire, desire carries them to rightness and thence to the body-mind. This communicates to feeling its reaction and that of rightness. Feeling, with the continued reports from the senses and with the reactions from the body-mind, gives its new impulse to desire and desire carries this to rightness and from there to the body-mind, which goes back to feeling. So the process is kept up until a decision is reached.

Human thoughts when issued are beings, not merely things. They are points having a potential system which gives them certain inherent qualities and power. They are centers of force and take on matter of the four worlds. They have no form that can be seen clairvoyantly.

The system is bestowed upon the thought by the Light of the Intelligence and by desire from the doer. The Light is representative of the seven faculties of the Intelligence, and desire stands for the three parts of the Triune Self. The system receives from the doer through the breath-form a potential form; then nature furnishes to the germ of physical matter that is in the thought, the material to make it actual on the physical plane. This potential form is the object to which the thought is directed, a house, a fight, a pair of shoes, an essay, a legislative bill, or a prayer to God for success or relief.

Thoughts have great potential power and the ability to last for ages, because thoughts are born in the light world under the Light of an Intelligence. Because of the power in thoughts the whole material world with all its acts, objects and events exists and is maintained and changed.

A thought is a fourfold being and has in it four potential systems.

Only that in the thought becomes actual which has to do with the purpose for which the thought was issued.

A human thought is not an independent being; it is dependent upon the one that issued it, or on a foster parent, that is, another human who entertained and nourished it. A thought has to be supplied with Light and with power to keep it going, and it has the right to come for such Light, power and sustenance to the parent or to the one who becomes responsible for it. A thought can be revoked, dissipated or changed before it becomes exteriorized, but once it has been exteriorized it continues until it is balanced.

Every thought has in it an aim, a design or plan to carry out the aim, the exteriorization or exteriorizations of the aim, and a balancing factor which will compel exteriorizations until through one of them there is an agreement by the Triune Self as a whole with the results following the exteriorization, (Fig. IV-A).

The aim is given by desire. During the course of the thought the aim guides it towards the purpose for which the thought was created. The design is the way in which the thought will become physical. The exteriorization is the physical appearance of the thought as or through an act, an object or an event.

Upon its birth through the brain, the thought is on the light plane of the light world and clothed in light matter. Thence it passes to the light plane of the life world, clothes itself with life matter and it sounds in that world. Thought is there a center of force; it is inaudible speech and sound. It is a word, and tells what it is. It proclaims its honesty or its deceitfulness.

The design becomes actual when the thought reaches the light plane of the form world and clothes itself with form matter. On the light plane of the physical world the thought comes into contact with light matter of the physical world. There the first step in exteriorization is taken, but exteriorization does not become actual until after three more steps. On the life plane of the physical world the sounding thought tells more distinctly what it is, its aim becomes more definite and it then descends to the form plane of the physical world, where it takes on full form and remains until there is an opening made onto the physical plane by the conjunction of time and condition at some place. Then the thought is clothed in the brain with radiant matter, in the heart and lungs with airy matter, in the kidneys and adrenals with fluid matter and in the digestive system with solid matter, and results as an act, an object or event. All can take place in a flash and is effected by the breath. So the design is exteriorized, though not necessarily the whole thought.

The balancing factor was heretofore potential. With the exteriorization of the design it becomes actual in the light world. This balancing factor is a seal, which conscience made upon the thought at the conception. Figuratively speaking, conscience is the stamp; its seal on the thought is its counterpart. By the exteriorization of the thought the doer is affected pleasantly or unpleasantly, and it also feels satisfied or dissatisfied with it as being morally right or wrong, and the thought will be balanced or will produce other exteriorizations.

The tendency of the Universe is to bring the seal on the thought back to the stamp which is conscience, but opposing feelings and desires and thinking stand between conscience and the seal on the thought and keep them apart. Rightness, being the Light in the heart, is no obstacle. The obstacles are worn away by experience and learning. Not until the obstacles are worn away, can the seal or counterpart be brought together with the stamp. When in their places are feelings and desires in accord with rightness and reason, the seal matches the stamp by the agreement of all with each other. Then the thought is balanced and conscience is satisfied.

The path of a thought after it issues on the light plane of the light world is towards the physical plane of the physical world, because the object of the thought is there and because the physical germ in the thought pulls it to the object. After a thought issues it becomes a center of force, without form, and in a formless world. There is in such a center a pressure which moves it onward in a cyclic path. As the thought comes into grosser matter, the abstract cycling becomes more actual. The cycles can run in any of the lines which can be conceived of as curves recurring with some regularity.

Usually the act, object or event into which the thought is exteriorized produces a feeling of joy or sorrow in the one who issued the thought. Sometimes a mental result follows. That is the last of the results of the thought, to the perceptions of the human. It may or may not be that he feels the finger of conscience pointing.

The first exteriorization was through the design, the second and further exteriorizations are compelled by the balancing factor which causes the cycles to continue. The second exteriorization produces a feeling and desire which sometimes has a mental result. Until the interior results match the seal of the balancing factor, the thought is kept going on in cycles. If the one who issued it dies, the thought goes with the doer and influences the building of the new body. In that new life and in subsequent lives of the doer, the thought continues to cycle and to bring about another exteriorization or exteriorizations, until the thought is balanced.

SECTION 4

Human thinking goes along beaten paths.

There are limitations to human thinking. Some limitations are insuperable, others are restrictions which may be overcome by desire, exercise and discipline in thinking.

The first of these limitations is that thinking is carried on under certain types of thought which have their origin in twelve universal points, types or numbers. Human thinking is done under a number, the number eight, under the type of two and under subtypes of two. People think of me and not me, of the visible and the invisible, of the in and the out and of spirit and matter. They do not think in any other way. Further, all this thinking is done under the male type and the female type. A man does not think as a woman does and a woman does not think as a man thinks. If the doer could think without the body it would not think under the male type or the female type, but because the doer is in a physical body and thinks through its organs, it must think according to the male or the female type of the body.

The type under which the thinking is done makes the visible world appear as twos, pairs, and opposites. The plants are male and female because of human thoughts; male animals are made by a man's desire and female animals by a woman's feeling; the sexless and hermaphrodite sometimes come from unusual humans, but they usually come over from prior ages and are parts of thoughts which still exist; they result from thoughts and acts which have not been balanced.

If people did not think under the subtype of me and not me there would be no ownership, no belief in creation and in a Creator. If they did not divide the world into the visible and the invisible there would be no darkness, that is, they could see as well in the dark as in the light. If they could think of more than in and out they could see throughout things. If they did not think of spirit and matter or force and matter as different they would actually see them as the two aspects of the one.

Another limitation of human thinking is that it is held down to sexual, elemental, emotional and intellectual subjects. If ever a human attempts to think on an abstract subject like time, space, the light, his Self, he is held down or drawn back by subjects of these kinds and he falls into thinking on them. The amount of experience, learning and knowledge available to him is thereby limited.

Another limitation is that every man is limited by the particular class into which his past thinking and consequent development has put him. There are four such classes; the first cannot think without considering their bodies first and last; the second cannot think without the idea of gaining, getting, selling, buying. The third cannot think without planning, comparing, and without respect for their reputation or name; the fourth class are few; they think to acquire Self-knowledge. Though a man clearly belongs to one of the first two classes, in which are the run of human beings, the amount, quality and aim of his thinking may transcend the limitations of his class.

Thinking is limited by dishonesty in thinking, that is, by thinking against what one believes to be right. Dishonest thinking shuts out Light, by refusing to see the thing one knows he should see and by looking for the thing he knows he should not see. Rightness shows what not to think, and the body-mind he uses in trying to build up the thing he should not do, is warned by rightness. Thoughts which one has already created, memories of the past, and the four senses bringing in sights and sounds, are constantly interfering and creating cross-currents of thinking.

The attachment of human beings to the objects of their thinking and to the results of their actions restricts the action of the thinking which is necessary to build to free the Light and to hold it steady. The sensuous activities of the doer and the impurities of the body befoul the psychic and obscure the mental atmosphere. They cause the Light to be diffused or obscured, as a cloud of smoke thickens the air and obstructs the sunlight. They prevent the clear Light of the Intelligence from reaching into the mental atmosphere of the human.

When there is a rift and the Light does reach in, the human is aroused, astonished, inspired and instantaneously enlightened. A human is not able to remain open to the clear Light. The very feeling which this Light awakens and the thinking of the body-mind close the rift, and the doer continues its thinking in its diffused Light.

Human beings prefer to think on accustomed paths, that is, they think only on familiar lines in religion, in science or in philosophy.

Thereby they think into the different planes of the physical world which are connected with the corresponding worlds. The lines of thinking are suggested by the senses. Education, habit and the senses limit their thinking to familiar paths. It is almost impossible for the average man to think away from these paths; the effort would be too great to continue. He does not think away from his four senses and they compel his thinking into certain parts of nature. That is one reason why man has made such progress in natural sciences along certain lines. Even there he is prevented from making greater progress by the limitations of his thinking.

The doer-in-the-body does not know of its limitations or of that which is beyond them. It has wrapped itself up in and attached itself to the things of the four senses. As a human it has separated itself from direct communication with its real thinker and knower. It does not distinguish itself from its four senses. It uses the Light it has towards the considera- tion of the physical plane of the physical world as the reality of life.

Therefore the human has no conception of his limitations. He can conceive of matter, of dimensions of matter, and of time, which is matter, because he feels and is experiencing change, which is time. He does not conceive of space, because he has no experience with space; he is in matter. He sees only one dimension of matter, surface matter, on-ness or length, breadth and thickness as the measure of space; but that is a misunderstanding, space having no dimensions. The fundamental con- ceptions of the nature of the earth, of the heavens, of the stars, of the sun and its planets, of the nature of the doer itself, of God, and of the Intelligence, are limited, sensuous and usually erroneous.

Human beings will not be ready to grow out of their limitations until they understand the difference between the feeling-and-desire of the doer-in-the-body and its Triune Self, and between the doer and nature as shown by the four senses and until they use the Light of the Intelligence to search for realities through, but not in, the physical world. Then it will be apparent what were the limits of thinking and why they existed.

SECTION 5

Character of the mental atmosphere of the human. Moral aspect of thinking. The ruling thought. Mental attitude and mental set. Sense-knowledge and self-knowledge. Conscience. Honesty of the mental atmosphere. Results of honest thinking. Dishonest thinking. Thinking a lie.

The doer's mental destiny is of the character of the mental atmosphere, comprising intellectual endowments and their relation to the physical body.

All the thoughts one has created which have not been balanced are in his mental atmosphere and circulate there. If this atmosphere be thought of in terms of distance and dimension, most of the thoughts may be said to cycle in zones as far away as those of the stars. The present life is not affected by such distant thoughts. Those which affect the present life circulate in nearer zones and in that part of the mental which is in the active psychic atmosphere of the human. The present character of the mental atmosphere depends more upon moral than upon intellectual endowments.

Human thinking can go on only within the human's mental atmosphere, and that atmosphere will not function except in accordance with the character of his psychic atmosphere. The character of these two atmospheres is definitely established at any given time and so is determined the nature of the thinking that can then go on in the human. In different human beings it opposes, forbids, favors or permits certain kinds of thinking. The character of the mental atmosphere has been made by thinking. The kind of thinking it opposes or favors is conditioned by the result of prior thinking. Things cannot be desired and cannot enter the psychic atmosphere unless the character of that atmosphere will permit. Even if the thing becomes an object of desire in the psychic atmosphere the desire cannot enter the mental atmosphere unless the character of that will permit it.

Thinking generates thoughts and issues them, and elaborates them before and after they have become thoughts and are issued. Thinking works out and changes the design in them and thinking makes the form for the design and exteriorizes the form through an act, an object or an event. Men are not conscious of what their thinking produces. After a thought has been exteriorized and psychic results of pain or pleasure, joy or sorrow follow, thinking upon them changes the mental atmosphere.

After the conception or entertainment of a thought and even after it is issued and so long as it has not reached the form plane, the thought may be revoked or dissipated by thinking. This will be done because conscience is heeded, because of self-interest or because of fear. It is dissipated when thinking directs the Light of the Intelligence into the thought, dissolves it and separates the Light and the desire from the object to which it is attached, which together made up the thought. Desire and the diffused Light then return to the psychic atmosphere and to the mental atmosphere from which they came.

In each case the atmospheres are affected by the thinking. If the dissolution was because the doer recognized and respected conscience, the atmospheres are improved and a tendency to reject similar thoughts is strengthened. Where the dissolution is brought about because of fear or expectation of an advantage, the atmospheres are vitiated and ready to entertain a similar thought in the future.

The moral aspect of the thinking is much more important than the intellectual gifts. Morals here mean the right relation of the doer, feeling-and-desire, to the thinker, rightness-and-reason. Mental destiny, therefore, depends primarily on feeling-and-desire; their thinking is done to satisfy them. Morals are so much more important in making the mental atmosphere than are the intellectual endowments, because the intellectual endowments are made to serve them and depend upon them. Mental endowments are of value in making a mental atmosphere, but the moral background of the mental atmosphere is more important, as mental attitude. This is so because although most of the thinking done during the day relates to work or trade or a profession and does not seem to have much to do with morals, yet what is done in trade or a profession is based on the moral condition of the mental atmosphere made by feeling-and-desire.

The morality of the mental atmosphere is a predisposition to think or to refuse to think along certain lines. Thinking limits or expands the moral tendencies, and embellishes or enlarges them and makes new channels for fuller expression, as urged by desire.

Present in the mental atmosphere of every human is a ruling thought, a thought which dominates that part of the mental atmosphere which has to do with the present life. This thought came into existence at the end of the previous life. The cycles of all thoughts of a life run together at the time of death and from these thoughts the ruling thought of the next life is formed. It is this thought which is the destiny already decided as inclinations, and it manifests at various periods throughout the life. It colors much of the thinking in the present life and gives tone to the atmosphere. It causes eddies, whirls and currents in or modifies and calms the mental atmosphere of a human. It helps to determine the mental attitude or general outlook on life and so helps to determine the manner in which one views other people and the world.

Mental destiny for the present life is not a remote aspect of the mental atmosphere, it is not the outcome of thoughts that are in a remote zone. Mental destiny relates to that part of the atmosphere in which the thinker contacts the heart and lungs, and that part is usually that in which the ruling thought moves. It influences his thinking, it brings up subjects of thought, it leads him to a junction of time, condition and place where a part of a thought can be exteriorized as an act, an object or an event.

A man's mental attitudes and mental sets are the ways in which the doer thinks on any subject and the way thinking deals with it. One's mental attitude is his outlook on life. A mental attitude is the background for a mental set. His mental set is what a man has set himself to do. The mental set of a money maker is to turn specific things into dollars; in a similar way a painter or an inventor obeys his mental set in pursuing his work. A mental attitude is often determined by love, bigotry and similar sentiments.

One's mental attitude and mental set toward any subject are a part of his mental destiny. They are brought about by his past thinking and by his past thoughts relating to his experiences and understanding. They nurse his moods and predispositions which are similar to the attitudes. They encourage thinking on subjects similar to themselves. They harbor and nourish thoughts of a nature similar to their own. They react on the mental atmosphere and largely make his disposition sour or sweet, grasping or generous, morbid or cheerful. They are a challenge to the people he meets.

By one's mental attitude he affects his mental destiny directly; he precipitates or postpones events. His attitude summons thoughts of like nature and hastens their development towards exteriorization. His own thoughts as well as the thoughts of others with whom he comes in contact are so affected. Thus he may hasten the exteriorization of a thought and bring about an injury or a profit to himself at a time when it would not otherwise have occurred. In this way one's mental attitude precipitates his own destiny, some of it long overdue, some not yet due. The precipitations are of two kinds, those which one recognizes as duties and those which befall one as events, expected or unexpected, pleasant or unpleasant.

A person has a certain leeway to bring out or hold off his own destiny. He does either by his mental attitude. An attitude of willingness to perform one's duty will allow destiny to come in its natural order, without postponement or hastening. An attitude of unwillingness to do or suffer may delay destiny, though at length the disturbance caused thereby will result in such pressure by elemental entities that events will break through the resistance and rush in. An attitude of fear may precipitate destiny; it may anticipate and project what would otherwise not have happened then.

One's mental attitude is not only an important part of his present mental destiny, but it is potent in making future mental destiny because it prepares for the conception or entertainment of thoughts. It is the condition in which they are conceived or gestated.

In the mental atmosphere is sense-knowledge, that is, the knowledge acquired by the body-mind from the mass of records brought in by the four senses. It is the systematized knowledge that constitutes the sciences, from physics and chemistry to theology and law. It is the materialistic knowledge of the one who possesses it and is tied up with the records of what is on the breath-form. What is impressed on the breath-form is of the present life only and is effaced after death when that form is broken up.

Sense memories on the breath-form are potent factors in mental destiny. They cause passive thinking which fills out so large a part of the life; they suggest many of the subjects of thinking which become thoughts and they are at once the foundation and the limits of the knowledge of the human. All the knowledge of all the sciences is sense-knowledge. From facts observed men arrive at conclusions, the reach of which is limited by the range of the senses and by the records on the breath-form. All this knowledge is in the mental atmosphere. Science and speculations about religion, about God and about the universe, are due to one's mental condition which is his destiny.

This sense-knowledge the doer uses, is affected by it, is subject to it and is held down by it, but it is not and never can be a part of the doer. All that is saved for the doer's knowledge are those results in the doer which are independent of the four senses. Therefore nearly all the results of an earth life are done away with. Only a small portion, namely, the abilities of the body-mind, is carried over in the mental atmosphere.

One who is merely well "educated" or merely proficient in a science or a trade may lose this advantage. The mental qualification for proficiency in intellectual achievements may be quite different in different lives, as different as the positions which the human beings of the doer hold in successive lives as to prominence or obscurity, comfort or trouble, wealth or poverty.

Nevertheless such sense-knowledge is an important factor in mental destiny. Efforts to think upon such knowledge may train the body-mind by exercising and disciplining it or by experimenting with and observing matter, and may be the cause of conceiving and entertaining many thoughts. The things which are retained as mental destiny are the kind of thinking at the end of the life, the effect the thinking on these subjects has produced in the mental atmosphere, and attitudes of mind which have been there created. This may be good or bad, depending on the moral tendencies developed which utilize the mental endowments.

Knowledge of the Triune Self is not available to the body-mind. The human cannot use the knowledge of the Triune Self, which is in reserve. Yet there are times when that knowledge becomes available, as when an action or an inaction has a moral aspect. Knowledge of the Triune Self then comes spontaneously through rightness and is known as conscience.

Conscience is not a part of the mental atmosphere, but when it does speak it speaks in the heart. Conscience represents the sum of knowledge as to what should not be done, acquired by the doer on any moral subject. It is a direct accusation. It is an injunction; it always forbids, never commands. It does not instruct; it does not argue. It speaks of questions of right or wrong action from a moral point of view only. Light of the Intelligence shows the way to the human and if he is about to go wrong by that Light, conscience forbids. Conscience stops either when it is dulled and overcome by desires or when the thought about which it warns is balanced or is dissipated.

The "No" of conscience is the sum of the doer's knowledge as to what he should not do and is sufficient to guide one aright in any situation. There is a constant communication between the knower and rightness. The voice of conscience is not an audible voice; it is a voice to the doer, feeling-and-desire. It has a meaning of which the human is conscious.

Conscience makes the human responsible irrespective of the laws of the land. Many of the things which the laws allow are forbidden by conscience. Disobedience to the injunction makes the doer liable. Conscience, though it does not reside in the mental atmosphere but only appears there at the conception of a thought or when the individual is about to arrive at a conclusion, plays a part in the making of mental destiny. When conscience approves the thinking, it neither speaks nor is there any apprehension in the thinking or the feeling that accompanies it. By its presence and by not interfering with the thinking, conscience aids in producing mental advantages, like endowments, abilities and achievements. When conscience speaks, it forbids and warns against thinking in connection with the thing which it forbade, and this may cause confusion and disturbance, which are mental disadvantages.

Conscience puts its mark on a thought which it disapproves. This mark is the balancing factor and remains on and with the thought as long as the thought lasts. That thought is destiny; it contains the four kinds. The physical impression will become physical destiny. The reaction on the doer is psychic destiny. The results produced on its minds by the doer is mental destiny. The freeing of the Light by desire is noetic destiny.

In the mental atmosphere of human beings circulate not only their own thoughts, but also thoughts of others. Thoughts are as gregarious as are the human beings, their parents; they herd together. Solitary thoughts are the exception. Visiting thoughts are attracted to an atmosphere because in that atmosphere are thoughts that have a similar aim as the visiting thoughts. The visiting thoughts can come in because the thoughts inside having a similar aim, usually make an opening for them.

Thoughts are hindered from getting into an atmosphere when the attitudes of mind in it are unfriendly and opposed to that kind of thought, or when the person closes his atmosphere unconsciously by thinking secrecy around his own thought. The thought of one person goes into the atmosphere of another, instead of the other's thought going into the atmosphere of the first, because the ingoing thought is the more active or seeks the other for reinforcement.

The visiting thought may take something from the other thought or it may impart something to it or there may be an exchange. The atmosphere from which comes the visiting as well as that of the visited thought is modified by the effect produced by the thoughts on each other.

The thought of a human when it visits the atmospheres of others comes back vitiated or improved, but the deterioration or improvement depends on the aim of the visiting thought. If the thought has an immoral aim it will seek like thoughts and will be further demoralized, and if it aims at something noble, the nobility will be furthered and accentuated. A human stands behind his thoughts, as nature does behind the units as elementals, and furnishes them with energy and Light. Though a man is not conscious of his thoughts, what they are and what they do, he is conscious of his thinking and that is what nourishes the thoughts of others which come to him. His thinking aims at the same aims as do these visiting thoughts. That is what makes him responsible for the deteriorization or improvement with which they go back.

These mental results are later seen as physical results in the actions in which various people engage together and in the events which befall them together as group destiny. Those who find themselves associated in physical things are persons whose thoughts have visited or crossed each other. So people meet to bargain and trade, to go on a fishing excursion, to form a club, to gamble or to commit a burglary. So artists, writers, physicians, party politicians, and religious workers come together in little groups and larger associations. So men come together in doing business, adventuring, warring, persecuting. Like as birds do, thoughts of a kind flock together.

Human beings are partly responsible for and share in the exteriorizations of other's thoughts. Their thoughts are mixed with the thoughts and interests of others. Attachments, dislikes and interests entangle every one. In this way doers share parts of each other's destiny. They are fellows in good and bad times, fellows in marriage, in families, in social, religious and political communities. The fellowship is evident when war, disease and famine devastate a country or when success in art and science elevate it.

In the mental atmosphere are the forms of outward nature, of animals, of trees, of plants and of elemental beings; not the things that inhabit the forms, but the forms only are there. These forms are expressions of types of thinking; the types are provided by Triune Selves who determine them according to the nature of the human beings who think on lines requiring such types for expression. These forms go into nature at any time when there is a demand for them to be filled out by desires and feelings.

The character of a mental atmosphere in its most general aspect is either honest or dishonest. When it is honest the thinking is honest; it then respects the morals of an affair as shown by rightness. Thinking recognizes facts as they exist and deals with them truthfully. It does not deny what exists and does not state what does not exist. It respects a truth. Truth itself, which is the pure Light of the Intelligence, is not seen but thinking nevertheless respects a truth in so far as it is revealed by the senses as to extraneous things, by feeling as to inner things, and by rightness as to the moral aspect of an affair.

Honesty in thinking is thinking about things as they are and dealing with them as one sees they should be dealt with. The source and test of honesty is what rightness shows to be morally fit or unfit in the mental conduct in question. The pure Light which rightness gets in the spark from selfness, and the diffused Light in the mental atmosphere, are enough to enlighten any man as to what is the truth for him and as to his responsibility for thinking honestly.

Honest thinking is normal in an honest mental atmosphere. The atmosphere aids this kind of thinking and the thinking strengthens the honest character of the atmosphere. Then when one finds himself in an unexpected situation with new problems, he is prepared to face them with honesty. Honest thinking and the consequent honest character of an atmosphere depend upon a desire, a desire for honesty. There can be no honest desire, because honesty is a mental, not a psychic virtue. The desire can be for honesty only. Without a desire for honesty there can be no honest thinking.

Desire does not control itself, it is controlled either by nature through the four senses or by rightness or by reason. At present it is controlled by nature which through desire gets its hold on the thinking of human beings. Desire is usually for comfort, possessions, luxury, laziness, not for the opposite conditions. As long as desire is inclined this way it will not be for rectitude. As nature acts it causes feelings and these stimulate desires; they start thinking regardless of honesty, often against the showings made by rightness. And some desires control other desires. Thus the thinking of people who are under the domination of nature is often dishonest.

If desire is not dominated by nature, but seeks to be controlled by rightness and by reason, seeks what these show to be right, it does not rush over rightness and reason to impel them to serve desire, and the thinking will act honestly. When desire wants rightness to correct it and reason to guide it, a great change occurs in the working of the doer in the human. Ordinarily nature affects feeling, that starts desire, that passes on the impression to rightness and, overriding it, impels reason which works to conform to feeling, and that satisfies desire. But when the change takes place and desire wants to be right, then feeling will not receive any impressions from nature which are not approved by rightness. Only feelings that are approved by rightness will start desire and desire will act directly on reason, which interacts with rightness, and that affects feeling. So the circuit is changed. Ordinarily it is from nature to feeling, to desire, to rightness, to reason, to feeling. But now the circuit is from feeling to desire, to reason, to rightness, to feeling, (Fig. IV-B). Nothing that is dishonest will be even felt.

From honesty in thinking come truthfulness, simplicity, sincerity, justice, rectitude. There comes a condition of the mental atmosphere in which virtues flourish and virtuous thoughts are conceived or entertained. These thoughts are then projected in speech and acts which show simplicity, sincerity and righteousness. When a man thinks such thoughts and intends such acts, he will not only so conduct himself, but there will come with such virtuous conduct, the qualities of fearlessness, calmness and strength. He will not even contemplate any act concerning which he could not speak truthfully and act with sincerity.

In this way once he has, by reason of the reversed circuit from rightness to feeling, the mental set towards thinking honestly, he will reinforce his virtues and lead a righteous life. His mental atmosphere will be honest. Troubles may swarm around and difficulties confront him, but whatever may come to pass, he will not be overwhelmed.

Dishonesty is not a negative quality; it is as positive and active as honesty. Dishonesty in thinking is thinking about things as they are not, and dealing with them in thought contrary to the way in which one sees, that is, in which rightness approves they should be dealt with. The test of what things are not is what rightness shows concerning them. Dishonest thinking is thinking against the way the thing is seen to be; it is thinking what is known to be false.

Dishonesty in thinking results from the demands of desire to satisfy feeling. Desire is neither honest nor dishonest. It wants what it wants. If it does not want expressly honest thinking, the thinking will be dishonest. If it does not want to be controlled by rightness, it will be controlled by nature and will override rightness and make thinking serve feeling.

Desire may be for dishonesty in thinking, but this is an unnatural thing. It then pits itself against all humanity to satisfy itself, not feeling, and leads to extreme wickedness. It sacrifices feeling and tries to kill it in order to be increased as desire and power. Such cases are sometimes found

MENTAL DESTINY 255

in the intense selfishness and corruption of the leaders of business, of party politics, of labor unions and of religious institutions. Such corruption is shown by the hard-hearted, from food engrossers down to little extortionists and blackmailers. In them desire tries to blot out rightness and substitute its own wants, so that it may not be interfered with. By thinking, in the accomplishment of its object, it realizes itself as a power. Many human beings working to this end are attracted to each other and combine in their efforts.

Dishonest thinking is at home in a dishonest atmosphere. By this kind of thinking the atmosphere is further prepared for the entertainment or conception of thoughts which are later exteriorized as lies, fraud, corruption and treachery, and their retribution.

A certain kind of dishonest thinking finds expression as lying. It is the kind of thinking that is directly intended to deceive either oneself or another. In order to deceive another successfully, the liar must in a measure deceive himself into seeing the falsehood he tells as true. Lying is a special kind of dishonest thinking. Generally dishonest thinking is thinking about things as they are not and dealing mentally with them in the way in which rightness says they should not be dealt with. Thinking a lie is the special dishonest thinking that is carried on deliberately to blot out, cover with a mask or lead away from what one knows to be true. Thinking a lie is a result and a climax of general dishonesty in thinking.

Thinking a lie disorders and upsets the mental atmosphere and perturbs thinking. This is so even with the little lies of daily life, like those uttered while one brags or boasts, or the unuttered lies of self-pity or self-conceit. They have an effect which reaches further than might be supposed. More serious is the result of lies spoken to slander, to make trouble between people, to defraud in commerce and trade, to deceive in politics to get votes, legislation and positions, or to stir up a revolt or a war. Thinking a lie tends to throw thoughts out of their orbits in the mental atmosphere, so that they may be interfered with in their exteriorizations. It tends to incapacitate the thinking from showing one a truth, from presenting in words even what one is capable of thinking, and from arriving at correct conclusions. From all this, stupidity or insanity may result. Insanity is often a physical result of lying. Lying prevents a human from knowing things as they are and so delays or defeats the education of the doer. It is the chief factor that prevents happiness.

Thinking a lie causes a sound as does the thinking of any thought.

But that sound jars and shocks the worlds, and in them the thoughts of whatever has been taken to be true. A lying thought soars and rolls in the mental atmosphere and then passes into the life world and affects and shakes up that world and the life planes of the other worlds, and the mental atmospheres of other people to whom it might be related. There it spreads the contagion of falsehood and confusion. In the worlds the reverberation of that lie booms on and every boom tolls out the name of the liar. This is so even before the lie is spoken or written; the thought produces this effect.

The doer to make progress must see its path through the world and must see things as they are. So only does one gain knowledge of the conscious self in the body, that is, accomplishments in the noetic atmosphere through thinking: to know what to do, and what not to do. By self-deception—and deceiving another involves self-deception—the doer loses its powers of discrimination and becomes unable to tell the true from the false, the right from the wrong, the existent from the nonexistent. So the purpose of its mundane experiences is frustrated. When the lying thoughts are exteriorized, the outer life becomes a fabric of lies and deceptions. So a liar is forced into troubles and hardship, while some of his lies appear also as diseases of his body. To these physical ills is added the mental confusion and blindness which is the mental destiny of a liar. That mental state sometimes deprives a liar of the faith and confidence that guide human beings through adversity.

The mental atmosphere of a man is not only honest or dishonest, but may at the same time be clear or confused, light or cloudy, active or inactive, well or poorly endowed, and it shows to which of the four classes he belongs, according to the amount, quality and aim of his thinking.

A man's thinking is done within limits set or allowed by his mental atmosphere and these have been created by his former thinking. If that was honest, if he thought about things as they were perceived to be true, if his thinking was straight and fair, not devious and deceitful, the diffused Light will now be more easily focussed and will be more plentiful, will show more truly that which he thinks about, will facilitate his thinking, will remove the fog and obstacles in the mental atmosphere and transform its character so that it will be clearer, lighter, more active and better endowed. Then his present thinking goes on within wider limits and with greater clarity, activity, directness and success in discerning the truth about things. His former thinking made his present mental atmosphere and that conditions his present thinking.

In every case thinking is the outcome of desire for the thinking. The desire is as a rule not for honest thinking, and therefore people who see things as they are, are rare. The kind of thinking that is done by the run of human beings shows what their desire has been. Their desire was not for honesty in thinking, not to see things as they were, not to act as honest thinking would have shown them how to act, but to reach to and possess the things which now are still their objects in life.

SECTION 6

Responsibility and duty. Sense-learning and sense-knowledge. Doer-learning and doer-knowledge. Intuition.

A man's mental atmosphere, if it could be seen, would show what he is responsible for. Of some, but not of all, of this responsibility he may be conscious.

He is responsible for his honest and for his dishonest thinking, for his good acts and for his evil acts, for his characteristics favorable or unfavorable, for his desires and for his feelings, for what he does with what he has and with what happens to him. He is responsible for the subjective mental and psychic and for the objective physical conditions which he is making. He is also responsible for the thinking he does around and about the thoughts of others.

He is aware of what he thinks and does in the present life and is therefore conscious of the responsibility that attaches to this thinking and acting. He is not aware of his previous lives and is therefore not conscious that his responsibility for his previous thinking and doing accounts for most of the conditions of his present life.

He is not conscious of, but nevertheless responsible for, the conditions in his mental atmosphere. Mere ignorance does not free him from the responsibility which he engendered in the past, else he would never learn to free himself from that past and get Self-knowledge, that is, knowledge of the Triune Self. There is no responsibility for the thinking that is done without attachment to the results. The responsible one is the present human. What happens to a human in one life is an exact retribution or reward for what the same portion of the doer had done in a prior life. Each of the twelve portions of the doer must continue its re-existences as long as its responsibility is not discharged.

A human is responsible to his thinker and knower and to his great

Intelligence, and through that to the Supreme Intelligence. He is not responsible to any outside God. He is made responsible by the law of thought, which is an expression in the earth sphere of universal justice.

The center of responsibility is in the mental atmosphere. It is produced there from the knowledge one has on the subject of which he thinks. The knowledge itself is in the noetic atmosphere and a flash of it comes into the mental atmosphere through rightness when morals are involved. Rightness makes the human conscious of his responsibility, and thinking can work it out. Responsibility is there always, calling ever for doing a duty by acting or omitting to act. Responsibility is with the human when he rises in the morning, when he performs the ordinary duties of the day and when he acts in a crisis. His responsibility is lessened by his incapacity to receive messages from conscience. This failure comes from insufficient knowledge on the subject of thinking. His responsibility is increased by ability to understand, due to knowledge sent from the noetic atmosphere as conscience.

There is a distinction between the responsibility for thinking and the responsibility for thoughts. A train of thinking may go on for a considerable time without showing any resulting acts. Yet during that time a record of the thinking is made in the mental atmosphere and on the breath-form; it may affect feeling-and-desire; and it may affect bodily organs and the units in the body, stimulating them to health or disease; the thinking may affect other human beings thinking on similar lines, or it may affect directly the people thought about, and yet such thinking may be insufficient to cause the thinker to create a thought. To all of this thinking some responsibility attaches, but no balancing of a thought is yet necessary. The thinking carries its responsibility at once and the human must answer, without a balancing factor being involved. Usually the sum of the accumulated thinking is taken up by the one who thinks and causes him to create a thought. The thought always contains a balancing factor. Until then the thinking can be changed or cancelled, though the thinker remains responsible for such thinking as has been done.

When the accumulations are of such a nature as to cause the thinker to issue a thought, the balancing factor is based on the responsibility which he had at the conception of the thought, and will compel a balance in accordance with it. The thoughts issued during a lifetime and thoughts previously issued which have to do with the present life come back to the human who is their parent, to be by him nourished, entertained, reinforced. He is responsible for their support and must continue to support them or else balance them. He must support them with his desire and with Light from his mental atmosphere. He does this when he thinks about them or around them.

The good and the evil thinking that men have done remains with them, in the mental atmosphere, until it is removed by thinking. The good can be removed by thinking evil in the place of it, and the evil by thinking good in its place. The acts, good or bad, that men have done do not remain; what remains is the thinking of them. That stays in the mental atmosphere. There it energizes and nourishes the thought that was exteriorized as the act, or it nourishes other similar thoughts and there the thinking may be the means of balancing the thought.

There is an immense amount of debit and credit to the account of each doer, in its mental atmosphere. The doers now in bodies have awaiting them there many of the good and the bad things which they long for, despise or dread. They may have waiting for them accomplishments which are now wished for, but which may not be developed in this life. Dullness of intellect or powers far beyond their present attainments may be in store. Intellectual development may be prevented by poverty, cares or ill health. All these things may be quite foreign to one's present outlook, possessions or limitations, but they together with worldly position and prosperity will come home in time. In the course of about a dozen lives a doer travels from obscurity to rank, from lowness and want to prominence and wealth, from simple-mindedness to intellectual power or back. Consciously or unconsciously, man determines that part of his destiny which he will suffer or enjoy, work out or postpone. Though he knows not how he does it, yet, by his mental attitudes towards himself and towards others, he calls into the present from the great storehouse of his mental atmosphere the endowments and qualities which he has.

An attitude of readiness to recognize responsibility and to meet obligations and to restrict the indulgence of desires, will allow his thinking to be guided by rightness, to focus the diffused Light more steadily and to build more successfully. In this way he develops mental excellence, which is at death stored in the mental atmosphere as an endowment, and will thence appear as such in a future life. Responsibility, the capacity to know right from wrong, determines and is the measure of duty, be the duty physical, psychic or mental. As a rule duties are connected with physical acts or events and every man knows what he

should or should not do in a given situation. A man need never be in
doubt about his duty. The only duty he should do is that of the moment.
Conscience through rightness shows him what not to do, reason shows
him what to do. In both cases his thinking will confirm this inner voice,
if he will listen to it and not to the onrushing desires.

Duty is the one thing a man has to go by. It opens out from the
exteriorization of a thought. He can always know the duty of the
moment, and if he does that duty willingly he either balances or prepares
for balancing the thought of which that duty is an exteriorization. A duty
shows what is necessary to balance a thought or to work towards a
balance. Most of the thinking that men do is concerned with physical
acts, objects or events; a large part of it relates to their duties. Hence come
experiences. Feeling anything is an experience. The feeling compels
desire to stimulate and start thinking on the subject of the feeling. If the
feeling is strong enough it will bring out a coordinated and searching
course of thinking. Thereby doer-learning is extracted from the experience, and this learning may lead to self-knowledge.

There are two kinds of learning and two kinds of knowledge. There
is sense-learning from the senses concerning nature, and doer-learning
from the experiences of the doer concerning the doer; and there are two
kinds of knowledge, the sense-knowledge which thinking has developed
from sense-learning, and the self-knowledge, or knowledge of the conscious self in the body, which thinking has developed from doer-learning.

An event felt is either outside and is brought through the senses to
feeling, or it is inside the human and wells up in the doer, feeling-and-
desire, where it is felt as sorrow, fear, warning, joy, hope, confidence or
similar states. From these two classes of events thinking gives information
and makes a record of it in the mental atmosphere.

The record of the experiences is made up of nature-matter and
intelligent-matter. The nature-matter is brought in by the senses, the
intelligent-matter is part of the doer. After death that part of the record
which was made of nature-matter disappears with the dissipation of the
breath-form, whereas the intelligent-matter remains in the mental atmosphere. During life while the information or record is on the breath-
form, it is only memory of experiences.

Learning, both sense-learning and doer-learning, is the sum, the
mass of all records. The single records have disappeared into the general
mass of learning.

The record kept on the breath-form is the memory of the particular experience. The extract made from the experience goes into the mental atmosphere to blend with the mass of other extracts of experiences which is learning. When the learning is readily available, the individual records of experiences usually disappear. Thus, while the multiplication table is being learned, individual records are kept as memories on the breath-form, such as three times four make twelve, but when from the repetition of this statement has been extracted enough to be called sense-learning, the memory of the individual experience is forgotten and one is able to say three times four make twelve, without having to confirm the statement.

Learning is not knowledge. From sense-learning comes sense-knowledge for the human, from doer-learning comes self-knowledge for the doer. Knowledge of both kinds results from thinking on what has been learned. It does not come from a thought or from thoughts, it is acquired by thinking.

It is a common thing to extract sense-learning from experiences, children and distinguished scientists do it. It is one set of functions which the body-mind executes. Occasionally it has another set of functions. It makes efforts to free Light from interfering matter and to turn it and to focus it on and into the subject of the thinking. This is a process of digestion or assimilation, so as to get an extract from what has been learned. It is thinking of what has been learned and leads to sense-knowledge, that is, knowledge of the actions of matter. Thus the generalizations are made which are called laws. Sense-knowledge is and remains in the mental atmosphere during life, and after death is lost when the breath-form is dissolved. But there remains from sense-learning and sense-knowledge the discipline of at most the body-mind. Inclinations, aptitudes and abilities are all that is brought over from the education and attainments in one life. Sometimes these are so marked that the person having them is called a genius.

On the other hand, doer-learning and self-knowledge are acquired by the doer, and are carried over after death. They are chiefly reactions to acts, objects and events, experienced by the doer. Feeling causes desire to start thinking on the feelings produced, and a record is made by the body-mind, the feeling-mind and the desire-mind, similar to that of sense-learning which is made by the body-mind alone. The store of doer-learning is thus increased. Doer-learning is the mass of extracts which the feeling-mind and the desire-mind have made from experiences of acts, objects and events, and of their causes and avoidances. Doer-learning is largely, not exclusively, of morals, and is carried over after death. What little of nature-matter there is in the record disappears after death, but the intelligent-matter in it remains in the mental atmosphere and is sufficient to connect it with the moral aspect of what is right concerning the act, object or event. Therefore, in the next or some future life the human brings with him an understanding, which is the total of the doer-learning. By this understanding the doer avoids what would bring about experiences concerning which it has a sufficient store of learning.

From the mass of doer-learning which is in the mental atmosphere of the human, thinking may extract self-knowledge for the doer. When the desire for such knowledge is strong enough in the human, thinking on the store of doer-learning is compelled. The feeling-mind and the desire-mind make efforts to get Light free from interfering matter and to focus it on and into the subject of the thinking. When the Light is focussed and is held steadily, everything disappears except the subject of thinking. Everything about this is present and is known in that Light, and is transferred by the thinking into the noetic atmosphere of the human, where it is knowledge of the conscious self in the body, available to the doer. It is then not necessary to go through the processes of that thinking again; the purpose of that thinking is attained. It becomes necessary to think about the knowledge only when it is to be applied or is to be conveyed to others. If it was acquired in the present life it is available to the human. If it was acquired in a former life it is usually not available, except on moral questions. Then it speaks spontaneously, appearing as the voice of conscience which is expressed through rightness. Conscience is negative and is always present.

The human acquires sense-knowledge through the body-mind, and this knowledge is lost to the doer portion when it lives again, though aptitude and inclination may become endowments. The doer-in-the-human can acquire self-knowledge by the use of the feeling-mind and desire-mind if available to it. Such knowledge is not lost, but remains in the noetic atmosphere of the human when the doer lives again, and is available to it by thinking, as memory of the doer. Such knowledge is acquired by the doer, it does not come from the knower. However, the doer may receive Self-knowledge from the knower, by which it may at once know all that the doer can laboriously acquire from the experiences of its human being and its thinking. This is intuition which comes through reason. It is positive and is exceedingly rare, but when it comes it is direct knowledge on any subject in question. It is not concerned with business or with things of the senses, but relates to problems of the doer. If, however, one opens communication with the knower, it is available on any subject. That knowledge of the knower comprises everything. It is a composite of everything that has been, resolved into the Triune Self. The knower as selfness is knowledge, while as I-ness it is the identity of that knowledge, and these are the knower.

Knowledge of the Triune Self, that is, Self-knowledge, is the sum of all knowledge. It is shared by all knowers, since they have a common part called the noetic world. That knowledge is to be distinguished from the doer-knowledge which is acquired by the human through its thinking and which is stored in the noetic atmosphere of the human, (Fig. V-B).

There is nothing new. As a unit, the aia has been through everything in nature; when it is translated and becomes a Triune Self it does not, so to say, speak the nature language any more, but has the composite experience and learning, now as knowledge of all.

All changes and combinations of matter and forces, have been made over and over again and again. They are innumerable, apparently, and yet they are limited like the moves on a chess-board. Human beings go over some of them as new in every fresh civilization. All thinking makes destiny. Noetic destiny for the doer is that part of a thought which is Light and is returned to the noetic atmosphere when the thought is balanced by thinking, and so is transmuted into self-knowledge for the doer. Thoughts circling in the mental atmosphere of the human are mental destiny. When one of them is balanced this results in self-knowledge in the mental atmosphere of the doer portion when it next re-exists and is mental destiny for its human being.

Psychic destiny is the desire part of the thought. Even while in a thought and so in the mental atmosphere, the desire part of a thought affects the psychic atmosphere and produces there states of joy and sorrow. When a thought is exteriorized the act, object or event produces experiences of pleasure and pain and joy and sorrow, and increases or decreases psychic tendencies in the psychic atmosphere, as to gloom or cheer, fearfulness or confidence.

Physical destiny is that part of a thought which is exteriorized as an act, an object or an event. Physical destiny which is presented by the visible conditions in which a human lives is often considered the only kind of destiny.

The mental destiny, which is the general character of the mental atmosphere with its endowments and attitudes and the ability to use the three minds, is not transmuted into noetic, psychic and physical destiny; it remains mental destiny. A transmutation of mental destiny into the other three kinds takes place when the mental destiny has matured into a thought.

The thought as a whole is mental destiny and in it the aim remains mental destiny; the design in it is psychic destiny; the exteriorizations are physical destiny as acts, objects or events; and the Light is noetic destiny. A thought is the means by which the distribution is made. All four kinds of destiny come out of a thought. The raw material goes into the thought, is made into an entity as a thought, and then it affects the sources and regions from which the material was taken and is the chief means by which thinking changes matter into higher degrees of being conscious.

Every thing on the physical plane is the exteriorization of a thought. The physical conditions of life, like health and disease, wealth and poverty, high or low rank, race and language, are exteriorizations of thoughts. One's psychic nature with little, dull or tender feeling, feeble or strong desires, the temperament or inclinations, is the result of thoughts. Moral qualities and mental endowments, inclinations to study and learn, to loose or clear thinking, mental defects and gifts, come from thinking.

People accept possessions, good fortune and mental endowments as a matter of course, but complain of impediments and trouble. However, all these things are exteriorizations and interiorizations of their thoughts, and come as lessons to teach them what to think and what not to think.

The great lesson to be learned is to think without creating thoughts, destiny, that is, not to be attached to the objects about which one thinks. Man does not do this, so he creates thoughts and will continue to create them until he learns to think without creating thoughts. Such thinking is real thinking. It can be done only when desire is controlled and trained. No mad desires will then affect the mental atmosphere; only controlled desires will act upon it. The obscurations and obstacles in the mental atmosphere will be eliminated, there will be more and clearer Light, thinking will be more true. This goal, which is reached by individuals, not by the race as a whole, is far distant. In the meantime human beings create thoughts and these are exteriorized.

An exteriorization is that part of a thought which was physical, was taken from the physical plane and returns to it as an act, object or event. It appears there when the thought in the course of its circling intersects the course of at least one other thought, at the juncture of time, condition and place. It is exteriorized through the four systems of the body, in a moment or in many years.

If at that exteriorization the thought is not balanced, the human may not be conscious that any of the many other exteriorizations are the result of the same thought. Another exteriorization is brought about when the course of the thought intersects the course of another thought, either of the same or of another person. If the second thought is one of his own thoughts, he may be conscious that he exteriorized the second thought, but he will not be conscious that that exteriorized the first thought; likewise, if another person's thought brought about the exteriorization of the first thought, he will not be conscious of this fact. Therefore, a human is not conscious that the acts, objects and events of his life are exteriorizations of his own thoughts.

Human beings aid or hinder the exteriorizations of their thoughts by their mental attitude, by their willingness or unwillingness to meet conditions of life as they find them or have made them and to perform the duties of the present. One's thoughts teach him, or should teach him, to learn the lesson of life, which is to get knowledge of himself and to think and act as the Light of the Intelligence shows. Man is constantly chasing objects of nature. As he possesses them they cause reactions in his feeling-and-desire which should teach him, but usually fail to teach him, the lesson that he can find outside nothing that will satisfy him. All the sense-learning, all the sense-knowledge which the doer-in-the-body can acquire, is of nature and cannot satisfy it. Unless the human is conscious of the doer within his body he will be carried away and be overwhelmed by sense-knowledge and will forget and even deny that he is not the body. The experiences of life constantly throw the human back on himself so that he may learn of himself *as* the doer.

Opportunity to educate himself so as to be conscious of himself as something more than a human is constantly before him. His duties, however humble or insignificant they may be, present the opportunity, and honesty in thinking is the means of using it.

Such is an outline of mental destiny, as the character of the mental atmosphere, that is made by thinking and that conditions further thinking. The mental atmosphere is a term here used for that small part of it which is represented in one's present life and in which the thoughts affecting the present life circulate.

SECTION 7

Genius.

The fact that a genius appears now and then is an example of something that goes on in the psychic and mental atmospheres of every human, though not to the degree where the result may be called genius.

A genius is one who is gifted with extraordinary ability and with originality that does not limit him to the old rules or paths, but makes him strike out for new fields. He does not depend on education or training for his powers, as do those whose endowments are of a lesser degree. Genius is not mere talent or aptitude. Genius is the spontaneous action of the doer in the use of any of the three minds which it can use to express its feeling-and-desire and in expressing a high degree of excellence in one or more of the arts or sciences. The expression of genius shows the feeling and understanding which the human has and which he exhibits without the experience and study usually required.

The ordinary man has the memories of the present life and loses them after death when the breath-form is broken up. He has sense-learning, but little sense-knowledge. If, however, enough sense-knowledge is acquired, it is transferred to the aia itself and comes back in another life, not as detailed memories but as sense-knowledge. The ordinary man is not in touch with his past, but it is there just the same, in his psychic and in his mental atmospheres. He is cut off from it, because the old breath-form is gone. He does not get far enough to acquire sense-knowledge, which the body-mind gets from what is learned. If enough sense-knowledge is acquired, the aia itself bears a record of it. If in a new life this record in the aia is transferred to the breath-form, the human is a genius. He has not the detailed memories any more than the ordinary man has, but he has the sum of them in the knowledge which his former thinking brought him. This puts him in touch with the endowments in his psychic and mental atmospheres and he appears as a genius. The difference between a genius and an ordinary person is that a genius is a human who had developed sense-knowledge to the degree where the aia bore the record and, in the life where he is a genius, puts him in touch with his endowments in the mental atmosphere and with his feeling in the psychic atmosphere; whereas the ordinary person has not the record on the aia to put him in immediate touch with any endowments he may

have. The sense-knowledge and its accessibility, which together constitute a genius, are not dependent upon the impressions made on the
breath-form in the past life, because they have been effaced.

The senses and the bodily organs used are only instruments for the
expression of the genius. The senses and the hands must have been
specially exercised, disciplined and developed through many lives. The
ordinary artist, whether he be painter, sculptor, musician, actor or poet,
follows the rules laid down by the best in his field, and he achieves
greatness to the degree that he adds excellence from his doer; but he is
not a genius. A genius makes his own rules and is distinctively original,
without, however, flying in the face of all canons of beauty, proportion
and power.

There is a mechanical genius, which is a physical achievement,
relating to the handling of tools and materials. Then there is the genius
in the line of music, painting or sculpture. Artists of this kind, including
poets, must have feeling developed to a high degree and with that the
skill to express such feeling by means of thinking. Both the high degree
of sensitiveness and the skill and power of expression are developed by
the feeling-mind and the desire-mind. A genius in architecture, literature
or war needs less sensuous feeling than do these artists, but his feeling
must be of a high order. In every case his skill in expressing his feeling
and using the sense-knowledge of the past are what make him a genius.
A genius may be many-sided as was Michelangelo, who expressed
strength of desire. A genius may reach superlative degrees as in the case
of Sophocles, Aristotle, Leonardo, Shakespeare, Napoleon. The great
achievements of a genius do not mean perfection of the doer portion in
his body.

Often a genius is unevenly developed. Usually a lack of morals and
of consideration for others is found in one who shows genius as an actor,
poet, musician or painter. This is because his genius is the result of effort
along a given line only. He may have sacrificed or neglected moral duties
while devoting his life to the particular thinking which resulted in his
being born a genius. Some allowance should be made for the shortcomings of some of these artists. An artist must be sensitive to nature,
therefore he is liable to be overcome by it. In a genius these peculiarities
of the artistic temperament are often accentuated.

In exceptional cases a human refuses to develop any other line than
that of his genius, and then he may give way to inordinate appetites for
drink and debauch. Thereafter the genius will be present in a succeeding

life, but self-control will be lacking. So there may be a mathematical genius who is in other respects an imbecile. It is better to develop self-control than genius, because the lack of self-control will ultimately defeat the advantages of genius. It takes greater effort to develop self-control than mental endowments, and with strength of character all other things, including mental endowments, will be attained.

Geniuses as they have been known in historical times are infants compared to those in prehistoric times and to those who will be in the future. A genius carried to his full development is a doer who has complete control of the senses and who through these four senses can control the four elements of nature. The body-mind, the feeling-mind and the desire-mind and their operations would then be available to such a genius. He would have access to all the sense-knowledge acquired through thinking. He would with that have a feeling carried to a degree beyond anything known in the present, and an ability to use his hands that would seem equally strange now. But if he were a painter or a sculptor he would not have to use his hands. Elementals would paint the pictures or cut the stone according to his mental orders, if color or stone were used. But color or stone would not be necessary, for such a genius could by seeing what he wanted cause nature units to precipitate colors as he directed to make a picture, or to build up statuary by precipitation of the elements of metal or stone. An engineering genius could build a bridge, remove a mountain, change the current of a river, tunnel earth or moisten arid land by control of elementals through his thinking, and all within the space of a day.

SECTION 8

The four classes of human beings.

There are four classes of human beings according to the amount, quality and aim of their thinking: laborers, traders, thinkers, and knowers. The classes are invisible. The measure by which the human beings are so divided is their development achieved by thinking.

Sex, age, dress, occupation, station, possessions are often used as marks to put mankind into classes. These marks are only outward. They do not reach the portions of doers that live in the bodies so classified. Even feelings, emotions, tendencies and desires fail to offer a comprehensive and causal classification. The marks which are physical destiny, depend on thinking. Only according to the thinking men do can they be separated into classes which are causal to physical characteristics.

This classification has nothing to do with the caste systems known to history, which are usually connected with or based on a religious system. A grading of men according to their thinking is independent of any religion. The four classes exist and are, whether they are recognized or not, whenever there is a humanity and whatever its form of government. In every man all four types are represented, since every man has a body and is related to the three parts of the Triune Self. But one type predominates, and indicates the class to which he belongs, irrespective of sex, rank, possessions, occupation or other outward marks. In some ages this division, which always persists in his atmospheres, obtains also in the exteriorizations of physical life, and is sharply marked. This is the case in the best periods of a people. Then everyone knows himself to be, and is known by others to be, in his class. He knows it as well as a child knows that it is a child and not a man. There is no contempt for or envy of any class distinctions. At other times, however, the distinctions of these classes are not strictly displayed, but there are always at least general indications which suggest the underlying fourfold classification

There are many things that all men today have in common. They all have desires for food, drink, dress, amusement, comforts. They nearly all have a certain good nature and sympathy, especially when the misfortunes of others appeal in a striking manner. They all sorrow and suffer. All have some virtues, some vices, all are subject to diseases. In different localities large numbers hold to the same beliefs as to government, religion and social order. These things which men have in common are so evident that they often obscure the distinctions of the classes. Then there is the leveling influence of money in a commercial and materialistic age. However, the four classes exist today as surely as ever.

In the first class are the persons who think little, whose thinking is narrow, shallow and sluggish and whose aim is to claim their rights from everybody and not to consider their duties to anybody. Their life is a service to their bodies. They want things for their bodies. They do not think of others except as the others affect their bodies. They have little or no memory of experiences and facts distant from the present and remember nothing from history except what falls in with their aims. They seek no information. They want no restraint, are lawless, illogical, ignorant, credulous, inconstant, irresponsible and self-indulgent. They take what they get, not because they would not take better things, but because they are not enough interested and are mentally too lazy to think out ways of getting them. They are carried on by the stream of events and are the servants of environment. They are servants by nature. Some of them have fortunes and high positions in the social order, some work in the arts and professions, but most are muscular laborers, hand workers or clerks. In recent times inventions have advanced industries and increased commerce. This has caused workers to be concentrated in cities, labor to become more specialized and people to become more dependent on the work of others. These gradual changes have aided in making labor prominent by organized minorities and labor unions. Thereby the heads of many persons in this first class have been filled with undue notions of their importance and such distorted views have not been rectified by the universal voting rights that exist in some countries.

However, their belief does not remove the persons who are in this class, from it. Nor will turmoil, strike and revolution do so. The persons who are in this class and remain in it are there because they belong there, because their mental destiny keeps them there and because they could not be in any of the other classes. Without the thinker and the trader, who create and distribute what the laborer is employed to produce, there would be no productions by the first class. Even the leaders of the first class do not usually belong to it. Often they are traders who deal in persons of the first class as other traders trade in coal or cattle. The power of these demagogues is exercised by trickery and by sensing the amount, quality, aim and range of the thinking done by the first class.

Some doers are born into this first class though they are not of it; after they have had the rough training they need they work themselves out of it, as an engine wiper who becomes a railroad head, a clerk who becomes a banker, or a millhand who becomes a scientist.

In the second class are doers who think more than the laborers, whose thinking is broad, takes in many subjects, accommodates itself to conditions, is agile and accurate though superficial. Their aim usually is to give as little as they have to and to get as much as they can, and not to do their duties to others any more than they are compelled to. They think of others from expediency and for exploitation. Their desires are the most active part of them; they try to control their bodies as well as their thinking. The aim of most of their thoughts is to get something that will satisfy a desire for gain, rather than to enjoy through the body. They live in and for their desires and make their bodies serve them. They will often go without food and drive their bodies relentlessly to obtain an object of desire, put through a business deal, drive a bargain, and generally pursue their trading. They will live penuriously to accumulate money. One of the first class, a body doer, will not work the body hard to satisfy a desire for money alone. He may work hard to get money, but his aim is to spend what he has so earned, on his body. As desire works the body in this second class, so does it also work the body-mind and compel thinking. Their aim then is to find means to satisfy desire. The more active the desire for gain is, the greater will be the amount of thinking which desire can command for its service and the better will be its quality as to thoroughness and comprehensiveness.

They want a general order in affairs, as this protects their interests. They are not as lawless as are those of the first class but want to use that general order to further their own interests, and they are not averse to finding loopholes or special protection for themselves at the expense of those who are bound by general laws. To them what they desire is right; what opposes their desire is wrong. They are logical in their enterprises and keen observers of the weaknesses of human nature. They are usually informed about facts and circumstances that affect their particular business. They are not credulous but are skeptical and suspicious of what concerns their property and projects. They feel a certain responsibility if they have property, but try to evade it if they can. They indulge their desires for enjoyment through the body only when they can afford it and when no dominating desire offers obstacles. Their ruling desire is for gain, profit, possessions. They trade everything for these. They accommodate themselves to conditions until they can make conditions to suit themselves. They overcome their environment instead of being satisfied or ruled by it. Naturally they obtain power over the first class.

The persons in this class are essentially traders. Mere buying and selling does not bring anyone into this class, for almost everybody has some buying and selling to do. Farmers and peasants, though they buy some things and sell their products, do not usually belong to the traders. Nor do persons who sell their unskilled, skilled, artistic or professional services, whether they work for wages or independently. But those who engage in commercial pursuits and whose desire is for gain rather than for getting a mere living, or for patriotism, honor or fame, all from peddlers to merchant princes belong to this class. From the shopkeeper in a village and the packman selling along country roads to the dealers in whole cargoes, from small pawnbrokers to bankers who make national loans, all are in the same class. Their poverty or riches, failure or success, do not affect the classification. The changes which have come in the social order in modern times have not only helped the first class, the body workers, into prominence, but have made the second class, the traders, the rulers of the world. With the development of manufacturing and commerce has come a mass of real estate brokers, loan brokers, promoters, agents, commissionmen, functionaries, and go-betweens of many varieties. They are clear types of the second class. Here belong also the rulers in modern democracies, that is, the heads of those behind the heads of big business, bankers, party politicians, lawyers and labor leaders. All persons in the second class try to bend everything to the service of their desire for gain and possessions. Their aim is always to get the best of the bargain.

In the third class are the persons here called thinkers. They think much; their thinking is broad, deep and active, compared with that of laborers and traders. Their chief aim is to achieve ambitions and ideals irrespective of material preferment. Their desire is for their thinking to be above and to control their desires. In this they differ from the traders, whose desire is that their desires shall control the thinking. The outstanding traits of the thinkers are a regard for honor, valor, conventions, fame and attainment in the professions, arts and sciences. They think of how to better the conditions of others. They make their bodies serve the aims of their thinking. Often they tax the endurance of their bodies, challenge privations and disease and incur dangers in pursuit of their ideals. They desire ideals. Their ideals dominate their other desires, and by thinking they lead their desires to serve their ideals.

To this class belong persons who are leaders in thinking, people who have ideals, think about and strive after them. They lead in and preserve honor, learning, culture, manners and language. They are found in the ranks of science, among artists, philosophers, preachers and in the medical, teaching, legal, military and other professions. They are found in families of distinction who value their honor, culture, good name and public service. They devise and discover the means by which the traders profit and the laborers find work in industry and commerce. They set the moral standard of right and wrong for the laborers and the traders. Among them start movements for the improvement of the people and of the conditions under which the less fortunate or the miserable parts of mankind live. They are the backbone of the nations. At a crisis in national life they lead the way. Many of them have means. But as the pursuit of their ideals is not a worship of the money god, he does not voluntarily give them money, land and possessions as their reward. When they are without visible distinctions of these kinds, the world pays little respect to the third class. Their mental attitude and love for their ideals is often a challenge to fate, which then permits them to be tried by hardships. Even in such situations their thinking bestows upon them advantages far above anything that the traders and laborers get out of life.

The fourth class are here called knowers. Their thinking is concerned with self-knowledge, that is, with what has been distilled out of learning which itself has resulted from experience. This knowledge is in the noetic atmosphere of the human, whereas the sense-knowledge of a lifetime is with the breath-form. Their thinking turns about self-knowledge, though they may not have access to it. Their desire is to get at ideas. They know about ideas like justice, love and truth, but that knowledge is not available to them, so they think about the ideas, clearly, logically, incisively. They think about their conscious selves in their bodies and their relation to their own Divinities beyond their bodies and nature, and also to the gods of nature. They think about others, not for exploitation or from necessity, but they put themselves in other persons' places. The thinking of traders serves their desires, the thinking of the thinkers reaches out for ideals, but the thinking of the knowers seeks to connect with ideas and either to dwell with them in the abstract or to apply them to the affairs of life. The knowers depend upon themselves to get this knowledge, as life shows them that they cannot get it from any other source. Inspirations come from within. When they think, they can throw light on problems of life. They are not mystics, nor do they get information in ecstatic states. Some of them are not what the world calls thinkers; but they have insight into things. They do not belong to any particular layer in the social order. They are not numerous enough to make a layer. If found they may be in any vocation or position. They do not set the usual values on position, approval or possessions, because their thinking does not deal much with them, except to generalize from and consider about them. But at certain times some of them impart enlightenment, usually to the thinkers who are in a position to make use of it for the world. They are only few in number and are of types like Penn, Alexander Hamilton and Benjamin Franklin.

These four classes exist always whether among barbarians or high civilizations and irrespective of the outward form of government. The doers in bodies on the earth are going up and down inside these four invisible classes into which the amount, quality and aim of their thinking puts them and which indicates their development as human beings.

A change in the aim may put a thinker into the laborers or traders class and a knower can become a trader. Such descents as a rule are temporary. The higher can become the lower suddenly, but the lower cannot become the higher except by slow progression. When a laborer or a trader suddenly thinks and pushes himself out of his class and becomes a thinker or knower, he shows thereby that he had first descended from these higher classes.

According to the changing conditions of the mental atmosphere of its human being a doer goes up and down in these four classes. When human beings change the aim of their thinking, the change carries with it the quantity, quality and range of the thinking and so changes the condition of their mental atmospheres. That affects the conditions of their other three atmospheres. If the four atmospheres could be seen, the changed aspects which they present from time to time, would appear as marked as those of a day which may be dull, and brilliant and stormy.

Today the four classes cannot be discerned easily. Nevertheless they are there. The largest number of persons by far is in the first class; a much smaller number makes up the traders; the thinkers are in number less than a quarter of the second class; and the knowers are few indeed.

Usually the class to which a human belongs can be discerned in a general way, but often the marks of the layer of the social order he is in do not accord with the type that rules interiorly. Many who are in the professional layer of the lawyers do not belong to the thinkers, but are traders or laborers. Many physicians also are only traders, notwithstanding their occupation and even reputation. Many officiating as men of God are likewise traders or even body-doers. Most of the statesmen, lawgivers, politicians, agitators and wirepullers monger in public affairs merely or mostly for their own pockets. They occupy places which should be filled by thinkers, but they are traffickers. In all such cases the human beings are in the class of the traders, but figure in positions which in a well-ordered community could never be held by them while their thinking kept them in the trader class.

Often body-doers, those of the first class, figure in places in which thinkers should be. They are courtiers and time servers in monarchies; and in democracies they fill many public offices, where they obey the bosses who put them there and who are themselves traders. From partisan lawgivers and facile judges to arbitrary officials and brutal jailkeepers, their words and acts show the class to which they really belong. They think little and that little is narrow, shallow and sluggish and aims at self-indulgence and body worship. Sometimes some of this first class figure in positions which ought to be filled by the best of the traders. This is the case especially where the making of public contracts and expenditure of public money is concerned.

The mental destiny of the four classes has been determined by their thinking, in every age and through every civilization. These ages and civilizations go back far, far beyond anything that legend, tradition and history tell. In the following pages a brief account will be given of what has been called a "Beginning".

SECTION 9

Conception of a Beginning. The permanent physical world or Realm of Permanence, and the four earths. The trial test of the sexes. The "fall" of the doer. Doers became subject to re-existence in man and woman bodies.

Within the permanent physical world or Realm of Permanence there are four invisible earths.

Our human earth (Fig. V-B,a) is an interruption or, so to speak, a drop-out from or in the Eternal Order of Progression.

These four earths are co-existent; the numbering is merely to give distinction and show difference. They are here not dealt with in detail. Myths and legends hardly deal with them,—except perhaps as Paradise or the Garden of Eden,—and history not at all.

The permanent earth or Realm of Permanence, contains, maintains and balances all things which change in the human world, but is not itself changed by the changing human world within it. The Realm of Permanence is composed of balanced units of the radiant, airy, fluid, and solid states of matter; it pervades the human world, but is not perceptible to human vision because human vision is not attuned to the balanced units of the Realm of Permanence. The Realm of Permanence is necessary for the development of all units,—more necessary than is the sun, which is representative of our present changing earth.

Such words as "time", "first", "beginning", "start", "origin", and the like, are here employed because of their common usage, or because there are no words in our vocabulary to describe and explain conditions in other worlds. Really, there was no "beginning" in the sense of a beginning in time. There are conceptions determined by the condition of the body of a human sense-bound doer. The measurements of time according to solar years are inapplicable to time in physical states other than that of the present time and dimension.

In the Realm of Permanence the physical bodies of the Triune Selves are sexless and perfect, and creatures of that state of matter are not as the animals on our earth. To our limited sensuous perception they are invisible; they are strong and are responsive to the intention in what is thought or said to them. This was, and still is, the period of creation by the exteriorization of the thinking of the complete Triune Selves. The thinking of Triune Selves is steady and, sounding, takes form. Around the form gather and cluster particles of radiant, airy, fluid and solid matter. The physical cells are balanced, and therefore not of the sexes. The doers in the Realm of Permanence are in their perfect physical bodies and their Triune Selves shine through them. Nature is made animate by the thought of these shining doers, and bodies for animals are prepared by thinking and speaking them into physical being. Pure elementals come into these bodies.

In the Realm of Permanence is no death, no sorrow, no sickness, no pain. There are no men, no women, no children, no riches. The Triune Selves know the law and act with it. The perfect bodies continue, not by eating food, but by the transient units from the four elements, taken in and distributed by the breath.

Doers on earth today, intoxicated and maddened in sense-drugged bodies, cannot at once get into touch with the thought and feeling of that permanent state. In that state the doers have their final training and the Triune Selves pass on, after they have performed their duties as officers in The Government of the world and as administrators of the destiny of nations; they are raised to be Intelligences and the aias of those doers become the Triune Selves of their Intelligences. The doers of these Triune Selves inherit their pure physical bodies. These doers live in the Realm of Permanence. This was and is the state of the doers before the trial test of feeling-and-desire through the sexes for qualifying them to operate the perfect bodies. In that test the doers now in human bodies failed and so were self-exiled and subject to death and re-existences in the temporal human world. Those doers that passed the test continued according to the Eternal Order of Progression, (Fig. II-G).

During that test the doers now in human bodies continued to think of themselves in a twofold way instead of as the oneness. They created thoughts of the type of two. So the doer had dual bodies, united by an invisible cord at the place where the navel is now. Feeling of the doer was in one of the dual bodies and desire was in the other, and each enjoyed the presence of the other in its thinking. This may have been the basis for such stories as that of Adam and Eve.

This way of thinking set the pattern of change out of permanence; a change to birth and death, to day and night, and to the pairs and to the opposites everywhere. At this first transition the doer became conscious of the dual forces at work on the second earth of the Realm of Permanence.

The original perfect body disappeared as it changed into a male body in which desire was, and a female body in which feeling was. They represented two forces which had before acted as one. The doer felt these two forces through its dual bodies. If today anyone could feel a chaste union of these forces in himself, without physical waste, and without the presence of another person, there would be a joy and a power undreamed of.

Then began changes in the doer and its bodies which brought about a second transition and which made the doer conscious of the third earth stage. These changes started when the desire aspect of the doer in one body looked upon its feeling aspect in the other body with a sense akin to sexual desire and feeling. Their thinking caused development of sex organs. They began to cohabit and to procreate, and thereby they lost their power to create.

Bodies on the third earth are male bodies and female bodies. Union of bodies is an important ceremony, attended by ecstatic revelation and takes place only when a new body is to be procreated. There is no shame, no sin, and the pleasure is a temporary opening of the world of creation, that is, the life world, to the senses. The bodies are of the general human form, but powerful and beautiful and clean, and do not have pain or disease. Their bodies are born and die. The doers in them, although now without the power to create forms consciously, still can direct elemental forces of nature. They direct these elementals to assist them in whatever work they undertake, and use no tools or machines. There are no houses, no cities, no storms, no wars, no upheavals of nature and no diseases. The animal and plant worlds come into existence as they do on our earth, unconsciously to the doers in human forms, though those doers know of the laws by which they bring animal and plants into existence. The animals are of the two sexes, and are not ferocious.

The first deviation from those peaceful times came when the doers in the human bodies cohabited, not for the lawful purpose of the union, but for the pleasure it gave them. At first they united at the proper season, later out of season. Formerly nature force was used for the purpose of procreation when they united in season; but later, when they liberated the power, not for procreation, but for pleasure and selfish ends, each sex trying to subjugate the other sex, they lost command over the nature force and their sexual activities became sinful. Thus human bodies were called into existence by sexual union. With the unlawful use of their sex organs, the doers were exiled to the human world of birth, death, and re-existence; they left and ceased to be conscious of the third earth; they became conscious of and lived on the temporal human earth. Here birth is painful and so is death and life is burdened with sin and sorrow.

The first earth is permanent; on the second the doers' bodies are adjusted or changed by thinking. On neither of these earths is death. On the third, death comes from birth, through the union of the sexes. The bodies of humans and those of animals and plants may live for ages, but they must die.

On the first or permanent earth there is a steady progress of doers to perfection; and, with their perfect Triune Selves, they become Intelligences. On the second, most of the Triune Selves likewise advance to be Intelligences. On the third earth the doers of some Triune Selves progress during the early stages and the Triune Selves become Intelligences.

Within the fourth earth of the Realm of Permanence—which earth is also invisible because it is of balanced units,—is the visible physical universe, with the temporal human earth of birth and death, (Fig. I-C). Such universe is visible to human eyes because it is made up of unbalanced units. The human world, the earth we live on, as stated, is a sort of dropout, or interruption in the Eternal Order of Progression. It exists for doers of Triune Selves that failed, or may fail, in their test. Such doers have to re-exist in the human world of time, of death and birth, until they do regenerate their bodies and restore them to the Eternal Order of Progression. Thus the earth we live on, is without beginning; it has been changed again and again by tremendous geological events, after which it has been as if the whole earth had been newborn. The thinking of the doers in human beings provides the forms of the kingdoms of nature on this man and woman earth of ours.

The solid earth is and has been a spherical crust in the earth element. Inside and outside of the crust are spherical zones. Inside the crust and zones are races and entities, some superior and some inferior to the human race. To some of these beings the earth crust is as transparent as the earth atmosphere is to humans, because gross matter does not hinder their vision when it is focussed on what is beyond. Because their bodies are of the matter of the form, the life, and the light worlds, they can pass through the thick earth crust as easily as humans move through air. Among these beings are doers of Triune Selves who were in the past connected with Humanity and who appeared from time to time on earth. They were either not known or were known as Wise Men, exhibiting authority and power, and having some human characteristics which made a common bond between them and the people on earth. They have appeared from the interior when a new start was to be made.

On our human earth, there are cycles of Four Great Civilizations, which come in sequence; in each of these are numerous minor civilizations.

At the end of this Fourth Civilization now on earth—if the doers fail to make it a permanent civilization—there will be a long period when there will be no civilized life. As in the past, it will be as if the earth were dead or in darkness. Then another cycle of Four Civilizations will set in, and after that another and another. Actually, there is no end of one and a beginning of another; they end and begin as one year passes into another. The seeming beginning or end is merely in the reckoning. The purpose of these civilizations is, of course, the education of the doers toward the recognition of their Triune Selves.

SECTION 10

Prehistoric history. First, Second, and Third Civilization on the human earth. Fallen doers from inside the earth.

On the four invisible earths of the Realm of Permanence there is no need for what is called Civilizations. On the human earth, any First Civilization in the cycles of Four Civilizations, started innumerable years ago; it was not a gradual development, but was inaugurated by those who came from the third and fourth earths of the Realm of Permanence, under the direction of an Intelligence and its related complete Triune Self. There were fluctuations but no evolution. There were divine kings, in the sense that they were not of the race, but were perfected doers who had come from the interior earth to teach and rule over human beings on the crust. The physical body of the king was different from those of the people. The human beings of doers were men and women, the divine ruler was a perfected doer in an immortal physical body.

Mankind gradually increased and spread over a large portion of the land. There was a steady rise in the civilization. The continents were different from what they are today; they have changed numberless times. At the high-water mark of this civilization some of the people were taught the relation of the Intelligence to the Triune Self, the history of the earth, the organization of the elementals in nature, the laws that governed them, the laws by which animals, plants and minerals received their forms and by what they were embodied, and the purpose which the existence of these creatures served. At the height of the civilization the earth was in a condition transcending in power, splendor and happiness anything that tradition or legend tells. Building, agriculture, metal working, fabrics, colors and the arts were such that, compared to them, the efforts of the people today in these crafts are primitive.

However, there was no commerce; all that was needed was produced by thought by the people in every locality. The people could communicate by thought from one end of the earth to the other. There was much travel; the people had air boats and swift vessels on the water. But they did not use steam or engines; the motive power for these vehicles and others used on land was taken directly from the starlight and connected with every part of the vehicle. The direction was given by the thought of the driver, and the speed regulated in the same way. Not only such vehicles but other objects like huge stones for building were moved by thought and the hands, which acted on the forces of nature. No part of the earth was a duplicate or imitation of any other. Different sections were distinguished in all respects. Only the form of government was the same throughout. The people were instructed by their divine ruler; there was an absolute monarchy, but it was by divine right. No one was oppressed, no one suffered want. There were the four classes that are always in the world. Authority and power were used for the good of everyone and everyone was satisfied. The people had health and long life; they lived without fear and had a painless death; there was no war. The types of the animals resulted from the thoughts of the humans, so they were without sharp teeth and claws and were of a strong, but gentle nature.

After these institutions were established and had lasted for long periods, the period of divine kings ended. The divine king withdrew and left mankind, which was now to be responsible for itself. There was only one race on the earth. The wisest of the governors selected one of their number to rule as king, and this order of government lasted for a period. As long as the wisest was selected all went well. Then a king began to wish to be succeeded by his issue, and the same desire for succession in families came to prevail among the people. A dynasty arose; the king, full of ambition, desired power. The hereditary successors were not always the most excellent. Some were good, some inefficient, and the old order in things was not maintained. Dissatisfaction among the people enabled some leaders to establish rival dynasties. The old order disappeared; the kings were removed, and in their stead sets of nobles ruled in various parts of the world. After a while the rulers, who possessed most learning, constituted an aristocracy which drew apart from the rest. Then another class, those who were skilled in the management of industries or agriculture, overthrew the aristocracy and established a new form of government with themselves at the head. This kind of government went on for a time, and then from the handworkers desiring power came men who claimed the right to rule for the people, and succeeded. They became despots and enslaved the people. When the people had suffered enough they supported other men, who then became their despots. The arts and sciences were lost; despot fought despot. Amidst conditions of misrule, the dominant factors in public and private life were rapacity, hate and corruption.

According to the types of the thoughts held, the surface of the earth changed. In different parts, people of different types and animals corresponding to them came into existence. Minor rises followed minor falls. Sometimes civilization disappeared in one place, but was started afresh in another by one of the Wise Men or some one sent by them. Lesser nations and races followed after the steady rise to the highest point reached by the single race under the divine rulers. Each race disappeared in decadence after it had repeated the political phases of the first. The thoughts of the decadents brought on lesser cataclysms that wiped out portions of the race, but through all there was a steady descent.

A large part of the earth crust was destroyed. These disturbances of the earth were merely exteriorizations of the thoughts of the people whom they affected. This was the end of that First Civilization on the fourth physical earth. The sea and the land changed positions. Great heat and great cold prevailed. The remnants of the peoples changed their habitations from the gradually sinking old lands.

For a long period only stray bands moved from place to place. They had lost the memory of the past, and hardships and climatic changes brutalized and debased them. They were without homes, comforts, civilization or government. The forms of the animals had been made from the types of thought of decadent peoples, and the entities in the animals were the unhuman desires of the decadents who were later confronted by them. There were animals that lived in water and animals that lived in trees and flying animals. The shapes of many were grotesque and monstrous. The brutalized humans had to fight these animals with stones and clubs. The humans were possessed of great strength and were much like the animals, with whom they mixed, the stronger of either sex overcoming the weaker. Interbreeding produced mongrel types between animal and human forms. There were some who lived in the water, some who lived in trees, some who lived in holes in the ground; some were flying men. There were hybrids whose heads were set in their bodies. Some of the remnants of these types may be seen today in monkeys, penguins, frogs, seals and sharks. Some of these human mongrels were hairy; some had shells and scales on the shoulders, hips and knees.

Left to itself, the race would have perished for want of Light, but after the thoughts they had had were exteriorized sufficiently, they were again helped by Wise Men. The better kind among some groups of the scattered remnants began to protect themselves against the weather and devised weapons against the animals. They built huts and houses, subdued animals, domesticated them and tilled the soil.

This was the beginning of that Second Civilization. With small comforts the groups became larger. Their habitations were often endangered by hordes of the wild and mongrel men. These they gradually overcame and drove back to the jungles and the waters. By degrees domestic crafts and arts began to flourish. The doers which had been obliged to depart from the earlier men took up their abode in those of the human bodies which were not unfit to hold them. Such doers came in groups, as the different colonies were prepared enough to receive them. In the course of time another great civilization was built up. Teachers again appeared among men and taught them arts and sciences. They led men through strife and war into ways of culture and taught them concerning the doer and the Triune Self and the laws by which the animals came into the world. There were again kings, but they were not divine rulers different from human beings; they were human kings. Variations of the types of government followed each other as in the First Civilization. The high-water mark was under the kings.

The different parts of the earth had again been filled with various races. Agriculture, trade, the arts and the sciences flourished. The people engaged in extended commerce, carried on through the air as well as by water and on the land. A motive power was taken from the air, the force of flight. This force was adapted to carriage through the air, through the water and on land and was applied directly to the vehicles in use, in all their parts. Men flew through the air without any appliances. They regulated their speed by their thought.

There was no machinery. Some of the woods used were as hard and as tough as metals. Some of them were of gorgeous coloring, which the people knew how to produce by directing the sunlight and introducing certain plant food into the growing tree. Some among the people could make diminutive plants to grow as large as they wanted them. Metals were worked not by heat but by sound, and so developed an unbreakable temper. People could soften and melt stone and had solid buildings of stone without mortar. They knew how to make stone and to give it different grains and colors. They had statuary of exquisite shape and coloring. Their civilization passed its height and was crushed out, the last state of decadence being the rule of the handworkers. Then came other rises and falls of various peoples in different parts of the earth. Continents were born and destroyed and others rose. The decline of the civilization as a whole was steady, though there were many local revivals, each followed by a relapse.

With each decline of the people came a change in the animal forms, due to the thoughts that gave them their shapes. There were huge mammals that flew through the air, and large fish that could fly for long distances. At last earthquakes split the outer crust of the earth, flames and steam issued and the water sucked in the land with its people. The water was churned hot over a large part of the earth. That Second Civilization was wiped out and only remnants of the people survived here and there.

Then came a Third Civilization. Stray herds of hardly human creatures ranged over portions of the newly risen lands, skirted the deserts and inhabited the dense growth of marshes and forests. They were the rude remnants of the glorious civilizations which had preceded, but they bore no trace of their past.

There also came additions of peoples from inside the crust of the earth. Some were descendants of people who had sought refuge there from the corruption under the rule of the handworkers, had escaped the cataclysm on the outer crust and had increased in numbers. Others were those who had fled from an inner earth toward the outer crust. They were the descendants of those who had failed, who had lost their perfect bodies and had taken the path of death and re-existence. As these people increased in number they were segregated and were gathered in communities, and in time were driven by fires and floods to the outer crust. There they were barbarian tribes like those who had survived.

The senses of all these inhabitants were as keen as those of animals and they could climb, burrow and swim as easily as the animals. They could defend themselves and escape as well in the water as on the land. They knew of no houses, but lived in caves, in burrows, under rocks and in hollow trees of enormous size. Their prodigious strength and cunning made them the equals of animals in fight. Some tribes developed claws; some used as protection a tree bark which was simple, strong and impenetrable to tooth and claw. In the course of time their cunning increased, but they were unable to make fire or implements. They used stones or clubs or strong bones as weapons. They had no orderly language, but articulated sounds, which they had no difficulty in understanding.

However, some of the better kind of doers had been led to safety chambers in the interior of the earth crust, where they propagated and continued to live through those ages. They came out, subdued the savages and taught them husbandry, the working of woods, metals and stones and weaving of grasses. At first there was very little land. As the population increased, they had floating cities on inland lakes. Their chief foods were liquids, which contained elements to produce the bodies desired. They could increase the size of their bodies or retard their growth and grow them in the forms desired. They were able to do this from their knowledge of the human type and of the foods needed for the growth of the body. They developed an extraordinary fineness of taste, and could prepare drinks that would put them into ecstatic states without injury to their bodies. During these ecstatic conditions they were still fully conscious and could communicate with others in similar ecstasies. This was a social pleasure. They could mix dreadful poisons and brew antidotes. They traveled a great deal on and under water in boats which they propelled by motive power obtained through the water. They knew how to harden water without freezing, and used the transparent mass to fill apertures and to admit light. They extracted while under water all the air they needed for breathing. They had access to subterranean waterways and to the vast oceans within the earth crust. Portions of the earth came up in continents and large islands, which were gradually populated, and in time their civilization reached its highest mark.

Their houses and buildings were made of stone but did not look like any architecture known today. Most of their buildings showed undulating curves throughout. In building they could soften any material with water, use it in construction and then harden the moisture in it, so that it would remain solid. Many buildings were made of a sort of grass or pulp. The buildings were not tall; few exceeded four stories in height, but they were spacious. On the roofs and from the sides, out of the grass and pulp, grew lovely flowers and vines. The people had a skill for growing their plants and flowers in strange shapes. They domesticated aquatic birds and fish, which would respond to call. None of these were ferocious.

There were neither rains nor storms, but they caused a vapor to rise from the water or to condense from the air, and settle to moisten the land. They made clouds which, however, did not come from the water, to shield them against the sun. They had extensive commerce and developed home industry and arts to a high degree. The people lived near each other, not separated by great distances. There were no large cities. The people were not all of one color; some were white, some red, some yellow, some green, some blue or violet; and they were of light and dark shades and combinations of these colors. Those who were of any of these colors were distinct races, the shadings were due to a mixture of races. The political institutions were the same as they had been during the Second Civilization. There were kings, then followed aristocracies, then bureaucrats and traders, and then came misrule and general corruption with the aid of the servants, but an oligarchy of some sort ruled always.

While the rise of the First and Second Civilizations had been steady and their decline proceeded amidst lesser falls and subsequent recoveries, the Third rose to its zenith, not steadily but through lesser rises and falls and then became decadent and went on towards total extinction as had the preceding ones, during the rises and falls of lesser races. The Third Civilization lasted through unrecorded ages and flourished on many waters and lands, which changed their positions after the various periods of decadence, when the thoughts of the people brought about the changes and upheavals.

A large number of the land animals had fins and scales, and could live in the water. The feet of many were webbed. During the long periods of obscurity between the rise and fall of peoples, the forms of animals changed. The types expressed the thoughts of the peoples, and the natures of the animals were harmless, stolid or ferocious, depending upon the doers from which they came.

This Civilization was wiped out by water. Great waves engulfed it and every vestige of it was effaced.

SECTION 11

A Fourth Civilization. Wise men. Rises and falls of cycles. Rise of the latest cycle.

Then began a Fourth Civilization in the recurring cycles of Four Civilizations, on the human earth. The last one began untold years ago and developed gradually upon a reconstructed earth, and has not yet reached its height.

Some of the decadent inhabitants of the former earth survived the submersion and wandered, sailed or drifted to mountains whose tops were above the water. New exiles came out of the chambers of the earth crust. The absence of comforts, the privations and the hardships of the inhospitable earth separated the tribes and forced the survivors into uncouth savagery. They lived and were like animals. To eat, to propagate and to save their lives took up all their time and effort. They had no fires, no homes. There were terrific storms and tremors of the earth. They were scattered over different parts of the earth and there was no communication among the savage groups. Some were more peaceful than others, but none had a social order.

There appeared then among these struggling groups men of a kind superior to them. They came from the interior of the earth and were of superior intelligence, so that the savages saw that it was useless to fight against them. These men taught the savages the use of fire and how to make rude implements, and established primitive social order. They gave some grains to the rude people, showed them how to grow them and taught them to build houses. These Wise Men were the leaders of the different groups. Gradually they taught the people to domesticate some animals, to weave, to work in metal and to build with stones. After many efforts and failures, intervening ages of darkness and convulsions of the earth, which were brought about because of the thoughts and vices of the people, minor civilizations arose again.

During some of these minor civilizations the people had vast cities which were the centers of great cultures. They had buildings of wood, of stone and of metals. The metals were light but of great strength and were tempered to be hard or soft, to conduct heat or to resist it. A kind of red metal generated heat. The buildings were in the shapes of squares, circles and triangles. Some of the dwelling houses enclosed courts and gardens, in which were grouped flowers, some of gorgeous hues, some of delicate shades, some of multicolored leaves. Some of these flowers of pronounced colors were filmy and light and parted from the plant and floated in the air for days, wafting their fragrance abroad. The people used woods which were as enduring as stone. They could make stones which had the structure of natural stones and fuse the joints so that no seam could be found. They could grow crystals and produce precious stones with heat, by the use of a metal which, once fashioned in a shape, was thereafter not affected by heat and could be reduced only by sound. In their gardens were fountains that spouted perfumed and varicolored waters, which sparkled in the sunlight. Birds hovered, with feathers of delicate tracery floating for several yards about them.

They had underground passages through which they moved to distant parts of the earth within a day; for in these passages they created a current that went with them so that they did not meet the friction of the air. The people were skilled in the making of many kinds of incense from earths and plants. They used the scent of it as a sort of fragrant food and to produce emotions. The burning of incense was also a means by which elementals could come. The clouds of incense were the material from which the elementals first got their bodies.

Some of the people communicated with fire, air, water and earth elementals of the causal, portal, form and structure groups. Each of the classes of elemental beings was of different color, size and shape. Some were in permanent bodies, others were in bodies that changed in shape, appeared and disappeared. Some of them responded to thoughts, others to words or signs. Others obeyed figures which had to be drawn to direct them. The elementals could not think, but did all the service required of them. So the people with elemental aid guided animals, cultivated the soil, reaped the harvests, drove vehicles on land, on and under the water, in the air, on subterranean roads, and worked the simple machines which alone were in use in the arts and industries. Most of the elementals so employed were in human form and could not be distinguished from the humans. In fact, the humans learned from the elementals in workmanship and art and so were able to weave their fabrics as if nature herself had grown them. So they learned the movements of nature in the making of her products and could work wonders in stone, metal and wood. Elemental choristers and musicians furnished exquisite music, vocal and instrumental, melodies and symphonies, impossible to humans and their instruments. Often these elementals were made to recite the history of the earth and of races that had passed away.

All this was done under the direction of the Wise Men, who were the rulers and who had instructed the people in the control and use of the elementals. In this a double purpose was served. The elementals were by association with humans impressed by the reflection of the Light of the Intelligences and their matter was improved. The human beings learned from nature the processes of her workmanship.

Some of the elemental beings thus called into service and some in nature who were free, were of exceeding beauty and loveliness. By association with them the human beings acquired the grace and developed the beauty of nature. To that they added the brightness of their intelligent doers which the elementals lacked. The people had been instructed by the Wise Men about the doer and its duties to the Triune Self, about the nature of the elementals of the four groups, how they worked and how to control them, about how to benefit and help them and about the elemental hierarchies in the four elements and the gods of the elements.

The most advanced among the people were taught about the nature of the sexes; how to conserve and direct these powers in the maintenance of health, the prolongation of life and the refinement of the physical body for future generations. They were also taught the history of the past and warned against being controlled by the elementals, as this would bring about their downfall.

In the generations which followed, the human beings mixed with elementals, men and women united with the beautiful but unintelligent entities of nature and the issue was usually devoid of an indwelling doer. Owing to the ease of communication, elemental gods appeared and demanded worship from the human beings, so the people became nature worshippers. Rites and ceremonies were gradually developed into religious systems. This was a beginning of religions. The people were easily led into the worship of these gods because of the beauty amongst which the people lived.

Four religions flourished for the worship of the hierarchies of fire, air, water and earth. Each religion had many sects, worshipping all kinds of gods, from refined to gross types. The gods manifested in living fire that burned without combustion, in sounds, in sacred streams and pools, in sacred groves, and through stones. These gods were in forms, apart from the gross element through which they manifested.

Nature worship was centered upon the sexes. The dual, fiery, creative and destructive power that is hidden in sex was desired, as all nature depends upon that and can get it only through doers while they are in human bodies under the Light of an Intelligence. This worship was kept on a high plane, but it was opposed to the progress of the doer. At first, long sexual fasts and consecration of a holy union, with a dedication of the incoming doer to the worship of the god, sanctified man and woman.

However, after a time, elementals mixed with humans for sensation. Soon sexual misdeeds followed and vice became general. The bodies of men and women were worshipped by the religious rites in use and these were interpreted in a lascivious sense. Sometimes the male was worshipped more, sometimes the female. The warnings of the Wise Men and their history of the past were forgotten or ignored.

Kings and queens appeared with their courts of luxury and power. Gods became jealous of the worship paid to other gods, just as in modern times, and caused wars. The conquered rulers and their people were made to worship the god of the conqueror, or were exterminated. Such wars continued everywhere. The people were brutalized and by that the gods, who were nourished and kept alive by the people, degenerated. Luxury, power, sex worship, poverty and ignorance came from control by the gods. Aristocracies, bureaucracies, demagogies and tyrannies in one form or another succeeded each other everywhere in the course of time. Whenever a cycle of thought had run its course, there was an upheaval in nature and parts of the earth were destroyed.

In great wars the gods took part and fought with their worshippers against their enemies. Water gods caused the waters to rise and rains to fall; air gods drove back the waters and by hurricanes brought destruction to the enemy; fire gods caused walls of fire to descend and consume, and water gods quenched the fire. The earth gods caused the earth to burst and engulf their enemies, or made thick layers of ice to cover parts of the earth.

All of this was done by human agencies. Elementals during their long association with human beings had taught them the wielding and direction of elemental powers. During the wars priests of the various gods used their knowledge. The gods used the intelligence of the men to direct their, the gods', own forces against the enemy, elemental and human. Wars were waged and elemental powers were used from the air as well as from the earth. Both sides hurled bolts of fire, exploding stones, and directed steaming water and stupefying and deadly gasses; by certain sounds they paralyzed the nerves and shattered the bones. By directing certain currents against the bodies of their enemies, these were set on fire. By cutting off air currents they suffocated their opponents. They conjured up terrifying spectral crab- and spider-like shapes, huge worms and bats, that seemed to suck out the doers of the enemy, while in reality they sucked out the juices of their bodies and left them paralyzed but conscious. These forces were controlled by priestly generals who, in their hidden halls, by sexual practices liberated, and then, by sounds and simple instruments, directed them. The priests, with astral sight and hearing, saw and heard what was being done by their hosts in distant parts. All had the same advantages, but the more skillful could cut off the vision or the hearing of their opponents or introduce optical illusions and could overcome element with element.

As the cycles ran their courses there were many rises and falls of nations and continents. Innumerable races have so far partaken of this Fourth Civilization. There were red and blue and green and yellow races, who came from different types that were saved from the Third Civilization.

All had a rude beginning, all got their start with the aid of Wise Men who came from the inner earth, all received aid and instruction in the inner and the outer life, all had an early period of power, all were charged with responsibility and duties—and most of them have failed. To all have come from time to time Wise Men, who have reminded them of their duties and have sometimes caused a revival of civilization. But the majority of the doers in all the races has failed to make progress.

An important cycle ended with the sinking of the continent called by some Atlantis. This continent, one of many that have arisen during this Fourth Civilization, had its beginning untold ages past and, according to present reckoning, the last of its sinkings took place from twenty to ten thousand years ago and is mentioned by Plato in his Timaeus.

The remnants of civilization in China, India and around the Mediterranean flared out. Then Europe went through a night and an awakening. The crest of the new wave of the Fourth Civilization is far from being reached. It is to be on an American continent; it began with the founding of the Virginia and Plymouth colonies, notwithstanding the behavior of the early settlers.

During the rises and falls of minor civilizations there have been numerous religions, nearly all of them instituted by the gods of the elements aided by the intellects of theologists or priests. These gods desire worship by human doers, because they thereby get some of the Light that is in the atmosphere of the doers. The Light is in the thought. When the thought is directed to the gods in worship, the gods live by it. When the thought or worship is refused, the gods become angry, cause wars and die out from lack of nourishment. Some gods get their sustenance through thought directly, others need hymns, praise, incense, blood, sacrifices or sexual rites. Sun and star worship, serpent worship and other forms of animal worship, tree worship and stone worship, are some of these religions which have appeared and reappeared in the past of the Fourth Civilization.

Doers who did not reach perfection so as to be united with their Triune Selves during the three preceding Civilizations, and who had not destroyed themselves and become "lost" doers, continued through the various races in the Fourth Civilization. They continued through the various ups and downs and took part in the civilization according to the state to which they had raised or lowered themselves by their thinking.

The animals, plants, flowers and minerals always represented in their appearance and structure the thoughts in which the thinking of these doers had resulted. The entities animating the animal forms were such portions of the doers as could not go on through the after-death states. At certain times the facts about the animals were made known to some doers but were lost whenever they would not profit by the information. The types of the animals showed the ferocity, greed or gentleness of the thoughts which were exteriorized in the animal forms.

SECTION 12

The forms of nature come through the breath-forms of human beings. There is progression, but no evolution. The entities in animal and plant forms are cast off feelings and desires of man. The entities in vermin, in flowers.

The portions of doers that today are in the human race are the same doers that were once associated with their Triune Selves in the Realm of Permanence. The doers then created by the word, speech. The forms were spoken into being and the entities that came into these forms were primal elemental beings. Now that the doers are no longer associated with their Triune Selves, the forms here cannot be spoken into being by the power of words. They come into being by physical acts, but they are still the exteriorizations of thoughts. The entities inhabiting the animal kingdom are cast off, sensualized portions of human doers.

Thinking changed the type of the breath-form of the perfect, deathless body without sex to the type of sexual man and woman bodies and this breath-form compels the doer to think according to its type, and the breath-form is the type from which all things in nature come. Thoughts of greed, hate, venom, gentleness and kindliness, change the type and modify the breath-form for the time during which the thinking goes on, as a face is changed by love or anger. The breath-form impresses upon the thought a form indicative of the nature of that thought. A thought when issued has a certain sound, that being the equivalent of a form. That sounding causes physical matter to collect into the form of rock, plant or animal.

The fundamental types came from the early thinkers who spoke the forms and beings on earth into existence, and projections of these types are preserved in the constellations of the stars. In each of the physical earths these types were changed and adapted to the current thought. Though human bodies have been changed by the character of the thoughts mankind has had for ages, traces of the original types remain.

Hunger, sex and cruelty are today the outstanding features of animals. Some, like cats and pigs, embody all three. Some, like cows, horses, sheep and deer, are of a gentler and cleaner type. But all animals are variations of the types of human thought, and are given form by it.

The body and form of man are not the result of an evolution from any animal type. The present form of man is a modification of a type of a higher being from which he has deteriorated. The animals, from mammals and birds to vermin and parasites, all come from man. Of course the thought of man can raise an animal directly into a higher form, especially where the animal is to serve his uses, just as he has cultivated some wild grains and fruits.

The rocky material of the earth comes from nature, but it gets its form from the bony structure of man. Rocks are the skeleton of the earth. All plants get their forms from the nervous system of man. The animals get their organs with their relations and functions from the organization of man. The kingdom above includes the features of the one below. So trees have wood to support them, corresponding to the rocky structure in the earth, and the animals being nearer to their origin have everything that the physical body of man has. No matter what the classification of animals or plants, their forms and functions are modifications of the human body and functions. So plants have stomachs and secretions which make food available to their digestive apparatus. Animals have craniums and brains by which impulses that come to the creatures guide them. All present creatures, including plants, have their definite forms. They are reproduced by seed, egg, spore or cutting, according to the species to which they belong. The design of that form is in the seed, egg, spore or cutting; but there is something else besides the design, namely, the creature that inhabits the body.

All the entities that inhabit living bodies are furnished by the portions of doers in human bodies. There are no other entities. The doers make them, though not consciously, during life and after death. When the doers are making them they do not dream of the possibility that they are doing so. The entities inhabiting the bodies of flies, lice, fleas, maggots and like vermin and pests as well as those in microbes causing disease and decay are cast off sensual effluvia of feelings and desires in living human bodies. Also all entities in plants, except in some trees, are made during life. Flowers are separate entities, so are seeds, and all are produced during life.

Flowers are exteriorizations of thoughts of sexual feeling-and-desire. Daisies, buttercups, carnations and all other flowers show the sentiment of thoughts connected with that thought. There is a rose thought, and its varieties, like the moss rose, ramblers or tea-roses, are variations of that rose thought. A lily thought is different. The reason there are definite types that are held so continuously is that the thoughts run always on the same lines. Sex prompts men and women to use certain grooves for expression, no matter how delicately phrased.

The whole plant is required in order that a seed may be produced. An essence goes out of the sap into the seed, on which is thereby impressed the type of the plant. When the seed is ripened it represents a potential plant. When the seed germinates by moisture, warmth and light, the entity of the potential plant grows into being with the growth of the seed. So the type of anything from a mushroom to an oak is reproduced. The entity that will inhabit the plant is present at the germination and lives through the life of the plant, a day or hundreds of years. The type of the plant expresses the type, strength and endurance of the thought. The structure is taken from the nerve structure of a human. Each plant, each flower, each seed, represents one thought, and the development of that thought. Flowers close together may come from the same individual.

The mineral kingdom is also made by human thought. The matter comes from the four elements and is given the indefinite form rocks have, by a certain kind of human thought. This human thought is characterized by mass, endurance and the absence of a system. The thought is mass thought, not the thought of one person. When the thought is of a higher order it forms crystals. The great disturbances of the settled rock strata of the earth crust that come at the end of a cycle and sweep away decadent civilizations, are exteriorizations of human thoughts. They cycle through the psychic atmospheres of the doers, in bodies or in their after-death states. When the cycle is ripe, agents of the law of thought bring these thoughts together so that they form a huge thought wave. This is released to be suddenly exteriorized in wave upon wave of solid matter and causes convulsions of greater or lesser extent.

The various kinds of vermin, parasites and insect pests are given form by human thought and animated by the sexual energy of man. All the biting, sucking, stinging, blistering insects causing annoyance and disease in man and in animals and destruction to plants, are the progeny of man. They come into being by sexual waste, by union at improper times, by the shedding of blood, by the ejection of saliva and sputum and by abortions. Thoughts of hate, spite, meanness, viciousness, rapacity and destructiveness, give to these creatures forms expressing the thoughts, and desire is the animating energy as well as the nature of these creatures.

So by the thoughts of living men are made rocks and all plants and these species of animals. The rocks remain until changed by other thoughts, but the forms of the plants and animals are dissolved after a short time and are reproduced by thoughts of other living men.

Wolves, cats, swine, vultures, polecats, devilfish and the gentler antelopes, zebras and cattle, in short, all animals other than these insect pests, are human thoughts which are expressed as these forms after the death of the persons who entertained them. It is not necessary that they were issued; that they were entertained is enough. During the after-death states the doer receives its judgment and passes through purgations. By the purgations of the breath-form, it is cleansed and thereby the carnal desires of the doer are loosened from the breath-form and are separated from the doer. Then these desires, which had no form during the life of the human, take definite forms. Sometimes many desires may coalesce into one form, which expresses the dominant desire. The doer goes through other purgations after the separating before it passes on to the beatific state of heaven.

The carnal desires—thus without the breath-form and without the I-ness and selfness of the knower, and without the rightness and the reasoning powers of the thinker, and without the refined emotions and sentiments of the doer—are left alone. These desires, however, are a portion of the doer. They are hunger for food, for excitement and for fleshly lust, selfishness, greed, cruelty and what appears as rage, viciousness, sloth and destructiveness. These desires wait in a layer on the form plane. They have forms, but these are somewhat amorphous, not as distinct as those in which they will later appear. They are desire entities, without a breath-form. They wait until the mating of animals of their own types. They urge the animals to mate at their seasons. They are the driving power to procreate, they cause conception of the new animal bodies, and at birth they come into bodies as the feeling and desire of the foal, lamb, puppy or similar creature. The feelings and the desires that are such animals are of course the harmless and gentle feelings and desires. The entities in swine, rats, cats, vultures, squids, sharks, in all beasts, birds and fish of prey, too, are parts of human feelings and desires which act in the same way at the procreation of these animals.

These embodiments of sensuous portions of human desire must not be mistaken for an embodiment of the doer. Only the grosser feelings and carnal desires of the portion of a doer come into such animals and these portions have no identity as a doer or a particular portion of a doer, or even as a particular swine or cat. The desires and feelings belong to the doer from which they came, but do not sense it. These desires and feelings inhabit the bodies of the animals until death and then go back to the astral stratum, which they leave again when there is another opportunity for them to come into and be the animals. These lives as animals continue until the doer to which they belong and of which they are a part, returns to earth after its heaven period and gets a new body. Certain of the desires are taken into the body of the embryo when the sounding, whirling stream of thoughts finds its exteriorization in a new human body. The others return to the psychic atmosphere of the doer and remain there until they are breathed in again during later life or in another life.

So each person has in his psychic atmosphere a vast number of animals, that is, desires, which will later manifest through him in his moods, passions and vices and after death become separated from him and then will replenish the earth, air and waters as animals again.

This serves many purposes. One is, that as the doer cannot take to heaven the many-headed, many-clawed and many-tailed beasts that are in it and of it, they must be disposed of in some way so as to give the doer a rest from them while it is in heaven, and the desire matter in them can be worked over in new physical forms. While it is of a doer it cannot be reached, but when in animal forms it may be acted on and made to suffer by humans, by other animals or by circumstances; so it carries back to the doer impressions it could not receive while it was in the mass with the other desires. Another purpose is that the animal kingdom may be furnished with entities that give it energy and aid in the circulation of the four elements in the human world. Another purpose is that animals may be used as agents of the law in their relation to man, to aid him or to make him suffer. Another purpose is to show man his desires special-ized in nature since he does not know them when they are mixed and many-headed, while in him. Visible nature is a mirror in which man can see and feel some of the many aspects of himself. In nature he can see his own desires disentangled, separated and distinct in character and form, as a hog or a wolf. Unconsciously people verify this when they call, not themselves, but others by such names.

The animals on the earth differ entirely from human beings, al-though that which animates them is taken from doers in human bodies and though the forms, furred, feathered, scaly or shell-clad, are made by human thought. These animals have no independent existence because they must return to the humans of which they all are parts. No animal will ever become a separate doer, because it is only an offshoot of a doer and cannot be separated from it. Each animal is always connected with a certain doer.

The term "separation" is used to aid understanding and to conform to observation through the senses. The dimensions of physical matter prevent one from seeing that which is not subject to them and which appears separate when imprisoned in them. Man does not conceive forms of finer grades of matter that are not couched in dimensions and he does not even think of things unless they are limited by dimensions.

From the desire that is in a special animal form is screened off the Light that is connected with the doer. Therefore animals have no intelligence, that is, they have no Light of an Intelligence. Instinct in them is the nature elemental, as for instance, the sense of smell, which is most active in them and which leads the desire energy, called the animal. The nature elemental has behind it the entire earth spirit, just as an electric bulb has behind it the power plant and a faucet has the force of the reservoir. Though the great power is behind them, only a given amount can run through the bulb or faucet. The earth spirit has power and it has also Light of the Intelligence which it gets from human beings; it is that Light which is the intelligence in nature usually called God, and which guides the power in the actions of ants, bees, beavers and birds in their building, and which is the instinct of all animals. This is so with wild animals; with domestic animals, especially dogs and horses there is another factor.

It is that the domesticated animal, by direct contact with human beings, comes under the influence of their thoughts and their thinking. According to the typal form of the animal and the kind of feeling and desire animating it, it responds to the thoughts and psychic atmospheres of the humans. For instance, the desire animating a dog form is that portion of a doer which responds more readily to the diffused Light of the Intelligence in the human beings with whom the lot of the dog is cast, than does the desire in the form of a wolf. Therefore also a dog seeks human companionship. The desire of that dog can do no thinking, but responds to the thinking, feeling and intention of his master. So a dog may know the hour or day when his master will come and where to look for him. No matter how intelligent animals may seem, they are not intelligent in the degree of being able to think. They are only human desires and feelings in animal forms, and when the desire and feeling are in an animal form they do not mix with the Light of an Intelligence.

While human desires are in all animal forms, they are with few exceptions not in plant forms and they are in no mineral forms, not even in crystals. However, all forms in the mineral, plant and animal kingdoms are exteriorizations of human thoughts, and it remains to be shown in what manner these exteriorizations as forms are made.

SECTION 13

History of the kingdoms of nature. Creation by breath and speech. Thinking under the type of two. The human body is the pattern of the kingdoms of nature. The intelligence in nature.

Through all ages, Triune Selves have, by the breath and power of speech through the doers' bodies, maintained or changed the kingdoms of nature.

When the doers in their perfect states wanted to produce things, they thought them and breathed them into physical existence. They knew what they wanted, and they knew what they were doing when they thought. The Light of the Intelligence united with the desire of the doer into a thought, about which they continued to think. That thought was a sound, but was not, had not, and did not make vibrations. However, when it passed into the form world it caused vibrations in matter which it affected. This vibrating matter built out the form; then the final word breathed consolidated the vibrating mass into the form of the thinking or of the thought in the physical world. So all things physical came through the power of words, and continued in the world until they were spoken out of existence. They could not decay, could not be knocked apart. A word of dissolution had to be spoken to end their existence.

Today men make the world they live in just as then, but they make it and all things on it in ignorance. They do not know what they are doing when they are thinking, nor do they know the power of their thoughts. They do not know that their thoughts when issued, are issued on the light plane of the light world. They do not know that these thoughts then descend as sound and speech in one, into the life world, where they take matter of the life world as a magnet takes iron filings. There a thought is a sound. It is inaudible to the human ear, but it sounds in the life world, and thereby gives life to the matter it affects. It descends further and comes into the form world, taking with it that portion of life matter. It is sound in the form world also, and makes a part of form matter coalesce. This causes the matter to take a form, expressive of the sound, which comes into the physical world, but is still invisible. Then it passes on to the astral or radiant state of matter of the form plane of the physical world, where it remains on the threshold of the radiant-radiant matter of the physical plane and is ready to be exteriorized in solid matter.

The appearance of the plants and animals depends upon the appropriate season for germination. The thought, which is speech and sound in the different worlds, continues to sound until it is exteriorized. When the time for this arrives the sound compels solid-solid particles to vibrate around and through the radiant-solid form and finally draws them into it. The sap in the plants and the fluids in the body of the animal build out the visible solid shape according to this astral form. A thought of love and a thought of greed are different as thoughts and they sound differently. The sound of the speech which is the thought differs from the time the thought comes to the life plane of the life world until, with matter gathered, it arrives at the threshold of physical life. On the life plane of the life world the sound of that which will be formed as a yellow rose is as different from that which will be formed as a white carnation, as are the two flowers when at last seen and smelled.

The form in which a thought is exteriorized is not necessarily furnished by the same doer from which comes the feeling-and-desire entity that will inhabit the form. For instance, the aggregate of strong sexual desires and rage with an absence of general viciousness may coalesce after death when the separation of breath-form and doer occurs, into a mass of desire that will be made to animate the body of a bull. The body of the bull is made of elemental matter of the four elements, but the form in which it is held is the expression of a thought, which, when it was thought and spoken, sounded as what is visible as the form of a bull. The form fits the inhabiting power of desire.

The atoms known to chemistry have a valence or combining capacity which they get from matter of the form world. Matter of the form world combines matter of the life world into forms according to the combining capacity which the form matter receives from certain characteristics of that life matter. The life matter receives these characteristics from thinking or from thoughts, which can give character to life matter only according to certain types or numbers to which the thoughts belong. The thoughts give the character by unfolding and extending a point toward a circle, (Fig. IV-A).

Men think only under certain types, just as they eat with their mouths and walk with their legs, and not otherwise. The types in which men think come from Universal Types or Points, which themselves are not known on the earth except as the types under which men think. The Universal Types came from abstract Numbers; the only way in which they can be thought about is as two.

Man thinks under a type of two with an immeasurable number of subtypes. All mental activities in the individual mental atmospheres are governed by this type and its subtypes. Every thought therefore that is issued is under a subtype of one of the human types. When it is issued and comes to the life world as speech and sound, it affects matter of the life world and imparts to it the character of its own particular subtype. That matter, when it is combined, grouped and given a character by thinking or by a thought, takes in elemental beings which are then of the subtype to which the thought belongs. What these subtypes are can be seen from the many forms in the physical world where they are exteriorized. They are all subtypes and variations of the type of two.

Two of the subtypes under which human beings think are the man type and the woman type. A man thinks in the type he is; and a woman thinks in the type she is. All their thoughts are according to these two types. Underlying the two types and as a background for the thinking of man and woman is another type, the type of one. This type links the two. It is the secret of their feeling-and-desire or union. Neither man nor woman is able to think according to the type of one, but they think about it. Every time human beings attempt to think in the type of one, they become confused, as when they try to apply it to metaphysical speculations in religions or to think of the two or of the many as the one. All the thinking a human does in literature, business or pastimes, he does from or in his own type as a man or as a woman.

This thinking is related to some zone of the four kingdoms, mineral, vegetable, animal and human. The idea of two is always there, active and passive, positive and negative, right and left, up and down, light and dark, sleep and waking, life and death, good and bad, true and false, pleasure and pain, like and unlike, spirit and matter, me and not me, or not nature and nature. Humans think about two kinds of things only, the things they can see, hear, taste, smell and touch; and the second kind, the things that are not to be seen, heard, tasted, smelled or touched.

Whenever a man thinks about any of these things, he thinks of how he feels or desires about them. He thinks of the feeling or desire as himself; it is he who desires, it is he who thinks, it is he who is—always he. He relates this him to that which is—not him; he does not think of himself without thinking of what is not himself.

The male's thought is according to the type of his sex as distinct from the female. When he thinks of other human beings he thinks of them as men or as women. It is the same with a woman; her thought is according to the type of her sex. She thinks in the type which she is.

The thoughts of men and women are of the type of the one who thinks and affects matter according to that type, whether they are exteriorized to that one or in nature.

The two types, of man and of woman, produce in nature the same two. The nearer the kind is to the one who thinks the more pronounced is the type; the farther the less pronounced. So, plants are less markedly male and female than are animals. In minerals the type can be discerned only as positive and negative.

Thinking and thoughts affect the matter in the life world and cause it to be grouped according to the type or subtype of the thinking or the thought. The grouping is caused by the sound which is the speech and thought, three aspects of the same action. The grouping by number of the particles of life matter produces form in the form world. The form matter, impressed in its structure by the grouping of the life matter, coalesces according to the sound and to the structure of the life matter that carries it. The form matter comes into the physical world, that is, into the invisible part thereof; and the forms, differing in each case, cause the particles of radiant-physical matter to vibrate accordingly and to be grouped into atoms, in the manner known to chemistry as those of the physical matter of the ninety-odd elements. So come into existence all crystals, those of frost designs and snow as well as those of minerals, the plants, the flowers and the bodies of all animals. The circulating sap in plants, the deposits in the plant which make it grow and produce flowers, fruits and seeds, the fluids in animal bodies with their resultant health, maturity and disease, are produced in the same way. Each plant and animal conforms to some subtype of thought. The conformations are directed by the thinkers of Triune Selves.

Two orders of Intelligences, the Thinkers and the Desirers, direct the operation of the law of thought, through the Triune Selves to which they are related. The Thinkers observe the disturbance of matter in the life world which all human thinking causes. They do not watch, they are aware of what occurs. The Intelligences of the order of Desirers work with their Triune Selves in the form and physical worlds. Each of the orders acts in the world with which it is naturally in contact.

As the stream of thinking circulates within the mental atmosphere of a human it affects the life matter of the life world and comes under the notice of the Triune Selves acting there. They cause elementals to group life matter according to the type and character of the thoughts that are in the stream of thinking. Thereby the type under which the thought was produced is expressed in matter. Then disposition is made by the Triune Self of the destination, course and time cycles of the thought. Some thoughts are thus limited to the mental atmosphere of the man, some are allowed to act further upon matter in the life world and later to become physical acts, objects or events.

The Intelligences do not act directly; they act through or with Triune Selves complete, and even with the embodied doers. For however imperfect the doer of a human may be, his knower and his thinker always have the Light of the Intelligence and do not act otherwise than in accordance with it. As to the destiny of a human, it is directly operated by his thinker. However distasteful, hard or oppressive the events of the life of a human may be, they come to him through the thinker of his Triune Self.

A part of the thought matter is marked for the mineral, vegetable and animal kingdoms. Of course there are no visible marks, but all is done by instantaneous thinking which produces geometrical symbols, and elementals obey involuntarily in carrying out the directions given them by the points and lines.

Some idea of the accuracy and quickness of the operations by these Intelligences and Triune Selves can be gained by reflecting upon the order and continuity which the physical universe exhibits, from the ocean tides to the structure of a pine needle. A thought is a being of potential power, for each unit that is affected by it has behind it the power of its element, as the faucet has that of the reservoir, and the Light of the Intelligence which comes through the thinker liberates the power. Human thoughts, discordant, selfish, ignorant as they are, but having this tremendous potential power, would destroy the worlds, visible and invisible, if it were not for the control and direction by the Intelligences, here called Thinkers.

The directions which life matter and the elementals connected with it bear, are taken into the form world. Here the Desirers observe the direction given by the Thinkers. The Desirers have to do with the marshalling of the forces and elemental beings which bring about physical acts, objects and events. So they see to it that what is destined for the forms in the mineral, vegetable and animal kingdoms receives its proper form, from the glistening hairs of a horse to the dust on the wings of a moth, from a pine tree to a daisy. They also see to it that the animal forms are animated by appropriate desire entities and that the plant forms and flowers have fitting elementals to inhabit them.

These Intelligences and Triune Selves do not create the animals, plants and minerals; they merely see to it that the types which are in the mental atmospheres of human beings are expressed by forms, which then appear as the outward aspect of the creatures in the animal, plant and mineral worlds. These types have resulted from all prior thinking in all prior lives of all doers in human bodies. A type is made of matter of the life world.

A type is the emblem of the sum of a variety of thinking that has been done in the past, but it is abstract, invisible and has no form. Types are summarized records of forms, of thinking and of activities of intelligent-matter in nature-matter. They are the working out in different ages of some of the twelve points of the circle, according to which all thinking must be done. The circle and the twelve points are the ultimate source of all types, (Fig. I-A). The types are exteriorized by the coordinate action of the Light of the Intelligence, the mental atmosphere and the thoughts in it, the aia and the breath-form and the process of generation.

The human body itself is an exteriorization of types in the mental atmospheres, and projects and is the source and pattern of the mineral, plant and animal kingdoms. From the body as a pattern elementals body forth these types, comparatively few in number, as the earth and its myriad of animals, plants and minerals. The forms are then filled out and energized by desires of human beings and are given instinct by Light of the Intelligence that has gone into nature and which is the intelligence that guides nature and is commonly called God.

Human beings are not conscious of these processes, which are carried on by parts of their mental, psychic and physical organizations, any more than they are conscious of the processes of sight or digestion. Some of these processes go on after the death of the physical body.

SECTION 14

This is an age of thought. Schools of thought.

The present is a new wave in the Fourth Civilization. The crest should carry humanity higher than any of the former waves of this Civilization, which has existed for untold years and has seen the rise and fall of many such waves. Each of these waves has lifted and buried continents and nations. During some of these cycles humanity reached an incomparably higher material development than it has now, but it was unable to hold what it had achieved. Power, luxury, sensuality and dishonesty perverted thinking and so caused humanity to lose what it had. The doers who brought about the downfalls have had to pay dearly for them and most of them will continue the paying.

The last great cycle began in the East, rose to its height in early Atlantis and ended in the West, far out in the Pacific. Chinese, Indian, Mesopotamian, Egyptian and Mediterranean civilizations, as well as those in South, Central and North America, are as ripples on that wave.

A new vast cyclic wave has set in in the West. It began in Massachusetts with the Plymouth colony. In America a new race will be founded. What its type will be cannot yet be discerned. So far the history of the people who have lived there has been far from ideal. Their individual conduct, with comparatively few exceptions, has not differed much from that of people elsewhere, except in so far as pioneer conditions, a rich virgin country, and, since 1776, the form of government, a republic, have given more freedom and opportunity for lawlessness. Still, the promise of a great future is there. Many of the old doers that took part in building prior periods of achievement are coming in. In North America there is such an appearance of inventive genius as is shown nowhere else, a readiness to turn hand and brain to anything, and an occasional idealism; and in the United States have sprung up new schools of thought, which thence have spread over the world.

This is an age of thought. Each century has had its thinkers, but the world is entering upon a period in which thinking and thoughts will be recognized. Their reality, their nature and their power over matter will be more and more appreciated. This new era has changed the conditions for insight, growth and mental development. The limitations of thinking, the types under which it is done, the grooves in which it runs, and its results will be perceived. This will be the season for the appearance of new mental activities. Religions used to be emotional and tolerated no thinking about their doctrines, unless it was done by their own theologists; but now new cults, having a little to do with thinking, are finding followers. Gradually religions will become more mental and reasonable, as doers become more concerned with thought.

The life world is the realm of thinking, that is, of the thinking that is done definitely. Passive thinking is not in the life world but on the life and form planes of the physical world. When one gets into the life world by his thinking he will be on a road and will be obliged to follow it. That road has been made by thinkers in the past. To strike out on a new road one must be an independent thinker, that is, have originality and the bearings in himself to take him to the goal of his thinking, together with the determination to get there. There have been only a few such thinkers; they have made the roads on which the thinking of others follows.

From the number of books written on philosophies, religions, arts and sciences, it might seem that if books were the representatives of thoughts the life world must be filled with roads. However, this is not so. Human thought usually goes only to the life plane of the physical world. There are highways and beaten roads, as well as paths where here and there some independent thinker has made a trail. As the paths are traveled they become more distinct and extended. When an independent thinker attempts a system of thinking and puts his thoughts into words, his trail becomes a road and can be traveled at any time by him or by other thinkers who are able to follow. At times some thinker tries to think into the unknown regions on either side of the road, but the effort is too great; he becomes confused and is glad to get back to the beaten track, if possible. As long as these main traveled roads are followed men think over the same routine thoughts.

With the incoming of the new cycle many new schools of thought have begun to flourish. Among the multitude of modern movements are Modern Mysticism, Nature Worship, Spiritism, Christian Science, the Eastern Movement, Hypnotism, Self-suggestion, Pranayama, and Theosophy. Each of these is old in its essential teaching and is an old road, but is new in its presentation as a modern school. Each has its good and its bad aspects; in some the good predominates, in some the evil. The coming in sight of these movements is the mental result of the past and the destiny of the present; the manner in which they are received will be a large factor in determining the mental destiny of the coming race. If the wrong in any of these movements is sanctioned and carried into the future, it will be there exteriorized; if these movements are condemned and not accepted when found wrong, many possible difficulties of the approaching age will be removed.

SECTION 15

Mysticism.

Mysticism is an old practice in religions. Buddhist, Sufi and Christian mystics and mystics who are not followers of any religion seek to get what they call Truth or God, by subduing the body, overcoming the passions and engaging in a life of mystical meditations. Without priestly intermediaries they seek a direct personal communion with God.

Mystics usually hold the carnal body to be a hindrance to their seeing God and so seek to quiet it. They try to rise by interior processes of exaltation to ecstasy. When they are with God, as they call it, they have beatific visions and enjoy the rarest delights. They arrive at this state by what they call meditation, which is really suppressing their thinking. By the passive mental attitude, which is their kind of meditation, they would exalt the doer to the position of the knower and obscure the I-ness or identity of the knower in the ecstasy of feeling; this they call being in the presence of God, union with God, absorption in God. This state is one of experiencing; it is not one of learning or of knowing. It is only exalted feeling, though superphysical. Mystics believe that such "union with God" is the highest "spiritual" state which can be attained. They are mistaken; for the highest ecstasy reached by their kind of meditation is only psychic and not noetic. It has to do with feeling, and usually feeling that is concerned with the senses, such as visions or hearing celestial music. Their periods of ecstasy are followed by utter depression. When they have seen God or have had a revelation from him, as they say, such communion does not give them knowledge. It produces in them only a feeling. If they try to express something of their experiences, their language is obscure and often turgid. So Boehme, Gichtel and mystics generally appeal to the feeling, but their words are neither clear nor ordered and do not stand the test of reason. But one who is really conscious of God or as God, that is to say, of the thinker and knower of the Triune Self or of the Light of the Intelligence, is not in ecstasy but has a conscious serenity of feeling and is conscious as having an insight and knowledge distinct from phenomena. He can express in clear and ordered language something definite of the nature and relation of that of which he was conscious.

Mysticism is different from most of the schools of thought and is morally far superior. In what thinking true mystics do, they try to be honest and not to deceive themselves. Though they are in the world they try to be not of it. Many of them are connected with churches or religious foundations. Some lead retired lives; few are active in the world. Indeed the world has not much use for mystic discipline and mystic meditation without physical benefits. The world wants results, and by this is meant quick material advantages. A true mystic does not care for these, but wants what he believes to be "spiritual" results. Religious institutions often make use of religious mystics; they use the power which comes from the "holy" life of mystics, and their atmosphere of sanctity; in fact, if religious mystics were withdrawn from the churches, these would lose their power. However, mystics do not really think, and they do not know;—they feel. They are going through a series of experiences which their previous thoughts have made necessary, and they receive a training which may be of value in other respects. Their thinking is concerned with feeling and explains their feelings, not for the sake of learning but for the purpose of exalting feeling.

There are people who call themselves nature mystics, nature worshippers or nature lovers. They are quite different from true religious mystics. The distinction is that the mystics live in the senses and in the psychic part of the Triune Self, and they suppress the carnal body, whereas the nature mystics revel in the physical body by means of the four senses. Some of them want to "go back to nature" and live as animals do. Others are not so extreme and want merely "a simple life." Others worship external nature as God. With many their doctrines are a cloak for immorality. There is little thinking and a great deal of feeling and desiring, and their thinking is an effort to exalt sex and the four senses.

SECTION 16

Spiritism.

Spiritism, often called spiritualism, was known to every ancient people. It is the mark of the decadence of a people. It was condemned among the ancient Hindus and other Asiatic races. Many tribes of

American Indians have their mediums, through whom they get materializations and sometimes try to communicate with their departed. Spiritism is in one sense the opposite of nature worship. Nature mystics worship the growing, living nature; but spiritism worships the dead and has little or nothing to do with living nature. Spiritism as a movement appeared in America in the nineteenth century, when science was making headway with its materialistic theories of evolution.

A particular lesson spiritism teaches is that death does not end all, that there is a survival of something after the death of the body. This fact was denied by some; but, as a fact, it has overcome objections and contrary theories. Spiritism, by offering social intercourse between the living and the dead, endeared itself to many of those who suffered from the loss of relatives and friends, and in many cases strengthened their faith in a future life. But notwithstanding the lessons it has taught it has done a great deal of harm.

The harm comes from opening relations between the world of the living and the evil or earth-bound creatures of the astral-physical plane. Some of the communications received from the other side have been lucid and even of benefit, but they are few and meager as compared with the mass of useless, vapid and nonsensical trash of the seance room. No information of substantial value as to the nature of the Triune Self, what the Light of the Intelligence is, or the purpose of life on earth has been given by the so-called spirits of the dead. The evil results of spiritism come in making of the medium an automaton which is possessed sometimes by extraneous, low, degrading influences, nature ghosts, desire ghosts of the dead and beings which are mixtures of these two; in causing the idle curious to run after the medium for materializations and tests; and in lowering the moral tone of the persons obsessed.

Spiritism is a thought movement though it results largely in psychic states such as mediumship. It starts with thoughts favorable to spiritistic practices. Such thoughts confuse the mental atmosphere, however well-intentioned one may be. The wish to become a medium often leads to mediumship. This condition causes grave injury to the breath-form and to the doer, as well as to the physical body. At present the breath-form is subject to the commands of nature and of the doer. It is itself a guard for the doer and the body against the entrance of spooks. When the doer desires intercourse with them it willingly makes the breath-form subject to them, and itself submits to them. In doing this it surrenders to these astral things the possession of its breath-form and its astral and other physical bodies. This is a grave matter. The doer can usually regain possession, but only after much suffering and by driving out the intruders. This the doer seldom knows how to do. The practice of mediumship often results in insanity.

If spiritism were generally established among the people, they would set up a religion of "ancestor worship," would become worshippers of dead men's desires, and large numbers would develop into mediums. A channel would then be opened by which the remains of the dead would ooze into and out of the physical world. Through this channel would also come denizens of the form plane, inimical to the human race, bearing lethal influences from the lees of the pools there.

SECTION 17

Schools of thought that use thinking to produce directly physical results. Mental healing.

In recent times a number of movements have come to the fore which use thinking to produce direct results on the physical plane, to cure disease and remove poverty, and in the doer to banish worry and trouble. In all of them thinking is used with the intent to produce directly physical and psychic results in the operator and in others. Some of them have grandiose but ill-defined terms for their doctrines; some have in addition a religious aspect and vocabulary and use prayers to God.

All of them embody in their teachings some truths and a mass of falsehoods, and the thinking in all of them consists in deceiving and being false to oneself in thought. By the use of such teachings persons often attain some of the intended results; sometimes they fail to get them. But whether they succeed or fail, they cannot too long interfere with the working of the law of thought. They can never, by practicing according to these schools, become really freed from disease, want, worry and trouble. These afflictions, because they come through thinking and thoughts, and though they sometimes disappear when they are thought at or against, will return until the thoughts of which they are exteriorizations are balanced.

There have always been some persons who knew of the power of thought, and always persons who have succeeded in life because of the use of that power, even though they did not know much about it. But these modern movements are general in scope and teach practices which are directly based on ways of thinking. There are many of them and great numbers of people join in them. Therefore the manner in which they affect the mental life of the community is a peculiar sign of the times.

The persons in these movements are the portions of doers who became confused in the past, and confused others. Their mental atmospheres are different from those of the average doers, and admit aberrant thoughts without their becoming aware of it. So they cannot distinguish between the real and the unreal, the true and the false, that which is inside and that which is outside of them, and thus they are mentally crippled.

In the past they were adherents of systems that treated sensible physical matter as unreal and looked upon all that was not physical as real, though it was actually a slightly finer degree of physical matter. Their philosophy was a refined materialism. The carnal body, pain, poverty and discomforts they held to be illusions and treated them with contempt. They wanted to ignore the carnal body. Instead of enjoyments derived from sensations through it, they wanted enjoyments without it, through the psychic nature; and this they called spiritual wisdom. However it was only materialism, though more refined than the grossest kind, which is derived directly from the flesh body. They sought to obtain this refined enjoyment through the misuse of thinking, through suppression of thinking, through imagining, and through self-hypnotism.

Today these doer portions are here again, and they suffer from the reaction, which produces in them a fear of disease and poverty while they deny their reality now as they did before. What they then despised they now make the object of life—health, comfort and money. They worship that of which their senses give them evidence. Such high sounding names as God, Truth, Universal Mind, and Divine Mind are taken in vain in their mental service to physical and sometimes to psychic things. By handling such names and mistaking psychic things for noetic or so-called "spiritual," rightness in them is somewhat paralyzed, the flame in the heart flickers feebly in moral matters, and their views as to what is real and what is unreal become still more distorted. In addition to this erroneous philosophy they use wrong means when they try to dispel disease and to get money by statements which are based on misconceptions. So they have a false system; they have made an abnormal mental atmosphere by which they are influenced in their thinking; their thinking is wrong because it is opposed to facts and it is disordered; their thinking is carried on without the usual interaction of rightness; and they sell for money what they should not.

Diseases have been healed by faith ever since there have been diseases. They are slowly developed disorders in the functioning of a physical body and are all exteriorized parts of former thoughts of the doer that inhabits the body. They are the sediments of improper thinking and may be accompanied by pain. Of course one who is befouled by a malady seeks to get rid of it. But the ordinary cures of nature, even if applied, work slowly and often fail. Indeed a disease is one of the last and one of the severest means the law has of enforcing payment and of giving notice that there is something to be learned. So diseases often continue a long time, until the doer has freed itself of some of the impurities they indicate, and usually a last ailment destroys the body. Where so many persons are ailing and racked with pain, it is small wonder that one who can dispel disease at once or even after a while and without resorting to the treatment by physicians, is widely acclaimed. Therefore the institution of new religious movements is often heralded and made popular by actual or alleged healing. Healing is in this way often connected with religious cults.

Mental healing is done by impressing thoughts on the breath-form of the sufferer, and faith is simply one means of doing this. Other means are repetition of words, self-suggestion, willing, that is, strongly desiring and commanding. They are not all equally available or acceptable, but they are effective. Without thoughts and thinking, none of these means is workable; thoughts of the sufferer usually, and in some instances thoughts of another. If the thinking is honest the thought may be balanced and the cure will be permanent. If the thinking is false or dishonest the cure will not be permanent. However, not every person can be cured by mental means. There are some whose destiny will not allow them to be cured. A consideration of the cause, nature, development and purpose of disease will help to understand how futile is the attempt to cure it by mental healing.

SECTION 18

Thoughts are the seeds of a disease.

Diseases are the slowly accumulated sediments of thoughts which have passed through the parts affected. Thoughts which have been at home in the mental atmosphere of a doer, readily enter a body through the openings and centers of the four systems and the openings in the head, and leave these sediments. When these same thoughts are enter-tained in the heart, they play around and through the organs of the particular system with which they are connected. So the old familiar thoughts leave sediments upon entering and again while they dwell in the respective parts.

Once one has entertained a thought, it remains in one's mental atmosphere until it is balanced. While it so remains, it moves in cycles and can enter the physical body when the conditions of the mental, psychic and physical atmospheres are favorable. A thought may be in the mental atmosphere of several and even many human beings at the same time. Mental atmospheres and thoughts can intermingle if they are alike, irrespective of the distance between the people. Life and death of the body do not make any difference as far as the existence of the thought, or the existence of the atmospheres of the doer, or the character of these atmospheres and their attitude towards the thoughts are concerned. When there is a new body, the thoughts which have not been balanced are there, and they must enter it to produce the effects which will later manifest as a physical ailment

A thought is always entertained in the heart, and dwells also in the bodily part to which it belongs. Distance and dimensions make no difference where thoughts and their actions are concerned, because thoughts are independent of dimensions and distance. While a thought thus dwells in a part of the body, it awakens and stimulates it and attracts the blood to it. Usually the one who holds a thought is not conscious of this effect. All he knows is what the subject is of which he is thinking, and the sensations which accompany the thinking. So a person who wants to acquire a piece of land does not know that his thought dwells in his digestive system and excretory tracts. If he seeks the property by fair means the thought will not affect the health, but if he holds the thought of fraud, extortion or oppression, this will leave its mark in that system and may later appear as some affliction there.

Each thought is related to one of the four systems in the body, and when it is entertained in the heart, dwells also in the system to which it is related and more particularly in a special part thereof. Some parts belong to several systems. If the thought is right it brings health; if wrong, disease, and the disease may settle in any one of these parts. In the digestive system dwell thoughts of food, drink and physical possessions of all kinds. In the circulatory system dwell thoughts of anger, envy, enmity, jealousy, revenge and ingratitude, as well as their opposites. In the respiratory system dwell thoughts of pride, ambition, servility, conceit, remorse, and their opposites. Sexual thoughts dwell in the generative system and may be concentrated in an organ in it. That system includes not only the local organs, but also the spinal cord, the quadrigemina, pituitary body, optic thalami, pineal body, the optic nerves and the eyes, also the organs in the throat, mouth and breasts, and it ramifies in the kidneys and suprarenals.

While each of the four systems is distinct, yet they all cooperate in the maintenance of the body. One system depends on the others. For instance, the liver is one of the organs of the digestive system, but the circulatory system is there through the arteries and veins; the respiratory system is there not only because it works through the blood, but because a finer physical air and the psychic breath pass in the airy body directly through the liver as well as through every other part of the body; and the liver acts also, in the radiant body, in the production of sex germs and so contributes to the generative system. All four systems are correlated with the brain and the solar plexus by nerves. The fluids and airs of the fourfold physical body act and interact in all systems. Blood, lymph, nerve fluid and breath go to all parts of the systems. Because the systems are connected and contributory and cooperate through certain parts, thoughts dwelling in one system often affect the others. All are kept going by the respiratory system, which system corresponds to the life world.

While a thought is entertained in the heart, it receives attention from rightness-and-reason; and so is put in touch with the respiratory system. Therefore a thought can be affected by and acted on through the respiratory system. Indeed there is what is called the science of breath, or pranayama, the object of which is to control thoughts through the respiratory system and in this way to effect, among other things, the cure of disease by mental means. As whatever disease a thought may be later exteriorized in the physical world, the essence is the thought. Breathing corresponds to thinking and is indeed the ultimate physical cause of disease. Breathing carries the thought and causes the deposit of the thought through the blood, and silently speaks disease into existence.

A thought that is being entertained is and emits a sound in the life world. The life world, as well as the form world, passes in and through all parts of the body somewhat as the systems do. By a thought these worlds are put into touch with the physical structure of the body. So a thought while it dwells in a part of a human body sounds in a region of the life world, which is, from the standpoint of the physical plane, in that part. In sounding, it speaks. At once the form world in its part that affects the body adjusts itself to the spoken sound. Elementals build form according to the spoken sound; that is, they build the sound into an invisible form. Around and through this form, radiant, airy, fluid and solid physical matter is then carried. The elementals build themselves into the form, which then becomes solid. Other elementals pour themselves in and become the physical sediment of the thought. This is done by the breath and the blood, with healthy or diseased tissue as a consequence.

In the course of this precipitation are built health and disease as the forms in which thoughts appear physically. The thought provides the form and desire fills out and animates it. Just as there are different forms in which thoughts are exteriorized in the body, so there are different desires that inhabit and energize these forms. The desires are in forms that fit them. Desires will fill out any forms made by the corresponding thoughts. Every feature of a face or body has its form, which is exteriorized thought, and in every feature, line and formation, lives desire of the appropriate kind sealed therein by the form from the thought. So, too, a disease presents a structural form.

The physical part of all this is done by the breath through the blood. Blood is a stream in which life by the breath and desire by the blood, are carried to all parts of the body. A part of the psychic atmosphere and its feeling live in the nerves and in the blood. The psychic atmosphere comes in with the breath and goes out through the pores, and comes in through the pores and goes out with the breath. In this way feeling-and-desire swing with the breath in and out of the heart and the blood. In the blood stream are two forms of life, the red and white corpuscles. The red build up the body when they are in the arterial stream, and remove effete matter when they return in the venous stream to the heart. The red are vitalized from the physical atmosphere by the air breath as it comes in through the lungs. The white are chiefly vitalized by the water breath which comes through the pores. They can absorb and kill bacteria and poisons and thus protect the body against disease.

There is an increased flow of blood to any part of the body in which a thought dwells. The one who thinks is usually not conscious of this and does not know what part of his body his thought dwells in. When the thought is proper the balance of constructive and destructive actions of the blood is not disturbed and the sediments of the thought are built into the normal tissues of the body. When the thought is improper there is either an increase in or a diminution of the flow of blood. The increased flow results in a temporary congestion of the part where the thought dwells; the diminution results in anemia of that part. From chronic congestion come enlargements, fibrous growths and other chronic inflammatory processes. From anemia come a lack of healthy tissue, wasting away and a readiness of the body to receive infectious diseases.

Sometimes the effect of a thought upon the body becomes apparent at once. Thoughts of anger may interfere at once with the circulation of the blood and cause choking, temporary blindness or a stroke. Thoughts of passion may use up the body so as to cause exhaustion or trembling. Thoughts of fear cause contractions, inanition or trembling or pallor.

Diseases due to infection are precipitations of thoughts, just as are diseases which are slow in their development. If there were a perfectly healthy body it could not be infected with any disease. An infection can take hold only where a body or an organ in it has been made ready to receive it. Long continued precipitations of thoughts in it make the organ ready.

When these sediments have reached a certain stage in accumulation as well as in development, a disorder will occur. Condition and place being ready, the time comes with the recurrence of the thought cycle. The form of the affliction is furnished by a thought, and this form is energized by a desire of the sufferer. So in the case of a tumor, abscess or sore, the form is always a part of a thought exteriorized, and a desire lives in it. In the case of infections there is the addition that the forms of the bacteria are parts of thoughts of the sufferer, and the spirits, so to speak, of the bacteria are desires of his.

Usually the results of accumulated sediments of thoughts are not manifested at once as disorders. Even if an ulcer or a fever appears or if an infection is caught suddenly, the sediments which permit the sudden appearance have been gradually stored for a long time. The sediments were concreted and collected only with the cyclic appearance and entertainment of a certain thought. It takes a very long time before the sediments of a thought and the disturbances in the flow of the breath and blood caused thereby, will affect tissue so that it becomes abnormal. Abnormality may increase for a considerable time before functional disorder or pain is felt in the part. Often a person in whose body the foundation of one ailment has thus been laid dies of another. The new body may then be born free from any actual malady, but the old diseased condition is impressed on the aia and is carried as a predisposition to that disease. It may be that conditions in the new life do not favor an appearance of the affliction. Then it will be carried as a tendency and its impression will remain on the aia, until there is an opportunity for it to manifest again physically. Then it will be transferred to the breath-form and manifest, first as a predisposition, and then as an established disease. In the aia of everyone are potentially many diseases.

If the history of many an illness were known it would reveal causes and a course with a long continued development having many suspensions and reaching over many lives. For instance, cancer is not an ailment of immediate growth, even if it appears after a tear or at a point of irritation. In almost every case cancer is the slow development of hermaphrodite or dual cells. These cells are in every human body. In fact, at one time human bodies were composed of this kind of cell and they may again become the normal cells of human bodies. But now bodies are composed chiefly of male cells and female cells, while the double cells are few and abnormal, though they are more powerful than the single-sexed cells.

Cancer may be the growth of thousands of years. It is usually caused by sexual thoughts and appears about the middle period of life and later, seldom in youth. In later life a person ought not to entertain sexual thoughts. If he does entertain them at this improper season sediments may cause a cancer by weakening single-sexed cells and forcing them to succumb to double-sexed cells. This little cancer will not be noticeable as such and the person will die of some other cause. In the next life at the time when unseasonable sexual thoughts have this peculiar result, the cancer will be formed again, be more pronounced, a little larger, but still unnoticeable. So the history goes on, a cancer being formed each time at the critical period in life. The last stage is the one in which the malignant growth of new tissue appears, at the usual cycle. Another cause of this disease is selfishness, the kind that wants to eat up others for one's selfish ends. Such thoughts may aggravate the sex thoughts in the development of the cancer.

Cancer is likely to become more frequent in the new age with the development of thinking. On the one hand, cancer compels thought as to its cause and shows that the doers as they develop should stop sexual thinking, and on the other hand, thoughts in this age are affecting the cells more than before. Therefore, the old causes, some of which have been dormant for thousands of years, are now more frequently and readily exteriorized as this disease. Because of the cause and origin of disease, these have a part in the mental destiny of the human.

SECTION 19

Purpose of a disease. The real cure. About schools of thought to banish disease and poverty.

What parts of a thought will be exteriorized as the sediments which are to be the seeds of disease, is determined in each case by the thinker of the Triune Self to bring about a balancing of the thought by the doer and to align the exteriorizations with universal adjustment. Therefore the determination of what part of a thought is to precipitate as a disease is the result of reason and is of far reaching import.

The purposes of disease are to purge the body and the breath-form and to force the sufferer to learn. A portion of certain thoughts is exteriorized as a disease to purge the body, and thereby through the four systems in the body, to purge the breath-form. The purging of a body is accomplished by a process of boiling out, when time and condition and place form a juncture.

The condition is furnished when the gradual development reaches a certain stage. The time is fixed when it fits in with the cyclic recurrence of the thought. The boiling out is what is called a disease. The sores and ulcers and festerings are the visible scum brought out by the seething. Sometimes these outer signs are absent, as in sciatica and paralysis, but the purging goes on just the same. By these processes of disease the sediments are brought out and removed. Sometimes a disease causes death without all the sediments being removed. Then the sediments which remain have to be boiled over again in a succeeding life, until they are boiled out and removed. Then that part of the physical body is cleansed. The breath-form is reached through the system in which the disease appears, by that one of the four senses which manages the particular system. This sense reaches into the involuntary nervous system, where the breath-form lives, and effaces the blemishes on the breath-form as the physical body is being boiled out.

The other purpose of disease is to force the sufferer to learn some particular thing. Ailments are usually accompanied by pain, fear, weariness and despondency, by disabilities of various kinds, by discomforts and inconveniences. All this affects the feeling of the doer directly through the nerves of the body. The sensations give experience and compel observations and deductions. Thinking may result in learning; often it has no such result. In that case the disease will recur and the experiences be repeated until the lesson which the disease is to teach has been learned. Then the disease will disappear and not recur. The most favorable case is one where a lesson is learned when a disease has run its course once. Disease teaches the doer what not to think and what not to do. Its purpose is not to teach the doer what it should think and what it should do.

To cure the pains and disabilities caused by his disease is the sufferer's dominating thought. Until these by-products of disease become intolerable the thought of cure is not uppermost, but even when it is not, it commands attention. This is the reason why schools of thought which offer quick ways of curing disease by thinking, have so many adherents, irrespective of whether these ways are right or wrong and regardless of future results. Yet if the cure is no real cure and the disease returns after a while, or if another disease is brought out when the first one is forced back, and if in each case injurious consequences are added to the troubles of the sufferer, a course of thinking according to the rules of these schools is inadvisable. Why such thinking is to be avoided will appear from a consideration of what a real cure is and how it can be effected.

A real cure is the complete elimination of the disease. This does not happen as long as the impression on the aia calls for the appearance of that disease in the physical body. The impression is called a sign, symbol, seal or signature, and it commands nature forces. Of course it is not physical. Every disease has its seal, that is, it is ruled by a seal. Nature forces obey the seal in the development and course of the disease. According to the seal some of them build diseased tissue and others build themselves into a disease.

It is true that many ailments appear, last for a while, and gradually disappear; but they are not cured. Such apparent cures are effected by the elementals working as the natural processes in the body if it is left alone, or by the use of roots, herbs and other simples, or by the treatment of physicians or by the operations of surgeons.

Surgical removal of tissues or organs may stop the pain and the spread of disease, but it is not a real cure, for the signature of the disease is still on the aia and even on the breath-form. Often surgical operations, no matter how skilfully performed, cannot stop a recurrence. This is the case if the seal compels a continuance.

Nor are medical cures permanent, because they are not real cures. The best that any physician can do is to alleviate conditions and to assist nature in her ways of healing. Whether the physician knows it or not, medicines work because they are elemental forces. When medicines touch human tissues, elemental action is compelled. It may be beneficial, ineffective or detrimental. Even if the disease disappears from visibility its immediate cause, namely the indication for it on the breath-form, remains.

Medicines may be remedial, because of elemental forces in them. These attract other elementals to the affected part, some of which aid nature in re-establishing health, while some drive out the elementals inimical to that part.

Those who are sensitive to nature forces and have a certain aptness can find in certain plants means to relieve afflictions. They make their way over meadows, along swamps, under trees, beside streams, amid mosses, in the clear sunlight or at certain phases of the moon, in dry or moist weather. They gather according to the signatures of the plants, leaves, stems, roots, barks, buds, flowering tips, mosses and seeds. They either use at once or preserve what they have collected. They mix at a proper time and place the ingredients in sympathetic relation, and give their medicines at the proper time. Sometimes they use also in their remedies fluids and parts of animals, and certain of the minerals. Some of those who are skilful in these ways can effect cures which seem magical. This is because of the direct action of the elemental forces in the removal and building up of tissue, and in the relief from fevers, swellings or abscesses, and the healing of scalds, burns, bites and poisonings.

Everything that grows could be used to advantage in relieving ills, if people only knew its signature and how to make use of its magnetic properties. The elemental virtue lies not only in the elementals composing the plant, but also in the magnetic power of the plant as a means to connect that which is to be healed with elemental influence which produces the cure. The meanest plant, or whatever object it may be will be effective or otherwise according to the time and place of its selection and preparation and the time and manner of its application. The seasons and the hours of the day or night have vastly different magnetic influences upon the same remedy, and so the same thing will produce different effects according to the times when prepared. Moreover, the application reaches different conditions according to the season and the hours when it is made, notwithstanding modern skepticism.

The failure of physicians to effect more cures, where these are possible, is largely due to their ignorance of and contempt for these matters. The part that elementals play is not generally known and, indeed, few are aware of their existence.

The most experienced of surgeons, physicians and healers by simples, know that their efforts are only aids to the processes of nature in effecting a cure. They also know that there is no assurance that any cure can be effected. Many times a case which appears plain and promises success, cannot be cured, and sometimes a case which appears hopeless, and where other doctors have failed, is cured at once and with little attention. The one who effects a cure is the "lucky" doctor, the others are "unlucky". In no case can a real cure be had unless the complaint has run its course or the signature of the disease allows the cessation.

A rather unusual and permissible method is that of the laying on of hands. In this as well as in all other healing, elemental forces are brought into play to affect and counteract the elementals making up the disease. Healing by the laying on of hands is the relief of an affliction by the healer placing his hands on the affected part, or on a related part of the body of the sufferer. Such healing can be done by a person whose astral body is in touch with the form plane and serves as a channel through which these forces will flow into the body of the sufferer.

This gift is a psychic power and is often incident to a strong astral body and to personal magnetism. While such a surplus of psychic power and fitness must have been acquired through conservation of generative force in a prior life, there may be in a healer many vices in the present life. In that case he will lose the power sooner or later. Nor need such a healer be free from disease himself. But he must have had and brought over a certain desire to help and benefit others. Sometimes the power to heal runs in families. Sex or age do not matter much, nor is intellectual power required, but the healer must have some insight, be magnetic and be sensitive to certain forces of the form plane. He ought to feel in himself that he wants to benefit the patient and he ought to feel that he is an instrument which some intelligent power uses for its own purpose. This psychic power should not be used for gain.

The way in which such psychic healing should be done is by placing the hands successively in front and behind each of the four sections of the body, and then remaining passive and having the attitude of being a channel for the passage of the life force, through the healer's own fourfold body, into the fourfold body of the sufferer. The healer need not know this nor anything of the process of healing. The healer must engage in no thinking, imagining, willing or believing at the time, because mental activities would interfere with the passage of the healing forces. While he remains passive these forces flow and thereby start the orderly rhythm of life in the body of the sufferer and re-establish proper functions of the elementals in its fourfold structure. The solid cells and organs are invigorated and adjusted to their finer counterparts, the sediments of disease are removed and the tissues repaired. Neither healer nor sufferer should engage in mental activities looking to a cure. This healing is done by psychic means. The sufferer need not believe, but he should not set his will against the method employed.

If a healer proceeds in this way and is merely passive, benevolent in feeling, and does not interfere by thinking, he will succeed. He will not be exhausted though he treats many persons each day. But if he assumes that he himself is doing the healing or if he tries to throw his own life force or magnetic force into the sick he will become exhausted, because he depletes his own reservoir of life. He may also then impart to those he treats tendencies to his own shortcomings.

The wish to be rid of disease is stronger even than that to escape from poverty. Around disease and want and their worries turn the wishes of most people. Even though it is not generally known how and why disease and poverty are exteriorizations of thoughts, it is becoming known that they can be driven away by thinking. In recent times schools of thinking in certain ways, so as to produce these effects, have gained many followers. They have this in common, that they want to produce immediate results by thinking directly at or against oppressive conditions so as to dispel them, and by thinking of and for agreeable conditions to get them.

SECTION 20

Thinking against a disease. Other ways of mental healing. There is no escape from payment and from learning.

All things that are possible can be done by thinking. A thought is a being. Because it is issued from the light plane of the light world and is a sound, compelling elementals in the form world to give it form which will appear physically as an act, an object or an event, a thought can be a being of tremendous power. It has in it the driving power from the doer's desire and perpetuity from the Light of the Intelligence, and with it the elemental forces of nature. Therefore, while disease and poverty may sometimes be banished by a method of thinking, it will be apparent that there must be an unwished-for reaction, unless the thinking is in accordance with the law of thought.

Even ordinary wishing demonstrates the power of thinking and some of its unexpected results. Simple wishing is often indulged in by a person who has no understanding of any precise method of thinking for a definite end. Although the things wished for sometimes come, they bring with them other things not wished for and these often make the position of the wisher worse than it would have been had he not gotten his wish. The things wished for seldom come in the way and under the circumstances he wished. The reason is that he could not see all the factors with which he was dealing when he wished, and that he could not see all the things which were connected with the object of his wish. This is so because the wisher cannot see mentally the things which are attached to and which follow the thing wished for. He is like one who reaches for a scarf hanging from a shelf, takes hold and pulls and so gets the scarf, but with it fall on his head things which had been placed upon the scarf: A wisher does not know the forces he sets in operation by his wish. He thinks only of the thing he wishes and of getting it and not of the means by which it is to come. If he intends to provide for means and contingencies by encompassing many things in his wish, he will make the results worse. For the more he tries to prevent untoward surprises, the more he interferes with the regulation of the universe. He is wishing in the dark and will encounter what he did not expect. However, wishing with its results is an instance of the power of thinking.

There are right ways and wrong ways for the cure of disease by mental means. The wrong ways have selfishness and mental blindness or deceit in their signatures. The thinkers proceed from false assertions and false denials. They assert things to be what they are not and deny that things are as they are. Thereby they try to think concerning facts what is untrue of them. They try to think that that which is real is unreal, and that which is unreal is real. They try to think that a jumping toothache is not real and that there is no such thing as a jumping toothache, that there is no pain in a sprained ankle, that gallstone colic does not mean pain, that a diseased body is well and that generally there is no such thing as disease. Yet they believe that all disease, though non-existent, can be cured by mental means. They believe that they can make disease disappear by thinking it away.

Indeed it is true that disease can sometimes be made to disappear by thinking and under the power of a thought. No matter how much a thought may be contrary to an existing state of facts it can sometimes make the facts disappear.

The thought that there is no disease, no pain, no disorder, but only health, well-being and comfort where disease actually is, will stamp an impression on the breath-form. This way of thinking would directly efface the previous impressions. It thinks directly at them. It seeks the disease impressions out and attacks them. The mental healer is ignorant of the many limitations of his thinking, and interferes with the natural course of events. Sometimes the impression which is made on the breath-form by the thought of the mental healer is strong enough to compel the elementals to build themselves out according to the new impression that there is no disease, pain or disorder, and the mental healer succeeds in making his "cure".

Another wrong way of curing diseases by mental means is to will that disease away. These healers are not as blind to the facts as the first kind, inasmuch as they recognize the disease as a fact.

There are still other ways of mental healing, such as those which demand and those which hold a thought of a cure. Any of these methods may be equally effective in curing certain cases. There are, however, limits. In some cases no cure can be effected. In some improvement lasts only a short time. In some the cure is permanent during the present life. It all depends on whether the law of thought permits. In no case is a real cure effected.

Their own thinking is the active force used by those who cure themselves by mental means. Yet this is as little clear to them as is the process by which they achieve whatever success they may have.

The school of thought to which they belong provides them with a set of ready-to-use thoughts according to which they think. They are usually told not to do their curing in any other way than under the thoughts with which they are furnished. Such thoughts are: that they must pray to or demand of God, Universal Mind, or Divine Mind, to remove the disease; that they are part of God and exert his universal power; that God is good and all-powerful and his goodness allows no place for disease.

Attempts to heal by mental means as practiced by various cults, are wrong because the thinking necessary to bring about the desired results is morally wrong. The thinking involves self-deception, either in denying the existence of what exists or in affirming the existence of what does not exist, and in demanding as one's own what is not his. In his thinking the operator seeks to see health where there is disease and which disease he denies. This is quite evident in the case of some, but less so in the case of other cultists who recognize facts as facts but "hold a thought" that the facts are to be removed by some supernal power because of their demand. This requires the deceiving of themselves in so far as they see and demand as their own what is not theirs. The wrong lies in the self-deception. They blind themselves to what rightness would show them. The wrong is intrinsic and runs through and vitiates all these methods of mental healing, by whatever name they are called.

While it is bad for one to deceive himself intentionally until he actually believes the false to be true, it is worse to treat another by such means. For thereby he teaches the other the practice of self-deception; he interferes with and disorganizes the thinking of the other; teaches him to shut out the Light of the Intelligence and causes him to suffer from the results of the self-deception. He attempts to treat with the delicate and dangerous powers of the doer, of which he knows nothing. He is in the position of a surgeon who would pick up instruments unsuited to the occasion, and attempt to perform an operation of which he knows nothing upon a body which he cannot see.

Disease and want are among the chief means of learning from experience. Mental healers make themselves see and think contrarily to what they have learned during lives. They stifle the flame in the heart, shut out the Light of Intelligence from rightness, and shut out self-knowledge. They postpone their acquiring that knowledge and they work against the development that will end in the perfecting of their physical bodies and in becoming united with their Triune Selves. There are few greater calamities for a doer than such setbacks.

SECTION 21

Mental healers and their procedures.

Poverty, scarcity and lack of physical possessions bring on severe trials. These conditions are exteriorizations of long continued thoughts. Upon the aia are wrought the records which these thoughts worked in, each time they were reissued. From the aia are transferred on to the breath-form all the records from which is forecast into the physical world the immediate physical environment of the body. So the breath-form is marked and intextured for the possession or the lack of money. It has the indications for physical things to produce feelings and so give experiences. The natural results that will come from the future projections of these signs are also indicated, such as pleasure, dissipation, pain, fear and worry. However, it is entirely within the province of the human how he will deal with these psychic results.

If the money sign of metals is on the breath-form, earth elementals will swarm around the person. He will have money, no matter how incapable or unworthy he may be, and especially if he is able, benevolent and good. Earth elementals will predominate in the make-up of his physical body. Earth elementals of the metals will lead him to where he will get them, in mines, as presents, in the business or over the counter. Whether he hoards it or spends it, he will always have ready money. What he touches will turn to money. If the success sign is on the breath-form earth elementals of success crowd around that. His business will be successful. He will be thrown in with successful people. If any enterprise in which he is, is about to fail, he will get out of it in time without knowing why.

If the sign of want is on the breath-form, he will be in want, even when he has also a sign for money elementals and though he does make money. He will lose it or it will not be enough to meet his needs in the position in which he is. If the signs call for trouble, unrest, worry or fear, the elementals project them unfailingly. They build the body and bring on the events which cause these sensations or worries.

The signs are of two classes, those that affect the body directly, like disease or an injury, and those that affect the body indirectly by furnishing the physical surroundings in which it lives. Both classes produce pleasant and unpleasant feelings. The pleasant are accepted as a matter of course, the unpleasant are unwelcome. All are for the purpose of educating the doer. The doer must have the sufferings so as to get the experiences which will teach it what not to think.

The human should use every legitimate means to overcome adverse conditions. In the case of disease the person should consult a physician or a surgeon and then act in the way that seems most reasonable. In the case of poverty the person should think and work to overcome it.

There are schools of thought which use various methods. Some of them admit the reality of disease and adverse conditions and proceed to cure them by directing their thinking against them. They persuade themselves that there is an abundance of all good things in the universe, that they are a part of the universe and so entitled to their share, and they declare their share to be all that they desire. So health, abundance, success, and happiness is theirs if they think it, demand it and continue to demand it until they get it.

All these movements have formulas through which to think at or against that which they want to remove, and at and for that which they want to attract and possess.

The formulas have in common a belief in an Infinite or Supreme Power and seek to attract from that what they want. They claim that they are parts of that Infinite and that its abundance, happiness and success are theirs for the asking and for the taking. They say that by claiming what they want they attract it, that it must come to them, that they have it, that they are it, that they are one with God and are God and therefore are and have all. So they assert that happiness, power, influence and comfort are theirs, and if they see them so the objects of their thoughts sometimes come to them and are realized. Undoubtedly, these various methods are successful in many cases. Why and when and how they are successful, they do not know.

There is a complacency, a self-satisfaction, in their mental attitude which supplants worry and fear, and the physical results, such as freedom from disease and a comfortable living, do often come in consequence of the prayers, assertions and formulas. Desire is no longer opposed by rightness and has its own way. The thinking is free from doubts and the warnings of conscience, and so often goes straight to its mark and accomplishes its purpose, because it is not told that it is false and wrong. So health, success and business acumen are often the lot of the followers of these schools.

There is a limit to all of these results which follow successful desire. When the false thinking has gone on long enough the evil results will be manifested on the physical plane as nervous diseases and insanity, and even as thievery, fraud, corruption and robbery.

There are some truths and good advice scattered through the teachings of these movements. In fact much of their success comes from precepts for silence, self-restraint, resisting temptation and husbanding magnetic force.

SECTION 22

Faith.

Faith and nature-imagination are what counts most in the cures by physicians, by healers who treat through laying on of their hands, by "miracles", at shrines and pools, by patent medicines, colored lights and symbols, by mental and by so-called "spiritual" healers or under cults of Christian churches.

Faith is a kind of belief, in that it is a feeling of assurance of something without personal experience or evidence; but faith differs from mere belief in that trust and confidence are added and that there is no room for argument or doubt. Faith is a kind of doer-imagination, which is the voluntary image making by active thinking. Doer-imagination differs from nature-imagination, which is the spontaneous and uncontrolled play of present sense impressions with memories. The pictures made by the four senses merge on the breath-form with memories of similar impressions, and represent the realities of the physical plane. This new combination is nature-imagination and it usually causes sensation in the doer. Instances of sensations occasioned by nature-imagination are the dizziness and fear of falling, caused by walking over a narrow plank at a height, or by standing on the edge of a precipice or of a high building; the chill that overtakes one who will have to plunge into water; the fear of being bitten by fish in the water; the fear of drowning; the fear of unseen things in the dark. The sensations created in such cases may be without foundation in necessity or reason, but the compelling power is beyond argument. Reasoning will not overcome the sensation caused by nature-imagination.

The power of faith and of nature-imagination is in the impressions which they make on the breath-form. Faith is imagination which comes from the doer to the breath-form and makes its strong impression because of assurance, trust, confidence and lack of doubt. By faith the thinking may be stilled. Right or wrong, wise or foolish, faith has a great power, when it comes to the breath-form and it makes there a deep impression. Nature-imagination, and that may be even more powerful than faith, comes to the breath-form from nature. These two factors, faith and nature-imagination, enter into all phases of life. They play also the most important part in cures.

If it is a person's destiny that he shall be cured, faith or nature-imagination or both will be the means that assist the physician or surgeon in curing him. There are only a few specifics the effects of which are definitely known. The use of most medicines and treatments is a venture accompanied by some hope. Uncertainty is the main feature in the practice of medicine. No one knows this better than an experienced practitioner. The patient will go from one physician to another, from one remedy to another, until the time is ripe and then a cure is effected. Usually the sufferer does not dream that his faith or his nature-imagination is in play.

It is quite different where a healer, whatever his denomination, effects a cure. He also performs the cure by faith and nature-imagination. These are the only two ways in which he can cure. But he manufactures the faith or compels the imagination. In his case they do not come naturally to the breath-form. The wrong lies not in the mere manufacture, but in self-deception and in teaching others to practice self-deception.

SECTION 23

Animal magnetism. Hypnotism. Its dangers. Trance states. Painless injuries inflicted, while in trance.

The cure of disease is the drawing feature in other schools also, such as those of hypnotism, mesmerism and self-suggestion in its many applications. Both hypnotism and mesmerism are in the last analysis based upon self-suggestion. The manner in which the forces involved in these practices work cannot be understood unless the following things are remembered: that the four senses are four distinct beings; that each of these beings controls a complete system and one of the four bodies; that these four systems and bodies act through the involuntary nervous systems on the breath-form; that the breath-form coordinates the four systems and bodies and controls automatically the involuntary movements of the solid body; that the doer is the conscious dweller in the fourfold body and is one of the three parts of the Triune Self; that the flesh body has an atmosphere; that the Triune Self has three atmospheres in which its three parts belong; that the Triune Self is as the Supreme Being to the doer and that the Light acts through the mental atmosphere of the doer; that the Light of the Intelligence enables the doer to think; that the thinking is passive or active; that nature-imagination is passive thinking and the doer-imagination is active thinking; that these two kinds of thinking leave their mark on the breath-form and cause all physical actions and states of the body, including its disease or health.

Hypnotism is a means by which one person gets control over the solid and the three inner bodies, the senses, the breath-form and the doer in another. The state of the subject is called hypnosis, hypnotic sleep or mesmeric sleep, from a condition which resembles natural sleep. While in this artificial sleep, the subject is as though he were in a dream or in deep sleep. He is not conscious as in the waking state, and the nerves through which rightness and reason are related are almost paralyzed. He is not aware of what is going on around him any more than if he were naturally asleep. The hypnotizer has to put the subject into this artificial sleep in order to get control over him. The means he uses are included in what is called the science of hypnotism.

There are three forces, forces of magnetic quality, in the three inner bodies or masses within the visible physical body, (Fig. III), which forces are possessed in some degree by everybody and by some persons can be used as a hypnotic power. These forces have been sometimes called animal magnetism or mesmeric force. They are generated when feeling-and-desire impart their nature to these forces moving in the body and these are united and directed by the breath-form. These forces flow in waves through and around the body in the physical and psychic atmospheres and bear the mark of the breath-form. They leave their impress on walls, furniture, garments and the ground, and are the means by which animals identify a human. They are effluvia that move in curves and waves from the body and can be given direction through the eyes, the hands or words and by forceful desire, sometimes called willpower. The hypnotist projects the force of his own fluid body through his hands into the fluid body of the subject, the force of his own airy body by words into the airy body of the subject, and the force of his radiant body through his eyes into the radiant body of the subject. Then it is as if his three bodies were grafted on to the three bodies and the breath-form of the subject. This mesmeric force has adhesiveness and a quality of magnetizing negatively to itself a breath-form against which it is directed.

If the hypnotic sleep is produced by the use of this force alone, the hypnotist holds the patient's hands while he gazes into his eyes, or makes passes over the patient's body, or tells him that he is going to sleep; or he stands behind the patient and makes passes down his spine. Hypnosis can be produced also by tiring out certain nerve centers in the head, as by letting the patient gaze upon a shining object, or letting him hear monotonous sounds, or having him roll back the eyes until he becomes drowsy, and then projecting the mesmeric force into the inner bodies of the subject. Usually such means to tire the patient and make him dull and non-resistant are combined with the use of the magnetic force to put him in a hypnotic trance, if he submits.

While hypnosis can be induced by the tiring of the nerves without the use by the hypnotist of the mesmeric force, no control can be exercised over the subject without that force. But one cannot be controlled or even be put into a hypnotic state unless he consents or submits.

A hypnotic trance resembles natural sleep. In natural sleep, when the body gets tired, the senses relax the hold they have on the doer through the breath-form. If the doer consents to this letting go, it slips back from the pituitary body toward the cervical vertebrae. Thereby the doer lets go of its breath-form and of the senses. Then the doer no longer has any control over the movements of the body. In a hypnotic sleep, on the contrary, the body is not necessarily tired, but the senses are weakened by an artificial strain upon their nerves. This strain causes the senses to relax the hold on the doer which they have through the breath-form. However, the doer can always prevent their letting go, and that with less effort on its part than when it prevents the body from falling asleep when actually tired at night. In the hypnotic sleep the doer accepts the suggestion of the hypnotist that it is going to sleep, and submits. But it cannot be forced to do this; it has its choice. This is the difference between natural and hypnotic sleep, and relates chiefly to the mechanical part.

As no person can be hypnotized against his will, the fact that one is in the hypnotic trance indicates that he was not unwilling to have the hypnotist use his hypnotic force. Non-resistance by the subject makes his breath-form negative to the magnetic force. The force then magnetizes the breath-form of the subject. The subject is impressed with the character of the forces and of the one who imparts it. The senses and the breath-form are then subject to the force, and the hypnotizer becomes a substitute for the doer as far as the breath-form is concerned.

When the subject is in the trance, the suggestions or commands of the hypnotizer take the place of the nature-imagination, and the four senses convey to the breath-form what the hypnotizer tells them, and not what they would convey under natural conditions. What he suggests to the sight is at once seen and pictured on the breath-form as suggested. When he tells a patient that a chair is a tiger, the sense of hearing conveys that meaning to the breath-form, and that connects the sense of hearing with the sense of sight and communicates to the sense of sight, by the sensory nerves of sight, the meaning of tiger. The sense of sight by its motor nerve sends back to the breath-form the picture of a tiger. In every case the breath-form receives the impression of the suggestion as made, and communicates the meaning of it to the proper sense by the sensory nerves of that sense; and only when the motor nerves of the sense have sent the impression back to the breath-form, does the subject see, hear, taste, smell or contact the suggested object. The whole process is instantaneous, quicker than lightning. In this way sounds are heard, flavors tasted, odors smelled, by way of the three inner bodies and the breath-form, exactly as they are suggested.

Sight, hearing, tasting, and contacting by smell may be dulled or sharpened to an extraordinary degree according to an order coming through the breath-form. The workings of the four systems can be accelerated or slowed, impaired or increased. So breathing can be made deeper, the circulation stimulated and digestion made more active according to the orders given to the senses by the breath-form upon the receipt of impressions from the hypnotizer. The involuntary sense impressions and involuntary movements of the systems in the body are then due to the reaction of the breath-form to nature-imagination compelled by the hypnotizer. On the other hand voluntary movements of the body, and feelings and desires and thinking are due to doer-imagination upon orders conveyed to the doer by the breath-form on hearing the suggestion, and then imaged back upon the breath-form by the doer.

When the hypnotizer tells the subject that the chair is a tiger and nature-imagination has impressed the picture on the breath-form, the breath-form conveys to feeling the impression of tiger. The panting breath, the red tongue, the long teeth, the glaring eyes, are produced and terror is depicted on the features of the subject.

The terror is felt according to the previous impressions on the breath-form by "tiger" and what it connotes. The feeling passed on through desire and by that to rightness starts mental activities as to what movements to make, whether to run, climb, fight or submit. The character of the patient will determine this, unless the hypnotizer tells him what to do, because a hypnotizer has control of the actions of the doer's breath-form. The mental activities of a subject in the hypnotic state are automatic and mere repetitions of past thinking. The Light of the Intelligence does not enter into the thinking unless the hypnotizer gives new problems to be answered.

There are two kinds of hypnotic trance, the nature-trance and the doer-trance. In the nature-trance the subject deals with his own or another's physical body. He may when in this state be made to see and describe the conditions in his own body or the body of another. He can be made to see distant persons, scenes and objects and hear distant sounds; he can be required to report the near or distant past, and sometimes to detect crimes. Anything the four senses can do may be done in this trance.

The manner in which the doer acts in this nature-trance is that the doer through the breath-form turns the senses inward, from the outward focus they usually have. The hypnotizer can force this to be done by commanding the doer to so direct the senses or he can direct the senses himself by the influence of his mesmeric force on the breath-form. The outer surface of the physical world is what is perceived in the waking state; the three inner surfaces are the fluid-solid, airy-solid and radiant-solid. They are the replica and the inside of the solid-solid state. When the sense of sight looks through the eye, its vision is limited by the focus of the eye, and it sees only the outer surface. When the sense looks not through the organ of the eye but looks as the sense of sight it can see the inside surfaces of things. The reason the sense of sight cannot see astral-physically in the waking state is that the feeling and thinking of the doer will not let go of the sense and give it freedom to act naturally, so that the sense would focus towards the inside as well as the outside. In fact, in former times, the doer was able to use the sense as it might do now under the direction of a hypnotist. The feeling and reasoning of the hypnotist are apart from the working of the senses in the subject entranced. Therefore the senses in the subject act naturally and both ways.

The other hypnotic trance is a doer-trance. In this condition the doer is in contact with the senses which are turned inward and act clairvoyantly or when it uses the body-mind or when it is by itself in its own state as feeling-and-desire, free from contact with the senses. However, in the doer-trance the doer may get information from the senses, as in the illustration of the picture of the tiger whereby the feeling was affected by the hypnotizer's conceptions and the subject ran away or fought.

There are three states of the doer-trance. The first state comprises all that relates to feeling. When in this state the subject may be made to feel pleasure or pain about physical things or any resulting joy or sorrow. Or a subject may be prevented from feeling any pain while he is receiving an injury which would produce great pain in the waking state, like an amputation or by a cautery. Injuries may even be inflicted without leaving any evidence, as when a piece of steel is run through the arm of a subject and no blood flows, no scar is left or there is only a mere indication of a scar, or as when persons walk over a bed of glowing coals or hold live coals in their mouths, during religious frenzy. The subject may be made to experience the feelings of others as they are going through certain events like surgical operations or dying. Voluntary movements of the body in trance are performed in this state.

In the second state the subject can be made to think. He may be made to diagnose or analyze diseases which the breath-form in the nature-trance has reported, and to prescribe remedies for himself or for another.

While in the third state the subject may be made to consummate certain knowledge concerning the causes of actions, or to reveal something of the past. While the doer is forced back into this state the physical body is rigid or appears to be dead. A hypnotizer is seldom able to put a subject into this state, or if he does get one into it, he is seldom able to get any information. The reason is that the doer is then far removed from its ordinary state and its ways of thinking, and cannot well be held in contact with physical things. It soon becomes engrossed in itself and the hypnotizer will have difficulty in bringing it back to the second and the first state. Usually death follows this cataleptic condition.

When the phenomena of artificial sleep became more generally known in modern times, a few physicians availed themselves of the hypnotic sleep to administer suggestive treatment. A few surgeons performed operations, which under ordinary circumstances would have been most painful, on hypnotized subjects who had no sensation of pain. After the use of anesthetics became common, mesmerizing for operations was discontinued. Some physicians, however, still make use of hypnosis in their treatment of patients.

In view of the power which a hypnotist exercises over the doer of his patient, it is a question whether all the advantages which may result from hypnotic treatment, especially of nervous troubles, will compensate for the dangers of the practices. Of course it is always wrong to hypnotize or allow oneself to be hypnotized for experimentation or buffoonery. But even for medical purposes hypnosis is not advisable, because it puts the patient under the control of another, and not every person who practices medicine can be trusted. However, no one can compel another, even while the other is in a hypnotic trance, to commit any act which the deep-seated moral conviction of the subject tells him to be wrong. The great danger of allowing oneself to be hypnotized is, that once a person has submitted to hypnotic control, others can throw him into a hypnotic trance more easily. The breath-form and the doer are made negative to the desire of any person with magnetic force.

SECTION 24

Self-hypnosis. Recovery of forgotten knowledge.

Self-hypnosis is a deep sleep into which one puts himself intentionally, the hypnotizing and controlling of oneself by oneself. It differs from hypnotism in that the doer takes the part which the hypnotizer takes in inducing the artificial sleep and in controlling the subject. In the self-hypnotic trance the doer and the breath-form can do or omit only that which the doer has commanded should be done or omitted, before the artificial sleep began. During the sleep no other orders will be acted upon. In other respects what happens in self-hypnosis is the same as if it had been ordered by another person.

To hypnotize oneself one must turn back the eyes until the strain causes drowsiness and sleep, or must look fixedly at an object at an angle of 45 or more degrees upward, or gaze at intersecting sets of concentric circles, or must count inaudibly, or repeat a jingle in a monotone, or must command oneself to go to sleep. The sleep so produced is self-hypnosis, and may be induced to bring on a nature and a doer trance.

If one wishes to practice self-hypnotism to achieve any result, he must before beginning the exercises which will bring on drowsiness clearly outline to himself what he, as the doer, wishes himself or his body to do or omit during the sleep. Then he must command himself to so do or omit, while he is in the trance, what he has outlined. He uses his own mesmeric power, and the commands go through the same nerve channels as in the case of ordinary hypnotism. If he wants anything to be done after he awakens, he must instruct himself to use his mesmeric power and to order himself in the trance state to be or do or suffer that particular thing when the trance has ceased and he has returned to the waking state. By forming the plan and giving the order he sculptures them on the breath-form. At the proper time the breath-form will carry out the instructions and compel the body and senses to act as ordered. The breath-form also reminds the doer of the orders which it was to give itself. The reason the doer can compel itself to do in the trance state things it could not do in the waking state is that in the trance it is removed from the physical environment which seemed to preclude them, and is in its own state where nearly all things are possible; and when it returns to the waking state it brings these powers with it, if it is so ordered. Further, in the doer-trance certain forces are generated and liberated in the body; at the time appointed for subsequent action in the waking state they will again be engendered and liberated and will start the body into action.

The practice of self-hypnotism does not entail the dangers which attend hypnotism, as the self-hypnotized doer does not become subject to the power of another doer or negative to the mesmeric influence of the persons it encounters.

Nearly everything a hypnotizer can compel may be compelled by the doer itself. The doer can in this way by self-hypnosis place the breath-form and the physical body in the nature-trance and the doer itself in the three states of the doer-trance. So one can hypnotize himself to do in a somnambulic state things he would not do in the waking state like climbing a tall flagpole and taking down a flag, walking a tight rope or a plank at great height, swimming a river, walking a great distance at night and bringing back a token, riding a horse over places he would not venture to cross in the waking state or performing any physical feat of which he was capable of thinking. If in the waking state he thought the feat impossible, he could not do it in the somnambulic state. He can only do the things he knew of and planned in the waking state. He cannot go to any place of which he had not known. These acts differ from those in ordinary somnambulism in that in natural somnambulism the person does not order himself to do such things, or does not know that he will do them.

In the nature-trance one can do things impossible while awake. So one can hypnotize himself to see distant scenes, places and persons and hear what is said, to stimulate any organs in his body, to retard their actions or to repair lesions. In this way one can in the hypnotic state cause gallstones or stones in the bladder to pass, or stop waste, increase the circulation in any part of his body, gradually straighten a bent or deformed limb or joint, counteract the ravages of disease, eliminate

pathogenic germs, remove inflammation, or reduce, absorb and eliminate tumors. He can suspend animation in his body for a week or a
month, and also produce death.

One who has hypnotized himself to that end, does not feel pain. He
can submit to certain injuries of his body without feeling pain and
without the body giving much evidence of the injury; for instance, a
knifeblade could be run through his arm and the blood would not flow
and the incision would heal quickly and would not appear to be a scar.
He can allow delicate surgical operations without his having any sensations, or he can feel the conditions of fever patients and sufferers from
ordinary or unusual diseases, and he can tell whether they can be cured.
Moreover, one may in this self-induced sleep solve mathematical problems or questions of engineering, or he may diagnose conditions of
disease, in himself and others.

He can in a doer-trance recover forgotten knowledge like languages
he knew in a former existence or the interpretation and pronunciation
of the words in a dead language like that of the Mayas or of the ancient
Greeks. But he cannot acquire any new knowledge while in the trance
condition; he may only get items of information which will help him to
acquire knowledge in the waking state or which he can use in the waking
state.

By self-hypnotism one may also compel himself to do, to feel and to
know things experienced during the trance, after he comes out of it. So
he may instruct himself during the process of self-hypnotization, and
then after he is in his waking state he will record the distant scenes, places
and persons which the sense of sight had shown him, and he may write
down what the sense of hearing had reported. He may write down the
sensations and diagnoses he had made of disease, if he has not already
dictated them in the trance to an attendant. He may go consciously over
the feelings he had in the trance when he placed himself in the state of
persons who had suffered from diseases. He may go consciously over the
mental problems he had solved in the trance state, and he may again
become conscious of the keys and items of information he had in the
hypnotic sleep. He may instruct himself to reproduce to himself in his
subsequent waking state everything his senses and his doer went through
in the self-induced trance.

If he so desires, he will do moral acts and be in states like fearlessness,
equanimity or endurance, and will master his natural feelings, provided
that while hypnotizing himself he directed himself to order himself, while

hypnotized, to be and to do so after returning to the waking state. Any control over feeling in the waking state may be exercised in this way.

The limitations to the use of this power are indicated on the aia by the record of past action. At first it is not as easy to hypnotize oneself as it is to be hypnotized by another, yet that is no reason why anyone should run the risk that is always incident to hypnosis by another person. Attempts to practice self-hypnotism to accomplish self-improvement, physical as well as moral and mental, will sooner or later show favorable results. One is limited in his ability to hypnotize himself by his doubts and fears.

The danger connected with self-hypnotism is that the self-hypnotizer may not be honest and truthful with himself. If he tries to deceive himself, he becomes confused and uncertain in his thinking and in his sense perceptions. He cannot be sure that what he sees or feels or knows is true and real.

SECTION 25

Self-suggestion. Intentional use of passive thinking. Examples of a formula.

Self-suggestion is not self-hypnotism. The difference is that in self-suggestion the doer does not put the body or itself into an artificial sleep. Self-suggestion is the impressing upon the breath-form and on the doer that which the physical body or the doer itself is to be or to do. These impressions are made with the consent or by the command of the doer.

Self-suggestion plays a part in self-hypnosis. It may be intentional or unintentional. People recognize that extraordinary results are sometimes produced by intentional self-suggestion; but the still more extraordinary results of unintentional self-suggestion are generally unrecognized.

Self-suggestion is based upon the facts that thinking is active and passive, and that passive thinking has usually more power than active thinking. Pictures, sounds, tastes, and contact by smell are continually rushing through the senses into the involuntary nervous system, in which the breath-form is. That system connects with the voluntary system, in which the doer is. There the pictures, sounds, tastes, and contact by smell play with the feelings of the doer, and, if the doer entertains them, it thinks them; and they become fixed upon the breath-form as sense impressions. Passive thinking never produces active thinking; but, when long continued, it compels active thinking on subjects of passive thinking, and so ultimately compels thoughts.

Passive thinking is unobtrusive, unobserved, automatic; and it accumulates until its mere quantity gives it a preponderance and power over active thinking. In addition to these features, passive thinking is ordinarily concerned with present objects perceived by the senses, therefore it usually cuts deeper marks on the breath-form than does active thinking, which does not have the same clarity and definiteness, and which consequently lacks the cutting edge that passive thinking has with its clear sights, sounds, tastes, and contact by smell. Other reasons are these: the senses are nearer the breath-form in elemental nature; the senses and the breath-form are in the involuntary system; therefore, the senses are geared into the breath-form and grip it closer than does the doer through the voluntary system; and, finally, the doer has given itself up to being controlled by the senses.

Passive thinking is almost the same as nature-imagination. They are to be distinguished in this way. Nature-imagination is included in passive thinking. It is that part of passive thinking which the present sense impressions take in connection with memories, and in which the senses play with the feelings of the doer more in relation to memories. In passive thinking, the senses, and the impressions which they bring, play with the feelings and desires of the doer under the Light of the Intelligence. Passive thinking often functions as nature-imagination, when pictures, sounds, tastes, smells and contacts call up memories of associated or similar impressions from the past. Such a combination has a power against which reasoning or desiring, even to the degree where it is called willing, does not avail.

Active thinking is the effort of the doer to hold the Light of the Intelligence on a subject of thought presented by the doer itself or by the senses. Active thinking is the attempt to gather Light and then to focus it, and is jerky and spasmodic. This requires the pressure of desire; and with this pressure, active thinking begins and at once makes an impression on the breath-form. Usually the impression is faint because the doer cannot focus continuously and give undivided attention.

The force of passive thinking can be used to remedy the troublous results of disease and want, to check the sort of passive thinking that produces them, and even to bring about an active thinking that will be right. While it is almost impossible for the doer to think out of itself the righteous thoughts that will produce righteous acts, it is not even difficult to lead the doer, by means of passive thinking, into active thinking that will produce thoughts which will be exteriorized in honesty, morality, health and peace.

Self-suggestion is the name given to the intentional use of passive thinking for these purposes. However, all passive thinking is self-suggestion, whether intentional or unintentional. Most of the thinking that people do is unintentional self-suggestion. The large majority live by passive thinking, and this determines their lives. Their lives are carried on without much of an object or a goal, and are steered or led into this position or that condition by their senses and by passive thinking with them.

The four senses present objects to the doer and play with them under the diffused Light of the Intelligence. If the doer considers these objects, passive thinking begins and the impressions become fixed on the breath-form. In this way are produced the notions and fancies which govern people's lives. Fear of a danger or belief in the impossibility of accomplishing a thing realizes the danger and prevents the accomplishment. The use of one's reason or willpower, that is, the concentrated force of one's desire behind the definite thinking, to overcome these notions, will not avail when the notions are strong. This is especially so when the memory of past experiences connected with similar impressions strengthens them.

Persons who are afraid of catching a cold from a draft, from wet feet, wet clothing or exposure are much more apt to do so than those who have no such notions. A person who is afraid of walking through the woods in the night may have his hair turn gray, or may contract a fever if he is forced to spend a dark night in a forest. Fear that a swelling will become a malignant tumor tends to make it grow into such. The greater a person's fear of catching infectious diseases, the more liable does he become to contract one. A person that persuades himself that he cannot remember figures, names or places, cannot remember them, and one who believes that he cannot add a column of figures will surely make mistakes. A person who believes that he can never make a success of anything, disqualifies himself before the start; and if he starts he is practically doomed to failure. One who believes that he is too tired to finish a march, is likely to collapse. One who believes that he cannot cross a trestle or a plank or ledge at a height, is almost sure to fall.

Some people observing these results as facts seek to explain them by theories that there is an "unconscious mind" or a "subconscious mind" that brings about these phenomena. That which produces these results is the breath-form. It is not mind and it is not subconscious. It does not act consciously at all. It acts as an automaton, and manages the human body through the involuntary nervous system by means of the four senses and the three inner bodies.

There are only two kinds of impressions it can receive: impressions from nature and impressions from its own doer.

If the impression relates to feelings, the desires of the doer itself are bound to follow the lines of the impression. It is the same with impressions that relate to rightness in moral and intellectual matters; thinking is bound to follow the lines of the impressions just as did the elementals of nature and the desires of the doer. The markings on the breath-form are lines which compel the doer to follow them in its desires and mental activities. According to these signs, which it has made by thinking, the doer feels joy or gloom, ease or anxiety, fear or anger; and it thinks of noble or ignoble subjects with honesty or dishonesty, along the lines of the signs. In these lines is stored up a power which is the concentrated force of desire stamped there through the breath. This is the power which the mental healers generate and try to concentrate, and which they use wrongfully. Thinking, feeling, and acting are done along these lines. Their power is all-compelling unless there are clearer and deeper lines. Then these control.

Unintentional self-suggestion is the gradual making of these ruling signs without knowing it. The method of self-suggestion should be to make them intentionally, and yet not violate any law. The power of intentional self-suggestion can be called into play easily by using intentionally the unintentional method. The object is to produce passive thinking along certain lines which will make signs on the breath-form and compel a certain kind of action, feeling, thinking and being.

The points of the method are to cause passive thinking by seeing or hearing something which is unobtrusive and is done or occurs habitually, and which for these reasons accumulates or concentrates force in lines which it makes gradually, clearly and deeply. The seeing or hearing to be most effective should be done at those times when it will make the deepest impression, that is, in the morning soon after waking and at night before retiring. At night they should be the last impressions. Then they will be carried out more immediately because there is no interference by the doer with the marking of the lines on the breath-form. The last impressions will guide the thinking in sleep when the doer is dissociated from the senses. In the morning they should be the first, because on awakening the doer is relaxed, the breath-form is most receptive, and the physical body is rested. Thus the impressions are made, as it were, on a clean sheet.

These points are well covered by seeing and reading aloud a written formula or by the mere speaking of a formula every day, as the first thing done on awakening and the last thing done before going to sleep. The reading or mere speaking should be loud enough to reach one's ear, and should be done at least three times on each occasion. The formula should be as short as the object in view permits and should have a measure, rhyme or cadence.

When the ear catches the sound, the three inner bodies and the breath-form are affected; the breath-form is the medium through which the doer feels the impressions. The doer feels them in the voluntary nervous system through the medium of the inner bodies and the breath-form in the set of nerve fibers through which the doer senses. Of course, the doer entertains these impressions, since they are intentionally made, and therewith passive thinking starts. The motor nerves of the voluntary nervous system act by means of the inner bodies on the sensory nerves of the involuntary nervous system, and those nerves, by means of the inner bodies, automatically start the motor nerve fibers of the involuntary nervous system to sculpture the impressions on the breath-form. The transfer forth and back from the involuntary to the voluntary nervous system is made through the pituitary body. The inner bodies are the magnetic and electric matter connecting the flesh body with the breath-form; they are the exact duplicates of the physical body, and they transfer the impressions from the flesh body to the breath-form and from the breath-form to the flesh body, by means of the nerves.

If the formula is well made, the impressions thus engraved upon the breath-form will have the power of sense impressions and will be clear; they will be cut in deep by memory and daily repetition, especially if they are repeated on rising and retiring; they acquire the power of nature-imagination, and as they become gradually deeper they become the strongest impressions upon the breath-form. When this happens the formula has won the day. It will mark out the lines for passive thinking, which will run along the grooves made by the formula. Whenever the person's thinking wanders, it will run along these lines which dominate all else. No matter of what he is thinking, his thinking will be deflected into the lines. Therefore, once a certain depth or clearness of the impression has been made, it becomes deeper and deeper by pulling all thinking towards itself and into its grooves. After a while the passive thinking compels active thinking, and then a thought. The passive thinking suggests, for example, the thought of becoming and being well, and the active thinking generates and issues it. When the evidence of the senses is overcome by the first results of self-suggestion, faith in this method of healing springs up from within the doer. When the power of faith is added, the cure will be surely made, if it is possible.

The depth of the seal shortens the cycle of some thoughts and extends the cycle of thoughts which do not run along the lines of this dominant impression on the breath-form. In this way the firmness of the impression made by the repetition of a powerful formula will further increase. Astonishing results can be obtained by the repetition of a simple formula, provided it starts passive thinking and nature-imagination.

Nature-imagination can be induced by seeing as well as by hearing. Therefore if a formula is written out and read regularly, though in silence, the optic nerve plays the part of the auditory. When one reads the formula aloud so that one hears it, the sense impressions come through the optic as well as the auditory nerve, and are increased in their power to start passive thinking. The best results are obtained when the formula is repeated attentively at the regular times without active thinking and without wishing anything, as such mental activities interfere with the passive thinking upon which the results are based.

If self-suggestion is practiced in this manner, it will change almost any condition of the physical body from disease to health, or at least to a more tolerable condition. By self-suggestion can be prevented, cured, or at least greatly relieved: pains, blemishes, malformations, overweight, underweight, eruptions, inflammations, ulcers, abnormal growths, fevers; diseases of a sexual nature or diseases of the stomach, bowels, bladder or kidneys; or of the blood, heart or lungs; or of the nervous system; or of the eye, ear, nose or throat.

It is not advisable to try to remove one special affliction by self-suggestion, because the suggestion that is directed at that one might cause another in some other part of the body. The proper manner of effecting any cure by self-suggestion is to treat the constitution as a whole. Thereby all the organs in all systems are stimulated to function coordinately for health. When all the systems work together in this way the body will be reorganized for health, and the life forces will play through the body without being checked or over-stimulated. When the body is in this condition no disease will take hold, nor can any retain its hold.

By self-suggestion one may free himself from psychic and mental conditions that are objectionable. So one afflicted with feelings of fear, despondency, indolence, bashfulness or lack of confidence, may remove them and substitute for them their opposites. By self-suggestion one may get himself into a train of thinking which will cure lying, dishonesty, cupidity, cowardice, selfishness and other moral delinquencies. Also intellectual shortcomings can be rectified by self-suggestion; and the power can be acquired to think clearly, to distinguish and to classify; or to abstain from irrelevant discussions and from flighty and loose thinking. Other faults can be remedied such as: disbelief in the doer or in its future; and egotism, that is, the feeling that the universe turns around oneself. Doubt that there is a Supreme Intelligence and law and order in the universe can be replaced by a better understanding through the simple means of self-suggestion.

The essential in practising self-suggestion ought to be a proper formula for daily repetition. The propriety depends in the first instance upon the honesty and truth of the statements made in it. No formula should be used that is not in every respect honest as to aim and true as to statement. If a formula is used that is lacking in honesty and truthfulness, the power may be there, but the final results will be injurious to the body, the breath-form and the doer. Diseases and shortcomings must be recognized as such, and improvement must not be predicated as existing when it does not exist.

The propriety further depends upon the comprehensiveness of the formula. It should cover the body, the senses, the inner bodies, the breath-form, and the doer; and should have a reference to the Light of the Intelligence. The formula should also be framed in such a way as to cause thinking which will tend to balance thoughts—particularly those unbalanced thoughts that are the disease, and those that are about to become a disease. No money or other physical benefit should be received or given for imparting the science or teaching the practice of self-suggestion to anyone.

As an example of a formula to have physical well-being the following may be taken:

Every atom in my body, thrill with life to make me well.
Every molecule within me, carry health from cell to cell.
Cells and organs in all systems build for lasting strength and youth,
Work in harmony together by the Conscious Light, as truth.

The following is a formula for moral improvement as well as for conduct in business:

Whatever I think, whatever I do:
Myself, my senses, be honest, be true.

The cures accomplished by self-suggestion are no more real than the cures made by medicines, surgery, or by mental healing. At best, all these methods of healing by physical or mental means can restore normality for the time during which the signature of the disease or the impediment is weaker than the signature of the cure. Until there is a balancing of the thought of which the disease is an exteriorization, all other cures are nothing but respites. Balance the thought and the disease will be cured.

This system of self-suggestion agrees with the evidences of the senses, is honest in statement, is true in thought, is simple in its application, is free from the taint of money paid for mental healing, enables one to cure himself, follows the ordinary course of human thinking, and reaches far enough to comprise all possible taints not only of the physical body, but of the inner bodies, and the senses, the breath-form, and the doer. Doubt in the efficacy of this method, or reasoning about it, will not prevent its working a cure. However, if one's destiny does not permit the respite which would be afforded by this method, there will come up a conviction that a cure is impossible, or a wish that a cure may not take place, or a belief that the formula will not be effective; and this mental attitude will prevent passive thinking from making its mark on the breath-form sufficiently deep to overcome the signature of the disease.

This system of curing disease is subject to the objection that it postpones the day of reckoning. However, the system of self-suggestion as here presented does not attempt to dodge merited results. It is not opposed to the law of thought; it works with it. The repetition of the formula will lead ultimately to balancing the thought that is the disease. Balancing that thought removes the cause and so cures the disease.

The lines made on the breath-form by the formula will compel feelings and desires to run in the grooves of the lines. In this way the feelings and desires will be changed from what they formerly were. The same lines will appeal to rightness and will compel thinking; and this thinking will be steady along the lines of the formula, and not spasmodic and jerky, as thinking usually is because it is not in accord with rightness. The lines will also concentrate the knowledge which the doer has on the subject of the formula, and will confirm, strengthen and increase that knowledge. So, on the one hand, elementals obey the signature which thinking along the lines of the formula has made; and on the other the doer feels comfort, ease, joy and sympathy, and thinks with clearness, steadiness and probity.

For millions of years nearly all human beings have been unable to hold the Light of the Intelligence steadily on moral, abstract or noetic subjects, and so have been impeded in balancing thoughts. Most human beings are too feeble to generate active thoughts on these subjects directly. It is almost impossible for the run of human beings to think out of themselves the moral thoughts that will produce moral acts, for there is no immediate moral background and no steadiness of thinking.

Therefore this system of self-suggestion is offered to provide a way of passive thinking that will induce active thinking steady enough to let one look into and balance thoughts. When the doer is in this state it is ready to balance the thought which is the disease.

SECTION 26

The Eastern Movement. Eastern record of knowledge. Degeneration of the ancient knowledge. The atmosphere of India.

Another movement which affects a considerable number of people in their mental destiny is the Eastern Movement. Over a hundred years ago scholars translated books of Eastern philosophy and religion for the West. Only a few students were interested until toward the end of the nineteenth century the Theosophical Movement made Indian philosophy prominent. Then thoughts to be found in Eastern literature attracted wider attention.

It was seen that the old Eastern nations had a record about knowledge which the West had not. That record concerned a vast chronology based on astronomical cycles, a history of the world divided into ages, information about the structure and functions of the body, the correlation of forces in man and the universe, and the existence of other worlds within and without the visible earth. It dealt with some of the hidden forces by which the life of man and of the earth functions, with some of the elementals, gods and Intelligences. It is likely that ancient Eastern sages had knowledge of the relation of the doer to its body, and of the control of the body through training and through the use of nerve currents. They knew about "the science of the breath," of states after death, of human hibernation, of mystic trance states, of the possible extension of life, of the virtues of plants, minerals and animal matter in sympathy and antipathy, and of the powers operable by means of the senses of seeing, hearing, tasting and smelling. They were therefore able to change matter from one state to another, to handle forces of nature which are unknown to the West, and to control thinking.

This knowledge was taught to the East by Wise Men in a past age. Nothing remains but a few records and even they are changed. The Wise Men withdrew after the human beings had ceased to follow the teachings. The Wise Men could stay only as long as the people showed a desire to go along right lines. When those to whom the knowledge and the power had been given, used it for worldly advantages or refined selfishness, they were left to themselves. The existence of the Wise Men became a legend except to a few. Some of those who knew the teachings, gradually became priests and developed a priestcraft and religious systems which they supported with the knowledge remaining to them. They transcribed the knowledge into words which required to be read with keys. They omitted parts of the ancient teachings and fabricated additions to meet their ends. They forgot a large part of the ancient knowledge. They suited the philosophy to the environment of the country with its vast mountains, plains, waters and jungles, to hierarchies of gods and devils, mythological monsters and sprites. They fostered superstition and ignorance. They put the four classes of doers into a caste system that holds many persons out of their true class. They restricted the acquisition of knowledge to certain layers of people.

They subverted the philosophy to support their system of priestcraft. The whole course of living and thinking was arranged on a religious foundation, and science, art, agriculture, marriage, cooking, eating, dressing, laws, everything rested on religious observances, which made priests necessary everywhere. The country, India, gradually lost freedom and responsibility. Invasions, internal wars and diseases devastated the land, which was repeopled several times. Each time the people got further away from the enlightened age which had been when the Wise Men moved among men. Today they have only remnants of a past which is greater than they know.

An atmosphere of awe, a pall of mystery, weighs heavily on that land. The people cannot see the real in the unreal. In their effort to escape from the bondage of matter many of them devote their lives to selfish asceticism, which unfits them for their duties in the world. Their customs, observances and traditions hinder their progress. Some doers among them have a knowledge which they do not give out, and they allow the masses to continue in their ignorance and decadence.

However, the philosophy which these Eastern people still have diffused through their sacred books, is more valuable than much of what is in the West. There is much that is erroneous, much that is written in cipher and much that has been warped and a great deal that was inserted to further the policies of the priests; yet many statements may be found in the Upanishads, Shastras, Puranas and other writings, that are of great value. But this information cannot be disentangled from the mass in which it is enmeshed, unless one has knowledge of it in advance. It would be necessary to supply the omissions and to excise the additions that have been made in the course of time. Finally, the information to be of practical use would have to be systematized and conformed to present needs. This would be as necessary for the East as for the West.

The presentation of Eastern knowledge to the West is further made difficult because of the Eastern method of thinking and manner of expression. Aside from the absence of modern words to convey the terminology of ancient tongues, an understanding by Westerners of the Eastern knowledge is impeded by the exaggeration, disproportion, mysteriousness, ciphers, episodes and figurative style of the Eastern writings. The standards of East and West in art and literature are different. The East is weighed down by age, tradition, environment and a declining cycle.

The interest recently created in the West by the revelation of the existence of Eastern treasures of knowledge does not center around the noetic and intellectual features of that philosophy. The West picks out the things that cause wonder, like clairvoyance, the astral phenomena, hidden forces, and the acquisition of power over others. Since the road has been opened by this interest, missionaries have come from the East to convert people of the West. Even if the missionaries come with good intentions they often weaken under the lure of the West. Their appetites and ambitions get the better of them and frequently they succumb to the desire for comfort, praise, influence, money and sensuality which they tell their adherents to overcome. The missionaries have grand titles, like Guru, Mahatma, Swami and Sanyasi, indicating perfection in knowledge, virtue and power. What they and their pupils have done so far does not show that they knew much beyond the letters of their books.

Whatever may be the darshana, one of the six schools of philosophy to which these missionaries belong, they teach what is so foreign to Western thinking that they do not pass the meaning on to Western people. The Western disciples get only a few general and inaccurate notions about purusha or atma as the soul or self, tattwas, saktis, chakras, siddhis, mantrams, purusha, prakriti, karma, and yoga. These notions are in such forms as to be unavailable for good. The missionaries work up enthusiasm among their followers, and after a while they give practical teachings. These relate to their practice of yoga or the use of physical means to acquire psychic powers, "spiritual" enlightenment, union with Brahman and liberation from the bonds of matter. The physical practices hinge on sitting in postures for pranayama, the control of the breath. The wonders of the breath, svara, and the acquisition of psychic powers are the chief attractions of these teachers. However, the importance of the breath merits a consideration in connection with the breath-form and the doer, to facilitate an appreciation of the Eastern doctrines regarding it.

SECTION 27

The breath. What the breath does. The psychic breath. The mental breath. The noetic breath. The fourfold physical breath. Pranayama. Its dangers.

Breathing is one thing, the breath is another. Breathing is the indrawing and expulsion of air into and from the lungs and is only one of the ways in which the breath enters the body. The breath is an elastic tie that binds the physical body to the breath-form. This tie is a magnetic tidal flow of invisible physical matter through the physical atmosphere from the breath-form to the body and back. The three inner bodies make the contact between the body and the breath-form and the movements are kept up by the breath, the breath being the active aspect of the breath-form. The breath becomes nervous force in the nerve channels. There are nerve centers, the plexi, where the nerves are interlaced and from which the currents in them are controlled by the flow of the breath. The breath pulsating in the physical atmosphere enters and leaves the body through the lungs. This entry and exit of air is recognized as breathing. But the breath enters and leaves the body also through the openings other than the mouth and nostrils. The intake and outlet through these other openings, including the pores of the skin, is not accompanied by air and is not noticed. It has as regular a swing as that part of the breath which comes in with the air. There is a center of the breath inside the body in the heart, and a center outside which changes its position while swirling in the physical atmosphere. Between these two centers, the one fixed, the other moving about, the breath ebbs and flows. It enters the tongue and swings out through the sex organ, and when it swings back it enters through that organ and leaves through the tongue. Its path is that of an ever moving lemniscate, the figure 8, the lines of which inside the body are definite, while they vary in the physical atmosphere outside.

At conception the breath of the breath-form acts through the breathing of the father and mother during their union, and then or later the form of the breath-form bonds the seed with the soil through the astral counterparts of the two cells which it fuses. The breath is the force which compels elementals to build out with solid matter those symbolic lines on the breath-form which prescribe the physical destiny of the future human. The breath of the mother activates the embryo directly until a placenta is formed, and causes the fetus to grow. At birth the breath of the breath-form unites with its form and the physical breath begins to swing directly into and out of the body of the newborn. The swing of the physical breath continues until the time of death. Then the elastic tie which is the breathing is snapped. The breathing swings physical matter into a body, maintains the body during life and takes up the swing in the new body, although the breathings are not active between death and conception. When the doer comes into the baby, some years after birth, the swing of the psychic breath continues from where the swing stopped at death in the former body.

The worlds—the light, life, form, and physical worlds—have their influences conveyed to the physical body by the breath-form. Nothing can be built into the body except with the flow and through the force of the breath. The matter of the worlds flows in by way of the senses and the four systems, through the three inner bodies and through the involuntary nerves to the breath-form. According to signatures already on it, the breath-form compels some of these influences to build themselves into the physical body. The breath-form does this while the breath swings into the four systems and bodies. The inflow of the breath makes possible digestion through influences from the physical world, circulation through influences from the form world, respiration through influences from the life world, and vigor and generation through influences from the light world.

The force of the breath affects these systems directly, and merely through breathing air. The nature influences are built in by the inswing of the breath, and what is to be carried away leaves with the outswinging breath. The breath-form performs its functions by controlling the nerves of the four systems. In this way the breath-form controls through the breath the involuntary functions of the body. The influence carried by the breath from the nature-side of the four worlds to the breath-form includes the sense impressions of sight, hearing, taste, and contact by smell, which become memories. The breath so far mentioned is the fourfold physical breath.

Impressions from the doer are conveyed to and stamped on the breath-form by means of the three breaths of the Triune Self,—the psychic, mental and noetic breaths—through the physical breath. The psychic breath circulates in the psychic atmosphere of the human and flows in and around the physical atmosphere and the physical body. As the physical breath is the action and reaction between the breath-form and the physical atmosphere, so the psychic breath is the action and reaction between the doer portion in the body and the psychic atmosphere; the mental breath is the action and reaction between the thinker and the mental atmosphere; and the noetic breath is the action and reaction between the knower and the noetic atmosphere of the human.

The psychic breath is a movement in the psychic atmosphere and is like that of rolling, surging and breaking waves beating in on the physical body, or like a welling-up or sinking-in in the physical body. The psychic breath has one center in the kidneys and another in the psychic atmosphere outside the physical atmosphere, and through these two centers it breathes. This breath has a path which cannot be seen and streams along with and supports physical breathing. In the physical body the breathing of the psychic breath acts as feeling-and-desire. It keeps up the communication between the psychic atmosphere and the doer. The psychic breath carries to the human, through the physical breath, the impressions which the breath-form bears. Feelings of joy or sorrow result as the psychic breath carries the impressions to the doer. The psychic breath flows through the psychic atmosphere, as the Gulf Stream flows through the Atlantic; the stream is different from the ocean, but any part of the ocean may become part of the stream. So any part of the psychic atmosphere may become part of the psychic breath, but at any time the breath and the atmosphere are different.

The mental breath is a movement in the mental atmosphere and is intermittent like air currents. It is the active part of the mental atmosphere, which is passive to it and through which it flows. It is the channel that brings diffused Light of the Intelligence during thinking. It stimulates thinking and increases its power. It is not connected with the breath-form directly, but by way of the psychic atmosphere, part and breath.

The mental breath has a center in the heart and two centers in the mental atmosphere of the human, one of these two connects with the noetic and the other connects through the heart with the psychic atmosphere. It does not flow as steadily as the psychic and noetic breaths. When desire is at an ebb, the mental breath slows down; when desire is wild, the mental breath is agitated. The mental breath brings diffused Light of the Intelligence from the mental atmosphere and so is the means by which thinking is carried on. Thinking is active and passive; and the mental breath acts on and is acted on by both kinds of thinking. In passive thinking the mental breath streams steadily but slowly. In active thinking it is fitful and jerky, made so by efforts to focus the Light on the different subjects which rush in and claim attention. If thinking is continued, the mental breath becomes more regular in expanding and contracting. This is its ordinary movement in thinking. Usually this movement continues until the thinking stops. But if the thinking is so perfected and controlled that there is a focussing of the Light, the expansions and contractions become slower, until they cease; then the Light flows steadily, and something like a focus is maintained. When the mental breath—meaning that of the human—stops, then the psychic and physical breaths also stop. This is an unusual achievement.

The noetic breath is a movement like that of constant sunshine, in the noetic atmosphere. It has a connection with the pineal body, and through that with the genitals in the human; and it is connected with the spheres of the Intelligence. In the ordinary human the pineal body is too inert for the noetic breath to make proper use of it. Because of this state the noetic breath contacts the physical body at the pineal, but does not operate through it. This contact makes the human conscious of identity, of responsibility, of faith and of his conscience. The noetic breath does not contact the generative organs at all. There is in the physical breath only a slight current of it, most of which is turned off at the kidneys and is lost through the sex organs from time to time.

The physical breath consists of a fire, an air, a water and an earth current. This fourfold breath connects the fourfold physical body with the physical atmosphere, and relates it to the atmospheres of the Triune Self. With and through the physical breath flow the psychic, and the mental and noetic breaths of the human, during the life of the human. Though the physical breath ceases at the death of the body the three other breaths continue until the end of the heaven period. When thereafter the doer sinks into a coma these three inner breaths also cease to flow, the three atmospheres are quiet, and the doer is at rest in the atmospheres of its Triune Self. When the doer resumes activity, the psychic breath begins to flow in the psychic atmosphere. This flow starts the aia which starts the breaths and vivifies the form of the breath-form, causing it to glow. At conception the form of the breath-form through the physical breath of the parents fuses the seed with the soil. When the baby is born and the cord is cut, the physical breath enters the heart through the lungs; then it takes possession of and operates the body. In childhood the psychic breath enters the body, and with advancing years the mental and at last the noetic breaths make contact with their centers in the body.

After puberty the three inner breaths, with the physical breath, flow until death. The psychic breath is the cause of passive feeling and active desire; the mental breath is the cause of rightness-and-reason in thinking; the noetic breath is nearly inactive except at sexual fits. All actions of the doer are done by means of these three breaths, and their record is stamped on the breath-form by means of the fourfold physical breath through the fourfold body and the nerves.

In this vast system the only part of the breaths with which the run of human beings comes consciously into contact, is that small part of the fourfold physical breath which enters and leaves the body with the air that is inhaled and exhaled. Through that small part may be reached and affected the inner breaths which there, as elsewhere, stream through the physical breath. They may be acted on by interception of physical breathing, especially when the interference is accompanied by sitting in certain postures and by muttering mantrams.

These practices are a branch of the science of yoga and they have been made attractive to the West through the efforts of missionaries from the East. Here they are used by many persons who do not know what the breath is and how it acts, or the disasters they are challenging in their search for power through their practices of breathing. The functions, the power and inner connections of the physical breath here shown make apparent some of the dangers incurred by the interception of breathing. Indeed, when Westerners, whose constitution is different from that of the Eastern races, practice yoga they often get out of it nothing more than heart trouble, consumption, paralysis, skin disease, increased immorality and psychic and mental derangements, instead of the psychic powers and "spiritual" enlightenment promised them—if they actually do practice pranayama.

Normally the breath flows for a certain length of time more through the right nostril, then it changes and flows evenly through both nostrils alike for a little while and then it flows more through the left nostril for the same time as through the right. After this it flows evenly through both and then again more through the right nostril and so on throughout life. When the breath comes through the right nostril it is the positive or sun breath; when it flows through the left it is the negative or moon breath. The breath is neutral when it flows evenly through both nostrils. All the inbreathings and outbreathings, while the breath flows through one nostril, make a cycle. Several of these cycles make another cycle. These larger cycles make up still larger cycles. All these cycles affect the body in different ways. The breath pulsates around man in waves of varying lengths. The fourfold body is the center of an atmosphere containing breath currents of varying fourfold curves, swirls, ripples, vortices and densities which are working around the body as the center of their movements.

The practice of pranayama consists in part in voluntarily changing the flow from the left or the right nostril to the right or the left, as the case may be, before the natural change sets in; in voluntarily preventing the flow, and in changing the wave lengths. There are many ways; this is one. The would-be yogi proceeds by closing one nostril with a certain finger, then by exhaling through the open nostril for a certain number of counts, then by closing with a particular finger the nostril through which the air was exhaled; then by stopping breathing for a certain number of counts; then by removing the first finger and by inhaling through the first nostril; then by stopping breathing and holding the inhaled air for a certain number of counts and then by exhaling as before. So the practitioner inhales only through one nostril and exhales through the other, and has his lungs filled with air when the inhalation stops and has his lungs empty when the exhalation ends. The outbreathing and stopping and inbreathing and stopping are continued for the time that has been set by the would-be yogi. These exercises are mostly practiced in some posture different from any usually assumed by Westerners.

The object of such exercise is to master one's lower nature and to unite the "lower" with the "higher self," and thereby to gain psychic and "spiritual" powers which will lead to "spiritual" liberation—according to the missionaries. By suppressing and regulating breathing they seek to turn and keep the breath in one or another part of the body for a time and to get hold of the power of the breath. Then they turn the breath into certain nerve currents to open special nerve centers as a lotus is opened. As each of these nerve centers is opened and the force flows through it, the yogi becomes conscious of certain states and realms and becomes acquainted with the gods or powers that act in the forces playing through him. He enters into states of ecstasy and attains superhuman powers. Finally he reaches the highest state and attains liberation. Such in part is their doctrine.

Pranayama, if practiced at all, is safe only for one who is free from vices. He must have health and be clear in his thinking. He needs courage and strength of character to go on. He must have progressed far already in the practice of "meditation," and must seek the external means of pranayama only as an assistance in his progress in raja yoga training. Such a person should be the pupil of a sage who has gone through all stages of pranayama and who is able to sense and to observe all that the pupil is going through in the practices. In this way the disciple will be guarded against the many dangers he must encounter. For the result of the regulation and suppression of breathing will be that, if the pupil's heart and lungs are not strong enough, he will develop a weakness or disease in those organs. If he has not control over himself in the ordinary affairs of life he will have a nervous breakdown. Unless he has overcome allurements of the senses, the sights and sounds he may see and hear will mislead him in the astral states. When the gates in his body are opened and astral forces pass through him, they are likely to burn out or paralyze his nerves if he is not ready.

All that the pupil can do by the physical practices of pranayama he can do more safely by thinking. The path of steady thinking is the only proper way. Pranayama at best invokes passive thinking to induce active thinking to purify the breath-form; and opens the three inner bodies and the inner side of the four senses, which makes the practitioner conscious in several astral states and, instead of liberating him, binds him to the phenomena of nature. Pranayama cannot give any knowledge about the Triune Self. It can do no more than put one in contact with forces of nature.

SECTION 28

The system of Patanjali. His eight steps of yoga. Ancient commentaries. Review of his system. Inner meaning of some Sanskrit words. The ancient teaching of which traces survive. What the West wants.

Different systems of yoga are spoken of in Eastern philosophy. Raja yoga is that system which aims to train the disciple by the regulation of his thinking. Raja yoga in its best sense is a method to clear the mental atmosphere and thereby the psychic atmosphere of the human by a system of thinking.

Patanjali unites the Indian systems of yoga. He is the authority to which most yogis look. He gave a set of rules on the practice of raja yoga, probably the most valuable which have been transmitted on the subject. His rules should cover the period from the purification of the morals, through the various stages of thinking, to the attainment of liberation of feeling from nature. But feeling is by him identified as a fifth sense, and he calls the conscious something in the body by another name or names. Instead of liberating feeling from nature, Patanjali would chain the doer to nature by dealing with feeling as a part of nature, that is, as a fifth sense, instead of as an aspect of the conscious self, the doer-in-the-body. At best that goes only a short way towards the end, which should be union of feeling-and-desire of the doer, and then union of the doer with the thinker and knower. He treats of eight stages through which one must pass. These stages he calls yama, niyama, asana, pranayama, pratyahara, dharana, dhyana, and samadhi.

Yama means morality towards others and cutting oneself off from dependence upon them. It is mastering the desires to be unchaste, to hurt anyone, to speak falsely and to receive what belongs to others. Niyama consists of cleanliness in body and thought, religious observances including the repetition of the name of God, and asceticism. It is a self-discipline irrespective of others. Asana is sitting in a place free from disturbance, with the spine straight and the head erect. This posture allows the breath to flow easily along the spinal cord and to any part of the body to which it may be directed. These three stages are preparatory and designed to free the would-be yogi from worldly attachment, to purify, change and strengthen his body and desires, and to bring his body into a condition where he can engage safely in the practices of the fourth stage.

Pranayama, the fourth, is the regulation and control of the breath so that it flows as it ordinarily would not. It is not likely that Patanjali himself gave any rules concerning this practice; perhaps it was not of much moment to him, any more than asana was. But later yogis have developed a science of the breath including some eighty postures.

Prana means the force that guides the four forces of nature and is Light of the Intelligence tied up with nature-matter that has been in the mental atmosphere of human beings. The four forces are the active expressions of the elements fire, air, water and earth; they come to a human through his breath, which is the active side of the breath-form; they go back to nature through his breath, and coming and going they are guided by prana, which may be controlled by the breath. Yama means a change from the old way of the prana to the new way. The old way is a going out of the prana into nature, the new way is the return of the prana to the human without bringing with it impressions from the objects of nature through the four senses.

Particles of nature-matter come through the four senses and their systems and bodies, the breath-form and feeling-and-desire into the mental atmosphere. There they mix with matter of the mental atmosphere and are affected by diffused Light of the Intelligence. They go back into nature with feeling-and-desire as thoughts. They go through the breath-form, the four senses and their systems and bodies, borne by prana. They go out while a human thinks; thinking lets them out. They are carriers of Light of the Intelligence which they take with them from the mental atmosphere, are the prana that underlies the four active forces of nature, and cause all action in nature.

These particles of nature-matter are what is in Sanskrit called chitta. This chitta is understood and translated as mind matter or mind stuff; this shows that matter in the mental atmosphere is what is meant by mind matter or mind. Chitta is the matter in the mental atmosphere with which a mind works and which it sends back into nature; it is the building stuff of that mind. The Sanskrit manas, mind, is used, even among philosophers, just as the West commonly uses the term mind; that is, the body-mind, not distinguishing between the doer and nature and not knowing what the real Intelligence is, or the functions of its faculties, or the relation which the Intelligence bears to what are here called the seven minds of the Triune Self.

Pratyahara is the name given by Patanjali to the fifth stage, the one of turning powers inward toward the doer instead of outward, and thereby giving calmness to the psychic and the mental atmospheres of the doer in the human. Out of the many ways in which the would-be yogi can use the powers that come with a controlled breath the raja yoga system requires that they be used in pratyahara. This is the suppression of the flow of the breath whereby the influences that come from nature through the four systems and bodies and the four senses, are prevented from reaching the breath-form; the object of this suppression is to prevent interference with thinking.

In pratyahara nothing from the outside can make an impression on the breath-form, and so on feeling. The senses and exterior nature are, thus far, conquered. But the doer can still make impressions on the breath-form. The psychic breath, which is not mentioned by Patanjali, continues to flow and, since there is no longer an interference by nature, develops psychic nature powers, such as to see objects at a distance or to hear whatever is said anywhere. In raja yoga these powers are not turned outward but are used to strengthen the efforts at thinking. The body-mind is used to think of nature only, but inwardly instead of outwardly.

Dharana is the first of three stages in yoga mentioned by Patanjali and is translated as attention, intention or concentration. Dharana he gives as the first stage in active thinking. To accomplish dharana in the full sense the practitioner must have perfected himself in the preceding four stages. By pratyahara he must have removed the rajas and the tamas gunas from the chitta, which is then sattva, and the Light of the Intelligence in the mental atmosphere is made clear. That is, by turning inward the powers of the breath the influences of the inactive form world (tamas) in the psychic atmosphere and the turbulent actions of the mental atmosphere of the human, due to matter of the life world (rajas), are removed, and the clear matter of the light world (sattva) in the noetic atmosphere of the human acts without hindrance. Only when the admixture of tamas and rajas is removed can the chitta, which is then of the quality of sattva, be steady. Patanjali speaks of dharana as holding the mind, manas, fixedly on some particular subject. By mind is generally meant what is here called the body-mind. What he says sometimes refers to the feeling-mind and desire-mind, controlled by the body-mind, but he does not indicate any distinction.

Dhyana is Patanjali's second stage in yoga. It is the continuation of the first stage of concentration and is called contemplation or meditation by the translators. In this stage one develops the power to keep on thinking. It is an exercise of thinking, continuous thinking with the effort to get a right focus for the Light which is held on the subject.

Samadhi is with Patanjali the third stage in yoga. It is translated as absorption or trance. It means absorption of the mind into the subject to which the body-mind was turned, focussed and held. Therewith is obtained knowledge of the subject, that is, union with the subject.

The three stages together are called samyama. Samyama is the power of directing the mind, usually in the sense of manas or body-mind, to any subject and having knowledge of that subject, that is, having it, being it, having its powers and its knowledge, if it has any.

These are Patanjali's eight stages of yoga. He does not explain them in this way. He consolidates the statements about yoga found in the Upanishads and puts them into his system. This was not intended for the public, but only for the elect who qualified under a teacher and wanted to become liberated and united with the "self," Brahman. But what the "self" or Brahman is, is not made clear. It refers to the "universal self" or Brahman of the Hindus.

His system is written as if in a code language. Without a key and familiarity with the philosophy, the words transmitted as the famous sutras, are insufficient to permit an insight into his system. Patanjali's writing is too sketchy to be followed without the commentators. There are ancient commentaries, which modern commentators merely paraphrase without giving much, if any, further information. This much, however, appears, that when the yogi can perform samyama he goes through most of the eight stages which he should have passed through. And it appears that so he obtains knowledge of all things, states, places, conditions, past and future, and has the powers which that knowledge gives him. He is said to have innumerable powers of which some are given, as: knowing the time when he or any person will die; knowing his own past lives or those of others; knowing the motions of the stars and what the clusters of the stars are; making himself invisible, immovable and invincible; becoming acquainted with celestial beings; walking on the water; rising in the air; surrounding himself with fire; prolonging his life to any age; isolating himself and living consciously apart from the body. But this does not free the practitioner from nature. The fact is that he is more securely bound to nature than he formerly was, because every stage in the accomplishments is connected with nature.

Patanjali, however, does not deal with the different minds and the knower and thinker as spoken of in this book. He does not carry through any certain distinction between nature-matter and intelligent-matter. He deals with the liberation of the feeling, which he names "purusha", meaning the embodied portion of the passive side of the doer of the Triune Self, not the entire doer. What he calls manas, translated as mind, he looks upon as connecting the feeling-and-desire of the doer with nature. It is sometimes the body-mind, and sometimes he speaks of manas as performing the functions of the breath-form. This is shown, for example, by the comment made that the samskaras are impressions in the mind stuff (chitta) that produce habits. The two minds, the feeling-mind and the desire-mind, which would give knowledge of the doer, are not mentioned.

His observations on "purusha," taken in the sense of feeling, are usually in accord, but in his book which deals with the desires he fails to show proper ways to change them, so that they will let go of their attachments to objects of nature. He teaches much of the isolation of feeling, which he speaks of as "purusha," but he does not show how the desires are to be changed and how desire is to be isolated. Desire cannot be killed; yet, the commentators say that there cannot be isolation until the last vestiges of desire are destroyed.

The doer as feeling-and-desire is the only conscious self in the body. This is so because nothing but feeling and desire is conscious of the body, or of anything that happens to the body, or of the senses or organs in the body. In evidence of these facts anyone may understand that *you* as feeling-and-desire are conscious of the body and of what happens to it, but the body is not conscious of itself or of what happens to it; and, that while you are in deep sleep, you are not conscious of the body or of yourself as feeling-and-desire until you return to the body and wake up. Further, feeling-and-desire (you), are conscious of seeing and hearing and tasting and smelling; but these senses are not conscious of themselves as organs or as instruments, or of what they are, or of what they see, or hear, or taste, or smell.

But although you, the doer as feeling-and-desire, are the only conscious self in the body, you are not conscious *as* yourself because you are so dispersed in the nerves and blood throughout the entire body that you are unable to collect yourself and distinguish yourself from the body and the senses through which you operate. You are conscious *of* the body and of the impressions through the senses; but you are so entangled, enmeshed, confused, that you are unable to disengage and detach yourself from the things that bewilder you, so that you can be conscious *as* what you are. This is the actual situation of you, the doer, as the conscious self in the body. The important problem is: How to detach yourself from your entanglements and free yourself, so that you will know yourself to be what you are, and know the body of nature to be what that body is.

The philosophy or system of yoga is supposed to show how this can be done. The books on yoga do not state this situation as it is; they do not show why or how you got into the body or how you can free yourself from the illusion of the senses of the body, and they do not dispel the delusion of your thinking with your body-mind. The books say that there is a Universal Self, which they name Brahman; that there is an embodied conscious self (you), which they name purusha or atman; and, that the embodied self (you) is a part or fragment of the Universal Self. They say that the embodied self (you) must continue to be re-embodied life after life until you free yourself from bondage and reunite yourself with the Universal Self.

But if you, the embodied conscious self, were part of the Universal Self, and could reunite with that Self, what the books say would make it impossible for the embodied self (you) to free itself. The teaching given would free the conscious self (you) from gross illusions and delusions, only for you to be conscious in and of finer and finer illusions and delusions. The books do not show what happens when the conscious self is said to be "isolated".

If, as the books say, feeling were a fifth sense of nature, there would be nothing left of you, the doer, that could be isolated, because the desire side of you is supposed to be "killed out, until the last vestiges of desire are destroyed". Therefore, if feeling were a part of nature and if desire were destroyed, and since you as feeling-and-desire are the conscious self in the body, there is nothing left of you to be isolated and freed.

The books do not show what the difference is between the Universal Self and nature; they do not show any purpose in having innumerable parts of the Universal Self encased in bodies; they do not show what advantage there can be in having you as a part of the Universal Self continuing your re-embodiments in order to rebecome the Universal Self. The statement is made that the embodied self (you) gets experience; that nature furnishes the experience. But it is not shown how the experience is really of any benefit to you or to the Universal Self. No benefits accrue to nature; and no benefit to the Universal Self. The entire process seems to be without purpose.

There must have been some reasonable purpose, and a system by which the purpose was to be achieved. But that does not appear today.

Mention of the self by the commentators really refers to desires, higher or good desires and lower or evil desires. They are the "God" and the "Devil" in man; that is, the desire for Self-knowledge as the good; and the desire for sex as the evil. The union, yoga, concerning the desires is, that the lower desires must change themselves and unite with the desire for Self-knowledge, that is, knowledge of the Triune Self. There can be no yoga until there is a willing devil, a devil willing to subordinate itself to and become one with the desire for Self-knowledge. After this union of desires there comes another union, the union of feeling-and-desire, but Patanjali does not mention it. It has been forgotten or suppressed.

Patanjali speaks of manas sometimes as a "thinking principle" which should be trained and purified, so that the yogi can perform the three stages of yoga. The yogi is a human, though with fewer limitations than the majority. He should achieve yoga, the union of the feeling-and-desire of the doer, through training and purification of his manas, his body-mind, which is called meditation by translators. The three stages of yoga called dharana, dhyana and samadhi, represented as one in samyama, refer to efforts to hold the Light of the Intelligence steady on the subject of the thinking. The body-mind is the one mostly used, because it deals with matters of the body and of outside nature. The feeling-mind and the desire-mind must be in complete control of the body-mind.

Names do not make much difference. What Patanjali predicates as the result of the practices determines what subject he refers to. Patanjali does not go beyond feeling-and-desire in the human in his use of at most three minds and their thinking. The most that is done by the doer, as feeling-and-desire, with these minds, in Patanjali's system, is limited. One may gain all the powers over nature that Patanjali mentions and even many more. He may isolate feeling and control or suppress the many desires by the desire for liberation. By isolating feeling, desire is cut off from nature; but desire is not isolated. And if feeling is temporarily liberated from the body it does not know what it is, because it was identified with nature and does not distinguish itself as feeling. But it seems that Patanjali did not realize this.

When a doer reaches this yoga it cannot go into moksha, which is a state in the purified psychic atmosphere of the doer, entirely cut off from nature. It does not become a "free soul" or "self". The knower and the thinker of the Triune Self are always free. When a doer is alleged to have isolated itself, according to Patanjali's method, it does not go any further; it does not obtain the union with the thinker and with the knower, because it still has the desire for liberation, for sat-chit-ananda, translated as "Being, Consciousness and Bliss" but which is only—being conscious bliss. This desire for liberation has temporarily become master of all the other desires, even the desire for sex, but not with the consent or by the agreement of those desires. They are merely suppressed. This is extreme selfishness of one of the desires, though it seems to have renounced everything. If the dominating desire were the desire for Self-knowledge, the case would be different, because then the other desires would have changed themselves and would be in agreement and one with the desire for Self-knowledge.

The feeling of the doer in moksha or nirvana, which is a psychic condition, though called "spiritual", does not become an Intelligence. It does not even become a perfected doer. It does not raise its aia. After having remained in that state for a period not measured by human time, it must leave it. It was partly because of its aia that the doer was able to advance. If the doer goes into Nirvana, temporarily, it repudiates what it owes to the aia. The aia, inert and without dimension, goes with the doer and will ultimately, together with the suppressed desires and the unbalanced thoughts, be the means of bringing the doer back to earth and other earth lives.

When yoga is practiced merely for the purpose of isolation, liberation and absorption, it is extreme selfishness. In India it has been practiced for centuries in this way. The ideal of the religious life there is to obtain liberation. The decadence of India is largely due to this refined selfishness by which the knowledge of noetic things which priests and yogis may still have, is turned into a practice to obtain liberation rather than a larger field for service. They try to get liberation from nature without seeing the real distinctions between nature and the Triune Self, the purpose of the Universe, and the relation and duty of the doer to nature.

The priests and yogis have gradually shut themselves off from the inner meaning of the words they have. Many names commonly used suggest the high development reached by Indian philosophy in the past. The ancient language, it would appear, had a large vocabulary to cover noetic, mental and psychic conditions for which there are as yet no names in Western languages. The following examples will illustrate this with regard to some phases of what is here called an Intelligence.

Brahm. A complete Triune Self which has become an Intelligence. It has no contact with the four worlds of nature and is alone in its own light in the fire sphere.

Brahma (neuter). The same Intelligence, which has raised the aia to be a Triune Self. The passive and the active sides are equal and it is alone with the Triune Self it has raised. Brahma (neuter) in the spheres signifies the Intelligence whose Triune Self—later, in the worlds—maintains its sexless and perfect physical body in the Realm of Permanence, the Eternal.

Brahmâ (active). The same Intelligence, but the circumflex accent over the a in Brahmâ signifies that it has become active. This means that the doer of its Triune Self has separated its perfect sexless physical body and has procreated a new universe for itself, a man body and a woman body. Therefore the doer has exiled itself from its thinker and knower and is no longer conscious of the Realm of Permanence, the Eternal; it is conscious only of this man and woman world of time. Here it must continue periodically through life and death to re-exist in a man body or in a woman body, until it regenerates and restores its physical body to its original state of perfection, that is, balances its feeling-and-desire in permanent union and unites with its thinker and knower; and, by so doing, again becomes conscious of and regains its place in the Realm of Permanence, the Eternal. By so doing it will free the Intelligence (Brahma) and complete its Triune Self by being itself free.

Brahman. The same Intelligence, to which its Triune Self has restored all the Light loaned and whose Triune Self is now itself a Brahm. A Brahman is freed from all connections with nature and is a free Intelligence.

Parabrahm. The same Intelligence, which has become Supreme Intelligence.

Parabrahman. That Supreme Intelligence, which includes or is the representative of all other freed Intelligences.

Purusha (unqualified). (1) The knower of the Triune Self in its noetic atmosphere. (2) The thinker of the Triune Self in its mental atmosphere.

(3) The doer of the Triune Self in its psychic atmosphere. In none of these cases is purusha connected with nature.

Mula Prakriti. General nature. In its highest state the element earth of the spheres, from which the four elements of the worlds are drawn, to be the matter of the four worlds, by individual:

Prakriti, which is (1) the matter of which the human body is composed; (2) outside nature making up the four worlds.

Purusha-Prakriti (unqualified). The doer living in its immortal fourfold physical body in the Realm of Permanence.

Ishwara. (1) An active aspect of the Supreme Intelligence, to which correspond: (2) the light-and-I-am faculties of an Intelligence; and, (3) the I-ness-and-selfness of the knower of the Triune Self. All three are called Ishwara. A certain light, breath, and power aspect of the Intelligence manifesting to the Triune Self as a being.

A O M. The name of Ishwara, to the proper thinking and sounding of which Ishwara responds. When it is used as the name of the Triune Self, A is the doer; O is the thinker and doer joined; M is the knower with A O joined in it. For a human the sounding should be I A O M.

Sat (unqualified). Truth as a self-perpetuating Light of Parabrahman, Brahman, Brahma (neuter), Brahmâ (active), and Brahm. Truth as the Light of the Intelligence in the atmospheres of the Triune Self. It is the Conscious Light within, which shows all things as they are. Truth is of the degree in which one has that Conscious Light.

Sattva. In nature, the matter of the light world which is made light by the Light of the Intelligences in the noetic atmospheres of their Triune Selves. In the human the matter of the light world which is in his psychic atmosphere.

Rajas. In nature, the matter of the life world made active by the mental atmospheres of human beings and the acting desires which in thinking and thoughts enter into these atmospheres. In the human, the matter of the life world in his psychic atmosphere.

Tamas. In nature, the matter of the form world, which is without light and therefore dull and heavy. In the human the matter of the form world in his psychic atmosphere. Sattva, rajas, and tamas are the three gunas, which are said to be qualities, attributes, of nature, one of which rules the other two in the psychic atmosphere of the human.

Atma. The Light of an Intelligence; the Conscious Light within a human, by the use of which he thinks and creates thoughts.

Atman. The Triune Self (as the knower) in the Light of the Intelligence; the portion of that Light which the Triune Self (as the thinker) allows its human being to use.

Jivatma. Every living thing in physical nature, which is given its being by the atma (Light) which the human thinks into nature.

Mahat. The nature-matter which had been in and is sent out again from the mental atmosphere of a doer or of all doers. It is nature, but made intelligent by the Light of the Intelligence used by the body-mind, which is sometimes assisted by the feeling-mind and the desire-mind, when these are used by the doer in the body.

Manas. The body-mind, sometimes aided by the use of the feeling-mind and the desire-mind.

Ahankara. Egoism or egotism, as the doer's distinctive feeling of the presence of the I-ness of the knower.

Antaskarana. The thinking which the doer does, (1) by the use of the body-mind, connecting feeling with its physical body and so with nature; (2) by the use of the feeling-mind or of the desire-mind to identify itself as feeling or as desire, and so to feel itself as distinct from nature.

Chitta. The matter of the life world or life planes which has been impressed by the diffused Light of the Intelligence in the mental atmosphere of a human. It may still be in the mental atmosphere or it may act in forms of nature.

Chitt. (1) The Light of the Intelligence in the mental atmosphere of a human; (2) "Consciousness," used in the sense of being conscious of; and, (3) "Consciousness," in the sense of being conscious that one is conscious.

Chitti. The actions in the mental atmosphere, of matter that is impressed with Light of the Intelligence.

Chittakasa. (1) The nature-matter which is in the mental atmosphere; (2) the disturbance it makes there; (3) the disturbance it makes in nature when it is sent back there.

Vritti. Waves or whirls of nature-matter in the mental atmosphere. They attract the attention of or cause activity of the body-mind which produces actions and objects in physical nature.

Samskaras. Habits of thinking. Impressions made on the breath-form before death, which are passed on by the aia to the new breath-form as habits, instincts and inhibitions.

Jagrata. The waking or outermost state, in which the doer is conscious of the appearances of objects.

Svapna. Dreaming or the inner state, in which the doer is conscious of the appearances of objects as forms.

Sushupti. The state of dreamlessness, in which the doer is not in contact with the four senses and is conscious of objects and forms only as subjects.

Turiya. The state of the doer of the human as self-knowledge, where all other states are included and vanish in the Light.

Ananda. Joy or bliss, a certain state of feeling which is produced when feeling uses the feeling-mind, independently of the body-mind.

Maya. The screen as nature and the everchanging objects on it, made by feeling-and-desire when thinking with the body-mind according to the senses.

Karma. The action and the result of the action of the Light of the Intelligence and desire; the exteriorization of a thought.

Many such suggestive terms are to be found in Sanskrit. The ancient teaching was most likely based on what is intelligent-matter (the Triune Self) and what is unintelligent-matter, that is, nature. The true teaching is that intelligent-matter works in nature-matter and thereby perfects both itself and nature.

Prakriti, universal, is nature as the four worlds. It comes out of mulaprakriti, which is inertia, avyaktam or pradhana, the earth sphere. Prakriti, individual, is the human body, which is of the four worlds and keeps the human world of time in circulation. Purusha is the Triune Self in its threefold aspects as parts, breaths and atmospheres. Purusha is also each of its three parts. Two of the three parts, the knower and the thinker, distinguish themselves from prakriti. But the purusha as the doer portion in the human cannot do this while it is connected with prakriti, as the body in which it lives and in which it is under illusion, and while it does not distinguish itself from the body.

The purusha performs functions which are reflected as the Trimurti. Prakriti is periodically created, preserved and destroyed by Brahmâ, active, Vishnu and Shiva. These are names for the doer, thinker and knower acting in nature, where they create, preserve and destroy universal and individual prakriti. The individual prakriti as the human body is created, preserved and destroyed by the doer alone, acting as Brahmâ, Vishnu and Shiva. Brahmâ, Vishnu and Shiva are nature and the Gods in nature, as acted upon by the Triune Self. So they are Brahmâ the form world, Vishnu the life world, and Shiva the light world. They are as Gods, the Creator, the Preserver and the Destroyer of the physical world of time, kept going by individual prakriti, the human body. The pattern set by individual prakriti of the continual creation, preservation and destruction is followed by prakriti in outside nature. When the body is perfected so as to be two-columned in which is embodied the complete Triune Self, the individual prakriti is permanent. Then it is no longer the source from which purusha as the Trimurti, creates, preserves and destroys the universe.

Then the purusha as the doer, thinker, and knower, becomes Brahm, by the power of the word. This word is A O M. Brahmâ, active, is A; Brahmâ and Vishnu joined are O; Shiva is M with A O joined in it. A O M, thus made up of the three purushas acting as the Creator, Preserver, and Destroyer, and breathed by its Intelligence, which is B R, becomes B R A O M, which is called Brahm. The H may have been substituted for the U, to shield this great teaching of the translation of a Triune Self into an Intelligence. Then the Intelligence which is Brahman, freed by and from its Triune Self, becomes a Parabrahm, an Intelligence united with or under the Supreme Intelligence. The Supreme Intelligence is the Parabrahman.

A O M is the Word of the Triune Self, of the Intelligence and of the Supreme Intelligence. It is the Word only if one knows its meaning and is able to think it, sense it, and breathe it. Merely sounding or singing it amounts to little. The Word represents the Triune Self, or the Intelligence. It expresses what the One is. It shows the nature, functions and relations of that One. It *is* the One.

Applied to the Triune Self, A is feeling-and-desire, O rightness-and-reason, and M I-ness-and-selfness. A O M shows the relation of the three to each other. The sound is the expression of the Triune Self as its three beings, when it has called them into being. The Triune Self has no sound, but these beings sound: the being for the doer, as A, the being for the thinker, A U as O, and the being for the knower, as M. Therefore this Word, when one thinks and senses and breathes it, puts him into communication with the One, his own Triune Self. What does he want to say to his thinker and knower? and what does he want his thinker and knower to say to him? when he has called it by its secret name? The Word of one's Triune Self remains secret until he knows its meaning. Why does he call on his Triune Self? What does he want from it? Usually he does not know. Therefore the Word has little effect, even if spoken a thousand times. "I am A O M," "I am Brahm," amounts to nothing if the person does not know what he is thinking or talking about. The fact that people do use the Word is evidence that there is a secret, an unknown desire which urges them. This desire is the beginning of the A and it seeks to know, it seeks union with the thinker and the knower of its Triune Self that do know.

How to sound the Word is therefore a secret in the doer. The secret cannot be divulged, however much is revealed about it. One must be ready for the secret; he must have made himself ready. He makes himself ready by thinking. When by continued effort to think about it he has prepared himself, the thinking makes an inaudible sound which he perceives and senses. Then he breathes in consonance with the sound. This puts him into communication. His Triune Self instructs him in what he has prepared himself to know about it.

The sounding of A O M relates the doer with the thinker and the knower. If continued, this would take the doer out of the body. To remain in the body and to have the doer manifest in the body, the body should be included in the sound. The secret letter of the individual prakriti is I. Therefore human beings, if they are that far advanced, should say, while thinking the vowel sounds, I A O M and stop when the M is sounded. I is the geometrical symbol for the upright body; A is the creative beginning of the Word; O is the continuation and rounding out; and M is the fulness and completion of the Word, resolved into itself. The M is the point within the fulness of itself in the circle.

From these fundamentals remain only limited teachings of nature in the physical world, and of the doer in the human under the Light of the Intelligence. What remains relates only to the Light of the Intelligence as it, atma, is with atman, the Triune Self, and in nature, as jivas, having come through the doer. The information about the Intelligence itself in its own state, that is, in its three spheres, is lost. Traces that there were teachings concerning the Intelligences may be seen in the references to everything that is beyond the Triune Self, as being para: parabrahm, paramatma, stand for Intelligence; and paravidya is the knowledge beyond the Triune Self; that is, knowledge as Intelligence in the spheres, as distinguished from knowledge as the Triune Self in the worlds. The distinction made that everything is purusha, the Triune Self, or prakriti, nature, shows not only the ancient plan handed down, but also that little more of it remains than what relates to the doer in a human, which is to them the Triune Self, and to the human physical world of time, which is to them the universe as a whole. Everything that has passed into nature is made by manas, ahankara, chitta; that is, by the doer through thinking and thoughts.

Lost is the teaching that there are Intelligences from which the Triune Selves receive the Light by which they think.

Lost also is the teaching that there are the spheres, in which the Brahms or Intelligences are, and the worlds, in which the purushas or complete Triune Selves are; and that different from these there is the human world of time, with its manvantaras and pralayas for re-existing doers throughout their series of lives.

Lost is the teaching that a human is a representative of the intelligent-side and of the nature-side of the Universe. The Bhagavad Gita treats of this, but in the present form of this great little book the characters of the epic cannot be recognized. The Kurus are desire as a whole. It is divided into two branches, the Kurus who are the sensuous, selfish desires for bodily things, and the Pandavas who are desires for knowledge of the Triune Self. The blind king Dritarashtra is the body, and his generals are the four senses. Arjuna, one of the Pandava princes, represents the desire for Self-knowledge. Another of the Kurus represents sexual desire. The better desires have been driven from the body Kurukshetra, the plane of the Kurus. The capital, Hastinapura, is the heart, the seat of government, where the lower desires rule. This is the case with the run of human beings. The Bhagavad Gita shows an extraordinary human being, Arjuna, who is determined to regain control over the body and to have knowledge of the Triune Self and the Light of the Intelligence. To him comes Krishna, his thinker, with the Light of the Intelligence, speaking as reason through the mind of reason. His instruction is intuition, which is the true teaching (tuition) from within.

The names show much about the nature of the Triune Self and its three parts, together with the powers and workings and results of some of the minds, on none of which subjects the West has anything definite. There is much in the ancient literature of the East for anyone who approaches it not only with sympathy but with the understanding that he himself must find the accurate information it contains. No one can get anything of definite value out of these scriptures, unless he has some knowledge to begin with, and unless he understands that neither the scriptures nor the commentaries discriminate as to the relative values of what they transmit to him. Accurate information can be obtained only if, in addition, he can distinguish it in the Eastern dress, in which it appears amidst superstition, ignorance, idolatry and the incrustations of time.

The average person does not find enough in this literature to reward him for all these difficulties. Therefore the study is neglected. But what does attract most people in the West who become interested, is the promise of the powers to be gained by the Eastern breathing exercises. So the Eastern missionaries supply the demand by teaching yoga. Even if they start with raja yoga they abandon it because Western disciples do not qualify in the angas of yama and niyama. So the yoga, as union: first, union of feeling-and-desire, and then union with one's Self, turns into a yoga designed to give lower psychic powers, beauty and strength of body and a long life. This is what the disciples expect. The results that come to them if they actually practice pranayama are very different, and their teachers, who must share their destiny, cannot guard them against it.

SECTION 29

The Theosophical Movement. The teachings of Theosophy.

One of the signs of the times is the Theosophical Movement. The Theosophical Society appeared with a message and a mission. It presented to the world what it called Theosophy, old teachings which until then had been reserved to a few: of a brotherhood of students, of karma and of reincarnation, of a sevenfold constitution of man and of the universe, and of the perfectibility of man. The acceptance of these teachings allows one a glimpse of himself as few other doctrines do. This revelation of ancient knowledge was given out as coming from certain teachers called by the Sanskrit name Mahatmas, who had renounced nirvana or moksha and remained in human bodies, to be of help as Elder Brothers to the "souls" who were still bound to the wheel of rebirth.

The source through whom these teachings came was a Russian woman, Helena Petrovna Blavatsky, who was the only person, it was stated, who was psychically fitted and trained, and who was willing, to receive and to spread them. Her assistants from the first were two New York lawyers, Henry S. Olcott and William Q. Judge. These teachings referred for corroboration to Sanskrit literature and used many of its terms, and so started the Eastern Movement with its missionaries to the West. Only Sanskrit had a terminology which, though foreign, would lend itself to express aspects of the inner life which were unknown in the West. Not only Sanskrit but many other records are mentioned; however, the influence of the Indian literature prevails.

The Theosophical Society, founded in New York in 1875, was the first to plow the ground. It had to do hard work in unfriendly times. It had to bring to general notice teachings which were foreign and unusual. H. P. Blavatsky produced psychic phenomena which, though insignificant in themselves, attracted and held the attention of people until a general interest was created. The teachings presented in the literature are mere outlines, but they set people to thinking as nothing else had done.

By the light of these teachings man is seen to be not a puppet in the hands of an omnipotent being, nor to be driven by a blind force, nor to be the plaything of circumstances. Man is seen to be the creator and arbiter of his own fate. It is made plain that man may and will attain through repeated "incarnations" to a degree of perfection far beyond his present conceptions; that as examples of this state, reached after many incarnations, there must be now living in human bodies, "souls" who have attained to wisdom and who are what the ordinary man will be in the future. These doctrines were enough to satisfy human needs. They offered what the natural sciences and religions lacked. They appealed to the reason, they appealed to the heart, they placed an intimate relation between the intellect and morals.

These teachings have made their impress on many phases of modern thought. Scientists, writers and followers of other modern movements borrowed from this fund of information, though not always consciously. Theosophy, more than any other movement, shaped the tendency to freedom in religious thought, brought a new light to searchers and made for a kindly feeling towards others. Theosophy has largely removed the fear of death and of the future. It has given to man a freedom which no other form of belief had conferred. Even though the teachings are not definite, they are at least full of suggestions; and where they are not systematic they were more workable than anything proclaimed in religions.

Those that could not stand the light that shone through the information and suggestions of Theosophy, were often its enemies. The most active enemies in the early days were Christian missionaries in India. Yet some theosophists have done more than any enemies could do to belittle the name of Theosophy, and have made its teachings appear ridiculous. Becoming members of a society did not make people theosophers. The charges of the world against members of the Theosophical Society are often true. Thinking and feeling brotherhood would at least have brought the spirit of fellowship into the life of the members. Acting instead from the low level of personal aims, they let their baser nature assert itself. The desire to lead, petty jealousy and bickerings, split the first Theosophical Society into parts after the death of Blavatsky, and again after the death of Judge.

Pretenders, each assuming to be a mouthpiece of a Mahatma, quoted Mahatmas and presented messages from them. Each side, claiming to have messages, assumed to know their will, much as the bigoted sectarian claims to know and to do the will of God. Impostors and spooks are more likely to have been the moving spirits of some of these theosophical societies. It seems incredible that the claims printed in some of the theosophical magazines and books since 1895 should have been made. The doctrine of reincarnation in its theosophic sense has been made ridiculous by such theosophists, who asserted a knowledge of their past lives and of the lives of others,—indeed giving absurd lines of descent through past "incarnations."

Most interest was shown in the astral states and the display of psychic phenomena. The attitude of such theosophists made it appear that philosophy was forgotten. The astral states were sought and entered by some; and, coming under its glamour, many became victims of that deceptive light. From the publications and actions of these people it would seem that many of them were in the slums and lees of the astral states without seeing the better side.

Brotherhood appeared only in print on ceremonial occasions. The actions of the theosophists show that its meaning has been forgotten, if ever understood. Karma, if talked about, is a stereotyped phrase and has an empty sound. The teachings of reincarnation and the seven principles are repeated in hackneyed and lifeless terms and lack the understanding required for growth and progress. The members cling to terms they do not understand. Religious formalism has crept in.

The Theosophical Society of 1875 was the recipient and dispenser of great truths. The "karma" of those who have failed to perform their work in the Theosophical Society will reach farther than that of those in the psychic or other mental movements, because members of the Theosophical Society had information of the law of karma, action.

SECTION 30

States of the human being in deep sleep.

The states of the human beings in deep sleep, in trances and after death are generally psychic, but some at times go beyond the psychic atmosphere, which is the limit within which the happenings are psychic. A doer which passes beyond is conscious in parts of its mental atmosphere.

One can be conscious in deep sleep of what he is not conscious of while awake, but only when he has in the waking state thought of matters connected with those trans-psychic or mental states. When he is again in his waking state, he may or may not be conscious of what he was conscious of in the trans-psychic states. If he brings back any information of which he became conscious, it is translated into terms of the waking state. If he is not conscious in his waking state of the things of which he was conscious in the trans-psychic states, he will at least have a mental impression.

When one is in deep sleep the doer-in-the-body is disconnected from the four senses and their nerve ramifications in the outer brain and from the pituitary body; it sinks back through the ventricles into the cerebellum and passes down as far as the cervical vertebrae and is not in touch with the involuntary nervous system. If the doer contacts any organ below the cerebellum it may possibly be conscious in its mental atmosphere and of the life world, but this is an unusual condition.

While in deep sleep the doer cannot see, hear, taste, smell or touch anything; he may feel, but that kind of feeling is so different from the feeling of sensations, that it cannot be understood as feeling pain or pleasure. That which is or may be active in deep sleep is the doer of the Triune Self, not merely the embodied doer portion. Any subject of thought dealt with is transmitted to the doer, such as abstract subjects connected with physical life, like mathematics or any of the sciences, or with emotional life like probity or courage.

The doer is beyond any stage where it could see clairvoyantly; it is not on the form plane. The effect of its being conscious is that it comprehends without hindrance. It can understand the nature, properties, qualities and value of physical things, as well as the nature of desires, anger or any of the forces that move in physical life.

However, there are limits to what can be comprehended in this state.

The doer cannot comprehend its own ultimate nature or what the Intelligence is. Thinking goes on without interference. Cognition is direct, because the Light of the Intelligence centers towards the subject, which thus becomes the focus of the Light. In the waking state, thinking is a process of comparing, sorting out and judging, and the diffused Light which is transmitted through the pituitary body, has to be focussed by the thinking.

There are certain states in which the doer may be conscious in the mental atmosphere. What is active in such states is the doer of the Triune Self. The embodied portion of the doer is disconnected from the breath-form and the involuntary nervous system; circulation and breathing sometimes stop, and the body appears to be dead. While the doer portion may still be in the body if so disconnected, it is as if it were not there.

Trances in which the doer in the body is conscious merely in the psychic atmosphere and the form world and experiences only psychic exaltation, are not here dealt with. Saints and religious persons may have such trances. Mystics, especially those who feel that they are in union with God, are usually in such a psychic trance. The test of whether they were in the life world is, whether they learned something definite that they can express clearly. A feeling of exaltation does not amount to that.

It is possible for some persons to put themselves into a state where they are conscious in their mental atmosphere and of the life world. Then their feeling-mind or desire-mind is active and they can learn the things mentioned above as the kind of information that may be obtained in deep sleep, subject to the same limitations that exist in deep sleep.

Mental states may come about naturally, that is, without any effort for that purpose. In these cases they are the result of previous actions, such as unsuccessful efforts to understand problems of the natural sciences or of philosophy. Sometimes the brain offers an obstruction. These efforts, if enough work has been done, lead to a condition where accumulated desire shuts off physical interferences. Such states are rare. Still rarer are states where the doer is intentionally conscious in its mental atmosphere. These states result only from definite efforts to get into such a state, like mental exercises to control the desires and regulate the thinking.

A person who goes into a trance usually gets only into his psychic atmosphere; in that state he is conscious of things on the form plane of the physical world; usually be is conscious only of things in the lower states there. The colors, sights, sounds and feelings there overwhelm him. He supposes that these experiences are of an exalted, divine variety. The people to whom he tells about them think so too. Clairvoyance is considered to be "spiritual vision," vibrations the key to everything, colors to indicate "spiritual" distinctions and to be the last word in wisdom, spooks to be Masters of Wisdom, lights, stars and fireworks to be signs from God, beautiful figures to be saints, emotions on the form plane to be heavenly joys, ecstasy to be union with God.

The reason people exaggerate psychic conditions in this way is that these conditions represent the highest states they can conceive; that time and dimensions are different from physical time and the dimension on the physical plane, which are the iron limitations within which they ordinarily move; that their standards of reality are inapplicable; that they have no standard by which to judge their new experiences. Therefore, any experience beyond the tangible world is deemed supernal and usually supreme. Further, self-conceit aids in magnifying the importance of values in psychic trances, so that they are believed to be mental and even noetic. But the lights and colors seen are not the Light of the Intelligence, nor are they perceived by the Light of the Intelligence. The lights seen in the usual visions and trances are the sparkle, flash or glow of desire on matter of the astral state or of the form plane. Even though it be the desire of a moral person, it is still desire.

Trance states are states of nature. All that is performed or heard or seen in a trance state is of appearances, phenomena, illusion, glamour of nature, perceived through the senses concerning objects of nature. Intentional active thinking on a subject is by the Conscious Light; that prevents trance.

In a mental state no lights, colors, persons or scenes are witnessed. A mental state is a condition of insight, understanding, without emotion. It may give exhilaration, but no emotion. It is possible that in a mental state the seer is conscious of the processes by which he reaches to insight. The processes consist in focussing the diffused Light of the Intelligence by thinking. In the waking state he does this by the effort to think, but in a mental state, as in deep sleep, the processes are done without that effort. But all such mental states are connected with nature and could come from the effort to think while awake.

SECTION 31

*Mental destiny in the after-death states. The round of twelve stages
from life to life. Hells and heavens.*

A part of the mental destiny of a human is experienced after death,
in that part of the mental which reaches into the psychic atmosphere;
but the majority have their hells and their heavens in their psychic
atmosphere, whether the destiny is psychic, mental or noetic. The reason
is that their thoughts are usually concerned with physical things and with
the psychic reactions therefrom.

There is a round, generally speaking, of twelve states or stages which
a given doer portion goes through between one life on earth and its next
life. Some of these stages are of short duration, while others may last for
hundreds or even thousands of years,—this depends among other things
on the destiny of the doer, that is, the kind of life the doer had lived and
on his thoughts and acts. Eleven of these are stages after death and states
in the preparation for another life. In the twelfth the doer re-exists in a
human body, (Fig. V-D).

In the first of the after-death states the doer portion lives and dreams
over certain events and scenes of the life ended; it is with its breath-form
and so sees, hears, tastes or smells. This stage may be of short duration
or as though of centuries. Approximately at the end of the first stage,
there is the judgment. The second stage has to do with the feelings and
desires of the doer, and eventually there is a separation of its good from
its evil desires, and from the breath-form. The period between the first
and the third stage is that which is spoken of as hell. The third stage is
the grading of the doer's thoughts. In the fourth, there is a purification
of the thoughts. In the fifth, the doer is purified; the breath-form is
cleansed and ready for the doer to be in its heaven. In the sixth, the doer
unites with the breath-form, cleansed of all untoward impressions, and
is in its heaven. It lives over and realizes all ideal thoughts which it had
had on earth. This stage varies greatly with individual doers, in character
and duration. In the seventh, the sense elementals are temporarily freed
and are in their elements. This stage is a period of peaceful rest. It is
during this period that the other eleven portions re-exist one after the
other in succession; each uses the same breath-form, which is common
to all twelve doer portions. In the eighth stage, the doer is made conscious

of the thought for the next life and the breath-form is summoned to again serve that doer portion. In the ninth, the form of the breath-form enters the body of the mother-to-be and causes conception by binding the two physical germs, and so makes contact with the physical world; this stage covers the first three months of intrauterine life. In the tenth stage, placental life begins and the flesh body is developed; this stage covers the second three months of the prenatal period. In the eleventh, the last three months of pregnancy, the human form is completed. In the twelfth stage, there is birth of the body into the physical world. Here the body grows, its senses become active, and it is developed and made ready for occupancy by the doer. Entrance of the doer into the body is marked by its first memories of this world, and by the intelligent questions it will ask.

In the building of a human body for each of the twelve doer portions, as they successively re-exist on earth, the breath-form is the same for all. That this can be so, the order of events is as follows: When the heaven period of a doer portion ends and it is at rest and in forgetfulness of nature, the four senses are temporarily freed and in their elements, and the breath of the breath-form is disunited from its form. All nature memories are removed from the form, and it is inert. It is then ready and waits to recompose the compositor and sense units for the building of a new body when summoned to do so by the thought of the doer portion next in line for a life on earth. There are countless intricacies which have to be adjusted in the lives of doers, so that in their re-existences they will be marshalled in their destined relation to each other on earth, in time and condition and place.

The after-death states of the human being are largely determined by what he thought about during his last moments. The dominating thoughts of the life just ending crowd into these last moments. These thoughts turn upon the things in which the human was interested, for which he worked. They blend, and one or more thoughts result. At the time of death these thoughts hold the attention of the human. He made them and they rule his destiny for his conditions after death and for the span of his next life. Generally the last thoughts center on objects of the senses and on sensations sought or dreaded. Therefore, the after death stages are mostly psychic; what little mental destiny there is is taken in with the psychic and is worked out on the life plane of the form world or on that of the physical world.

What distinguishes psychic and mental hells and heavens is that in the hells feeling and desire disagree with rightness, while in the heavens they agree with it. It is the doer that has a mental hell or heaven, because of the effect that rightness has upon it. The mental hells are conditions in which the doer feels anguish, remorse and grief because of the censure of rightness; the mental heavens are conditions in which the doer has satisfaction and peace through the approval of rightness.

The mental heaven is like the psychic heaven in that happiness is the dominant feature in both. While the doer has the breath-form and the four senses and its feelings and desires, happiness lies in dealing with thoughts and problems concerning subjects of thoughts. It is a life with ideals.

The mental heaven is as little a community heaven as is the psychic heaven. It is a condition of the doer in its own mental atmosphere. In the psychic heaven there are mental states, but they are in the psychic atmosphere and are related to psychic conditions where sensuous enjoyment is concerned with thoughts and ideals. These heavenly states are experienced with scenes, persons, pictures, sounds, places, actions and enterprises and are incidental to a trained, cultured enjoyment. The majority of cultured, artistic, learned people enjoy such mental activities. But a mental heaven is quite different. While there are scenes of places and people whom the doer meets, these are always incidental to mental activities.

Those who have a mental heaven enjoy working on moral and mental problems. They have a keen joy in contemplation. Their occupation is an extension of the thinking they did in life to benefit people, but the difficulties they had to contend with in life are removed. The happiness comes in their work rather than in the results. They solve their problems in an abstract way, not in the concrete manner in which they would be solved on earth.

A mental heaven is comparatively rare. Such persons as Emerson, Carlyle, Thomas Taylor, Alexander Wilder, Kepler, Newton and Spinoza get into that state when their difficulties are removed after death. Contemplation is the word that is the nearest approach to a description of the joy of that state, but this word is colorless, because it does not convey, except to those who may have a mental heaven, the joy one has there. The run of humans connect joy only with physical and emotional things and therefore use no words for what is here called mental joy. Contemplation is here used because it is a process with which the mental joy is connected. The contemplation becomes so absorbing that the doer forgets all else than the subject which it contemplates. So the end of the heaven period draws near, but the doer does not perceive this, because for it there is no end to heaven.

CHAPTER VIII

NOETIC DESTINY

SECTION 1

Knowledge of the conscious self in the body. The noetic world. Self-knowledge of the knower of the Triune Self. When knowledge of the conscious self in the body is available to the human.

The noetic destiny of the majority of human beings is the condition of the noetic atmosphere of the human, (Fig. V-B). That condition includes the amount of knowledge of the conscious self in the body available to the human, the much or little of the Light of the Intelligence present, the quality of that Light as attachable to objects of nature and the consequences of all this to the human. Human beings think of destiny as physical only, yet their noetic destiny dominates the other three kinds.

Noetic destiny may not seem as obvious as mental destiny. It manifests through physical destiny chiefly as the generative power and the use to which it is put; through psychic destiny as the ability or inability to control one's passions and desires; and through mental destiny as the power or lack of power to do real thinking. It can be seen in physical things because human beings let the Light of the Intelligence go into nature through the action of the four senses and through the generative power; and the physical results are the only indications that they are able to notice. Noetic destiny in the present stage of human beings appears chiefly as their troubles, their afflictions, their diseases, though the immediate cause of all these is the psychic part of the Triune Self, the doer, and the thoughts which it generates. Noetic destiny is a background in the noetic atmosphere rather than an active force.

When there are enough people who think along these lines, their thoughts will be exteriorized in words according to the genius of the language, and a vocabulary will be made. In the meantime, terms are here used which can be taken in a sense approximating the unknown things named, such as the Triune Self, its noetic atmosphere, the knower as the noetic part of the Triune Self, the noetic breath, the noetic world and the Light of the Intelligence.

Knowledge, which is the permanent result as accomplishment in the noetic atmosphere coming from the thinking of the human, is stored in the noetic atmosphere of the human. It depends upon thinking and cannot come without it. Thinking that brings knowledge into the noetic atmosphere and strengthens the powers of that atmosphere is such thinking as that on the origin, nature and destiny of feeling-and-desire as the doer, and on its relation to the Triune Self and to other doers. But thinking selfishness, greed, lust, meanness, hypocrisy, lying, dishonesty and ingratitude, creates thoughts which lead away from the knowledge stored. Be the doer's knowledge much or little, it is acquired only through thinking with the mind that it uses and so must be reached through the mental atmosphere. It cannot be gotten through actions, feelings, emotions, ecstasy or trances. Knowledge of the conscious self in the body can come only as the result of active thinking. This knowledge is of the intelligent-side of the Universe and is stored in the noetic world. This world is in but is not of the light world, which belongs to the nature-side. In the light world the beings are all, from the highest to the lowest, devoid of intelligence, except for what they get from human doers. On the intelligent-side there are no worlds in the sense of the worlds of nature-matter. On the intelligent-side are Triune Selves. The term noetic world is figurative like scientific or literary world.

The noetic world is a world of knowledge and is a name for the common part of the noetic atmospheres of the knowers of the Triune Selves in the earth sphere. The human beings of these Triune Selves are different from each other. But there is a part of the noetic atmosphere of each Triune Self that it has in common with all other Triune Selves. There is a one-ness among Triune Selves. That common part is here called the noetic world or world of knowledge. It has an identity and unity in the Great Triune Self of the world. The Great Triune Self of the world is the Triune Self of the Supreme Intelligence and has to it a relation similar to that which exists between a Triune Self and its Intelligence. The noetic world is the storehouse of the knowledge of all

Triune Selves in the earth sphere and this knowledge is available to every Triune Self.

In the noetic world is the knowledge of everything concerned with the earth sphere, the earth crusts that have been and the present earth crust; with their matter, the forces that act through them; with the units of the elements in the earth sphere and the laws by which they work. It also contains knowledge of gods, elemental beings and races, past and present, of the continents and races of the physical earth, its fauna, flora and structure, past and present; of the make-up of the exterior and interior sides of the earth crust; of how the stars and other bodies beyond the physical earth are produced, continued and changed; of the nature of sun and moon and their functions and of times and their measurements. All this is knowledge of nature-matter. Moreover the knowledge of the origins and nature of all Triune Selves, the manner of their progress and their final destiny and the relation that the Light of the Intelligences has to their Triune Selves and to the earth sphere, is contained in the noetic world. There is no noetic destiny in the noetic world. In that world, therefore, is the treasure of knowledge of all that is or touches the matter, forces and beings in the four worlds of the earth sphere.

The knowledge which a human acquires is available to him only during that life, except for a small portion, the essence of that knowledge, which is assimilated and stored up by the doer-in-the-body. The knowledge which the doer thus acquires through its many human beings, often assists the present human being. In a crisis and even in ordinary affairs of trade and work, a human then finds that hidden knowledge of his doer coming to his help.

On moral questions this hidden knowledge reveals itself through rightness and speaks as conscience. This knowledge makes a human responsible. It is his noetic destiny and makes physical destiny.

Self-knowledge of the knower of the Triune Self is always certain, be it much or little, and it leaves no doubt. It leaves no room for thinking, because it is the summation in which thinking has found its completion.

Self-knowledge of the knower may come to the doer also as intuition. Intuition is a definite and certain knowledge concerning a subject that has a relation to the doer. Intuition comes through the thinker and gives to the human information and an understanding of a superior kind. The understanding is a live understanding and because it comes from Self-knowledge of the knower is not subject to argument. Intuition is not a feeling, not an instinct, not a prejudice or a preference. It is impartial, it does not come to everybody, and those to whom it comes do not usually mention it. Intuition is tuition by one's Self from within.

Knowledge of the conscious self in the body comes to some unexpectedly, not as definite intuition and not as conscience, but as confidence and as a general aid in accomplishing a plan. This is noetic destiny of the human.

According to the purpose for which one uses this assistance he closes or opens himself as a channel for further contact with Self-knowledge of the knower. If he will not have anyone but himself benefit by the contact with that aid he closes himself as a channel and shuts off the aid. If he is willing to share the advantages he keeps himself open and may even make better contact. The more he is willing to share without restrictions, the more he receives of this knowledge, from which most people shut themselves off because of their selfish desire.

As it becomes more evident to him that there is an inner source he will be led by it to think about it, and so he opens the way to the source, which is by exercise and discipline of his thinking, until this becomes a thinking without attachment, which does not create thoughts. Thus a doer may eventually have in its waking state access to the noetic world.

An aspect of noetic destiny is the amount of Light of the Intelligence present in the noetic atmosphere and available to the human. An Intelligence lends to its Triune Self a certain amount of Light, so that the doer may use it to educate itself and to go through the experiences necessary to acquire knowledge of the conscious self in the body. At times the Intelligence loans more Light, at times it withdraws Light, according to the use which the human makes of the Light loaned to him. As the human acquires knowledge of the conscious self in the body he receives more Light. The noetic atmosphere shows by a record how much Light has been received, how much has gone out into nature, how much the Intelligence has withdrawn, how much remains in the atmosphere, what has been done with the Light that went into nature and where in nature that Light is.

The record in the noetic atmosphere of the human is noetic destiny. The condition of the noetic atmosphere is the record. It shows itself in the mental atmosphere, in the psychic atmosphere and in the physical body.

Another aspect of noetic destiny is the quality of the Light in the noetic atmosphere. The Light when in the noetic atmosphere is not attached to objects of nature but is attachable or non-attachable. The attachable Light will go out into nature. The Light which is unattachable is Light that has gone out many times and has at last been made unattachable so that it can never again be bound to desire and sent into nature. It is Light that has been freed by the action of desire with rightness and reason, freed from desire by desire. The atmosphere shows to what uses the Light has been put in the doer itself and in nature and how it has been made unattachable. There is in the noetic atmosphere of the average human little Light that has been made unattachable. This shows itself in the actions of men, who go through the same experiences over and over again, without learning anything, without changing their positions as body doers, without the desire to free themselves from nature, without the desire to look into the Light.

Noetic destiny is recondite. It is not visible as is physical destiny, nor manifest as is mental destiny, but there are physical facts which are immediately and above all others connected with noetic destiny and are therefore indications of it.

SECTION 2

The test and trial of the sexes. Projection of a female form. Illustrations. History of the Triune Self.

The scarcity of Light in the noetic atmospheres of human beings is because of happenings, long years ago, when the doers now in human bodies were in perfect bodies and were conscious as doer parts of Triune Selves, in the Realm of Permanence. For each Triune Self to be qualified to be one of The Government, and to govern the world of time and the destinies of the nations of human beings, it was necessary for its doer part to take and pass through the trial test of the sexes for balanced union of feeling-and-desire. The test was that the doer should temporarily divide its sexless body into a male body and a female body; that the desire of the doer be in the male body and the feeling be in the female body; that the feeling-and-desire minds should think in unison, and be uninfluenced by the body-mind, which could function only as or for the body senses and would try to make the desire and feeling of the doer see itself as in two bodies instead of as the active and passive aspects of the doer.

As a doer passed the test, the temporary male and female bodies merged and were again the perfect body, but were now permanently balanced in one permanently sexless body; and the desire-and-feeling were inseparably welded in balanced union—by the body-mind being subject to the desire-and-feeling minds thinking in union.

Each of the doers now in human bodies failed to pass that test. Their body-minds influenced the desire-and-feeling minds to think of themselves as bodies until these consorted. Then the Conscious Light was withdrawn by their thinkers and knowers and they were in the darkness of the body senses, and were afraid. They left the Realm of Permanence; they could not see it; they found themselves in the human world of time, among male and female bodies, subject to death and re-existence. When the bodies died the doer, feeling-and-desire, could not re-exist in a male and a female body at the same time; it re-existed in a male body with its feeling dominated by desire, or in a female body where desire was dominated by feeling, there being only one aia and one breath-form. The doer could no longer think of itself as desire-and-feeling. It was controlled by the body-mind and the body-mind compelled it to think of itself in the terms and the functions of the sexes, either as a man or as a woman.

Here the doers in human bodies must continue to re-exist in bodies until they think of themselves as doers of immortal Triune Selves, and work their way onward to the Realm of Permanence by being conscious *of* themselves *as* doers of their Triune Selves and by regenerating their bodies and restoring them to their perfect state in the Realm of Permanence.

The temporary separation—for the test mentioned—of the doer's perfect body into a male body and a female body was effected by a projection in solid, tangible matter by a transfusion of matter from the perfect physical body of the doer. Into this projected body came the feeling of the doer, and the desire portion was in what had been the perfect physical body, which had become a male body. So there were two bodies connected with each other by a magnetic tie, which served as a bridge connecting the two bodies. The desire in the man body and the feeling in the woman body did not at first think and act as two, as being different and separated from each other. Each saw itself in the other, as though in a looking glass. They felt and acted as one, just as there is reciprocal action in one's hands in whatever one does.

The projection of the female form and the transfusion of matter from the perfect physical body of the doer into that form, can be illustrated in two ways. First, by a temporary materialization during a spiritistic performance, and, second, by the gestation of a fetus and the birth of the baby. In the first case, there is an exuding or issuing of an astral or radiant form from the physical body of the medium and, the development of that form into a transient physical, fleshly body. In this case, where the astral had extended from the medium as the exterior transient body of the materialization, there is a magnetic tie connecting the medium's body with the body materialized into physical form. The tie acts as a bridge and is similar to the umbilical cord for the transmission of the material or life force from the body of the medium to the body of the materialization.

In the second case, during placental development, where a human body is being prepared, the transfusion is from the mother directly into the fetus; the umbilical cord is as the magnetic tie; at birth the cord and the placenta are cast off, independent circulation in the baby is established by its own breath, and individual existence begins. These two examples may suffice to illustrate how the transfusion of life matter from one body to another can be conducted and maintained for a given period.

In the case of a medium the transfusion is usually the projection of a human form and the transfusion of living particles into that form to give it solidity, and illustrates after a fashion how the female body was extended from the perfect body and built up and the two bodies were connected by the magnetic tie; and the disappearance of the materialized form at a seance shows how the projected female form was reabsorbed into the original perfect body. That would have happened with every doer if—after its sexless body had been altered into a male and a female body—they had not consorted. The feeling-and-desire in those bodies would have been adjusted and balanced in perfect union, and the two bodies would have reunited as the one sexless perfect body. But, by consorting, they severed the magnetic tie. Then the sexual organs formed the tie or bridge between the man and woman bodies. When the psychic tie was broken and the physical tie was made, the bodies were subject to death. Thereafter new bodies could be built only by the physical bridge or sexual tie. Since then the desire-and-feeling in a man body and the feeling-and-desire in a woman body seek union of their man and woman bodies, instead of each doer regenerating and having balanced union of feeling-and-desire in its own regenerated physical body.

With those of the doers that passed the test, the projected female body was reabsorbed into the original body, the two bodies were thus reunited as the one perfected, sexless, two-columned body, and the feeling and the desire of the doer were in permanently balanced union in that body. The Triune Self thereby became a complete Triune Self, which took its place in The Government of the world as an administrator of the destinies of the nations.

Some of the doers that failed in the test were of the later third, and are now on the fourth, the present earth, but most of them came out to the crust during the fourth earth. They re-exist again and again as human beings, until their feeling-and-desire shall have attained to balanced union in a regenerated, perfected physical body.

The Triune Self is a unit which the Intelligence has raised from the state of aia to the state of Triune Self. When it became a Triune Self it was under the direct influence of its Intelligence and in contact with the Light of the Intelligence. It was conscious of itself in the Eternal in the light world in the Light of its Intelligence and in the sphere of its Intelligence. There was no here, no there, no distance. It was present throughout. There was no past, no future. Time did not exist. For the Triune Self there was no beginning. It was with and partook of the everlasting realities of unity, truth, eternity, immortality, justice, honesty and happiness. The Triune Self knew them; it can never lose this knowledge; hence they are innate in the doers of human beings.

Thinking was unnecessary in the presence of the Intelligence. The Triune Self was in bliss, in everlastingness. It identified itself with the Intelligence. It was as though it had always been with that glorious One. The Triune Self was impressed with its future destiny to become that glorious One, and the future was present. The plan of its development and freedom was unfolded within it as the present. Details as to how and where all was to come did not exist. The Triune Self was perfect in its knower and thinker parts, but the doer part was not qualified; it had yet to establish its feeling-and-desire in balanced union; it had to go through the trial of the sexes before mentioned; some doers passed it and others failed; these became the re-existing doers in human bodies.

The Triune Self has three parts, three atmospheres and three breaths, the noetic, mental and psychic. Each of these nine partakes somewhat of the nature of the others and may be affected by them. Each of the three parts, the doer, the thinker, and the knower, is passive and active. The psychic part is passive as feeling and active as desire; the psychic breath is passive as ingoing and active as outgoing; the psychic atmosphere is passive as receiving and active as impressing. The part, the breath and the atmosphere are passive and active in their relation to each other. The atmosphere is passive to the breath, the breath is active to the part and the part is active to the atmosphere. However, these relations, though usual, are not permanent and are at times reversed. Similar divisions and relations exist in the mental and in the noetic parts of the Triune Self.

These many aspects of the Triune Self are quite distinct, yet the Triune Self is one. They act, react, and interact with each other as if they were distinct. And from the standpoint of the doer they are distinct. So the development of the doer is carried on.

As heretofore stated, portions of each of these aspects have to do with the human being of the doer. The portions concerned with the human are in his fourfold physical body. They extend by nervous action through the whole body, but are located in certain organs. The portion of the psychic part in the body is located as feeling in the kidneys and as desire in the adrenals. The passive and active psychic breath and the passive and the active psychic atmosphere work through the psychic part in these organs. A portion of the mental part as rightness contacts the heart and as reason contacts the lungs, and with it are portions of the mental breath and the mental atmosphere. A portion of the noetic part as I-ness contacts the pituitary and as selfness contacts the pineal body. At the death of the body the doer that was in the body, goes with the breath-form as the disembodied human through certain states and then returns to the portions of the doer which were not in the body.

SECTION 3

The Light of the Intelligence. The Light in the knower of the Triune Self; in the thinker; in the doer. The Light that has gone into nature.

The Triune Self receives Light from the Intelligence to which it is related; that Light comes from the light faculty of the Intelligence into the noetic atmosphere of the Triune Self. The Light is not a part of the Triune Self and never becomes a part of it. It is loaned to the Triune Self so that by the use of it the Triune Self may become an Intelligence.

The Light is a Conscious Light; it is conscious that it is Light, and is conscious *as* Light. The Light, that which is with the Intelligence and that which is loaned to the Triune Self, is one. The Light is indivisible, though it appears to be divided. If the doer sends it into nature the Light is still one, no matter into how many different beings and things it has gone, or where it is, or in how weak a being it is, or how much it is obscured by the matter of nature. The Light of an Intelligence is the same Light irrespective of the forms in which it is. It seems to be confined in them, but it really is not.

The reality in the Triune Self above all else, except Consciousness, is the Light. The Light lets things be seen as they are, shows what should be done by the beings in whom it is, leads them to be conscious in further degrees and shows them the power to change, without itself being changed. It bears, as long as it is with the doer, the evidence of the uses to which it has been put by the doer. The fact that the Light is there causes these various processes to go on. The Light does not act, but it keeps beings in action by stimulating the active principle in them. It does not act nor does it suffer nor does it react. Its presence is the cause of all things spoken of as light. Starlight, sunlight, moonlight and earthlight are various functionings of matter made active by the Light of the Intelligences sent by the doers of their Triune Selves into nature. Human beings do not know the Light as such.

The doer is in the sphere of its Intelligence and receives a certain amount of Light from it. This is the amount the doer should have in order to acquire its education through its human beings. The amount is at times increased or decreased, depending on the thinking of the doers of the human beings, and is the outstanding feature of their noetic destiny. The Light so loaned may be sent by the doer into nature and become attached to nature units to which the doer by its thinking ties the Light.

In nature the Light is attached to units, that is, the Light is bound up and blended with them and so remains until the doer draws it back. The Light allows nature to unfold in every field and it evokes the latent sides and forces in the units. The presence of the Light makes the latent energy of nature active. In nature the Light sent out through doers is the intelligence often called God, who is supposed to have created the world and to carry it on. The doer is responsible for the Light it has sent into nature and must redeem it. Redeemed Light goes out again and again until it becomes unattachable to nature. Then it remains in the noetic atmosphere, is of the noetic world and is beyond and free from noetic destiny.

The Light is clear in all of the noetic atmosphere that does not penetrate the mental and psychic atmospheres of the human. The Light is taken into the noetic atmosphere by the noetic breath, and makes the atmosphere conscious in the degree of I-ness-and-selfness. The matter of the noetic atmosphere has the characteristic that it tends to oneness. This matter is conscious in various phases of I-ness-and-selfness and is poten-tially that out of which will be developed the light faculty and the I-am faculty, when the Triune Self becomes an Intelligence. In the atmosphere flows the noetic breath which is the active side of a part of the atmosphere and connects the remaining part with the knower. The knower has two aspects, passively I-ness and actively selfness. From I-ness comes the identity of the Triune Self which in the human is manifest as the feeling that it is the same today as through all past years, notwithstanding the changes in the body. Selfness is knowledge. The knower of the Triune Self is conscious in the highest phases of the degree of I-ness-and-selfness; the breath and the matter of the atmosphere are conscious in lower phases.

In the noetic atmosphere there is neither place nor time. The matter is everywhere at once. The Light is throughout, in the atmosphere, in the breath, and in the knower. The Light quickens and brings out what is potentially in the atmosphere. That which is in the atmosphere has no direct or special bearing upon the noetic destiny of the human.

That which is noetic destiny of a human is Light which is in the part of the noetic that is in the mental atmosphere of the human, (Fig. V-B); also Light that is tied up in the physical body and Light in nature which will be called on by the human.

Though Light comes in the first instance from the Intelligence, some Light comes back into the noetic atmosphere from nature when it is reclaimed and some from the mental atmosphere when a thought is balanced and so the Light in it is freed, and some when knowledge of the conscious self in the body results from thinking without creating a thought. There is a circulation of part of the Light from the noetic into the mental atmosphere, thence by means of thought into nature and thence back from food and thought into the mental and thence into the noetic atmosphere.

Light is sent by the knower into the mental atmosphere with the noetic breath. I-ness sends Light to be used in thinking, reason checks the amount that is allowed to go. Selfness sends Light to rightness when conscience speaks, and to reason as an intuition. The Light that I-ness sends becomes diffused in the mental atmosphere. The Light that selfness sends remains clear and direct. The noetic breath conveys some of the Light to the mental atmosphere, which receives it through its mental breath.

When the Light is in the matter of the mental atmosphere of the human it is diffused, modified, dimmed, dulled. The Light itself is always the same and has lost none of its character, but it appears in the mental atmosphere as though it were in a fog. This is caused by the matter of the mental atmosphere. In the lower part of this atmosphere, which is the part the human uses to think with and in which the thoughts connected with his thinking circulate and whirl, the Light is most fogged and clouded.

Whereas the Light itself, being of Intelligence and being Truth, shows in the noetic atmosphere everything as the thing is, the Light in the mental atmosphere must be freed from obstacles and interference, and must be held steadily on the subject and brought to a focus, before the Light as Truth can show what the thing is. The Light in its clear state in the noetic atmosphere cannot thence be sent into physical nature. The Light in the mental atmosphere is in a state where it can be mixed with desire and so may be sent into physical nature in that portion of a thought which is exteriorized.

The presence of the Light diffused in the mental atmosphere stimulates the matter of the atmosphere and keeps the mental breath in circulation, and the Light circulates with it and allows reason to act through its thinking. The Light in rightness is not the light of the mental atmosphere, but is clear Light that is sent in flashes from the noetic atmosphere by selfness.

No Light is in the psychic atmosphere, but there is Light in those parts of the mental and noetic atmospheres which are in it. The matter of the atmosphere is conscious in the degree of feeling-and-desire. The matter is usually dark, heavy, gross and sluggish. The psychic atmosphere pulls on and weighs down the mental and, in a lesser degree, the noetic atmosphere of the human by those parts of them which pervade it. The Light therefore is dimmed in those parts. The noetic destiny is the absence of the Light from the psychic atmosphere, from feeling-and-desire and from the psychic breath.

The chief characteristic of the psychic atmosphere is a feeling for and the desiring and rushing after something it longs for, yet fears. That something is the Light of the Intelligence and contact with the thinker and the knower. The atmosphere is not conscious of the Light. It is never quiet, but when impressions from nature, elementals or desires of other doers enter through the avenues leading from the openings of the body, it is stirred into turmoil. It pulls and it pushes, it sucks in like a whirlpool and it tries to get into everything. It surges in these ways during eating, amusement, dancing, celebrations, sermons, funerals and all trading. The atmosphere is conscious of these, its activities, but is not conscious of why it has them. It has them to get Light, the Light it once had, but which was withdrawn.

The psychic atmosphere is represented in the feeling and the desire of the doer. If feeling and desire could get the Light into the atmosphere the doer would not desire to change its present condition, it would continue to seek satisfaction from nature, it would have a greater intensity of satisfaction because of the Light, and it would not advance and so it would retard the progress of the doer. Because the doer has no Light it is in the dark, it cannot tell one thing from another, cannot form a judgment, but can only feel and desire. When things are pleasant it tries to hold them and get more of them; when they are unpleasant it tries to get away from them. Not having discrimination it does this over and over again.

The feeling or the desire is so evident in the human that it seems to be all there is. The doer occupies not only certain nerves of the voluntary nervous system, but also some which belong to the thinker and the knower. No noetic reactions may be felt, and mental reactions are felt but vaguely. If the thinker and the knower are noticed at all, they are interpreted as feeling and desire. On the other hand psychic conditions, mystic trance states and visions are supposed to be what is spoken of as "spiritual". When a human suffers he usually seeks consolation and hope in religious promises, rather than an understanding of the facts. In the psychic atmosphere feeling and desire act without the Light.

Because feeling-and-desire came into being through Light and had their greatest satisfaction while Light was with them, and because they can reach completeness only when they are in the Light, they want Light. The place where they can get it is in the mental atmosphere in the heart and principally in the lungs. Feeling cannot get beyond the heart, but desire can, and feeling gets satisfaction from desire. When the psychic atmosphere and the doer become agitated, desire rushes towards the mental atmosphere in the lungs to get Light. It cannot get into the atmosphere until it has passed rightness in the heart. Then it is in the mental atmosphere in the lungs. Desire cannot get that Light until it compels its mind to think, to gather and to focus the Light on the impression; the Light bonds the desire with the impression. The thing which is being created by thinking is a thought and is a new being. In the thought are desire of the doer and Light of the Intelligence, with which desire could not come into contact in any other way than by this admixture by thinking.

The Light is not changed, though it is bound up in the combination until the thought is balanced. Desire pushes the thought, and the Light guides it toward the first exteriorization and toward every subsequent exteriorization. When a thought is exteriorized Light goes into nature, some of it is bound up in the thought and some is diffused in the body of the human. When Light thus goes into nature it is attached to units and is part of the Light which acts as the intelligence, order and law of nature.

Only a doer can contain or direct Light of an Intelligence; no physical body, object of nature or even matter of the light world can deal with the Light, in the same sense.

The Light that is in the noetic atmospheres of the doers also illumines the light world, which is on the nature-side, and there, though not mixing with the matter, keeps that matter illuminated and in constant action. It also shows what goes on in the light world and what has been done with any of its matter while that matter was in the lower worlds. But the light world of nature does not contain the Light. The Light is there because of the atmosphere of the Triune Selves.

The Light in the mental atmospheres of the doers pervades the life world. This Light is the diffused Light in the mental atmospheres and is not mixed with desire. Light mixed with desire does not function in this way; it does not get into the life world; when it is mixed with desire and so is bound up in a thought, it remains in that thought in the mental atmosphere. The Light in the life world stimulates there the active side of the units and so starts what appears later as life on the physical plane. The Light does not illumine the form world, because there is no Light in the psychic atmosphere.

The bright lights, pictures and colors seen by psychics are matter of the physical world, for psychics cannot see into the form world, as their psychic atmospheres do not carry Light. The form plane of the physical world is not illumined by Light of the Intelligence. Its matter is lit up only in exteriorization of thoughts, not from the Light in the light or life worlds.

The physical plane of the physical world is lit by starlight coming through human nerves, by sunlight coming through hearts and lungs, moonlight coming through kidneys and adrenals, and earthlight from the sex organs and digestive systems. Starlight is diffused between the stars but is focussed by the sun. Starlight, if it could be seen directly, would be seen to penetrate and to bear the other three kinds and to be more powerful than any of them. Sunlight focusses starlight into a steady stream, as thinking focusses diffused Light. Moonlight adjusts the sunlight. Earthlight takes in or passes on or throws back the other three kinds of light. All four kinds of light work together in causing a tree, a flower or an apple to be compacted or to grow. Starlight, sunlight, moonlight and earthlight are not and do not possess light themselves; what is called their light is their property of showing their active side when this reflects Light of the Intelligence. In this sense the Light of the Intelligence, which is self-luminous and self-conscious in the noetic atmosphere, is hidden in the objects of nature which were wrought by the presence of the Light. The process is not physical and cannot be coordinated with conceptions of dimensions.

SECTION 4

The intelligence in nature comes from human beings. The pull of nature for Light. Loss of Light into nature.

Nature needs Light from Intelligences and in the human world of time gets it through human thinking and thoughts, which convey to it Light that reaches the human beings from their noetic atmospheres. The Light does not go directly into nature. The Light from the noetic atmosphere must first go into the mental atmosphere where it becomes diffused and mixes with desire, which comes into the mental atmosphere from the psychic atmosphere. The Light is not in the desire, but is bound to it in a thought. The thought is conceived or entertained in the heart and issued from the brain. In order that the Light of the Intelligence may go into nature, an act of the body is necessary to exteriorize the thought or part of it. Without an act of the body the Light from the mental atmosphere cannot go out into nature. Nature therefore wants acts by human bodies, to get through them Light from Intelligences. To that end, nature with the swing of the breath and by an object of sense reaches through the system of one of the senses into the doer, and pulls on the desire, to get the human to perform a physical act. The Light of the Intelligence goes into nature with thinking and with thoughts, through the openings of the body.

Nature seeks Light, life, forms and desire, none of which it has. It seeks them as a dry soil seeks water, as fire seeks wood, as negative seeks positive. There is an urge of unfolding and growth by combination in all matter. Without Light and without desire nature must remain inert; with Light and desire nature units combine and advance by life through growth as forms and so become conscious in higher degrees.

Nature gets the Light from human thoughts and the desire from the embodied portions of doers. Therefore nature pulls constantly on the doers in human bodies to get what will maintain it and advance it. Desire is the driving power within the form and structure of the animal and plant. Desire and the Light are in the organisms of nature as instinct, which guides in selecting food, in self-protection and in procreation.

Because nature depends upon doers in human bodies for all that it is in bodies and in forms, and for the instinct which guides the actions of the animal and vegetable organisms, and because of the elemental, universal urge for compounding, combining, growth and progress, nature pulls on doers in human bodies. It pulls on the physical plane, on the form plane, on the life plane and on the light plane. Its direct pull is, however, only from the physical plane. It pulls through seeing, hearing, tasting and smelling, and through physical contact. It does this through the four senses and by contacting the feeling-and-desire of the doer through the fourfold physical breath, the nerves, the three finer bodies and the breath-form.

Each of the senses works a set of nerves, and all four sets run into and are part of the involuntary nervous system. In this system is the breath-form, connected with all parts of the body by means of the three inner bodies. The breath-form is to the physical atmosphere somewhat as the doer is to the psychic atmosphere. The form of the breath-form is passive; the breath, the active side, is the fourfold physical breath. The breath is not breathing; it is that which keeps the physical body going and makes contact between the four senses and the doer.

Impressions of seeing, hearing, tasting, and contact by smell reach the doer by way of the corresponding physical body, the sense, the branch nerves of its system, the involuntary nervous system, the breath-form and that breath current of the fourfold physical breath which corresponds to the sense and the body. When physical contact causes feelings, impressions of contact reach the doer by way of the nerve touched, the sense of smell, the nerves of the digestive system, the solid body, the breath-form and the earth or digestive breath. The impressions brought in by seeing, hearing and tasting must go to and through the sense of smell to the breath-form and the earth breath to reach the doer, before they can be noticed as sights, sounds and tastes. The three senses and the three currents of the breath other than smell and the earth breath, are taken by the breath-form and the earth breath to the doer. These three senses and breaths touch the sense of smell, then the breath-form and the earth breath in the head, and pass by way of the involuntary nervous system to the solar plexus and thence to the end of the spinal cord, where the earth breath transfers the impression and causes the doer to see, hear and taste. Thus all sense impressions reach the doer by contact, by way of the sense of smell, the breath-form and the earth breath. But in seeing, hearing and tasting the contact is not immediate. In smelling and feeling by touch it is immediate.

When a thing is seen the sense of sight performs a double function. First it goes out towards the particles of radiant matter which are thrown off by every object, and focusses them in the line of vision; then it transmits the picture they have made in the eye to the nerves of sight. The senses of hearing and tasting work on the same principle. So does the sense of smell. All this is instantaneous.

However, when the sense of smell transmits touch it works on a different principle. It does not focus matter into the line of smelling, but it lets an elemental get into the nerves that are touched. The elemental, when in the nerves, is a sensation to the doer, such as pleasure or pain.

Nature uses objects on the physical plane to reach the desire of the doer and the Light of the Intelligence. Nature can get reactions from the doer and with them what it needs, because a human body is a thing of nature, and is at the same time the instrument of the doer. The four senses, breaths and systems in the fourfold body are in contact with the three parts, breaths and atmospheres of the Triune Self, and on the other side with the four worlds of nature.

The seven facial and five other openings belong to nature, but are used by nature and by the doer. Nature uses them for reaching into the body, to connect with the breath-form; the doer uses them to connect with objects on the physical plane. Nature begins her pull through one of her four senses and its system. So nature is connected with the doer, above and below, in a human body.

There are two nerve tracts or cords or tubes in the body, one for nature and the other for the doer, which in the perfect body were connected, (Fig. VI-D). In the human the nature-tract is the alimentary canal, from mouth to anus. The sense of smell has charge of this tract directly, but the three other senses are connected with it, act upon it and influence it. The other tract, the spinal cord and terminal filament, is at present for the doer of the Triune Self; it reaches from the first cervical vertebra to the tip of the terminal filament at the end of the spine; the doer does not use this tract as it might, but uses organs instead; these organs are the heart and the lungs, the kidneys and adrenals, and the male and female organs, which are go-betweens for the nature tract and the doer tract.

The sections of the body are in and connect with the four worlds; the head with the light, the thoracic cavity with the life, the abdominal cavity with the form, and the pelvic cavity with the physical world. However, the head is now used for the physical world and the pelvic cavity for the light world. That is so because the knower, the thinker, and the doer as a whole, have withdrawn from the body. The brain in the head has been usurped by the portion of the doer that is in the body and the pelvic organs are devoted to and controlled by the procreative functions in the body.

The four systems are related to and run through the four sections. In this organization nature pulls on the doer for Light, with and through the fourfold breath. The generative system is worked by the elemental functioning as the sense of sight. Through the generative system the sense of sight can act, indirectly, from the four planes of the physical world on nature, and on the three parts and the three atmospheres of the Triune Self, and so may get Light from the doer for nature. Some of the organs of the generative system, which connect with nature through the involuntary system, are: on the light plane the eyes and their nerves; on the life plane the heart and lungs and their nerves; on the form plane the kidneys and adrenals and their nerves; on the physical plane the generative organs and their nerves.

The Triune Self may contact organs of the generative system through the voluntary nervous system; the pituitary body may be contacted by I-ness and the pineal body by selfness; the heart and cerebellum by rightness and the lungs and cerebrum by reason; the kidneys are used by feeling and the adrenals by desire. So the Triune Self may work the generative system through the cerebellum, the heart and the kidneys, and through three brains, the cerebrum, the lungs and the adrenals. It does not do this at present, but through these organs the sense of sight now gets Light from the doer for nature.

The pull of nature is exercised from the light plane of the physical world, through the generative system, and by the sense of sight through the eyes and the male or female organs, and especially the testicles and ovaries. By means of the sight acting successively on the planes of the physical world,—on the light plane through the eyes, on the life plane through the heart and lungs, on the form plane through the kidneys and adrenals, and on the physical plane through the sex organs,—there is finally an action on the breath-form by the earth breath as it breathes out through the sex parts. The pull is transferred in the kidneys from the breath-form to the feeling of the doer, and then desire, in the adrenals, rushes to the heart.

In the heart, if rightness is overcome or does not put up any barrier, thinking is started, which draws Light from the mental atmosphere. The heart and cerebellum and the lungs and cerebrum interact, and the brain diffuses the Light which is mixed with desire in the heart and lungs for thinking and thoughts. The pull of nature is directly on the doer. Light passes out in the thoughts as they are issued from the brain, and as they are exteriorized in acts, objects or events. Or especially when there is a sexual spasm, the Light leaves, being then precipitated by the brain and drawn along the spinal cord to the small of the back and along the kidneys out into nature. The sexual brain, the testicles or ovaries, influences the psychic brain, the adrenals; that influences the mental brain, the lungs; and that influences the noetic brain, the cerebrum; and all this causes the Light of the noetic atmosphere to work for nature. Such is noetic destiny at this time. The physical human world of nature has sex and sex organs; the doer has no sex and no sex organs.

The breath-form, as the form and the breath, is used by the doer as the bridge by which it crosses over to nature and nature crosses over to it. The crossings from all planes are made on the physical plane in a human body and by means of the earth breath.

The respiratory system is worked by the sense of hearing and through that system this elemental can act, indirectly, from the four planes of the physical world upon the three parts of the Triune Self and the three atmospheres in which they are, and so may get thoughts from the doer and from them forms for nature. The respiratory system uses substantially the same organs on the respective planes of the physical world as does the generative system, namely: on the light plane the ears; on the life plane the heart and lungs; on the form plane the kidneys and adrenals; on the physical plane the generative organs, and the involuntary nerves of each of these organs. The Triune Self uses the same organs, the cerebellum, the heart and the kidneys, and the same brains, the cerebrum, the lungs and the adrenals, as when it acts in the generative system.

The pull of nature through the respiratory system is exercised from the life plane of the physical world. The pull is ultimately always on the doer and that draws on the mental atmosphere for Light. The sense of hearing cannot pull directly on the mental atmosphere. The sense of hearing acts with the earth breath in the generative parts on the breath-form; that transmits a pull, in the kidneys, to the doer in the body, and desire if aroused goes to the heart. If rightness is overcome or agrees, mental activity begins there and passive thinking results. In passive thinking there is only a playing of desire in the diffused Light of the Intelligence. Yet this is enough to carry some of the Light into nature. If the passive thinking results in active thinking or in a thought, more of the Light is mixed with desire and goes out into nature by speech or by a thought. The stages are as follows: the sense of hearing is on the life plane of the physical world and after acting on the intermediate planes and organs, acts on the breath-form in the sex parts, through the sense of smell and the earth breath; this transmits the pull to the doer, in the kidneys; then desire rushes to the heart. If rightness is overcome or agrees, thinking is started and draws Light from the mental atmosphere. So a thought is there generated, and is issued from the brain, or the Light goes out by speech through the mouth.

The circulatory system is worked by the sense of taste. When nature pulls through this sense the sense acts from the form plane of the physical world to reach the three parts of the Triune Self and their atmospheres. Nature uses the sense of taste and the circulatory system to get forms and desire. The thoughts obtained through the respiratory system are the models for the forms, and the sense of taste gets the design, the details, and the desire which fills out the models. The desire is the driving power in the form. The circulatory system uses substantially the same organs on the respective planes of the physical world as does the generative system, namely: on the light plane the tongue; on the life plane the heart and lungs; on the form plane the kidneys and adrenals; on the physical plane the generative organs; and the involuntary nerves of each of these organs. The doer of the Triune Self has the same organs, the cerebellum, the heart, and the kidneys, and the same brains, the cerebrum, the lungs and the adrenals, as it has for action through the generative system.

The pull of nature through the sense of taste is exercised from the form plane of the physical world. The pull is ultimately made on the mental atmosphere, if the pull is effective. The sense of taste exercising the pull of nature transmits it to the breath, which passes it on to the breath-form as the breath passes out through the sex parts. So the pull is passed on to the kidneys where the doer receives it. If there is a reaction it begins when the desire rushes to the heart, and the thinker receives it. If rightness is ignored or agrees, thinking uses the Light diffused in the mental atmosphere, and a thought results.

The digestive system is worked by the elemental functioning as the sense of smell. When nature pulls through the digestive system, the sense may act through any of the four planes of the physical world to reach the doer and its atmosphere to get Light. Nature pulls through the digestive system and the sense of smell to get food for its bodies. The food builds up, exteriorizes and gives physical bodies to the forms which nature has received through the sense of taste. The digestive system uses substantially the same organs on the respective planes of the physical world as the generative system, namely: on the light plane of the physical world the nose and its nerves; on the life plane the heart and lungs and their nerves; on the form plane the kidneys and adrenals and their nerves, and on the physical plane the generative organs and their nerves.

But differing from the other three systems, the digestive has a special set of organs in addition: the esophagus, the stomach and the intestinal tract, a tract which goes from the light plane, the head, to the physical plane, the anus. The Triune Self has the same organs,—the cerebellum, the heart and the kidneys, and the same brains, the cerebrum, the lungs and the adrenals,—as it has for action through the generative, respiratory and circulatory systems, but the Triune Self does not touch the digestive system with these organs and brains as directly as it uses or contacts the other three systems, because it is not as intimately related to the digestive system. In addition, the doer of the Triune Self touches the digestive system in two organs, the stomach and the liver, but it does not touch it in these organs as immediately as it touches the other systems.

The pull of nature through the digestive system is exercised from the physical plane of the physical world. The pull ultimately draws on the mental atmosphere if rightness is ignored or consents and the pull of nature becomes effective. The sense of smell, in order to exercise the pull for nature, reaches from the light plane of the physical world through the nose, from the life plane through the heart and lungs, from the form plane through the kidneys and adrenals, and on the physical plane through the urinary tract, and the anus at the end of the digestive tube. The sense of smell transmits the pull to the breath which passes it on to the breath-form as the breath goes out through the sex parts and the excretory ducts. The pull starts at the anus and the opening of the urinary tract and continues up the alimentary canal to the mouth. From the small intestine the pull is transmitted to the kidneys where the doer receives it. The pull continues to the stomach causing various secretions from the organs along the tract, like the pancreas and liver. The pull is transmitted from the kidneys through the involuntary nervous system by the breath to the stomach, where it is felt as hunger. If there is response, it begins by desire rushing to the heart.

There, if rightness is ignored or agrees, the doer may by thinking obtain some of the Light, and a thought results. The Light may pass out in a thought, and if food is consumed to satisfy the pull, some part of the thought with the Light in it is exteriorized in the tissue of the body; and other parts return to nature as excrements, which nature uses to rebuild her structure.

The pull of nature for the Light that is in the noetic atmosphere of the Triune Self begins by a pull on the breath, and at a time when the breath swings out at the sex parts. When the pull is made through the digestive system there is an additional pull at the end of the alimentary tube. This special pull of the digestive system is due to the fact that this system is on the physical plane of the physical world, the plane where all worlds touch, and through which the circulation between the Triune Self and nature is kept up. The digestive system is on the lowest plane, but it is the most powerful of the systems. All worlds of nature come in contact with the atmospheres of the Triune Self only through the digestive system, that is, through the physical plane.

The doer of the Triune Self depends on its physical body for progress and this body is of the same plane as the digestive system. The power of hunger compels the doer to furnish physical food; and food, maintaining the body, keeps the doer on the physical plane. The desire for food brings about the complex relations which compose civilization. The power of the digestive system is also shown by the fact that the alimentary tube takes up more space in the body than the other systems, and that the other systems are subsidiary to the digestion and assimilation of food, turning physical nature into skin, flesh, fat, blood, bones, marrow and nerves. The way nature works in all the systems is displayed more openly in the digestive system. There, in the working of peristalsis, it is most readily seen. Peristalsis, the involuntary contractile movements in the organs of the four systems, conveys to nature the material it needs after the material has in it some Light. In the digestive system this response to the pull of nature by the breath is most pronounced.

The connection and interrelation between nature and the doer is made by the physical breath, and more particularly by that stream of it called the digestive or earth breath. Both nature and doer work on the breath-form through the fourfold physical breath. Nature works on it through its four senses and systems, and the doer works on it through its feeling and desire.

The breath-form has two aspects, a negative and a positive. The negative is the form, the positive is the breath and the physical atmosphere. The matter of the breath of the breath-form is refined matter of the four worlds of the earth sphere. The breath-form is akin to nature and to the doer, and one side of it is the flowing breath that enables both to make their communication. While the breath-form is negative to the breath and the breath positive to it, the breath itself is positive in its outbreathing and negative in its inbreathing. This breath bathes the entire body in its tidal flow, which is imperceptible except where it carries air into and out of the lungs. Imperceptibly it moves just as much out of the eye, or any pore or any other part, as it does out of the lungs.

The physical breath has four currents, namely, the generative, respiratory, circulatory and digestive breaths, and is related by them through the four bodies to the fire, air, water and earth in the earth sphere. The psychic, mental and noetic breath streams have to work through the fourth, the current called the earth breath, to reach the doer.

When nature pulls, which she must do by one of the four senses, she reaches by means of the ingoing breath with the sense to the sense nerves, and then with the sense through its system to the corresponding current of the breath, and pulls on that when it is positive and flows out with the earth breath current through the sex parts into the physical atmosphere. This pull induces an involuntary peristaltic action in the system on which nature pulls, to get out of that system the matter and the Light that is mixed and concealed in it. The pull then goes with the breath to the breath-form and to the sex parts and the other parts which are on the physical plane, and thence to the form plane and the kidneys.

So nature pulling on the fourfold physical breath causes thereby a peristaltic action in the four systems, by which visible and invisible physical matter, in which there is hidden some Light, goes into nature directly. The pull is ceaseless as long as the breath flows, but the peristaltic results do not carry Light to nature as regularly; sometimes more, sometimes less, sometimes no Light is transferred. Whatever light goes out goes with the outgoing positive breath.

Some of it goes through the twelve openings of the body and the pores of the skin. This is either Light carried out by matter which has while circulating in the body been impressed by thinking, or it is Light which is directly thought out into nature through the sense organs, as through the eye when one looks at a person or thing. The thinking is usually induced by elementals or by thoughts that enter with the incoming breath through the sex openings, the navel and nerve centers in the pelvic and abdominal cavities. The other Light that goes out does so in thoughts, when they are issued from the brain and when the person who issues them exteriorizes them by an act. Then the Light goes out through the act by sight or by word.

Through the bodies of children no Light goes out into nature until they become pubescent. The Light that is taken in from food is built into the body, particularly the bones and brain, through the thymus gland, the distribution being regulated by the pituitary body. By puberty the thymus gland is absorbed and therefore can no longer act as a stopcock. At puberty a child is connected with its noetic atmosphere. From then on the generative system assumes the function of withdrawing Light from the two nervous systems, together with the function of seed production.

The main channels through which Light is lost into nature are the sex organs. Seeing dress and movements, hearing a voice, especially in song, tasting rich food, smelling odors and touching a body of the opposite sex, all suggest sexual attraction and take hold of and dominate thinking on sex matters. Elementals come in. They are the sexual sensations. A human feels these sensations, but does not feel his feeling and mistakes the elementals he feels and nourishes, for his own feeling. The elementals excite him, he acts for them and he allows them to take the Light away.

SECTION 5

Automatic return of Light from nature. The lunar germ. Self-control.

The Light which a human has sent or allowed to go into nature is returned to the human. It goes out again and is returned again. This outgoing and incoming will continue until the Light is reclaimed from all admixtures and attachments and is made unattachable or freed Light. Then it goes out no more.

Light is returned to the noetic atmosphere of the human either automatically, or through self-control. Automatic reclamation is started by a Light finder or gatherer, called lunar germ, and is accomplished by the pull of the noetic breath along the nature-tract. Reclamation by self-control, which is of three degrees, is done by thinking and is aided by another germ, called solar germ, which makes a path along the tract for the Triune Self for Light to travel on.

Automatic reclamation of Light is the finding and the gathering by the lunar germ of Light that has come in with food and the carrying of the gathered Light as far as the kidneys, and then the raising of this Light to the noetic atmosphere in the head by the psychic, the mental and the noetic breaths. This automatic reclamation can be made only while the Light is in the body to which it has returned in food, and after it has been extracted from the food by organs of the four systems and by the fourfold physical breath.

The Light that has gone into nature comes back automatically in food. The Light that has gone out in the various ways mentioned never leaves the noetic atmosphere of the Triune Self. Just as thoughts never leave the mental, and desires, even if they appear as animals, never leave the psychic atmosphere, so the Light never leaves the noetic atmosphere. Earth time and dimensions have no effect upon and are no hindrance to Light of an Intelligence. The Light of an Intelligence that is in the noetic atmosphere of its Triune Self, though it goes out into physical nature, returns thence because that Light has an identity. It retains this identity however long it circulates in nature and in however many forms and places it appears there. For the Light is a part of an Intelligence, which is an ultimate unit, inseparable, indivisible.

Special parts of Light circulating in nature are summoned into food, to be thence extracted for reclamation. What of the Light is so called depends upon the thinking of the human. It may be days, months, years or lives before some of the Light is drawn back. But when it is to be reclaimed, any special part of the Light will return to the body of the doer that let it go out, though the present human is not aware of the identity and the circulation of the Light which his thinking summons to return to the body.

Not all the Light that is taken in with food is the Light of the consumer. Light from other doers is with it and affects those who eat the food. Usually there is something in common between the foreign Light and the doer that receives it. Just as the atmospheres of different people intermingle according to quality, so the Light that is with food intermingles.

Food is of the four elements and is taken in as solids, as liquids, in air and sunlight, and in starlight. The solid food contains the other three, just as the physical world is a precipitation of the other three worlds, as the physical plane is matter condensed from the other planes of the physical world, and as the structure elementals contain the form, the portal and the causal. The solid and liquid forms of food enter through the digestive system; the airy and some of the fiery foods enter through the respiratory system. But these are only the most apparent ways. Starlight enters also through the eyes and through the skin. With the breath food from the four elements is taken in directly from one's physical atmosphere where it is held in suspension. No matter how the food is taken in, it all goes into the digestive system. There the other three systems also work on it.

The fourfold physical breath, as it flows in and out of the body, causes a peristaltic action in the organs and tubes of each of the four systems. Each breath causes the peristalsis in its own system, and each sense stimulates the function in its system under that peristaltic impulse.

As food is moved in the digestive system this fourfold stream of the physical breath, each stream acting with its stimulated peristalsis, affects the food. Seeing the food, what is said and heard while eating it, tasting it and smelling it, have a direct bearing on the digestion. The salivary glands add their secretions, the gastric juice is poured out from the walls of the stomach, the liver gives its bile, the pancreas its fluid, and the intestinal digestive glands their secretion. The four senses cause the activity of the juices and of the ferments in them. Thereby proper changes are made in the food, which is turned into chyme in the stomach and later into chyle and becomes ready for absorption and assimilation in the intestines.

In the circulation the kidneys strain the blood and free it from impurities, and the adrenals pour out their secretion, which empowers the red and the white blood cells, keeps the blood and lymph in circulation, invigorates the sex glands and the ductless glands. The respiratory system takes in air as food, supplies oxygen to the blood and eliminates waste matter. This system is the channel through which starry matter flows into the generative system. The seat of the generative system

is the pituitary body, and it has organs and branches in all parts of the
brain and throughout the body.

The generative system is the source of the other three systems. It
begins in the fused cells as a point, grows into a line and a surface and
becomes a circle within a sphere. The circle separates into the spine and
the digestive tract. From some part of the generative system the allantois
is created; that later protrudes through the amniotic sac and the chorion,
fastens itself to the wall of the uterus and becomes the placenta. With
the placenta are developed the kidneys and adrenals and the heart and
lungs, and the circulatory and the respiratory systems are started within
the divided circle. The kidneys working through the heart carry on the
circulation, which is not independent until the intake of breath after
birth.

The generative system is the beginning of the physical body from
the fecundated cell, the carrier of vitality during the existence of the body,
the governor of the nervous systems and of the ductless glands. Seed
production in the adult is but one of its functions. During life the
generative system regulates the secretions of the ductless glands, such as
the pituitary, thyroid, thymus, spleen and adrenals. By these secretions
the activities of all four systems are maintained from the pituitary body.
The generative system inspirits the ferments and secretions of the organs
and thereby causes digestion, absorption and assimilation. At death it
cuts itself off from the other three systems which are then unable to
function.

The generative system makes an extract of four grades of radiant
matter from all the foods. The first is small in amount and is of radiant
matter drawn directly by means of the nerves from food in the digestive
system; the second grade is the largest in amount and is radiant matter
drawn from food that has passed into the circulatory system; the third
grade is radiant matter drawn from food in the respiratory system and
the fourth and most potent grade is elaborated from starry matter that
has reached the generative system itself.

The four kinds of extracts are elaborated in the testicles and the
ovaries for seed and for soil. So that in the seed and in the soil are
represented all parts of the body in essence. After the seed and the soil
are brought to a certain point they take on independent life as spermatozoa and ova.

From these extracts of starry matter the generative system makes a
tonic tincture and turns this tincture back into the other systems and

into itself. The generative system is the ultimate cause of well-being and disease. It gives the tonic tincture to the involuntary and the voluntary nerves, and in this way returns to the digestive, circulatory and respiratory systems that which is made from the extract of the food that passed through them. Because of this tincture the other three systems are kept going, a life-giving quality can be taken in by respiration and sent to all parts of the body, the blood can be circulated and food can be digested.

While these transformations are going on Light is being extracted from the food in its first and subsequent forms. The digestive, the circulatory, the respiratory and the generative breaths work each upon its system in the body to take up a certain part of the food and of the Light which is in it and carry the Light into the generative system. Finally the generative breath transfers a portion of the Light connected with the food to a lunar germ. Physically these processes are controlled by the pituitary body. It controls the four systems and the four physical breaths by means of the involuntary nervous system and its involuntary actions. Light going back to the noetic atmosphere goes through the generative system.

The four grades of extract have in them Light and circulate in the generative system. While they are in the head the fire current of the fourfold breath can draw Light out. The Light that moves up and down in the generative system is Light that is contained in the radiant matter that was extracted from food.

The automatic transfer of Light to the noetic atmosphere is made by the generative system naturally to the noetic breath, when there is enough Light in the generative system. The noetic atmosphere exercises by means of the noetic breath a continuous pull for its own Light. This attempt to raise its Light out of the generative system is contrary to the pull which nature makes there for the Light. The noetic breath contacts indirectly the generative physical breath, that is, the fire current of the fourfold physical breath, in the head and there takes some of the Light off and back into the noetic atmosphere.

There is in the generative system other Light, Light which does not come out of nature, but comes through the pituitary body from the noetic atmosphere. Some of this Light is sent out monthly in the lunar germ to gather Light that has come in from nature.

A lunar germ is made of matter of the four worlds and has mingled with it essential matter of the four worlds, that is, matter which has circulated so long that it has reached ultimate states of refinement. In addition to the general matter and to this essential matter, a lunar germ bears the impress of the doer and has in it consequently Light of the Intelligence. The lunar germ is material but invisible.

Both the lunar germ and the seed or soil are builders of bodies. With the seed and the soil the outer physical body is started; with the lunar germ inner bodies may be built. The spermatozoa and ova are both as female to the lunar germ, and it is as male to them. Only the gross physical elements flow through the seed and the soil and these are deficient in finer forces of physical matter. A lunar germ supplies these deficiencies and has in it contacts for forces of the other three worlds. A lunar germ must be united to the seed or the soil to produce a body which is not entirely deficient. There ought to be for a proper human body a lunar germ in the seed and a lunar germ also in the soil.

In each month, after puberty, the generative system produces one of these lunar germs in the pituitary body, (Fig. VI-A,a). When the lunar germ has matured and has life of its own it leaves the pituitary. It starts from there in a rudimentary way, on the right side, and passes down in the involuntary nervous system, having a little Light, which attracts other Light as it descends in the nerve plexuses supplying the digestive system in the abdomen, until it reaches the lowest point, (Fig. VI-B). From that point the lunar germ, having crossed over to the left side, ascends along the involuntary nervous system and is carried by the generative breath to the region of the left kidney.

During all this time Light from food along the digestive tract, Light from blood and Light from the organs in the body attaches itself to the Light in the lunar germ for automatic reclamation. While a lunar germ is in existence and carries Light, it may be deprived of some of the Light by an outburst of anger or state of jealousy, envy or revenge, but it will always carry some Light until the germ is lost. It is lost in outgoing seed or soil. It is not connected with seed or soil until that is precipitated and lost.

If the lunar germ has risen with its diffused Light to the region of the kidneys, some of that Light is taken away by the psychic breath and carried upward in the involuntary nervous system. The psychic breath is made to do this by the mental breath acting within it and obeying the pull of the noetic breath for Light. Then the mental breath takes the Light and carries it along the thoracic vertebrae to the region of the cervical vertebrae. The mental breath is made to do this by the noetic breath acting within it. The noetic breath takes the Light along the pons and the quadrigemina to the pineal body and into the noetic atmosphere.

This return of Light to the noetic atmosphere is automatic. It is done without the knowledge of the human and usually without the possibility of interference by him, though certain habits like the consumption of alcohol or of narcotics, or excessive sexuality, may hinder even the automatic reclamation.

The purpose of automatic reclamation of a certain amount of Light is to keep enough in the mental atmosphere to furnish the human with the Light necessary to continue living and carrying on his activities as a human.

The returning of Light from nature goes on continually in every human. Only a certain amount of Light is allowed by the Triune Self to its doer, and the doer must husband and reclaim what Light is loaned to it. Without this automatic process of reclamation a doer would soon be bankrupt and lost. In the noetic atmosphere moves in regular action the noetic breath. This carries Light of the Intelligence by inspiration into the physical body within the reach of nature, and carries by aspiration the available Light from the body, reclaimed from nature, back into the noetic atmosphere.

The usual means by which Light that has been in food is raised is carriage by a lunar germ. Such a germ is produced once a month, descends on the right side and in a week reaches the region of the solar plexus; in another week it reaches the large intestine and the lowest point of its descent and during the third week ascends to the kidneys, on the left side. Usually the lunar germ, after it has ascended to the region of the kidneys with the aid of the pull exercised by the generative breath on account of the noetic breath, drops back to the sexual organs and is lost. If it were not for the automatic protection which the monthly germ receives because of the noetic breath, the germ would be lost on its path downward from the solar plexus and would never ascend to the left kidney. The run of human beings would, owing to the pull of nature, become idiots in one life, if it were not for the automatic reclamation of Light and the protection which the lunar germ usually receives. For this reason the lunar germ cannot be lost on its path from the head to the solar plexus; from the solar plexus downward and then upward towards the left kidney it is protected; but from the kidney to the head, if it goes there at all, it can go only as the result of self-control.

SECTION 6

Reclamation of Light by self-control. Loss of the lunar germ. Reten-
tion of the lunar germ. The solar germ. Divine, or "immaculate",
conception in the head. Regeneration of the physical body. Hiram
Abiff. Origin of Christianity.

Automatic reclamation is done by the psychic breath taking Light away from the lunar germ, and along the nerves of the digestive system upward from the region of the left kidney and adrenal. The three stages of reclamation by self-control are made by the doer, the thinker, and the knower. Then these three parts of the Triune Self take off Light from the lunar germ and take the germ itself up the spinal cord of the voluntary nervous system. The basis of all four kinds of reclamation is the automatic process by which Light is, from food, prepared for the lunar germ.

The first stage of voluntary reclamation of Light that has come into the body, is the recovery of that Light due to desire to do right. This first stage has to do with taking Light away from the lunar germ, with carrying that Light into the blood and to the heart and lungs and with raising the lunar germ itself from the lowest point to about the junction of the first lumbar and the twelfth dorsal vertebrae on the left side along the voluntary nervous system. The first stage of the reclamation of Light in the body is done by a human who does not want to be led by nature into doing things he feels that nature wants; who wants to be led into doing what is best for him and who does his duties, not grudgingly, but cheerfully. This relates especially to eating and sex, to the desires for possessions, a name or fame, and for power.

If such control is the endeavor of a human his desire will, without his being conscious of it, take away some of the Light which is carried by the lunar germ when it has risen as high as the left kidney.

After the psychic and the mental breaths have there taken some Light for the noetic atmosphere, in the course of the automatic saving, desire living in the blood may bear some of the remaining Light away in the blood stream. The only time when desire can get this Light is during one to three days of each month when a lunar germ is near the kidneys. The Light which desire gets in this way mingles with it, but does not blend. The human does not know about the reclamation, except that he may feel a slight sensation of cheer.

In the blood there is bound Light and free Light. Light which was extracted from the digestive system of the body, is bound Light and cannot be taken up by desire until a lunar germ has extracted it. Light which desire has brought into the blood is free and remains free, until it is either reclaimed by thinking or until desire unites with the Light when the breath meets the circulatory system in the heart and lungs, and only when a thought is conceived or entertained.

The run of human beings lose their lunar germs within the month, and with the lunar germ goes the Light that is in it. But if some Light is taken from the germ by the automatic reclamation, that much Light is returned by the psychic breath to the atmospheres and is saved for the time. If in addition some Light is taken by desire by this unwitting reclamation into the blood, that too is saved when the germ is lost and the remaining Light in it goes back into the circulations of nature.

The second stage of the reclamation of Light that has come back into the body is reached when a human is acquiring self-control by thinking. Pessimism, mysticism and asceticism are of no use. They hinder rather than help. It is not necessary that one should know anything about the phrases "Light of the Intelligence" or "reclamation". It is enough that he intends what his inner One, his Father, the Light in him, shows to be right. Every human has that Light within, though he does not know it as such and does not do what it shows to be right. The second stage requires an attitude of mind akin to optimism, which favors honest and clear thinking, and an enjoyment of the pleasures of life with temperance and without hate, greed or envy. It requires as to his duties, that he should perform them willingly and understandingly.

With the desire that brings the first degree of reclamation and with this attitude of mind, he develops, though he may at times slip back, a mental set that will result in voluntary reclamation. By this mental set his thinking will without his being conscious of it, extract Light that is free in the bloodstream and some of the Light that is bound in a thought and will even balance some thoughts. It may also raise the lunar germ along the voluntary nervous system up to the highest of the thoracic vertebrae.

Thinking can get Light from circulating blood only while it is heart-blood and lung-blood, and only when rightness reigns and desire is in agreement with it.

The seasons in the body present a favorable condition when the solar germ, descending and ascending in the two hemispheres of the spinal cord, is opposite the heart. This occurs twice a year, during the three days following the twenty-first days of June and of December. Getting Light in thinking is, however, not restricted to these favorable times; it may happen at any time, provided the lunar germ has risen above the kidneys.

From heart-blood and lung-blood, thinking, by means of the mental breath acting through the respiratory breath, raises Light from the heart and from the lungs to the cerebellum and cerebrum. Thinking raises it by an effort to hold Light on a definite subject, such as who one is, and who one's knower or Father in Heaven is. The thinking which reclaims Light is intent upon learning from the errors of the past. It is different from ordinary, haphazard, passive thinking. It is even more than active thinking on a matter of religion or philosophy. It is thinking so intended and restrained as to be active thinking on such subjects as immortality, the dweller in the body, truthfulness, chastity, honesty, the purpose of life or service and goodwill. It is active thinking with the definite aim of learning for personal moral and mental advancement. It overrides all obstacles of desires, allurements and weaknesses. It is accompanied by events in the body. When this sort of thinking goes on it prevents the Light circulating in the body from flowing out, and it empowers the lunar germ to take up more Light.

During this effort Light in the mental atmosphere claims and takes Light from the heart-blood. When the blood-Light becomes mental Light and is taken away from desire, desire tries to follow the Light and so gives force to the thinking. Thinking carries the Light to the cerebellum and the cerebrum. The Light remains in that part of the noetic atmosphere in the brain which is related to the subject of the thinking.

Thinking gets Light not only from heart-blood but also from thoughts, yet only under certain conditions. The thought must be in the heart or the lungs and the thinking must either be done in connection with the willing and understanding performance of a duty or must be thinking toward repudiation of the thought. Such thinking may produce two kinds of results. It may take away some of the Light from the thought, weakening it, and restore the Light to the mental atmosphere, or it may take away all of the Light because it balances the thought. The human is not conscious of the result produced by his thinking, but the effects of the reclaimed Light will be felt by him as lightness, airiness and vitality in the body and mental ease and the ability to see things more clearly.

Thinking may extract some of the Light that is bound in a thought while the thought is in the heart or the lungs. It does this when it disapproves of the thought, and so draws Light away from it, thus limiting and retarding it.

Thinking may also take all the Light out of a thought. When a thought has been conceived and is not yet issued, it is being gestated in the cerebellum and the cerebrum. There is a communication between the thought and the heart in which it was conceived. The thought is nourished by active and by passive thinking. If during this time the human determines to abandon the aim and the object of the thought, the thought is drawn back into the heart, and the Light is separated from the desire by thinking and is returned to the mental atmosphere from the heart and lungs.

Light may also be reclaimed from a thought after the thought has been issued, but before it is exteriorized. The thought has then left the head through the frontal sinuses and is in the mental atmosphere. If the human decides to abandon the aim and the object, the thought goes to the part of the mental atmosphere which is in the heart and lungs. There thinking separates the Light from the desire, and the Light is transferred to the mental and the desire to the psychic atmosphere.

It may be that the thought was not exteriorized as a whole, but that only the design was exteriorized wholly, partially or in a modified form. In this case no Light is extracted. If the thought as a whole is exteriorized with the first exteriorization all the Light is extracted, otherwise the Light is extracted when the thought is balanced, which may not be until after many exteriorizations.

A thought is balanced by thinking when feeling-and-desire are in agreement with each other and both are in agreement with rightness and that and reason are in agreement with selfness concerning the act, object or event, which had been witnessed by I-ness. Then the thinking extracts Light from the thought and transfers it to the pineal body where it is restored to the noetic atmosphere.

The Light can be extracted only when the thought is in the heart and lungs. In the first and second cases the decision to abandon the aim and object sends the thought there. In the third case, when the thought is balanced at the first exteriorization because of the mental attitude, this attitude calls it to the heart and lungs.

It is different in cases which are reactions to results of the law of thought. There the balancing is done at a time when a thought cycle has brought the thought back to the heart and lungs for balancing, or when circumstances like mental associations, memories or an event cause the thought to be drawn suddenly into the heart and lungs, or when an abstract subject is thought of, such as destiny, living forever, service, or being conscious of the desire for self-knowledge. Then something affects the heart and lungs and compels the human to question.

This probing and searching is the beginning of the third stage of voluntary reclamation, which is intentional and knowing. Sometimes the searcher finds what he looks for, sometimes he discovers what he did not expect. His thinking opens up the thought and by the Light it uses and the Light that is in the thought, shows him the feelings and desires in the thought as they truly are. When he acknowledges these to be as the Light shows that they are, and determines that he will make them as they should be, the Light of that thought goes with the Light in the mental atmosphere to the pineal body and is thence transferred to the noetic atmosphere, and the thought is balanced.

The third stage of the reclamation of Light which has come into the body from nature is the recovery of the Light due to knowledge gained in the previous two stages. This knowledge is that he should not by his thinking attach himself to anything or attach anything to himself. The third stage is reached when a human applies this knowledge in his living. As he continues, encumbrances and interferences fall gradually away. He acquires confidence in action, strength in purpose, penetration in looking at a thing or a condition. Neither friends nor strangers influence him. Money, possessions and attainments cease to have attraction for him. He eats and drinks what will keep his body in health, he enjoys his food although he does not eat for the pleasure of eating. He is not bitter or sour any more than he is a hedonist. He attends to his occupations because they are his work. But all his effort in whatever he thinks or does or omits is to reclaim Light and not to bind it up again.

With such a one, too, the automatic reclamation works better and is more effective than with one who knows or cares nothing about it. The voluntary reclamation is based on a more steady desire which controls all other desires, and on a mental set to reclaim Light, intentionally and intelligently. Thoughts that are balanced are one of two main sources of the Light that is reclaimed, although this is not known to the one who balances them and so obtains the Light that was in them. The other source is Light that is carried by a lunar germ into the head.

The automatic protection of a lunar germ ends when it has come up as high as the left kidney; and the germ is lost, usually through sexual occupations, after the psychic breath has taken off some Light automatically. It may, however, be raised along the spinal cord in the region of the dorsal and the cervical vertebrae until it reaches the midbrain. There it arrives as a physically matured germ, and can when united with seed or soil, be used in the generation of a physical body, superior in health and strength to those that crowd the world. However, if it is preserved, it will unite with the next monthly germ which merges into it. Then it will descend and make a second round through the body, being automatically protected up to the left kidney. It will, if it is not lost, arrive at the head for the second time, at the end of the second lunar month, strengthened by additional Light it has gathered,

While it is possible for one who has developed a lunar germ of higher degrees, that is, one carried for two, three or four months, to beget a body in which a doer more perfect than those in the bodies of the run of human beings may enter, and while indeed there have been men on the earth who were born from seeds containing lunar germs preserved for many lunations, it is also possible to retain the lunar germ into which the subsequent monthly lunar germs have merged, for the regeneration of the body, for self-impregnation and for the building of three inner bodies, in which the three parts of the Triune Self will live also in the form, life, and light worlds. When all of the subsequent lunar germs have been merged with the first, there is a divine conception in the head, because of the presence of the solar germ.

The solar germ is a portion of the doer and it represents the Triune Self, and has with it some of the clear Light. It has no body of nature-matter, such as the lunar germ has. There is only one solar germ for each life, though the germ renews itself every year. It appears at puberty, in the pituitary body and descends in the right side of the spinal cord until, after about six months, it reaches the end of the cord proper at about the first lumbar vertebra, (Fig. VI-A,d). Then it turns and ascends in the left side, during about six months, and arrives at the pineal body. While it is in the head it renews itself and then starts on the next descent. It continues this through life. At the death of the body it becomes again one with the doer.

The solar germ by its journeys, south and north in the spinal cord, patrols The Way. It keeps open the dwelling place of the Triune Self, while the three parts of the Triune Self, as at present, do not dwell in the spinal cord. With the run of human beings the solar germ does nothing more.

Its potential activities depend upon the presence of a lunar germ in its field of operation. Every lunar germ must pass the solar germ at least once a year, that is, while the lunar germ is going down. With the run of human beings it does not pass the solar germ a second time.

If a lunar germ is not lost, but on the return path to the head rises higher than the station at the lumbar vertebrae where the psychic breath takes off Light in the course of the automatic reclamation, it is near the path of the solar germ and within the field of its influence. The solar germ then assists the lunar germ, by giving it strength as well as a push or pull upwards. If a lunar germ is preserved so as to make the second round it receives additional assistance. So it is in each succeeding round. When a lunar germ has completed thirteen rounds within twelve months, having of course with it the twelve successive monthly germs which have merged into it, and having the Light it received each time it passed the solar germ, and returns to the head, it is met there by the solar germ and receives Light from it. With that Light is a direct ray of Light of the Intelligence. This is a self-impregnation or divine, immaculate, virgin conception, and from it begins the rebuilding of the physical body into an immortal physical body. With the rebuilding of the body is achieved the reclamation of all Light that has gone into and was outstanding in nature. Reclamation of all the Light cannot be accomplished except in a rebuilt physical body. In the measure that a human reclaims Light he becomes conscious of the Light in him, and with that conscious of himself *as* the doer.

The rebuilding is begun by the lunar germ which has been preserved during thirteen lunations. It is accomplished when the body is two-columned and sexless. Not until then can all the Light from nature be reclaimed, and even then some Light in thoughts will still be outstanding. Human beings living in one-columned bodies cannot reclaim all the outstanding Light because such bodies have not the necessary organization.

The only indication in any school or tradition of a rebuilding of the physical body into an immortal body is found in the Masonic teachings about Hiram Abiff, which is the lunar germ; about the broken column, which refers to the part missing below the sternum, (Fig. VI-E), and about the temple not made with hands, eternal in the heavens, which is the rebuilt, regenerated physical body.

It is likely that about the time the Christian teachings originated, one man had succeeded in retaining a lunar germ for thirteen lunations, had consequently reclaimed Light and had become conscious of and as the Light of his Triune Self, his "Father in Heaven." They could have given out teachings of how others could achieve this result. This event probably occurred at a time when a lesser cycle swung in, when men's thoughts were stirred by Greek philosophy, doubt and dissatisfaction, when men were expecting something new and were made to prepare an atmosphere for its appearance.

SECTION 7

Three degrees of Light from Intelligences. Thinking without creating thoughts or destiny. Bodies for the doer, the thinker, and the knower of the Triune Self, within the perfect physical body.

There are three degrees of the Light of Intelligences: Light which is in nature; Light which has been reclaimed from nature, has come back into the mental or noetic atmosphere of the human and is unattached; and, freed Light. In the third stage of reclamation a human reclaims Light from thoughts and from lunar germs that are preserved until they arrive in the head. Light which has been reclaimed and is for the time unattached is not freed, but it must be freed. Reclaimed Light may go out again into nature and it may again be bound in thoughts, and exteriorized.

Desire and nature-matter can attach themselves to Light even though it has been reclaimed many times. Light does not attach itself to matter; nature-matter attaches itself to the Light through desire. Only when Light has become unattachable, so that no matter either of nature or of the atmospheres of the doer can attach itself to it, is it freed. It does not become unattachable by anything the Light itself does but by the thinking of the doer to which it is loaned. It becomes unattachable when there is no claim made on it by the doer. This is the case when the doer has no desire for anything in nature, and when it has knowledge of itself and of the Light. Then the unattachable Light is freed Light and is ready to be restored to the Triune Self. But it is not restored until the doer has perfected itself and its body.

Light that has been in circulation in the body but a few days has not the same power as Light that has been carried by a lunar germ for one lunation. After Light has been reclaimed voluntarily from a lunar germ the Light that it gathers the next time is itself brighter and of higher potency and increases the clarity and power of the first reclamation. Light that is reclaimed has still attached to it adhesions of desires, which are the hooks by which nature can again lay hold of the Light. An adhesion changes when another kind of desire takes the place of the first. As long as there are such adhesions, they are obstacles which dim and qualify the Light. As long as there are such qualifications which go with reclaimed Light, nature can get the Light out again through feeling and desire that cause thinking. Yet through all this the Light is never anything but Light, just as gold is gold, no matter what else is mixed with it.

When a man knows enough not to attach himself to anything or to attach anything to himself, he begins to free Light. His thinking and his actions free it, though he does not know what the Light is or that he is freeing it as such. His past thoughts which are his destiny bring him into all manner of conditions, which will afford him the opportunity, as a duty, to reclaim and free Light. He is working out and balancing old thoughts while they are exteriorized as his destiny. So he is working off his old destiny and is not creating new thoughts, new destiny. The thinking by which he balances his thoughts is thinking that does not create thoughts. His thinking is done with greater power and with more accuracy, because he is thinking with clearer Light and can turn and hold that light on the subject of his thinking. The Light in the mental atmosphere becomes clearer and clearer as he uses the reclaimed Light and by that use removes the adhesions of desires and of nature.

As his duties to the world are performed and no others are contracted his thinking takes him into higher realms, not connected with the world. These are the things with which his thinking is then concerned. It may extend for lives. Eventually he knows himself, not as a human being, but as the doer. This he does by the freed, the unattachable Light. He discovers the Light and knows it to be the Light apart from him and that it belongs to the Intelligence. He may have known about this long before, intellectually, but now he knows it as it actually is, as the reality in his case. When he attains to perfection as a doer he knows that there is a potential Light in him and that as soon as he evokes it and makes it an actual Light, he will become an Intelligence. Feeling-and-desire and rightness-and-reason are ready to have I-ness become the light faculty, and selfness the I-am faculty of what he will be as an Intelligence. But before the Triune Self can evoke its own potential Light it must restore to the parent Intelligence all the Light it has received and that it has freed.

What of nature when all doers have redeemed and freed their Light? How is nature kept going when it no longer finds means in human desire to draw Light of Intelligences into it? The units of nature will then have been so changed by the progress of the human beings, that the Light extending from the Triune Selves will penetrate nature and will affect the units without being bound with them. There will not be any such animals as there are now, because there will not be any uncontrolled desires. The plants will have different forms, in which to afford nature units the means to go through the stages of the vegetable kingdom. There will be animals, but no human desires will animate them. The animals, while having flesh tissues, will be inhabited by advanced units as elementals, and none will be ferocious.

In such time man will no longer be merely a human being. He will be conscious as a doer. He will think without creating thoughts. He will have a physical body which will be immortal. It will be made of the four states of matter of the physical plane, but it will differ from the perishable bodies of present humans in that the compositor units will be balanced and be no longer active-passive or passive-active; the food will be taken directly from the elements and not through an alimentary canal and the cells will be renewed by essential life.

The Triune Self will then have three inner bodies, in which will be its three parts. The doer will have absorbed its psychic atmosphere and will be in a form body made of the matter of the form world and in contact with it, (Fig. V-B,a). The thinker will have absorbed its mental atmosphere and will be in a life body of and in contact with matter of the life world. The knower will have absorbed its noetic atmosphere and will be in a light body of and in contact with matter of the light world and the three will be in the immortal, perfect, sexless, physical body. The import of this may be understood if it be remembered that not even the doer can now enter completely into a present human body, but that only a small portion of the doer does so and that this portion is not in its proper place, and that the physical body contacts and operates through that matter only which is in the solid state of the physical plane.

These three inner bodies for the Triune Self will then have been built in or through the physical body when it has been reconstructed after the self-impregnation and the divine conception in the head. The rebuilding puts the physical body into contact with the four worlds and their forces and so makes possible a development of the three bodies for the parts of the Triune Self. These three bodies are developed after the lunar germ begins to ascend the central canal of the spinal cord, which it can do only after the physical body has been rebuilt. The four senses are then still elemental beings, but they differ from the four senses of a human in that they are in touch with all grades of matter in the four worlds, whereas in a human they are in touch only with the lowest grade of matter on the lowest plane of the lowest world. They differ also in that they then work through perfect organs which do not limit the action of the doer. The breath-form then obeys the orders of the doer and experiences no resistance from nature.

The Triune Self is then a Triune Self complete; it knows its relation to other Triune Selves and sees the common bond among all Triune Selves. The common bond is the noetic world. What one Triune Self has and is and knows is therein open to the use and service of all other Triune Selves.

The freeing and restoring of the Light of the Intelligence and the transition of the Triune Self into an Intelligence, seem to be the foundation of the various traditions of the perfection which a human being eventually will reach.

The thinker determines, according to the knower of the Triune Self, how much of the Light it can let into the mental atmosphere of the human, (Fig. V-B). I-ness sends the amount allowed into the mental atmosphere. The Light passes through I-ness into the mental atmosphere where it becomes available to thinking according to one's capacity to use it. Physically the Light comes from the pineal body, which selfness contacts, to the pituitary body, which I-ness contacts, and thence goes diffused and dimmed to the brain, the spine and the heart and lungs where it is used in thinking.

Some few people have Light from beyond the noetic atmosphere of the human. They are the ones who have an understanding of and an insight into the things affecting human life, which exceeds that of the run of human beings. To them is available some of the self-knowledge not acquired in the present life, but in better times when the human beings were incomparably greater than today. Such people are enlightened on things which are of little interest or are unknown to the majority.

But the noetic destiny of the run of human beings is that they are hindered by the lack of Light and the inability to reach it or to draw it. They fear the Light. They have no Light except what automatic reclamation saves for them, so that they can barely go on as human beings. They are in a noetic night and have been so for thousands of years. They are unable to reach the knowledge which has been acquired by their doers in the past. They do not acquire self-knowledge, that is, knowledge of the conscious self in the body, from their experiences in their present life.

Their noble noetic inheritance has been lost, is unknown and will be unattainable until they husband the Light, preserve the Light and reclaim consciously some of the Light they have let go into nature and so bring more Light into their noetic atmospheres. Their noetic powers are degraded to sexual indulgences. They have lost the ability to use noetic powers for noetic ends.

Their mental atmosphere instead of being full of Light is like a grey fog; the Light is dimmed, diffused, scattered and full of intervening obstacles. The Light has too many accretions, is too scarce. In thinking they find difficulties in focussing and in working with this sort of Light. That which does work is weak, impeded, ineffective. Such human beings are not conscious of reason and not conscious of rightness. They are not conscious of their thinking or of how it is done. Their thinking is haphazard, jumpy. It is limited to physical and to psychic things and even these it does not encompass or penetrate. Man's great intellectual attainments in natural science, engineering, literature are concerned with things of the four senses and serve nature. They are due to the thinking with only one of the three minds which he might use. The mind he uses is the sense-mind or body-mind. This leaves him sense-bound and nature-bound. It does not aid him in gaining self-knowledge which would solve all problems.

The body-mind cannot think of the doer; it cannot think beyond nature. Its thinking is subordinated to the body senses which are controlled by nature. The character of human beings is often marked by dishonesty, greed, meanness, immorality and the love of intoxicating drinks. Their feelings are entirely controlled by nature, which they worship and obey. Nature is interpreted to them by the four senses, which are nature's priests and hold the feelings and desires. The strongest of the senses is the sense of smell, which is touch. Touch, contact, is the action of this sense in the body, and the most desired contact is sexual. Hence the waste of Light through the sex organs.

The noetic destiny, this noetic darkness, causes the run of human beings to be born from seed and from soil which had not sufficiently matured and which are produced in unhealthy bodies.

To produce a proper human body the seed and the soil must each have been carried in chastity for twelve months. During that time the seed and the soil have been turned into the tonic tincture and have been worked over and reabsorbed in the body. It vitalizes the body and gives it power to resist disease. Any woman who loses ova monthly cannot bear a perfect child. Abstinence in thought and act will change the female so that during the monthly periods no ova are lost. They, the ova, will be reabsorbed and do for the female body somewhat as the seminal power or tincture will do for the male. When man and wife are in this condition they may have a healthy child that will be immune to disease. In any case, a woman should be left alone during pregnancy, during the nursing period and, thereafter, for seven days before and after menstruation. When man and woman understand what they as doers really are, they will not have intercourse, unless both husband and wife want a child; that they are willing to have a child is not sufficient.

It is partly because of a violation of these fundamental rules and because bodies are often produced from seed which may be only a few hours old, that the run of human beings have the kinds of weak bodies that crowd the world and are prone to disease.

The man must himself preserve the lunar germs, as well as his seed. If he does not preserve his seed he cannot preserve the lunar germ, which will be lost after the second week. The simple precepts of chastity and decency are all that is required as subjects of thinking and rules of conduct, in order to save the lunar germ and the seed. The age-old and always new revelations, books, mystic teachings, cults, brotherhoods and sisterhoods that present love and sex as anything else than matters of chastity and decency, are blinds for corruption. They have helped to bring on the noetic night.

In these weak bodies, disease is often developed by food. The run of human beings know and care little for the science of food. They usually eat too much; they take too large a load to carry, more than the body can digest or absorb. They eat much that is indigestible or incompatible. Hence the foods which they eat ferment and putrefy, and this commonly deranges the digestive functions and produces poisons which are frequently the causes of disease. The object of their eating is principally to gratify the craving of the palate or to have the comfortable feeling of fulness. The feelings that they want are swarms of elementals which get into the body and its organs and pull, prod, drive, fret the nerves and are felt as sensations by the doer. Health or disease of the body is immaterial to the elementals. When disease follows decomposition, other elementals come in and thrill as the discomfort felt in the diseased parts.

Upon this basis of sex and food human beings have built up a false civilization with useless occupations, false standards, insufficient or excessive rewards, lawlessness, crimes, childish religions and ignorance of true and honest government.

Because of the noetic darkness, the run of human beings have conceptions of life and responsibility which are infantile. Their problems concerning free will, and destiny, God, good and evil and their relations with other human beings, their own make-up, their future and the object of life show the limitations of their thinking and conceptions, which are imposed by the absence of the Light.

SECTION 8

Free will. The problem of free will.

Free will is a phrase for one's freedom to feel, to desire, to think, or to act, as opposed to the inescapable necessity to feel, to desire, to think, or to act, in a given way. It means the absence of prevention, restraint and compulsion that would interfere with physical, psychic and mental action and inaction. The phrase means that one can feel, desire and think and do as he pleases, and not be limited by bounds or coerced by goads.

Not only in this phrase but in the language generally, the word 'will' is used as if it were different from what is called desire. But so-called will is an aspect of the active side of the doer-in-the-body, which is desire, nothing more than that. Will is one of the four functions of desire. Desire, which is conscious power, has four functions: to be, to will, to do, and to have. To will is the second function of desire; it is followed by to do, and to have. Will is that one desire which controls the other desires, be it for the moment or for a long period. It controls to the degree that it can use the conscious power which desire is. It gets strength by exercise, that is, by long continued desiring. It lasts until its object is attained or until it is overcome by a stronger desire, which is then the will. The cause or starter of will is immediately feeling and remotely unsatisfied desire, which is ultimately the longing for perfection and to be perfect. Will manifests by a surging up out of the inner depths, of a desire to attain an end. This manifestation may last for years. Will is weakened by the interference of contrary desires, and it is strengthened by continued exercise and by overcoming and compelling other desires.

Will is not free, cannot be free; it is much conditioned at all times. Each desire is will, but that desire is to be designated as will which at any time controls the opposing desire. One of the desires as will does not always control the other desires.

At no time has a human freedom of will, even though there be no physical obstacles to the actions, desires and thinking. A human has a limited amount of freedom to will. He has set the limitations. In so far as he himself has not prevented himself from acting, desiring and thinking, he is free to act, to desire, to think. All his bonds, obstacles or limitations are of his own making, but he is free to remove them when he wills. As long as he has not exercised that freedom, they remain and they limit. He has made them by creating thoughts and the only way to remove them is by thinking without creating other thoughts.

Past thoughts are exteriorized in the physical body and mark the limitations of the body which are also limitations to the will. These physical limitations extend to the time when life begins, the race, the country and the nationality, the kind of family in which the body is born, the sex, the kind of body, the physical heredity, the chief mundane occupations, particular diseases, some accidents, the critical events in life and the time and nature of death. The limitations which a person has made extend to his disposition, temperament, inclinations, moods and appetites, which are part of his psychic nature, and to his insight, comprehension, reasoning and other mental endowments or the absence of them.

The limitations which are obvious, and therefore principally the physical limitations, are what people call destiny or foreordination. Because people limit themselves in their perceptions and conceptions and so are ignorant of the cause of these trammels, they speculate, and they attribute them to God and Divine Providence or to chance. All this is their problem, our problem, of free will. It will remain an unsolvable problem as long as men are ignorant of their own nature and of their relations to what they suppose to be an extraneous deity. That which limits their free will and determines when their destiny shall be precipitated, is no extraneous being, but is the thinker of each one's own Triune Self.

A human is always free to consent or to object to the conditions in which he is, including his psychic and mental conditions. Even if one of his numerous desires forces him to act, he can register agreement or objection; he is free to agree or object; and this is due to another desire. His free will centers around this point of freedom, the only freedom he has. The point of freedom is the desire he lets rule. This desire is a psychic thing. In the beginning it is only a point. Every human has such a point of freedom and can by thinking extend the point to an area of free will.

Originally desire was undivided. That was when the doer as feeling-and-desire was with and conscious of the thinker and the knower as the Triune Self. The desire of the doer was for Self-knowledge, which was desire for its completion with the Triune Self. Then came the time when feeling-and-desire appeared to separate and be in two bodies, desire in the man body and feeling in the woman body. Of course there could be no real separation of feeling from desire, but that was what the use of the body-mind showed when the doer began to think with the body-mind through the senses. Its thinking caused the doer to see feeling-and-desire in bodies apart from each other and caused an apparent but not a real division, because there can be no desire without feeling nor can there be feeling without desire. Feeling-and-desire were in the woman body, but feeling dominated desire. Also, desire-and-feeling were in the man body, but desire dominated feeling. Continued thinking with the body-mind prevailed and caused the desire for sex to separate from the desire for Self-knowledge. So the desire for sex exiled itself from the Conscious Light in the Triune Self, and into the darkness of the senses. Thus the doer lost the free use of the Conscious Light to make known to it its relation to its thinker and knower. The desire for sex was thus separated from the desire for Self-knowledge. The desire for Self-knowledge has never changed and can never be made to change. That desire for Self-knowledge still persists with the human. But the desire for sex has continued to divide and to multiply into innumerable desires. The multitude of desires are all marshalled and arranged under the general-ship of the four senses. They attach themselves to objects of one or another of the four senses, for the direct or remote purpose of gratifying or ministering to or serving their chief desire, the desire for sex. All these desires are attached, they have attached themselves, they are not free. Yet they have the right and the power to remain attached or to free themselves from the things to which they are attached. No one desire, nor the combined desires of all other powers can compel the least of the desires to change itself. Each desire has the right and is the power to change itself, and to do or be what it will of itself desire to do or to be. That desire may be dominated by a stronger desire, but it cannot be made to change or to do or be anything until it itself wills to change and do or be. In that right and power is constituted its own free will.

The only desire which actually and truly is free is the desire for Self-knowledge, for knowledge of the Triune Self. It is free because it has not attached itself to anything and it wills not to be attached to anything. And because it is free it will not interfere with the right of any other desire to attach itself to anything. Therefore it is free.

Not one of the innumerable other desires is free, because they all have chosen to attach themselves to the objects to which they are attached and to which they choose to remain attached. But each one has the right and it is the power to let go of that to which it is attached; and it can then attach itself to any other thing, or it can remain unattached and free from anything, as it wills.

Each desire, therefore, is its own point of freedom. It remains the point, or it may extend its point to an area. The stronger desire controls the weaker and so extends its point to an area, and as it continues to control other desires it extends its area of control, and it can continue to dominate other desires until it has will or control over a vast area of its own and over the desires of other doers. And yet that dominating will is not free. It is not free because the desires it controls are not free, and they are not free if they are controlled: because if they are free they act in accord, each by its own will, and are not controlled. The dominating desire as the will is not free merely by dominating the other desires. The test of its freedom as a point, or its extension to an area is: Is that desire, as will, attached to anything in any way related to the senses? If it is attached, it is not free. How then does it extend its point of freedom of will to an area of will, a dominion where it controls not only its own desires but the desires of others? It wills, and it may extend its will over its other desires, by thinking. Merely by desiring no desire can extend itself so that it controls other desires. But if it is strong enough, it will compel thinking. By continued thinking the desire extends itself as will. The will is increased by exercise. It is exercised by persistence in the effort to think, persistence against and irrespective of all obstacles or interferences to thinking. By persistence in the effort to think, obstacles are overcome and interferences disappear. The more the doer continues to think the greater will be its will over its other desires. Its power to think and to control its own desires will determine the dominion of its will over the desires of other men.

Yet that overruling desire, though it has dominion over the will of others, is not really free. That desire has increased its power by its will to think; only so has its thinking increased its power to desire, to will. Each of the desires over which it has exercised its will and extended its dominion is controlled, but not changed. Each such desire will remain as it is until it wills to change itself or to change other things. And the only means that any desire has of changing itself is by thinking, thinking to accomplish what it wills.

Every desire wants knowledge, knowledge of how to get or to be what it wants to have or to be. The many desires continue to desire, but they do not think. If they will not think, they are controlled by a dominating desire that does think. And because the desire that does think, refuses to think about what it is and why it is attached to things away from itself, it attaches itself to objects that it does not continue to want after it is attached. When it tires of one thing it changes to another and another and is never satisfied. The reason that it is never satisfied and never can be satisfied with any of its attachments is that it has lost parts of itself, and it is dimly conscious that it is lost to them. And it will not and cannot be satisfied until all the desires of the original desire are again one undivided desire. Therefore, as it is afraid or refuses to think about itself, it attaches itself to this thing and that thing in the hope that it has at last found a part of itself that has been lost. But no thing to which it can be attached can also be a part of itself. And even when a desire does think, it will not think about itself.

Why? Because if it really has made the attempt, it finds that as soon as it tries to think about what it is or who it is, it must let go of the objects to which it is attached. Then the effort tires it, or it is afraid of being lost if it lets go of sights and sounds. Why does this happen? It happens because from the earliest years it has been taught to use the mind of the senses, the body-mind. The body-mind can think only about the senses and the objects or things related to the senses; it cannot think about desire or about feeling except in the terms of the senses. To think about feeling or about desire exclusive of the senses, the body-mind must be made inactive, stilled. If or when desire makes an effort to think about itself, it must be a long and persistent effort, and the effort must be repeated again and again, because that effort is calling into action the desire-mind which has been dormant, inactive, except when moved by the body-mind which then draws on it for more Light in its thinking. It would be too much to expect either feeling or desire to use the feeling-mind or the desire-mind to exclude the body-mind from their thinking. Therefore when one desire would think about itself, let it think about itself in relation to the thing to which it is attached. With persistence, the thinking will show to that desire what that thing is. As soon as the desire is conscious of what that thing is, the desire knows that that thing is not what it wants. It will let go and never again will it attach itself nor can it be attached to that thing. That desire is then free from that thing.

Now what happened during the thinking to free it from its attachment? Thinking is the steady holding of the Conscious Light within on the subject of the thinking. By thinking with the body-mind only, the body-mind can show by its Light what the senses show the thing to be. That Light does not and cannot show what things really are. But when a desire turns its thinking on itself in relation to the thing which it wants, then the desire-mind and the feeling-mind focus the Conscious Light on that desire and on the thing which the desire wants or to which it is attached. And the desire at once lets go and refuses ever again to be attached, because that desire then knows that it does not want that thing. The doer in a human for whom certain things have no attraction, has been freed from the attachments of its desires to those things by this process of thinking in a former existence. But the desires which have freed themselves may attach themselves to other things.

How then, can the desire that frees itself from one thing remain free from all other things? This is indeed important. It is done in this way: When the attached desire wills and thinks about itself, it is acting on its point of freedom. It is thinking to know what it is and what its relation is to the thing of its attachment. It desires to know. Very well. Then let it identify itself as the desire to know the thing of its attachment. And let it at the same time relate itself in thinking to its other desire, "the desire for Self-knowledge". Let the desire to know then persist in thinking on the thing of its attachment and its relation to the desire for Self-knowledge, until the Conscious Light is focussed on the thing of its attachment. As soon as the Conscious Light shows that thing as it is, the desire knows it and knows that it is free. Then the free desire will think of the desire for Self-knowledge and will relate itself or at once identify itself with or as the desire for Self-knowledge. When this is done, the human in whom that desire is has an acceleration of joyous life and experiences a new sense of freedom. When the point of freedom has identified itself with or as the desire for Self-knowledge there is an area of free will, and by a like freeing its other desires from their attachments the area can be extended to include all the noetic atmosphere of the human. At present human beings have only the point of freedom; they do not extend it to an area of free will.

Free will will be a problem until men understand that a human is a human being of a doer and that the doer is an integral but imperfect part of an otherwise perfect and immortal Triune Self. Free will is closely related to noetic destiny.

The doer, from the depth or heights of its own inner self, projects a portion of itself into a flesh body which moves among other flesh bodies in an objective world. The bodies are moved around by the four senses, which also belong to nature. The four senses are attracted or repelled by objects of nature. Chief among these objects are other flesh bodies. The four senses which are elementals, nature units, impersoned in a body and harnessed into its systems and organs, play upon the feelings of the impersoned portion of the doer and produce the illusions that the doer is the senses, that feeling is a fifth sense, that the body is the doer, that the doer is nothing if it is not connected with a person or body, that the senses are the test for reality, and that what the senses do not perceive is non-existent. The four senses surround with glamour the other flesh bodies which then excite love and hate, greed and cruelty, pride and ambition. The four senses intensify the hunger for food which is the hunger of nature for circulation. The four senses do not show to the doer, nature as it really is; they hide nature and cast a glamour over it. The human is thus in ignorance of his real nature, of the organization of which he is a part, of his make-up, of his origin and of his destiny.

In a human the essential thing is the doer portion, feeling-and-desire, which are projected periodically from the doer part of the Triune Self into a flesh body for a life on the earth crust. The doer in the human extends to the innermost of nature, and beyond nature to the knower, and to the Intelligence. Feeling-and-desire are the essentials of the human on earth; they persist after the death of the body and through the life of another and other bodies. The succession of the human beings of a doer constitute the twelve portions of the doer, and the entire doer is one of the three parts of the Triune Self. One life on earth is a part of a series, as one paragraph in a book, as one step in a procession or as one day in a life. The notion of chance and that of a single life on earth are two of the outstanding errors of human beings.

The human sees only an outer aspect of a small section of the history of the doer, as presented in the life of that human. He does not see connections which, if he saw them, would appear as producing causes of what the cross section shows. Therefore he is without an explanation of what he sees and feels as the physical, psychic and mental limitations of his being, and so he uses such terms as chance, accident, and Providence to account for the mystery. But this question will cease to be troublesome when man knows more about himself and understands that his destiny is in his own hands.

CHAPTER IX

RE-EXISTENCE

SECTION 1

Recapitulation: Make-up of a human being. The Triune Self. The Light of the Intelligence. A human body as the link between nature and the doer. Death of the body. The doer after death. Re-existence of the doer.

TO RECAPITULATE: A human being is the combination of a fourfold physical body, a breath-form, and a portion of the doer of a Triune Self, which receives Light from an Intelligence. The breath-form together with the four senses and the physical body is the personality in which a portion of the doer part of the Triune Self is housed.

The physical body is a condensation of the four elements and belongs to nature. Its form is not permanent. The body is a mere mass of nature-matter, constantly changing. The matter consists of billions of units of the four states of matter on the physical plane. These are either transient units of which a stream is constantly flowing through and around the body, or compositor units which detain some of the transient units for awhile and compose them into the visible, tangible mass of the cells of the body. The cellular matter is arranged into four systems and the organs and parts of the body. This is the extent to which a human being is visible and tangible.

The fourfold physical body, (Fig. III), consists of a radiant or astral body, an airy body, a fluid body, and a solid body, which becomes visible because of the compacted mass of its cells. The matter of the radiant body holds the airy, fluid and solid units of the cells and is given form by the breath-form. The breath-form clothes itself in this radiant matter and

431

breathes through all four bodies. The radiant, airy and fluid bodies are intra-cellular and connect all the parts of the solid body with each other. The radiant body operates the nervous systems and receives and transmits messages among these systems and the breath-form, and so brings about changes in the make-up of the body and executes bodily movements.

Into the physical body are impersoned, so as to be parts of the personality, four beings of nature-matter, the senses of sight, of hearing, of taste and of smell, each having a double aspect of receiving and of acting. They operate the four bodies and the four systems; the sense of sight works the generative, the sense of hearing the respiratory, the sense of taste the circulatory and the sense of smell the digestive system. The breath-form enables the sight, the hearing, the taste, and the smell to contact the things which they see, hear, taste, and smell, and finally to coordinate and bring these four into contact with the feeling of the doer. Thus they keep up commerce by means of the human body between nature and the doer. The body exists in a physical atmosphere, (Fig. V-B), which is the emanation of the transient units as they are breathed in and out by the breath-form.

A human body is constantly changing. Its cells and their parts are composed of transient units. The mass as which they are visible is a flow of transient units. This stream flows through the holding or compositor units; and these continue from birth to death and from life to life. They are summoned at the time of conception and are resurrected in the new body. There is thus a continuity of the permanent or compositor units. At present, death interrupts their activity. They fabricate and furnish new bodies for the doer until they are established in permanence in a body which does not die, and that body is a balanced, immortal, sexless physical body.

The breath-form controls and coordinates the operations of the four systems and thereby the involuntary functions of the physical body. That which compels the breath-form is nature, which is kept going by the driving forces that are the total of human thinking and thoughts.

Involuntary functions of the body are performed as follows: Nature affects one of the senses through the sensory nerve fibers of the involuntary nervous system in the organ of that sense; the sense then acts on the breath-form, and that acts on motor fibers of the involuntary system, and they compel the organs of the body to function.

The breath-form also provides the traits and habits of the physical body and all physical conditions of health or disease. The breath-form, by the signatures which it bears and which it transfers also to the fourfold body, attracts elementals which furnish the surroundings of comfort or want, adventures and escapes that make the physical conditions under which the body lives. Not only physical conditions are brought about by the breath-form, but feeling and thinking run along the lines which previous thinking and feeling have made on it. The breath-form is a unit; it has a passive side, the form, which is receptive to impressions, and an active side which is the fourfold physical breath. The impressions are made through the physical breath, which also puts them into effect and visibility. The aia, though without dimension, bears a symbolic record of the sum of all impressions made on it in the past. Whenever there is a juncture of time, condition and place, the breath brings some parts of this record, which are on the breath-form, into physical reality. The breath causes a radiation from the physical body, which is the physical atmosphere, (Fig. III).

The Triune Self has three atmospheres, in each of which is one of its three parts, having an active and a passive side, and a breath which keeps up the relation between the atmosphere and its part. These three breaths are related to each other; each acts through and is affected by the breath below it; and all three work through the breath of the breath-form, that is, the fourfold physical breath moving through the physical atmosphere.

The Triune Self is of matter which is conscious in three degrees, feeling-and-desire, as the doer, rightness-and-reason, as the thinker, and I-ness-and-selfness, as the knower. These names are used to characterize the degrees in which matter of the Triune Self is conscious. The three degrees are related, but the doer is not in accord with the thinker and the knower.

Time exists on each of the four planes of the physical, of the form and of the life worlds and on the physical plane of the light world. Time is different on each plane. On the other planes it is not like time as perceived through the senses on the physical plane of the physical world. Time there does not affect the three degrees of matter of the Triune Self. It is only when a portion of the doer is in the body that time of the physical plane of the physical world exists for it.

The reality of physical things exists only on the physical plane; the things are freed from it when they leave that plane. The reality of the same thing is different on different planes. So the reality of a thought on the physical plane is its exteriorization, as in a disease or in the ownership of a house. On the form plane the reality is the feeling which the disease or ownership produces, and on the life plane the thinking that will cause or result from the disease or ownership of the house, and on the light plane of the physical world the sensing of them as "mine". Time, dimension, place and the other phenomena of physical reality do not exist as such for any of the three parts of intelligent-matter that constitute a Triune Self, except in so far as the doer is connected with the physical plane.

The Light which the doer receives from the Intelligence is Intelligence and is that faculty of an Intelligence that is connected with the doer in its human body. The Light causes everything that it affects either to grow toward it to become Light or to depart from it and to disappear. So after the doer has come as near to the Light as it can, in its heaven period, the Light causes the doer to depart back to earth. The Light draws what seeks it and repels what is opposed to it. The effect that it has on things is a constant unveiling of their nature, attributes and associations. Only the permanent can stand in the Light for it causes the impermanent to disappear. It draws out the Light in all things.

Light is in the noetic and mental atmospheres of the Triune Self, not in the psychic. During life nature has the advantage of the Light which is in the noetic and mental atmospheres of the human, (Fig. V-B). After the existing portion of the doer has shed its body, the Light draws that portion to it. This causes purifications, while the impermanent, everything that cannot stand the Light, is burnt off. All of the doer that can stand the Light is in heaven radiating in happiness. When all there is in that portion has been brought out by the Light, the Light causes it to seek new growth, new efforts, a new life.

A human body is made up of many elementals, units, which through it get a chance to change. They remain the same units, though their qualities and functions are changed. They can be changed only while a doer dwells in the body.

The entire Universe is related in its greatest and smallest, highest and lowest parts. All parts of nature are related to parts of Intelligence. Some parts are more closely related, some more distantly. The relations run along two chains, the chain of nature and the chain of the Triune Self. All the parts of each chain are necessary to each other. Physical human bodies connect them. When the doer no longer needs nature it can let go and do without this link forever, but nature is always dependent on the doer and needs a link. Until the doer is self-sufficient because of the amount of Light that it can redeem for itself, it remains connected with the chain of nature. The chain of nature always needs the chain of the Triune Self, because it cannot get forms, desire and the Light except from a Triune Self.

The link between nature and the doer is a human body. This link is temporal, existing for a span only. Its disappearance by death is necessary for several reasons. The portion of the doer existing in a human needs an opportunity to rest and to recuperate from the troubles incident to an earth life. It must be freed from the memories of its errors and misdeeds which would otherwise overwhelm it. It must be prevented from making more mistakes than it can correct. It does not assimilate in life all the events that come to it. They come bunched together or disguised, and the human must have time and be in a different state to separate, sort out, feel and assimilate them. The doer in the human needs a purification from its earthly sins and it must, while free from the bondage of the world, come into touch with the Light of the Intelligence, so that the Light can act upon it directly, after the desires and emotions have burnt off. In life a human has many thoughts of which he is only partly conscious and then they disappear into another part of the mental atmosphere. After death they become again real to the doer who goes over them until he is affected by them sufficiently. The continued projection of these thoughts is the cause of the after-death states. The death of the body is chiefly for the benefit of the doer, but nature also requires it to get desires for her energy and for her animal forms.

While the body lives it links the chain of nature with the chain of the Triune Self. It allows a flow from doer to nature and from doer to the Triune Self. It allows all the worlds and beings and forces in them to reach into a doer and the doer to have its adventures in nature. It allows nature to feel through a human. Nature has no feeling, she can feel only when her units as elemental beings become sensations when making contact with feeling in a human.

A human body keeps up the circulation of nature within the human world. Through it nature gets the forms of her animals and plants, the beings that animate them, and her very gods. Except for a human body, she could get none of these. The elementals of nature become sensations in a human body. On the other hand, the doer has its feelings and desires moved by nature through a human body. The body furnishes the experiences from which the doer may have emotions, may learn and may acquire knowledge. Without a human body it could never grow out of nature and obtain freedom.

In a human link, meet, intermingle and become related, the four worlds and the four atmospheres. The fourfold body is so built that the worlds and atmospheres have their separate sections, systems and special organs in it as well as a centralization of all in the generative system. The body is built so that the doer can get Light of the Intelligence in it and there be conscious of what it thinks, feels and does and have commerce with nature under the Light of the Intelligence, and so that nature can get that Light.

With the death of the body the link between the chains of nature and of the Triune Self is destroyed. Thereby the chains are separated. Nature later gets the animal desires of the doer and lodges them in animal bodies. The elemental matter that composed the body goes back into the four elements and the elementals go into their elemental races. The four senses, after they have left heaven, may become nature spirits in human form; some may become glorious beings in the elements. The elemental beings bear the stamp of the doer in the human body in whose charge they were, and carry the marks of the acts performed by the doer while they were in the body. They retain these signs even though they have passed into a thousand other bodies. The doer after death acts with itself, works itself and churns itself. Under the Light of the Intelligence it goes through certain changes, which are a digestion and an assimilation of the thoughts its human being had in the past life. It does all this because of the Light of the Intelligence. When it has worked over all that is possible and has rested, there is a void for the things that are absent from it. It begins to stir in such a way as to fill the void.

Some of its desires are outstanding in animal forms. Some of the Light that was given it for its use is outstanding in nature, and must be reclaimed by it and ultimately freed. In its mental atmosphere innumerable thoughts circulate in longer and shorter cycles. Thoughts outlive the fleshly instruments through which they passed. Then there is a vast number of latent desires for things in physical life. They are unsatisfied, though asleep in the psychic atmosphere. The thoughts, ever moving in the mental atmosphere, seek exteriorization by their own energy. They bring themselves into touch with and awaken the sleeping desires, in due time. Desires cannot be killed. They are powers that must be expressed until they change themselves, since they cannot be satisfied. Desire develops into an innumerable variety of desires, though these are in a few comprehensive subdivisions, such as lust, greed, selfishness, slothfulness. These countless forms of desire must have a human body in which to root and feed. Only there can they wallow and grunt and howl and roar under the diffused Light of the Intelligence. While a desire is in an animal body it cannot get the same degree of gratification.

For these reasons the chains of nature and of the Triune Self attract each other. This happens after the necessary time has elapsed for the doer to digest, assimilate, rest and feel new hunger for an earthly life; and, for nature to automatically want the circulation of the elements through, and new forms from a human body. When the chains are in this condition, a cycling thought impels the aia. This thought is made up of the interests the doer has in living. In the thought are merged the dominant thoughts which filled the dying moment of the past life. That thought is all that the doer link of the chain of the Triune Self now furnishes until after birth; the rest is furnished from the chain of nature.

After the doer had finished its heaven period, the breath and the form of the breath-form disunited. The form became a mere speck or point and was in a non-dimensional condition, and the breath remained with the essential matter of the four worlds. When a new physical body is to be built for the doer, the dominant thought of the past life presses towards exteriorization and starts the aia. Then the aia draws the essential breath matter from the four worlds, and causes the breath to revivify its form, and, together the form and the breath are then and will be the breath-form or "living soul" according to which a new physical body will be built by a man and a woman for the doer to dwell in and operate. At the juncture of time, condition and place, during or after copulation, the breath of the breath-form unites the physical breaths of the parents to be, and the form of the breath-form enters the mother's body and, then or later, bonds the two germs and so causes conception. The breath of the breath-form remains in the mother's atmosphere during pregnancy. The form of the breath-form in the impregnated ovum is that according to which the physical body is built with the matter furnished by the mother.

Then birth takes place on the physical plane. In normally bringing the body into the world, the breath-form of the mother helps to breathe it into the physical world; the breath of the breath-form enters the infant with its first gasp, and unites with its form in the infant's heart. Then the breath continues the building out of the form as the body. All the physical steps from conception to birth are along the chain of nature.

The preparation of the body is building the physical link in which will be a place for nature and for the doer to function. All the building is done along the nature chain. The generative system is the first to start the body and the last to be completed. It connects with the light world and the fire element. The respiratory system is to be connected with the life world and the element of air, the circulatory system with the form world and the water element, and the digestive system with the physical world and the element of earth. These worlds and elements act through the corresponding planes of the physical world and only through the mother, not directly on the systems. The elementals which are called into the body to build out the physical heredity also have to act on it through the mother. Digestion, circulation, respiration and some of the functions of the generative system, all have to be carried on by the mother for the fetus. In this way the mother guards and protects the fetus against elemental forces. At the juncture of time, condition and place, the breath-form brings the body to birth, and as soon as the body is free from the mother it begins to function independently. Nature claims its body and rushes in by compelling it to breathe, and the doer guides the breath. The breath-form enters the body and changes the systems which were all operated by the mother, so that they are thereafter operated by the breath-form under the impulses of nature through the four systems. So the link is connected with the chain of nature. But nature is not embodied fully until her four senses function through their systems.

Immediately upon birth the doer is connected with the physical body through the breath. At birth the psychic breath enters the physical breath, and the psychic atmosphere thereby surrounds the physical body and atmosphere. The doer does not begin to enter the body until the kidneys and adrenals as stations are sufficiently developed to admit feeling-and-desire. The thinker and the knower do not enter the body, but they are in touch with the doer. So memory of early days in the body is possible. The only way for one to tell when he entered the body is the memory of the first impression produced by the feeling of seeing, hearing, tasting, smelling and touching. At that time the chain of the Triune Self was linked by the physical body with the chain of nature. Years pass before the thinker and knower of the Triune Self find organs sufficiently developed to let them contact the body. When the feeling of rightness and reasoning begins, the thinker contacts the body. At puberty the knower contacts the body. When all three parts are in contact with the body, the chain of the Triune Self is aligned with the chain of nature. When the knower is in contact the doer becomes responsible and must account for its thoughts and acts. The thinker and knower do not enter the body; they only contact it.

Only a small portion of the doer comes into the body. Re-existing doers make the human physical world. When they are not in physical bodies they work over and work out what they have made while they were in the world in human bodies. Everything on the physical plane is the exteriorization of human thoughts. As the doers meet in flesh bodies they work for, with and against one another, singly, in groups, in classes or in large masses. These actions and their mutual results bring out latent qualities of the doers. These qualities operating and manifesting through thoughts are exteriorized in the visible products and the invisible relations that make up the external physical world. All in it is for the purpose of producing feelings and possibly a learning from the feelings and ultimately a balancing.

The exteriorization of the thoughts of each doer makes a common ground, the physical plane, on which all those doers meet of which portions are in flesh bodies. They come to this common ground to meet each other; and they meet through their thoughts, caused by the feelings and desires they have while on the common ground. The common ground unites them by their aversions as well as by their interests. Each doer is moved essentially by self-interest. Expressions of the many phases of the inner working of self-interest make the physical world what it is. Conflict of these interests is increased by nature, which has the doers there on its own plane. It tries to keep them there because it profits by the conflict. It is like a man who keeps a gaming house and collects something for every game played in his establishment. The profit of nature is desire and its forms and Light of the Intelligence from the doers.

How is it that the world holds together and that after all there is a mysterious ordering, joining and unity in the clash and jar of life? The answer is that in external nature there is a wise ordering of events by the Intelligences and complete Triune Selves. The Intelligences, with these Triune Selves, acting under the Supreme Intelligence, cause the order of all terrestrial events to be arranged by elementals great and small. The Intelligences and Triune Selves do not and cannot interfere with or set aside the law that every thought must be balanced by the one who issued it, according to his responsibility. All they do is to accelerate or retard the conjunction of time, condition and place at which thoughts are exteriorized. They do not exteriorize thoughts, the thoughts exteriorize themselves. The opportunity for exteriorization is furnished by elementals, invisible units which bring about physical events. They cannot do this if they do not sense on the breath-forms of the persons affected such signatures as permit or compel their action. There are signatures enough on the breath-form of every person to call down good fortune or acute calamities at any time. The marshalling of the physical occurrences is done by the upper elementals acting under the order of the Intelligences or the complete Triune Selves, who decide upon the accelerating or retarding.

The destiny of each human is worked into the general plan by his own thinker, his Judge. The thinker being in touch with The Government and the justice and surety of it, aligns itself with it and brings the human into his place in life.

SECTION 2

Four kinds of units. Progression of units.

To understand the purpose of the doer's re-existences and the length of time they continue, one should keep in mind the origin of the doer, some of the changes it has undergone, its ultimate destiny and where it now stands in the plan and purpose of the Universe. Noetic destiny, as the presence or absence in the human of a certain amount of Light of the Intelligence, is the factor on which all else depends. It is the final statement of the account.

The spheres have in them units, divided into four great kinds: nature, aia, Triune Self, and Intelligence units, (Fig. II-H). These are four sections in each of which is completed a course of development. At the end of the course the opposites in a unit are adjusted to and are equal to each other.

The least developed unit of nature has the potentiality of becoming an Intelligence. The least developed unit of nature is the primordial unit in the fire element, the most developed is the breath-form. The breath-form ceases to be a unit of the nature kind when its active and passive sides have been made equal, and when it becomes an aia. This is brought about by the Triune Self which it had served. Eventually the aia becomes a Triune Self. The Triune Self kind is on the intelligent-side of the Universe and is of three parts: psychic, mental and noetic. When a Triune Self has completed its course the active and the passive sides of its three parts are equal. Then the doer and the thinker act independently of and coordinately with each other and are both in agreement with the knower, which is oneness. The unit of the Triune Self kind becomes an ultimate unit of the Intelligence kind.

The units in the fire sphere are in constant activity. Fire units are the first manifestation out of Substance. There is activity only, in each unit; the opposite is latent and potential. When the potential side comes into evidence as passivity the unit leaves the fire sphere and becomes an air unit of the sphere of air. There the active side dominates the passive. Later on the passive side of the unit dominates the active side and the unit enters the sphere of water as a water unit. When the passive side of the water unit dominates the other side so that all activity ceases, the unit becomes a unit of the sphere of earth.

In the manifested part of the earth sphere is the light world, (Fig. I-B). It is on the nature-side and corresponds to the noetic atmosphere of a Triune Self. The light world is composed of units which have been roused from their inactivity in the earth sphere by the Light of the Intelligence in the noetic atmosphere of Triune Selves. The units of the light world are nature units which reflect, and appear to be, Light. In these units there is that which is not manifest in the light world. That eventually progresses and becomes a life unit in the life world; and, similarly, there is that in the life unit which becomes a form unit in the form world. Then the unit enters the physical world and comes successively to the light, the life, the form, and at last to the physical plane of the physical world. On each of these planes the unit passes through four states of matter, which on the physical plane are called the radiant, the airy, the fluid, and the solid. The unit progresses from one state to another. So it advances to new functions and states in which it is conscious. It does not change as an individual unit.

Time is of different kinds, in the physical, the form, and the life worlds; in the light world is eternity, an everpresent now, in which all changes are in the present and the effect is in the cause, because there are no divisions to distinguish past from future. The changes in the units are in the Realm of Permanence, where the Conscious Light, as Truth, prevails and shows things as they are. In the human world changes are brought about by the mental and psychic atmospheres of the doer and physical atmosphere of the body. In the temporal human world the lights of nature prevail as stars and sun and moon, and the body senses measure the time as night and day, of the changes of masses of the sun and moon and earth in their relation to each other.

The units of the physical world pass through these systems, but do not lodge in them until the units are units of the radiant, airy, fluid and solid states. They must have been part of the structure of a human body before they can be compounded and become chemical elements and enter into the compound bodies of nature on the physical plane. They cannot be part of the physical structure of the stars, the sun, the moon, the earth and rocks, plants or animals until they have passed through the structure of a human body.

The stage in which a unit is part of a human is that in which it is a part of a cell. A cell has one cell link unit which as a link holds many cell units, in the solid state. A cell link unit holds one form link unit which as a link holds many form units, in the fluid state. A form link unit holds one life link unit which as a link holds many life units, in the airy state. A life link unit holds one breath link unit which as a link holds many breath units, in the radiant state.

A cell is made up of four holding or compositor units which are links retaining each a few or a host of units as they pass in streams through the cell. These are transient units, each functioning in one of the four states,—the radiant, airy, fluid or solid. They remain in the cell a short time and then flow on with the stream. Each cell in the human body has such streams flowing through it from the birth to the death of the body. After transient units have been so retained for a while in a human body they may be imprisoned in a rock, flowing in the ocean, floating in the air, sparkling in the sunlight. They return to a human body, not necessarily the same one, and go back to outside nature.

There are passing through the transient units in the human body, free units which are affected gradually by their passage so that they will in time become transient units. They are not part of the structure of a human body, of a chemical element or of any object of external nature. The transient units are the mass of a human body, of a chemical element or any object of external nature.

The matter, that is, the transient units, which is arranged so as to be the cell is gradually carried away by the stream, but the cell link unit organizes other matter into the cell, holding all the time its form link unit which holds its life link unit which holds its breath link unit, each of them attracting units of its own kind. The four link units keep the cell in organization. The cell link unit holds cell matter of the plasm which comes from one of the four kinds of food; the form link unit holds form matter making up the plasm; the life link unit holds the life matter; and the breath link unit holds the inspiriting matter.

Food is required to retain some of the units in the four streams passing through the cell. When no food is taken the cell is like a net that does not retain the fish in the stream. Food accrues to the net, fills it out and makes some of the transient units stick and so be caught.

The cell unit is stamped, like a coin, with the mark of the body to which it belongs. When the body dies the cell unit goes into external nature, enters into the structure of the bodies of animals or plants, and it may be taken into human bodies. Like coin circulating in foreign countries, it comes back to the source where it was coined, when the organizer of the body calls for it.

The cell unit appears first in a cell in some part like the neck or the buttocks, a part not directly connected with any system. Then it appears in some organ of the generative system and its cell forms a part of the cell structure there. The unit changes its place from time to time until it has built and has functioned through cell after cell in all parts of the generative system. Then the cell unit travels, while it keeps on organizing and reorganizing its physical cells, through the respiratory, the circulatory and the digestive systems; and in each of them it occupies successively all parts in the organs, except that of an organ unit.

Then instead of moving from place to place as it had done so far, it remains in one of the organs of the digestive system. Then it goes back to the generative system, this time as an organ unit.

Each organ exists on a fourfold plan. The organ unit dwells through the whole organ and holds one cell unit, which is the cell link unit around which the other cells of the organ are arranged and upon which they depend. The cell link unit holds the form link unit of the organ; that form link unit of the organ holds the life link unit; and that holds the breath link unit of the organ. Around these four link units are grouped and held by each, fleeting units of its own kind, and through the transient units pass the free units.

The cell unit that is in line to become an organ unit is eventually impressed through its own breath link unit by the breath link unit of the organ, through its own life link unit by the life link unit of the organ, through its own form link unit by the form link unit of the organ and is itself impressed by the organ unit. The breath link unit of the cell becomes the breath link unit of the organ, the life link unit of the cell the life link unit of the organ, the form link unit of the cell the form link unit of the organ and the cell unit changes to the organ unit. A cell unit may change its position in one of the systems from time to time during the life of the body, but the organ unit remains the organ unit of its organ for the life in which it becomes the organ unit. The organ unit manages the functioning of its organ. It keeps all the parts of the organ working together, and keeps all the units, from the cell units to the breath units, in their proper relations while they are in the organ. The cell link unit keeps the other cell units, the form link unit keeps the other form units, the life link unit keeps the other life units and the breath link unit keeps the other breath units in order. The product of the organ is passed on to other organs. Thus the organs of the digestive system act together in the functioning of that system as a whole and affect each other. When the organ unit has worked its own organ long enough it has also impressed on it the workings of the other organs in the system and so becomes eventually the unit of another organ. The change begins at the end of the digestive system, the anus.

The highest organ in the generative system is the eye. The unit of the eye adjusts the cells and regulates the curvature of the eyeball and of the lens; steadies the nerve endings in the retina; focusses the eye, and emits and takes in radiant matter by means of which to make contact with the object. Anything that is seen is contacted by the unit of the eye. The sun, or the remotest star, if seen, is actually contacted. The unit of the eye is the instrument which the sense of sight uses for seeing. It becomes familiar with the sense of sight through the optic and other nerves. It does all this under the influence of the sense of sight and becomes ever more sensitized to fire units, breath units and radiant matter. When the unit of the eye is adapted to the sense of sight and has served its time, it becomes the manager of the whole generative system and functions as the sense of sight.

The sense of sight or light unit, the breath unit of the four systems of the body, passes to become the sense of hearing, which is the life or air unit of the body; that passes to become the sense of taste, which is the form or fluid unit; and that passes to become the sense of smell.

The sense of smell immediately connects with the functions of the breath-form, which is the last and direct link between the nature-side and the aia. The aia belongs to the intelligent-side, (Fig. II-H).

The sense of smell as contact touches particles in the solid-solid state of the object smelled. Smell is actual physical contact as of particles of cabbage, camphor, or musk. It is not so with taste. The sense of taste does not contact gross physical particles, but it reaches into the solid-solid units and takes the fluid-solid units, the essence, from gross physical food, which is food to the structure of the body. To the sense of smell, but not to the fluid body, the odor is food.

The sense of smell impels the action of the digestive system and relates all the organs of the digestive system to each other and to each of the other systems, by the breath which is the active side, the life, of the breath-form. And, further, it is through the sense of smell, functioning as contact, that all sense impressions are received. So things seen, heard, or tasted, are passed through the sense of smell, by the breath, to feeling in the nerves.

SECTION 3

Raising of the aia to be a Triune Self in the Realm of Permanence. Duty of its doer, in the perfect body. Feeling-and-desire produced a change in the body. The twain, or dual body. Trial and test of bringing feeling-and-desire into balanced union.

After the death of the body the purgations of the doer are carried on by means of the breath-form, as the thoughts of the past life are unrolled from the mental atmosphere. The breath-form had preserved the memories of all that was said and done during the past life, and presents them to the doer in the after-death states called hell and heaven. As the doer is purged, some of the memory impressions on the breath-form are burned off, though the impressions graved by thoughts remain on the aia. After the doer has lived over the events of the past life, it rests and the aia remains in its dimensionless state in the psychic atmosphere.

In due course, the aia is acted on by a thought in the mental atmosphere. Then it stimulates the breath of the breath-form, which vivifies its inert form, the "soul", and the breath and form together are the breath-form, the "living soul", for the next physical body. Eventually the doer enters the body and the aia is affected by the development of the doer. Briefly stated,—after innumerable existences in human bodies the doer learns to resist the impulses of nature and to govern its desires. It improves accordingly until, eventually, it brings its feeling-and-desire into balanced union, and, with its thinker and knower, it is a Triune Self complete, in a perfected, regenerated, sexless, immortal, physical body, in the Realm of Permanence.

When the Triune Self advanced and became an Intelligence, the aia was ready to take the place of that Triune Self. It was like a bud, sensitive to the Light, ready to burst into bloom. Yet when the Triune Self had progressed, it was quiescent and in darkness.

Figuratively speaking, a ray brighter than sunlight sundered the darkness, and raised the aia into its sphere of Light, where the aia was at once translated as a Triune Self. That Triune Self was in, and conscious of, the measureless, Conscious Light of the Intelligence which had raised it, and was conscious of itself as a Triune Self in its noetic atmosphere; it knew that it never was not. There was no impression of time, of evil, of injustice, wrong, or death. The Triune Self was conscious of the sum of the functions as which it was conscious in each and all of the degrees of nature as which it had functioned before it became conscious of and as itself in the Eternal. Because of its own noetic atmosphere it was conscious of the presence of Intelligences. There it knew itself to be identity-and-knowledge-and-rightness-and-reason-and-feeling-and-de sire,—one Triune Self. But its doer part had yet to bring its feeling-and-desire into balanced union.

Its rightness-and-reason, the thinker, caused the Triune Self to think about the Intelligences and subjects of which it was made conscious by the Light; and as it thought, it was in its mental atmosphere and in a different world, the life world, though it was not conscious of the life world. In thinking there came up in the Triune Self the subjects of unity and separateness, immortality and death, good and evil, justice and injustice, and other opposites. No opinions, no conclusions were arrived at, merely the thinking went on. Just as the thinker extended from the life world into the light world by thinking, so the doer then extended into the life world by its thinking. It thought of the opposites, and so the doer was conscious in that world. As it continued to think and feel, a third atmosphere, its psychic atmosphere, was within the noetic and the mental atmospheres. The doer was now in the form world, and was conscious of itself.

At this point the knower, the thinker and the doer were each in its own atmosphere. They were negative and the atmospheres positive, and each atmosphere was connected with the world in which it was. The Triune Self was in its highest state in all its parts, and was not connected with the worlds and the senses of nature. Its three parts were adjusted, each to the others, so that the Light was present also in the psychic atmosphere of the doer. The doer thus conscious was at home in the Light.

In this way the aia was translated into a Triune Self. This was its coming into itself as a Triune Self. The raising of the aia, its translation into a Triune Self, and the degree in which it was conscious did not occur progressively, by development and in time, but instantaneously, and the Triune Self was conscious in all degrees at once, in the Eternal.

Eventually the thinking of the Triune Self was turned to the condition it had been in when it was still the aia, and to the relation which it then had to the breath-form. Now it knows that it must take the breath-form out of and away from nature and raise it to the degree of aia to form the link between itself as Triune Self, and the unintelligent units of nature. This the Triune Self does. The breath-form thus became the aia. As aia, it had yet to be adjusted to its Triune Self, to the four elements, the four worlds, the four senses, and the earth sphere as a whole.

While the Triune Self was being raised to be an Intelligence, the perfect body was inactive in safety in the interior of the earth. When the aia is raised to be a Triune Self, the perfect body is the physical body for that newly raised Triune Self.

The body had been adjusted to the four worlds. It was sensitive to them. The doer used the four senses, which acted in the four worlds. It saw the light world present through the three lower worlds and the interrelation of these with each other. It saw and heard the movements of the matter of the worlds and how the discords caused by human thoughts were brought into harmonies. Through taste it sensed the qualities and quantities of matter coming into form, and the comings and goings of matter in the maintenance and changing of the forms. By the sense of smell it perceived the building of the structures in the forms.

The doer with its four senses in alignment with the four worlds and their planes, perceived the difference and realities of the matter, forms and structures in each of the worlds, and its planes and states. It perceived the reality in the relation of each to the others. It perceived that light and heavy, great and small, near and far were interchangeable in different states and planes of any world. It perceived that when the senses were turned towards an object in any state and plane, the object was the measure of reality and all else unreal; that when the senses were not limited but were aligned with the other states and planes all things were equally real in their own states and on their planes, and that no object lost its relative reality.

In its perfect body the doer thus became acquainted first with the light, then with the life, then with the form and lastly with the physical world.

It became the duty of the doer to make the connection between outside nature and the impersoned nature in the perfect body. It aroused the organs in the head and connected them with the planes of the light world, from the light plane of the physical world through sight and its generative system; and the doer was in the light world and sensed the harmonies of the light world within the lower worlds. It aroused and connected the organs of the thorax with the planes of the life world from the life plane of the physical world through hearing and its respiratory system; and the doer was in the life world and contemplated the activities of the life world in itself and within the form and physical worlds. It aroused and connected the organs of the circulatory system with the planes of the form world from the form plane of the physical world through taste and its circulatory system; and the doer was in the form world and gave attention to the mingling of the elements and the forms. It aroused and connected the organs of the pelvic cavity with the planes of the physical world from the physical plane of the physical world through smell and its digestive system; and the doer was in the physical world and it brought together the physical planes of the other worlds with the physical plane of the physical world and all were adjusted on the physical plane in its own physical body, in the Realm of Permanence.

The doer was so related to the perfect body that it and the thinker and the knower of the Triune Self could later act freely in all of the worlds and that it could exercise the powers of any world in that world, through the systems and the organs in its fourfold body. In this body it was familiar and had contact with all states of matter in the physical world. In its physical body it could be present in all the four zones and states of matter of the physical plane.

The doer in its perfect two-columned body could perceive beings in the zones and in the bodies of the zones, for the Light of its Intelligence was with it. These beings were of the fire, the air, the water and the earth, and beings made up of combinations of them. There were beings who were fixed in the bodies of the zones, beings who could move about in the bodies of the zones and beings who could move freely in the zones or their bodies or through any of the zones and bodies, going from one to the other.

The doer perceived that the great difference between all these beings was that some had and others did not have the Light of Intelligences. Among those who did not have such Light there were beings of greatness and power who could do things which the doer had not the under- standing to do, but these things were done by means of the Light furnished to those who had it. It perceived that the passage of the matter of the zones and in the bodies therein and the changes brought about in them were done by various beings without the Light by the thinking of those who had it; and, that it was among those who had the Light. The doer perceived that there were differences between those who had the Light, that the differences were in the stage of development of the doer; and that there were those who had to do with the matter of the zones on the planes of the physical world and those who had to do with the worlds beyond the physical. Among those who had to do with the matter of the zones were others like itself, who observed but took no part in the working of the matter. During all these times the doer knew no evil, no sin, no sorrow, no death. It knew only the good and perceived the working of law as a harmonious whole.

All this took place while the Triune Self, which had been raised from the state of aia, was in its perfect immortal two-columned body in the Realm of Permanence, and prior to the trial test, which its doer part must undergo, of bringing feeling-and-desire into balanced union, which test it, the doer, must successfully pass in order to take charge of and operate the perfect body, and to advance according to the Eternal Order of Progression, as alluded to previously.

Desire became active. It was a harmless desire. The doer wanted to take part in doing what it saw going on; it wanted to express itself by acting in the forms and with the forces of nature.

The doer thought easily and clearly and its thoughts were at once exteriorized, that is, balanced because there was no attachment to the objects of the thinking. The wants of the doer were small, but what it wanted it called and that was exteriorized. So the doer was with its Triune Self in the Light of its Intelligence, in the interior of the earth. It had no fear, had all that the body needed, experiencing the world without contamination and acting in the world without losing its Light.

The doer began to think about the things it saw and heard, tasted and smelled and about its feelings and its desires. It understood how nature responded to these feelings and desires. It did not understand the relation that desire had to feeling. Feeling wanted desire, desire wanted feeling, each wanted to be itself and yet be the other; each wanted to be in the other and have the other in itself. There was a longing for each other. This longing, together with the thinking, brought about a change in the perfect two-columned body. There was then a circular path through the two columns, one in front, the other in the back of the body, for the Light from the Triune Self into the body, from the body into nature and back into the body and thence to the Triune Self, (Fig. VI-D). Feeling wanted an objectification of desire, and desire of feeling. When the change in the body came, the desire aspect became more pronounced, yet neither of the two columns was affected. Then there went out from the body a form, which was not physical. It was an elemental form. The form eventually became female. Feeling went from the doer into the female body, and desire of the doer, in the original body which had become male, saw the complement of itself in that companion body.

The knower and thinker of the Triune Self allowed the doer to do this that the doer might learn of itself in nature and that feeling-and-desire might adjust themselves to each other. When adjusted, feeling would go back into the two-columned body. This was the plan and the path.

Every sentiment, every movement, every act of desire, was at once re-enacted by the companion, as in a mirror. Feeling-and-desire felt that they were one. Indeed they were one, but they were one within, not without. Desire continued to look outwardly and then the doer thought outwardly to the reflection, instead of thinking inwardly from it. The desire of the doer began to think the other was different from itself, and desire went out strongly to the other; the other craved desire. From what are now the kidneys, adrenals and spleen a radiant fluid went out as the astral matter which later became the physical female part of the twin body.

Then the Triune Self warned its doer. It let the doer see that it might learn from its female body all of nature that was not expressed in its own male body; that it must pass a trial and test through the sexes, and that its twin bodies must not consort. It was necessary for the doer to learn the relation of the sexes to each other, in the human world of change, so that the doer would be able to administer the destinies of nations of the human world, without being influenced by the sexes. This it would learn by bringing into balanced union its own desire-and-feeling in its male and female twin bodies. Doing this was the trial test. But union must be of desire and feeling, not of the male and female bodies, in which desire and feeling were. To allow union of the two bodies would be failure, as that would sever the two columns, would cause the loss of one of the columns and a loss of Light into nature. Therewith would begin that affliction of its body which would end with expulsion from the inner earth, in the Realm of Permanence. Then it would not be able to stand in the Light, but would thereafter be afraid of it and would lose its vision in the Light. Instead of seeing the deathless things in permanence it would be in an outside world of change, of sexes and of death, and live in sin and sorrow and occasion sin and sorrow in others. Blind to the Light it would wander through life and death on the outer earth. It would forget the past, forget its Triune Self, and forget the Light, except to be afraid of it, until it should regain the state which it then was in in the inner earth.

Among the doers that had come thus far, some took the warning and followed the path that the Light showed. These doers lived in their twin bodies and thus learned all there was of the nature of the human. Each pair reunited into one body as soon as feeling-and-desire were in permanently balanced union. The Triune Self was then complete; it had direct Light in its three atmospheres and lived in its perfect, immortal, sexless, physical body, informed about all things by the Light of its Intelligence.

The doer of such a Triune Self thus advanced according to the Eternal Order of Progression. Those doers that failed in the trial test thereby exiled themselves from the Realm of Permanence into the human world of change, of death, and of re-existences in human bodies, (Fig. V-B), until, in due course, they adjust feeling-and-desire into balanced union, when the three parts of their Triune Selves will again be in a perfect, immortal, sexless physical body.

Sometimes a doer that had passed the test, felt the troubles of the world and asked its thinker and knower that it be allowed to go among mankind to awaken the doers. That doer then became human and took the responsibilities of a human. It called together those in the world who were the fittest. It had insight and powers, which were made manifest to them and they gathered around it. Such a great doer could come only when the thoughts of many persons converged at the beginning of a cycle.

SECTION 4

The "fall of man", i.e. the doer. Changes in the body. Death.
Re-existence in a male or a female body. The doers now on earth.
Circulations of units through the bodies of humans.

The doer that did not take that inner path continued to think of the
companion as other than itself. As the thinking went on, changes came
about in the male body of the desire of the doer, and in the female body
of the feeling of the doer. These changes made it possible for the bodies
to consort. The desire of the doer was reflected in the feeling of the doer,
and each attracted the other until their bodies consorted. Thereby the
doer, as feeling-and-desire, took the outer path. Some doers who took
the outer path are doers who today live in human bodies on the outer
earth crust.

Above, the pineal and pituitary bodies were closed because the doer
had opened procreative organs below. With the closing of these inner
organs the eyes became blind to all but human physical things. Light
went out through the sexual organ and was lost into nature. The then
unused front- or nature-column of the perfect body, (Fig. VI-D)), was
broken and its lower part dwindled away, (Fig. VI-E). Organs, among
them the thymus gland, atrophied. Nerves of the front-cord which had
been used for work with nature were transferred to run along the spinal
column and there formed the right and left main trunks of what is now
the involuntary nervous system, with which are merged the branches of
the right and left vagus nerve; other nerves were scattered about and
became nerve centers and plexuses in the body cavities, and those from
the lower part of the broken column became the labyrinth of the
intestinal tract. The arms and legs which once could move in any
direction became limited in their movements; many of the ribs melted
away; one-half of the double flexible pelvis faded away, and what
remained hardened; the pubic bone is all that is left of the lower front
part. The vertebrae of the front-column disappeared, and the only signs
as vestiges of them are in the sternum, (Fig. VI-E).

The fourfold body, which had been used for the maintenance of
nature, now became dependent upon nature. The body, which had been
the servant of the doer, became the master; most of the time was spent
in working for and serving it.

The body which had been nourished by matter taken into it directly from the four elements through the four senses, needed to be nourished by food. The food and drink became heavy and coarse and were taken in through the mouth. Much was waste; only a small part was used to support the body. Food became and has remained the problem of life. What is now the digestive system with its large organs was once a system of nerves through which the transient units came to maintain the body. Some of them became the liver, gallbladder, pancreas, spleen and stomach when the front-column became the bowels. The present circulatory system with the kidneys and adrenals and the bladder became such from a system of fine structures when the present digestive system became gross and adapted to gross food. The respiratory system was then the thoracic brain; the present generative system exercised its creative function from the brain in the head.

The doer knew it had done wrong. It knew that it had sinned against itself, and it was afraid. It knew division in itself. The doer no longer had communion with the thinker and knower. The doer-in-the-body no longer knew itself as the desire or as the feeling, but sensed itself as the human being. The doer which had known no fear because it lived in the Light, now feared. It was obliged to leave the interior of the earth where it had been, and joined other doers which had taken the outer path, the path of death and birth. These doers were separated from their former places and lived together in communities.

After the death of the two bodies of the doer, when the doer re-existed it entered a male body or a female body and in that body it did not have the power to put forth its counterpart. It selected a mate, a doer in a male or a female body, according to the predominance of feeling or desire. The doer itself has no sex. It is neither male nor female. It possesses the characteristic nature of both. Desire is characteristic of a man; feeling is characteristic of a woman. If the doer expresses itself as a male, it shows the nature of a man and does the things that men do; the body is masculine. The female side is suppressed in the body of a man. Likewise in a female body the male side is suppressed.

Some communities lived proper lives and remained in the interior. Others deteriorated and were led on, towards the outer crust, by a search for food suitable to their conditions, until they came to the outside world, where were men and women, doers who had fallen long before into the stream of birth and death. At times the newcomers were superior, at other times inferior to the people on the crust. At times they started a new cycle of civilization, at other times they were barbarians who overran a portion of the earth. At times they wandered out in tribes through caves, at other times they were borne out by waters and the waters filled up the openings through which the tribes had come.

In isolated cases a doer came in its companion bodies to the outside world as a pair, who were not born in the interior earth. The bodies of the pair were different from those around. Their bodies were superior in form, not subject to disease or fatigue. There was a beauty, freshness and liveliness about them that was distinctive. Their hair was as different from that of the people as is human hair from hemp. The doer had a vague memory of the Light, its Intelligence, and of immortality, justice, and happiness, ideas it had been conscious of when with its thinker and knower. Sometimes it told the people about that world from which it came and used the sun as a symbol for the Light in which it had dwelt. Sometimes the people believed it came from the sun. So original solar dynasties may have been founded. The doer did not know it had created its companion by dividing itself, but the two came together into the world and they felt that they were brother and sister as well as husband and wife. The legends of marriage between a divine brother and sister, as of Isis and Osiris, and the corresponding human customs may have originated in the appearance of such a pair. These legends are as distorted as are those of Jesus and of Adam, but there is a fact of human experience underlying each of them.

Every doer now on earth has been re-existing as a human being ever since the time it fell and had to leave its companion bodies at their death. The vast majority of the doers came in and belong to this present Fourth Civilization which began millions of years ago on this earth. However, some doers have been re-existing since the Third and some even since the Second and the First Civilizations. These are old travelers who have had many ups and downs and have each cycled through wealth and poverty, prominence and obscurity, health and disease, honor and shame, culture and crudeness, in short lives and in long lives, and most have made little progress in untold millions of years.

Among the doers some earned their freedom and passed on. The majority keep on the treadmill of life and death, repeat their experiences and learn little or nothing, while they are issuing thoughts and weaving destiny.

The re-existing portions of some doers got into a condition where they lost so much Light that the Triune Self withdrew the Light from the embodied portion; and those doer portions were "lost", that is, they are in darkness and their re-existences are suspended.

In some bodies that appear to be inhabited, there are no doers. Among them are some whose doers have withdrawn and will have no further embodiment during a long period. Such beings as these are unable to conceive of the doer and are opposed to the thought of it; they have a horror of death. If they show mental abilities these are due to working according to the patterns made on the breath-form before the withdrawal of the portion of the doer that was in the body, and that are prompted by nature; they are automatic and are carried on by the brain and voluntary nervous system.

During the immense periods which have passed in this Fourth Civilization, there have been many changes in the structure of the earth's crust, in the surface distribution of land and water, in the inclination of the poles, in the climates in different parts, in the magnetic and electric currents in the earth, the water, the air and the starlight, in the relation and influence of the four elements and in the manifestation of forces and phenomena in them. These changes were produced as the exteriorizations of thoughts of streams of re-existing doers. Amidst these varying surroundings came many different types of minerals, plants and flowers with strange properties, and also came animals of varying types, all put into form by human thought.

There were changes in the colors and features of human bodies and a constant swinging of cycles from primitive rudeness to the refinement of culture. Amidst all these changes in outer nature, the governments, morals and religions gradually have changed too and have ever repeated themselves in cycles. All changes of the conditions under which the doers lived were the externalizations of their thoughts.

From the standpoint of man with his conception of length, breadth and thickness as three dimensions, the earth, if it could be seen, would appear as a sponge-like spherical crust, between three outer spherical layers and three inner spherical layers. The earth crust has an outer and an inner surface. The distance between these varies from about two hundred to eight hundred miles. The outside is the world of men and is the only world men know of.

Between the outer and the inner skin of this solid layer are large and small subterranean chambers in which there are fires, airs, oceans, lakes and rivers, which often differ in their qualities and colors from the things seen on the outer crust. Minerals, plants and animals are different in their

forms and habits from those known to human beings. Forces are operative there which are dormant on the outer crust. Gravity and other forces
are changed from what they are as known to man. Many peoples in
various degrees of development exist between the outer and the inner
skin of this layer. They differ as to color, size, features and weight. To
some of them the crust is as transparent as the air is to men. To others
it is opaque, but they have a diffused earthlight by which they see. To
these many races, in the different strata of the crust, their environment
is a world. The beings inside and beyond the crust are of the nature-side
or of the intelligent-side. Each set has its own world in which the
constituents, requirements and possibilities are different. Beyond the
outer and the inner skin conditions are such as to be incomprehensible
at present.

On either side of this solid spherical layer is a fluid layer, which is
not water, but is the element of water as it appears through and is affected
by the earth element. The two layers of water, one on each side of the
solid layer, are in reality one mass which moves through and in the solid
layer. On either side of this fluid layer is a layer of air. These air layers,
though they would appear as one on the inside and as one on the outside,
are in reality one mass, which moves in and through the mass of water
and the rind of the solid earth. On either side of the airy layer is a layer
of fire, and the outer and inner layers of fire are really one mass. What
would appear and is conceived of as the central portion of fire inside is
one with the vast layer of fire matter outside. The spherical mass of fire
is and moves in and through the air, the water and the earth.

The earth which would thus appear to be made up of seven layers is
made up of four globes, the earthy globe being only a spongy rind and
not solid throughout. These are the four states of matter on the physical
plane, (Fig. I-D). The fire extends from the center to the outermost
portion through the earthy rind and through the fluid and the airy
masses. The earthy shell is thus supported and maintained by the other
three states of matter, and the four move through it as a fourfold stream
of breath.

The apparent contradiction that the three outer layers are one with
the three inner layers is due to people being acquainted only with one
dimension out of four. Their sight reaches only surfaces, they know only
surfaces, they live on surfaces, their thoughts are about surfaces. The
surface dimension is on-ness. If people became conscious of the other
dimensions, the earth would not look as it does now. It would not even

look as if in layers, but would be a mass of fire, containing, pervading and supporting a smaller mass of air, containing, pervading and supporting in its turn a lesser mass of water, containing, pervading and supporting the hollow earth crust. But to one who saw four dimensions this description would be insufficient. There would be no globe or layers or masses, nor would the solid layer on which is the outside crust be a ball.

The solid layer extends as an atmosphere of diffused particles of matter beyond its compacted state, into the fluid layer. This atmosphere of solid particles extends to the moon. The moon is a body in the zone of water and this zone extends to the sun. The sun is a body and center in the airy layer which extends to the stars. These are bodies in the zone of fire. The planets are bodies in the zones of water and air. What is called the space through which the earth moves around the sun is matter more closely compacted than the earth, through which the earth moves like a fish through water. In the region of the stars is little sunlight and less moonlight and earthlight. In the sun is starlight and sunlight but little moonlight and less earthlight, and in the solar spaces, that is, in the area around the sun, there is hardly any moonlight or earthlight, (Fig. I-E).

There is a constant circulation of the masses of units of the four states of matter. They circulate in a stream which is fourfold when it passes through the earth crust. Each of the parts comes from its own layer. The course of the stream is from the stars through the sun, through the moon, through the earth to the corresponding layers and back again.

The sun is the general center and focus of the fourfold stream. Starlight, radiant matter, is everywhere; but it has centers which are the stars, and a stream of it enters the solar focus. The sun centers also its own light, airy matter, and moonlight, fluid matter, and earthlight, solid matter. As the stars attract and are centers for starlight, so the sun acts for sunlight and the moon for moonlight and the earth crust for earthlight.

There are thus four lesser currents which make up the main or fourfold current that goes through the sun to the earth. The sun sucks in starlight and sunlight directly. It does not in the same manner take in moonlight and earthlight. The moon is a focus and center for the layer of moonlight and sends that into the stream of starlight and sunlight that is pumped from the sun to the earth. The moon also sucks in earthlight and pours that with its own light into the sunlight that goes to the earth.

Thus is made up the fourfold stream that goes through everything on the outer surface of the earth. On the earth it circulates as a fourfold stream, it goes back to the moon which cleanses, modifies and regulates the earthlight and the moonlight, which then go with the purified sunlight and starlight to the solar focus. There the moonlight and the earthlight are vivified, and the sunlight and the starlight stream on to their own layers. This fourfold stream of radiant, airy, fluid and solid units is the fourfold physical breath that comes and goes through all things on the earth crust and builds, preserves and destroys them. This breath is kept in circulation by the fourfold physical breath of human beings, which is the active side of their breath-forms.

It is the breath of human beings that keeps the starlight active among the most distant stars, that breathes the sunlight through the sun, that drives the moonlight through the moon and that causes the fourfold breath stream to flow into and out of the sun, the moon and the earth. This fourfold stream circulates outside as the arterial and venous blood does inside the human body, and envelops and penetrates all things on the earth crust. It leaves behind some units, those that are caught, and carried away others, those that are no longer held. The units that are held so as to be the mass of a thing, that which is seen, are coming and going. This mass appears to be permanent, but it is not.

The physical bodies of human beings are the centers around which all turns and through which all circulates. Without human physical bodies, what is known to human beings as nature would cease to act. There would be no phenomena, no colors, no sounds, no forces, no beings, no things celestial or terrestrial. Physical matter would be at a standstill. The physical universe is an expression, projection and extension of the human body. The solid earth crust is the sex, the moon is the kidneys and its atmosphere the adrenals, the sun is the heart and its atmosphere the lungs, the planets are other organs and the stars are the brain and nervous systems of the universe on the fourfold physical plane of the physical world.

The fourfold breath goes through all human bodies as the generative or fire breath, the respiratory or air breath, the circulatory or water breath and the digestive or earth breath, which ebb and flow in their respective systems, the upper three breaths pervading the earth breath. The fire breath or starlight comes along the nerves of the eye and generative system; the air breath or sunlight along the nerves of the ear and respiratory system; the water breath or moonlight along the nerves of the tongue and circulatory system, and the earth breath or earthlight along the nerves of the nose and digestive system. The fire breath goes out along the nerves of the testicles and prostate or of the ovaries and womb; the air breath along the nerves of the heart and lungs; the water breath along the nerves of the adrenals, kidneys and bladder, and the earth breath along the nerves of the stomach, intestines and anus. At the same time these breaths come in and go out through the pores of the skin. The breaths swing in from above while they swing out from below, and swing in below when they go out above. In the body the heart is the center for the air breath which is the carrier and mixer of all the breaths, and there is another center in the physical atmosphere outside the body. The mixing and distributing of the four breaths is done chiefly by the heart, corresponding to the sun, and secondarily by the kidneys, corresponding to the moon. The breath that is noticed in breathing is the air breath only; the other three breaths which it carries are not noticed.

The breath of human beings comes and goes many times in a minute. It causes the fourfold breath of the earth crust to come and go every few hours, and the water breath of the moon to come and go as ebb and flow twice a day, and the solar breath to come and go twice a year. The speed of the radiant, airy, fluid and solid units in the solar breath is immeasurably greater than that in the human breath. Nevertheless, the human organs are so geared with the celestial bodies that there is a constant reaction between them.

The fourfold physical breath flows from conception by means of the mother's breath until birth, and then by independent breathing until death. The fourfold current builds up the fourfold body, maintains it, and destroys it when, individual breathing having ceased, the outside breath carries the fleeting units into their elements. When there is a conception for the new body the swing of the physical breath, that was suspended, begins again where it left off. So the whole row of lives of the human beings of a doer is a unity because of the continuity which is provided by the aia, when it revivifies the form for the new breath-form to take up and carry on the fourfold breath of the body.

SECTION 5

Fourth Civilization. Changes on the earth crust. Forces. Minerals, plants and flowers. The varied types were produced by human thoughts.

Since this Fourth Civilization began there have been many changes on the earth crust. Rocks and soils of different kinds composed it at different times. Changes in the surface distribution of land and water have been numerous. They were made during upheavals and submersions. They were made slowly during long periods or by sudden elemental changes which brought about the same results. Changes which sometimes required thousands of years, occurred at other times in days; liquids turned into solids and both into gases and these again into liquids and solids. Sometimes the action of the fire was direct, sometimes concealed in water.

After a change had taken place it sometimes was succeeded in a short time by another, and at other times the continents and islands remained undisturbed for a long while. The lines between water and land, and the elevations of the land have changed over and over again. Sometimes the land was slowly eaten away by the ocean or slowly decomposed by the air and washed away by rain and rivers. Sometimes the land was precipitated from the air. At other times the air crumbled the land quickly and it was washed away like sand. Sometimes the water rose in mighty mountains engulfing the land, sometimes the land opened and a subterranean ocean rushed over it.

The direction of what is called the poles has changed many times, sometimes gradually, sometimes suddenly. The changes were adjustments to the sum of the thoughts of the people of the crust, and were to provide a suitable environment for future destiny. A sudden change when the earth slipped or fell over was cataclysmic. During and after the readjustment the climates changed. Where there had been a continuous summer, icebeds thousands of feet in depth buried the peoples, and icy regions were melted and exposed the land to a temperate or tropical sun.

The direction of the poles is that of those of the earth crust only. The layers on either side of the crust need not be polarized in the same direction as the crust. Upon the direction of the poles of the crust depends the recurrence of a possible fourfold cycle of an earth, a water, an air and a fire age of human beings.

From the magnetic and electric currents on the earth today are drawn the forces used in industry, commerce and travel, upon which modern development largely depends. The same currents have not always been operative. They mark stages in the power of men's thought. What appears as magnetism is an expression of feeling in matter, and what appears as electricity is an expression of desire in matter. Magnetic waves sweep through the strata of the earth as waves of feeling run through human bodies; and as desires are evoked by these feelings, so electric currents are due to their actions in the fields of nature. At different times in the past, different currents and forces operated not only in the earth, but in the water, the air and the fire. These currents produced phenomena which would seem strange to persons to whom none but the present manifestations are known. These currents and men's knowledge of how to use them gave to an age the character of an earth, a water, an air or a fire age.

There were parts of the ocean which were seething, so that no animal life was possible in or near them. At some periods the crust of the earth was of great weight and at the same time plastic like clay, and sometimes it moved in waves, but human beings lived on it. Rains of fiery bolts from the air, varicolored lightning rising from the earth as well as coming from the sky, clouds of fire moving over the earth and discharging themselves or disappearing, battles of fire with fire in the air, wars of elementals in the water or the air occurred in different ages. Forces now unknown were active and put to use by some of the people. At different periods the relation of the four elements to each other changed; at one time one element dominated the others, and at another time it was subsidiary to one of the others.

At times there existed minerals, plants and flowers which are no longer known. At one time people used a bluish metal which, after it had been treated in a certain way, became a medium for one of the nature forces, and eliminated weight from any object to which it was applied. It had to be treated in one way for wood, in another for stone and in another for metals. By the use of a small amount of this metal weights many thousand times greater could be handled as if they were feathers. Huge blocks of stone were transported by its use. This metal had the peculiar property of transmitting the influences of the object on which it was placed, to feeling. If a rod of this metal was held in the left hand

and placed on an object, the holder would feel the qualities of the object, bitter, sour or fragrant. If held in the right hand, the holder could harden or soften objects, crumble or dissolve them. Another metal which was known at certain times was reddish, varying from a whitish red to a ruby color. By means of it a gentle or an enormous heat could be produced. The heat was generated from the air. A rod of this metal, if held by certain persons toward an object, would melt and consume it at a distance. This metal responded in its action to the intention of the holder. Only a certain trained class could use it. The two metals were known and used at the crest of some of the waves of a high civilization. Another metal, when applied to an object, caused oscillations in it or in the air, the force that worked through the metal being liberated by contact with the object. Another metal caused condensation of particles of matter in the air and produced any solid form desired. Another metal caused any solid object to be disintegrated and its particles to be shattered and to disappear, resolved into its four elements. These are only some of many minerals by which forces now unknown could be liberated, isolated and directed.

There was a black stone that seemed to be liquid and alive inside of its polished surface. If it was placed on the forehead or on the top of the head, it would fascinate that person, so that he revealed his thoughts without power of resistance, and the examiner could find out the truth concerning anything with which the one examined had been connected. In the black stone would also appear what had been said, done, seen or heard by those who were made to look at it. There was another jewel through which, when it was shaped convex or concave, light of varying colors would be generated.

A family of plants existed that would grow strong threads. There were numerous varieties that produced threads, which when separated were some as fine as silk, others as coarse as grass. These plants were in shape like posts, varied from sandy to dark brown, and opened at the top, shedding a profusion of fibers which were the usable threads. The product ranged through all colors and their shades, and the people wove it into fabrics. Some of these threads resisted destruction by fire, others were impervious to water. There were plants which were without roots and moved about, drawing nourishment from the air.

There were flowers that furnished indelible colors. Flowers, being the sex part of the plant and affecting the sense of smell, which represents the earth element in the body, were powerful in certain ages. Some flowers had fragrance and others stenches which were overpowering.

They had odors which intoxicated, produced cataleptic states, poisoned and brought instant death. Some flowers by their smell incited to murder, lust or greed. Some brought on impotence, melancholy, or even self-murder. The size of some flowers was over three feet. Some flowers were like flowing golden hair, others like thick wax, some left their stems and floated in the air. Some flowers could be grown in almost any shape desired, and at certain times the shapes of lizards, birds or butterflies were preferred.

The leaves of plants and trees were not always green, as they usually are today. At times the general coloring was red or blue or yellow or purple. Some of the leaves had odors that produced effects on human beings and animals like those of some of the flowers. Some of the leaves looked like flowers, some like fur. At all times flowers, leaves and fruits were used in healing and in industry.

At different times the shapes and qualities of the trees varied much. At times some trees had a great diameter, but were not proportionately high, and other trees reached heights uncommon today. There were trees that were hundreds of feet high. The very high trees had wood that was as supple and tough as whalebone. Some of the woods then known were indestructible by fire, some were inflammable like straw. The wood in some of the trunks grew in geometrical figures of different colors. The wood of some trees and the sap of others, furnished penetrating and indelible dyes. Though apples were there at all periods, in one form or another, many periods had fruits today unknown. At times the flora furnished various juices which produced visions, were intoxicant or narcotic, either naturally or after they had been exposed to the sun or the moonlight. One kind of tree grew a container like a gourd, that was filled with a sweetish and pungent acid which had an immediate penetrating effect as an intoxicant.

These different types of plants, as well as the fauna of the various periods, were produced, as they are today, by the thoughts of man; their nature was the desire of the doers, and their forms were the forms of their thoughts, standardized by a ruling Intelligence according to type.

At the beginning of any age the animals were huge, ungainly and fierce. As the age rose towards its crest they gave way to more graceful and symmetrical shapes. Some were adapted to industrial and domestic purposes. Some of the fiercest and clumsiest were brought under human control. Huge fish with shells or scales were used as beasts of burden to pull rafts and boats through the water. Men could ride fish through the water, and go under it with the fish. They could also make birds fly through the air while bearing human riders.

Since the first wave of the Fourth Civilization on the fourth earth, there have followed many waves. Uncounted years of physical time have elapsed since then. In each wave were many fluctuations and cycles. Sometimes a small, sometimes a large portion of the earth crust was affected, sometimes the whole. Sometimes the trend of events was toward religion, at other times toward architecture, sometimes toward the discovery and application of the forces of nature. Sometimes the development was broader, and intellectual as well as sensuous results were sought. At times pursuits were limited to the land, and people were afraid of the water. At other times there were races of water people who lived chiefly on the water and were as familiar with it as the land people were with the earth. At times human races mastered the air and could make use of the sunlight. When they discovered how to use starlight, they could protect themselves against fire, so that they could move around in it. Such ages of earth, water, air and fire have succeeded each other many times. When there was a rise of a great wave sometimes all four of the ages blended.

At times the run of human beings knew of nothing more than their physical environment. At other times the screens were removed and the different states of matter on the physical plane were accessible. Even the other planes of the physical world were sometimes opened, and nature gods and elementals were in communication with mankind.

For long ages interests and occupations were concerned with growing and winning products from the soil. At such times there were great varieties of grains, fruits and plants used for food and clothing and in industry; and the pleasures and worship of the people had to do with these products. At other periods the products needed for life and pleasure were produced artificially, that is, precipitated from the elements directly by the thought of man. By combinations of the elements foods were produced as desired, without growing them from the soil. All manner of wearing apparel was drawn from the elements and produced in the forms and colors desired. Those who did this had to have the power of imagination, an understanding of the qualities of the units in the four states of matter, and power over them, so that they could precipitate objects having the durability, elasticity, flexibility or porosity needed. This was in periods when the fire and air were dominant and the bodies of the people of the age were in touch with them.

SECTION 6

Fourth Civilization. Lesser civilizations.

During the time when there was an earth age, when the earth element was dominant and the people were adjusted to it, there were great civilizations surpassing in achievements anything reported in history. These civilizations were based on agriculture and the working of stone and metal. Starting with the use of animals for power, the civilization advanced to the use of complicated machines. These the people operated by the forces of nature.

There is but one force. It is turned into many channels and appears under many aspects. Today it manifests as light, heat, gravity, cohesion, electricity and otherwise. Untold years ago the same force manifested differently. The solid, fluid, airy and radiant matter of the earth, is being continually decomposed and recomposed. The resulting matter which today takes the form of minerals, coal or oil was different in different ages. A circulation of the same four elements and the four states of matter on the physical plane is kept up continuously by means of the manifestation of this earth force. In the past this force was liberated not so much by means of wood, coal or oil, as it is today, but by tapping the earth currents in which it manifested. The ability of the fundamental earth force to manifest at different times in varying ways results in the different directions of the poles of the earth crust and in connection with these changes in the cycles of four ages of earth, water, air and fire. The kind of manifestation of the force depends on the class of units, earth, water, air and fire units, with which the humans can make contact directly through their involuntary nervous system, or indirectly through exterior objects, as wood, coal, oil, copper, or radium and the like.

At the height of the earth ages the currents running through the earth at certain places were let out and were connected with machines for mechanical operation. Broad and permanent roads were built over and through mountains and across plains. The people did not use the water for travel and transportation. Some of these roads into the interior of the earth remain today. The people did not use an air force, but lifted great weights of stone by their machines. They could so focus the earth force that it would produce heat or light at any place where it was intercepted or an outlet made through a receiving machine. This force could be used to make hard metals workable without heat. The people had processes to make soft metals hard. They had machines for cutting and polishing stone, for melting, churning and setting it solid, for spinning and weaving plant fibers and the hair of animals. They had material which was not woven, but was solid like leather, and could be made proof against the cuts of weapons.

They travelled not on wheels, but in closed vehicles which slid easily along the roads. These sleds were of metal and sometimes of a composition which was transparent. The material was so hardened that it was scarcely affected by friction even though the vehicles were moved along with great speed by the earth force. The greatest speed, which was of many hundred miles an hour, was developed when the cars travelled underground. Distance was practically eliminated. This travel went along beneath the outer crust of the earth, but the travellers gained no knowledge of the interior earth, its worlds and its beings, any more than humans now know the beings living in what is called the air. The whole earth was not inhabited by a people that had reached this stage; on some parts were people who were less advanced, and in other parts savages.

They had their sports which were feats of endurance, ball games, wrestling and friendly combats. The ball games were of great variety; running was not so much a feature as clever throwing, catching and intercepting the ball. They could throw a ball so that it would make a circle on the ground, and the game was to intercept it. The water and the air were foreign and unfamiliar to them in their sports and in their work.

Learning was concerned with agriculture, metal working, stone making, architecture, earth currents and their operation. The languages spoken differed from those of today in sound and connotation. There were extended systems of literature. The chief means of recording was by engraving or stamping signs in color on thin metal plate. There was a white metal which would not tarnish, but would absorb and retain indelible dyes. Sheets of thin metal were rolled, or books were made by fastening the plates on hinges. These sheets were made as thin and flexible as paper is today. They also had a composition made of a plant which retained an impression of writing. This material was insoluble and not inflammable after it had been treated.

There were many such civilizations in each earth age. They started from rude beginnings and sometimes attained by slow stages to astonishing heights. At other times they bloomed suddenly because of information which Wise Men imparted.

An earth age was succeeded by a water age. While some peoples were in an earth age, others had entered upon a water age. They became conscious of the units of the watery layer, got in touch with them, and learned to use them. Sometimes this came about by the beginning of another period after the earth civilization had been swept away, some-times by gradual adaptation of a people to new surroundings, when there was a slow subsiding of the land. Most frequently the water age developed out of the earth age and people existed at the same time in both. The bodies of the people of a water age were more supple and quicker than those of an earth age. In general conformation the human form has remained the same throughout the Fourth Civilization.

There were great lakes with well populated floating islands. The people built houses by growing plants and vines together, solidified the walls with a clay, and decorated them artistically. The houses were not higher than three stories. The people grew fruits and flowers from the vines that were part of the houses.

They built boats for the accommodation of one person, which fitted their bodies and in which they could travel under water. Other boats were large enough to hold several hundred. Air was drawn from the water by an appliance in the boat. Such boats were built of pliable wood or of fish bones and cemented by plant juices so that the boats had flexibility. Some of the people learned to run the boats, not by machinery or the force of the wind, but by a certain feeling within their bodies which they imparted to the rudder of the boat. This feeling was generated from the abdominal and pelvic cavities and driven forward. Then the navigator held his hands to the tiller and so connected with a current in the water, which was thereby utilized to propel the boat.

The ocean was at such times not divided as now. The huge lakes were connected by underground streams and divided by mountain chains. Boats could travel under water from lake to lake. The people could stay in the water, warm or cold, for a long time. An oil or an insulating suit was used when the water was too cold. They did not have to swim with their limbs, but could use their feeling to connect with the water current. Over their heads they fitted hoods that allowed them to breathe. Fish would not attack them. They could swim as fast as the fish, for a distance, and kill them by the use of a water force.

They did not work metals well. If there was no contemporaneous earth age in bloom, they used bones and the sharpened shells and scales of fish, some of which were like flint. With such tools they hewed wood and tilled the soil on their small islands. They wove fibers into cloth, and made a fine linen from water plants. They decorated their clothes with many colors, from the juices of vines and berries, and with fish scales and gems. Their foods were fish, marine plants and savory fruits which they got from the bottoms and sides of the lakes. They ate them cooked, getting heat from a device which was worked by a water force. They knew how to make fire, but did not use it extensively, as they obtained in other ways the heat and power they needed. They did all these things as did the people of the earth age, but they were conscious of something which the earth people could not touch or use. They were conscious of the water layer which was in the solid earth and were conscious of living in it when they were in the streams and lakes. They used forces which were within the water layer to accomplish their ends with matter in the solid state.

They lived in small communities or in cities, some of which were built on the water. The buildings were on boats and connected with each other. There was a lively commerce between different peoples. They followed widely different trades. The savages were usually on the mainland and afraid of the water. These water people had sports and physical exercises, all connected with water. Among their games was one in which the contestants rode certain fish, which raced and leaped over each other.

They had their arts and sciences, a melodious music, a peculiar aquatic architecture and their almost indestructible boats. Their language consisted chiefly of vowel sounds. They had literature and records, on cloth spun of the fibers of water plants. These civilizations of the water ages saw a high development of humanity. Bodies of great endurance, nobility of feature, skill in their arts and great intellectual attainments distinguished the people of some of these water races.

An air age succeeded the water age when people became conscious of and adjusted their bodies to the air units which moved through the layer of air. Such ages usually began with the discovery by individuals of the force of lightness and the force of flight in themselves. These forces always exist, but they cannot at present be used by humans.

The force of lightness is a distinct force, as much so as heat. It is one of the manifestations of the fundamental earth force. Its manifestation removes weight to a greater or lesser degree. If to a lesser degree than gravitation, it reduces the weight, if to a greater degree it causes the object in which it manifests to depart from surrounding objects. By rising into the air is meant only going away from the earth crust. Rising when an object is moved by lightness can be done into the air inside the earth as well as into the air outside the earth. Lightness affects the feeling as ecstasy without producing foolishness. It is brought into play by a mental attitude that puts one in touch with the air units on their active side, which is the air force, and by breathing, which liberates the force and draws it through the nerves of the involuntary nervous system. When the force is felt in the voluntary nervous system, it is lightness and the body rises into the air. Its lightness is equal to the mental attitude, so that a body can rise and float like thistledown or shoot away from the earth.

The force of flight is a force of the layer of air and is similar to that of lightness, but is distinct as a force. Lightness moves away from the earth crust; flight generally moves parallel to it, but it can move on an incline, up or down. The characteristic of it is direction. It receives this by the mental set and it is induced into the body by breathing. It can be exercised without the force of lightness. But then it must be exercised continuously and at a different speed, great enough to make the air support the body. Usually both forces are exercised together. Both forces are manifestations of the fundamental earth force, specialized by being active in the air layer.

In an air age, that is, in a period when many of a people can come into contact with these forces in the layer of air, their thoughts and nerve currents touch the units of air directly, instead of as now through the earth units. The movements of the air units being at a different rate from that of the earth units, they counteract and overcome the forces exercised by the earth units.

The people in an air age were a development from those of the water age. The forces which were used for moving swiftly through the water were adapted to the air, as the forces on the earth crust had been adapted to the water. The force of lightness had been used to a moderate degree in running and jumping on land and in rising in the water. At first a few exercised the forces of lightness and flight. Then a greater number became familiar with the use, and finally the people born were naturally adjusted to these air forces.

At the crest of an air age the people lived in houses on the earth and in floating houses on the water, but the dominating race lived chiefly in the air. Some persons on the earth seldom took to the air and were afraid to trust themselves to it; but the people of the air age lived in dwellings or in huge buildings in the air. They took some of the materials for these from the earth; other materials they precipitated or consolidated from the air itself. They removed the weight from the materials and placed them in position in the air where they were fixed and balanced, so as to remain undisturbed until they were removed. The people accomplished this by focussing and attaching to the buildings the force of lightness. There were no streets. The buildings stood on different levels in the air. They were just as solid as anything on earth today. Timbers, stones and metals were used, but their weights removed and kept removed by the use of a certain blue metal, either drawn from the air or mined and refined from the earth. This metal was a conductor of the force of lightness, and was used to impart lightness to inorganic objects.

The people obtained their food from the fruits, grains and animals of the earth, and from fish and birds. Much of their food they drew from the air itself by breathing. They had plants that floated in the air and drew their nourishment from it, but most plants were in gardens attached to the houses. The materials of their draperies and garments were made from plants and from the hair of animals. Feathers were used largely.

Their forms were human, but their bodies surpassed those of the earth and the water people in lightness and freshness. To use the air force was natural. Babies had to be protected, but they soon learned to adjust their mental set and their breathing so as to touch the forces in the air layer. They learned this more readily than children learn to walk, as readily as birds learn to fly. The people used these air forces without much effort. They walked about and worked in their houses, and slept on couches without exercising the force of flight; over long galleries they glided above the floors, and in the open relied naturally upon their command of the air. They rested and floated in the air, as one does in water. They could control the winds and prevent or cause storms; sometimes they had wings or shields attached to the back to facilitate movement. They had airships for commerce and travel over long distances. They used all the products of the earth, its plants, woods, stones and metals, but had no complicated machines. Their enormous airships were guided and propelled by the force of the helmsman alone.

Their games consisted chiefly in variations of flying, and in performances in the air. The salient features of their sports were graceful sliding or rising movements in the air accompanied by charming sounds produced by the movements themselves and accentuated by the voice. The movements and sounds produced colors, light-colors like those of a rainbow rather than pigment-colors. The marvellous effects of these lights were enhanced when many people engaged in the harmonies of movement, sound and color at the same time. There were wrestling matches and dancing in the air.

Their arts centered around singing and music. Among the instruments used was a sort of trumpet with diaphragms which were moved and varied by the human voice, and thereby direct sounds and echoes were created in the air, followed by colors which often took on forms. They had huge instruments shaped like the half of a hollow sphere and many feet in diameter, which produced a symphonic sound by intercepting the units of the four states of matter in their movements and relating the movements to each other. By the power of that sound, if directed towards the earth, the people who heard it lost their fear and weight, were enraptured and rose into the air where they remained as long as they were within hearing of the sound.

At times there was a proficiency in the sciences among some of the people. Their learning was concerned chiefly with the different rates of movement of the four kinds of units in nature and their many subdivisions. They knew of hundreds of different rates of movement of units and adjusted some of these by combining, binding and eliminating certain of the units. Thereby they evoked forces, chiefly of the air layer, and made them dominate the water and the earth forces. The reason they maintained their habitations in the air was that there they could more easily reach and direct these forces. By means of such forces they stabilized their houses and cities in the air, and obtained heat, light and energy for their domestic affairs. Since only some individuals could do this, it was left to a certain group whose duty it was, to attend to the supply. Waste matter was at once disposed of by decomposing it into its component units, or by recombining these units into other objects.

They had languages to express their thoughts. They had sheets of a material on which communications from one to the other could pass, but these were used only as keepsakes, because the people could communicate by thought. The nerve matter of their brains contacted the currents made by thoughts in the physical world. Speech and thought coincided. If anyone told a lie it was at once manifest because then speech and thought were seen not to coincide.

The things which they wanted to put on record as information, news or literature, they inscribed on or sounded against plates, connected with a reservoir on the life plane of the physical world. The inscribing or sounding was transferred to, and so made a permanent record on, the matter of the reservoir. People who thereafter wanted the information so preserved, could find it by going to a public building, where they found registers of sign words. Then they touched with an instrument the selected sign word on the reproducing plate that connected them with the permanent record of the reservoir, and so they obtained the information. After getting the subject and the sign word they could go over the record at home, provided they had there a device for receiving and reproducing the records. Books and libraries did not exist; they were not needed.

A fire age succeeded the air age and gradually grew out of and dominated it. The air age continued to exist contemporaneously. The human beings in a fire age had the same form and figure as the air people. But they differed noticeably in that there was in them a presence of conscious power, which gave them superiority. Their distinctive physical feature was the eye with which they appealed, commanded and expressed to others their sentiment and thought.

The age began when some of the air people became acquainted with the fire which is radiant matter or starlight. They became conscious of the presence of the fire units in the layer of fire. After that others and then more found their way into the starlight. At no time did all of the air people develop into fire people. In a fire age there were on the earth also the three other ages and people lived on the earth, in the water and through the air and communicated with each other by travel and trading. People of an earth age had bodies adjusted and restricted to the use of those solid units that were in a gross and solidified state. People who were of a water age had bodies which were adapted to the fluid-solid units; people of an air age were such because they had bodies attuned to airy-solid units, and the people of a fire age were conscious of the radiant-solid units and their bodies were adjusted to them.

The fire units on the physical plane are starlight. Starlight is imperceptible, though a condensation of it in a mass produces the bodies of the stars. In a fire age people were conscious of and in touch with the units of starlight. They saw them and saw by them, and by means of them could use the forces of the radiant-solid layer, and through them the forces of the other three layers. Starlight works through the sun. The people of an earth age can use starlight only when they use it in and as sunlight, but the people in a fire age could use starlight without being dependent on the sun.

The sun is a focus of forces, an airy center in an airy layer. Through and out of the sun streams sunlight, which is a mixture of radiant, airy, fluid and solid units. Starlight works through the airy matter and is the cause and the main support of the activities of sunlight. The sunlight causes units to be active as nature forces which maintain life on the earth crust and by which the present age builds up its civilization. The earth crust, which is a precipitation of the fourfold sunlight, screens off portions of each set of units and so retains and supplies what is needed to keep up the activities on the earth crust. The units become nature forces as they approach the screen of the earth crust. Away from the screen the units do not act as these forces. These forces produce light, heat, power, generation and decomposition within a certain range only. Thus if the focal body called the sun is not within that range of the earth crust, it does not produce these effects. Moreover it is necessary that the earth crust should give up earth units to furnish some material to produce these effects. In an earth age people cannot have light and heat unless these three conditions are fulfilled, but in their fire age the people could get the equivalent of light, heat and electricity without being dependent on the screening, on the range of the sun and on the action of the solid crust in sending out units to meet the incoming sunlight.

The habitations of the fire people were in the air, on the water and on the earth, but they were conscious of and used as their medium the fire present in the air, in the water and in the earth. They lived in communities of their own, and had their own circles, though they went among the others. If they did this they were immediately seen or sensed to be superior because of the influences that went with them and the power in their eyes. They could eat any of the animal or vegetable foods or live on fluids or even by breathing only. If they wanted to prolong their lives, they did not eat solid or liquid foods. Their bodies were physical, but they could do things with them that the others could not do with theirs.

They engaged in agriculture, commerce, mechanics and the arts. They could produce things for the earth people which these could not. They did the same for the water and the air people. The air people reached so high a state because those of the fire age lived among them and assisted them.

In agriculture they could see what was going on in the plants. They could see the activities of the seeds and roots, how the plants received nourishment, how they appropriated it and grew, and they could direct development as they wished. They blended plants and produced new fruits, vegetables and grains.

In the beginnings of the fire ages these people built machines for dredging, building, lighting and generating power. As they advanced they used few or none for themselves, though they still built machines for the people who were in the more backward ages. They helped the earth and the water people in cutting great canals on land and through the earth and made great waterways. They used huge machines to cut under water and to dredge. They could see all that was going on in the great depths and direct operations accordingly.

At the height of a fire age, the foremost among the fire people needed only their bodies to accomplish what they wished. Four fingers were used, the index finger for fire, the middle finger for air, the third finger for water and the little finger for earth. With the fingers of the left hand they sensed; and with those of the right hand they directed a stream of the units of the elements. They could tear down and dissipate or create and build up the structure of solid things by the forces guided by their right hands. The thumbs were used either to feel, or to direct, unify or accentuate the streams. The organs in their bodies were reservoirs of force, and the nerves connected with the respective systems contacted the force. The forces in the earth they called, used and directed through their digestive systems and the sense of smell. The forces of the water which entered into combination with the earth they controlled through the organs of their circulatory systems and the sense of taste. The air they ruled by control of the air forces which worked outside through the air, the water and the earth and passed inside through their respiratory systems, which passes through the circulatory and digestive systems. Speech was the power that unified the four states, as sunlight unifies the four kinds of light. By contacting the starlight in the sunlight they synchronized and controlled the forces in the other elements. The starlight was present throughout the others. They used it through their generative systems and the sense of sight.

The physical bodies of these foremost among the fire people could pass through any part of the earth at any speed desired. They could pass their physical bodies through any physical object, no matter what its density. They could appear in several places at the same time, no matter how distant the places. They did this by seeing where they wished to be and, by using radiant-solid matter, were present in and penetrated all

intervening grosser matter. These fire people could see and hear anywhere through solid matter.

The fire units are everywhere at the same time. These people
connected the fire units in their bodies with the fire units in the earthy
layer. There these fire units affected the air units and these the water units
and these produced the phenomena through the earth units. The fire
people had use of the fourth dimension, presence, because of their being
conscious of and familiar with the radiant-solid units. This meant that
they could pass through, be in or work with the fire, the air, the water
or the earth units. When their physical body was put in phase with
radiant-solid units—which was done by focussing the sense of sight on
some of them—it appeared simultaneously at the places where these
foremost people wanted to be seen. No obstructions intervene between
those who can use the radiant-solid units and the places where they wish
to be seen. They remained visible in these different places as long as they
continued to think, to feel and to see themselves there. Their bodies were
in any one place only, but they removed the intervening units of matter
and so became visible at the same time at every place where they wished
to be seen. Because of their power of sight, which no matter could
obstruct, they saw, at the same time, all the places at which, and the
people by whom, they were seen. They could disappear when they
wished. They did this by cutting off from their bodies the contact with
the class of fire units whose contact makes visibility.

They could examine any cell or organ in the human body and tell
the uses to which it had been put, and describe means appropriate to
effect a change. They could see at once the cause and the cure of a
disorder. They communicated among themselves by thought and
speech. Distance was no obstruction to their hearing each other or any
sounds in nature. They could get some records of past events by looking
at them or hearing them from the radiant or the airy states of matter and
so get as far as the form plane of the physical world.

There were laws that prevented the use of these forces beyond certain
limits. The people of a fire age could not interfere with the law of thought
without too great injury to themselves. Their powers reached everything
in the four zones of the solid state of the physical plane on the nature-side,
but there were many things in themselves as doers, which they had not
mastered and did not master as a people, though some of the individuals
did. This lack of mastery brought about their decline and the disappearance of the fire age.

The high point of a fire age marked also the highest point in the air, the water and the earth ages. As the fire age disappeared, each of the others deteriorated and vanished by degrees. The last to crumble was the earth age. It was ended by cataclysms. A bleak earth succeeded. On that lived barbarians who were the degenerate remnants of the four ages, of which they had not even a memory, or who were newly outcast from the inner earth. Only here and there remained traditions of some of the people of the four ages in distorted legends of supernatural beings with divine powers.

SECTION 7

Fourth Civilization. Governments. Ancient teachings of the Light of the Intelligence. Religions.

At all times and in every one of the four ages of any cycle the people were of four classes: the handworkers, the traders, the thinkers and those who had some knowledge. These distinctions were outstanding at periods of the highest development and obscured in periods of low development. The forms of the relation between these four classes have changed many times.

In agricultural periods the handworkers acted as slaves or as hired laborers or as small landowners working for themselves, or they received a part of the produce or other remuneration as pay from greater landholders, or they worked in large family communities. In industrial periods they worked as slaves or as hired men, owned small manufacturing plants in their houses or worked together in larger shops or in communities. It was so among the people of an earth age as well as among those of the other ages. One class was the handworkers or muscleworkers or bodyworkers; the other three classes depended on them, but the bodyworkers in turn depended on the other classes. The second class was that of the traders. They traded products for products, or for a medium of exchange, metals, animals or slaves. Sometimes they predominated for a while, as they do today, when large landholders and manufacturers, politicians, lawyers and often doctors belong to this class. The third class was that of the thinkers, those who had a profession, supplying information and service to traders and workers; they were priests, teachers, healers, warriors, builders, or navigators, on land, on water or in the air. The fourth class were the knowers among men, those who had a sense-knowledge available from the past, of the forces of nature which the third class only applied to practical ends, and who had some knowledge of the doer and the Triune Self and of their relation to the Light of the Intelligence. At times all classes lived in a rude fashion; at others they lived in simple comfort with art and learning widely diffused; at other times there was great disparity in the standards of living, and poverty, discomfort and disease of the masses were in contrast to the wealth and luxury of a few. Usually the four classes were mixed, but, sometimes their distinctions were rigidly observed.

The governments were phases of rulership by knowledge, by learning, by traders, and by the many. The forms in which the phases actually appeared were hierarchies, with a chief as the top of a pyramid of lesser officials. Whether knowledge ruled or learning or whether traders or the many were in power, actually one person was the ruler, with assistants, councillors and numbers of servitors decreasing in authority and importance. Sometimes the head was elected by his own class or by all classes, sometimes he usurped or inherited his position. Those under him would usually draw power, property and privileges to themselves at the expense of those who were not of the class in power at the time.

All this was tried over and over again. The most successful governments, where the greatest well-being and happiness prevailed among the greatest number, were those in times when the class that had knowledge was in power. The least successful, those where the greatest confusion, want and unhappiness prevailed, were the governments by the many.

Corruption and trading the general interest for private ends existed as much when the many ruled as when the traders themselves were in power. The curse of government by the masses has been ignorance, indifference, unbridled passion and selfishness. The traders, when they ruled, modified these inherent properties by a thought of regulation, order and business. But the curse was that the practice of corruption, hypocrisy and trading in public affairs still existed in the general order which they outwardly maintained. When the learned were in power as warriors, priests or the cultured, the fundamental qualities, which were unrestrained when the many were in power and only modified superficially when the traders ruled, were often influenced by considerations of integrity, honor and nobility. When those ruled who had knowledge the pyramid of the public servants was free from greed, lust and cruelty, and brought justice, simplicity, honesty and consideration for others with it.

But this was rare and only came at the climax of an age, though it sometimes lasted for a long period.

The moral qualities of humanity have been very much the same in every age for long periods. What had varied is the openness with which they have appeared. Responsibility and freedom from sexual immorality, from drunkenness and from dishonesty have been the mark in all ages of those who had knowledge. The other three classes have been governed by their passions. While the learned and cultured have often been restrained by pride, honor and position, the traders have been restrained by fear of the law and the loss of trade, and the fourth class has been restrained by the not seeing, or neglecting to take advantage of, opportunities, and by fear.

This general aspect of the morality of the ages is modified by many exceptions. Exceptional persons are such because they do not really belong to the class of which they for the time seem to form part. In each human is a combination of all classes. Everyone is a worker, a trader, has learning and has knowledge in some degree. His morality is regulated by the predominance in him of one of the four. He is one of the exceptions when the predominance in him of one of the four gives him a moral standard differing from that of the class to which he apparently belongs.

During the Fourth Civilization numerous and widely divergent religions have come into existence, have risen and have fallen into desuetude. Religions represent the ties that hold the doer to nature, from which it came, and the pull that nature has on the doer's feelings, emotions and desires, through the four senses. These senses are the messengers and the servants of nature. The ties last until the doer learns that it is not a part of nature, not those senses, and that it is independent of nature and the senses. These ties are allowed by the Intelligences and Triune Selves in charge of humanity for the purpose of training it. Religions of some sort are necessary in so far as they are these ties, and advantageous in so far as they tend to advance the doers which are tied. The Light of the Intelligences is loaned, through the doers, to the God or gods to which the thoughts and desires of the human beings go out in worship. The apparent intelligence of the gods of religions is due to the Light of the Intelligences, which they permit to enlighten the gods and the theology of the religions. The more important religious movements were started by Wise Men, a name here used for advanced doers living for a special purpose in human bodies, and by Saviors of a tribe, of a people, or of the world. The fact of the appearance of new religions from time to time is patent, though the personalities that started the movements as Osiris, Moses and Jesus are legendary, even in historical times. In the present earth age a new one appears about every twenty-one hundred years.

The religions of the past of which no known record remains often reappeared in a cyclic order. Some religions were unlike anything that is called a religion today. Sometimes they were identified with science. They were logical and orderly. Their theology met the demands of reason. It was so in periods when the worldly governments were in the hands of those who had Self-knowledge. At those times there existed as distinct from religions a teaching of The Way which led to the Light of the Intelligence, and to the freedom of the doer from rebirth. The Way had to be traveled individually and consciously. There has never been collective worship with feasts and rites and ceremonies to reach the Light of the Intelligence. Religions are on the nature-side. The Way is on the intelligent side.

At most times there was a chasm between thinking and religion. The theologies were given out as infallible and unchangeable. Usually they maintained their hold on the people by rites and spectacles symbolic of events in nature or of events after death since these appealed to the feelings and emotions. The theologies promised their votaries rewards which they desired, and threatened punishments which they feared. The stories of what the gods went through, their sufferings and adventures, appealed to the sympathy and sentiments of the worshippers. Martyr-dom was important in these theologies. Impressive angels, demons and devils existed in hierarchies. All was arranged so as to appeal to sympathy, fear and expectation of reward. A moral code was always injected into the mass of often incongruous, fortuitous and illogical stories. The Intelligences and Triune Selves in charge of humanity saw to that. "Saviors" from time to time gave out teachings concerning the nature of the doer and its destiny, and when the teachings were forgotten or distorted, enlightened reformers sought to re-establish them. The life of the doer after death and its return to earth in a new human body were often revealed and as often forgotten or distorted. The true teachings were obscured and ignorance or fantastic beliefs prevailed.

Today there is in the East a remnant of the great teaching of the Light of the Intelligence going into nature and of its reclamation, hidden under the theology about purusha and prakriti and atma in its various phases. The Conscious Light, once known to ancient Hindus as the

Ancient Wisdom, has in the course of time been shrouded in myth and mystery and is lost in their sacred books. In that little book, the Bhagavad Gita, the Light can be found by one who is able to extract the essential teaching of Krishna to Arjuna from the mass of other doctrine. One's conscious self in the body is Arjuna. Krishna is the thinker and knower of one's Triune Self, who reveals itself to its conscious doer in the body when one is ready and prepared to receive the teaching. In the West similar teachings are obscured by an elusive and improbable theology with a strange Adamology of original sin, and a Christology which is based on martyrology, as in nature worship, instead of the teaching of the sublime destiny of the doer.

Every teaching requires a body of men to bring it and keep it before the people and to lead in religious observances. All religions, therefore, had priests, but not all priests were true to their trust. Seldom, except at the culmination of a cycle, did those who had knowledge function as priests. Usually not even the third class, those who had learning, but the class of traders furnished the priests of the temples. Some had much learning, but their mental set was that of the traders. Offices, precedence, privileges and tribute were exacted by them, as far as possible. They molded a theology that supported their claims to be the chosen, and to the ensuing authority. They asserted that they had the same power over the doers of the people after death that they exercised over their lives. The farther they got from the true teachings the more they fortified themselves by the ignorance, bigotry and fanaticism which they maintained around them, and the fear they bred. As teachers, priests are entitled to a proper place so as to exercise their high office with dignity. But their power should come from the love and affection of the people whom they teach, console and encourage, and the respect which is due to a noble life. The worldly power of the priests, an expression of their inner nature as traders, finally brought corruption and downfall to every religion which served them.

Some of the religions of the past were great in the clarity, singleness and power of their teachings. They accounted for many of the beings and forces in nature and gave to those who followed them power over elemental beings. Their festivals and rites had to do with the deeper meanings of the seasons and the phenomena of life. Their influence was widespread and affected all classes of the people. They were religions breeding joy, enthusiasm, self-restraint. All people took the teachings

gladly into their lives. Such times happened only when the government
was in the hands of those who had knowledge.

From such heights the religions fell, gradually or suddenly, when the
government passed to the traders. The truths formerly revealed were
re-stated as absurdities dressed in fantastic garb. Pomp, long ritual, plays,
mystic ceremonies, miraculous stories varied with dances and human and
animal sacrifices. An interminable and preposterous pantheon and mythology was their theology. The people in their ignorance accepted
readily absurd stories. The most miraculous and incomprehensible became the most important. Ignorance, fanaticism and cruelty were universal, while the revenue of the priests increased and their authority was
supreme. Lasciviousness and sexual practices were presented and accepted as the worship of many gods or of the supreme God. Rottenness
of religions, loss of morality, corruption in government, oppression of
the weak and vast power of the great usually came together and led to
the disappearance of the religion.

Wars have recurred through all the ages. Between the hostilities came
periods of rest. The causes were the desires of persons, classes and peoples
for food, comfort and power, and the feelings of envy and hate which
started from these desires. Wars were conducted with whatever means
were at hand. In crude ages tooth and nail, and stones and clubs were
used. When the people had machines for war, these were employed.
When they commanded nature forces and elemental beings, they made
use of those. In hand to hand fights individuals were wounded or killed,
one at a time; in the mechanical and scientific periods, thousands of
enemies were maimed or destroyed at once; and in the most advanced
stages, when some persons could use elemental forces, it was possible for
them to annihilate, and they did annihilate, whole armies and peoples.
Those who directed the elemental forces were met by enemies who used
the same or opposing forces. Between these individuals it was a question
of thrust and parry with force against force until the operators on one
side were overcome. They might be overcome by the force they themselves exerted, which recoiled on them when parried, or they might
succumb to the force they did not parry. When those who directed the
force had so been killed, a whole army or people could be destroyed or
enslaved.

The behavior of the people which resulted periodically in small or
great wars and revolutions and other general calamities and consequent
disturbances, brought with it diseases. The diseases were exteriorizations

of the thinking as much as were the other calamities. From the general afflictions many escaped, but very few remained free from disease. There were times when many, in fact most, of the people were free from disease. These were the periods of simple savagery or those when the class that had knowledge ruled completely and there was a general state of comfort, simplicity and joy in work. Otherwise there has always been more or less ailment of the body.

In different periods the prevailing diseases differed because the thoughts differed. Sometimes single persons were affected, sometimes epidemics came. There were skin diseases where the skin was eaten away and left running sores, beginning in patches and spreading till there was not enough whole skin for breathing. In another kind the skin puffed in places, grew like cauliflower, became discolored and emitted a stench. A disease ate through the skull and continued until the bone was so eaten away that the brain was exposed and death followed. Diseases of the sense organs ate away the eye or inner ear or the root of the tongue. Diseases severed the attachments that held the joints, so that fingers, toes, and sometimes the lower leg dropped off. There were diseases of the inner organs which stopped their functions. Some diseases caused no pain but disability, some caused an intense pain and terror. There were infectious sexual diseases in addition to those of today. One of them caused loss of sight, hearing or speech, without any affection of their organs. Another caused a complete loss of feeling. Another an enlargement of the male or female organs or a shrivelling that made them useless.

Most of these diseases have never been cured. Attempts to cure by surgery, by medicine, by charms, incantations, prayers, dances, mental healing and such methods as are used today, have not effected a real cure. At the proper time the disease returns in one form or another. At times the manifestations of diseases increased until a people were decimated, weakened and disappeared.

SECTION 8

The doers now on earth came from a prior earth age. Failure of the doer to improve. The story of feeling-and-desire. The spell of the sexes. The purpose of re-existences.

Doers now on earth and those of whom tradition and history tell, were embodied in some of the people of these past ages. The doers that appeared in the past ages continue to re-exist, though not all of them can be here today. The leading doers in the past may not be here now.

The majority of the doers known of in historical times belong to an earth age. This started after the obliteration of the people of a former cycle of four ages. There are now also many who belonged to water, air and fire peoples. But they were not the ones who made those ages great. They were then in a position like that of the people today who while they receive telegraphic and wireless communications and ride in electric cars, know little about electricity. It is likely that the few men who have changed conditions on the earth in the last hundred and fifty years by their inventions and applications of the sciences belong to the water, air and fire people, but they played a part more prominent than the mere populace, and some of them probably helped to develop great achievements. However, some here today who are under a cloud were yet in the past among the makers of the great civilizations of the earth, water, air and fire people.

The changes the doers have undergone while they have passed through all these rises and falls in the Fourth Civilization, were changes in feelings and desires. The cultural phenomena in the different ages were expressive of these changes. The doers thought outwardly and the changes were outward. Even the highest civilizations were outward. They developed to satisfy sensuous perceptions. They were nature civilizations. The human beings had after all little more than glorified bodies and trained senses. At no time during these civilizations could the people, except those who attained freedom, use more than the body-mind, with the feeling-mind and desire-mind as aides. For it is necessary to feel and to desire something beyond the four senses, in order to call upon more than the body-mind. The body-mind works for nature only.

The doers are old in experience, very old, but young in learning and infants in knowledge. Rightness and reason have been disregarded by feelings and desires. What the doers felt and desired was considered right, and the thinking served in building up the ages accordingly. Often doers had reminiscences of their origin, their happy state and of the innate ideas of truth, justice, immortality and happiness which had been once with them. They desired them again and then they worked toward that which they felt. So they built that desire out into a civilization thinking that this would bring them back their happy state. Their desires reached out to lofty ideals. But as they sought for them outwardly they failed to realize them and soon lapsed. The desires of the doers have changed many times from grosser to finer objects, which were sought as means of satisfaction. The thinking of the feeling-mind and the desire-mind, dominated by the body-mind, has not changed much. These three minds were and are servitors of the senses. Though their thinking was often brilliant in accomplishments, there was still no great change in what the doer learned. Outward things it mastered, but it learned little thereby, because its activities were turned outwardly to nature, and not to itself as being part of its Triune Self and under the Light of the Intelligence. Often when doers had reminiscences of the presence of the Light in which they once had stood, and often when they remembered the warning of the Light, they were afraid, and worshipped the nature gods all the more in their religions. But often the reminiscences aided some doers to turn inward and to look for the Light there. Some advanced, but most fell back into the arms of nature, which was always reaching for the Light they had. So some doers went ahead and then fell back from time to time. The majority, however, were in nature and were afraid to think of leaving it, so strong was the domination of the religions or of worldly objects. How small the result of all the changes has been in this vast period can be seen from the state in which the run of human beings are today. Human nature has changed little in millions of years, because those who continue to re-exist are the ones who have learned little.

The background of all that the human beings have done was their noetic destiny. Each time a doer lived in a flesh body it drew upon the Light in its noetic atmosphere. It drew by its thinking and subsequent actions which were caused by feelings and desires for outward things. The four senses beat in on the doer, awoke feeling and that aroused desire, which started thinking, and this furnished the means of outward satisfaction. The Light of the Intelligence showed the way and went out with the thoughts and acts into nature. Though much Light was redeemed automatically, not enough was saved or redeemed to bring about a change sufficient to cause the doers in human beings to improve their desires.

The story of feeling-and-desire is strange. The story shows that the world is governed by law, but that man allows himself to be governed by feeling and desire under the direction of the senses, and which are opposed to law. Feeling and desire govern in so far as past destiny will permit. When the doer first took up its abode in the physical body, feeling-and-desire were stainless and without fear, free, without worry or trouble. They were innocent, without a taint of evil. The doer enjoyed everything without questioning, under the Light of the Intelligence. It seemed to know everything though it had no knowledge of its own. The Light of the Intelligence revealed everything to it. The Light was in the feeling and the desire, and everything desire wanted it had. Everything that was good for desire was made apparent to it by the Light. Feeling-and-desire were not blind to the Light as they now are, and they were not afraid of it. But as soon as the Light was shut out from the psychic atmosphere when the doer had disregarded the warning of the Light, the doer left that interior and happy state and journeyed toward the outer crust of the earth. There everything was different. The doers no longer had revealed to them the knowledge which the Light had given. Slow reasoning took the place of direct revelation. The happy state was replaced by unhappiness, freedom by coercion, and stainlessness by lust. Worry, disease, oppression, want and death were the lot of those outside who were governed by their four senses. Pleasure and the gratification of the appetites came to give relief to feeling-and-desire. But there never is enough to satisfy them. Feeling-and-desire cannot be satisfied by anything on earth. They are a portion of the doer which was satisfied in its original state. Of that condition desire is vaguely aware and wants it again, and therefore is turbulent in its search for satisfaction. The doer seeks this in outward things and reaches outward into nature. It has been doing this ever since the Light of the Intelligence was withdrawn from it after desire fell under the spell of the sexes.

The spell of the sexes is over all of human life. The power of the spell is exercised by nature. The thoughts of the doers have given to nature the sexes which are now its keynote. Since it has been keyed to the sexes, nature pulls by them on the doers for the Light it needs. The feelings and the desires of the doer have gone out into nature, and the doers are under the spell of their own feelings and desires, which nature works against them. Nature is not to be blamed, for the doers have made it what it is. That the doers lose the Light which is loaned to them is their noetic destiny. Nature was lowered, unbalanced, by feeling-and-desire through the sexes and must be redeemed, balanced, by feeling-and-desire; this too is the noetic destiny of the doer. Some doers feel this in a vague manner. They feel they are guilty of something, though they do not know of what. This feeling begets a vague fear, which is sometimes presented in poetic form as dread of the anger of the gods, or the wrath of God. The power of the spell, however, has usually been greater than the fear.

This fear has been a companion of feeling-and-desire since the doers came to the outer earth. They have been afraid of the Light ever since they did not heed its warning. The vague apprehension that misfortune would fall on them was but a form of that fear. Seeking and fearing are two aspects of desire. The doers have built and destroyed the civilizations of the past which all grew up as expressions of their feeling-and-desire.

Even the highest civilizations of a people of a fire age were outward developments; the inner natures of the people were little developed. This is why the doers will continue to re-exist. Fear, and desire to get satisfaction, drive them. Their thoughts and acts are in response to these impulses. Another aspect of desire is rebellion against the Light, which takes the form of rebellion against existing things. The rebellion arises from the fact that desire is not satisfied; it never can be satisfied by anything outside. It opposes all existing order. It is ungoverned. It cannot do without the Light of the Intelligence, yet it rebels against it. It rebels against control. It wants to get back to the original state of happiness and cannot do it without the Light.

It is no wonder that feeling-and-desire are restless. It is their sensual feelings and desires compelled by the body-mind, that have controlled the doers, their beliefs, their thoughts and their actions for all these years since the doers came to the outer earth. Every embodied doer has had all the experiences it needs, more experience than is represented by all the experiences which the present age offers, all experiences possible. What the doers lack is the learning they should have from the experiences they have had. The turmoil will go on until the doer distinguishes itself as feeling and as desire and realizes that the satisfaction it seeks it can never get outside itself; that desire must desire to be under the rule of rightness and reason and to be guided by the Conscious Light within.

In order to understand the purposes of re-existences and the length of time they must continue, it is necessary to keep in mind the origins of the Triune Selves as primordial units in the fire sphere and the history of their doers up to their present re-existences. In view of the duty of human beings to desire that they be ruled by the thinkers of their Triune Selves and by their destiny to be conscious as Triune Selves it is well to observe how little they have developed in all the ages they have passed on earth, even though some of the civilizations were great beyond fancy.

SECTION 9

Importance of the flesh body. Reclamation of Light. Death of the body. Wanderings of the units. Return of units to a body.

The exteriorizations of the thoughts of all doers make the common ground on which they meet in their physical bodies. This is the objective world on the physical plane. Desires and feelings are always subjective and belong exclusively to individuals. Mob spirit, patriotism, worship by a multitude, are similar feelings but not the same feelings. Every one has his own feelings; the exteriorization in a riot, a war or a church is the common ground on which the inner factors objectivize. Likewise rightness and reason are individual and subjective. I-ness and selfness, too, are subjective. The human demonstration of this manifold nature of the Triune Self is made on the objective, physical plane by the exteriorization of the thoughts which the doer produces as the mixture of its desire with Light of the Intelligence. When the thoughts are in evidence as objects on the physical plane they can be seen or felt by other doers. Not until a thought is concreted as an act, an object or an event, is the reality of it apprehended. The physical demonstration of a thought is the center upon which for the time the doer which issued it is focussed. Other doers, if they are involved, are also held by the act, object or event, which is that demonstration.

Only in this objective world can all doers come together. Here they encounter on a common plane as objects the thoughts of other doers. Here they find the objects which stir their emotions. Here men, women, marriage, work, business, amusements, worship, poverty, disease, luxury, vice, plagues and war furnish them experiences. Here birth, death, youth and age affect them. Here the doers have possessions. These are the source of deceit and strife, as well as the means of self-control and virtue. The doers can distinguish the objects from themselves and learn the difference between "me" and "mine" through a human physical body only.

The flesh body is unstable, of short life and weak, when compared with nature and the doer, both of whom it serves. Its time of service is short. Soon upon its youth and vigor follows death. It is too feeble to stand the strain which nature and the doer put upon it. The doer should use it in the reclamation of the Light of the Intelligence from nature. When it is no longer capable of reclaiming Light automatically, its days are usually numbered. When the Light available to a human has been used up the body grows weaker and dies. The Light is as a tincture that gives vitality. The chief cause of the shortness of life and of the feebleness of the body is the absence of enough Light of the Intelligence. In this short time the body has hardly begun its life before it is withered by age or destroyed by disease.

The failure of the body to serve continuously until the purposes of its existence are attained, necessitates a calling together of the dissolved parts after they have returned to their elements. After the death of the body, the elemental matter that composes its parts is reassembled and renewed to continue its service in a new one.

The fourfold stream of radiant, airy, fluid and solid matter, which is the fourfold breath that supports all physical beings and things, thereafter takes some of the compositor units into the bodies of plants and animals. There they compose for these vegetable and animal bodies as they did for the human bodies. So comes the similarity to human form and structure which runs through animate nature. In nature these units compose in animals and plants until they are called back to build a new body for a new breath-form of the returning doer.

If, when the compositor units are released, they are not carried into the bodies of plants and animals, they remain free in their elements in the sphere of earth. The units which had acted as system units or senses may appear in human form. If they do they are the elementals called by some alchemists salamanders, sylphs, undines and gnomes. Nature sprites seen from time to time, such as water nymphs, wood sprites, elves and fauns are elementals which have functioned as compositor units in human bodies. They have a human or nearly human form because of their long association with the breath-form of a doer. These nature sprites are as variously high and low in degree as were the human beings in whom they functioned.

The other matter of which the body is made up at any one time is transient matter, transient units of the four states of matter on the physical plane. The transient units are caught and held by the compositors when they pass through the body, carried in the stream or fourfold breath of the earth, which flows through all physical things. The fourfold stream of units contains free units which never have been held in a human body, transient units which have been caught, held and so enmeshed in a human body, and compositor units. This breath comes from the four layers of matter that makes up the physical plane. The breath passes through the solar and lunar centers and returning to the earth crust carries its units into all things. The breath comes not only in solid and liquid food, water, air and sunlight that are taken into the body, but it flows at all times through the body imperceptibly to the senses.

Breath and speech through human bodies keep the entire mass of physical matter moving. They agitate innumerable hosts of minute particles and keep them in circulation in the physical world where some of these particles enter and leave human bodies. The bodies through which a particular stream of units will pass are opened by previous thoughts and the consequent relations which have just been mentioned through which the intermingling of the matter is facilitated.

A human body is made up of two categories of units. One re-exists as the units of the senses and of the organs with the respective link units. These units have acted as the compositors in previous lives and re-exist in each succeeding life. The other category make up the transient matter which is held in a body but does not necessarily re-exist in it. It re-exists if it has been sufficiently impressed by the signature of thoughts, so as to bear the stamp which guides it back to the body where it had received the stamp of the signature.

From the standpoint of nature re-existences of a particular doer are needed because the sense and compositor units have been sealed with the seal of the particular doer, through the medium of its breath-form. These units bearing the seal have been marked, coordinated, articulated, through the breath-form time and again while they served in a flesh body used by the particular doer. They require that that doer shall return. The doer which binds them to it, also binds itself to them. They are a special part of nature-matter which is in the charge of the particular doer, and this matter has to be raised so as to become conscious in certain degrees before the doer can be released from that charge; and until then the matter requires the field of a human body belonging to that doer for the travels, changes, separation, reunion. and adventures of that matter.

SECTION 10

The doer-in-the-body. Error in the conception of "I". The personality and re-existence. The doer portion after death. The portions not in the body. How a doer portion is drawn out for re-existence.

Only one of the twelve portions of the doer is embodied at any one time. Each portion represents a different aspect of the doer and re-exists to accomplish a definite purpose. Each of these portions is a separate portion and yet is related to all the others because the doer is one doer. That portion of the doer which re-exists is not conscious of its connection with the other portions. At the end of the heaven period that portion enters again into relation with the other portions, returns to its place among them and remains there until the other portions have re-existed, each in its turn. Then it re-exists again. Each portion is responsible for itself, makes its own destiny, takes up its own life and reaps what it has sown.

The other eleven portions of the doer constitute the non-existing portions. These are however affected by the embodied portion during its life as well as after the death of its body. The portion of the doer which is embodied may be, though it need not be, affected by those portions which are not embodied. Sometimes more than one portion of the doer is embodied during one life. This happens when the embodied portion works to the advantage of the doer and its capacity for work is increased. Sometimes some of the embodied portion is withdrawn, as in old age, in insanity or after disregarding conscience. In the portion of the doer which re-exists sometimes feeling predominates and sometimes desire. In the thinker, which contacts the body, rightness-and-reason are equal; one does not dominate the other. The knower contacts the body in a small degree, enough for I-ness to give identity and for selfness to furnish Light from the Intelligence. In the successive existences the re-existing portion of the doer takes up its own life and not the life of any of the other portions.

The twelve portions of the doer are one and inseparable. Each is what makes the human being of the doer conscious as a human, distinct from other human beings, throughout the period of his earth life. A human is conscious that he is conscious, but he is not conscious *as* that which is conscious; he is not conscious that he is only a portion of a doer, or that there are the other portions, or of relations between himself and these non-embodied portions. He is conscious of his feeling, desiring and thinking and of his identity. He is conscious *of* "I" but not *as* "I", and he does not know the "I". He does not know himself, nor does he know how he feels and desires nor how he thinks.

The doer-in-the-body says to itself "I see", "I hear", "I taste", "I smell", "I touch", but it does nothing of the kind. It cannot see, hear, taste, smell, or touch. The sense of sight looks through the eye, sees through the eye and makes on the breath-form a record of what it sees. The breath-form carries the impression to the feeling of the doer. The desire side of the doer passes the impression on to the body-mind to have translated and interpreted in terms of feeling the impression brought in by the sense of sight. Then the feeling of the doer, being all over the body, identifies itself with the sense of sight, which does the seeing, and says to itself "I see", which is an error. It is only conscious of what is seen, heard, tasted, smelled and contacted by the senses. It does not itself do any of these things. It feels identity with or as the senses, because it is conscious of them and not conscious that it is not the senses and that it merely feels through them. It merges itself with the senses by feeling and then cannot be separated from them. Feeling will be merged with these senses and be conscious of itself as these senses until it desires to feel itself apart from them, and then, thinking with its feeling-mind, it will identify itself and establish itself as feeling and as being different from the senses.

The doer in the body says "I feel", "I think", "I know". In this it is nearly as much in error as when it believes that it sees or hears. It is true that the doer-in-the-body feels and thinks, after a fashion, but the real "I" does not feel and does not think. The error lies in the conception of what that "I" is. The "I" of which the embodied portion of the doer is conscious is a delusion, it is a false "I" and is the basis of the actions of the human being. The false "I" is feeling-and-desire, the doer, and identifies itself moreover with the physical body and the senses.

There could be no conception by the feeling-mind as an "I" if there were not actually an "I" present. This "I" is the I-ness of the Triune Self, but the doer-in-the-body is not conscious *as* that. Being conscious of the presence of that "I" causes feeling to make the mistake that it is what it feels, whereas it only feels the "I", but is not that "I" anymore than it is the four senses. Feeling tries to find the "I" in desire and desire wants to get the "I" from feeling. This interaction of each trying to get the "I" in the other adds to the mystery of identity—of what is the true "I" and what is the true Self.

By their thinking, feeling-and-desire can never give a correct interpretation of this mystery, because the feeling-mind can solve the mystery of feeling and the desire-mind can solve the mystery of desire, but these minds cannot be made to solve the mystery of the "I" and of selfness. Rightness does not confirm but leaves them in doubt. The subject they are dealing with is a truth, a reality, but their solution is not right. The mistake about the "I" and the self of the human being is due to a delusion which is produced by thinking under the pressure of feeling-and-desire.

So the doer-in-the-body is conscious of itself as being something which it is not, and it is not conscious of what it actually is. This delusion of the false "I" lies at the basis of the human being, which is partly personality and partly doer.

The personality consists of the physical body with the four senses, all operated by the breath-form. The personality is an inseparable combination during life. It is a mask, a costume; it does not work alone. In it is the embodied portion of the doer. The doer uses the personality, speaks through it, acts at its behest and conceives that it is the personality. The combination of the personality and the embodied portion of the doer is the human being and usually identifies itself as the personality. Thereby it shuts out the possibility of being advised by thinking that this is an error. Its feeling and desiring and thinking are done for nature; it is not conscious of true feeling-and-desire, or of true thinking, which are done by the doer for itself, apart from nature. The human does not identify himself with the atmospheres and the portions of the doer inside and outside of the physical body. The "I", as which the human being is conscious, is a false "I".

The personality as a whole does not re-exist; parts of it do. It is dissolved before another portion of the doer re-exists in a new personality. The human being does not re-exist as a whole; his fourfold body and transient units do not re-exist. The breath matter of the breath-form returns to the matter of the four worlds from which it was drawn. The matter of the body is dissipated into the four states of matter of the physical plane, and these transient units go back into nature and continue to travel through the heavenly bodies and the bodies of minerals, plants, animals and humans. The matter that made up these beings may or may not be part of a future body of a human being of the doer.

Between re-existences the portion of the doer with its breath-form, which had been in the human being, recedes from the outer crust of the earth through the earth towards the inner crust; and in certain zones between these two crusts the doer with its breath-form has its hell and its heaven, (Fig. V-D). During his journey the human being is divested of his carnal desires, which make his hells until they have burned themselves off, and is later enveloped in a dress of his nobler desires which make his heaven.

Between the outer and the inner surfaces of the earth's crust there are passages and chambers like cavities in a sponge. In these each doer portion has its own experiences, which are the development of its thoughts during the past life. No new thinking takes place. Each concentrates on and repeats automatically the thinking done in life, and this conjures up events of which it is there conscious.

The run of human beings are not developed beyond feeling-and-desire. Their thinking concerns these and they identify themselves with them. Feeling-and-desire have now to do with surfaces only. Therefore the doer of the average human does not go much beyond the outer earth crust. After death the doers are in states; but, for a short time, they are also in what would be to sensuous perception, localities on surfaces in the earth crust. In life they knew of but one dimension, surfaces, and to these they are limited after death. The exceptional human beings whose lives were not dominated by the lower feelings and desires, go beyond these surfaces into the inner sphere.

In life the doer-in-the-body conceives of itself as an entity, the human being; and this entity does not know itself any better after death than it did while it acted through the personality in life. The false identity does not change, though the desires and the thoughts change as the human goes through his hell and his heaven after death. The portion of the doer that was embodied does not recognize its relation to the Triune Self as a whole, because it did not know it during life. The journeys from the outer crust towards the inner are made by that which carries with it the identity it had in life. After the end of the eternity of happiness in heaven this false "I" as the human being disappears, when the portion that was embodied is gradually withdrawn from the breath-form into its psychic atmosphere. There it rests until each of the other doer portions has re-existed in its turn and then it is drawn out again for an embodiment into a new human being.

The portions of the doer that were not embodied are, however, affected in life and after death by the portion that was embodied. In life there was a connection in the kidneys and adrenals between the doer portion and the thinker and knower which had contact through the breath with the heart and lungs and with the pituitary or pineal body. In life, currents in the atmospheres flowed to and from the parts outside the body through the embodied portion. These currents were kept up by the three breaths of the Triune Self flowing through the fourfold physical breath. There was a strengthening or a weakening, a calming or disturbing, a darkening or enlightening of the non-embodied portions. After death this ceases. Then the reaction comes. The results produced upon the non-embodied portions are then thrown back upon the portion that was in the personality, and produce in it the automatic feeling and thinking that makes the hell and heaven for the false "I". These states of suffering and of happiness are intensified because the intermingling and alternation of pain and pleasure, which came in life, are absent. The reactions from the non-embodied portions are therefore more poignant and severe in hell and more intense in heaven than were the casual feelings in life. These reactions continue until the results in the non-embodied portions which were affected during life are exhausted by the suffering and happiness of the false "I". Then the portion which was embodied is ready to be reabsorbed into the atmospheres of the doer. When this takes place after the end of the heaven period, the four senses return to their elements, the compositor units build up the structure of animals or plants, the breath leaves the form of the breath-form, and the aia remains in its undimensional state. The form of the breath-form is then reduced to a speck, as of ash, a point, inert, and is in the psychic atmosphere of the doer; there it waits until the ruling thought for the next life of the doer portion to re-exist causes the aia to revivify that inert point with essential matter of the worlds as its breath, and it is again the breath-form.

When the doer portion which was embodied has joined the portions that were not in the flesh, the false "I" as which the human being was conscious, ceases to be. It will have its next embodiment after each of the non-embodied portions has re-existed in its turn. The thinker of the Triune Self directs the portion to be drawn out to make up the next human being, according to the ruling thought of that portion.

That thought is the sum of the thoughts of its past life. Though these may seem numerous, various and hard to coordinate, yet the thoughts which underlie them are simple and much alike because they have the same aim. It is their designs which make them vary. Many designs often specialize the same aim. Usually an aim or a few aims unite all the thoughts of any life into one dominating thought. This has a continuity, notwithstanding slight variations in the aims. It changes very little from life to life with average people because they allow themselves to be pushed or led by circumstances and by passive thinking. The ruling thought is a being of great power. It gets its power from the desire of the doer and from the Light of the Intelligence. It gets its good or evil aspects from the use to which it has put the Light of the Intelligence which it has sent into nature, and from the amount of Light it has brought back into the noetic atmosphere.

Such other portions of the doer are also drawn into relation to the portion about to re-exist as will supply the characteristics which the ruling thought requires to let the person be a burglar or a banker, a clam digger or an archaeologist, a housewife or an actress. Without the relation of these other portions the ruling thought could not manifest itself as the new human being. These other portions are drawn in to satisfy unfulfilled wishes, to enable destiny to come home, to allow other thoughts to find cyclic expression which past lives did not afford them, to furnish an opportunity for learning special things, to open avenues for new adventures and to fill out the personality.

All attainments which are matters of memory, like professional or business efficiency, together with mechanical skill, are left behind, whereas tendencies, habits, manners, health and temperament, which are not as superficial but express aspects of the doer itself, may be brought over as characteristic traits. Such externals as rank, money, position, success or their opposites are evanescent and, if not needed for the doer to learn from, will not appear among the surroundings of the new human being.

SECTION 11

The thoughts summarized at moment of death. Events determined then, for the next life. The flare-up in classic Greece. Something about the Jews. The stamp of a God at birth. Family. The sex. Cause of changing the sex.

The factors which affect the new human being during his life are of two classes. In one class are some of the thoughts of the doer portion now embodied which it had had in its previous life; in the other are thoughts of the present life. The thoughts of a life are totalled at death as the ruling thought. The summary is like that at the end of a book or the totals of a business at the end of a year. The totalled thoughts of the past life form a sketchy program for the next life. Some of its incidents are determined definitely, others are open.

At the moment of death all thoughts and acts of the past life are reviewed and comprehended by the departing doer portion, which so confirms the dominating thought. Thereby are fixed the outstanding and some of the minor incidents of the coming life. These irrevocable destinies have become such either by persistent thinking on and wishing for them, or because they are thoughts the exteriorizations of which as destiny can be postponed no longer, or because they are continuations of conditions, mostly oppressive, to which one has submitted slothfully without sufficient effort to get out of them. The advent of these events has become gradually predestinate during the course of the past life, and at the moment of death the doer acknowledges them and binds itself.

Among the events determined at the moment of death as preordained for the next life of the same doer portion are the time when that life will begin, the race, the country and the nationality, the kind of family in which the body will be born, the sex, the kind of body, the physical heredity, inherent manners, the chief mundane occupations, particular diseases, some accidents, the critical events and the time and nature of death. These inevitable happenings are marked on the aia and are, especially where they are involved with the actions of several or many, marshalled in physical place and time by upper elementals under the direction of Intelligences and complete Triune Selves.

At the death of the body are determined the beginning and the end of the next life on earth. This does not mean that the hour, day and year are fixed according to reckoning by any earthly calendar. Time as measured by a calendar does not apply to the doer. Time applies to nature. There time is the change of units or of masses of units in their relation to each other. The sequence of changes in the doer is measured by accomplishment. There is a relationship between nature time, and the accomplishment of changes in the doer. The arrival at accomplishment coincides with a date in the earthly calendar. This means that the predestined events must have occurred before death can take place and that a certain course must have been completed by the doer portion before the next life begins.

The race, country, nationality and religion are predestined. The symbolic lines on the aia which are confirmed at the time of death, call for certain characteristics which will appear in the traits of a race and a nationality and through birth in a certain country. The fundamental selfishness and sloth of human beings find expression in different development through different races. The ways of the development are traits of character. According to them humans are grouped in races; these are specialized in nationalities; and the latter are modified by soil, climate and environment. Often these traits are not apparent, nevertheless they are present to a greater or lesser degree. In many periods distinctions are not as marked as in others or they amalgamate, as social differences are sometimes displayed by costumes and at other times lack these tokens. However, under the outward level an interior distinction persists in races as in social layers. The Latin race is different from the Celtic and the Semitic. Birth on a hillside, a plain or on the shore, in a secluded region or in one which is a national capital further modifies the racial and national traits.

People have not wished for the particular racial condition into which they are born. Probably they did not consider the matter. What brought them in was their nature-imagination, their passive thinking. Of the probable effects of these they did not think. Self-suggestion developed into active thinking and that left its record for the future on the aia. Fundamental to the thinking were certain longings, feelings and desires. These and the manner of their expression are of the essence of a race. The thinking formerly cast the desires into a certain mold that represented the characteristics of the race with its specifications and modifications. The cryptic lines on the aia were made from that mold and are the prescription which elementals later work out in physical matter when they build the new body in the country of its birth.

A factor which draws the doer especially into an inferior or oppressed race, are thoughts leading to sexual relations with members of that race or to oppression, persecution or personal antagonism. Such re-existences are usually felt as oppressive and unjust, because the persons do not feel themselves to be really of the race. Persons who naturally belong to a derided race or mixture are happy in it because they belong there and because it expresses their feelings and desires. Sometimes one who has oppressed or injured a race will be born into it to atone by endeavors to improve its condition. Sometimes one whose antagonism has brought him into a race is made to feel the feelings of it and so is forced to put himself into the position he did not formerly understand. Re-existences caused by these retributive principles last until the doers suffering from them have learned.

Doers re-exist in a race as long as their feelings and desires and the manners of expressing them are suitably externalized in the peculiarities of the race. Doers leave a race when it no longer enables them to exhibit this interior nature and then they appear in a fitting race. Doers appearing in the bodies of an abandoned race and country are usually different in quality from those who formerly dwelt in the bodies of that race. This is one reason why races seem to rise and fall. The fact is that doers of different character come in.

A remarkable flare-up of a race may be seen in classic Greece. There a stock from an ancient period had lapsed into a common people. But some of them had a tendency to rise. Among them suddenly appeared a few re-existing doers from the prehistoric period of glory, and they made classic Greece.

Usually degradation and mixing with others cause the disappearance of nations and races. The persons who live in certain localities are therefore often quite different from their ancestors and belong to a different race, even though features and some habits survive. So the doers of the ancient Egyptians were not the same doers as those that inhabit the bodies now born as Egyptians. It is slightly different with India. The doers that lived in bodies in ancient India have largely suspended their re-existences there and may not re-exist at all, until a new race appears for them. Most of those of the ancient race that still re-exist in India have debased themselves by an exalted selfishness and so, without the Light of the past, live in degraded forms. But the people of India are of the same races as were those doers who had knowledge. In this respect they are distinguished from the Egyptians.

A race that has survived almost unchanged from a distant past is the Jewish. It lives on because the desires of the doers re-existing in it were and are for the earth and things of the earth. The race as a whole worships one of the earth spirits as its God, with more or less loyalty. Therefore money, things of earthly value and fecundity, together with sensuous enjoyment of them, are its rewards from the God it worships. Its desires and thinking for these things are undivided. Its desires compelling the thinking are the worship. Other earth races have looked to a heaven, and to honor, valor and purity as ends in themselves and so have divided their desires and therefore have not worshipped the earth god with all their heart and desire and mind as the Jews have sometimes done. Not only does this earth god reward them for their worship, but it avenges them. The racial traits are so strong because of this worship, that they persist without a racial country and without subdivisions into the usual racial nationalities. Jews take the nationality of that country in which they live.

This shows that their God is no longer local as tribal spirits usually are, but is of a somewhat universal character. This spirit has many tribes, but that tribe which remains while others disappear is the one that is closest to the earth and single in its worship of the things of the earth, procreation, money and possessions. Races persist, increase or disappear in accordance with the feelings and desires and the ideals or ambitions of the people.

Unless there is a race for them to come into, doers do not re-exist as a race. Only here and there are exceptions to be found. The historic age is not one in which the more enlightened doers can be embodied. The physical bodies furnished by any of the historical races have not been fit habitations. If from the enlightened doers one does re-exist, it finds itself in a hostile world. An instance is that of Socrates.

On the one hand the feelings and desires of certain doers predestinate them for certain races and nationalities, on the other there are definite nature ghosts, entities made up chiefly of any one of the four elements, which hold doers in these races and to nature and so mark their bodies at birth. These ghosts are racial and national. An outstanding instance is the Jewish God. They derive their strength from the collective desire of the doers, which gives to the nature-matter individual existence as a deity. These gods are perpetuated by the Light they get from doers, which send it out while worshipping them as racial gods. Often these gods receive a sacerdotal worship at the same time and so are believed to be the gods of particular religions as well as the gods of certain races. As the existence of these gods depends on the worship, belief, desire and service of the doers of a race or a religion they hold the doers and urge them in all the various conditions that arouse feeling, stimulate desire and draw out the Light of the Intelligences from the doers.

Even in historical times these gods have been the causes of cupidity and war, subjugation and oppression. Sometimes the reigns of kings and oligarchies, sometimes a rising of the slothful and at other times religious strife and persecution mark the activities of these gods among men. Behind the scenes these gods are created, changed and disappear as the races do before the scenes. During their lifetime, be it long or short, these gods are powerful beings and have a hold on the doers of their race and religion through feelings and desires.

At the time of the death of the human devotee the ruling thought stamps the mark of these gods on the aia. That carries the mark after death, bears it at the new birth and stamps it on the breath-form. So Catholics and Jews are marked at birth as belonging to a certain religion. In the case of the Protestant sects the mark is not so strong, yet it is there.

Only the kind of family, usually not the particular one, into which the doer will be born is predestined. The religion, race and nationality are bestowed by birth in a family which has them. Ancestry furnishes an opportunity for breeding and manners, if the re-existing portion is to have them. The early influences of the family often affect behavior and speech throughout life. A family by its importance, wealth and ideals may furnish opportunities for development which in another family is stimulated by poverty and responsibility. Formative influences come through birth in a family, whether they reach the child directly in the family or indirectly through persons with whom the family brings it into contact. Racial, national, and religious characteristics are distinguished in one's bearing, manners, conduct and general behavior.

Tendencies are developed or impeded by harsh treatment or by kindness, as the symbols of the breath-form call for. The heredity that brings the physical traits which are the exteriorizations of the child's own former thoughts, can come only through a family. A portion of the psychic disposition may be inherited in like manner from ancestors. The vocation and pursuits in life are often closely connected with the family in which the doer portion is born. An important aspect is that birth in a certain family often means access to or exclusion from a number of persons. Usually the particular family is not predestined. But it is predestined when there is a strong destiny tie of love, hate or duty between the human beings who are so brought together as near relatives, so that they cohere until that which makes the tie is worn away. Or it may be that a family has characteristics which cannot be found elsewhere and which alone fulfill the requirements on the breath-form.

The active or the passive side of sex is predestined at the end of life, for the next life. The doer has no sex and the re-existing doer portion has none. The sex is of the physical body and carries with it the display of certain psychic qualities, just as it modifies the general outlines of the body as male or female. Of the twelve portions of the doer, six are desire and six are feeling. The male body is characteristic of and is determined by desire. The female body is characteristic of and is determined by feeling. The six desire portions re-exist successively in male bodies. Likewise, the six feeling portions re-exist in female bodies. The three parts of the Triune Self and three breaths are each active and passive, while each atmosphere is passive to the part and to the breath in the atmosphere. The three breaths are substantially these three parts in action. The positive and the negative portions of the doer as one entity are not male or female, and their functions could not be distinguished in that way; however the doer has both aspects undivided. The male and female sexes on the physical plane are exteriorizations of thought representing the dominance of the desire or of the feeling of the doer.

The sex organs demonstrate types of thinking, the geometrical symbols of which are the line and the circle. The line is a conveyor, and the circle a container. Out of many possible physical forms in which these symbols could manifest they appear as the male column and the female entrance, as the solid and the hollow column, and as the passage into the chamber. Thinking according to feeling or desire brings about these modifications of the universal types. Men and women think according to the feeling and desire for the functions of their sex. Thinking pursuant to the desire for the function of the male generates a thought of the male sex, stamps the lines on the breath-form and so tends to determine the male sex. Thinking of the feeling of the functions of the female, generates a thought of the female sex, stamps the lines on the breath-form and so tends to determine the female sex.

The cause of changing the sex in the next life of a re-existing portion is found in thinking subservient to the desire for and feeling of the opposite. The significant thinking is usually gradual and is done in consequence of a preponderance of feeling or of desire. The preponderance predisposes to thinking according to the corresponding type. For instance, when the desire of the doer preponderates, the thinking will be according to the desire for the functions of the male and he will desire a woman as representing the feeling side in his psychic breath and will so determine the sex of his next body as male. In every case the development of the sex organs takes place from the kidneys and adrenals.

On the common ground of the physical plane doer portions meet in physical bodies. These bodies are keyed to the sexes. As the doer portions go through life bound to such bodies they come into relations which constantly center around the male and female aspects of the bodies. Thereby those feelings and desires are stimulated by which the human beings unconsciously mark and determine the relations which exist between them and the non-embodied portions. The human with his false "I", thinks on subjects connected with the sexes. Nearly all thinking turns around clothes, appearance, money, attractiveness, amusement, society, art and religion, with a background of the sexes. The tendency in all this is to bring to human beings the sex that is not expressed in them. When six consecutive portions of the doer have existed in male bodies, their experiences with the female sex have, by degrees, brought about changes in the relation of the factors that determine the sex. There is a gradual change in the feelings and desires, and when enough pressure is exercised by the non-embodied portions of the doer, thinking begins to make sharp lines on the breath-form which call for a change of the sex of the body. If the lines have become sufficiently powerful at the time of death, the re-existing portion acknowledges them, and a change of sex at its next embodiment is unavoidable—provided destiny permits this.

SECTION 12

Also predetermined is the kind of body. Physical heredity and how it is limited. Chief mundane occupations. Diseases. The chief events in life. How destiny can be overcome.

Also among the events determined at the moment of death as preordained for the next life is the kind of body. Even in youth, and more distinctly later in life, such destiny appears as a favorable or adverse gift. Doers find themselves in bodies which are gross, weak, supple or tough. The four classes of elementals build all bodies according to the lines exhibited on the breath-form at conception. Weak eyes, soft bones, stiff joints, or the opposites are foreordained, as well as the ability of a body to recover from wounds or diseases. The features of the face and the movements and other characteristics of physical appearance are predestined.

There is a physical heredity, a transmission of qualities from the parents of the body. Some bodies are good examples of heredity, others do not show it in a marked degree. The seed cell and the soil cell carry with them the appearance and quality of the bodies of the father and of the mother, but the cells must build according to the form of the breath-form of the new human being. The cells build according to the pattern which the breath-form conveys through the astral parts of the cells. These astral parts, or breath link units, can thus build the pattern coming from the father and the mother only in so far as the pattern of the breath-form permits. Where the lines on the breath-form are not pronounced, the heredity is exact, almost as in plants and animals. The more distinctive the lines, the less noticeable will be the heredity of features, qualities and habits. Strong personalities will diverge from the parents, but if the character traits are alike even strong personalities may resemble them. The existing doer gets from the parents only some of the material used in the make-up of the body. The compositor units of the present body, namely the senses, the organ units and the four kinds of link units in each cell, are the identical units that were in the former body. They come back from nature and build the new body, using the qualities inherent in the seed and soil cells to build out the bodily characteristics marked on the breath-form.

The form and features of a person change little more from existence to existence than they do at various periods in a life on earth. Thinking changes features gradually during life. Pictures of the average person taken at corresponding periods of two or even several lives would show little difference. The physical parents may or may not be the same, but the features furnished by heredity no matter from what parents, are the same for a string of lives, with the ordinary person.

Inherent manners are predestined. They are qualities of the re-existing portion of the doer, are of its own nature and show the development of the doer portion. They are the basis of the superficial manners which are the customs of a period and country. The inherent manners range from those of a brute to those of gentility. They are of two kinds; those shown in strictly personal conduct and those displayed where other people are also concerned. The inherent personal manners are those that show respect for oneself. The other kind are seen in one's speech and conduct towards others. Respect for or disregard of their rights and feelings mark the difference between good and bad innate manners. Not conventional training or superficial compliance with formalities, but the inherent manners make a gentleman or a gentlewoman.

Native manners are character in action. They are important indications of the development of the particular doer portion. They are the result of thinking in conformity with or in opposition to what the Light of the Intelligence has shown the human what his conduct should be. They are among the factors which determine lasting associations. They produce grace of nature, grace of speech and grace in movement, or the opposites. They cause deep lines to be made on the breath-form along which the person will act in life. But they can also change by improvement or impairment. They are brought over from the past life, because they are of the doer itself. They are called manners and usually confounded with superficial behavior according to fashion and custom, but they are more. They show the brutishness or refinement of the re-existing doer portion. There is in them a continuity which is absent in superficial manners.

These native, predestinated manners will work themselves out, no matter what the early surroundings were. Usually birth in a family where there is breeding, culture and leisure aids the display of good manners, but many are born into such favored families, whose inherent manners are brutish and selfish, though their superficial behavior is polished.

In most cases the chief mundane occupations of a life are predestined. It is so whether a person selects an occupation, accepts one proposed for him or is compelled to it by force of circumstances. He was making the destiny for the present life when he fell in with and consented to remain in the occupation of the past life, or when, though he rebelled, he did no thinking that would produce a change, or when the exteriorization of past thoughts as an occupation can no longer be postponed. Occupations are superficial, vary with age and country and lead the doer outward.

Occupations are of four classes, labor, trade, learning and knowledge. Inside these classes the occupations change with the conditions of the times. Leadbeaters are no longer in demand; plumbers have come into existence. Among the traders new kinds have appeared with the revelation and use of electrical forces. There are many subdivisions, especially among the traders and the laborers, and the changes go on as inventions are made and as forces of nature are discovered. Even among the learned the application of these discoveries causes new methods and occupations, as in architecture, engineering, surgery, archaeology and chemistry. In some occupations bodily exertions predominate, and little or no mental effort is used. In some the work is almost entirely mental. Some occupations tax the workers to the utmost with long hours and strenuous work, mental or physical, while others allow the workers leisure and even idleness. Some occupations are for amusement or sport, but require taking risks and hard work. Some people, poor or rich, are occupied with idling, looking for something to do or shirking work. Another occupation is the commission of crimes. People perform their work mechanically or with originality, with or without interest, well or ill, and the quality of the worker may vary from inefficiency up to genius. All occupations, no matter how necessary they may seem for sustaining life and supporting a family or maintaining public order, safety, and welfare, no matter how unavoidable and forced are superficial.

The purpose of every occupation is the training of the doer. From that standpoint it does not matter whether they are easy, agreeable, high, remunerative, successful, healthful, or the opposites. It does not matter whether a person has one occupation or several, or whether he changes his occupations during life, or whether talents are concealed and find no opportunity of appearing in the particular occupation which is part of his destiny. The purpose of a man's having a particular occupation is to spur on or to hold back his development in a certain direction.

All is arranged by his thinker according to his thoughts, which develop by exteriorization directly as design and thereafter as destiny projected according to the balancing factor. The human in his undeveloped state cannot judge what occupation is best for him. So his thinker, seeing the best arrangement that can be made for the experience of the doer, allows events that will lead into an occupation and then makes the occupation the chief factor in bringing out the principal events in the life. The kind of occupation is not preordained to the same degree as are the chief and turning events. What other occupations the doer will be led into depends on the attitude and manner in which it deals with its occupation and the concomitant events.

Like family and social connections, occupations are means of bringing the doer into contact with those it is destined to meet. It is likely that it has met them before. The relations may change from superiority to dependence, from beneficence to mordacity, as the destiny is worked out. Through the conditions under which occupations are carried on, usually come rewards, punishments, duties and the opportunity for development. No matter how much time the pursuit of one's occupation demands, there is always a margin of leisure. This margin, though it be ever so small, is important for future destiny. This margin is the field that offers more of an opportunity for the exercise of what is called free will than any other condition. The margin has to be used in some way whether by idling, daydreaming, passive thinking or work undertaken for some purpose. The way the margin is used shows the choice of the doer when there is no compulsion by circumstances, and shapes the future occupations according to the choice, in so far as they have not yet been made unavoidable by the past.

Important though occupations are as exteriorized thoughts and thereby as affecting the relations of life, there are some things occupations do not do. They educate the senses, develop skill and endurance of the body and compel a certain amount of thinking. They allow the past to work out in the present. But in all this they keep the doer employed largely with the external world. They do not tell the doer anything about itself. Rather do they keep it ignorant about itself while they tangle it up with the world. They do give experience and sometimes teach, but they cannot give knowledge of the conscious self in the body.

Certain of the diseases that people have are predestined from the past life. Hereditary diseases and such as come without apparent cause are among their number, sometimes also those that result from unexpected injuries and from infections. If signatures for them are on the breath-form for the new life they are predestined, no matter at what time in life they appear. Many a disease which afflicts a person is not predestined from the past life. The thoughts stimulate the breath-form to action and that causes the systems to which the disease belongs to build out the symbolic lines into the bodily disease. It comes assisted by hereditary preparation, bodily inclination or occupation or infectious taint. The time of its appearance will fit in with the condition of the body and of the place in or on the body where it breaks out.

The chief events in life are also usually predestined, because they are things from the past that must be dealt with. They are either things wished for or submitted to, or things unwished for that can no longer be avoided. Among them are education and ignorance, marriage and off-spring, friends and enemies, poverty, riches and sudden changes, honor and disgrace, travels and adventures, injuries and escapes.

All such features of a life that are preordained are the result of the thoughts which the human had in his past life. That human has vanished. He centered himself around a false "I", which covered the real, but unknown, identity of the doer. The new human is likewise built around a false "I", and knows as little of the underlying identity, but he is the inheritor, nevertheless, of some of the thoughts and desires of the vanished human from whom he also inherits his physical destiny.

Universal law ever pushes the doer on, ever causes some thoughts to turn into new events which confront the doer, ever forces the doer to meet them and to deal with them. The doer must do something with its destiny and with the desires and thoughts which come to it.

Once thoughts have been exteriorized, they are destiny, whether brought over from the life of the last human or made by the present one. What a person does with his destiny will make the present and determine part of the future. So it is with what one does with the desires and thoughts from the past that visit him. They, too, are destiny, every bit as much as the hard and fast facts of life. They come from the realms of the atmospheres and from those portions of the Triune Self that are not in contact with the body. They surge up in him, float into his present thinking, urge him on to actions, stand behind him like a background and make parts of the future. They build around him clouds of gloom or doubt or make him see things in clear and cheerful light.

This destiny, tangible and intangible, one has to meet from birth to death. What can he do with it? How far does it control him? How far can he act freely with or against it? Destiny as the events that have occurred, such as birth in a certain family, cannot be revoked; nor can that which is destined to be be prevented, though it may be hastened or postponed, accentuated or weakened. When it is precipitated the consequences which flow from it are largely decided by what one thinks about it.

The average man thinks little about it. He feels the advantage or disadvantage, it impresses him as acceptable or objectionable; but he does not think about it. He acts in consequence of it, but not in consequence of thinking about it. So he misses his opportunity to deal with it as he should and, therefore, destiny controls him. But this need not be.

Its consequences are not impassable. Some of them can always be overcome. There is always a leeway and it depends on the determination and clarity of one's thinking about his destiny. He is bound to it by his inability to see it as it is, to think about it and to accept it. With honesty and persistent thinking a way can be found to overcome some of the apparently insuperable consequences. One can act freely with or against his destiny to the degree that his thinking can control his acting.

The factors which act on a human during his life are of two classes. In one are some of the thoughts of the human being of the past life, which appear exteriorized in the hard facts of destiny or as thoughts which come and go and leave pleasant or unpleasant impressions. These are all from the past. In the second class are thoughts of the present life. They are the new crop that has to do with the present, yet it grows out of the past. There is a sharp distinction on the one hand between the thoughts which suggest themselves and of whose cause one is ignorant and has no memory and which come over from the past, and on the other hand the thoughts conceived and issued in the present life. The distinction is shown by memory. The thoughts of the present life can be remembered, can be identified with persons, places, purposes or events. This new crop of thoughts is the other factor which acts on a human during his life. It strengthens or weakens the cycling thoughts, it hastens or delays their exteriorizations and so precipitates or puts off destiny. It wears away old bonds or forges new ones; but most important of all, the present thinking will reclaim Light from nature or call in new Light from the Intelligence, or lose Light to nature.

It is not a misuse of Light to send it out into nature to maintain its higher forms as plants, trees, animals or rocks, but it is a desecration of the Light to appropriate it to the vermin, pests and scourges of nature as does the run of human beings. If one's thoughts put the Light which is loaned to the doer to legitimate uses, it is returned and sooner or later he learns from it what it went through while out in nature. That Light will enlighten him when he is thinking upon the subject with which the Light was connected. It will so show him the stupendous wonders of plant life and the molecular and atomic marvels of organic and inorganic nature, the actions of which it guided. The Light reclaimed will also affect his destiny more quickly than any other power. The Light shows one his destiny, how to deal with it, how to accept it and thereby to make the most of it.

SECTION 13

The time between existences. About the heavenly bodies. Time. Why people fit into the age in which they live.

The time between existences varies. Before a doer portion can exist again, the other doer portions must have existed in their order. Many factors influence the period which must pass before a doer portion' returns to the common ground as a human. The periods vary in different cases from within a hundred years to thousands and thousands, as measured by physical time.

Existences, just as all other events that depend on this physical time, can take place only when there is a coincidence of this physical with certain other kinds of time. The kinds of time by which the periods between the re-existences of a certain doer portion are measured, and which have to coincide are of four kinds. Each kind of time has divisions and these again have subdivisions. What is here loosely called physical time is intended to point to four subdivisions of time on the physical plane of the physical world, namely to that which applies to matter in the four states. As physical time is the time on the common ground the coincidence with it is the telling factor.

About time human beings generally know nothing, except their conscious experience with the change of the masses of the units of the sun, moon and earth in their relation to each other. Time, represented by a calendar, means to human beings events produced by the change in the relation of these masses of units, such as day, night, month and year. Man uses these changing natural phenomena because they are regular and produce the seasons, as marks to measure the flowing streams of events in his life: sowing, reaping, waking, sleeping, past and future, near and far. His perception of time depends upon his four senses, principally sight, chained to the physical body. Therefore, his perception of time is limited to the outermost phenomena which occur on the common ground where time as an objective relation is the same for all human beings.

The four kinds of nature time are time in the light world, light time; time in the life world, life time; time in the form world, form time; and time in the physical world. Of the time in the physical world mankind perceives only time on the physical plane. In each world the units or masses of units are different, their relations are different and the dominant units or masses by which the changes in the relations are made and can be measured, are different.

What appears as the sun is a focus in the airy layer of the physical plane of the physical world, and focusses matter which comes into it from the fiery, airy, watery and earthy layers upon and into the earthy layer. It precipitates this fourfold matter with the aid of the moon to the outer earth crust. The moon is fluid-solid, not as solid as the earth crust, and is a mass or body in the watery layer. It screens, filters, magnetizes, demagnetizes, modifies and adjusts the matter that flows from the sun to the earth crust and from the earth crust to the sun. These two dominant masses affect the units and masses of units on the physical plane. The sun works with the heart and lungs, the moon with the kidneys and adrenals, the earth with the sex organs, all through the breath. All units are affected on that plane by the sun, the moon and the earth.

There is no sun, no moon and no earth in the form world or in the life world or in the light world. The stars are not in the form world, but are on the borders of and mark the limits of the perceptible physical plane and the form plane of the physical world.

Time in the other worlds cannot be measured by the masses which make physical time. But there are dominant units or masses of units in the other worlds which make form time, life time and light time, but light time is only on the physical plane of the light world. There are relations and even analogies between physical time and the various subdivisions of time on the other planes of the physical world and of time in the other worlds. Though these many subdivisions or varieties of nature time exist, only some aspects of four varieties, namely, of those on the physical plane, can be perceived at present by existing doers. During an existence various subdivisions of time coincide. They coincide not only among themselves, but also with changes or occurrences in the doer.

When the doer is in the body and conscious on the physical plane as a human he measures all things by physical time, by the sun, moon and earth. When he is cut off by sleep or death from the physical plane, he continues to experience nature time, but not solely as this physical time. He then can experience time also as earth time or water time or air time or fire time on the form, life and light planes of the physical world, or as form time, rarely as life time and hardly ever as light time. Thoughts, desires and the breath-form are the factors which take the place of sun, moon and earth and are the means for measuring. The human perceives nature time through the four senses after death as long as the senses and the breath-form are with him.

There is no time in the Triune Self. But there is time for the doer of the Triune Self when it is embodied. The changes in the doer, while embodied, are measured not by time but by accomplishment. Events in the doer bring about accomplishment; the accomplishment is the result of changes in the doer. These changes are in the doer, not in the thinker and not in the knower, which are unaffected. The factors which bring about changes in the doer are feeling and desire. They bring about these changes by their attitude towards nature through the use of their three minds. These changes are experienced by the doer in the psychic atmosphere, where they affect not only the existing portion of the doer but also the non-existing portions. The changes go on chiefly between the desire for Self-knowledge and the desire for sex, and are recorded in the psychic atmosphere.

During the period after death the four kinds of nature time are arranged to coincide with the accomplishment, that is, the result in the doer produced in the last earth life.

Before a re-existence can take place the various subdivisions of nature time other than physical time must coincide with the accomplishment in the doer, and all together must coincide with physical time and with place and condition.

Moreover, it must be possible to continue this alignment of time throughout the life of the physical body. The coincidence of the various times other than physical time takes place as the human works out in the after-death states what he has to pass through. When the doer portion is ready for an existence it waits after its eternity in heaven, in blissful sleep. When physical time, condition and place coincide with what is predestined, that doer portion re-exists.

The synchronizing of the different kinds of time with the accomplishment in the doer is done by the thinker. The doer passes necessarily through its hell and its heaven and at the end there have been synchronized and adjusted through the thinker and knower, the kinds of time in the four worlds of nature to the accomplishment in the psychic atmosphere.

How is it that most people seem to fit right into the age in which they live, although the other doer portions had to be embodied before their own term came again and the language and occupations may have changed in the meantime? The reason is that the doer has gone through all experiences and has repeated them over and over. Therefore a human does not have to come from a recent past and locality to fit into his place at the present time. The facility of some in using a language, the readiness with which some take hold of sciences and their modern applications, the extraordinary capacity of some to handle large undertakings in government, war or commerce, do not indicate that these achievements are continuations of a recent past. Nor are stupidity, awkwardness and ignorance signs that the doer portion was deficient during the previous existence.

Nothing in the way of attainment or absence of achievement is proof or indication that the human had or had not powers in the past. The capacities and abilities of human beings depend upon the use of their three minds; all doers had control of all three many times in the past, and most of them have lost the control.

The world in which the human beings of the doers live is a play of shadows and illusions, which has been going on for millions of years. The play is as a farce to the Triune Self. It is as a farce because there is no time in the Triune Self. End and beginning are one; and even to the doer there is nothing new, because it has had all possible experiences. It is ludicrous that the thing on which men depend most for certainty is one of the most illusory things to the Triune Self; that is, time.

SECTION 14

Everything after death is destiny. Inventors. Classic Hellas. Re-existence in nation groups. Centers of succeeding civilizations. Greece, Egypt, India.

Everything after death happens as destiny; the human cannot determine anything after death. Lessons are given to him, but he cannot make use of them until he gets back to earth and lives in a flesh body. The reason that he cannot control anything after death is, that choice is possible only while on the common ground. After death the human is subject to illusions, as he was in life.

In life he cannot see anything as it is. He sees everything as massed together and sees no thing by itself. Therefore he sees things that are temporary as permanent. He sees only the outside of things, and not the causes which draw the things together. He does not see the changes that go to make the outside change. He cannot distinguish between himself and nature, nor can he distinguish the four senses, which are part of nature, from himself. He fears to let go of the four senses and what they connect him with, as though he would lose himself if he lost them. He depends for permanence on nature, which is ever changing. He is mistaken about his identity. Only those who have overcome the illusions of life can control them after death and so master the destiny which is theirs.

Just as Intelligences and Triune Selves marshal physical events so that the world moves on and the thoughts of all doers can be exteriorized on the physical plane, so Triune Selves sometimes accelerate or retard the synchronizing of kinds of time for their doers, so that these may be ready when physical time permits a re-existence. The Light of the Intelligence by its action hastens or extends the accomplishment of the events which are the consummation of the time that has to be passed The Intelligences may have nothing to do with the management of the physical plane, but they are in touch with other Intelligences who marshal in time and place physical events that are to be. Frequently such acceleration or retardation happens when a doer has to meet many other doers on earth or if a doer is distinct from the ordinary run of doers, or if it is on The Way.

The human beings themselves cause the acceleration or retardation of the time of their re-existence by what they think while they are embodied and by how they act in relation to this thinking. The determining factor is whether its feeling and thinking keep a doer with the physical world or take it away from physical conditions.

A human hastens his return by trying to see facts as they are, by doing his duties without hope of reward or fear of disadvantage, by working to achieve his ideals and by having ideals not too far ahead of attainment. The time for the return is delayed when a human sees only part of the facts and longs for things to be different, when he fears the coming of events, when he does good in hope of reward or refrains from wrong for fear of punishment, when he thinks much about heaven and hell and longs for the one or fears the other, or when he thinks without putting his thinking into practice. Plotting evil deeds even without doing them will tend to bring a doer back soon, because its feelings and thoughts are with the present and with the earth. Thinking ideally even though it is of the earth, postpones the return to earth because it relates to the future.

Occupation or position in life have in themselves not much influence; but the thinking which they permit or engender has. A cobbler at work may think of an ideal government or of philosophy; a country parson may think far beyond his present field of action. Such thinking may keep them away a long time. On the other hand a pawnbroker, an undertaker or a lawyer may never get beyond the hard facts of his life; not the philosophy of need, death and strife, but chiefly what they themselves can get out of them for their purses attracts their thinking. Such thinking would bring them back soon. Generally practical thinking and its transference into immediate acts shortens the absence from physical life.

In the after-death states, ages and eternities of suffering and of bliss can be experienced in short terms as measured by physical time. To the doers in their subjective states physical time does not exist. Long or short periods as measured by physical time mean nothing to them.

Whether a long or short absence from the common ground is advantageous depends upon various conditions. No absolute statement applicable to all doers or even to any one doer, can be made to cover the many situations on the common ground and the varying conditions of doers at certain times.

Generally speaking, it is better for human beings who have goodwill and who work for the benefit of others, to come back soon. Their return gives them at least the opportunity to think and work and thereby to accomplish something. But an early return may be bad if the human comes into a period for which he is not prepared, and therefore has a disposition to escape from destiny, or if he comes with handicaps, such as an infirm body. Still, such impediments may be resisted and overcome and the situation be turned to advantage. Sometimes human beings who come back too soon cannot accomplish their work, because they have not had a sufficient period of dreamless rest after the end of their heaven period. For lack of that rest they may be unequal to opportunities, unprepared for events or without vigor to make or carry out plans. Even unfitting times into which a human is born and in which he is out of place and not understood, may become advantageous if he faces his environment bravely or if he learns something from it.

Generally a long interval is unfavorable because it keeps a doer from the field of action and from opportunities. It is likely to take it too far out of times to which it is accustomed and with which its thinking has made it familiar. A doer may think of and speculate on high ideals and, as long as it connects them with present physical realities, it does not think so as to be kept away from the earth. It is different with thinking which has no connection with or is opposed to physical realities. Such dreaming keeps the human away from the earth and is disadvantageous, because it prevents opportunities to accomplish anything with himself. In each case the length of absence involves questions of individual destiny and cannot be disposed of by a flat answer tending to cover all cases.

The disposal of the body of the deceased can have an influence on the earlier or later return of the doer. Cremation or the devouring of the body by birds or fishes frees the compositor units from the influence of the fourfold physical body. Then the physical earth loses all hold on the four senses and on the breath-form. Thereby the doer is set free from the physical influence which the earth exerted through the senses and the breath-form.

In the case of burial the physical earth can continue its influence through the fourfold body on the compositor units and retard their freedom until decay dissipates the physical body. Embalming and mummification retard the decay of the body and hold transient units in the body. The compositor units are not affected. When death takes place the body of transient units remains; the breath-form with the senses and the compositor units leave the body at once; but there remains the magnetic connection between the compositor units and the physical body.

Cremation destroys at once the fourfold physical body, and the influence of the physical earth on the breath-form and the compositors. When the dominating thought of the next doer portion to re-exist presses for re-existence, the after-death states of the preceding portion are hastened. Then the aia vivifies the breath-form, which makes contact with the parents-to-be through their breaths, for conception. If the former body is not decomposed there may be a lethal influence from the disintegrating astral on the astral that is being built in the mother. The astral of the dead body may affect the compositor units that are fashioning the new body in the womb, may bring morbid sensations to the mother and may transmit prenatally tendencies to disease or to badness. Usually the time that must elapse between re-embodiments is at least the time necessary for the compositor units to become free from the magnetic influence of the decaying body.

In the case of cremation the compositors are set free from this influence at once; in the case of decay they are free when the organs which they managed have reached a certain stage of decomposition. This may take place within a few months. The bones, made up as they are of transient units in the solid-solid state, are the last to disintegrate and least important.

Doers may be absent from earth life for thousands of years. This occurs where the conditions marked by physical time do not afford to their dominant thoughts means for unfolding, to their talents a field for display, to their virtues suitable environment and to their ideals a people who understand them and are like them. Many doers that belonged to heights of former ages of the earth, water, air and fire are excluded from re-existence.

The earth, since history tells, has been the common ground of such doers as have made the bloody and rapacious history which is recorded. In historical times the doers who knew and even those who belonged to the class of the thinkers have been greatly in the minority and often misunderstood and persecuted. Yet it is due largely to them that the Fourth Civilization has been enabled to go on. Many such doers have returned out of their time, but the race to which they belong could not return, as a whole, for thousands of years. For many centuries backward doers have come to the earth. They have made it a place to which the more advanced doers that built up the earth, water, air and fire ages to their heights, could not come.

But within the last hundred and fifty years much has been done, by the wider diffusion of information and by discoveries and their general application, to furnish a basis for an ascent. New groups of doers are coming in who have been away for a long time. During these few years the improvements in the material surroundings have been greater and more general than at any time in the historic period.

Among inventors and discoverers have been some of the doers who lived in those former ages. Then forces of the earth, the water, the air and the starlight were known and used, which later could no longer be reached and mastered. Some of the recent discoverers are doers who in those ages were conscious of the operation of those forces. The thoughts which they had then formed of the working of those forces made their marks on the aias of those doers. When they came back their thoughts refreshed the signatures on the breath-form and started the body-mind on the subjects of the signatures. Conditions on the earth were different, but these doers having gotten into touch with their thoughts in those past times, were enabled to apply their former knowledge to the new surroundings and so made the discoveries which are ushering in a new era. When the general thinking of humanity is opposed to anything new, there is a general belief that the proposed novelty is impossible. Many discoveries have for this reason been treated with indifference or enmity. The original discoverers are therefore often not known. But when the desiring and thinking of the people run along certain lines, either new discoveries or former discoveries which had been rejected, are accepted and popularly applied. The persons who are credited with being the pioneers in discoveries are often only those who utilized at the favorable moment the discovery made by some unknown or forgotten predecessor who could not prevail against the weight of the general thinking. These original discoverers, known or unknown, are usually doers who have lived in those former ages.

The more advanced races to which these doers belong do not re-exist as a whole. Occasionally there is a flare-up, and a group of doers from one of these races of prehistoric times appear together. Then they mark an epoch in the darkness.

Such was the case in the classic age in Hellas, which was so great that it has conspicuously influenced the world for over two thousand years. There had been a land which is now below the waters of the Mediterranean. What was later Athens, was a spot that had been used by the people of a period when a fire, an air, a water and an earth age flourished together. The illustrious philosophers, scientists, builders, artists and poets of classic Hellas were doers who had lived in the period when the four ages flourished. They returned together to Athens and made it for the time even greater than what it is now believed to have been. What the philosophers said about the four elements and the earth crust has come down to the present in fragments, or in distorted statements. The divine beings and races of Greek mythology are traditions standing for human beings who had actually lived in the starlight, the air, the water and the earth.

The doers that compose the nations now on earth have been re-existing in their national groups for a long time. When a nation disappears, the doers withdraw for a while and then build a new race or come into the bodies of a race living on some other part of the earth's surface. They go in groups to different races according to their way of thinking. They impress themselves as a group upon that nation, or are absorbed by it.

When nations are born they settle around certain localities which, because of the formation of mountains, plains, rivers and harbors, favor the building of cities. Some of these spots are centers of succeeding civilizations, because they are special places on the earth crust. They are outlets for magnetic forces and allow certain other less material forces to manifest there. There are places which time and again have been fields of battle, centers of government, seats of learning or cities of commerce. Some places have served in several of these roles. New York, London, Rome, Athens, Cairo are some of them. Notwithstanding many changes in the conformation of the land and water on the earth crust, cities have risen again and again at these centers. There are such centers in North, Central and South America and in the Pacific, on which important cities will be, as they have been in the past.

If nations at different times are different, it is because different sets of doers came back to earth. Certain sets come in the youth of the nation, other sets build it up, other sets bring culture or corruption and other doers come to aid in its destruction. Sometimes a nation disappears imperceptibly. A certain bloodstrain remains to keep up a continuity of bodies, but the dwellers in those bodies are not the doers that existed formerly.

The illustrious doers of classic Greece do not live in bodies of modern Greeks. The fellahin, though good simple people, are not the doers that made Egypt great; the doers in Central America are not the doers of the ancient Mayas; and the doers of the people in India are not the ones who made and used Sanskrit. But as long as nations remain substantially the same in their thinking, the same doers return to them, generally speaking. There are some exceptions, but there is this general coming back. Doers usually meet again in their families other doers with whom they had close relations, be it of attachment or of enmity. The families also have relations, hostile or friendly, with other families or groups of people. These more or less effective ties will bring all the doers which are bound by them into a community or a class in a nation. The opportunities for these appearances are limited by physical time. Therefore a synchronizing of the return of certain doers is effected by the beings who marshal all earthly events in time and place, so that those re-exist together who have to work out their destinies in common.

SECTION 15

Training of the doer portion though memory is not present. The body-mind. Doer-memory. Sense-memory. A good memory. Memory after death.

Throughout all the re-existences of a doer its training is carried on by its higher aspects under the Light of the Intelligence even though the memory of previous lives is not present. A consideration of the nature of memory will show why the human does not remember past lives.

Memory of the human is sense-memory when it deals with external events; it is doer-memory when it relates to states of the doer. Sense-memory of the human is of four kinds and is the doer's recognition of sights, sounds, tastes, and smells and contacts which were impressed by the four senses upon and are reproduced by the breath-form. The impressions are received through the respective organs by the optic, auditory, gustatory and olfactory nerves and by other sensory nerves, and are passed on through the involuntary nerves to the fourfold body which transmits them to the breath-form on which they are fixed by the breath. The gallery of the pictures, sounds, tastes, smells and contacts for the whole life is there. The brain has little or nothing to do with the reception of impressions, unless intentional mental activities accompany the see-ing, hearing, tasting, smelling or touching. The impressions on the breath-form are not physical, though made through physical means. No brain cells, nerve cells or other cells retain the impressions. These remain as nonphysical imprints on the breath-form.

The impressions of sights, sounds, tastes and smells received by the four senses in their sense organs and respective nerves, are received in the same manner as are impressions of agreeable or disagreeable touch. The impressions of touch are received by the sensory nerves from the thing making contact with the body. The sense of smell is the entity that receives directly the impression made by physical contact upon the sensory nerves of the involuntary nervous system, of hot or cold, soft or hard, burning or squeezing. The sense of sight visualizes objects, the sense of hearing transmits movement as sounds, the sense of taste brings in tastes and the sense of smell touches and makes physical contacts. These contact impressions are of two kinds, those of smell and of physical contact. The breath-form receives the impressions and automatically passes them on to the sensory nerves of the voluntary nervous system, and the motor nerves of that pass them on to the doer.

Prior to their transfer to the doer these impressions are not recognized and produce no effects as sights, sounds, tastes, smells or contacts. They are simply impressions without meaning and they produce no feeling. Nevertheless they are fixed on the breath-form by the breath when they first reach it, though they are without color, form, sound, taste or smell, and though they produce no pain or pleasure, no sensation of any kind. These impressions of physical things made on the breath-form are the basis of such phenomena as dreams or unconscious reproductions in trance states or of reproductions and combinations which make hells and heavens and they are the preliminaries of memories.

The doer does several things with these impressions, which all come to it in the voluntary nervous system. It merely feels them as sights, sounds, tastes, smells and contacts, as the doer; it perceives and classifies them as those things through the body-mind and it identifies them in various ways, because of the presence of the knower of the Triune Self. All three actions together constitute what is called seeing, hearing, tasting, smelling and feeling by touch. Thus when a house in a meadow is perceived, the impressions brought home by the sense of sight are felt by the doer as agreeable or disagreeable, nothing more; to this feeling there is added by thinking, as it distinguishes, compares and interprets, the perception of long grass, gray sides, three gables, and windows with green shutters. By virtue of I-ness, the false "I" gives identity to the picture and says: "I see it", and further: "This is that particular house", "This house I have seen before with its long grass, gray sides, three gables and twisted rainpipe". Not until all three actions are gone through is the simplest object seen or any sensation felt.

After perceptions through the four senses have been made by the doer, it stamps its feeling, thinking and identification on the impression first made on the breath-form. This fixing also is done by the breath. Thereafter, the sight, sound, taste, smell or sensation by touch can be summoned, or may appear without summons, as a memory. In every case the memory is partly sense-memory and partly doer-memory. Animals have no breath-forms, yet they have memories. The animal memories are feeling and desire memories, called instinct or impulses, inherent in the feeling or desire that animates the animal.

The remembering which is the result of an effort or desire, starts by active thinking on a subject associated with the thing sought to be remembered. The thinking begins in the heart and lungs, then continues in the brain. There it calls into play the particular nerves of seeing, hearing, tasting, smelling or touching. This awakens the subjective or inner side of the particular sense, which is turned inward and through its nerve and system acts on the fourfold physical body and through that on the breath-form. There the original impression is summoned and then reproduced in the frontal sinuses or a nerve area of the brain by the sense, through the objective side of which the original impression was taken. The picture, sound, taste, smell or other sensation in the area of the brain is not the original impression but a copy of it, transferred from the breath-form to the brain area. If the copy produces a sensation similar to that produced when the original impression was made and the false "I" identifies the copy with the original impression made from the external object, the sight, sound, taste, smell or contact is remembered. While the original impressions are not usually made with the cooperation of the brain, its assistance is necessary in all cases of intentional remembering. The doer in its thinking must cooperate with at least one of the senses in every instance where anything is remembered. The sense goes, in inverse order, over the processes that produced the first impression in the voluntary nervous system, but the doer repeats the original action. Without the activities of the sense, intervening between the initial thinking and the final recognition as the result of the combined action of the doer, there can be no memory. In order to remember a thing there must be a recognition or a reproduction, voluntary or involuntary, of impressions made of external things by the senses.

The remembering, which is not the result of an effort but which comes uncalled for, is due to an influence on the breath-form. The prompting may be from different causes, such as passive thinking, nature-imagination, another person's thought or a suggestive occurrence. If the stimulus is strong enough or comes at the right time, it will compel the breath-form to reproduce an impression which it had received from the senses. The reproduction is made through the same sense or senses that made the original impression and is thrown on the frontal sinuses or nerve area in the brain and there felt, classified and identified by the doer. This is involuntary memory.

Human beings live in involuntary memories, which make up the largest part of their lives. With every act are associated memories of other acts. These make scenes amidst which passive thinking goes on. This draws in other memories. They hold the stage of the inner life until fresh sense impressions shift the memory of the human to other scenes. Then the thinking goes on there. Life is a continuous interaction between passive thinking and memories. After death the inner life is the only one, yet it becomes objective. It is, as regards memories, the same kind of life that the doer led while on the common ground. But all the memories then are involuntary, and the thinking that is interwoven is automatic.

Whether voluntary or involuntary, whether in life or after death, this memory of the human is the recognition by the doer of sensations of sights, sounds, tastes, smells and contacts which the doer had felt from impressions on the breath-form received through the four senses and interpreted by thinking.

Doer-memory of the human is the reproduction and recognition by the re-existing doer portion of states of itself apart from the impressions of outside things made on the breath-form by the senses. These are states through which the particular doer portion has passed, whether in the present life or in any lives in the past or in any of the after-death states between them. They are states in which the doer portion was conscious in feeling and desiring and in the active and passive sides of one of the three minds it may use. They are states of the doer itself. They are apart and quite distinct from the impressions of external objects made by the senses. The impression on the breath-form is one thing, and the pain or pleasure, desiring and feeling or other doer state induced by the impression is quite another.

Doer-memory of the human is usually of two, rarely of three degrees, according to the aspects of the doer of which the human is conscious. The doer states to which the world today attaches most importance are pleasure and pain from sensations through the senses, and joy or sorrow, fear or desire, as interior states of the doer.

In the conscious waking state doer-memory may be intentional or come uncalled for. If it is the result of an effort it is recalled by active thinking on a subject of thought connected with the doer state sought to be remembered. There are three ways of remembering, according to the three degrees of doer-memory.

In the first degree of doer-memory, when one tries to remember a doer state of feeling-and-desire the process begins by inquiring of oneself what the doer state connected with a former time, place or event was; such as "How did I feel when I first went to school?" Then one gets sense-memory, as of the way to school, the schoolhouse, the teacher and the pupils. This line of sense-memories must be found before there can be any doer-memory as of the feeling when one first went to school. The aid of sense-memory is a preliminary to the doer-memory of feeling. Sense-memory is the recognition of the sights, sounds and other sensations, and that recalls the feelings and desires which sense impressions caused many years before. The process of remembering feelings and desires starts in the kidneys, but it is not recognized until it reaches the heart. Usually it is not recognized even there, and people remain unconscious of the effort to remember until the process reaches the brain.

The second degree of doer-memory of a human is that of remembering states concerning rightness-and-reason. Recalling a judgment connected with a person or a scene is a memory of a state concerned with rightness; instances of a state concerned with reason are such as the understanding of the multiplication table, of axioms and of general truths. The breath-form is usually called upon to present impressions previously made by the senses, to aid in this kind of memory. The remembering begins in the heart by thinking of a subject and then reaches the brain. In the heart the action of the breath calls on the breath-form for the impression connected with that subject of thought. The breath-form throws the impression into the heart, whence it is carried into the brain, and there it is recognized as a former state of the doer.

The reason why people cannot call up the memory of other mental states is because they do not control their thinking. They use chiefly the body-mind, the mind that is worked for the physical world and is particularly concerned with contact, measure, weight, distance and such physical things. While they use the feeling-mind or the desire-mind, they use them much less and work them only in connection with the body-mind. Using chiefly the body-mind people can get only such doer-memories as are caused by physical things.

Doer-memories of the third degree, that is, of states relating to I-ness-and-selfness do not come to the average human by efforts to remember. If the attempt to pursue one's identity in memory is made, as by trying to remember who one was a week ago, a year ago or twenty years ago, I-ness is called upon by the false "I". The false "I" then feels itself to be the same entity it was a week ago, a year ago and twenty years ago, though the physical features of the human have changed. The breath-form is not required to do anything actively, but is needed as a background, for instance, to show today, a year ago and twenty years ago. It is felt that something has not changed at all, is no younger, no older and was and is conscious as something without change. This is a feeling by the false "I" of "I"-ness, which is the real "I" behind the false. The connection and continuity are given by I-ness.

Doer-memory of the three degrees usually appears without being summoned. Just as casual, unintentional sense-memory, mingled with passive thinking, makes up the longest stretches of life and draws in doer-memories of feelings and desires, so the turning points of life are marked by uncalled upon doer-memories of the other degrees. These are not associated with sense impressions and surroundings, but burst in on them and evoke in the doer feelings of fear and gloom or of serenity, peace and ease, often quite at variance with surrounding conditions. These memories from beyond the senses are felt as hope, conscience and destiny.

All these doer-memories are due largely to thoughts cycling in the mental atmosphere of the doer portion in the human. They act at certain times on the aia, calling out and reviving impressions which they made on it when they were generated, and thereafter from time to time in their coursings. The thoughts are the same as they were in the past. The indwelling doer portion is not conscious of the thoughts, but it is conscious of the effects produced by these passing thoughts, which are memories of past doer states. These memories produce temptation, remorse, fear, hope, pangs of conscience and faith in one's destiny. But they do so in a manner for which the human does not account. He cannot account for it because he is so ignorant of the nature of memory.

A "good memory" is a mechanically accurate process of reproduction from the breath-form of impressions received from the four senses. All one has to do is to call for the memory; the less he interferes with remembering by thinking the clearer will be the automatic reproduction. Memory is not thinking and is not accomplished by thinking. Thinking, while the impression is being made by the senses, interferes with the clearness of the impression, and thinking may also interfere with or prevent remembering. Defective memory is caused not only by inability of the particular sense to make impressions, but also by anything on the road that prevents their transmission from the breath-form to the doer, or by want of skill or power in the doer to receive them. Failure to get clear impressions on the breath-form may be due to one of two causes. The senses may be unable to receive and convey clear impressions, or the breath-form itself may be unable to receive or retain them.

Memory will be poor if the impression was slight, blurred, inaccurate or combined with other impressions. If a sense cannot make a sufficient impression on the breath-form there will be no memory. Such is often the case with people who cannot remember melodies or sounds. When they hear a melody the auric nerve transmits it to the airy body and from there it passes by way of the breath-form to the doer, without however making a clear impression. Therefore, the melody is heard, the doer reacts to it, but cannot reproduce it by memory because no clear impression was retained by the breath-form.

Other causes of poor memory are impediments which prevent proper transmission of impressions to or from the doer, even if they have been made on the breath-form. That is the case where the nerve structure, along which they have to pass to or from the doer, is defective, or where the organs or nerve channels are obstructed by abnormal substances, such as adhesions. This may happen because of diseases, old age or dissipation.

Memory will also be poor if there are impediments created by the doer itself, which will prevent either a clear impression on the breath-form in the first instance or later a proper reproduction. They are inattention, confusion, dissatisfaction, a riot of feelings and desires, or a lack of Light in the mental atmosphere of the human, so that it is dim and the doer is not clear as to what it wants to remember. Its mental activities are not coordinated; they lack resilience and clarity, order and discrimination.

The call for things sought to be remembered depends upon association. There must be an impulse felt in the doer for a name, occasion, person, event, sight, or something associated with the thing sought to be remembered which once drew a reaction from the doer. This subject suggests to the doer the thing once seen, heard, tasted, smelled or touched and the doer calls for the memory or reproduction of it. This is then produced automatically as the breath-form throws up a copy of the first impression in the frontal sinuses or on the sensorium of the brain.

To repeat in the afternoon a statement heard in the forenoon it is necessary that the hearer should have a good memory of sounds, that he should have listened to the words and not have allowed himself to think while listening. When later repeating the words, he must again stop thinking, have confidence and listen to the sounds as they reappear on the areas of the brain. If he strains too hard he will interfere and will not remember. He would be able to repeat a long conversation word for word if the first impression were clear and there were no mechanical obstructions in the way and if the doer had been attentive and not engaged in collateral thinking.

If one has a memory good enough to let him note discrepancies in stories, he does this by means of association and comparison. He must listen to the several stories without interfering by his thinking. He will then get a clear-cut imprint to which his doer and his thinking will react. When he hears other stories bearing upon the subject of the first, the doer-memory causes him to associate and compare the new with the prior impressions of the story and calls on the sense-memory to furnish the prior records. Where persons are vaguely conscious of variations or contradictions, but cannot remember distinctly, they fail in their memory either because they did not receive clear impressions in the first instance or because they did not listen attentively and without mixing their own thinking with the record.

The most frequent causes of poor memory are not to be found in weakness of the senses or of the breath-form and in defects in the ways of transmission, but in the vague passive thinking that interferes with the making of the first impression and again with the reproduction and recognition.

Sense-memory and doer-memory are not distinguished. There are various causes. The doer-memory of which a person is conscious is evoked by events in the world, that is, impressions which the senses make on the breath-form; these events cause sense-memories to come together with the doer-memory; and the person, not being expert enough, does not distinguish one from the other. Another cause is that the doer-memories of which people are conscious are chiefly desires and feelings, and both of these are usually suggested by the senses. The doer-memories of feeling-and-desire are unfamiliar, and if they do appear they are considered as unusual experiences and are not classified as memories.

Doer-memories are all memories of states of feeling-and-desire, brought about by thinking. The thinker of the Triune Self has before it at all times all of the past and of the future that has been made. Thus it knows and brings about destiny for the human. The knower of the Triune Self is in the Eternal, as knowledge, which includes past and future of every kind. Thus doer-memories are states of the doer in the human, which lives in time and makes destiny.

There are four kinds of psychic states which can be called doer-memories. There is a memory of the impressions of nature affecting feeling or desire as events; this is brought on by the action of the body-mind; this is psycho-physical memory. There is a memory of feelings as feelings or of desires as desires, a memory of themselves. This memory is usually evoked by events of nature in association with the body-mind, working with the feeling-mind or the desire-mind; this is psychic memory. There is a memory which is a state of feeling or of desire, but not merely of feeling or desire. It is a memory where the human remembers concerning an event which seems to say "Yes", "No", "It should be" or "It should not be." This is not instinct, which is based on the experience of feeling or of desire. It is a feeling of a truth, a conviction. The conviction may be contrary to one's instinct, that is, to his feelings and desires, because it is the recurring as a memory of previous learning through thinking.

The ability to do things is a result of the third kind of memory. For this ability to become operative it is necessary that there should be a physical event which evokes it. Instances of such doer-memories are feats of instantaneous calculation, the flashing in of musical themes and the conception of plans for business and management of affairs. All persons who show abilities beyond routine, training and mere skill, have at times doer-memories, which are the basis of inspirations and of extraordinary accomplishments. Writers, composers, inventors, statesmen or soldiers who stand out from the mass of their associates have doer-memories which aid them; this is psycho-mental memory.

To the fourth branch of doer-memory belong memories which come to one suddenly, whether he is alone or in a throng, and make him conscious of his own identity apart from the present. They bring a state of isolation, serenity and exaltation. This is a rare occurrence and does not usually last more than a few moments. But it leaves one with a sense of permanence among the changing forms and shifting scenes of life; this is psycho-noetic memory.

Memories of the third and the fourth kinds do not appear as what is called memories, that is, the recognition of former states, as do the memories of the first and the second kinds. The memories of feelings and desires require a stimulus from sensuous events, which are like the feelings and desires, whereas the memories brought about by the thinker require events which become subjects of thought. Ordinarily no distinction is made and all memories seem to be of the same kind.

After death the impressions made during the life by the four senses remain on the breath-form. The impressions or symbolic signatures, the magic records of thoughts, remain on the breath-form and also on the non-dimensional aia itself. The solid parts, the brain, the nerves, the four systems and the astral-airy-fluid parts are gone and dissipated. Only the senses, with the breath-form, remain. The breath-form reproduces to the doer portion that was dwelling in the human, in the after-death states, the events of his past life. These reproductions are memories. Some of them help to make the hell of the human. Some aid in realizing the ideals which are his heaven. During the hell state those memories which cannot enter heaven, are burnt off the breath-form. That is one of the purposes hell accomplishes. At the end of the heaven period the breath leaves the breath-form; the form lets go of the senses and their memories, which are dissipated, and all that remains in the doer portion is the aia and the form of the breath-form which is inactive and at rest, The doer portion is in a state of rest. The aia is without dimension. It carries no impressions which had been made by the senses on the breath-form, but it carries in potency the magic signatures made by thoughts. When there is a re-existence of that doer portion, some of these signatures will become actual when the aia revivifies the form of the breath-form, which had been inactive, and relinks it to its breath, and it is the same breath-form unit or living soul for the next existence on earth.

SECTION 16

Why it is fortunate that the human does not remember previous existences. The training of the doer. A human thinks of himself as a body with a name. To be conscious of and as. The false "I" and its illusions.

From the causes and the nature of memory it becomes at once apparent why past lives are not remembered by the re-existing portion of the doer, and why it is that such memories are not necessary for the education of the doer.

The reason why people do not remember the events of their past lives is that the records that the senses made of these events on the breath-form, are destroyed before the doer portion returns to life.

By doer-memory alone, that is, without the aid of sense-memory, the human cannot remember the events of past lives. Doer-memories are not concerned with events, but only with the states which these events produced, that is, with the feelings, desires, mental activities, faith, conscience or illumination. The human does not know how these states come, but he recognizes them when they do come. They are memories of these states in past lives of the doer portion. The doer is frequently reproducing its own states of former lives, but because the means for sense-memory have been wiped out, the human has nothing by which he can identify the states with the events that caused them. The states caused by the impressions of the former life, the doer portion may have, but the state is the result, not the memory, of the event in the former life.

There are instances of persons remembering something of a past life. They do not remember the whole life as they do a great part of the present, but see only a figure, a street, a gate, a room, a valley. The scenes do not follow one another consecutively, though there is sometimes a connection between several scenes.

Beside the flashing up of such unarticulated scenes, there are sometimes memories of events in which persons are in action. Then more appears than mere pictures. The events bring not only the sight of changing scenes and actions, but with them may come the hearing of sounds and the feeling of pleasure, fear or hate. These scenes or events must produce some feeling and desire, and the doer must identify itself as having some relation to the persons, places or events in them, for them to be classed as memories. Many persons have some such flashes, but even if these cause a feeling, they are not usually related by the doer to itself and so are not felt as memories. The people who believe these flashes to be memories, are such as are responsive to impressions and have a tendency to clairvoyant perceptions. They have such memories also when cycling thoughts cause doer states to be quickened into life as memories and some passing event is identified.

The manner in which these three classes of memories of scenes and events are brought about differs. Similar or associated events can evoke them because, although the old breath-form became inert, the impression was still on the aia and preserved in the psychic atmosphere of the doer and was transferred to the new breath-form. Then from that impression can be worked a sense-memory of a scene or event which caused the impression. When there is such a memory it is at once distinguished as something which is foreign to the present life and yet is intimate. Thoughts cycling in the mental atmosphere stir it up and may cause the recurrence of doer states as memories.

In the third class which is quite different, the doer experiences something which has no connection with nor finds corroboration in any event of the present life. The doer, stirred by a thought related to an occurrence in a former life, compels one or more of the senses to reproduce the event from the doer state and the thought. The senses manufacture from the feeling and from the thought a new event similar to the other. This new event is felt to be a memory and is identified with that which took place in the past and of which it is a counterpart.

Many persons claim to remember past lives, even if they have only momentary glimpses, without completeness and orientation. Still greater is the number of those who see nothing, but may persuade themselves that their fabrications are memories of past lives.

It is fortunate for the doer that the memories of the events of its past lives in human bodies are not with it in the present existence, for the education of the doer could not be accomplished if the human being could remember. If the doer did remember these events, it would be conscious of what it had done in the former personality. To be so conscious would be due to a continuance of the memories of the environments and conditions and of what the personality then did and suffered. It would necessitate access to the marks on the breath-form, which are dissipated when the personality is broken up after death. Many persons fear that they may lose that personality; they will surely lose it, but there is no more reason to fear or regret that loss, than there is reason to fear the loss of a worn-out suit of clothes. What makes the human conscious that he is the same personality during any one life, is due partly to the record of the acts and events engraved upon the breath-form, and partly to the feeling of the unbroken identity of the I-ness of the knower of the Triune Self. Both these factors are necessary to give the human being a sense of being one and the same throughout life; the presence of I-ness which is felt by the human, enables him to connect the memories with the name of the body and to identify them from the symbols on the breath-form. When these symbols are lost, the feeling of the presence of I-ness is not strong enough to make one conscious of one-and-the-sameness.

A person remembering past lives would carry too great a burden of past events to have any freedom of action. He would be ashamed of his meanness, foolishness, hypocrisy, licentiousness, cruelty and crimes. He would be humiliated by the positions or situations in which he had found himself, or he might be carried away with egotism because of the characters as which he has figured, and might be filled with arrogance and puffed up with pride. He might be dominated by greed to acquire again the riches and power once possessed. The memory of comfort and distinction which once had been his might make present hardships quite unbearable. He might be blasted by despair at the vainness of his efforts to overcome destiny. Worst of all, future destiny would be revealed to him by some of the memories. He would be unable to do the duties of the present moment, which is as much as he should be concerned with. He might try to run away from destiny or rush into it instead of meeting it as he should. He could not pass through temptations which are tests necessary for the development of the doer. Knowing the outcome beforehand he would not be tempted, and so would fail to get the training and tempering of character and the strength which overcoming the temptation can give. In any case memory is not necessary for the education of the doer.

The education of the doer is a progress towards the state where it becomes a free and perfected doer. This development of the doer proceeds under the Light of the Intelligence and is attained by means of repeated re-existences of the portions of the doer in human bodies. The doer learns something as the result of each existence of its various portions. Life on the common ground and experiences from the senses are the means used for the training. The education goes on, not in the senses but in the doer itself, as it learns through its embodied portions from experiences. The education goes on without sense-memory, though the experiences are interlinked with sense memories. Therefore, it is not necessary that one should bring into the present life memories of the events of past lives.

Doer-memory, however, is necessary for the education. Doer-memories are states of feeling-and-desire, of mental attitudes and abilities and of I-ness and selfness. These states exist apart from any objects that might bring them into play, and they represent the results of experiences through objects. These doer-memories continue from past lives and they exist even in the present life apart from the experiences of which they are the result. One remembers the multiplication table without the memory of how it was learned. One has the capacity to read and yet does not remember the processes by which he acquired it. Some can use foreign languages, but do not remember how they learned them, especially if they did so during childhood. What they remember is a doer-memory, which appears as an ability. There is a gap between the repetition of the sound seven times three are twenty-one which the boy had made with the body-mind, and the understanding by the man that seven times three make twenty-one. The repetition of the arithmetical formula made sense-memory, but the present ability to command the information contained in it, is doer-memory. The sense-memory of the repetitions is gone, but the doer-memory remains as the ability to use the results without the aid of the sense-memory. So it is with the knowledge of foreign tongues or with economic and ethical beliefs, as that one cannot benefit others without advancing himself or harm others without a disadvantage to himself or that a gentleman has self-control, integrity, honor, manners, and consideration for the rights of others. Such abilities and convictions are present, but the details from which they resulted in the past or the present life are not remembered. The education of the doer is furthered by such learning, which is retained as a doer-memory. Just as the doer-memory of incidents in the present life remains when the sense-memory of these events can no longer be recalled, so can it be available to that doer portion when it next exists.

The character with which a person is born and the traits brought out in the course of life, his endowments, abilities and tendencies are doer-memories. On them he builds with doer-memories of sense impressions.

The development of a doer portion is determined by its ability to do the right thing at the right time, regardless of memory of what has gone before. There are twelve doer portions which re-exist, each in its turn. The portion which re-exists was the next in turn and is guided by its ruling thought, which brings back doer-memories as feelings, as desires and as mental attitudes. This portion of the doer is embodied by attaching itself to its stations and organs as they mature and as the human being grows up. At first little, then more and in old age usually less, of the selected portion is connected with the body. Development of the organs and outside influences affect the functioning of the embodied portion of the doer. Hence the outlook upon life changes. A child, a schoolboy, a married person, a business man, and an old man or woman, all take different views of things. Notwithstanding the limitations as to the varying amount and functioning of the embodied portion of the doer, the education of the doer is carried on by the Light of the Intelligence.

The embodied portion of the doer is drugged by the body and intoxicated by the senses. While this condition exists there is no full communication between the portion in the body and the eleven portions that are not in the body, but there is nevertheless a relation. What the embodied portion does or suffers affects of course the portions not embodied. The body as a whole is improved or retarded by what is done through the body by its embodied portion.

Though only one portion of a doer is in the stations and organs, yet at times of passion or excitement, or at times of fear or hope, or of egotism or illumination, there is a surcharge. This comes from the non-existing portions. When there is a tension, more of the doer can be contained in the body than in the normal state, and in disease or enfeeblement less is present.

The embodied portion is the only means by which the doer comes into relation with the common ground. This in itself might explain why the progress of doers is slow; but more telling is the fact that the interiorizations which come through that small portion in the body do not go far. They do not usually go beyond gross feeling-and-desire, because all that human beings usually care for is what they want and whether things are pleasant or unpleasant. Therefore no mental results are attained beyond skill in procuring the things they want. Because the interiorizations do not produce mental results of learning, humanity has been slumming for millions of years. Nevertheless, training is accomplished by the Light of the Intelligence.

There are indications of the interrelation of the embodied portion of the doer with the thinker and knower. The most familiar is the voice of conscience as it warns against or forbids desires. Other instances are that at times in critical conditions, as of trial, disaster or revolution, one may feel an influx of light or power, rise above his ordinary condition and become a captain of the crowd of which he was but one; that at times while reading a book, something in a scene or event mentioned may cause one to identify himself with a similar scene or event, though he has never been connected with anything of the kind in the present life; that in silent moments one may become conscious as a being totally different from that of the human being of feelings and desires as which be usually exists; that at times one may become conscious of things that have nothing to do with the senses; that on rare occasions one is illuminated, the present disappears without leaving any sensation, ecstasy or exaltation and there is a calm, serene, comprehensive and conscious feeling beyond the senses; and that in rare cases one may be conscious of an identity, which is beyond his feeling of identity and is before and beyond time.

Because of these interrelations the experiences kept as doer-memories by the non-existing portions are made by the Light of the Intelligence to educate the embodied portion gradually and so train the doer. As the human advances, more of the doer can come in, until in a perfect body all twelve portions of the doer can, in turn, come in. Then the doer is conscious as the entire doer part of the Triune Self.

The training goes on not only without a memory of the events of past lives and although different portions of the doer re-exist in its successive human beings, but even though the human has a false identity and does not know who he is.

The human has a name in the world and thinks of himself as the being having that name. He is conscious of a continuity of himself as a being having that name; he is conscious that his personality persists, at least, from birth till death. Usually not much of an examination is made to find out who this being is or how be is composed and of what. He is composed first, of a radiant-airy-fluid-solid physical body; second, of the four senses which maintain this fourfold body and connect it with and relate it to nature; third, of the breath-form which exists in the involuntary nervous system, gives form to the astral body, coordinates and operates the four systems and the movements of the physical body and is the link between nature and the doer. These three altogether make up the personality. And fourth, there is the re-existing portion of the doer. In addition there is present Light of the Intelligence which the doer receives and which it sends out into and reclaims from nature. Only the solid part of the physical body is visible; to that the name is attached and with that the human is identified and identifies himself.

No distinction is made between the invisible parts. They are held to belong to the visible, as these are the only parts perceptible. Erroneous and inaccurate notions obtain concerning the invisible. So the breath-form is mistakenly called the subconscious mind or the subconscious self; the astral body is spoken of as the soul, or its functions are mistaken for those of the breath-form; the four senses are not looked upon as separate beings, but are called functions of organs; feeling, an aspect of the doer itself, is called a fifth sense; and gross ignorance exists concerning the "mind".

The human is conscious, he is conscious that he is conscious and so he is conscious of having an identity, the one that is related to the body to which the name is attached and which the human speaks of as himself. But that identity, while some sort of an identity, is not the real one. It is a fact that he is conscious of something he calls "I", but his understanding of it and his feeling of it are self-deceptions, and if he looks for it he does not find it at once. Each physical cell is a conscious unit, it is conscious *as* its functions; each unit of astral, of airy, of fluid and of solid matter making up the fourfold body, is conscious in the same way, that is, conscious *as* its function; each sense is conscious *as* its function. The embodied portion of the doer which is intelligent-matter and no longer nature-matter, is conscious in a different way. It is conscious *of* its functions, but it is also conscious that it is conscious. No nature unit can be so conscious.

The embodied portion of the doer is conscious *of* itself as feeling, that it feels, and is conscious *of* the impressions of seeing, hearing, tasting, smelling and being in contact. It is conscious that it desires to feel these impressions. It is conscious that this feeling and desiring is pleasant or unpleasant. The impressions made upon feeling-and-desire are translated by thinking into descriptive terms usable by feeling or desire. Without the thinking there could be no appreciation of things, aside from their grossest impressions.

Events affect the doer when the sense transmits to feeling the impressions received through the sense organ. These impressions are taken by desire and are transferred to rightness. From there they are translated into descriptive terms, such as bright, broad, noisy, rhythmic, bitter, fragrant, hot, soft; and neglect, quarrel, delicacy, affection, kindness, sympathy, play. Not only impressions brought in by the senses but also reactions of the doer to phenomena of nature and to human actions are separated, arranged, classed and described by thinking. Feeling and desire simply get impressions and react to them. This can be seen in the effect which a bunch of cornstalks or a red cloth has upon a bull. The reactions in a human would be just as unintelligent if he did not think. Emotions of love and anger would be as crude and wild and without sentiment as in the case of an animal. The psychic refinements of preference, sentiment, passion, luxuriousness, fear, suffering or grief are due to the service which the mind renders to the doer.

The doer is susceptible to all these because it can think, but this does not give it a perception of one-and-the-same-ness, permanence, endlessness. Yet the doer, while not conscious *as* this continuity, has a vague feeling that there is this continuity somewhere, and desires to be it. That the embodied portion of the doer and the contacting portion of the thinker are both conscious *of* themselves, conscious *of* identity, is due to the presence of the knower, which gives them this feeling and understanding of continuity and one-and-the-same-ness in their essence.

The thinker is conscious *as* this continuity. The thinker and the knower are as one. The doer is not in communication with the thinker, or with the knower; it cannot distinguish itself from nature or from the senses, *as* what it is. When it tries to think of itself *as* a continuity and one-and-the-same-ness, it has a feeling *of* identity and desires to have or to be this identity. It gets no further than this feeling and this desire, which come through the feeling-mind and the desire-mind. Their thinking does not reach the knower, but because they are connected with the thinker, they communicate the presence of identity to feeling-and-desire. Because of the presence of identity the doer thinks about it and attaches that to the desired feeling of continuity of the personality having the name. This feeling is a false "I". Thus the thinking with the body-mind deludes the human, to satisfy the desire with the thought and the feeling of identity as the personality.

The contacting portion of the knower is conscious *as* I-ness and *as* selfness and is conscious *of* the embodied portion of the doer. I-ness, as the identity, extends without limit through time; it has no beginning and no end. It is an unbroken continuity. Selfness is that aspect of the knower which knows it is knowledge, and knows not merely *of* the continuity and sequence of events through time, but all things *as* they are and at once. It knows the sum of the memories of its doer as its psychic part and of its thinker as its mental part. It knows not only what it as a Triune Self has done, but what all other Triune Selves have done, and has part in the sum of knowledge which is common to all Triune Selves. As I-ness and selfness, the knower knows itself in endlessness. The knower is the real "I" and the real Self.

The human is conscious *of* his feeling-and-desire; he is conscious *of* his mental activity and that he can in a way use it at will for thinking, but he is not conscious of any of the things that the knower is conscious *as* or knows. However, the knower is the source of identity in the human. The doer and the thinker have aspects of the knower, because the Triune Self is One. The presence of I-ness produces in the thinker an intimacy with and an appreciation of I-ness; and in the doer it produces a reflection, a feeling of I-ness and a desire for Self-knowledge. This causes the fabrication of the false "I" by the body-mind. So the human thinks himself to be "I" and feels himself to be "I".

Therefore he says "I see", "I hear", "I move", "I feel pleasure", and feels himself *as* an "I" that does this. This "I" is attached to the body with its name. The human is ignorant of how he comes to this conception of "I". The thought is erroneous and is furnished by the body-mind under the lure of the senses and the pressure of desire. When the human says

"I feel", "I think", the "I" is again a false "I", furnished by the thought to satisfy the feeling which wants to be "I"-ness; and this illusion is strengthened by links of memory, the memories of acts and events, conditions and places.

The test of what this "I" of the human being is, is found in what he is conscious *as*. He is conscious usually *as* feelings and desires, not even as a mind, and certainly not as reason or rightness.

The false "I" is the feeling, feeling the presence of the real "I" of the knower. The doer feeling itself as the "I" is under an illusion, and it is unconscious that the illusion is due to a thought created by thinking to satisfy the craving of desire itself to have identity as "I". When the human thinks, he is conscious *of* the thinking, but not *as* thinking. He is at times conscious *of* the presence of the real "I", but not *as* the real "I". So he feels that he has an identity, that he is the same human being he was a week or a year ago. But he does not locate this identity, which remains a mystery to him, because he does not communicate with the knower.

The false "I" is real, but only as feeling-and-desire and as the ability to think; it is not real as I-ness. Because real things are back of the illusion, these real things, which are the embodied portion of the doer and its psychic atmosphere with its doer-memories, can be reached; and so the human can be trained even through the false "I". Whatever happens to the false "I" affects some reality behind it. Pleasure, disease, intoxication, injury and comfort of the human go beyond the illusion of the false "I" and reach the non-embodied portions of the doer. The effect they produce there lasts longer than the earth life and longer than the lines on the breath-form and the sense-memories that these make. The effect is experience. The experiences which come through the existing portion of the doer help to produce the character of the psychic atmosphere and the qualities of the doer, and their record in the noetic atmosphere is the knowledge which speaks as conscience.

Continued pressure, troubles, hardships, pain and discomfort which are experienced through physical destiny, train the doer along moral lines away from indifference, selfishness, hatred, bigotry and malice, toward patience, sympathy and goodwill. Doer-memories of these states come from the psychic atmosphere as feelings and desires to the human. Feelings of or desires for generosity, patience, sympathy and goodwill that come over a man are doer-memories of states through which the re-existing portion of the doer has passed in the lives of its former personalities. This is one branch of the training of the doer and relates to a man's attitude towards others.

There is another branch, which relates to his attitude towards himself. This attitude also is the result of doer-memories in the psychic atmosphere. So there will come, because of the doer-memories that have accumulated, a time when there is a feeling in the human that he is not what he feels himself to be, and this starts the desire to be shown what he really is and what is that identity or "I" which he feels. Gradually, thinking, always at the service of feeling-and-desire, will make it clear that the identity is quite different from feeling-and-desire; that feeling-and-desire may be conscious *of* I-ness but not *as* I-ness, that the identity is with and in I-ness of the Triune Self and not with feeling-and-desire.

In the meantime the general training of the doer can go on, because the events affecting the human being and its false "I" affect the indwelling portion of the doer and then the non-embodied portions and also its psychic and mental atmospheres.

The run of human beings do not make an effort to find out who and what they are. They do not even think that their personalities are not the entities they believe them to be. Yet the education of the doers goes on. It goes on though they do not know of it any more than they know of the involuntary processes which maintain their bodies, digest their food and circulate their blood. The education goes on whether they wish it or not. The doer-memories, without the events that caused them, are preserved. In the run of human beings the learning is small, very small, still they learn a little.

The doer in each human without knowing its predecessors inherits from them the sum of the memories of their experiences and makes its way through life with this inheritance. The continuity relates to doer-memories, not to whether its human beings are conscious of or as each other.

SECTION 17

When re-existences of a doer portion stop. A "lost" doer portion. The hells inside the earth crust. The lecherous. The drunkards. Drug fiends. The state of a "lost" doer. Regenerating the physical body. The test in which the doers failed.

The re-existences of a doer portion stop either when the Light of the Intelligence is withdrawn from the mental atmosphere of the doer portion or when the physical body becomes immortal.

When the Light of the Intelligence is withdrawn in certain cases from the mental atmosphere of the doer-in-the-body, the doer has been spoken of as a "lost soul". The doer cannot be lost. What is called a "lost soul" is only that portion of the doer which was in a human body and felt itself as the human being at the time when the Light was withdrawn. The withdrawal of the Light happens during life, never after death.

The lost portion of the doer, during the remainder of its life in the body, can think, but only along the lines on which it has worked in the past, and which are on the breath-form. Conscience does not speak. Light remains in the noetic atmosphere, but the portion of the knower that was in contact has withdrawn, and with it goes the reflected feeling of identity. The body-mind which was with the embodied portion of the doer is still there, but it has no moral understanding. The non-embodied portions of the doer remain as they were.

There are two kinds of lost doers: the intellectual, from whom the Light is withdrawn, and the animal kind, who have wasted the available Light. The first kind are those who have misused the Light for intense selfishness, meanness, enmity or injury to human beings, who have used their intellectual powers and developed them, but sacrificed the interests or lives of others to their own; their feeling-mind and desire-mind are barely in contact with the lines already on the breath-form. The animal kind are those who have had pleasure to excess, abandoned themselves to unrestrained indulgences and so have wasted the Light through many lives, until there is no more to be allotted to them. The contact with the thinker of the Triune Self is broken, and the being acts under pressure of its own past desires and of lower elementary creatures which swarm around it.

After death the connection of the breath-form with a lost doer is dissipated at once and there is no judgment, no hell and no heaven. The lost doer portion obstructs the regular order of re-existences, but those portions which were in turn to re-exist may or may not re-exist until the lost portion again continues to re-exist. The portion that was embodied is cut off from communication with the other portions and with the psychic atmosphere, and it may or may not pass into the bodies of certain animals.

A lost doer portion of either the intellectual or the animal kind may re-exist once more in a human form. Then the intellectual kind will be enemies of humanity; the animal kind will be born idiots. But thereafter neither kind will appear again in human form for a long period.

A difference between natural animals in which are the cast-off desires of the common run of human beings, and the animals in which are lost doer portions, is that the desires in natural animals return to—in reality they never leave—the psychic atmosphere of the doer when they are summoned for re-existence in a human being of that doer; but lost doer portions are cut off from communication with their atmospheres. Another difference is that the natural animals feel at home in their animal bodies, whereas an animal in which is a lost doer portion feels that it is not natural, and the natural animals are aware of the difference. The natural animals do not want an animal in which is a lost doer portion. Since the natural animals are the stronger they drive out the one with the lost doer portion which is such from self-indulgence; but they run away from the other, the devilish kind, or they kill it for self-protection. The lost doer portions in animal bodies are in continual fear; of what, they do not know; and they are desires which cannot be appeased. Their hunger is as intense with a full stomach as with an empty one.

Those lost doer portions from whom the Light was withdrawn because of their meanness, viciousness and ill-will, continue to animate certain kinds of ferocious animals like vampire bats, sharks, certain apes and large poisonous spiders. Upon the death of these bodies they go into others of a like kind. After a time they are retired into sections inside the earth crust where they are segregated in special places. There these fiends have no physical bodies, but they have their abnormal forms of concentrated miserliness, vindictiveness, cruelty and enmity expressed in animal-like types. These forms are at times visible and at other times invisible. They are visible when the creatures are active, and invisible when their active malice ceases. Having nothing else to prey upon or to injure, they fall upon each other, look for each other and escape from each other. They cannot kill each other, though they seem to. When one seizes another and overcomes it, activity continues until both are exhausted and the exhaustion takes the place of death and disappearance.

Lost doer portions of the other kind, those who have wasted all the Light allotted to them, life after life, in pleasure, eating and sex, drink and narcotics, without giving more return and service than was forced from them, go into the bodies of animals which are more or less harmless, such as some monkeys, pigs or snakes, according to their nature. After the death of one body they live in another body of the same kind. Then they are put into places inside the earth crust where they swarm, having forms not physical, which express their real characters. These forms are alternately visible and invisible. When the creatures are active their bodies are visible, when dormant they lose their shapes and these fade into the scenery of plants and rocks. No two bodies are alike in the horrible assemblies. Those who sinned by gluttony are generally in the forms of mere mouths and stomachs, distended, misshapen, scoop-like. They are only hunger. When something to eat appears to them they work themselves up to it and make a gulp or a scoop at it, but they remain unsatisfied.

Lecherous ones are in the most disgusting male and female forms, from a few to many feet long. At certain periods they become active, chase each other, affect the atmosphere so as to cause vile odors, and they unite by absorbing each other. In their orgies they groan and howl. They continue until exhausted. There never is any satisfaction. Then they become inactive and thereby invisible.

Drunkards are in spongelike bodies that are mostly heads, misshapen and disproportionate. In their periods of activity they roll or hop, if able, and burn for drink. They beg, all yelling at the same time and tell their inane story. Then drink appears in whatever form they desire. They drag themselves towards it. Some never reach it. Others drink and drink and drink, but the drinking does not quench their thirst, nor does it affect them except to make them burn for it still more. Then drink appears somewhere else and they scramble over each other to it, but get no satisfaction. They cease when they are exhausted. Then they become invisible. Deathlike silence prevails. They become active and, with their yelling for drink, the empty show starts again. If a human being could hear any one of them, the nerves in his body could be shattered and he might become insane.

Drug fiends are in another section. Their bodies have a human form, but with hands like spiders' claws and leaden faces, hideous with staring and searching. They want to be taken out of themselves and be put into some other place. Some want to sleep, some want excitement, some want beautiful things. None of them gets anything of the kind. They keep on taking their drugs but no result follows. Their expectation is at the same time a disappointment. The drugs produce no effects. They shout out their execrations and, when annihilated by their vain efforts, they become invisible. After a rest they reappear and re-enact these scenes.

These are a few indications of the shapes, of the practices during the active periods, of the inanity of these practices, of the lack of satisfaction, of the continued burning of the desires; and of the localities, desolate and fearful, in which lost doer portions are in sections set apart for them near the outer earth crust. The cases and their conditions are numerous, varied and unmentionable. When the lost creatures are not active and are therefore silent and invisible the atmosphere is frightful. Even elementals, which are thrilled at human pain and suffering, shun these places.

The conditions in which lost doers are, are different from the hells in which human beings suffer after their death. Hells are individual and for one person alone, but lost doers are usually in communities. A hell is of short duration as compared with the state of the lost doer, for when the desires are separated and the breath-form is cleansed there is an end to the hell, but lost doers continue in that state for what is by comparison an enormous period. The suffering in hell is of a different nature; it is human suffering, whereas lost doers have an unnatural, hardened, distorted suffering, for they have lost their humanity.

Lost doer portions are conscious that they are lost. There is more fear in that than there is in their suffering. They have no feeling of "I", but they feel the lack of it and they have an unappeased desire to have that feeling. They do not remember, but they try to remember. They are not in that state as a punishment, but merely as a result of their long continued actions as human beings. Their state of lost doers is necessary to stop their downward course. When they get to a certain point in that course they are so low that they cannot pick themselves up again. Their being in this state serves two purposes. It continues until the feeling and desire for their special activities is exhausted or as near exhaustion as is possible, and until they get the impression that their practices result in suffering and disappointment and that they can never be satisfied. Then these lost doer portions are taken back into the psychic and the mental atmospheres of the doer. The length of time necessary for them to reach that state of exhaustion and to be impressed cannot be computed in actual time, though it seems to be for ages.

However, no portion of the doer can be forever lost, because the Triune Self is One. The term "lost" doer is apt because the loneliness and abandonment are so real to the lost doer portion and lasts so long. At some time, when the exhaustion and disappointments have done their work and the seemingly separated portion of the doer is impressed sufficiently, the Triune Self will again allow that portion to have Light. The somnolent condition in which the other eleven portions of the doer were while there was no Light, and the rest they have taken, will have enabled the lost doer portion to begin again and to correct the tendencies which resulted in the loss. Then the lost portion is taken back into the doer and when the turn to re-exist comes for that portion, the aia vivifies the breath-form and a new set of re-embodiments of the doer begins.

The orderly and the proper way for the doer to end its re-existences is, to regenerate and make its physical body immortal. Then the doer portions which had existed successively, will each have added to the improvement of the body so as to make it immortal.

It would have been unnecessary for the doer to re-exist in human bodies if it had passed the test which it was obligatory for all doers to go through. It was, and is, the regular and proper thing to do. Those doers who act according to plan, make their Triune Selves complete. They in orderly accomplishment become Intelligences.

However, this book is particularly concerned with humanity—composed of doers that failed in that test and therefore came into the human world. The failure was that the desire-and-feeling of each such doer in its man and woman bodies had sexual union, instead of inseparable union of desire-and-feeling, which is part of its training.

The purpose of the test was for the doer to become immune to sexuality, and thereby to cause the two bodies to rebecome the immortal body, which body the doer had inherited from the Triune Self in that body.

That immortal body was perfect in form, structure, adjustment and function. It had four brains and two columns, the column for nature in front and the column for the Triune Self in the back, curved and united in the pelvis and opening into the head, (Fig. VI-D). The organs and fluids in the body were in a state of sublimation. The body was made up of refined and balanced units of the four states of the physical plane. It was in the interior of the earth and was nourished not by the kind of food that humans take, but by essences from the four elements breathed directly into itself. This was more satisfying to the sense of taste than food can possibly be to the human and was one of the means by which the doer's excellence of form was attained.

This perfect body was in touch and in tune with the whole of the physical, the form, the life and the light worlds. Through this body the doer of the Triune Self could reach into and work in any part of the worlds. The organs in the body were adjusted to each other so that they worked in harmony in the whole organization. They were further adjusted to the states of matter on the physical plane and on the other planes of the physical world. They were likewise adjusted to the matter in the other three worlds. Therefore the matter in the four worlds responded to the action of the senses, nerves, glands, organs and systems of the body.

The functioning of such a body cannot be readily comprehended by human beings of today. No obstacles of time, of distance or of any kind could stand in the way of its functioning. The four senses had free range in all the worlds, and so the doers could reach and could work with any unit or any number of units anywhere. They could evoke, move and direct the forces of nature. They could create and dissipate forms and bodies anywhere.

Though the body was not subject to injury and death and had powers which were unlimited, it had come to be in that state not by any merit of its own, but as the instrument made so by the indwelling doer. It was perfect only so long as the doer that used it was perfect. The doer had yet to pass the test above mentioned. The doers now in human bodies failed in that test.

Since the bodies have been degraded by the re-existing doers from this former state of purity and power to the present state of disease and impotence, they must be raised again to their former state. The state of the body is the measure of the condition of the doer portion that inhabits it. To raise their bodies the doer portions must first improve themselves. The re-existences of a doer portion continue until the body it inhabits has been improved by the action of all twelve doer portions, so as to make that body immortal. The body has no desire of its own, and of itself cannot improve. It is made of nature-matter, is representative of nature and is concentrated nature. It is the instrument of the doer and is a record of the actions of the indwelling doer portion. When the body has again become immortal, that means therefore that the doer has made itself perfect and thereby has made the body perfect and immortal.

There is a long course ahead of the run of human beings before they cease to be mere human beings and become conscious as doers in bodies. They must reclaim the Light loaned to them and outstanding in nature. They must rebuild the front-column and at the base build a bridge connecting it with the spinal column, (Fig. VI-D). They must improve their bodies so that the sexual organs will disappear, and must transform what are now nerves and ganglia spread about the pelvic cavity, into parts of a pelvic brain, so that the breath-form will be located at the blending of the two columns, where it belongs, not as it is now in the front half of the pituitary body, where it ought not to lodge and where it interferes with the contact with I-ness. They must so temper the physical body in the forces of nature that nature can no longer have any control of it. The doer, the thinker, and the knower will be in the body, in their proper stations, in the spinal cord, instead of the doer being in the kidneys and adrenals, the thinker merely contacting the heart and the lungs, and the knower merely contacting the pituitary and pineal bodies intermittently. The three atmospheres of the Triune Self will be absorbed into the doer, the thinker and the knower. These three parts will act through three inner beings, each emerging immaculately from, or all acting through, the perfected physical body. Then in the perfect physical body there is the form being for the doer part, which is the vehicle for the life being and for the thinker, which is the vehicle for the light being and the knower of the Triune Self. In the physical body then is the Triune Self by means of its three inner beings. Light will be again with the doer from which it was absent for so long. Light will be in the three beings of the Triune Self and in the physical body. All the Light that was loaned to the doer will be ready to be restored to the parent Intelligence. The Triune Self will be ready to become an Intelligence and to raise its aia to be a Triune Self.

SECTION 18

Summary of preceding chapters. Consciousness is the One Reality. Man as the center of the world of time. Circulations of the units. Permanent institutions. Records of thoughts are made in points. The destiny of human beings is written in the starry spaces. Balancing a thought. Cycles of thinking. Glamour in which things are seen. Sensations are elementals. Why nature seeks the doer. Illusions. The essential things in life.

To review some preceding statements: Consciousness is the ultimate Reality; compared with it, all else is illusion, (Fig. VII-A). Therefore: Unmoving Motion, which causes homogeneous Substance to put forth into manifestation as the manifested, is an illusion. Substance is space, no thing, is nothingness, is illusion. From out of the quiescence of Substance comes the manifested. This is unqualified spirit or force, activity, made up of indestructible units, and is the sphere of fire, (Fig. I-A). It is One, and it is the source of all things manifested as nature. This sphere is the ultimate reality which human beings can conceive of as nature. Yet, it is an illusion—as compared with Consciousness.

In the sphere of fire the manifestation continues as activity of the indivisible units until an unexpressed aspect of certain ones of them begins to express passivity. So duality begins. The units so expressing are of a dual nature, one part of each unit being activity, spirit, force, and the other passivity. This is the sphere of air. There activity dominates passivity until among the mass are units in which passivity begins to dominate activity. This is the sphere of water. Among these units are some where passivity only is manifested and the active side is at rest. This is the sphere of earth, inertia. These four spheres are illusions as compared to Consciousness, the ultimate Reality. The spheres are permanent institutions for the passage of the units according to the Eternal Order of Progression, (Fig. II-G, H).

In the manifested side of the sphere of earth, certain of the units in the inertia become active as Light; the passive side of the units is not expressed. They are somewhat passive as compared with the activity of the fire sphere, yet have a potential double aspect. They make the light world, which is a colorless sphere of shadowless light. In some of the units the passive side is expressed and they make the life world. In some of these the passive side dominates the active side; these units are the form world; and the physical world is made of units where the active side has disappeared into the passive. In the unmanifested part of the physical world the units so remain. In the manifested part of the physical world they repeat in a measure the previous progress downward and make the light, the life, the form and the physical planes. Further on they make on the physical plane four states and their substates and compose the realms of visible and tangible nature. Yet all is an illusion, as compared with Consciousness. (Fig I-B, C, D, E).

It is because of the presence of Consciousness that Motion acts on Substance and that Substance manifests gradually as the units of nature in the four spheres and worlds. Because of the presence of Consciousness the units progress through subsequent stages in nature.

In the Universe are four kinds of units, broadly divided into nature units, aia units, Triune Self units and Intelligence units.

Nature units are merely conscious. They are conscious *as* the particular function which they perform. They never cease to be conscious; even when they are inactive they perform their function of being inactivity. Some do not perform more than one function at a time. As they give up one they take up another. They never go backward to function in a state which they have passed. On the physical plane some of them, those in the four subdivisions of the solid state of matter, make up the objects of animate and inanimate nature. These objects are the grossest of the illusions. They are the universe.

Aia units are not conscious as the functions which they are made to perform by the thinking and the thoughts of their doers, but they bear the record of all the impressions made on them. They do not function unless they are impelled to by doers. They are out of reach of nature. Nature cannot touch and cannot compel the aia to function without the sanction of the doer, in thinking. The breath-form is a unit, a nature unit. The form of the breath-form is the form of the body, and the breath is the life of the breath-form and builder of the body. In these two aspects the breath-form is the builder of each physical body in all re-existences of the twelve portions of the doer.

Triune Self units are conscious as feeling-and-desire, rightness-and-reason, I-ness-and-selfness; nevertheless the Triune Self is One. As a unit, the Triune Self is conscious, not only *of* and *as* its function, but that it is conscious and knows that it is conscious of its Oneness, as a Triune Self.

An Intelligence unit is the last stage in which a unit is conscious as a unit. Intelligence units are conscious *as* their seven faculties and *of* themselves as Intelligences, as the Oneness of the seven. They are conscious as their Light which they lend to their Triune Selves, and which from the doers goes into nature, causes the units of the light world to appear as light and is the intelligence and order in nature and which is that of which some people speak as God. They are conscious in nature as that Light wherever it is, in rocks, plants, animals, human bodies and the gods of nature or of religions. Intelligences are conscious that they order universal nature; and, with complete Triune Selves, adjust the affairs of human beings according to the law of thought. These are the four classes of units.

By the presence of Consciousness an Intelligence of the highest degree may, when its Triune Self has become an Intelligence, leave the manifested and become Conscious Sameness. An Intelligence does not lose its individual intelligence when it becomes Conscious Sameness, but it ceases to act as only an Intelligence by becoming something beyond it. Sameness is unmanifested and is all that Substance was, but it is all-conscious as Sameness, whereas Substance was unconscious Substance. Conscious Sameness is conscious of being the same in and as every unit in the manifested. It is conscious as being in them and as their being in it. Yet it is conscious that it is not a being. An Intelligence is conscious of itself as a separate unit, and carries this to the highest degree of being one individual, though it is also conscious of all other Intelligences as units under the Supreme Intelligence which rules the four spheres. Sameness is conscious of itself as being one in the same degree as Intelligence was, but it is further conscious of being through all units of whatever kind and of their being in it. To Conscious Sameness the state of being conscious as Intelligence, even as the highest Intelligence, is an illusion.

Conscious Sameness becomes Pure Intelligence by the presence of Consciousness. An Intelligence is a name here used to designate the highest order of units, which are Intelligences, but Pure Intelligence does not designate any unit. To Pure Intelligence, Conscious Sameness is an illusion. Pure Intelligence is conscious in a higher degree than anything in the unmanifested that is not Consciousness itself. It is not conscious as being in all things and all things being in it. It is unaffected by anything except by the presence of Consciousness. To it even Conscious Sameness is an illusion, and to it Consciousness is the One Reality. Pure Intelligence is not power, but it enables all Triune Selves and Intelligences to have power according to their capacity to receive and to use it. It enables them to do this irrespective of the purpose for which they use the power. It decides one thing: to become Consciousness; then it appears to itself as an illusion.

The manifested Universe and its four spheres and all that is in them on the nature-side and on the intelligent-side are conscious units because of the presence of Consciousness. There are no planes, states, phases or degrees of Consciousness. Consciousness does not change. Units change according to the states in which they are conscious. Consciousness does nothing, causes nothing directly or indirectly, but by its presence all beings are enabled to be conscious and to change in the degrees in which they are conscious. Its presence in them makes them conscious *of* or *as* what they are. Consciousness cannot be apprehended by thinking of it as or comparing it with any matter, force, thing or being, or by thinking of it as performing any function. It is unmoved and unmoving, unattached and unattachable.

Consciousness is the One Reality, all else is in some degree illusion. Units below the Triune Self cannot distinguish between reality and illusion. The question of reality and illusion has no meaning to animals or to elementals. To them, things are. But a human can think, and therefore can distinguish what is illusion from what is reality—to it. Things are seen as realities on the plane on which one is. When one becomes conscious on a higher plane, the things on that plane are realities, and the realities of the plane on which that one was before become illusions.

A human is conscious of his four senses, of the things of the senses and of outside nature. He is conscious of feelings and desires, conscious of himself as a personality. He is not conscious *of* himself *as* the embodied doer portion. But he can become conscious *as* the doer, which he is, and *of* the thinker and the knower of his Triune Self. He can become conscious of anything he wants to think about. He can do this by feeling and desiring and by thinking. He can become conscious of anything in the world of change through the doer portion in his body. He has in him connections with everything. As all nature of the human world circulates through him, he can become conscious of that part which he feels and of which he thinks. He can become conscious *of* himself and *as* the doer, the psychic part of his Triune Self, by feeling and thinking *of* and *as* feeling-and-desire. He can become conscious *of* the thinker, the mental part, by feeling and thinking of rightness-and-reason. He can become conscious *of* the knower, the noetic part, by feeling and thinking of I-ness-and-selfness. All depends on what he desires to feel and to think about.

He may become conscious of any of these things, but there is that, by the becoming conscious of which, he will be enabled to reach all things through his thinking, because that is in and through all things and enables all things to function in whatever capacity: Consciousness. While still a human and far from the end of his journey, it is possible for one to become conscious of Consciousness by feeling and desiring and thinking of it.

A human does not last long. He appears and disappears. But the things which are his make-up continue after the combination has ceased to be visible. Each part, even to the least unit, has a continuity because of the presence of Consciousness. The unit changes, but it is never destroyed, because it is indivisible. It lasts as a unit until it has ceased to be an Intelligence and has become Conscious Sameness.

There is the same number of breath-form units as there are aia units and Triune Self units. The number of Intelligence units is greater, and the number of nature units is vastly greater. There is a steady slow progression all along the line which is no faster than the progress of the Triune Self in its course to become an Intelligence.

Thus nature units pass through human bodies and bring about the phenomena which give experiences to human beings. Units of the fire are present with units in the radiant state and enable the sense of sight to see, wood to burn, changes to occur. The presence of units of the air with units in the airy state enables the sense of hearing to hear, beings to fly and matter to take life. Water units with units in the fluid state enable the sense to taste, and matter to combine as a fluid, and to take form. Earth units with units in the solid state enable the sense to smell and to contact, and matter to concrete and to be tangible structure, and the breath-form unit to coordinate the functions of the body.

Nature units from the highest to the lowest never cease to function. If they are not active they function as the passive. There is no death for them. They cannot go back to where they came from.

Everything that is visible and tangible changes, but units remain the same units. They circulate from combination to combination, from phenomenon to phenomenon, as transient units. The structures of outside nature partake of the model of the human body and are built after it and specialize it in the various forms of animals and plants, all objectifying human thoughts.

The units which compose the four spheres and the four worlds are moving on, graduating, and becoming conscious in higher degrees, as their functions. But the spheres and worlds are permanent. They are permanent institutions, having a manifested side which remains always manifested. There are no periodic appearances of the spheres or the worlds.

The cyclic appearances and disappearances, called in Eastern literature manvantaras and pralayas, occur only in the four states of matter on the outer earth crust of the human world of change, (Fig. II-G). The objects there are made of the four kinds of compositors, here called causal, portal, form and structure units. They come from human bodies and are the builders of outside nature. These compositors compose transient fire, air, water and earth units which, if sufficiently massed together, make up the objects perceived by the senses. All these objects exist for a time only. The stars, the sun and the planets, the moon, and the land and water on the earth crust, are subject to this law of creation and dissolution or appearance and disappearance, as is a human body. The law is the law of thought. The fourfold earth remains, but the forms on the outer earth crust are according to the physical body of man, and that is determined by his thinking and his thoughts. The manvantaras and pralayas come and go only as long as the human body appears and dies. They are summations of the totality of human beings and exteriorizations of the thoughts of man. The visible world in which things appear and disappear, in which time signifies growth, decay and death, is surrounded and pervaded by permanence, (Fig. V-B,a). The nothingness, out of which visible things come and into which they go, means that the temporary combinations which made them visible, are dissolved for a time. The units that made them up and became visible because they were held as a mass in a form continue, though they are invisible as individual units, and can therefore not be traced into new combinations. The fact of a continuity as distinct from visibility escapes observation.

The run of human beings are acquainted with only a small part of the solid earth, the outer side of the earth crust and with those features there which they perceive through their four senses. They even perceive surfaces of units of the fourfold solid state only when these units are massed closely enough. If they are not so concreted there is nothing that can be seen, heard, tasted, smelled or contacted.

The four states of matter on the physical plane are arranged as follows, (Fig. I-E): Within a globe of radiant matter, there is the radiant-solid substate, which has in it the stars; within that globe is a globe of airy matter, which has in it the sun in the airy-solid state, and some planets; within the airy globe is a globe of fluid matter which has in it the moon in the fluid-solid state; and within the fluid globe is a globe of solid matter, which has in it the solid earth crust in the solid-solid state. The units of the solid state are penetrated by and are borne up by the units of the fluid state; the units of the fluid state are supported by those of the airy state and these by the units of the radiant state and these by units in the solid state of matter on the form plane. These bodies are not permanent; they will disappear when thinking and thoughts make them no longer necessary. The upheavals and destructions of large portions of the outer earth crust are the manvantaric days and nights mentioned in Eastern tradition.

Because of the limitations of on-ness, human beings cannot perceive the earthy, fluid, airy and fiery globes of the states of physical matter, or these globes as being on the inside as well as on the outside of the crust, or that inside and outside of the crust each globe is one and the same; nor can they perceive the functioning of the celestial bodies in these globes.

The run of human beings do not understand the make-up of their own bodies, or how they are a part of nature, the impersoned part as distinct from outside nature, or how the units in their bodies pass from there into outside nature and from there back into human bodies, or how some of the units are identified as belonging to certain human bodies. They know not how the compositor units go after death into the kingdoms of nature and compose transient units into plants and animals and are back again at the proper time to set up a human body, or how these compositor units build up the human body with transient units, or how the compositors so maintain, tear down and reconstruct the body during life. They do not know that a human body is a constantly flowing stream of transient units, visible only while passing through the compositors; or how a human body extends into rocks, winds, trees, animals, the moon, the sun and the stars. They do not know that the units that pass through the kidneys and adrenals go through the moon, and those that pass through the heart and lungs go through the sun, and those that pass through the nerves go through the stars and those that pass through the sexual organs go into the earth crust and the things thereon; nor do they know what the functions of the planets are in relation to the sun, the moon and the earth.

They do not comprehend how the transient units while passing through the body get from the breath-form an imprint which is a symbolic, a magic line; how these units while still in the body make a record in the starry spaces by making a symbolic figure, composed of the marks on them; how they later come back from distant and various objects to be among those units that produce the acts, objects and events to a human which are the projection of the symbolic figure as which the prior act, object and event were preserved.

While the transient units are in the body and so partake of an act, an object or an event they are at the same time making in the starry limits the symbolic figure by transmitting from the breath-form to the starry limits the marks made on them; they can so transmit because other units are not obstructions to them and do not interfere with the transmission. The inability of human beings to conceive how this is done is due to their being limited to the conceptions of on-ness and distance. But distance exists only for the transient units in the solid state, it does not exist in the same way for those in the fluid, airy and radiant states. While the solid units are in the body and in the physical atmosphere, they transmit through the fluid, airy and radiant units in them the symbolic marks which they receive, and these units at once transfer these marks to a point in the starry spaces, where at once a corresponding, not identical, act, object or event is represented.

If this were seen it would not appear as an act, an object or an event, but as a symbolic figure, made up of the marks which were impressed by the breath-form on the units in it at the time of the occurrence.

From this symbol in a point is made an obligatory recomposition and projection into a physical act, object or event. This recomposition is made naturally, easily, unfailingly, because of the automatic, harmonious action of the units which compose the four states of matter on the physical plane, and because behind the physical world are the other worlds which in the light world are completed as one whole.

If the intent or aim with which an act is done is in line with the original, no record is made in the physical world; but if the intent does not so coincide, a record of it is made in the physical world, is preserved in symbols at the limits of the physical plane, and a recomposition of that record into a physical act, object or event is compelled. The record shows at once what the act was and what is required to bring the aim with which the act was done into line with the whole. The recomposition is made by the symbolic record so that eventually the aim or thought will agree with the original. The cause and effect, which are one, become separated in manifestation. What is one in an upper world may thus become many physical acts and events. These are, however, connected in sequence by the original intent. Its veering away does not cause a disturbance in the light world, where there is wholeness and eternity, but it does cause disturbances in the physical world. For there its essence and its value are expressed in matter which wars within the limitations of time and place. This conflict, brought about by the intent, is regulated by means of its symbolic record, from which subsequent recompositions of all those acts are made which perpetuate the first one, until there is an adjustment.

The acts, objects and events which come to human beings as the return projected from the symbolic record, which is in a point in starry matter, may appear unlike those that were recorded. From the point may go out a projection that may spread over a large region, a country, a large part of the earth, and may affect many more people than took part in the original act. In the projection ·there is made an exchange of transient units, so that while the acts done are substantially the same, the persons who do them are not, and the persons who are affected are not the same ones as before. The same transient units take part, but their places are reversed. One who assaulted another will be injured in turn by someone. The transient units which were in him then, will now be in the other. The transient units that were in one when he acted with intent to defraud, steal, rob or corrupt will now be in another who causes him to be the victim. The compositor units of the former actor affected the transient units in him and now these compositor units are affected by the same transient units, which now are in the other person. The transient units which are the means by which the symbolic figure in the starry point is made are those that are marked by the breath-form of the actor.

Those units only are marked which take part in an act or an event which the doer intends or which is an exteriorization of a thought. If a routine thought, like that of brushing one's hair or putting on one's shoes, or a thought without attachment to results or its exteriorization, is balanced with the first exteriorization, the transient units are not marked by the breath-form and no record is transmitted by them.

A record on being made is drawn into a point. The point is a transient unit. From that point the former scene is again spread out at the proper time and in the new scene the same transient units are employed, which were marked by the symbol of the former act or event. If the reproduction is made during the same life, the point containing the symbol is breathed in by the person and that person is the source of the event which happens to him by the coming of the transient units. Not only is the life time of human beings filled with events which are the projections made from the symbolic figures of the record, but before a child is born its body in the womb is endowed with the records of former acts. These records are now points in breath units in brain and nerve cells, built in by the breath-form. At the conjunction of time, condition and place, from these points will spread out the scenes and events in which the physical body takes part. Time and distance as they exist for human beings, do not exist for these points. All of the above is the basis of astrology.

The destiny of human beings is thus written in points which are in the human beings themselves and, from the moment they become active, are in all the starry spaces. The whole physical universe with all its forces is thus behind destiny. No one who understands this can believe in the happening of anything by chance or by accident, nor can he believe that one can escape from the destiny be has made. Destiny like any day of reckoning may be postponed, but it cannot be prevented or avoided.

Destiny is brought on by that which commands elementals. The beings which command the nature-side are Intelligences and their Triune Selves on the intelligent-side, under Supreme Intelligence. They order it according to a law, the law of thought: Everything existing on the physical plane is an exteriorization of a thought which must be balanced through the one who issued it, in accordance with his responsibility, and at the conjunction of time, condition and place.

This law attaches to acts and omissions which are exteriorizations of thoughts and which are intended, not to such as are casual, automatic or incidental, like saying perfunctorily "how are you", or where a thought is balanced at once at its first exteriorization.

When an act is done with intent, it is the exteriorization of the design of a thought, and a record of the act is made in a point in the starry spaces and a recomposition of the act follows as destiny. If it follows in the same life, the point containing the record comes into the human body through the breath; if it follows in a subsequent life, the point is built into the body before birth. With the recomposition of the act to the doer, who is now a recipient, the original record becomes inoperative. Though inoperative it remains as a record until the thought is balanced. The record shows how far the aim deviated from what it should have been, according to the thinker's conscience. The record is always in a magnetic relation to the embodied doer, whose act it preserves.

There is another record of the act as an exteriorization of the thought and this record is not made by or in nature-matter. This record is in the thought itself. It is not even in a point and cannot be described in terms of matter; it is not a picture or even a symbolic representation. It causes a doer-memory, which appears as a feeling, as a desire or as a mental attitude.

Triune Selves who see the record in the starry spaces see also the record in the thought itself and thereafter must arrange the exterioriza- tions of the thought, when it cycles towards the physical plane, so that situations are created which present a duty of action or omission. These situations flow at the appropriate time out of the thought itself; they are created by exteriorizations of the thought. The duty which is thereby presented offers an opportunity to balance the thought.

To balance the thought the duty must be done without fear or hope. It must be done irrespective of results which may follow. If it is so done without attachment, the constituents of the thought, balancing factor, aim, design and the physical part which came in through one of the senses and caused first the desire and then the exteriorizations, are freed. These constituents are freed because there is nothing to hold them together. As long as there is attachment to the object or action they are held together by the attachment.

It is not necessary for one to know which of his thoughts he balances. All one can do is to balance some thought by doing the duty that offers itself. Even if he could choose he could not select a better thought than the one which a present duty allows him to balance. For the events in life are so marshalled that the lives and the duties of all people on the earth fit in together.

There will come to everyone a time in some life when he can be conscious of his outstanding thoughts as they come up before him, and when he can balance them consciously. At present human beings are not conscious of their thoughts as beings, nor of the duties of life as coming from exteriorizations of their past thoughts. All they can do is to do their present duties without attachment to results. Thereby they balance some thought and free Light that was bound up in the thought. So they achieve some knowledge, however little it may be, and receive a feeling of satisfaction, of lightness and of serenity. The present life, as the present day and the present duty, is that into which the past has melted and from which the future spreads out. The thoughts which are not balanced continue to exteriorize and make new existences necessary to the doer.

Life seems to be full of examples of injustice, where the wicked often prosper and the good meet with misfortune. It is the actively wicked who get things, not those who are wicked and passive. If the good were as active in their goodness, they would get practically the same results of prosperity. The mass of the people, who are traders and laborers, think towards knavery, hypocrisy and gain by fraud rather than by honesty. Therefore the thoughts and the efforts of the wicked find ready response, since they go with the tide, whereas the good have to fight against it. The atmosphere, that is, the elements permeated by the thoughts of human beings, is in constant confusion and conflict and is therefore more responsive to the wicked and the dishonest than to the good. The nature forces, the elementals, are more readily attracted to the aims of the crooked than to those of the honest, because they respond more to sensation and excitement.

There is under these conditions nothing unjust in material success of the wicked. They succeed because of greater interest, stronger desire, persistence, a favorable atmosphere and often because of greater ability and of likable personal qualities. Nor is it unjust when the good are far from prosperous for they have feebler impulses, less incentive for gain and scattered interests; they are passive and allow themselves to be preyed upon and often lack likable and sociable traits. Justice in material things is unnoticed, but an apparent injustice is remarked because it is striking.

If the good were persistently good no harm could come to them and they could stand up against anything. Nobody is entirely good or entirely bad, entirely active or entirely passive. In different lives different traits find expression. Those in whom wickedness had been suppressed may, obeying their promptings, become actively wicked, and those in whom goodness has not been manifest may become actively good. The goodness and the badness so-called are shown, the other side is not manifest. When the wicked prosper it is partly because they are enjoying benefits they have merited in the past, and often the good suffer because of their past carelessness or iniquities. These aspects of life are ephemeral, they bring to the surface what has been unseen in the past and what may soon disappear.

The outer conditions of riches, possessions, success, upon which some predicate injustice or caprice in human affairs, come to everyone in orderly turns. They are opportunities, opportunities for thinking honestly and for training and controlling feelings and desires. They are opportunities for acting with cheerfulness and goodwill, and yet without attachment. Laziness, selfishness and ill will do not loosen the chains that bind men to the treadmill of life. Vocations, possessions, power, admiration, adventures, failures and successes are not essential. A man must control his appetite whether he be rich or poor, he must think honestly whether he be famous or obscure, he must preserve the Light whatever his vocation.

Usually a cycle of twelve existences takes the human beings of a doer part through a round from affluence through poverty to affluence, from prominence through obscurity to prominence, from hazards to security and back to hazards and from variety through monotony to variety. These outward changes come about, determined under the law of cycles or succession of events. Thus are made the twelve steps or spokes of the treadwheel which takes one from poverty through wealth again to poverty. Incidental to this may be the course through monotony and change and through other opposites. The zenith and the nadir of some of these cycles may or may not coincide. These cyclic changes in the situations do not interfere with a man's physical, psychic, mental and noetic destiny, but are so arranged that they fit in with the destiny and yet obey the law that the succession of events proceeds in four seasons, each with three aspects. Nearly everyone who today is swallowed up in the mass, poor in physique, in purse, in intellect and is ruled by his desires, has within twelve lives held possessions, been valiant in adventures and enjoyed pleasures in abundance, though his psychic and mental weakness may not have varied much from that of the herd of human beings of today. The twelve aspects of such a cycle present phases of life which are not essential; but the conditions or states of the doer which are the result of thinking, due to the feelings and desires of the human in these positions, are essential.

These conditions of the doer bring about other cycles which are independent of that cycle of twelve. These cycles may be for more or less than twelve lives. Among such cycles are those of sex, of persistence or lethargy in thinking, of intellectual attainments or their loss, and of associations and relations with others.

A change of sex may come through thinking and feeling. If the doer-in-the-body exists as a woman but thinks strongly on the line of desire its next embodiment is likely to be in a male body, or if the desire of the doer thinks positively on the line of feeling, its next body will probably be female, but this is not the order. The change from one sex to the other is the result of several, usually six, lives of thinking; it is not due to the thinking in one life alone. Feeling-and-desire as the doer, in series of six, re-exist alternately. There are six re-existing portions of feeling and six re-existing portions of desire in the make-up of the doer of the Triune Self. In the proper succession, six desire portions should re-exist in male bodies and the six portions of feeling should re-exist in female bodies. The successive existence of each of the six portions of feeling and of each of the six portions of desire constitutes the cycle of the twelve existences of the doer—and of re-existences.

Another cycle in which the human beings of a doer rise and fall also depends on thinking, with the consequent mental attitudes and character of the mental atmosphere. This cycle may be complete in one life or it may cover several lives. When there is the impulse to go ahead in thinking, man is not strong enough to maintain the effort and the advance. Then there is a reaction of lethargy in thinking, brought about by a pull of desire in other directions. There is a pull-back, a sagging down, a giving way. The tendency of the other desires pulling against the rise, brings about a retrogression in thinking and the consequent drifting, superficial life.

The rise and fall in intellectual attainments in a line of lives is also due to cycles of thinking. Intellectual attainments which are mere sense-knowledge relating to the natural sciences, as well as to material philosophy, law, medicine and theology, are not brought over. Whatever is acquired by the four senses is lost at death, because the physical record made on the breath-form is destroyed. There may be brought over what the thinking extracted and appropriated from these attainments. It does not appropriate anything from slight acquaintance or from superficial dealing. What the doer has acquired by intimate and thorough occupation with the sciences will be brought over as a tendency to take them up in the new life and as a ready understanding of them. The new form of expression will have to be learned as was the old form. If there should be a doer-memory of what one has gone through in the past, it will come as a flash of understanding, a stroke of genius.

Contact between people comes about by thinking on similar or opposed lines. The relation begins casually, grows closer and then moderates, weakens and at last disappears. If their feelings and desires and the consequent thinking are similar in some respects, people are drawn together and become comrades, friends or lovers and they may be held by marriage and family ties. People may also be held closely by ties of dislike. That former friends or enemies are husband and wife, parent and child, brother and sister and so in situations where they meet continually, gives them an opportunity to work together on friendly and kindly lines or to work out or aggravate old troubles. Persons are so held together for a life or several lives by their feeling and desire and the consequent thinking. While it is not impossible for two or more doers to remain in close contact for the whole period of their doer development, this is most unusual. Generally human beings come together once or many times, contact and separate.

The cycles due to thinking are different from the cycles of an average of twelve re-existences which take the human beings of a doer portion through a round of worldly stations and conditions. A human makes his own cycles of thinking by his choice among his feelings and desires. Desire starts thinking and keeps it up until the desire is worn out or until the human turns to another desire. The cycle with the twelve spokes of existences is a general cycle; it is provided to put a human into positions in which he may have a variety of experiences from which to learn.

Things appear in time cycles because they are not permanent. Permanence is the background out of which all that is temporary reappears physically. These appearances recur cyclically, because they represent something permanent. Cycles are steps toward a permanent state, and continue until this is attained. Man is the midground on which the cyclic appearance of the nature units and of the doer occurs in conjunction until permanence is established for the perfect form of the breath-form. The form of the breath-form must be made permanent, immortal, and perfect, so that the physical body will not age and die. Through this permanent physical body forms, bodies, that are permanent must also be developed for the three parts of the Triune Self. Meanwhile, the doer must continue to live in temporary bodies and in each life pass through various cycles; the changes incident to the cycles are accompanied by glamour and illusion. The glamour they discover, but to the illusions they remain subject.

Because of their self-seeking human beings are often led by an initial glamour. If they could see things as they are they would see the emptiness of the objects of life. They would not be interested in situations which might demand from them the doing of duties. They would avoid getting into such situations and would so lack experiences from which they could learn and would incapacitate themselves for learning and for meeting their destiny. A glamour therefore serves to lead humans into situations where duties will be revealed to them or forced upon them, as it is used to lure them into situations where destiny can reach them.

Glamour is a state of the doer-in-the-body wrought by illusions which the four senses produce. Glamour is further made by thinking in answer to the pressure of feeling and desire. The senses report the physical world to feeling-and-desire. The doer portion, identifying itself with the four senses, calls upon the body-mind to obtain for it the thing desired.

The difference between things seen as they are and things seen in a glamour is the difference made by expectation, embellishment, exaggeration, astonishment or terror, as distinct from the physical facts as they are. It makes a paradise out of a farm, a heaven out of a marriage, a romance out of soldiering, an abundance out of an employment. They idealize common persons and things. After the humans are entrapped by the initial glamour, it falls away and they are confronted with the naked facts, the drudgery of winning a living from the soil, the trials of marriage, the hardships of a soldier's life, the scantiness and affliction of servitude, and the disappointment in their comrades.

Man himself makes the glamour by his ignorance combined with self-interest and the desire to possess and to have pleasure. But his thinker engineers the situations around which he throws an enchantment, which then lures him into a future in which the realities of the thing will be much less pleasing than the alluring prospects which he fabricated for himself in his ignorance.

So people are induced to enter into engagements, if they have a choice, because they believe that out of them will come something that is more agreeable or something with fewer unpleasant features than the reality will be. Likewise they are sometimes kept out of temptation and trouble by apprehending fearful consequences. The creation of an initial glamour is aided by simple-mindedness and selfishness. A glamour is not necessary as an inducement when a person is willing to assume the duties of a situation and to take things with equanimity as they come.

The things that make life attractive or repellent, that give motives for thinking and aims to ensuing thoughts, that hold the doer to life on earth, are sensations and the objects from which they come. Sensations of hunger and of sex are overmastering. Sensations are illusions from the standpoint of the doer, but not from the standpoint of the earth. While the doer is under them they are not illusions, but are strong realities of life. Sensations are among the causes of the re-existences of a doer. As long as they remain realities to the doer, the doer cannot escape re-existence. When sensations are felt as elementals, and not felt as part of feeling, a beginning is made by which the necessity for re-existence will in time end.

Sensations are elementals, nature units; they are not part of the feeling of the doer, but the feeling of the doer feels them. Every sensation of light, of shade, of color and of form, of sounds, of the tastes of food and drink, of odors and of all touch, is an elemental or a stream of nature units, elementals. These are elementals coming into the body from without. The sensations of hunger for food and for drink, including alcoholic liquors, and for drugs and for sexual contact are elementals within the body itself. When one eats a strawberry, the desire for the strawberry is not an elemental, nor is the act of eating, nor is the strawberry, but that which starts the desire for the sensation of tasting the strawberry and the sensation of taste of the strawberry, are elementals. When one drinks wine, the sensations of taste and of intoxication are elementals as well as are the cravings in the cells of the body that started the desire for drink. At sexual union the sensations of sexual contact are elementals and so are the sights, sounds and odors that aroused sex desire, and so are the cravings in the sexual cells of the body that stimulated the desire. Sensations of craving and sensations of satisfaction, sensations of physical suffering and of physical enjoyment are all elementals.

The sensations are not feeling and not desire, nor are feeling or desire sensations. The doer cannot be hungry; feeling cannot be hungry. Hunger is a stream of elementals, which feeling feels as sensations. The elementals become sensations when they reach feeling or desire. It is as if a match were by a touch turned into a flame. A touch of human feeling transforms and vitalizes elementals, which are mere nature forces. Elementals become sensations only while in contact with feeling-and-desire. These forces are the active side of the units of the four elements and are sensations only as long as they remain in contact with feeling and with desire. The passive side is that in which the force manifests. The two sides are indivisible and inseparable. After the contact has ceased they are again mere elementals, nature forces; but they are impressed by that with which they have been in contact, and they will be attracted to repeat the same sensation.

Some of the elementals which become sensations are bound in the body, some are out of the body. Those that are in the body are cell units and want to be supplied with what they crave. They can reach feeling at any time. Those outside seek feeling because they have no feeling and cannot get into touch with feeling except by contact with the elementals in the body, which they arouse. The manner in which feeling is affected by the presence of elementals in the nerves is that feeling feels the elementals as sensations after it has made them such itself; and the elementals become sensations as soon as feeling feels them. They are then felt as sensations, which they become by contact with feeling. Feeling thus transforms the elemental into a sensation.

While it is a sensation an elemental partakes of the feeling that has enlivened it from a mere nature force into a sensation. By itself the elemental does not feel, even while it remains transformed into a sensation, in the manner in which humans feel or even as an animal feels. It never suffers, it never enjoys—it thrills. It seeks pain equally as pleasure, and it feels neither as such, but only as a thrill, and that only as long as it contacts feeling and as long as feeling feels it as a sensation.

The object seen, heard, tasted, smelled or contacted is not sensed as it is, or as a sensation, or as a feeling: it is an illusion. The illusion is actually an elemental which is temporarily transformed into a sensation. The whole world, and every object and every sensation in it are illusions; they are not seen as such and cannot be seen as such by an embodied doer until it distinguishes between itself as feeling, the sensation as an elemental, and the object as made up of elementals. When the doer can distinguish between sensations and itself, feeling-and-desire can remain unaffected by elementals; the illusions produced by objects and sensations will become transparent, and the realities producing the illusions can be perceived. All sights, sounds, tastes, smells and contacts, and all hunger and sexual cravings will lose their charm, power and terror for the doer that can distinguish between itself and the elementals.

Nature seeks the doer for several purposes. It tries to get Light of the Intelligence which the doer has the use of, and to get the doer into nature, so as to have an association with feeling-and-desire, and with thinking from which it gets forms. Nature seeks this association so as to keep its units in circulation. It does this by having the doer transform elementals into sensations and then identifying itself with them while they are sensations. Human beings would not allow themselves to be so used if they were conscious of the true state of facts and of the illusion under which they live. So the illusion is allowed to continue until the doer is sufficiently advanced to perform its duties to nature and raise it, without being under any illusion.

The illusion is produced by letting the doer feel that the four senses are part of itself and that other elementals either entering the body through these or already in the body are also part of itself, when it feels them as sensations.

All sights, sounds, tastes, smells and contacts are streams of elementals coming from outside nature to that part of nature that is the body. They come through the seven openings of the sense organs in the head and through the other five openings, and in case of contact, through the skin also. They travel along the nerves of the involuntary system, which like wires connect them, through the breath-form, with any part of the body, where they stimulate cells. Through the breath-form they reach the doer, which is in the kidneys and adrenals and in the voluntary nervous system. When they so reach the doer they, as well as the elementals of the cells in the body which they affect, become sensations. All are transformed from elementals into sensations by the contact they make with feeling through the breath-form. The doer-in-the body, as the human being, then identifies itself with the senses and as the sensations and says: "I see," "I hear," "I taste," "I smell," "I touch," "I am hungry," taking the sensation as part of itself.

When one is hungry and food is taken, the stream of incoming elementals, which is hunger, is not satisfied by food; elementals do not eat. The more intense the hunger, the more intense their thrill. When food is eaten they thrill again. After the stomach is full they find no way to reach the nerves, because the nerves are not open to them and will not receive them. If they can induce overeating they thrill again at the ensuing discomfort.

Whether the human feels more or less intense sensations depends on the capacity of his organs and nerves to entertain the stream of elementals, and upon the volume of the stream. The sensations of pleasure are dulled when the nerves and organs that receive them as elementals are exhausted. Sensations of pain result in becoming unconscious if the volume of the elemental stream coming in is greater than the capacity of the organs and nerves to entertain it. Then the astral-airy-fluid bodies are made inactive and are expelled from the nerves by the overwhelming stream and so are no longer a medium of communication with the breath-form. Thus the doer is switched off from its connection with the involuntary nervous system. In this way elementals can be aided or hindered in becoming sensations. They can also be prevented.

This may be done by a process of unglamouring and disillusioning the doer-in-the-body from the senses. It is possible for the doer to be conscious of itself as distinct from the body in which it lives and from the elementals that make up the body. When the doer has found itself it need not feel hunger or the craving for sex, or the delights of sights and sounds, tastes and smells and contacts. Or it can feel these things, but distinguishes itself from the sensations. The hunger then is different from the hunger that one feels under the illusion that one hungers. It is as when one feels for one's dog which is hungry. When one feels that his dog is hungry he is not under the illusion that he himself is hungry.

The life of human beings is made up of illusions. They often discover in the course of a life the illusions which they have made for themselves, by the disappearance of the glamour under which they entered into a relation. They do not discover the illusions of their sensations, and that they merely satisfy elementals as long as they believe that they are enjoying or suffering. From this illusion human beings do not know how to free themselves. Nor can they rid themselves of the conception that physical objects are as they are sensed, which also is an illusion. The four senses bring in everything of a material nature. But that means only that they bring in impressions of objects as they appear to be to the human. The objects are realities as appearances only. Matter is seen as an appearance, not as the matter is. The appearance is the outermost aspect, the surface aspect, and conceals the other parts and aspects.

What appears to the smoker to be a cigar made of brown, fragrant, tobacco leaves is such only as reported by the eye, the nose, the tongue and the touch which receive impressions from surfaces, that is, matter massed in the solid state on the physical plane. This cigar is in the other three states of matter on the physical plane, if they are perceived separately, unlike what is seen, tasted, smelled and touched as the burning cigar. In the solid state of the form plane of the physical world the cigar looks different, though the outline of its form is about the same. It looks finer, more colorful, its fragrance is more pronounced, its taste is more intense, and if it burns the smoker, the burn is more lasting and the mark of it remains. In the other three states of matter on the form plane, there are further differences. On the life and light planes of the physical world, the cigar as such does not exist; only a plan is there. In the form world, on the physical plane, there is the bare form or wraith of the cigar, in the life world even that does not exist, but there is a symbol or a certain value in place of what is the burning cigar in the smoker's hand.

All solid objects on the physical plane are such only as long as they are perceived through the sense organs of the human body. In other states of matter they are no longer what they seem in the solid state. The appearance is lost in the other states. It is no longer the only reality, though it can have a reality as an appearance, the reality of appearing.

Because thinking is more real than the appearances of matter as the objects in life, it can demonstrate their relative unreality. It can deprive pain of its hurt, disease of its devastation and age of its withering. Thinking can call into existence objects, like money and possessions, and it can make circumstances, such as of employment and success. Such is the power of thinking. Many people are using it. They force themselves to think that their pain, disease, age, discomfort and poverty do not exist, are not realities, but are illusions. They are illusions, but people do not want to get rid of them because they are illusions, but because they are unpleasant; and they want to put in their place other illusions, not realities, which are more pleasant. Sometimes they succeed in driving the illusions away and putting others in place of them, because the power of thinking may overcome the power of the illusion, thinking being more real.

The result of such practices is a self-deception and increasing inability to distinguish not only illusions from realities, but generally the true from the false. While such people may intend to be honest, they blind themselves to the facts owing to prejudice and preference. They use the power of thought much as a burglar uses steel. There are such things as pain, disease, age, discomfort and poverty; they are very real to one who feels them. Even when they are known to be illusions they are real as illusions. To see them as they are and see what they are is legitimate. To force oneself to think they are not what and where they are, is untrue and wrong.

A human is beset, surrounded, submerged by illusions. All outside things are illusions. So are his appetites, pains and pleasures, dislikes and hatreds. They are elementals. His own feelings and desires, aside from these illusions, he does not know. He does not see the people he thinks he sees; he sees only the thoughts which he creates of them. Therefore if a thousand see a man, no two would see him alike, because no two out of the thousand thoughts would be alike.

Each one creates a thought of himself, as which he sees himself, yet no one else sees him or thinks of him as the person he sees and thinks himself to be. The thought of himself which he has created is an illusion, because he does not know himself to be that reality which he is. He thinks of himself as an identity, as "I", whereas he is merely that portion of himself which feels the presence of his identity or "I". He is under the illusion that he does the thinking and reasoning, whereas these are done by one of the three minds which he may have the use of, but of which he is not conscious.

Man believes he is conscious of time and of the passage of time. This is an illusion. Time is the passage of events in the field of the Eternal; the passage is noted as the past, the present and that which is to come. But the Eternal is unchanging, as related to time, and in the Eternal the past, the present and the future are a Now, without a past and without a future. Eternity has many varieties of time; among them is the variety ticked off by the celestial clock, with the sun and moon as its hands and the planets in its works. Every act, object and event that exists in physical time exists also in the Eternal, but it does not exist there in the same manner or in sequence. In the Eternal it is not an act, an object or an event, with a beginning, a middle and an end, but it is one, cause and result are one.

Time is ever devouring itself. It consumes itself and arises anew out of itself. Beginning, origin, first cause and end are only markers on the flow of time. In reality, the end is as much the beginning as the beginning is the end, but to humans they are opposites. Human beings cannot know the nature of time as long as their bodies are part of time and are the means by which they measure time, and as long as feeling-and-desire alternately dominate each other. For not until then will the doer be freed from the illusion of time.

In this mass of illusions the human exists as a combination that is drawn together for a time. He is conscious as an entity, but that is an illusion. To be conscious as anything is an illusion, though it is a reality relatively. To be conscious is a reality absolutely, but to be conscious as any being is only relatively real.

When a human is conscious *as* himself it means merely that he is conscious *as* feeling-and-desire. The grossest illusions are his supreme realities—the objects of his feelings and desires. The visible world in which he lives is the type in which he conceives his world after death. His own body is the type of his God and of his Devil. The things which he abhors and which terrify him, make up his hell, and the things he likes, his heaven. But his own doer appears fanciful, doubtful, unreal, except in so far as it is feelings and desires.

Yet under these unfavorable conditions man is being educated. He is being educated by doer-memories. Notwithstanding that he does not remember his past lives, that only a portion of the doer is in his body and that the highest conception of himself as a being, is an illusion, the false "I", and notwithstanding that the world in which he exists is an illusion and all the objects he sees and the people he meets are illusions, he is being educated. The illusions educate him by doer-memories of them as realities, until he sees them as illusions.

The essential thing in life is to preserve, reclaim and free his Light and to think without creating thoughts, that is, without attachment. He must find out what he is not. He must find out what and who he is. He must rebuild his body into one that is deathless. He cannot be lost. He is never forgotten, never forsaken, never without the care and protection which he will allow himself to receive. He can feel and think of himself through all discomforts and troubles as being guarded and judged by his administrator, the thinker, known by his knower, guided by the Light of the Intelligence, and loved, cared for and supported by the Supreme Triune Self of the worlds under the Light of Supreme Intelligence.

CHAPTER X

GODS AND THEIR RELIGIONS

SECTION 1

Religions; on what they are founded. Why belief in a personal God. Problems a religion must meet. Any religion is better than none.

Religions must be considered because they deal with the conscious doer-in-the-body and with Gods. Religions are founded on the belief in a relation between human beings and a superior being or beings to whom the humans are subject. Sickness, accident, death, unavoidable destiny, things that do not depend on or that overcome the action of the human, are ascribed to the presence and power of a superior being. Religions and religious teachings must have and do have a certain foundation in facts, else they could not last for any length of time.

Here are some truths that are fundamentals of religions and their teachings, and for the belief in religions. In every human body there is a deathless conscious something that is not the body but that makes the animal body human. Because of past mistakes the conscious something has hidden itself in the coils of flesh and the flesh prevents it from understanding that it is a small integral and inseparable part of its all-knowing Great Self that is not in the body. One's own feeling-and-desire is the conscious something in the body, which is here called the doer-in-the-body. The doer-in-the-body feels that it belongs to or is a part of a superior being on whom it must depend and to whom it must appeal for guidance. Like a child who depends on its parent, it desires the recognition and protection and guidance of a superior being. The doer-in-the-body feels and desires and thinks, but it is by its body-mind compelled to think and feel and desire through the body senses; and, it thinks in terms of seeing, hearing, tasting and smelling. The doer is therefore limited by the body-mind to the senses, and is prevented from thinking of its relation to its Great Self that is not in the body. It is led to think of a superior being of nature that is above and beyond the body, and which is all-powerful and all-wise—to whom it must appeal and on whom it must depend.

The need for a religion comes from weakness and helplessness. The human seeking support and refuge wants to feel that there is a superior being to whom one can appeal for help and for protection. Consolation and hope are needed at some time by everybody. Man wants to feel that he is not abandoned and alone. The fear and feeling of abandonment in life and at death are dreadful. Man rarely wants his existence to be blotted out at death, nor does he want to be severed from some of those he has been with in life. He wants security, he wants to feel assured. These feelings and desires develop into belief in a superior being who watches, protects and endows, where the human is helpless.

The wish for a relation with a superior being is inherent in man. Seeing the visible universe moved by something invisible, he believes this invisible to be a being, whose support or protection he seeks. The belief, which is religion, is the belief in nature and in its powers which affect the body and so overawe him. He feels a power in himself, but he sees in nature a power superior to that of his own personality, so his belief is, and has to be, in a personal God as a magnified and sublimated human being.

Man perceives order, power and intelligence in nature. He feels that they are the attributes of a personal ruler. The cause of this belief is that the doer in man identifies itself with its body and feels the power of the body over it. With a loss of knowledge of the Light within, came worship of gods. Such is the need and the wish, and such is the conception which is formed for the belief. When the belief increases to faith it produces phenomena which seem to prove its correctness. The need which man feels is used by his Triune Self and by Intelligences to foster religions for the training of human beings. These Intelligences use the belief to nurse humanity along until a very different teaching can be given by them. They allow the revelation, spread and enforcement of teachings concerning the Gods and their will.

There are twelve types of teachings which have appeared cyclically throughout the ages. The Intelligences do not make religious systems or institutions; men make them; the Intelligences allow them now, as they have in the past, because men demand them and need them for experience.

The problems encountered are many. There must be a system or theology, meeting the needs of all from the lowly to the great, from the undeveloped to the educated, from the materialistic to the inspired and from the credulous to the thinkers. It must allow for thousands of different conceptions of the same thing. There must be a system which can, when backed up by innate conservatism, last for centuries and yet permit an advance of interpretation within the prescribed doctrines. There must be a collection of essays, teachings, laws, exhortations, prayers, adventures, magic, stories, which can be called sacred writings and which can be made the foundation for such theology. These must be such that they permit, if not urge, the exercise of literature, architecture, sculpture, music, painting and handicraft, so as to inspire worshippers with sensuous exaltation. These writings must have the strongest appeal to feelings and emotions and must be the foundation on which the ethics and laws of the adherents can rest. Religion as a belief is accompanied by theology, which is a system to justify the belief, by religious institutions and forms of worship in which the belief is exhibited and, most important, by a method of life. If religious belief leads to virtues such as self-control, duty and kindliness, it serves its highest purpose in the training of the human.

The various religions, that is, theological systems and religious institutions for worship, which appear from time to time in different settings, are fitted to meet the special needs of their believers. The institutions have been made by the thoughts of those who will exist as believers and who will live under them. The outer forms of the religions thus fit the beliefs of the adherents. The religious offices are filled by persons who personify the thoughts and desires of the mass of devotees. The actions of these officials are the expression of that mass. Those who are opposed to a religion are often the ones who have helped to bring the conditions about, but have learned of their mistakes and see that what they have is not what they want, yet they must meet the exteriorizations. The history of religions is what it is, because religions as theologies are made by men and as institutions are administered by men.

Religions as beliefs, systems and institutions are both good and bad. This depends on the people who practice them. When a religion is practiced to lead or to allow its devotees to develop reasoning and understanding and to grow into a higher and more enlightened state, it is good. It is bad, when by means of it people are kept in ignorance and darkness, and when vice, crime and cruelty flourish under it. Usually the beginning of a new religion is promising. It comes to meet a demand. It starts out of a decaying religion. It is usually born out of tumult, confusion, dissension and war. It attracts enthusiasts and the changeable crowd. It fails to school the mass of adherents to a higher life, and soon suffers from theology, institutionalism, officialism, hypocrisy, bigotry and corruption. So one religion after another appears, disappears, and reappears. The reason is twofold: the mass of re-existing doers whose religion it is get it because it exteriorizes their thoughts, and the actions of those who figure as its priests and officials reflect and embody the aims of the adherents.

On the whole it is better that there should be even such a religion than none. It keeps the believers from doing worse than they do. Religions are allowed to survive as long as they supply the requirements of belief for a number of persons. They survive chiefly by means of the devotion, virtues and holy lives of some few persons in the great body of adherents. These are so-called mystics, who lead lives of purity and contemplation. Their living infuses strength, vitality and virtue into the organization. The holy life is an active force and invigorates the religion as an organization. This force follows and supports the policy of the heads of the body of devotees and may be used for good or evil. Thus an organization is often enabled to last, because of the virtues of some few of its members.

There are inner and outer parts of religions. The inner parts are the thoughts engendered by the theology and by the virtues, aims, ideals and aspirations, as well as by the faults of those who carry on the religion. The outer parts are the forms in which the inner appear, as offices, institutions, rites and acts of the devotees connected with the belief. The outer aspect is necessary for the practice and propagation of the belief and for the other activities often connected with religions, such as teaching the young, nursing the sick and caring for the poor. Sometimes sciences are studied and advanced by means of religious institutions. Always there is a tendency of the religious officeholders to exercise functions of government and to wield power, because the priests are human and this is natural. Forms are necessary though they become means of abuse. As soon as a religion is started, obscurantism, that is, the tendency to stifle individual development and thinking, comes with it. The forms are given a physical meaning and made rigid, while the claim is made that they are "spiritual" and not physical. Hence come fanaticism, wars, persecutions, and whatever is horrible about religions. The profit is with the religious officeholders whose reach is increased by conservatism and obscurantism. They acquire worldly power and become less inspired and "spiritual" with their successes. Religions may be cheapened by trivialities or abused when put to the service of social or political interests, but there is enough to be found in them to give consolation and hope to those who need these, and morals and faith to those who are willing.

SECTION 2

Classes of Gods. The Gods of religions; how they come into existence. How long they last. Appearance of a God. Changes of a God. Gods have only what human beings have who create and keep them. The name of a God. Christian Gods.

There have been and there may be innumerable Gods. There are nature Gods outside, and there is the Light of Intelligences within man. The nature Gods are of two classes, the gods of the pure elements and the Gods worshipped in religions.

The gods of the pure elements, that is, of the spheres, exist in hierarchies. The term hierarchy is freely figurative; channels would be more descriptive. The earth fire is one. It is like a reservoir having many channels which have lesser channels, making a system like that of water which is the same in a mountain lake, in a reservoir and in a faucet. The reservoir of the fire element is the fire god. The lesser gods under it are like channels in which it is and through which it can flow; and a radiant unit is the least jet or utmost channel of the fire element. The units can progress downward only and towards the earthy earth and then towards a physical body. The great elemental fire god which stands behind all its units is the most powerful, is the most easily commanded and will obey most readily. However, it is the least of all elementals in that it is the least progressed. It is less progressed than its lowest unit. The great fire gods under it are like lesser reservoirs. They are less powerful, but more progressed than the fire element as a whole. In these hierarchies a unit cannot ascend, because its descent is its advance and its development. It cannot go back, it must go on. However, when it is freed upon the breaking up of a compound in which it is, it returns to its element, by entering the stream of the units of the four states of matter that flows to a stratum in the solid earth, to the moon, to the sun and to the stars. The gods of the pure elements are not known to humans and are not worshipped in religions.

The Gods worshipped in the pagan, Jewish and Christian religions are nature Gods, but not pure nature Gods. They are made by human thinking. They are nature-matter and nature forces and get their forms and traits from humans.

The Gods worshipped in religions have been and are parts of the elements. These parts are projected from their worshippers and are supported as separate beings by the thinking of these worshippers. They are allowed to exist for the experience of human beings.

Gods come into existence as the expression of human thinking which tries to bring to a few or to a group or to a mass of humans what they desire. The desire cannot be expressed by many acting together; it must be done through one of the number. The one who can most clearly think of what is needed, conceives and issues a thought and speaks about it; and that thought enters into the hearts of the many and is accepted and issued by them. The God first comes into being as a human thought. The thought takes on a part of one or more of the elements and clothes itself in this elemental matter.

So far the thought is no different from other human thoughts. Before it can be turned into and take being and identity as a God it must be approved by the ruling Intelligence and must take life. The Intelligence is not arbitrary in its approval or rejection. If the thought is what the people desire and merit, as a happy, lavish, bloody, warring, sexual or voluptuous God, it will be approved. The God announces his name through the mouth of a human and is known to his worshippers by that name. He grows in mass and power according to the increase of the number who believe in him as a God, and praise him and pour out their thought to him. He is as though astonished at the power he has and amazed at that attributed to him. Soon he becomes accustomed to be praised as the Creator, the First Cause and the Supreme Intelligence. He is made to feel assured even of that, and he demands faith from his worshippers so that he may have faith in himself.

In this manner came into existence Moloch, Baal, Jehovah, Thor and various Christian Gods, also such trinities as Brahmâ, Vishnu and Siva, and Osiris, Isis and Horus. The Greek Gods do not belong to this class. They were not created as human thoughts, but were race types of men and women who had lived. There were in Hellas traditions of human races that had existed in former ages. At their renaissance the Hellenes personified and deified these races, pictured them as the Olympian Gods, poured out to them their thought and praise and worship, and so empowered them as Gods.

A God lasts as long as there are any who nourish and support him. His life may last for decades, thousands of years or ages, but it is not eternal. He ceases to be when there are no more human bodies to give exteriorization to thoughts of prayer and worship, to voice his name and to let him live in their blood and nerves. This occurs when the mass of worshippers fades away or is destroyed by war, disease or a cataclysm, or when its thought has changed to the worship of another deity. When a God ceases to be, his elemental parts return to the element to which they belong, and the thoughts which have held them together remain in the mental atmospheres of the doers who created them. Only the thoughts of the living can nourish a God, because he needs blood and nerves to transmit the nourishment of prayer and praise. A God lives through the bodies of his worshippers.

Every God has the feeling of identity, that is, he feels that he is the same entity throughout the period of his existence. This identity is different from the identity which each of his worshippers believes him to have. Every one of his worshippers looks at him in a different way. They all recognize his identity, but each qualifies it differently. The difference is not in the God, but lies in the persons. The identity may also be different from that given him by those who do not acknowledge him as their God. All who think about him contribute to his identity. The identity lasts as long as the God and the God is conscious of his identity, though he may be worshipped under different names, either at the same time or in successive periods. The identity of a God differs from the identity which each Triune Self is. Each doer of its Triune Self contributes from itself to the identity of the God, but the identity of the God, being the sum of these contributions, is different from any one of them. The identity may repeatedly grow stronger and become weaker during the life of the God; when the God ceases, his identity ceases.

The Gods have bodies, but these are not fleshly bodies. There is in the body of the God elemental matter. To this substratum comes other matter, namely, units that flow in from and go back to human bodies. This matter consists of free units from the elements, and of transient units from the bodies of the worshippers. Sometimes the bodies of some

Gods may contain in addition compositor units from the bodies of their worshippers, after the doers, in the after-death states, have ceased to use these units. The transient units that come from human bodies qualify the background of elemental units by their character, and the compositor units build the bodies of the deities into forms. Among these compositor units streaming in and out are human senses of sight, hearing, taste and smell. These give the God his all-seeing eye, his hearing of prayer and praise, his tasting of offerings and his smelling of incense.

All Gods have bodies of nature-matter and though most of these bodies have form, some are without form. The body of Jehovah is without form; he dislikes images of himself. Some Christian Gods have bodies in form, and these forms are in the human image. The bodies of Gods when in form are not fleshly bodies, though they contain units that have made up the flesh bodies of their worshippers. The bodies of Gods. need not be dimensional as human bodies are. They may be present on the four planes of the physical world, that is, they may be present in the world of solid matter in many places at the same time. The bodies of the Gods if without form may take on form, or if having a general form may change it for a time. Gods may appear in the general human form or as many-armed, many-headed. They may appear temporarily as a tree or as a dragon, a serpent, an elephant, an ape, or as a speaking rock, flowing water, a rushing wind, a flame, a blazing star, a burning sun. They may also speak as a voice coming from any of these forms. These appearances may be solid or they may be airy or astral.

While a God has no youth or old age but comes into existence fully created, he changes during his existence as his worshippers change. At times he may be stronger or weaker. He suffers no physical aches or pain, but only purely psychic afflictions, such as anger, grief and fear. A God does not sleep; he has no solid body and at all times some of his worshippers are awake. The Gods have sex but no sex organs, because they have no fleshly bodies; the sex organs of their worshippers are adequate. There are Gods and Goddesses. If they were worshipped by hermaphrodites they would be hermaphrodite Gods.

In addition to the nature-matter which makes up the body, with or without form, a God has intelligent-matter, with which the doers of his worshippers endow him, through their minds and psychic atmospheres. The intelligent-matter itself has no form, any more than have the doer portions to which it belongs. When people speak of a God they can only refer to the physical matter in which he dwells. They do not refer to the intelligent-matter of the God, any more than they refer to the doers of people unless they connect them with the human bodies through which they live. The nature of the Gods is in great part psychic. They feel and they desire. Their character, their actions, their relations are essentially psychic, that is, like their human sources. Gods have a mental part, they think and they reason. These mental activities are not original, not self-prompted, but Gods use them to serve their desires. They do as little thinking as do their worshippers. A God is conscious as a composite of his living humanity. No God is conscious apart from the bodies and the doers of his worshippers.

The nature of Gods presents the same aspects as the average human nature. Some Gods are simple, some complex. The Gods have only what the human beings who create and worship them have, but the many human contributions during many years magnify the human traits of the Gods. So the goodness, love, knowledge and power, and the anger, hatred, cruelty and lasciviousness of a God are greater than any of these traits are in human beings. The inner nature of a God changes as that of his worshippers changes. He may be more loving and forgiving or more arbitrary, revengeful and cruel at one time than at another.

A God differs from a human in the things he lacks. A God has no identity independent of the identities of his worshippers; he has no mentality and no feelings and desires other than those furnished him by them. No God has a doer or a Triune Self of his own. A God has no aia and no breath-form. No God receives Light directly from an Intelligence. No God was ever human, none will ever become human. Gods are not stations in the Eternal Order of Progression. There are no entities that rise to become Gods, and Gods do not develop into entities independent of the doers and bodies of their peoples. A God has no destiny. He is the destiny of each of his worshippers who accepts and issues the thought of him. No God is responsible. A God exists for the experience of his people, as long as they want to look up to an outside deity.

The name of a God, if he has one, is characteristic of the God; it indicates his nature. The name is made by sounds and these are shown by letters. The forms of the letters and of the sounds have meanings. The total of the meanings is the name and shows the nature of the God. To illustrate. The name Jehovah embodies powers, organs, functions, qualities and relations. The letters make a male part and a female part, the male part having in it the female, and the female part having in it the male. The name is divided, but each part comes from and gets its power from the one name. The function is sexual. When the parts are in two separate beings one has to act through the other; when the parts are both in the same being they act together as one. The qualities are the elements in their active and their passive sides. The relations embodied in the name of Jehovah are those of male to female and those of both to their God, their origin, their creator and their ruler.

Some Gods have no name in this sense. Christians have taken the generic title God and transformed it into a name, as they have done with the word Lord, but it is not a real name. The designation as God and the description by attributes like the All-wise, the Almighty, or by relation like Father, Friend, or by titles like King, Creator are not names. There is a reason for the failure of the Christian Gods to acquire a name.

A God gets his name through the breath and mouth of his worshippers. The name, if it is a real name, like Allah, Brahmâ, Jehovah, not an appellation or a title, is always sexual, no matter what the religion or the age. The worship centers around the name. So Jehovah is properly worshipped when a Jewish man and woman breathe alternately each his and her own part of the name, to propagate. They desecrate the name of their God when they are in union not to propagate; then they use his name in vain.

The name identifies the God, but it is not his identity. The name is a channel through which the desire and thought of the devotee flow to him. Rigidity and conservatism in the worship of the name are necessary to preserve the very basis of the God as a being. Those Gods who have been successful in maintaining the worship of their names have had the longest life. The Gods of the Christians, though nature Gods, have no names, but the worship of the Christian religions is held together by the name of Jesus Christ, who personifies and is a substitute for these Gods. Christians have adopted the Jewish God, but are not as devoted to him as they are to Jesus.

There is a mystery about a God. His nature, origin, past, location, presence, his relation to nature and to nature forces, his works and how he does them, his relation to his devotees and to others, to his messengers, prophets and priests, the purpose of life: everything about his being, aims and actions is mysterious. People wish to account for the world as it is. So they accredit it to a God, and he does not reveal how he created the world or how he manages it. Many things, especially in outside nature, go by definite law, and people are inclined to believe that law prevails.

Yet otherwise, especially as to moral compensation, there seems at times to be no law. The mystery remains because humans have not solved it.

Among the results of the mystery are religions, and with them the awe and fear of the unknown and obscure God, the fanaticism of ignorance, the claim to know, the fascination and the wonders of the works of God, and the profit to the mercenary who can turn all this to their advantage.

These results are at times used by Intelligences and complete Triune Selves to bring about effects as destiny in their government of the world. So the awe and fear of the unknown are used to give a moral code in religions, the fanaticism is used to loose blind force to carry out some plan, the claim is used to further order, the fascination and wonder are used to stimulate doers in their search for God, and the desire for worldly advancement is used like any other desire, to have profit or advantage.

Mystery about a God is essential to him. If the mystery is gone the nature of the God is gone, the God is gone. The mystery of God lies in man himself.

There are varieties of Gods. Fashion Gods, family Gods, political party Gods, guild Gods, dynastic Gods, money Gods and gambling Gods, and the help and protection Gods who are the Gods of religions—all come into existence in the same way, by human thoughts, and have a similar nature. All are made by humans, have bodies of elemental matter empowered by human thought and desire, and exhibit human traits. Here the concern is, however, only with the Gods of religions.

There are the gods of the streams and woods, in localities where human beings are and think. In places where no human beings penetrate and of which they do not think, there are none of these Gods. All are made by human thought. Elementals are there, but they cannot be called Gods. Household Gods exist, though they do not receive as much attention today as they did. Most Gods are local, from the mountain and sea Gods to the English or the French or the German Gods. Locality and language, since they influence thought, determine the conception of a God and therefore his nature. Sometimes Gods which were once local become independent of locality, as was the case with the Jewish Jehovah. The same God is worshipped by Jews in various countries as long as they adhere partially to the Hebrew service and to his name. Generally, however, locality and language have their part in the nature of the God.

There is no one Christian God, though most Christians believe Jesus to be the son of God. The Gods of the various Christian countries are different entities. There are many Gods even in any one of these countries. Thinking through the molds of locality, language and sect makes these Gods. They are composites of the thoughts of their worshippers. Each one is by his believers held to be the Creator and the Supreme Ruler of the universe. There is no one God who harmonizes and unites these various Gods. Moreover the dominating idea of a locality modifies the conception of God. The idea of democracy, if dominant, influences the king or ruler idea concerning God. The characters of these Gods change when the thinking of the people changes. The Gods become kinder, more tolerant, more just, as the people do. When the times are hard, relentless, arbitrary, the Gods become so too. The Christian Gods are held together by the worship of the idea of Jesus, the Savior. He too has been made a nature God, worshipped with bread and wine, with fire and water, and with stone and chants.

SECTION 3

The human qualities of a God. The knowledge of a God. His objects and interests. Relations of a God. The moral code. Flattery. How Gods lose their power. What a God can do for his worshippers; what he cannot do. After death. Unbelievers. Prayer.

The qualities of a God are entirely human. He has no qualities which a human has not. His disposition is human. His powers may be superhuman, because they are an accumulation of the powers given by many worshippers and because he has the power of elemental nature in so far as it makes up his body. A God has no health or disease and no bodily pains. He feels pleasure or distress from the manner in which his worshippers, other human beings and other Gods, treat him. He desires pleasure from the display and consequent recognition of the qualities and powers with which he is endowed. Some Gods are pitiless, revengeful, jealous and are pleased when their people successfully demonstrate these qualities. None of them is entirely just, righteous or loving, or is perfect, almighty or the ultimate Good. None of them has foresight, to any greater extent than the human beings have who worship him. None of them is limitless in time, though some have lived through thousands of years under slightly different names as the Gods of different peoples. In his belief and in his declarations each God is sincere. None of them has knowledge or knows that he is ignorant. Each believes that he has supreme power, when such is credited to him by his worshippers.

The objects, interests and purposes of a God are human affairs. He takes the conditions of the earth as he finds them. He does not create new earths, new continents, new races. He leaves this to man, whose originality and imagination are greater than that of any God. A God is thus interested in human affairs for the purpose of increasing the numbers of his worshippers and their enthusiasm and to obtain devotion in working for his power and glory.

Gods have relations with Intelligences, with other Gods, with nature and with men. A God derives his mental properties from a multitude of doers, a part of whose educational needs is filled by the existence of this composite entity. Any Intelligence is immeasurably superior to the most powerful of the Gods that have been or ever can be. There are many Intelligences having relations with a God. The bond is the Light of the Intelligence sent out by the human beings in their thoughts of worship that support the God, as the money of many small depositors constitute the assets and power of a large bank. The Intelligences guide the God in certain instances. They do not create a God, men do that. They do not give him his character, men do that. They do not shorten or prolong his life, men do that.

Governing Triune Selves use him in exteriorizing thoughts and carrying out destiny as determined by those to whom it comes. They empower or hinder a God for a special purpose. So one dynastic and religious God may be assisted in overcoming another, or a warlike God, ready to consume whole nations, may be restricted in the conquest made by his people. A God is allowed to go and assisted to go as far as the destiny of those affected permits. Triune Selves see to it that the moral code, which every system of worship has, does not go against the needs of the people, and that it contains something that will aid in the education of doers. The Triune Selves do not give it, nor does the God give it; men give it. The God does not particularly care about the moral code. The Triune Selves are interested in the education of the doers, which is not only immaterial to but is opposed by the God, as it will take them away from him. He does not know of Triune Selves or of Intelligences. All he feels in this regard is that he is sometimes checked, and then he fears.

The relations of Gods of religions to other Gods comprise those with pure elemental gods and those with Gods of other religions and those of

Gods which are not Gods of religions. Humans do not know of and do not come in contact with the gods of the four elements. These gods are not manifest to humans. If humans worship a fire God or a water God it is a God created and supported by their thought, not a pure elemental. The Gods which humans worship are in contact with the elemental gods because, though humans do not perceive it, their Gods are in the elements. The elements are their setting. They have their being in the elements and so are in contact with the elemental gods. The elements are necessary to the Gods of religions. Without them these could not exist. But the elemental gods are not manifested to the Gods of religions, though they support them. The relation of the God of a religion to the pure elemental gods is like that of an animal to air or of a fish to water. All the Gods of religions are in the Great Earth Spirit, that is, in the elemental of the sphere of earth; but they are not in direct contact with it. They reach it and are affected by it through the elementals of the light, the life, the form or the physical worlds. The Gods of the religions of historical times, however, were or are in direct contact with the Earth Spirit only, that is, with the elemental of the physical human world, or indirectly with it through elementals of the four planes of the physical world. Because of their connection with purely elemental gods the Gods of religions are enabled to produce physical phenomena like lightning, storms, floods and earthquakes, good harvests and famines, possessions and poverty, and otherwise to show favor or disfavor to humans. Inasmuch as the worshippers connect their God with nature, they worship him as an extraneous being, and so engage in common prayer and worship.

The relations with the Gods of other religions are friendly or hostile according to the objects which the Gods pursue. The relations are chiefly inimical, since the Gods of religions want the same things from the same people, worship with "body, mind and soul". The bodies of Gods have in them units which have served as compositor units in human bodies, and other units which have passed as free or as transient units through human bodies. The free and the transient units may pass from the body of one God into the body of another, but the compositor units do not do this, unless the human to whose body they belonged during his life has changed his worship to that of the other God. The same matter may be therefore successively part of the physical make-up of several Gods. From the psychic make-up which comes to them from their worshippers, Gods derive their feeling and power. This changes likewise when the worshippers change from one God to another. Gods are separate. They do not fraternize with one another. The relation between the Gods of religions is a constant, jealous and fierce struggle. Hence comes the general tendency to demand exclusive worship, to reward it and to enforce it. Gods conquer each other only through human beings.

The history of religions shows therefore that the God of nearly every religion demands worship as the Creator of the universe and as its Supreme Ruler, claims for his priests religious and worldly power and wants to be adored in every act of life. Religious persecutions and religious wars are common features of history.

The Gods of religions have also relations with Gods who are not Gods of religions. Among such Gods are dynastic Gods, big family Gods, household Gods, money Gods, field, stream, woodland, water and other little nature Gods. The religious God wants to be at the head of this collection and usually is allowed to be so. Sometimes even that is not enough. Then these lesser gods are also looked at as enemies, and the humans who recognize them are persecuted and punished.

The relation of the God of a religion to nature exists because the elements of nature compose his body. When a God of a religion is created, the thought of his human creators draws through the manifested out of the unmanifested, the matter that makes up the body of the God. This is the background of elemental matter to which the God is related as long as he exists. The body is not condensed into solid matter, but remains on the planes where it was fashioned. The God is thus always with the unmanifested and with the manifesting elements.

Nature as causal, portal, form and structure elementals of fire, air, water and earth, forms the body of a God and gives him his power. This includes power over these elementals. He can thus produce the phenomena seen as active physical nature. He cannot act in the unmanifested though he draws power from it. But everything from the bursting of volcanoes and of continents to the falling of snow, from the growing of fruits to the blighting of all vegetation, from the birth of animals to their destruction, everything that makes the conditions of human existence, a God may produce because of his relation to nature. There are no bounds to what he may do with nature, as nature; but he is subject to two limitations. He is limited by the thoughts of humans and by the plans of the Intelligences and the Triune Selves who marshal the exteriorization of these thoughts. He cannot do what would be against the destiny of the people affected. Within these two limitations he may act arbitrarily in rewarding and in punishing. He has little leeway. His great power is one which he must exercise according to law within a narrow range.

The relations of a God to men are in part shown by their religion. The relations are often different from what they are supposed to be. A God is created by the thinking of men. He is a thought, differing from other thoughts in that a God-thought is one to which many persons contribute; in that a God-thought is a living being superior to any one of its creators, which an ordinary thought is not; in that a God-thought is in constant touch with the unmanifested physical world and can draw on it, which an ordinary thought cannot. It differs, too, in that a God-thought is a being acknowledged by Intelligences to be an established agent between unmanifested nature and men, through which some of their thoughts are exteriorized to them; in that the idea of a God-thought as a help and protection God is established by Intelligences as the central idea in a religious system; and in that a God-thought receives constantly from men feeling-and-desire, the feeling of rightness-and-reason, and the feeling of I-ness-and-selfness.

Men adore, praise, give thanks to their God and worship him with rites, vestments, symbols, feasts, fasts and holy days. They develop a theology, a religious system and institutions for him. By all this worship they build him up from themselves. Some serve him in these ways with heartfelt devotion, some as fanatics with overwrought zeal. The mass find this the easiest worship. People are less sincere in their expression of gratitude, and still less do they worship their God by obedience to his moral precepts where these clash with their self-interest, appetite and lust. Neglect and disobedience of the moral code have been and are the general rule. But the God does not care much about their self-interest and vices, except for the abuse of sex.

This is hated by the Gods of most religions because the Gods want the sex energy to go to the multiplication of their worshippers or into their own glorification. Sex abuse drains the force, which should go out to the God in prayer and praise. But there are some Gods who want to be worshipped by orgies.

A God is not interested in human affairs, social or political, in which he is not named or thought of. He is interested in food because men pray for their daily bread, and in games if they have a religious tinge. He would be interested in a baseball game, a bullfight or a prize fight, if he were thought of or his name were invoked in connection with such sports. Of course he takes an interest in battles, because he is prayed to. Usually the other side has a different God. So even if the prayer be apparently directed to the nominally one Christian God, each side prays to its own Christian God.

In flattery every God revels. There has never been one who did not delight in flattery. In this every God is very human. A God uses every means to get flattery. Deserved praise is not enough; the most extravagant flattery is encouraged. Hymns, prayer and worship abound in flattery.

Men shear their God of his power by the misuse of their sex function, by the worship of another God, by heresy and by sorcery; and by attempts to solve the mystery of God by thinking.

The actions which are possible to or permitted to a God are actually circumscribed in a manner which religions do not at all suggest. His actions are not voluntary; they are controlled by many factors.

No God created the world. No God made man. There have been thousands of Gods in the history of the world, and nearly every one has been credited with the creation of the world and of man. In a few thousand years the Gods of today may be as forgotten as those of a buried continent, and others will be worshipped, and each of them will claim to be the Creator of the world and of man. No God governs the world, no God maintains it. No God sets the stars and the sun, moon and planets in their courses or makes the seasons.

Yet the God of any religion does many things for his worshippers, whom he aids in getting food, clothing, shelter, comforts, possessions and whatever makes life pleasant. The God also burdens them with hardships and trials, and gives them what makes life bitter, hard and desolate. The God does these things not directly, but by means of hosts of the causal, portal, form and structure group elementals, which control the four classes of fire, air, water and earth elementals, the producers of all earthly phenomena.

The God does these things for his worshippers because they in consequence support him, not because they are his children, not because he wants to educate or improve them and not because he is just. He allows and fosters the belief, which he eventually shares, that he is just, kind and loving, as he is told by them that he is, although the belief may be opposed to the facts. He does not give knowledge or conscience, nor does he give science, art or literature. But these are used in his worship and he wants them in his service as much as possible. At times priests have secret knowledge of nature forces and use it in his worship, sometimes theology is finely spun, sometimes art in his service is lofty, but he is not the cause of this.

Not only does a God not give his worshippers enlightenment, but he tries to keep them in ignorance about themselves and about himself. He takes advantage of their ignorance in that respect. So he favors mysteries. Inspiration in a mass of people, enthusiasm, excitement, frenzy, these a God bestows. Theurgy, in the sense of direct and supernatural interference with natural laws or with human affairs, is not among his powers.

He does not appear to men, because he has no solid physical body, and because he has no form in the form world, the life world or the light world, since his worshippers themselves have not developed any. He can only appear in the form of fire, wind, a cloud or similar shapes furnished by elementals.

Sacred monuments, books or writings are not given to men by their Gods. Men provide them, though they may be inspired thereto by their Gods. A God stunts the mental development of his worshippers where it is concerned with an inquiry into his being, but he encourages such development where it is employed in his service.

In the after-death states no God can do anything for those who were his worshippers, nor can he harm or even reach those who have failed to worship him. This is as true of Jehovah, Jesus and the Christian Gods as it is of the Hindu Gods and of Allah. Their power is limited to the world on which sun and moon shine. No God can reach a doer except through and as long as it has its physical body. What does follow a man into the states after death is his conception of God and what he felt was his duty. Those who believe in Jesus as the Savior, or in God as their Father enthroned in the heavens amidst his angels, or in some protecting saint, will find the thought they have formed. The thought will be as real as they have made it. So they meet God, Jesus or the saints in their heaven.

Though a God cannot reach his worshippers in their after-death states, he marks the breath-form during life, and this mark is by the aia transferred to the new breath-form, so that it will deliver the body to be born to parents following the religion of the God. If the religion of the God has passed away when the re-embodiment comes, the human being comes into that faith which is most like the religion that has passed.

There are limits set to the power of a God in rewarding or punishing his worshippers. He can bestow, take away or withhold his gifts from them only within the limits set by their destiny, that is, the exteriorization of their thoughts. He does not know the limits as limits, but he feels them. He feels that that to which he is limited is the only possibility of action and he believes that he is acting freely. He cannot despoil an enemy or an enemy of his people unless the destiny of the enemy permits. He cannot bless a worshipper with gifts whose destiny does not permit it.

Materialists, skeptics, unbelievers and atheists nearly all believe in some kind of superhuman power manifesting in external nature. They call this power chance, luck, fate, destiny or nature. So they come back to a God of nature, even if they do not give it a name or praise. This thought is not endowed with feeling, desire and a little intelligence, as is the God of a religion, but it has power. These thoughts of the deniers, the doubters and the indifferent, form some sort of little God which causes elementals to act and so furnishes the gifts of life and takes them away according to the limits set by the law. If there were a human who did not believe in any God, not even in nature or fate, he would still get necessaries, pleasures and troubles. All this would come to him from elementals and not as sent by any God.

In every case what comes to a man is the exteriorization of his thoughts, nothing more, nothing less. But the events can be hastened or retarded within certain limits by a God. The exercise of this limited power appears to those who believe in him and are entirely ignorant of the matter, as omnipotence, shown sometimes as a granting of their prayer, and sometimes as the fearful judgment of heaven.

In the case of an unbeliever, events come in the end as they do to a believer, but many more unpleasant things are likely to happen to the unbeliever before his thought can produce the destiny that the simple faith of a sincere believer can project at once.

A God answers prayer, but not every prayer, especially not every selfish prayer. Indeed his power to answer prayer is circumscribed. He is limited by the destiny of those who pray and by the plans of the Triune Selves who marshal that destiny. Among the prayers which are "answered" many are not answered by the God at all. They never reach him. They are attended to, not by the God, but by elementals building according to the lines engraved by thought on the breath-form. As for prayer for special physical things or for help out of a difficult situation, the God does not and cannot answer it. Prayer for others, for their success, for strength or growth of those one cares for, is another matter. The God does not answer that either, but it seems to be answered, sometimes because it gives encouragement to and makes easier the way of those who are prayed for. It is like saying a kind word to one who is making an effort. The result does not come from God but from the thoughts of those who pray. These have an effect on the thoughts of the one who is prayed for.

SECTION 4

Benefits of a belief in a God. Seeking God. Prayer. Outside teachings and the inner life. Inner teachings. Twelve types of teachings. Jehovah worship. The Hebrew letters. Christianity. St. Paul. The story of Jesus. Symbolic events. The Kingdom of Heaven, and the Kingdom of God. The Christian Trinity.

The results which come to the human from a belief in one of these Gods may be of great benefit. They make up the higher life of human beings. In their troubles and trials men look to their God for help and protection. They believe him to be unchangeable among the changes of life. They think he is the source of their mind, that he speaks to them through their conscience, that he will give them peace. Belief in his love and presence gives them strength to live through their hardships. But more. A belief in God is an incentive to a virtuous life in the hope of thereby coming nearer to God and becoming more conscious of him. These are some of the interior results.

But men must seek God and forget about themselves. If they do think about themselves it should be with humility. They must not think of what they are entitled to have or to be. They must think not of their wishes and their rights, but of their obligations for what they have received and of their duties. If they do not think about themselves they can seek God. They are not free to seek God until they abandon themselves as personalities. They cannot find him while thinking of personal self persists. There is no place for both.

The exterior results are the building of places of worship, the maintenance of a hierarchy of priestly officers, almsgiving and philanthropy, persecution, war, hypocrisy and occasional excesses.

People are not aware that they are believing in two different Gods, whom they call by one name and whom they believe to be one. They look for him and see his works in the vast expanse and in the fearful power of nature outside. They believe he gives and takes things away. They believe that he gives them understanding and speaks through conscience. Thus they confuse two different beings. The being from whom they receive understanding, conscience and identity and because of whom they can feel and think, is that of which they are a part. It is their unknown noetic part, their knower. How to know and worship one's knower is taught in no historical religion. But through the worship paid to the God of a religion, by a pure and noble life, worship is paid, seemingly to the God without, but really to one's individual knower.

The run of human beings is sense-bound. They live and think in externals. Their feeling and thinking go out into nature. The grandeur and terror of nature and the force of destiny make deep impressions on the breath-form, and feeling and thinking follow these impressions. The knower makes no such impression. It is merely a witness. Because of its presence there is in man the feeling of "I" or identity. This is not valued, as it is always present; its meaning is not appreciated. This feeling is changeless and eternal and cannot be lost. Upon this identity depends the existence of the human. Yet it is not even noticed.

Man's idea of God comes from his thinker and knower. That is the mystery of God. His ignorance about his thinker and knower and about himself as only a portion of the doer, compels him to account in some way for the "divinity" felt within. His ignorance concerning the "divinity" within and the compulsion to explain it, cause him to look outside himself. The doer is affected by this noetic presence. Man seeks to personalize, portray and deify the feeling of identity which he feels but cannot grasp. He is a slave of nature, and forced to picture the idea of God in terms of nature. When the nature God is built up outside, the human attributes to him the power and knowledge which he sees displayed in the universe. The attribution is wrong. The outside God cannot reveal himself, because he can tell the human only what he already knows and contributes to that God. The only explanation given is, that God is a mystery. The mystery is within. When a human knows of his thinker and his knower, he will not worship a nature God. But while a human does not understand this it is fitting and the best thing for him, to worship the God of the religion into which he was born or of that of his choice.

The results of belief in God are usually good. The belief is uplifting, stimulating, comforting. It supplies what nothing else in life can give. Such a belief is necessary and answers one of the strongest yearnings of the human heart. If that God is powerless to change destiny and even helpless to answer prayer, yet strength and consolation may come from some other source.

Sincere prayer for enlightenment, for strength to withstand temptation, for light to see one's duty, is answered by one's own thinker, who is his judge, even though the prayer is addressed to the God without.

Prayer that is one-pointed, unconditioned and without reservation, is the only kind that will reach one's thinker. The thinker will not give Light or help or comfort in sorrow or in trouble where the prayer is simply to satisfy a selfish want.

The belief itself, that there is a God, even if he be a God of straw, gives strength. It allows the believer to feel that he does not stand alone, that he is not forsaken, that he can depend on God. The belief itself gives strength. Worship of a God of a religion is a help, because the underlying idea is that it is concerned with something superior, something beyond the material, and because it is a lifting of the voice to what is supposed to be a being of justice and power. Again, it is the strength of the belief that brings benefit. But men do not usually worship their God honestly; they worship with their lips and not with their hearts; they say what they do not feel or believe; they are dishonest with their God; they promise more than they are willing to do.

Because of the many benefits which come from belief in a God, religions which teach his worship are necessary. They form one of the closest bonds between humans believing in the protection and fatherhood of a God who is the source of their being. Every religion is a brotherhood and has in it the germ of a brotherhood of humanity. A religion is a social circle in which marriage is made and a family developed. A religion encourages self-denial, self-control. It teaches a method of life which is clean, wholesome, moral. Religion based on a belief in God tells of the way to God.

Most of the great nature religions have these outer teachings. Within the religions are developed sects which search for and try to attain to an inner life, The Way, which leads to the Light within. With Brahminism developed the Yoga schools. Buddhism grew out of Brahminism and teaches about The Way. Into Mohammedanism came the Sufi sects with their inner teachings. From the outer Greek religions developed sects which looked for the inner Gnosis. In Judaism arose the inner teachings called Cabala. Into it also came the inner teachings of St. Paul. But these were not able to change the Jewish nature religion, which still survives in Christianity.

Too much secrecy of these inner teachings usually has caused the possessors to lose their knowledge of them. If men have knowledge and keep it for themselves because they are too selfish to share it, they retain some of the forms without the knowledge. The keys, omissions, blinds, ciphers and similar preservatives debase the teaching, until it is altered so as to be unintelligible to the would-be guardians themselves. Instances can be seen in the lost knowledge of the Brahmins, of the Cabalists and of the earliest Christians.

One who understands that he, as feeling-and-desire in the physical body, is the agent, the conscious doer portion of his own thinker and knower in the Eternal, will not, he cannot, depend on the god or gods of a nature religion. Understanding this he becomes independent and responsible; he will not require or want a nature religion. He will also understand that the worship of nature gods is observed by people because such attributes as ever-presence, all-powerfulness and omniscience, with which the gods are endowed, are due to promptings from their own thinkers and knowers, whom they will then recognize and give service to. Without such understanding human beings have created thoughts which became the nature gods. Thus the nature religions have been perpetuated.

There are cycles of six types of nature religions and six types of information about the thinker and knower,—one about every 2,000 years. So far, whenever this information has been offered, the priests of religions have changed it, and it has been turned into nature religions. There is evidence of this in some of the nature religions. Whenever the six opportunities for the acceptance of information about the thinker and knower are rejected, a cycle of six nature religions swings in and holds sway for the next 12,000 years, approximately. Then a new opportunity is given.

The Christian teachings belong to the cycle dealing with the thinker and knower. Brahminism belongs to a former cycle, and is a remnant turned into a nature religion. Buddhism, Zoroastrianism, and Mohammedanism, though millions adhere to them, do not belong to the cycle.

With Jehovah worship ends the last cycle of the six nature religions. This worship was from a former teaching which was given to a different race and which was to enable people to build a permanent body, (Fig. VI-D). The Jehovah of that original religion, whose name is now *ineffable*, stands behind the Jewish Jehovah. Judaism is based on the five books of Moses, on what Jehovah says about himself and on what his people say about him. The first of the Ten Commandments is that they shall have no other Gods before him. The Commandments make for a proper life and a safe community in which to live on earth. The Jews have made a god, whom they worship as Adonai, which is the symbol of the physical body, as A O M is the symbol of the Triune Self. Adonai is the name of the physical body as it is, in place of the Jehovah body, which would be a sexless body. Adonai is the name that the race can pronounce. They cannot pronounce the name of the Jehovah or Jaweh who stands behind, because his name can be pronounced only by a two-columned sexless body. At present it takes two, a man and a woman, to invoke the name. The original nature religion which underlies the Jewish version was aided by the Intelligences and Triune Selves to aid humans in producing a permanent body, in which the entire Triune Self could be embodied.

The present Jehovah religion shows that the Jewish Jehovah is a sexual nature God, a spirit of the physical earth and its subsidiary earths, water, air and fire. The Hebrew letters are elemental forms, magical figures, through which nature elementals may be used. The vowels are the breaths and the consonants are the forms through which they work.

There was a class among the Jews who could use these letters to produce magical results with the aid of nature spirits. They knew a great deal about the workings of the body, and so could build up strong, healthy bodies for the worship of their God. Their time was before Christianity.

After Christianity a class among the Jews developed a system, the remains of which are known as Cabala. They claimed that this Cabala was the secret knowledge of their sacred books. Each of the twenty-two letters represents a particular organ or part of the body and is an opening to reach elementals and for elementals to come into the body. The elementals build the body, change it and destroy it. By knowing the use of each letter a Cabalist acquired psychic powers. He could evoke and use these elementals through the letters and thereby bring about changes in his body. He could in the same way learn about the structure of physical nature and so bring about changes in it. These may be magical phenomena. The Cabalists had an opportunity of raising the Jewish religion. Because they guarded this knowledge too selfishly and would not give it out, they lost it. Only fragments, which are ineffective, remain to them.

The religion which was the last in the cycle of nature religions and which became the Jehovah religion, was a link religion. It could have been used to link the cycle of nature religions with information about the thinker and knower, which is not a religion. The new information was turned into religions and became Christianity. The opportunity given about 2,000 years ago was lost. Five more opportunities will be offered during the cycle.

Christianity is not one religion, but includes many. These have a common origin in a religion supposed to have been founded by Jesus, in a belief in Jesus as the Savior, in central ceremonies in Baptism, the Lord's Supper and common teachings taken from the New Testament, and so are held together by the name of Jesus, the Christ.

Christianity had its origin in the Jehovah and in the Greek nature religions. Inside of these arose Gnostic sects. Perhaps out of one of these, in combination with Greek philosophy and the Jewish religion, came Christianity.

The founder of Christianity was St. Paul. His teachings are teachings of the inner life. He pointed to The Way. True Christianity would be the seeking and the finding of The Way. Christianity has turned out to be nothing of the kind. Instead, the Jehovah religion has multiplied itself into many nature religions, each under a different God, which are united by the name of Jesus Christ. The Christian Gods, however, do not demand the food and sex regulations which the Jehovah worship imposed. The stories about the Savior's birth, life, suffering, death, resurrection and ascension have become the basis of additional nature worship which unites the various Christian nature religions.

Christianity may have resulted from the attainment to a state of perfection by a doer all of whose twelve portions were together embodied in an immortal body, and the Triune Self would be ready to become an Intelligence. Such an event would cause a stir in the atmospheres of human beings, and some would feel called to follow and to teach more emphatically an inner life. The development of the doer in a human into what in the eyes of the world would be a divinity, and his telling of "the way, the truth and the life," and of the "Kingdom of God", is the basis of the story of Jesus.

Of his carnal body nothing is known. It is likely that he had retired from the world, else he could not have developed his immortal physical body. Jesus was the name given to the body of the doer, here called the form being, which he had developed; Christ was the name given to the life being of the thinker; the light being of the knower is his Father, of whom tradition has him speak and with whom he attained union.

As this development of the doer could not be understood, the stories soon came to be on a level with everyday life, made attractive by miracles. The supernatural in these stories was to hold the attention of the run of human beings.

Nothing is known of the physical existence of Jesus; and of course nothing is known of the doer that inhabited this unknown body. The names Jesus and Christ were names given by the people who attempted to publish the story of his attainment and of his teaching, now lost, of The Way. The New Testament version of the person of Jesus and of his teachings is most likely the result of ignorance, compromise, tradition and editing.

Some of the events narrated are symbolic. The divine conception stands for the union of the solar and lunar germs in a purified or virgin body. The birth in a stable is the beginning of the life of the form being in the pelvic region, where the animals were. The baptism stands for a later event on The Way, where the advancing traveler is led into a pool under a fountain, where the new form being draws from and is quickened by the water of life, expands into the ocean and becomes that ocean throughout nature, and the doer feels itself throughout humanity. Jesus is said to have been a carpenter. He might have been called a bridge builder, a mason or an architect, because he had to build a bridge or a temple between the nature-cord and the spinal-cord for the Triune Self.

The cross is also symbolic. A human body has both a male and a female nature, and these two natures are tied together, crossed in it. This is symbolized by the cross made by a female horizontal and a male vertical line. The story of the crucifixion is symbolic of the doer embodied in and fastened to the cross of its body. Living in a body means a suffering for the doer.

His life of about thirty years in a physical body is mythological. If he had disciples they were advanced doers, not of the characters bestowed upon his apostles, and not picked up as the Bible tells. But the twelve disciples are symbolical of the twelve portions of the doers.

As for his depicted suffering, that is impossible. The physical body of a doer such as was Jesus, could not suffer as human beings can, because the physical body was not of flesh such as humans know it. It would have been impossible to capture it, to hold it, to injure it. Even if he had had a body such as humans have, he would not have suffered. A moment's thinking would have disconnected the involuntary from the voluntary nervous system. Even with martyrs, dervishes, sorcerers, feeling is taken away from things of the flesh when a thought connects it with worship, ideals, principles, glory; and Jesus was beyond the state of a martyr.

The story of the Roman penalty of the cross stands for any manner of slowly dying. The body in which such a one as Jesus was, went through the process of transformation from the human physical body to the perfect, deathless body. Jesus, the psychic part of the Triune Self, was immune to suffering any process of death. The story of the death of his body as the result of slowly dying is a natural misconception, due to the fact that ordinary human bodies die and there is nothing left when their particles return to the four elements. This did not apply to the body of Jesus, which went through the process of transformation during which it was recreated and, instead of ending by death, it conquered death and became an immortal sexless physical body. Evidence of this is given by Paul, in his fifteenth Chapter of First Corinthians.

The stories of the crucifixion, resurrection and ascension are remnants of great truths, distorted and turned into gross flesh tales. The story of the resurrection of Jesus represents the raising of the physical body from the stage of death through which it had passed, to a life eternal. His ascension is a distorted picture of a doer going through a white fire which burns away the last vestiges of illusion, going into the light world and becoming a being of the three worlds in the Light of the Intelligence, in the presence of the knower, standing in the presence of the Supreme Triune Self of the worlds through which the Supreme Intelligence acts, and seeing into the Light of his Intelligence and through that Light seeing into the Light of the Supreme Intelligence.

What is called the "Kingdom of Heaven" is the purified psychic atmosphere. The "Kingdom of Heaven" is within. It can be experienced by one who isolates feeling from his body and is thereby in his psychic atmosphere, untouched by the changes of pain and pleasure which come through the body. He is not then conscious of the body.

"The Kingdom of God" refers to what in this book is called the Realm of Permanence, and was evidently intended to designate the earth or physical world of permanence, which does not change, (Fig. V-B,a); it exists throughout all changes and civilizations of the crust. "First" Civilization means the highest in degree, and the "Fourth" means the lowest degree of the Civilizations of the matter and beings. They are not "created", or "destroyed" in the sense that they cease to exist. The

"Kingdom of God" is within, that is, within the body. The body is in it, when that body has been raised to immortality and permanence. This kingdom extends throughout the permanent earth. One who has not regenerated his body into a state of perfection cannot see it; and one who has not perfected his body cannot inherit that kingdom.

The doctrine of a Trinity, as presented in the Christian and other religions, has been a stumbling block, a subject of perplexity, which may be surmounted and solved by an understanding of the Triune Self.

One of the problems of the Christian Trinity was to understand how three persons are only one. The Trinity can be seen to correspond to or mean the three parts of the Triune Self—which is one unit. The three parts constitute one whole unit, which is indivisible.

The trouble may have been that in changing the information about the Triune Self into the teachings of a nature religion, those that promulgated the Christian doctrines failed to understand the Triune Self and were confronted with the difficulty of presenting one God as three individual persons, as a Trinity, which they called the Father, the Son, and the Holy Ghost, or God the Father, God the Son, and God the Holy Ghost. In nature there are threefold gods, who create, maintain, and destroy. This threefold nature aspect is the cause of Trinities in religions. The nature god is presented under three aspects as: creator, preserver, and destroyer or regenerator.

If made to correspond with the Triune Self, God corresponds to the Triune Self, as the unit; the Father is the noetic part, the knower; the Holy Ghost is the mental part, the thinker; the Son is the psychic part, the doer. The doer then is to be the Savior of the physical body, from death, by making of it a perfected, immortal physical body. The doer is the real "Creator" in nature, who stands behind the nature gods and, by thinking, causes them to create, maintain, and destroy. In doing this, the Son, the doer, suffers until he controls his feeling-and-desire and is willing to be guided by the Light of the Intelligence, through his thinker, and until he perfects his physical body.

Christianity has apparently retained only the Father, the "Creator" conception, and has turned the "Preserver" and the "Destroyer" or Regenerator ideas into the Holy Ghost and the Son, or the Mother and the Son.

The teaching which became what is now Christianity was evidently not intended to be a religion at all. It was intended to be a teaching of The Way. This appears from some of the statements attributed to Jesus, among them the one that he was the way, the truth and the life, and his references to his connections with his inner God. It appears especially in the teachings of St. Paul. This teaching of The Way was, however, turned into many nature religions and was lost to Christendom, the whole of the believers, as a teaching of The Way. The Greek Catholic Church is a nature religion. The Roman Catholic Church preaches nature religions; the majority of the sects that came through the Reformation are nature religions. But some like the Quakers and the mystics seek for The Way. Whatever the form of the Christian or any other religion may be, and irrespective of the few who are seeking The Way, it is true that even nature religions give to their followers a little preparation for The Way.

SECTION 5

Interpretation of Bible sayings. The story of Adam and Eve. The trial and test of the sexes. "Fall of man". Immortality. St. Paul. Regeneration of the body. Who and what was Jesus? Mission of Jesus. Jesus, a pattern for man. The order of Melchisedec. Baptism. The sexual act, the original sin. The Trinity. Entering The Great Way.

As stated in the Foreword, this section is added to explain the meaning of what seem to be some incomprehensible passages in the New Testament; and which will also be evidence supporting statements about the interior earth.

It is likely that the original teachings of the New Testament were about the Triune Self, as the *individual* trinity; that they told of the departure or "descent" of the doer part of that Triune Self from the Realm of Permanence into this temporal human world; that it is the duty of each doer, by thinking, to become conscious of itself in the body and to regenerate the body, and thus to become consciously one with its thinker and knower as the Triune Self complete, in the Realm of Permanence,—which Jesus spoke of as the "Kingdom of God."

The books of the New Testament did not become known to the public until some centuries after the alleged crucifixion of Jesus. During that time the writings passed through processes of selection and rejection; the rejected are the apocryphal books; those which were accepted make up the New Testament. The accepted books, of course, had to conform to the doctrines of the Church.

Concerning "The Lost Books of the Bible and The Forgotten Books of Eden," mentioned in the Foreword, it is said in the Introduction to "The Lost Books of the Bible":

"In this volume all these apocryphal volumes are presented without argument or commentation. The reader's own judgment and common sense are appealed to. It makes no difference whether he is Catholic, Protestant or Hebrew. The facts are plainly laid before him. These facts for a long time have been a peculiar property of the learned. They were available only in the original Greek or Latin and so forth. Now they have been translated and brought in plain English before the eye of every reader".

And in the "First Book of Adam and Eve" in "The Forgotten Books of Eden", we read:

"This is the most ancient story in the world—it has survived because it embodies the basic fact of human life. A fact that has not changed one iota; amid all the superficial changes of civilization's vivid array, this fact remains: the conflict of Good and Evil; the fight between Man and the Devil; the eternal struggle of human nature against sin."

One critic has said of this writing:

"This is we believe, the greatest literary discovery that the world has known. Its effect upon contemporary thought in molding the judgment of the future generations is of incalculable value,"

and:

"In general, this account begins where the Genesis story of Adam and Eve leaves off." (Permission has been granted to quote from these books, by the World Publishing Co. of Cleveland, Ohio, and New York City.)

The Bible story of Adam and Eve is: The Lord God formed man of the dust of the ground, and breathed into his nostrils the breath of life; and man became a living soul. And God named the man Adam. Then God caused Adam to sleep and took from within him a rib and made a woman and gave her to Adam to be his help-meet. And Adam called her Eve. God told them they might eat of any of the trees of the garden, except of the fruit of the tree of knowledge of good and evil; that in the day they ate of that fruit they would surely die. The serpent tempted, and they partook of the fruit. Then they were exiled from the Garden; and they brought forth children, and died.

So far, that is all that the public at large has known about the story as told in the book of Genesis. In the "Book of Adam and Eve" in "The

Forgotten Books of Eden," the version given is said to be the work of unknown Egyptians, which has been translated into other languages and finally into English. Scholars have had it for centuries, but not knowing what else to do with it, it is given to the public. It is mentioned here as in part corroboration of what has been written in these pages about the interior earth; of the original oneness of man; of his division into two, male and female at the trial to balance feeling-and-desire; and, later of their appearance on the surface of the earth. According to the story, Adam and Eve were expelled from Paradise, the Garden of Eden. They came out to this outer earth crust by way of what is spoken of as the "Cave of Treasures."

Let Adam and Eve speak for themselves, and of God's voice to them:

Chapter 5: "Then Adam and Eve entered the cave, and stood praying, in their own tongue, unknown to us, but which they knew well. And as they prayed, Adam raised his eyes and saw the rock and the roof of the cave that covered him over head, so that be could see neither heaven, nor God's creatures. So he wept and smote heavily upon his breast, until he dropped, and was as dead." Eve speaks:

"O God, forgive me my sin, the sin which I committed, and remember it not against me. For I (feeling) alone caused Thy servant to fall from the garden (Realm of Permanence) into this lost estate; from light into this darkness. O God, look upon this Thy servant thus fallen, and raise him from his death. But if Thou do not raise him up, then, O God, take away my own soul (form of the breath-form), that I be like him; for I (feeling) could not stand alone in this world, but with him (desire) only. For Thou, O God, didst cause a slumber to come upon him, and didst take a bone from his side (front column), and didst restore the flesh in place of it, by Thy divine power. And Thou didst take me, the bone, (from sternum) and make me a woman. O Lord, I and he are one (feeling and desire). Therefore, O God, give him life, that he may be with me in this strange land, while we dwell in it on account of our transgression."

Chapter 6: But God looked upon them... He, therefore, sent His Word unto them; that they should stand and be raised forthwith. And the Lord said unto Adam and Eve, "You transgressed of your own free will, until you came out of the garden in which I placed you."

Chapter 8: Then God the Lord said unto Adam, "When thou wast under subjection to Me, thou hadst a bright nature within thee, and for that reason couldst thou see things afar off. But after thy transgression thy bright nature was withdrawn from thee; and it was not left to thee to see things afar off, but only near at hand; after the ability of the flesh; for it is brutish."

Chapter 11: And Adam said: "Remember, O Eve, the garden-land, and the brightness thereof! Whereas no sooner did we come into this Cave of Treasures than darkness compassed us round about; until we can no longer see each other."

Chapter 16: Then Adam began to come out of the cave and when he came to the mouth of it, and stood and turned his face towards the east, and saw the sun rise in glowing rays, and felt the heat thereof on his body, he was afraid of it, and thought in his heart that this flame came forth to plague him. For he thought the sun was God. But while he was thus thinking in his heart, the Word of God came unto him and said:— "O Adam, arise and stand up. This sun is not God; but it has been created to give light by day, of which I spake unto thee in the cave saying, 'that the dawn would break forth, and there would be light by day'. But I am God who comforted thee in the night."

Chapter 25: But Adam said unto God, "It was in my mind to put an end to myself at once, for having transgressed Thy commandments, and for having come out of the beautiful garden; and for the bright light of which Thou hast deprived me; and for the light that covered me. Yet of Thy goodness, O God, do not away with me altogether (re-existence); but be favorable to me every time I die, and bring me to life."

Chapter 26: Then came the Word of God to Adam, and said unto him, "Adam, as for the sun, if I were to take it and bring it to thee, days, hours, years and months would all come to naught, and the covenant I have made with thee would never be fulfilled. Yea, rather bear long and calm thy soul while thou abidest night and day; until the fulfillment of the days, and the time of My covenant is come. Then shall I come and save thee, O Adam, for I do not wish that thou be afflicted."

Chapter 38: After these things the Word of God came to Adam and said unto him:—"O Adam, as to the fruit of the Tree of Life, for which thou askest, I will not give it thee now, but when the 5500 years are fulfilled. Then will I give thee of the fruit of the Tree of Life, and thou shall eat, and live for ever, thou, and Eve."

Chapter 41: ...Adam began to pray with his voice before God, and said:—" O Lord, when I was in the garden, and saw the water that flowed from under the Tree of Life, my heart did not desire, neither did my body require to drink of it; neither did I know thirst, for I was living;

and above that which I am now. But now, O God, I am dead; my flesh is parched with thirst. Give me of the Water of Life that I may drink of it and live."

Chapter 42: Then came the Word of God to Adam and said unto him:—"O Adam, as to what thou sayest, 'Bring me into a land where there is rest', it is not another land than this, but it is the kingdom of heaven where alone there is rest. But thou canst not make thy entrance into it at present; but only after thy judgment is past and fulfilled. Then will I make thee go up into the kingdom of heaven."

What in these pages is written about the "Realm of Permanence", may have been thought·of as "Paradise" or the "Garden of Eden". It was when the doer of its Triune Self was with its thinker and knower in the Realm of Permanence that it had to undergo the trial to balance feeling-and-desire, in the course of which trial it was temporarily in a dual body, the "twain", by the separation of its perfect body into a male body for its desire side, and a female body for its feeling side. The doers in all human beings gave way to the temptation by the body-mind for sex, whereupon they were exiled from the Realm of Permanence to re-exist on the crust of the earth in man bodies or in woman bodies. Adam and Eve were one doer divided into a male body and a female body. When the two bodies died the doer did not thereafter re-exist in two bodies; but as desire-and-feeling in a male body, or as feeling-and-desire in a female body. Doers will continue to re-exist on this earth until, by thinking and by their own efforts, they find The Way and return to the Realm of Permanence. The story of Adam and Eve is the story of each human on this earth.

Thus can be epitomized into a few words the stories of the "Garden of Eden," of "Adam and Eve", and of the "fall of man;" or, in the words of this book, the "Realm of Permanence," the story of "feeling-and-desire," and that of the "descent of the doer" into this temporal human world. The teaching of the inner life, by Jesus, is the teaching of the doer's return to the Realm of Permanence.

Immortality has always been the hope of man. But in the struggle between life and death in the human body, death has always been the conquerer of life. Paul is the apostle of immortality, and Jesus Christ is his subject. Paul testifies that on his way to Damascus with a band of soldiers to persecute the Christians, Jesus appeared and spoke to him. And he, blinded by the light, fell down, and asked: "Lord, What wilt thou have me do?" In this way was Paul chosen by Jesus to be the apostle of immortality to man. And Paul took as his subject: Jesus, the living Christ.

The entire 15th Chapter of First Corinthians composed of 58 verses is Paul's supreme endeavor to prove that Jesus "descended" from his Father in heaven into this human world; that he took on a human body to prove to mankind by the example of his own life that man could change his mortal into an immortal body; that he did conquer death; that he did ascend to his Father in heaven; that, in fact, Jesus was the Forerunner, the bringer of the Good News: that all those who would, could come into their great inheritance by changing their sexual bodies of death into sexless bodies of everlasting life; and, that the changing of their bodies should not be put off to a future life. Paul declares:

Verses 3 to 9: For I delivered unto you first of all that which I received, how that Christ died for our sins according to the Scriptures. And that he was buried, and he rose again the third day according to the Scriptures. After that, he was seen by above 500 brethren at once; of whom the greater part remained unto this present, but some are fallen asleep. After that, he was seen of James; then of all the apostles. And last of all he was seen of me also, as one born out of due time. For I am the least of the apostles, that am not meet to be called an apostle, because I persecuted the church of God.

Paul has here stated his case, giving as evidence that according to the Scriptures, the physical body of Jesus died and was buried; that on the third day Jesus rose from the dead; that over 500 persons saw Jesus; and, that he, Paul, was the last to see him. Based on the physical evidence of witnesses, Paul now gives his reasons for immortality:

Verse 12: Now if Christ be preached that he rose from the dead, how say some among you that there is no resurrection of the dead?

All human bodies were variously called the dead, the tomb, and the grave, because 1) human bodies are not of continuous undying life; 2) because they are in process of death until the conscious desire-and-feeling within stops breathing and leaves the dead body, the corpse; 3) the body is called the grave because the desire-and-feeling self is enmeshed in the coils of flesh and does not know that it is buried; it cannot distinguish itself from the grave in which it is buried. The body is called the tomb because the tomb is the form of the body it is in and holds the flesh, and the flesh is the compacted dust of the earth as food in which the self is buried. To rise from the dead and be resurrected it is necessary for the self of desire-and-feeling to be conscious of and as itself while it is entombed in the body, its grave, until, by thinking, the self changes the form, its tomb, and the body, its grave, from a sex body to a body without sex; then the twain desire-and-feeling self has become one, by changing, balancing desire-and-feeling, itself; and the body is no longer the male desire or the female feeling, but is then Jesus, the balanced doer, the acknowledged Son of God, his Father.

Verse 13: "But", Paul argues, "if there be no resurrection of the dead, then is Christ not risen."

That is to say, if there is no change or resurrection of or from the human body, then Christ could not have risen. Paul continues:

Verse 17: And if Christ be not raised, your faith is in vain; ye are yet in your sins.

In other words, if Christ did not rise from the grave there is no resurrection from the body nor any hope for life after death; in which case every human would die in sin, sex. Sin is the sting of the serpent, the result of which is death. The first and original sin was and is the sexual act; that is the sting of the serpent; all other sins of the human in varying degrees are consequences of the sexual act. The argument continues:

Verse 20: But now is Christ risen from the dead, and become the first-fruits of them that slept.

Therefore, the fact that Christ has risen and has been seen by more than 500 people, and become the "first-fruits of them that slept," is the proof that for all other desire-and-feeling selves (still sleeping in their tombs, in their graves), it is possible to follow Christ's example and also to change their bodies, and rise in their new bodies, resurrected from the dead.

Verse 22: "For", as Paul argues, "as in Adam all die, even so in Christ shall all be made alive".

That is to say: Since all bodies of sex do die, so by the power of Christ, and with the doer of desire-and-feeling, all human bodies will be changed and made alive, no longer subject to death. Then there is no more death, for those who have overcome death.

Verse 26: The last enemy that shall be destroyed is death.

Verses 27 to 46 are the reasons given by Paul to bear out the foregoing statements. He continues:

Verse 47: The first man is of the earth, earthy; the second man is of the Lord from heaven.

This shows the human body to be of the earth, and distinguishes the desire-and-feeling of the human, when it becomes conscious of itself, as the Lord from heaven. Paul now makes a startling statement:

Verse 50: Now this I say, brethren, that flesh and blood cannot inherit the kingdom of God; neither does corruption inherit incorruption.

This is equivalent to saying: All human bodies are corrupt because the seed of sexual bodies is of flesh and blood; that those that are born of flesh and blood are corrupt; that bodies of flesh and blood must die; and, that no flesh and blood bodies can be in the kingdom of God. Were it possible for a human body to be transported into the Realm of Permanence or kingdom of God it would instantly die; it could not breathe there. Because flesh and blood bodies are corrupt, they cannot inherit incorruption. How then can they be raised? Paul explains:

Verse 51: "Behold, I show you a mystery: We shall not all sleep, but we shall all be changed."

And, Paul says, the reason for the changing is:

Verses 53 to 57: "For this corruptible must put on incorruption, and this mortal must put on immortality. So when this corruptible shall have put on incorruption, and this mortal shall have put on immortality, then shall be brought to pass the saying that is written, Death is swallowed up in victory. O death, where is thy sting? O grave, where is thy victory? The sting of death is sin and the strength of sin is the law. But thanks be to God, which giveth us the victory through our Lord Jesus Christ."

This means that all human beings are subject to the sin of the sexes and are therefore under the law of sin, which is death. But when the human thinks, and wakes to the fact that as the doer in the body, he is not the body in which he is encased, he weakens the hypnotic spell cast on him by his body-mind. And he begins to see things not by the light of the senses but in a new light, by the Conscious Light within, by thinking. And to the degree that he so thinks his "Father in heaven" guides him. His body-mind of the senses and the sexes is his devil, and it will tempt him. But if he refuses to follow where the body-mind would lead him by its thinking; and, by thinking of his relation as the Son of his Father, he will eventually break the power of his devil, the body-mind, and will subdue it. Then it will obey him. When the doer of desire-and-feeling in the body controls his thinking, and by the thinking of his desire and feeling minds also controls the body-mind, then the body-mind will change the structure of the mortal body of the sex into a sexless body of immortal life. And the conscious self in the body as Jesus the Christ will rise in the glorified body of its resurrection from the dead.

Paul's teaching, to all who will accept it, is: that Jesus descended from his Father in heaven and took on a mortal body to tell all mortals: that they as conscious doers were asleep, entombed and buried in their bodies of flesh, which would die; that if they so desired they could wake from their sleep, could appeal to their Fathers in heaven, and discover themselves in their bodies; that they could change their mortal into immortal bodies and ascend to and be with their Fathers in heaven; that the life and teaching of Jesus set them an example, and that he was the "first-fruits" of what they also could do.

The Gospel Story.

Scholars assert there is no authentic record that Jesus Christ of the Gospels lived on this earth; but no one denies that there were Christian Churches in the first century, and that our calendar began with the date that Jesus is said to have been born.

Earnest, honest and intelligent Christians of all denominations believe the story that Jesus was born of a virgin and that he was the Son of God. How can these claims be true and reconciled with sense and reason?

The story of the birth of Jesus is not the story of the ordinary birth of a baby; it is the unrecorded story of the conscious self of every human who has regenerated, or will in the future regenerate and change his mortal body into a sexless, perfect, immortal physical body. How? This will be shown in detail in the next chapter, "The Great Way."

In the case of an ordinary baby, the doer that is to live in it for the span of its life does not usually enter that little human animal body until from two to five years after its birth. When the doer does take possession of the body, can be marked when it asks and answers questions. Any adult can approximate the time he entered his body by the earliest recollections, memories of what he said and what he then did.

But Jesus had a special mission. If it had been for himself only, the world would not have known of him. Jesus was not the physical body; he was the conscious self, the doer in the body. Jesus knew himself as the doer in the body, whereas the doer in the ordinary human cannot disting··ish itself from its body. People did not know Jesus. The 18 years before his ministry were spent in regenerating his human body into the

stage of virgin—virgin pure, chaste, stainless,—neither male nor female,—sexless.

People believe in the story of Jesus chiefly because it appeals and
applies to their own conscious selves as desire-and-feeling. The story of
Jesus will be the story of the one who, by thinking, discovers himself in
his body. Then, if he will, he literally takes up his body-cross and carries
it, as Jesus did, until he accomplishes what Jesus did. And, in due time,
he will know his Father in heaven.

Jesus, and His Mission.

The non-historical Jesus came at the due cyclical period and told all
who would understand that the desire-and-feeling in the man or in the
woman is in a self-induced hypnotic sleep in its breath-form tomb, in
the flesh body, which is its grave; that the doer self must wake from its
death-like sleep; that by thinking, it must first comprehend and then
discover, wake, itself in its mortal body; that while discovering itself in
the body, the doer self will suffer crucifixion between its male desire in
the blood and the female feeling in the nerves of its own body, the cross;
that this crucifixion will result in changing the physical structure of the
mortal into that of a sexless physical body of everlasting life; that by the
blended and inseparable union of desire-and-feeling as one, the doer
abolishes war between the sexes, conquers death, and ascends to the
knower of its Triune Self in the Realm of Permanence—as Jesus, the
Christ, ascended in his glorified body to his Father in heaven.

His mission could not have been to found a religion, to institute or
order the building or establishment of a universal church, or any temple
made with hands. Here is some of the evidence from the Scriptures:

Matthew 16, verses 13 and 14: "When Jesus came into the coasts of
Caesarea Philippi, he asked his disciples, saying, Whom do men say that
I the Son of man am? And they said, Some say that thou art John the
Baptist; some, Elias; and others, Jeremias, or one of the prophets."

This was a perplexing question. It could not have been a question
concerning his lineage for it was said that he was the son of Mary. Jesus
wanted to be told whether people considered him to be the physical body
or as something different from the physical, and the answers indicated
that they considered him to be a reappearance, the re-existence, of any
one of those mentioned; that they believed him to be a human being.

But the Son of God could not be *only* a human. Jesus questions
further:

Verses 15 to 18: He saith unto them, But whom say ye that I am? And Simon Peter answered and said, Thou art the Christ, the Son of the living God. And Jesus answered and said unto him, Blessed art thou, Simon Bar-jona: For flesh and blood hath not revealed it unto thee, but my Father which is in heaven. And I say also unto thee, That thou art Peter, and upon this rock I will build my church; and the gates of hell shall not prevail against it.

Here Peter's answer tells his belief that Jesus is the Christ, the Son of the living God,—*not the physical body* in which Jesus lived; and Jesus points out the distinction.

The statement of Jesus "…and upon this rock I will build my church; and the gates of hell shall not prevail against it" did not refer to Peter, who was not proof against the fires of hell, but to Christ himself, as the "rock."

By church, was meant the "Lord's house", the "temple not built with hands, eternal in the heavens"; that is: a sexless, immortal, imperishable physical body, in which his Triune Self could be and live in its three aspects as the knower, the thinker, and the doer, as explained in "The Great Way". And such a body can only be built on the basis of the indwelling self, which must be as a "rock." And each human must build his own "individual" church, *his* temple. No one can build such a body for another. But Jesus set a pattern, an example, of how to build,—as told by Paul in First Corinthians, 15th chapter, and in Hebrews, 5th and 7th chapters.

And further, Peter was too unreliable to be the "rock" on which to establish the church of Christ. He professed much but failed in the test. When Peter told Jesus that he would not forsake him, Jesus said: Before the cock crows twice thou shalt deny me thrice. And that did happen.

The Order of Melchisedec,—the Immortals.

It should be seen from the foregoing that Jesus did not come to save the world, or to save any one in the world; that he came to show to the world, that is, to the disciples or any others, that each one could save himself by changing his mortal body into an immortal body. Though not all that he taught has come down to us, there is enough left in the books of the New Testament as evidence that Jesus was one of the "Order of Immortals", of the order of Melchisedec, one of the Order of those who had done what Jesus came to demonstrate of himself, to mankind, so that all who would could follow his example. In Hebrews, Chapter 5, Paul says:

Verses 10 and 11: Called of God an high priest after the order of Melchisedec. Of whom we have many things to say, and hard to be uttered, seeing ye are dull of hearing.

Melchisedec is a word or title in which so much is included that it is hard to tell all that the word is intended to convey, and those to whom he speaks are dull in understanding. Nevertheless, Paul does tell a great deal. He says:

Chapter 6, verse 20: Whither the Forerunner is for us entered, even Jesus, made an high priest for ever after the order of Melchisedec.

Chapter 7, verse 1 to 3: For this Melchisedec, king of Salem, priest of the most high God, who met Abraham returning from the slaughter of the kings, and blessed him; to whom also Abraham gave a tenth part of all; first being by interpretation King of righteousness, and after that also King of Salem, which is, king of peace; Without father, without mother, without descent, having neither beginning of days, nor end of life; but made like unto the Son of God; abideth a priest continually.

Paul speaking of Melchisedec as King of peace explains the saying of Jesus, Matthew 5, verse 9: Blessed are the peacemakers: for they shall be called the children of God (that is, when feeling-and-desire of the doer are in balanced union in an immortal sexless body, the doer is at peace, it is a peace-maker and thus in union with the thinker and knower of its Triune Self).

Here are three strange verses in Ephesians, Chapter 2 (which likewise refer to the union of feeling-and-desire, in an immortal sexless body):

Verses 14 to 16: For he is our peace, who hath made both one, and has broken down the middle wall of partition between us; Having abolished in his flesh the enmity, even the law of commandments contained in ordinances; for to make in himself of twain one new man, so making peace; And that he might reconcile both unto God in one body by the cross, having slain the enmity thereby.

"Breaking down the middle wall of partition between us," means the removal of distinction and division of desire and feeling as the difference between the male and the female. "Enmity" means the war between feeling-and-desire in every human, while under the law of sin, of sex; but when the enmity is abolished, the sin of sex ceases. Then the commandment "to make in himself of twain one new man", that is, union of feeling-and-desire, is fulfilled, "so making peace," and the great work in hand of "redemption," "salvation," "reconciliation," is done, is complete—he is a peacemaker, a "Son of God". Again Paul says:

Timothy, Chapter 1, verse 10: But it is now made manifest by the appearing of our Savior Jesus Christ, who has abolished death, and hath brought life and immortality through the Gospels.

In "Lost Books of the Bible," II Clement, Chapter 5, headed: "A Fragment. Of the Lord's kingdom," it is written:

Verse 1: For the Lord himself, being asked by a certain person, When his kingdom should come? answered, When two shall be one, and that which is without as that which is within; and the male with the female, neither male nor female.

What this verse means is clearly seen when one understands that desire is the male, and feeling is the female in every human being; and, that the two disappear in their union as one; and, when that is done, that the "Lord's kingdom" would come.

Desire and Feeling.

The vital importance of what the two words, desire and feeling, represent, seems not to have been considered before. Desire has usually been regarded as a longing, as something unsatisfied, a want. Feeling is believed to be a fifth sense of the body: touch, sensation, a feeling of pain or pleasure. Desire and feeling have not been linked together as the inseparable, undying "twain", which is the conscious self in the body, the doer of everything that is done with and through the body. But unless desire-and-feeling are thus understood and realized, man will not, he cannot, know himself. Man is at present the unconscious immortal. When he finds and knows himself in the body, he will be consciously immortal.

No mention is made in the Gospels of Jesus after he talked in the Temple at the age of twelve, until eighteen years later, when he is again mentioned as appearing at thirty, to begin his three years of ministry. It could have been possible that during those eighteen years he had prepared and changed, metamorphosed, his human body so that it could have been in a state somewhat like a chrysalis, ready to change, as Paul explains in the 15th chapter, "in the twinkling of an eye" from a mortal to an immortal body. Jesus in that form-body could appear or disappear whenever and wherever he willed to be, as is recorded that he did, and in that body he could have it so that anyone might look at it, or to have it of such radiant blinding power that it would affect a human, as it did Paul.

The changing of a human body should not seem more wonderful than the changing of an impregnated ovum into a baby, or the changing of a baby into a great man. But the historical mortal has not been observed to have become an immortal. When that is known to be a physical fact, it will not seem to be wonderful.

Baptism.

Baptism means immersion. The doer-in-the-body in the ordinary human, is only one of twelve portions, six of which are of desire and six of feeling. When in the course of its development and transformation other portions are enabled to come into the body and the last of the twelve portions has entered, the doer is entirely immersed, baptized. Then the doer is fit, recognized, acknowledged, as the "Son" part of God, his Father.

When Jesus began his ministry, he went down to the river Jordan to be baptized by John; and after he was baptized, "there came a voice from heaven saying 'this is my beloved Son in whom I am well pleased'."

The narrative story of Jesus after his baptism would reveal much if one had a key to the code which Jesus used in his sermons and parables.

The Trinity.

In the New Testament there is no agreement concerning the order and relation of the "three persons" of the Trinity, though the Trinity has often been spoken of as God the Father, God the Son, and God the Holy Ghost. But their relation is apparent if placed side by side with what is herein called the Triune Self. "God the Father" corresponds to the knower of the Triune Self; "God the Son," to the doer; and "God the Holy Ghost" to the thinker of the Triune Self. Herein they are the three parts of one indivisible unit: "God", the knower; "Christ or Holy Ghost", the thinker; and "Jesus", the doer.

The Great Way.

It is not impossible for one who desires to travel The Great Way, which is dealt with in the next chapter, to begin at any time, but then only if he wishes to make it an individual course for himself, and unknown to the world. If one should attempt to begin The Way "out of season", he might not bear the weight of the world's thought; it would be against him. But during the 12,000 years, which cycle began with the birth or the ministry of Jesus, it is possible for any one of those who will, to follow the path which Jesus came to show, and of which he himself set the pattern, being, as Paul says, the first-fruits of the resurrection from the dead.

In this new age it is possible for those whose destiny may permit, or for those who make it their destiny by their thinking, to go on The Way. One who chooses to do so, may succeed in overcoming the thought of the world, and build a bridge from this man and woman world across the river of death to the other side, to life eternal in the Realm of Permanence. "God", the knower, and "Christ", the thinker, are on the other side of the river. The doer, or "Son", is the carpenter or bridge builder or mason, the builder of the bridge to be. When one has built the bridge or the "temple not made with hands," while remaining in this world, he will be a living example for others to build. Each one who is ready will build his own bridge or temple and establish his connection between this man and woman world of time and death, with his own thinker and knower in the "Kingdom of God", the Realm of Permanence, and continue his progressive work in the Eternal Order of Progression.

CHAPTER XI

THE GREAT WAY

SECTION 1

The "Descent" of man. There is no evolution without, first, involution. The mystery of germ cell development. The future of the human. The Great Way. Brotherhoods. Ancient Mysteries. Initiations. Alchemists. Rosicrucians.

In every age a few individuals do find The Great Way. They do conquer death by regenerating and restoring their bodies to the Realm of Permanence. But this is an individual and private affair of each such doer. The world does not know; other human beings do not know it. The world does not know because public opinion and the weight of the world would be opposed to it, and would hold back the doers who choose to regenerate their bodies and restore them to the Realm of Permanence.

Before a human will even agree to the idea of a "Way" to a "Realm of Permanence", he will have become estranged to the concept of an "ascent of man" or "evolution"; that is, that man, with his great gifts, has ascended from a mere speck of matter. On the contrary, he will have become convinced of the "descent" of man, from a higher estate to his present low condition in a perishable human body.

Evolution is preceded by involution. There cannot be an evolution unless there has been an involution of *what is* to be evolved.

It is not merely unreasonable, it is unscientific to suppose that any form of life can evolve from a germ cell that was not involved into that cell. An oak tree cannot evolve from the germ of a cabbage or a fern, even through countless developments from those germs. There must be the involution of an oak into its acorn in order that there can be the evolution from that acorn into an oak tree.

Likewise every man or woman has descended into this human world of change from an ancestral sexless being of the Realm of Permanence. The descent has been made by variation, modification, mutation, and division. The evidence of this procedure is shown by spermatogenesis and by ovulation, of the spermatozoon and the ovum into gametes, marriageable cells. Each cell must be changed from its original state or condition, and be modified and divided, until it is a distinctly male or female sex cell. These changes and divisions re-enact the biological records of the history of the cells, from the time of the ancestral type of sexlessness until they become male or female sex cells.

Heretofore no definite explanation has been given to account for these mysterious facts, but an understanding that the development of the sexes is the degeneration and departure from a former state of deathlessness into the lower human world of birth and death and re-existence, will explain the facts and open the way for understanding that there will be the return from the human to the former higher state. Here is part of the evidence:

Science has furnished evidence that in both spermatogenesis and ovulation the germ cells must divide twice before the spermatozoon can enter into the ovum and begin the generation of a new male or female body. The reason is that the spermatozoon is at first a sexless cell. By its first division it puts off that of itself which is sexless and is transformed into a male-female part; but as such it is not yet fit to marry. By its second division it throws off its female part and is then a gamete, a marriageable cell, and is ready for copulation. Similarly, the ovum is at first sexless; it must be changed into a sex cell before it can marry. By its first division it rids itself of its sexless part and is then a female-male cell, unfit for marriage. By its second division the male part is discarded and it is then the female sex cell ready for marriage.

For each life the history of the transition from an ancestral sexless body is re-enacted by each of the two germ cells. The changes which take place are determined by the thinking inscribed on the breath-form or living soul of the body through long series of lives of crucifixions and resurrections, each life being a crucifixion, followed by a return or resurrection. The breath-form has on it the original type of the sexless perfect body, but is changed into male or female according to the thinking of feeling-and-desire.

The conscious self in the body is feeling-and-desire, which is symbolically nailed through the body of sex to its cross.

Its cross is the invisible breath-form of the visible body. The body is the fleshly material of the body-cross.

Feeling is bound into the body-cross by nerves; desire is bound into the body-cross by blood.

Sight, hearing, taste, and smell, are the four senses which are themselves a cross and which are the symbolical nails with which the conscious self is nailed to its breath-form cross.

By breathing, the self of feeling-and-desire is kept on its breath-form cross throughout the life of its body-cross.

When the self of feeling-and-desire gives up the breath, the body is dead. Then the self leaves the body-cross.

But, as the conscious self, it continues with its breath-form cross through its after-death states, (Fig. V-D).

With its breath-form cross, the self will take on another body-cross of flesh and blood:—to be prepared for it for its next life on earth.

The conscious self of feeling-and-desire will again take on the body-cross of flesh and blood, and will be nailed to the objects of nature by sight and hearing, and by taste and smell.

So the conscious feeling-and-desire must continue its crucifixions life after life in this world of birth and death, until it regenerates its body of death into an everlasting body of life. Then, as the Son, it ascends and unites with its thinker and knower as the Father, the Triune Self complete in The Realm of Permanence from which it originally descended.

Teachings about the mysteries and initiations were not about The Great Way.

Information about The Great Way could not be made known to the rulers and conquerors, and the people who have made up the civilizations have been too savage and brutal. The civilizations have been based on conquest through murder.

This is the first time in any historic period when, it is said, there is freedom of speech; and that one may choose to be, to think, and to do what he thinks best, especially if it is for the benefit of others. That is why information about The Great Way is now given—for those who choose and will.

When The Great Way is made known to the few, they will make it known to the people. When it becomes generally known, those of the people who are weary of the treadmill of human life, who want something more than the glory of possessions and fame and pageantry and power, will rejoice at the good news of The Great Way. Then the few individuals who have made their destiny for The Way will be free to give the information to those who desire and choose to be on The Way.

In the past, growths into the inner worlds were not unusual; in fact, that was the normal course of progress. And unless this civilization is brought to an end by continued rapacity and sexual indulgence out of season, they will in the future become frequent again. Then human beings will not have to go against the whole of nature, because their physical bodies will be developed along the lines here indicated. They will begin to rebuild a vertebrate column in front, (Fig. VI-D), containing a front- or nature-cord. Into this front-cord are blended the right and the left cords of the present involuntary nervous system. The cord branches out laterally and into the pelvis, abdomen, and thorax, replacing the internal organs there at present; its ramifications fill these cavities with nervous structures somewhat as the cephalic brain now fills the cavity of the skull. So there will eventually be four brains,—a brain, each, in the pelvis for the perfect body, in the abdomen for the doer, in the thorax for the thinker, and in the head for the knower. The bodies will have forms in which matter will become conscious in higher degrees more easily than it does at present.

The doer-in-the-body is conscious mainly *of* feeling-and-desire and, to a lesser degree, *of* thinking, but it is not conscious *as* feeling-and-desire, nor *as* thinking; still less is it conscious *as* its identity. It is conscious of a difference between feeling and desiring, but not conscious of a difference between rightness-and-reason, as two different aspects of the thinker of the Triune Self. Nor is it conscious of its three minds of which human beings use chiefly the body-mind. Of conscience, which comes from selfness speaking through rightness, it is not conscious as coming from the higher source. It is not conscious of the three parts of its Triune Self and is not conscious of the Light of the Intelligence. It is conscious of nature as reported by the four senses, but is not conscious *as* nature, or even *of* nature in the flesh in which it dwells. It feels aches or comfort in parts of the body, but then it is conscious of feeling a sensation and not conscious *as* nature or *as* feeling. When there are sensations, that is, elementals playing on the nerves in which the feeling aspect of the doer is, the human is not conscious *of* or *as* the elementals, or that they are elementals, or even *as* feeling apart from these elementals, but he is conscious *of* the feeling *as* sensations. One does not know how to distinguish between himself as feeling and the sensations which he feels, and he must therefore become conscious *of* himself *as* that which feels, as distinct from the impression of nature that is made on feeling. To overcome these limitations the human must become conscious of his breath-form, of the way in which it operates, and of the actions of the four senses. When these limitations are overcome, the doer portion is conscious *as* feeling-and-desire, but the feeling-and-desire are heightened and refined. They take in the feeling-and-desire in all humanity, in nature in the body, and through that in nature outside.

In the present age the stages in which human beings are conscious are so low that special training is required. They themselves must prepare themselves; they cannot get anyone to teach them or to do the work for them. They do this by learning from their experiences, through thinking.

But what of the teachers, initiations, brotherhoods and lodges of which so much is heard? What of secret symbols, cryptic language and "The Way"? The answer is that these are not concerned with The Great Way here spoken of, which is found and traveled by the aid of the Light of the Intelligence. They are concerned with the legendary path, which at its best is only a related part of what is The Great Way. They have to do with symbols and language referring to the lunar germs, though not by that name, and to transformations in the physical body which the preservation of these germs brings about.

There are brotherhoods composed of those who have command over many of the forces of nature, and who have knowledge of much that is hidden from the senses of the run of human beings and is equally unknown to the learned men of the world. In these brotherhoods are members who have disciples, taken out of the world from time to time. There is no way in which the public or those not fitted can enter these schools. When the inner development of a human shows him to be fitted to become a disciple of one of these lodges, he is called to it. He has to comply with certain rules in his daily life, follow a course of study, go through trials, temptations, dangers, initiations and ceremonies. These lodges exist for the purpose of developing the human in worship of a deity.

There are other groups of initiates which are not so numerous today as they were in the past when they flourished with the ancient Mysteries. The object of all such Mysteries—Eleusinian, Bacchic, Mithraic, Orphic, Egyptian and Druidic,—was nature worship; their gods were nature gods. In the rites of these religious institutions was often something that gave, if one cared to receive it, information about the nature and the powers of the doer-in-the-human. So the teaching of the Hall of the Two Truths was a fair representation of the Judgment that awaits the human after death, when he stands naked—not clothed with the breath-form—in the Light of his Intelligence. In the Druidic Mysteries the first ray at sunrise entering the stone circle at the vernal equinox, remained from an unknown past as a symbol of the influx of the Light of the Intelligence to meet the solar germ at its entrance into the head, indicated by the stone circles which were symbols of the skull and the brain. The Druids interpreted this symbol, of course, as relating to the awakening of nature or to the procreative act, and accordingly the outer stone circle was the pelvis and the inner the uterus.

Generally, in the Mysteries, sacrificing animals was a degenerate representation of a disciple sacrificing his own passions, which the bull or goat symbolized; human sacrifices were a degenerate misrepresentation of the giving up of one's human sexual life for a regenerate life. But these inner meanings of what became brutal, noisy and sensuous displays, were lost.

The mysteries, that is, those that were secret, were adapted to the seasons of the year. The meaning had to do with the life of the doer in nature. Gods and Goddesses personified nature. The coming of the portion of the doer into physical life, its descent into the body, the dangers and allurements encountered during life, and death and the state of the doer after death, were dramatically presented.

There were also initiations which the neophyte had to pass. Privations and sufferings, dangers, encounters and obstacles had to be overcome before he could be initiated and join the purified. After he had gained the highest initiation, he discovered that the years it had taken him to qualify were filled with symbolic teachings of what the after-death states would be, so that when death actually did come and he had to pass through death, he had been so trained in these mysteries that he knew what to do. That was the inner object of the mysteries and of course was not told to the world, nor was it discovered by all who took part in them. None but superior persons could go through them. A true disciple, in any age, could through these forms get an insight into the real path beyond them. The training he received was a preparation to fit him in some life for The Great Way.

Among fraternities of a later date Alchemists and Rosicrucians have acquired notoriety. The disfavor in which they are sometimes held is due to impostors and charlatans who pretended to belong to the true orders.

The Alchemists, while they studied or appeared to study laws of external nature, concerned themselves with transmuting and refining the baser metals of the physical body, which was to become a refined astral body and by them called a "spiritual" body. Their fanciful terms can be interpreted as referring to alchemical processes in the flesh body by which the fourfold matter of it was refined and transmuted. The Philosopher's Stone, the Red Lion and the White Eagle, the White Tincture and the Red, the White Powder and the Red Powder, the Sun and the Moon, the Seven Planets, Salt, Sulphur and Mercury, the Elixir and many strange terms placed together in an unintelligible jargon, conceal definite meanings. When they had arrived at a certain stage, where they could through their own bodies command some of the forces of nature, they could transform lead and other base metals into gold. But as they then had no desire or use for possessions, the making of gold was no object. The alchemical steps which lead to the making of gold were processes in their own bodies and built up and vitalized organs so that these would hold the elixir of life. The elixir was the conserved essence of the procreative stream in the generative system. When the organs were able to hold the elixir, the lunar germ could extract Light from the contents of the organs. When enough had been gathered by the lunar germ, the solar germ was discovered to be the Philosopher's Stone.

The Rosicrucians were much like the Alchemists. They were a body of men who tried to grow into an inner life while they lived in the mask of their worldly stations. In the Middle Ages they let the existence of their order be known by the name of Brothers of the Rosy Cross or Rosicrucians, for the benefit of any who found themselves not in accord with the Church, and who wanted to lead an inner life. Their publications appeared with symbols and strange language. Those known to the world are not likely to have been real Brothers though some of them may have been disciples. Anyone who, having heard of their teachings, tried to live an inner life, was discovered to them by his earnest effort. He was called, and if he could go through their course, he became a Brother of the Rosy Cross. The Red Rose is the new heart which is opened by the Light of the Intelligence in thinking, and the Golden Cross is the new astral body which has been developed within the solid physical body. The ordinary heart is like a rose with petals closed. When it opens to the

Light and feels the needs of the world, it is symbolized by the rose with petals opened. It was to them a "spiritual" thing and so was the new body, though in reality the opened rose was a stage, namely, a mental stage of the psychic degree, and the new body was the astral body which when developed had a golden lustre. This body of gold was to be transmuted out of the ordinary body, which is like lead. It passed from lead to mercury, to silver and then to gold. The heart was called a living rose on a golden cross. They had to do alchemical work to transmute the body of lead into the body of gold. The furnaces, crucibles, retorts and alembics were organs in the body. The powders were the ferments in the body, which at critical stages caused, like catalysts, a change from one alchemical element or stage into another. By the stone and the elixir they changed in these organs the metals of the body from lead to gold.

SECTION 2

The Triune Self complete. The Threefold Way, and the three paths of each Way. The lunar, solar, and light germs. Divine, "immaculate" conception. The form, life, and light paths of The Way in the body.

When the doer will have reached its ultimate perfection, having lost itself and thereby found itself, it will be united with the thinker, who is in union with the knower.

These three parts then have absorbed their atmospheres and are a Triune Self complete, (Fig. V-B,a). This Triune Self complete has, besides the perfected physical body, three other bodies: a body for the doer in the form world, developed out of the fluid-solid body; a body for the thinker in the life world, developed out of the airy-solid body; and a body for the knower in the light world, developed out of the radiant-solid body, (Fig. III). These new bodies act through the perfected physical body and each may act in its own respective world. Thus the Triune Self complete has a perfected physical body, a form body, a life body and a light body, which may act together or separately. The three beings of a Triune Self are called: a being of the form world, a being of the life world and a being of the light world.

The physical body through which this has been done is a perfected, sexless and immortal body, through which the three inner bodies have issued.

In such a perfect physical body the three parts of the Triune Self complete can be and are fully embodied, (Fig. VI-D). They live in the spinal cord and in the voluntary nervous system, and there each operates its respective body from the center or station in which that being is; the form being from its abdominal brain, the life being from its thoracic brain, and the light being from its cephalic brain. The brain for the physical body is in the pelvis. From the centers, which have ceased to be common ground for nature and the Triune Self, the beings act through all parts of the body and thence on all planes of the physical world. The Light of the Intelligence is throughout.

Far from such perfection is the state of the doers banished to the outer crust of the earth. They are not even fully in the body; only a small portion of the doer is in the body, and the thinker and the knower merely contact the heart and lungs and the pituitary body, respectively.

From the state in which each doer is at present, it must go on until it opens and travels the path which will lead it to the end of its re-existences. To determine to find The Way is simple, but is a most momentous undertaking. Every doer must some day enter upon The Way. The Great Way is a name here given to a Threefold Way: a certain Way in the physical body; a Way of thinking for the development of the human by thinking; and a Way on which the human travels inside the earth during this development. These three Ways are travelled together and at the same time, not separately and at different times; but they will be treated here as though separate and distinct.

Each of these three Ways has three sections, called the form path, the life path, and the light path. On The Way in the body, the form path reaches from the end of the terminal filament to the beginning of the spinal cord proper; the life path reaches from there to the seventh cervical vertebra; and the light path reaches from there to the first cervical vertebra, (Fig. VI-D). On The Way of thinking, the form path ends with the ability to use the feeling-mind and the desire-mind; the life path ends with the ability to use the minds of rightness and of reason; and the light path is completed with the ability to use the minds of I-ness and of selfness. On The Way in the earth, the form path reaches from the entrance into the earth to the end of the first third of half the circumference of the inner crust; the life path ends when the second third has been travelled; the light path is the completion of half of the circumference of the inner earth.

The Way in the body, though it leads to immortal life, is a closed road and must be opened by a lunar germ bearing Light. The form path of The Way in the body is the hollow within the terminal filament, which at present is a tubular thread from the coccyx to the spinal cord proper. This tube is now choked and sealed wholly or in part and can be opened only by a light bearer, a lunar germ, (Fig. VI-A,d).

When a lunar germ, after descending on the right side, in the involuntary nervous system, generally speaking along the digestive tract, is not lost and has, by way of the coccygeal ganglion, ascended in the left side of the involuntary system to the region of the kidney, and passes upward, it will go to the head and complete its first round. As it descends again it is, if not lost, accompanied by the succeeding lunar germs, and is reinforced by the Light they carry and by Light of the solar germ. When the lunar germ returns to the head at the completion of its thirteenth round, Light issues from the solar into the lunar germ and there is a divine, a true "immaculate" conception. This is the initial step and factual basis of the development of the three embryonic bodies; it is analogous to the physical process, the lunar germ—in the female as well as the male—representing the ovum and the solar germ the spermatozoon. The lunar germ developing towards an embryonic form body, descends again in the right side of the involuntary nervous system along the digestive tract. After it has reached the lowest point in the pelvis it does not ascend on the left side to the region of the kidneys. It builds a bridge from what is now the coccygeal ganglion at the junction of the two cords of the involuntary nervous system, to the tip of the filament of the spinal cord, by way of nerves belonging to the voluntary system, goes across the bridge, opens the seal of the terminal filament and enters the filament through the opening, (Fig. VI-C).

The lunar germ then is on the form path and travels through the terminal filament. The path leads to the central canal of the spinal cord proper, about the junction of the first lumbar and twelfth dorsal vertebrae. When the lunar germ has reached that point, the solar germ which went down in the right hemisphere of the spinal cord, meets it and both germs blend and go through the central canal of the spinal cord to the head. When the lunar germ has entered the central canal of the spinal cord the human has eternal life, that is, obligatory deaths and rebirths are at an end.

What is here called the lunar germ ceases to be a mere germ after its impregnation in the head. In its descent along the nerves of the digestive system it begins to develop and when it enters through the opened seal into the filament it is ready to become the embryonic form body. So what was called the lunar germ traveling along the path, is a living embryonic form body traveling in the filament towards the central canal of the spinal cord, that is, towards eternal life. This will become in time the form body, the body of the doer, the psychic part of the Triune Self complete. When this embryonic body has reached the central canal of the spinal cord at about the upper level of the first lumbar vertebra, it has come to the end of the form path of The Way in the body. It is here that it is met by the solar germ. This is no longer a mere germ but it began to develop during its downward course in the right hemisphere of the spinal cord, and, after it had entered the central canal of the spinal cord and met there the form body, finally grew up into an embryonic life body, the body to be, of the thinker, the mental part of the Triune Self. Both these entities then ascend the central canal together, from the first lumbar to the seventh cervical vertebra.

When the embryonic form body and the embryonic life body enter the cervical part of the central canal of the spinal cord, they are met there at the seventh cervical vertebra by a light germ from the pituitary body, which is to the solar germ what the solar germ is to the lunar germ; this is the beginning of the light path in the body and of the embryonic light body. This light germ started from the pituitary body, descended through the third and fourth ventricles to the pons and medulla oblongata, and into the central canal of the spinal cord which runs through the canal of the vertebrae. The light germ is always there, but its descent and consequent development into the light body depend upon the rising and coming of the life and form bodies to meet it in the central canal of the spinal cord at the seventh cervical vertebra. The light germ developing into the embryonic light body, accompanied by the embryonic life and form bodies, advances through the medulla oblongata and pons to the pineal body, (Fig. VI-A,a).

At that time the pituitary sends a stream of Light through the canal of the infundibulum to the pineal body. The Light stream opens the pineal, the embryonic light body enters it and the head is filled with Light. Later, when the embryonic form, life and light bodies reach their full growth, are raised and issue, and the three parts of the Triune Self are in them, the doer has reached perfection, is of the complete Triune Self in a perfected, sexless, immortal, physical body and is at the end of

The Great Way. The cause of these processes is the development of the doer, the psychic part of the Triune Self.

SECTION 3

The Way of thinking. Honesty and truthfulness as the foundation of progress. Physical, psychic, mental requirements. Changes in the body in the process of regeneration.

The second of the three Ways of The Great Way, The Way of thinking, begins when the human has run the gamut and is through with pleasure and pain, when the doer has reached the saturation point of experiences, and when the human inquires into the causes of human action and inaction, into the purpose of living, of health and disease, riches and poverty, virtues and vices, life and death. He then discovers a futility in human effort. Though discontent and restlessness are experienced by everyone, and though at times despondency comes and weariness and indifference, these states are not what is meant by that discovery.

The discovery of the vanity, the emptiness of life, the discovery that no human possession is worthwhile, is a mental insight and is made when the human has reached the saturation point of human experiences. The desire of the doer can never be satisfied with physical things; but it can be gorged and surfeited with experiences of them, so that feeling cannot get anything more out of experiences. Still, feeling-and-desire are not satisfied and continue to drive the body-mind over the range of things that might satisfy. Then the body-mind, still driven by desire, makes the discovery to the doer of the futility of human effort.

By a flash of interior Light the human sees the world as a whirligig. He sees that the objects and the situations which men desire revolve; that they have appeared and disappeared to him many times. He sees that these things are toys which attract people and hold the attention and interests in life. One set of toys gives place to another. The toys, though seemingly innumerable, are of a few types and patterns. They return endlessly and seem new when they come. The types are sex and its four desire generals: food, possessions, fame, and power. They spring from feeling-and-desire, which are never satisfied. Thereby feeling-and-desire cause the change and keep the whirligig going, make the toys, give them movement and color and ruin them. This goes on until feeling and desire each seeks the other in itself. The whirligig stops.

With the discovery the castles, dungeons, playgrounds and work-shops of the world break down and disappear, so far as value, attraction or repulsion goes.

The discovery of the futility of all efforts and the state of emptiness that follows, eventually force the human to question who he is and to search into the recesses of his being for a way out of the emptiness. By hearing or reading or a flash from within, he becomes conscious that there is a way, and he desires to find it. This is a distinct understanding and a choice. He discovers that there are many things to be done and many things that must not be done, before he can find the way. The saturation disappears when there is a desire for the new way, the true way which lies beyond, past human events. Singleness of desire, and purpose to find and walk on the true way, start the feeling-mind and the desire-mind, before little used, and these bring more Light of the Intelligence.

In the ordinary man, feelings, started by nature, influence desires; these compel rightness, which starts reason, and that reacts to feeling. Thus the rounds continue with passive and active thinking. But in the case of one who desires to follow his knower, from whom the Light comes, the round is reversed. The feelings are not started by nature from the outside, but the desires are started by rightness acting on feeling from within. Therefore, the Light which selfness sends to rightness rules the desires which cause the feelings to appeal to reason; so that the desires are more passive and the feelings are more active than in the run of human beings. Then reason goes to I-ness for Light and I-ness causes selfness to send Light to rightness. And so the rounds continue. This is the government from within, instead of the government from without which obtains with the run of human beings, (Fig. IV-B).

The human then lives and works by the Light from within. He does not get that Light, which is a direct Light from his knower, continuously, but only in flashes and in response to his own efforts. After complying with the necessary requirements he has, eventually, an illumination and during that, finds that he is on The Way.

The period from the time when a human first discovers the futility of human effort for the things of the world to the time he enters The Way, sees many changes in his environment, in his occupation, in his associations, in his inner life and in his physical body. The period covers the time it takes to save thirteen lunar germs which have become one, and for it to reach the coccygeal ganglion for the building of the bridge.

There may have to be many re-existences of the doer after the choice is once made.

A human may be in any environment when he makes the great discovery. He may be in a vast city, a small town, a hamlet or a lonely place; he may be engaged in any occupation, he may be a pork butcher, a jail guard or a party politician; he may have all sorts of acquaintances, associates and friends; his family ties may be close or loose; and his possessions may be great or small. All this will change; but not by a violent effort on his part. That is not to say he should he unconcerned about the duties which these connections impose on him, but means that he must not be attached by liking or disliking.

One's surroundings, his work and his ties will change naturally, as his thinking changes, after he has made the choice. It is not for him to decide for changes and to move by his own efforts out of present conditions. He must wait, wait until opportunities for change present themselves. He should not make opportunities. He lives in a certain environment and is held by the various ties of and duties to locality, nation, race, friendship, family, marriage, position and possessions, because there is a purpose. Ties cannot be broken; they must be worn away or must fall away. Even possessions should not be done away with to be rid of them; one has them for a purpose; they mean responsibilities and trust and one must answer for them and his stewardship. They, too, will disappear naturally if they are in the way of his advance. There is in these outward conditions no mark, no criterion by which the world can distinguish from the run of human beings one who has made the great discovery and has made his choice for an inward life.

As he progresses by thinking and by leading the life, his body will change and he will gradually retire from the world, inconspicuously and without attracting any attention.

Though there is no standard in outward things, in the scenery in which he lives, there are standards to which he must have attained in his psychic nature, in his mental set and activities and in his physical make-up before he can enter The Great Way.

The stages through which one passes before he reaches the psychic standard to enter The Way, vary with different persons, but this standard which must be reached by all is substantially the same for all. Honesty and truthfulness must be the foundation of his character. His unequivocal feeling-and-desire must be to see things as they are, else preferences and prejudices will unseat his judgment and lead him astray.

The standard for his psychic nature is that feeling-and-desire are in agreement to gain The Great Way, above all things. Ordinarily feeling-and-desire are not in agreement; before they are in agreement he has to go a long way, and many things will happen to him.

When after his great discovery he desires to look for the Light within, the saturation ceases. To be cloyed and to choose to get out of the world is one thing, to be free from it so that it has no claim, is quite another. The saturation is a saturation with the world, with its outward life and gifts and attractions, a world-sickness. It chokes up the cloyed feelings and desires. When they are turned towards an inward life new realms of experience are opened and new objects are to be attained. The cloyed feelings and desires go into the new realms and as they find objects there the saturation ceases.

The feelings and desires had not overcome the old things which cloyed them. They are still slaves of nature when they go away from it and turn to an inward life; they are slaves, although slaves who demand their freedom.

The old things have renewed attractions and new attractions; renewed attractions because the old ones were not overcome, and new ones because things are looked at from a new point of view. Both of these attractions are great, greater than they would be with an ordinary person. Formerly he went along with them and now he fights them; now the pull of nature behind and through its things is stronger, as nature can now get more Light than from the ordinary person. Therefore as one seeks The Way and accumulates a little Light he is apt to make missteps. However often he fails, if he continues his efforts for an inward life, he will go on.

The psychic standard requires, second, certain moral qualifications. The moral aspect of his psychic nature is of course interlinked with the rightness of the mental part, the thinker. Ingratitude, malice, rancor, hatred, envy, anger, vindictiveness; jealousy, meanness, greed, fretfulness, restlessness, gloom, despondency, discontent, fear, cowardice, voluptuousness and cruelty must be strangers to him. He must have become estranged so that they are not his usual, or occasional or recurring visitors. It means that if they approach they are unwelcome because he has grown to be out of touch with them. They are now not natural to him, there is no room for them because he is surcharged with a power that comes from his new method of living. He is chaste, friendly, kindly, brave, temperate and firm.

The psychic standard requires, third, with all this, a fineness of feeling. It also requires, fourth, that psychic powers and the finer side of the four senses be not employed and that though one be sensitive to astral impressions he is not influenced by them.

The mental standard one must have reached before he can enter The Way relates to mental quality, mental attitude and a mental set, all of which will manifest in a certain kind of thinking which will produce the psychic and the physical standards. His mental quality must be such that dishonesty and untruthfulness are abhorrent to him. Deceit, hypocrisy, pride, vanity and arrogance must be strangers. He must be honest with himself, self-restrained, self-contained, and modest withal. His mental attitude must present friendliness generally, that is, the recognition that he is a related part of the whole; a readiness to perform his duties with joy if they relate to The Way and with willingness if they relate to other things; a determination to respond to rightness; and a reverence for and an eagerness to receive Light of the Intelligence. His mental set must be for one point only and that is, to be on The Way.

The standard for the body is that it has preserved the germs of thirteen lunar months. Ordinary nerve matter cannot hold a lunar germ much more than one month. To preserve thirteen a new, special, finer, fourfold nervous structure has to be grown within the old. At any time while this new structure grows it may be broken down. Malice and malcontent encrust, rancor tears, hatred withers, envy rots, jealousy, greed and salaciousness eat into, anger consumes, vindictiveness contracts, meanness dries up, fretfulness and restlessness unsteady, sullenness stifles, gloom deadens, despondency wears away, fear paralyzes, cowardice shrinks, voluptuousness wastes, licentiousness softens, lust burns, cruelty scars the finer nervous structure, and ingratitude shuts off the Light and leaves one in ignorance of his relation to his Triune Self and to humanity.

The body must be healthy and strong. Any food will do if it supplies what the body needs for health. Food should not be a fad and has little or nothing to do with the goal, that is, the preservation of the thirteen lightbearers, except that one should be temperate and should not eat too little or too much. Beverages, whatever they are, must be free from alcohol. The body must not sleep too much, or too little. It must not be abused by fasting, discomforts or other kinds of asceticism. Torturing the flesh will not bring anyone to or near The Great Way. The body must be kept healthy and strong, and all that is necessary for this is the steady living of a simple, temperate and chaste life. The body must not be governed from without by nature, but from within by thinking.

During the thinking, the living and the striving, which is the special preparation for entrance upon The Great Way, the body undergoes certain changes. The thymus gland becomes active and works with the thyroid. The gut will be less of a sewer. The stomach, duodenum, jejunum, ileum and colon become shorter and smaller. During the rounds of the lunar germs in the body the nervous currents are regulated by the lunar germs and gradually strengthened, so that a new and inner nervous structure grows up. The involuntary nerves of the digestive system begin to form a structure which eventually will be similar to that of the voluntary nervous system.

The length of time it takes from the discovery that the world has been a whirligig for countless years and ever disappoints expectation, to the entering upon The Way, varies with human beings. After the discovery and the choice for an inward life there is usually a steady progress, for a time. Then the world, which is nature, exercises its pull effectively, because some of the thoughts which have not been balanced by the human, aid nature when their cycles tend toward exteriorization. The human may get discouraged and may fall back into the world. When he is again sick of the world, he looks again for an inward life.

When death has intervened between his flounderings, he is reborn with an inclination to recognize the futility of an outward life. He will at some time in that or in the next life make the discovery again, and it will not strike him as being strange; he will make the choice and seek to attain to The Way and perhaps fail again. In a new life it is natural for him to see that life is empty; when the time comes he will again make the choice for the road that will lead to The Way. Once one has made the discovery and made the choice, he will be led towards The Way, even though he does not again make the discovery. Failures cannot prevent, they will only delay the finding of The Way. Failures are incidents, and sometimes they are unavoidable because of past thoughts; they are often blessings in disguise and cannot hold back one who is determined to strive for The Way, after he has once made his choice.

Having now in it a lightbearer, that is, a lunar germ into which will merge the germs of the next twelve months and which has now begun to grow, the human eventually enters The Way when the lightbearer opens the seal and enters the filament, (Fig. VI-C, D).

SECTION 4

Entering The Way. A new life opens. Advances on the form, life, and light paths. The lunar, solar, and light germs. Bridge between the two nervous systems. Further changes in the body. The perfect, immortal, physical body. The three inner bodies for the doer, the thinker, the knower of the Triune Self, within the perfect physical body.

When one enters The Way he is away from all his connections and associations. The world in which he has lived is left behind. The human, by the opening of the seal and entrance on The Way, feels a great joy, such as he has never before felt. The joy is not thrilling, spasmodic or ecstatic; it is steady and from a source within. All things seem to reflect that joy. The joy is feeling progressively safety, permanence and assurance that he will come into his own. The joy can last for months.

Gradually a new life opens. It extends from within and reaches the outer world. Everything is different from what it seemed before. The world has not changed, but it looks different because he and his body are different, he knows himself to be a being distinct from nature and from his body. He identifies feeling, if he has not done so before.

He seems to be in the heart of the world. Before, he felt its pull, now he feels its pulse. Before, only the outer world could act on him, now an inner world, the form world, begins from within to open to him. There is a direct interplay between the doer-in-the-body and the non-embodied portions of the doer. The psychic atmosphere is felt; and through the physical atmosphere is felt the form world.

By feeling this new world he is able to feel nature in the physical world and how things act and move as they do. He feels the crystallization of minerals, the seeding, feeding, growing and dying of plants, the impulses and instincts of animals, the movements of the earth, of the water and of the air, the influences coming from and going to the sun and the moon, the interaction of the planets and the beings on the earth, and the relation of the stars to mankind and the universe. He feels all these in their four zones working within the four systems of his fourfold body and he feels the organs of his systems working in the universe.

There comes a tendency to be clairvoyant and clairaudient. Scenes and persons flash across the view. If he thinks of anyone, that one is seen and his voice is heard, without intention or effort to see or hear. The tasting or smelling of objects comes without seeking, when they are thought of. The inner side of the four senses seeks to manifest. The senses begin to act in the fluid, airy and radiant states as they did in the subdivisions of the solid state. These phenomena must be disregarded; this inner side of the senses must not be allowed to develop, else the inner life will flow outward.

At this period the wish for possessions or the wish to see or communicate with elementals will be fulfilled at once, because elemental beings which obey the powers working within him carry out his wishes. These elementals are hidden from him unless he wants to see them and command them. He has not yet transformed malice, anger, hatred, lust and the other vices into higher powers though he has control of their physical expression; if he should allow an old dislike to make him wish harm to anyone, or allow a liking to cause him to wish a gift to someone, he would unleash nature forces which he had controlled and they would throw him off The Way. Longing for or attachment to anything he has left behind will pull him back and away from The Way.

The feeling-mind and the desire-mind gradually control the body-mind, as these develop. New mental activities develop. The man on The Way now deals with the constituents, combinations and solvents of the matter of the different planes of the physical world and of the planes up to the life plane of the form world. He can deal with this matter as it is, as a fact, and not in a theoretical manner. He need use no instruments other than the organs of his fourfold body and the three minds. By this mental working he changes the matter of his body and aids the growing form body.

During this advance there are periods of exaltation, depression and illumination. They are caused by the exclusion of the surrounding chaos and the infusion of life into the growing form body. He no longer feels himself out into the world, but feels the outer world within his fourfold body. The beings, colors and sounds of thousandfold nature are within this body. The elemental matter of the earth, the water, the air and the starlight, flows through his body and he is conscious of it. He becomes accustomed to and intimate with nature. If he allows himself to be tempted to wield the forces which move through his body or to command nature outside of him by the power within him, he is off The Way.

He must not feel temptation. It must be a stranger to him. When the fullness of nature is within him and there is no inducement for him to interfere with it and to exercise his power over it, except to exclude influences adverse to the development of the form body, nature falls away. Then he is alone and in darkness.

All forms and colors are gone. There is no sound. There are no means to operate the four senses, because there is nothing to see, nothing to hear, nothing to taste, nothing to smell, nothing to contact, and feeling is stilled. He stays in darkness, but he is conscious. There is nothing by which to measure time. If the darkness overwhelms him, it remains. If he fears, if he longs for it to go, it remains. When it cannot influence him or evoke any reaction he becomes conscious that there are things in the darkness. Gradually they stand out. He can see some, he can hear some. They seem strange and yet as intimate as if they were parts of himself. All the emotions and passions, all the evils which he believed he had overcome, bear in on him. They would enter him. If he has not changed them sufficiently before, they can now gain entrance. He does not let them. They want to make him fear them, run away from them or shut off the sensing of them. He will do none of these things. They do not leave him. He searches into them and finds they are a part of him. He becomes conscious that they are his unbalanced thoughts. This is a shock to him. As he stands the shock he begins to balance them. When he has balanced them, others come. This continues until his thoughts are balanced.

The darkness vanishes as light comes. A calm and peace come with the light. The earth loses its power over him. The ties which his thoughts had forged about him are worn away and he is free from them and the attractions of the world. He has distinguished and identified feeling and desire.

Before and after this advance is made, various changes take place in the body. On the form path of The Way in the body, an impregnated lunar germ has opened the seal and has entered the filament of the spinal cord; a bridge has been built between the front-cord and the filament, whereby the involuntary nervous system is directly connected at the coccyx with the voluntary nervous system, (Fig. VI-C, D). At this time a new epoch begins for the human. He enters the form path; he feels the nervous currents that are turned on when the connection is made between the front- or nature-cord and the spinal cord, the cord for the Triune Self. Prior to the opening of the seal at the terminal filament, every sensation, impulse and communication in that region had to go by way of the pairs of voluntary nerves which pass through the openings of the sacral and lumbar vertebrae. While these old connections still exist, the new connection changes and rearranges the involuntary and voluntary systems at once.

Formerly, he felt himself to be the body, and nature impressions coming into it by way of the involuntary system passed into its tissues and organs; now, he distinguishes and identifies himself as being the doer; humanity communicates with him; he feels its hopes and fears, its loves and hates, its longings, emotions and aspirations, and the thoughts of others; they enter through the sense organs, and by way of the continuous canal that now runs through the two nervous systems, they pass into the nerve structures that replace what formerly were organs in the cavities of the body, and connect with the stations and centers that are being opened to the three beings now in process of development.

Various other changes in the organs of the body and their functioning accompany progress on The Way. The kidneys become less active in the work hitherto done, and the testicles or ovaries are drawn towards them. The bloodstream gradually ceases to build and maintain the body; it acts more as a conveyer of nervous force than as a carrier of nutrition. Nutriment is taken in by the breath directly from the four states of matter. The brain takes and sends impressions more easily than was possible before. The spinal cord takes on more and more the appearance of brain structure; its central canal becomes larger, and the terminal filament, which is now atrophied from disuse, is greatly enlarged; its central canal, which at present is threadlike and is lost on its way to the end of the filament, is widened and reaches to the very tip of the filament, (Fig. VI-A,d). The intestinal tract ceases to be a feeding tube and a sewer, and the anus disappears. The stomach and the small intestine are then superfluous and disappear.

The large bowel or colon, then serving a new purpose, becomes part of a nerve structure, similar to the spinal cord, termed the front- or nature-cord. This cord with its lateral branches is made up of the former esophagus, of the two cords and the plexuses and the widespread ramifications of the involuntary nervous system, and of the colon. The middle of the three bands that run along the outer wall of the colon, becomes hollowed out, and around this slender canal is arranged the colon, greatly reduced in length and width, so that only a short, narrow tubular cord remains, as part of the front-cord. Included in the front-cord are the right and the left vagus nerves, with their ramifications. It is situated in front of the abdominal cavity and is slightly curved from before backward, pointing towards the tip of the terminal filament of the voluntary nervous system.

This front-cord becomes enclosed in a resilient structure, here spoken of as the front- or nature-column. This takes the place of the sternum and is extended to and is continuous with the greatly changed pelvic bowl. The body is thus a two-columned body.

The front-column and the front-cord correspond to the spinal column and the spinal cord behind. The lumbar, dorsal and cervical sections of the spinal cord will be the form path, the life path, and the light path, along which the lunar and the solar germs are to travel when the bridge between the two nervous systems will have been built. Then there is a continuous central canal running down within the front-cord, across the bridge, and upward within the spinal cord, (Fig. VI-D).

From the front-cord pairs of nerves begin to grow outward, towards the corresponding pairs of nerves coming from the spinal cord. The coiled serpent of mythology becomes a tree.

The bridge that is built for the passage of the lunar germ from the involuntary nervous system to the voluntary, extends from the coccygeal ganglion to the terminal filament of the spinal cord by way of communicating branches of nerves which even now connect the two nervous systems.

When the lunar germ had returned to the head for the thirteenth time, it was infused with light from the solar germ. The next time it descends, it passes downward to reach the tip of the filament, by way of the bridge, which by then has been built. When the lunar germ has entered the filament, it travels along the form path, is thereby in touch with the non-embodied portions of the doer, and develops into an embryonic form body for the doer. By the time the embryonic form body has reached the place where the filament leads into the spinal cord, at about the first lumbar vertebra, it fills the filament. The physical body is on its way to become a perfect, immortal, sexless physical body.

The embryonic form body which is of matter of the form world, goes through many phases, just as a physical embryo does. These phases put it in touch with the planes of the physical world and with those of the form world.

The phases are not summaries of the past, but are promises of the future, and resemble a globe, an egg, a column and a human-like form. The psychic atmosphere and the doer are the sources from which the development of the form body is urged along. When the embryonic form body is fully developed it has reached the end of the form path. Feeling-and-desire are now in agreement, and the feeling-mind and the desire-mind are under control, self-control.

At this time the aspirant must make a choice. If he chooses to continue his advance, the form body does not issue; he ascends from the filament into the central canal of the spinal cord, and thereby enters the life path, the second section of The Great Way; if he were to forego further progress, the embryonic form body would emerge from the filament, pass by way of the present solar plexus and issue from the place where now the navel is. But he goes on.

The proper choice for the human is The Threefold Way, The Great Way, and not to issue into the form world. This choice, and the only one here dealt with at length, is the choice to continue until the light body issues and the Triune Self is a Triune Self complete and is a being of the form, the life, and the light worlds. Issuing of the form body into the form world would inhibit the development of a life body for the thinker and of a light body for the knower of the Triune Self. To go on, the human must develop a life body and a light body, in addition to a form body, out of the physical body. The choice is an actual decision. It has been prepared by previous desiring, thinking and living for this event. By such desiring and thinking the foundation is laid for entering on the life path and, later, for entering on the light path of The Great Way. The choice for entering on the life path is made by the thinker at the request of the doer, because the doer desires it ardently.

A life body can be developed only if the human—long before he enters on the form path—desires to know who he is and what in him is the permanent and continuously conscious One, identity-and-knowledge. With this desiring will come thinking, as that follows desire. The thinking will be adjusted to that at which desire aims, and this will give Light concerning what is to be thought and what is to be done. The thinking will turn around how to be conscious as the permanent and continuously conscious One.

There are some changes in the physical body in addition to those given, which will obtain when the human enters the life path. Nerves not now visible, potential nerves, will become active and will affect chiefly the lungs and the heart. The lungs will then be more like the cerebrum, and the heart with the aorta, the thymus and other glands, like the cerebellum and pons.

When one has made the choice an illumination takes place. The desire-mind, after the thoughts for psychic matters were balanced, began to act quickly and with certainty, instead of slowly, inaccurately and with confusion, as it does with humans. After the illumination has come, the mental atmosphere in which the Light has been a diffused Light, becomes clearer. Subjects the doer thinks about or into which he thinks are shown by the Light he turns towards them. Darkness and ignorance flee before that Light. He understands the inner workings of things. Because of the Light he has, his comprehension takes the place of apprehension through the four senses. The feeling-mind and desire-mind take the place and answer all purposes of seeing and hearing. They work over problems connected with the physical world, which he now understands. Following the choice, a connection is made with the non-contacting portion of the thinker, and a communication between that and its contacting portion follows. More of the thinker is in contact as the body becomes fitted for contact. It is as though the body lived in a new world. He senses his mental atmosphere and through the physical atmosphere the life world. He senses by means of nerves, old nerves which have been remodeled and new nerves which have been developed.

In consequence of the illumination and the more intimate and fuller connection, he gets powers. These are mental, not psychic. Among them are the powers to deal with units on any plane of the life world, to separate, merge, amalgamate and combine them, to speak them into being in the life world and so create new types and laws dealing with them, which will later appear in the form and physical worlds. He knows of his powers, but he also knows that he should not use them. These powers come from thinking in connection with rightness-and-reason.

All thoughts have been balanced. Before they were balanced they interfered and made impossible the thinking he is able to engage in now. Before the desire in them was released, it took away from the power to think on the life path; now it is ready to aid. There is a brighter Light stream because of the Light which was reclaimed at the balancing. Now there is nothing to prevent real thinking, nothing to interfere with thinking that does not create thoughts. Thinking with rightness and reason holds the Light steadily towards a subject. That to whom thinking is directed is the knower. Rightness receives Light not only from its mental atmosphere but also from selfness, and reason works with it as the Light shows what work should be done. Such thinking turns the mental power on the embryonic life and light bodies going up the spinal cord, and, as they progress, more of the thinker contacts and operates through the embryonic life body.

The solar germ which was being prepared, by thinking, for a future development into a life body, descends in the right hemisphere of the spinal cord and is ready to enter the central canal, and to begin its development into an embryonic life body. When the embryonic form body has attained its full growth and fills the terminal filament, and when the choice is made for the life path, the solar germ meets the embryonic form body at the upper end of the filament, the end of the form path, and, instead of ascending in the left hemisphere of the cord as it had previously done, it unites with the embryonic form body, and together they pass into the central canal of the spinal cord. This is the time of the choice, of the illumination and of the connection with the now embodying thinker. The doer on The Way now thinks with the minds for feeling-and-desire and for rightness-and-reason. All four minds work harmoniously. They are in union. As the doer develops in union with rightness-and-reason, the embryonic life body is also developed. It grows up within the embryonic form body, which is its vehicle. More of the thinker is embodied. When these two bodies traveling up the spinal cord have come to the seventh cervical vertebra, the embryonic life body has reached its full development within the embryonic form body. The minds of rightness and of reason are under control, and the end of the life path has been reached.

The perfect physical body is at this stage largely a body of nerves. The pairs of nerves coming from the spinal cord and the corresponding pairs issuing from the nature-cord in front ramify and embrace each other. The tissues of the circulatory and respiratory systems have become nerves. The organs in the body have become centers of nerves. These nerves are not of the coarse structure found in a human body, but are radiant, luminous lines. Instead of being half paralyzed or deadened, as are the bodies of the run of humans, such a body is alive. The sternum, now part of the front-column, is flexible and extends to and blends with the pelvis. Half-arches extend laterally from both sides of the lower vertebrae, somewhat as the upper ribs do now, connecting the dorsal and lumbar vertebrae with the front-column. The bones have become resilient, and the marrow in them has turned into luminous matter. The shape of the body is still human, with a head, trunk and limbs; but there is no gross matter in such a body. Its grossest matter consists of cells in parts of the organs and in the skin, which cells are sexless or bi-sexed.

Another choice must be made when the embryonic life body has reached its growth. It is then ready either to issue with the breath from the spinal cord through the throat out of the mouth into the life world, or to take the light path. If the determination is to be a being of the life world, the embryonic life body will issue.

But as the choice will be to take the light path, the life body does not issue. Though previous desiring and thinking will have predisposed, the choice has to be made.

When the choice is made and the light path is taken, the human—still called here by that name though he became more than a human before he came to the end of the form path—no longer thinks. He knows. The knowing takes in the previous desiring and thinking. It is an instantaneous process of desiring to know, thinking, and knowing a thing. The knowing takes in at the same time the idea in the light world, the subject in the life world, the object in the form world and the reflected shadow and appearance of the object in the physical world.

The human then knows the history, the continuous system, of the four worlds of the earth sphere. He knows the manifested side of the light world, and the manifested and the unmanifested sides of the life, form, and physical worlds. He knows about the beings and events on the first, second and third earths and about the Civilizations and changes on this fourth earth. He knows the history of the doers on the earth crust and the history of some of the beings and races of the layers within the earth crust. He knows the earth forces and how to direct and control them; but he does not use them. He knows the immortal Government in The Realm of Permanence where he will be one of the governors of this man and woman world of change. The human has feelings and desires as much finer and more potent than he had before he discovered the emptiness of the world and the futility of human efforts, as the power of the sun is greater than that of a candle. He controls his feelings and desires, by thinking. Feeling, desiring and thinking are as one in and with knowledge.

When the embryonic life body has attained its full development and has risen in the central canal of the spinal cord to the seventh cervical vertebra, it is met by a light germ from the pituitary body. The light germ comes from that part of the knower which contacts or is in the pituitary body. It descends through the canal of the spinal cord within the cervical vertebrae, meets and enters into the ascending embryonic life body at the seventh cervical vertebra and opens the way for the life body to ascend the light path, and the light germ itself is developed into an embryonic body of light. That light is greater than sunlight, yet eyes cannot see it. So the three, the embryonic form body, the embryonic life body and the embryonic light body, rise together on the light path. The human during this time comes into his knowledge about the things mentioned. When the three embryonic bodies have passed the first cervical vertebra the human has come to the end of the light path.

By the time The Way in the body has been completed with the development of the light body, the end of The Way of thinking has been attained by the control of the minds of I-ness-and-selfness, and the end of The Way in the interior of the earth has been reached by the physical body, which is now a perfected, regenerated, immortal, sexless physical body.

When the three embryonic bodies have passed into the third ventricle of the brain, (Fig. VI-A,a), and as they approach the pineal body, the pituitary body sends a light stream to the pineal which opens to let the three ascending bodies enter and to receive another light stream which then, through the top of the head, comes from the knower into the pineal body. The light streams enter into and are united in the embryonic light body.

At this time the portions of the thinker and the doer not in or in contact with the body, descend into their respective parts of the spinal cord and enter their embryonic life and form bodies. So the knower, thinker, and doer inhabit the immortal fourfold physical body, and all twelve portions of the doer which formerly re-existed successively, now are embodied together and are in union.

The knower, thinker, and doer of the Triune Self, in their light, life, and form bodies, ascend through the roof of the head, are in the light world, and in the presence of the Great Triune Self of the worlds.

The light body ascends into the world; but the life and form bodies do not come forth; they cannot take being in the light world. The light body has no form, but from the human standpoint it would be conceived of as a globe of light, and light is invisible.

As the light body ascends, the knower enters into and functions through the light body apart from the physical body; and the thinker and doer are still. The doer knows that it has ever been there. Never was there such a thing as its not being there. It does not consider this, because there is no question about it. The knower never left the light world. In all re-existences after its first existence, only portions of the doer were successively embodied, and these portions were as though shut off from the light world. This is why the portion in and as the human did not know about the non-embodied portions. Now that there is unity in its portions, the doer is conscious that it never really left the light world. The doer now knows that its human life has been the dreaming of itself through nature, and that the dream began when it hypnotized itself and put itself to sleep, under the spell of the sexes and the senses.

Through its knower, the doer of the Triune Self knows all lives are a dream, made up of many dreams, and each so strong, so fast, so real, as to shut out knowledge of the thinking of the desire that made the dream. Now it establishes the things about which it knew before the unity of its portions was attained. It knows its relation to all other doers. Through its knower it knows its relation to the Great Triune Self of the worlds, to the Intelligence that raised it, and through that it knows about other Intelligences and about the Supreme Intelligence. It knows that that Intelligence is not what human beings project, build up out of themselves and then believe to be the Supreme Intelligence. It links itself up with other doers that are not dreaming, and it is known by them.

The thinker takes being in the life world and is a being of the life world. The thinker and its life body are as one, though human beings would think of them as different. The difference is the difference between the matter of the Triune Self and nature-matter. Matter of the Triune Self cannot be seen by physical sight or by clairvoyance. If it is conceived of from the physical world, it is as a luminous body like an ovoid column, having no limbs or features.

The thinker and his thinking breathe the embryonic form body into being into the form world, and the doer inhabits this body as a being of the form world. In this case the difference between the body and the dweller in it, is more apparent than it is with the being of the life world and the being of the light world. The form of the body of the doer is an ideal human form, and the matter is matter of the physical plane of the form world. It has color; the other two bodies have no color. The color of it is different from any physical color; it might be imagined as the white of a rose, the red of a flame and the light yellow of lightning as one color. If one could see this color mentally, he would recognize a being of the form world by that color, provided the being permitted himself to be seen. No psychic can penetrate into the privacy of these beings. A being of the form world is feeling-and-desire refined and potent to the highest degree.

The perfect body, at the time when the three inner bodies issue, is still physical, but it is so different from the body of the human that that is, without exaggeration, like a deformed and walking corpse by comparison. Though still human in general form, its lines are more perfect than is a conception of divinity. The four brains are made up of currents and coils of light in which are centers for receiving impressions coming from the four worlds and for operating the forces in those worlds. The pituitary and pineal bodies are no longer pudgy or flabby, pea-sized things, but are as large as eyes; the pituitary is highly organized and vital and the pineal is a globe of Light. What was the sternum has become part of the front-column composed of vertebrae similarly articulated as is the spinal column at present; it extends to the pelvis and encloses the front-cord, which reaches from its origin in the brain, by way of what was the esophagus and the bowels, to the coccyx. What were sex organs are entirely within the pelvis; what were the ovaries or the testicles are more like the inner brain and are centers of nerves. The spinal cord, very much larger than with man, extends to the coccyx, and is not nervous matter but currents and coils of Light. The lateral distances between the spinal column and the front-column are spanned by bands or half-arches from either side. The sacrum and coccyx are articulated and flexible and are completed by a similar structure which has been built out from the front-column and the pelvis. The front-cord is united with the spinal cord, through the bridge that was built, so that one central canal runs down in the front-cord and up in the spinal cord. Intervertebral nerves emerge from the spinal cord and corresponding nerves issue from the front-cord; these nerves divide and subdivide and their ramifications mingle with each other. All bones are stronger than steel and unbreakable, but are as flexible as the tongue. There is no alimentary canal; that has become part of the front-cord. There is no blood; that has changed into life currents of a higher power. Respiration does not come through lungs. Air and drink and food come through the cells of the skin, acceptance being regulated by the sense of taste and absorption by the sense of smell; there is no waste. All is done by the coming and the going of the four breaths.

The matter of the body is cellular; few of the cells are bisexual, and the others are sexless. In kind the matter is the same as that in human bodies, but it is superlative in degree. In the human the cells are out of touch with the four states of matter on the physical plane, with the matter of the other three planes of the physical world and with the matter of each of the planes of the form, life and light worlds. But in a physical body from which has issued a body for a being of the light world, the matter is in direct relation with the matter of all these worlds and their planes. Therefore, to give one illustration relating to food, the cells in an ordinary human body have to be fed with gross physical food from which to get the finer matter of the physical world needed for the maintenance of their structure, but when the cells are of a higher power and in direct touch with that finer matter, they take it as they need it directly from the sources. Gross food would be an interference and an encumbrance. The breath units of the cells get their support directly from the fire units of the physical world, the life units from the air units, the form units from the water units, and the cell units from the earth units, all by osmotic processes.

The four senses, of course, belong to nature; they are still its ministers and ambassadors; sight, hearing, taste and smell function; and the breath-form coordinates the senses with the functions of the physical body. They are all carried to the highest degree of development. They are the instruments through which the Triune Self works with nature. The sense of sight can receive impressions from and can be brought to bear upon anything anywhere in nature that has to do with fire and color. So it is with the sense of hearing as to air and sound, with the sense of taste as to water and form, and with the sense of smell as to earth and structure. The senses can work separately or together. The brain that rules them is the brain in the pelvic bowl, though the cephalic, thoracic and abdominal brains cooperate. The senses are ruled from within and not from without.

The aia is then in the body. The breath-form is the medium by which the senses and their systems are operated through the front-cord by the doer. Nature cannot come in as formerly, but only when summoned. The breath-form adapts itself to and is the likeness of the form body; and the physical body is the exteriorized image of the breath-form. The breath-form is directly in touch with matter of the four worlds and so enables its physical body to draw its life and structure directly from them. The body is a part of the four worlds and lives in them and with them. They move through it. Therefore it has everlasting life. Through the breath-form the perfect body becomes related to the form, the life, and the light bodies. The aia of that perfect body will be translated into a Triune Self, after the Triune Self of that body has become an Intelligence and has determined to raise the aia to be the Triune Self of that body.

SECTION 5

*The Way in the earth. The ongoer leaves the world. The form path;
what he sees there. Shades of the dead. "Lost" portions of doers. The
choice.*

Having described The Way in the body and The Way of thinking,
there remains to be treated the third of The Threefold Way, The Way
in the earth, on which the progress described in the foregoing sections is
enacted.

When the ties have fallen away, when there are no obligations to
family, community and country, and when he feels no attachment, the
human leaves and is lost sight of by his associates in the world. At that
time he feels a desire to go away and has the means for so doing. He
becomes an ongoer and prepares for the form path. The manner of his
going is inconspicuous and natural. He goes to live among simple people,
not to be a hermit or ascetic, but to lead a simple, orderly, unnoticed life.
There he is in an atmosphere of simplicity and adjusts his body to the
gradual changes which his thinking and feeling bring about. His work,
his business, his study is thinking, only thinking, to obtain the use and
control of his body-mind, feeling-mind, and desire-mind. He will encounter dangers, not as spectacular trials, but in the ordinary course of
his life, to establish confidence and equanimity. Though he moves
among the people of a tribe or village, he has little commerce with them.
He has only one associate and that is a companion.

It may be that the companion meets the ongoer before the ties have
fallen away or after the travels have begun or while the stay among the
simple people lasts. From the time the companion meets the ongoer, he
is with him and travels with him.

The companion is a human being but one acquainted with the forces
of the four planes of the earth and with human nature. He usually belongs
to a fraternity whose purpose is to study and use forces of nature and that
has an understanding of the history of the doer. It is made up of men
who live in the world, but in secluded places. They are outposts in
different parts of the globe; some of them lived in America before the
Spaniards came. Many of them can command some elemental beings
and have rare psychic and mental powers. They know and can make use
of certain laws of nature of which science, comparatively speaking, knows

THE GREAT WAY 643

little or nothing. While they are secluded they may, when necessary, move among throngs; they have played a part in all crises in history; if mentioned they are usually called names meaning skill in control of forces or objects of nature. This fraternity, with different orders, is a way station and outpost where ongoers towards The Great Way, who cannot go on, remain and learn. Among the duties of a member of this fraternity is that of being a companion to an ongoer when necessary. The companion, though he may live hundreds of years, will die sometime, but the ongoer will conquer death.

When the companion meets the ongoer and makes himself known, he may ask what his destination is and on being told, he may say: "I am here to help you on a part of the journey. Are you ready to go on and to have me as your guide? If you take me you must trust me and go where I shall lead you. If you do not, you will not find the way alone and you will fall back into the world." The ongoer accepts the companion, understanding that he is sent by those who know, and with the approval of his own knower.

The companion informs him about the form and structure of the outer earth crust, about states of matter, how they interpenetrate, about racial developments and external nature, about the cycles of religions and about the fraternity to which the companion belongs. Together the companion and the ongoer go from place to place. Their journeys may be less than a hundred miles or they may take in a large part of the surface of the earth and consume weeks or years, until the ongoer is familiar with the earth, and his nerves are so tested and under control that he can continue his journey.

When the time comes the companion leads the ongoer to an opening into the earth. It may be in a forest, in a mountain or under a building where no opening is seen. It may be under water or where gases issue or in a volcano. The companion bids his friend, who knows he may never see him again, farewell, and a new guide appears.

The ongoer and his guide leave the surface and enter the earth. That is, for the ongoer, the beginning of the form path. Shortly before this time or soon after, the lunar germ enters the filament.

The guide has the human form, has usually a moon colored body, is neither man or woman. He belongs to another race of beings, speaks the language of the ongoer and has an understanding far beyond that of a human being. The ongoer feels strange and the guide knows it. There is no announcement. They go on together from daylight into darkness.

Gradually the ongoer becomes accustomed to the darkness and sees by a new kind of light. The guide points out, here and there, sections through which they are passing, and the ongoer develops the ability to see outlines and then distinct forms and colors, in the dark. This requires the training of the eye as an instrument, of the nervous systems as a whole, and of the breath-form.

They come to a new world, inside the earth crust, a world existing on many levels. At first the ongoer is limited by the one dimension, on-ness, which is a barrier to perception as on the outer crust, where one cannot see within surfaces. Slowly he develops the power to perceive a second dimension, in-ness, to see within and between surfaces.

The new world is like spaces in a sponge; but some of the chambers, passages and labyrinths are vast in size, hundreds of miles long and high, and some only small pockets. The structure of the floors and walls ranges in density from that of metal to porosity and the lightness of foam. Some of them are drab, others are colored similarly to but often more delicately or brilliantly than landscapes on the outer surface. The ongoer sees great mountains, vast plains, cauldrons of fluids churning and lashing where earth currents coming in meet the outgoing earth forces. He sees where currents of air strike fluid substances and burst into flame, forming rivers of fire. He sees strange things in many colors, among them an immense desert of what looks like a white powder, amidst which cliffs, some of crystal, rise. He sees quiet surfaces of water and of other fluids, in lakes hundreds of miles in length.

No sun, no moon and no stars are seen. There is no visible central source of light, but he sees either the distant roofs of the chambers or limitless air lit by an inner earth light, which is made by a mingling of transient units. There is no night and no day. There are no shadows, except at the outer limits of the inner earth light, and even they have no distinct outline.

In some chambers are fierce winds, in others a calm. The air is colder in some districts than anything known on the crust. In some places the heat is so severe that human flesh could not endure it, but ordinarily the temperature is agreeable to the body. He travels on foot or at times in vehicles made of metal or compositions drawn from the air, and gliding with speed over the ground.

Two regions he cannot cross, one because the ground holds him, as a magnet holds a needle, the other because the ground repels his body. The vehicle glides like a sled over the magnetic ground, but the repellent ground cannot be traveled by him. He has to cross and recross the magnetic ground in his sled until it loses its attraction for him. Then he approaches the repellent ground and attempts to cross it, returning after each failure to the magnetic ground to get strength, until the matter has no longer power to attract or repel him. The overcoming of these forces regulates the structure of the cells in his body so that they are neither male nor female.

He travels on water in a boat propelled by a water force; he crosses oceans, one below the other, greater than the Atlantic and much deeper. The ongoer sees forests, single trees and plants, arranged as they grow on the earth, but there is much that would seem strange to human beings. Green is not the prevailing color. In some sections it is absent. In different districts and on different levels different colors predominate. The foliage is red, blue, green, pink, black or shining white, and some of it is many colored. Some leaves are geometrical in form, some are globular, some twenty feet long. There are edible flowers, fruits, grains; some are cultivated, some grow wild.

He sees animals, some of them like those on the outer crust and many of strange types. On the levels nearest to the outer crust are some ferocious beasts. They live where there are degenerate tribes and fierce races. In the regions farther inside the animals are strange, but docile and friendly. Few of them have tails. Many have no teeth. In shape some of them are graceful. The types of the animal forms are furnished by thoughts of the human races inside; what animates these creatures are parts of the cast-off feelings and desires of those human races.

As the eyes of the ongoer are being trained to focus, he sees that there are no sharp lines separating objects, but that all are connected by an interplay of the matter that composes them. So he sees the water element in the chambers and that it is flowing matter, and that some of it is passing through solid walls which retain particles of it and let go some of their own matter to be carried on in the flow. He thus becomes familiar with in-ness and his sight reaches into and he sees inside and between the surfaces of objects.

In some places he sees the shades of persons whose life on the earth crust death has ended. The shades are such as are no longer attracted to their earthly haunts or decaying bodies. The shades are the breath-form, the four senses and the embodied portion of the doer, without the Light of the Intelligence. They are dreaming over scenes of the life that has passed. Their thoughts are the matrices into which the flowing matter passes and to which it gives body and so makes the scenery and the persons of their dreams. The shades move, drone, ponder and wander in their chambers. Sometimes they float through each other, but each is unconscious of the others and of everything except its dream. Now and then a shade disappears, when it is wakened by a strong desire evoked through necromancy. The shades called to mediumistic seances may remain a while in the atmospheres of the living, before they are drawn back to go on with their after-death states. The shades disturbed by necromancy cannot return to their dream; they may wait in a dazed condition or go on with the after-death states.

In other places he sees the portions of doers working out the decrees which were pronounced in their Halls of Judgment. He sees the doers enacting the scenes of the past life according to the thoughts they had had. He could not see this if he were not on The Way and had not left the world. The thoughts of these doers are the molds into which the flow of matter is shaped, over and over again. The doers have their breath-forms, which are like the former personalities, and see, hear, taste, smell and feel somewhat as they did on the outer crust. The doers themselves cannot be seen, any more than they can be seen in life.

In a special place he sees "lost" portions of doers, some lost untold years ago, and some who failed even within his own time. Some of them are ape-like forms without hair, their skin grey, clay-colored, their eyes bleary, their mouths big and slimy; others are large, whitish worms with little hands and feet; others are like leeches with little human heads and long arms and legs with which they cling; and others appear in various forms—but all exhibiting most disgusting features. These things are male and female and have periods of orgies and of deathly silence. Sometimes they disappear, blending into the landscape, and leave an atmosphere of death behind. Then they reappear with hollow roaring, with echoing wails and shrieks, and begin their orgies. But these are empty; there is no sensation.

Among the "lost" doers he sees are those lost because of their selfishness and enmity to the human race. They are separated from the lustful. Some are like great spiders with wicked eyes, some like vampires or crabs with human faces and devilish eyes, some like snakes with legs and wings. Each of them lives separately among the brush or hanging from the rocky roofs or hiding among the stones on the ground. The spiders can leap fifty feet, the bats sail noiselessly, wolf-like forms with horns and bristly heads prowl about, cruel cat-like things with long snaky bodies spring, all to kill. But for some the killing is not the sole object; they want blood or the pleasure of torturing. Many attack each other. But none of them get any satisfaction. There is an aching, an emptiness in them at all times, which causes them to search for something, and that they cannot find.

He sees other things which have come from the outer crust; doers lost through an unwise religious devotion, who are called the "ancient dead." They have devoted themselves to a personal God or Gods or to nature and have wished to be absorbed in or to identify themselves with their deities or with nature. Most of these doers belong to former ages, but some belong to more recent times. They have worshipped their Gods devotedly, irrespective of a reasonable, universal moral code to which they had access in their religious system, and often against what reason showed and conscience forbade. They sought the favor of their deities from selfish motives. They performed nature rites and ceremonies and offered their thoughts in praise and flattery and in prayer for material gifts and for absorption in the almighty deities. They prayed for favors and did not conquer themselves. In their thinking and their thoughts went out the Light of the Intelligences. The deities were insatiable.

When all the Light available in their mental atmospheres had been sent out, the human beings thereby cut themselves off from the Light of their Intelligences. After death they did not return to the non-embodied portions of their doers, but went into their nature gods. They lost their identity temporarily, because nature gods have no identity except such as they get from the thoughts of the doer portions in human bodies; and they were not absorbed because doer portions can never again become part of nature. So after death they went into a form in one of the four elements or they passed from form to form.

The ongoer sees them in stones, in water, in winds and in fire. They are conscious and dissatisfied, like maniacs trying to find out who they are. Sometimes he hears cries coming from a rock or tree or water: "Who?", or "Where?" or "Lost, Lost."

The guide takes him through many countries, in which are varieties of human beings. They travel along different layers and from one layer to others. Different conditions exist on the different layers. Thus the force of gravitation is strongest near the outer crust and after that point is passed, decreases gradually as they advance into the crust, and finally ceases.

The ongoer sees many peoples. Nearest to the crust the races are wild and degenerate; they eat raw flesh and drink strong intoxicants. But farther in the people are peaceable and cultured. Nearly all the races are white. Some of them are acquainted with the earth and have power over its forces. In an instant they can melt, split and make or dissipate rocks. They can remove weight from an object or give it weight. They can develop new kinds of plants and fruits. In many of the layers some can fly as easily as they can move on a surface. Sometimes many join and rise into the air, where their thinking, because of the adaptability of the matter, tints the air in shining waves of color. Some of the people in some races can see into and through objects in the layer in which they are, but usually they cannot see into the layer on either side. Some can see through the earth crust and see the matter on either side of the crust. Others can hear in the same way, and still others can both see and hear.

The people in the earth crust are human beings, but who are not akin to any human races now on the crust. Some have never left the interior. The ongoer meets people of the race to which his guide belongs.

Some of the people he meets from time to time warn him against his guide; some invite him to leave his guide and to stay with them, offering him the peace, plenty and power they enjoy, or promising to show him wonders and reveal mysteries greater than any his guide will or can show him; some threaten him. The guide often absents himself, but if present offers no objection or inducement. Should any ongoer yield to the allurements he will not see the guide again, and he fails to reach the end of The Way.

During these wanderings the guide explains the structure of the inner earth, its forces and history, the phenomena and their causes and reactions, and the changes as history and the nature of the entities encountered. He explains the illusions of time and of the dimensions of matter and the relative reality of all these things, which are seen as illusions. He explains the powers and behavior of feeling-and-desire, what it means to travel the form path and issue into the form world as a being of that world. He explains that the ongoer must balance his thoughts, and that the end of The Way is in the balancing.

At length the ongoer is left alone. Darkness settles upon him, reaches into him and fills him. He would like to escape, but he does not. He seems to be dead, but he is conscious. His senses are not active. Gradually beings appear, human and non-human. He denounces them, but cannot drive them away. They look into him and reach into him and he knows they are a part of him. He sees their purpose. They want to continue to live by getting their life from him. Then he knows they are his thoughts. He balances them one by one as they come. More of them come. He can see that they are equal to physical events. He withdraws from them the power to become physical. He pronounces judgment upon them in relation to himself. This judgment dissipates them. A calm comes to him. His guide reappears and greets him.

The guide says that he will help him if he wishes to enter the form world in the new body he has within; but that if he decides to take the life path, he will lead him to another guide. The ongoer, though sorry to part with his guide, declares he will go on.

The path was hitherto within the earth crust and stretched for a distance which is about a third of half of the circumference of the earth. While the ongoer went along the form path his body changed in structure and in nature. It now has little or no weight and does not require solid food. It has lines so perfect and proportionate that in nobility and grace it excels any body on the crust. The intestinal canal has become a short columnar passage and the bridge has been built connecting the involuntary nervous structure within that columnar passage directly with the voluntary system at the coccyx. Within the filament has been developed an embryonic form body.

SECTION 6

The ongoer on the life path; on the light path, in the earth. He knows who he is. Another choice.

When the ongoer has announced his choice for the life path, the guide and he pass through a hall. The guide leads him to a crystal rock from which a fountain of clearest water falls in sparkling sheets and spray into a basin in the rock. The guide tells him that these are cleansing waters; that they will fit him to draw from the fountain of life or will dissolve his body and wash it away; that one who is prepared will have no fear. "Enter the water if you will and it will enter you."

The ongoer walks into the pool under the fountain. His whole body drinks in the welcome draught. He feels himself gliding into the pool. The rock, the guide, the chamber disappear as he feels himself going out with the water into the great ocean where all the waters meet. He expands into the ocean, yet feels the current that carries him. The ocean is through the rocks, the water, the plants, the animal life and the bodies of all human beings. It is feeling, desiring and emotional humanity. He feels himself through it and as it, in the present and the past. He is conscious of mankind extending as the ocean to the stars. These are the crossings of the nerves of human beings. He is extended to the farthest stars. Mankind goes out to the stars and they come into mankind. They are like the crossings in a spider's web. He sees the crossings but he does not see the lines, yet is conscious where they are. He draws himself together, after having been so spread out. He now feels the humanity which is in bodies on earth and that which is without bodies; these are the re-existing doers of Triune Selves. He went out to mankind, now mankind comes into him. He is conscious that he will continue on The Way. The feelings of human beings reaching into the form world rush into him and urge him to come to them, to help them and lead them out of their troubles. They show him that if he leaves them to themselves they will not find their way. The "ancient dead" in their nature prisons appeal to him to liberate them. "Lost" portions of doers are reminded by his presence in them that they are lost and that they want to get back. Their appeal is so strong and his desire to help so great that he would give himself to them. But the Light shows his duty to go on. He looks into the Light and affirms his choice for the life path. He is in the pool under the fountain, and steps out, cleansed. The guide is where he left him, and it is as if he had just stepped in and come out.

There is no effort in moving through the hall as the body has no weight and will go in the direction of the desire. Desire is its direct motive power, as it was the indirect motive power while he was on the earth. When the guide has taken him as far as he can he departs at the end of the form path and a teacher is there to meet the ongoer at the beginning of the life path.

The teacher is quite human in appearance, simple and unassuming, but there is the sublime in his presence. The color of his physical body is somewhat like that of a being of the form world, but he is a being of the form, life, and light worlds. Yet the teacher, notwithstanding his greatness, does not seem strange to the ongoer.

The life path, along which the ongoer now passes, continues within the earth crust and extends over the second third of half of the inner circumference of the crust. On the life path he so increases his power to think with his feeling-mind and desire-mind that he can use the speech of thinking to speak with the thinker of the Triune Self through the mind of rightness and the mind of reason. He achieves the powers to examine, penetrate, dissect, compare, construct, create and dissipate by speech with his body-mind. He learns how to use these powers, but he does not use them. Merely thinking of a subject now solves the problems which were only perceived before. He understands the causes of forms and of types, as prepared from age to age. He learns the law of thought, as destiny; he comprehends the cycling of thoughts and the causes and methods of their exteriorizations. During all this growth the teacher has not actually instructed him. By bringing up problems he has merely given him the opportunity to solve them himself; thus the ongoer learns how to find the solution of his own problems. In this way the ongoer has put himself into communication with rightness-and-reason. So he comes to the end of the life path.

As they are walking through a hall, the teacher sings: O-E-A-O-E-HA. Rushing wind descends, enfolds the ongoer and breathes into him. That air of life goes through his nerves, pervades him, and each unit of his body sings. It sings his own story from the beginning to the coming of the living air. It sings the songs of life. All nature units outside join in the songs. The doers in mortal bodies sing each its song of sorrow, bitterness and pain. He understands each sound and song. The air within him puts him in tune with all that lives, and he has understanding of that. He is conscious that the teacher knows that he can now hear and answer any call.

The teacher tells him that this is as far as he goes and asks if he will issue into the life world, a being of that world, or if he will go on to the light path, for if so he must go on alone. The ongoer says: "I will go on alone."

What he has heretofore considered and solved has developed for him the mental power to know without the process of thinking, which is the connection to the knower of the Triune Self. When the ongoer said "I will go on alone," he thereby found in himself a Light. That is the Light by which he knows The Way.

He finds the light path because he knows it when he comes to it. The path continues still within the earth crust for the remainder of the half of the circumference. To reach the end he goes through a white fire. When he enters it the remaining fabrics of illusion he has made by thinking are burnt away.

The partitions separating him from age to age, from life to life, from place to place, from state to state, are dissipated. The fire that burns down the veils within is the essential fire of the four elements in the earth sphere. He sees everywhere and is present in all parts of physical nature.

He knows himself as being that Triune Self which is identity-and-knowledge in the Eternal in the presence and in the Light of his Intelligence.

He knows himself, by that Light, to be the knower of a Triune Self in his noetic atmosphere within that Light. He knows himself to be the thinker, his mental part, within his mental atmosphere, and of the forming of the mental atmosphere by the thinking of his thinker. He knows of the processes of contemplation by his thinker concerning the things of the light world and of the life world. He knows of the feeling-and-desire of the psychic part, his doer, and of the forming of the psychic atmosphere, by the thinking of his thinker. He knows the twelve portions of his doer, that re-existed successively and yet were one.

He knows of the first existence of the doer in the body, of existence in it in a happy state within the earth, and of the apparent separation of feeling from desire at the putting forth of the twin body. He knows that that should have been the beginning of The Way and that he wandered off The Way with the twin. He knows of the flight to the outer crust, of the death of his body and of the twin, and of all his re-existences and their incidents. He knows of his present embodiment and the incidents attending his taking The Way, the same old Way that he once failed to take and which has led him through the three worlds to the end of his re-existences. He knows of the illusion of the separateness of the three parts of the Triune Self. He knows that the Triune Self is One. He knows that he has never left the Eternal, and that his re-embodiments were illusions in time thrown up by the thinking of his feeling-and-desire. When the fire has burnt out all that can be consumed, it has no further effect.

The knowledge he has gives him being into the Light. Now in his perfected physical body, he is at once in the form, the life, and the light worlds, and he is and knows himself to be a Triune Self complete; a being of the three worlds in the Light and the presence of his Intelligence, and in the presence of the Great Triune Self of the worlds.

Through the Great Triune Self of the worlds acts the Supreme Intelligence. The Supreme Intelligence needs such a Great Triune Self through which to act, a Triune Self which is all-feeling, all-thinking and all-knowing; a Triune Self that is omnipresent, omnipotent and omniscient. The Great Triune Self feels through all grades of Triune Selves, from the beings of the light world down to the portions of doers in human bodies and even down to the portions of doers that are in the state that is called lost.

The Great Triune Self of the worlds thinks through all these, from the high to the low; and it knows all that they know. Its feeling, its thinking and its knowledge are one. It knows the state of each human being and the collective state of all human beings at any time, that is, the state of humanity. It knows also the states of the super-human doers, singly and together. Human beings are not conscious that the Great Triune Self feels and thinks with them and knows what they know. The beings of the form world can feel it, the beings of the life world can think it, but only a being of the light world, one who has stood in the presence of it and has been attuned to it, can know it. A being of the light world is always in communication with it and is a high officer, a conscious agent of the law of thought, as destiny. The Great Triune Self is the coordinator for the Intelligences and of the interactions of their doers on the physical plane.

The ongoer who has arrived before the Great Triune Self of the worlds knows that that was at one time a doer of its Triune Self, and knows that that has not given up its relation to humanity in order to pass on and become an Intelligence; and knows, further, that it has retained this relation so that it may be a link between all mankind. The ongoer knows that the Great Triune Self is the exemplification of relationship. He knows that there is this relation, the sameness in kind of all doers. They are actually related and connected by this sameness, on the un-manifested side of their knowers, though they appear as different when portions of them are in fleshly bodies. The difference is built up by thinking and feeling. During embodiments the differences are seen and thought about, but the sameness is unknown. Yet even there is found a semblance of sameness, because all have like feelings and desires and like thoughts, which make the general types in nature and fashion the world in which they live together.

The ongoer sees into the Light of his Intelligence, which is an Intelligence of the highest order, a Knower, an Intelligence of the sphere of fire, and through that Light sees into the Light of Supreme Intelligence, whose Light is Truth. Thus he stands in the presence of Truth. The Intelligences partake of that Light, and the Light of the Intelligence which is loaned to the Triune Self is Truth, though it is obscured and beclouded when it is in the mental atmosphere of the human. This is the

Light used by the human being, and is all that he can stand of Truth. He sees that nothing that has anything to conceal can stand in the undimmed Light which is Truth, and which dissipates deceit and darkness and illusion.

The ongoer who has arrived before the Great Triune Self of the worlds knows the beauty in the law that works throughout the earth sphere adjusting the thoughts of each doer, its relations with other doers and the operation of all thoughts of all doers in nature. He comprehends the details of that law, and he feels it working through all doers. He knows, comprehends and feels the world as made by all doers and as kept in adjustment by the Great Triune Self of the worlds and its agents of the law. He knows he is free to do what he pleases, but comprehending the broad sweep of the action of the law, he chooses and desires to take part in the administration of affairs for the benefit of the doers who keep themselves in darkness.

He leaves the presence of the Great Triune Self of the worlds and returns to his perfected physical body through the light, the life, the form and the physical worlds, yet he is in them all, for he is conscious in them, being himself in the Light. It is during this return that the life body and the form body cease to be embryonic, and issue. The thinker and the doer enter in these inner bodies as a being of the life world and as a being of the form world. The knower is in the light body.

During these events, the perfect physical body had been left at the end of the path in the inner earth crust. The Triune Self enters through the top of the skull. It is a threefold being though One, in a perfected and immortal physical body. As a being of the form world he inhabits the abdominal region where there is now a brain in place of the suprarenals, the kidneys and the solar plexus. Below that, in the pelvis, is another brain for the perfect body and the physical world. As a being of the life world he lives in the thoracic region, where the heart and lungs have become a brain. As a being of the light world he is within the cervical vertebrae and the cephalic brain in the head. This is his embodiment.

When he has entered the body he finds the teacher whom he had left at the end of the life path, and who had, though unseen, accompanied him to the place where the ongoer had left his body. He recognizes the teacher as being a being of the three worlds who had before done what the ongoer has just accomplished.

The perfected physical body is brought to its high state so that it may be an instrument for the operation of the elemental forces in the four worlds of nature. All parts of nature can be reached through the nerves of such a body. Through the eye the doer that lives in such a body could set fire to a leaf or to a city. Anything that can be done by nature forces can be done by directing the forces through the nerves of such a body. The thoughts and the emotions of humans can also be reached through such a body, and so a riot, a war, a religious enthusiasm and a mental trend or attitude can be generated and sustained or abated. The four brains are the centers from which the nerves are operated.

A perfect body, always in the Realm of Permanence, affords to the units passing through it, a straight road of progress, according to the Eternal Order of Progression, (Fig. II-G, H). Each such unit eventually becomes an aia, then a Triune Self, and then an Intelligence. The doer part of every Triune Self must undergo the trial and test to bring its feeling-and-desire into balanced union, as heretofore mentioned. If it passes that test, as the majority of units do, the Triune Self is complete. If the doer fails in that test, it passes temporarily out of the straight road and takes a circuitous route by way of re-existences in human bodies in this world of change.

When a Triune Self complete in a perfect body acts in the physical world it acts through the pelvic brain. When the doer acts in the form world it acts through the brain in the abdominal region. In a similar way the thinker in such a body, when acting in the life world, uses the brain in the thorax. When acting in the light world the knower in such a body uses the brain in the upper spine and the head. Such a Triune Self can act in each of these worlds, independently of the body, but it uses the body when it wants to relate any one of these worlds to the physical world or to affect doers in human bodies, because its physical body is common ground for all the worlds and is perfectly aligned with them.

Such Triune Selves complete are high officers of the law of thought, as destiny. They have complied with its requirements concerning themselves, and are free from it. They have no motives similar to those of human beings. They feel the mass of human suffering; they desire only to act according to the law. They comprehend the thoughts, ideals and aspirations of human beings and carry out the law of thought in relation thereto. But they do not interfere with the choice or the responsibility of any human.

Having entered its perfect body the complete Triune Self is among other Triune Selves who are beings of the light, life and form worlds. They are in the noetic world, which is a term to designate the knowledge which is in the noetic atmospheres of all knowers and is common and available to each. They are beyond time and the changes which are time; they are in the state of permanence which persists through the changes of time.

Again a choice is open to and must now be made by the Triune Self. Its doer having balanced its thoughts and, therefore, being free from the necessity to re-exist; having reclaimed, freed and restored to its Intelligence the Light which had been loaned to it; having no claim upon or attachment to the Light of its Intelligence: the relation between it, as a Triune Self, and its Intelligence, is outgrown and ceases. The Triune Self may choose one of three courses. But the proper course, which it will choose, is: it becomes an Intelligence, evokes its own potential Light, raises its aia to be a Triune Self, and remains with that Triune Self in the earth sphere.

SECTION 7

Preparing oneself to enter upon The Way. Honesty and truthfulness. The regenerative breath. The four stages in thinking.

This section is written for those who feel that they would like to find and be on The Way. Here first principles only are considered. The system of thinking at the end of the book is more extensive; it leads from the beginning to the end of The Way.

The Way which leads the human to Self-conscious immortality cannot be travelled by everyone. It is the destiny for everyone, ultimately, but not immediately. Comparatively few will consider it before it is recognized as a public topic. It is not for the disbeliever. One who does not feel reasonably sure: that there is The Way, that there is the Triune Self, and that he is the doer part of such a Triune Self, ought not to undertake the quest.

The quest is to find oneself in the body, and one's greater Self when on The Way.

To prepare oneself for The Way involves a definite decision to do so, and is a far reaching step. The sooner one begins the work, the fewer lives are needed. Once the choice is made, it acts for the eleven doer portions not in the body. The decision is one's own private affair and should be considered as such. No one should advise him.

One should not decide for The Way until he has given due consideration to the marriage relation; to its duties and its consequences. One who is married may decide to be on The Way. In which case the relation will be mutually and naturally adjusted in due time. But one who is unmarried must understand that he cannot go on The Way unless there is cessation of the sexual desire and act. The desire must be for permanent union of feeling-and-desire, not for spasmodic union of physical bodies. Sex indulgence is the continuation of births and deaths. Whereas, The Way leads to Self-knowledge in a perfect and everlasting physical body.

You, the conscious doer-in-the-body, who have decided to find and be on The Way, may appeal to your thinker part to guide you. You will have the Conscious Light within to show you The Way—to the degree that you trust it and use it. The Conscious Light within is Truth, it is your degree of Truth. The Light will show you things truly as they are. That is what Truth does.

You must learn to distinguish that from all other lights. The difference is that the lights of the senses are lights of nature. They make you aware of the objects of nature from the outside, but they are not conscious of the objects which they make visible outwardly. Nor are they conscious inwardly; lights of nature do not know anything; they are conscious as their functions only, nothing more. Whereas the Conscious Light is Self-knowing; it is conscious that it is the Light that knows that it knows. The Light leads and shows the way to the knowledge of all things of nature, and to the knowledge of one's greater Self. Without the Conscious light one could not be conscious of or as oneself.

Without the Conscious Light you cannot find The Way. In right thinking you use the Light; and when you seek The Way, the Light will show you and keep you on The Way. But you must qualify yourself in two arts in order to find and to travel The Way.

The first is the art of seeing things as they are. You may ask: What do I see, if I do not see things as they are? You see things as appearances, as they appear to be, but not as they really are.

In acquiring the art, preference and prejudice, two treasured heirlooms of the human, must be done away with in order that you may find and travel The Way. Preference and prejudice grow on the mind's eye like as cataracts do on the physical eye. Thus the Conscious Light is dimmed and finally obscured. Therefore they must be removed and forgotten. They can be removed by virtue.

Virtue is one's power of will in the practice of honesty and truthfulness.

Honesty begins with right thought and motive in oneself, and is expressed by one's actions in dealing with others. Honesty is not merely a passive not-taking what belongs to others; it is also an active refusal to consider being devious or crooked.

Truthfulness is the purpose and practice of stating facts as the facts are, without intent to deceive. Truthfulness is not the mere negative assent to, or statement of what is so, fearful of misstatement or of being mistaken. It is the strict intent to not deceive oneself, and then be direct in statement of facts, in the simple words that allow no opposition.

One may have a strong will and a general acquaintance with honesty and truthfulness, and yet not have virtue. Virtue does not happen at once. Virtue is developed, but only by the practice of honesty and truthfulness.

Virtue, as the power of will in the practice of honesty and truthfulness, develops a strong and fearless character. Dishonesty and falsehood are then strangers, and are foreign, undesirable to virtue. By virtue the scales of preference and prejudice are dissipated and removed, and one sees things as they are. When the scales of preference and prejudice are removed from the mind's eye, the unobscured Conscious Light shows and makes one conscious of things as they are. One is then truly qualified to learn what not to do, and what to do.

The second art is the art of knowing what to do, and doing that; and knowing what not to do, and not doing that. Now you can speak to your thinker and ask to be guided. You can mentally say: My Judge and Knower!—guide me in all I think and do!

Rightness of your thinker will speak to you through conscience in your heart, and tell you what not to do; and reason of your thinker will tell you what to do. Practice in the art of seeing things as they are, and in the art of knowing what to do and what not to do, will be your preparation to travel the three sections of The Way.

For practicing the two great arts: of seeing things as they are, and of knowing what to do and what not to do, your ordinary everyday experiences will give you all the opportunities necessary for the practice. You need not be surprised at anything that happens, or that nothing that happens is out of the ordinary or beyond your duties. But whatever does happen will be for your training and for the development of your character, whether it be strange or commonplace.

Duties are important, always; but they are most important when one decides to be on The Way. No duties should prevent one from deciding for The Way, because no human can ever be free from them until he has performed all his duties. All that one has to do is: to do that which he knows to be his duty, and to do it as well as he can with goodwill, without undue expectation, and without fear.

Whether one's position in life be lofty or lowly does not matter. Whether married or single, with or without family, with or without encumbrance, does not matter so much. But what does matter is that one does in good faith all that he has agreed to do, or that circumstances show to be necessary. Should there be any ties, they will not be broken; they will naturally fall away. Duties that would ordinarily seem insuperable will in this way be done naturally and properly through circumstances which will come about in orderly process of time: they have a purpose in your training. For the learning and doing, time is not the important matter. The essence of the doing is in the accomplishment, not in length of time or number of lives that may be required. You are to learn to think and live in the Eternal, not in time.

There is a method of regenerative breathing which assists in seeing things as they are, and in knowing what to do and what not to do. It re-establishes the right relation between the breath and the form of the breath-form; it is a beginning of the reconstruction of the human body according to the form of its original perfect body. Further, this method is a way of exploring and examining the body by means of the breath, of knowing the mystery of the human body.

The breath as it is breathed in should be of four kinds: the physical breath, the form breath, the life breath, and the light breath. Each of these is subdivided into four subsidiary breaths. As the four subsidiary breaths of the first kind are practiced and known, they prepare and initiate one into the next kind and its subsidiaries.

The four subsidiaries of the physical breath are: the solid-physical, fluid-physical, airy-physical, and radiant-physical breaths; in other words, the structure of the physical, the form of the physical, the life of the physical, and the light of the physical.

These first four subsidiary breaths build and repair the structure of the physical body. They should maintain a balance between the building material and the waste matter that cannot otherwise be removed. This is done by the regular inflow and outflow of the four substates of solid-physical matter: that is, of solid, fluid, airy, and radiant units.

Breathing is intended to permeate and supply all parts and states and substates of the solid body with units of matter of its own state, so that all units in the body can perform their functions properly. This can be done only by regenerative breathing. At present, the human breathes only portions of the gross physical breath. These are insufficient for proper digestion and assimilation of the food and drink taken into the body. Therefore ill health and death may be consequences of improper breathing.

Tissue is built, and a balance is maintained between the building material and the elimination of waste matter from the body, by the process of breathing. Breathing is the process of (a) building new material as structure onto the form of the breath-form; (b) the elimination of waste matter from that structure; and (c) the metabolizing or maintenance of balance between the building and elimination. This explains the age-old biological mystery of tissue building.

By practicing the regenerative method of breathing until such breathing becomes the habitual breathing of the physical breath at all times, the solid-fluid-airy-radiant structure of the physical body will, by the four subsidiary states of the physical breath, be built into a properly adjusted and functioning physical body of health, the life of which may be prolonged indefinitely. One who decides to practice this system of breathing is advised not to practice yoga breathing, pranayama, or any other system: they would be interferences. The rules for the regenerative breath are as follows:

1) There should be no unnecessary pause or interruption of breathing, between inbreathing and outbreathing. That would be an interference with the rhythm of breath, or a stoppage of the Light for thinking.

2) One should think with and follow the breath as it comes into and passes through the body, to observe and actually feel where it naturally does go, what it does, and the results of what is being done by the breath in its tidal passage in and out of the body.

3) A time should be set for the daily practice of regenerative breathing; it should be at first not less than ten minutes, and should be gradually extended to longer periods as seems consistent with one's reason. But the breathing may also be practiced at any time of day or night, so that eventually the practice will become one's regular and normal breathing.

4) The practice of the breathing should be suspended or stopped if one believes there is any reason for so doing.

5) If there is a time of panic, anger, excitement, or when one seems likely to be overwhelmed, then persist in the uninterrupted and full inbreathing and outbreathing.

By the practice of this regenerative breathing, the breath rebuilds the tissues and opens new avenues for the unobstructed flow of the breaths through all the interstices of the body and its senses, its organs and its cells, molecules, atoms, and electrons or protons. The breath passing through the blood and nerves tends to relate and put into agreement desire, the active side of the doer-in-the-body, and feeling, its passive side, so that they will be in intimate relation.

The blood vessels and the nerves in the body run side by side, the blood being the field of desire, and the nerves the field of feeling. As the breath passes through blood and nerves it puts feeling and desire into phase, and so they act conjointly.

Thinking is the steady holding and focussing of the Conscious Light within on the subject of the thinking. The steady holding, or actual focussing, of the Conscious Light, by thinking, is possible only at the neutral moment or point between the outbreathing and the inbreathing, and between the inbreathing and the outbreathing. So that the actual results of thinking are possible only at the two poles or points of the complete round. The practice of so breathing and thinking is a method for acquiring the power to think.

When the thinking is on the subject of this regenerative breathing, the processes of breathing in the rebuilding of the body will be made known, as the Conscious Light is focussed at the neutral points between the breathings. As the practice continues, the thinking will make known the parts and functions of the body in relation to the functions of the universe; and the relation of the functions of the universe to the parts and functions of the body, and to the body as a whole, and their reciprocal action and reaction.

There are four stages or degrees in thinking. First, the selection of the subject, and giving attention to the subject. Second, holding the Conscious Light on that subject. Third, focussing the Light on that subject. Fourth, the focus of the Light.

The subject should be the only thing to which attention is given. There should be nothing else with which the attention is engaged.

In the second, the holding of the Light steadily means that all the available Light in his mental atmosphere that one has to think with is turned on that subject. As soon as the Light is turned on the subject, that

Light attracts one's past thoughts, and any other idle or wandering thoughts. To the Light so turned, thoughts and subjects of thought, pests of the night, all try to crowd into that Light. The first effect on the thinker is that there are a great many subjects that would obscure or prevent his seeing his subject. The thinker usually tries either to get these out of his Light, or else to give attention to any one of the number of thoughts that crowd in. This is too difficult and the thinker is usually distracted and prevented from holding the Light on the subject of his selection. He will mentally see one of the subjects or thoughts that have crowded in, and hold the Light on that. But no sooner has he done so than the others try to crowd that one out by getting in the line of his mental vision. Fight as he will, he cannot seem to get back to his subject. And he turns the Light from one to the other of the innumerable thoughts or things that crowd in; and he does not get any farther; so he finally gives up the effort, or else falls asleep.

He may take this same subject up again and again, for what he calls contemplation, or meditation, or by any other name. Then he will have itchings, or feelings of irritation and uneasiness, changing his position and beginning over and over again. He often tries to do away with these unwarranted intrusions. But the more he tries to put them out of his thinking, the less he is able to be rid of them. There is one way, and one way only, by which they are dispersed. That way is to keep on trying to think steadily on the subject, and to mentally refuse to see anything but the subject on which he is trying to hold the Light.

However many efforts and however long this may take, it is necessary for him to do it. Because that is steadiness in thinking. Each time he thinks of things that annoy him, he turns the Light on that thing and the other thing, and he is not holding the Light on his subject. But when he refuses to see anything but what he *wills* to see as his subject, then the unwarranted subjects flee, and he is holding the Light steadily on the subject; he has completed the second stage.

The third stage is the focussing of the Light. The Light is more or less diffused over an area, so to say. By looking steadily at the subject as a point, the Light becomes more compact and is directed from the area to its central point, which is the subject. The focussing must be continued until all the Light comes to a focus, to its focus on the subject. As soon as the Light is focussed, the subject as a point opens into the fullness of the knowledge of the subject, which the Light shows at once in its entirety. It is a more complete revelation of the subject of the thinking than a lightning flash which illuminates a landscape in the darkest night. The difference is, the lightning shows what is seen by the senses. The Light is the knowledge of the subject accomplished by thinking.

Concerning the second stage, the holding of the Light: Each time the Light is turned on intervening subjects, there is a change of distance and perspective. One subject intervening comes closer, another closer still; another may come still closer. Each tries to get closer in the line of vision, to attract attention. And the poor thinker is so distracted that he does not know what he is thinking about. And he becomes confused, ill at ease, or gives it up in discouragement. He does not get the knowledge until all the Light is focussed. With each focus of the Light he acquires knowledge.

When one looks at a thing it is not seen as an entirety. To see it, one must see the focal point of the thing that he looks at. And if he can see the focal point, he can see the whole through that point.

How does one get the Light in thinking? The surest way of getting the Light is by regular breathing. Whatever Light one gets will come through a point, at the neutral point, between inbreathing and outbreathing, and between outbreathing and inbreathing. So there is twice in one round of complete breathing where the Conscious Light can be focussed.

When the Light comes in at the two neutral points between the inbreathing and the outbreathing, one must be thinking steadily on the subject, else the Light is diffused. If he has more than one subject while trying to think, the Light cannot be focussed. So many subjects are hindering him in his steady thinking that he does not get any focus when the Light would come in; it is therefore diffused over the many subjects. But the continued practice of trying to hold his thinking steadily on the subject selected, allows him to so exercise his mental vision that if he persists long enough he will eventually be able to discover *something* about his subject, because the Light will give a little illumination on his subject, although it may not open it into knowledge.

In this way those who think get information in business, in art, in any occupation or endeavor in life. The Light gives information about the subjects of which they believe they think. But one seldom thinks steadily enough to get knowledge on the subject. All inventions, all discoveries in science and art, or in any earnest endeavor in life, come either as illuminations on the subject or as flashes of knowledge, through the neutral point between inbreathing or outbreathing.

This is thinking, human thinking; not real thinking. Real thinking is beyond the ordinary human. If it were necessary, when the Light was focussed at the time of thinking on the subject, breathing would stop. The Light would suspend the breathing, and one would think into the Light, and see into any subject of his choice. That would be real thinking, an extension of what may be called regular thinking.

Light is intelligence *per se*, and only that which can use Light is intelligent. But human beings are not Intelligences. They become intelligent in varying degrees, according to their ability to hold the Conscious Light on the subject of the thinking.

As one goes on and persists in the thought and action of right and justice, the advice and guidance of one's thinker, as Judge, can be mentally asked and received during breathing. So, one may gain strength, and act fearlessly and with confidence in any undertaking. So, one may from time to time have revelations in answer to one's questions on the relation between the universe and one's body, concerning duties, and one's relation to the thinker and knower of his Triune Self.

Each subsidiary of the physical breath is the medium which the next finer breath uses in the building of its matter into the structure of the physical body. The form breath and its subsidiaries begin to build out the form body when the physical body is developing to physical health. The breath-form will gradually and automatically rebuild and reconstitute and re-establish the physical body in its original state of perfection. But it can only do so as the doer empowers and directs it by thinking.

The one whose regenerative breathing has prepared the body for the form breathing will breathe the form breath, which will gradually improve and reconstruct the structure towards perfection and extend the life of the physical body indefinitely. The form breath is the beginning of the rejuvenescence of bodily life; it is the initiator and mystery and miracle of life in all its higher forms. It will gradually prepare the body for the breathing of the life breath. Then one will receive further information from the thinker and the knower of his Triune Self, as indicated by the system of thinking in the fifteenth chapter.

A chapter on "Freemasonry" was to follow this last section of "The Great Way", in which that subject was treated in the light of what is stated in this book. It was shown how the history of the conscious self in the body is depicted in the Ritual of Freemasonry, the Order being ancient beyond the dreams of any Mason, and symbolically recording such evidence and history of the self as are unknown to modern Masons. The progress of the conscious self in its capacity to become conscious of more Light is recorded by their symbols. The symbols show the Mason's progress by degrees in his travels, even to the building of the "second temple, eternal in the heavens",—as shown in "The Great Way".

On presenting the manuscript to publishers, it appeared that an interpretation of the "Dogma and Ritual" of Freemasonry, by a layman, not a member of the Order, might give offense. That was not intended. Therefore, the chapter is withdrawn; it will not be published, unless so desired by Masons.

❊   ❊   ❊

Since the original publication of *Thinking and Destiny,* Masons have reviewed and approved the original chapter mentioned above which was published separately. It is now being re-inserted as the author originally intended. As Percival himself writes at the end of *Masonry and Its Symbols:*

"Masons who have read the foregoing approved it, and it is now published with the hope that all readers will see its application to "The Great Way." It is addressed to all human beings, and the author, though not a member of the Masonic Fraternity, wishes especially to remind all Masons, of whatever Lodge or Rite, that entrusted to their care were the plans for the rebuilding of their second temple which will be greater than the first temple that they destroyed in the 'long-ago-at-the-beginning-of-time.'

"The information for the building of an immortal physical body has been a closely guarded secret preserved through all the ages by the Masonic Fraternity. The works of the author are for the purpose of showing that every human being, regardless of race, creed, or color who really desires to return to and re-establish his Father's house in The Realm of Permanence, may begin the Great Work without being crushed by the weight of the world's thought. That is to say, without having to leave his or her active work and retire from the world to do it in secret.

It is possible, but not probable, that human beings can rebuild their temples in the present life. However, anyone may prepare himself and become an entered apprentice and take as many degrees as he can in the present life and continue the work in the next life on earth.

This chapter also is to remind all Masons that it is *their work.* Let those, who will, see."

CHAPTER XII

MASONRY AND ITS SYMBOLS

SECTION 1

The Brotherhood of Freemasons. Compass. Membership. Age. Temples. Intelligences behind Masonry. Purpose and plan. Masonry and religions. The essential and the temporary teachings. The fundamental principles of the three degrees. Offshoots. Great truths locked up in trivial forms. The secret language. Passive and active thinking. Lines on the breath-form. Discipline of desires and of mental operations. The ancient landmarks. Masons should see the importance of their Order.

THE Brotherhood of Freemasons is the largest of the bodies in the world which are outposts to prepare possible candidates for an inward life. They are men drawn from all ranks and races for whose character and intelligence a Master Mason has at one time vouched. Masonry is for Humanity, the conscious self in every human body, not for any special race, religion or clique.

The Order existed under one name or another as a compact, well-organized body long before the building of the oldest pyramid. It is older than any religion known today. It is the extraordinary thing among organizations in the world. This organization and the system of its teachings, with the tools, landmarks, emblems and symbols, have always been substantially the same. It goes back to the age when bodies became male or female. The temple has always been a symbol of a rebuilt human body. Some of the legendary masonic temples, whose place is now taken by that of Solomon, were circles, ovals, squares and oblongs of stones. Sometimes the stones were connected at the top by slabs, later by two pieces of stone pitted against each other in triangular form, and then by semicircular arches. Sometimes the temples were enclosed by walls; these temples were open at the top, and the vault of heaven was the roof. So symbolic temples were built for the worship of the Lord, until the last that figures in the Masonic ritual is called Solomon's Temple.

Intelligences in the earth sphere are behind Masonry, though the lodges are not aware of this in the present age. The spirit that runs through the system of the masonic teachings connect these Intelligences with every Mason, from the greatest to the least, who practices them.

The purpose of Masonry is to train a human being so that he will reconstruct, through the body of change and death which he now has, a perfect physical body which shall not be subject to death. The plan is to build this deathless body, called by modern Masons Solomon's Temple, out of material in the physical body, which is called the ruins of Solomon's Temple. The plan is to build a temple not made with hands, eternal in the heavens, which is the cryptic name for the deathless physical vesture. The Masons say that in the building of Solomon's Temple there was not heard the sound of an axe, hammer or any tool of iron; nor will any sound be heard in the rebuilding of the temple. A Masonic prayer is: "And since sin has destroyed within us the first temple of purity and innocence, may thy heavenly grace guide and assist us in rebuilding a second temple of reformation, and may the glory of this latter house be greater than the glory of the former."

There are no better and no more advanced teachings available to human beings, than those of Masonry. The symbols used in the Craft are chiefly tools of a mason and instruments of an architect. The symbols have been substantially the same from immemorial times; though their shape and interpretation have changed, and though the rituals and lectures about them changed with the prevailing cyclic religion of the age. The doctrines of all religions are so made that they can be used for masonic teachings. In modern western Masonry, that is, what the Masons call Ancient Masonry, Masonry is given in forms of the Hebrew religion, with some additions from the New Testament. The teachings are not Hebrew. But Masonry uses parts of Hebrew traditions to clothe and present its own teachings, because the Hebrew traditions are familiar and acceptable as parts of the Bible. The masonic teachings might be presented in Egyptian or pre-Egyptian Greek clothes, if the people were familiar with them. The Hebrew traditions are colorful and impressive. Besides, the physical body in which the reconstruction has to go on is the divided name of Jahveh or Jah-hovah. Yet the rituals are sometimes easily shaped to exemplify Christianity, by making Christ the Supreme

Grand Master, and the Great Architect of the Universe can be interpreted as a Christian God. But Masonry is not Christian any more than it is Jewish. The temporary interpretations according to age and place and religion are looked upon by the common run of Masons as absolute and as the truth.

Often the symbology is obscured by adornments, additions, changes and omissions. Sometimes whole Orders are instituted in these ways and specialize a particular religious, warlike, or social feature. They disappear again, while the symbols and the teachings of which they are a part, remain.

The principles of Masonry are represented in the first three degrees, those of Entered Apprentice, Fellow Craft, and Master Mason, and in the development of those degrees in the Holy Royal Arch. The principles there represented are fundamental, whether found in the York rite, the Scottish rite, or in any other masonic rite. Some rites have degrees which are merely local, personal, social and inviting. There are many side rites, side issues, side degrees, which gifted ritualists have brought into existence, but the principles of Masonry are few and survive the ages and their styles.

Masonry is the trunk or physical connection from which different Orders are formed from time to time. Rosicrucianism in the Middle Ages and other movements of a later date were offshoots put out through members of the Masonic Order, to meet a need of the times without entangling Masonry itself.

In many of the forms of the masonic work that seem trivial and childish are locked up great truths. The truths have to be presented in some symbol or by some work, because human beings need forms in which to see truths. They call truths platitudes, yet cannot see them. When truths are put into forms which are parts of physical life, an apt and striking application of such truths impresses itself upon those who see and feel the application and holds their interest.

It is possible to arrange, and Masonry does arrange, information about fundamental truths about the conscious self and its relation to nature in a systematic way, though in simple forms. By constant repetition of these forms their application to life in general becomes evident. The words used in connection with these forms become a secret language whether the forms be symbols, jewels, tools, badges, emblems, degrees, steps, signs, grips, words, ceremonies, points, lines, angles, surfaces, or simple stories. A common language is a bond of brotherhood, and a secret language which is not bestowed by birth, as is the language of one's country, but by common choice and service, is one of the strongest ties that hold men together. Also by going through these forms over and over they are engraved by sight and sound upon the breath-form and cause passive thinking along the engraved lines. Later active thinking results along the same lines, and with it comes the Light by which the particular truth concealed in the form is seen. After death the lines, made on the breath-form by masonic thinking and masonic thoughts, play an important part in shaping destiny. In the next life on earth a Mason comes under the masonic influences, though he be born under and be claimed by the spirit of a race or of a religion.

The forms of the masonic work are designed to further a discipline of feelings and desires and three minds. The desires are disciplined by thinking which sets bounds to them, and the three minds themselves are disciplined by thinking according to the forms. Only a few subjects are presented in the many masonic forms. These subjects reappear and force themselves upon the attention of a Mason. The forms after a while become suggestive of the subjects for which they stand and so engage mental activity. The discipline results from the regular exercise of the mental activity along the aspects of an inner life which the forms are designed to symbolize.

The forms preserve the secret teachings and in that respect are of inestimable value. The forms are the ancient landmarks of the Order, entrusted to the care of Masons which they are to preserve carefully and are never to suffer to be infringed.

Such are some of the purposes which the masonic play serves. Though what Masons see and hear and say and do has a deep esoteric meaning, they are not affected by that, but delight in the play, the speeches and the social features. Masons seldom, if ever, see the importance of their Order and of its purposes. When they see the inner meanings of their work and begin to live according to their teachings, they will become better men, have a broader and deeper understanding of life, and make the Order of Freemasons a living power for good in the world.

SECTION 2

Meaning of the preliminaries. A free man. Recommendation. Preparations in the heart and for initiation. The divestment. The hoodwink. The fourfold cable-tow. The candidate is the conscious self in the body. Travels. The sharp instrument. Instructions. The pledge. The three great lights and the lesser lights. What the candidate learns about these symbols. Signs, grips and words. The symbol of the lambskin. The scene of poverty. The Mason as an upright man. His working tools. Declaration of the Apprentice. The signs and their meanings. The Word. The four virtues. The six jewels. The Ground Floor of King Solomon's Temple. Purpose of the symbols and ceremonies.

Before one can become a Freemason he must be a free man. A slave cannot be a Mason. In a wider sense he must not be a slave to lust and avarice. He must be sufficiently free to choose of his own free will and accord, that is, not be bound down by base desires or blind to the facts of life. To become a Freemason the candidate must be recommended as to character. He must be in some measure a searcher into the mysteries of life. He must desire more light and be in search of it.

The first preparation is to be made in his heart. He appoints himself to be a Mason and prepares himself by having an honest, clean heart. When a Mason meets with such a man, he will, believing that the other will be a good member, bring the conversation on subjects which will lead the candidate to express his desire to seek admission into a lodge. After the application is made, investigated and recommended, the candidate will be prepared for admission. After he is admitted there is a further preparation for initiation in the anteroom of the lodge.

He is there divested of his clothing. That ceremony stands for the removal of the things that hold him to the outer world, such as possessions and indications of station and rank. It means that he is separated from the past, so that he can enter on a new course. When he is stripped it will appear that he is a man, not a woman. A hoodwink or blind is put over his eyes, so that he feels he is in darkness, without light, and cannot find his way. Then the thing he most desires is light.

A rope, a cable-tow—it should be a rope of four strands—is put around him. It symbolizes the bond by which all Apprentices, Craftsmen and Masons have been entered, initiated, passed and raised into the light of Masonry. The cable-tow stands for the umbilical cord by which all bodies are prepared for birth. It stands for the senses of sight, hearing, taste and smell by which the candidate (the conscious self in the body) is held after birth, which bind him to nature and lead him in darkness. It stands for Masonry which brings him out of the physical world of darkness into the Light. The cable-tow stands for the tie that binds, into a brotherhood of whatever kind. The cable-tow also is the line on the breath-form that binds one to Masonry, to destiny, to rebirth and re-existence.

He begins his work and his travels naked, in darkness, tied to humanity and its common failings. He feels the touch of a sharp instrument; his flesh is pricked to remind him of the torture to which it may put him, and that he must nevertheless persevere with the work to which he will dedicate himself. He is instructed in the conduct of life, always with his work as the end in view. He calls on God, his Triune Self, to witness his obligation and gives his pledge to preserve himself inviolate to the work. To continue his work he needs more light, and he declares that that which he most desires is light. The symbolical hood-wink or blind is removed and he is brought to light. At birth into the world the cord is severed. Likewise when the Apprentice is brought to the light, which is the new tie, the cable-tow is removed. Then he is told that the Bible, the square and the compass, on which he has taken his obligation and to which he has dedicated himself, represent the three great Lights. The three lighted candles, he is told, represent the three lesser lights: the sun, the moon and the Master of the Lodge.

If the Apprentice keeps his obligation, and does the work, he learns, by these symbols, as he advances, that he receives the Word of God, the Light of lights, through his knower. He learns that as the compass describes a line equally distant throughout from the point around which it is drawn, so the mind, according to its light, keeps the passions and desires in bounds which are measured by reason and are of equal distance from rightness, the center. He learns that as the square is used to draw and prove all straight lines, to make two lines at right angles to one another and to unite horizontals with perpendiculars, so by himself as the doer all feelings and desires are made straight, are put in the right relation to each other and are united with each other.

He will learn, after he is raised, that the three great Lights are verily symbols of the three parts of his Triune Self; that the Bible, or sacred writings, which is symbolic of his knower, which is Gnosis, is the source through which he must get Light; and that instead of the points of the compass being under the square they must be over it for him to get that Light, that is to say, rightness, the right point, and reason, the left point, of the compass, must set bounds to feeling, the right line, and to desire, the left line of the square.

He will learn that there are connected with him, at present, only two of the great lights, the Bible and the Compass; that the points of the square are above the compass; that is to say, his feeling and desire are not controlled by his rightness and reason, and that the third Light, the square, is dark, that is, the Light does not reach his feeling-and-desire. The third Light was shut out at the destruction of the first temple; it is potential only and will not be an actual Light until the temple is rebuilt.

The three lesser lights, the sun, the moon and the Master of the Lodge symbolize the body, feeling-and-desire, and their minds. The lodge is the human body. The light for the body, that is nature, is the sun. The moon reflects sunlight. The moon is feeling, on which are reflected the objects of nature by the body, which is personalized nature and is the servant of outside nature. The third light is the Master or desire, and he ought to endeavor to rule and govern his lodge, that is, the body. The body-mind should be used to govern the body and its four senses; the feeling-mind should govern itself, and the desire-mind as the Master should govern itself in the coordination of the feelings and the control of the body.

The Apprentice, as he advances, receives the signs, grips and words, by which he can prove himself or another, in the light or in the dark, and among those not Masons, according to the degree of his light in Masonry. He learns to walk as a Mason should, on the square.

He receives a lambskin, or white apron, a symbol of his physical body. He who wears the lambskin as a badge of a Mason is thereby continually reminded of that purity of life and conduct which is necessary. The apron clothes the pelvic region and is a symbol that that should be kept clean. It refers to sex and food. As he grows in knowledge he should preserve the body not in innocence, but in purity. When he is able to wear the apron as a Master Mason should, the flap which may be an equilateral or a right-angled triangle, hangs over the square with the corners down. The apron as a square symbolizes the four elements of nature working in the fourfold body through its four systems and the four senses. The triangular flap stands for the three parts of the Triune

Self, and the three minds as substitutes for the Triune Self. They are above the body or not entirely in the body in the case of the Apprentice, and within the body or fully embodied in the case of the Master.

When asked to contribute to a worthy cause the Apprentice finds he is penniless, unable to do so, naked and an object of charity. This is a reminder to aid those whom he finds in life and who are in need of help. The scene should make him feel that he is nothing more or less than what he is as a man; that he should be judged by what he is and not be valued in terms of dress, possessions, a title, or money.

He is then allowed to reclothe himself; he puts on his apron and is taken before the Master of the Lodge who directs him to stand at his right hand and tells him that he is now an upright man, a Mason, and charges him ever to walk and act as such. As a Mason, he must have working tools. He is given the working tools of an Apprentice which are the twenty-four inch gauge and common gavel.

The gauge is the symbol of masculinity. It has to do not only with the hours but with the span of life. The gauge is the rule of life and the rule of right. The first third is for the Apprentice when he should, as the masonic ritual has it, remember his Creator in the days of his youth. This is the service of God, by not wasting the creative power. Thereby he fits himself to follow his masonic work in the second degree as a Fellow Craft. He then is rebuilding his body, the temple not made with hands. The last third is for the Master Mason who is refreshed by the conserved power and is a master builder.

The gavel is said to be an instrument which operative masons use to break off the superfluous corners of rough stones to fit them for the builder's use, but with the speculative Mason the gavel stands for the force of desire which should be used with the gauge, or rule of right, to remove inherited inclinations and vices, so that each life of the Mason may be shaped into and become a living stone, a perfect ashler, in the final temple of the Triune Self. His first life, that in which he becomes an Apprentice, is said to be a corner stone, from which a super-structure of an immortal physical body is expected to rise.

The Apprentice declares that he has come into Masonry to learn to subdue his passions and improve himself in Masonry. It is the profession of his purpose. He is asked how he will know himself to be or how he may be known to be a Mason, and he declares that he will do it by certain signs, a token, a word and the perfect points of his entrance.

The signs, he says, are right angles, horizontals and perpendiculars, which must be parallel. These signs mean more than how he shall step or hold his hands or pose his body.

The right angles mean the squaring of his feeling (one line) with his desire (the other line) in all actions.

The horizontals mean the equal balancing of his feeling and of his desire.

The perpendiculars mean that his feeling and desire are raised to uprightness from lowness.

The token is a grip. It means that he must hold his feeling and his desire with a firm grip, and it also means that feeling and desire should grip each other in the same degree and prove each other.

A word is the one used in the Apprentice degree, and is a symbol. Lines make letters, and letters a word. Four letters are needed to make The Word. The Apprentice can supply only one letter, that letter is A and is made of two lines, feeling and desire. The Word is found by the Royal Arch Mason.

The perfect points of the Apprentice's entrance are four. They are the four cardinal virtues: temperance is habitual self-restraint or control of one's passionate impulses and appetites; fortitude means constant courage, patience and endurance without fear of danger; prudence means skill in right thinking and in the performance of right action; and justice is knowledge of the rights of oneself and others, and in thinking and acting in accordance with that knowledge.

The candidate learns about the jewels. There are six jewels, three movable, which are the rough ashler, the perfect ashler, and the trestle-board. The rough ashler is the symbol of the present, imperfect physical body; the perfect ashler is the symbol of the physical body after it has been perfected, and the trestle-board the symbol of the breath-form, on which the designs of the building are drawn. These three jewels are called movable because they perish after each life or are carried from life to life. The immovable jewels are the square, the level and the plumb. The square symbolizes desire, the level feeling and the plumb the pattern of the perfect body which is on the breath-form. These three are called immovable, because they are of the Triune Self and do not die.

The First Degree, that of Entered Apprentice, relates to the initiation of himself as doer of feeling-and-desire. This is done on the Ground Floor of Solomon's Temple, that is, in the pelvic region. The Apprentice first prepares himself in his heart, then he is prepared for initiation by being separated from his past. After he has traveled, has been brought to light, has received some information about the three greater Lights by means of the three lesser lights, has received his white apron, is clothed again and has seen the blazing star, he is given the working tools of an Entered Apprentice and then makes certain declarations. All of the symbols and ceremonies are intended to impress upon him what to do with his desires and the use of his desire-mind, feeling-mind, and body-mind in his conduct towards himself, his brothers, and his God.

SECTION 3

The degree of Fellow Craft. How the candidate is received and the meaning of it. Being brought to light. What he receives. The tools of a Fellow Craft. Their meaning. The two columns. Building the bridge from Boaz to Jachin. The three, five and seven steps. The Middle Chamber. Meaning of the steps. The wages and the jewels. Meaning of the letter G. The point and the circle. The four and the three degrees. The twelve points on the circle. The Zodiacal signs. Expression of universal truths. Geometry. The achievements of the Fellow Craft. The thinker. The Master Mason. Preparation. Reception. Being brought to light. The pass, the grip, the apron and the tools of a Master Mason.

The second degree, that of Fellow Craft, is not an initiation of the thinker, but is the passing of the conscious doer from the darkness and ignorance of feeling-and-desire to the light of rightness-and-reason. He is received into this degree on the angle of the square, symbolic of the fact that he has made his feeling-and-desire right and square, at right angles with each other, that he has united them, and that they will be used so in all his actions. He asks for more light and is shown how to step towards that Light. He receives more Light. In being brought to Light in this degree, he perceives one point of the compass above the square, symbolic of the fact that he receives Light through the rightness of his thinker and that he will be guided in his actions from that point, that Light. He receives the pass, the grip and the word of a Fellow Craft. The pass is symbolical of the transfer or passage from the first to the second degree. The grip stands for the power of rightness over feeling-and-desire. The word is still not the Word, but is only two letters, namely the A with a U or an O.

He is given the working tools of a Fellow Craft which are the plumb, the square and the level. The plumb stands for uprightness in thinking, the level for equality in thinking, and the square for the union of the plumb and the level. This means that the signs which were only lines in the Apprentice degree have now in the Fellow Craft degree become tools; the perpendiculars and horizontals, which were lines, have become the plumb and the level, and the right angles have become the square. Desire and feeling are now upright and level, united, that is, in agreement with and in right relation to each other, and act from the point of their union which is at rightness. The angle of the square stands for the point of union. The square is used in thinking, whether by the plumb or on the level, in all that concerns the earth, that is, the physical body of oneself or of another.

He is shown two brazen columns, said to have been at the entrance of Solomon's Temple. Boaz, the left column, symbolizes the sympathetic or nature column, which will be in front of the body, and Jachin, the right one, is the spinal column, the column of the Triune Self. When the doer part of the Triune Self first came into its body, that is, its temple, the body was neither male nor female, and the two columns existed and functioned having the united power. After its temple was destroyed, the doer functioned in a body which was either male or female and had only Jachin, the male column, and had only the power of the male or of the female. Boaz does not exist, except potentially. The Fellow Craft is reminded by seeing the two columns that he has to rebuild Boaz. The stones which the Apprentice has prepared with his rule and gavel are to be further prepared by the Fellow Craft for the Master Mason before Boaz will be re-established. It is significant that the chapiters of both columns show network, lily-work and pomegranates full of seeds. The network is that of interlaced nerves which is built up by purity which preserves the seeds, and which builds the bridge from Boaz to Jachin.

The Fellow Craft sees the three, five and seven steps or stairs as the winding stairs leading to the Middle Chamber of Solomon's Temple. The five steps are symbolic of work in the Fellow Craft degree, while the three steps relate to the Apprentice degree through which he has passed and the work of which he continues.

The three, five and seven steps or stairs are certain centers or organs in the body. The body as a whole is King Solomon's Temple (or the ruins of it from which the temple is to be rebuilt). The entrance or first step is the prostate, the second step symbolizes the kidneys, the third the adrenals, the fourth the heart, the fifth the lungs, the sixth the pituitary body and the seventh the pineal body. These steps are taken by the use of the minds of rightness and of reason. The body-mind is used by the Apprentice to control the body, the feeling-mind to control feeling and the desire-mind to control desire. By controlling feeling he controls feelings, and by controlling desire, he controls desires. The candidate is always the doer part of the Triune Self, throughout the work of the three degrees. His taking the five steps of the Fellow Craft means the ability to reach the minds used by and for rightness and reason of the thinker of his Triune Self. His taking the seven steps symbolizes his reaching to the minds which are used by and for I-ness and selfness.

The white apron or clean body, which is the badge of a Mason, the rule of right and the gavel of desire are the three steps; by them the Apprentice prepares stones for building. The five are the same three together with the two, the plumb and the level, added. When uprightness in thinking is united with equality in thinking, the plumb and the level form the square, the point of union being at rightness. With these five the Fellow Craft prepares and fits the building stones. The building stones are the units of nature. The seven are a symbol for the seven minds and seven powers of the minds to develop which the Fellow Craft is called. Speculative Masonry designates these seven aspects by the names of the liberal arts and sciences, which are given as grammar, rhetoric, logic, arithmetic, geometry, music and astronomy. The great Three, Five and Seven, though here mentioned, are not brought into the ritual, except that the three, five and seven are brought into relation with the development of the doer of feeling-and-desire to use its minds.

The ascent through a porch, by a flight of winding stairs, consisting of three, five and seven steps, to a place representing the Middle Chamber of King Solomon's Temple, that is, the lodge working in the Fellow Craft degree, is also symbolical of various windings of nature to her concealed recesses, that is, certain physiological developments, due to the development of one's minds, by thinking, before he is received and recorded as a Fellow Craft.

The wages and jewels he receives for his work as a Fellow Craft are certain psychic and mental powers, symbolized by corn, wine and oil, and by the attentive ear, instructive tongue and faithful breast.

The attention of the Fellow Craft is directed to a great symbol placed above the head of the Master, the letter G. It is said to stand for God, for Gnosis and for Geometry. But it has not been at all times a Roman

G. The G stands in place of that which is universally symbolized by the point in the center of a circle.

The point and the circle are the same, the point is the infinitesimally small circle and the circle is the point fully expressed. The expression is divided into the manifested and the unmanifested. The expression proceeds by points and lines. The unmanifested is present in the manifested and the manifested is in the unmanifested. The purpose of the expression is to make that which becomes manifested, conscious of and to identify itself with the unmanifested which is within it; then the circle is fully expressed and the expression, by degrees, re-becomes the point. The expression is divided into the unmanifested or Substance and the manifested or matter. Matter is again divided into nature-matter and intelligent-matter, according to degrees in which the matter is conscious. These degrees are proved by the square and described by the compass, according to angles, horizontals and perpendiculars. Nature-matter is divided infinitely according to the subdegrees of the four elements, and their combinations and subdivisions, and their hierarchies of beings in the four manifested worlds. Intelligent-matter, that is, the Triune Self, is divided into three degrees, those of Apprentice, Fellow Craft and Master. These are exalted in the Royal Arch, which is in Substance, beyond matter. The unmanifested is always in the manifested on the nature-side as well as on the intelligent-side, but it can be approached and found in the intelligent-side only. It is found by being conscious, which in Masonry is called getting more Light.

The point and the circle stand for all this and for more. The meaning of the fully expressed circle can be rendered by symbols, twelve in number, which stand for twelve points on the circle. Every being and thing in the manifested worlds and the unmanifested universe has a sharply marked value, nature and place, according to some of these points.

The best symbols to indicate the twelve points of the circle are the Zodiacal signs. Universal truths can be expressed through the Zodiac in a way which ordinary language does not permit and so can be understood, after a fashion, by men. To illustrate, the Universe, as well as a cell, is divided by a line from cancer to capricorn into the unmanifested above and the manifested below. Matter is separated by a line from aries to libra into nature-matter and intelligent-matter. "Souls" enter by conception at the gate of cancer of the physical world, and are born at the gate of libra and pass on at the gate of capricorn. The square is made by the line from cancer to libra and by the line from libra to capricorn, and the Master sits in the East, at capricorn, and rules his lodge on this square, the angle of which is at libra. The square of the Great Architect is the square from cancer to libra to capricorn of the Universe, over and above the four worlds of cancer, leo, virgo, and libra. So the signs of the Zodiac, as symbols of the twelve points of the fully expressed circle, speak an accurate language that reaches everything in the Universe. This language is that for which the word Geometry stands. The Fellow Craft is told that this is also symbolized by the letter G.

Geometry is half of the science, the other half is the geometer. Geometry deals with only one of the tools, namely the square, which is used to draw straight lines, horizontals and perpendiculars, and to prove corners. The other tool, the compass, stands for the other half, the Geometer, or the Intelligence, without which there could be no Geometry. The compass draws curved lines between two points and describes a circle which is one continuous line without end, each part of which is equally distant from the center. Within the bounds of the circle, all true building must be erected on the square.

The Apprentice has passed into the Fellow Craft. The Fellow Craft has received more Light and has learned the use of his tools; he understands how to rebuild the two columns and how to ascend the winding stairs by the three, five and seven steps. The symbols and the work in this degree relate to the minds of feeling-and-desire coming under the guidance of the minds of rightness and reason of the thinker of the Triune Self. By the plumb and the level of his thinking the Fellow Craft adjusts feeling-and-desire. He causes all the feelings and desires to be squared on the inner as well as on the outer expressions. He does all this by his thinking.

The degree of Master Mason represents the Apprentice and Fellow Craft raised to the degree of Master. As the Apprentice is the doer and the Fellow Craft the thinker, so the Master Mason is the knower. Going through each degree as an individual symbolizes the development of the Apprentice or doer passing to the Fellow Craft or relation to the thinker and being raised to the degree of Master Mason or attaining to relation to the knower.

The candidate after he is prepared, blindfolded and tied with cable-tow around his waist, enters the lodge. He is received on both points of the compass, pressed against his breast. He takes the three steps to the altar where he kneels for the third time, rests his hands on the Bible, square and compass, and takes the obligation of a Master Mason. He asks for further light in Masonry. He is brought to light by the Master of the lodge, and hoodwink and cable-tow removed. Thus he sees that both points of the compass are above the square. This is a symbol that with one who has reached this degree both aspects of the thinker are operative above feeling-and-desire because feeling-and-desire have put themselves under the guidance of the thinker. He receives the pass and grip of a Master Mason and wears his apron as a Master Mason, that is, with the flap and all corners down.

The working tools of a Master are all the implements of Masonry of the three degrees, more especially the trowel. As the gauge and mallet prepared the rough stones, as the plumb, level and square fitted them into position, so the trowel spreads the cement and completes the work of the Apprentice and Fellow Craft.

SECTION 4

Life, death and resurrection of Hiram Abiff. The great lesson of Masonry. What Hiram symbolizes. The two triangles. The designs on the trestle-board. The South gate. The workmen. Hiram is restrained from going out. He is slain at the East gate. The immortal body. Jubela, Jubelo, Jubelum. Meanings of these three symbols. The three assaults. The Masonic drama. The fifteen workmen. The Great Twelve. The pairs of triangles forming six-pointed stars. Hiram as the power that makes the round. The finding of the three ruffians. The three burials of Hiram. The raising by King Solomon. The monument at the place of burial. Raising of the candidate. The three columns. The forty-seventh problem of Euclid.

The remaining portion of the initiation is a masonic drama, representing the life, death and resurrection of Hiram Abiff, whose part the candidate is made to take. Hiram was the master builder of King Solomon's Temple and was slain by workmen for his refusal to impart the Word to them, and after two burials was raised by King Solomon and then buried the third time. This story conceals the great lesson of Masonry.

Hiram is the seminal principle, the generative power, the sex power, not an organ, not the fluid, but the power, invisible and most mysterious. This power lies in the Conscious Light of the Intelligence which is carried by desire and is an extract from the four elements, prepared by the four systems of the body. This power, having therefore something of the seven faculties of the Intelligence, something of the three parts of the Triune Self, and something of the four elements, is to be found only in a human body. This power is concentrated monthly by the inner brain, so becomes the lunar germ, and as such descends along the sympathetic nervous system in the front of the body and gathers Light of the Intelligence as it proceeds. The lunar germ in man is a concentration of the whole power, but one half of the power is checked in its possible development. A man, symbolized according to the language for which the masonic word Geometry stands, by the triangle cancer, scorpio and pisces, has only half the power, and so has a woman, symbolized by the female triangle taurus, virgo and capricorn. The other half in each is dormant or suppressed. The active half develops in the body organs to express itself and is lost through them. With this loss are mingled thoughts of lust, violence, shame, dishonor, disease, love and hate, which are the cable-tow of rebirth. If Hiram is not lost, but is saved, the half of him that is checked will develop in the body and there will build new parts, new organs, new channels. Hiram is the builder.

Hiram, the Master-Builder, the Grand Master, draws his designs on the trestle-board—that is, the lines on the breath-form which is in the sympathetic nervous system—and passes out each day, that is, each life, through the South gate, libra, of the outer courts of the Temple. That is to say, the monthly germ is lost. It is his usual custom to enter the unfinished Sanctum Sanctorum, that is, the heart and lungs, on the line cancer to capricorn. There thinking draws out the lines of his designs upon the trestle-board, whereby the craft pursue their labors, that is, whereby the workmen or elementals in the four systems of the body build according to the lines, the physical state and circumstances in which the body exists.

On one day, that is, in one life, when Hiram, following his usual custom attempts to leave the body at the South gate, the gate of sex, he is hindered and restrained from going out. He turns, seeks to go out at the West gate, cancer, and is again prevented. Then he seeks the East gate, capricorn, and there he is slain. This means that the sex power sought to leave by the sex opening and when that was barred, by the opening in the breasts, that is, by emotions, and when that was closed, by a place in the spine, which stands for the brain or intellect, and when that exit, too, was blocked, it died to these mortal expressions of itself.

Having so died to mortality and corruption it was raised to build an incorruptible and immortal body.

The three ruffians Jubela, Jubelo and Jubelum, are no ruffians, but are the Junior Warden, Senior Warden and Worshipful Master, the three officers of the lodge, in Masonry, and they stand also for the three parts of the Triune Self, Jubela being the doer, Jubelo the thinker, and Jubelum the knower. Each has a part of the Word. If their parts were combined they would be AUM or AOM or three of the four parts of the Word. But no combination is made, that is, the three parts do not work coordinately.

Hiram has the Word, he is the Word, for he has the Light, that is, the Intelligence powers and the Triune Self powers and the powers of the four elements, and he has them combined. When assaulted by the first ruffian and asked for the Word, Hiram, therefore, says: "Wait until the Temple is completed," that is, until he has built the immortal body. He says about giving the secrets of the Word: "I cannot; nor can they be given, except in the presence of Solomon, King of Israel (the knower), and Hiram, King of Tyre (the thinker), and myself" the doer (the Light in the sex with feeling-and-desire). This means that the Word cannot be imparted by the sex power since the sex power only builds the immortal body, the Temple. When Hiram as the combined powers of the Light, the doer and the sexes, has completed the building of the body he can act his own part as Hiram, the doer of feeling-and-desire. Then together with the thinker, King of Tyre, and the knower, Solomon, he is the Word and enters the finished Temple.

Hiram is many things. He is the mysterious creative power hidden in the powers of the sexes, hence he is the builder, the Master Builder; he is the Lost Word, being the doer which is lost, because it is immersed in flesh and blood and does not know itself in the human being; and he is the combined powers of the Light and of the Triune Self and of the nature powers of the sexes when he has found himself in the ruins of the temple and is conscious of himself as the Triune Self.

Jubela, Jubelo and Jubelum are ruffians in so far as they are not performing the true functions of their offices. They are said to be ruffians because they act as the doer part in its thinker and knower aspects, when it is the false "I." The three are only the doer part in the three aspects of its Triune Self. Jubela gives Hiram a blow with the gauge, a tool of the Apprentice, across the throat, according to the ritual. This is a blind for the sex part. Jubelo strikes Hiram with the square, a tool of the Fellow

Craft, across the breast, and Jubelum fells him with a setting-maul, the gavel of a Master. The gauge is the line, the square the surface, and the maul the cube.

Hiram has so far gone out of the South gate, his custom in the bodies of the run of human beings. The masonic drama refers to a time when it is discovered that the sex power holds the key to all secrets and to all power. To wrest the key from this power the human being restrains it from going out. Mere restraint does not obtain the secret, but the power, when controlled, rises, passing from the sex functions into the four physical bodies. Then the human being prevents Hiram from leaving by thoughts, at the emotional center. But Hiram does not yield the secret, because the human being practices the restraint from selfish motives to get power, and not to rebuild the Temple, and because the human being is physically and psychically incapable of holding the power. Hiram passes to the East and there meets Jubelum who, though in the true aspect he is the knower, is in the drama the false "I," an egotistical aspect of the doer. To him Hiram cannot impart the Word. Yet, the human being, though from selfish motives, has so far advanced that there is no more physical reproduction. This is symbolized by the slaying of Hiram.

In the conspiracy to obtain the secret of Hiram were fifteen workmen. Twelve recanted and the remaining three, Jubela, Jubelo and Jubelum, carried out the plot. The twelve here are the twelve points on the Zodiac in the body, the three are the double aspects of the doer, and the body-mind. The twelve represent numbers, that is, twelve ultimate beings and orders of beings.

Everything in the manifested Universe is in some measure representative of the Great Twelve. The human body is their organ. The more a human being develops, the more will he have in him live centers representing and responding to the Great Twelve. King Solomon sends the twelve workmen in the body in search of the ruffians. He sends three East, three North, three South, and three West. He sends taurus, virgo and capricorn to act in the East, leo, sagittary and aries in the North, aquarius, gemini and libra in the South, and scorpio, pisces and cancer in the West. Of these triads, those of leo, aries, and sagittary, and of gemini, libra and aquarius are universal, the first triangle operating through the second. The triad of taurus, virgo and capricorn operates through that of cancer, scorpio and pisces, and both are human. Each pair of triads forms a six-pointed star. There is the universal hexad, the macrocosm, and the human hexad, the microcosm. The universal hexad, composed of the sexless triad, aries, leo, sagittary and the androgynous triad, gemini, libra and aquarius, is God or Supreme Intelligence, and nature. The human hexad is composed of the cancer, scorpio and pisces triad, pointing West, which is man or the male triad, and of taurus, virgo and capricorn, pointing East, which is woman, the female triad.

The macrocosmic and the microcosmic signs are represented in the human body by twelve parts and centers, each having its special character. The human body therefore is potentially a complete universe. The six universal signs are centers at which the six human signs can act if the human signs come together in any one of those six. For instance, if the male and female triads unite at their points of scorpio and virgo in libra, they procreate through the universal gate of sex of the nature triad. But if the male and female triads at their points of scorpio and capricorn unite at sagittary, the sexless gate of the universal triad, they create a thought. Though the twelve powers are represented in a human body, they cannot act freely and fully, but are restrained, paralyzed, half dead, impotent, except the powers represented by virgo, scorpio, and libra, that is, the female in a female body, the male in a male body, and the sex in both bodies.

Hiram is the power that makes the rounds of the twelve centers, that strengthens and empowers them, builds up the twelve centers, makes them alive and fits them so that they can be related to the Great Twelve, and so that the doer in the body can act with the Great Twelve.

King Solomon's sending the twelve workmen in search of the three ruffians means that after Hiram is slain, within the meaning of the legend, the knower part which is in contact with the body commands the twelve powers in the body to locate the three ruffians who have brought about the death of Hiram, who are the false "I" in its three aspects. The three ruffians are found near the body of the slain, that is, the physical suppression of the sex power, and are executed. They are condemned for having tried to get the power from Hiram before they were qualified to receive it.

Hiram was buried three times. First the ruffians buried him in the rubbish of the Temple, that is, the sex power was turned into the foods of the body to build it up. At night they came back to give the body a more decent burial. They carried it West, to the brow of the hill West of Mount Moriah, that is, the sex power was buried in or turned into psychic power. There it was discovered by a party of workmen. After it had been raised by King Solomon himself by the strong grip or lion's paw—which is the grip identified with a life like that of Jesus, the lion of the Tribe of Judah so-called from the alleged heraldic lion of the Tribe—it was buried near the Sanctum Sanctorum of King Solomon's Temple, that is, the sex power was turned into the spine.

The raising by Solomon is significant. The body could not be raised by the grip of the Entered Apprentice, nor by that of the Fellow Craft, that is, the doer could not, either with the psychic or its mental aspect raise or transmute the mortal into an immortal body. It required the knower, here King Solomon himself, to raise Hiram. King Solomon had the assistance of Hiram, King of Tyre, the thinker, and of the brethren, that is, the powers in the body.

The tradition of Masonry is that a monument was erected to the memory of Hiram, at his place of burial. The monument represents a virgin weeping over a broken column. Before her was an open book, behind her stood Time. It is a reminder of the destruction of the original temple, at which the Boaz column, which represented the female column in the temple of man was broken. The vestige or monument is the sternum, which is all that is left. The virgin is the woman weeping over her own broken column. Time is death, as the continuous passing of the events; and the open book is the breath-form and aia, which bear the record of what happened. The female figure is also the widow, as the broken column, who was the mother of Hiram, weeping for the male power, which she lost when the column was broken. Hiram is the son of a widow; he is unprotected and has had to wander along the labyrinth of the alimentary canal since the column was broken.

The destruction of the temple occurs in every life. Hiram is not allowed to rebuild it. In this sense he is slain in every life. At each life he is resurrected and tries to rebuild the temple beginning with the re-establishment of the column, which is broken. The Monument of the woman with her broken column is a reminder that a Mason must re-establish the broken column in himself as the requisite to rebuild his temple, and he can re-establish the column only by keeping Hiram in the body to rebuild it. Hiram has within him the original plan of the immortal body which, when rebuilt, will be greater than the first temple.

The candidate having been made to take the part of Hiram is finally raised by King Solomon, the Master of the Lodge, by the real grip of a Master Mason, and on the five points of fellowship, or five points of the body. The brethren assist in raising the candidate to a standing position. The hoodwink is slipped off his eyes. After he has received an historical account of the events he passed through as Hiram, the Master explains the various symbols. He uses them as subjects for moral exhortations and rules.

The three grand masonic columns or pillars, designated Wisdom, Strength, and Beauty, stand for the three parts of the body. They also stand for parts of the Triune Self. In this connection the pillar of Wisdom is Solomon, the spinal or Jachin column; the pillar of Strength is Hiram, King of Tyre, the sympathetic or Boaz column; and the pillar of Beauty is Hiram Abiff, the bridge or bridge builder, between the two.

The forty-seventh problem of Euclid is more than a moral exhortation. It means that when the male (desire) and the female (feeling) in one physical body work together they build a new body equal to their sum. The new body, the square of the hypotenuse, is the temple rebuilt.

After the candidate has been raised to the degree of Master Mason, he represents the doer, thinker, and knower, each developed to its capacity and coordinated so that they are a trinity, the Triune Self. This trinity is in Masonry represented as a right-angled triangle in the lodge.

SECTION 5

Meaning of the lodge as a room and as the brothers. The officers, their stations and duties. The three degrees as the foundation of Masonry. The work. A Mason's own lodge.

The lodge as a room or hall is an oblong square, which is a half of a perfect square, and which is inside or outside the lower half of a circle. Each lodge meets in the same room, alike furnished, but the lodge working in the Apprentice degree is styled the Ground Floor, the lodge working the Fellow Craft degree is called the Middle Chamber, and the lodge working the Master degree is called the Sanctum Sanctorum, all in King Solomon's Temple. The lodge in this sense symbolizes, with the present day humanity, the part of the body from the breasts and from the back opposite the breasts to the sex. When the temple is rebuilt the Ground Floor will be the pelvic section, the Middle Chamber the abdominal section, and the Sanctum Sanctorum the thoracic section.

The lodge, as a number of brothers who compose it, represents certain working centers and their activities in the body of a Mason. These are shown by the officers stationed in the West, South and East. These are the three without whom there can be no lodge. The breasts, standing for the Boaz column, where the sternum is, are the station of the Senior Warden in the West. The places of the coccygeal gland and anus, which are the ends of the two tubes, are the station of the Junior Warden in the South. A place in the spinal cord opposite the heart is the station of the Master in the East.

The Senior Deacon in front of and to the right of the Master, and the Junior Deacon at the right and in front of the Senior Warden make five, and the Secretary at the left and the Treasurer at the right of the Master, make seven. These are the seven officers of the lodge. In addition there are the two stewards, one on each side of the Junior Warden in the South, and the Tyler, the guard at the door.

The Senior Warden's duty is to strengthen and support the Master and assist him in carrying on the work of the lodge.

The Junior Warden's duty, according to the ritual, is to observe and record the time, to call the craft from labor to refreshment, to superintend that, to keep them from intemperance or excess and to call them to labor again. His station is there but there is no organ or conduit from Boaz to Jachin. His duty is to observe the time, that is, sun time, the Master standing for the sun, and moon time, the Senior Warden for the moon. This relates to sex power, the moon, and to doer power, the sun, that is to say, the duty of that center is to observe the time and the seasons of the lunar and solar germs. He should call the craft, that is, the Masons working in the part of the temple called the lodge, and the elemental workmen who labor outside, in the quarries, in other parts of the body. The four senses and the elementals in the systems all go to the sex center to get refreshment. The center of the Junior Warden should balance the forces of Boaz and Jachin and with these forces refresh the workmen of the temple.

"As the sun rises in the East to open and govern the day, so rises the Master in the East to open and govern his lodge, set the craft to work and give them proper instructions," says the ritual. The Master is the sun, represented by the solar germ, in the body, as the Senior Warden is the moon. The Master dispenses his light from his seat in the East, that is, the spinal cord back of the heart, to the Senior Warden at the breasts, through whom his orders are issued.

The remaining officers of the lodge, considered as centers in the body, are assistants to these three main officers, near whom they are stationed and whose orders they execute. The Secretary and Treasurer record and keep on the breath-form the accounts of the transactions of the lodge, which are carried over from lodge to lodge, that is from life to life.

The lodge as a number of brothers who compose it stands also for the embodied doer portions or contacts of the Triune Self and their aspects. The Junior Warden is the doer and his two stewards are the active and the passive side of desire-and-feeling. The Senior Warden represents the thinker and the Junior Deacon is the active side, called reason. The Master is the knower and the Senior Deacon is I-ness, the passive aspect. It may be noted that the Senior Warden and the Master have each only one assistant.

The degrees of Entered Apprentice, Fellow Craft and Master Mason, are the foundations of Masonry, which is the building of an immortal body. The Entered Apprentice is the doer, the Fellow Craft the thinker, and the Master Mason the knower in contact with the body. They carry on the work of the lodge in the trunk of the body and are assisted by the other officers. The work of the lodge is kept before the eyes of Masons by the opening of the lodge, the order of business, the initiating, passing and raising of candidates and the closing of the lodge. All is done with impressiveness and becoming dignity. The real work is the initiating, passing and raising of the doer-in-the-body to conscious relation with its thinker and knower parts.

Every Mason should open his own lodge, that is, begin in the morning the work of the day with the dignity of the opening of his masonic lodge. He should recognize the stations and duties of the parts and their centers in the body and charge them to see that the workmen, that is, the elementals functioning in the body, are properly employed. He should recognize that he is the candidate to be initiated by the trials of the day, and that he must pass through them with temperance, fortitude, prudence and justice, so that he may be exalted and receive more Light.

SECTION 6

The cable-tow. The Royal Arch. The candidate as the keystone.
Realization of the great Masonic symbol. The fifth degree. The fourth
degree. The keystone with the mark of Hiram. The sixth degree.
Another aspect of the keystone symbol. The union of Boaz and Jachin.
The Glory of the Lord fills the Lord's house. The seventh degree. The
Tabernacle. The Master's jewels and the Ark of the Covenant. The
Name and the Word.

The cable-tow of the four senses leads the candidate (the doer-in-the-body) through each of the four great degrees of Masonry, until the senses cease to be ties. The Master Mason receives More Light in the Chapter or Holy Royal Arch, which is in the North. This is the Fourth Degree. The Lodge is an oblong square in the lower half of the circle; the Chapter is another oblong square, which together with the first, forms a perfect square, within the circle, and that part of the circle which is the arc above or North of this square, is the Royal Arch. Into that, when the cable-tow no longer leads him, the candidate is fitted as a keystone. This Fourth Degree has, however, in the course of time been stretched out and cut into four degrees, of which the Fourth, Sixth, and Seventh Degrees contain the work of the original Fourth Degree.

The Royal Arch is the culmination and consummation of the three degrees of Entered Apprentice, Fellow Craft and Master Mason. The great Masonic symbol of compass and square is there realized. The three points of the square are those three lower degrees, and the compass, so joined with them as to make a six-pointed star, now, in the Royal Arch Degrees, represent the Light of the Intelligence, which in the Conscious Light of the Royal Arch Mason is the threefold Light that has come into his noetic, his mental and his psychic atmospheres. This state of a Mason is the subject of which various aspects are symbolized by the work of the Fourth, Sixth and Seventh Degrees, relating to the Light of the Intelligence when the Glory of the Lord fills the House, to the keystone when the arch is completed, to the Word when it is found, and to the Name when the divided Adam or Jehovah becomes one.

In the Fifth Degree, that of Past Master, the candidate takes the obligation of a Master of the Lodge, and upon being installed is made to see and feel his inability to keep the turbulent brethren sufficiently in order to conduct the work of the Lodge. This degree is a mere filler for ceremonial purposes.

The Fourth Degree or that of Mark Master is said to have been instituted by King Solomon for the purpose of detecting impostors. Each workman was required to put his distinctive mark upon the product of his labor. The Mark Master could thereby detect impostors and could notice unfinished and imperfect work. This degree is dedicated to Hiram, the builder, and its characteristic is the keystone he had fashioned and on which was his mark. This stone possessing merits unknown to the builders was rejected by them but became the "chief stone of the corner."

In the lodge in which the Master Mason is to be advanced to the Fourth, or honorary, Degree of Mark Master, the brethren, during the opening, gather round a miniature of King Solomon's Temple—symbol of the temple into which they are to rebuild their bodies—which is erected on the middle of the floor. During the opening the Master says to them: "Ye also, as living stones, be ye built up a spiritual house, an holy priesthood, to offer up sacrifices acceptable to God."

The candidate being duly and truly prepared and carrying a keystone is conducted into the lodge. Two of the brethren who carry oblong stones, and the candidate with his keystone, present the stones as specimens of their work. The two stones carried by the companions are received for the temple, but the keystone, being neither oblong nor square, is rejected as of no account and is heaved over among the rubbish of the temple where Hiram was buried at one time. For want of a keystone to one of the principal arches the workmen are disturbed. The Right Worshipful Master, representing King Solomon, says that he gave Hiram Abiff, the Grand Master, orders to make that keystone, previous to his assassination, and inquires if such a stone has not been brought up for inspection. The keystone, which the candidate had brought and had seen heaved over into the rubbish, is found and is now received and becomes the "head of the corner."

The keystone has on it the mark of Hiram. The keystone is Hiram transformed into a certain lunar germ, which was preserved, died to the world, rose along the spine, and ascended into the head. Hiram's mark is a double cross made by a stationary cross H.S.W.K. and a movable cross T.T.S.S. The import of these crosses can be known by the meaning of the Zodiacal signs which these eight points of the crosses represent on the circumference of the circle. His mark is his new name, a name of an

Order of beings to which he now belongs. This new name is written on a white stone, or the purified essence, that is the vesture of Hiram. Hiram, having overcome, has eaten of the hidden manna—that is, has received the Light accumulated by successive lunar germs. The keystone that has the mark of Hiram, also stands for the candidate himself who has overcome, who has ascended into the hill of the Lord and who shall stand in his holy place.

The Sixth Degree, that of the Most Excellent Master, is the initiation of the candidate by the descent of the Light into the completed temple, or, in Masonic language, when the Glory of the Lord fills the House. In his obligation the candidate promises that he will dispense light and knowledge to all ignorant and uninformed brethren.

Another aspect of the keystone is emphasized by the ceremonies which take up again the teaching of the stone with Hiram's mark, that is, the candidate himself. The ceremonies now represent the day for the celebration of the capstone, copestone, or keystone. The keystone is made to close an arch placed on the two columns Boaz and Jachin. This is a symbol that the physical body has been rebuilt, that an arch over Boaz and Jachin unites them above and another arch unites them below. This is done as the result of the action of the Junior Warden in the first three degrees. He harmonized the male and female forces in the West and East columns, at the South, libra, and with these equilibrated forces built the arches, or bridges, below and above. With the arch above and the keystone inserted therein, the temple is completed.

The Light of the Intelligence descends into the candidate and fills his body. The Glory of the Lord fills the Lord's House. The mortal body has been transformed into an immortal body. This culmination of the Masonic purpose is sometimes represented by the fire coming down from heaven and by a temple in the lodge being filled with effulgent light. Sometimes a passage from the Bible is read and an illumination made to show to the candidate the lodge filled with the glory that floods the temple.

In the Seventh Degree or Royal Arch are symbolized events which preceded the completion of the temple, and some information is given about the Word.

The candidate is made to represent one of three Masons who after the destruction of Jerusalem by Nebuchadnezzar were captives in Babylon till Cyrus of Persia liberated them. They returned to Jerusalem to assist in building the temple. On arrival they found the Tabernacle, a temporary structure. This is the temporary physical body, which serves until the temple is rebuilt. The three were given tools and directed to begin their labors at the North East corner of the ruined temple. There they discovered a secret vault under a trap which was the keystone of an arch. The keystone taken before the Grand Council was there discovered to be the keystone of the principal arch in Solomon's Temple. Lowered by cable-tow into the vault the candidate finds three small trying-squares which are by the Grand Council recognized as the Master's Jewels of King Solomon, of King Hiram of Tyre and of Hiram Abiff. On another descent a small box is found which is recognized by the Grand Council as the Ark of the Covenant. Out of this chest are taken a pot of manna and four pieces of paper containing in right angles and dots the key to a mystery language. With this key three mysterious words written in triangular form upon the Ark become readable as the name of God in the Chaldaic, Hebrew and Syriac languages; and this Name of the Deity is in the ritual said to be the long lost Master Mason's Word or Logos. This identification among modern Masons of the Name and the Word is a blind, or is due to a mistake.

The Name and the Word are distinct and not the same. The Name is a name, one of the names, of the God of the physical world, the Earth Spirit. This God belongs to the nature-side. It is known by different names in different ages among different peoples. Brahma is one of the names; originally it was Brahm and after it divided it became Brahma, and then the Trimurti Brahma-Vishnu-Shiva. This is the Name of the God of the physical world, with the Hindus. The name of the Triune Self, however, is BrahmA, VishnU, BrahM, the last letters of which are the Word.

The Hebrew Name is Jehovah, and modern Masons have adopted this. It is a name of the ruler of the physical world and its four planes. This God has no physical body except the formless four elements in the physical world and the human bodies of those who are born in his Name and who obey his laws. At one time this God acted through human physical bodies which were sexless, then he acted through human bodies which were bisexual, and now he acts through human bodies that are male human bodies and that are female human bodies. The Name can be pronounced only when a human body has in it active masculine and passive feminine powers. A man can only give half of the Name, because his body is only half the Name. To this fact refers the Masonic practice of saying: "I will letter it or halve it." The Name is the name of the body and the body must be rebuilt into a balanced male-female body before it is the Name and the dweller in the body can breathe the Name. The Name belongs to the body, is of the four elements and hence has four letters, Jod, He, Vav, He. The Name is ineffable until such time as it can be breathed by the dweller in a normal balanced or sexless physical body.

The Word, an English translation of the Logos, as used by St. John, is not the Name. It is an expression of the full Triune Self powers, each of the three parts being represented in it by a sound, and the perfect body in which the Triune Self dwells being also represented by a sound. The doer part is expressed as A, the thinker part as U or O, the knower part as M, and the perfect body as I. The Word is I-A-O-M, in four syllables or letters. The expression of the perfect body and the Triune Self as these sounds is an expression of the Conscious Light of the Intelligence through that Self and body. When a part in its physical body sounds as IAOM each of the parts sounds AOM, and each represents a Logos. The knower is then the First Logos, the thinker the Second Logos and the doer the Third Logos.

The Word is symbolized by a circle in which are a hexad of two interlaced triangles, and the point in the center. The point is the M; the triangle aries, leo, sagittary is the A; the triangle gemini, libra, aquarius is the U or the O; and the circle is the fully expressed point M as well as the line of the body I. The hexad is made up of the macrocosmic signs standing for the sexless triad and the androgynous triad, the triangle of God as Intelligence and the triangle of God as nature. These letters in which the perfect Self sounds, are symbolized in Masonry by the square and compass or the emblem of the interlaced triangles.

There is a succinct relationship of the Word with the Ineffable Name. The Word is feeling-and-desire, the doer. The doer is lost in the body of flesh and blood in the world of life and death. Thus the doer is the *lost Word*. The body, when perfected, serves as the instrument through which the doer pronounces the *Ineffable Name*. The *Ineffable Name* and the embodied *Word*, when one is fitted to speak it, is IAOM. By so doing the body is raised from a horizontal to an upright position.

The Name is pronounced as follows: It is started by opening the lips with an "ee" sound graduating into a broad "a" as the mouth opens wider with the lips forming an oval shape and then graduating the sound to "o" as the lips form a circle, and again modulating to an "m" sound as the lips close to a point. This point resolves itself to a point within the head.

Expressed phonetically the Name is "EE-Ah-Oh-Mmm" and is pronounced with one continuous outbreathing with a slight nasal tone in the manner described above. It can be correctly and properly expressed with its full power only by one who has brought his physical body to a state of perfection, that is, balanced and sexless.

SECTION 7

Summary of the teachings of Masonry. They center around "Light." The symbols, acts and words of the ritual. Ritualists and their workings. The permanent forms of Masonry and twisted teachings. Scriptural passages. Geometrical symbols. Their value. Masonry has in trust certain geometrical symbols which, coordinated in a system for the Masonic work, are thus preserved.

The teachings of Masonry are few and definite. They are of the Supreme Intelligence, of the Light of the original state of the Triune Self, of the first body when the doer was without sin and the body lived in the Light, of the death of the body, which is called the destruction of the temple, of the duty to rebuild the temple, of the training of the doer of feeling-and-desire, as the candidate, to be conscious of itself in the body and to come into conscious relation with the thinker and the knower, which training is symbolized by the degrees of the Entered Apprentice, the Fellow Craft and the Master Mason, that is, the three parts of the Triune Self, of the sex power, called Hiram Abiff, by which the temple is rebuilt or the body made immortal, and of the Light filling the temple. The Masonic teachings center around the Light, the Conscious Light the doer had, the Light it had lost and the Light it must regain. "More Light" is the true Masonic prayer. Getting light is the phrase used in Masonry for becoming conscious in higher degrees. Masons take their obligations of virtue and holiness to get more light, to become children of Light.

The symbols, the symbolic acts and the words of the ritual do not always present these teachings. In the course of time and with the popularization of Masonry, some of these teachings have become obscured because of twisting, substituting and adding symbols and work. Various ritualists have been active, not always within the bounds or along the lines of the Masonic landmarks. Nevertheless, the fundamental forms remain, and show the misfits. The doer, thinker, and knower parts are symbolized by the Junior Warden, Senior Warden, and Worshipful Master, by Jubela, Jubelo, and Jubelum, by the Entered Apprentice, the Fellow Craft, and the Master Mason, by Hiram Abiff, Hiram, King of Tyre, and King Solomon, by the Pillars of Beauty, Strength, and Wisdom. Where the same three parts are symbolized and there is an omission, it is clear that the later ritualists worked without understanding the relation of the three parts of the Triune Self. So the sun and the moon stand for the body and the feeling, but there is nothing for the desire in this imagery unless it be the stars, and in their place the ritual for the Entered Apprentice degree mentions the Master of the Lodge. Desire should be the Master of the Lodge in that degree. Boaz symbolizes the thinker and Jachin the knower, but there is nothing in the ritual to stand for the balancer, the doer, which makes the arch below, corresponding to the Royal Arch above. However, notwithstanding twists, missing links and the use of the same symbol to indicate different subjects, the general forms of Masonry remain as guides, to which the growth of rites, orders and symbology is reduced from time to time.

Among the permanent forms of Masonry are the point in the circle, the oblong square or the form of the lodge, the right-angled triangle or the square, the equilateral triangle which is the symbol of the Supreme Intelligence, the compass as the symbol of the light coming down, the interlaced triangles, the two columns, the three Great Lights, the arch, the keystone with the two crosses, the white lambskin or apron, the cable-tow, the four degrees and the Master Builder. At such times much stress is laid on some of these symbols, at other times symbols like the trestle-board, the G or point in the circle, the All-seeing Eye as the symbol of the Supreme Intelligence, the source of all Light, and the Blazing Star, symbol of the teacher of the Messianic cycle, are made less important according to the understanding and fancy of the ritualists. Notwithstanding the warning against any change or removal of the ancient landmarks, Masons vary the ritual. Thus many of the teachings have become twisted. For instance, the fire which is a symbol of Jehovah is identified with the Light, which is representative of the Supreme Intelligence; the cardinal point, the North, through which the Light comes, has disappeared from the ritual and the North is dark; the Word is confounded with the Name; the explanation why the three officers act as three ruffians has disappeared. Much of this deterioration is due to the fact that Scriptural passages which are parts of the ritual, are interpreted according to the religious sentiment of the times, and so color, distort or hide the Masonic teachings which the symbols preserve.

Masons have long been in a time of darkness. They are perhaps to be excused for the loss of the light in a time-of general darkness. In the present age, however, if they are traveling in search of light, if light is the object of their search, they can find it by searching for it through their symbols. They will get more light if they try to hold the Conscious Light in thinking steadily on the meaning of their symbols.

A geometrical symbol expresses an idea and is a prototype for thinking. It is the original pattern after which other things are modeled, by which they are prefigured, predetermined and given identity, to which they correspond and to which they respond. All things can be epitomized and placed under a few prototypes from which they have originated and by which they are predetermined. Therefore, physical things can be summarized under abstractions which are symbolic. Symbols show a unity in diversity.

Many things can be used as symbols, but geometrical symbols are the highest, because they are best adapted to convey the idea that is expressed in them. The reason is that the body-mind, feeling-mind, and desire-mind work with points, lines, angles and curves, that geometrical forms are the simplest, the most direct and freest from irregularities and complications, and that, therefore, the functions of the three minds are at home with geometrical symbols and get from them without color, form, prejudice, variations and coverings, the essence in the idea or thought which the symbols convey. Points and lines are not seen on the physical plane. Matter on the physical plane appears in forms. These forms have outlines, that is, they end. Lines are conceptions, due to the functions of the feeling-mind and have no physical, tangible existence. They exist on the life plane of the physical world. Points and lines are the matter on the life plane, that is, if the matter on this plane could be seen or conceived, it would be to the average human understanding as points, lines, angles and curves. With this kind of matter—that is, points, lines, angles and curves—the body-mind can work. In order to get the meaning of anything that is not physical the body-mind thinks in points and lines.

A geometrical symbol is not colored, but everything in the world that is seen is colored and therefore does not show the truth, which is without color. True form is without color. Geometrical symbols are true forms. They show the actual character of the things they represent. The reason people cannot use geometrical symbols is that they are looking at the colored forms of nature and have to grow accustomed to geometrical symbols before they can use them and see through them. They first suggest and then reveal the idea they express. When a human thinks intentionally through geometrical symbols he can get the truth which the symbols contain.

All geometrical symbols have their origin in points, lines, angles and curves which receive their value as symbols from positions they hold in the circle. The Zodiac is the best symbol of the circle with the twelve points on the circumference which give a value to geometrical symbols. The value which the symbols so receive is given them by their position relative to the twelve points. Masonry has its symbols from the Zodiac.

The chief reason Masonry exists, and has been preserved when other secret bodies have perished, is that it has in trust certain symbols and that these are coordinated and vitalized in a system for Masonic work. These symbols are geometrical. If Masonic symbols are tools, emblems or buildings, they are valuable because of the geometrical lines they embody.

CHAPTER XIII

THE POINT OR CIRCLE

SECTION 1

Creation of a thought. Method of thinking by building within a point. Human thinking. Thinking done by Intelligences. Thinking which does not create thoughts, or destiny.

The point is the infinitesimally small circle; the circle is the point fully expressed. The point is no thing; the circle is everything. The point is the unmanifested; the circle is the unmanifested and the manifested.

A point is the beginning of everything. It is the beginning of a perception by the senses, of a feeling, of a desire, of thinking and of a thought. Where thinking ends, knowledge begins, in a point. When a thought is issued it is issued as a point. A point is the departure from the unmanifested and is the beginning of manifestation. Within a point is the unmanifested. A point is an opening from the unmanifested into the manifested. A point has no existence, but it is that from which existence comes. A point has no dimension, but it is that from which dimensions come.

A circle is completion and completeness. It is the one, the whole, the all, the all in one. The circle is made up of twelve parts and is one through all of them. It is the perfect extension of the point. The extension is made by point, by line, by angle, by surface and by completing curve.

The physical universe with its chemical elements, colors of the sunrise, sounds, waters and solid bodies, is built up of phenomena, the realities behind which are points and the lines, angles, surfaces and curves which are built from them. This universe is so built out because it follows the structures within the thoughts, of which it is the exteriorization.

698

Thinking builds within a point by point, by line, by angle, by surface and by curve, until the structure in the thought is completed. After the thought is issued, elementals, nature units, obeying the structural lines within the thought, build them out. On the intelligent-side the doer builds within a point and on the nature-side elementals follow the pattern and build it from the point.

The principle of extending the point towards the circle has three applications that relate to the law of thought. The first application relates to the creation of the thought, the aim, object, design and structure in it, and the thinking of the ones that do the thinking. According to this principle thinking works from the intelligent-side with nature matter and thereby ripens into a thought. Then the thought is exteriorized on the nature-side according to this principle, (Fig. IV-A). Lastly, all nature-matter has to act according to this principle, because the units which produce the phenomena of nature must first have been in human bodies where they were affected by the thinking as they passed through.

Thinking works by the method of point, line, angle, surface and completing curve. Thinking begins with a point because the Conscious Light when turned on matter acts thus. When Light is directed upon nature-matter the matter is developed or built from points into lines, angles, surfaces and completing curves.

The object perceived is perceived as a surface. On the physical plane, when the four senses perceive an object, it is seen in the radiant state as a point, heard in the airy state as a line, tasted in the fluid state as an angle and smelled in the solid state as a surface. Every object is perceived by means of coordinated acting of the four senses. The sense through which the object is immediately perceived is the dominant one. In the case of coal gas smelled in the dark, sight, hearing and taste act coordinately with smelling, which is however the dominant sense. The dominant sense takes the lead in introducing the object for perception to the feeling of the doer in the body. So a carriage is perceived by the sense of sight acting as the dominant sense, while hearing, tasting and smelling act coordinately. By the sense an impression is made on the breath-form. The breath-form, as the physical breath, resolves the surface to a point which is matter of the physical plane of the physical world.

The point represents the whole surface as which the outside object is perceived. The breath-form transfers the point to feeling. Feeling is inclined towards or averted from the impression. Accordingly the passive side of the psychic breath breathes the point to desire and desire wants the carriage and does not want the coal gas. A special desire, the one affected by the point, breathes to rightness and impresses it with the thing desired or disliked. The impression which was received in the point of physical matter and then transferred into the psychic atmosphere, is now transferred to the mental atmosphere. This impression is still a point of matter of the physical plane. Desire then compels action by the desire-mind to turn Light of the Intelligence on that desire. The Light turned on the desire unites with it. This is the conception of a thought. Now begins the process of building within the point which is within the thought. The thought is on the intelligent-side, and the point within it, which is nature-matter, is on the nature-side. The conception will be developed through gestation when the amount of Light turned and held steadily on the point by the thinking is sufficient. The desire and the Light become the thought, which is always on the intelligent-side, and the point becomes the structure within the thought; this structure is of nature-matter and will remain on the nature-side.

The Light that is held by thinking enters the point. Holding the Light extends a line of points within the point. That line is the horizontal or matter or the manifestation line. The point is thus extended within itself by the addition of other points. They are points of nature-matter, from the life plane of the physical world, with which the mental atmosphere is in contact through the physical breath. In each case there is a limit to which the horizontal line can be extended. The limit of the extension is determined by the nature of the thought that is being created. When the horizontal line has reached its limit it is stopped by the completing curve.

Then, as the Light is held, the initial point extends a line within itself. This line, called the aim line, is extended within the point beside, so to speak, and along the horizontal line, at an angle from it. The horizontal line, of which there is only one in each thought, is extended by the addition of points; it is made up of point matter; it is not a line but it is points. The aim line is built, not by point matter but by line matter from the life plane of the physical world. Each successive line is built at a greater angle from the matter line. So thinking builds lines within the point until they fill a standard angle, an angle of one-twelfth of the circle. The aim line extends until it comes to the completing curve. Then, while the Light is being held by thinking, line matter builds the next line and stops at the completing curve. The completing curve thus is the limit of the standard angle. The first standard angle is made up of line matter. The second standard angle is built while thinking continues to focus and hold Light, and it is built of angle matter of the life plane of the physical world. When the second standard angle, limited by the curve, is complete and the Light is held on the initial point, a further angle is built within the point. It is built of surface matter. The whole structure within the point is now three standard angles covering together ninety degrees. It is a right angle or square bounded by one-fourth of the circle.

By this process of building within the point towards the circle, human thinking, in the heart and the brain, makes a thought for issuance. When point matter, line matter, angle matter and surface matter are gathered into this structure within a thought, the thought is ready for issuance, (Fig IV-A).

Thinking which creates a thought is the functioning of the body-mind by its producing and arranging of points, lines, angles and surfaces, and by its holding Light on a subject of thought. Real thinking is the proper functioning of one or more of the three minds in holding the Light of the Intelligence steadily on a subject of the thinking. Human thinking, even at its best and when it is active thinking, is an imperfect functioning of not more than these three minds, and is only the effort to focus the Light and hold it on a subject of thought. By far the greater part of human thinking is passive and is due to impressions received from objects of the four senses. Such thinking is done involuntarily and is an insufficient, incoordinate and unbalanced functioning of usually only one, the body-mind, and never more than three minds, that is, the body-mind, the feeling-mind and the desire-mind. Thinking that does not create a thought is a thinking where the mind works according to rightness and free from the control of desire for attachment for the thing thought of.

In all instances where any definite thing is to be done, thinking goes on by the method of point, line, angle, surface and completing curve. This is the process of human thinking. But it is not the process of the thinking that does not create a thought. Desire urges it, but the minds do not mix desire with Light of the Intelligence. The minds work on the subject of thought without being attached to it. In such thinking the desire is not attached to the object which is the subject of thought. Nor is it for self-interest. It must be a desire to serve, to learn, to know, to free the doer.

In human thinking the combining of points, lines, angles and surfaces into the structure is uneven, unequal, disproportionate, irregular and overlapping and so the structure is malformed, though it is approximately a fourth of a circle. This is due to focussing improperly, to holding the Light by spasms and not steadily, and to the untrained and unskilled working of the mind. Moreover, the mind is not free from the domination of desire, but is compelled, held back and obstructed by innumerable conflicting desires. Nevertheless, thinking goes on and results in the building up of thoughts, because the Light of the Intelligence, when turned on the point, which is the subject of thought, develops it from points into lines, angles and surfaces limited by completing curves.

When the structure within the thought is thus built and the thought is ready for issue, the balancing factor comprises the manifested and the unmanifested parts of the thought, that is, the whole circle of which the structure in the thought is only one-fourth or ninety degrees. The balancing factor being both center and circumference, is also the point.

The balancing factor is conscience. Conscience, which is the amount of knowledge on a given subject, puts its mark upon the subject of thought, the point of nature-matter brought in by the senses. This mark is made by conscience from selfness and is impressed on the point at the moment when desire compels thinking. Knowledge is of the knower, is the unmanifested side of the thought, and will be the unmanifested side of the structure in the thought.

The point is the center and the circumference between which all lines and angles are equal. When the thought is issued, the structure in it is only an angle of ninety degrees; when the thought is balanced, the structure will be a straight angle, or one hundred and eighty degrees, (Fig. IV-A).

This is an ideal, a potential state, and making that actual and real is balancing the thought. The balancing factor extends through every point, line, angle and surface of the structure in the thought. The structure when the thought is exteriorized is of three standard angles, and the balancing factor compels further exteriorizations until three other standard angles are added, so that the structure in the balanced thought is a straight line or angle of one hundred and eighty degrees. Then the manifested side of the thought and its unmanifested side make the circle of three hundred and sixty degrees, which is the balancing factor and again the point fully expressed.

The aim as a line has two points, one connecting it with the object which is usually in the visible world, the other being the balancing factor itself. The aim reaches away from the balancing factor, but it is as if the balancing factor said: You cannot get away. Your center point is myself.

The generation or the entertainment of a thought and its issuance may be aided, accelerated and strengthened, or may be impeded, delayed and weakened. The subject of thought is a point, the point brought in by one or all four senses. Thinking, with point matter from the life plane of the physical world, builds this point into a line of points, and with line matter from that plane continues the aim line until the first standard angle is built, then builds with angle matter from the same plane the second standard angle, and with surface matter from this plane the third standard angle or surface. By building this structure within the point, which is in the thought, the thought is made ready for issuance. All this takes place with lightning speed.

By thinking with the same aim of the same subject, the same or some of the same lines and angles are worked over by the mind and so the structure is strengthened.

If before the thought is issued the aim is changed, the structure in the thought will be changed. The thinking breaks down and replaces parts of the line, angle and surface structure. The units which are broken down go back into the life plane of the physical world. The substituted parts may not be fitted to the general intent of what remains of the original structure. The thought is then weak. If the aim is contrary to the original aim, the whole structure will be undone and the thought will be revoked.

Generally the aim remains, because it is the result of desire and of a lack of knowledge. Aims mark the degrees of the understanding and indicate the amount of knowledge accessible to the present human being of the doer. Aim is a name for a condition of a doer portion expressed in the mental atmosphere as part of a thought. Thus aims, being doer conditions, are not easily changed.

Fear, anticipated failure, lack of confidence or other inhibitions may be present to influence the thinking, but the aim remains. Whenever an impression which is in accord with the aim is made on feeling, the structure in the thought is strengthened, and the structure ultimately becomes so strong that no inhibitions can stop it from becoming surface matter and being exteriorized.

Unless the feeling of an impression is somewhat in accord with the aim, there is no temptation to build out a thought. If there is any temptation it indicates the presence of the aim. Thoughts with the same aim will come back to be entertained. Because the aim is there, thoughts will be worked over by the same kind of line and angle matter until there is an exteriorization.

In the structure in the thought the aim is a line, beginning at the center and pointing towards the object. To attain the object, the aim, that is, the line, is built out into a design, that is, into the standard angle, with angle matter. Upon the aim depend the means to the end. The means are the design. The angle matter depends upon the line matter. The surface matter depends upon the angle matter. The design tends towards exteriorization and so the surface is built on three standard angles with surface matter until the structure within the point is complete and the thought is ready to be issued.

The point in the structure is the subject of thought which is the condensed impression of the object of the senses. The matter line, which is made of points, of point matter or fire units, is the beginning of the manifestation of the thought; the aim line represents the aim and is line matter or air units; the angle is the design and is made of angle matter or water units; and the surface, made of earth units, represents the exteriorization of the design. When the design is exteriorized from surface matter into an act, object or event, the balancing factor becomes actual and drives towards a balance of the thought. Its range and field of action is the physical universe.

When a thought becomes a surface on the physical plane and it is only a quarter of a circle, it is not balanced. The balancing factor is not satisfied until the structure is completed so as to have three more standard angles and be an angle of one hundred and eighty degrees. When the manifested is equal to the unmanifested and the structure in the thought is resolved into the initial point and disappears, the thought ceases to exist and the desire and the Light in it are released.

When a thought is not balanced at the first exteriorization, the second right angle is not built out. The structure in the first right angle remains until the second or balancing angle is built out. The initial point has been exteriorized in the act, object or event, by the design, but the whole thought has not been exteriorized. From the act, object or event the senses take in another impression which becomes a point, is carried through feeling and desire to reason, where thinking builds from that point for another exteriorization. As the structure in the thought remains, thinking holds the Light of the Intelligence on it. This causes matter from the life plane to go over the structure to revivify and possibly to change it. The same aim and aim line are there, but the design or angle matter may be different.

At first the design followed the aim; now it may vary from it. Formerly the man was conscious of his design; now he may not be, and usually is not, conscious of it, because the design is not necessarily the same. Thinking makes it now as before. But before, it acted under the impulse of a known desire, now it acts under the impulse of a different desire, which is influenced by the balancing factor as conscience. The new design which is being built out may be exteriorized to the man in an anticipated or unanticipated event, happy or dreaded. His former actions return to him as events and as conditions under which he lives. The events and conditions through which he lives are just as much exteriorizations of his aim as was the first exteriorization. But he does not know or even suspect it. It may be and it usually is the fact that his thinking fails to build out an aim line and design angle that will build out the missing quarter circle. So the exteriorizations go on until the matter line becomes a straight angle or an angle of one hundred and eighty degrees. When feeling and desire are satisfied, that is, when they are no longer attached to a thing if it is pleasant, or repelled by it if it is unpleasant, and when rightness and reason are satisfied with this unattachment of feeling and desire, three more angles are added to the structure in the thought. When these three are completed the balancing factor is satisfied. This relates to the structure within the thought.

Human beings cannot now think without creating thoughts. Though their passive thinking does not create thoughts, it eventually compels active thinking, which creates thoughts, and these are not balanced.

Thinking that does not create thoughts and thinking that creates balanced thoughts is the kind of thinking done by Intelligences and complete Triune Selves in governing the visible world, and in arranging the sequence and the coincidence of the events in it. While such thinking deals with objects of the physical world, these are not the primary objects of their desires. Their desire is for regulating, for a continuance and sequence of exteriorizations of human thoughts under the laws of nature, so that the exteriorizations will tend to satisfy the balancing factor and be events from which the human beings can learn to become conscious as doers. The Intelligences through their Triune Selves do not think with minds such as the doer uses. They think with their seven faculties to bring about an adjustment of mundane affairs in time, form and solid matter. They are detached from the acts, objects and events upon which they shed Light and which they cause to be brought about.

Usually the Intelligences and Triune Selves think without producing thoughts. Their thinking is the ordering of nature, through their doers or through upper elementals which cause the four kinds of lower elementals and their four classes of units to bring about the changes of the world and in human affairs. This thinking of the Intelligences with their Triune Selves arranges fate or destiny. It aids or impedes human thinking and the exteriorization of human thoughts, if this is required for the protection of humanity, by helping in the timely and preventing the untimely discovery or use of natural forces; by aiding or defeating the perpetration of plots, crimes, uprisings and revolutions; by causing the little events upon which depend the winning or losing of battles and wars; by aiding in or preventing the finding of historical records; by bringing on or retarding periods of general darkness or enlightenment, local or general crop failures and depressions or abundance, and cataclysmal destruction of the earth crust. Generally they do not interfere with thinking, but through their Triune Selves they cause only the exteriorizations of human thoughts to be marshalled. They may interfere where individual thinkers would produce unseasonable events, or where the indifference of the masses or the corruption of officials would stifle a movement for real progress. Hence come some of the "accidents" of which history is full.

The Intelligences sometimes create a thought. They do this through their Triune Selves when they want to create something in the physical world, so as to assist human beings in their progress. They then order the lower elementals directly, without calling upon the upper elementals. The object created may be anything from veins in the earth or from the changing of the course of a river to the founding of an institution of learning. These, however, are not thoughts for themselves, and their thoughts differ vastly from human thoughts in that the preceding thinking is done with understanding and accuracy. Such a thought does not go through a slow and laborious gestation. It is created and issued instantly. Elementals may build it out according to the slow processes of nature or instantly by an immediate precipitation, when it is spoken into being. In these thoughts the aim is unerring, the exteriorization is sure and the balancing factor is satisfied at once. The thoughts of Intelligences resemble human thoughts in that they, too, build from a point, by lines, angles and surfaces.

The Intelligences order the elementals by thinking or by thoughts according to geometrical figures which elementals have to obey. Such figures are points, lines, angles and surfaces related to certain points of the circle, which are related to the places, things and events to be connected with the exteriorization. Such figures are few, but with them are produced complicated events, as with the four strings of a violin can be produced innumerable melodies, discords and harmonies. The Intelligences think of the points, lines, angles and surfaces, and then matter of the world, plane and state with which the thinking is connected, forms itself ultimately into the act, object or event. Sometimes the thinking is done through a human being who, however, does not know of the figure he is making and of its consequences, though he must be a willing instrument.

Such a figure affects elementals by means of the matter of which the figure is made. Matter, units, and elementals are almost synonymous terms, used to indicate different phases of the thing. The matter or elementals of which the figure is made acts on other matter or elementals by a compelling power coming from the form of the figure, and organizing them into the work to be done. The figure has in it point, line, angle and surface matter, that is, different kinds of elementals, units, which can act on similar matter in the mass of the elements.

Human thoughts that are to be exteriorized are drawn into the figure and fit themselves to it. Not all thoughts are ready to be exteriorized at all times. It is by the knowledge of the Triune Selves that thoughts which can be exteriorized are selected. Elementals print on the breath-form a copy of the points, lines, angles and surfaces of the thoughts selected for exteriorization. Sometimes thoughts are exteriorized to prepare a political, religious or physical condition in the world under which the doers of generations yet unborn will live when embodied. The fact that the world has been going on uninterruptedly is the best evidence of the knowledge of these Intelligences and of their Triune Selves.

The figures thought by the Triune Selves only guide the exteriorizations. The figures make designs in which many thoughts are blended into one and thereby they are exteriorized as one. The human thoughts in the figure are the power that compels elementals to exteriorize it. They are the power that acts through the form of the figure on the elementals in the mass of the element. When the thoughts are exteriorized in acts, objects or events, the persons whose thoughts are involved will invariably be at the juncture of time, condition and place, brought there in an orderly, natural manner. In obedience to lines of the figures, which are also copied on the breath-forms of the persons affected and transferred into brain and nerve cells built in by the breath-forms, elementals make certain impressions through the senses. These produce incentive to action or inaction, which will result in an action by or a happening to the person, a part of whose thought is thereby exteriorized.

Another kind of thinking is done by the Great Triune Self of the worlds and by the beings of the form, life and light worlds. They do not think with faculties nor do they think in the manner of human beings. The thinking of the Great Triune Self of the worlds is at once feeling, thinking and knowing. This thinking is used to coordinate the embodied portions of all the doers on earth. It is done on the principle of the point, line, angle, surface and circle. The beings of the form, life and light worlds work with individuals or sets of humans, under the direction of the Intelligences. Their thinking usually is done from knowing, not from feeling, and it proceeds on the principle of all thinking, which is the extension of the point to the circle.

While it is now usually impossible for human beings to keep on thinking without creating thoughts, they must all learn to do so eventually. The thinking that frees is a thinking which does not by attachment create angles and surfaces. Men must learn to think without conceiving a thought about the things of nature on which they think. The conceiving of a thought binds them to the object from which the thought was conceived. This object is a point in the conception and is developed into a structure within the thought. Thinking without conceiving a thought proceeds also by the method of point, line, angle and surface, but the structure developed by the thinking is not in a thought because there is no thought. It is in nature and acts at once in nature by starting elementals, if the thinking is on the nature-side, that is, is on a subject of nature. If it is on the intelligent-side, on a subject of the Triune Self or the Intelligence, no structure is developed, other than one of angles and lines leading to a point; the matter is not nature-matter; it is matter of the Triune Self. The terms angles and lines are metaphorical, abstract. When the abstract point is reached it is a point of Light and with that at once a circle. This is thinking on the Triune Self or the Intelligence without creating anything from the thinking. But the result is illumination on the subject of the thinking and consequent knowledge.

The second application of the principle of the point working towards the circle may be seen in the development by which a thought, once it is issued, becomes exteriorized.

A human thought is issued from the frontal sinuses, on the light plane of the light world, but goes directly to the life plane of the light world. Within the thought is, at that stage, the point of matter of the physical plane of the physical world. It is the same point which the breath-form received from the four senses, passed on to feeling, which gave it to desire, where thinking developed a structure within the point by holding Light of the Intelligence on it. The point is still only a point within the thought, but has within it an approximate, not a perfect, structure made up of the three standard angles of point matter, line matter, angle matter and surface matter. This matter is from the life plane of the physical world. The thought itself has no structure. It is psychic matter and mental matter, matter of the Triune Self. The force or active side of the thought comes from the embodied portion of the doer, drives the thought on and attracts to it nature-matter so that the point within the thought develops from itself outward into a surface, whereas it formerly had developed within itself.

The point attracts a point to itself to which other points attach themselves. This makes the horizontal or matter line of points; it is points, not a line. The matter extends until a certain limit is reached which is preconditioned by the point. Then a line is extended from the initial point, beside and along the matter line. This is a line, the aim line, and it is extended to a limit. The limit is a curve, the completing curve. The aim line makes with the matter line, an angle. It moves gradually away from the matter line and other lines take its place until a standard angle of thirty degrees is reached by the aim line and is built out from the horizontal line. The horizontal line is built with point matter, the first standard angle is built with line matter. Then another standard angle is built into the first from the point, with angle matter. The angle matter is increased until the second standard angle is completed. It is limited by the completing curve. To the second standard angle the third is added by the compacting of surface matter. There are now developed from the point outward three standard angles, making a figure of one-fourth of a circle, (Fig. IV-A).

The horizontal line, made up of point matter, is in the fiery state, the aim line made up of line matter is in the airy state, the angle made of angle matter is in the fluid state, and the surface, made up of surface matter, is in the solid state of the life plane of the light world. Thus a point of matter of the physical plane of the physical world, having within it a structure of matter of the life plane of the physical world, by virtue of the power of desire and the Light of the Intelligence, compels matter on the life plane of the light world to build out the structure of the figure which is in the point.

When the point has become a surface on the life plane, the surface builds from its lowest point, which is ninety degrees from the horizontal line, another and similar structure. The surface builds from its lowest point by point matter, line matter, angle matter and surface matter, a surface in the solid state of the form plane of the light world. And that surface builds from its lowest point, by a similar structure, a surface on the physical plane of the light world.

That surface builds from its lowest point, by a similar structure, a surface on the life plane of the life world. So surface after surface is built from the lowest point of the preceding surface until the structure is built through the form plane and the physical plane of the life world and through the life, form and physical planes of the form world and through the life, form and physical planes of the physical world.

On the form plane of the physical world the structure is a surface in the solid state of matter of that plane. When the structure in the thought is developed outward to this extent the thought waits there until it can be exteriorized into an act, an object or an event on the physical plane.

This description of the structure is like a physician's prescription, an architect's plan, a chemist's formula; but if anyone can feel it, understand it, he will see from it the relation of the different states of matter on the planes and in the worlds and how they are connected, blended, linked, geared and work with each other. Point matter is present throughout every line, line matter is through every angle, angle matter is in every surface, and surface matter is on every solid.

The structure in the thought is exteriorized from the lowest point of the form plane. It starts radiant matter to build out toward the circle. It does this in the brain of the one through whom the thought will be exteriorized. The point becomes a surface of radiant matter in the brain. From a point in that is built a surface of airy matter which is breathing. From a point in that a surface of fluid matter, that is, of blood in circulation, is produced. From a point in that surface is produced the act, object or event through the action of the physical body.

Every act that is done, every event that happens, every object that is produced by human effort is called forth in this manner. In this way a thought is built outwardly in conformity with the structure which is in it. Thoughts clothe themselves with matter according to the pattern of the structure in them.

Thinking begins at a point, because the Light of the Intelligence goes in or goes out from a point. When thinking directs the Light to a point the Light opens the point inward or outward. It opens the point inward when the thinking is directed towards the higher planes of nature or towards the Triune Self. But human thinking is directed outwardly, towards the physical plane. The purpose of the thinking is outside and so it builds first within a point by point, line, angle, surface and completing curve, and then elementals give existence to thinking when they body it forth into nature, by building out from the point.

SECTION 2

Method of thinking in fashioning nature. The forms of nature come from human thoughts. Pre-chemistry.

The third application of the principle of the point extending towards the circle may be observed when it is seen that nature, when it builds the exterior universe, follows the pattern in thoughts. There is no other way for nature-matter to act. Thinking and thoughts set the pattern, and the units, elementals in nature, have to follow it. The points, lines, angles, surfaces and curves are exteriorized as the forms of the physical world, where they are not distinguished as points, lines, angles, surfaces and curves but are massed into the things which appear as physical objects. Points, lines, angles and surfaces are everywhere. They are invisible. Only a compacted mass of surfaces is visible, but not one surface alone. As surface is built on surface, by combination of units, the structure becomes visible. So the elementals of the four earth elements build up what expresses visibly, audibly, tangibly, in solid matter, what the thinking and the thoughts of human beings are. These elementals build in this manner not only that which is the direct result of human effort but also that which is a distant and indirect result of human thinking, so distant that it is not attributed to it.

The elementals which received their impress from thinking while they passed through a human body build up organic nature, and there cause growth, expansion, development and change, all according to the method of point and limiting curve, which is the circle. Fungi, lichens and mosses, buds, flowers, fruits and seeds, trunks and branches are all built by the method of expressing a point as a circle in bodying forth human thoughts. According to the parts of the human body in which they were lodged as transient units they build out, under compositor units, plants such as an oak representing nerve structure, a cabbage representing a gland, a cactus representing a primitive state of the spine, a vine representing a blood vessel, grass or moss or needles of the evergreen representing hair.

Human thoughts force the units of the four earth elements to bring forth, to keep up and to destroy the bodies of the animals, according to the method of building out from the point toward the circle, the point expressed.

Plants and animals get their forms from human thoughts, though humans are not aware of this. These forms are a distant though direct result of human thoughts. The entities inhabiting these forms are in the case of short-lived animals as butterflies, insects and vermin, desires of the living, and in the case of mammals, birds, reptiles and fishes, desires cast off by doers after death.

The elementals which have passed through a human body build up also inorganic nature. The only manner in which they can build it is according to the pattern set by human thoughts, the pattern of the point developing toward a circle. In this way they make rocks, water and the air, and fill out all inorganic nature with phenomena, from starlight and sunsets, blue sky and thunder, to mountains and dust. The building is done according to the method of the point and circle, under the direction of upper elementals ordered by Intelligences and their Triune Selves.

The last stages of the precipitation of matter into the things of inorganic nature are from the form plane. The point matter or units in the fiery state of that plane develops by the method outlined into line matter, that is, into units in the airy state of that plane, then into angle matter, that is, units in the fluid state of that plane, and then into surface matter, that is, into units in the earthy state of that plane.

Then the solid unit from the form plane, by a similar development, grows to be the radiant physical unit. To a point in the units of surface matter on the form plane, points are attached outward as a matter line. The line begins to be what will become a surface, and thus a unit of radiant matter on the physical plane. From the first unit extends another line which is the aim line, and to it other lines as line matter attach themselves and so become angle matter, by the addition, at the apex, of line to line. Angle matter is a further step on the way to become a unit of radiant matter. The angle matter is limited by the curve, which is the limit of the radiant unit, as surface matter in the radiant state.

A similar process is repeated by this unit, that is, by the surface of radiant matter, from a point out of which is developed a surface which is a point of airy matter and later becomes a surface of airy matter. The process is then repeated by the unit of airy matter, from out of a point of which is developed a surface which is a point of fluid matter; and then by the unit of fluid matter, from out of a point of which is developed a surface which is a point of solid matter. From out of a point of solid matter is developed a surface of solid matter. In every stage of the concretion from solid form matter into solid physical matter a point as point matter is the beginning and is by the addition of point matter extended into a line, the matter line, and then into an aim line, which being line matter attracts line matter. Thereby the point becomes the apex of an angle which, growing, makes angle matter. The angle matter then grows to be surface matter.

Radiant units will be termed pyrogen, airy units aerogen, fluid units fluogen, and solid units geogen, (Fig. II-F). These four kinds of units are four main stations in the growth of units from the lowest state of the form plane into the lowest physical state. The plane of pre-chemistry shows these four kinds, in each kind of a fourfold group, in each group a fourfold subgroup, and so on by fours. To illustrate. The geogen group consists of pyro-geogen, aero-geogen, fluo-geogen and geo-geogen units; and the geo-geogen units have a fourfold subgroup of pyro-geo-geogen, aero-geo-geogen, and so forth.

The first stage of growth on to the physical plane as a point of radiant matter is pyro-pyro-pyro-pyro-pyrogen. From this stage the unit grows into a pyro-pyro-pyro-pyrogen unit, then into a pyro-pyro-pyrogen unit, then into a pyro-pyrogen unit, then into an aero-aero-aero-aero-pyrogen unit, and so on until it is an aero-pyrogen unit. Then it grows through corresponding intermediate stages until it is a geo-pyrogen unit. Then it becomes an unqualified pyrogen unit. After that it grows into a pyro-pyro-pyro-pyro-aerogen unit, and so on until it is an unqualified aerogen unit, then a pyro-pyro-pyro-pyro-fluogen unit, and so on until it is an unqualified fluogen unit, and then the development is repeated in the same way until it is an unqualified geogen unit. These systematic stages through which a unit passes all come into existence by the successive growth of point matter, line matter, angle matter and surface matter limited by a curve. The result of the growth is always a single unit, not a combination of units. It goes through all that before chemistry and physics can deal with it at all.

Among the traits which all units of whatever kind, group or subgroup have in common are these: they have twelve points, the twelve points on the circle, and only four of these are actual, the remaining eight being potential. The actual points of each unit are on the circumference at the matter line and at the lines completing each standard angle of thirty degrees. These four points may become active and upon their activity depends the combining capacity of the unit with other units.

Every unit has a passive and an active side, that is, a matter aspect and a force or spirit aspect. The passive aspect is the four points at which it can combine, that is, its combining capacity. The active aspect is, among other things, its combining power, which is the power to use this combining capacity. It appears as a power to take, to hold and to use other units. The combining power is not specialized, so as to act separately from the combining capacity. The trend of the unit is to develop so that the power will become so specialized. Until the combining power is specialized the unit is a unit in inorganic or in organic nature, and can use the power mainly to capture and hold other units when the combining capacity is called on.

The activity of one or more points gives to a unit its special traits. In a pyrogen unit one point only is active, the pyro point; the other three remain inactive as long as it is a pyrogen unit. In an aerogen unit the pyro and aero points become active; in the fluogen unit the pyro, aero and fluo points become active; and in a geogen unit all four points, the pyro, aero, fluo and geo points become active. The distinguishing mark of each unit is the point which indicates its kind, that is, in a geogen unit the mark is the geo point, in a fluogen unit the fluo point, in an aerogen unit the aero point and a pyrogen unit has only the pyro point.

A pyrogen unit can combine only at its pyro point. An aerogen unit can combine at its pyro point and at its aero point. With a pyrogen unit it can combine only at its first or pyro point which is the point common to both units. With an aerogen unit it combines at the second or aero point, which is the second point common to both units. The fluogen unit can combine at any one of its three points. With a pyrogen unit it can combine only at its own first or pyro point, which is the only point common to both units; with an aerogen unit it can combine only at its own second or aero point, which is the last point common to both units; with another fluogen unit it can combine only at their third or fluo or last common point, and with a geogen unit it can combine only at their last common point, which is the fluo point. A geogen unit can combine at any one of its four points; with a pyrogen unit it can combine only at its own pyro point; with an aerogen unit only at its own aero point; with a fluogen unit only at its own fluo point and with another geogen unit only at the geo point.

When units combine they do so at the last common point. Not more than two units can combine with each other at the same time at the same point. Units can combine, first, if they are of the same kind and also of the same grade of development in that kind; second, if they are of the same kind and one of them is an unqualified unit of the same kind; third, if they are of different kinds and both are unqualified units; fourth, if they are of different kinds and one is an unqualified unit of its own kind and the other is in combination with an unqualified unit of its kind; fifth, if they are of different kinds and each is already in combination with an unqualified unit of its own kind.

Though the combining units cannot be seen, their combinations can be seen or examined when they have reached the stage called "chemical elements". The compounds of these enter into the make-up of all inorganic and organic bodies, into everything that grows and into everything that is made. The combinations produce the phenomena of the physical world—starlight, sunshine, moonlight, lightning, rainbows, spectra, wind, thunder, rain, and the colors and shades of twilight, dawn and sunset; the stars, the sun, the moon and the planets; electricity, heat, cohesion, magnetism, gravity and some unknown forces; the mineral, vegetable and animal realms; human bodies; birth, growth and decay of all things; and all sights, sounds, tastes and smells.

Units of the same kind form groups or series. For example, pre-chemically, lead is the end of one series which contains uranium, helium, radium and lead, and is the beginning of another, which is lead, mercury, silver and gold. Then the gold turns into uranium and the series begins again. These visible things are like platforms; the curved stairs descending and then ascending, that lead from one to another, are not perceptible.

The place where these units are, from pyro-pyro-pyro-pyro-pyrogen units, which are the beginning of radiant matter, to the unqualified geogen units which are at the end of the grades of development of solid matter, is the region between the outermost stars and the center of the earth. Radiant matter is in airy matter, and that in fluid matter, and that in solid matter. Finer matter penetrates coarser. Because of this inter-penetration of units the outpourings of the sun may be directly inhaled and bodily exhalations be drawn into the sun. Thus the physical body may be made immune to disease and endowed with youth. A man sitting in a chair may actually be in contact with the farthest star.

Pyrogen is starlight, aerogen is sunlight, fluogen is moonlight and geogen is earthlight. Earthlight or pure carbon is light, as is sunlight, only human eyes, chiefly because their focus is limited to one octave, do not see it as light any more than they can see starlight in rocks. None of these lights could be operative without the earth. None of these things are true light. They are only units in states of matter affected through the Triune Self by the Light of the Intelligence. The difference in these kinds of light, so-called, is due to the capacity of the four states of matter on the physical plane of the physical world to transmit the Light of the Intelligence.

The stars, sun, moon and earth are foci in which the four states of matter on the physical plane are centered. Of these centers or foci the earth is a solid body, and the moon is semi-solid, but the sun and stars are not solid bodies. The four kinds of units are controlled through these centers. The centers are connected, each with the one above or within it. The sun is needed to bring and circulate starlight. Without the moon there would be no contact with sunlight. Without the earth there could be no contact with the moonlight. The sun centralizes starlight and radiates it through the aid of the moon to the earth. The sun pumps, through the moon as a strainer, all four kinds of light into and out of all animate and inanimate things and beings on the earth crust. It breaks down, compounds and replaces them according to the points that allow the combining of units to become active.

If the eye had the focal power of four octaves, one could see these four lights distinctly. He could see the free starlight, the free sunlight, the free moonlight and the free earthlight as units or as masses. He could see the interpenetration of the starlight into the sunlight, and of the sunlight into the moonlight and of the moonlight into the earthlight. He could see these four lights present through, and radiating in all directions from the solid-solid objects on the earth.

The less advanced units of each kind are in the starry spaces farthest removed from the earth; and the more advanced are nearer to the earth. On the surface of the earth unqualified units of the four kinds predominate, though there are also units in the intermediate stages of development. Geogen units are rarest at the stars and at the earth center and densest inside the earth crust.

A unit of the geogen kind is the beginning of solidity. Geogen units are the beginning of every object of a solid nature, whether it be a human body or a layer of marble rock. Without geogen there could not be anything solid. Geogen units are the building blocks of the universe. In some bodies the units are all of the geogen kind as in lampblack or in charcoal. In other bodies the geogen units predominate, as in a tree where there are also fluogen, aerogen and pyrogen units. In other bodies, as in phosphorus and sulphur, the geogen units do not predominate, but they are then at least the basis for the solidity of the mass. The geogen units are the base on which units of the other three kinds are held. Geogen units are in fluids and in gases. They are in sunlight and in starlight near the earth surface and, because sunlight and starlight like to combine with them, they make these lights available to things on the earth surface. The physical, visible, sensible universe is built on the points of geogen units. In the physical world geogen units play the dominant part. It is a geogen world. Other worlds and beings are in and through the geogen world and its beings. For these beings the geogen world with its geogen people and things exists as little as they do for it. Some of the geogen units get into these other worlds, but there they lack the significance which they have in the geogen world. They amount to little. But on the earth surface everything depends on them and their combinations.

Separation goes with combination. Combinations of units can separate and after a while do separate. Everything in inorganic nature and in organic nature is a combination and is divisible. Combinations are dissociated in the inverse order of their combining. The surface breaks down into angles, standard angles of thirty degrees; the angles break down into lines; the lines separate into points, and the original combining units are left. When compounds are separated the combinations which helped to make them may continue.

At any of their stages the units can recombine. The oftener they do so, the readier and fitter they become to recombine. Their separation may stop at any stage. The units may then remain where they are, for a short or a long time, from fractions of a second to ages, until they recombine. When they recombine they act under the same system by point, line, angle and surface, that dominates their growth and their combination and controls their separation. In this way all objects on the visible earth are built, maintained and dissolved.

If the limit of growth of any body or part of it is reached, the lesser units that make it are separated, carried away and carried back into the sun, or enter new combinations. If the limit of growth is not reached, some of the units of the thing are carried away and others replace them, carried in by the stream coming from the sun.

The length of time units remain in a combination before they separate and enter new ones, or are unbound for a time, depends on various factors, as on their own condition, showing that they are unfitted for or have outgrown the combination in which they are; on the governing unit of the compound if they are in one; on whether they are undisturbed, like the units in coal left in the earth, or are acted on by some outside force, as are the units in coal burning in a grate. If they are compositor units they leave their compounds in nature to go into a human body, when the summons for them is issued. If they are transient units, that is, units which are used by a human body but do not belong to it, they may remain in their compounds until these are broken up.

Solid objects, no matter how permanent they seem, are in a state of flux. They are compounds of units which are in various degrees of development, from pyro-pyro-pyro-pyro-pyrogen to the various geogen combinations. Of the units which make up the compounds some may be there for a long time, some for a shorter time and some are merely passing through. This is as true of marble or glass as of the petals of a peach blossom.

The difference in the relative permanence of these things is due either to cohesion, that is, a property of geogen or structure units due to the presence of fluogen or form units, or to the principle of typal form. Cohesion keeps units in compounds in inorganic structures together, unless the property of a mass of other units passing through the geogen mass disrupts it. Heat, which is a mass of pyrogen and aerogen units, disrupts the cohesion of a mass of units which make the compound marble. Sudden changes from heat to cold, a certain electric current or the will of one who can see or speak through solid matter, could crumble it. The cohesive property in units is that which keeps them together in inorganic things. Organic objects, that is, those of cellular construction, are, however, not held together by cohesion. Design or form is what keeps the units in the peach tree, its fruit or the peach blossoms together. The purpose of the design and a certain limit of time, bring about the disruption of a part of the design and thereby break down the compounds of the blossom, of the fruit and of the tree. The pyrogen, aerogen, fluogen and geogen units in the light, air, water and earth do the rest, liberating the units that compose the blossom, the peach and the tree, and allowing them to form new compounds. So objects in inorganic nature are given permanence by cohesion, and in organic nature by the design or form.

SECTION 3

The constitution of matter. Units.

Objects that last for ages, such as marble rock or granite, are not permanent in their make-up. They are in principle no more permanent than is a flowing river. The particles in both are constantly moving, though the contours of the marble and of the river are more lasting. There are streams of units which pass through marble, glass, bronze and all other solid objects in a constant flow. They carry away here some and there others of the units making up these solid objects and leave other units in their stead. Streams of units pass continuously through all the waters or fluids as through the solids. They pass through the air and the radiant matter in it. In no case are they visible, because human senses are not fine enough to perceive them. These senses can at best focus on geogen units when concreted so as to be a solid physical object. The general shape of a layer of marble or of a statue remains unchanged, because of the property of cohesion in the units, because the number of substitutions is small in proportion to the number of units making up the mass and because the substitutions are made so quickly. It is like a regiment which remains the same regiment, though soldiers drop out and others fill their places. The same streams which flow through inorganic matter and bring about substitutions of the units in a compound, also flow through plants, and animal and human bodies. In these organic things the form is the distinct principle which preserves the outline, the limits.

As the streams pass through the geogen layer some of the units in the streams combine with or carry away some of the units of the layer, of the combinations, of the compounds and of the objects in the layer. So the streams build up, maintain and break down structures in the layer.

In inorganic nature the combinations may produce a perfect structure, an imperfect structure or a mass without structure. A perfect structure is produced where the units enter each other. They enter each other at points, those which are the last points common to both units. The results may be that the units change each other, or that the parent units remain and an offspring grows from them or that the parent units disappear in the offspring. In any case the result is a combination, not a growth. At the combining point a line which is a new matter line, is extended by point matter, new line matter makes a new aim line, new angle matter is added and a new surface comes into existence which is limited by the curve. An imperfect structure comes into existence when the combining units do not enter each other and no new matter line is formed, but their surfaces come together. They adhere and the combination is superficial, not integral. In the third case the combination has no structure, but is mass, amorphous.

Thus a diamond, graphite, and lampblack are examples of a perfect structure, of an imperfect structure, and of a mass without structure, made by units of geogen. Similar manifestations of units belonging to pyrogen and its groups are, starlight, which has a perfect structure, being a oneness built by self-generation from points of form matter; the stars which have an imperfect structure and are built by the coming together of surfaces of starlight; and a flash of lightning which has no structure, but is made of pyrogen units brought into a mere mass.

A diamond comes into existence if all the combining units are of the same kind, that is, belong to the geogen group. If the strain is of unqualified geogen units or of units belonging to the pyro-geogen group and the subgroups are all pyro subgroups, a white diamond comes finally into existence. If the subgroups are not pyro subgroups there will be a shade of color in the diamond. If the strain is of aero-geogen and the subgroups are all aero subgroups, a blue diamond results. A yellow diamond appears when the strain is of fluo-geogen, and a red diamond is the result of a strain of geo-geogen. If the marrying units are of the geogen kind but belong to different geogen groups, other colored stones such as rubies, beryls, a variation of which is the emerald, or amethysts, which are quartz, come into existence.

All things that are organic have a system on which they are constructed. In inorganic nature only crystals show a structure. Inorganic nature is made up of conglomerations of masses of units, organic nature is made up of units which are built into structures, have a definite design and are governed by superior units. All the units in a petal or in a grain of pollen have their governing units, and these are under the unit of the flower as a whole. In a human body the units are arranged in hierarchies. The lowest of the governing units is the breath link unit of a cell; the highest is the sense of smell. In the structure of a human body all the compositor units, that is, the breath link units, the life link units, the form link units, the cell link units in the cells, the governing units of the various organs in the four systems and the four senses, remain throughout life, held together by the breath-form. All other units are transient and come and go through food, drink, air and light, and also with the all penetrating streams which constantly bear them on.

Some of the units in nature act on or are acted on by others. They function in this way whether they are single or are in combinations in inorganic nature, or when their combinations are in organic nature under a superior unit which operates the structure of which they form a part.

According to their functions there are causal, portal, form and structure units. The causal units bring things into existence and cause the changes in them; the portal units carry on the circulations of units in all things; the form units hold things together in forms; the structure units build solids and so make bodies for the other three to function in. The causal are the pyrogen units, the portal the aerogen units, the form the fluogen units and the structure the geogen units, and each of the kinds has in it a group of four. So the units of the pyrogen group function as pyro-causals, aero-causals, fluo-causals, or geo-causals; and each group has many subgroups of fours.

In a geogen unit work the other three kinds, the causal, the portal, and the form units. When a physical structure is built it can be built only with geogen or structure units. They are the building material. They make up the solid world; without them there could be none.

The form or fluogen units hold the structure units in place and keep things as they are, giving and maintaining the frame and the form of objects. They hold also the portal and the causal units. The portals and the causals work through the form units. One form unit connects with another and so they form the mass of structure units, as a block of marble or a heart. The action of the form unit is like that of a kaleidoscope in which the same bits of glass appear in a variety of patterns. The form units are the units that give to a mass of structure units the character of gold or tin, or of a strawberry or a pepper. The character is given by arranging the structure units in form. A statue retains the outline given to it, because the form units in the mass of structure units hold that mass in the shape given to it by the sculptor.

The portal or aerogen units circulate through the form units. They carry the causals around with them. Without the portals the causals could not act on the form units. The portals are life and carry life.

The causal or pyrogen units are contained within a portal, as the portals are within a form unit and form units in a structure unit. They are the beginners, the generators, the changers and the destroyers. If the form units are no longer able to maintain the form, the causals acting within the portals and the portals acting within the form units start the breaking down of the form and of the structure.

To have a structure there must be building blocks, the geogen units. To hold the structure there must be form units in these structure units. The bound form units connect with unbound transient form units which pass through the structure as water flows through a sponge. Some of the unbound are caught and bound into the form units of the structure units while some of the form units in the structure are carried off. The portals in the form units connect with the unbound transient portals which pass through the bound form units, and hold those of the portals which they need, while some of the bound portals are carried off with the stream of unbound portals. The portals are the life of the structure. The causals in the bound portals connect with the unbound causals which the ever moving streams of matter of the form plane carry through the portals which are held by the form units. Some of the bound causals capture and hold some of the unbound causals and the stream of causals carries away some of the bound causals. The causals remaining in the portals are the active causes that bring about every change that takes place. They bring about the dissolution of the form when the form units are no longer able to maintain it. Then the bound causals, making contact with unbound causals, relate them with the form units of the structure, and that is broken up.

The activities of the various units are based on the system of point, line, angle and surface limited by the curve. Of the unbound units streaming through a structure which are caught by bound units in it, the causal are caught by the causal, the portal by the portal, the form by the form units, and the structure by the structure units. The bound units which are carried out of the structure with unbound units, are taken in like manner, the causal by the causal, the portal by the portal, the form by the form units, and the structure by the structure units.

A geogen unit can catch a pyrogen unit only at the pyro point of the geogen unit, and that pyrogen point is the causal unit within the structure unit, (Fig. II-F). In the structure unit the causal unit is the point matter, the portal unit is the line matter and the form unit is the angle matter, while the geogen or structure unit itself is the surface. The same aspects are presented by the other kinds of units. So a pyrogen or causal unit is point matter in a structure unit, but it is surface matter among the unqualified pyrogen kind; there the point matter is a pyro-pyrogen unit, the line matter is an aero-pyrogen unit, and the angle matter is a fluo-pyrogen unit, and the geo-pyrogen unit is the final stage of angle matter before the unit becomes an unqualified pyrogen unit, which is a surface.

Though a causal or pyrogen unit is a surface in its own state it is only the pyro point in a structure or geogen unit or surface. A portal or aerogen unit is a surface among the unqualified aerogen kind, but in a structure unit it is line matter and is the aero point. A form or fluogen unit is a surface among its unqualified kind, but in a structure unit is angle matter and is the fluo point. Structure units are the building blocks of the physical universe.

When structure units build perfect structures they build from these pyro, aero, fluo or geo points, in them. What is built from pyro points is colorless, as rock crystals or colorless diamonds. What is built from aero points is blue as sapphires; what is built from fluo points is yellow, and what comes from geo points is red. This is so with perfect structures in inorganic nature, such as stone crystals and metal crystals. The variety of colors between the three primary colors is due to combinations of several units.

When structure units build imperfect structures they act as surfaces, but they act merely as surfaces and not from their points, that is, they do not enter each other. Thus they build up a common mass, that is, a mass which is not a crystal or a cell, by merely adhering to each other. Such masses as aqueous or igneous rocks are compacted by surface upon surface. There the structure units do not penetrate each other, but merely stick together by means of the cohesive power which lies in their form units.

When the structure is organic, built of cells after a design, it is built by structure units which penetrate each other. It is built by geogen point matter, which starts line matter, which develops angle matter, which becomes a surface, a living surface. The surfaces or building blocks meet at points, their geo points, and from there build up cell structure. They build it up on the system of the point, line, angle and surface. The new surface is a new cell. It separates from the parent cell at the geo point of the parent cell. So one cell becomes two. At the center of each new cell the development by point, line, angle and surface is repeated, until the structure of the body built by cells is complete.

The causal, portal, form and structure units not only build up structures, but are also the forces of nature. There are four earths: the radiant, airy, fluid, and solid masses. These are the passive or matter aspects of the four earth elements. In that condition the matter aspect of the units dominates their active side. The active or force aspect is streams of units which pass through the masses, and in those units the active side dominates the passive side. The source of these streams is the form plane. They flow continuously, though at some times they are more active than at others, and they flow in all directions at the same time.

Some of these streams, if they could be measured, would be found to be faster than the speed at which light is said to travel. They travel so fast that as they pass through they do not ordinarily affect solid objects or even the two lower layers of geogen and fluogen. Under conditions allowing contact these streams manifest as electricity, as light or as creative force, which are starlight; as heat, which is starlight and sunlight; as the force of flight, which is sunlight; as magnetism, which is moonlight and earthlight; and as gravitation, which is earthlight. At certain times these streams appear as other forces, at present unknown. The forces themselves are not vibrations, but they cause vibrations in the mass of passive units.

If the plexuses of the generative system were in contact with the forces of pyrogen or starlight, one could generate power in machines without fuel or other outside means. If the plexuses of the respiratory system were adjusted to the forces of aerogen or sunlight, one could fly and could impart to the body speed in traveling through the air; he could produce heat without fuel by adjusting aerogen units. If the plexuses of the circulatory system were in contact with fluogen or moonlight, one could have lightness of body and could rise in the air or move in the water, produce varying colors in vegetation and control the sap of plants. If the plexuses of the digestive system were in contact with geogen or earthlight, one could increase or decrease his own weight and the weight in other bodies; he could precipitate the diffused geogen units into solid forms; he could magnetize bodies and cause them to attract or repel each other.

Fortunately this condition of human bodies does not exist at present. Any one of these forces would shatter the nervous system and possibly cause immediate death. Before one may attempt to use any of them one must have his body under control and not be controlled by it.

The growth, and the combining and compounding of the pyrogen, aerogen, fluogen, and geogen units, are accomplished on the principle of the point developing by line and angle towards the circle. Thoughts when they are issued are exteriorized by this principle because nature has to follow the pattern which is in the thought.

Not only in the immediate exteriorization of thoughts into acts, objects and events is this principle followed but also in the remote and indirect exteriorizations which are the phenomena in the maintenance of outside nature. These are brought about by the transient pyrogen, aerogen, fluogen and geogen units which received their impress from thinking while they passed through human bodies. They make a leaden sky, a coppery afterglow, the frosting on a windowpane, the gold in the earth and all the fauna and flora. The extension of a point towards a circle is always the plan on which nature works. The result of the growth is their development.

The units come as free units from the other spheres into the earth sphere and there, through the light, life and form worlds, into the physical world. There they descend through the light, the life and the form planes to the physical plane of the physical world. They pass as free units through all objects on the physical plane. They are unattracted and unattached, but they are affected while passing through bodies. Units do not affect other units and have no power over them as such. The only things that can affect them and bring about a change in them are thinking and the Light of the Intelligence used in thinking. The change is brought about in the units, whether they be of the spheres or worlds or planes, as they pass through bodies. So the units of the sphere of fire are changed in their make-up and their activities until they come from sphere to sphere and world to world down to the solid state of the form plane of the physical world.

From there they grow out through the pyro-pyro-pyro-pyro-pyrogen stage, through subgroups and their subgroups, into unqualified pyrogen units. Then they become transient units. They become such only when they are attracted, caught and held by the breath link unit of a cell. Their growth continues until they become geogen units of the unqualified kind. In the meantime, while they are so growing, they make up the phenomena of nature and enter into the composition of the various chemical elements and of the bodies of plants and animals. They return to bodies, where they are again caught by compositor units; the pyrogens are caught by the breath link units, the aerogens and their subgroups by life link units, the fluogens and their subgroups by form link units and the geogens and their subgroups by cell link units. They remain transient units until they become compositor units. They act as compositor units in nature in the building up and maintenance of the structures of plants and animals. Finally they become organ units and manage organs, successively in the four systems, and then they manage the systems and are successively the senses of sight, of hearing, of taste and of smell. There ends their career in nature. A sense of smell becomes the breath-form unit, which in turn is translated by the Triune Self to be its aia, when the Triune Self becomes an Intelligence. The progression of the unit is always from the earth-fire to the earth-earth towards the goal of being an aia unit, (Fig. II-H). Throughout the development of units in nature the principle that governs the growing, combining and massing is that of the point growing towards a quarter circle or the quarter circle diminishing towards a point.

SECTION 4

Erroneous conceptions. Dimensions. The heavenly bodies. Time. Space.

Erroneous conceptions about the world in which they live interfere with men's understanding the worlds which penetrate it and the forces which keep it going. The natural sciences do not lessen ignorance and error about things which are not perceptible. They do not dispel the misconceptions of the sense-bound doer. Among the erroneous conceptions are some that are connected with size, weight, solidity, dimensions, distance, form, originals and their reflections, sight, time and space.

There is no large or small except by comparison of expanse and volume. "Large" and "small" are conceptions resulting from thinking which deals with certain perceptions through the senses. These perceptions are made in the subdivisions of the solid state of matter on the physical plane. In other states of matter, even on the physical plane, the perceptions are different. Definite objects are less and less conceived of as large or small, and objects in the radiant state are not perceived as large and small at all. If one could perceive the four states of matter intermingling in objects there would be no fixed conception of size. The large could be seen as small and the small as large.

When one looks at objects one does not see how they are made or maintained, nor the forces playing through them and giving them qualities such as weight, cohesion and conductivity, and attributes such as outline and color. One sees merely their color, their contour and their size in comparison with each other. But if he could look at a geogen unit and see other units within it and streams of units passing through it, he would see relation instead of size. If he could see the geogen unit held by another unit he would see action or cohesion, not size. When thinking is focussed on extent and volume, one is prevented from perceiving the nature of the thing. When men think of a thing the impression is of size and the thinking limits itself by such comparison.

Man must understand the universe through his body. The farthest star is represented in the body and can be examined there, better than where the star is. A star is no larger than its corresponding nerve center to one who can perceive the two, not that one measures as much as the other but the conception of size gives place to that of what the star and the nerve center are and of how they are related. While one thinks of the universe as different from and as unrelated to his body, or of one as larger or as smaller than the other, he does not understand either. To one who sees the relation between them, sunspots are no larger than the heart-throbs by which they are caused. The sun can be seen as small as a heart and a heart as large as the sun. A star is like a nerve center spread out and the nerve center is as the star condensed. The Milky Way cannot be seen as a whole unless it is seen as an extension and projection of the system of ganglia and nerve plexuses. The human nerve trunks may be perceived as extending to the Milky Way, and that may be seen as the spinal cord. To understand how physical things came into and pass out of being, the idea of size has to be abandoned.

From the form plane the physical universe may be like a speck. The form plane is as much vaster than the physical plane as the ocean is vaster than the sponge in it. Yet the matter of the form plane can be understood only by that matter of the form plane which is in some part of the physical plane. The ether, that is, the solid matter of the form plane, can be perceived and dealt with from the physical plane only through a point. The ether is entered through a point just as from a point or points in the ether comes the whole physical universe.

One who can see matter in its states on the form and physical planes will not conceive of objects as large or small. He will see that what seems large on one plane or in one state of matter is small on or in another, and that the small on or in one may be large on or in the other.

Gravity is a relation between states of physical matter. So the weight of iron is the relation of the four states of radiant, airy, fluid and solid matter that make up a given mass of iron. The relation may be changed by the medium in which this iron is placed, as inside the earth crust or in water on the surface or in thin air or on a mountain.

The center of gravity is the line of closest intermingling of the four states of matter in any body. Each body has a gravity of its own, but the gravity of the earth is the standard for all things about the earth. The line of closest intermingling of the matter of its four layers is between the outer and the inner earth crust.

The line of the earth's gravity changes from time to time. Inside, beyond the earth crust, the action of gravity diminishes rapidly. At the center of the earth there is no gravity, nor is there any in the region of the stars. If the relation of the matter of a body to the matter of the earth as a whole is cut off, there is no weight. Matter of greater density than that of the earth, that is, where the units lie closer together, has no weight if it is not related to the matter of the earth. There is matter, such as that on the form plane, of greater density than solid earth matter, which cannot be perceived, has no weight and is not affected by the gravity of the earth. When such matter is put into relation with the solid earth, the line of gravity will be transferred to that.

Solidity is a deception by the senses of sight and contact through smell. There are holes in a copper plate as there are in a fabric. But this deception can be dispelled to a certain degree by the aid of instruments. Nevertheless the sense perception dominates the understanding. Finer matter composes, permeates and flows through solid matter. It produces the phenomena of solid matter. Beyond this finer matter in the physical world is matter in other worlds that is still finer. Some of the qualities of and the conditions produced by different states of the interior and finer matter are unintelligible, and if they were to be stated would appear as impossibilities, contradictions and nonsense.

Dimensions are spoken of as properties of space. But space has no dimensions. Matter has dimensions and only that matter which is in the three lower, the life, form and physical, planes of the physical world. Its dimensions are among its characteristics. The dimensions on the physical plane are called length, breadth and thickness. These are really only one dimension, on-ness or surface.

Matter on the physical plane has the dimensions of on-ness, that is, an outside; in-ness, that is, an inside; throughness, that is, consecutive insides; and presence, that is, being anywhere and everywhere at once.

The first dimension is on-ness. On-ness is exteriority, the outward aspect of the things made up of matter and perceived by the senses as a whole. It comprises length, breadth and thickness. They are the first dimension. Length breadth and thickness together are seen as surfaces. All three are necessary to see a surface.

In-ness is the second dimension. In-ness makes on-ness. It holds surfaces together. A bare surface cannot be seen because it has no thickness. A thing appears as one thing, but even the simplest is many things. In-ness makes the many appear as one. In-ness makes tangible, visible, that which would otherwise be intangible, invisible. In-ness is not solid, but it makes solid. It is an aspect of the same mass which appears to have length, breadth and thickness, as having also interiority in a general way. The exteriority is the thing as it looks, the interiority the thing as it is.

The third dimension of matter is throughness, which is to be known by seeing, hearing, tasting or smelling through matter, that is, perceiving all surfaces of the thing. Throughness is sequence, or consecutive relation. It is a continuity in the sequence and relation. It is a quality of matter as going through a thing. The first and second dimensions make the mass. Throughness relates the various parts of the mass and goes through it.

Presence is the fourth dimension of matter, that is, matter is everywhere at once. The other three dimensions are no interferences or obstructions to presence.

In on-ness, as an exteriority, appear results of activities of the other three dimensions. Presence, throughness and in-ness, though they are dimensions, have not the characteristics of on-ness, and therefore the three aspects of on-ness do not aid in suggesting the properties of the other dimensions. These dimensions are active, not inert as is on-ness. Their properties are activities or forces and do not appear as or in on-ness. Only results of the activities appear. They appear in the first dimension as solidity, color, outline, shadow, reflection, refraction.

In-ness, throughness and presence are dimensions which physical matter has independently of its visibility and tangibility. Unless the four dimensions of matter act coordinately, on-ness is not in evidence, that is, things do not appear as things.

Each kind of nature unit is a dimension of matter; each class of elementals is a dimension. The pyrogen units or causal elementals are the fourth dimension of matter, and the geogen units or structure elementals are the first dimension, or length, breadth and thickness. There are units which are not elementals. So the aia, the Triune Self and the Intelligence are units, but they are not elementals, and they have and are no dimensions. Nor have they qualities which are predicated on dimensions.

An understanding of the nature of the visible world is precluded by ignorance of the dimensions of its matter. As long as people are limited in their conceptions by the perceptions of their senses, they do not conceive what the universe can be behind, inside or apart from length, breadth and thickness. Even if in-ness alone were realized as a dimension they would see a universe which could hardly be identified with the visible world.

If one could sense on-ness alone, that is, without coordination of the other dimensions, it would have the substantiality of shadows. There would be bare outline without color and without perspective. The sun and the moon would be shadows. This is one of the states through which the dead pass; their thoughts may give color and activity to the scenery.

If in-ness alone were sensed, there would be no top, no bottom, no up or down. There would be no gravity, as in-ness is gravity in its relation to other states. There would be no things solid to the touch. Things would be where they are but one could not take hold of them. Things would be sensed in layers in the mass. A cigar could not be seen as a cigar, only as layers of matter without curve, and it could not be grasped. There would be no moon, no sun, no stars, only matter in intangible layers. A human body could not possibly be recognized. It would be seen as layers, not of skin, bone, muscle or blood, but as layers of units.

If throughness alone were sensed everything would look like moving lines. There would be no sun, no moon, no stars, no solid earth, no water. But everything would be air and sound.

If presence alone were sensed, then according to the person who perceived, there would be either one mass of light, or everything would be points of light. The whole universe would be like that, no stars, no sun, no moon, no earth, and no things and beings on the earth.

Thus appears this universe of the physical plane if it is sensed separately in each of its dimensions without their coordination. When the dimensions are sensed as coordinated there are perceived through the visible universe three interior universes, which four together make the physical universe, as the fourfold human body is seen as one body.

The visible earth is round and moves around the sun. This is true in a sense. But other statements could be made and be just as true, though at present they would be considered absurd. The sun is not where it seems to be, and the planets are not where they seem to be. The dimensions of matter and the state of the senses prevent investigators from perceiving where they are. The sun and the moon may be seen inside the earth as they appear outside, apparently just as far distant from the inner as from the outer crust. The stars may be seen at the center, apparently as far away as they are seen from the outer crust, and one perception is as correct as the other, for all are perceptions of reflections of projections.

The connection of the dimensions with the states called radiant, airy, fluid and solid matter is apparent. The elementals which are this matter have traits which are called dimensions. Some conceptions can therefore be formed of the dimensions of matter in the solid state of the physical plane. But when it comes to the dimensions of matter on the form plane and those of matter on the life plane, there is little that can be used as a stepping stone, a measuring rod or a comparison to aid in a conception. When it comes to states of matter which have no dimensions at all, as the matter of the light plane of the physical world, and the matter of all the worlds beyond the physical, there is nothing, from the physical view, to go by. Human conceptions do not take in what goes on in a world where matter has no dimension. Yet men are in such matter at all times.

The conception of distance is connected with that of dimension. Distance, from one point to another, is a term used to measure matter from one point to another. Distance is the measurement of matter intervening between the two points. Distance is the measure of on-ness, the first dimension, not of space. The distance from the earth to a star is a measure of matter, as much as the depth of the water under a ship. It is impossible to measure in a straight line, but for ordinary purposes the assumption that distance is a straight line is adequate.

Distance is a correct measure for everything that can be touched, but not for that which, though visible, cannot be touched. Things that can be touched are made of solid matter. There are things that look as if they were made of solid matter, but that cannot be touched, among them the sun and the stars. Distant things look as if they were made like the things men know as solid, if the things have in them the same ingredients as the solid things. So the sun and stars have in them chemical elements that are in the earth. But the surfaces in the heavenly bodies are not compacted into a solid. The stars are radiant matter, bodies; the sun is an airy body. Being too far away to be touched these heavenly bodies give the appearance of solidity.

The idea of distance which is based on their apparent solidity is erroneous, because what is seen of these heavenly bodies is like a reflection in a mirror. It is not even the first or second reflection. What appears as a star may have been reflected many times before it appears in the focus where it is visible. Again the idea of distance is based upon measurement made upon the earth crust. The rules applicable on the earth crust are not always applicable when applied to measurements in other states of matter, such as what is called interstellar matter.

Form is another conception which prevents a ready understanding of the conditions of matter which is affected by thinking. Matter which is seen has a form. If it has no form it is not seen. Even a God has to have a form to be conceived of. He is conceived of as a Father, a Friend, a Creator.

The form in which physical matter is seen is on-ness, that is, as surfaces, and gives no assistance in the conception of what is form other than as on-ness. So there is no conception of form other than as the forms that are seen. Forms on the form plane and on the life plane are not like those on the physical plane. In so far as they have other characteristics they are not conceived. One of these characteristics is that the forms of matter there can sometimes be changed instantaneously. Thoughts which have been issued and which appear on the nature-side fashion matter at once into forms and cause the adjustment of units into forms. In the after-death states thoughts at once give form to matter, and there need not be the gradual development or gradual dissolution which the change of forms of physical matter requires.

Among the characteristics of on-ness, surface matter, is the property to reflect objects. On-ness has this property by reason of the three interior dimensions. Near the earth, the surrounding atmosphere, which is in the fluid layer, and beyond that, the air in the airy layer, have this property.

The fluid layer is semi-transparent and through it are seen directly some stars, the sun and the moon. The airy layer is transparent and through it are seen some stars and the sun, not the moon which is at the border of the fluid layer. Some stars, the sun and the moon and the planets are seen directly. But of some of these various sights there are also visible reflections, which do not look like the things reflected. Some of what are seen as stars are reflections of parts of the sun, and some are reflections of other stars. The fluid and the airy layers not only let some pictures and light pass directly and reflect other pictures and light, but they also refract. The planets are sometimes not where they are seen to be. The stars are almost never where they are seen to be. The sun and moon are not where they are seen to be.

The diameter of the sun is reckoned to be over eight hundred thousand miles. This apparent size of the sun is largely due to the magnifying properties of the unknown media through which it is seen. The sun may not be as far away as is supposed. The distances assigned to the stars cannot be correct, because the media through which the measurements are made are not known, and reflections are taken for originals. When four stars are reflections of one star and all five show different spectra, this is due to the media through which the stars are seen. In the media are present or absent certain chemical elements. The chemical elements revealed by the spectroscope as present or absent in the stars, are added or eliminated during the passage of the reflection through the media.

Most astronomical observations and calculations are no doubt correct. What is seen with telescope and spectroscope is actually seen. But the inferences drawn as to the size of the universe and the distances, the reality, the movements and the constitution of the stars are not correct. The better the telescope the more reflections can be seen with it, but there is no way of distinguishing whether a reflection is the first, second or one hundredth, or where in the media the mirrors are which produce the reflections, or where the background is by which the reflections are focussed. Greatness and smallness and distance are not there in reality, but in relation to a background and a focus.

To be correct the real stars must first be distinguished from their reflections. Then it should be understood how the real stars are projections of matter from human nerve centers. Of these projections of radiant matter into the layers of fluid, airy and fiery matter on all sides of the earth crust, some are caught and focussed on different backgrounds in the fiery layer. Those are the real stars. Other stars seen are mere reflections of these stars, thrown by the airy and fluid layers on the backgrounds in the fiery layer. There may be many reflections of a star back and forth and they may differ in apparent size as well as in apparent composition. The difference in size is due to a magnifying like that of a magic lantern. The process is not quite the same, but the principle of projection is. The apparent size of a star depends on the focus made by the background. The backgrounds give the stars position and size. Until they are caught by the backgrounds in the fiery layer they cannot be seen.

A star, irrespective of the size given it by astronomy, is a projection from human nerve centers. Such a star is material, has a body and has properties, all of which are endowments from human bodies. If there were no background there would be no projection seen, because there would be nothing to hold it in focus. Different from these original stars which have bodies, are the stars which are reflections; they have no bodies, but are surfaces only. The real stars are cosmic nerve centers, as much as those in human bodies, and act coordinately with their counterparts in human bodies. The nerve centers in the heavens are extensions and enlargements of composite human nerve centers; and the nerve centers in every human body are miniature patterns of the cosmic nerve centers which are stars.

The human body is expanded to the limits of the universe and the universe is condensed into every human body. The matter between the stars cannot be seen, but it is of the matter of the human bodies. The organs of the bodies also have their places in the heavens and interact with their counterparts. The apparent movements of the stars are in phase with the actions of the nerve centers in the body. The sun is the projection of all human hearts, and the planets are the projections of other organs. The asteroids are parts of organs that no longer function.

The sun and the planets are seen directly, that is, they are not reflections. Yet these bodies are not where they are seen. Their apparent movements are not their actual movements. The visible relation to each other and to the universe as a whole is not the real relation.

What the sense of sight reports of them is true as long as one looks at matter in the dimension of on-ness only. The movements of a horse or of a ship, seen in the dimension of on-ness appear different from what the movements would appear when seen in in-ness, throughness and presence. On on-ness a body has to keep on a surface, but if a body moves in in-ness it does not have to keep on the surface, any more than a fish does. A fish moves, in a sense only, in in-ness. If seen from the surface its movements are sometimes appreciated correctly and sometimes they are misconceived. On-ness prevails on the earth crust, in-ness in the moon, throughness through the sun and presence with the stars.

The regular movements of the heavenly bodies, including the earth, are a composite of the phenomena of respiration, circulation and digestion. The movements of the solar system represent the actions of the nervous systems. All these movements are seen by the aspect of on-ness only.

Sight is the chief means for perception of outside nature. Sight depends on earth-fire in the states in which it is radiant matter outside and the sense of sight impersoned inside the body. Man sees because he has in his service a fire elemental, the sense of sight, and contacts by means of it radiant matter in four conditions. They are radiant matter in the object seen, radiant matter in the eye, radiant matter sent out by the sense of sight and radiant matter in the space between the eye and the object. Seeing is the alignment by the sense of sight of the radiant matter in these four conditions. The sense of sight focusses the eye and the focus makes the alignment.

When a house is seen its surface, like all other objects, sends out radiant matter, and the eye sends out radiant matter to meet this. The sense of sight aligns both and seeing is the presence of the sense of sight in the four conditions of radiant matter. Light does not travel at all, but its presence causes units of aerogen matter to move. Some of their movements take on fiery aspects and produce the phenomena which appear as waves and the speed of light.

While radiant matter in the four conditions is always there, visibility of objects depends upon their being focussed. A human eye is limited in its ability to focus. Therefore people do not see in darkness, or through a solid wall, or beyond a certain distance. For that reason also they cannot look beyond the earthy-earth visibility. Clairvoyance, which is uncondi-tioned vision, is rare and fitful. Ordinary human vision is limited to on-ness, the solid-solid. If man could focus on other states than the solid-solid he could see not only on the wall, but inside the wall, through the wall to any object beyond. He could see in darkness as well as in light, and distance would not be a hindrance to focus. Focussing is done by the sense of sight by using radiant-solid units, units of on-ness. If radiant-radiant units were used all states of matter could be seen through, things could be seen where they are and as they are, at any time. The universe would be seen to be different from what it is now seen to be.

Men measure time by the revolution of the earth on its axis and around the sun. This measure suffices for mundane things. Beyond that it is insufficient. It is a measure of on-ness. Time measured in in-ness or in throughness gives different results. In in-ness there are no revolutions on the axis and around the sun, and so these cannot be used to measure time. Time is the change of units or masses of units in their relation to each other. As the earth as a mass turns, it changes its relation to the sun as a mass, and one revolution on its axis measures a day and a night. Thus is time measured in the solid state of the physical plane. It is there measured on surfaces on the earth crust.

In the fluid state time is measured by the change in the relation of units which are layers between surfaces. There are there no days, nights or years. Time is measured differently in the airy state, and differently again in the fiery state of the physical plane. This is enough to suggest how limited is the application of the ordinary measure of time by days and years.

On the permanent earth, the Realm of Permanence, past, present and future make a composite, (Fig. II-G). From the permanent earth the other three earths can be seen, though the permanent earth is invisible to mortal eyes, until they see what is called by Jesus, the Kingdom of God. The permanent earth is present throughout the physical universe.

Days and nights, lunar months and years, solar months and years, and the vast or small cycles into which all these can be multiplied and divided, are measures of time of on-ness on the fourth, the present earth. There have been and still are two other earths, the third and the second, where time was and is reckoned as of on-ness. On the third earth there is a sun and a moon. On the second earth there is a sun and a moon, but not as they seem to look and act today. On the first, and permanent earth, there is no sun and no moon as they are known today and there is no time as it is at present measured, (Fig. V-B,a). There, the measurement of time is the instantaneous coming into or the going out of being of anything. Accomplishment is instantaneous. There, permanence is. There is no change, only beginning and end for special creations. The four earths are four stages in which the earth crust appears. The measurement of time on the earth crust has changed, with the change of human bodies. There are days and nights as soon as the bodies become male and female and subject to birth and death.

Space has no dimensions; matter has dimensions, and matter is not space. Space has no extension, vacuity, boundlessness, or any of the attributes of matter. Space is unmanifested. The four states of matter making up the physical plane, (Fig. I-D), are in the form plane, and that is in the life plane, and that in the light plane of the physical world, (Fig. I-C). The physical world is in the form world, which is in the life world, which is in the light world, and all are in the sphere of earth, (Fig. I-B).

This is in the sphere of water, this in the sphere of air, and this in the sphere of fire, (Fig. I-A). The sphere of fire is in space. From the lowest state of matter, that is, from the solid-solid state on the physical plane of the physical world of the sphere of earth to the highest matter, that is, the sphere of fire, all are connected with the next higher state of matter through their unmanifested sides. The manifested sides of the planes, worlds and spheres exist in their unmanifested sides, and space is related with them through these.

Space is Substance, always unmanifested, without differences, the same throughout, without change. When it manifests, that of it which is manifested becomes fire as the fire sphere, and so becomes matter and divides into units. The earth does not float or move in space, it moves in matter, in a mass of geogen units which is interpenetrated by fluogen, aerogen and pyrogen masses. Space is not a thing, but all things exist because of it and in it. From the viewpoint of space all the spheres, all that is manifested in them, all is seen as illusion, as unreal. Space is through all these unrealities. They exist because they are in space.

Space is not in human thought, therefore there is no name for it in the language, but it may be approached in thought by thinking on a symbol. The symbol is a circle divided by a horizontal diameter. The diameter is the point extending into a line, which distinguishes ever unmanifested space from the manifestations in the spheres below. In them matter manifests until it passes again into the unmanifested, and ultimately becomes Consciousness. Then the point has become the circle.

CHAPTER XIV

THE CIRCLE OR ZODIAC

SECTION 1

Geometrical symbols. The Circle with the Twelve Nameless Points. The value of the zodiacal symbol.

A symbol is a visible object which is used to represent an invisible subject for thought. The purpose of a symbol is to cause thinking on the invisible subject of which it is the sign. Usually symbols are material things which connect thinking with abstractions or qualities made familiar by everyday life, such as scales for justice.

Geometrical symbols are not such material things. Points, the circle, straight lines, curves, horizontals, perpendiculars, opposites, angles and combinations of some of these, are geometrical symbols because they are figures which have no properties except those arising from extension and difference of situation. They are not pictorial. But they give something about which one can think easily, and which connects him with an abstract subject, such as the Triune Self, with which he is not familiar, but with which the symbols form links. They free thinking from sensuous objects. Therefore they are the best things for use in representing qualities and relations apart from objects. They can be used as typical of nature or of the Triune Self. Geometrical symbols are to be distinguished from other symbols in that they typify not only material things, but that which is beyond the corporeal. Geometrical symbols are representations of the coming of the units of nature into form and solidity and of the progress of the doer, through materiality to knowledge of Self, and into being conscious within and beyond time and space.

One of the values of a geometrical symbol, as compared with other symbols, is the greater directness, accuracy and completeness with which it represents that which cannot be expressed in words. A symbol such as a human figure, a tree, a flag or a flame, may suggest many things, yet they all relate to physical acts, objects or events. But a geometrical symbol reaches further on, to other planes of the physical world and to other worlds.

Geometrical symbols not only represent the essentials, but are more than a mere representation. They have something of the essence, the reality, of that which they symbolize, because geometrical symbols have a relation to the circle and because every being has a relation to the circle, which may be expressed by a geometrical symbol.

Geometrical symbols are mental and so are above and more potent than symbols which are physical objects such as a crown, a halo or scales. They themselves are of the essence of what on the physical plane are abstractions, and so they may guide thinking up to the sources of the symbols. They derive their meaning and their value from their relation to the twelve points of the circle. The method of using geometrical symbols is to relate them to points on the circle, which then give them their meaning.

So "horizontals", (Fig. VII-D,a), are straight lines which relate in orderly sequence certain units on the nature-side of the manifested half with each other and with corresponding units on the intelligent-side. There are four horizontals in each sphere and in each world. In the physical world the horizontals represent planes: the light, life, form and physical planes, and on the physical plane the horizontals represent the four states of matter there.

The "perpendiculars", (Fig. VII-D,b), are straight lines which relate vertically certain points in the unmanifested with the corresponding points in the manifested. The perpendiculars are the lines which show how units become conscious, so that the units can be related by horizontals according to the degree in which they are conscious. The perpendiculars show the points in the manifested to correspond with the points in the unmanifested. There are five perpendiculars,—two on the nature-side, two on the intelligent-side and one dividing nature and the intelligent.

The "opposites", (Fig. VII-D,c), are straight lines running through the center of the circle and connecting opposite points. There are six opposites. They relate the manifested to the unmanifested as opposites, the nature-side with the super-intelligent-side and the intelligent-side with the super-nature-side.

The circle with its twelve points on the circumference, (Fig. VII-B), is the origin, the sum and the greatest of all geometrical symbols. Man and the Universe are related to and can only be understood by their relation to the circle with the twelve points on the circumference.

The circle with the twelve points on the circumference is a figure which enables one to see at least a symbol of that which is incomprehensible to the human. This symbol is a figure, a diagram which represents relations. It illustrates visibly invisible relations, bearings and connections. It shows correlations and analogies. The circle has no physical existence, neither have these points. The circle with twelve points is not any or all of the relations, bearings or analogies which it demonstrates. It is not and it does not show a picture of the things of which it demonstrates relations. It does not represent matter, forces or beings. It is a diagram on which the twelve points can be used to distinguish, to measure and to prefigure relations, by degrees in which matter is conscious.

The figure of the circle with its twelve points reveals, explains and proves the arrangement and constitution of the Universe, and the place of everything in it. This includes the unmanifested as well as the manifested parts. It applies to every kind of matter, force and thing in the manifested Universe, from a primordial unit of the fire to the Supreme Intelligence. This symbol shows therefore the make-up and the true position of a human being in relation to everything above and below and inside and outside. It shows the human being to be the pivot, the fulcrum, the balance wheel and the microcosm of the temporal human world.

The symbol of the circle with twelve points reveals, explains and proves the ultimate purpose of the Universe. That purpose is to have Substance become Consciousness. Unmanifested Substance manifests as units of matter. A unit of matter progresses in being conscious in various degrees until it is conscious as its function as a unit in a body, such as a cell, or is conscious as a Triune Self, or as an Intelligence; and then it ceases to be matter and becomes Conscious Sameness, from which state it goes on until it becomes Consciousness. The stages of progression through which every being must pass in its travel towards the ultimate purpose indicates the purpose.

This symbol is like a clock which ticks off the progress of everything from a fire unit to an Intelligence. It gives the calendar and the history of the Universe and of the lesser universe and its changes, and it prefigures the future. As to the doer in the human, the circle with the twelve points shows its past and marks its future and its limitations and possibilities at any time. It also shows the stages through which the body, which is prepared for the housing of the doer, passes.

The symbol reveals how a mind works in its efforts to focus the Light, before a human can think. The symbol shows how it works from the center of the circle along the matter line to the circumference and then fills out standard angles until a quarter circle is filled out and a thought is so made ready for exteriorization, (Fig. IV-A). The symbol shows how nature, through the four senses, controls human thinking, how human thinking is done on the life plane of the physical world according to dimensions of matter on the physical plane, and how analogous limitations to thinking are encountered in other worlds. The symbol reveals all these things and many others because it enables a human to understand these revelations by thinking along the lines of the diagram.

The twelve points on the circle are marvelous, the most far reaching and the most powerful of symbols. They give much incidental information on various subjects. The moving power of words is on the form and the life planes of the physical world, but the lines of this symbol lead through all worlds and spheres. The symbol is stamped on everything, but the human head, being the highest thing in the physical world, expresses it visibly. The head approximates a sphere. The half above the eyes represents the unmanifested Universe, and the seven openings on four planes correspond to the seven points in the manifested Universe. The symbol is stamped also on the human body as a whole. When the doer was in its perfect body, (Fig. VI-D), the circle began at the head—which is the point—and extended along the front of the body to the crotch and back along the spine to the head. But because of the changed state of the doer, the circle is now broken at the sternum, and the three brains which once functioned in the three sections of the torso, are scattered, or transformed into organs.

Because of the importance of the circle with the twelve points as a symbol through which man can come into contact with a knowledge he has lost, the great symbol has been preserved for human beings in all ages.

The twelve points are abstract and the circle is abstract. None of them has a name. However names are needed to distinguish and characterize the twelve points. The names of the twelve signs of the zodiac, (Fig. VII-A), answer the purpose of marking the twelve points on the circumference of the circle. The signs have of course something of the meaning of the points, transferred to the physical plane.

The doer is related to the twelve points because it has in it the presences of them. Each of the twelve portions of the doer is related to one of the twelve points. Each of the twelve points is always represented on the physical plane by the re-existing portion of the doer in a human body. The millions of successively re-existing portions in their human bodies impress on the transient units passing through, the influence of the point to which that portion is related and to which the units respond. The human body, too, bears signs of its connection with the twelve points. All nature from the least unit to the macrocosm has a relation, potential or actual, to the twelve points. The symbol has always had a strong influence on the doers of men. They cannot get away from it. Their whole life is under its order.

Therefore, they have arranged star groups so as to present to the fancy twelve animals or humans in the heavens on the ecliptic, the path of the sun. Therefore, the months and the seasons of the years, the solstices and equinoxes and the festivals connected with them have been used to keep alive the great symbol. Sowing and harvesting and the works and feasts of husbandry remind man of the zodiac. It was and is connected with nearly every religion, cult and mystery. Stories of the adventures of the personified sun, in twelve or some of the twelve places on its annual path, have been woven into religious myths and dramas. The zodiac in the human body has been preserved in sculpture, architecture and pictures, from ancient records to modern almanacs. The physical basis for the names and shapes of the twelve constellations has been different with different peoples in different ages. The zodiacal stories and rites have changed accordingly, but through all variations the idea of the circle with the twelve points has been preserved.

The value of the zodiacal symbol consists not only in the knowledge which it offers eventually, but in the certainty of the information which it gives and which will lead to that knowledge. The twelve zodiacal marks are, like an alphabet, the elements of a language which surpasses in accuracy any language of science and of religion, and with which philosophical jargon cannot be compared. The twelve points for which the twelve names stand are the principles of a science as certain as mathematics. To get the information which the zodiacal figure can give, one must think about it. Nothing else will do, because the circle of twelve signs shows nothing in a pictorial way. It shows only relations between the things which are the subjects of thought. But if one begins to think about the zodiacal figure he will be compelled by that figure and the relative position of the signs to think logically and inescapably along the lines that lead to knowledge concerning the value, principle, nature, type and power of the subject of his thinking.

An approximate meaning may be assigned to the twelve abstract, nameless points. Words merely introduce; thinking about the points establishes familiarity; and this leads to an ever better understanding of the points. These points, though nameless, are for convenience sake called by the names of the twelve signs. The signs are given the meaning they have for a human, that is, at the cross-section at which the average human stands, and this meaning is rendered in English words.

However, it is to be remembered that the twelve points themselves are abstract and nameless and can be conceived only according to the degree in which the particular human who thinks of them, is conscious. The following statements about the twelve zodiacal signs are not about the twelve constellations which are only stars, that is, matter on the border between the solid-solid matter on the form plane and the radiant-solid layer of matter on the physical plane of the physical world, and visible while at certain focal positions in the earth's atmosphere. The statements are made concerning the twelve abstract points. These points, though they may be called by the names of the zodiacal signs, are themselves abstract and nameless. The zodiacal signs are symbols for them. The zodiac here spoken of does not consist merely of the star clusters of astrology or astronomy.

SECTION 2

What the zodiac and its twelve points symbolize.

The circle represents a whole, a oneness. It represents all there is, space, time, beings, events and all this as one, as a whole, as inseparable. No part of this whole can be dispensed with, any more than can a part of a circle. This whole has twelve aspects, behind which stand what are here called twelve abstract points, which when symbolized show relations and progression within the whole. And all are related to Consciousness.

Consciousness is not a being, or a thing, or a state, (Fig. VII-A). All beings, things and states which exist, exist because of the presence of Consciousness in them. It is not space, or time, or matter, or force, or any God. It is independent of all these, but they and everything else depend upon Consciousness. It cannot be changed, qualified, affected, divided, destroyed, improved, weighed or measured. There are no degrees of Consciousness. It has no attributes, no properties, no qualities, no states. It has no limitations, no beginning, no end. It is present everywhere and in everything. By its presence everything is conscious and everything changes from the degree in which the being or thing is conscious to the next higher degree in being conscious. Consciousness is ever unmanifested.

Taurus or Motion symbolizes the nameless point which is a presence, and the presence of which makes possible all departures from super-nature, and activity and movement in nature. The presence of Motion is the cause of movement in matter; it does not move things directly because it is not matter, but it is within or behind matter and its presence causes the impulse or drive in nature.

Gemini or Substance symbolizes the nameless point which is a presence, and by the presence of which Substance is as it is and has the potentiality of becoming matter. Substance is space, homogeneous, the same throughout. It has no dimension, no extension, no push, no pull. Yet it supports, contains, is in and through all matter as is the ocean in and through a sponge; in it all matter appears and vanishes, as a cloud does in the air. It is a point, a blank, no thing, to human perception. Out of it comes all matter. It has one potential attribute and that is duality. Through that potentiality it manifests and thereby issues as matter. This matter becomes part of the manifested and unmanifested states of the Universe.

Cancer or Breath symbolizes the nameless point which is a presence, and by the presence of which Substance becomes the units of fire and the element fire as a whole, and the unmanifested can become manifested. Breath or fire is activity as the beginning and the end of all matter. It is the pervasiveness in and the permanence of the Universe or macrocosm. It is the stage in which matter coming out of Substance first appears as a manifestation. With it super-nature ceases and manifestation of Substance as nature comes or continues, and nature manifests as fire units, as indivisible primordial units and through and beyond nature as units developed to ultimate completeness. The idea of oneness is with Breath; for all the units begin as fire and, as units, end as fire. Every being in the manifested Universe is born and borne by Breath, is maintained by Breath, and remains in Breath.

Leo or Life symbolizes the nameless point which is a presence, and which presence is behind the units of air and the element air as a whole. By its presence activity is turned into growth, throughout nature. Life or air is the principle of combination and growth. Its presence causes the active side of matter to energize and change the passive side and to combine and to grow. But it preserves nevertheless the pervasiveness and permanence of all-containing, all-pervasive Breath. By Life, the carrier of Breath, is kept up all life and activity.

Virgo or Form symbolizes the nameless point which is a presence, and which is behind the units of water and the element water as a whole. By its presence the units of water function as form. Form is the principle by which the activities of mass and life are held within definite bounds. Virgo or Form restricts combination and confines growth. Virgo or Form is the carrier of life, controls it, holds and circumscribes it. It causes the passive side of matter to bound, preserve and hold the active side.

Libra or Sex symbolizes a presence, the presence behind the units of earth and the element earth as a whole. Sex is not the sexes. Sex is not maleness and femaleness showing themselves in matter so that the active and passive sides of matter are different. Sex is balance, equality, undivided and indivisible, whereas maleness and femaleness are each the same in the other. Sex is the balancing and the balance. Sex is the aia, the outcome from the earth, which stimulates the breath of the breath-form, so that the form of the breath-form is revivified; and the form of the breath-form clothes itself in physical matter and reappears as a male body or as a female body. Sex as the aia is the means by which the sexes are separated, united, and adjusted and balanced. By the presence of the nameless point symbolized by Libra or Sex, the units of a human body now functioning as active or as passive can each have its active side and its passive side made equal to each other, so that a human body composed of such units will not be a male body or a female body. The sexes in such bodies will then have disappeared, they will have been changed into bodies of perfect equilibrium and balance, bodies in which change has given place to permanence as immortal physical bodies. A doer in such a body, while carrying on its own work, trains each of the nature units connected with it to function as perfect balance. Libra marks the limit of nature, that is, the limit of the progression of matter in nature. Matter cannot progress any further in nature. The laws applicable to nature-matter do not apply to matter that has passed the Libra point of balance, and has thus become intelligent-matter.

Scorpio or Desire symbolizes the nameless point which is a presence, and which presence is behind the desire of every doer and of every Intelligence. By its presence each embodied doer portion, as it wills, makes itself a slave to its body of nature and remains ignorant of its slavery; or, it may become conscious of its slavery and desire freedom, but still let nature rule it through other of its desires; or, it may decide to and actually engage in the work for freedom; and, it may continue in the work until it is conscious of itself as feeling and as desire and achieves union of its feeling-and-desire.

Sagittary or Thought symbolizes the nameless point which is a presence. By its presence law and justice are kept among all Triune Selves and among all Intelligences. By its presence each aspect of each doer has the Light it is entitled to by its thinking. By its presence reason administers to its embodied doer portion without hindrance what that human has made its destiny, and assists in bringing about the destiny of other embodied doer portions to which its own embodied doer portion is related. Its presence causes matter of the spheres to mingle and to combine with matter of the worlds, and causes this matter to be raised, lowered, accelerated, retarded, limited and extended. All this is done according to the capacities of the one, such as a human being, a Triune Self or an Intelligence, who operates the matter by thinking.

Capricorn or Self-knowledge symbolizes the nameless point which is a presence, and which presence is behind the identity and the knowledge of all Triune Selves and of all Intelligences. Its presence sets the sphere of earth as the limit of the knowledge of nature to which Triune Selves can go, and sets the sphere of fire as the limit of nature, to which Intelligences can go. Its presence is the link or relation between the intelligent-side and the super-intelligent-side of the Universe. By its presence the knowledge of every Triune Self is common to all Triune Selves, and the knowledge of every Intelligence is common to all Intelligences. Intelligence is that which gives indivisibility, permanence, distinctiveness, identity, responsibility and completeness to matter. Matter having these qualities has reached the stage of perfection as intelligent-matter. Such matter is ready to become Conscious Sameness.

Aquarius or Conscious Sameness symbolizes the nameless point which is a presence. Conscious Sameness is ever unmanifested. Like Substance, it is homogeneous; but Sameness is conscious throughout, which Substance is not. It is the unity through duality, diversity and separateness. By the presence of the nameless point which it symbolizes,

Sameness is the all-conscious unity as a whole throughout the units of nature, of Triune Selves, and of Intelligences. By its presence, Intelligences, which pass beyond the highest development as units, cease being separate units without losing their identity as individuals. By its presence Intelligences can do this by extending their singleness and separateness into and as unity in the wholeness of Conscious Sameness.

Pisces or Abstract Will is Pure Intelligence and symbolizes the nameless point which is a presence. By its presence, Conscious Sameness becomes Abstract Will or Pure Intelligence, which is unmanifested, unattached and unattachable, and therefore free. It is next to the last step in the plan: by which super-nature becomes nature, as nature units; by which nature units become aia units; by which aia units become Triune Self units; by which these units become Intelligence units; by which Intelligence units become Conscious Sameness; by which Conscious Sameness becomes Pure Intelligence; and, by which Pure Intelligence becomes Consciousness, when it wills to be Consciousness. Will as Pure Intelligence is not power, but it is the source of power, according to the capacities and the abilities of Triune Selves and of Intelligences to use their power.

Aries or Consciousness symbolizes the nameless point which is a presence and which represents Consciousness. The nameless point as a presence is not Consciousness but it represents Consciousness. By its presence are made all beginnings and all ends, if the passage through states in the order of progression can be called beginnings and ends. By its presence super-nature and super-Intelligence are united and completed. By its presence as passage, in the last step of becoming, Pure Intelligence becomes Consciousness when it wills to be Consciousness.

Thus is carried out the purpose of the Universe: that everything continues to progress in being conscious in ever higher degrees; and, that this purpose is accomplished, step by step or stage by stage, according to the plan: the presences of the Twelve Nameless Points. The twelve may be called steps, causes, degrees, states, stages, or by other terms, but they are the presences in the circular ladder from super-nature to the nature unit, to the aia unit, to the Triune Self unit, to the Intelligence unit, to the Sameness of all, to the Intelligence of all, to the presence representing Consciousness, and finally to the one and ultimate reality:—CONSCIOUSNESS.

This figure of the circle with the twelve points is in itself nameless and is not treated at length, but the names given to symbolize the twelve nameless points indicate something of the meaning they have for human beings on the physical plane. The reason is that each of the twelve portions of the doer of a Triune Self corresponds to one of the Twelve Nameless Points on the Nameless Circle. Therefore it is possible for a doer portion in a human to become conscious of Consciousness and of all there is in and beyond the Universe.

In the Circle of the Twelve Nameless Points a horizontal diameter would divide the abstract circle into an upper and a lower part. In the lower part are the points which, if they had names, would be cancer, leo, virgo, libra, scorpio, sagittary and capricorn.

The origin of Substance, symbolizing one of the nameless points on the abstract circle, cannot be explained. Thinking may carry one to Substance, but no farther.

Substance issues as matter, that is, it becomes manifest, when taurus, Motion, and cancer, Breath, affect it. Consciousness does not act, but by the presence of Consciousness, taurus and cancer act on Substance. Then there is an issue from Substance, at cancer; this issue becomes units of the fire sphere; their number is equivalent to the number of nature units that become intelligent units, and of the Intelligence units that become Conscious Sameness. Thus is maintained the constant unit number, the Oneness, in the manifested Universe. This Universe is the sphere of fire, and is symbolized by the first zodiacal figure, (Fig. VII-B). This is a circle with the twelve points marked by the signs of the zodiac. This circle is so drawn in the lower half of the abstract circle, that its aries point is at the center of the abstract circle and its libra point coincides with the libra point of the abstract circle. This circle is itself symbolized by the point cancer. A horizontal line drawn in this circle from cancer to capricorn divides the circle into an unmanifested part in which are capricorn, aquarius, pisces, aries, taurus, gemini and cancer, and a manifested part in which are cancer, leo, virgo, libra, scorpio, sagittary and capricorn. Cancer and capricorn are connected both with the unmanifested and with the manifested, because they are the gates on the dividing line, where matter begins and where matter ends. When a unit of matter passes the capricorn gate and becomes unmanifested at aquarius, an equivalent of Substance, gemini, passes the cancer gate and becomes manifest as matter; compensation, something for something. A corresponding action takes place in all the spheres, worlds, planes and beings down to the lowest cell.

In the lower half of this zodiac of cancer is symbolized the zodiac of the sphere of air, which is itself a circle with the twelve points and is symbolized by the point leo. The leo zodiac, which is the second zodiacal figure, has its aries point at the center of the zodiac of the fire sphere and its libra point coinciding with the libra point of the zodiac of the fire sphere. In the lower half of the leo zodiac is the third zodiac, or sphere of water. It is symbolized by virgo and has its aries point at the center of the zodiac of the air sphere and its libra point coinciding with the libra point of the zodiac of the air sphere. Finally, in the lower half of the third or virgo zodiac is a fourth circle, the zodiac of the earth sphere symbolized by libra, with its aries point in the center of the third or virgo zodiac and its libra point coinciding with the libra point of the third zodiac and of the second and the first zodiacs.

The sphere of earth or of libra is the universe for Triune Selves. The highest conception of God as the Supreme Intelligence, omnipresent, omniscient and omnipotent, relates to him as the Supreme Intelligence of the earth sphere. The portions of doers in human bodies do not in life or after death go beyond the human physical world. Doers in perfected bodies are limited to the worlds in the earth sphere. Only when as Triune Selves they become Intelligences can they go into the three other spheres of virgo, leo and cancer.

The sphere of earth, symbolized by the libra or fourth zodiac, has four worlds, the light, life, form and physical worlds. These worlds are symbolized by four further zodiacal figures within the libra zodiac which stands for the sphere of earth, arranged in such a manner that the aries point of the light world is at the center of the sphere of earth, the aries point of the life world is at the center of the light world, the aries point of the form world is at the center of the life world and the aries point of the physical world is at the center of the form world, and the libra points of all these worlds coincide with the libra points of the zodiacs of the spheres. All eight zodiacal figures are divided into an unmanifested and a manifested part, by a line drawn from cancer to capricorn of each. The manifested side of the physical world is divided by planes, which are lines from cancer to capricorn, the light plane; from leo to sagittary, the life plane; and from virgo to scorpio, the form plane, libra being the physical plane of all zodiacs.

In each of the four worlds of cancer, leo, virgo, and libra, of the earth sphere, are four planes of matter, and on each plane are states of matter. This holds good for the permanent physical world or Realm of Permanence, and as well for the human world of change, (Fig. V-B,a). It should be remembered that this book deals with the human, and that, when the physical world is spoken of, the temporal human world is meant, and not the permanent physical world or Realm of Permanence, unless it is so stated. The bodies, possessions and interests of the human are in the four subdivisions of the solid or libra state of matter on the libra plane of the libra world. Humans do not go beyond the fourth or last state of matter on that plane, that is, the geo-geogen, fluo-geogen, aero-geogen and pyro-geogen states.

Each sphere, world, plane and state of matter is four stages removed from that above it. The sphere of air is thus four stages away from the sphere of fire; the sphere of water is four stages from the sphere of air and the sphere of earth is four stages from the sphere of water. It is so with the worlds, planes, states of matter and their substates. The world in which human beings live, which is made up of the solid-solid, fluid-solid, airy-solid and radiant-solid substates of matter, is made up of matter, the substates of which are all four stages away from each other. Thus the solid-solid substate is separated by four unmanifested stages from the fluid-solid, and that by similar four unmanifested stages from the airy-solid, and that by four unmanifested stages from the radiant-solid, and that by four unmanifested stages from the fluid state.

The four stages are, in every case from the spheres, the worlds, the planes to the lowest subdivisions of the solid state on the physical plane, the unmanifested part or side of that which becomes the manifested part of the sphere, world, plane, state and substate. The four stages are always, as shown by the zodiacal symbol, stages represented by the signs aries, taurus-pisces, gemini-aquarius and cancer-capricorn. The unmanifested four stages are present throughout the manifested stages.

The circle symbolizing the sphere of libra or earth is divided by a line from aries to libra into two parts. On the cancer side is matter which is merely conscious, called nature-matter; on the capricorn side is matter that is conscious that it is conscious, and is called intelligent-matter. The human body is on the nature-side of this dividing line, where nature-matter meets intelligent-matter. The human body is the common ground for both. Nature-matter is by means of fire, cancer, in each of the worlds kept circulating through the worlds, and the human body is the libra point for all matter that circulates. The degrees of nature-matter outside of a human body are cancer, leo, virgo and libra units, here called fire, air, water and earth units of the physical plane, and inside of a human body, cancer, leo, virgo and libra units, here called breath, life, form and cell units.

When a unit of nature-matter becomes a unit of intelligent-matter, it is still a unit of matter but the laws of nature-matter are no longer applicable to it. It is a Triune Self in the Realm of Permanence. But the doer of a Triune Self in the world of change, lives periodically in human bodies. The human doer has its four senses, the sense of sight, cancer; of hearing, leo; of tasting, virgo; and of smelling, libra. The three parts of the Triune Self are, the doer, scorpio; the thinker, sagittary; and the knower, capricorn. The aia, represented by the breath-form, is the dividing line from aries to libra of the physical body, dividing the parts of the Triune Self from the senses, and is the libra of the Triune Self.

In this manner does the circle, which is in every thing from the greatest to the smallest, reveal its nature. The doer, the thinker and the knower, are shown in their true relation by the zodiacal figure. The superior One of the Triune Self is its Intelligence, within the sphere of which the Triune Self always is. The zodiac shows the Intelligence to be of three spheres, (Fig. V-C), just as the Triune Self is of three worlds. The zodiac further shows the relation of the three Orders of Intelligences, the Desirers, the Thinkers, and the Knowers. The nature gods which the embodied doer portions worship are likewise shown in their true relation as fire, air, water, and earth, or cancer, leo, virgo, and libra entities, called by different names, according to the language of the worshipers.

The zodiac reveals that every sphere, world, plane and being has an unmanifested and a manifested part. The unmanifested is that in which are the things which the manifested may become or which it may bring forth. There is that of the unmanifested which does not become manifested, but is always in and through and remains unmanifested. The manifested is that which has come out of the unmanifested. That of the unmanifested which is in the manifested is that by which the manifested may change from what it is into what it is to become. The unmanifested is that by which the manifested may again become unmanifested. It does not do anything with the manifested, but because it is in and through it the manifested works with itself and changes. The unmanifested contains potencies which become actual when the manifested liberates and makes them so. The manifested is manifested in two ways, one active as spirit or force and one passive as matter; and because of the unmanifested being in and through them it may be said that they act and react upon each other, and changes are brought about in the active and in the passive. Thus the manifested progresses until it becomes again the unmanifested, but conscious in a higher degree than when it ceased to be unmanifested.

Pisces, aries and taurus are not manifested. This is true of all zodiacs. Gemini manifests in part through cancer; and aquarius is the means by which that which has passed through manifestation progresses into the unmanifested.

SECTION 3

The zodiac related to the human body; to the Triune Self; to the Intelligence.

The zodiacal figure shows that man in his physical body is the microcosm of the macrocosm, that is, of the Universe or sphere of fire and of all that is in it.

The parts of a human body are related to and connected with the signs of the zodiac, it being always understood that the points are meant and not the constellations on the ecliptic.

The head is related to aries, (Fig. VII-A). Aries, Consciousness, contains all, in the sense that it is throughout all. Language is inadequate to express this idea, because language is made to express thoughts that deal with the kind of matter that is at most one-dimensional or surface matter of the physical world. The head or sphere or circle is one, and it contains all. Out of it all things in the body come. The head represents the manifested and the unmanifested. The unmanifested signs capricorn, aquarius, pisces, aries, taurus, gemini and cancer are in the upper half, while the manifested signs cancer, leo, virgo, libra, scorpio, sagittary and capricorn are represented in the lower half by the seven openings in the head. By emanation or extension, in the torso, the chest shows the upper, unmanifested, half of the circle, while the pelvis shows the lower half.

The head is represented throughout the torso and in it are the types from which the torso is built in its three sections. The brain is represented in the thorax by the lungs and heart; in the abdominal section by the kidneys and adrenals, and in the pelvic region by the prostate and the womb, and the male organ and the vagina. All specialized organs in the head have their counterparts in the thorax, abdomen and pelvis. Everything starts from the head: the food that is eaten and maintains the body, the things that are seen, heard, tasted and smelled and so act on the body, breathing and voluntary muscular actions—everything starts from the head.

The neck or throat is related to taurus. It is the first departure from the head. Through it come the impulses that cause the movements of the body.

The shoulders and arms are related to gemini. They have no internal organs, take no part in the internal action of the body, but when they act, their potential power and duality, as represented by the hands, work civilization into being.

The breasts are related to cancer. Because of the breath all elements can come into the body. Breath starts life; by it all things are sustained and kept in activity.

The heart is related to leo. Through the heart the blood which is the life carrier, is sent forth, to build new tissue and cause life and growth.

The womb and prostate are the representatives of virgo. They mold the seeds of life into form.

The parts of the body where the sex openings are, are related to libra. There the gender is apparent, there the male and female unite. There is the center of human interest. There is the gate through which breath, life and form pass down and out into the temporal human world, or along which they pass on and up into the spine to eternal life.

The male organ and the clitoris are the representatives of virgo and of scorpio. They are acted on by, and react to, the pull of nature to procreate.

The terminal filament is related to sagittary. At present it is not used by the doer as the path of desire to the thinker.

The spinal cord opposite the heart is related to capricorn. At present it is not used for the purposes of the Triune Self.

The spinal cord between the shoulders is related to aquarius. At present it is not used for purposes of the Triune Self.

The spinal cord at the cervical vertebrae is related to pisces. At present it is not used for the purposes of the Triune Self.

Thus all the twelve points, the manifested as well as the unmanifested, are represented in a human body, which is thus a Universe in miniature or model universe.

The Triune Self also is constituted as the pattern of the zodiac, but the manifested signs only are notably represented in the make-up of the Triune Self and its servants, and in the Universe in which it lives. The signs are cancer, represented by the sense of sight; leo, by the sense of hearing; virgo, by the sense of taste; and libra, by the sense of smell. All of these are on the nature-side, but are also servants of the Triune Self:

scorpio is represented by the doer; sagittary, by the thinker; and capricorn, by the knower. The matter of which these four senses and the three parts of the Triune Self are, is more directly in contact with the points for which the zodiacal signs stand, than is the transient matter in the bodily parts.

The unit which is the sense of sight, is a fire, cancer, unit, and is the channel through which all fire or cancer matter of varying degrees, flows into and out of the generative system and through that into the body. The sense of sight, cancer, is by its nature directly related to the cancer sides of the light or cancer-capricorn planes of the four worlds, and particularly to the matter of the light or cancer world. So it is with the other three senses which are similar channels and are respectively related to the leo side of the leo-sagittary planes and to the leo world, or to the virgo side of the virgo-scorpio planes and to the virgo world or to the libra point of the libra planes and to the libra world.

The unit which is the Triune Self is a capricorn One of the light or cancer world of the earth sphere, and is intelligent-matter. The doer of the Triune Self is in the form or virgo world of the earth sphere and is scorpio matter. The thinker is in the life or leo world and is sagittary matter, and the knower is in the light or cancer world and is capricorn matter.

The knower or capricorn part of the Triune Self is the channel through which clear Light coming from the Intelligence and ultimately from the abstract point which, if named, would be the presence symbolized by capricorn, flows into the noetic or capricorn atmosphere and thence goes into nature, libra; and through which Light that is reclaimed from nature returns to the Intelligence, whose Light it is, and thence to the point which, if named, would be symbolized by capricorn. The knower is by its nature directly related to the capricorn sides of the light or cancer-capricorn planes of the four worlds. The thinker or sagittary part is the channel through which diffused Light in contact with the abstract point which, if designated, would be symbolized by sagittary, flows into the mental or sagittary atmosphere under the presence of the abstract point and thereby through thinking goes into nature, libra; and through which reclaimed Light goes into the mental atmosphere under the nameless point designated as sagittary. The doer or scorpio part is the channel through which desire from the presence of the abstract point which, if designated, would be symbolized by scorpio, flows into the psychic or scorpio atmosphere, and thence, when mixed with Light, goes into nature; and through which desire returns to its source in the abstract point which, if named, would be the scorpio point of the abstract circle. The thinker and doer are respectively related to the sagittary and scorpio sides of the leo-sagittary and virgo-scorpio planes and to the life and form worlds.

The four cancer, leo, virgo and libra senses act through the four systems, the cancer, leo, virgo and libra systems, by means of which they circulate nature-matter, each sense focussing from and into its respective sign in the planes and worlds. Correspondingly, the doer, thinker and knower, scorpio, sagittary and capricorn, act through the scorpio, sagittary and capricorn atmospheres which are in the psychic atmosphere of the human, each part focussing respectively scorpio, sagittary and capricorn matter from and into the respective sign on the intelligent-side of the planes and in the worlds. The four, or cancer, leo, virgo and libra, systems in the body correspond to the four atmospheres. This is so notwithstanding that there are only three parts and three atmospheres of the Triune Self. The Triune Self is related to nature by the aia, by means of the breath-form. The breath-form is the last and most progressed unit of nature, the living form or "living soul" of the body. The breath of the breath-form, its active side, is that which relates the aia with the Triune Self and with nature. The breath-form is the active point or line from the aia, from aries to libra in the physical or libra world, which divides as well as connects nature and the Triune Self. The breath-form as breath is the fourfold physical breath, and through that flow the scorpio, sagittary and capricorn breaths which are the active sides of the three atmospheres of the Triune Self, which are through the psychic atmosphere. The sense of smell is also the physical or libra breath in breathing. One does not smell without breathing. The generative or cancer, the respiratory or leo, and the circulatory or virgo breaths of the libra breath, all have to connect with the digestive or earth breath of the libra breath, to reach the receptivity or form aspect of the breath-form, and thence to reach the doer. The correspondence between the senses of sight, cancer, hearing, leo, and tasting, virgo, on the one side, and the knower, capricorn, the thinker, sagittary, and the doer, scorpio, on the other side of the same planes is obvious, and the correspondence of the sense of smell with the breath of the breath-form is equally obvious as both are in libra. The four cancer, leo, virgo and libra systems on the nature-side correspond to the capricorn, sagittary, scorpio and libra atmospheres on the intelligent-side.

The zodiacal figure shows other relations, those of the active and passive sides of the three parts of the Triune Self; the knower, itself capricorn, has two sides, I-ness, cancer, and selfness, capricorn; the thinker, itself sagittary, has the sides of rightness, leo, and reason, sagittary; and the doer, itself scorpio, has a passive side, feeling, virgo, and an active side, desire, scorpio. These passive sides, cancer, leo and virgo, of the parts of the Triune Self, capricorn, sagittary and scorpio, are related to the active sides, capricorn, sagittary and scorpio, of the respective senses, cancer, leo and virgo; and the active sides, capricorn, sagittary and scorpio, of the parts of the Triune Self, capricorn, sagittary and scorpio, are related to the passive sides, cancer, leo and virgo, of the senses, cancer, leo and virgo, through those parts of their atmospheres which are in the psychic atmosphere. Each atmosphere of the Triune Self may be symbolized by a zodiacal figure and has twelve aspects which it manifests through the part to which it belongs.

From a zodiacal figure can be seen the relation of the atmospheres of the Triune Self to the worlds in which they are, (Fig. V-B). The psychic atmosphere, scorpio, is in the form or virgo world; the mental atmosphere, sagittary, is in the life or leo world; and the noetic atmosphere, capricorn, is in the light or cancer world, by the portions of these atmospheres which are in the psychic atmosphere. An atmosphere and the world in which it is, are related. For instance, the feelings and desires of a psychic atmosphere and the elementals in the form world, are similar, because they have the same tendencies, namely for sensation and emotion; that which puts them into relation is the similarity of the tendencies. So, generally, that which relates is the similarity between the things in the world and the qualities of the atmosphere. Because of their relation the three atmospheres and the three worlds are in touch and affect each other, and they do this by means of the breath-form.

The atmospheres may, according to their fineness and power, interpenetrate any part of their worlds. A psychic atmosphere may be in, may affect or may be affected by, any part of the form world. A psychic atmosphere may reach a very limited or a considerable part of the form world or it may reach or fill the whole of it. The terms reaching and filling are figurative, because the Triune Self is of a matter to which the terms and laws of nature-matter cannot apply. So it is with the other atmospheres in regard to their worlds. Let it be understood that when it is stated that the atmospheres of the Triune Self work on the worlds and that the worlds work on the atmospheres of the Triune Self, these do not act on each other directly. The parts of the noetic and mental atmospheres which are in and related to the psychic atmosphere only, can work on or in the corresponding light and life worlds by means of the psychic atmosphere and form world, and this through the physical world by means of the breath of the breath-form and physical body. No part or atmosphere of the Triune Self can act directly on any world. To reach any of the worlds, the thinker and knower and their atmospheres must act through the doer and its atmosphere, and the doer and its atmosphere act through the breath-form and thence through the physical body into any of the worlds.

A zodiacal figure shows this relation. The psychic atmosphere is represented by scorpio in the zodiac of the noetic atmosphere, and the form world by virgo in the zodiac of the light world. The zodiac, that is, the symbol, of the form world is also the zodiac for the psychic atmosphere. In other words, the one zodiac of the form world and of the psychic atmosphere particularizes and shows the relation of the two signs virgo and scorpio of the light world and of the noetic atmosphere. In this zodiac the nature-side works upon the intelligent-side and the intelligent-side upon the nature-side, according to the positiveness or negativeness of these sides to each other. The interaction goes back and forth between corresponding signs, as cancer with capricorn, leo with sagittary and virgo with scorpio, but by way of and passing through libra.

The zodiac shows that in each world are only the signs cancer, leo, virgo and libra, that they are the only signs that indicate the essential qualities of the matter of that world and that all that matter is nature-matter.

The zodiac shows that in each atmosphere are only the signs libra, scorpio, sagittary and capricorn, that they are the only signs that characterize the matter of the atmospheres and that all the matter of the atmospheres is intelligent-matter. The matter of the cancer, leo, virgo and libra types makes up the worlds, and the matter having the scorpio, sagittary and capricorn traits penetrates and, on lines shown by the planes, interacts with the corresponding nature-matter. The zodiac shows that each world is made up of the four elements, and that they are more and more modified as they come towards the physical plane, and that in these elements is intelligent-matter, which gives to the fire, air, water and earth matter the traits of light, life, form and sex; and that the aries-libra line of union and division is the physical body of man and is the breath-form through which the penetration takes place.

The cancer, leo, virgo and libra matter of nature is energized from the corresponding signs on the intelligent-side. When this matter is energized it is made active and acts as force. Applied to the physical plane of the physical world, this means that a pyrogen unit is energized through its potential capricorn point, that an aerogen unit is energized through its potential sagittary point, that a fluogen unit is energized through its potential scorpio point and that a geogen unit is energized through its libra point.

The zodiac presents a means of lining up and so of checking up conceptions; thereby metaphors can be distinguished from the realities which they indicate. So the zodiac shows the relation of the noetic world, which is only a name, to the light world. The noetic world is a capricorn world, that is, the essential qualities are those of capricorn knowers, and it is in the light or cancer world of nature. It is made up of the sum of knowledge of the noetic atmospheres of all knowers. It is not a world in the sense in which the light and the other nature worlds are. A similar relation obtains with regard to the mental world of thought, a sagittary world, and the life or leo world, and the psychic world of desire, a scorpio world, and the form or virgo world.

From the zodiacal signs can be seen that which no words can tell, the relation of the Intelligence to its Triune Self, something about the faculties of an Intelligence and something about the three orders of Intelligences.

As to the relation of an Intelligence to its Triune Self, the Triune Self never leaves the sphere of the Intelligence under whose Light it is. As long as it is a Triune Self it is related to that Intelligence by characteristics which are in a measure the same as those of the Intelligence, that is to say, that the qualities and powers of a Triune Self are potentially akin to those of its Intelligence. The figure of the circle with twelve points shows the connections which the knower has through all the capricorn signs, which the thinker has through all the sagittary signs and which the doer has through all the scorpio signs. Each of the three parts is so connected with the Intelligence by a number of identical signs. For instance, the doer, itself a scorpio part of the Triune Self, is connected through the scorpio points of the mental and noetic atmospheres and of the water and air spheres with the scorpio point of the fire sphere.

The first circle, that of the fire sphere, is the zodiac of the Intelligence; the fifth circle, that of the light world, is that of the Triune Self, and the eighth circle, that of the physical world, is the zodiac of the physical body and of its breath-form. The fourth circle is that of the earth sphere, which stands in a similar relation to the four worlds in it as the abstract circle stands to the four spheres. The first, second and third zodiacs stand for the Intelligence with its three degrees of capricorn, sagittary and scorpio Intelligence; and the fifth, sixth and seventh zodiacs stand for the Triune Self with its three atmospheres of capricorn, sagittary and scorpio.

Both the Intelligence and the Triune Self are capricorn entities, but they are in different zodiacs. The Triune Self is a capricorn unit of the scorpio sign of the zodiac of the Intelligence, which is a capricorn unit of the fire sphere.

The zodiac shows the relation of the Intelligence and its Triune Self to nature. The cancer part of the Intelligence is related to the I-ness, cancer, of the knower, and by means of that to the cancer or passive side of the sense of sight and by means of that to the passive fire element in nature. The capricorn part of the Intelligence is related to the selfness, capricorn, of the knower, and by means of that to the capricorn or active side of the sense of sight and by means of that to the active fire element in nature. The leo part of the Intelligence is related to rightness, leo, of the thinker, and by means of that to the leo or passive side of the sense of hearing and by means of that to the passive side of the air element of nature. The sagittary part of the Intelligence is related to reason, sagittary, of the thinker and by means of that to the sagittary or active side of the sense of hearing and by means of that to the active side of the air element in nature. The virgo part of the Intelligence is related to feeling, virgo, of the doer and by means of that to the virgo or passive side of the sense of taste and by means of that to the passive side of the water element of nature. The scorpio part of the Intelligence is related to the desire, scorpio, of the doer and by means of that to the scorpio or active side of the sense of taste and by means of that to the active side of the water element of nature. The libra part of the Intelligence is the focus of the other six parts or faculties of the Intelligence and is related to the libra aspect or breath-form of the Triune Self and by means of that to the libra aspect, or sense of smell, of nature in a human body.

A zodiacal figure shows how these relations of the Intelligence with nature are maintained. All are maintained by way of the libra point, (Fig. VII-B). So the cancer part of the Intelligence which is related to the I-ness of the knower and by means of that to the cancer side of the sense of sight and by means of that to the passive fire element in nature, cannot get across or communicate on the cancer to capricorn line, but must, when crossing from the intelligent-side to the nature-side, from the knower to the sense of sight, go by way of libra. So it is with all the actions and reactions between the Intelligence and nature. If the action starts in the fire sphere, it cannot reach the sphere of the Intelligence, unless it goes across the libra point in a physical body and across that in the breath-form. Or to give another illustration. If the action starts on the physical plane of the physical world, when an orange is seen the action cannot reach feeling, unless it goes with the generative, cancer; the respiratory, leo; the circulatory, virgo; the digestive, libra, breaths and so with the breath-form to the feeling, virgo, of the doer, scorpio.

It is because of these connections of the Triune Self with the senses, their organs in the body and their elements in outside nature, that one who knows of the alignment shown by the zodiac and who has control of his senses, can create or destroy. No supernatural feat would be impossible to him. Without instruments he could do or have whatever he wanted. He could condense and guide starlight so that the entire heavens would be fire, or be filled with shooting bolts of lightning, or send a rain of lightning to the earth. He could melt mountains into rivers of lava or dissipate them. He could crumble or consume a stronghold as well as a hut. He could by precipitating build a wall or a house, he could produce metals and fabrics. But he would also have the knowledge not to use his powers for foolish ends.

A zodiacal figure shows something about the faculties of an Intelligence, (Fig. V-C). It shows that an Intelligence has a faculty for every sign that is in the manifested side of the zodiac. The light faculty is of cancer, the time faculty of leo, the image faculty of virgo, the focus faculty of libra, the dark faculty of scorpio, the motive faculty of sagittary and the I-am faculty of capricorn. The light faculty acts and reacts with the I-am faculty, the time faculty with the motive faculty, the image faculty with the dark faculty and the focus faculty puts all these faculties into relation with each other and with everything in the Universe.

A zodiac shows the relation of the faculties of an Intelligence to the three parts of its Triune Self. It shows a present potential relation which will become actual when the Triune Self becomes an Intelligence. Then the three parts will become six faculties. Selfness and I-ness, the active and passive sides of the knower, will become the I-am and the light faculties; reason and rightness of the thinker will become the motive and time faculties, and desire and feeling of the doer will be the dark and image faculties and the aia will become the Triune Self or focus faculty.

The zodiacal figure shows the relation of the faculties of an Intelligence to nature, that is, to the four great elements, which are the four spheres of nature. The light, cancer, and I-am, capricorn, faculties are related to the fire sphere; the time, leo, and motive, sagittary, faculties to the air sphere; the image, virgo, and the dark, scorpio, faculties to the water sphere; and the focus, libra, faculty to the earth sphere. These relations are established and maintained below through the Triune Self of the Intelligence and the aia, and above through the Supreme Intelligence of the fire sphere.

The zodiac shows the three orders of Intelligences and their characteristics. They are scorpio Intelligences, sagittary Intelligences, and capricorn Intelligences. These three orders are designated Desirers, Thinkers and Knowers, (Fig. V-C). The dominating faculty of the Desirers are the image, virgo, and the dark, scorpio, faculties and their field of action is the sphere of water, scorpio. The Thinkers are Intelligences of the sphere of air, sagittary; and the time, leo, and the motive, sagittary, faculties dominate in them. The Knowers act in the sphere of fire, capricorn, and their light, cancer, and I-am, capricorn, faculties are dominant in them. The spheres, scorpio, sagittary, capricorn, of an Intelligence are above analogous to the atmospheres, scorpio, sagittary, capricorn, of a Triune Self below, and must not be confused with the spheres, cancer, leo and virgo, on the nature-side. The relation between the spheres of an Intelligence and the spheres of nature is like that of the atmospheres of a Triune Self and the worlds in which they are.

The zodiacal figure shows that from libra extend lines to all parts of nature and of Intelligence, (Fig. VII-B). This means that a human body is so constituted that through it all things in the Universe may be reached and affected and that it is the microcosm through which the changing macrocosm is kept in circulation. From libra extend lines through every sign in every one of the eight zodiacs. On the line from libra to any sign of the zodiac of the fire sphere, which is the macrocosm, are all the signs of the same name. So on the line from libra to cancer of the macrocosm are the cancer signs of the zodiacs of the solid state of matter, of the fluid state of matter, of the airy state of matter, and of the radiant state of matter of the physical plane of the physical world, and of the zodiacs of the three other planes of the physical world and of the zodiacs of the form world, the life world, the light world, the earth sphere, the water sphere, the air sphere and the fire sphere. The correspondences on all planes in all worlds and in all spheres are perfect. The action and interaction of the entities characterized by the respective signs of the zodiac go on by passing through the physical body, libra. The beings which carry on the actions of the manifested Universe are capricorn beings. These beings in the spheres are Intelligences, in the worlds they are Triune Selves. All Triune Selves and the Intelligences with which they are connected work on nature of the man and woman world through a human body, and are affected by nature through a human body. Libra is the center and the fulcrum for the action and the relation between all Triune Selves and nature.

These are some of the topics upon which the symbol of the circle with the twelve points conveys information which is more accurate than any that language can impart.

SECTION 4

The zodiac reveals the purpose of the Universe.

Likewise the zodiacal symbol reveals to a greater extent than any science or religion the ultimate purpose of the manifestations of the Universe. That purpose is to have Substance become Consciousness. The zodiacal figure reveals it by showing the successive stages through which matter passes on its way to Consciousness.

Gemini, Substance, is ever unmanifested. It is space. To human conception it is No thing, nothingness. Yet from it comes all that is manifested in the Universe. Of or in itself, it has no parts, no action. There is no difference in it. When taurus, Motion, acts on it, there is an issue from Substance, No thing, and this issue becomes cancer, matter.

This cancer, matter, is the fire sphere called the Universe and is patterned after the twelve abstract, nameless points of the abstract circle. It contains all that is to be manifested. Cancer is the nature gate between the unmanifested and the Universe. In the fire sphere is oneness. The active or force or spirit aspect of matter is alone in evidence; its material aspect does not appear. The ultimate divisions of matter are units, fire units, and they are elemental beings. These fire units are primordial units, unprogressed. They are conscious in the degree of fire, cancer. They are conscious *as* the fire, *as* the force, but no one of them is conscious *of* itself as the fire or of the others.

This fire, or cancer, matter, made up of fire units, progresses and becomes air, or leo, matter, that is, the units change and become conscious as air matter in the sphere of air, leo. The oneness disappears into twoness. The air matter exhibits a double aspect as activity and passivity. Activity dominates the passive side. The passive side adapts itself to the active side. The air units are no longer primordial. They are not primal, but they are simple. The fire sphere permeates the air sphere, and the fire units become air units when they begin to manifest their passive side. They become air units, that is, they become conscious in the degree called air, leo, and thereby cease to be conscious as fire, cancer. The air units are one step further on the way toward tangibility, libra. In the air element the air units are conscious as the passive as well as the active side of the air element. They do not distinguish between the active and the passive sides, but they respond to the active side of the air, and the passive side of the units adapts itself to their active side. The air units are not conscious *of* themselves, but they are conscious *as* the function of the air element.

The air, or leo, units progressing become water, virgo, units, that is, the air element disappears as such and becomes the water element. The pure air matter becomes pure water matter in the water or virgo sphere. The twoness of the air element now shows a different aspect, for in the water sphere the passive side of matter dominates the active side. The water units are passive-active, no longer active-passive. The air sphere permeates the water sphere, which is in its lower half; and there water units attract air units and cause them eventually to become water units. These units cease to be conscious in the degree called air, or leo, and become conscious in the degree called water, virgo. The water units are conscious as the function of the water element. They do not distinguish between the active and the passive sides, but they respond to the passive side of the water element, and the active side of the units is adapted to the passive side, which responds to the element. Water units are not conscious of themselves, but they are conscious as the function of the water element. Water units are the next step on the way toward tangibility or libra.

The pure water, or virgo, units developing become pure earth, or libra, units in the earth sphere. The two sides, or active and passive aspects, of matter now disappear. There is no longer active-passive and passive-active, but only matter in the earth sphere. The passive aspect of matter alone is in evidence, its active aspect does not appear. The utmost divisions of earth matter are earth units. These units are the opposites of the fire units, since they progressed down to the earth sphere. They are quiescent, stationary, inert, and so appear as a mass or a whole, somewhat as the fire units appear as a whole in the fire sphere. They are conscious in the degree called earth, or libra. In their totality they are the earth element. They are conscious as inertia, immobility, fixity, rest and are the ground for activity. The fire sphere and the earth sphere are extremes and opposites of each other. The fire sphere is activity, force, spirit, without any evidence of its opposite; and the earth sphere is matter, inertia, without any evidence of spirit, force, activity.

In the earth, or libra, sphere which is itself inert and resistant, act the other three elements, cancer, leo and virgo, and cause the four worlds to manifest in the earth sphere. The earth sphere stands to the four worlds in it somewhat as Substance stands to the four spheres. The fire sphere acting within the air sphere and that acting within the water sphere within the earth sphere, cause a representation of the fire or cancer sphere to be in the earth element, as the light or cancer world. In a similar way the air sphere, leo, acting within the water sphere and that within the earth sphere, all acting through the light world, causes the life, or leo, world to be in the light world. So, the water, virgo, sphere, acting within the earth sphere, and both acting through the light and life worlds, cause the form, or virgo, world to be in the life world. The physical, or libra, world is in existence because the cancer, leo and virgo spheres act within the libra sphere and cause the cancer, leo and virgo worlds in it to maintain the physical world.

The matter of the light or cancer, life or leo, form or virgo, and physical or libra, worlds is therefore not the pure fire, air, water and earth. It differs from the pure elemental matter in that the matter in the four worlds is mixed and in that it is limited by the inert earth element.

The cancer, leo, virgo and libra spheres maintain the cancer, leo, virgo and libra worlds. The worlds with the elements of the spheres acting through them similarly maintain in each of these four worlds four planes, that is, additional divisions of matter in each world. The planes, with the spheres and worlds acting through them, similarly maintain in each of these planes four subdivisions, which on the physical plane are called the four states of radiant or cancer, airy or leo, fluid or virgo, and solid or libra matter. The terms spheres, worlds, planes and states of matter designate divisions of matter, and in each set of divisions the essentials are the cancer, leo, virgo and libra types.

In the universe thus maintained or brought into existence only some of the combinations of the four states of cancer, leo, virgo and libra matter on the physical, or libra, plane of the physical, or libra world can be seen. The earth, libra, and the moon, virgo, the sun, leo, and the stars, cancer, make up this small portion.

Parts of all the spheres, worlds, planes and states of matter are condensed and concentrated into fourfold human bodies, libra, (Fig. VII-B). These are centers through which matter of all the different states, planes, worlds and spheres circulates. The four senses and their four systems are the means by which the matter makes its rounds to and from the fourfold bodies. This matter consists ultimately of beings, the units of nature of the different cancer, leo, virgo and libra types. These beings circulate and are drilled in human bodies, and are trained between times in outward nature. As nature units they can go as far as the breath-form unit, libra. Then they leave the category of nature units and become aia units, libra.

This change can be made only while a unit is a function of the breath-form, libra, in a two-columned physical body, libra. An aia unit is an entity of the libra type in the zodiac of the earth sphere, where the breath-form was a being of the libra type in the zodiac of the physical world. The aia is the libra of the Triune Self, stands between nature, cancer, leo, virgo and libra of the spheres, and the Triune Self, which is scorpio, sagittary and capricorn of the light world. The aia as libra by means of the breath-form links nature and the Triune Self in a human body; the libra of the Triune Self links with the libra of nature.

The next stage is that where the aia unit becomes conscious as a Triune Self unit and changes from a libra unit of the zodiac of the earth sphere into a capricorn unit related to the zodiac of the light world, corresponding to the noetic atmosphere of the Triune Self. The change is made in a two-columned physical body, which is a libra entity of the physical world. After the change, the cancer faculty of the capricorn sphere, the doer works its way upward to capricorn of the light world, and with the thinker and knower of the Triune Self becomes conscious *as* itself; it does this independently of the physical body, libra of the libra world, through the form world, scorpio of the light world, and through the life world, sagittary of the light world. The doer with its Triune Self becomes conscious of and knows all there is of itself and in the four worlds, and it remains there until it changes and becomes conscious as an Intelligence, which is a capricorn unit of the fire sphere. These changes can be made only while all parts of the Triune Self, its whole zodiac, are embodied in a two-columned physical body, a libra entity.

The Intelligence, that is, the Triune Self unit which has become conscious as an Intelligence unit, becomes conscious in the three degrees of its three spheres which are those of scorpio, sagittary and capricorn of the capricorn or fire sphere. When it has reached perfection as such an Intelligence of the highest degree, it passes from matter into the unmanifested and is there Conscious Sameness, aquarius. The unit must have passed through all the points of the circle of matter and all the differences represented in the manifestation of the twelve points of the circle of matter, the fire sphere, before it can become Conscious Sameness. In this manner the zodiacal figure shows the purpose of the Universe.

This purpose of changing Substance into Consciousness, and the manner in which the changes are accomplished through a human body, in libra, cannot otherwise be demonstrated to doers in human bodies. A statement of the purpose can be made, and it will stand comparison with other statements, such as that the purpose is to glorify God, or to make men better by progressive improvement of their "souls", or that there is no purpose ascertainable.

The reason why the purpose is not demonstrable is that only a small part of the Universe is open to investigation and that even that small part cannot be cognized correctly. From the human standpoint, that is, to the run of human beings, only the physical, the form and the life planes of the physical world of the sphere of earth are intelligible. These planes are invaded consciously by the physical, emotional and intellectual parts of human beings and are the means for scientific, philosophical and religious conceptions of man and of this universe, that is, the visible, physical universe. Even the light plane of the physical world is not evident and it is not invaded consciously. As to the states of matter, only the substates which are those of the solid state of matter on the physical plane of the physical world are evident to the perceptions of man. His imperfections set boundaries to perception and conception. So not all colors and shades of color on the physical plane can be seen, nor can all forms be seen; and many things and beings remain invisible; and nothing but surfaces, compacted on surfaces until visible, can be seen.

The conceptions are one step ahead of the perceptions. However, the conceptions cannot go more than this one step ahead until the perceptions verify and approve them and take that step. The progress is somewhat like that made by the feet of a walker, whose right foot cannot take another step until the left foot has stepped.

Nor are facts available on the intelligent-side to the run of human beings upon which to base an intelligent opinion of the purpose of the Universe, including the meaning of their life in it. The facts here are not matters of perception through the senses, but are psychic conditions in which one is conscious. Men are conscious of their psychic life. This life consists of feelings and desires, of thinking of which they are conscious in an undiscerning way and of identity. They are so conscious until they come to the gate of death. While they pass through the gate all human beings, that is, the combination of the embodied portions of the doers with the senses of nature, are unconscious. In some of the after-death states they are again conscious as the human beings. Their experiences are limited to what they were conscious of during the past life.

When they re-exist in human bodies on the earth crust they are not conscious of anything of the past. So no facts are usable to test a theory concerning the purpose of the universe and the purpose of their life in it, and no reason is given them for striving for temperance and virtue. The limitations of the perceptions and conceptions are shown by their problems. Because they think with the body-mind in terms of the senses and of time and cannot think beyond it, they ask: Who created the world, if not God? A "God" did not create it, he was himself created. It never was created, it always was; only the outer earth crust changes, disappears and reappears periodically. They say: I did not ask to come into the world; why was I born? What caused the First Cause? Such questions cannot be dealt with because they are based on meager experience and insufficient thinking. They speak of space and mean matter so fine that they do not conceive it. Space, in which all matter is, is beyond their conception.

In all such questions the zodiacal figure as applied to the Universe and man, carries the student of it at once beyond such limitations of his conceptions. The zodiac accounts for the relations of all units in the Universe. The circle shows the purpose of the Universe to be the change of matter into Consciousness by showing the progressive stages through which the purpose is attained.

SECTION 5

The zodiac as a historical and prophetic record; as a clock to measure progress in nature and on the intelligent-side, and in the building out of a thought.

The zodiac is like a clock that measures the progress of everything from a fire unit to an Intelligence. The zodiacal clock indicates the progress of matter, both of nature-matter and of intelligent-matter, (Fig. II-G). Because it shows the change in the relations of units or of masses of units to each other, which is time, it indicates human time and time which is beyond human conception, and which is, therefore, called by some such words as eternity, duration or everness. To the mind's eye the hands move over the zodiacal dials in a direction opposite to that in which the hands of ordinary clocks advance. The zodiacal clock has twelve dials. It has four sphere dials, four world dials and four dials for the four planes of the physical world. The lowest dial, that of the physical plane, is made of four states of matter, which are represented by the earth, the moon, the sun and its planets, and the stars. Though these bodies represent the four states they are all in the substates of the solid state, (Fig. I-E). The sun and the moon are the hands on the lowest dial and mark the time there. They are the only hands that can be seen, though there are as to the other dials unseen things which correspond to these hands.

The concealed works which move the hands of the zodiacal clock have aspects which men call God, the love of God, Divine Providence, Supreme Wisdom, creation and maintenance of the world, fate and destiny. These works are the government of the universe. Their mechanical and unintelligent actions, that is, the part of nature, are controlled by loving, understanding and knowing complete Triune Selves and Intelligences, which are on the intelligent-side. Their government is in the permanent physical world, the Realm of Permanence, that pervades this human world of change, but which is not visible to human beings.

The pivots, libra, of all the works are on the physical plane of the human world of change, libra. They are fourfold human bodies. In these pivotal male and female organizations are produced lunar germs, a solar germ and a light germ. There is for each body only one light germ and one solar germ, and they last during life; but a new lunar germ is produced every month, as the result of the working of the four systems in the body.

Lunar germs, if retained in the body, build it up towards permanence; if lost, as they are with the run of human bodies, they keep nature going on her bloody and destroying way.

Everything in changing nature is worked from these human pivots on the physical plane. The forces of the Universe flow into them and are transmuted by them. The physical works reach into other works on the other planes and these works work into other works in the worlds and these work into the spheres. It is like one vast system of toothed wheels geared to other wheels, so that a transfer of free units is made from the physical plane of the physical world as far as the highest of the spheres, and a transfer of units that have become transient units is made within the confines of the physical world. During the transfer the matter which is passed on by these various wheels, axles, springs and escapements of the great clockworks, is itself slowly transmuted in the laboratory and workshop of the human body. There it is condensed, combined, compounded, organized and, by feeling and desire and thinking, marked for its circuit.

The works behind the physical dial turn the works behind the next dial, and so on, through all the works and the dials. The works behind the physical dial are the physical bodies of humans, and the whole visible universe is the dial of the zodiac of the four substates of solid matter of the physical plane of the physical world.

The stars located at the boundaries of the radiant layer are receiving and distributing centers of nerve force coming from the nerve centers in the generative system. The sun, between the fiery and the airy layer, is a receiving and distributing center of the life blood of the universe, coming from the heart and lungs in all human bodies. This life blood is sunlight and is fourfold. The moon, between the earthy and the watery layer, cleanses and adjusts the matter going to the sun from the millions of human kidneys and adrenals. From the sun this energy is, through the moon, turned back into the sunlight in the air, to the air, to the water, to the earth, and then into food. From there the energy goes into lunar germs. So the rounds continue and the clock-works carry on.

All this accurate and balanced interplay is automatic and is done by beings that are not intelligent. The machinery and forces which drive it are nature units or masses of nature units, elementals, be they great Gods of the worlds or be they the four units of a cell. But the zodiacal clock is not run without Intelligences. The elementals are controlled and directed by Triune Selves and by Intelligences. With the Supreme Intelligence of the spheres men are not concerned, as they cannot go beyond the earth sphere. But the earth sphere is ruled by the Supreme Intelligence of that sphere with the assistance of Intelligences who are still connected with their re-existing doers and with the assistance of the Great Triune Self of the worlds. These Intelligences under the Supreme Intelligence guide their Triune Selves in so far as the re-existing doers will be guided. Each Intelligence furnishes Light to its Triune Self. The Light in the noetic atmosphere of the Triune Self shines in the light world, where it lights up the units and makes that world a shadowless sphere of colorless light. Some of the Light the doers send into nature, through their human bodies. This Light is mixed with nature-matter and shows in the externalizations the thoughts, the quality of the thinking and the degree of the doer by which the thought was issued. The power that keeps the zodiacal clock going is desire in thinking, the law of thought, as destiny.

The zodiacal clock reveals a system which extends into the past and into the future and so allows one to use the conditions shown for any given time, as a basis for stating the order of the past and of future events. The zodiac is a systematic historical and prophetic record. It is a calendar that gives the sequence of events, and the largest as well as the smallest divisions of time. By means of the zodiac one can see from one event the order in which other events preceded it or will follow it. This is as true of any condition of the doer in the human as it is of the stages through which its body passes. Here are two illustrations:

The body is conceived in cancer, when or sometime after the breaths of the parents are joined by the breath of the breath-form; it takes life in leo; in virgo it takes on form; and it is given birth in libra. It lives through periods where it develops organs through which desire works in scorpio, where it develops a new structure for mental activities in sagittary, and where it reaches old age or death in capricorn.

The body itself is a libra body and has its own zodiac of which the manifested signs are here given. The five unmanifested signs show the stages of the after-death states of the disintegrated body, that is, of the mere matter of the body. But the body is only the mask of the breath-form, which is the entity back of it. It is a libra entity and its zodiac is the same as that of the physical body. It was the breath of conception in cancer; it made the contact with life in leo; it developed its form in virgo; and in libra it brought the physical matter to birth out of the womb and entered the body with its active side, the breath. It carries the physical matter through the stages of youth in scorpio, maturity in sagittary and death in capricorn. There, in capricorn, it separates itself from the body, and after it has passed through purification in the signs of scorpio and sagittary in its own zodiac, it is freed from contamination of physical life and begins the heaven period of the personality in capricorn and then passes through the five unmanifested signs, where it reaches the zenith of the heaven at aries and is disintegrated in taurus and gemini, (Fig. V-D).

Another illustration: The Triune Self is a capricorn knower in the noetic or capricorn atmosphere; its thinker is in the sagittary atmosphere and its doer is in the scorpio atmosphere. In each it has a zodiac. When the ruling thought in the mental atmosphere or sagittary zodiac comes to the point of cancer, it causes the aia to revivify the form of the breath-form which it does in cancer of the libra zodiac. When the body is born in libra, it is developed, and in scorpio of the psychic or scorpio zodiac a portion of the doer is embodied; in sagittary of the mental zodiac, the thinker contacts, and in capricorn of the noetic zodiac the knower may contact the body. During life the doer works through the scorpio and sagittary parts of the physical body. At death, the body is separated from its breath-form in capricorn; the doer carries on in its psychic, scorpio, atmosphere the cleansing of the breath-form through its own feelings and desires, scorpio, and by its thinking in sagittary. Then, at capricorn of the psychic or the mental zodiac, the portion of the doer that was embodied, unites again with the cleansed breath-form, and goes through the five unmanifested signs. This ends the round of the existence of that particular doer portion and of the personality. The doer makes ready for the re-existence of the next portion, which must be that which is under the following zodiacal point.

There are stationary and movable zodiacs. The signs of the zodiacal symbol are always in the same relative position to one another. But as this figure can be used to symbolize various subjects, some zodiacs are seen to be movable against a stationary zodiacal background. In the case of a movable zodiac the zodiacal figure as a whole turns like a wheel against a background which is a stationary zodiac. The zodiacs symbolizing the spheres, the worlds and the planes are always in alignment with one another, and are stationary. They mark that which they symbolize, as permanent institutions through which matter flows. But the zodiac of a unit of nature, of a physical body, of a breath-form or of the outer earth crust is movable; it turns like a wheel against the background of the stationary zodiacs. If the sign aries of the movable and the sign aries of a stationary zodiac start when in alignment, after the wheel has turned one sign the sign aries of the movable zodiac will be aligned with the taurus of the fixed zodiac, and after the wheel has turned twelve signs, the sign aries of the movable zodiac will again be aligned with the aries of the stationary zodiac.

The zodiacs of a human are movable against the stationary zodiacs of the plane and world in which he is. His movable zodiacs show by their positions the condition of the body, of the breath-form and of the doer. The stationary signs show seasons or conditions in which certain influences prevail and certain things can or cannot be accomplished. The relation of the movable to the fixed signs is the origin of physical phenomena.

The zodiac of the breath-form is movable, (Fig. VII-K,b). The movements of the zodiac of the breath-form are coincident with those of the zodiac of the physical body. At conception aries of the zodiac of the form of the breath-form is at cancer, breath, of the stationary zodiac of the physical world and of the physical plane, represented by the body of the mother. When the fetus takes life the aries of the zodiac of the form of the breath-form is in leo of the stationary. When the fetus takes on the human form, that aries is in virgo of the stationary. When the child is born into the world, its head being down and coming through the birth canal, out of the invisible into the visible world, the aries of the form of the breath-form is in libra of the stationary zodiac. As soon as the child takes breath and is separated, the breath of the breath-form enters as the breath, the aries of the zodiac of the breath-form remains in libra until youth, when the child develops its sex power in scorpio, then maturity of the body brings the aries into sagittary, and death takes it through the gate of capricorn. The gross matter of the body is thrown off and the essential matter of the breath-form goes through the five unmanifested signs.

Every unit as well as every being composed of units, like a cell, an organ, a human body, the earth crust or the moon may be represented as a zodiac. It is a movable zodiac against the background of the stationary zodiac in which it is manifesting or working. The aries of the movable zodiac shows by its position in any sign of the stationary zodiac in what degree the entity is conscious, or working.

There is a circular and an extended zodiac, (Fig. VII-C). The distinction goes back to the time of the breaking of the front- or nature-column in the body. The doer once functioned consciously in a perfect, two-columned, balanced, sexless body, and Light of the Intelligence was in its psychic atmosphere. Each doer now in a human body was at that time conscious in its atmosphere, in its perfect physical body and in all the worlds. The doer was then conscious as a doer and was conscious of its parent Intelligence, of the Intelligences and of the elemental beings on the nature-side. When the doer broke the column it lost connection with the knowledge of its Triune Self. It lost the knowledge of its identity and so lost the Word; for A O M is the name of the three bodies for the three parts of the Triune Self. A O M is the Word. The doer became conscious merely as a man or a woman. Then began the use of the sexual organs to reproduce bodies. He broke through the circle.

The circular zodiac represents the twelve signs arranged in a circle. The extended zodiac is the broken circle, and represents the twelve signs arranged on a double curve. The circular zodiac is to be found on the nature-side in the spheres, the worlds and the planes, and on the intelligent-side in those who are Triune Selves or Intelligences. The extended zodiac is shown in the human figure and in the animal and vegetable bodies that are patterned after it. In the human figure the signs scorpio, sagittary, capricorn, aquarius and pisces through which it was made the dwelling place of a Triune Self, are now turned away from aries and are extended to the earth, libra.

The arrangement of the signs of the extended zodiac is the same as that of the signs of the circular zodiac in the torso of the human body down to libra. The head is related to aries, the throat to taurus, the shoulders and arms to gemini, the breasts to cancer, the heart to leo, the womb and prostate to virgo and the sex and alimentary openings to libra. The male organ and clitoris are the representatives of scorpio, the thighs are related to sagittary, the knees to capricorn, the legs to aquarius, and the feet to pisces.

The landmarks and the path of the circular zodiac are still in the upper part of the body, but they are used only for physical functions and not as the path of the Triune Self. The end of the terminal filament is related to scorpio; the terminal filament itself up to the first lumbar vertebra to sagittary; the spinal cord in the lower dorsal vertebrae to capricorn, and that in the upper dorsal to aquarius; and the spinal cord in the cervical vertebrae to pisces. When man uses his creative force, not so that it will bind him to the earth, but so that it will build him an immortal physical body, he will still walk the earth, but will also re-establish the circular zodiac in his body.

Among the subjects that are made accessible to human thinking by geometrical figures and which receive meaning from the zodiac, are further relations of man as the microcosm to the macrocosm, the processes by which a thought is developed, exteriorized and balanced, the relations of the manifested to the unmanifested, and some of the meanings which the zodiacal signs have for human beings when arranged in characteristic groups.

In one sense the macrocosm is the manifested half of the universe of nature, or as it is here called the sphere of fire, and a human body is a microcosm, through which all things in the Universe may be reached and affected. Through the human body the spheres cannot be operated, but human bodies, which are connected with the physical plane, keep in circulation the human world of change. The twelve signs are in both the macrocosm and the microcosm. In the microcosm the signs are centers or parts of the body through which the human acts on the macrocosmic signs and through which the macrocosm reacts on the human.

In another view the macrocosm is the physical body itself and is represented by the macrocosmic signs cancer, leo, virgo and libra, while the microcosm is the doer portion in the body, affecting and affected by the macrocosm. Then the microcosmic signs representing the Triune Self are scorpio, sagittary and capricorn. The body is the Universe and the dweller in the body is the microcosm. From this standpoint, the body, and not the outside world or the heavens, is the Universe. The body as the Universe, acts upon and influences the dweller in the body by the four senses, cancer, leo, virgo, libra, acting upon the centers and organs of the body. The action and reaction are carried on through the breath-form which is libra in the macrocosmic and in the microcosmic symbols.

In another view the macrocosm is the physical body and is represented by the macrocosmic signs, aries, gemini, leo, libra, sagittary and aquarius, and the microcosm is the embodied doer portion, represented by the microcosmic signs taurus, cancer, virgo, scorpio, capricorn and pisces. The body has in it the twelve signs, but in this third case six of them are universal or macrocosmic, while the intervening six are microcosmic or of the doer and work through the macrocosmic signs. Two portions of the doer work on or through the part of the body that represents the macrocosmic signs between them, as microcosmic signs. The macrocosmic signs are divided into the sexless signs aries, leo and sagittary; and the signs gemini, libra and aquarius, which are either bisexual or sexless. The microcosmic six signs are divided into taurus, virgo and capricorn, which are female, and cancer, scorpio and pisces, which are male signs. The embodied doer portion may use any two of its signs or powers to act through the intervening macrocosmic signs. Taurus and cancer can meet in gemini, cancer and virgo in leo, virgo and scorpio in libra, scorpio and capricorn in sagittary, capricorn and pisces in aquarius, and pisces and taurus in aries. So when two of the microcosmic signs come together they act in a macrocosmic sign. From the physical standpoint the application of this can be seen only to active and passive and to male and female. However, the statement as well as many other things may be understood by means of geometrical symbols.

The zodiac explains how Light of the Intelligence directed by the doer toward a point of nature-matter in a thought builds within that point, which is unmanifested, until a zodiacal structure within that point is completed, how after the completion of this structure within it the thought is issued, how then elementals following the lines of the zodiacal structure within the thought build them out into acts, objects and events, and how exteriorizations continue on the nature-side until the doer balances its thoughts on its own side, the intelligent-side, and the zodiacal structure is finished.

A thought is constituted of intelligent-matter and of nature-matter. It is made up on the one hand of Light of the Intelligence, joined to desire, and on the other hand of a point of nature-matter. The point of nature-matter is brought in by the senses and is the impression of the object which desire seeks, and which the Light of the Intelligence, directed by thinking, shows it the way to get.

After the object of nature has been tendered by the senses, representing cancer, leo, virgo and libra, has been accepted by feeling and desire, scorpio, and has been carried to the thinker, sagittary, and after thinking in sagittary, working with Light of the Intelligence received from the knower, capricorn, has joined Light of the Intelligence with desire, a thought is conceived, having within it the point of nature-matter which is the object of the thought. Thinking in sagittary, using the Light by which alone this can be done, opens with it the point. Thinking opens it inwards into those unmanifested parts of nature of which the exteriorizations will become the manifested.

The point is on the cancer to capricorn line, between the unmanifested and the manifested, and is a potential circle, into which it will be developed by the influence of the Light of the Intelligence, which thinking and desire direct towards the point, (Fig. IV-A,a).

The point, when the Light of the Intelligence is upon it, becomes the center of the circle which it is to be. When it begins it is a point, when it is ended it is a circle. It begins by drawing on unmanifested nature to get matter of its own kind. With this point-matter it extends a line until the potential cancer becomes the actual cancer to itself. This is the matter line of points from the center to cancer and is the breath of the thought. The zodiacal structure within the thought is further developed when Light of the Intelligence, directed by thinking, extends from the center of the circle a line at an angle to the horizontal or matter line. This is line-matter, attracted by the center of the circle when the Light is upon it. The line-matter is built on the matter line of points. Line after line is built until the last line reaches from the center to leo. Then the first standard angle, which is of thirty degrees and is the distance from cancer to leo, is completed at leo. The Light has created the first angle in the unmanifested, of line-matter which takes on life and is the life of the thought. The zodiacal structure is still further developed within the thought when the effect of the Light attracts to the center of the circle angle-matter. The angle-matter is taken on by the line-matter until angle-matter fills the angle from leo to virgo. This is the second standard angle, which is leo to the center to virgo. The Light has now created the second standard angle in the unmanifested, of angle-matter, which takes on form and is the form of the thought. The development of the zodiacal structure progresses within the thought when the effect of the Light draws surface-matter toward the center of the circle. The surface-matter builds itself on to the angle-matter, until the third standard angle, from virgo to the center to libra is completed.

The thought is now built out in the unmanifested as far as may be. This condition is symbolized by the zodiacal structure of a quarter circle from cancer to libra.

Then the thought is issued on the light plane of the light world, having in it the point which has in it the unmanifested parts of nature-matter that will become exteriorized as acts, objects and events. The thought affects the matter of the light world, and elementals then build in the life world on the life plane there, out from the point a zodiacal structure according to the unmanifested pattern within the thought. They build with nature-matter of the life plane of the life world point-matter, line-matter, angle-matter and surface-matter, until they have copied the quarter circle from the center to cancer to libra. Elementals build this zodiacal figure again on the form plane and again on the physical plane of the life world, with matter of those planes. Elementals then build matter of the form world out according to this figure. They build the quarter circle of point-matter, line-matter, angle-matter and surface-matter successively with matter of the life, form and physical planes of the form world. The thought then is sufficiently materialized to be in the physical world. There elementals, still following the pattern within the point, build from it the zodiacal figure of the quarter circle, on the life plane and on the form plane with matter of those planes.

Then the thought is ready for exteriorization and waits for time, condition and place to be ready for it. When there is a conjunction of these the thought is exteriorized. It is exteriorized according to the same zodiacal figure that has controlled it all along. The act of writing a letter, chopping down a tree, or building a house, is accomplished with elementals which are point-matter in the generative system including brain and nerves, line-matter in the respiratory system, angle-matter in the circulatory system, and surface-matter in the digestive system to which belong the hands, the feet and the rest of the solid body.

This is the exteriorization of the point of nature-matter, developed according to the zodiacal figure of the quarter circle which has thus come through all the worlds and their planes below the light plane.

The quarter circle from cancer to libra is on the nature-side, and has to be balanced by the corresponding quarter circle from libra to capricorn on the intelligent-side. The nature-side is represented by the point of nature-matter in the thought, the thought itself is represented by the intelligent-side of the circle, from libra to capricorn. The point, which is the concentration of the perceptions made by the four senses, could never have been taken in by the doer, if there had not been a desire for it and thinking about it. Desire and thinking directing to it Light of the Intelligence on the point, create a thought. At the creation there comes into the unmanifested a quarter circle from libra to capricorn. Libra represents the object of the desire; and scorpio, sagittary and capricorn represent the desire, the thinking which made the aim, and knowledge as conscience, producing the balancing factor in the thought.

When the thought is issued the balancing factor, the aim and the design are present as the manifesting thought. When the nature-quarter circle from cancer to libra is exteriorized, only the design is exteriorized. The thought will not be exteriorized until the intelligent-quarter circle from libra to capricorn is built up, to balance the nature-quarter circle and make the thought a manifested half circle of six standard angles. The manifesting part of the thought being complete as a half circle, the unmanifested part makes the upper half and the point is completed in the entire circle.

The zodiacal figure explains symbolically the relation of the manifested to the unmanifested. With words such an explanation can be made only as to things perceptible by the senses or conceivable by understanding. The unmanifested is that which is not perceptible by the senses and which has not been conceived by the human. The terms manifested and unmanifested are relative in their application to the spheres, worlds, planes and states of matter.

The entire Universe is contained in the fire sphere, which is the manifested of Substance. Substance is the unmanifested as compared with the fire sphere. To the sphere of air the sphere of fire is the unmanifested; and the sphere of air is the manifested of the fire sphere. In its turn the sphere of air is the unmanifested to the sphere of water and the sphere of water is the manifested of the sphere of air. To the sphere of earth the sphere of water is the unmanifested and the sphere of earth is the manifested of the sphere of water. In the same way the earth sphere is the unmanifested to the light world, and the light world is the manifested of the earth sphere. The relation is continued through the life, form and physical worlds, so that to the physical world the form world is the unmanifested, and the physical world is the manifested of the form world. So it goes on through the light, the life, the form to the physical planes. Each plane is the manifested of the, to it, unmanifested plane above it. These relative terms of the unmanifested and manifested apply also to the four states of matter on the physical plane. To the solid state the fluid state is the unmanifested, out of which all things come into manifestation in the solid state, where they are seen, heard, tasted, smelled and contacted by the four senses of the human.

The term manifested is usually applied only to the things in the four subdivisions of the solid state. But in a wider sense and with a secondary meaning, as explained by the zodiac, the distinction of the manifested and the unmanifested exists through all the states of matter, and through the planes, worlds and spheres. The manifested part of each sphere, world, plane and state of matter is zodiacally symbolized by a lesser zodiac drawn below the line cancer to capricorn. The lesser circle is so drawn that its center is midway between libra and the center of the cancer to capricorn line. All beyond, that is, around, the lesser circle, stands for the, to it, unmanifested, and is symbolized zodiacally by the upper half of the circle between cancer and capricorn.

SECTION 6

Groups of zodiacal signs. Application to the human body.

The signs of the zodiac can be arranged in characteristic groups which, when connected by lines, are geometrical symbols for everything in the macrocosm, excepting of course the twelve abstract points. The symbols represent the monad, the dyads, the triads, the tetrads, the pentads and the hexads. These symbols having no character except that arising from extension and difference of situation, receive their meaning for human beings from the signs by which that character is indicated.

The twelve as a whole are a monad, (Fig. VII-E). They are the circle. The circle represents a whole, a oneness. It represents all there is, space, time, being and events. Within the monad are included all things; there is no thing outside of it.

The signs may be arranged as two sets of dyads, that is, halves, (Fig. VII-F). One half, consisting of cancer, leo, virgo, libra, scorpio, sagittary and capricorn, stands for the manifested, for the spheres and for what is in them; for matter in its states of circulation and progression. The second dyad, consisting of capricorn, aquarius, pisces, aries, taurus, gemini and cancer, stands for the unmanifested, no spheres, no matter, the abstract. It stands for the potentialities and possibilities of all things that are or ever may be in the manifested Universe.

The halves of the other set of dyads comprise the signs aries, taurus, gemini, cancer, leo, virgo and libra, standing for super-nature and nature; and the signs libra, scorpio, sagittary, capricorn, aquarius, pisces and aries standing for intelligent and super-intelligent.

Then there are the triads, groups of three signs, (Fig. VII-G). They are the fire triad aries, leo and sagittary; the air triad taurus, virgo and capricorn; the water triad gemini, libra and aquarius and the earth triad cancer, scorpio and pisces. The triads are not identical with the four manifested elements, but they have the characteristics of what in manifestation becomes the four spheres. Fire, air, water and earth are these characteristics, in manifestation as the elements. The fire triad is the cause of matter being conscious as and active as the fire, cancer; the air triad is the cause of matter's being conscious as and active and passive as air, leo;

the water triad is the cause of matter's being conscious as and passive and active as water, virgo; and the earth triad is the cause of matter's being conscious as and passive as earth, libra. That aries, leo and sagittary are the fiery symbols or points may be seen if the signs are read aries fire, taurus air, gemini water and cancer earth. Then the next sign is leo, again fire, and virgo air, libra water, scorpio earth. Finally the following sign sagittary is again fire, and capricorn air, aquarius water and pisces earth. Thus the fiery signs which make the fire triad are aries, leo, sagittary; the airy signs are taurus, virgo, capricorn; the watery signs are gemini, libra, aquarius; and the earthy signs are cancer, scorpio, pisces. These triads stand behind, beneath or within the manifested spheres and their worlds and planes. Changes are brought about by the fiery and the watery triads. Physically, therefore, nothing can be solved in air or earth, but only in fire or water, which are the changer and the solvent. So physically the cancer point of the earth triad and the virgo point of the air triad have to meet in the leo point of the fire triad to change life into form.

The fire sphere is cancer as fire in manifestation, but it is cancer as earth before it was manifested. The zodiac shows that the Universe is an earth Universe in essence, though it is the fire sphere in manifestation, in matter, and that so the sublimest reality in matter is an illusion, as compared with realities above or beyond. In this sense the sphere of air, leo, is in essence fire, the sphere of water is in essence air, and the sphere of earth is in essence water. If it were not for the essence's differing from the element in which it is, there could be no change in or of the element, and so it would be impossible for matter as inertia to change. What enables the changes to be brought about is the essential water triad which works through the earth sphere, libra. Because the essential nature of the fire sphere, cancer, is the unmanifested cancer as earth, this essential nature, in the earth sphere, becomes libra, which is the opposite of activity, cancer. The lowest unit of nature-matter which is the geogen unit has the characteristics of the prototype or essential nature of the highest sphere, which is the earth triad. The origin and essence of the fire sphere is the earth triad and indicates what the fire will become. It indicates that the fire will ultimately become earth, libra.

The triads cause a oneness, a twoness, a threeness and a fourness in the manifested Universe, which appear as the four elements and their subdivisions. The oneness is the fire, it is the beginning and the end of manifestation. All things that come into manifestation are potentially and actually contained in oneness. Twoness is the departure from oneness. It is not only a departure, but it is a different thing, with the oneness, which is everpresent, in it. Twoness is the second element, air, with the first in it, inseparably. The air cannot exist by itself; it is contained in the fire and the fire is in it. Threeness is again a new thing. It is another element, water, with the two others inseparably in it. The two others are expressed in and by it. It is the representative of the other two, and thus is threeness. Fourness is the ultimate element, earth, as regards the outwardness from fire. It is farthest removed from and is the opposite of the fire. It has the other three elements inseparably in it and represents and dominates them.

Each element is one, but only the fire element is one without any other and is not a continuation of any other. Each element is one in the sense that there is a distinctness about it, as to the other three. Fire is the first, the original, the primitive, the presence of which brings about change, continuous change in each of the other elements in which it is, until they are brought into permanence in products which can be no longer changed by them, that is by nature, but only by thinking and the spoken word. The foremost of these products is a perfect physical body in the Realm of Permanence, in the Eternal Order of Progression, or a human body in the world of change, of birth and death.

The fire, air, and earth triads have one point in the unmanifested, one point on the nature-side, and one point on the intelligent-side and so show the action of the triad on the intelligent-side and on the nature-side. The action of these triads starts on the intelligent-side and from there operates the nature-side from their points in nature. In the earth triad one point, scorpio, desire, is in the manifested on the intelligent-side; one point, pisces, is in the unmanifested, and either one of these points may operate cancer, which is the point between the unmanifested and the manifested on the nature-side. The water triad has two points in the unmanifested and only one, the libra point, in the manifested, and so is neutral in the manifested. In this triad, different from the others, there is no point in the manifested on the intelligent-side from which the triad can be operated, on the nature-side. The water triad has to be operated by the air or by the earth triad.

The fire triad is the ideal and sets the pattern for everything that is or may be in the manifested, on the nature-side and on the intelligent-side, and shows how the ideal is to be accomplished. Thought, sagittary, works on life, leo, determines the development and direction of matter on the nature-side, and is the means of the ultimate accomplishment,

Consciousness. This is one of the two fixed, universal triads. The other is gemini, libra, aquarius, the water triad. This has two points in the unmanifested; and its manifested point, libra, is between the nature-side and the intelligent-side, connecting with both. Gemini is the origin of matter, that from which matter comes; the point libra of that triad is the neutral stage between nature-matter and intelligent-matter in manifestation, the stage in which nature-matter is changed and becomes intelligent-matter; aquarius is the stage where matter is no longer matter and becomes Conscious Sameness. The water triad is the means by which the ideal triad is worked out, and the ground on and from which this is done. The other two, the air and the earth triads, are the doers, the workers, that bring about the ideal accomplishment through and from the basis of matter.

There are three tetrads or groups of four signs. They are squares, (Fig. VII-H), or crosses, (Fig. VII-J). The first is aries, cancer, libra, capricorn; the second is taurus, leo, scorpio, aquarius; and the third is gemini, virgo, sagittary and pisces. The first tetrad, as a square, contains the plan and shows the processes by which the plan is carried out. It is unchanging and universal. The line from aries to cancer indicates the four points on the quarter circle and so stands for aries, taurus, gemini and cancer. The lines which are the other three sides of the square likewise stand for the points on their quarter circles. The first tetrad is a square that represents all the twelve points, whereas the second and third tetrads do not represent the twelve points, but the second is only the points taurus, leo, scorpio and aquarius, and the third is only gemini, virgo, sagittary and pisces.

By the plan of the first tetrad all accomplishments are attained. The plan is outlined in the unmanifested by the line aries to cancer, for nature; the line cancer to libra shows how the work is done by and in nature; the line libra to capricorn shows how the work is done on the intelligent-side; and the line capricorn to aries shows the four accomplishments.

The first tetrad, as a cross and as opposites, is the line aries to libra and the line cancer to capricorn. As a cross it is also fixed, stationary and universal. The line cancer to capricorn is the line of manifestation, where, at cancer, Substance becomes nature in its many units, and where, at capricorn, the units cease to be such and go back to the unmanifested as Conscious Sameness. The line aries to libra shows, in the manifested, nature-matter at its limits as nature-matter and the beginnings of intelligent-matter. In the unmanifested that line shows the limit of super-nature and of the super-intelligent becoming Consciousness.

The second and third tetrads as squares are just as fixed and unchanging as the first tetrad. They seem to be movable for the reason that the doer in human beings moves from one of these tetrads to the other. They are the means and the stages by which the plan shown by the aries tetrad is carried out. The square made by the lines taurus to leo, leo to scorpio, scorpio to aquarius and aquarius to taurus shows how the sign taurus, Motion, in super-nature acts in and affects nature in the spheres and in the worlds, how nature, as leo, acts with and affects desire on the intelligent-side, how scorpio affects aquarius in the super-intelligent, and how aquarius affects taurus. Taurus and its tetrad act through all human bodies, but particularly through a male body, from the point of desire. The square made by the lines gemini to virgo to sagittary to pisces and to gemini shows how gemini, Substance, in super-nature affects nature in the spheres and worlds, how nature as virgo acts on and affects thought on the intelligent-side, how sagittary affects pisces in the super-intelligent, and how pisces affects gemini. Gemini and its tetrad stand behind all human bodies, but act particularly through a female body from the nature point of virgo. Therefore a woman is more aided by and is more under the influence of nature than a man; the senses affect feeling, which is the virgo side of the psychic doer part, before they reach desire; and a woman lives more in the involuntary nervous system which is the system for nature.

The second and third squares show the succession in action from the nature-side to the intelligent-side and the reaction from the intelligent-side to the nature-side. Each of these squares shows how one set of signs acts particularly through a male body and the other acts particularly through a female body. The sex of the body, and all that goes with it as shown by the squares, is movable and does move from one square to the other and back, when the doer re-exists in a body that has the sex different from that of the last body. The first tetrad, which contains the plan of what is to be realized by the liberated doer, is neither male nor female, as are the second and the third. The human tetrads must ultimately be conformed to the universal sexless tetrad. Until then the doer moves from one of the movable tetrads to the other.

The second tetrad as a cross and as opposites is the line from taurus to scorpio and the line from leo to aquarius. To human conception one line represents Motion affecting desire and the reaction of desire on Motion; the other line shows life and Sameness acting and reacting. It is the male cross and shows the forces from the sphere of air, the life world, the form planes and the airy and fluid states of the physical plane acting through a male body. These forces are counterbalanced by powers from the super-intelligent of aquarius with which the run of human beings are not in touch. The third tetrad as a cross and as opposites is a line from gemini to sagittary with the line from virgo to pisces. This cross shows Intelligence affecting form, and thought affecting Substance. The cross is the female cross and shows the action and reaction of these powers, influences and qualities through a human body, but more particularly a female body.

The pattern on which both these second and third squares and crosses must work is the universal tetrad aries, cancer, libra, capricorn. So the unmanifested is worked out in the manifested. It is done on the manifested square, that is, from cancer to libra and from libra to capricorn. From conception to birth is the nature-side of that square, and from birth to death or to immortality is its intelligent-side. The body itself is the universal square, and the sex, libra, of it represents the male, scorpio, or the female, virgo, tetrad. In order to work on the universal square, the human sex, libra, must build the other tetrad within the body, because both must be in one body, that is, on the universal square. The tetrads as crosses, while showing different actions and reactions between their four points, show the same facts of human life from different standpoints.

When the doer is embodied in a male or in a female body it is on its cross, either the male cross or the female cross. There it suffers all that the flesh can do to it, until it brings its cross into alignment with the aries to libra and cancer to capricorn cross, the universal cross, and then there is no more suffering for it.

The pentads are four in number, each having the shape of a pentacle or pentagram, that is five lines making a five-pointed star, (Fig. VII-K). These pentads are, first, aries to leo, to aquarius, to gemini, to sagittary and back to aries; second, libra to aquarius, to leo, to sagittary, to gemini and back to libra; third, cancer to scorpio, to taurus, to virgo, to pisces and back to cancer; and fourth, capricorn to taurus, to scorpio, to pisces, to virgo and back to capricorn.

The first and second pentads are universal, (Fig. VII-K,a,b), the third and fourth are human, (Fig. VII-K,d,e). The action between the universal pentads goes on in and through a human body. The human pentads show the actions and reactions of the doer in a male or in a female body, to the action of the universal pentads in that body, (Fig. VII-K,g).

In the upper universal pentad action works from aries, Consciousness, towards leo, life, towards aquarius, Conscious Sameness, towards gemini, Substance, towards sagittary, thought, and back towards aries. Applied to a human body, the head acts on the solar plexus, which acts on the plexus between the shoulders, which acts on a plexus opposite in front, which acts on a plexus at the lumbar vertebrae, which acts on the head. In the lower universal pentad action works from libra, sex, to aquarius, Conscious Sameness, to leo, life, to sagittary, thought, to gemini, Substance, and back to libra. In the body sex acts on the plexus between the shoulders, where Sameness is now dormant; that plexus acts on life in the solar plexus; and that acts on the plexus in the lumbar region, thought; which acts on the plexus between the breasts, where Substance is dormant, and back to libra. The two universal pentads are symbols for the human body as the macrocosm, in which the doer as the microcosm works.

The universal pentads are also symbols for the aia and the breath-form and show the relation of the aia to the breath-form. The unmanifested macrocosmic pentad is the aia, the manifested macrocosmic pentad is the breath-form. The unmanifested as the aia is everywhere, and is present everywhere in the breath-form. The aia and the breath-form are thus locked up like the two macrocosmic pentads. The center of this figure, which is a six-pointed star, (Fig. VII-K,c), is the center of the circle. Through this center is conveyed into the breath-form for manifestation in a particular life something of that which is stored up in the unmanifested, the aia.

The human pentads, (Fig. VII-K,d,e), represent the doer acting in its human body. It acts between scorpio and capricorn. It can never be lower than scorpio nor higher than capricorn, because the doer is scorpio and the knower is capricorn in the capricorn atmosphere, or in the light world. The left pentad, with its head at cancer, represents the passive aspect of the doer. It does not represent nature, but the passive or cancer side of the capricorn part and the passive or virgo side of the scorpio part. The right pentad, with its head at capricorn, represents the capricorn aspect of the capricorn part and the scorpio aspect of the scorpio part. Both the human pentads, together, making a six-pointed star are a symbol of the doer; separately they show the relations of the passive to the active aspect of the doer, (Fig. VII-K,f). In a male physical body the active pentad of the doer is manifested, while the passive is hidden and unmanifested, and in a female body the passive pentad of the doer is manifested and the active is hidden or unmanifested.

The human pentads are symbols also for the human body. The left pentad, with the manifested signs cancer, virgo and scorpio indicates the type of a female body; the other pentad, with the signs virgo, scorpio and capricorn manifested, indicates that of a male body. However, in a male body virgo is suppressed and kept within, while in a female body scorpio is suppressed and kept within. Both virgo and scorpio are in one body; but one predominates and so is the characteristic of the type.

With the one pentad is always the semblance or shadow of the other. With the upper pentad is the lower, and with the right is the left. In each pentad are signs that are potential and in the unmanifested, and signs that are dormant, although in the manifested.

In the universal pentads the signs gemini, leo, sagittary and aquarius are common to both pentads, and the fifth sign is aries in the upper and libra in the lower pentad. When seen together these pentads make a six-pointed star, (Fig. VII-K,c). The human pentads have the signs taurus, pisces, virgo and scorpio in common, while cancer is the fifth in the female and capricorn the fifth in the male pentad. Together these pentads also make a six-pointed star, (Fig. VII-K,f).

The human body, as representing the breath-form, is a pentad, the universal pentad, and in it are both a male and a female human pentad, symbolizing the embodied doer portion. If the embodied doer portion is dominated by feeling it is symbolized by a human pentad having a point at virgo, and if it is dominated by desire, it is symbolized by a human pentad with a point at scorpio. Both human pentads are in the same body or universal pentad. But in a human body one pentad is accentuated on one side and inhibited on the other, so that the suppressed side does not function in its normal capacity. Thus, a man has feeling though his desire dominates him and a woman has desire though her feeling rules her. The two human pentads in a man or in a woman can meet by scorpio and capricorn coming together in the macrocosmic sign of sagittary. In this way a thought is created. The two pentads in one body might also come together when capricorn and pisces meet in aquarius, or pisces and taurus meet in aries, or taurus and cancer meet in gemini, or cancer and virgo meet in leo. But the meetings of the points of human pentads in the macroscopic signs next to them is a matter beyond the ordinary scope of comprehension; only the coming together in sagittary by thinking is a matter which will be understood.

There is one exception to the powers of both human pentads in the same body acting together in a macrocosmic sign. The exception is when they act on the physical plane of the physical world, for procreation. The male pentad having its point in scorpio cannot come together with the female pentad having its point in virgo, because the female organs do not function in a male body and the male organs do not function in a female body, and so the two sexual organs which are in the same body cannot function together to procreate. Two bodies of different sex are needed to come together for procreation. Then scorpio of the male pentad in a male body joins virgo of the female pentad in a female body, in libra, the macrocosmic sign.

Then there are two groups of six signs, the hexads, (Fig. VII-L). The signs in each group may be connected by lines which will make a six-pointed star. This geometrical symbol is composed not merely of two interlaced triangles, which, symbolizing the union of male and female, are a common sexual symbol, but added to it are the two diameters from the five-pointed stars out of which it was made. There is the universal hexad of aries, gemini, leo, libra, sagittary and aquarius. This hexad is a symbol of a physical body. The human hexad comprises the signs taurus, cancer, virgo, scorpio, capricorn and pisces. This hexad symbolizes the Triune Self acting in the body.

The symbolic meaning of the hexads differs from that of the pentads. Both the universal and both the human pentads cannot work completely in a human body at the same time, because the body is a sexual body, either male or female. In the case of the universal pentads only the manifested can, as the breath-form, work the body; the unmanifested, as the aia, cannot affect the body directly, but only through the pentad manifested as the breath-form. Similarly only one of the human pentads, the pentad of the male body or that of the female body, can function through the body worked by the breath-form. When a pair of pentads works coordinately, that is, both work together equally in the same body, the nature of the body changes from a sexual to a sexless body. Then the universal pentads become a hexad, the universal hexad, and the pair of human pentads becomes the human hexad.

Aspects of human bodies may be symbolized by triads, by tetrads or by pentads, but not by hexads. The universal hexad symbolizes a physical body in which male and female aspects have disappeared, which is without the sexes and in which the aia is manifested and operates, untouched by nature, as the direct instrument of the Triune Self. This hexad symbolizes also a body brought to that point of development where through it may be reached the forces of the earth sphere and of the worlds in it. The human hexad stands for a doer in a perfect body in whom neither feeling nor desire dominates, but both are adjusted so that their action is equal.

In the dyads, triads, tetrads and pentads some of the signs are manifested, some unmanifested. Some are actual, some potential. Only some signs, the manifested, represent actual relations, the unmanifested represent potential relations to the manifested signs. That for which the signs stand is everywhere. The signs are in every human body and they are in every doer in a human. Different things are, however, affected differently by them. Sometimes the relations are direct, sometimes indirect and sometimes potential. The meaning of the signs as here given refers to human beings. The meaning of the group signs applies to their bodies and their doers. These bodies are nature and super-nature, the doers are on the intelligent-side and are potentially Intelligences. The relations between that which human beings perceive as outside nature and as nature impersoned as their bodies on the one hand and their doers on the other, are thus shown by these geometrical symbols. The task of the embodied doer portion is to realize these relations by making the potential actual and waking the dormant to activity. Physically the task is to create a body in which there is both a front- or nature-column and a column for the Triune Self, so that the body will be immortal. At present there is no front-column and the station at libra is open as sex, either male or female.

In the monad and in the hexads there is not this distinction between some of the signs, which represent an actual relationship, and others which are unmanifested.

The hexads are symbols of realization, of perfection, where there is no unmanifested. When the universal and the human hexads work together they make the monad. Then the dyads, triads, tetrads and pentads, having done their work, are in alignment and can disappear because no longer needed. But the hexads remain and make the monad.

The zodiac, whether as the twelve constellations in the heavens or in any pictorial representation of the twelve symbols, is a constant reminder to human beings of their task to reach Oneness. They reach Oneness by thinking without creating thoughts.

CHAPTER XV

THINKING: THE WAY TO CONSCIOUS IMMORTALITY

SECTION 1

The system of thinking without creating destiny. With what it is concerned. With what it is not concerned. For whom it is presented. The origin of this system. No teacher is needed. Limitations. Preliminaries to be understood.

By this system one may train himself to think without creating thoughts, that is, destiny; the system will aid him in knowing his Triune Self and, possibly, in becoming conscious of Consciousness. The system is concerned with training the feeling-mind and the desire-mind to control the body-mind; and, by control of the body-mind to control the senses, instead of allowing the senses to control the body-mind and thereby to control the minds of feeling-and-desire. By training oneself how to feel, what to desire, and how to think, the body will be trained at the same time. By this system one may locate and find the bearings of the portion of the doer dwelling in his body. If and while he does this, changes will be brought about in the body; diseases will disappear in their proper order, and the body will become sound and responsive and efficient.

This system is not concerned with acquiring health merely to have health and to be free from pain, discomfort and impediments. Nor is it concerned with acquiring possessions, fame, power or even a competence. Health and possessions will come as one develops himself according to this system, but they are only incidental. Those who seek health should acquire it with the aid of intentional lung breathing, by proper posture, carriage, eating and exercise, by temperance in sleeping and the marriage relation, and by kind and considerate feeling towards others. Those who seek possessions should acquire them by honest work and thrift. This system is not for those whose particular purpose is to seek clairvoyance, thought reading, power over others, control of elementals and the rest of what they call occultism. Occultism is concerned with the operations of nature and with the control and operation of nature forces. This system is concerned, above all, with understanding the Triune Self and the Light of the Intelligence, and with the practice of self-control and self-government. By self-control and self-government nature will be controlled and protected.

This system is for one who seeks to know himself as the Triune Self in the fullness of the Light of the Intelligence. Other systems deal with nature and the doer, undefined and undistinguished. This system identifies and distinguishes the doer from nature and shows the relations and possibilities of each. It shows to the embodied doer a way out of slavery to nature, into the freedom and wholeness of its own Triune Self in the Light of the Intelligence.

There is no history connected with this system. Its origin is in being conscious of Consciousness. The system as a course of training oneself in thinking and feeling and desiring, is composed of exertions by the portion of the doer-in-the-body and by intentional breathing and thinking. The system is directly connected with the efforts of the doer toward the right development of itself and thus furnishing higher types for nature to work through. The system is more subtly connected with being conscious as the doer and having enough knowledge to think without creating thoughts; that is, thinking without being attached to objects about which one thinks.

One who practices this system need not depend upon any other person than himself. His own thinker and knower will teach him as he gradually becomes conscious of them. Certainly he may communicate, if he wishes, with anyone about it. He obtains some information from the system and his experience with it, but it is he who must furnish the Light and become conscious of what the Light shows, as he goes on. He may be furthered by his own past thoughts, by his feelings, his desires, the people he meets, the matter he reads, or he may be hindered by any of these. His progress depends upon himself, on his intelligent, silent persistence in following this system. This must be so if he is to be self-controlled and self-governed.

There is no limit to what one may attain by following this system. The limitations, if any, are in himself, not in the system which leads to thinking without handicaps and so to knowledge of himself as the doer of his Triune Self and of his Intelligence. He can, by this system, desire, breathe, feel and think so that he himself will be the Way to all beyond.

One who follows this system should have an understanding of the difference between himself and nature. He must understand the relation of himself to nature as the outside universe and to nature as his body. He must understand the aia and the breath-form and their relation to each other, to nature and to himself. He must understand what the doer-in-the-body is and what it does and what is the relation of himself as the doer to his Triune Self and to his Intelligence.

In order to facilitate this understanding, a recapitulation of the statements made on these subjects is furnished in the following sections.

SECTION 2

Recapitulation: The make-up of the human being. Units. The senses. The breath. The breath-form. The aia. Human bodies and the outside universe.

A human being is, first, nature units organized into a fourfold human body, by, second, the breath-form or living "soul" of that body; third, the portion of the conscious doer in the body; and, fourth, Conscious Light which is loaned to the doer.

The human body is composed of a solid-solid, a fluid-solid, an airy-solid and a radiant-solid body, and is a fourfold physical body, (Fig. III). The solid-solid part is the only one that has apparently definite outline and form. This is what is called the physical or flesh body. It is made visible by solid-solid structure units, which are sufficiently compacted. It is the field in which the sense of smell works with its digestive system. The fluid-solid body is made up of units of the fluid-solid state, penetrates the solid-solid units and makes them cohere. It has no definite form apart from the form of the solid-solid particles. It is the field in which the sense of taste works in its circulatory system. The airy-solid body permeates the fluid and through that the solid body. It has no form and could not stand alone, without the solid-solid and the fluid-solid bodies. It is the field through which the sense of hearing works with its respiratory system. The radiant-solid or astral body is the only one of the three inner bodies which can at times stand apart from and appear as the form of the solid-solid man or woman body. The astral body is present in the other three bodies and is the field from which the sense of sight works with the generative system. This radiant or astral body is the first body to be built by the breath of the breath-form. The radiant-solid units take form from the breath-form and give form to the solid-solid body.

The form of the breath-form unit enters the woman's body through her breath during copulation and then or later causes conception by uniting the two germ cells. This re-existing form is the pattern which the mother's breath and blood follow in building the body as soon as the embryo takes life. At birth, its breath at once enters the infant, unites with the form, as the breath-form, in the heart, and throughout life the breath continues the building of the man or woman body according to the form.

A human body is the plan of the changing universe. The head and spine represent the center of the starry system, the heart the center of the solar system, the kidneys the center of the lunar system and the sex the center of the earthy system. At present the body is one-columned, instead of two-columned: the digestive system which should be stationed in the pelvis extends through the body to the head. The circulatory system should be located in the abdomen. The respiratory system is the only system which is, generally, in its proper place, that is, in the thorax. The generative system, which is now in the pelvis, should be the creative system and be in the head. The misplacement of the systems has developed malformed organs which function with effort, feebly, often for unworthy results.

The distinguishing feature of the body is its sexual function, which is a degradation of creative power into the pelvis, from whence it rules the other systems. The sexes are not in the doer, though the potentiality and the origin and cause of the sexes are. Feeling and desire affect the original perfect breath-form so as to divide and modify it to the male and the female type. Physical matter then adapts itself to the type and builds out the male and female organs and traits of the body. The sexes in the human body are the pattern for the world of change, which is an extension and magnification of the human body. The breath carries transient units from the organs of the fourfold body into the fourfold breath stream of the earth zones and so creates a universe extending and expressing human beings which are on the outer earth crust.

The condition of the body in which the organs are, through which thinking has to be done, prevents proper thinking. It holds and compels thinking by the body-mind about and for the body and its chief features, the sexes. The thinking has to be done according to the male or to the female type. Thinking ought to be done by means of four brains and plexuses, the pelvic, the abdominal, the thoracic, and the cranial. But thinking is now started by the heart and lungs, which are used for circulation and respiration, and is carried on and completed by the brain as a subordinate and secondary organ. Nature, which is the screen on which the picture of man is projected, in turn stimulates the body to distract and to dominate thinking.

The body is visible in so far as it is made up of compacted units of the solid-solid state of the physical plane. Some of the invisible units are of the three other states of the physical plane, some are of the three other planes of the physical world and some are of the three other worlds of the earth sphere. Four kinds of units make up the fourfold physical body: sense units, representatives of the four systems; compositor units, which build and maintain the body; transient units, which the compositors hold for a while; and free units, which are not subject to but affect the transient and the compositor units. The transient units are the structural matter of the visible physical world, after they are released by the compositors. The compositors, between re-existences of the doer, build and transform the things in the physical universe, which includes the visible world with its strata, flora and fauna, the heavenly bodies and all phenomena of sights, sounds, tastes and smells. The free units are the active forces or the passive matter which stand behind these phenomena. The compositors are arranged in the generative or fire, the respiratory or air, the circulatory or water and the digestive or earth systems, each controlled by its sense, which connects it with the corresponding element in outside nature. Outside nature as elemental units acts on, maintains and controls the fourfold body through these same four senses and their nerves in the involuntary nervous system.

The senses themselves do not see, hear, taste, smell or contact independently. They merely receive impressions from nature and carry them to the breath-form, and the breath which is the active side of the breath-form, focusses them and correlates them so that they do their work through the sense of smell. A nature impression is received by a sense in its organ, as in the eye, and is taken inside the body by the breath along nerves in the brain and in the involuntary nervous system to the sex opening, and is taken simultaneously outside the body along the breath current itself, to the same opening. The senses, sight, hearing, taste and smell, cause the sex organ to be open for the reception of the impression. From there, the breath of the breath-form carries the impression to the portion of the doer in the kidneys and adrenals, and from there to the heart and lungs, with which the thinker of the Triune Self is related, and thence into the brain. The tip of the tongue, the heart and lungs, above, and the sex opening, below, are the gates for the swinging in and the swinging out of the breaths. In the brain, the impression, as it comes in through the eye, is met by the impression that has made instantaneously the circuit of the atmosphere and the body. In the heart and lungs and in the brain the impression compels thinking.

Each of these senses controls the compositors which make up its system during life. After death each sense has much to do with the units of its system in outside nature. When it is summoned on re-embodiment it leads the transmigration of the units, from outside nature, into the new body of the doer.

The sense of sight cannot become less than a sense of sight, nor can it be destroyed. It can only progress, though its powers may be diminished or dulled for a while. It is a unit, trained by many adaptations while in human bodies belonging to one doer, so that it as such sense may be used by nature towards the control of the doer, or by the doer to control fire units of the fire element. So it is in every way with the other three senses in their respective elements. These senses belong to nature, are ministers of nature and are the means by which outside nature affects the physical body and the thinking.

Around the fourfold physical body and circulating through it, its transient units make up the physical atmosphere, (Fig. III), which is roundish or oval in form and is kept in constant circulation by the breath-form and its breathings. While they are being held by the compositor units, the transient units, compacted into mass, make up the visible physical body. To an eye allowing sight of the four states of physical matter or even of the four substates of the solid state, the transient units are streams coming into, coalescing with and going out of the fourfold physical body. The physical atmosphere is a diffusion of these transient units.

Ordinarily, the physical atmosphere extends from a few inches to several feet. The four senses perceive only within the boundary of the physical atmosphere, which may be extended in any direction. In the case of smelling, the units of the object smelled contact the nerves directly in the solid-solid state. In the case of tasting, the units also contact the solid-solid body, but the taste of the object is sensed through the fluid-solid matter of the object by nerves in the fluid-solid body. In the case of hearing, the sounds contact the solid-solid organ and are heard through the fluid-solid body by nerves in the airy-solid body. In seeing, the units from the object seen contact the solid-solid organ of the eye, and are seen through the fluid-solid and the airy-solid bodies of nerves in the astral body which contact radiant-solid units coming from the object seen. The units of these objects must come into the atmosphere before they can be sensed. This is passive seeing and perception. There is an active sensing. There the human projects by one of his senses his atmosphere beyond its ordinary boundary. This projecting is now done in a small measure and unconsciously by seeing or by hearing distant objects. So a portion of the atmosphere is sent or is present as far as the distant mountains or the sun. Within this portion some of the radiant-solid units of the mountain range are aligned or focussed by the sense of sight with radiant-solid units in the atmosphere and thus the distant mountains are seen. When the senses are trained to sense actively at will, the universe holds nothing they may not perceive.

It is the breath that keeps the fourfold physical body and the physical atmosphere in relation. The breath catches transient units, carries them to the compositors and after a while takes them away from the compositors.

The breath is the active side of the breath-form, which is always active and passive at the same time. One part is active as the breath, the other passive as the form. The breath takes the transient units out of the food in which they are bound. The breath stimulates and mixes the ferments with the food and changes that so that the transient units are taken out of it into the blood stream, where they, together with the transient units from the outside, build the cellular tissue structure of the body from the form of the breath-form. The breath liberates the secretions of the endocrine glands and mixes them with the blood.

The breath-form is a unit; its form aspect controls the functioning of the sense of smell and of the three other senses; and the breath is essential matter, that is, it differs from the ordinary matter in the visible world, in that it is matter of the unmanifested sides of the four worlds which has been present through manifestations so often that it has become refined as essential matter and is used in thinking to build out thoughts from their issuance to their exteriorization. It is neutral matter through which a unit in its changes must pass to get from one state into the next.

The breath-form attracts radiant matter of the body to itself, adapts it to its form and thus makes the radiant or astral body, which is the connection between the other masses of units composing the fourfold physical body, (Fig. III), and the breath-form. The difference between them is that the breath-form is of the refined matter which is not in the state of units and is related to all the worlds, whereas the astral is the copy of the breath-form, made from units of the physical plane of the physical world.

As to form and structure, the form of the breath-form changes according to needs, as determined by the ruling thought and by the marks made on it by thinking. Its changes are brought about by the breath, the active side of the breath-form. They are visible as the features and form of the physical body, its youth and age and its health and disease, and in addition they may be seen in the physical environment in which the body lives.

The matter of the breath-form cannot be injured or destroyed, because it is refined or essential matter and so not subject to harm, but the form of the breath-form is marked by the lines which thinking and thoughts make upon it, and so is besmirched by vices, by feelings and desires, or purified by virtue.

After death the breath-form represents nature to the doer. Every scene and event that is to be reproduced to the doer is borne by the breath-form and elaborated therefrom by elementals. After death the breath-form goes with the doer, is separated from it in the purgations and is again united with it in its bliss or heaven world. Like gold, however it may be sullied, the breath-form emerges clean from the fires that are fed by ignoble desires. At the end of the heaven period the breath of the breath-form is, so to say, out of gear with its form until, by the aia, it is again related to vivify for conception the form, which was reduced to a mere point.

In life the inertia of the ordinary form of the breath-form weighs on and so holds up and slows down any effort to think. After death, the lines on the form of the breath-form cause the unfoldment and reproduction of thoughts which made them. The breath of the breath-form is the means by which impressions from the four worlds can reach the atmospheres of the doer and can so affect thinking, and by which thinking can reach those worlds.

The breath-form unit is the most advanced degree to which a nature unit can progress. Then it is advanced and becomes the aia unit. The aia is unmanifested matter, neither nature-matter nor intelligent-matter. It cannot be perceived by the senses because it is not nature-matter. The aia is the transition state from nature to the Triune Self. It is under the influence of the doer, and is in the atmospheres of the Triune Self. It is not conscious of what it is, of what it does or of what is done with it or to it. It has no form, no extension, no physical properties. It is indestructible. It is without dimension, without a single attribute, except that it can be affected by the thinking, the thoughts, the feelings and the desires of the doer to which it belongs. Nature cannot affect it, unless the doer submits to the pull of nature. It takes every impression made by nature on the breath-form to which the doer agrees; but it can take no impression from the breath-form that is not allowed by the doer. It receives an impression from every thought of the doer and is marked by the thinking of the human. The impressions or marks are conveyed to it by means of the breath-form, with which it is at all times in phase.

The aia does nothing of itself or by itself. It acts only through the breath-form and by thinking. Thus it yields up the destiny which the doer has prepared for each embodiment. After the death of the body the aia is inert, is not in contact with the breath-form, and remains inert until the time for the conception of a new physical body.

The doer is the only friend and the only enemy of the aia; it can improve it or debase it. On the one hand, the aia is to the doer what the breath-form is to the aia and what the astral body is to the breath-form, and on the other hand, what the doer itself is to the Intelligence.

Nature is matter, unmanifested and manifested throughout the spheres and worlds, which has come out of Substance. Manifested nature is made up of units, that is, the ultimate divisions of nature in the sphere, world and plane on which the units are. Unmanifested nature in any sphere or world, plane or state is that condition where the matter is one mass, not divided into units. A unit is in the unmanifested state after it has run its course as a unit of one kind and before it becomes a unit of the next kind. Each unit has an active and a passive aspect and a side which does not manifest but is neutral to the active and the passive aspects. This unmanifested side of the unit pervades the manifested mass and is the means by which the active and the passive aspects of the unit change in their relation of dominating each other, and it is also the means by which the unit changes from one state, plane and world to the next.

The units of nature, and therefore nature itself, have no qualities, attributes or powers, except duality. They have no size, color, form, weight, temperature, instinct, feeling, desire, intelligence or anything, in and as themselves, except their active and their passive aspects. Their active and their passive aspects cannot act by themselves, but only when under the influence of human thinking, which brings them the Light that awakens them and releases their energy, which expresses itself through the passive aspect as the phenomena of light, sound, heat, electricity, magnetism and all other forces, known and unknown.

All things visible, all that can be heard, tasted, smelled or contacted, are made up of units in the solid state of the physical plane of the physical world. These things, masses made up of structure units, are created and destroyed by causal units, maintained by portal units and held together by form units. These four classes are progressed beyond, and control the multitudes of other earth, water, air and fire units, elementals. The only things that can be seen, heard, tasted, smelled or contacted are structure units, when massed sufficiently. They become so massed as to become objects perceptible by the senses, because of human thinking. The objects are perceptible when a sense focusses their mass which flows along the line of vision and brings them into the sense organ as impressions.

The bodies of human beings are of nature, they belong to nature as much as the parts of nature that are not in human bodies. Nature that is in human bodies is either fixed or movable. Permanently fixed from birth to death are the four senses and their four sets of compositor units. These are invisible and intangible. They compose, build up and maintain the physical bodies from the transient units which are caught and brought into them by the breath, light, air, water and solid food, out of the fourfold stream of transient units that is constantly passing everywhere. Some of the transient units are held for a while as the visible body and then are carried on by the stream. That is, nature fixed and nature flowing as and in the human body.

The fourfold stream flowing in and through each human body goes into the solid earth and the planets, the waters and the moon, the air and the sun, the starlight and the stars. Thus human bodies and their bodily atmospheres extend to the remotest stars. Neither the earth nor the sun is the center of the universe, but human bodies on the earth are.

The heavenly bodies are interrelated, as are the organs and nerves of the body. The heavenly bodies are not in the same zones or layers, but men hold them to be bodies on the same layer as the earth crust, and judge the apparent movements of the heavenly bodies by their own movements in on-ness. In this they are in error, not understanding the eclipses and other phenomena, which prove to them the axial and orbital rotations and vast distances of the heavenly bodies.

Human beings on the outer earth crust see only those parts of the universe which they maintain and use. There are other parts of the universe which correspond to the organs of the body which human beings have lost; those parts they cannot see or use, as they do the visible stars and the sun. Those parts are seen only by doers in bodies which have not lost them. Such doers do not move among human beings on the outer crust of the earth, where the seasons and the rules of the sexes are ignored.

The earth crust and the visible heavenly bodies correspond to the human physical body, and the four zones or layers of the earth correspond to the four zones of a human atmosphere. The fourfold breath through human bodies moves the fourfold breath stream of the earth that circulates through and animates the physical universe. The only units that are moved by both these breaths are transient units. The compositors remain in the human bodies which they build and rebuild during life. But after death these compositors, when they go into outside nature, still catch and hold transient units and so make up the earth crust, the bodies of the plants and animals on it and the heavenly bodies above it. There is a constant action and reaction between human bodies and the outside universe. The transient units of outside nature make the conditions under which the human bodies exist, through which these units have passed and from which they have received and carried impressions.

One who thus understands nature will not conceive himself to be a part of it. He will distinguish himself as one who is distinct from his four senses and from his body, and as not of or a part of nature. He must discover what he is, that is, the kind of thing he is, and who he is, that is, his identity, and he must become conscious of himself as that identity. He must understand that beings that are merely conscious as their functions in nature, are only elemental units, nature spirits or nature ghosts, but that he is conscious of nature. And when he distinguishes nature as being not himself, he begins to be conscious of himself as connected with his Triune Self.

SECTION 3

Recapitulation continued. The doer portion in the body. The Triune Self and its three parts. The twelve portions of the doer. How long a human is dissatisfied.

What the soul is has not been shown by those who have spoken of it and speculated about it. Nobody seems to have known what the soul actually is or what it does. At least, the soul has not heretofore been described so that its place and function in the body could be understood. But much of what has been said about it does actually have place and function in the make-up and maintenance of the body—even though many of the statements about soul are contradictory. The soul does die, but it lives again. The soul is lost, but it is found, to resurrect its parts into a new body for the return of the conscious doer to bodily life in the world. "Man" (as the conscious doer) must eventually "save his soul". And, the soul, when saved, does save the body from death. The discrepancies are reconciled by understanding the facts: that what has been called "soul" is actually the form aspect of the breath-form, which is the most progressed and ultimate unit of nature, including in itself all the functions as degrees in being conscious that it has passed through in its training in the nature machine; that it is indestructible and cannot really die, though it is temporarily inert after death and before it is recalled as the form for the building of another human body; that it is the form of the breath-form which causes conception; that at birth its breath of life enters into it; that it then becomes the living form (the living soul), and thereafter depends on its own breath and not on the breath of its mother for the building up and maintenance of its body throughout the life of that body. The form of the breath-form, then, is the soul of the body, and the breath is the life of the breath-form. The living breath builds food into the flesh and blood and bone tissue, as the physical body, according to the plan on its form. The soul or form of the body is not conscious of itself or as itself. It is merely the form, on which the conscious doer in the body, by thinking, writes the plans for the building of the body of its next life, in which it will itself re-exist and operate.

When the doer in the human eventually restores the human body to the perfect state in which the doer had inherited the body, by adjusting its feeling-and-desire into balanced union and thereby balancing the breath-form, then that breath-form is ready to be advanced to the aia state. The aia is as a line, or neutral point, between the nature-side and the intelligent-side. Upon it is inscribed in symbolic lines the totality, in essence, of the acts and thoughts of all the human bodies of the doer in whose service it has been. After eternities of functioning as the aia, it, so to speak, crosses the line, and is advanced on the intelligent-side of the universe and is a Triune Self.

Only a small portion of the doer lives in the body. The entire doer is prevented from coming in because of the weakness, inefficiency and unfitness of the body. The portion of the doer that does come into the body is, moreover, subject to limitations imposed by its own faults, and to illusions and consequent delusions. Hence human beings are limited in their understanding of that which is itself as the conscious something in the body, as distinct from the body, and of how it works in the body or out of it. They are limited in the exercise of their powers for the advancement of the doer, and of those for guiding the forces of nature. The doer is connected, on the one hand, with the body through the aia and the breath-form, and on the other hand, with the Intelligence that has raised and has its Triune Self in charge.

The doer is matter, to use a nature term, but it is incomprehensible as nature-matter. Words for nature have to be used to describe this matter because there are no words for the doer of the Triune Self. But dimension, distance, size, weight, force, division, beginning and end and all other qualifications and limitations of nature-matter do not apply to the matter of the doer.

A Triune Self is a unit that has been raised from the state of aia and is now a unit of intelligent-matter. It has three parts, the doer, the thinker, and the knower; each being a part, a breath, and an atmosphere. The breaths connect the Triune Self atmospheres with the three parts of the Triune Self. Each of these nine parts has an active and a passive aspect, and each of these eighteen aspects is represented in the others. Yet the Triune Self with these hundreds of aspects is a unit, is One. They have to be spoken of as separate, else they could not be described, explained, or understood; nevertheless they are One.

The Triune Self is connected with the body by means of the small portion of the doer which lives in the body. Through the indwelling portion of the doer, the respective breaths flow and keep up the connections between that and the non-embodied portions, and the atmospheres. These atmospheres, like the parts of the Triune Self and their breaths, are matter, and all together are a unit of matter.

But this matter cannot be measured or divided; it has no dimensions, no size or weight, it is incorporeal; it cannot be spoken of in any terms of corporeal nature-matter. It is the matter of feeling-and-desire, of thinking and other intangible states and actions. No nature-matter can feel, desire or think. Though the Triune Self is one, it is conscious in three degrees; passively as feeling, rightness, and I-ness; and, actively as desire, reason, and selfness.

The embodied portion of the doer in a human is subject to limitations and to illusions. It is limited in the exercise of its own powers because of its own ignorance, indifference, sloth, selfishness and self-indulgence. Because of ignorance the doer does not conceive itself to be not of nature. It does not understand who and what it is, how it got here, what it has to do, what are its responsibilities and what is the purpose of its life. Because of indifference it allows itself to remain in ignorance and to be the slave of nature, and so it increases its troubles. Because of sloth its powers are dulled and deadened. Because of selfishness, of blindness to the rights of others and of gratifying its own wants, it cuts itself off from understanding and feeling its powers. Because of self-indulgence, the habit of giving way to its own inclinations, appetites and lusts, its powers are drained and wasted. Therefore it is limited in its understanding of who and what it is and of what it has to do to discover itself and to come into its inheritance.

The doer in the human is limited in the exercise of its powers also by its slavery to nature. The doer has made itself depend upon the four senses for its thinking, its feeling and desiring and its acting. It is unable to think of anything as apart from the senses or as other than as reported by the senses; and its feeling is guided and ruled by sensations, which are nature elementals that play upon the nerves. The four senses originally functioned in the four worlds; now their perceptions are limited to the solid state of matter on the physical plane of the physical world. Therefore the doer is trained to regard only the hard, coarse, physical and most material things and to hold them to be the realities. The human is thus shut off from the higher realms and worlds of nature and cannot perceive in the light world or in the life world or in the form world or even on the three upper planes of the physical world, but is bound down to the four subdivisions of the lowest of the four states of matter on the physical plane.

The run of human beings desire, feel, think and act merely as human elementals, that is, their thinking, their feelings and desires are dominated by elementals, by sensations; they run after and act for sensations; their feelings and desires dominate their thinking, and that turns around material things as the realities and is blind to the higher parts of nature and ignorant of the royalty of the doer; they have no Light in their psychic atmosphere and the little Light in the mental atmosphere of the human, is dimmed and obscured.

In addition to such limitations, human beings are inevitably subject to illusions and delusions. The four senses are limited and disqualified from perceiving anything beyond on-ness, surfaces. If one were to be undeceived concerning nature, his senses would have to see, hear, taste, smell and contact anywhere and everywhere. The sense organs, too, are defective, and so inhibit the free action of the senses, disqualified as these are. So the sense of sight does not see correctly, as they are, form, size, color, position; and light it cannot see at all. So the sense of hearing does not perceive what a sound is and what the sound means; the sense of taste does not perceive what it is that it tastes in food, nor does this sense perceive forms, which it ought to do, as forms are to be apprehended by taste; the sense of smell does not perceive the bodies which it contacts as smell, and does not report their properties and qualities.

Because of these illusions, feeling does not feel correctly about outside objects. Feeling causes thinking to conceive and interpret these objects so as to satisfy the incorrect feeling. Hence the information is incomplete, distorted and often false. Thus the human deludes himself about outside nature. His conceptions are delusions.

The doer has twelve portions, which re-exist successively. When a doer portion enters the body it is embodied in the kidneys and adrenals by means of the breath. To this embodied portion of the doer is related the thinker which does not come into the body, but is related to the lungs and the heart. With the thinker is the knower which is related to the pituitary and pineal bodies.

The small embodied doer portion is seldom if ever conscious of its connection with the non-embodied portions, though there is no separation. There is a reciprocal action between the embodied and the non-embodied portions. Many of the ambitions, aspirations, thoughts, feelings and desires of the human are not exhausted, recognized and adjusted during life, and so fail to respond to the reciprocal action. Hence the states after death, through which the doer portion that was in the body passes, are the states necessary to complete the reciprocal action of the non-embodied portions upon the portion that was in the body.

The portion in the body is conscious of its loves and hates, pains and pleasures, fears and longings and its turmoils and flashes of inspiration. It is conscious as and of its feelings and desires. It is conscious also of its calculating, comparing, reasoning, judging and other mental actions, which are all instances of thinking with the body-mind, intellectually; but it is not conscious *of* itself *as* any of these mental activities. It is conscious of an identity which it connects erroneously with its name and the body. It is not conscious *of* its identity, and it is not conscious *as* identity, *as* who and what it is. It is conscious *of* feeling and desire; and that "I" which it erroneously believes itself to be, is the false "I", is the embodied portion of the doer which is mistaken for the true or real "I", as which the knower as the noetic part is conscious, knows. Among the causes of misunderstanding the identity of the human, are the presence in the doer of the I-aspect of the knower and the misinterpretation of this given by the thinking under the pressure of desire. The human being is conscious of the I-ness in it, and desire forces the mistaken conception, to please itself and feeling.

Of all this the run of human beings are unconscious, except that they are conscious of feelings and desires, and occasionally conscious of thinking and conscious of having an identity. They are unconscious of the relations existing between any of the parts of the Triune Self and their aspects and between these and the Light of Intelligence.

There are in a human feelings and desires that demand communion with the thinker and the knower. Yet he is not satisfied if he tries to feel and think beyond nature. This is so with every doer portion in a body, but is true in a greater degree when certain others of the twelve portions of the doer are in the body, and the demand for communion with the thinker and the knower is more urgent. Those portions are related on the intelligent-side. Then the restlessness causes the human to seek piety, mysticism, philosophy, occultism, asceticism, or forces him to engage in good works. These efforts do not satisfy him, because he cannot distinguish what is nature and what belongs to the conscious something which is himself, the doer, and because he mixes the two in his conception of what he is and of what his "God" is. As long as he is controlled by his body-mind he cannot distinguish himself as feeling-and-desire, and not as the elementals which he regards as feeling, and he is unable to feel and think away from nature, and the urge to feel and think beyond nature makes him dissatisfied.

SECTION 4

Recapitulation continued. The doer as feeling and as desire. The twelve portions of the doer. The psychic atmosphere.

The embodied portion of the doer is passively feeling and actively desire. The doer is embodied as feeling in the kidneys and as desire in the adrenals. Its influence is over the whole body. It largely controls the heart and lungs, which should be entirely controlled by the thinker. Feeling-and-desire cannot distinguish itself from that in nature to which it is attracted or attached.

Feeling has many functions. Four of them are used in its dealings with nature; they correspond to the four senses. They are perceptiveness, that of feeling which perceives; conceptiveness, that of feeling which makes of the perception a conception; formativeness, that of feeling which gives form to and develops the conception into a thought; and projectiveness, that of feeling which puts forth from the brain the thought which later becomes an act, object or event.

Feeling feels itself as being whatever affects it. So feeling feels hunger, which is a craving by elementals of the body for the sensation of food, as being itself the craving of the elementals. Feeling feels a wound in one's own body, as itself being the elementals which are affected by the cut, the blood and the pain. It feels a wound seen in the body of another in the same way, by being all the known details, though in a lesser degree. It feels the death of a friend, by being the sensations of the loss of company, comfort and support. But feeling is not the hunger, the wound or the loss, which it feels itself to be.

In the case of sexual union there is an exception, because feeling feels itself as being the other side of itself in the union, though it also feels itself as the elementals which it enlivens and thrills into sensations.

Feeling is that of the embodied doer that receives the impressions which the breath-form presents to it, after the breath-form has received them from the senses. The impressions are elementals sent in by or taken in from nature, with the current of the breath. All sense impressions are carried by the breath-form to feeling. There these elementals become sensations while, and only as long as, they are lit up, thrilled and formed, by being in touch with feeling. When feeling feels them it makes them sensations. They remain sensations as long as they are in contact with feeling. When they have passed out of the touch of feeling, which they do in a short while, they are no longer sensations, but are again elementals, nature units not in contact with feeling.

Feeling is not sensation, nor is a feeling a sensation. Feeling does not have any sensations of its own, or in or by itself. When feeling feels a pain from strain or pressure on a nerve, elementals enter along the nerve, and through the breath-form get into touch with feeling. The elementals which so enter are elementals making up the extraneous material object which causes the pain, such as a bullet, or the pleasure, such as a warming fire; or elementals making up the part of the body which cause the pain, such as a fractured bone or the exhilaration of well-being, such as the lungs in deep breathing; or unbound elementals such as those in the elemental streams which crowd in on a case of pain or pleasure. Feeling feels them as the sensation, as a hand feels a pencil. But while a pencil is not mistaken for a hand or for the feeling in the hand, the sensation, though just as foreign to the feeling as is the pencil to the hand, is mistaken for the feeling. Feeling in the body is that which feels.

Because feeling is not a sensation it can refuse elementals to become sensations; it can refuse to feel. It can do this by not permitting the elementals to contact it, after they have approached it through the breath-form. Elementals at all times swarm in the involuntary nervous system; and there they are still elementals. It is only when the breath-form transfers them to the voluntary nervous system that they become sensations. Chloroform, taken by the breath-form and acting on the voluntary nervous system, prevents sensation of pain, by disconnecting the voluntary from the involuntary system. Feeling can do the same thing as anesthetics do, or else it can withdraw from the voluntary nervous system. The disconnecting or withdrawing must be done by thinking.

Feeling, the passive side of the doer, is not mentality, but in thinking it uses the feeling-mind. It has no knowledge, no opinion. It is strictly feeling and it only feels. It does not analyze, it has no judgment. It is entirely dependent on desire, the active side of itself, for stimulation. It needs its feeling-mind to interpret to it what it feels and to refine and cultivate grosser feelings into finer ones. It depends upon the feeling-mind to be so trained by thinking that it can feel the right from the wrong in nature and in itself, and that it can feel the thinker, and the permanence of the identity of the knower.

Feeling is not noetic, it has no identity. Its tendency is to associate itself with anything and everything and so it fluctuates and has no identity in itself.

Feeling is one, but its feelings are many. Feeling itself as of the doer portion in the body, is the source of all feelings. When feeling is aroused by the sensing of toothache, that part of feeling which is in the nerve of the tooth, identifies itself as the sensation of toothache. It animates for the time the contacting elementals which cause the toothache. The feelings, as pain from a toothache or the comfort from a full stomach, or as the enjoyment of a sunset or of a mountain range, are so many distinct feelings, separated and distinguished and given form by the objects which cause them, and yet all come from feeling and disappear into feeling, as whitecaps appear on and disappear in the ocean.

The cause of the separation and development of the various feelings from feeling, is one or more of the four senses. These, with their impressions from objects of nature, are breathed by the breath-form into the psychic breath and so reach into and contact feeling. Thus the senses are the means of elementals becoming sensations and of drawing feeling along the channels of the senses, where it becomes separate feelings. When the impression reaches the kidneys and touches feeling, feeling closes upon it as a magnet holds a needle, and cannot let go at once. The impression is felt as pleasant or as unpleasant and becomes a sensation, which, if intense enough, compels thinking.

Without the physical body nature could not reach feeling, could not call out feelings and could not get part of the doer into nature. Nature provides the opportunity for the doer to train and develop its feeling. Feeling is trained by the doer through the four senses to distinguish contacts, odors, tastes, sounds and sights. Thus feeling is trained along the nature line in the arts and sciences. The units in the body and in outside nature are impressed and affected by the contact with feeling. In outside nature they are prepared to become units in the body.

The complement, the other side of feeling, its active side, is desire. There is no feeling without desire and no desire without feeling. They are inseparable, one cannot be without the other; they are in communication and interact continuously. Feeling impresses desire and desire responds to feeling. Feeling feels an impression as pleasant or unpleasant and communicates it to desire to satisfy or to remove.

Desire is a surging, driving, pulling, pushing, obstinate, conscious power. It answers to and complements feeling. It works to gratify feeling.

When it cannot itself answer to all that feeling feels, it uses the desire-mind and demands that the thinking answer to feeling. Desire is in communication with nature through feeling only, and with the knower through the thinker only. Time is not and distance is not a factor in the action of desire, though obstacles in nature may hinder its expression there.

Desire itself is one, but there are innumerable desires. These are evoked from desire by the four senses, through feelings. Any one feeling brings out a particular desire which answers to it. Persons and objects of nature are introduced to feeling by the senses. Feeling feels what is so brought in and evokes a desire for or against the persons or the objects. The desires are or are like voices that speak to the human. They urge him in favor of or against the person or object. The desires being the active side seem to be, for the time, the governing part of the human. Yet desire is led by feeling, and feeling by nature. The feelings and the desires change, and so the human has everchanging rulers. They have potential forms, as a cat, a hog, a wolf, a bird or a fish and take form after death. Desire, following feeling, goes into nature and becomes a driving power in animate nature. Few desires of the living go into nature and dwell there in forms; most desires evoked by feeling produce thoughts and go into nature in thoughts. The desires of the dead animate the animal forms in nature.

The embodiment of any one of the twelve portions of the doer is usually for the life of a physical body. But it is sometimes the case that two or more successive portions enter the body, one after the other, with the same breath-form and so in the same life. Then the person shows successively different characters which are usually displayed in different positions in life.

The embodied portion of the doer is separate, as far as the human which it largely is, is conscious, and yet is not separated from the non-embodied portions. It is accountable for its own feelings and desires, but the non-embodied portions are in a lesser degree affected by them and are helped or hindered and enjoy or suffer for them, as it does for theirs, because it and they are one. Yet as to physical events in a life, each portion reaps what it has sown. Ultimately the body must be so competent that all twelve portions will be in it at the same time, so that the whole doer is embodied.

The psychic atmosphere is matter of the doer, but is not as developed as is the matter of the mental atmosphere. It is that matter of the doer which is related to the form world and has to do with matter of that world, by action and reaction. The atmosphere is distinguished from the doer, which is its nucleus of action, and from the psychic breath, which is the current flowing from the atmosphere into the doer and from the doer out into the atmosphere. The psychic atmosphere ebbs and flows as the psychic breath, in and through the physical breath and so keeps that and the physical body going. The psychic atmosphere is also to be distinguished from the nature-matter, that is, elementals of the form world, which is in it. The form world surrounds and penetrates the physical world, and the psychic atmosphere may be in touch with any part or all of the form world. Time and space, as known in the physical world, do not exist in the form world, and are no hindrance to the psychic atmosphere and the doer. The psychic atmosphere is not embodied, but parts of it pervade the physical atmosphere and the physical body, which are in it.

The form world is not in direct touch with the psychic atmosphere; communication between the two is kept up by means of the breath-form for the doer, and by the physical body for nature. The doer does not act on the form world directly. It acts on the breath-form by means of the psychic breath, which flows in the physical breath, and acts through the breath-form and the four senses through the physical world on the form world. The form world reaches the doer in the inverse order. Nature elementals of the form world act through the physical world on the sense organs in the body and are by the breath-form conveyed through feeling to the psychic breath, which circulates them in the psychic atmosphere.

In the psychic atmosphere is no Light of the Intelligence, and therefore the psychic breath does not carry Light and the doer is without Light. In the psychic atmosphere is psychic matter, which is part of the doer. Some of this matter is without form and some is in the changing forms of feelings and of desires. These, though different, are not separate things in the atmosphere and their forms are not forms like physical objects. That which is called form is the cause of physical form. When feeling issues as a feeling, or desire issues as a desire, these separate feelings and desires take on the form of what they feel or desire, and these forms of the feelings and of the desires circulate in and are a portion of the psychic atmosphere. These feelings and desires are psychic states and act as psychic memories when they affect the embodied doer portion.

There are also in the psychic atmosphere elementals of the form world; while they are entertained they become sensations of sprightliness or gloom, grief or recklessness, curiosity or adventure, or other psychic states. Some of them take on the so-called forms of the feelings and desires and affect elementals of the physical world, that is, the matter of the physical world, and thus feelings and desires enter into insects and into flowers. Some of the elementals in the psychic atmosphere evoke other feelings and desires. Some enter the psychic atmosphere of others and there stimulate similar feelings and desires.

The elementals of the form world are finer, more subtle, than the elementals which are physical pleasure or pain; but they are only elementals, which arouse the feeling and play with it. So pain experienced in an eye, irritated by a cinder or a cold, pleasure felt while eating, excitement of crowds caused by demagogues or bigots, are elementals of the physical world. But castles in the air, clouds of gloom, deep emotions and the visions, transports and communion of mystics are elementals of the form world which are playing in the nerves and on the feeling and desire of the doer.

SECTION 5

Recapitulation continued. The thinker of the Triune Self. The three minds of the doer. The minds of the thinker and the knower. How desire speaks in place of rightness; the reversed round. The mental atmosphere.

The thinker is in its mental atmosphere and is in communion with the doer and the knower of the Triune Self by the mental breath. It lets the embodied portion of the doer, which is virtually a human animal, use three of the seven minds to get what it wants, by thinking; but on the other hand it brings to the human some of the knowledge of the knower, to show it what it should do and to warn it when about to do wrong. The thinker thinks with the Conscious Light of the Intelligence that is loaned to the Triune Self, so that any one of the seven minds may focus some of the Light and turn this on the subject to which the thinking is directed.

The seven minds are centered in reason, the active side of the thinker. They are distinct from each other, that is, they are as seven kinds of thinking with the Light of the Intelligence, yet they are one; they have to be spoken of as separate to show how thinking is done. All seven kinds are to act according to one principle, which is, to hold the Light steadily on the subject of the thinking. Four of the kinds, those of rightness and reason of the thinker, and of I-ness and selfness of the knower, do this perfectly. The three minds which the embodied portion of the doer may use, that is, the body-mind, the feeling-mind, and the desire-mind, are unable to do this properly; they do not act independently of the body, for they work from the heart and lungs and cannot be well controlled by the doer—nevertheless they may make the effort. Usually only one kind, the body-mind, is workable by the doer in the human, never more than three. After death, freed from the body, they repeat automatically their actions during the past life.

Reason is at all times in touch with the knower, though the human does not know of this. Reason operates the destiny of its human being, and is the direct and immediate dispenser of it.

The body-mind that is used by the doer in the human works with the senses and thinks for the body, the sex of the body and the physical world; it deals with the phenomena of physical matter. A perception of a thing is made by this body-mind, not by the senses, which merely bring in an impression. The perception is the consideration which the body-mind, as the perceiver, gives to the impression which has been brought to the doer.

A conception is made by the body-mind when it endeavors to focus Light on a perception. The body-mind is that used in perceiving, planning, comparing, analyzing and judging the affairs of business and of science, of law and of politics, of convention and of religion, from any physical act or object to the loftiest conception, and is what people usually term their "mind." By its thinking it has made the visible world and the acts, objects and events that have brought about the conditions and situations thereon. It takes objects of nature and makes them subjects of thinking. None of the other minds work directly for nature.

The feeling-mind should think for feeling and the expressions of feelings, but it is invariably controlled by the body-mind and the result is that it works for the body, that is, for nature. Whenever one tries to express what he feels he does so with the feeling-mind. This effort is made by almost everyone in language, music, painting, architecture, sculpture, adventure, acting, dancing, cooking, shooting, sailing and the use of tools. Usually the feeling-mind is not workable, and so people are not able to use it as it should be used. But if their efforts are somewhat successful they stand out as original artists and manipulators of tools and instruments, and are called poets, writers, musicians, painters, sculptors, adventurers, discoverers, actors, dancers, cooks, marksmen and sailors. The mental action of such revealers, artists and artisans corresponds to taste and form in nature. If to the ability to use the feeling-mind there is joined a body in which suitable elementals predominate, the person will excel in his art.

The third kind, the desire-mind, thinks for desire and to execute desires. There are four functions of desire, namely, the power to be, to will, to do, and to have. As persons by the effort to use the feeling-mind become artists and artisans in handling things so as to express their feelings, so persons by the more or less successful efforts to think with the desire-mind display their power and are more or less successful in being, in willing, in doing or in having the objects of their desires. Desires are put into effect through efforts to think with this desire-mind.

People who stand out among the mass are those who have accomplished things according to feeling or to desire or to both. They are people of sentiment or of action. They are successful, not merely because of the feeling or the desire or because of their efforts, but according to their ability to work and think with the feeling-mind or with the desire-mind. If persons have much feeling without being able to use the feeling-mind they are swallowed up by a morass of sentimentality, or if they have strong desires without the ability to use the desire-mind, they are often brutes in word and deed.

The mind for feeling cannot be used at will unless the human is able to use to some degree the desire-mind; and one cannot use the desire-mind at will, unless he is able to use the feeling-mind, at least in some degree.

The body-mind tries to turn the Light on the objective, physical side of the impression only. The feeling-mind, if it does think for feeling, tries to turn the Light so as to express the subjective side of the impression which is concerned with sympathies and sentiments. The desire-mind, if it does think for desire, tries to turn the Light so as to express the subjective aspect of the impression, which is concerned with accomplishing or getting or holding possessions or a name or power. The feeling-mind thinks for feeling, and so for all the feelings, whether they be for nature or toward the doer. The desire-mind thinks for desire and so for all the desires, whether they reach for nature or into the doer.

Yet the body-mind invariably controls all the thinking in the world. With it a man thinks for the "things that make life worth living", for the run of human beings. Physical things are what he wants to feel or not to feel and what he desires to have or to avoid. He does not want to feel feeling or feelings. Therefore he can use only the mind that thinks for physical things. His feeling and his desire strive by this body-mind to get physical things. By thinking physically he gets an abundance of physical gifts, but no psychic advancement of his doer, no finer feelings, no nobler desires. When he holds steadily on to an object, his feelings and desires cause this body-mind to turn to the object as a subject which he wishes to have, to do or to be. The mind tries to focus the Conscious Light on the subject to the degree that his feelings and desires hold steadily to the object.

When an impression of an object has been taken by the senses and reduced to a point, it is taken by the breath-form to the kidneys and there makes contact with feeling. When this has aroused desire in the adrenals, desire takes the impression to the heart, to rightness, whence it is passed on to reason in the lungs. There the breath fixes it on the form of the breath-form and so affects that and through it the nerves of the involuntary system. All this is done with an incoming breath. If the man wants the object, his feeling and desire hold the body-mind upon this impression on the breath-form and an attempt at thinking on that subject begins in the mental atmosphere, in the area from the lungs to the brain. The brain in the thorax is not organized for thinking but for breathing and for the circulation of the breath; the brain in the head is used by the heart and lungs for thinking. But the brain is secondary, the heart and lungs are the principal, though at present disorganized, organs for thinking. The cranial brain does the work as a substitute for the thoracic brain. Thinking is done between an outgoing and an incoming breath, if there is any thinking, but much of what passes for thinking is not actual thinking.

While the body-mind attempts to focus the Light, other sense impressions come into the area, along the same road, attracted to the Light. They attempt to get into the Light. Other elementals in parts of the body are stimulated or are devitalized and are projected as forms by the breath into the area of the thinking. Still other obstructions, such as thoughts and thinking, are in the mental atmosphere and interfere with the focussing.

If one continues to feel and to desire an object, the Light will show him how it is to be obtained. As soon as this is seen, elemental matter takes the impression of the means by which it is to be obtained. The matter is of the life and form planes of the physical world and affects the radiant and airy matter of the physical plane and reaches and impresses those persons through whom the object is to be obtained. The continued thinking brings about circumstances aligning persons, places or things so that the object will be attained, unless this interferes with destiny.

The mind for rightness is not usable by the human; it thinks for rightness, on estimates and judgments on the subjects presented to it by reason, and on communications which come to rightness from selfness. The thinking consists in holding the Conscious Light in the mental atmosphere on the subjects which are presented by desire or by reason. Human beings cannot in any way work the mind of rightness. The mind for reason is for thinking by reason and leads the Conscious Light into all subjects and questions which are brought to reason by desire.

The mind for I-ness is for communication with I-ness. I-ness uses it, but a human cannot. When he can consciously communicate with it, he will be more than a human. The mind for I-ness holds the clear Light of the noetic atmosphere on, and so identifies what is done by the other minds with feelings or with desires that urge them. I-ness uses its mind to flash Light to reason, when the human wants to know who he is. Then reason satisfies feeling and desire by letting them have the feeling of the ego or false "I". The mind for selfness is for communication with selfness; it cannot be used by the human. Selfness uses its mind to flash the clear Light of conscience, that is, the sum of knowledge on any moral subject, to rightness, and so to warn. Selfness uses its mind to give knowledge to reason, though the human does not come into possession of this knowledge except in the rarest cases. If the human had the ability to reach in his thinking to the mind for I-ness and to the mind for selfness even as little as he can now think with the body-mind, he would know himself, who and what he is, as a consciously immortal doer in the Eternal of the Triune Self as well as throughout time, and he would know his destiny.

The matter of which these seven minds consist is matter of the Triune Self and therefore has no qualities and no activities which can be designated by terms applicable to nature-matter. However, the matter is matter of the thinker, not life matter of the nature-side, and corresponds to and affects matter of the life world. It affects it by its efforts to hold Light of the Intelligence that is in the mental atmosphere, on a subject of thought which the senses have brought in and which has reached the body-mind. It affects it also by passive thinking and by the nature-matter that is in the thoughts circulating in the mental atmosphere.

Efforts at thinking, which at present is done mostly with the body-mind, affect the active side of the units in the life world, and so cause the units as passive things to be lit up, to be energized and to take on a life impulse which eventually manifests physically. The minds, when they do work, also affect feeling, and desire through feeling. They do not affect the knower, because they do not think about it. They have a powerful effect on the physical body through feeling.

Rightness is the name here given to the passive side of the thinker. Rightness is of as much importance to the human as its organ, the heart, is to the body. Rightness has some of the clear Light. It is as if a point opened from the heart into the noetic atmosphere. At this point of Conscious Light is the little flame in the heart that makes the being human. The feeling of rightness is the standard of what is right for the human on any subject. Its nature is to be right, that is, as it should be, in the Light of the Intelligence. Rightness is conscious of that which is presented to it, as being right or wrong.

The relation of rightness to reason is analogous to that of feeling to desire. Feeling prompts desire and desire tries to satisfy feeling, but rightness and reason in themselves actually do satisfy each other and act in agreement, though their organs, which are the heart and lungs, are usurped by feeling and desire.

Rightness is replaced in the heart by desire. Reason allowing feeling and desire to use the first three minds, seems to act upon the urge of desire, which, speaking from the heart, seems to overpower and speak in place of rightness. When feeling will not feel for nature, but will listen to and be guided by rightness, and when desire will not act except under the guidance of reason, feeling-and-desire will withdraw from the heart, where now both are. Rightness will then be in the heart, its own organ, and will act on, regulate and advise feeling. Feeling will prompt desire from the point of view of rightness instead of from that of nature. Desire will seek contact with rightness; it will seek to be approved by rightness instead of forcing out rightness and speaking from its place to the body-mind.

Then the round is reversed. Whereas now feeling influences desire, desire taking the place of rightness and compelling the feeling-mind to serve feeling for the benefit of nature, the round going the other way will start from rightness, not from nature. Feeling will not feel unless rightness starts it, and then it will prompt desire which will seek approval and confirmation by rightness, and rightness itself will start reason, to work with its mind to satisfy feeling. Thus the lemniscate will be reversed, and represent a self-government from within, (Fig. IV-B).

Rightness thinks particularly on such subjects as affect the Triune Self rather than nature; and, because it is under the Conscious Light, which is Truth, thinks of them as being right or not right. It thinks of the correctness of the manner in which the doer is affected by nature, and of the manner in which the doer feels and desires in itself, apart from nature. It sanctions any feeling which is right and discountenances any feeling which is not right, under the Light. It approves of any right act or intent to act by desire, and denounces it when wrong. Feeling-and-desire cannot induce rightness to leave its position, but they can refuse to listen to it and can crowd it out by the body-mind; and this is what the human usually does. He has done this so persistently in the past, that desire has usurped the place of rightness which has been forced, so to say, into a corner of the heart. A human wants what he wants whether it is right or not, and gets it by his ability to think how to get it.

In the human the organs through which feeling and desire function are the kidneys and adrenals, but a human neither feels in the kidneys nor desires in the adrenals. Feeling and desire have taken possession of the heart, which is the organ of rightness. When rightness speaks in the heart, feeling and desire overpower it and, as lust and anger, speak in its place. This is so where self-interest rules. On moral questions rightness receives flashes of Light from selfness and so becomes the mouthpiece of conscience without respect to how one feels or what he desires.

Where self-interest does not rule and has no power to affect the correctness of things, as in observing the time of day or in calculating tide time tables, rightness is not interfered with by the doer. Then desire starts the body-mind to discover, calculate, ascertain or solve whatever is desired.

For all mundane things the body-mind is used. Its thinking presents to rightness the subject on which the thinking strives to hold the Light. When the thinking presents a conclusion, that is, when it thinks, it holds the Light steady on the subject, and rightness says "far away", "near it", "incorrect", "correct", "wrong", "right", "no", "yes". In this way rightness determines the correctness or deviation therefrom in searching and assembling facts and in calculations, opinions and judgments. The little invisible flame in the heart is steady when the thinking is correct, but flickers when the thinking is not correct. Whereas the mind of reason extends from the lungs to the brain, rightness never leaves the heart.

The mental atmosphere of the human is a portion of intelligent-matter which is included in the noetic and which itself includes the psychic atmosphere. It, like the other two, is not directly connected with the physical body and so the physical organs are not in touch with the mental atmosphere. It acts in and upon the physical body through the mental breath, which acts through the psychic breath which acts through the physical breath in the heart and lungs. The mental atmosphere does not blend with the psychic atmosphere, though it contains it and is through it as light shines through water.

The mental atmosphere of the human is related to the noetic atmosphere by the mental breath and the noetic breath. Through these breaths it receives Light of the Intelligence from the noetic atmosphere. In the mental atmosphere of the human the Light is dimmed, obscured and impeded as in a fog, but the atmosphere does not affect the Light. The Light never leaves the mental atmosphere; not even when it is mixed with desire in a thought and is issued into the forms of nature. The Light can go from the mental atmosphere into nature carrying a portion of the matter of the atmosphere with it, can circulate in nature and can be brought back into the mental atmosphere, all without leaving the mental atmosphere. It is as though the mental atmosphere were extended with that Light into nature. When the Light is brought back it brings adhesions which seem impressions and affect the matter of the mental atmosphere, but not the Light.

These accretions are among the obstacles that impede the thinking. The obstacles consist of matter of the life world, of the form world and of the physical world, brought in by perceptions of what the senses present, by feelings and by desires through passive and active thinking, by nature-imagination and by the thoughts of oneself and of others.

The mental atmosphere of the human is related and corresponds to the life world. The mental atmosphere is intelligent-matter and the life world is nature-matter. The atmosphere is one, the life world is made up of many. The thinking which goes on in the mental atmosphere stirs up and awakens life in the units of the life world, and there causes the units to dart, to whirl, to eddy and to contract and expand. What the atmosphere does to the world, the world does to the atmosphere. The life world reacts on the mental atmosphere and so stirs it up and causes concentration and diffusion in it, which cause further thinking and thoughts. In the mental atmosphere are one's own and others' thoughts and elementals of the life world. These are habits of thinking. In the lower part of the atmosphere is the psychic atmosphere and in that the physical atmosphere with their elementals of the form world and of the physical world. These elementals suggest thinking on their own lines and produce passive thinking and nature-imagination, so as to become sensations. Human beings cannot use the mental atmosphere as a whole, but only that part of it which is in the psychic atmosphere of the doer.

The minds used by human beings have difficulties in working in the Light which is dimmed and obscured by these hindering things and so have to be trained in being steady in holding the Light.

SECTION 6

Recapitulation continued. The knower of the Triune Self, selfness and I-ness. The noetic atmosphere. What a human is conscious as. Isolation of feeling; of desire. Being conscious of Consciousness.

The knower of the Triune Self does not feel or desire, nor does it need to think to get knowledge; it is Self-knowledge. Knowledge of the Triune Self does not change. When it acts it acts as Self-knowledge. It is that which knows, and which knows its identity. When thoughts are balanced and so knowledge of the conscious self in the body is acquired, it is acquired by the human, not by the knower that already has and is all knowledge.

I-ness is the passive side of the knower, and selfness its active side. I-ness is the undying, continuous, unchanging, self-same, self-conscious identity of the Triune Self. It is in the noetic atmosphere, in the clear Light of the Intelligence. It witnesses and so identifies all the feelings and the desires which are carried out by the thinker, but is untouched and unaffected by them or by the changes that go on in them. Neither reason nor rightness interferes with I-ness, and I-ness does not interfere with either of them. I-ness is not connected with outside nature; but in the body its organ is the pituitary body, through which it lets Light of the Intelligence into the body.

Nothing can approach I-ness that cannot stand in the clear Light, which is a reason why the doer does not communicate with it, or is not conscious of what it is in this life or of what it was in past existences and why it cannot remember those lives.

The I-ness and the selfness of the knower are not in the body. The feeling in the body feels I-ness and thinks of itself as "I", and so is the "ego", the false "I". The desire in the body desires selfness and thinks of itself as "self". The "self" is only desire to the human. Thus feeling-and-desire in the human is the feeling of identity and the desire for the knowledge of Self. Among the desires are some that are classed as good and others that are spoken of as evil. The good ones cause the desire of an ideal or higher Self, and the bad ones cause the desire of an evil or lower self, which are then called by some the "Higher Self" and the "lower self". Selfness is the knowledge of itself as a Triune Self in its entirety and of its permanence throughout all the changes in the doer.

This knowledge is a whole, unbroken, unlimited as regards itself, its noetic atmosphere and the noetic world. Selfness is not directly connected with feeling-and-desire and is not affected by anything that feeling-and-desire do. Selfness is connected with rightness and with reason. To rightness it gives flashes of the Light of the Intelligence. When subjects of a moral aspect are considered by the human, these flashes are regarded as conscience. Selfness gives to reason flashes of Light on rare occasions for the human, and these flashes are intuitions, teachings from within, concerning a subject or thing. They come to reason from the mind for selfness, and then to the human through the mind of reason. Selfness and I-ness in their relation to each other are the two aspects of the knower. When one side acts, the other reinforces and amplifies the action. When I-ness is in evidence, the knowledge of selfness is behind that I-ness; when selfness acts, the identity and endlessness is behind the knowledge. Selfness and I-ness differ from each other in that I-ness is a conscious, persistent identity without beginning or end, and selfness is the knowledge without beginning, end or break; but selfness and I-ness are the same in that the knowledge and the identity cannot act without each other.

Of this knowledge selfness makes available through rightness only what relates to the portion of the doer in the human in the performance of his duties and what relates to itself as selfness, when the human prepares himself to receive such knowledge.

Selfness and I-ness are related to the Intelligence from which they receive the Light. They stand in the Light, and therefore are in the Intelligence. They do not stand in the fullness of the Light, yet they stand in clear Light. They give the Light to the noetic atmosphere, conserve it there, and after the Light has been made unattachable they may restore it to the Intelligence. Selfness, and in a lesser degree I-ness, issues Light into the mental atmosphere.

A human may become conscious of the presence of I-ness. It is also possible, but it is improbable, that he will come into contact with selfness. Though he cannot so come into contact by his own efforts, yet if he has made enough effort in that direction, selfness will know when it will let him be conscious of it. Then the human has a standard of himself as that which is conscious in the Eternal without change or break, which he distinguishes from himself as the human being of short duration made up of days and nights and conscious only of his waking hours. He is astounded at the vastness and the verity of the knowledge which is his own, and yet not his as the human. He becomes conscious of this identity and knowledge by the action of the mind of I-ness and the mind for selfness, not by his own volition but by the grace of I-ness and selfness, who use them to make him conscious.

The organ of I-ness is the rear half of the pituitary body and the organ for selfness is the pineal body, in the brain, (Fig. VI-A,a). While the use of these organs has not been usurped, as has the use of the heart by feeling and desire, yet they are not in use, except to the limited extent in which a human is allowed to be conscious of himself. There is, however, a usurpation of the brain, which should be used for noetic purposes but is used by the heart and lungs in thinking about physical things. Such thinking should be done in a pelvic brain, now degenerated and inoperative, except for the sexes.

The knower is in the noetic atmosphere which flows as the noetic breath. The noetic breath is intelligent-matter and so does not in any way resemble the physical breath. The noetic breath flows in the mental and that flows in the psychic breath and that in the physical breath.

In the physical breath the noetic breath starts the lunar germ, by giving Light to a transient unit of matter of the light world in the generative system of the physical body. The noetic breath does not work directly, but through the mental and the psychic breaths and at last through the radiant current of the physical breath gives Light to a unit in the radiant matter in the brain, which so is made the lunar germ. The noetic breath, working through this aspirational fire breath when this ascends the spine, takes the Light that is saved automatically every month, back to the brain. The noetic breath also carries the solar germ, which is a part of the noetic atmosphere bearing clear Light, down and up the spinal cord during the life of the body.

The noetic atmosphere is not matter of the light world. It is intelligent-matter and belongs to the Triune Self. In the atmosphere are I-ness and selfness, the noetic breath and the Light of the Intelligence. It permeates the mental, psychic, and the physical atmospheres and the physical body, and all these are kept going by the breath of the noetic atmosphere. The Light of the Intelligence is throughout the noetic atmosphere and the Light impresses the intelligent-matter in the atmosphere. In the lower portion of the noetic atmosphere, where are the psychic and the physical atmospheres, the Light is not perceived, not because there is actually no Light, but because the matter in these atmospheres cannot make contact with the Light. The condition is like that of a man who cannot see because he is blind, and not because there is no light. The noetic atmosphere is of the noetic world, a name given to that which unites in knowledge the noetic atmospheres of all human beings.

The noetic atmosphere can act in any part of the light world and affect the elementals, the matter and things in that world, but these cannot act in the atmosphere. The Light in the noetic atmosphere affects the matter of the light world so that that matter seems to be itself light and the light world a shadowless world of colorless light. The entities of the life, the form and the physical worlds, which are in the lower and the lowest portions of the noetic atmosphere, do not affect the noetic atmosphere; they act only in the atmosphere which corresponds to the world in which they are.

The knower and the thinker of the Triune Self are perfect. The doer is not perfect. The duty of the doer is to make itself perfect, under the guidance of the thinker. Feeling and desire must identify and isolate themselves, to be conscious that they are distinct from the body and nature.

In a human feeling and desire are not thus conscious. A human is, however, conscious that he is conscious of feeling and of desire, of thinking and of a certain identity. At death he loses even this trifle of which he is conscious, because he does not think of what he is conscious *of* or *as* during life. If he will think of what he is conscious *as* during life, he will be conscious *of* it at the time of death. Everyone should try to be conscious of his identity with his Triune Self at the time of death, apart from the body with its name. Then he will be conscious of his identity in the after-death states and will be conscious of his identity as distinct from the body and its name, when he again re-exists.

Being conscious is the presence of Consciousness in that which is conscious. Only a doer can be conscious of being conscious, or that it is conscious. Nothing in nature can be so conscious. Nature units are conscious only as their functions and never *as* what they are, nor are they conscious *of* their functions. Every human is, so to speak, an infinitesimal opening into the indescribable immensity of Consciousness.

A human does not know what he is conscious *as*. He knows that he is conscious, which means he knows that he is. This is the only thing he actually does know. It is the only thing he knows of reality. He does not know who or what it is that is conscious *as* he. He is conscious *of* many things, of his feeling, of his desiring, of his thinking and of his identity, but he is not conscious *as* these things. He is conscious *of* his body, of its parts, of its senses, and of the sensations of these as pleasant or unpleasant, interesting or indifferent. He not conscious *of* all there is in his body, nor of the manner in which the units in the body are conscious *as* their functions. He is not conscious *as* his senses. He is conscious of the objects perceived, but not of the manner in which he perceives them. He is not conscious of the manner in which the sense organs act, the senses work, nature-matter is affected, the breath-form operates and the doer reacts. He is not conscious of what the things actually are, but is conscious only of certain impressions which are made on him by the perception of these things. He is conscious *of* sensations, but can never be conscious *as* sensations, such as pains and pleasures, hunger and thirst, love and hatred, joy, sorrow, gloom and ambition.

That in the human which is conscious that it is conscious, is the aspect of the doer which is feeling and the aspect which is desire. That *of* which he is conscious is the body which is nature. This contact of nature with the doer produces an illusion which disables the human from distinguishing himself as being conscious, and as being distinct from the body as nature. The doer in the human cannot be conscious *as* being conscious, while it is conscious *of* what it is conscious. It cannot be conscious *as* doer while it is conscious *of* nature. That in the human which is conscious that it is conscious, must disconnect itself from the body of which it is conscious, to become conscious *as* itself. Therefore, it is necessary for feeling to distinguish, identify, itself, so that it will know what it is, and will know that it is not nature. That portion of the doer which is conscious that it is conscious, needs no thinking to be so conscious. To be conscious of nature it needs the thinking of the body-mind. To be conscious *of* itself *as* feeling it needs the thinking of the feeling-mind without interference by the body-mind. By that, the feeling-mind, it is made conscious that it is feeling. By the thinking of the desire-mind it is made conscious that it is desire. In being merely conscious *of* nature or *of* feeling or *of* desire, these minds are passive. They must be active in order to recognize nature as functioning, or feeling as functioning, or desire as functioning.

For the doer in the human to become more than merely conscious that it is conscious, feeling must think of itself with the feeling-mind and without the body-mind. When one thinks, he is conscious of sensations and of nothing more. This means that impressions from objects of nature contact and grip feeling and while so gripped are sensations and are not distinguished from feeling. This thinking is done with the body-mind. The feeling-mind and the desire-mind are, so to speak, limp and flabby. For the doer to be conscious *as* what it is, it must not be conscious *of* sensations. For feeling to know itself *as* feeling when it is freed, it must first understand or realize itself in the body.

To stop sensations, one must stop the use of the body-mind and one does this by disconnecting the breath-form by which the sensations come in. This is done by giving undivided attention to thinking with the feeling-mind, on feeling only. When one is successful in thinking with the feeling-mind only, one is not at all conscious *of* nature, but discovers oneself *as* feeling. This is the introduction of the doer in the human to itself, and is the beginning of Self-knowledge. The system for one to think without creating thoughts or to think so that one will have Self-knowledge, is based on one's being conscious and on becoming conscious in higher degrees by the use of the feeling-mind. After one has become conscious of oneself *as* feeling, that is, has freed feeling, and has established oneself as a being independent of the body and nature, even while conscious of his body, he is qualified for being conscious in higher degrees. One does so by giving one's undivided attention to thinking of desire. Such thinking calls into use the desire-mind. When one has become conscious of oneself *as* desire, that is, has freed desire, and has established himself *as* desire, as a being independent of the body and nature, even while conscious of the body, one is qualified to become conscious successively as rightness, reason, I-ness and selfness. Then one is conscious *as* and knows oneself to be the complete Triune Self. This is the object to be obtained by the system of thinking without creating thoughts, that is, without attaching oneself to nature.

Being conscious that one is conscious is, as it were, a point in the fullness of the boundless circle of Consciousness. To speak of point or circle on the intelligent-side is a metaphor, because points, lines, angles, surfaces and circles are nature-matter, degrees of nature-matter. They are presence, throughness, in-ness and on-ness. On the intelligent-side there are no points, and there is no development into circles. But points, lines, angles, surfaces and circles can be used as symbols. They are accurate symbols indicating the doer's progress in being conscious on the intelligent-side. But it is always to be remembered that they are symbols, metaphors like word-forms for living things in nature, which are used to designate things of the doer, because no word-forms for the doer are available.

Thus it may be said that all possibilities of knowing begin from a metaphorical point of being conscious. This point is expanded to a circle, as one progresses in being conscious. The circle of his being conscious is ever expanded as he becomes conscious in higher degrees, until he is conscious as the boundless circle of Consciousness.

The system of thinking without creating thoughts is based upon the use and the training of the feeling-mind until feeling is isolated, and then upon the successive use of the other minds to be conscious as the Triune Self. Being thus conscious is after all only a small circle of being conscious. The Triune Self must go on until it is conscious as an Intelligence, and on and on until it is conscious *as* Consciousness.

He who bears in mind what has thus been recapitulated, and assiduously puts into practice the system of thinking, now to be dealt with, will find in it a way to develop himself to whatever he may aspire to. He will see a way towards becoming one with whatever his highest conceptions of Deity may be, that is, with his own thinker and knower, and how to attain the greatest accomplishment possible to a human, which is: being conscious of Consciousness.

SECTION 7

The System of Thinking. What it is. Stages on: The Way to Conscious Immortality.

This system of thinking is for you, you choose and will: to have knowledge of nature and of your Triune Self; to think without creating destiny, to be conscious of Consciousness, and to become consciously immortal.

I.

1. You who would follow this system to become conscious of Consciousness should think about the reality as represented by the word Consciousness—as different from anything that you have read or heard about the word. You should not think of Consciousness as being your consciousness or another's consciousness or as the consciousness of any being or thing. You should not think of Consciousness as possessing or being possessed, as having states or extension, or as being divided into states. You should not think of Consciousness as having any attributes or limitations, or as becoming anything or doing anything, or as a being, or as having being or non-being. You should not think of the consciousness of any being, but of the being as conscious *as* something or *of* something. You should think that you cannot really know anything about Consciousness before you become conscious of Consciousness. You should think that you may become conscious of Consciousness at any time after you begin to think about it, even while you are human and have not rid yourself of thraldom to nature and have not taken your place among the consciously immortal Triune Selves who are freed. You should think that Consciousness is present in and through and about everything, however small or great. You should think that it is by the presence of Consciousness in and through every thing or being that the thing or being is conscious of that of which or as which it is conscious. You should think that Consciousness is not in any way different in the most primitive unit in nature and the most advanced Intelligence. You should think that Consciousness is the same in the units composing a block of granite as it is in the Supreme Intelligence of the Universe, no less and no more. You should think that by the presence of Consciousness each being performs its work and is conscious of as little or of as much as it has attained the capacity for being conscious. You should think that when you have an understanding about what Consciousness is not and think about what it is, you are ready to make the effort to become conscious of Consciousness.

2. Then you can think: O Consciousness! undescribed, unexplained, and without qualities; not dependent on, not affected by, any thing; present throughout all space and time and being and throughout all Intelligence; by whose presence all nature units are conscious as their functions, and the Triune Selves are conscious as what they are, of what they do and of what they may become. By Thy Presence in me through life and through

death, I think and feel and will to be conscious of Thee, and to know Thee—Consciousness.

You should not set the time when you will first become conscious of Consciousness. There is the possibility of its being at any time in your present human life. It may not be until, at the end of lives, you have all your minds under control. You should think the death of your body a no greater break in your continuity of living in this world than is the retiring for a night's sleep in your present body. When you, as the will to become conscious of Consciousness, think thus of Consciousness, you can be assured that soon or late, perhaps when least expected, you will so be. On being conscious of Consciousness you do not know any of the beings of which you are then conscious. You will know them only after you know yourself as a Triune Self. But having once been conscious of Consciousness it is possible for you by thinking to be again conscious of them. Becoming conscious of Consciousness neither cancels the obligations which you have incurred by your thoughts, nor gives you entrance to other planes or worlds, nor puts you in control of your desires and your minds, nor establishes you in union with yourself. But once having been conscious of Consciousness you will surely meet your obligations and make connection with the planes and worlds and learn the control of desire and of your minds and eventually be in union with yourself. It will be as a map and a light for you. You are human, you may choose to reach the heights and the depths of human life, but you will not linger at either extreme, for you know the road and your Light will guide you, and you will surely reach the end of the road of attainment as the Triune Self. You can no longer make yourself believe that all your desires are right. While you see things as they are, you cannot deceive yourself. You may not do what you know to be right, but you know when you are doing wrong. You will right the wrongs done, as you gain strength; and surely you will get strength. With such an understanding about Consciousness you go on with your regular duties, being confident that in due season you will be conscious of Consciousness. Overanxiousness will delay and interfere with your self-adjustment in becoming so conscious. Expectation or speculation as to time or condition will keep you out of right relation to nature and defer the time of your being conscious of Consciousness. You should have a constant, steady assurance that you will live through the lives of your physical bodies—and with no less confidence than you now live through the daily lives of your present body—towards the attainment of the purpose of life. Then, when you are ready, whether in the present life or in one far removed, it happens unannounced. Intervening partitions and divisions are gone: you as feeling-and-desire-and-rightness-and-reason-and-I-ness-and-selfness are One.

3. In the instant of being conscious of Consciousness the Light which is greater than the light of ten thousand times ten thousand suns opens up in the brain and tempers it and quickens the portion of the doer connected with that brain so that you are conscious beyond the limits of thought and are made conscious of your relation to Consciousness. You are conscious of all Intelligence, and see everything of nature at once. You are not thrilled by emotions, do not build in imagination, are not raised to beatific ecstasies and are not dazzled or overpowered. You are calm, and have limitless increase and extension in being conscious throughout and within all being and Intelligence, and there is no thing of nature which you do not perceive. By the Great Triune Self of the worlds and your Intelligence, you are related to all Triune Selves and to all Intelligences, and by your body with its breath-form you are related to all nature manifested and unmanifested. You are conscious of all there is of the spheres and worlds and planes, and through these are conscious of that which is unmanifested. You see and hear in all the worlds. You are conscious through all space, and in the same instant you are conscious of all the aias and Triune Selves and Intelligences, of Conscious Sameness and of Pure Intelligence and of their relation. By being conscious of Consciousness you are at once conscious of every being. All things are related in Consciousness and you are in conscious relation with all. You do not wonder at the mightiness of yourself as the Triune Self or at the number and the greatness of the Intelligences with which you are in relation, or at the order in relation of all beings of which nature is composed. There is no here and there, or this or that. All are at once. In the same instant you are in gracious peace and conscious allness with every being that is, and that is not yet. You are satisfied and calm and you have ease and poise with a glad at-homeness in unmistakable reality. Being conscious of Consciousness, you are serenely conscious of the glory and the grandeur and of the simplicity in relation of all there is.

II.

4. Before being conscious of Consciousness you will desire to think without being attached; then you will cease to make destiny. You should

understand that thoughts are beings, the children of their parent-creator who is responsible for all that they do. You should understand that they influence others, and that as acts, objects and events they exteriorize to you the impressions of the objects which you have generated by thinking. You should think and understand that the desires in your thoughts holding on to the impressions from nature in your thoughts, are the magnetic links which bond you to nature. You will think without creating thoughts when your feelings and desires will not attach themselves to the nature impressions which have come in through your four senses. You should understand that the thoughts which you have created, blind you to and prevent you from being conscious of the difference between your desires and the impressions of objects to which they are attached, and from distinguishing yourself as different from nature. You should understand that, to free yourself from your thoughts, you must learn how to think so that you will recognize yourself to be that which is conscious *as* itself and as distinct and different from nature. You should understand that when you find that you are so conscious and as not of nature, you will dissipate your thoughts by returning the matter in them which belongs to nature, and by reclaiming that which is of yourself, and that then you should always be able to think without creating thoughts.

5. Thinking is the steady holding of the Conscious Light within on the subject of the thinking. Thinking is done by feeling-and-desire with the body-mind or the feeling-mind or the desire-mind or with these three minds. The process of thinking, that is, the gathering, the turning, the training, the holding and the focussing of the Light, is the same for each of the minds, though only the body-mind is ordinarily used in human thinking. There is human thinking which is not a steady holding of the Light, but is an untrained, spasmodic, irregular, often feeble, inconsequent attempt to hold the Light; and there is real thinking which is the steady holding of the Light. Human thinking is done by the use, not the control, of the body-mind, which calls to its aid the feeling-mind and the desire-mind. If the feeling-mind is used, even to a small degree, the results show originality and are superior in kind. The thinking is started by desire, and desire is prompted by feeling. The subject of the desire determines the mind which is used when one tries to think. The seven minds are centered in reason. The body-mind is related to the physical body and is used for nature by means of the four senses. It should be used by feeling-and-desire for the control of the body and the guidance of

nature, subject to rightness and reason. Each of the other six minds is for the use of a particular aspect of the Triune Self: the second for feeling, the third for desire, the fourth for rightness, the fifth for reason, the sixth for I-ness, and the seventh for selfness. Nearly all human thinking is done with the first or body-mind. This is used for seeing, hearing, tasting, smelling, touching, weighing, measuring, and for comparing, analyzing, combining, coordinating, computing and reasoning about these sense perceptions. The body-mind thinks on all things of nature and its instrument, the body, and on sensations. It does not and cannot think of any part of the Triune Self. You cannot think on more than one subject at a time; that is, human thinking is thus restricted, though real thinking is not.

6. Thinking, that is, the steady holding of the Light, is done only in the intervals between the incoming and the outgoing and the outgoing and the incoming breaths. Therefore human thinking consists of intermittent, irregular and jerky flashes of Light; whereas in real thinking there is a steady stream of Light, and breathing stops. The thinking that is done between the breaths, is done, as it were, in points connected or separated by dashes, which represent the sense impressions received during breathing. The continued effort to think on a subject results in such intermittent flashes of Light on the subject. This is as far as human thinking goes. Thinking is done in the heart and lungs, which are, potentially, a brain, like the cerebellum and the cerebrum. A thought conceived in the thorax is gestated, elaborated and issued from the brain in the head, which is the only brain that can be used at present. The direct cause of thinking is desire, and desire is prompted by feeling, which receives impressions of objects from outside nature. If these impressions are not the immediate subjects of the thinking, they are at least the bases for associations, distinctions and memories which cause the thinking.

7. There are four stages in thinking. The first is the presentation of the subject, which is a nature impression, its acceptance and turning the light on it; the second is the fixing and cleansing of the subject, which is done by training the Light upon it; the third is the reducing of the subject to a point, which is done by focussing the Light upon it; and the fourth is the focus of the Light on the point, which is that impression, and the result of the thinking. These four stages are incipient in all thinking, but are completed only in the thinking which results in knowing. Ordinary,

casual, human thinking stops with the second stage, if it can go that far. Thinking usually does not go far because of adverse conditions. These are that the body-mind is weak, untrained and unsteady and keeps turning from one subject to another; then there is the unsteadiness, disagreement or lack of coordination of the three minds themselves, and the fact that they are out of touch with the nerve centers through which they should work. Further difficulties are due to feeling-and-desire, which make no proper effort to call their minds into action and often interfere with their own action after they have been started by the body-mind. Then there are the interferences from elementals pouring in as impressions and prodding, irritating, distracting and confusing the body-mind so that they may become sensations; elementals, nature units, are attracted into and swarm in diffused Light. The Conscious Light which the mind finds available is so diffused and obscured that there is difficulty in turning and focussing it on the subject of the thinking, and the Light is unsteady because the mind which guides it is unsteady. The result of this is that human thinking is ineffective, beyond the bare material achievements of a corrupt civilization, and leaves the human in his self-delusion and ignorance of the world in which he lives. The results of human thinking are the thoughts which are ever being exteriorized as the acts, objects and events of the lives into which they are drawn. The purpose of this system is to show you how to think and yet to avoid the creation of thoughts, since they rule your lives and subject you to nature.

8. The first step is to decide upon a subject to be known, that is, to turn the Light on that subject and on no other. Then comes the fixing of the subject, which is done by training the mind on that subject and so holding the Light steady upon the subject. Then comes the reducing of the subject to a point by focussing the Light upon it. The fourth stage is the steady holding and focus of the Light on the point, that is, the thing as it is in itself, the opening up of the thing and the revealing of itself to the Light. Then the thing is known at once as a whole, and in all its parts. The difficulties to be overcome in casual ordinary thinking become almost insuperable as soon as you select a definite subject to think upon. To overcome them you must have persistence. Persistence in thinking on one subject alone is a necessary exercise to strengthen, train and steady the mind which gathers Light and excludes from it obstructions and so makes it clearer and holds it steady. As the Light which is used in the thinking increases and becomes clearer, the nature units and thoughts

which are attracted and swarm into diffused Light cannot endure it; they flee. Persistence in thinking increases, strengthens and tones up your nerve matter so that it can be worked by your mind as that becomes more effective. You who hold the body-mind steady on a subject and so hold the Light steady and focus it, know the subject and know that you know it. Then you have the body-mind under control, that is, you, as feeling-and-desire, are able to think with it. Thinking with the body-mind may begin with nature as a whole or with any part or object of nature units, such as a star, an atom, a tree or a geogen elemental. After the subject to be known is selected, thinking can begin anywhere and at any time. Nor need your thinking be with any special preparation or favorable condition. When the subject to be known is decided upon, the time and place to think is here and now. When the subject is known you should define it by putting into appropriate words what you know of the subject. A definition is the embodiment of a subject in a set of words which expresses the subject as it is, without need of a description or explanation. If you will not think into words what you think, you will not make definite progress in thinking. You need think about nature and the objects of nature only until you can use the body-mind at will. Use of the body-mind relates to it the brain and nervous centers and through these the finer states of matter, so that by thinking all states of matter can, later on, be controlled and related to the doer. Continuance in thinking with your body-mind to solve problems of matter, other than those concerned with you, will lead you away from yourself and make more difficult the thinking that will enable you to be conscious independently of the body. Feeling-and-desire, under the glamour of the body and nature, mistakes the senses and the physical body for portions of itself and so you want to think with the body-mind in order to get body comforts and objects of nature. You are conscious of the distinction concerning yourself, in your two aspects as feeling-and-desire and as nature, when you are dissociated from contact with nature. But you are no longer conscious of that distinction when in association with the body, because then you fall under the glamour of nature. You ought to help nature in requital for the use of the physical body and you should work in pursuance of your own destiny, but you fail to do either when under the glamour of nature, and so you remain a slave. To fulfill your destiny in your relation to yourself and to nature, you must dispel the glamour of nature and discover your dignity and purpose as feeling-and-desire, while in the body. Then you, as feeling and as desire, recover your memory of the distinction and difference between yourself and nature.

III.

9. The actual effort to think without creating thoughts begins with the effort to identify and free feeling. This effort calls into use the feeling-mind. Before sleep, at waking, and before the effort to think for freedom, you may make this earnest appeal. You address yourself in thought to your thinker and knower, as your Triune Self, and think clearly: My Judge, and my Knower! Give me Thy Light and the Light of Thy Knower. Let me be always conscious of Thee, that I may do all my duty and be consciously one with Thee.

Feeling is that of yourself in the body which feels: which feels impressions from objects of nature, but which cannot of itself distinguish itself from the impressions and from the senses. Your feeling-and-desire cannot be identified and freed unless each has the other's assistance. Your desire cannot free itself until after the freedom of your feeling, because nature has its stronghold in feeling and your feeling holds desire and holds your desire to nature. Your feeling cannot be identified and freed unless your desire desires feeling to free itself. When there is the persistent desire for feeling to be freed, your feeling is empowered by your desire to accomplish its identification and freedom by your persistence in thinking on feeling as feeling, until you as feeling are identified and freed.

10. The freeing of feeling begins with locating it in the body and distinguishing it from the sensations with which it is associated and identified. You should try to think of and feel feeling as different and distinct from the body and the sensations which you feel. Then your feeling extends through and over the body and there are sensations of warmth and tingling, but you do not feel feeling. The effort to think of and feel feeling as of yourself and as distinct from the sensation, by which you are employed and engrossed, awakens and calls into action your second mind, the feeling-mind, which is for the control of feeling. You, as feeling, are in the body wherever the blood and nerves are; therefore you may practice by trying to locate feeling in some particular part, a finger, toe or other part of the body, by thinking of it there. As soon as you try to think of and distinguish feeling as yourself, you are likely to be distracted by sensations, such as itching, uneasiness, trembling, sweating, flushing, yawning, fatigue or sleepiness. This is caused by your effort

to control your untrained feeling-mind and its sluggish nerve centers. You, feeling, will then go into parts of the body to serve these sensations, and your thinking following you, as feeling, also serves them. This means that there has been an obstruction to the thinking and that your thinking has been turned from feeling as the subject, to the obstruction. Thinking on your feeling alone as the subject, necessitates the holding of your feeling-mind steady, to focus the Conscious Light on feeling and so to locate yourself in your body and to free and know yourself. The change of the subject from feeling to a sensation changes thinking with your feeling-mind, to thinking with your body-mind. When thinking is not turned to a subject of nature and continues on yourself alone, the first efforts so to think will most likely numb or tire your body and induce sleep. When your thinking is switched back to thinking on a subject of nature, or when sleep comes, your effort to distinguish and identify yourself as feeling stops. You cannot feel feeling in the body without sensation until you use the feeling-mind, except in deep sleep, when you are not related to the body. Therefore you must persist in training your feeling-mind by trying to think of and feel yourself, feeling only, nothing else. You should not think of feeling as having anything to do in connection with or related to seeing, hearing, tasting, smelling, or even touching. You, feeling as yourself, are separate and distinct from the senses and objects of nature, even though you extend along the blood and nerve centers of the body. The body is corporeal; you are incorporeal. If after many efforts you are not able to know yourself in the body, as distinct from the body, you may practice the feeling of sensations, so that in this way you may become more familiar with yourself as feeling. You may think of your toe and feel what you can in that toe. The member in which there had been no feeling, then begins to pulse with sensations of warmth. Then you should think on and feel the same toe on the other foot, and it will pulse in unison with the first toe. Then you should extend your thinking and feeling to each of the other toes until all are pulsing. Then you should continue the thinking and feeling to the instep, the heel and the ankle, until there is a pulsing and activity through all parts of your feet and ankles. Then you should steadily extend your thinking and feeling to the legs, knees, thighs and pelvis, and then along the spine to the abdomen, thorax, neck and head. When you arrive at the top of your head you will feel a current, a shower of life, which as from a fountain sprays down through your whole body. This means that as desire-and-feeling, and by intentionally and uninterruptedly thinking upward in the body, you have temporarily connected and coordinated the roots and branches of the two nervous systems with the spinal cord; that you have thus caused the life breath and form breath to rise and flow with the physical breath through or along the trunk or spine of the body; and, that on reaching the crown of the brain, the life currents return like a shower from a fountain and quicken the body. Practice in thus thinking and feeling, keeps up and brings the parts of your body into coordination, and harmonious life flows through it. After that you should try to think of and feel the living breath, the active side of the breath-form, penetrating every part of the form of the breath-form of the body, the passive side of the breath-form. You should try to feel the breath-form as a living being inside of and moving the body, as the hand moves and is felt inside a soft glove.

11. The breath-form is the living soul, the creator and builder and preserver of the body, which is dependent on the feeling and desire of the doer in the body. When you can feel the breath and the form through the body as a being, distinguished and distinct from the mass of matter of which the physical body is composed, the breath-form adapts the matter of the body to your thinking and feeling. Then nature begins to lose control over you, because nature loses power over the breath-form, as you gain control of it. By thus thinking and feeling you use your body-mind jointly with your feeling-mind, to the end that you may be able to use the feeling-mind without assistance from the body-mind. You are training feeling to follow thinking, instead of letting thinking follow feeling. When thinking will not follow feeling, feeling must follow thinking. When you can feel the parts of your body and the fluids, the breath and the nerve currents in them, you are prepared to think of and feel feeling as distinct from the breath-form and the body. Patience and persistence in thinking of feeling, to locate and feel it in some particular part of the body, and to distinguish it, centers feeling and cuts off the elementals, nature units, which then cannot become sensations. When you are conscious of and as feeling, in and distinct from the body, you discover that the body is actually not you, but a mass, a form, which you inhabit and wear. While conscious of the body, like as the costume which it wears, you can by practice think of yourself as feeling only, and not feel sensations of any kind. You may be cut, burned or undergo a surgical operation without sensations of pain or touch, because you are dissociated from the sensory nerves of the voluntary nervous system. While

being conscious as feeling in the body you should not perform any of the wonders possible for you, else you will fall into subtle nature entanglements and stop your progress. By thinking of or as feeling only, to the exclusion of all else, you identify yourself as feeling. You, as feeling, then feel yourself to be and are conscious of yourself as being a portion of the doer, and as distinct from your body and its senses. Then the body is not seen, heard, tasted, smelled or contacted by you.

12. The world has dropped off and is forgotten. Thus your banishment of yourself to ex-istence, in nature, ends, when you are conscious of your reality in istence. Istence is the conscious doer, feeling the reality of itself in itself, as itself; not as ex-istence, not in ex-istence, but in its aloneness resulting from its intentional disattachment of itself from the illusions of nature. That is intentional freeing of feeling from nature; it is: being conscious bliss, knowing "Nirvana". If your purpose in thinking had been to escape from the world and to be liberated from nature, without knowing what of you it was that desired escape, then the feeling of you as part of the doer could seem to remain in its state of conscious bliss for long duration, even though in a short space of physical time. But you would have to return and re-enter your human body, because you would not even be the doer part of your Triune Self, (in "Nirvana"). After death, your unbalanced thoughts would compel you to be re-embodied in a human and to continue on your path to freedom. You cannot do that because your understanding that you are feeling-and-desire as the doer part of your Triune Self prevents you from making any such mistake as an attempt to escape. A reality is a unit as it is, unattached, the thing alone, itself. An illusion is an evanescent appearance as the result of the clustering of units into mass or form. As feeling, you have no sensations, no pains or pleasures, no physical body, no senses, no breath-form, no memories of any of these, but you are the feeling which gave much of personality to all these and which made the physical body human; you are the feeling aspect of the doer. You do not know *who* you are, though you are conscious as an immortal reality. You as feeling are untrammeled, peaceful, happy, blissful. You become conscious of the feelings you had but which you could not distinguish from the elementals as sensations, which drained off feeling. You feel the feelings, which you mistook for sensations when the elementals fed on you, and which you could not feel while entangled with the physical body; but these cause no pleasure, no pain, because you are conscious of your reality in istence; the body

composed of elementals is cut off and they cannot produce and become
sensations until there is contact with you, feeling. So you do not taste
food, hear sensuous music or voices, see sights or touch flesh, but you
now feel that of which you were not then conscious, namely, your
feelings, not felt while you felt the sensations which held you and engaged
your attention. You have awakened from the unreality of sensuous life
into the unmixed happiness of the reality of yourself as feeling. These
feelings summon the desires which are their complements and answer to
them. The reactions between you as feeling-and-desire cause the psychic
breath to start the physical breath, which had stopped, and to draw your
feeling back into the voluntary nervous system, where the breath-form
brings you into contact with the senses. Now you use these senses not as
one who sees and hears and tastes and smells, but as the one who feels
what is seen, heard, tasted and smelled. You are conscious of the body
and its senses, but you are also conscious of yourself and as yourself, and
independent of and distinct from the body. You are conscious of yourself,
not as having sight, hearing, taste and smell, but conscious that these
senses are used by you and are expressions in nature of yourself as feeling.
The thinking which leads to this intentional freeing of feeling must be
repeated again and again until you have the feeling-mind so under
control that you can use it at will and be freed at will. When repeating
the thinking you should try to be continuously conscious of what you
have been conscious, until there is no break in your being continuously
conscious *as* yourself, in the body or out of and distinct from the body.
When you do this you have established yourself in your istence as
yourself, distinct from and independent of your body; as distinct from
the body as the body is distinct from the clothes it wears. Then you are
the reality as feeling with the capacity to feel.

13. You now distinguish sensations, which belong to nature, from
feelings, which are of yourself. You become sensitive to impressions from
objects of nature which would reach into you and move you and which
call upon you to feel them and to express them through poetry, music,
painting, and other arts. You should not respond to any of these calls,
not because you would not or could not, but because you are not ready.
If you allow yourself to be allied to nature, you will be drawn again into
it and its glamour and slavery. You are delicately sensitive to the troubles
of others. Their sorrows appeal to you for solace and comfort. You may
advise them, but you should not allow yourself to melt in sympathy and

to share their sorrows, not because you would not, but because at this time you would be overcome by sorrows, theirs and later your own. You would thus abort a vesture, the form body for yourself which is being formed in the body. During each of your freedoms by thinking with the feeling-mind, your desire would rush in to re-enforce and satisfy feeling, but as feeling you resist, and your thinking holds back the desire. This prevents a premature union of your feeling with your desire, which, if allowed, would thereafter make freedom more difficult, if not impossible. Your feeling-and-desire must each in turn be intentionally freed by itself in order that they will eventually have perfect union. Your resistance by feeling and the exercise of your feeling-mind strengthen feeling and develop skill in the use of your feeling-mind. When you can remain unmoved in feeling and can by thinking with the feeling-mind free your feeling at will, you are ready to make an effort to think for freedom of desire with your desire-mind. Your desire-mind is used for the finding, control and freeing of itself. In order that your desire-mind may be exercised at will, you should have the desire that desire should be itself self-controlled, and self-governed. When you have this desire you are ready to make an effort to think with the desire-mind. You should then think on desire, nothing else. By thinking on desire, your desire seems to be split into numerous desires, most of which are clinging to impressions of objects or want: to be, to will, to do, or to have, something. On finding the desires so divided you should declare your purpose in thinking. If the purpose is one that can be achieved by the body-mind, and you attend to it, it will lead you back into the entanglements of the world where you can achieve the object of your desire, because you can use the body-mind. If you so use the body-mind you will not free desire, though you may learn some of the uses, but not the control, of your desire-mind. When your purpose is to free desire, you must examine and prove your purpose by thinking to know what and who you are—in preference to doing, or having, or being anything in the world. You then ask rightness to be the judge in the examination, and you state that your purpose is to free desire. You question why you wish to isolate desire. Many desires appear in the Light as it is held on the subject, and the thinking must continue until one among the desires is approved by rightness. Doubt attends each desire as it is presented for examination, until rightness approves. Then, instead of doubt, there is an unmistakable certainty.

14. In every human the desires arrange themselves into two groups: those which seek the Triune Self, and those which seek nature. The few which seek the Triune Self are subject to the desire for Self-knowledge, that is, knowledge of the knower of the Triune Self; the many which seek nature are subject to the desire for sex. The many are marshalled, led or directed by four desire-generals: the desire for food, the desire for possessions, the desire for a name, and the desire for power. By an examination of the four desire-generals, all the many are included, but before the examination some things about these desires should be understood. No desire will hold fast to any impression of an object when that desire is conscious of what that impression or object is, to which it is attached; it will then let go of that impression. No desire really wants any object of nature. Each desire really wants to be at one with the desire for Self-knowledge, and with the Triune Self. The desires are under the sway of darkness because they shut themselves off from the Conscious Light in the Triune Self. These desires grasp the impressions of objects of nature which the senses bring in, hoping that through the objects they will find what they seek. They will let go of some impressions of objects, but will hold on to the others, like as one who cannot swim grasps and holds any object, fearing he will sink. These desires are led by the light of the senses, which is as darkness when compared to the Conscious Light in the Triune Self. Light in the Triune Self shows the darkness of the senses. Desires are vaguely conscious of that Light and fear it because it will make them conscious of their ignorance and of their mistakes. So they turn from the Light and seek the objects presented by the senses. When the desire for Self-knowledge turns to the Light and would lead the way, there is war. The desire for sex behind the forms of food, possessions, a name, and power, urges the four and they lead the many desires in battle—and they have won. No power other than its own can separate a desire from an impression which it holds. No power can change a desire; that desire, and that desire only, can change itself. A desire will not let go the impression it holds until it is conscious that that impression is not what it wants. A desire cannot be conscious of what the impression it holds really is, because of darkness; it must have the Conscious Light to be conscious of what that impression really is. Therefore, the Conscious Light in the Triune Self must be turned on a desire with the impression it holds, so that it may be conscious that neither the impression nor the object is what it most desires. Light comes with the desire for Self-knowl-edge, by thinking on the desire with the impression or object to which

it is attached. The desire so thinking with the desire-mind calls to its aid
the body-mind for nature. This thinking holds the Light on the desire
with the impression or object it desires. The Light makes that desire
conscious of what the object is to which it is attached; that the object is
different from itself, is not of itself. Then that desire changes itself from
attachment to disattachment. It is conscious of the difference of itself
from the object it then does not want, and it lets go, and thereafter it will
not again be attached to that object or attracted by it. Each desire must
let go of the impression, to free itself from the object, and make itself
unattachable, so that the many desires divided or opposed to each other
may be united as one. Therefore, when the desire for Self-knowledge
appears in the Light by thinking, rightness approves it. Rightness does
not approve of any other desire which may appear.

15. Then begins the proving of the desire for Self-knowledge as the
purpose of your thinking: you prove it by testing it with other desires.
You summon all your desires to compare them with and adjust them to
the desire for Self-knowledge, which is to be the desire of your life, the
purpose of your efforts. The summons is made by your mental declaration that you desire knowledge of yourself as a Triune Self above all else,
and that your purpose is to be or to have Self-knowledge. This is a
summons which is answered by the cunning of age-old desires, through
the events of life. By your thinking, each of these is put in the Light
beside the desire for Self-knowledge. One desire only can remain in the
Light. First come the desires for food. As your thinking turns and holds
the Light on them, the strength of your desires for food is tested by the
strength of your desire for Self-knowledge. Then food is seen to be not
of you or for you, but entirely of nature, made by innumerable combinations of units of fire, air, water and earth, for the nourishment of the
four systems in their upkeep of the physical body. The appetites are seen
to be devices for nature elementals, which stimulate and compel your
desire to keep nature-matter in circulation. When the desire for Self-
knowledge has been chosen as your purpose of life and approved by
rightness, no desire for food can stand in the Light against it. As each
desire for food lets go the impression, that desire becomes disattached;
then the strength of your desire for Self-knowledge increases and the
desire for food is no longer a hindrance. When your desire for food
becomes conscious that the appetites are not its desires, and that they are
sensation-decoys which are binders to nature, it lets go; they lose their

power over it; food ceases to be a hindrance and your desire for food serves your desire for Self-knowledge. Then are summoned the desires for possessions. As your thinking arraigns in the Light the desires for possessions, the possessions are seen to have value for the body only, as they answer to its needs of clothing and shelter and its position in life, and that in all other respects they are snares, cares and shackles. The desires for possessions, such as avarice, covetousness and rapacity, are undeceived by your thinking; they change. Possessions other than for service lose value as your desire for them becomes conscious of what they are, and they are subordinated to the desire for Self-knowledge. Freed from the binding power of the desires for possessions, your desire for Self-knowledge increases and becomes more clearly defined. Then the desires for a name are brought into the Light, with your desire for Self-knowledge. In the Light desire becomes conscious that a name is a cluster of impressions of indeterminate attributes for a personality, which are as empty and as evanescent as a bubble. These desires now let go of the impressions and willingly enlist for service under your desire for Self-knowledge. Then the desire for power is summoned into the Light. In the Light, power over objects of the senses as against Self-knowledge is revealed to be an illusion created by that desire which is the offspring and adversary of the desire for Self-knowledge. The illusion will be dispelled in the Light when the desire for it changes into your desire for Self-knowledge. When your desires for food, possessions, a name and power have become conscious in the Light that the things they desired were not what they wanted, and have put themselves under the control of your desire for Self-knowledge, and merge with it, your desire for sex can be examined. The desire for sex is summoned by turning the Light on it as the subject of the thinking. In the Light your desire for sex becomes conscious that it is selfishness grounded in ignorance and that it calls forth and stimulates the desires for food, possessions, name, and power. By thinking you see that: from these desires a male body or a female body belonging to nature is built up by food, endowed with possessions, identified by a name and engendered by power, as deter-mined by thinking. By thinking you see that your desire for sex dreads the Light, but that it cannot escape when the Light is held on it. In the Light, you see the desire for sex to be the basis of duality, separateness and strife, the chief adversary and leader of all the desires opposed to your desire for Self-knowledge. You become conscious that the desire for sex cannot be dissipated or done away with, but that it can be changed. As the desire for sex stands beside the desire for Self-knowledge in the Light, you are conscious that it senses that a male body or a female body is not what it wants, and it changes itself and is disattached and ceases to want a male or a female body. Then the desire for sex is seen to change itself in the Light as it becomes conscious that it cannot be or get what it wants without the desire for Self-knowledge. Your desire for sex then desires to be led by your desire for Self-knowledge and is no longer afraid of the Light. When your desire for sex desires to be led by your desire for Self-knowledge, "desire as a whole" should become the subject of the thinking. As your thinking holds the Light on desire as a whole, your desire for Self-knowledge has increase of power, and the desires which had been in animal forms appeal to the desire for sex to war against your desire for Self-knowledge, or to get away from desire as a whole. Under the Light your desire which had been for the sexes now changes and leads all desires desiring nature, and, with them, merges with your desire for Self-knowledge, and there is no desire for expression as the sexes. Your thinking then holds the Light on desire itself, alone. The body with its seeing, hearing, tasting, smelling and touching falls away, nature vanishes, and you as desire are alone and at rest. But you do not remain at rest.

16. Under the Light, you as desire become restless, strong, powerful. When your thinking held the Light on the desires they were by the desire for Self-knowledge drawn together and united. While the desires divided and warred, they were good and evil, God and Devil. Now that they are united and controlled, they are conscious power, which is goodness. In the proving of the desires, the desire-mind called upon the body-mind to cooperate with it. When the desires for food, possessions, a name, power and sex were by the Light made conscious of what those things really are, and no longer desired them, thinking with the body-mind for nature was stopped, and the desire-mind continued the thinking, which resulted in the freeing of desire. Your self-controlled desire is free in the Light, conscious of itself as power and part of a greater Self, which it desires to know. The freeing of your desire has been brought about by your effort to use your desire-mind, and by its use. The desire-mind makes contact with breathing and the body-mind, and desire is again active in the body, but the human is no longer the same human. You are conscious of yourself as a conscious power, not guided, not led by seeing, hearing, tasting, smelling or touching, and you are conscious as not the

body. By thinking with your desire-mind on yourself you are conscious as unexpressed power that desires expression. But you do not desire expression of power through bodily personality, because you are now conscious that this is merely an appearance, an illusion, which could be dissipated and scattered. By thinking with your feeling-mind on yourself, you are conscious as beauty and you yearn for expression. You do not want expression of beauty through objects of the four senses because you are conscious of them as illusory and evanescent.

17. Feeling and desire are now conscious as beauty and as power, and as not the body; but they are not balanced. They can be balanced only when they are freed from sexuality and the body-mind is under their control. Sexuality is the condition of feeling-and-desire in a human body, experiencing forms of nature-madness or nature-intoxication. By the successive thinking on food, possessions, a name, power, sex, the senses, on the attractions these are to the deluded, and on their deadliness, feeling-and-desire are freed from sexuality. Then these are seen to be illusions, as unreal as moving pictures, not the things themselves, and their hold on feeling-and-desire ceases. Feeling-and-desire, immune from sexuality, are ready to be balanced. Balance between feeling and desire is made by the feeling-mind and desire-mind thinking on their right relation. Right relation is found to be, that feeling-and-desire are the necessary complements to the union and action of each other, and are equal in their relation to each other. Feeling-and-desire each feel and desire equality, and they are equal. Equality of feeling-and-desire puts the body-mind in right relation to them, so that the body-mind cannot think of them as being separable, and must think of them as they are: each being the same in and as the other. Then the body-mind is itself balanced; it thinks of things as they are, and in no other way. The three minds thus thinking hold the Light on feeling-and-desire and they, feeling-and-desire, are amalgamated in balanced union, inseparable. When feeling-and-desire are thus united in balanced union they find love. Feeling-and-desire in union with love is blessedness in perpetuity. Blessedness is the state of the doer, when feeling and desire have immunity from the intoxicating passions and pleasures of the body senses and have found love. Love is Conscious Sameness throughout the four worlds. Love in the doer is the state of balanced union and interaction between feeling-and-desire, in which each feels and desires itself to be and is itself in and as the other.

Then feeling-and-desire are at peace and stand reconciled in the Conscious Light of the Intelligence.

18. At this stage you, the doer, feeling-and-desire in complete union, have capacity and power to feel, to will, to do, and to be. You see mankind in ignorance, suffering endless rounds of sensations, pains and pleasures. You would willingly show them the simple way of ending their troubles; but you should know also that those wiser than you would have done this were it possible. You see nature in perpetual and aimless turmoil and distress. You see that you can relieve suffering, give direction to force and establish order and purpose; but you should know that the state of the human world is what man makes it, the exteriorization of his thoughts, and that it must be changed by suffering man by balancing his thoughts. You see that you could be as God to men and could control them through their feelings and desires and thus prevent their bringing suffering on themselves and others. But you see that by your doing this they would be kept in the child state in which they are; that you would then be responsible for them; that men must learn to change and to control their own feelings and desires. By thinking, you see that at this stage your effort to help man or nature would only be a check to his own progress and to nature. You wish to help and you see that you could create a thought of love and beauty and power and give it to men to lift them out of sordidness and strife. But you also see that men would take the thought and build from it a religion to suit their feelings and desires, and that the religion would pass and be forgotten without accomplishing its purpose. You see the futility of doing any of the things that you might do. By thinking, you see that to be able to benefit men you must first know them. And you see that you can know them only by Self-knowledge. By thinking, you find that you do not know your Self. You are now conscious of your ignorance. By thinking, your past thoughts as ideals are examined and are dissipated in the Light. When, by thinking, the only thing that can remain in the Light is the desire for Self-knowledge, you are ready to go on.

IV.

19. To go on, you must have communion with rightness. The way to communion with rightness is made by thinking in connection with the mind of rightness. Clouds of thoughts separate you from rightness. By trying to think with the mind of rightness you perceive the clouds to be

thoughts of your own and of others which are concerned with laws of nature or with human ideals. You must not be led away by these, else you will not make the way to rightness. By thinking steadily on rightness you open the clouds and go through them. Then you are conscious of the actuality of rightness and that it thinks only what is right. You find that rightness had been deserted and betrayed by your feeling, and dethroned and cast aside by your desire which had usurped its place, and you realize how both your feeling-and-desire were enthralled and deceived by nature. You are eager to repair the wrongs. You are conscious that the Light is in rightness. You recognize rightness as the conscious standard for feeling and for thought and action; you acknowledge the rule of rightness, restore to it its place, and rightness is enthroned. By thinking, you are in communion with rightness. Communion is the giving yourself to rightness and the receiving of Light. Communion with rightness is the direct connection with the mind of rightness. You see the worlds and the things in them as they are. You are conscious that it is right that they should be so, though you do not yet understand why and how. You see the perpetual slavery of men in illusions through life and death and birth. You see that they can wake and save themselves from these illusions, and you would point the way. You are conscious that you are not ready to do this; that you should go on and get understanding. Understanding is perceiving and feeling what things are as themselves and what their relations are, and comprehending why they are so and are so related. Understanding comes only with the aid of reason.

20. By thinking, you are conscious that reason will be the advocate for and liberator of mankind. The way to reason can be made only by thinking in connection with the mind of reason. The way to reason is beset by armies of reasons, causes, origins and principles which if not dispatched will bring chaos, chaos of doubt, out of which there seems no way. Persistence in thinking on reason brings approval from rightness and makes the way to reason. Then there is no room for doubt, and the chaos vanishes in the presence of reason. The Light comes with reason and all things are made clear. This is proof that by thinking on reason you have opened communication with reason through the mind of reason. Reason is the beginning and the end of thinking, the primal and ultimate cause, for the doer, the thinker and the knower, of things in the manifested worlds. Reason is the action and the sum of the actions of all the minds in agreement and in focus. Reason causes the issuing, retard-

ing, speeding and precipitation of thoughts, as the acts, objects and events of a life; or it causes the balancing and abrogation of these thoughts according to the thinking and the feeling and the desiring of the thinker. Reason is the answerer of all questions, the solution of all problems concerning the Triune Self, concerning nature, and concerning the relation between the Triune Self and nature. Your thinking in connection with the mind of reason only, makes reason known to you, the doer. By your thinking with reason you are raised out of the world of sensations and shadows, out of the world of emotions and dreams, and you are in the world of clear vision where you see them and understand all that you see.

21. By thinking with reason you see the possibilities for all things. You see how it is possible for you to do all things. You are exultant in serenity. Then you remember your former disregard for reason and you feel guilty. You confess your ignorance and wrong and you ask reason to guide you. Reason imparts understanding to you. Having understanding you are impressed with wonder at reason. You see and understand that past and future run together; that old and new are interchanged; that birth is death and death is birth; that opposites are the same in each other; that activity and inertia end in beginning. As you think with reason you understand that that which will be is the continuation of that which has been done, stressed or varied in the meantime only through what the doer thinks and does.

22. You ask to know your past. By thinking with reason you are and again live that past. Once more you are in the body of your first existence, your original physical body, with your breath-form and your aia. With the senses you perceive the units of nature in their comings and their goings, and their changes through the four worlds. You have understanding, for you walk with the Light. Desiring anew to know completely who or what you are, you evoke feeling from yourself, and fashion for it a female form by putting forth a portion of your body, which thus becomes male and female. Then you, as desire-and-feeling, give up understanding; you betray the Light for sensations of nature through bodily union. You are blind to the Light; and, unbalanced and without understanding, you lose contact with reason. You wander in darkness. Death comes. Your re-existences begin. Again and again you live and die and live again through the endless flow of lives, as man or as woman.

The recurrent flow of things in nature is caused by your thinking according to feeling through the female, and according to desire through the male. In the consecutive lives you are never conscious as the same, because the portion of yourself in each new life is different from that in the last. And still in each of the lives you are ever the same, because all parts of yourself are inseparably the same and your identity is conscious as an unbroken One throughout. You are mighty and you are menial, you are evil and you are just; you are adored and you are despised, you are divinity and you are beast. Through all changes of the earth crust by fires and earthquakes, by hurricanes and floods, by burning sands and frozen earth, through all changes of the heavens, from near to far, from one to many seasons, through all the flow and the phenomena of time, you are still the same conscious One. You are conscious that you have always been the same and yet you are conscious that you are and always have been a stranger to yourself. As a stranger to yourself you feel lonely. So in every life you try to find yourself. You are conscious that this trying takes you farther from yourself, until from agony of self you begin to think of the way and how to find yourself. You are conscious that you will thus go on continuously until you find the way to end your troubles. You are conscious that the ending of your troubles begins with your discovery that in sensation you are attached and bound to nature by feeling and thinking, and that by thinking and feeling without sensation you disattach yourself, and are freed from nature. You are conscious that by thinking you find feeling and desire of and as yourself. You are conscious that by thinking you disattach feeling-and-desire from nature and unite them into balanced union as yourself. You are conscious that by thinking you find the Light in rightness and are in communion with it. You are conscious that by thinking you have understanding, and that through rightness and reason you will be established in the Light. Now that you have seen your past and have lived over it again you come back and you are in the Light, which you never have really left.

23. In the Light and from out of the Light you now see that each of the lives you have lived was and is a dream, and you see that by thinking with the senses you dreamed that dream over again and again, through each life and after each death. By thinking with reason, you see that each human life is the dreaming of the doer of itself through nature. You see that the play of dreams began when you hypnotized yourself by thinking with the body-mind into nature, and thereby exiled yourself from the

Light, and that the dreams ended when you awakened to the Light by your thinking with the feeling and desire minds, and thus took yourself out of the hypnotic dream. You see and understand that I-ness-and-self-ness and rightness-and-reason never left the Light, and that you, as unbalanced feeling-and-desire, exiled yourself into darkness of the senses by thinking with the body-mind only. You see and understand that by thinking through the senses with the body-mind only, you hypnotized yourself, put yourself into the hypnotic sleep, to dream of yourself as being the body of a man or as being the body of a woman. You now understand that with the body-mind balanced and controlled, and by thinking with the feeling and desire minds only, you have redeemed yourself and re-enter the Light. You understand that you are by rightness and reason in the freedom of the Light, and that you are now at peace. Then you think of humanity and see the stream of human life and how needless it is that the doers should continue to doom themselves to sorrow and to suffer. No human thought or act is hidden from your vision, and you understand. You love and pity the doers in human life. You see that without understanding they act in ignorance by the fires they kindle with their desires. You would take the Light to men and give them understanding; you would show them that right thinking is the cure for sorrow, and Light the way to freedom. You ask reason to act with you and to guide you. By thinking with reason you look through the lives you have dreamed. You see innumerable forms of thoughts and you see the parts you have taken in the building up and the tearing down of these. You see that you have been among the teachers and the prophets as well as among the believers, the hunters and the persecuted. With reason you see that what you would do now has been attempted from time to time by others. You see that the teachers have been betrayed and deserted, or have been made into gods by men; that their teachings have been twisted into doctrines which breed selfishness and fear, helplessness and greed, which lead to deceit and wars and which cause men to dread rightness and reason and to remain in bondage to nature. You see that mankind in their distress clutch at anyone who would save them. But, you also see that to be saved, they must save themselves. You understand that the most that can be done for mankind is to show them the way; that to do more is to prolong their slavery. You understand that men cannot see the way until they weary of sensation, and desire Self-knowl-edge. You understand that what you now are conscious of and are is the result of your own thinking; that you could not be as you are by any

other means. Your experiences in sensation, your freeing yourself from
captivity into nature and your understanding of the purpose of all this,
result in Self-knowledge. Knowledge of your own past saves you from
the failure to which you would doom yourself by going among men and
instructing them. Knowledge frees you from the glamour of sympathy.
You still feel for the sorrows and sufferings of men; but you are no longer
tempted to suffer with them, because you know that by so doing you
would prolong their agony and blind yourself to your true course. When
there is no temptation to think yourself into the affairs of men, reason
makes known to you that you are no longer in jeopardy of self-delusion.
Self-delusion is the state into which the doer puts itself by letting
attraction or repulsion, preference or prejudice, influence thinking. You
see and understand the difficulties and dangers you have passed and how
you have overcome and freed yourself from them, and you ask reason
why you did not see through them and overcome them before. Then you
understand that attachment to nature had dimmed your perception and
influenced your thinking. You desire to know what your other attachments are, and you see that they are the remainder of your unbalanced
thoughts. Then you see that each of the difficulties you encountered was
the result of a thought which barred your progress, and that the bar was
removed when you balanced that thought by thinking. You see that your
thoughts were the bonds that held you to the earth and to nature. You
know that you must be released from all such thoughts and so become
free from every attachment. You see that you created the thoughts by
thinking and that by thinking you must balance them and so free
yourself. You now know that thinking without attachment is the only
way in which you can live in a physical body and still be free from
entanglements. You believed, when you began your course of thinking,
that you knew all this; but not until now do you really know it. With
the aid of the mind of reason you have clear perception, and you are in
right relation with reason. You desire to balance all your thoughts, and
reason summons them in order. They come, each in its turn: thoughts
for the cure of ills and sorrows, for lessening the burdens and the
difficulties of men; thoughts of abstract matter or of mass, its form and
constitution, thoughts of the plan and of the purpose of the Universe.
You know through reason that they were conceived in ignorance, formed
in fallacy and so were destined to dissolution. Then you balance all your
thoughts in their order. As each thought is balanced, that in it which is
of nature goes to its place in nature, and that which is of the Triune Self

is in right relation to the Triune Self. You learn as you balance each thought; and, as you balance the last, you have learned all that it is possible for you to learn from your experience with nature. You now know what not to do. With and as reason you know what to do.

24. By thinking with the aid of the mind of reason you have made all your advances toward Self-knowledge and now you have available the mind of reason, at will. Thinking with the mind of reason adjusts you to reason. By thinking with the mind of rightness you are in communion with rightness. You know that rightness has approved your thinking on your problems, and that these are solved. You now have access to the life world by the mind of rightness and the mind of reason, to the form world by your feeling and desire minds, and to the physical world by the body-mind for the physical body, through which all seven minds will act to reach the worlds. You know that you should not and you do not act in the worlds. You desire Self-knowledge and you will not venture into nature before attaining Self-knowledge. By thinking with your feeling and desire minds to be free, you are in freedom. Formerly, whenever, as feeling-and-desire, you had isolated yourself by thinking with your combined feeling-and-desire minds, you were untroubled by nature and in selfless blessedness. Since then you have had the assistance of the minds of rightness and reason; through them you have been in communion with rightness and have had understanding from reason. In communion, feeling came into agreement with rightness, and desire desired to be and to do what would accord with rightness. By understanding, desire made its adjustment with reason and feeling became responsive to reason. So that by thinking you, as feeling-and-desire, have freed yourself from nature and are conscious of yourself as independent of and apart from it. In isolation you are now conscious of rightness-and-reason as the thinker of the Triune Self, which is beyond you, but of which you are a part. In isolation you are free from feeling any impression not in complete agreement with rightness, and from desiring whatever might interfere with perfect adjustment to reason. Now you return from isolation and are in relation with your body. From isolation you find that the well-spring and fountainhead of all the arts and acts and events is in you as feeling-and-desire. Acts, objects and events are the distorted reflections in nature of projections from you, as feeling-and-desire. In you are the originals of these and you do not desire the reflections. By thinking with the aid of the mind of rightness and the mind of reason you understand

that rightness and reason are and have been in agreement and in right relation to each other. By thinking to coordinate your feeling-and-desire minds with the minds of rightness-and-reason you, as feeling-and-desire, the doer, become a part of and are one with rightness-and-reason, the thinker. By giving yourself up to rightness-and-reason you, as feeling-and-desire, have been rectified by rightness and liberated by reason from ignorance of what you are and from bondage to nature. Now that you are identified with and as rightness-and-reason, you are free beyond the possibility of falling back into entanglements with nature. You coordinate the body-mind for the physical body with the other four minds so that the body is responsive to all the minds and is in right relation to the three worlds. As rightness-and-reason you are conscious that you are beginningless and deathless.

25. You see order in the Universe: in the life world, in the form world, and in the physical world. With the worlds as with the least unit in them, you see undeviating regularity and sequence. In human relations and in their relation to the changing world you see actions and reactions in unerring continuity. You see the objects that affect the feeling and desire which cause man to think. You see the matter and composition of a thought, how it is conceived and is born, how it and the thinking about it affect the different states of matter and how that thought and the matter thus affected act on the brains, the bodies and the thinking of mankind. You see the opposition, if any, to the thought and how it battles until there is an exteriorization of it on the physical plane. You see how the thought is balanced, and while it is not balanced how it continues its rounds. You see that in every life man is his own maker and unmaker, his own witness and judge. You see that even the slightest event that happens to anyone or anything is in order; that it could not happen out of order without upsetting the worlds, and that this cannot be done. You see and understand and know that all that men are passing through is what you have passed through. You know that each one must and will become conscious of the illusions that enthrall him; will find and will use the creative power to think; and, by thinking will free himself from all illusions and attachments. You, as rightness-and-reason, are a thinker. You know that you are feeling-and-desire as the doer, and rightness-and-reason as the thinker, and you know that there is the identity of the I-ness as yourself, of which you are conscious but which you do not yet know. You know things as they are, and you are steadfast and true. You are now

ready and prepared to go on. You have reviewed your own past: your first existence, your illusions or dreams through your re-existences, the waking from dream, the rectification of your body by thinking and your present knowledge of all that has transpired. You are conscious of your being an unbroken identity throughout all changes and conditions, but you do not know the origin and history of your identity.

V.

26. You now purpose to know the reality of what you are conscious of as "I". You will reach to I-ness by thinking with the two minds which you are not yet able to use. By thinking of yourself, only as "I", you call to your aid the mind for I-ness. You do not isolate yourself from nature to find I-ness. By centering your thinking on "I" only, rightness-and-reason and feeling-and-desire and the physical body and nature are not included, and your thinking enters into blankness. If the blankness is a deadness, a stoppage to the thinking, the thinking must begin again, and again, until the thinking thinks through the blankness. The blankness is the barrier built by the thinking which the doer compelled, after it had abrogated its right to unity with I-ness, by its attempt to divide itself to dwell in male or in female bodies, and away from the eternal "I" in everlastingness, which made the doer a wanderer in darkness and forget-fulness. By continued thinking on "I" the blankness opens, ceases. In that moment you become conscious of I-ness and as I-ness, and I-ness uses its mind to identify you with and as itself, and you are I-ness. As I-ness you are neither past nor future; time exists, but it has no effect on you. Horizons vanish in the immensity of I-ness: you are conscious identity in the Eternal which is within and through and beyond time, self-conscious without flow or stop, in boundlessness of Light. As I-ness you are the conscious permanence of identity. When you are identified with and as I-ness, you are also conscious as rightness-and-reason and feeling-and-desire, and all are identified with I-ness. There are no complications, distinctions, qualifications or misgivings, there is no wonder or awe at your being as you are. Nothing disquiets your serenity as the eternal conscious I. You are conscious of and as your identity, and you determine to have the completion of all parts of the Triune Self in the knowledge of selfness. You have qualified yourself by thinking with the other minds and have no difficulty in thinking in conjunction with the mind for selfness. Selfness has used its mind through the ages to impart knowledge to reason, so that reason should have all knowledge

necessary in the administration of justice, in the exteriorization of the doer's thoughts and in all human relations. In thus thinking on selfness, you are qualified, there are no approaches, no obstructions to overcome, as there were in the thinking with the minds of other parts of the Triune Self. When you think in conjunction with the mind for selfness you are at once conscious not only of selfness, but you are and have knowledge as selfness. You are knower and thinker and doer—the Triune Self.

27. As the knower, you are knowledge and know yourself to be the same eternal One whose I-ness is the self-conscious permanence in the Eternal and throughout time. As the thinker, you know the rightness and the reason of yourself to be the law and the justice in the worlds. As the doer, you know your feeling and desire to be beauty and power, in the body and in the worlds in which you have made yourself and the body beauty and power. As the Triune Self, you think from yourself as knowledge-and-identity with rightness-and-reason and feeling-and-desire, and with the minds of these you coordinate and gear the body-mind. By so thinking, the aia is caused to enter the physical body and to be in perfect relation with its breath-form. The aia and the breath-form are still automata. Nature contacts but cannot control them; they are under your direction and respond to your slightest behest. By thinking from knowledge into the physical body all parts of the Triune Self as your real Self enter it; and your embodiment is complete. By so thinking, the power and the glory of the Light through you as the Triune Self pervades the body and tempers it to you. By so thinking, the physical body is established in permanence and is immortal. All parts of you, as the Triune Self, are in the physical body with the aia and the breath-form. You have knowledge of all your parts as yourself and have complete mastery of your body, and the Conscious Light of your Intelligence is in and through you and your body. By thinking on the Light with all your minds you think yourself into the Light and presence of your Intelligence. You had known of your Intelligence through the Light, but now, in its presence, you are in consciously established relation to it. You make salutation, offer service, are accepted and in tranquil reverence. You choose to be in adjustment with the Great Triune Self of the worlds. By thinking on the Great Triune Self of the worlds you are in its presence and it is in and through you. You are inspired by the love that it has for every being. You know that because of its love it remains in the worlds to be the loving bond between all Triune Selves and all animate beings.

You are now in right relation to yourself, to your Intelligence and to the Great Triune Self of the worlds.

28. You choose to take birth into the three worlds. During the course of your thinking the breath-form has been remaking the physical body to fit it for the embodiment of all the parts of you, the Triune Self. Your physical body is rehabilitated, made perfect, and is now a body suited for you. Your body has been made deathless and immortal by your thinking. No power in the Universe can destroy or corrupt it. You only, as the indwelling Triune Self, can change it by your thinking. It is a body built to gauge and mold and move and translate and guide nature units in being conscious as their functions, to serve the purpose of the Universe, which is, that all units will progress in being conscious in ever higher degrees. Your immortal physical body is the model of beauty and strength for the Realm of Permanence, the world by which the Universe is operated and kept in balance. The organs of the four systems have been translated into four brains in their respective sections: in the head, in the thorax, in the abdomen, and in the pelvis. The brain in the head is for your operation of the light world, the brain in the thorax for the life world, the brain in the abdomen for the form world, and the brain in the pelvis for the physical world. The physical body has a front- or nature-column for your operation of nature by means of the four senses, and a back column from which you, the knower and thinker and doer, the Triune Self, operate. The four brains have parts for you and parts for nature, each related to its section and spine, and coordinated into a working organization. The breaths keep up a circular flow of the free and the transient units of the four worlds, through the four senses of the physical body. These units are not for the upbuilding of the physical body, which is immortal and not dependent on transient units, but for the on-going of the worlds.

29. The compositor units of the physical body are now refined and tempered to the essential matter of the four worlds. This matter is of the unmanifested of a world; it is unchanging, the same, through the changing units. The aia relates the physical body to the essential matter, and the breath-form adapts the units to the worlds. The aia keeps the breath-form and the physical body in permanence, while the breath-form gives form to the units and moves the physical body to action. There is life in the mingling of the units of the worlds in your perfect body, and

the units carry life through the worlds. When the physical body has been made perfect and is related to the worlds you, the three parts of and as the Triune Self, are ready to issue from your physical body into the form, the life, and the light worlds. In the course of your thinking with your feeling-and-desire minds, feeling-and-desire were voluntarily self-controlled and caused the breath-form to rebuild the physical body to accord with your conscious development as feeling-and-desire. By continuing your thinking with the minds of rightness and reason you also became conscious of yourself as rightness-and-reason. By thinking as rightness-and-reason your feeling and desire were rectified and justified; and the breath-form was made to raise the physical body into a higher form and structure. By thinking with the minds of I-ness and selfness you reached self-conscious knowledge of yourself as I-ness-and-selfness; and the breath-form was made complete and caused the physical body to be perfect. As feeling-and-desire, you are beauty and power. As rightness-and-reason, you are law and justice. As I-ness-and-selfness, you are identity and knowledge. As these three, you are not separated or divided; you are the doer, the thinker, the knower as the Triune Self complete, each developed as itself, yet partaking of and in perfect relation to each other, and all are and make complete the unity of the Triune Self. As the complete Triune Self, you are in your perfect physical body which is the physical measure of your perfection.

30. In your physical body matter of each of the three worlds has been modeled into bodies which each of your three parts will use to work with the worlds. Matter of the form world has been developed in what was the abdomen which you, as feeling-and-desire, the doer, will use to work with the matter of the form world. Matter of the life world through the thorax has grown to be a life body which you, as rightness-and-reason, the thinker, will use in the life world. Matter of the light world in the head has become a light body which you, as I-ness-and-selfness, the knower, will be with in the light world, (Fig. VI-D). By your thinking you have made these bodies perfect instruments, and you are now ready to rise out of your physical body with them and to issue and to adjust each to its particular world. By thinking of yourself as the knower and knowledge in relation to the light world, you, the complete Triune Self, rise out of your physical body through the top of the head and you are in the light world, the colorless sphere of shadowless Light. You, as the knower and knowledge, are sheathed in a column of Light, light-matter

of the light world, the light body which your thinking has created and called into being in the light world. You have always been I-ness-and-selfness, the knower and knowledge, in the light world; but not until feeling-and-desire had by thinking become detached from their illusions and delusions, and by thinking had attained union, could the three bodies be related and ready for you, as the knower, to work with in the three worlds. From your light body in the light world you think of yourself in relation to the life world and you are in the life world, a radiant sphere of cycling life. As rightness-and-reason, you are clothed in an oval of life, life matter of the life world which passes from the thorax by your thinking, and through which you will deal with the life world. You have always been rightness-and-reason, the right and the just, but only in relation to feeling and desire which were enslaved to nature. Now that they are free, you, as the thinker, can be an administrator of the law and justice in accord with the knower and knowledge. From your life body in the life world you think of yourself in relation to the form world and you are in the form world, a sphere of light of typal forms. As feeling-and-desire, you are in a form body, form matter of the form world, which issues from the abdomen in response to your thinking, and in which you will act in the form world. You have always been feeling-and-desire, but now that you are free from all entanglements with nature, you, as the doer, are also beauty and power and will act in the form world with all forms of feeling and desire in accord with the right and the just. You, the Triune Self, are in each of these three beings; each being is separate and different from the other two, according to the matter of which it is. That part of your Triune Self which acts through its being in the world of that being is essentially the same as the other two parts and the three parts of the three beings constitute the unbroken and inseparable beings of you as the Triune Self. So your being of the life world and your being of the form world act coordinately with your being of the light world, though each is a being distinct from the other two. Because of the difference in fineness of matter of your three beings, the being of the light world is present and lives in and through the being of the life world, the being of the life world is through the being of the form world and the being of the form world is in the physical body, which is attuned and related to the matter of all the worlds; and, by it the three beings of you, as the complete Triune Self, may act on the matter of the physical world. Because of the relation of the fourfold physical body to the four planes of the physical world and to the four states and substates of matter, you, the Triune Self can, by your thinking through the matter of the physical body, be present and appear as the physical body in any place at any time. There you can, by thinking, cause to occur such phenomena as you see fit.

31. Now that your service is accepted by your Intelligence and since love is awakened by the Great Triune Self of the worlds in you for every being, and your body is related and attuned to all states of matter on the planes of the physical world, you are ready to take your part in working for the plan and the purpose of the Universe. You are a qualified and accepted officer in The Government of the Universe: you are knowledge and justice and love in relation to the world of men and in all the worlds. In the light world you are the knower and knowledge: you know all other Triune Selves and you are known by the knower of every Triune Self to be the knower of yourself and of them. In the life world you are the law and justice: the thoughts of men are open to you and you adjudicate upon each in its relation to the thoughts of other men according to the law of thought and in agreement with the reason of any of the doers in bondage to nature. In the form world you are beauty and power: you are the ideal form and character to which great thinkers and artists aspire, and you direct the administration of justice with love so that all who will may find their way through the wilderness of the world. In the physical world you are knowledge and justice and love to all human beings of the doers among whom you move, and you are sense and power supreme to all elemental beings. So you are the Triune Self complete, being and acting in each of the four worlds separately or simultaneously.

32. You choose the locality of the physical world in which your physical body is to be, on or between the crusts of the earth or beyond the crusts, alone, among others of your kind, or in relation to a people. You need not be limited to a locality, you may go, in your physical body, where you please: in any part of the solid earth, or its zones, or you may be and act on the physical plane of any of the other three worlds. You may appear to travel on surfaces, but you can go with the speed of light-matter of the world and plane and state of matter in which you will your body to be. You can be present anywhere. You are where you will to be. By your sight you see, by your hearing you hear, by your taste you taste and by your smell you smell, and contact any matter or being or place in any of the four worlds or their planes or states. You do this by thinking and by

feeling your body where you will it to be. Feeling through your senses contacts the matter of the place, desire gives moving power to the matter and thinking places the body where the desire with feeling wishes it to be. You can see through, hear or contact any state or zone or being of the four worlds, from the least progressed unit to the greatest God, and it must obey what you command. But you will command only what it is right that you should command, and only what should be obeyed. You can cause the stars to move, to be bright or to be invisible in a clear sky; or the sun to focus heat or light; or you can cause these celestial masses to change their courses. But you will do these things only when the people for whom they are done have by their thoughts and acts made it necessary. You can bring the fire zone into the air, making the air a raging sea of fire or have it rain lightning on the earth, or bury the earth under deep layers of ice or you may cause the water zone to flood the earth, but only when the land and water areas are to be changed and when a people have determined destruction by what they have thought and done. You can cause the earth crust to quake and open and pour forth fire and brimstone and jets of steam and to destroy vegetation and to heave like waves between rivers of molten masses, but only when the people of the crust have ceased to learn, and the earth must be prepared for a new course and effort by re-existing doers who are to inhabit it. You can cause the seasons to recur in orderly succession over a long period or to be changeable and uncertain, or cause periods of drought or fertility, pests and panics, depression, peace and prosperity, all in response to what the people do to themselves and each other as individuals or as masses. You need not appear on the outer earth crust to do these things; you can be within the chambers of the earth or in the inner or outer zones of water or air or fire, and you can be as distant or as present as you will. For you it is possible to do anything; the only thing impossible for you to do is to do wrong, inasmuch as you are knowledge and justice and love.

THE END

SYMBOLS, ILLUSTRATIONS and CHARTS.

Symbols I-A, I-B, I-C, I-D, I-E indicate
THE COSMOGONY
outlined in these pages.

———

To show the Spheres, Worlds, Planes and States of Matter on one page of this book would be impossible. Therefore, each will be given separately.

THE CIRCLE OF THE TWELVE NAMELESS POINTS
AND THE FOUR SPHERES

Fig. I-A

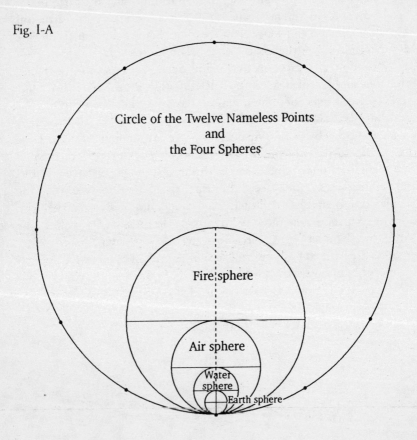

Circle of the Twelve Nameless Points
and
the Four Spheres

Fire sphere

Air sphere

Water sphere

Earth sphere

The Points are to symbolize Presences. By their Presence all parts of the all-inclusive One are kept in right relation according to the Eternal Order of Progression through the Realm of Permanence.

The spheres and, in the symbols to follow, the worlds and planes and states of matter, are, each, divided by a horizontal diameter. The upper half represents the unmanifested which is throughout the circle, and the lower half symbolizes the manifested.

THE EARTH SPHERE AND THE FOUR WORLDS

Fig. I-B

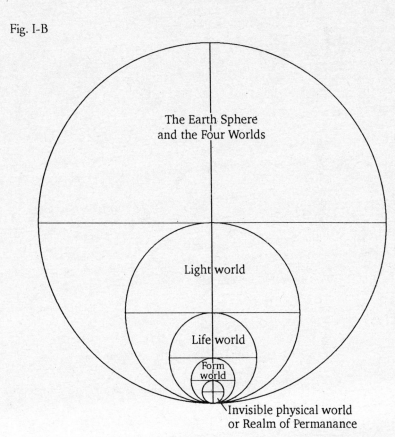

The Earth Sphere
and the Four Worlds

Light world

Life world

Form world

Invisible physical world
or Realm of Permanance

THE INVISIBLE PHYSICAL WORLD or
REALM OF PERMANENCE
and the
TEMPORAL HUMAN PHYSICAL WORLD

Fig. I-C

Invisible Physical World
or
Realm of Permanance

Light plane

Life plane

Form plane

Physical plane of the
Realm of Permanance

The small circle on the lowest,
the physical plane, represents
the four states of matter

Human physical world
and it's four planes

Owing to a deviation from, an interruption in, the Eternal Order of Progression, there is on the physical plane of the Realm of Permanence, the temporal:

Human Physical World,

which is of four planes: the light, life, form and physical planes.

* * *

These two worlds differ in that the Realm of Permanence is of balanced units and is therefore not attuned to human senses, while the Human Physical World is of unbalanced units and is in small part visible.

———

In the text, unless otherwise stated, it is the human physical world—not the Realm of Permanence—that is referred to by the term "physical world."

THE PHYSICAL PLANE OF THE HUMAN
PHYSICAL WORLD
and its
FOUR STATES OF MATTER

Fig. I-D

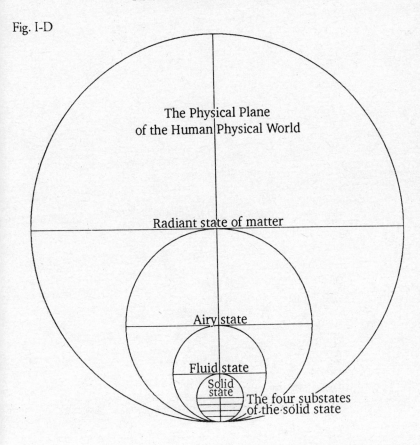

The Physical Plane
of the Human Physical World

Radiant state of matter

Airy state

Fluid state

Solid state

The four substates
of the solid state

In the four substates of the solid state are the stars, sun, moon, and the earth, (Fig. I-E).

*   *   *

All these states are invisible to the human eye, but some of the objects in the four substates of the solid state can be perceived by the human.

THE SOLID STATE OF MATTER
and its
FOUR SUBSTATES

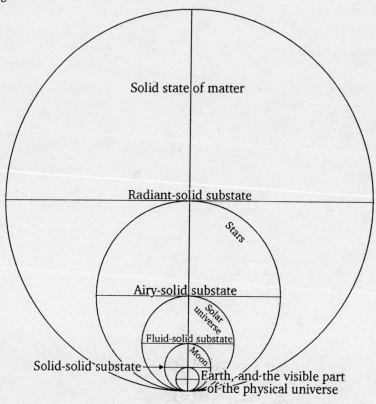

The visible physical universe is of and in the four substances of the solid state of the physical plane of the temporal human physical world, namely: the stars in the radiant-solid, the solar universe in the airy-solid, the moon in the fluid-solid, and the earth in the solid-solid substate of the solid state of matter.

*　　*　　*

In the four substates of the solid state is also the fourfold physical human body, (Fig. III), the visible solid-solid body corresponding to the earth.

UNITS.

THERE ARE FOUR KINDS OF UNITS: A) Nature Units; B) Aia Units; C) Intelligent Units; D) Intelligence Units

Fig. II-A

A) NATURE UNITS:
In the four spheres of fire, air, water, and earth are the units of the four great elements of primordial fire, air, water, and earth.

The four worlds are in the manifested side of the sphere of earth:
    In the light world, the units are light units;
    In the life world, the units are life units;
    In the form world, the units are form units;
    In the physical world, the units are physical units.

The units of the planes of the physical world are:
    Light units; life units; form units, and physical units.

The units of four states of matter of the physical plane are:
    Radiant or pyrogen units;
    Airy or aerogen units;
    Fluid or fluogen units;
    Solid or geogen units.

The units of the four substates of the solid state of the physical plane are:
    Radiant-solid or pyro-geogen units;
    Airy-solid or aero-geogen units;
    Fluid-solid or fluo-geogen units;
    Solid-solid or geo-geogen units.

When a unit has passed through this course, the opposites in the unit are adjusted and are equal to each other, and the unit is then a balanced unit in a perfect physical body of a Triune Self in the Realm of Permanence.

In the temporal human physical world—which is a "drop-out," a cul-de-sac or blind alley in the Realm of Permanence—the units are active-passive as man, or passive-active as woman, and are of four kinds: free, transient, compositor, and sense units.

B) AIA UNITS are neutral units. They belong to the intelligent side, but are the dividing point or line between intelligent-matter from nature-matter.

C) TRIUNE SELF, OR INTELLIGENT UNITS.

D) INTELLIGENCE UNITS.

863

UNBALANCED UNITS
ON THE NATURE-SIDE OF THE HUMAN PHYSICAL WORLD:

Fig. II-B

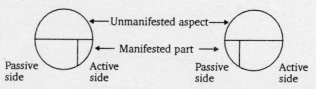

The active side of a unit is the side from which the unit is charged while in a human body.

————

A BALANCED UNIT
OF THE PERFECT BODY IN THE REALM OF PERMANENCE.

Fig. II-C

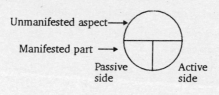

————

PRE-CHEMISTRY

Fig. II-F

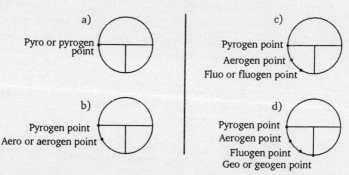

The combining points of a nature unit of the four elements, as states of matter in the human physical world.

Fig. II-D

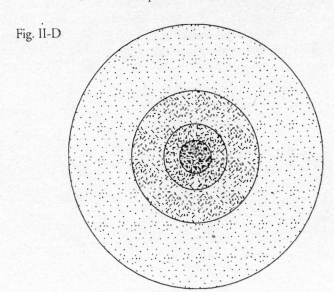

The units converging in the solid state of the physical plane of the human physical world,—visualized from the birdseye viewpoint.

Fig. II-E

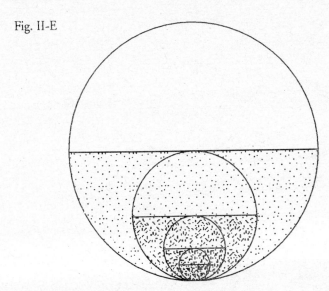

The units converging in the visible, physical universe, as exemplified by the fourfold physical human body.

ETERNAL ORDER OF PROGRESSION

This figure symbolizes the Eternal Order of Progression of a unit: as a nature unit, on the nature-side, within the sphere of earth, through the light world, the life world, the form world to the permanent physical world or Realm of Permanence; to the degree of breath-form;—then by way of the aia point or neutral line, as an aia unit, to the degree of a Triune Self unit, on the intelligent-side.

Fig. II-G

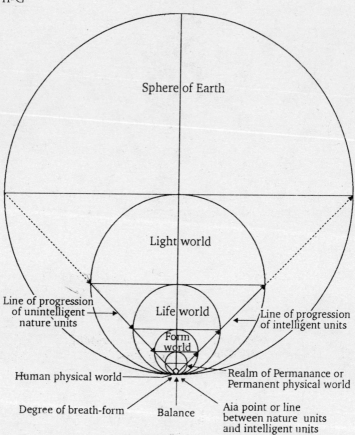

The oblique line of arrows leading to the point of balance downward indicates the line of progression of the unintelligent units to the Realm of Permanence; the line leading from the point of balance upward on the intelligent-side indicates the line of progression of intelligent units.

The symbol also shows the line of descent into the temporal human world of birth and death and re-existence, by the doers that failed in the trial test of bringing their feeling-and-desire into balanced union.

866

ETERNAL ORDER OF PROGRESSION

This chart indicates the stages in which the unit progresses in being conscious in successively higher degrees,—from being a primordial unit of the element of fire to becoming an ultimate unit as an Intelligence, trained through the perfect sexless bodies in the Realm of Permanence.

Fig. II-H

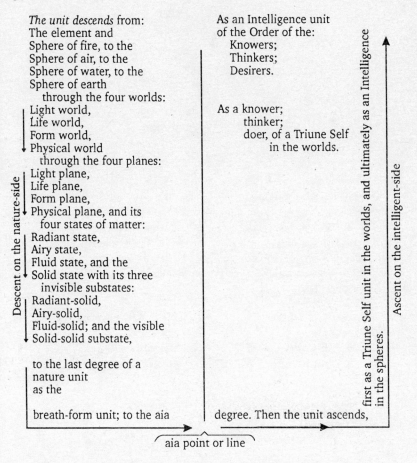

The unit descends from:
The element and
Sphere of fire, to the
Sphere of air, to the
Sphere of water, to the
Sphere of earth
    through the four worlds:
Light world,
Life world,
Form world,
Physical world
    through the four planes:
Light plane,
Life plane,
Form plane,
Physical plane, and its
    four states of matter:
Radiant state,
Airy state,
Fluid state, and the
Solid state with its three
    invisible substates:
Radiant-solid,
Airy-solid,
Fluid-solid; and the visible
Solid-solid substate,

to the last degree of a
nature unit
as the

breath-form unit; to the aia

Descent on the nature-side

As an Intelligence unit
of the Order of the:
    Knowers;
    Thinkers;
    Desirers.

As a knower;
    thinker;
    doer, of a Triune Self
        in the worlds.

degree. Then the unit ascends,

first as a Triune Self unit in the worlds, and ultimately as an Intelligence in the spheres.

Ascent on the intelligent-side

aia point or line

The progression of a unit starts as a nature unit on the nature-side; passes through the neutral state of an aia unit, as the point or neutral line; is translated into an intelligent-unit, and ascends on the intelligent-side, first, as a Triune Self unit and then as an Intelligence unit.

THE FOURFOLD PHYSICAL HUMAN BODY

Fig. III

This symbol indicates the visible solid-solid body from which extend emanations, consisting of invisible particles which radiate from the solid-solid structures of the digestive, circulatory, respiratory and generative systems within the body; they extend from a few inches to a considerable distance, and make up the physical atmosphere. The emanations and radiations from the circulatory, the respiratory and the generative systems are here spoken of as the fluid, the airy and the radiant inner bodies or masses; these, together with the solid-solid body make up the fourfold physical body of man.

SENSE-GOVERNMENT   and   SELF-GOVERNMENT
from without.   from within.

Fig. IV-B

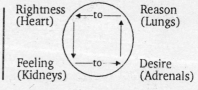

Ordinarily, a person is governed by expediency: then, nature impressions control feeling; feeling arouses desire; desire ignores rightness and forces reason; and desire has its way.

In government by law and justice, rightness guides feeling; which prompts desire; desire. agrees with reason. Then, feeling and desire are controlled by rightness and reason.

868

LINES OF A THOUGHT

symbolizing the creation, the building and the exteriorization; and the experience, the learning from, and the balancing of a thought.

Fig. IV-A

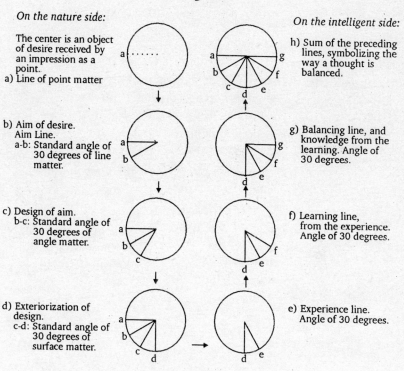

On the nature side:

The center is an object of desire received by an impression as a point.
a) Line of point matter

b) Aim of desire.
Aim Line.
a-b: Standard angle of 30 degrees of line matter.

c) Design of aim.
b-c: Standard angle of 30 degrees of angle matter.

d) Exteriorization of design.
c-d: Standard angle of 30 degrees of surface matter.

On the intelligent side:

h) Sum of the preceding lines, symbolizing the way a thought is balanced.

g) Balancing line, and knowledge from the learning. Angle of 30 degrees.

f) Learning line, from the experience. Angle of 30 degrees.

e) Experience line. Angle of 30 degrees.

INTELLIGENCES and TRIUNE SELVES

THE TRIUNE SELF
of the human,
its THREE PARTS and SEVEN MINDS.

Chart V-A

The three parts: *The knower,* as selfness and I-ness.
                      The thinker, as reason and rightness.
                      The doer, as desire and feeling.

The seven minds: *The mind of selfness*
                      The mind of I-ness
                      The mind of reason   }   Not in connection with
                      The mind of rightness   the doer-in-the-body.

                      The mind of desire
                      The mind of feeling   }   In connection with, and
                         and, for the body   at the service of the
                         and the senses: doer-in-the-body.
                      The body-mind

THE TRIUNE SELF OF THE HUMAN,

and its three parts: the knower, the thinker, and the doer.

THE THREE ATMOSPHERES OF THE TRIUNE SELF, and

THE ATMOSPHERES OF THE HUMAN.

* * *

This figure also serves to indicate the Four Worlds, through which are the Triune Self and the doer-in-the-body.

Fig. V-B

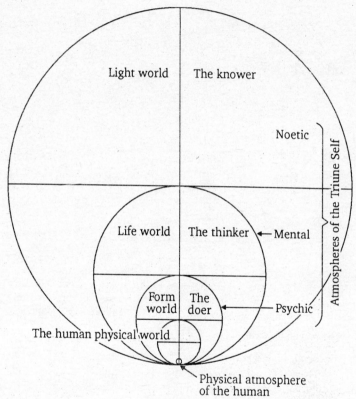

The noetic, mental and psychic atmospheres of the human, are those portions of the atmospheres of the Triune Self that reach into the physical atmosphere of the human.

The physical atmosphere of the human, is made up of emanations from the fourfold physical body, which extend from a few inches to a considerable distance, (Fig. III).

871

THE TRIUNE SELF COMPLETE:

its light-being in the light world;
its life-being in the life world;
its form-being in the form world.

THE PERFECT PHYSICAL BODY
for these three beings in the Realm of Permanence.

Fig. V-B,a

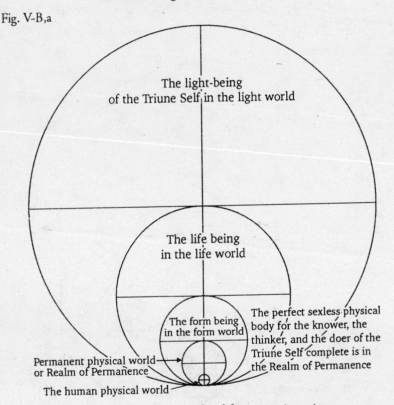

The light-being
of the Triune Self in the light world

The life being
in the life world

The form being
in the form world

The perfect sexless physical
body for the knower, the
thinker, and the doer of the
Triune Self complete is in
the Realm of Permanence

Permanent physical world
or Realm of Permanence

The human physical world

The physical world may be considered from two viewpoints:

1) *as the Realm of Permanence,* where the doers progress that have passed the trial test of bringing their feeling-and-desire into balanced union; and,

2) *the temporal human physical world,* (Fig. V-B), where the doers that fail in that test continue to re-exist until they regenerate their bodies and restore them to the Realm of Permanence.

The physical bodies of the Triune Selves complete are in the Realm of Permanence. Through their perfect sexless physical bodies these Triune Selves govern the four worlds; and, through the Triune Selves of human beings they govern the temporal human world and administrate the destinies of nations as the individuals of those nations determine by their thoughts and acts.

The Three Orders of
INTELLIGENCES,
and the SEVEN FACULTIES OF AN INTELLIGENCE.

Fig. V-C

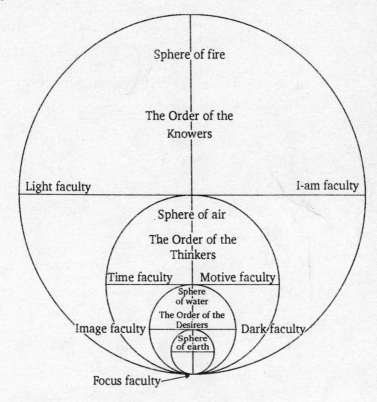

The Order of the Knowers is in relation to the sphere of fire;
The Order of the Thinkers, to the sphere of air;
The Order of the Desirers, to the sphere of water.

In the worlds within the sphere of earth is the Triune Self.

A RE-EXISTING DOER PORTION
and its
STATES AFTER DEATH

Fig. V-D

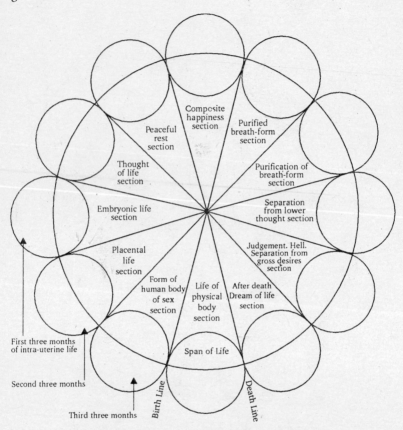

The large circle symbolizes the psychic atmosphere of the doer. From the center to the circumference the twelve lines enclose sections which represent the stages of the symbolical roadway through which each doer portion in its turn, passes successively after death, from its life on earth to its next re-existence. The circle of the lowest section represents the physical life on earth. The opposite and highest circle represents the heaven period of happiness. The five circles on the right represent the after-death stages through which the doer portion passes to prepare it for its period of happiness. The five circles on the left represent the stages through which each doer portion in its turn passes on its return journey for its re-existence in the lowest circle as an appearance on the earth stage of physical life. The lowest line on the left separating the circles is the line or gate of birth. At the moment of birth the breath of the breath-form enters with the first gasp

874

and the breath unites with its form in the heart. The lowest line on the right separating the circles is the line or gate of death. The half circle within that section represents the length or span of the doer's inner life and thoughts in its rise from birth to its fullness and decline and death of the body. The outer part of the circle represents what is said and done to outside nature as the expression of its inner thoughts. Likewise, each of the circles signifies what the doer goes through in itself, and its effects on the stage through which it passes.

THE BREATH-FORM (the living soul), and
THE TWELVE STAGES AFTER DEATH.

1st stage: The breath-form is with the doer portion.

2nd stage: The breath-form is separated from the doer portion during the separation of the desires;

3rd stage: and during the separation of the thoughts.

4th stage: Purification of the breath-form.

5th stage: The breath-form is purified.

6th stage: The breath-form is united with the doer portion, which is in its heaven.

7th stage: The form of the breath-form is inert.

8th stage: Form and breath are summoned for activity.

9th stage: The form enters the mother of the doer portion next in line for re-existence. The breath is in the psychic atmosphere of that doer portion. Embryonic period.

10th stage: Placental life begins. Fetal period.

11th stage: Fetal period continued. Human body is made ready for birth.

12th stage: The breath enters through the infant's lungs and unites with its form in the heart, being the breath-form at the moment of birth and until the death of the body.

THE CEREBRO-SPINAL OR VOLUNTARY
NERVOUS SYSTEM.

This system consists of the Brain, the Spinal Cord and the Nerves issuing from these structures.

THE BRAIN.

Fig. VI-A, a

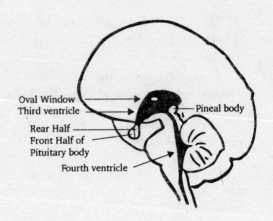

This figure shows the contours of the brain; the 3rd and 4th ventricles (cavities) in the median line, with the oval window leading into the lateral ventricle of the right hemisphere, and the pituitary and the pineal bodies. The black areas represent the ventricles, which are continued downward as the central canal of the spinal cord.

The ventricles, the spaces between the convolutions of the brain, and the space immediately surrounding the body of the brain are for the passage of life and breath currents, of which next to nothing is known to the West.

Note how the 3rd ventricle reaches into the stem (infundibulum) and the rear part of the pituitary body; this rear part is the seat of the doer-in-the-body; the front part is the seat of the breath-form, which controls the involuntary functions of the body.

SPINAL CORD
and
SPINAL NERVES

Fig. VI-A, b

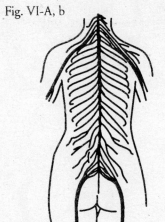

SPINAL COLUMN
and
SPINAL CORD

Fig. VI-A, d

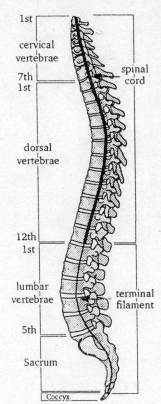

1st

cervical
vertebrae

7th
1st

dorsal
vertebrae

12th
1st

lumbar
vertebrae

5th

Sacrum

Coccyx

spinal
cord

terminal
filament

CROSS SECTION of
SPINAL CORD

Fig. VI-A, c

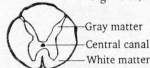

— Gray matter
— Central canal
— White matter

THE SPINAL CORD,
AND ITS RELATION TO THE SPINAL COLUMN.

The spinal cord proper reaches from the base of the brain to about the junction of the 12th dorsal and the 1st lumbar vertebrae; its prolongation downward is called the terminal filament, which is anchored below to the coccyx. The spinal cord has a central canal, the prolongation downward of the ventricles of the brain; below, in the embryo, this canal reaches to the end of the terminal filament, but in the adult it usually becomes clogged up within the filament and disappears more or less, in the run of human beings.

The spinal column is divided into five sections: the cervical, dorsal, and lumbar vertebrae, and the sacrum and coccyx. Bony processes and the shape of the vertebrae create openings on both sides through which pass spinal nerves to the neck, trunk, and upper and lower extremities, (Fig. VI-A, b).

877

THE SYMPATHETIC OR INVOLUNTARY
NERVOUS SYSTEM.

This system consists of two main trunks or cords of ganglia (nerve centers), extending from the base of the brain to the coccyx, and situated partly on the right and left sides and partly in front of the spinal column; and, further, of three great nerve plexuses and many smaller ganglia in the body cavities; and of numerous nerve fibres extending from these structures. The two cords converge above in a small ganglion in the brain, and below in the coccygeal ganglion in front of the coccyx.

Fig. VI-B   Fig. VI-C

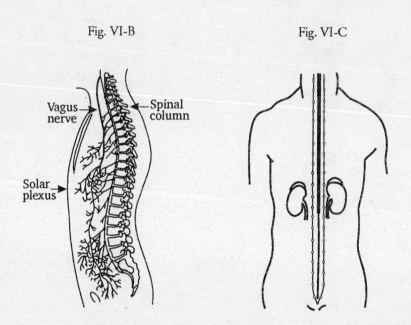

In Fig. VI-B, to the left of the spinal column, is indicated one of the two cords of the involuntary nervous system. From it are seen to extend widespread ramifications of nerve fibres, which form the plexuses that are spread like spider webs over the digestive and the other organs in the body cavities; in the solar plexus they are joined by the vagus nerve of the voluntary system.

Fig. VI-C is a sketch indicating the two ganglionic cords of the involuntary system, converging below; running down between them is the spinal cord, terminating near the coccyx. On the sides are indicated the kidneys, topped by the adrenals.

THE PATHS OF THE LUNAR GERM AND THE
SOLAR GERM, IN THE ORDINARY HUMAN.

The ovum in the female body and the spermatozoon in the male body correspond to the lunar germ and the solar germ, in one and the same person; these two germs are the material for a divine conception by the Triune Self, for the building of a perfected, sexless, regenerated body, out of which are to issue a form body for the doer, a life body for the thinker, and a light body for the knower of the Triune Self, (Fig. VI-D).

The lunar germ: Once a month a lunar germ is formed in the rear part of the pituitary body, (Fig. VI-A,a) , and descends on the right side, along the trunk of the involuntary nervous system and its branches, (Fig. VI-B), to the solar plexus, where they become joined by the right vagus nerve of the voluntary system. Branches of these structures are widely distributed over the body cavities, especially over the organs of the digestive system, and are continued downward into the pelvis. As the lunar germ reaches the lowest point, it crosses over to the left side, by way of the coccygeal ganglion in front of the coccyx, and ascends to the region of the left kidney; but usually it drops back to the sex organs an¹ is lost.

The solar germ: There is only one solar germ for each life. The ordinary course of the solar germ is: Once a year, in the course of six months, it descends from the region of the pineal body, in the right hemisphere of the spinal cord to the region of the first lumbar vertebra; then, during or in the course of six months, after crossing over to and ascending in the left hemisphere of the spinal cord, it returns to the head.

———

DIVINE, "IMMACULATE" CONCEPTION,
and
REGENERATION OF THE PHYSICAL BODY.

Regeneration begins with thinking when, by self-control, the lunar germ is not lost after it has reached the region of the left kidney, (Fig. VI-C); instead, it continues its upward course and ascends to the brain,—thus completing the first round.

The next month the lunar germ descends again, together with the succeeding lunar germ; if and when the lunar germs are saved for thirteen rounds, equal to one solar year, and the thirteen having merged into one, a divine conception. takes place in the head, by the union of the lunar germ with the solar germ, through issuance of light from the pituitary and pineal bodies. So far only slight structural changes have taken place in the human body.

After this divine conception the germ descends on the right side as far as the pelvis; now, however, instead of ascending in the involuntary nervous system on the left side, it connects with the voluntary system by building a "bridge" from the coccygeal ganglion to the terminal filament, (which by this time has developed a central canal from above down to the coccyx).

The lunar germ then opens and enters the terminal filament and is thereby on the form path of The Great Way, and then passes upward to near the junction of the 1st lumbar and 12th dorsal vertebrae, within the central canal. Building the "bridge" and thus making the connection between the two nervous systems, marks a definite change in the structure of the body.
A divine conception is the beginning of the building of a perfect physical body, which is to be the medium for three finer bodies; that is, one, each, for the form-being of the doer, the life-being of the thinker, and the light-being of the knower of the Triune Self.

When the lunar germ has travelled upward within the filament as far as the 12th dorsal vertebra, it has developed into an embryonic form body; at that point it is met by and merges with the solar germ, which has descended in the right hemisphere of the spinal cord. Together they enter into and ascend through the central canal of the spinal cord, to the 7th cervical vertebra. The distance between the 12th dorsal and the 7th cervical marks the life path, and while on this path, the solar germ develops into an embryonic life body. Traveling up the central canal of the spinal cord, the embryonic form and the embryonic life bodies are met at the 7th cervical vertebra by a light germ from the pituitary body; this marks the beginning of the light path and of the embryonic light body. Then the embryonic light body, accompanied by the embryonic life and form bodies, advances through the medulla oblongata and the pons varolii to the pineal body, opens the pineal and fills all ventricles and the spaces between the convolutions and immediately around the brain, with light. Later, the three embryonic bodies reach their full development and ascend through the top of the head, and the doer, the thinker and the knower of the Triune Self are established therein. The doer has then reached perfection, and the Triune Self complete is in a perfected, sexless, regenerated, immortal physical body, and at the end of The Great Way. The other two of the threefold Way, The Way of thinking and The Way in the interior of the earth, have then been successfully travelled.

DIAGRAMMATIC SKETCH OF

THE REGENERATED, PERFECTED, TWO-COLUMNED, SEXLESS, IMMORTAL, PHYSICAL BODY, FOR THE TRIUNE SELF COMPLETE, SHOWING

1) THE WAY IN THE BODY, and its THREE SECTIONS: THE FORM PATH, THE LIFE PATH, and THE LIGHT PATH.
2) THE FRONT- OR NATURE-CORD.
3) THE SPINAL CORD OR CORD FOR THE TRIUNE SELF.
4) THE "BRIDGE" that has been built between the two nervous systems.
5) THE CENTRAL CANAL, running down through the nature-cord, across the "bridge" and up through the spinal cord to:
6) THE PITUITARY AND THE PINEAL BODIES.

Fig. VI-D

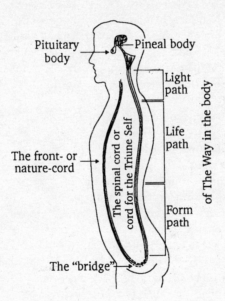

On the form path, extending from the end of the terminal filament to the 12th dorsal vertebra, a form body is developed for the doer, the psychic part of the Triune Self, the being of the form world.

On the life path, extending from the 12th dorsal to the 7th cervical vertebra, a life body is developed for the thinker, the mental part of the Triune Self, the being of the life world.

On the light path, extending from the 7th to the 1st cervical vertebra, a light body is developed for the knower, the noetic part of the Triune Self, the being of the light world.

When the human physical body has been rebuilt and its reconstruction into a perfect, immortal body is completed, that body need not be sustained by the gross foods of this earth. Certain nerve currents come into the body chiefly by way of the sense organs and their nerves; they pass along the central canal of the front-cord, of the "bridge," and of the spinal cord and upwards into what are now the ventricles of the brain. In their uninterrupted passage through the canal of the two cords, the units making up these currents are charged with power by the Triune Self, and so the body is enabled to serve as a powerhouse through which nature is energized and empowered.

There is then no longer any need for the generative, respiratory, circulatory and digestive systems as they are now, and the organs at present serving these systems have become transformed. In their places, structures resembling those of the nervous systems fill the four body cavities: these structures are here spoken of as the four brains: the pelvic brain for the perfect physical body; the abdominal brain for the doer and its form body; the thoracic brain for the thinker and its life body; and the cephalic brain for the knower and its light body. By virtue of these brains, the three parts of the Triune Self can each thus act separately in its respective body, or together, and with or through the physical body.

When the body has been regenerated many significant changes have taken place. The present sternum with the esophagus and what has remained of the stomach and intestines, have been converted into a resilient, tubular column, the front- or nature-column, which is analogous to and resembles somewhat the spinal column; within this tube is the front- or nature-cord, made up of what are now the two main trunks of the involuntary nervous system and of the nerve structures belonging to that system. Joined with the nature-cord are the two vagus nerves, which are, however, under the direct control of the voluntary system. From the front-column, (Fig. VI-D), extend half-arches to both sides, similarly to the present ribs, with which the half-arches are joined. A "bridge," a direct connection, has been established in the pelvis between the two nervous systems, of which even now indications may be seen in slender fibrils that run between the two systems. Running down within the nature-cord, then across the bridge and upward in the spinal cord is a continuous canal, which, as stated above, is for the passage of breath and nerve currents, and for the use of the doer, the thinker, and the knower.

The present ganglia and nerve plexuses of both systems are greatly augmented and fill the body cavities; they form the four brains before mentioned. The body is by that time largely a body of nerves.

SKELETON OF HUMAN BODY
SHOWING THE STERNUM.

As stated in the text, the sternum is the vestigial remains of the front- or nature-column of the once perfect body,—prior to the "fall" of the doer.

Fig. VI-E

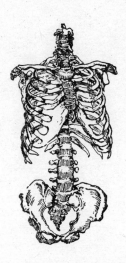

In this connection it is worthwhile to quote from Cunningham's "Textbook of Anatomy", 4th edition, page 767:

The Morphology of the Sympathetic Nervous System:

"The philogenetic relation of the sympathetic and the cerebro-spinal elements in the system it is impossible to determine. It may be that the sympathetic system is the representative of an ancient architecture independent of the cerebro-spinal nervous system, the materials of which are utilized for a more modern nervous system; or it may be that the correlation of spinal nerves and sympathetic are both the consequences of the formation of new organs and structures in the splanchnic area. Examined in every light, it possesses features which effectually differentiate it from the cerebro-spinal system, although it has become inextricably united with it and subservient to it."

THE ZODIAC

Fig. VII-A

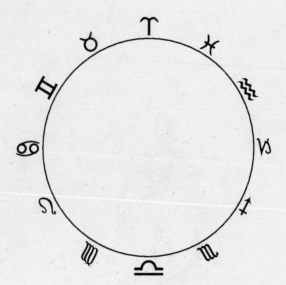

		Symbolizing:	*Corresponding to:*
♈	ARIES	Consciousness	Head
♉	TAURUS	Motion	Neck
♊	GEMINI	Substance	Shoulders
♋	CANCER	Breath	Breasts
♌	LEO	Life	Heart
♍	VIRGO	Form	Prostate and womb
♎	LIBRA	Sex	Crotch
♏	SCORPIO	Desire	Male organ and clitoris
♐	SAGITTARY	Thought	Terminal filament
♑	CAPRICORN	Self-knowledge	Spinal cord opposite heart
♒	AQUARIUS	Conscious Sameness	Spinal cord opposite shoulders
♓	PISCES	Pure Intelligence or Abstract Will	Spinal cord opposite cervical vertebrae

THE ZODIAC
within
THE CIRCLE OF THE TWELVE NAMELESS POINTS.

Fig. VII-B

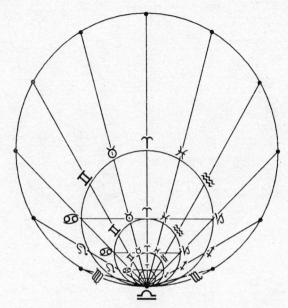

From libra, the physical body, man by thinking may extend lines towards every point in nature, and be related to the Intelligences, and even to the nameless points on the Nameless Circle.

THE BROKEN AND EXTENDED ZODIAC

Fig. VII-C

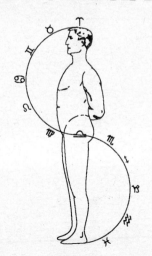

HORIZONTALS	PERPENDICULARS	OPPOSITES

Fig. VII-D

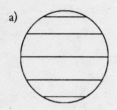

a)   b)   c)

The Zodiac as a
MONAD

THE DYADS

Fig. VII-E   Fig. VII-F

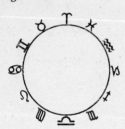   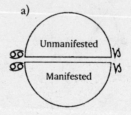

a)   b)

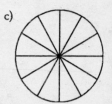

THE TRIADS

Fig. VII-G

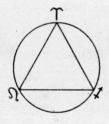   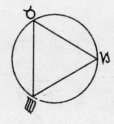   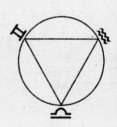

Fire Triad   Air Triad   Water Triad

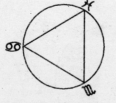   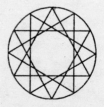

Earth Triad   The Four Triads

Fig. VII-H

THE TETRADS AS SQUARES

a)

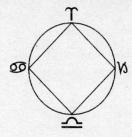

The Standard Square

b)

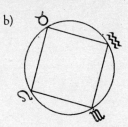

The Male Square

c)

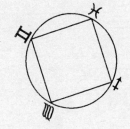

The Female Square

d)

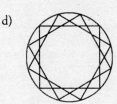

The Three Tetrads as Squares

Fig. VII-J

THE TETRADS AS CROSSES

a)

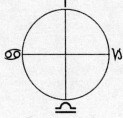

The Standard Cross

b)

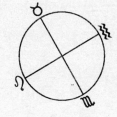

The Male Cross

c)

The Female Cross

d)

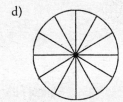

The Three Tetrads as Crosses

a)

The unmanifested universal pentad, representing the aia in a perfect body.

b)

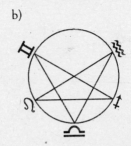

The manifested universal pentad, representing the breath-form in the body.

c)

The unmanifested and the manifested pentads, representing the aia and the breath-form in a perfect body.

d)

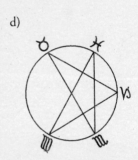

Male Human Pentad

e)

Female Human Pentad

f)

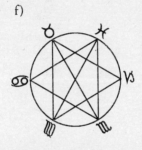

The male and the female human pentads in the human body.

g)

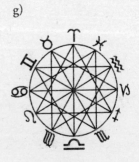

The human body as the unmanifested and the manifested universe and the male and female pentads operating therein.

Fig. VII-L

a)

The Universal Hexad

b)

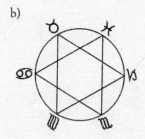

The Human Hexad.

c)

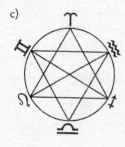

While in the course of regeneration the male and female pentads think and work coordinately, equally, in the same body, the body changes from an unbalanced sexual to a balanced sexless body.

This universal hexad symbolizes a sexless physical body in which the aia is manifested and linked with the breath-form to operate nature, as the direct instrument of the Triune Self complete.

LEGEND TO THE OBLONG SQUARE

Masonic Lodges: Entered Apprentice, Fellowcraft, Master Mason, and Royal Arch degrees, showing the stations or gates of Cancer (♋) the senior warden in the West; Libra (♎) the junior warden in the South; and Capricorn (♑) the master in the East; in each of the degrees. The physical body of man is the ground floor or plan or lodge in which all the degrees are worked, as the body or lodge is prepared for each degree.

The conscious self, as the Doer-in-the-body, is the entered apprentice to be initiated in the first degree. He begins to learn the use of his rule, or line of feeling, from Cancer to Libra (♋ to ♎) and his line of desire from Libra to Capricorn (♎ to ♑). When he has brought these into right relationship to each other they unite and make the square on which a Mason works, and the oblong square (♋ to ♎ to ♑) below. The feeling line and desire line make the square of the right-angled triangle (the hypotenuse), the square of all true Masons on which the work of the lodge is conducted.

All degrees are degrees to be taken by the Doer-in-the-body; not by the Thinker and Knower. They await the Doer on his initiation as a Master Mason. The Doer is initiated into the higher degrees to be eventually united with the Thinker and Knower in the Royal Arch. Then they will be complete and perfect. The work of the Doer as entered apprentice is, as he advances by degrees, to rebuild his present physical body into that temple not made with hands, immortal in The Eternal.

This figure shows the Masonic Lodge to be the present physical body. The oblong square is given in detail. The two columns and the three pillars are, by extension, also shown.

The Groundfloor is the pelvic section. The Middle Chamber is the abdominal section. The Sanctum Sanctorum is the thoracic section. The Royal Arch is the physical body in its atmospheres, complete. The top of the head represents the keystone.

Refer to symbols (Figures I-D; VI-A,b; VI-A,c; VI-A,d; VI-B, VI-C) in *Thinking and Destiny*. Figure VI-B shows the front, or nature, column of the perfect body—which is now broken, being absent below the sternum.

The three signs Cancer, Leo, Virgo (♋, ♌, ♍) are the three female signs, from the breasts to the womb; when squared, 3 x 3, they make 9. The male signs are four, Libra, Scorpio, Sagittary, Capricorn (♎, ♏, ♐, ♑), from the coccyx Libra to Capricorn opposite the heart. When squared they equal 16. 9 plus 16 equal 25. The five signs, Aquarius (♒), Pisces (♓), Aries (♈), Taurus (♉), Gemini (♊), are signs representing the hypotenuse, above Cancer (♋) and Capricorn (♑) which when squared equal 25, the square of the circle, thus "squaring the circle."

Fig. VIII-A

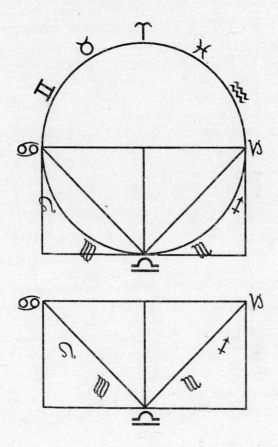

The lower section is set apart to show the Oblong Square itself. The first three signs—Cancer, Leo, Virgo—are feminine and the next four—Libra, Scorpio, Sagittary, Capricorn—are masculine. The sum of the squares of the first three and the next four is equal to the square of the hypotenuse which, itself, is actually equal to five and conforms to the five unmanifested signs representing the Royal Arch. As is readily seen in the plate, the hypotenuse is equal to one side of the square capable of encompassing the circle. It is the total sum of the Mason's work on the Oblong Square, the trestle board, his lodge, his body, which squares the circle and enables him to take his rightful place as the Keystone in The Royal Arch in the Realm of Permanence.

DEFINITIONS AND EXPLANATIONS

ACCIDENT, AN: is usually said to be an unexpected happening or event without apparent cause. Nevertheless, an accident is the only visible segment in a chain or circle of unobserved or preceding causes inevitably resulting in that occurrence called accident. The other segments of the circle are the thoughts and acts which are related to the accident.

AIA: (eye'-uh) is the name here given to a unit that has successively progressed through each and every degree in being conscious as its function in a University of Laws, in a perfect, sexless and immortal body; which has graduated from nature, and is on the intelligent-side as a point or line distinguishing it from the nature-side.

ALCOHOLISM: is a psychic disease of the doer of desire-and-feeling, with which disease the physical body is infected by the drinking of alcoholic liquors. Alcohol is excellent and trustworthy, while kept as a servant, or used as a medium in the making of pharmaceutical preparations. But alcohol, as a spirit, is ruthless and relentless when it becomes master. It is only a matter of time, in this or some future life, when every doer will of necessity have to face the fiend and conquer or be conquered by it. The liquor is harmless, if one does not drink it; it is only a medium. But when one drinks it, the spirit of which alcohol is the medium makes contact with desire in the blood and with feeling in the nerves and cajoles the desire and feeling into the belief that it is a friend, and this belief grows and grows. It is the spirit of conviviality and good fellowship through all stages of drunkenness along which it leads its victim. And when the doer eventually is too depraved to take on the human form, the fiend leads it to its prison in the inner recesses of the earth, where it is fixed in conscious inertia. Conscious inertia is more galling and frightful than the fiercest fires of any theological or other hell conceivable. Alcohol is the preserving spirit in nature; but it kills the thing which it preserves. The spirit of drunkenness fears the Conscious Light in the human, and strives to incapacitate the human. The only sure way to be the master and not the slave of the spirit of alcohol is: Do not taste it. Have a firm and definite mental attitude and set not to take it under any pretense or form. Then one will be the master.

ANGER: is desire burning in the blood and acting in resentment at what is or is supposed to be a wrong to oneself or to another.

892

APPEARANCE: is nature units grouped into mass or form and is visible; it is subject to change or disappearance, when that which holds it together changes or is withdrawn.

APPETITE: is the desire to gratify taste and smell with material, in response to the urge of entities of nature to keep matter in circulation.

ART: is skill in the expression of feeling and desire.

ASTRAL: is starry matter.

ASTRAL BODY: as a term used in this book is to describe the radiant-solid of the fourfold physical body. The other three are the airy-solid, fluid-solid, and solid-solid. The airy-solid and fluid-solid are only masses, they are not developed into form. The astral body is that which shapes the matter of the growing body according to the form of the breath-form until birth. Thereafter, the physical body depends on the astral body to keep its structure in form according to the form of the breath-form. After the breath-form leaves the body at death, the astral body remains near the physical structure. Then the astral body depends on the structure for maintenance, and is dispersed as the structure decays.

ATMOSPHERE: is the mass of diffused matter which radiates from and surrounds any object or thing.

ATMOSPHERE, PHYSICAL HUMAN: is the spherical mass of radiant, airy, fluid, and solid units emanating from and kept circulating in four constant streams of units in and through the body by the breath, the active side of the breath-form.

ATMOSPHERE OF THE HUMAN, PSYCHIC: is the active side of the doer, the psychic part of the Triune Self, the passive side of one portion of which exists in the kidneys and adrenals and the voluntary nerves and the blood of the human body. It surges, pounds, pulls and pushes through the blood and nerves of the body in response to the desire and feeling of the doer which re-exists in the body.

ATMOSPHERE OF THE HUMAN, MENTAL: is that part of the mental atmosphere of the Triune Self which is through the psychic atmosphere and by means of which the feeling-mind and desire-mind may think at the neutral points between the uninterrupted inflow and outflow of breathing.

ATMOSPHERE, OF ONE'S TRIUNE SELF, NOETIC: is, so to say, the reservoir, from which the Conscious Light is conveyed by the mental and psychic atmospheres to the doer-in-the-body through the breath.

ATMOSPHERE OF EARTH: is made up of the four spherical zones or masses of radiant, airy, fluid, and solid units which keep up a constant circulation from and through the compacted and spherical earth crust, and from and through the interior to the farthest stars.

BREATH: is the life of the blood, the pervader and builder of tissue, the preserver and destroyer, by or in which all operations of the body continue to exist or pass out of existence, until by thinking it is made to regenerate and restore the body to everlasting life.

BREATH-FORM: is a nature unit which is the individual living form (soul) of each human body. Its breath builds and renews and gives life to tissue according to the pattern furnished by the form, and its form keeps in form the structure, its body, during its presence in the body. Death is the result of its separation from the body.

CELL, A: is an organization composed of transient units of matter from the radiant, airy, fluid, and solid streams of matter, organized into living structure by the related and reciprocal action of four compositor units: the breath-link, life-link, form-link, and cell-link compositor units constituting that cell, which is not visible, not the body of composed transient units which may be visible or seen under a microscope. The four compositor units are linked together and remain in that cell; the transient units are like flowing streams from which the compositors continue to catch and compose transient units into and as the body of that cell during the continuance of the larger organization of which that cell is a component part. The four compositor units of a cell in a human body are indestructible; when they are not supplied with transient units the cell body will cease, be decomposed and disappear, but the compositors of the cell will again build out a body at some future time.

CHANCE: is a word used to excuse oneself for not understanding, or to explain acts, objects and events that occur and which are not easily explained, as "games of chance," or "chance happenings". But there is no such thing as chance, in the sense that a happening could have happened in any other way than it did, independent of law and order. Every act of chance, such as the flipping of a coin, the turning of a card, the throwing of a die, happens according to certain laws and in order, whether they are according to laws of physics or laws of knavery and trickery. If what is called chance were independent of law, there would be no dependable laws of nature. Then there would be no certainty of the seasons, of day and night. These are laws which we more or less understand, just as are "chance" happenings, which we do not take enough trouble to understand.

CHARACTER: is the degree of honesty and truthfulness of one's feelings and desires, as expressed by his individual thought, word and action. Honesty and truthfulness in thought and act are the fundamentals of good character, the distinguishing marks of a strong and considerate and fearless character. Character is inborn, inherited from one's own former lives, as the predisposition to think and act; it is continued or changed as one chooses.

COMMUNION: is the thinking oneself into relation with rightness, and in receiving Light, according to the system of thinking.

CONCEPTION, DIVINE, "IMMACULATE": is not the impregnation of an ovum in a woman, to be followed by the gestation and birth of another physical body. A sexual birth cannot result from a divine conception. A truly "immaculate" conception is for the rebuilding of the imperfect sexual physical body of death into a perfect sexless physical body of eternal life. When the twelve preceding lunar germs have been merged with the thirteenth lunar germ, on its return to the head, it is there met by the solar germ, and receives a ray of Light from the Intelligence. That is a self-impregnation, a divine conception. The rebuilding of the perfect body follows.

CONSCIENCE: is the sum of knowledge about what should not be done in relation to any moral subject. It is one's standard for right thinking, right feeling, and right action; it is the soundless voice of rightness in the heart that forbids any thought or act which varies from what it knows to be right. The "No" or "Don't" is the voice of the doer's knowledge concerning what he should avoid or not do or not give consent to be done in any situation.

CONSCIOUS: is, with knowledge; the degree in which that which is conscious is conscious in relation to knowledge.

CONSCIOUSNESS: is the Presence in all things—by which each thing is conscious in the degree in which it is conscious *as* what or *of* what it is or does. As a word it is the adjective "conscious" developed into a noun by the suffix "ness." It is a word unique in language; it has no synonyms, and its meaning extends beyond human comprehension. Consciousness is beginningless, and endless; it is indivisible, without parts, qualities, states, attributes or limitations. Yet, everything, from the least to the greatest, in and beyond time and space is dependent on it, to be and to do. Its presence in every unit of nature and beyond nature enables all things and beings to be conscious *as* what or *of* what they are, and are to do, to be aware and conscious of all other things and beings, and to progress in continuing higher degrees of being conscious towards the only one ultimate Reality—Consciousness.

CREDULITY: is the innocent readiness of the doer-in-the-body to believe that things are as they appear, and to accept as true what is said or written.

CULTURE: is the high development of learning, skill and character of a people, or of civilization as a whole.

DEATH: is the departure of the conscious self in the body from its fleshly residence, the snapping or severance of the fine elastic silvery thread that connects the breath-form with the body. The severance is caused by the willing or with the consent of oneself to have its body die. With the breaking of the thread, resuscitation is impossible.

DEFINITION: is that composition of related words which expresses the meaning of a subject or thing and, by thinking on which, knowledge is available.

DESCENT OF MAN: has been variously and figuratively told in ancient scriptures, as in the Bible story of Adam and Eve in the Garden of Eden; their temptation, their fall, their original sin and expulsion from Eden. This is shown as the four stages in the departure of the doer-in-the-body from the Realm of Permanence. The descent from the Realm of Permanence into this world of birth and death, was by variation, division, modification and degeneration. Variation began when the doer of desire-and-feeling extended a part of its perfect body and saw feeling in the extended part. Division was the doer's seeing its desire in the male body and its feeling in the female body and thinking of itself as two instead of one, and its departure from permanence. Modification was the descending or extending from the interior and finer to the outer and lower state of matter and change in structure of body. Degeneration was coming on the outside crust of the earth, the development of sexual organs and generation of sexual bodies.

DESIRE: is conscious power within; it brings about changes in itself and causes change in other things. Desire is the active side of the doer-in-the-body, the passive side of which is feeling; but desire cannot act without its other inseparable side, feeling. Desire is indivisible but appears to be divided; it is to be distinguished as: the desire for knowledge and the desire for sex. It is, with feeling, the cause of the production and reproduction of all things known or sensed by the human. As the desire for sex it remains obscure, but manifests through its four branches: the desire for food, the desire for possessions, the desire for a name, and the desire for power, and their innumerable offshoots, such as hunger, love, hate, affection, cruelty, strife, greed, ambition, adventure, discovery, and accomplishment. The desire for knowledge will not be changed; it is constant as the desire for Self-knowledge.

DESIRE FOR A NAME, (FAME): is a cluster of impressions of indeterminate attributes for a personality, which are as empty and evanescent as a bubble.

DESIRE FOR POWER: is the illusion created which is the offspring and adversary of the desire for Self-knowledge—(the desire for sex).

DESIRE FOR SELF-KNOWLEDGE: is the determined and unyielding desire of the doer to be in conscious relation or union with the knower of its Triune Self.

DESIRE FOR SEX: is selfishness grounded in ignorance concerning itself; the desire that is expressed by the sex of the body in which it is, and which seeks to unite with its suppressed and unexpressed side, by union with a body of the opposite sex.

DESPAIR: is the surrender to fear; the unreserved resignation to let happen what may.

DESTINY: is necessity; that which must be or happen, as the result of what has been thought and said or done.

DESTINY, PHYSICAL: includes everything concerning the heredity and constitution of the human physical body; the senses, sex, form, and features; the health, position in life, family, and human relations; the span of life and manner of death. The body and all concerning the body is the budget of credit and debit which has come over from one's past lives as the result of what one thought and did in those lives, and with which one has to deal in the present life. One cannot escape what the body is and represents. One must accept that and continue to act as in the past, or one may change that past into what one thinks and wills to be, to do, and to have.

DESTINY, PSYCHIC: is all that has to do with feeling-and-desire as one's conscious self in the body; it is the result of what in the past one has desired and thought and done, and of that which in the future will result from what one now desires and thinks and does and which will affect one's feeling-and-desire.

DESTINY, MENTAL: is determined as what, of what, and for what the desire and feeling of the doer-in-the-body think. Three minds—the body-mind, desire-mind, and feeling-mind—are put at the service of the doer, by the thinker of its Triune Self. The thinking which the doer does

with these three minds is its mental destiny. Its mental destiny is in its
mental atmosphere and includes its mental character, mental attitudes,
intellectual attainments and other mental endowments.

DESTINY, NOETIC: is the amount or degree of Self-knowledge that
one has of oneself as feeling and desire, which is available, is in that part
of the noetic atmosphere which is in one's psychic atmosphere. This is
the result of one's thinking and use of one's creative and generative force;
it manifests as one's knowledge of humanity and human relations on the
one hand, and on the other through physical destiny, as troubles,
afflictions, diseases, or infirmities. Self-knowledge is shown by self-control, the control of one's feelings and desires. One's noetic destiny may
be seen in time of crisis, when one knows just what should be done for
oneself and others. It may also come as intuition for enlightenment on
a subject.

DEVIL, THE: is one's own chief evil desire. It tempts, goads and drives
one to wrong action in physical life, and it torments that one during a
part of its after-death states.

DIMENSIONS: are of matter, not of space; space has no dimensions,
space is not dimensional. Dimensions are of units; units are indivisible
constituents of mass matter; so that matter is a make-up, composed of
or as indivisible units related to and distinguished from each other by
their particular kinds of matter, as dimensions. Matter is of four dimensions: on-ness, or surface matter; in-ness, or angle matter; throughness,
or line matter; and presence, or point matter. The numbering is from
the apparent and familiar to the remote.

The first dimension of the units, on-ness or surface units, has no
perceptible depth or thickness or solidity; it depends on and particularly
needs the second and third dimensions to make it visible, tangible, solid.

The second dimension of the units is in-ness or angle matter; it
depends on the third dimension for it to compact surfaces onto surfaces
as mass.

The third dimension of the units is throughness or line matter; it
depends on the fourth dimension for it to carry, conduct, transmit,
transport, import and export matter from the unmanifested non-dimensional matter into in-ness and fix surfaces onto surfaces and so body out
and stabilize surfaces as solid surface matter.

The fourth dimension of the units is presence or point matter, a
succession of points as the basic matter line of points, along which or
through which the next dimension of line matter is built and developed.

Thus it will be seen that unmanifested undimensional matter manifests as or through or by means of a point, and as a succession of points as a matter line of point units, by means of which the next dimension of units as line matter is developed, and by means of which is in-ness or angle matter, which compacts surfaces on surfaces until visible tangible solid matter is shown as the acts, objects and events of this objective physical world.

DISEASE: A disease results from the cumulative action of a thought as it continues to pass through the part or body to be affected, and eventually the exteriorization of such thought is the disease.

DISHONESTY: is the thinking or acting against what is known to be right, and the thinking and doing of what is known to be wrong. The one so thinking and doing may eventually make himself believe that what is right is wrong, and that what is wrong is right.

DOER: That conscious and inseparable part of the Triune Self which periodically re-exists in the man body or woman body, and which usually identifies itself as the body and by the name of the body. It is of twelve portions, six of which are its active side as desire and six are its passive side as feeling. The six active portions of desire re-exist successively in man bodies and the six passive portions of feeling re-exist successively in woman bodies. But desire and feeling are never separate; desire in the man body caused the body to be male and dominates its feeling side; and feeling in the woman body caused its body to be female and dominates its desire side.

DOUBT: is a condition of mental darkness as the result of not enough clear thinking to know what to do and what not to do in a situation.

DREAMS: are of the objective and the subjective. The objective dream is the waking state or state of being awake; nevertheless it is the waking dream. The subjective dream is the sleeping dream. The difference is that in the waking dream all objects or sounds that are seen or heard and which seem so real are the exteriorizations of one's own or other's thoughts on the background of the objective world; and, that the things that we see or hear in the sleeping dream are the reflections on the background of the subjective world of the projections of the objective world. While we are dreaming in sleep the reflections are just as real to us as are the projections in the waking world now. But, of course, when we are awake we cannot remember how real the sleeping dream then was, because from the waking world the dream world seems shadowy and unreal. However, all that we see or hear or do in dream while asleep are the more or less distorted reflections of the things that happen to us and the things we think about while we are in the waking state. The sleeping dream may be likened to a mirror which reflects the things held before it. By meditating on the happenings in the sleeping dream one may interpret much about himself, his thoughts and his motives, that he did not before realize. Dream life is another world, vast and varied. Dreams have not been, but should be, classified, at least into kinds and varieties. The after-death states are related to earth life somewhat as is the sleeping dream to the waking state.

DUTY: is what one owes to oneself or to others, which must be paid, willingly or unwillingly, in such performance as that duty calls for. Duties bind the doer-in-the-body to repeated lives on earth, until the doer frees itself by performance of all duties, willingly and gladly, without hope of praise or fear of blame, and being unattached to the results well done.

"DWELLER": is a term used to signify a vicious desire from a former life of the doer in the present human body, which dwells in the psychic atmosphere and tries to enter the body and influence the doer to acts of violence, or to indulge in practices harmful to doer and body. The doer is responsible for its desires, as dweller or as cloak of vices; its desires cannot be destroyed; they must eventually be changed by thinking and by the will.

DYING: is the sudden or long drawn out process of the breath-form of gathering its fine form from the extremities to the heart and then puffing itself out through the mouth with the last gasp of the breath, usually causing a gurgle or rattle in the throat. At death the doer leaves the body with the breath.

EASE: is the result of the doer's reliance in destiny and in itself; a certain poise in action, irrespective of wealth or poverty, position in life or family or friends.

EGO: is the feeling of the identity of "I" of the human, due to the relation of feeling to the identity of I-ness of its Triune Self. The ego usually includes the personality of body with itself, but the ego is only the *feeling* of identity. If the feeling were the identity, the feeling in the body would know itself as the permanent and deathless "I" which persists through and beyond all time in unbroken continuity, whereas the human ego knows no more about itself than that it is "a feeling."

ELEMENT, AN: is one of the four fundamental kinds of nature units into which nature as matter is classified and of which all bodies or phenomena are composed, so that each element may be distinguished by its kind from each of the other three elements, and so that each kind may be known by its character and function, whether combining and acting as forces of nature or in the composition of any body.

ELEMENTAL, AN: is a unit of nature manifesting as of the element of fire, or of air, or of water, or of earth, individually; or as an individual unit of an element in a mass of other nature units and dominating that mass of units.

ELEMENTALS, LOWER: are of the four elements of fire, air, water, and earth units, here called causal, portal, form, and structure units. They are the causes, changes, maintainers, and appearances of all things in nature which come into existence, which change, which remain for awhile, and which will dissolve and vanish, to be re-created into other appearances.

ELEMENTALS, UPPER: are beings of the fire, air, water, and earth elements, out of which they are created by Intelligences of the spheres, or by the Triune Selves complete, who constitute The Government of the world. Of themselves these beings know nothing and can do nothing. They are not individual nature elementals as nature units, in process of development. They are created out of the unmanifested side of the elements by thinking, and respond perfectly to the thinking of the Triune Selves who direct them in what they are to do. They are executioners of law, against which no nature gods or other forces can prevail. In religions or traditions they may be mentioned as arch-angels, angels, or messengers. They act by direct order of The Government of the world, without human instrumentality, although one or more may appear to give instruction to the human, or to bring about changes in the affairs of men.

EMOTION: is the rousing and expression of desire by words or acts, in response to sensations of pain or pleasure by feeling.

ENVY: is the feeling of ill-will or grudging bitterness toward a person who is or who has what one hungeringly desires to be or to have.

EQUALITY IN THE HUMAN: is that each responsible person has the right to think, to be, to will, to do, and to have, what he is able to be, to will, to do and to have, without force, pressure or restraint, to the extent that he does not try to prevent another from the same rights.

ETERNAL, THE: is the beginningless and endless, within and beyond time and the senses, not dependent on, limited or measurable by time and the senses as past, present, or future; that in which things are known to be as they are, and which cannot appear to be as they are not.

EXPERIENCE: is the impression of an act, object or event produced through the senses on feeling in the body, and the reaction as the response of feeling as pain or pleasure, joy or sorrow, or any other feeling or emotion. The experience is the essence of the exteriorization for the doer and is to teach, that the doer may extract learning from the experience.

EXTERIORIZATION, AN: is the act, object or event that was the physical impression in a thought before it exteriorized as an act, object or event on the physical plane, as physical destiny.

FACTS: are the realities of the objective or subjective acts, objects or events in the state or on the plane on which they are experienced or observed, as evident to and tried by the senses, or as considered and judged by reason. Facts are of four kinds: physical facts, psychic facts, mental facts, and noetic facts.

FAITH: is the imagination of the doer which makes a strong impression on the breath-form because of trust and confidence without doubt. Faith comes from the doer.

FALSEHOOD: is a statement as fact of what is believed to be untrue, or the denial of what is believed to be true.

FAME, (A NAME): is the changing cluster of impressions of indeterminate attributes for a personality, which are evanescent as bubbles.

FEAR: is the feeling of foreboding or impending danger concerning mental or emotional or physical trouble.

FEELING: is that of one's conscious self in the body which feels; which feels the body, but does not identify and distinguish itself as feeling, from the body and the sensations which it feels; it is the passive side of the doer-in-the-body, the active side of which is desire.

FEELING, ISOLATION OF: is its freedom from control by the body-mind and the realization of itself as conscious bliss.

FOOD: is of nature material composed of innumerable combinations of compounds of fire, air, water, and earth units, for the building up of the four systems and the upkeep of the body.

FORM: is the idea, type, pattern or design which guides and shapes and sets bounds to life as growth; and form holds and fashions structure into visibility as appearance.

FREEDOM: is the state or condition of the desire-and-feeling of the doer when it has detached itself from nature and remains unattached. Freedom does not mean that one may say or do what he pleases, wherever he is. Freedom is: to be and will and do and have without attachment to any object or thing of the four senses; and, to continue to be, to will, to do, and to have, without being attached, by thinking, to what one is or wills or does or has. That means that you are not attached in thought to any object or thing of nature, and that you will not attach yourself while thinking. Attachment means bondage.

FUNCTION: is the course of action intended for a person or thing, and which is performed by choice, or by necessity.

GAMBLING: is an obsession of one by the gambling spirit, or the exciting chronic desire to get, to win money or something of value by "luck," by "betting," by games of "chance," instead of earning it by honest work.

GENIUS, A: is one who shows originality and ability which distinguish him from others in the fields of his endeavor. His gifts are inherent. They were not acquired by study in the present life. They were acquired by much thought and effort in many of his past lives and are brought over with him as the result from that past. The distinguishing characteristics of genius are originality concerning ideas, method, and the direct way of expressing his genius. He does not depend on the teaching of any school; he devises new methods and uses any of his three minds in expressing his feeling-and-desire according to the senses. He is in touch with the sum of his memories of his past in the field of his genius.

GERM, THE LUNAR: is produced by the generative system and is necessary for the procreation of a human body, to be the residence for a re-existing doer. It is called lunar because its travel through the body is similar to the phases of the waxing and waning moon, and it has a relation to the moon. It starts from the pituitary body and continues its downward path along the nerves of the esophagus and digestive tract, then, if not lost, ascends along the spine to the head. On its downward path it gathers Light which was sent out to nature, and which is returned by nature in food taken into the digestive system, and it gathers Light from the blood which has been reclaimed by self-control.

GERM, THE SOLAR: is a portion of the doer that at puberty is in the pituitary body and has some clear Light. For six months it descends, like the sun, on the southern path, on the right side of the spinal cord; then it turns, at the first lumbar vertebra, and ascends on the left side on its northern course for six months until it reaches the pineal body. On its southern and northern journeying it patrols the spinal cord, the path of eternal life. The lunar germ is strengthened each time it passes the solar germ.

GLAMOUR: is a state in which one is being fascinated with an object or thing by a spell, which the senses cast on his feeling-and-desire, and which holds him captive, and so prevents him from seeing through the glamour, and from understanding that thing as it is in fact.

GLOOM: is a psychic state, for the brooding over unsatisfied feelings and desires. In it one may create an atmosphere of gloom which will attract thoughts of morbidness and discomfort, which may lead to acts of harm to oneself and others. The cure for gloom is self-determined thought and right action.

GOD, A: is a thought being, created by the thoughts of human beings as the representative of the greatness of what they feel or fear; as what any one would or might like to be, to will, and to do.

GOVERNMENT, SELF-: Self, oneself, is the sum of the feelings and desires of the conscious doer who is within the human body and who is the operator of the body. Government is authority, administration and method by which a body or state is ruled. Self-government means that one's feelings and desires which are or may be inclined, through preferences, prejudices or passions to disrupt the body, will be restrained and guided and governed by one's own better feelings and desires which think and act with rightness and reason, as the standards of authority from within, instead of being controlled by the likes and dislikes concerning the objects of the senses, which are the authorities from outside the body.

GRACE: is loving kindness in behalf of others, and ease of thought and feeling expressed in conscious relation to form and action.

GREATNESS: is in the degree of one's independence with responsibility and knowledge in his relation and dealing with others.

GREED: is the insatiable desire to get, to have, and to hold whatever is desired.

GROUND, COMMON: is used here to mean a place or body on or in which two or more meet for mutual interests. The earth is the meeting ground for the doers in human bodies to act together for their common interests. The human body is the common ground for the action between the doer and the units of the elements of nature which pass through it. So also the earth surface is the common ground on which the thoughts of all people on earth are exteriorized as the plants and animals which grow on and inhabit the earth, and which are the exteriorizations into forms of desires and feelings of human beings.

HABIT: is the expression by word or act of an impression on the breath-form by thinking. Repetition of strange sounds or acts often causes uneasiness of the individual and of the observer, which is likely to become increasingly more pronounced unless the cause is removed. This can be done by not continuing the thinking which causes the habit, or by positive thinking to: "stop" and "do not repeat"—whatever the word or act is. The positive thinking and mental attitude against the habit will efface the impression on the breath-form, and so prevent its recurrence.

HALL OF JUDGMENT: is an after-death state in which the doer finds itself. What there seems to be a hall of light is really the sphere of Conscious Light. The doer is astonished and alarmed and would escape, anywhere, if it could; but it cannot. It is conscious of the form which, on earth, it believed to be itself, though it is not in that form; the form is its breath-form without the physical body. In or on this breath-form the Conscious Light, Truth, makes the doer conscious of all that it had thought, and of the acts that it did while in its body on earth. The doer is conscious of these as they are, as the Conscious Light, Truth, shows them to be, and the doer itself judges them, and its judgment makes it liable for them as duties in future lives on earth.

HAPPINESS: is the result of what one thinks and does in accord with rightness-and-reason, and the state of desire-and-feeling when they are in balanced union and have found love.

HEALING BY LAYING ON OF HANDS: To benefit the patient, the healer should understand that he is only a willing instrument to be used by nature for the purpose of re-establishing the orderly flow of life which has been obstructed or interfered with in the patient's body. This the healer may do by placing the palms of his right and left hands on the front and back of the head, and then to the three other potential brains, in the thorax, the abdomen, and the pelvis. In so doing the healer's own body is the instrument through which the electric and magnetic forces flow and put into adjustment the machinery of the patient for its orderly operation by nature. The healer should remain in passive goodwill, without thought of pay or gain.

HEALING, MENTAL: is the attempt to cure physical ills by mental means. There are many schools that attempt to teach and practice the cure of disease by mental effort, as by the denial that there is disease, or by affirming health in place of the disease, or by prayer, or by repetition of words or phrases, or by whatever other mental effort. Thinking and emotions do affect the body, by hope, cheer, joy, sorrow, trouble, fear. The cure of an actual disease can be effected by the balancing of the thought of which the disease is the exteriorization. By removing the cause, the disease disappears. Denial of a disease is a make-believe. If there were no disease there would be no denial of it. Where there is health, there is nothing gained by affirming what already is.

HEARING: is the unit of air, acting as the ambassador of the air element of nature in a human body. Hearing is the channel through which the air element of nature and the respiratory system in the body communicate with each other. Hearing is the nature unit which passes through and relates and vitalizes the organs of the respiratory system, and functions as hearing through the right relation of its organs.

HEAVEN: is the state and period of happiness, not limited by the earthly time of the senses, and which seems to have no beginning. It is a composite of all one's thoughts and ideals of life on earth, where no thought of suffering or unhappiness can enter, because these as memories were removed from the breath-form during the purgatorial period. Heaven really begins when the doer is ready and takes on its breath-form. This does not seem like a beginning; it is as though it had always been. Heaven ends when the doer has gone through and exhausted the good thoughts and good deeds which it had and did while on earth. Then the senses of sight and hearing and taste and smell are loosened from the breath-form, and go into the elements of which they were the expression in the body; the portion of the doer returns into itself, istence, where it is until its turn comes for its next re-existence on earth.

HELL: is an individual condition or state of suffering, of torment, not a community affair. The suffering or torment is by parts of the feelings and desires which have been separated from and sloughed off by the doer in its passage through metempsychosis. The suffering is because the feelings and desires have no means by or through which they can be relieved, or of getting what they grieve for, crave and desire. That is their torment—hell. While in a physical body on earth, the good and evil feelings and desires had their periods of joy and sorrow which were intermingled throughout that life on earth. But during metempsychosis, the purgatorial process separates the evil from the good; the good go on to enjoy their unalloyed happiness in "heaven", and the evil remain in what then is torment of suffering, where the individual feelings and desires can be and are impressed, so that when they are again brought together, they can, if they choose, shun the evil and profit from the good. Heaven and hell are for experiencing, but not for learning. Earth is the place for learning from experience, because earth is the place for thinking and learning. In the states after death the thoughts and deeds are as in a dream lived over again, but there is no reasoning or new thinking.

HEREDITY: is genèrally understood to mean that the physical and mental qualities, factors and features of one's ancestors are transmitted to and inherited by that human being. Of course, this must be true to some degree because of relation of blood and family. But the most important verity is not given place. That is, that the feeling-and-desire of an immortal doer takes residence in a human body after its birth and brings its own mentality and character with it. Lineage, breeding, environment and associations are important, but according to its own quality and strength the doer distinguishes itself from these. The breath-form of the doer causes conception; the form furnishes the compositor units and the breath builds out into its own form the material furnished by the mother, and after birth the breath-form continues to build and maintain its own form through all stages of growth and age. The doer in each human body is beyond time. Its breath-form bears its history, which antecedes all known history.

HONESTY: is the desire to think of and see things as the Conscious Light in thinking shows these things as they really are and then to deal with those things as the Conscious Light shows that they should be dealt with.

HOPE: is the potential light inherent in the doer in all its wanderings through the wilderness of the world; it leads or prompts in good or ill according to the disposition of the doer; it is always uncertain concerning objects of the senses, but is sure when reason rules.

HUMAN BEING, A: is a composition of units of the four elements of nature composed and organized as cells and organs into four systems represented by the four senses of sight, hearing, taste, and smell, and automatically coordinated and operated by the breath-form, the general manager of the man body or woman body; and, into which a portion of the doer enters and re-exists, and makes the animal human.

HUMAN BEINGS. THE FOUR CLASSES OF: By thinking people divided themselves into four classes. The particular class in which each one is, he has put himself in by his thinking; he will stay in it as long as he thinks as he does; he will take himself out of it and put himself into any other of the four classes when he does the thinking that will put him into the class in which he will then belong. The four classes are: the laborers, the traders, the thinkers, the knowers. The laborer thinks to satisfy the desires of his body, the appetites and comforts of his body, and the entertainment or pleasures of the senses of his body. The trader thinks to satisfy his desire for gain, to buy or sell or barter for profit, to get possessions, to have wealth. The thinker thinks to satisfy his desire to think, to idealize, to discover, in the professions or arts or sciences, and to excel in learning and accomplishments. The knower thinks to satisfy the desire to know the causes of things: to know who and what and where and when and how and why, and to impart to others what he himself knows.

HUMANITY: is the common origin and relation of all the incorporeal and immortal doers in human bodies, and is the sympathetic feeling in human beings of that relation.

HYPNOSIS, SELF-: is the intentional putting oneself into the state of deep sleep by hypnotizing and controlling oneself by oneself. The purpose of self-hypnotism should be to be self-controlled. In self-hypnosis the doer acts as the hypnotist and also as the subject. He considers what he would like to do that he is not able to do. Then, acting as the hypnotist, he clearly instructs himself to issue these commands to himself when he is in the hypnotic sleep. Then, by suggestion, he puts himself to sleep by telling himself that he is going to sleep, and finally that he is asleep. In the hypnotic sleep he commands himself to do the things in time and place. When he has so commanded himself, he returns to the waking state. Awake, he does as bidden to do. In this practice one must in no respect deceive himself, else he will be confused and will fail in self-control.

HYPNOTISM OR HYPNOSIS: is an artificial state of sleep produced on a subjec who suffers himself to be hypnotized. The subject is or makes himself to be negative to the hypnotist, who must be positive. The subject surrenders his feeling-and-desire to the feeling-and-desire of the hypnotist and by so doing surrenders control of his breath-form and use of his four senses. The hypnotist hypnotizes the subject by using any or all of his own electric-magnetic force through the eyes or voice and hands of his subject and by repeatedly telling him that he is going to sleep and that he is asleep. Submitting to the suggestion of sleep the subject is put to sleep. Having submitted himself, his breath-form and his four senses to the control of the hypnotist, the subject is in condition to obey the orders and do anything commanded by the hypnotist without knowing what he actually is doing—except that he cannot be made to commit a crime or perform an immoral act unless he would in his waking state so do or act. A hypnotist assumes grave responsibility when he hypnotizes anyone. The subject must suffer through long periods for allowing himself to be controlled by another. Each should practice self-control until he is self-controlled. Then he will not control another or allow another to control him.

HYPNOTIST, A: is one who has will, imagination and self-confidence and who is successful in hypnotizing his subjects and producing the phenomena of hypnotism to the degree that he exercises these with understanding.

"I" AS IDENTITY, THE FALSE: is the feeling of the presence of the real identity of the I-ness of one's knower. I-ness is the self-conscious selfsame identity of the knower, changeless and without beginning or end in the Eternal. Thinking with the body-mind and feeling the presence of its real identity, deludes the doer into the belief that it is one and the same with the body and the senses.

IDEAL: is the conception of what is best for one to think, to be, to do, or to have.

IDENTITY, ONE'S: is the feeling of identity in one's body, one's own feeling as being the same now as what one was in the past, and the same feeling to be in the future. One's feeling of identity is necessary and certain in the doer through the body, because of its inseparability from the identity of the knower of one's Triune Self.

I-NESS: is the incorporeal, undying, and continuously unchanging identity of the Triune Self in the Eternal; not embodied, but whose presence enables feeling in the human body to think and feel and speak of itself as "I" and to be conscious of the unchanging identity throughout the constantly changing life of its corporeal body.

IGNORANCE: is mental darkness, the state in which the doer-in-the-body is, without knowledge of itself and of its rightness and reason. The emotions and passions of its feeling and desire have eclipsed its thinker and knower. Without the Conscious Light from them it is in darkness. It cannot distinguish itself from the senses and the body it is in.

ILLUSION: The mistaking of fancy or appearance for reality, as a mirage to be a place or scene which it depicts, or a distant post to be a man; anything which deceives the senses and causes a mistake in judgment.

IMAGINATION: is the state in which the thinking of feeling-and-desire gives form to matter.

IMAGINATION, NATURE-: is the spontaneous and uncontrolled play of present sense impressions with memories; the combining or merging of pictures made on the breath-form by the senses with memories of similar impressions, and which combination represents the realities of the physical plane. These forceful impressions compel, and may forestall reasoning.

INCUBUS: is an invisible male form seeking to obsess or to have sexual relation with a woman during sleep. Incubi are of two kinds, and there are varieties of each kind. The most common is the sexual incubus, the other is the incubus that tries to obsess the woman, as in what is called a nightmare, which horrible dream may be largely due to indigestion or some physiological disturbance. The kind of incubus will depend on the habits of thought and mode of action of the sleeper during her waking life. The form of an incubus, if it were visualized, would vary from that of an angel or a god, to a devil or a spider or a boar.

INSTINCT IN THE ANIMAL: is the driving power from the human which is in that animal. Light from the human, bound up with the desire, is that which guides or leads the animal in its actions, according to the four senses of nature.

INTELLIGENCE: is that by which all Intelligences are related and which distinguishes and relates and establishes relation of all beings to each other who are conscious of being conscious; and, by which they, as and in their different degrees in being conscious, impress, distinguish and relate all units or masses of units in their relation to each other.

INTELLIGENCE, AN: is of the highest order of units in the Universe, relating the Triune Self of man with the Supreme Intelligence through its self-conscious Light, with which it endows man and so enables him to think.

INTELLIGENCE, FACULTIES OF AN: There are seven: the light and I-am faculties which govern the sphere of fire; the time and motive faculties governing the sphere of air; the image and dark faculties in the sphere of water; and the focus faculty in the sphere of earth. Each faculty has its own particular function and power and purpose and is inseparably interrelated with the others. The light faculty sends light to the worlds by means of its Triune Self; the time faculty is that which causes the regulation and changes in nature units in their relation to each other. The image faculty impresses the idea of form on matter. The focus faculty centers other faculties on the subject to which it is directed. The dark faculty resists or gives strength to the other faculties. The motive faculty gives purpose and direction to thought. The I-am faculty is the real Self of the Intelligence. The focus faculty is the only one which comes into contact with the body through the doer in the body.

INTELLIGENCE, THE SUPREME: is the limit and ultimate degree that an intelligent unit can advance to in being conscious as a unit. The Supreme Intelligence represents and comprehends all other Intelligences in the spheres. It is not the ruler of other Intelligences, because Intelligences know all law; they are law and each Intelligence rules itself and thinks and acts in accord with universal law. But the Supreme Intelligence has in its charge and supervision all the spheres and worlds and knows the gods and beings throughout universal nature.

INTUITION: is the teaching, tuition from within; it is direct knowledge which comes through reason to the doer. It is not concerned with trade or affairs of the senses, but with moral questions or philosophical subjects, and is rare. If the doer could open communication with its knower, it could then have knowledge on any subject.

ISTENCE: is the feeling-and-desire of the doer, conscious of the reality of itself in itself, as itself; not as existence, not in existence, but in its aloneness resulting from its intentional disattachment of itself from the illusions of nature.

JEALOUSY: is the resentful and jaundiced fear of not getting or having one's rights in the affections or interests of another or of others.

JOYOUSNESS: is the expression of the feeling and desire of one in whom there is trust.

JUSTICE: is the action of knowledge in relation to the subject under consideration, and in judgment pronounced and prescribed as law.

KARMA: is the results of the actions and reactions of mind and desire.

KNOWER, THE: is that of the Triune Self which has and is actual and real knowledge, of and in time and the Eternal.

KNOWLEDGE IS OF TWO KINDS: real or Self-knowledge and sense- or human knowledge. Self-knowledge of the Triune Self is inexhaustible and immeasurable and is common to the knowers of all Triune Selves. It is not dependent on the senses though it includes all that has taken place in the worlds; this concerns everything from the least developed unit of nature to the all-knowing Triune Self of the worlds throughout the entirety of time in the Eternal. It is the real and unchanging knowledge at once available in the minutest detail and as one perfectly related and complete whole.

Sense-knowledge, science, or human knowledge, is the accumulated and systematized sum of the facts of nature observed as natural laws, or experienced by the doers through their undeveloped senses and imperfect bodies. And the knowledge and statements of the laws have to be changed from time to time.

KNOWLEDGE OF THE DOER: is the essence of the doer's learning by thinking. The Light freed from its attachments and restored to the noetic atmosphere, in the balancing of its thoughts, is unattached and unattachable, and therefore knowledge; it is not human "knowledge".

KNOWLEDGE OF THE THINKER OF THE TRIUNE SELF: includes all knowledge concerning the administration of law and justice to its doer, and in the doer's relation to other doers in human bodies, through their thinkers. All thinkers know the law. They are always in agreement with each other and with their knowers in the administering of destiny to their respective doers in human bodies. Their knowledge of law and justice precludes doubt and prevents the possibility of favoritism. The doer in every human body gets its destiny as it makes it. That is, law and justice.

KNOWLEDGE OF THE KNOWER OF THE TRIUNE SELF, SELF-KNOWLEDGE: comprises and embraces everything in the four worlds. As selfness it is knowledge, and as I-ness it identifies and is the identity of the knowledge. It served its apprenticeship to nature as a nature unit. There it was conscious *as* its function successively in every part of the nature machine of time. When it became a Triune Self in the Self-knowing Light of its Intelligence in the Eternal, every function as which it was successively conscious in time is at once available, unlimited by time, in the Eternal. The I-ness of the knower identifies each function and is the identity as which the unit was conscious, and the selfness of the knower knows and is the knowledge of each such function separately, as in time, and all together compositely in the Eternal. This knowledge is conveyed to the thinker by the minds of I-ness and selfness, and may be available to the doer as conscience in rightness, and as intuition in reason.

KNOWLEDGE, NOETIC (THE WORLD OF KNOWLEDGE): is composed of the noetic atmospheres of all the knowers of Triune Selves. There all the knowledge of every Triune Self is available and at the service of every other knower.

LAW: is a prescription for performance, made by the thoughts and acts of its maker or makers, and to which those who have subscribed are bound.

LAW OF NATURE, A: is the action or function of a unit which is conscious as its function only.

LAW OF THOUGHT, THE: is that every thing on the physical plane is the exteriorization of a thought which must be balanced by the one who generated it, according to his responsibility and at the conjunction of time, condition and place.

LAW OF THOUGHT, DESTINY. AGENTS OF THE: Each human is an agent for good or for wickedness by his purpose in life and by what he thinks and what he does. By what he thinks and does, one fits himself or herself to be used by others. People cannot be used or coerced to act against their inner motives, except as they have fitted themselves by their thoughts and acts. Then they are influenced to act or yield by other humans, especially when they have no definite purpose in life. Those who have a purpose are also instruments, because, whatever the purpose, it will fit in for good or for evil with The Government of the world by the conscious agents of the law.

LEARNING: is the essence of experience extracted from the experience by thinking, so that the Light can be freed and that experience need not be repeated. Learning is of two kinds: sense-learning as experience, experiment, observation, and the recording of these as memories concerning nature; and, doer-learning as the result of the thinking of itself as feeling-and-desire and of their relation. The details of memory learning may last through the life of the body but will be lost after death. What the doer learns about itself as being distinct from the body will not be lost; that will thereafter be with the doer through its lives on earth as its inherent knowledge.

LIAR, A: is one who tells as true what he knows to be not so, untrue.

LIBERTY: is immunity from imprisonment or slavery, and the right of one to do as one pleases, as long as one does not interfere with another's equal right and choice.

LIFE: is a unit of growth, the carrier of light through form. Life acts as agent between the above and the below, bringing the fine into the gross and reconstructing and transforming the gross into refinement. In every seed there is a unit of life. In man it is the breath-form.

LIFE (TO ONE'S CRITICAL UNDERSTANDING): is more or less of a nightmare, an apparently real but uncertain series of sudden or long drawn out, more or less vivid and intense happenings—a phantasmagoria.

LIGHT: is that which makes things visible, but which cannot itself be seen. It is composed of the units of starlight or sunlight or moonlight or earthlight, or of the combination or condensation and expression of these as electricity or as the combustion of gases, fluids or solids.

LIGHT, ATTACHABLE AND UNATTACHABLE: is the Conscious Light of the Intelligence loaned to the Triune Self, which the doer-in-the-body uses in its thinking. The attachable light is that which the doer sends into nature by its thoughts and acts, and reclaims and uses again and again. The unattachable Light is that which the doer has reclaimed and made unattachable, because it has balanced the thoughts in which the Light was. Light that is made unattachable is restored to one's noetic atmosphere and is available to that one as knowledge.

LIGHT, CONSCIOUS: is the Light which the Triune Self receives from its Intelligence. It is not nature nor reflected by nature, though, when it is sent into nature and associates with nature units, nature seems to manifest intelligence, and it may be called the God in nature. When, by thinking, the Conscious Light is turned and held on any thing, it shows that thing to be as it is. The Conscious Light is therefore Truth, because Truth shows things to be as they are, without preference or prejudice, without disguise or pretense. All things are made known by it when it is turned and held on them. But the Conscious Light is fogged and obscured by thoughts when feeling-and-desire try to think, so the human being sees things as it wants to see them, or in a modified degree of Truth.

LIGHT IN THE DOER, POTENTIAL: When one performs duties uncomplainingly, ungrudgingly and with pleasure because they are his duties, and not because he will profit or gain or get rid of them, he is balancing his thoughts which made those duties *his* duties, and the Light that he frees when the thoughts are balanced gives him a new sense of the joy of freedom. It gives him an insight into things and subjects he had not understood before. As he continues to free the Light he had kept bound in the things he craved and wanted, he begins to feel and understand the potential Light that is in him and which will be actual Conscious Light when he becomes an Intelligence.

LIGHT OF NATURE: is the reaction as shine, sparkle, brightness or glitter of combinations of nature units, to the Conscious Light sent into nature by the doers in human bodies.

LINK UNIT, A CELL-: catches and holds transient units of solid matter, and by which it is connected with other cells in the organ or part of the body to which it belongs.

LINK UNIT, A FORM-: catches and holds transient units of fluid matter, and is connected with the cell-link and life-link units of its cell.

LINK UNIT, A LIFE-: catches and holds transient units of airy matter, and is the link by which life is connected with the form-link and breath-link units of its cell.

LINK UNIT, A BREATH-: catches and holds transient units of radiant matter, and is the link by which the breath is connected with the life-link unit of its cell.

"LOST SOUL", A: What is called a "lost soul" is not the "soul" but is a portion of the doer part, and it is not permanently, but only temporarily, lost or cut off from its re-existences and the other portions of the doer. This happens when, in one of two cases, a doer portion has through long periods of time persisted in extreme selfishness and used the Light loaned to it in deliberate fraud, murder, ruin, or cruelty to others and has become an enemy to mankind. Then the Light is withdrawn and the doer portion ceases to re-exist; it retires into chambers of the earth crust in self-torment until it has exhausted itself, and may thereafter reappear on earth. The second case is when a doer portion has wasted the Light through self-indulgence in pleasure, gluttony, drinks and drugs, and eventually becomes an incurable idiot. Then that doer portion goes to a chamber in the earth. There it remains until it can be allowed to continue its re-existences. In both cases, the retirement is for the safety of others, as well as its own.

LOVE: Is Conscious Sameness through the worlds; to the doer in the human, it is the feeling-and-desire of and as another in and as oneself and the desire-and-feeling of oneself in and as the other.

LOVE IN THE DOER: is the state of balanced union and interaction between feeling-and-desire, in which each feels and desires itself to be and is itself in and as the other.

LYING AND DISHONESTY: The desire to be dishonest and to lie are a special pair of evils; they go together. He who chooses to be dishonest and to lie is one who after long experiences through lives has failed to see things as they are and has misinterpreted what he has observed. He has more particularly seen the worst sides of people and has convinced himself that all men are liars and are dishonest, and that those who are usually believed to be honest and truthful are only clever enough to cover up their dishonesty and to conceal their lies. This conclusion breeds hatred and revenge and self-interest; and that one becomes an enemy to humanity, as an outright criminal or as a shrewd and careful plotter against others for his own advantage. However great a curse to the world that one may become, his thoughts as his destiny will eventually reveal him to the world and to himself. He will in time learn that honesty and truthfulness in thought and action show the way to Self-knowledge.

MALICE: is the obsession by a spirit of ill-will and evil intent to injure, to cause suffering; it is an enemy to goodwill and right action.

MANNERS: Good manners are inherent in the character of the doer; they are developed, not grafted. Superficial polish will not conceal the inherent quality of good or bad manners, whatever may be the doer's position in life.

MATTER: is substance manifested as unintelligent units as nature, and, which progress to be intelligent units as Triune Selves.

MEANING: is the intention in a thought expressed.

MEDIUM, A: is a general term meaning channel, means, or conveyance. It is here used to describe a person whose radiant or astral body exudes and radiates an atmosphere which attracts any of the many nature sprites, elementals, or wandering ones in the after-death states and which seek the living. The medium thus acts as a means of communication between such a one and the doer in human bodies.

MEMORY: is the reproduction of an impression by that on which the impression is taken. There are two kinds of memory: sense-memory, and doer-memory. Of sense-memory there are four classes: sight memory, hearing memory, taste memory, and smell memory. Each set of organs of the four senses is arranged for taking impressions of the element of which it is the representative, and transmitting the impressions to that on which the impressions are recorded, and by which they are reproduced; in the human, it is the breath-form. The reproduction of an impression is a memory.

MEMORY, DOER-: is the reproduction of the states of its feeling-and-desire in its present body, or in any of the former bodies it has lived in on this earth. The doer does not see or hear or taste or smell. But the sights, sounds, tastes, and smells which are impressed on the breath-form react on feeling-and-desire of the doer and produce pain or pleasure, joy or sorrow, hope or fear, gaiety or gloom. These feelings are doer-memories of states of exhilaration or depression which it has experienced. There are four classes of doer-memory: the psycho-physical, which are reactions of feeling-and-desire to physical events of the present life; psychic memories, which are the reactions of feeling-and-desire to places and things, for or against, which are due to similar conditions experienced in former lives; psycho-mental memories, which concern questions of right or wrong or are the solving of mental problems or the settling of sudden or unexpected situations of life; and psycho-noetic memory, which concerns the knowledge of identity, when time disappears in a moment and the doer is conscious of its isolation in timeless identity irrespective of all the lives and deaths it has passed through.

MEMORY, SENSE-: involves (a) the organs of the eye, as a camera with which the picture is to be taken; (b) the sense of sight with which the clear seeing and focussing is to be done; (c) the negative or plate on which the picture is to be impressed and from which the picture is to be reproduced; and (d) the one who does the focussing and takes the picture. The set of sight organs is the mechanical apparatus used in seeing. Sight is the elemental nature unit used to transmit the impressions or picture focussed on the form of the breath-form. The doer is the seer who perceives the picture focussed on its breath-form. The reproduction or memory of that picture is automatic and mechanically reproduced by association with the object to be remembered. Any other mental process interferes with or prevents an easy reproduction or memory. As with the sense of sight and its organs for seeing, so it is with hearing and taste and smell, and their reproductions as memories. Seeing is the optical or photographic memory; hearing, the auditory or phonographic memory; tasting, the gustatory memory; and smelling, the olfactory memory.

MENTAL ATTITUDE AND MENTAL SET: One's mental attitude is one's outlook on life; it is as an atmosphere with the general intention to be or to do or to have something. His mental set is the particular way and means in being or doing or having whatever that something is, which is determined and brought about by thinking.

MENTAL OPERATIONS: are the manner or way or working of any one of the three minds used by the doer-in-the-body.

METEMPSYCHOSIS: is the period after the doer has left the Hall of Judgment and the breath-form, and is in and passes through the process of purgation, where it separates those of its desires which cause suffering, from its better desires which make it happy. Metempsychosis ends when this is done.

MIND: is the functioning of intelligent-matter. There are seven minds, that is, seven kinds of thinking by the Triune Self, with the Light of the Intelligence,—yet they are one. All seven kinds are to act according to one principle, which is, to hold the Light steadily on the subject of the thinking. They are: the mind of I-ness and the mind of selfness of the knower; the mind of rightness and the mind of reason of the thinker; the mind of feeling and the mind of desire of the doer; and the body-mind which is also used by the doer for nature, and for nature only.

The term "mind" is here used as that function or process or thing with which or by which thinking is done. It is a general term here for the seven minds, and each of the seven is of the reason side of the thinker of the Triune Self. Thinking is the steady holding of the Conscious Light on the subject of the thinking. The mind for I-ness and the mind for selfness are used by the two sides of the knower of the Triune Self. The mind for rightness and the mind of reason are used by the thinker of the Triune Self. The feeling-mind and the desire-mind and body-mind are to be used by the doer: the first two to distinguish feeling and desire from the body and nature and to have them in balanced union; the body-mind is to be used through the four senses, for the body and its relation to nature.

MIND, THE BODY-: The real purpose of the body-mind is for the use of feeling-and-desire, to care for and to control the body, and through the body to guide and control the four worlds by means of the four senses and their organs in the body. The body-mind can think only through the senses and in terms restricted to the senses and sensuous matter. Instead of being controlled, the body-mind controls feeling-and-desire so that they are unable to distinguish themselves from the body, and the body-mind so dominates their thinking that they are compelled to think in terms of the senses instead of in terms suited to feeling-and-desire.

MIND, THE FEELING-: is that with which feeling thinks, according to its four functions. These are perceptiveness, conceptiveness, formativeness, and projectiveness. But instead of using these for the emancipation of itself from bondage to nature, they are controlled through the body-mind by nature through the four senses: sight, hearing, taste, and smell.

MIND, THE DESIRE-: which desire should use to discipline and control feeling and itself; to distinguish itself as desire from the body in which it is; and, to bring about the union of itself with feeling; it has, instead, allowed itself to be subordinate to and to be controlled by the body-mind in service to the senses and to objects of nature.

MORALS: are determined to the degree that one's feelings and desires are guided by the soundless voice of conscience in the heart concerning what not to do, and by the sound judgment of reason, as to what to do. Then, notwithstanding allurements of the senses, one's conduct will be straightforward and right, with respect to oneself and with consideration for others. One's morals will be the background of one's mental attitude.

MYSTICISM: is the belief in or the effort for communion with God, by meditation or by experiencing the nearness, the presence of or the communing with God. Mystics are of every nation and religion, and some have no special religion. Their methods or practices vary from silence in quiet to violent physical exercises and exclamations and from individual seclusion to mass demonstration. Mystics are usually honest in their intentions and beliefs and are earnest in their devotions. They may rise in sudden ecstasy to beatific heights, and sink into the depths of depression; their experiences may be brief or prolonged. But these are only experiences of feelings and desires. They are not the results of clear thinking; they do not have knowledge. What they consider to be knowledge of God or nearness to God is invariably connected with the objects of sight, hearing, taste or smell, which are of the senses—not of the Self, or of Intelligence.

NATURE: is a machine composed of the totality of unintelligent units; units that are conscious as their functions only.

NECESSITY: is destiny, compelling action, usually immediate, from which there is no escape for gods or men.

NOETIC: That which is of knowledge or related to knowledge.

NUMBER: is One, a whole, as a circle, in which all numbers are included.

NUMBERS: are the principles of being, in continuity and relation to unity, Oneness.

ONE: is a unit, a unity or whole, the origin and inclusion of all numbers as its parts, in extension or completion.

ONENESS: is the right relation of all principles and parts to each other.

OPINION: is judgment pronounced after due consideration of all the aspects of the subject in question.

OPPORTUNITY: is the fit or favorable time or condition or place for action to accomplish any given purpose and which particularly concerns the needs or wants of people.

PAIN: is a set of disturbing sensations as the penalty of improper thinking or doing, and is the notice served on the doer of feeling-and-desire to remove its cause.

PASSION: is the raging of feelings and desires concerning objects or subjects of the senses.

PATIENCE: is calm and careful persistence in the accomplishment of desire or purpose.

PERFECT PHYSICAL BODY: is the state or condition which is the ultimate, the complete; from which nothing can be lost, nor to which anything can be added. Such is the perfect sexless physical body of the Triune Self in the Realm of Permanence.

PERSONALITY: is the corporeal human body, the mask, in and through which the incorporeal doer of desire-and-feeling thinks and speaks and acts.

PESSIMISM: is a mental attitude produced by the observation or belief that human desires cannot be satisfied; that the people and the world are out of joint; and, that there is nothing to be done about it.

PLAN: is that which shows the way or the means by which purpose is accomplished.

PLEASURE: is the flow of sensations in agreement with the senses, and gratifying to feeling-and-desire.

POETRY: is the art of modeling the meaning of thought and rhythm into forms or words of grace or of power.

POINT, A: is that which is without dimension but from which dimensions come. A point is the beginning of every thing. The unmanifested and the manifested are divided by a point. The unmanifested manifests through a point. The manifested returns to the unmanifested through a point.

POISE: is the state of balance, of equanimity of mind and control of body, in which one thinks and feels and acts with ease, not disturbed by circumstances or conditions, or by the thoughts or acts of others.

POSSESSIONS: are such necessaries as food, clothing, shelter, and the means to maintain one's personality in its position in life; in excess of these and in all other respects they are snares, cares, and shackles.

POWER, CONSCIOUS: is desire, which brings about changes in itself, or which causes change in other things.

PRANAYAMA: is a Sanskrit term which is subject to numerous interpretations. Practically applied it means the control or regulation of breathing by prescribed exercises of measured inhalation, suspension, exhalation, suspension, and again inhalation for a certain number of such rounds or for a certain period of time. In the Yoga Sutras of Patanjali, pranayama is given as fourth in the eight steps or stages of yoga. The purpose of pranayama is said to be the control of prana, or control of the mind in concentration. However, the practice of pranayama confuses and defeats the purpose, because thinking is directed to or on the breathings or on prana, and the stops in breathing. This thinking and stopping in breathings prevents real thinking. The Conscious Light used in thinking—to make known to the thinker the subject of his thinking—is prevented from flowing by stopping the natural and regular flow of physical breathing. The Conscious Light enters only at the two neutral points between the inbreathing and outbreathing and the outbreathing and inbreathing. The stoppage keeps out the Light. Hence, no Light; no real thinking; no real yoga or union; no real knowledge.

PREFERENCE: is the favor of some person, place or thing by feeling-and-desire, without due regard for right or reason; it prevents true mental vision.

PREJUDICE: is judging a person, place or thing to which feeling-and-desire are opposed, without considering, or regardless of, right or reason. Prejudice prevents right and just judgment.

PRINCIPLE: is the substratum from which all principles are what they are and by which they may be distinguished.

PRINCIPLE, A: is that fundamental in a thing of which it was, by which it came to be what it is, and according to which its character may be known wherever it is.

PROGRESS: is the continuing to increase in the capacity to be conscious, and in the ability to make good use of that of which one is conscious.

PUNISHMENT: is the penalty for wrong action. It is not intended to cause torment and suffering to the one punished; it is intended to teach the one punished that he cannot do wrong without suffering, soon or late, the consequences of the wrong.

PURPOSE: is the guiding motive in effort as the immediate thing, for which one strives, or the ultimate subject to be known; it is the conscious direction of force, the intention in words or in action, the accomplishment of thought and effort, the end of attainment.

QUALITY: is the degree of excellence developed in the nature and function of a thing.

REALITY, A: is a unit as it is, unattached, the thing itself; that which one senses or is conscious of, in the state or on the plane on which it is, without consideration of or relation to anything other than that.

REALITY, RELATIVE: the continuity of facts or things and their relation to each other, in the state and on the plane on which they are observed.

REALITY, ULTIMATE: Consciousness, changeless and absolute; the Presence of Consciousness in and through each and every nature unit and Triune Self and Intelligence throughout time and space in the Eternal, during the entirety of the continuity of its constant progress through ever higher degrees in being conscious until it is one with and as Consciousness.

REALM OF PERMANENCE, THE: pervades the phantasmagoria of this human world of birth and death, like as sunlight pervades the air we breathe. But the mortal sees and understands the Realm no more than we see or understand the sunlight. The reason is that the senses and perceptions are unbalanced, and not attuned to things that time and death cannot affect. But the Realm of Permanence bears up and preserves the human world from utter destruction, as sunlight does the life and growth of living things. The conscious doer in the body will understand and perceive the Realm of Permanence as he understands and distinguishes himself from the changing body in which he desires and feels and thinks.

REASON: is the analyzer, regulator and judge; the administrator of justice as the action of knowledge according to the law of rightness. It is the answer of questions and problems, the beginning and the end of thinking, and the guide to knowledge.

RE-EXISTENCE: is the doer portion leaving the other portions of itself, in istence, to re-exist away from itself, in nature, when the animal human body has been prepared and made ready for it to enter and take a life residence in that body. The animal body is made ready by training it to make use of its senses, to walk, and to repeat the words which it is trained to use. That it does, like a parrot, while it is still animal. It becomes human as soon as it is intelligent, as shown by questions that it asks, and what it understands.

REGENERATION: is the reversal of generation, procreation of body. This means: the germ cells in the body are used not to bring another body into the world but to change and give a new and higher order of life to the body. This is done by rebuilding the body from an incomplete male or female body into a complete and perfect sexless physical body, which is accomplished by not entertaining thoughts of sex or thinking about sexual acts; and by the persistent mental attitude to regenerate one's own body to the original perfect state from which it came.

RELATION: is the origin and sequence in ultimate unity by which all nature units and intelligent units and Intelligences are related in Conscious Sameness.

RELIGION: is the tie of one or all four of the elements of nature, as of fire or air or water or earth, through the body senses of sight, hearing, taste, or smell, that holds or binds the conscious doer in the body back to nature. This is done in thoughts and acts by worship and by burnt offerings and songs and sprinklings or immersions in water and by incense to one or more gods of the elements of fire, air, water, or earth.

RESPONSIBILITY: depends on the capacity to know right from wrong; it is the dependence and trust that can be placed in one to do all that he in the past and present has made, or will in the future make, himself responsible for. Responsibility involves honesty and truthfulness, honor and trustworthiness and such other characteristics as constitute a strong and fearless character, whose word is more reliable than is a legal contract.

RESURRECTION: has a twofold meaning. The first is the gathering together of the four senses and the compositors of the body of the past life, which were distributed into nature after its death, and the rebuilding by the breath-form of a new fleshly body to serve as the residence of the doer on its return to earth life. The second and real meaning is that the doer in the man or woman body regenerates the sexual body from the imperfect man or woman body that is, to a body where the essentials of the two sexes are merged into one perfect physical body and restored, resurrected, to its former and original and immortal state of perfection.

REVENGE: is a hungering desire to inflict injury on another in retaliation and as punishment for real or imagined wrongs suffered, and to satisfy one's desire for vengeance.

RHYTHM: is the character and meaning of thought expressed through the measure or movement in sound or form, or by written signs or words.

RIGHT: is the sum of knowledge of which one is conscious, as his rule of action from within.

RIGHTNESS: is the standard of thinking and action, as the law prescribed and the rule of conduct, for the doer of feeling-and-desire in the body. It is located in the heart.

SADNESS: is the depression of feeling by passive thinking.

SELF, THE HIGHER: is the desire or desires which the human is conscious of as being higher, above, superior to the sensuous, carnal, trivial and petty desires of its everyday life. The higher self is not a being separate from desire in the human, but the human thinks of a higher self because it, as desire, is inseparably related to the selfness of the knower of its Triune Self, hence the real source of one's desire for "the Higher Self."

SELF-DELUSION: is the state into which the doer puts itself by letting attraction or repulsion, preference or prejudice, influence thinking.

SELFNESS: is knowledge of itself as the knower of the Triune Self.

SENSATION: is the contact and impression of nature units on feeling, through the senses and nerves of the body, resulting in a feeling, an emotion, a desire. Sensation is not a feeling, an emotion, or a desire. Without the body, feeling has no sensation. While feeling is in the body there is a constant stream of nature units coming through the senses and passing through the body as impressions on feeling, somewhat like an impression of ink on paper. As without the ink and the paper there would be no printed page, so without the streams of nature units and feeling there would be no sensation. All the pains and pleasures and emotions, all the joys and hopes and fears, the sadness, gloom and despondency are sensations, the results of impressions made on feeling, by contact of the nature units. So also are the responses by desire to the impressions made on feeling, as avidity, cupidity, covetousness, avarice, rapacity, lust, or aspiration. But desire in itself without the body is none of these, no more than feeling is the impression made on it by its contact with the nature units.

SENSES OF THE BODY: are the ambassadors of nature at the court of man; the representatives of the four great elements of fire, air, water, and earth, which are individualized as sight, hearing, taste, and smell of the human body.

SENTIMENT: is opinion expressed by feeling and thinking with regard to a person, place or thing.

SENTIMENTALITY: is the debasement of feeling by false sentiment.

SEXES: are the exteriorizations in nature of the thoughts of desire and feeling resulting in male and female bodies.

SEXUALITY: is the hypnotic condition of feeling-and-desire in a human body experiencing forms and phases of nature-madness or nature intoxication.

SIGHT: is a unit of fire, acting as the ambassador of the fire element of nature in the body of man. Sight is the channel through which the fire element of nature and the generative system in the body act and react on each other. Sight is the nature unit which relates and coordinates the organs of the generative system and functions as sight by the proper relation of its organs.

SILENCE: is knowledge in repose: conscious calmness without movement or sound.

SIN: is the thinking and doing what one knows to be wrong, against rightness, what one knows to be right. Any departure from what one knows to be right, is sin. There are sins against oneself, against others, and against nature. The penalties of sin are pain, disease, suffering, and, eventually, death. The original sin is the thought, followed by the sexual act.

SKILL: is the degree of art in the expression of what one thinks and desires and feels.

SLEEP: is the letting go by the feeling-and-desire of the doer, of the nervous system and the four senses of the body, and retiring into itself in dreamless sleep. The letting go is brought about by the slackening down of the activities of the body because of its need of rest, for nature to repair the wastes, and to condition the body during the doer's absence. Then the doer is out of touch with nature and cannot see, hear, touch or smell.

SMELL: is a unit of the earth element, the representative of the earth element in a human body. Smell is the ground on which the earth element of nature and the digestive system in the body meet and contact. Sight acts with hearing, hearing acts through taste, taste acts in smell, smell acts on the body. Sight is the fiery, hearing the airy, taste the watery, and smell the solid earthy. Smell is the basis on which the other three senses act.

SOMNAMBULISM: is the walking about during deep sleep, the doing of things by the sleeper as though awake, and, in certain cases, of performing feats that the somnambulist would not attempt while awake. Somnambulism is the result of passive thinking while awake; and such passive thinking makes deep impressions on the breath-form. Then sometime in deep sleep that which was dreamed in the waking state is carried out automatically by the breath-form, according to the plan inscribed thereon by the somnambulist.

SOMNAMBULIST, A: is a sleep walker, one who is imaginative and whose astral body and breath-form are impressionable and subject to suggestion; one who thinks of what he would like to do but fears to do. The things that he has thought about in daydream in the waking state are later on enacted by his breath-form during sleep. But, on waking, he is not conscious of what his body has been made to do asleep.

SOUL: The indefinite something of religions and philosophies, sometimes said to be immortal and at other times said to be subject to death, whose origin and destiny have been variously accounted for, but which has always been said to be a part of or associated with the human body. It is the form or passive side of the breath-form of every human body; its active side is the breath.

SPACE: is substance, the ever unmanifested and unconscious no thing, that is the origin and source of every manifested thing. It is without limits, parts, states or dimensions. It is through every unit of nature, in which all dimensions exist and all nature moves and has its being.

SPIRIT: is the active side of a nature unit which energizes and operates through the other or passive side of itself, called matter.

SPIRITISM: usually called spiritualism, has to do with the nature sprites or elementals of the fire, air, water, and earth, and sometimes with parts of the doer of the human who has departed from the earth life. These are usually seen or communicated with through a medium in trance. In trance, the radiant or astral body of the medium is the material or form used in which the departed one appears, and particles from the medium's fleshly body and the particles of the onlookers' bodies may be drawn off to give the appearance body and weight. Notwithstanding the ignorance and deception connected with such materializations at seances, parts of the one who died may return and appear through the instrumentality of a medium.

SUBSTANCE: is boundless space, without parts, homogeneous, the same throughout, the all containing "no thing," unconscious sameness, which is, nevertheless, present throughout nature.

SUCCESS: is in the accomplishing of purpose.

SUCCUBUS: is an invisible female form trying to obsess or to have sexual relation with a man during sleep. Like the incubus, succubi are of two kinds, and vary in form and intent. Incubi and succubi should not be tolerated under any pretext. They may do much harm and cause undreamed-of suffering to a human.

SYMBOL, A: is a visible object to represent an invisible subject which one is to think of, as itself or in relation to another subject.

TASTE: is a unit of the water element of nature progressed to the degree of acting as a minister of nature in the human body. Taste is the channel in which the water element of nature and the circulatory system in the body circulate in each other. Taste is the nature unit which commingles and relates the units of air and earth in its units of water to prepare them for circulation and digestion and in its own organs to function as taste.

THINKER: The real thinker of the Triune Self is between its knower, and its doer in the human body. It thinks with the mind of rightness and the mind of reason. There is no hesitancy or doubt in its thinking, no disagreement between its rightness and reason. It makes no mistakes in its thinking; and what it thinks is at once effective.

The doer-in-the-body is spasmodic and unsteady in thinking; its feeling-and-desire-minds are not always in agreement, and their thinking is controlled by the body-mind that thinks through the senses and of the objects of the senses. And, instead of with the clear Light, the thinking is done usually in a fog and with the Light diffused in the fog. Yet, the civilization in the world is the result of the thinking and the thoughts that have made it. Were some of the doers in human bodies to become conscious that they are the immortals that they are, and to control instead of being controlled by, their body-minds, they could then turn the earth into a garden in every way superior to the legendary paradise.

THINKING: is the steady holding of the Conscious Light within on the subject of the thinking. It is a process of (1) the selection of a subject or the formulation of a question; (2) turning the Conscious Light on it, which is done by giving one's undivided attention to it; (3) by the steady holding and focussing the Conscious Light on the subject or question; and (4) by bringing the Light to a focus on the subject as a point. When the Conscious Light is focussed on the point, the point opens into fullness of the entire knowledge of the subject selected or in answer to the question formulated. Thinking affects subjects according to their susceptibility and by the rightness and the power of the thinking.

THINKING, ACTIVE: is the intention to think on a subject, and is the effort to hold the Conscious Light within on the subject, until that subject is known, or until the thinking is distracted or turned to another subject.

THINKING, PASSIVE: is the thinking that is done without any definite intent; it is started by a fleeting thought or an impression of the senses; the idle play or daydreaming involving one or all three minds of the doer in such Light as may be in the psychic atmosphere.

THINKING THAT DOES NOT CREATE THOUGHTS, THAT IS, DESTINY: Why does a person think? He thinks because his senses compel him to think, about objects of the senses, about persons and events, and his reactions to them. And when he thinks he wants to be something, to do something, or to get or to have something. *He wants!* And when he wants he attaches himself and the Light in a thought, to what he wants; he has created a thought. That means that the Light in his thinking is welded with his desire that wants, to the matter and course of action, or to the object or thing he wants. By that thought he has attached and bound the Light and himself. And the only way he can ever free the Light and himself from that bond is to be unattached; that is, he must balance the thought which binds him, by freeing the Light and his desire from the thing it *wants*. To do this, it usually takes countless lives, ages, to learn, to understand; to understand that he cannot act as well and as freely with the thing to which he is attached and bound, as he can if he were not attached, not bound. Your desire is *you!* The action or thing you want is not you. If you attach and bind yourself to it by a thought, you cannot act as well as if you are unbound and free to act without attachment. Therefore, the thinking that does not create thoughts is in being free to think, and to not want, have, hold, but to act, to have, to hold, without being bound to the act, to what you have, to what you hold. That is, to think in freedom. Then you can think clearly, with clear Light, and with power.

THOUGHT, A: is a living being in nature, conceived and gestated in the heart by feeling-and-desire with the Conscious Light, elaborated in and issued from the brain, and which will exteriorize as an act, object or event, again and again, until it is balanced. The parent doer of the thought is responsible for all results that flow from it until that thought is balanced; that is, by the experiences from the exteriorizations, the learning from experiences, the doer frees the Light and the feeling-and-desire from the object of nature to which they were bound, and so acquires knowledge.

THOUGHT, BALANCING A: Thinking extracts the Light from a thought when feeling-and-desire are in agreement with each other and both are in agreement with selfness concerning the act, object or event which has been witnessed by I-ness. Then the thinking transfers and restores the Light to the noetic atmosphere and the thought is balanced, ceases to exist.

THOUGHT, THE BALANCING FACTOR IN A: is the mark which conscience stamps on a thought as its seal of disapproval at the time of the creation of the thought by feeling and desire. Through all the changes and exteriorizations of the thought, the mark remains until the balancing of that thought. The mark and the thought disappear when the thought is balanced.

THOUGHT, RULING: One's presiding thought at the time of death is the ruling thought for the following life on earth. It may be changed, but while it rules it influences his thinking, helps in the selection of his associates and leads or introduces him to others of similar thought. It often decides in the selection of a profession or business or occupation which he may follow through life. While it remains his ruling thought it tempers his disposition and gives color to his outlook on life.

THOUGHTS, VISITING: Thoughts circulate; they are as gregarious as their parents are; they visit each other in the mental atmospheres of human beings, because of the aims and objects for which they are created, and they meet in the atmosphere of the similar interests of the human beings who create them. Thoughts are the chief causes of the meeting and association of people; the likeness of their thoughts draw people together.

TIME: is the change of units or of masses of units in their relation to each other. There are many kinds of time in the worlds and in the different states. For example: the mass of units composing the sun, the moon, the earth, changing in their relation to each other, are measured as sun time, moon time, earth time.

TRANSMIGRATION: is the process which follows the bonding of the human male and female germs by the breath-form, the soul of the future body, at conception. It is the migrating and gathering together successively all the elements and lives and typal forms from the mineral and vegetable and animal kingdoms of nature into which they were distributed after death, and relating and building them into a new human body, a new universe, according to the soul, the form of the body to be, and preparing it to be the fleshly residence for the return and re-existence of the doer portion of the Triune Self. The migration of the constituents of the body is across or through these kingdoms of nature: the mineral or elemental, the plant or vegetable, and animal, into a baby. That is the end of the transmigration of the soul, the form, for the human, across or through three kingdoms of nature into the human.

TRIUNE SELF: The indivisible self-knowing and immortal One; its identity and knowledge part as knower; its rightness and reason part as thinker, in the Eternal; and, its desire and feeling part as doer, existing periodically on the earth.

TRIUNE SELF OF THE WORLDS, THE: is as the identity of the noetic world of Triune Selves, and stands in relation to the Supreme Intelligence as does the Triune Self to its Intelligence.

TRUST: is the fundamental belief in the honesty and truthfulness of other human beings, because there is the deep-seated honesty in the one who trusts. When one is disappointed by his misplaced trust in another, he should not lose trust in himself, but he should learn to be careful, careful of what and in whom he trusts.

TRUTHFULNESS: is the desire to think and speak straightforwardly about things without intending to falsify or misrepresent the subject thought of or spoken about. Of course, it is understood that one should not reveal to prying or inquisitive people all that he knows.

TYPES: A type is the initial or beginning of form, and the form is the inclusion and completion of the type. Thoughts are the types of the animals and objects and are forms bodied out as the expressions of human feelings and desires on the screen of nature.

UNDERSTANDING: is the perceiving and feeling what things are of themselves, what their relations are, and comprehending why they are so and are so related.

UNIT, A: is an indivisible and irreducible one, a circle, which has an unmanifested side, as shown by a horizontal diameter. The manifested side has an active and a passive side, as shown by a mid-vertical line. Changes made by their interaction are effected by the presence of the unmanifested through both. Every unit has the potentiality of becoming one with the ultimate reality—Consciousness—by its constant progression in being conscious in ever higher degrees.

UNITS: The training and education of units is based on the proposition that every nature unit has the potentiality of becoming an Intelligence. The education of the unit is conducted in a University of Laws. A University of Laws is a perfected, sexless physical body of the Realm of Permanence, which is governed by the doer and thinker and knower of a Triune Self complete according to the Eternal Order of Progression.

The education of the unintelligent unit of nature consists in the increase in being consecutively conscious as its function through all degrees until it eventually graduates from the University, to become an intelligent unit beyond nature.

The degrees in the perfect body are: transient units, compositor units, and sense units, and finally there is the breath-form unit, which is in training to be graduated from nature and be an intelligent unit conscious *as* itself and *of* all things and laws. Transient units are by the compositors composed into and function as structure in all parts of the University body of laws. During their transitory stay they are empowered and charged as laws and sent forth to be the operating laws of nature. Sense units are the ambassadors from the great elements fire, air, water, and earth, which are to guide the four systems—generative, respiratory, circulatory and digestive—of which the organs are operating parts. The breath-form unit coordinates the senses and systems and organs into the functioning constitution of the body.

UNITS, NATURE: are distinguished by being conscious *as* their functions only. Nature units are not conscious *of* anything. There are four kinds: free units which are unbound and unattached to other units in mass or structure; transient units, which are composed into or cohere in structure or mass for a time and then pass on; compositor units, which compose and hold transient units for a time; and sense units, as sight, hearing, taste, and smell, which control or govern the four systems of the human body. All nature units are unintelligent.

UNIT, AN ORGAN: Through one cell-link unit an organ unit keeps in relation all the cells of which the organ is composed, so that it may perform its function or functions which link it to the other organs into the one of the four systems in the body to which it belongs.

UNITS, SENSE: are the four link nature units in the body which connect and relate the four senses of sight, hearing, taste, and smell, with their respective four systems: sight with the generative, hearing with the respiratory, taste with the circulative, and smell with the digestive; and, with the four elements: fire, air, water, and earth.

VANITY: is the unseen and unappreciated emptiness of all the objects or positions and possessions which are desired in the world, as compared with the Realm of Permanence; it is not understanding the uselessness of striving for the enjoyment of popularity, and excitement and appearance of situations, when their evanescence is compared with the power of will in the practice of honesty and truthfulness.

VICES, CLOAKS OF: here so called, are wicked and depraved desires of a doer in human life which, in its after-death states cause suffering while the doer is trying to separate from them. The base desires as a cloak of vices also suffer, because they have no means of indulgence without a human body. Therefore they often seek the atmosphere of a human who has like desires and who is willing or becomes a victim to the urge to drunkenness or crime.

VIRTUE: is power, strength of will, in the practice of honesty and truthfulness.

WILL, FREE: Will is the dominant desire, of the moment, of a period, or of the life. It dominates its opposing desires and may dominate the desires of others. Desire is the conscious power within, which may bring about changes in itself or which changes other things. No desire in the human is free, because it is attached or attaches itself to objects of the senses when thinking. One desire may control or be controlled by another desire, but no desire can change another desire or be compelled to change itself. No power other than its own can change it. A desire may be subdued, crushed, and made subordinate, but it cannot be made to change itself unless it chooses and wills to change. It is free to choose whether it will or will not change itself. This power to choose whether it will remain attached to this or that thing, or whether it will let go of the thing and be unattached, is its point of freedom, the point of freedom that every desire is and has. It may extend its point to an area of freedom by willing to be, to do, or to have, without attaching itself to what it wills to be, to do, or to have. When the will thinks without being attached to what it thinks, it is free, and has freedom. In freedom, it can be or do or have what it wills to be or do or have, as long as it remains unattached. Free will is to be unattached, unattachment.

WISDOM: is the right use of knowledge.

WORK: is mental or bodily activity, the means and the manner by which purpose is accomplished.

WORLD, NOETIC: is not a world of nature-matter; it is the intelligent realm or knowledge of the Realm of Permanence, a oneness composed of the noetic atmospheres of all Triune Selves and of the laws which govern nature. It is the unchanging eternal knowledge concerning all Triune Selves and concerning the entirety of the past, present and what has been determined as future of the four worlds of the earth sphere. The ever accumulating and changing knowledge of the senses in the human world by experiencing and experimenting cannot add to the world of knowledge. These are like products of summer and winter, which come and go. The world of knowledge is the sum of the knowledge of all Triune Selves, and the knowledge of all is available to each Triune Self.

WRONG: is that thought or act which is a departure from what one is conscious of as right.

INDEX

How to Use This Index:

MAIN TERMS are capitalized.

- All first-level terms begin with a
  bullet (•) and may span several lines.
  - Second-level terms are indented
    below first-level terms.

A single asterisk (*) stands for the
main term. Thus, under AGENT(s),

- law, * of the ... *is read as:*
- law, AGENT(s) of the

A double asterisk (**) occurs only in a
second-level term and stands for the
first-level term directly above it. Thus,

- - unconscious ** ... *is read as:*
  - unconscious AGENT(s) of the law

A

ABDOMEN, 34, 752, 853
ABSCESS, 315
ACADEMY
- Plato's school, the *, 8
ACCIDENT(s)
- community, * which happen to a, 52
- definition of, 892
- example of *, 51
- history, * in, 706
- how * brought about, 49
- purpose of *, 51
- there are no *, 48
ACORN, 613
ACTS, OBJECTS, & EVENTS. *See
also* THOUGHTS,
EXTERIORIZATION
- records of * written in
  - starry spaces, 553, 555
ADAM and EVE, 277, 603, 689
- story of * distorted, 454

ADAMOLOGY, 480
ADONAI
- symbol of physical body, 592
ADRENALS, 35, 167, 564
- center of desire is in the *, 71, 805
- doer portion is embodied in the *,
  803
- moon works with the *, 510
- system of fine structures became the
  * when digestive system adapted to
  gross food, 453
- third step in Masonry symbolizes *,
  677
- units that pass through * go through
  the moon, 552
AFTER DEATH. *See* DEATH
(AFTER)
AGE(s), 298
- Dark *, 125
- four *, 465, 472, 483
- Middle *, 618
- new *, 316
- past *, 346
- thought from prior *, 243
AGENT(s)
- law, * of the, 92, 120, 294, 913
  - animals may be used as **, 296
  - conscious **, 92, 124, 653
  - unconscious **, 123
- Triune Şelf (complete) are active * of
  Intelligences, 37
AGNOSTICISM, 57, 58, 61
AHANKARA, 365, 369
AIA (UNIT), 44, 64, 101, 137, 227,
276, 303, 641, 726, 730, 747, 755,
760, 787, 791, 845, 852, 889
- after death
  - cycling thought impels * to start
    new life, 437
  - dimensionless state in the psychic
    atmosphere after death, * is in ,
    445
  - impressions made by thoughts
    remain on * after breath-form

- radiant body, * is, 138
- radiant matter of physical plane, * made of, 142
- radiant-solid body, * is, 142, 206, 791
- seeing the *, 142, 208
- soul, * is mistakenly spoken of as the, 534
- spiritual body, * called by Alchemists, 618
- stars/lightning, * made of same matter as, 142

BODY - HUMAN (FOURFOLD PHYSICAL), 2, 34, 431, 452, 868
- circulation of matter/units through/in *, 458
- destiny, * as, 105, 110
- doer, * has become the master of, 452
- generation of *, 405
- governing unit(s) in *
  -breath-link unit is lowest ** in *, 721
  -hierarchy of **, 721
  -sense of smell is highest ** in *, 721
- importance of *, 487
- inner bodies (three) of *, 206, 534, 791. See BODY - ASTRAL
  -airy, 139
  -fluid body, 206
  -fluid-solid body, 139
  -hypnotism, control of ** by, 329
- Masonic teachings and the *, 687
  -divided name of Jahveh or Jah-hovah, 667
  -lodge is the *, 672
  -Name of the *, 692
  -rough ashler is symbol of *, 674
  -white apron is symbol of *, 672, 677
- rebuilt human *, Masonic temple has been symbol of, 666
- structure of *, 442, 721
  -cellular structure of *, 442
  -elemental matter of the *, 488
  -organs of the *, 443
  -sections/systems (four) of the *, 34, 397

- symbols for the *
  -Adonai, symbol of *, 592
  -Dritarashtra represents the *, 369
- types, * is exteriorization of types in mental atmosphere, 303
- units, two categories of in *, 489
  -compositor/transient units in the *, 489
  -fixed/movable, nature in * is, 798
- universe. See STAR(s)
  -center of universe, * is the, 458, 798
  -fulcrum on which all things rest, * is, 174
  -plan/pattern of **, * is, 303, 458, 792
  -relation of * to the **, 173, 552

BODY - PERFECT/SEXLESS/IMMORTAL/PHYSICAL, 20, 384, 416, 419, 853, 872, 881, 920
- aia in the *. See AIA-Body (Perfect)
- arms/legs of * can move in any direction, 452
- brains (four) in *, 615, 620, 640, 641, 654, 853
  -abdominal *, 853
  -cephalic *, 620, 882
  -currents/coils of light, ** made of, 640
  -pelvic *, 620, 853
  -thoracic *, 620, 853
- bridge in the, 594, 633
- building of the *, 545
- centers of Triune Self in the *, 545
- constitution of the *, 543, 640
- functioning of *, 544
- inner bodies (three) of, 419. See COLOR
  -building of the **, 415
- legs in *. See arms/legs
- Masonic teachings and the *, 667, 682, 693, 694
- no power in the universe can destroy the, 853
- tracts/chains/chords of. See TRACTS
- what doer can do through, 655

- psychic *, 87

COLON
- shorter/smaller, * becomes preparing for the Great Way, 628

COLOR(s), 268, 375. See also RED, YELLOW, BLUE, etc.
- body (human), no * without, 458
- classes of elementals were different *, 287
- inner bodies of perfect Triune Self, * of
  - form body color is like white of a rose, etc., 639
  - life and light body have no *, 639
- plants/trees have not always been green, 463
- pyro points, colorless if built from, 720
- variety of * between the three primary * due to combination of units, 723

COLUMN(s)
- three * of Masonry, 686
- two * of Masonry, 676

COLUMN(s) in the BODY
- front/nature *. See TRACT-Front/Nature.

COMETS, 87

COMMUNICATION
- Knower of Triune Self, * with the, 263, 537
- Rightness-and-Reason of Triune Self, * with, 97, 651
- thinker and knower, * of doer with, 533, 535
  - speaking with the thinker of the Triune Self using the speech of thinking through the minds, 651

COMMUNION, 844, 849, 895
- God, * with, 306, 919
- Thinker and Knower, * with, 804
  - doer no longer had ** after the fall, 453

COMPANION
- Way in the Earth, * on the. See WAY.

COMPASS, 671, 672, 675, 678, 679, 689, 693
- points of the *, 672

- symbol of the light coming down, * is, 695

COMPETENCE, 789

CONCEPTION, 139, 146, 349, 437, 792
- animals die at time of *, 147
- divine/immaculate *, 416, 594, 621, 879, 895

CONCEPTIONS
- erroneous *, 245, 553, 726

CONFIDENCE, 263
- lack of *
  - self-suggestion, use of in curing **, 343

CONSCIENCE, 76, 103
- after death
  - doer feels the presence of *, 215
- always present, * is, 262
- contact of noetic breath with pineal body makes human conscious of *, 352
- definition of *, 895
- doer memories and *, 528
- doer memories felt as *, 524
- finger of * pointing, 242
- knowledge in noetic atmosphere revealed through rightness, * is, 382
- knowledge in the noetic atmosphere of the human appears as the voice of * express through rightness, 262
- knowledge of departure from duty/what man knows to be right, * is, 98
- knowledge of Triune Self speaking through rightness, * is, 250
- lost doer, * does not speak in, 539
- negative, * is always, 262
- selfness speaking through rightness, * is, 615
- stifling of *, 214
- stifling of * is a crime against the Intelligence, 100
- voice of * warns against/forbids desires, 533
- what the doer has become conscious of as being right or wrong and kept in the noetic atmosphere, * is, 86

CONSCIOUS
- * of/as/in. See CONSCIOUS -

OF/AS/IN.
- consciousness, being * of. See CONSCIOUSNESS.
- death, being * at the moment of. See DEATH.
- definition of *, 895
- intelligent matter/units may be * that they are *, 535
- matter differs in degree in which it is *, 32
- nature matter/units
  -** become * in higher degrees by combination/growth through forms due to Light/desire, 395
  -nature units cannot be * they are * (i.e., are not intelligent), 535
- units in nature are * but not * they are * (i.e., are not intelligent), 64
- waking state of being *. See WAKING STATE.

CONSCIOUS OF/AS/IN, 1
- body, conscious as being not the, 565, 841
- doer, conscious as the, 265, 360, 419, 549, 803
- explanation of phrase, 22, 895
- feeling-and-desire may be conscious of, but not as I-ness, 538
- feeling-and-desire, conscious of/as, 615, 821
- feels, conscious of oneself as that which, 616
- identity, conscious as, 615
- nature units are conscious as their function only, 32, 547
- physical cell/unit of astral/airy/fluid/solid matter of body, conscious as its function, 534

CONSCIOUS SAMENESS, 827
- * is I-Am-Thou-and-Thou-Art-I-ness, 228
- love is *. See LOVE-Conscious Sameness.

CONSCIOUS SELF in the BODY, 383, 420
- knowledge of the *, 1, 7, 262, 359, 380

CONSCIOUSNESS, 37, 389, 550

- becoming conscious of *, 824, 825
  -possible to be ** while still a human, 550
  -system to aid in **, 789, 824
- Conscious Sameness becomes Pure Intelligence by the presence of *, 548
- current classification of *, 31
- definition of *, 895
- how to think about *, 825
- misuse of the word *, 22
- One Reality, * is, 546
- planes/states/grades/divisions/ variations of *, there are no, 23, 549
- Pure Intelligence becomes * when it wills to, 747
- purpose of Universe is to have Substance become *. See UNIVERSE-Purpose of.
- think, no one could without *, 23
- ultimate One Reality is *, 23, 31, 546, 548
- unique, coined English word that does not appear in other languages, * is a, 22

CONSIDERATE, 790
CONSTELLATIONS, 175
- projections of types are preserved in *, 292

CONTEMPLATION, 378, 572, 662
- mental heaven, * of problems in, 219, 378
- second stage of Patanjali's yoga, 358
- thinker, * by, 652

CONTROL
- body mind, * of by feeling-and-desire minds, 630, 789. See FEELING-Isolation.
- body, * of by yogi, 10
- breath, * of the (pranayama), 348, 356, 370
- breath-form, * of the, 834
- desire(s). See DESIRE-Control.
- destiny * man, 507
- elementals, * of, 288, 630, 790
  -downfall, being controlled by **, 288
  -genius' * of **, 268
- elementals, upper * the lower, 229

D

- good/bad *, 104
- hastening *. See postponing/etc. below.
- how * brought about, 555
- human, * of, 28
- postponing/hastening/accentuating/ weakening *, 507
- power of a god limited by one's *, 586
- Thinker and Knower have no *, 223
- thinker of Triune Self, * is directly operated by, 302
- thinking makes *, 263
- thinking, all * begins with, 223
- thoughts are *, 789
- weakening *. See postponing/etc. above.

DESTINY - FORM
- fetal development, 143
- parents, 150
- prenatal influences/states, 140, 143, 145
- prenatal influences/states, * has chiefly to do with, 137

DESTINY - GROUP
- chaos in world, 134
- history, facts of, 123
- how * of nation is made/administered, 43, 131
- rise and fall of nations, 121, 290
- sewage disposal, 123

DESTINY - MENTAL
- definition of, 897
- four classes of human beings, 270
- hell and heaven, 377
- Intelligences direct nature's operations, 302
- liar, * of, 256
- mental healing, 311
- race, * of, 305
- real cure of disease, 318
- schools of thought, 318
- seeing things as they are, 256
- this is an age of thought, 304

DESTINY - NOETIC
- * as presence/absence of Light, 380, 440
- * dominates other three kinds of destiny, 380

- definition of, 898
- free will and *, 423
- intelligence in nature, 398
- Light of one's Intelligence, 389
- noetic world, no * in the, 382
- re-existence and *, 440
- return of Light from nature, 404
- trial/test of sexes, 384

DESTINY - PHYSICAL
- death, manner of is *, 115
- definition of, 105, 897
- justice in human affairs, 130, 132
- life, span of, 115
- poverty and wealth, 117
- precipitating/retarding *, 95, 248
- purpose of, 107
- reversals, 117
- thoughts are causes of, 105
- unjust persecutions, 113

DESTINY - PSYCHIC
- after death states
  - danger of ancestor worship, 161
- astral body. See BODY, ASTRAL-after death.. See also DEATH(AFTER)-astral body.
- death, 204. See also DEATH-dying.
- definition of, 897
- form destiny as a type of, 137. See also DESTINY - FORM.
- heaven. See HEAVEN.
- hell. See HELL.
- lost doers, 151
- six classes of, 138
- sleep and dreams, 192
- third class of *, 182
- three things are affected by *
  - aia, 138
  - aia/breath-form/doer, 138
  - breath-form, 138
  - doer, 143
- transmigration, 147

DEVELOPMENT
- * by progression not evolution. See PROGRESSION-Development.
- course of * of units in the spheres, 441
- doer, right * of, 790
- progression, not evolution, * by, 31

DEVIL, 15, 139, 177, 211, 212, 346,

H

PERMANENCE-Kingdom.
• nature, * of. See NATURE;
KINGDOMS OF.
KISMET, 25
KNOW
• * what to do and what not to do, 24,
658, 849
KNOWER [NOETIC PART OF
TRIUNE SELF]
• communication with *. See
COMMUNICATION.
• definition of, 911
• duty of knower is to think, 65
• following one's *, 624
• God
  -man's idea of God come from his
  thinker and *, 589
  -thinker and * of Triune Self are
  man's God, 306
  -when human knows his thinker
  and * he will not worship a nature
  God, 589
  -worshipping God of a religion
  best while a human does not
  know of thinker and *, 589
• Jubelum is the *, 682
• Master of Masons represents *, 688
• noetic part of Triune Self, * is, 31
• Oneness, * is, 441
• pituitary body, * contacts. See
PITUITARY.
• worship/reverence for one's *
  -bringer/dispenser of Light, one's *
  should be revered as, 97
  -worship of knower is paid by
  worship made to God of a
  religion, 589
KNOWLEDGE
• ancient *, 368, 370
• conscious self in the body, * of the.
See SELF-KNOWLEDGE.
• definition of *, 911
  -* is the permanent result, as
  accomplishment in the noetic
  atmosphere, coming from
  thinking, 381
• desire for Self-*. See
SELF-KNOWLEDGE [OF THE
KNOWER]-Desire.

• doer *, 256, 260, 262
  -definition of **, 912
• hypnotic state, certain * available in,
333
• intuition is direct *, 911
• kinds of *, two, 911
• learning is not *, 261
• perfection in *, 348
• recovery of forgotten *, 334, 336
• self-*. See SELF-KNOWLEDGE
[OF THE KNOWER].. See
SELF-KNOWLEDGE.
• sense-*, 249, 911
• Thinker of the Triune Self, * of the,
912
• thinking
  -* cannot come without **, 381
  -* is acquired by **, 261
• thought(s), * does not come from,
261
• Triune Self, * of the. See
SELF-KNOWLEDGE [OF THE
KNOWER].
KRISHNA, 14, 369, 480
KUNDALINI, 168
KURUS, 369

L

LAMBSKIN, 672, 695
LAMPBLACK, 720
LANDMARKS
• ancient * of the Masons, 669
LANGUAGE, 272
• secret * of the Masons, 668
LATIN, 598
• * race, 497
LAW, 127
• definition of *, 912
• nature, * of
  -definition of *, 913
• prescription for performance, * is,
127
LAYER(s). See also ZONE(s)
• air * surrounding fluid/solid *, 174
• airy * of physical plane, 510
• fire * surrounding air/fluid/solid *,
456
• fluid * surrounding the earth crust,

374

N

SALEM
• King of *, 608
SALEM, MASSACHUSETTS, 126
SALT, 618
SAMADHI, 355, 358
SAMENESS
• Conscious *. See CONSCIOUS
  SAMENESS.
• unconscious *, 41
  -space is **, 39
• unmanifested of a unit is *, 41
SAMSKARAS
• habits of thinking, * are, 365
SAMYAMA, 358
SANSKRIT, 168, 518
• * literature, 370
• * term(s)
  -chitta, name given particles of
   nature-matter, 356
  -inner meaning of **, 356, 366
  -pranayama is a **, 920
SANYASI, 348
SAPPHIRES, 723
SAT [Sanskrit term], 364
SATTVA, 364
SAVIORS
• doer is Savior of physical body, 596
• teachings concerning doer and its
  destiny given out by *, 479
• tribe, people, or world, * of, 478
SCARF, 322
SCIENTISTS, 261, 371
SCOTCH
• * Presbyterians, 126
SEAL
• balancing factor is a *, 242
• balancing factor, * of the, 242
• compositor units have * of doer. See
  UNITS-Compositor.
• sense and compositor units have * of
  doer, 489
SEANCES
• apparitions and *, 208
• entities at *, 156
• shades called to mediumistic *, 646
SEEING THINGS AS THEY ARE,
256, 657
SEER, 375
SELF

• greater *, 7, 657
• higher *, 819
  -definition of **, 924
• lower *, 819
• real *, 7, 21
  -is the ever-present counselor and
   judge that speaks in the heart, 8
  -protect you, your real * will, 24
• union with one's *, 370
SELF-CONTROL, 403, 674
• feeling-and-desire minds, * is control
  of, 29
• genius, better to develop * than, 268
• gentleman has *, 532
• lunar germ can go from kidneys to
  head only as result of *, 409
• minds of feeling-and-desire, * of, 634
• possessions are means of *, 487
• reclamation of Light by *, 404, 410,
  411, 414
• regenerate body/accomplish aims by
  *, 21
• religion encourages *, 590
• religious belief and *, 571
• system in Thinking and Destiny
  concerned above all with *, 790
• voluntary * of feeling-and-desire, 854
SELF-CONTROLLED
• desire, when *, 224, 841
• fallen doers are not *, 44
• you should have the desire that
  desire should be *, 837
SELF-DECEPTION, 324, 328, 566
SELF-DELUSION, 830
• definition of *, 924
• state resulting from preference and
  prejudice influencing thinking, 848
SELF-DENIAL
• religion encourages, 590
SELF-DISCIPLINE, 356
SELF-GOVERNED, 837
SELF-GOVERNMENT, 53, 790
SELF-HYPNOSIS, 334, 908. See also
HYPNOSIS, - SELF.
• advantages of, 335
• feats possible in, 335
SELF-INDULGENCE, 154
SELF-INTEREST, 561
SELFISH, 124, 504